THE
MICHIGAN
FOUNDATION
DIRECTORY

Reb
061
F

1/12

Council of
Michigan
Foundations

Serving grantmakers. Advancing giving.

FOUNDATION
CENTER
Knowledge to build on.

17TH EDITION

THE
MICHIGAN
FOUNDATION
DIRECTORY

Council of Michigan Foundations
Foundation Center

INTRODUCTION

THE 2011 EDITION

The 17th edition of *The Michigan Foundation Directory* contains descriptive entries for foundations, corporate giving programs, or grantmaking public charities that accept applications and are either located in Michigan or have a stated funding interest that includes Michigan. Based on these criteria, there are 1,575 entries in the descriptive directory and its indexes, including 195 entries from grantmakers in 31 additional states.

The tables and data provided in this introduction reflect statistics beyond the contents of the descriptive directory. The information is based on the 2,433 private and community foundations with a primary address in Michigan, including those funders that do not accept applications, and excludes direct corporate giving programs, grantmaking public charities, and geographic affiliates of community foundations located within the state.

WHAT IS A FOUNDATION?

The Foundation Center defines a foundation as a nongovernmental, nonprofit 501(c)(3) organization with its own funds (from a single source, either an individual, family, corporation, or the community at large) and program managed by its own trustees and directors, that was established to maintain or aid educational, social, charitable, religious, or other activities serving the common welfare, primarily by making grants to other nonprofit organizations.

TYPES OF GRANTMAKERS

Grantmakers included in this volume fall into one of six categories:

Independent Foundation: A fund or endowment designated by the Internal Revenue Service as a private foundation under the law, the primary function of which is the making of grants. The assets of most independent foundations are derived from the gift of an individual or family. Some function under the direction of family members and are known as "family foundations." Depending on their range of giving, independent foundations may also be known as "general purpose" or "special purpose" foundations.

Company-Sponsored Foundation: A private foundation under the tax code that derives its funds from a profit-making company or corporation but is independently constituted, the purpose of which is to make grants, usually on a broad basis although not without regard for the business interests of the corporation. Company-sponsored foundations are legally distinct from contributions programs administered within the corporation directly from corporate funds.

Operating Foundation: A fund or endowment designated under the tax code by the Internal Revenue Service as a private operating foundation, the primary purpose of which is to operate research, social welfare, or other programs determined by its governing body or charter.

Community Foundation: In its general charitable purposes, a community foundation is much like a private foundation; its funds, however, are derived from many donors rather than a single source, as is usually the case with private foundations. Further, community foundations are classified under the tax code as public charities (see below) also known as public foundations and are therefore subject to different rules and regulations than those which govern private foundations.

Corporate Giving Program: Corporate giving programs make grants directly through the company. The grantmaking apparatus exists within the corporation and is administered by corporate personnel.

Public Charity: Public grantmaking charities, also known as public foundations, redistribute funds that have been raised primarily from the public-at-large. In most instances, the funds are raised through a fund-raising campaign or endowed gifts as in the case of community foundations.

SOURCES OF INFORMATION

Michigan foundations are researched using the newest and most complete information available. This information is either provided by the foundation itself, or it comes from available public records. The main source of information is the IRS information returns for private and community foundations (Forms 990 and 990-PF). Other public sources of information include updates from foundation web sites, annual reports, press releases and newspaper articles. In addition, the Foundation Center offers foundations several ways to provide newer and more current information. Profiles for the larger foundations are prepared and sent to them for verification. Foundations also may provide information updates via Foundation Center electronic reporting applications (Foundation Finder and Foundation Directory Online Updater) available on the Foundation Center's web site (foundationcenter.org).

A breakdown of the 2,433 Michigan private and community foundations in this analysis by fiscal year-end date reveals the following: 289 foundations (11.9 percent) with 2010 fiscal data, 1,962 foundations (80.6 percent) with 2009 fiscal data, 136 foundations (5.6 percent) with 2008 fiscal data, and 46 foundations (1.9 percent) with 2007 fiscal data. Thus, 2010 and 2009 fiscal information is reported for 2,251 foundations (92.5 percent).

LARGE AND SMALL FOUNDATIONS

In all, private and community foundations in Michigan hold over $24.4 billion in assets and make annual contributions close to $1.5 billion (Table 2). Most of these assets and funds are managed by a small portion of the 2,433 Michigan foundations described in this introduction (Table 1). Although they represent 11.6 percent of the private and community foundations located in Michigan, the 283 largest foundations—defined as holding assets of $5 million or more—account for close to $23 billion or 94 percent of the assets held and $1.3 billion or 86 percent of the total giving reported. In contrast, the 1,646 smallest foundations—defined as having assets under $1 million— account for only $406 million or 1.7 percent of the assets held and $109 million or 7.3 percent of the grants awarded, even though they comprise nearly 68 percent of the private and community foundations in Michigan.

Tables 3, 4, and 5 illustrate an analysis of independent, company-sponsored, and community foundations respectively. Sorted by assets, the tables also list foundation name, city of location, fiscal date, expenditures, and total giving.

Table 3 represents the top 50 independent foundations by assets, while tables 4 and 5, the tables for the top 33 company-sponsored and 55 community foundations respectively, list only those foundations with assets over $1 million.

GEOGRAPHIC DISTRIBUTION OF FOUNDATIONS BY COUNTY

Table 6 shows the distribution of Michigan private and community foundations by county with corresponding aggregate fiscal data. While 72 of Michigan's 83 counties are represented in The Michigan Foundation Directory (all except Alcona, Alger, Clare, Keweenaw, Lake, Luce, Montmorency, Ogemaw, Ontonagon, Oscoda, and Schoolcraft counties), the distribution of foundations across the state is uneven. Oakland County has the most foundations (663), followed by Wayne County (364) and Kent County (305). In contrast, 11 counties have one foundation each and 45 have fewer than ten.

Many of the foundations located in Michigan are national in scope and do not generally focus on or limit their funding to local organizations. At the same time, 1,983 of the 2,433 (81.5 percent) Michigan private and community foundations listed in this volume are considered local funders. Grantseekers should take careful note of any geographic limitation statements in order to gain a clear picture of funding patterns in their own area.

In comparing the size and grantmaking activities of Michigan foundations in urban versus towns and rural areas (Figure 1), there is a noticeable disparity. Michigan foundations in urban/metropolitan areas account for close to 90 percent of all foundations in Michigan, hold 96 percent of the overall Michigan foundation assets, and distribute 97 percent of all Michigan foundation grants.

ANALYSIS OF FOUNDATION GRANTS BY SUBJECT

A breakdown of the grants by Michigan foundations in the top 10 major subject areas (Table 7) reflects a broad scope of giving interests. Nearly 70 percent of the total dollar amount awarded fell into three broad categories: public affairs/society benefit ($241.5 million or 25.9 percent); human services ($201.9 million or 21.6 percent); and education ($199.9 million or 21.4 percent). Grants by out-of-state foundations (Table 8) show the additional foundation dollars that flow into Michigan. The three largest areas of giving, which make up 57 percent of total giving by out-of-state foundations to Michigan nonprofits, are education ($25.5 million or 22.6 percent); health ($23.6 million or 21.0 percent); and public affairs/society benefit ($15.8 million or 14.0 percent).

SNAPSHOT OF MICHIGAN FOUNDATION PHILANTHROPY

TABLE 1. Analysis of Michigan Grantmaking Foundations by Asset Categories (All dollar figures expressed in thousands)

Asset Category	Number of Foundations	%	Assets	%	Gifts Received	%	Expenditures	%	Total Giving	%
$100 million and over	28	1.2	$17,748,314	72.7	$111,416	19.5	$1,106,778	58.5	$ 882,976	59.3
$50 to $100 million	24	1.0	1,692,511	6.9	95,836	16.8	174,713	9.2	142,455	9.6
$25 to $50 million	38	1.6	1,379,337	5.6	84,868	14.8	129,764	6.9	98,825	6.6
$10 to $25 million	82	3.4	1,294,429	5.3	95,864	16.8	143,577	7.6	110,111	7.4
$5 to $10 million	111	4.6	796,754	3.3	26,007	4.5	65,821	3.5	51,638	3.5
$1 to $5 million	504	20.7	1,102,043	4.5	82,439	14.4	137,666	7.3	94,067	6.3
Under $1 million	1,646	67.7	406,591	1.7	75,501	13.2	134,828	7.1	109,046	7.3
Total	2,433	100.0	$24,419,978	100.0	$571,932	100.0	$1,893,148	100.0	$1,489,118	100.0

Note: Figures may not add up due to rounding.

TABLE 2. Aggregate Fiscal Data of Michigan Grantmaking Foundations by Foundation Type
(All dollar figures expressed in thousands)

Foundation Type	Number of Foundations	%	Assets	%	Gifts Received	%	Expenditures	%	Total Giving	%
Independent	2,095	86.1	$20,748,824	85.0	$320,778	56.1	$1,480,239	78.2	$1,218,847	81.9
Company-Sponsored	91	3.7	668,784	2.7	83,436	14.6	125,735	6.6	117,238	7.9
Community	65	2.7	2,177,997	8.9	125,885	22.0	180,496	9.5	142,657	9.6
Operating	182	7.5	824,373	3.4	41,833	7.3	106,678	5.6	10,376	0.7
Total	2,433	100.0	$24,419,978	100.0	$571,932	100.0	$1,893,148	100.0	$1,489,118	100.0

Note: Figures may not add up due to rounding.

TABLE 3. Top 50 Michigan Independent Foundations by Assets

Foundation Name	City	Fiscal Date	Assets	Expenditures	Total Giving
W. K. Kellogg Foundation	Battle Creek	8/31/2010	$ 7,238,160,845	$ 358,022,541	$270,011,667
The Kresge Foundation	Troy	12/31/2010	3,293,222,730	255,091,764	235,702,000
Charles Stewart Mott Foundation	Flint	12/31/2009	2,080,000,000	141,190,677	112,542,064
The Skillman Foundation	Detroit	12/31/2009	457,235,000	26,225,000	21,123,000
The Herbert H. and Grace A. Dow Foundation	Midland	12/31/2009	392,338,544	15,055,400	9,771,115
Max M. and Marjorie S. Fisher Foundation, Inc.	Southfield	12/31/2009	237,206,127	12,807,544	11,203,928
Van Andel Fund, Inc.	Grand Rapids	12/31/2009	211,173,677	3,388,698	2,402,500
Ruth Mott Foundation	Flint	12/31/2009	198,621,065	11,487,136	8,642,088
Dorothy D. and Joseph A. Moller Foundation	Hillsdale	12/31/2009	195,537,596	9,882,516	8,200,000
Irving S. Gilmore Foundation	Kalamazoo	12/31/2009	186,519,893	10,415,991	8,437,614
Arcus Foundation	Kalamazoo	12/31/2009	167,555,502	30,925,766	25,425,501
Hudson-Webber Foundation	Detroit	12/31/2009	150,553,592	7,644,215	5,823,313
The Rollin M. Gerstacker Foundation	Midland	12/31/2009	145,930,303	8,627,110	8,181,668
McGregor Fund	Detroit	6/30/2009	140,703,167	7,404,528	5,924,974
Herrick Foundation	Detroit	9/30/2009	134,750,486	10,517,997	7,227,673
The Samuel and Jean Frankel Jewish Heritage Foundation	Troy	12/31/2009	129,367,963	6,890,536	6,665,991
Frey Foundation	Grand Rapids	12/31/2009	123,390,443	5,518,694	3,193,712
Richard & Jane Manoogian Foundation	Taylor	6/30/2009	121,658,499	12,886,420	6,413,393
The Carls Foundation	Detroit	12/31/2009	103,060,613	4,976,727	3,957,275
Wege Foundation	Grand Rapids	12/31/2009	100,866,387	16,114,510	13,822,485
Fred A. and Barbara M. Erb Family Foundation	Birmingham	6/30/2010	97,079,085	5,044,282	4,511,278
Thompson Educational Foundation	Plymouth	12/31/2009	91,270,537	3,623,261	987,140
Manoogian Simone Foundation	Taylor	12/31/2009	89,494,805	5,739,142	5,647,604
The Richard and Helen DeVos Foundation	Grand Rapids	12/31/2009	89,446,796	52,844,411	46,457,200
Samuel & Jean Frankel Foundation	Troy	12/31/2009	85,645,093	4,053,499	3,784,174
The Meijer Foundation	Grand Rapids	9/30/2009	79,091,049	19,077,813	18,269,168
Elsa U. Pardee Foundation	Midland	12/31/2009	75,426,678	4,493,641	4,256,864
The Gerber Foundation	Fremont	12/31/2010	72,293,973	3,882,089	3,607,083
John E. Fetzer Memorial Trust Fund	Vicksburg	6/30/2009	66,915,152	4,631,808	528,999
Douglas & Maria DeVos Foundation	Grand Rapids	12/31/2009	61,992,136	11,627,818	10,433,131
Alex and Marie Manoogian Foundation	Taylor	12/31/2009	61,541,162	2,707,590	1,999,750
Ethel and James Flinn Foundation	Detroit	12/31/2009	55,368,771	3,016,683	2,901,201
Dick & Betsy DeVos Foundation	Grand Rapids	12/31/2009	54,829,634	8,135,254	7,600,422
Orville D. & Ruth A. Merillat Foundation	Adrian	2/28/2009	54,004,645	8,573,645	7,741,940
The Lloyd and Mabel Johnson Foundation	Brighton	9/30/2010	52,797,286	1,231,097	586,959
Christ Cares for Kids Foundation	Traverse City	1/31/2010	50,066,609	1,445,637	1,410,225
Sage Foundation	Brighton	12/31/2009	50,055,133	3,001,364	2,462,700
The Charles J. Strosacker Foundation	Midland	12/31/2009	49,996,011	2,793,012	2,711,549
The Isabel Foundation	Flint	6/30/2009	47,373,286	3,665,618	3,205,148
Steve & Cindy Van Andel Foundation	Ada	12/31/2009	46,882,242	2,804,307	625,062
Silverwing Foundation	Grand Rapids	12/31/2009	45,085,727	4,024,570	3,187,262
David and Carol Van Andel Foundation	Grand Rapids	12/31/2009	45,034,514	3,239,777	1,869,395
DeRoy Testamentary Foundation	Southfield	12/31/2009	42,513,567	2,605,048	1,967,816
Thompson Foundation	Plymouth	12/31/2009	42,455,999	1,801,831	1,682,301
The Harry A. and Margaret D. Towsley Foundation	Midland	12/31/2009	41,879,640	2,503,064	2,410,100
The Duffy Foundation	Ann Arbor	12/31/2009	40,028,383	2,857,795	2,758,500
Ted & Jane Von Voigtlander Foundation	Livonia	12/31/2009	38,978,881	2,108,443	1,631,193
Earhart Foundation	Ann Arbor	12/31/2009	35,723,529	6,154,181	5,049,476
The Wayne and Joan Webber Foundation	Clinton Township	12/31/2009	35,598,504	1,840,750	951,000
Harvey Randall Wickes Foundation	Saginaw	12/31/2009	35,177,457	2,031,364	1,768,248
TOTAL: 50			$17,541,898,716	$1,136,632,564	$927,674,849

TABLE 4. Top 33 Michigan Company-Sponsored Foundations by Assets

Foundation Name	City	Fiscal Date	Assets	Expenditures	Total Giving
General Motors Foundation, Inc.	Detroit	12/31/2009	$157,666,694	$ 9,011,341	$ 7,985,218
Steelcase Foundation	Grand Rapids	11/30/2009	82,069,885	5,233,695	4,395,581
Kellogg Company 25-Year Employees Fund, Inc.	Battle Creek	12/31/2009	63,547,168	3,120,556	2,588,658
Blue Cross Blue Shield of Michigan Foundation	Detroit	12/31/2009	49,886,689	2,801,465	1,562,936
Ford Motor Company Fund	Dearborn	12/31/2009	39,855,247	21,774,573	19,952,391
Kellogg's Corporate Citizenship Fund	Battle Creek	12/31/2009	39,303,021	8,756,433	8,351,486
DTE Energy Foundation	Detroit	12/31/2009	31,125,813	7,951,660	7,733,278
Dow Corning Foundation	Midland	12/31/2009	23,198,941	867,950	849,775
Robert C. Dart Foundation	Mason	10/31/2009	21,670,256	4,000,620	4,000,000
The Dow Chemical Company Foundation	Midland	12/31/2009	20,253,635	20,145,179	20,145,179
La-Z-Boy Foundation	Monroe	12/31/2009	18,672,629	1,021,467	918,800
Delphi Foundation, Inc.	Troy	12/31/2009	15,657,568	910,416	784,000
Masco Corporation Foundation	Taylor	12/31/2009	15,361,941	4,327,297	4,049,833
The Pokagon Fund, Inc.	New Buffalo	6/30/2010	9,857,943	1,038,124	804,070
DENSO North America Foundation	Southfield	12/31/2009	9,770,667	446,346	437,400
The Jubilee Foundation	Detroit	5/31/2010	6,745,347	2,410,122	2,410,122
Lear Corporation Charitable Foundation	Southfield	12/31/2009	6,293,442	308,999	300,000
The Alro Steel Foundation	Jackson	12/31/2009	5,914,865	1,088,601	1,088,252
Edward F. Redies Foundation, Inc.	Saline	12/31/2009	4,028,253	239,293	200,000
Consumers Energy Foundation	Jackson	12/31/2009	3,839,173	998,637	998,617
The Chrysler Foundation	Auburn Hills	12/31/2009	3,625,839	4,641,691	4,080,349
Zatkoff Family Foundation	Farmington Hills	12/31/2009	3,575,900	133,946	131,747
Wolverine World Wide Foundation	Rockford	12/31/2009	3,235,238	642,776	619,081
Whirlpool Foundation	Benton Harbor	12/31/2009	2,822,763	10,148,447	9,847,102
Hastings Mutual Insurance Company Charitable Foundation	Hastings	12/31/2009	2,609,969	115,390	112,227
Weingartz Family Foundation	Shelby Township	12/31/2009	2,036,826	484,740	483,685
The Batts Foundation	Grand Rapids	12/31/2009	1,945,153	66,385	49,650
Fabiano Foundation	Bay City	12/31/2009	1,635,135	236,236	236,100
MEEMIC Foundation for the Future of Education	Auburn Hills	12/31/2009	1,630,914	50,683	37,472
The Dart Energy Foundation, Inc.	Mason	12/31/2009	1,578,215	89,062	0
Felpausch Foundation	Hastings	12/31/2009	1,364,568	63,886	45,887
Amerisure Charitable Foundation, Inc.	Farmington Hills	12/31/2009	1,342,073	345,569	327,026
MAC Valves Foundation	Wixom	11/30/2009	1,153,674	77,017	75,500
TOTAL: 33			$653,275,444	$113,548,602	$105,601,422

TABLE 5. Top 55 Michigan Community Foundations by Assets

Foundation Name	City	Fiscal Date	Assets	Expenditures	Total Giving
Community Foundation for Southeast Michigan	Detroit	12/31/2009	$ 571,969,510	$ 71,893,574	$ 67,259,122
Kalamazoo Community Foundation	Kalamazoo	12/31/2009	266,354,216	14,545,272	11,337,891
Grand Rapids Community Foundation	Grand Rapids	6/30/2009	183,524,161	13,230,263	8,961,846
Fremont Area Community Foundation	Fremont	12/31/2010	178,178,821	8,756,558	7,057,861
Community Foundation of Greater Flint	Flint	12/31/2009	127,186,236	6,246,920	4,527,084
Community Foundation for Muskegon County	Muskegon	12/31/2008	88,425,309	5,743,732	3,245,846
Battle Creek Community Foundation	Battle Creek	3/31/2009	73,299,916	9,728,383	7,843,180
Midland Area Community Foundation	Midland	12/31/2009	59,173,628	2,587,083	1,180,412
Capital Region Community Foundation	Lansing	12/31/2008	49,812,103	3,983,738	2,879,556
Ann Arbor Area Community Foundation	Ann Arbor	12/31/2008	39,737,991	3,400,822	2,284,402
Grand Traverse Regional Community Foundation	Traverse City	12/31/2009	39,417,056	1,841,231	1,298,823
Grand Haven Area Community Foundation, Inc.	Grand Haven	12/31/2009	37,853,369	3,230,697	2,659,511
Saginaw Community Foundation	Saginaw	12/31/2009	36,344,180	2,752,188	1,234,409
Bay Area Community Foundation	Bay City	12/31/2009	32,105,535	1,824,124	955,590
The Community Foundation of the Holland/Zeeland Area	Holland	12/31/2008	31,700,171	2,683,811	2,195,111
Community Foundation of St. Clair County	Port Huron	12/31/2008	26,448,298	2,665,918	1,659,698
Berrien Community Foundation, Inc.	St. Joseph	12/31/2010	23,643,341	1,777,010	1,464,010
Community Foundation for Northeast Michigan	Alpena	9/30/2010	20,861,768	1,357,955	1,049,983
Charlevoix County Community Foundation	East Jordan	12/31/2009	20,256,212	1,401,786	1,051,580
Sturgis Area Community Foundation	Sturgis	3/31/2010	19,402,490	510,419	332,424
Petoskey-Harbor Springs Area Community Foundation	Petoskey	3/31/2010	18,549,457	778,551	427,043
Jackson Community Foundation	Jackson	12/31/2009	17,991,604	2,003,601	1,272,985
Community Foundation of the Upper Peninsula	Escanaba	12/31/2008	17,379,338	1,580,010	1,074,216
Lenawee Community Foundation	Tecumseh	9/30/2010	15,385,219	1,279,678	1,064,610
Barry Community Foundation	Hastings	6/30/2009	15,047,917	959,343	638,988
Greenville Area Community Foundation	Greenville	12/31/2009	13,844,185	812,585	523,961
Allegan County Community Foundation	Allegan	12/31/2009	11,838,171	526,722	246,250
Hillsdale County Community Foundation	Hillsdale	9/30/2009	9,622,042	648,033	311,426
Mount Pleasant Area Community Foundation	Mount Pleasant	12/31/2009	8,445,418	619,674	368,259
Four County Community Foundation	Almont	12/31/2009	8,385,458	486,544	291,060
Marshall Community Foundation	Marshall	9/30/2009	8,330,112	489,878	333,986
Tuscola County Community Foundation	Caro	12/31/2010	7,560,487	329,886	177,180
Lapeer County Community Foundation	Lapeer	12/31/2009	7,522,423	291,497	133,080
Marquette County Community Foundation	Marquette	12/31/2008	7,196,671	466,340	286,789
Gratiot County Community Foundation	Ithaca	9/30/2009	7,183,564	240,516	122,412
Community Foundation of Greater Rochester	Rochester	12/31/2009	6,346,009	718,248	346,548
Dickinson Area Community Foundation	Iron Mountain	4/30/2008	5,967,895	306,633	178,362
Cadillac Area Community Foundation	Cadillac	12/31/2009	5,419,051	595,616	451,840
Michigan Gateway Community Foundation	Buchanan	3/31/2009	5,013,319	537,890	274,083
Mackinac Island Community Foundation	Mackinac Island	12/31/2009	5,005,030	224,715	112,049
Roscommon County Community Foundation	Roscommon	12/31/2008	4,634,180	421,867	266,103
Frankenmuth Community Foundation	Frankenmuth	12/31/2009	4,453,583	281,145	253,917
M & M Area Community Foundation	Menominee	12/31/2008	4,210,606	470,906	200,904
Branch County Community Foundation	Coldwater	9/30/2009	4,206,109	472,620	347,345
Shiawassee Community Foundation	Owosso	9/30/2009	4,092,502	110,123	28,824
Community Foundation of Monroe County	Monroe	3/31/2009	3,778,021	824,347	222,528
Albion Community Foundation	Albion	12/31/2008	3,616,266	379,011	208,881
Keweenaw Community Foundation	Hancock	3/31/2009	3,462,112	163,910	42,180
Sanilac County Community Foundation	Sandusky	12/31/2008	2,601,293	151,035	94,737
Otsego County Community Foundation	Gaylord	12/31/2008	1,976,637	140,179	78,302
Leelanau Township Community Foundation, Inc.	Northport	12/31/2008	1,868,111	306,261	233,562
Huron County Community Foundation	Bad Axe	9/30/2009	1,854,041	105,317	47,450
Southfield Community Foundation	Southfield	6/30/2009	1,594,523	1,097,572	895,760
Canton Community Foundation	Canton	6/30/2009	1,396,996	245,712	36,763
Three Rivers Area Community Foundation	Three Rivers	12/31/2008	1,333,187	53,803	17,601
TOTAL: 55			$2,172,805,848	$179,281,252	$142,088,323

Table 6. Fiscal Data of Michigan Foundations by County

County	Number of Foundations	Assets	Gifts Received	Expenditures	Total Giving
Allegan	8	$ 16,241,087	$ 2,279,060	$ 1,592,608	$ 1,263,543
Alpena	7	49,607,739	1,685,238	3,295,700	2,013,340
Antrim	6	6,971,830	1,021,247	542,600	248,304
Arenac	1	674	2,194	1,524	1,500
Baraga	1	753,331	28,658	71,550	6,925
Barry	10	66,658,726	7,026,662	4,062,780	1,064,826
Bay	18	45,606,366	1,962,337	2,953,886	1,990,515
Benzie	5	21,552,642	0	3,393,299	3,253,355
Berrien	35	106,828,339	14,167,162	18,848,963	16,798,241
Branch	17	17,212,932	2,185,066	1,403,889	821,962
Calhoun	29	7,498,724,059	32,483,608	385,490,663	292,512,701
Cass	8	108,835,861	155,700	6,593,318	389,248
Charlevoix	7	29,845,962	1,541,977	2,578,130	2,168,477
Cheboygan	5	5,776,563	9,500	316,449	104,000
Chippewa	2	1,448,006	100	76,806	48,079
Clinton	2	603,398	20,850	51,320	49,062
Crawford	1	1	0	17,993	250
Delta	6	25,991,187	1,453,205	2,104,990	1,534,008
Dickinson	7	7,202,265	371,123	424,163	219,287
Eaton	10	5,003,608	136,016	314,931	259,707
Emmet	17	32,486,475	1,466,111	1,887,890	1,255,392
Genesee	129	2,632,054,518	9,210,592	174,858,965	137,361,957
Gladwin	1	62,041	30,000	26,632	26,414
Gogebic	1	197,369	0	15,062	10,140
Grand Traverse	37	143,934,499	4,261,931	10,265,871	8,666,727
Gratiot	7	15,016,184	4,165,756	4,135,138	3,926,015
Hillsdale	5	205,634,902	8,575,212	10,546,342	8,524,198
Houghton	3	4,707,602	431,234	241,074	63,980
Huron	7	4,820,273	748,144	323,389	216,709
Ingham	44	197,569,606	33,230,820	43,178,278	20,426,321
Ionia	3	1,488,530	937,206	922,329	70,000
Iosco	2	1,959,576	45,000	112,837	87,500
Iron	2	689,071	0	46,134	25,039
Isabella	5	47,903,378	5,009,885	2,833,551	2,110,558
Jackson	43	89,594,135	3,383,793	8,587,849	7,096,557
Kalamazoo	67	1,248,778,311	51,013,836	99,838,979	62,182,228
Kalkaska	3	617,514	131,819	65,860	34,109
Kent	305	1,513,249,549	130,470,367	203,083,645	170,822,191
Lapeer	4	15,923,815	416,453	785,756	429,100
Leelanau	7	3,557,582	235,572	444,889	352,061
Lenawee	24	97,215,784	2,844,314	11,742,982	10,087,103
Livingston	16	110,657,563	140,514	4,994,753	3,546,547
Mackinac	1	5,005,030	363,171	224,715	112,049
Macomb	83	157,425,808	7,503,799	17,594,715	14,602,247
Manistee	5	15,347,688	2,002,287	418,560	354,750
Marquette	9	13,156,496	454,705	821,350	590,599
Mason	2	2,661,284	1,446	152,401	139,277
Mecosta	1	80,736	0	2,966	2,500
Menominee	2	5,856,148	369,141	649,635	200,904
Midland	24	847,557,954	7,785,968	59,430,517	50,781,782
Missaukee	1	526,035	2,000	38,502	31,500
Monroe	17	42,282,018	946,752	4,563,221	3,685,709
Montcalm	6	23,754,279	2,677,856	1,281,219	917,720
Muskegon	12	110,671,698	4,369,877	7,282,537	4,602,837
Newaygo	10	258,484,640	4,100,211	13,338,896	10,923,010
Oakland	663	4,792,470,324	77,297,488	376,556,730	338,885,535
Oceana	3	3,959,273	1,150,000	623,208	583,581
Osceola	1	148,679	0	3,320	2,625
Otsego	2	1,991,139	71,684	144,235	81,687
Ottawa	87	218,168,382	17,442,099	24,431,257	21,533,764
Presque Isle	1	99,955	2,495	5,577	2,700
Roscommon	3	5,042,157	132,187	452,309	283,068
Saginaw	51	150,181,021	7,867,529	12,384,355	9,656,213
Sanilac	5	12,353,525	530,873	516,768	338,037
Shiawassee	7	18,352,125	123,862	1,040,215	568,204
St. Clair	23	50,566,167	1,878,461	4,099,055	2,753,252
St. Joseph	10	25,083,896	767,186	762,250	508,727
Tuscola	7	10,334,659	1,169,583	469,053	303,612
Van Buren	6	7,038,157	99,000	488,221	461,350
Washtenaw	109	256,610,678	29,003,828	41,291,337	23,552,334
Wayne	364	2,996,366,237	80,343,039	310,411,700	240,138,575
Wexford	1	5,419,051	196,827	595,616	451,840
TOTAL	**2,433**	**$24,419,978,092**	**$571,931,616**	**$1,893,148,207**	**$1,489,118,164**

TABLE 7. Grant Distribution In Major Subject Categories by Michigan Foundations, circa 2009

Subject	Amount	%	No. of Grants	%
Arts and Culture	$ 91,987,332	9.9	539	10.1
Education	199,984,389	21.4	1,107	20.7
Environment and Animals	64,447,422	6.9	396	7.4
Health	79,107,854	8.5	458	8.6
Human Services	201,941,241	21.6	1,301	24.3
International Affairs, Development, Peace, and Human Rights	12,544,064	1.3	105	2.0
Public Affairs/Society Benefit	241,518,205	25.9	1,127	21
Science and Technology	11,003,183	1.2	75	1.4
Social Sciences	11,282,185	1.2	108	2.0
Religion	17,057,313	1.8	133	2.5
Other	2,624,714	0.3	7	0.1
Total	$933,497,902	100.0	5,356	100.0

Source: The Foundation Center, 2011.

The Foundation Center's grants sample database (circa 2009) includes grants of $10,000 or more awarded to organizations by a sample of 1,384 larger foundations.

For community foundations, only discretionary and donor-advised grants are included. Grants to individuals are not included.

Grants included for the 41 Michigan foundations in the sample accounted for approximately three fifths of total giving reported by all Michigan foundations in 2009.

TABLE 8. Grant Distribution in Major Subject Categories by Out-of-State Foundations to Michigan Nonprofit Organizations, circa 2009

Subject	Amount	%	No. of Grants	%
Arts and Culture	$ 7,965,107	7.1	102	10.8
Education	25,470,206	22.6	189	20.1
Environment and Animals	3,781,100	3.4	39	4.1
Health	23,598,332	21.0	111	11.8
Human Services	12,072,066	10.7	229	24.3
International Affairs, Development, Peace, and Human Rights	12,904,318	11.5	14	1.5
Public Affairs/Society Benefit	15,782,333	14.0	148	15.7
Science and Technology	3,159,059	2.8	34	3.6
Social Sciences	2,629,199	2.3	29	3.1
Religion	5,203,795	4.6	47	5.0
Total	$112,565,515	100.0	942	100.0

Source: The Foundation Center, 2011.

The Foundation Center's grants sample database (circa 2009) includes grants of $10,000 or more awarded to organizations by a sample of 1,384 larger foundations.

For community foundations, only discretionary and donor-advised grants are included. Grants to individuals are not included.

Grants made by the 228 out-of-state foundations included in the sample accounted for approximately one fifth of total grant dollars awarded to Michigan nonprofit organizations in 2009

FIGURE 1. Share of Foundation Number, Assets, and Giving by Urban vs. Town and Rural Michigan Foundations*

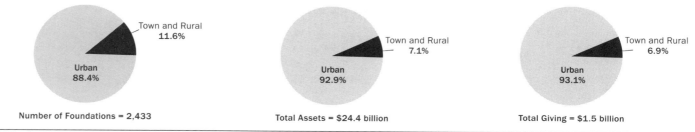

Town and Rural 11.6%
Urban 88.4%
Number of Foundations = 2,433

Town and Rural 7.1%
Urban 92.9%
Total Assets = $24.4 billion

Town and Rural 6.9%
Urban 93.1%
Total Giving = $1.5 billion

*"Urban" corresponds to Metropolitan Areas designated by the U.S. Office of Management and Budget (OMB).

"Town and Rural" include all locations outside the OMB-defined Metropolitan Areas.

DOING YOUR HOMEWORK: HOW TO RESEARCH A GRANTMAKER

Doing your homework will assure that your proposal will be sent to foundations or corporations that make grants to your type of organization, in the geographic area in which you function and for your field of interest. Foundations and corporations reject many of the proposals they receive because the proposals do not fit their guidelines. Be clear about your goals, the needs to be met by your project, the amount of money necessary to achieve objectives, and the availability of funds from other sources—especially local support.

If you represent a small organization or a new organization looking for funding for a project limited to the local community, first seek local funding through your own local constituency, community support and neighborhood business donations. Starting with community fund-raising efforts now may help secure funding for a larger, more important project in the future.

Foundation or corporate funding is not for everyone. A great deal of time, frustration, and disappointment will be saved if you assess the appropriateness of foundation/corporate funding in advance.

1. CHECK THESE SITES ON THE INTERNET

◆ Go to foundationcenter.org to learn about the *Foundation Center's Guide to Grantseeking on the Web* and link to Foundation Finder. For the most comprehensive and current data, turn to the *Foundation Directory Online* for all currently active U.S. grantmakers, over 101,000. It provides links to foundation 990 or 990-PF tax returns, facts on over 2.5 million recent grants, and over 523,000 key decision makers. Preview this fundraising tool at fconline.foundationcenter.org

◆ GuideStar: guidestar.org for a copy of a foundation 990 or 990-PF form, the annual filing required by the IRS.

◆ The Grantsmanship Center: tgci.com for training and resources on fundraising

◆ Idealist: idealist.org

◆ *The Chronicle of Philanthropy*: philanthropy.com

◆ *The Dorothy A. Johnson Center for Philanthropy & Nonprofit Leadership*: gvsu.edu/jcp

◆ State and federal grant information can be found at michigan.gov and grants.gov

◆ groundspring.org: an online fundraising resource.

2. USE THE MICHIGAN FOUNDATION DIRECTORY

Because almost all funding is local, start with foundations in Michigan. Most public libraries and each of the Foundation Center's Cooperating Collections listed in the next section have copies, or contact the Council of Michigan Foundations at michiganfoundations.org to purchase a copy of *The Michigan Foundation Directory*, 2011—available in print. Use the "Subject Index" and the "Geographic Index" to begin establishing a list. Using the main entries, note each foundation's and corporation's purposes and limitations to rule out those that are inappropriate. If the foundation or corporation publishes an annual report, see if it is available in the Cooperating Collection or online.

For further information on the grant records of Michigan foundations, consult the annual tax returns (Form 990-PF for private foundations, Form 990 for community foundations) filed with the Internal Revenue Service that include a complete list of grants for the year indicated. Many foundations include their return on their web site. You can also view the 990s and 990-PFs at foundationcenter.org or guidestar.org.

3. VISIT A FOUNDATION CENTER COOPERATING COLLECTION

The Foundation Center (foundationcenter.org) has established a network of free funding information centers in libraries, community foundations, and nonprofit centers in Michigan. We encourage you to visit one. Each of these centers has the same basic collection of information on state and national foundations (including 990-PF forms for Michigan private foundations) and corporate giving programs, along with supplementary materials (books, periodicals, annual reports, newsletters, and press clippings) on grantsmanship, fundraising and philanthropy. Please telephone individual sites for more information about their holdings and hours.

◆ **ALPENA COUNTY LIBRARY**
211 N. 1st St.
Alpena 49707
(989) 356-6188

◆ **UNIVERSITY OF MICHIGAN**
Harlan Hatcher Graduate Library
920 N. University
Ann Arbor 48109
(734) 615-8610

◆ **WILLARD PUBLIC LIBRARY**
Nonprofit and Funding Resource Collections
7 W. Van Buren St.
Battle Creek 49017
(269) 968-8166

◆ **WAYNE STATE UNIVERSITY**
Purdy/Kresge Library
134 Purdy/Kresge Library
Detroit 48202
(313) 577-6424

◆ **MICHIGAN STATE UNIVERSITY**
Funding Center
100 Library
East Lansing 48824
(517) 432-6123

◆ **FARMINGTON COMMUNITY LIBRARY**
32737 W. 12 Mile Rd.
Farmington Hills 48334
(248) 553-0300

◆ **FLINT PUBLIC LIBRARY**
1026 E. Kearsley St.
Flint 48502
(810) 232-7111

◆ **FREMONT AREA DISTRICT LIBRARY**
104 E. Main St.
Fremont 49412
(231) 924-3480

◆ **GRAND RAPIDS PUBLIC LIBRARY**
111 Library St. NE
Grand Rapids 49503
(616) 988-5400

◆ **PORTAGE LAKE DISTRICT LIBRARY**
58 Huron St.
Houghton 49931
(906) 482-4570

◆ **KALAMAZOO PUBLIC LIBRARY**
ONEplace
315 S. Rose St.
Kalamazoo 49007
(269) 553-7844

◆ **MASON COUNTY DISTRICT LIBRARY**
Ludington Library
217 E. Ludington Ave.
Ludington 49431
(231) 843-8465

◆ **PETER WHITE PUBLIC LIBRARY**
217 N. Front Street
Marquette 49855
(906) 226-4311

◆ **PETOSKEY PUBLIC LIBRARY**
500 E. Mitchell St.
Petoskey 49770
(231) 758-3100

◆ **LAKE SUPERIOR STATE UNIVERSITY**
Kenneth J. Shouldice Library
906 Ryan St.
Sault Ste. Marie, MI 49783
(906) 635-2815

◆ **HOYT PUBLIC LIBRARY**
505 Janes Ave.
Saginaw 48607
(989) 755-0904

◆ **TRAVERSE AREA DISTRICT LIBRARY**
610 Woodmere Ave.
Traverse City 49686
(231) 932-8500

◆ **ROMEO DISTRICT LIBRARY**
Graubner Library
5821 Van Dyke
Washington 48095
(586) 752-0603

THE COOPERATING COLLECTIONS' NATIONAL DIRECTORIES OF GRANTS TO ORGANIZATIONS

Check to see if the national directories contain any additional information on the Michigan foundations or corporations on your list. They can also be used to determine which non-Michigan foundations might give to Michigan organizations. (These non-Michigan grantmakers are included in *The Michigan Foundation Directory*, as well.)

The Foundation Directory describes 10,000 of the top foundations, including corporate foundations, by total giving. These largest foundations also award 89 percent of all U.S. grant dollars. This directory contains a statistical breakdown of the foundation community by geography, assets, and grants.

The Foundation Directory, Part 2 includes the next 10,000 largest foundations, those with grant programs between $125,000–$370,000. Complete coverage is provided on 10,000 foundations.

The Foundation Center's *National Directory of Corporate Giving*, 17th Edition, published in 2011, includes complete corporate giving profiles on over 3,300 company-sponsored foundations and over 1,680 corporate giving programs from close to 4,150 companies.

Begin your list of potential funding sources with those whose recent grants indicate a possible interest in your project, that are located or award grants in your geographic area and that have made grants in dollar amounts comparable to the amount you are seeking.

NATIONAL DIRECTORIES OF GRANTS TO INDIVIDUALS

Over 9,500 foundations that conduct ongoing grant programs for individuals are included in *Foundation Grants to Individuals*, 20th edition. (This publication is also available online at gtionline.foundationcenter.org.) Research can be done by subject, type of support, geography, company-related grants, and specific educational institutions. General welfare and medical assistance are included, as well as scholarships, loans, prizes, and travel grants. Program limitations are also described.

4. COMMUNICATE DIRECTLY WITH THE FOUNDATION OR CORPORATION

Call those foundations that are staffed or write to request an annual report or guidelines. Always check the foundation's web site.

ADVICE FROM A FOUNDATION PROGRAM OFFICER

THE PROPOSAL PROCESS

The business of foundations is to give away money to qualified organizations for the purposes approved by the foundations' board of trustees. To carry out their charitable mission, foundations need good ideas—good projects effectively presented in written proposals from nonprofit organizations. Foundations need nonprofits' problem-solving skills and ability as much as nonprofits need foundation financial support.

The process through which foundations award grants varies greatly. *The Michigan Foundation Directory* reveals the great diversity of programming interests and priorities among foundations. However, the basics of the proposal process are the same whether for community foundations, corporate foundations, or independent foundations and whether you apply via mail, email or online. Understanding both sides of the process, i.e. how the nonprofit requests funds and what the foundation's perspective is, will improve your proposal and the likelihood of foundation support. It will also help you realistically assess your chances and make decisions about whether or not to apply for a grant.

The proposal process has four essential phases: 1) Pre-Proposal Preparation, 2) The Proposal, 3) The Grant Decision, and 4) The Grant's Execution. Think through all four phases relative to your idea before writing and submitting the proposal.

PRE-PROPOSAL PREPARATION

Grants are made to qualified tax-exempt organizations under federal (not state) law, since foundation taxes and potential penalties are assessed by the federal government. "Tax-exempt" refers to Section 501(c)(3) of the Internal Revenue Code and to its classification that an organization is not a private foundation as defined under Section 509(a). Evidence of tax exemption may be requested with the proposal. Make sure it is current information and that the name on the Treasury Department's letter is the same as that on your organization's letterhead.

Foundations are permitted to make grants to individuals or to non-501(c)(3) organizations to carry out charitable activities. However, few foundations do so since the Internal Revenue Service requires them to exercise special "expenditure responsibility" over such grants. The few foundations that do make grants directly to individuals usually have special programs for this purpose.

Foundations scrutinize all indicators that help determine whether an organization is stable, has a strong board of directors, has adequate finances and related oversight, and, perhaps most importantly, has the capacity to successfully operate the proposed program. Therefore, the proposal writer must know the nonprofit organization well and be able to succinctly summarize its history, operations, mission, and sources of revenue.

Define the purpose of your funding request before researching foundations. Without a clear purpose, it is much more difficult to assess the likelihood of a particular foundation's interest. A foundation looks at the grant's purpose as well as the organization requesting the funds to determine whether a proposal fits within its funding guidelines and priorities. A foundation's program and geographic areas are usually published in its annual report, printed guidelines, and/or on its web site.

Make sure your proposal's purpose fits the foundation both programmatically and geographically. Learn what grants the foundation made in the past, which are listed in its annual report or Form 990-PF. This form is available at Foundation Center Cooperating Collections, on many foundation web sites, and at foundationcenter.org or guidestar.org. However, note that there is no guarantee that similar grants will be made in the future.

The Michigan Foundation Directory is a great place to begin foundation research, but try going directly to the foundation for a copy of its latest annual report or guidelines. Guidelines are subject to change. Follow the guidelines or the request may be denied on a technicality or not considered at all. If your program or organization doesn't fit the foundation's stated interests, it is a waste of time to send a proposal. Some foundations will respond to a letter of inquiry or discuss it at a meeting or over the phone, and some provide preview questions on their web sites.

Tailor your proposal to fit each foundation on your list. "Tailor" means knowing to whom to address the request at the foundation, understanding required information about the foundation's areas of interest, and then focusing your proposal to meet the foundation's funding priorities. In some cases, a foundation might completely fund your program. However, in many cases, you may want to ask different foundations to support different aspects or components of your program. Some are more willing to provide grants for furniture or computer equipment. Others emphasize support for construction and renovation of facilities. Still others limit their support to actual delivery of specific human services.

Start with foundations close to home. These will be more concerned with local organizations and problems than large foundations with national programs. Generally, the latter are looking for programs with national significance and solutions to problems that can be applied elsewhere. And local foundations generally have made a much larger investment in your community over time than national foundations.

Remember that foundation people exchange information about proposals and grantees, just as you exchange information about potential grantors with other nonprofits. Although it may be appropriate to directly contact trustees of family foundations and foundations which serve as extensions of the donor's personal philanthropy, it is not appropriate with staffed foundations. Trying to influence trustees can even have an adverse effect on your proposal. Professional staffs are employed to communicate with potential grantees. They will help you as much as they can.

THE PROPOSAL

There are many books and articles about how to write proposals that can be helpful. Some foundations have specific formats to follow. Some do not. Many Michigan grantmakers use a version of the Council of Michigan Foundations' *Common Grant Application Template* that can be found at the end of this section and on the web at michiganfoundations.org. Proposals can be elaborate or simply written in letter format. Foundations are increasingly using online application systems—if you apply online, be sure to follow the directions and pay attention to the recommended length of responses. In any event, brief (5-7 pages), tightly written proposals are preferred. But be sure to include all the information requested in a foundation's guidelines. If something is not applicable, say so and why not.

Follow the outline of the required information as contained in the guidelines. Do not include an administrative charge for items already accounted for in the budget. Avoid jargon and define terms. Assume the foundation is not familiar with your organization. Include a brief history, since most foundations will not take the time to learn more about it.

Proposals not only ask for a grant, but they build the case for awarding one to your organization. State why the organization is qualified to conduct the program, what long-lasting results will come of it, how the grant funds will be spent, the organization's past successes with similar efforts and the expertise of the

staff. Be sure to document any claims made; superlatives are ineffective. Avoid emotional language or stories that do not enhance a proposal.

Emphasize how the grant program's performance will be evaluated. Evaluation should be planned from the beginning with specific data collection and analysis outlined in the proposal. Make sure the organization can complete the grant's program and also document its outcomes. You may also use the Council of Michigan Foundations' *Common Report Form Template* found at the end of this section and on the web at michiganfoundations.org.

Foundations do not want to support a program over a long period nor do they want grantees to become dependent upon their funding. Foundations want to know how the program or purpose will be funded when the grant concludes. "Increased fundraising" is insufficient; list specific sources of future revenue or those likely to give to sustain the program.

THE GRANT DECISION

Many more proposals are denied than funded by any foundation. However, some grant requests may be deferred for a future decision. Some grants are awarded for a lesser amount than originally requested.

Letters of denial may not state specifically why a proposal was denied. However, it is rarely because there was something "wrong" with the proposal that if fixed would then result in a grant. Usually proposals are declined because: a) the foundation's grant budget was insufficient, b) the program or purpose wasn't a priority, or c) the organization did not demonstrate the capacity to carry out the proposal.

The letter confirming the award will include the foundation's conditions and expectations. Prompt acknowledgement and thanks on receipt of the grant letter is the right thing to do. The executive director or an officer of the organization may be asked to complete a grant contract confirming its tax-exempt status, the purpose for which the money will be used, and that the organization will refrain from activities that jeopardize its tax-exempt status. If the agreement is not adhered to, the foundation could ask for the grant's return. Many foundations also reserve the right to audit your financial records on a project.

THE GRANT'S EXECUTION

During the period of the grant, your organization is responsible for ensuring that every effort is made to conduct the program as outlined in the proposal. However, changes may be necessary. If so, contact the foundation and let them know of changes. They will appreciate knowing earlier rather than later. The foundation is interested in the program's progress. Send periodic reports every six months with copies of any publicity about the program, particularly if it mentions the foundation.

An accounting that confirms expenditure of the grant funds is due to the foundation at the close of the grant period. Share future plans for the program and how the organization plans to build upon progress made during the grant. Let the foundation know if other organizations are interested in your program.

CONCLUSION

The proposal process and the grant decision are not mysterious. Each foundation does its best to serve its community within the framework of its mission and funding guidelines. By doing your research, you will understand what foundations look for in terms of form and content. However, the original, creative idea of the proposal is still up to you. Foundation grant decisions are made in many different ways but never in a vacuum. Your proposal competes in a "marketplace of ideas." The proposal will ultimately succeed or fail on its own merits.

TYPICAL QUESTIONS A FOUNDATION MIGHT ASK ABOUT A GRANT APPLICATION

A foundation staff member or trustee may ask any combination of the following questions when considering a grant request. Consider how your proposal provides the answers. Does the application include:

- ◆ verification of 501(c)(3) non-profit charitable tax status?
- ◆ how the project addresses the Foundation's current priorities?
- ◆ a brief summary of the project?
- ◆ making a case for the need, including data if available?
- ◆ how constituents will be actively involved in planning and evaluating the project?
- ◆ demographics of the population served, staff, and board of trustees?
- ◆ if the project duplicates or overlaps other existing programs?
- ◆ evidence of collaboration with other nonprofits?
- ◆ request for new and innovative activities or for general operating support for an ongoing effort?
- ◆ measurable outcomes and provision for project evaluation?
- ◆ a one or multiple year budget?
- ◆ other potential and actual sources of support?
- ◆ information on the role of the executive director and other managers of the project?
- ◆ a listing of the board of directors with their organization affiliation?
- ◆ the current year's board-approved operating budget?
- ◆ the most recent audit?

COMMON GRANT APPLICATION TEMPLATE

The following form was composed by a committee of private, corporate and community foundations, all members of the Council of Michigan Foundations. The idea of the Common Grant Application is to eliminate the grantseeker's burden of creating multiple versions of a request in order to meet differing information requirements of grantmakers. It also offers funders more consistent information for evaluating a pool of requests. Many foundations now have their own application forms, with many using online forms.

Keep in mind that every grantmaker has different guidelines and priorities, as well as different deadlines and timetables, and any funder that has agreed to accept this form may request additional information. While many foundations have their own application form, this template can still serve as an excellent guide to writing a proposal. Although forms and styles may vary, this Form includes all the basics required for a complete proposal.

GRANT APPLICATION COVER SHEET
TEMPLATE

Date of Application: _____

Legal name of organization applying: _____
(Should be same as on IRS determination letter and as supplied on IRS Form 990)

Year Founded: _____ Current Operating Budget: _____

Executive Director: _____ E-mail Address: _____

Contact person/title/phone number:
(if different from executive director): _____

Address *(principal/administrative office):* _____

City/State/Zip: _____

Phone number: _____ Fax Number: _____
(include area code)   *(include area code)*

Web address: _____

List any previous support from this funder in the last 5 years: _____

_____

_____

Project Name: _____

Purpose of Grant *(one sentence):* _____

_____

_____

Dates of the Project: _____ Amount Requested: $_____

Total Project Cost: $_____

Geographic Area Served: _____

_____   _____
Signature, Chairperson, Board of Directors   ***Signature, Executive Director***

_____   _____
Typed Name and Title   ***Typed Name and Title***

_____   _____
Date   ***Date***

GRANT APPLICATION FORMAT

Please provide the following information in this order. Use these headings, subheadings and numbers provided in your own word processing format, thus leaving flexibility for length of response.

A. NARRATIVE

1. **Executive Summary**

   Begin with a half-page executive summary. Briefly explain why your agency is requesting this grant, what outcomes you hope to achieve, and how you will spend the funds if the grant is made.

2. **Purpose of Grant**

   Statement of needs/problems to be addressed; description of target population and how they will benefit.
   Description of project goals, measurable objectives, action plans, and statements as to whether this is a new or ongoing part of the sponsoring organization.
   Timetable for implementation.
   List of other partners in the project and their roles.
   List of similar existing projects or agencies, if any, and explain how your agency or proposal differs, and what effort will be made to work cooperatively.
   Description of the active involvement of constituents in defining problems to be addressed, making policy, and planning the program.
   Description of the qualifications of key staff and volunteers that will ensure the success of the program.
   List of specific staff training needs for this project.
   Long-term strategies for funding this project at end of grant period.

3. **Evaluation**

   Plans for evaluation including how success will be defined and measured.
   Description of how evaluation results will be used and/or disseminated and, if appropriate, how the project will be replicated.
   Description of the active involvement of constituents in evaluating the program.

4. **Budget Narrative/Justification**

   Grant budget; use the **Grant Budget Format** that follows, if appropriate.
   A plan (on a separate sheet) that shows how each budget item relates to the project and how the budgeted amount was calculated.
   List of amounts requested of other foundations, corporations and other funding sources to which this proposal has been submitted.
   List of priority items in the proposed in the proposed budget, in the event that we are unable to meet your full request.

5. **Organization Information**

   Brief summary of organization's history.
   Brief statement of organization's mission and goals.
   Description of current programs, activities and accomplishments.
   Organizational chart, including board, staff and volunteer involvement.

B. ATTACHMENTS

1. A copy of the current IRS determination letter indicating 501(c)(3) tax-exempt status.
2. List of Board of Directors with affiliations.
3. Finances:
   Organization's current annual operating budget, including expenses and revenue.
   Most recent annual financial statement (independently audited, if available; otherwise, attach Form 990).
4. Letters of support should verify project need and collaboration with other organizations. (Optional)
5. Annual report, if available.

GRANT BUDGET FORMAT

Below is a listing of standard budget items. Please provide the project budget in this format and in this order.

A. Organizational fiscal year: _____

B. Time period this budget covers: _____

C. For a CAPITAL request, substitute your format for listing expenses. These will likely include: architectural fees, land/building purchase, construction costs, and campaign expenses.

D. **Expenses:** include a *description and the total amount* for each of the following budget categories, in this order:

	Amount requested from this organization	Total project expenses
Salaries	$_____	$_____
Payroll Taxes	$_____	$_____
Fringe Benefits	$_____	$_____
Consultants and Professional Fees	$_____	$_____
Insurance	$_____	$_____
Travel	$_____	$_____
Equipment	$_____	$_____
Supplies	$_____	$_____
Printing and Copying	$_____	$_____
Telephone and Fax	$_____	$_____
Postage and Delivery	$_____	$_____
Rent	$_____	$_____
Utilities	$_____	$_____
Maintenance	$_____	$_____
Evaluation	$_____	$_____
Marketing	$_____	$_____
Other (specify)	$_____	$_____
Total amount requested	$_____ *Total project expenses*	$_____

E. **Revenue:** include a **description and the total amount** for each of the following budget categories, in this order; please indicate which sources of revenue are committed and which are pending.

	Committed	*Pending*
1. Grants/Contracts/Contributions		
Local Government	$_____	$_____
State Government	$_____	$_____
Federal Government	$_____	$_____
Foundations (itemize)	$_____	$_____
Corporations (itemize)	$_____	$_____
Individuals	$_____	$_____
Other (specify)	$_____	$_____
2. Earned Income		
Events	$_____	$_____
Publications and Products	$_____	$_____
3. Membership Income	$_____	$_____
4. In-Kind Support	$_____	$_____
5. Other *(specify)*	$_____	$_____
Total Revenue	$_____	$_____

COMMON REPORT FORM

COMMON REPORT FORM FORMAT
Cover Sheet

The purpose of the Common Report Form is to help grantees save time in reporting to you and to help grantmakers simplify the process of gathering standard grant evaluation information.

Date of Report: _____

Legal name of organization applying:_____
(Should be same as on IRS determination letter and as supplied on IRS Form 990.)

Executive Director: _____Phone number_____

Contact person/title/phone number
(if different from executive director): _____

_____

Address *(principal/administrative office):* _____

City/State/Zip: _____

Fax Number: _____E-mail Address:_____

Project/Program Name:_____

Purpose of Grant *(one sentence)*:_____

_____

_____

Dates of the Project:_____ Amount of Grant Awarded: $_____

Have there been any changes to your organization's IRS 501(c)(3) not-for-profit status since your request for this grant? *(yes or no)*:_____If yes, please explain:_____

_____

Dates covered by this report: from_____to_____.

Check one: ____ This is an interim report   ____ This is a final report

_____   _____
Signature, Executive Director   *Date*

_____
Typed Name and Title

COMMON REPORT FORM FORMAT
Narrative & Financials

I. *Narrative* — Two to five pages.

    A.   **Results**
1. List the original goals and objectives of the grant, and tell how they were met during this reporting period. Describe current status on meeting any special terms of this grant (e.g. challenges, contingencies, etc.).
2. If possible, explain results in outcome-based terms. For example, what difference did this grant make in your community and for the population you are serving?
3. Variance from original project plans often occurs. In what ways did the actual project vary from your initial plans? Describe how and why.
4. Describe any unanticipated benefits or challenges encountered with this project.
5. Describe how collaborative/cooperative efforts with individuals and organizations involved in planning, implementing, funding and/or evaluating this project/grant affected outcomes.

    B.   **Lessons Learned**
1. What are the most important outcomes and lessons learned from this project?
2. What recommendations would you make to the Foundation or to other project directors working in this area?
3. If you were to undertake this project again, would you do anything differently? If yes, please explain.
4. Other lessons?

    C.   **Future Plans**
1. What is your vision of this project over the next three years? Include plans and rationale for ongoing funding, expansion, replication or termination.

    D.   **Public Relations**
1. Provide a "human interest" story that helps explain the success of the project.
2. Attach any printed material relating to the funded project: press or news items, brochures, letters of support, photographs, etc.

II. *Financials*

    A.   Using the budget from the original application, provide detailed expenses and income for the project for this period. Provide narrative on any variances from the original projected budget.

    B.   Include a complete, detailed accounting of how the specific grant dollars from this grant were spent.

HOW TO USE THE MICHIGAN FOUNDATION DIRECTORY

ARRANGEMENT

The descriptive directory of *The Michigan Foundation Directory* is arranged in five sections: independent foundations, corporate funders, community foundations, public charities, and operating foundations. Within each grantmaker type section, the entries of both Michigan funders and out-of-state funders are arranged alphabetically by grantmaker name. Each entry is assigned a sequence number, and references in the indexes refer to these entry numbers.

WHAT'S IN AN ENTRY?

There are 37 basic data elements that could be included in a *Michigan Foundation Directory* entry. The content of entries varies widely due to differences in the grantmaker type, size, and nature of grantmaker programs and the availability of information from grantmakers. Specific data elements that could be included are:

1. The full legal **name of the grantmaker**.

2. Other names associated with the grantmaker, such as **former name**, **also known as**, and **doing business as**.

3. The **street address**, **city**, **zip code**, and **county** of the grantmaker's principal office.

4. The **telephone number** of the grantmaker.

5. The name and title of the **contact person** at the grantmakers.

6. Any **additional address** (such as a separate application address) supplied by the grantmaker. Additional telephone or fax numbers as well as e-mail and/or URL addresses also may be listed here.

7. **Establishment data**, including the legal form (usually a trust or corporation) and the year and state in which the grantmaker was established.

8. The **donor(s)** or principal contributor(s) to the grantmaker, including individuals, families, and corporations. If a donor is deceased, the symbol ‡ follows the name.

9. **Grantmaker type:** community, company-sponsored, independent, or operating foundation; corporate giving program; or public charity.

10. The **year-end date** of the grantmaker's accounting period for which financial data is supplied.

11. **Revenue:** the total amount of contributions and support received by a public charity, including investment income, program service revenue, net profits from sale of assets, etc.

12. **Assets:** the total value of the grantmaker's investments at the end of the accounting period. In a few instances, grantmakers that act as "pass-throughs" for annual corporate or individual gifts report zero assets.

13. **Asset type:** generally, assets are reported at market value (M) or ledger value (L).

14. **Gifts received:** the total amount of new capital received by the grantmaker in the year of record.

15. **Expenditures:** total disbursements of the grantmaker, including overhead expenses (salaries; investment, legal, and other professional fees; interest; rent; etc.) and federal excise taxes, as well as the total amount paid for grants, scholarships, and matching gifts.

16. **Total giving:** Gifts, contributions, grants paid; total amount for all grants and contributions during the year. This amount generally excludes loans and the costs of foundation-operated programs, but includes all other forms of support such as grants, scholarships, and employee matching gifts.

17. **Program services expenses:** includes all expenses by public charities that are directly involved in carrying out charitable activities, including total grants paid.

18. The total amount of **qualifying distributions** made by the grantmaker in the year of record. This figure includes all grants paid, qualifying administrative expenses, loans and program-related investments, set-asides, and amounts aid to acquire assets used directly in carrying out charitable purposes.

19. The dollar value and number of **grants paid** during the year, with the largest grant paid **(high)** and smallest grant paid **(low)**. When supplied by the grantmaker, the average range of grant payments is also indicated. Grant figures generally do not include commitments for future payment or amounts spent for grants to individuals, employee matching gifts, loans, or grantmaker-administered programs.

20. The total dollar value of **set-asides** made by the grantmaker during the year. Although set-asides count as qualifying distributions toward the foundation's annual payout requirement, they are distinct from any amounts listed as grants paid.

21. The total amount and number of **grants made directly to or on behalf of individuals**, including scholarships, fellowships, awards, and medical payments. When supplied by the grantmaker, high, low, and average range are also indicated.

22. The dollar amount and number of **employee matching gifts** awarded, generally by company-sponsored grantmakers.

23. The total dollars expended for **programs administered by the grantmaker** and the number of grantmaker-administered programs. These programs can include museums or other institutions supported exclusively by the grantmaker, research programs administered by the grantmaker, etc.

24. The dollar amount and number of **loans/program-related investments** made to nonprofit organizations by the grantmaker. These can include emergency loans to help nonprofits that are waiting for grants or other income payments, etc. When supplied by the grantmaker, high, low, and average range are also indicated.

25. The number of **loans to individuals** and the total amount loaned. When supplied by the grantmaker, high, low, and average range are also indicated.

26. The monetary value and number of **in-kind gifts**.

27. The **purpose and activities**, in general terms, of the grantmaker. This statement reflects funding interests as expressed by the grantmaker or, if no grantmaker statement is available, an analysis of the actual grants awarded by the grantmaker during the most recent period for which public records exist. Many grantmakers leave statements of purpose intentionally broad, indicating only the major program areas within which they fund. More specific areas of interest can often be found in the "Fields of Interest" section of the entry.

28. The **fields of interest** reflected in the grantmaker's giving program. The terminology used in this section conforms to the Foundation Center's Grants Classification System (GCS). The terms also provide access to grantmaker entries through the Subject Index at the back of the volume.

29. The **international giving interests** of the grantmaker.

30. The **types of support** (such as endowment funds, support for building/renovation, equipment, fellowships, etc.) offered by the grantmaker. Definitions of the terms used to describe the forms of support available are provided at the beginning of the Type of Support Index at the back of this volume.

31. Any stated **limitations** on the grantmaker's giving program, including geographic preferences, restrictions by subject focus or type of recipient, or specific types of support the grantmaker cannot provide.

32. **Publications** or other printed materials distributed by the grantmaker that describe its activities and giving program. These can include annual or multi-year reports, newsletters, corporate giving reports, informational brochures, grant lists, etc.

33. **Application information**, including the preferred form of application, the number of copies of proposals requested, application deadlines, frequency and dates of board meetings, and the general amount of time the grantmaker requires to notify applicants of the board's decision. Some grantmakers have indicated that their funds are currently committed to ongoing projects.

34. The names and titles of **officers**, **principal administrators**, **trustees**, **directors**, and members of other governing bodies. An asterisk following the individual's name indicates an officer who is also a trustee or director.

35. The number of professional and support **staff** employed by the grantmaker, and an indication of part-time or full-time status of these employees, as reported by the grantmaker.

36. **EIN:** the Employer Identification Number assigned to a foundation or public charity by the Internal Revenue Service for tax purposes. This number can be useful when ordering copies of the grantmaker's annual information return, Form 990-PF for foundations and Form 990 for public charities.

37. A list of **selected grants**, generally for those foundations with annual giving of at least $100,000. Up to ten grants reported during a given fiscal year may be provided. Grants to individuals are not included.

INDEXES

Five indexes to the descriptive entries are provided at the back of the book to assist grantseekers and other users of *The Michigan Foundation Directory*:

1. The **Grantmaker Name Index** is an alphabetical list of all grantmakers appearing in this edition of *The Michigan Foundation Directory*. Former, also known as, and doing business as names of grantmakers appear with "see" references to the appropriate entry numbers.

2. The **Types of Support Index** provides access to grantmaker entries by the specific types of support the grantmaker awards. A glossary of the forms of support listed appears at the beginning of the index. Under each type of support term, entry numbers are listed by state location and

abbreviated name of the grantmaker. Grantmakers that award grants on a national or international basis are indicated in bold type.

3. The **Subject Index** provides access to the giving interests of grantmakers based on the "Fields of Interest" sections of their entries. The terminology in the index conforms to the Foundation Center's Grants Classification System (GCS). A complete alphabetical list of the subject headings in the current edition is provided at the beginning of the index as well as "see also" references to related subject areas included in this volume. Under each subject term, entry numbers are listed by state location and abbreviated name of the grantmaker. As in the Types of Support Index, grantmakers that award grants on a national or international basis are indicated in bold type.

4. The **Geographic Index** references grantmaker entries by the state and city in which the grantmaker maintains its principal offices. Grantmakers that award grants on a national or international basis are indicated in bold type. The remaining grantmakers generally limit their giving to the county or city in which they are located.

5. The **Index to Donors, Officers, Trustees** is an alphabetical list of individual and corporate donors, officers, and members of governing boards whose names appear in *The Michigan Foundation Directory* entries. Many grantseekers find this index helpful in determining whether current or prospective members of their own governing boards, alumni of their schools, or current contributors are affiliated with any grantmakers.

DESCRIPTIVE DIRECTORY

INDEPENDENT FOUNDATIONS

1
41 Washington St. Foundation
914 S. Harbor Drive
Grand Haven, MI   49417-1745   (616) 850-1330
County: Ottawa
Contact: James P. Hovinga, Dir.

Established in 2003 in MI.
Donor: The James P. and Debra K. Hovinga Charitable Foundation.
Grantmaker type: Independent foundation.
Financial data (yr. ended 12/31/09): Assets, $1,282,648 (M); gifts received, $50,000; expenditures, $67,387; total giving, $58,000; qualifying distributions, $58,000; giving activities include $58,000 for 5 grants (high: $50,000; low: $1,000).
Fields of interest: Higher education, college; Education; Christian agencies & churches.
Limitations: Applications accepted. Giving primarily in Grand Rapids and Holland, MI.
Application information: Application form not required.
Deadline(s): None
Officer: Sue Boschma, Pres. and Treas.
Directors: Debra K. Hovinga; James P. Hovinga.
EIN: 611438980
Selected grants: The following grants were reported in 2006.
$25,000 to Kids Hope USA, Zeeland, MI.
$20,000 to Hope College, Holland, MI.
$10,000 to Western Theological Seminary, Holland, MI.
$5,000 to Bethany Christian Services, Grand Rapids, MI.
$3,000 to Words of Hope, Grand Rapids, MI.
$2,000 to Salvation Army, Port Huron, MI.
$1,000 to Christian Counseling Center, Grand Rapids, MI.
$500 to Alpine Chapel, Telluride, CO.
$500 to Safe Haven Ministries, Grand Rapids, MI.

2
Frances H. Abbott Memorial Foundation
c/o Fifth Third Bank
P.O. Box 3636
Grand Rapids, MI   49501-3636   (800) 400-0439
County: Kent
Application address: c/o Riverside-Brookfield High School, Attn.: Beth Augustine, 160 Ridgewood Rd., Riverside, IL 60546, tel.: (708) 442-7500

Established in IL.
Grantmaker type: Independent foundation.
Financial data (yr. ended 12/31/09): Assets, $17,477 (M); expenditures, $3,615; total giving, $0; qualifying distributions, $0.
Purpose and activities: Scholarship awards to graduating seniors of Riverside-Brookfield High School, Illinois.
Fields of interest: Higher education.
Type of support: Scholarships—to individuals.
Limitations: Giving limited to residents of Riverside, IL.
Application information:

Initial approach: Letter
Deadline(s): 1st Tuesday in May
Trustee: Fifth Third Bank.
EIN: 366672535

3
Edward & Marie Abele Memorial Fund
c/o Citizens Bank Wealth Management, N.A.
328 S. Saginaw St., MC 001065
Flint, MI   48502-1923
County: Genesee
Contact: Karen Schultz
Application address: c/o Abele Loan Comm., 5800 Weiss St., Saginaw, MI 48603-2762, tel.: (989) 799-7910

Established in MI.
Grantmaker type: Independent foundation.
Financial data (yr. ended 07/31/10): Assets, $396,017 (M); expenditures, $9,891; total giving, $0; qualifying distributions, $8,834.
Purpose and activities: Student loans to practicing Catholics in Saginaw County, Michigan.
Fields of interest: Education; Catholic agencies & churches.
Type of support: Student loans—to individuals.
Limitations: Applications accepted. Giving limited to Saginaw County, MI.
Application information: Application form required.
Initial approach: Request application form
Deadline(s): May 5
Trustee: Citizens Bank Wealth Management, N.A.
EIN: 386356628

4
Aboudane Family Foundation
5032 Parkwood Ct.
Flushing, MI   48433-1390
County: Genesee

Established in 2007 in MI.
Donor: Zakwan Aboudane.
Grantmaker type: Independent foundation.
Financial data (yr. ended 12/31/09): Assets, $29,184 (M); gifts received, $49,000; expenditures, $32,041; total giving, $28,144; qualifying distributions, $28,144; giving activities include $28,144 for 5 grants (high: $11,754; low: $2,260).
Limitations: Giving primarily in MI.
Officer: Zakwan Aboudane, Pres.
EIN: 261426333

5
Adray Foundation, Inc.
300 E. Long Lake Rd.
Ste. 200
Bloomfield Hills, MI   48304-2376
(248) 540-2300
County: Oakland
Contact: Joseph M. McGlynn, Dir.

Established in 1983 in MI.
Grantmaker type: Independent foundation.
Financial data (yr. ended 12/31/09): Assets, $607,282 (M); expenditures, $55,466; total giving, $34,606; qualifying distributions, $34,606; giving activities include $34,606 for 1 grant.
Purpose and activities: Giving for support for athletics with an emphasis on hockey leagues.
Fields of interest: Athletics/sports, amateur leagues; Athletics/sports, winter sports.
Type of support: General/operating support; Equipment; Endowments.
Limitations: Giving limited to MI.
Application information: Application form not required.
Initial approach: Proposal
Deadline(s): None
Directors: Deborah Adray; Louise Adray; Joseph M. McGlynn.
EIN: 382435251

6
The Akers Foundation
840 N. Lake Shore Dr., Ste. 403
Chicago, IL   60611-2489   (312) 475-1131
County: Cook
Contact: James Akers, Pres.

Established in 1958 in OH.
Donor: Phyllis M. Akers.
Grantmaker type: Independent foundation.
Financial data (yr. ended 12/31/09): Assets, $1,065,667 (M); expenditures, $63,650; total giving, $57,420; qualifying distributions, $59,334; giving activities include $57,420 for 47 grants (high: $10,000; low: $25).
Fields of interest: Higher education; Health organizations; Human services; Jewish federated giving programs; Jewish agencies & synagogues.
Type of support: General/operating support.
Limitations: Applications accepted. Giving primarily in MI and OH. No grants to individuals.
Application information: Application form not required.
Initial approach: Letter
Deadline(s): None
Officers: James Akers, Pres.; Joel Levine, Secy.
EIN: 346549129

7
The Aletheia Foundation
P.O. Box 127
Belmont, MI   49306-0127   (616) 784-7303
County: Kent
Contact: Connie Wynalda, V.P.

Established in 2004 in MI.
Grantmaker type: Independent foundation.
Financial data (yr. ended 12/31/09): Assets, $4,120 (M); expenditures, $670; total giving, $300; qualifying distributions, $300; giving activities include $300 for grants.
Limitations: Applications accepted. Giving primarily in MI. No grants to individuals.

Application information:
Initial approach: Letter
Deadline(s): None
Officers: Robert Wynalda, Pres. and Treas.; Connie
Wynalda, V.P. and Secy.
Director: Robert Wynalda III.
EIN: 201861132

8

Alexandrowski Family Foundation, Inc.
7633 Quackenbush Rd.
Reading, MI 49274-9625   (517) 283-3723
County: Hillsdale
Contact: Muriel F. Alexandrowski, Pres.

Established in MI.
Donor: Muriel F. Alexandrowski.
Grantmaker type: Independent foundation.
Financial data (yr. ended 12/31/09): Assets,
$22,518 (M); gifts received, $20,000;
expenditures, $9,531; total giving, $9,531;
qualifying distributions, $9,531; giving activities
include $9,531 for grants.
Fields of interest: Higher education.
Type of support: Scholarship funds.
Limitations: Giving primarily in Hillsdale, MI.
Application information:
Initial approach: Letter with college transcripts
Deadline(s): None
Officers: Muriel F. Alexandrowski, Pres.; Joseph A.
Alexandrowski, V.P.
EIN: 383443665

9

Allen Foundation, Inc.
P.O. Box 1606
Midland, MI 48641-1606
County: Midland
Contact: Dale Baum, Secy.
FAX: (989) 832-8842; URL: http://
www.allenfoundation.org/

Established in 1975 in MI.
Grantmaker type: Independent foundation.
Financial data (yr. ended 12/31/09): Assets,
$9,978,169 (M); expenditures, $571,362; total
giving, $517,847; qualifying distributions,
$517,847; giving activities include $517,847 for 13
grants (high: $77,300; low: $10,000).
Purpose and activities: The foundation focuses on
projects that benefit nutritional programs in the
areas of education, training and research. A lower
priority is given to proposals that help solve
immediate or emergency hunger and malnutrition
problems.
Fields of interest: Higher education; Hospitals
(general); Nutrition.
Limitations: Applications accepted. Giving on a
national basis. No grants to individuals.
Publications: Application guidelines; Annual report;
Grants list.
Application information: Application forms and
latest information available on foundation web site.
All applications are to be submitted online.
Application form not required.
Initial approach: See web site
Copies of proposal: 1
Deadline(s): Dec. 31
Board meeting date(s): Annually
Final notification: June

Officers and Trustees:* Gail E. Lanphear,* Chair.;
Mark Ostahowski, M.D.*, Pres.; William
Lauderbach,* V.P., Finance; Dale Baum, Ph.D.*,
Secy.; William James Allen; Laurie Bouwman; Leslie
Hildebrandt, Ph.D.; Ann F. Jay; Charles B. Kendall;
Mary M. Neely; Pat Oriel, Ph.D.
Number of staff: 1 part-time support.
EIN: 510152562
Selected grants: The following grants were reported
in 2008.
$76,304 to Childrens Hospital Los Angeles, Los
Angeles, CA.
$75,000 to La Maestra Family Clinic, San Diego, CA.
$50,000 to Cedar Crest College, Allentown, PA.
$43,530 to Central Michigan University, Office of
Research & Sponsored Programs, Mount Pleasant,
MI.
$40,000 to Doernbecher Childrens Hospital
Foundation, Portland, OR.
$28,105 to Florence Crittenton Home and Services,
Helena, MT.
$20,000 to Regional Food Bank of Northeastern
New York, Latham, NY.
$4,475 to Baptist Child and Family Services, San
Antonio, TX.

10

William & Louise Allen Scholarship Trust
P.O. Box 3636
Grand Rapids, MI 49501-3636   (630) 468-8946
County: Kent
Application address: c/o Fifth Third Bank, Trust
Dept., 9400 S. Cicero Ave., Oak Lawn, IL
60453-2536, tel.: (708) 857-3475

Established in 2002 in IN.
Donor: Georgia Louise Allen†.
Grantmaker type: Independent foundation.
Financial data (yr. ended 12/31/09): Assets,
$512,896 (M); expenditures, $69,638; total giving,
$64,000; qualifying distributions, $64,275; giving
activities include $64,000 for 64 grants to
individuals (high: $1,000; low: $1,000).
Purpose and activities: Scholarship awards to
residents of Lake County, Indiana.
Fields of interest: Higher education.
Type of support: Scholarships—to individuals.
Limitations: Giving limited to Lake County, IN.
Application information: Application form required.
Initial approach: Letter
Deadline(s): Mar. 15
Trustee: Fifth Third Bank.
EIN: 266010234

11

Alliance for Gifted Children
2200 Fuller Ct., Ste. 1101B
Ann Arbor, MI 48105-2381   (734) 995-0999
County: Washtenaw
Contact: David Klimek Ph.D., Pres.

Established in 2001 in MI.
Donor: Nagy Family Foundation.
Grantmaker type: Independent foundation.
Financial data (yr. ended 12/31/09): Assets,
$9,345 (L); gifts received, $63,000; expenditures,
$91,429; total giving, $1,650; qualifying
distributions, $62,316; giving activities include
$1,650 for grants.

Purpose and activities: Provides ongoing
psychological therapy for children, including parent
and teacher consultations.
Fields of interest: Mental health, counseling/
support groups; Children/youth.
Limitations: Giving primarily in Ann Arbor, MI.
Application information: Application form required.
Deadline(s): None
Officer: David Klimek, Ph.D., Pres.
Directors: James Gleason, J.D.; Kathy S. Nagy;
Rebecca Patrias, M.D.; Timothy Wadhams.
EIN: 383555369

12

Almansour Family Foundation
7072 Woods W. Dr.
Flushing, MI 48433-9463
County: Genesee

Established in 2007 in MI.
Donor: Muhammad Almansour.
Grantmaker type: Independent foundation.
Financial data (yr. ended 12/31/09): Assets,
$68,199 (M); gifts received, $50,000;
expenditures, $15,301; total giving, $15,301;
qualifying distributions, $15,301; giving activities
include $15,301 for grants.
Fields of interest: Islam.
Limitations: Giving primarily in MI.
Officer: Muhammad Almansour, Pres.
EIN: 261519863

13

Almont-Dickinson Foundation
c/o Jerry L. Jonker
4680 Bradford St. N.E.
Grand Rapids, MI 49525-7040   (616) 942-8885
County: Kent

Grantmaker type: Independent foundation.
Financial data (yr. ended 12/31/07): Assets,
$102,380 (L); expenditures, $13,165; total giving,
$2,500; qualifying distributions, $2,500; giving
activities include $2,500 for grants.
Trustees: David Cole; William Jones; Douglas
Mennie; Marty Sherman.
EIN: 916477249

14

E. Bryce & Harriet Alpern Foundation
8809 Cold Spring
Potomac, MD 20854-2430   (248) 647-0386
County: Montgomery
Contact: Harriet Alpern, Tr.

Established in MI.
Donors: E. Bryce Alpern†; Harriet Alpern.
Grantmaker type: Independent foundation.
Financial data (yr. ended 10/31/10): Assets,
$1,683,238 (M); expenditures, $64,140; total
giving, $55,000; qualifying distributions, $56,173;
giving activities include $55,000 for 32 grants (high:
$11,000; low: $300).
Fields of interest: Arts; Higher education; Hospitals
(general); Human services; Jewish federated giving
programs; Jewish agencies & synagogues; Women.
Limitations: Applications accepted. Giving primarily
in MI. No grants to individuals.
Application information:

Initial approach: Letter
Deadline(s): None
Trustee: Abbey Alpern*; Dwight Alpern*.
EIN: 237441861

15
Ambrosiani Foundation
4253 W. Herbison Rd.
Dewitt, MI 48820-9214 (517) 669-5509
County: Clinton
Contact: Sherrill Ambrosiani Kovach, Tr.

Established in 1992 in WV.
Donors: F. Peter Ambrosiani; Irene P. Ambrosiani.
Grantmaker type: Independent foundation.
Financial data (yr. ended 12/31/09): Assets, $590,705 (M); expenditures, $30,977; total giving, $29,862; qualifying distributions, $29,862; giving activities include $29,862 for 25 grants (high: $7,000; low: $62).
Fields of interest: Higher education, college; Hospitals (general); Cancer research; Salvation Army; Catholic agencies & churches.
Limitations: Applications accepted. Giving primarily in MI. No grants to individuals.
Application information: Application form not required.
Initial approach: Letter
Trustees: David Kovach; Sherrill Ambrosiani Kovach.
EIN: 550668197

16
Americana Foundation
28115 Meadowbrook Rd.
Novi, MI 48377-3128 (248) 347-3863
County: Oakland
Contact: Marlene J. Fluharty, Exec. Dir.
FAX: (248) 347-3349; E-mail: fluhart5@msu.edu; URL: http://www.americanafoundation.org

Established in 1978 in MI.
Donors: Adolph H. Meyer†; Ida M. Meyer†.
Grantmaker type: Independent foundation.
Financial data (yr. ended 12/31/09): Assets, $17,465,753 (M); expenditures, $937,634; total giving, $644,642; qualifying distributions, $644,642; giving activities include $644,642 for 30 grants (high: $78,481; low: $500).
Purpose and activities: Support for education and advocacy programs that address issues of conserving agriculture and natural resources, and the preservation of the American heritage.
Fields of interest: Museums (history); Historic preservation/historical societies; Environment; Agriculture.
Type of support: General/operating support; Building/renovation; Program development; Conferences/seminars; Publication; Internship funds; Technical assistance; Matching/challenge support.
Limitations: Applications accepted. Giving primarily in MI. No support for private foundations or for political purposes. No grants to individuals, or for fundraising events, tables, or scholarships.
Publications: Annual report (including application guidelines); Grants list; Informational brochure (including application guidelines).
Application information: Council of Michigan Foundations Application Form accepted. Application form not required.

Initial approach: Letter or telephone
Copies of proposal: 1
Deadline(s): Jan. 10, Apr. 10, July 10, and Oct. 10
Board meeting date(s): Quarterly
Final notification: 3 months
Officers and Trustees:* Robert Janson,* Pres.; Jonathan Thomas,* V.P.; Thomas F. Ranger,* Treas.; Marlene J. Fluharty, Exec. Dir.; Norman Brown; Kathryn Eckert; Kate Harper; Gary Rentrop.
Number of staff: 1 full-time professional; 1 part-time support.
EIN: 382269431
Selected grants: The following grants were reported in 2005.
$110,500 to Michigan State University, East Lansing, MI. For historic farmhouse and grounds maintenance.
$50,000 to Colonial Williamsburg, Williamsburg, VA. For curatorial internship support.
$50,000 to Metropolitan Museum of Art, New York, NY. For historic furniture exhibition.
$50,000 to Philadelphia Museum of Art, Philadelphia, PA. For furniture conservation internship.
$30,000 to Headwaters Land Conservancy, Gaylord, MI. For farmland protection.
$25,000 to Pewabic Pottery, Detroit, MI. For historic streetscape construction.
$20,000 to Land Information Access Association, Traverse City, MI. For land use planning.
$20,000 to Sierra Club Foundation, San Francisco, CA. For Michigan forest management.
$15,000 to Ecology Center, Ann Arbor, MI. For farmland preservation.
$2,500 to EARTH University, San Jose, Costa Rica. For agriculture education.

17
Amy Foundation
c/o The Amy Writing Awards
P.O. Box 16091
Lansing, MI 48901-6091
County: Ingham
E-mail: amyfoundtn@aol.com; URL: http://www.amyfound.org/

Established in 1976.
Donors: Walter J. Russell†; Phyllis M. Russell.
Grantmaker type: Independent foundation.
Financial data (yr. ended 12/31/09): Assets, $271,704 (M); gifts received, $181,562; expenditures, $184,896; total giving, $55,623; qualifying distributions, $182,779; giving activities include $21,623 for 11 grants (high: $4,800; low: $250), and $34,000 for grants to individuals.
Purpose and activities: The foundation sponsors the Amy Foundation Writing Awards program to recognize creative, skillful writing that applies in a sensitive, thought-provoking manner the biblical principles to issues affecting the world today, with an emphasis on discipling; support also for Christian organizations.
Fields of interest: Christian agencies & churches.
Type of support: Grants to individuals; General/operating support.
Limitations: Applications accepted. Giving primarily in MI.
Publications: Informational brochure; Newsletter.
Application information: Applications accepted for Amy Writing Awards program only; see foundation web site for instructions on submission by mail or online.

Officers: James A. Russell, Acting Pres.; Phyllis M. Russell, V.P.; Kathy Brooks, Secy.-Treas.
Number of staff: 2 full-time professional; 1 full-time support.
EIN: 237044543

18
Harold A. and Marilyn Kay Andersen Charitable Trust
4210 Abby Ct., S.W.
Grandville, MI 49418
County: Kent
Contact: Harold and Kay Andresen
Application address: 6740 Oakville Rd., Chadwick, IL 61014

Donors: Harold Andresen; Marilyn Andresen.
Grantmaker type: Independent foundation.
Financial data (yr. ended 12/31/09): Assets, $1,525 (M); gifts received, $25,000; expenditures, $23,521; total giving, $23,500; qualifying distributions, $23,521; giving activities include $14,500 for 5 grants (high: $11,000; low: $500), and $9,000 for 10 grants to individuals (high: $1,500; low: $500).
Application information:
Initial approach: Proposal
Deadline(s): None
Trustee: Pamela K. Slagh.
EIN: 266260717

19
Frank N. Andersen Foundation
P.O. Box 225
Bridgeport, MI 48722-0225
County: Saginaw
Contact: William F. McNally, Pres.

Established in 1955 in MI.
Donor: Frank N. Andersen†.
Grantmaker type: Independent foundation.
Financial data (yr. ended 12/31/09): Assets, $9,844,038 (M); expenditures, $825,067; total giving, $741,800; qualifying distributions, $741,800; giving activities include $741,800 for grants.
Purpose and activities: Emphasis on human services and higher education; support also for arts and humanities.
Fields of interest: Performing arts; Historic preservation/historical societies; Higher education; Education; Food services; Human services.
Type of support: Capital campaigns; Building/renovation; Equipment; Scholarship funds.
Limitations: Applications accepted. Giving limited to Saginaw and Bay counties, MI. No grants to individuals.
Publications: Annual report.
Application information: Application form required.
Initial approach: Letter requesting application form
Copies of proposal: 1
Deadline(s): None
Board meeting date(s): Quarterly
Officers and Trustees:* William F. McNally,* Pres.; Gerald Barber,* V.P.; John Gilmour; Arnold L. Johnson; Barbara Lincoln; Paul Wendler.
Number of staff: 3 part-time professional.
EIN: 386062616
Selected grants: The following grants were reported in 2009.

$100,000 to Saginaw, City of, Saginaw, MI.
$50,000 to Boy Scouts of America, Lake Huron Area Council, Auburn, MI.
$50,000 to Delta College, University Center, MI.
$50,000 to Health Delivery, Saginaw, MI.
$50,000 to Saginaw Valley State University, University Center, MI.
$25,000 to City Rescue Mission of Saginaw, Saginaw, MI.
$25,000 to YMCA, Bay Area Family, Bay City, MI.
$21,000 to Andersen Enrichment Center, Saginaw, MI.
$20,000 to Child Abuse and Neglect Council of Saginaw County, Saginaw, MI.
$20,000 to Teen Challenge of Saginaw, Saginaw, MI.

20
Andrew F. & Mary H. Anderson Charitable Foundation

1140 Rosemary Ln.
Essexville, MI 48732-2017 (989) 667-4900
County: Bay
Contact: Mary H. Anderson, Pres.
Application address: 1601 Marquette St., Bay City, MI 48706-4196, tel.: (989) 667-4900

Established in 2003 in MI.
Donor: Mary H. Anderson.
Grantmaker type: Independent foundation.
Financial data (yr. ended 12/31/09): Assets, $352,802 (M); expenditures, $45,101; total giving, $40,000; qualifying distributions, $40,000; giving activities include $20,000 for 6 grants (high: $8,500; low: $1,500), and $20,000 for 5 grants to individuals (high: $5,000; low: $2,500).
Purpose and activities: Giving primarily to community foundations in Bay County, Michigan. Scholarship awards to students at Delta College, including the Midland, Michigan campus, who are residents of Bay County; also for students of Northwood University without residency requirements. Preference will be given to students studying an automotive curriculum.
Fields of interest: Higher education; Foundations (community).
Type of support: General/operating support; Scholarships—to individuals.
Limitations: Applications accepted. Giving primarily in Midland and Bay County, MI.
Application information: Application form required.
  Deadline(s): Aug. 31
Officers: Mary H. Anderson, Pres.; Ashley Anderson, V.P.
Director: Lori Appold.
EIN: 200464768

21
Anderson Foundation

480 W. Dussel Dr.
P.O. Box 119
Maumee, OH 43537-0119
County: Lucas
FAX: (419) 242-5549; E-mail: fredi@toledocf.org; Application address: c/o Ms. Fredi Heywood, 300 Madison Ave., Ste. 1300, Toledo, OH 43604-1583, tel.: (419) 243-1706

Trust established in 1949 in OH.
Donor: Partners in The Andersons, Inc.
Grantmaker type: Independent foundation.

Financial data (yr. ended 12/31/09): Assets, $9,201,832 (M); gifts received, $130,000; expenditures, $444,193; total giving, $323,333; qualifying distributions, $338,220; giving activities include $323,333 for 80 grants (high: $50,000; low: $100).
Purpose and activities: Grants primarily for community funds, higher and secondary education, and cultural programs; support also for social service and youth agencies, civic and community efforts, educational and research associations, and religion.
Fields of interest: Arts; Education, association; Secondary school/education; Higher education; Education; Environment; Agriculture; Human services; Children/youth, services; Community/economic development; United Ways and Federated Giving Programs; Government/public administration; Religion.
Type of support: General/operating support; Annual campaigns; Capital campaigns; Building/renovation; Emergency funds; Program development; Conferences/seminars; Publication; Seed money; Scholarship funds; Research; Matching/challenge support.
Limitations: Applications accepted. Giving primarily in the greater Toledo, OH, area, including Maumee and Columbus. Giving also to organizations located within the areas of the Anderson plants in the following cities: Champaign, IL, Delphi and Dunkirk, IN, and Albion, Potterville, Webberville, and White Pigeon, MI. No support for private foundations, public high schools or elementary schools. No grants to individuals, or for endowment funds, travel, or building or operating funds for churches or elementary schools.
Publications: Application guidelines.
Application information: Application form not required.
  Initial approach: Proposal not exceeding 5 pages
  Copies of proposal: 1
  Deadline(s): 3 weeks before board meetings
  Board meeting date(s): Mar., June, Sept., and Dec., usually the 3rd Mon. of the month
  Final notification: Generally 3 months; depends on completeness of proposal
Officer and Trustees:* Matthew C. Anderson,* Chair.; Charles W. Anderson; Jeffrey W. Anderson; Richard M. Anderson; Richard P. Anderson; Dale W. Fallat; John P. Kraus.
EIN: 346528868
Selected grants: The following grants were reported in 2006.
$50,000 to COSI Toledo, Toledo, OH.
$36,667 to Sunshine Foundation, Maumee, OH.
$15,000 to Kids Unlimited, Rockford, IL.
$15,000 to Toledo Symphony, Toledo, OH.
$10,000 to American Red Cross, Greater Toledo Chapter, Toledo, OH.
$10,000 to Central City Ministries of Toledo, Toledo, OH.
$10,000 to Cherry Street Mission Ministries, Toledo, OH.
$6,000 to YMCA of Greater Toledo, Toledo, OH.
$3,250 to Future Farmers of America Foundation, National, Indianapolis, IN.
$3,000 to Boy Scouts of America. For Boy Scouts of America in Ohio, Illinois and Indiana.

22
Anderson Foundation

5158 Lakeshore Rd.
Fort Gratiot, MI 48059-3115
County: St. Clair

Established in 1996.
Grantmaker type: Independent foundation.
Financial data (yr. ended 12/31/09): Assets, $2,504 (M); expenditures, $1,520; total giving, $1,500; qualifying distributions, $1,500; giving activities include $1,500 for grants.
Fields of interest: Hospitals (general); Human services; Christian agencies & churches.
Limitations: Giving primarily in MI, with some emphasis on Port Huron.
Officer: Richard T. Anderson, Pres.; Linda Anderson, Secy.
EIN: 383294782

23
Olson L. Anderson and Catherine Bastow Anderson Scholarship Trust

2322 Tittabawassee Rd.
Saginaw, MI 48604-9476
County: Saginaw
Application address: c/o Central Michigan Univ., Financial Aid Office, 201 Warriner Hall, Mount Pleasant, MI 48859, tel.: (517) 774-3674

Established in 1987 MI.
Grantmaker type: Independent foundation.
Financial data (yr. ended 12/31/09): Assets, $1,021,852 (M); expenditures, $53,510; total giving, $41,280; qualifying distributions, $46,293; giving activities include $41,280 for 10 grants to individuals (high: $5,184; low: $3,408).
Purpose and activities: Scholarship awards only to full-time undergraduates at Central Michigan University, with a preference for students from Bay County.
Fields of interest: Higher education.
Type of support: Scholarships—to individuals.
Limitations: Applications accepted. Giving primarily to residents of Bay County, MI.
Application information: Application form required.
  Initial approach: Proposal
  Deadline(s): May 15
Trustee: PNC Bank, N.A.
EIN: 386345071

24
The Rhoda Burke Andrews Foundation

567 Purdy St.
Birmingham, MI 48009-1736 (248) 642-0910
County: Oakland
Contact: Edward F. Andrews, Jr., Pres.

Established in 1992 in MI.
Donor: Edward F. Andrews, Jr.
Grantmaker type: Independent foundation.
Financial data (yr. ended 12/31/09): Assets, $843,870 (M); gifts received, $100,000; expenditures, $83,219; total giving, $82,919; qualifying distributions, $82,919; giving activities include $82,919 for 14 grants (high: $11,000; low: $1,919).
Fields of interest: Economically disadvantaged.
Limitations: Applications accepted. Giving primarily in southeastern MI. No grants to individuals.
Application information:

Initial approach: Proposal
Deadline(s): None
Final notification: 2 months
Officers: Edward F. Andrews, Jr., Pres. and Treas.;
Colleen M. Andrews, V.P. and Secy.
EIN: 383017759

25

Ted Annis Foundation
2997 Devonshire Rd.
Ann Arbor, MI   48104-2859   (734) 975-4428
County: Washtenaw
Contact: Ted C. Annis, Chair.
URL: http://www.tedannisfoundation.org

Established in 1997 in MI.
Donor: Ted C. Annis.
Grantmaker type: Independent foundation.
Financial data (yr. ended 12/31/09): Assets,
$293,861 (M); expenditures, $14,991; total giving,
$11,500; qualifying distributions, $11,500; giving
activities include $11,500 for 3 grants (high:
$7,500; low: $500).
Fields of interest: Higher education; Hospitals
(general); Health care; Health organizations; Human
services; YM/YWCAs & YM/YWHAs; Economic
development; Community/economic development.
Type of support: General/operating support;
Building/renovation; Equipment; Endowments;
Scholarship funds.
Limitations: Giving primarily in MI, with emphasis on
Ann Arbor.
Application information: Application form not
required.
    Initial approach: Proposal
    Deadline(s): None
Officer and Trustees: * Ted C. Annis,* Chair. and
Pres.; Ann Annis.
EIN: 383346207

26

The Eugene Applebaum Family Foundation
39400 Woodward Ave., Ste. 100
Bloomfield Hills, MI   48304-5151
County: Oakland
Contact: Pamela Applebaum Wyett, Treas.

Donors: Pamela Applebaum Wyett; Lisa S.
Applebaum; Pamela Applebaum; Eugene
Applebaum; Eugene Applebaum Charitable Lead
Trust.
Grantmaker type: Independent foundation.
Financial data (yr. ended 11/30/09): Assets,
$6,496,706 (M); gifts received, $911,935;
expenditures, $665,317; total giving, $584,519;
qualifying distributions, $614,918; giving activities
include $584,519 for 134 grants (high: $100,000;
low: $25).
Purpose and activities: Giving primarily to Jewish
organizations, including federated giving programs;
support also for education, the arts, and health
care.
Fields of interest: Arts; Elementary/secondary
education; Higher education; Education; Health
care; Jewish federated giving programs; Jewish
agencies & synagogues.
Limitations: Giving primarily in MI, and New York,
NY.

Officers: Eugene Applebaum, Pres.; Marcia
Applebaum, V.P.; Lisa S. Applebaum, Secy.; Pamela
A. Applebaum, Treas.
EIN: 382782955
Selected grants: The following grants were reported
in 2008.
$1,200,000 to Mayo Foundation, Rochester, MN.
For education and research.
$400,000 to Detroit Institute of Arts, Detroit, MI. For
education and research.
$300,000 to Wayne State University, Detroit, MI.
For education and research.
$150,000 to Wayne State University, Detroit, MI.
For education and research.
$70,000 to Hillel Day School of Metropolitan
Detroit, Farmington Hills, MI. For education and
research.
$50,000 to Cranbrook Academy of Art, Bloomfield
Hills, MI. For education and research.
$50,000 to National Yiddish Book Center, Amherst,
MA. For education and research.
$35,000 to YM-YWHA, 92nd Street, New York, NY.
For education and research.
$25,000 to Jewish Community Center of
Metropolitan Detroit, West Bloomfield, MI. For
education and research.
$25,000 to Jewish Federation of Palm Beach
County, West Palm Beach, FL. For education and
research.
$20,000 to JARC, Farmington Hills, MI. For
education and research.
$20,000 to Kadima: Jewish Support Services for
Adults with Mental Illness, Southfield, MI. For
education and research.
$10,000 to Bnai Israel Synagogue, Rochester, MN.
For education and research.
$10,000 to Connecticut Public Television, Hartford,
CT. For education and research.

27

Arcus Foundation
(formerly Jon L. Stryker Foundation)
402 E. Michigan Ave.
Kalamazoo, MI   49007-3888   (269) 373-4373
County: Kalamazoo
Contact: Carol Snapp, Comms. Mgr.
FAX: (269) 373-0277;
E-mail: contact@arcusfoundation.org; New York
address: 44 W. 28th St., New York, NY 10011, tel.:
(212) 488-3000; URL: http://
www.arcusfoundation.org

Established in 1997 in MI.
Donor: Jon L. Stryker.
Grantmaker type: Independent foundation.
Financial data (yr. ended 12/31/09): Assets,
$167,555,502 (M); gifts received, $35,000,089;
expenditures, $30,925,766; total giving,
$25,425,501; qualifying distributions,
$30,532,858; giving activities include
$25,425,501 for 259 grants (high: $2,625,927;
low: $25), and $350,000 for 1 loan/
program-related investment.
Purpose and activities: The mission of the
foundation is to achieve social justice that is
inclusive of sexual orientation, gender identity and
race, and to ensure conservation and respect of the
great apes.
Fields of interest: Animals/wildlife, endangered
species; Animals/wildlife, sanctuaries; Animals/
wildlife, special services; Civil/human rights,
LGBTQ; Civil/human rights; LGBTQ.

Type of support: General/operating support;
Management development/capacity building;
Capital campaigns; Building/renovation;
Endowments; Program development; Conferences/
seminars; Publication; Curriculum development;
Technical assistance; Consulting services; Program
evaluation; Employee matching gifts; Matching/
challenge support.
Limitations: Applications accepted. Giving on a
national basis, with some emphasis on MI,
especially southwest MI. Giving on an international
basis, with emphasis on Africa, the Middle East and
Southeast Asia. No support for lobby groups or
political campaigns. No grants to individuals, or for
religious or political activities, scholarships, or for
medical research or film production projects.
Publications: Annual report (including application
guidelines); Newsletter.
Application information: Application Process: 1)
Please confirm that your organization is an eligible
tax-exempt organization under Sec. 501(c)(3) of the
IRS regulations (or as a non-US organization, can
you demonstrate an equivalent status and a
non-discrimination or EEO policy compliant); 2)
Contact appropriate foundation program officer to
discuss interest and ideas for your request; 3)
Submit a formal Letter of Inquiry to the foundation;
and 4) If invited, submit a full proposal. After
reviewing your LOI, the foundation will inform you as
to whether a full proposal is being invited.
Application form not required.
    Initial approach: Contact a foundation program
        officer and then submit a formal letter of inquiry
    Copies of proposal: 4
    Deadline(s): Rolling; Once the foundation accepts
        a Letter of Inquiry and invites a full proposal, a
        specific deadline for submission of the full
        proposal will then be provided in the letter of
        invitation sent by the foundation
    Board meeting date(s): Four board meetings
        annually
    Final notification: After board meetings; Grant
        recipients will receive a Grant Award Letter.
Officers and Directors: * Dr. Yvette C. Burton,
C.E.O.; Jon L. Stryker,* Pres.; Richard Burns,
C.O.O.; Kristine Stallone, C.F.O.; Stephen Bennett;
Cathy J. Cohen; Catherine Pino; Darren Walker.
Number of staff: 21
EIN: 383332791
Selected grants: The following grants were reported
in 2009.
$3,162,493 to Center for Captive Chimpanzee Care,
Save the Chimps, Fort Pierce, FL. For high quality
care of chimps in Florida and New Mexico
sanctuaries.
$2,100,000 to Kalamazoo College, Kalamazoo, MI.
For initial programming and operating support for
Arcus Center for Social Justice Leadership, payable
over 2.00 years.
$1,600,000 to National Gay and Lesbian Task Force
Foundation, Washington, DC. For general operating
support, payable over 2.00 years.
$500,000 to Equality Michigan, Detroit, MI. For
general operating support, payable over 2.00 years.
$310,000 to African Wildlife Foundation,
Washington, DC. For bonobo conservation in the
Lomako Forest Reserve, payable over 2.00 years.
$299,000 to International Institute for Environment
and Development, London, England. For Poverty and
Conservation Learning Group, payable over 2.50
years.
$200,000 to Tides Foundation, San Francisco, CA.
For ARC International-for Global Development Fund
For ARC International to advance recognition of

human rights based on sexual orientation and gender identity at international level through strategic planning, coalition and movement building, and advocacy, payable over 2.00 years.
$100,000 to Village Enterprise Fund, San Carlos, CA. For Integrated Conservation and Microenterprise Project to protect chimpanzee habitat in Uganda, payable over 2.00 years.
$93,345 to New Ways Ministry, Mount Rainier, MD. For Catholic Marriage Equality Program.

28
Richard and Mary Arden Foundation Trust
c/o Comerica Bank
P.O. Box 75000, MC 3302
Detroit, MI 48275-3302   (313) 222-6297
County: Wayne
Application address: c/o Joseph Powers, P.O. Box 7350, Portland, ME 04112-7350

Established in 2002 in NY.
Donors: Richard Arden; Mary Arden.
Grantmaker type: Independent foundation.
Financial data (yr. ended 11/30/09): Assets, $88,308 (M); expenditures, $6,134; total giving, $4,000; qualifying distributions, $4,550; giving activities include $4,000 for grants.
Purpose and activities: Scholarship awards to journalism students.
Fields of interest: Media, print publishing; Journalism school/education.
Type of support: Scholarship funds.
Application information: Application form required.
   Deadline(s): Dec. 31
Trustees: Mary Arden; Richard Arden; Comerica Bank.
EIN: 550807783

29
Edmund Armstrong Educational Corporation
(formerly Edmund Armstrong Foundation)
c/o Jack Burket
1011 Glenhurst Dr.
Birmingham, MI 48009-1156   (248) 258-4977
County: Oakland
Contact: Jack D. Burket

Grantmaker type: Independent foundation.
Financial data (yr. ended 07/31/10): Assets, $137,611 (M); expenditures, $3,043; total giving, $0; qualifying distributions, $0.
Fields of interest: Performing arts, education.
Limitations: Applications accepted. Giving primarily in Los Angeles, CA.
Application information:
   Initial approach: Letter
   Deadline(s): None
Directors: Jack Burket; Herbert Couf.
EIN: 351603618

30
The Arnold Family Foundation
3390 Clover Dr.
Saline, MI 48176-9539   (734) 429-4289
County: Washtenaw

Established in 2000 in MI.
Donor: Barbara J. Arnold Trust.
Grantmaker type: Independent foundation.

Financial data (yr. ended 10/31/09): Assets, $0; expenditures, $2,497; total giving, $1,677; qualifying distributions, $2,497; giving activities include $1,677 for 3 grants (high: $677; low: $500).
Limitations: Giving primarily in MI.
Officers: Charles B. Arnold, Pres.; Barbara J. Arnold, Secy.-Treas.
EIN: 383538451

31
Stanley and Blanche Ash Foundation
829 S. Lincoln St.
Greenville, MI 48838-2242
County: Montcalm
Contact: Blanche E. Ash, Pres.
Application address: P.O. Box 310, Greenville, MI 48838-0310

Established in 1991 in MI as successor to Stanley & Blanche Ash Foundation.
Donors: Blanche E. Ash; Stanley P. Ash‡; Greenville Tool and Die Co.
Grantmaker type: Independent foundation.
Financial data (yr. ended 12/31/09): Assets, $5,636,162 (M); expenditures, $331,326; total giving, $300,139; qualifying distributions, $300,139; giving activities include $300,139 for grants.
Purpose and activities: Giving to organizations that improve the quality of live for residents of West Michigan. Scholarship awards restricted to students in the Montcalm County, MI, area who show financial need and have satisfactory grades.
Fields of interest: Higher education; Higher education, university; Health organizations, association; Christian agencies & churches.
Type of support: Scholarship funds; Research; Scholarships—to individuals.
Limitations: Applications accepted. Giving limited to the western MI area.
Application information: Accepts Standard Scholarship Form used by the college of the applicant's choice. Application form required.
   Deadline(s): None
   Board meeting date(s): Quarterly
Officer and Directors:* Blanche E. Ash,* Pres.; Jennifer K. Ash; Robert Price.
Number of staff: None.
EIN: 382966745
Selected grants: The following grants were reported in 2005.
$40,000 to Montcalm Community College Foundation, Sidney, MI.
$25,000 to Saint Pauls Lutheran Church.
$10,000 to Greenville Area Community Center, Greenville, MI.
$5,000 to American Red Cross.
$5,000 to Greenville Area Community Foundation, Greenville, MI.
$3,000 to Salvation Army.
$2,000 to Salvation Army.
$500 to United Way.
$500 to United Way.
$50 to First Congregational Church.

32
Raymond V. Attanasio Charitable Trust
c/o Comerica Bank
P.O. Box 75000, MC 8280
Detroit, MI 48275-8280   (313) 222-6297
County: Wayne
Application address: c/o Beverly Suchenek, 500 Woodward Ave., 21st Fl., Detroit, MI 48226-3416, tel.: (313) 222-6297

Established in 2000 in NJ.
Donor: Raymond V. Attanasio.
Grantmaker type: Independent foundation.
Financial data (yr. ended 06/30/10): Assets, $693,530 (M); expenditures, $54,883; total giving, $41,000; qualifying distributions, $41,530; giving activities include $41,000 for 18 grants (high: $7,000; low: $500).
Fields of interest: Education; Catholic agencies & churches.
Limitations: Giving in the U.S., primarily in NJ and NY. No grants to individuals.
Application information:
   Initial approach: Letter
   Deadline(s): None
Director: Rev. Joseph Szulwach.
Trustee: Comerica Bank.
EIN: 226855593

33
AtWater Foundation
111 Willits St.
Birmingham, MI 48009-3326
County: Oakland
Contact: Vivian L. Carpenter, Pres.

Established in 1997 in MI.
Grantmaker type: Independent foundation.
Financial data (yr. ended 12/31/07): Assets, $580 (M); expenditures, $946; total giving, $0; qualifying distributions, $0.
Purpose and activities: Giving primarily for youth services and community development in Detroit, Michigan.
Fields of interest: Arts; Elementary/secondary education; Youth, services; Christian agencies & churches.
Type of support: Curriculum development.
Limitations: Giving limited to Detroit, MI. No grants to individuals, or for operating expenses.
Publications: Financial statement.
Application information: Application form not required.
   Copies of proposal: 1
Officer and Trustee:* Vivian L. Carpenter,* Pres.
EIN: 383219694

34
The Ayrshire Foundation
301 E. Colorado Blvd., No. 802
Pasadena, CA 91101-1917
County: Los Angeles
Contact: Margaret G. Boyer, Pres.
FAX: (626) 795-7689;
E-mail: info@AyrshireFoundation.org; URL: http://www.ayrshirefoundation.org

Established in 1998 in CA.
Donor: James N. Gamble‡.
Grantmaker type: Independent foundation.

Financial data (yr. ended 05/31/10): Assets, $16,516,022 (M); expenditures, $1,204,874; total giving, $1,052,200; qualifying distributions, $1,118,532; giving activities include $1,052,200 for 31 grants (high: $112,500; low: $10,000).

Purpose and activities: Giving primarily for health care, including a hospital, and a cancer center; some giving also for education, the arts, and youth and social services.

Fields of interest: Arts; Education; Environment; Health care; Children/youth, services; Community/economic development; Children/youth; Youth; Aging; Young adults; Disabilities, people with; Mentally disabled; Women.

Type of support: Capital campaigns; Building/renovation; Equipment; Land acquisition; Endowments; Program development; Conferences/seminars; Professorships; Film/video/radio; Seed money; Scholarship funds; Matching/challenge support.

Limitations: Applications accepted. Giving primarily in Pasadena, San Francisco, and Sonoma, CA; giving also in the Petoskey/Harbor Springs, MI, area. No grants for continuing support.

Publications: Annual report; Grants list.

Application information: Application form required.
  Initial approach: Varies
  Copies of proposal: 1
  Deadline(s): Mar. 15 and Sept. 15
  Board meeting date(s): May and Oct.
  Final notification: One month or less

Officers and Directors:* Margaret G. Boyer,* Pres.; Tracy G. Hirrel,* V.P.; Peter S. Boyer, Secy.; Richard J. Hirrel,* Treas.; Peter S. Boyer.

Number of staff: 1 full-time professional.

EIN: 954690418

Selected grants: The following grants were reported in 2006.
$150,000 to California Academy of Sciences, San Francisco, CA. For general support.
$150,000 to Kidspace, A Participatory Museum, Pasadena, CA. For general support.
$100,000 to Pacific Asia Museum, Pasadena, CA. For general support.
$100,000 to Rocky Mountain Institute, Snowmass, CO. For general support.
$75,000 to Hillsides, Pasadena, CA. For general support.
$50,000 to Pasadena Playhouse State Theater of California, Pasadena, CA. For general support.
$40,000 to Golden Gate National Parks Conservancy, San Francisco, CA. For general support.
$30,000 to California Institute of Technology, Pasadena, CA. For general support.
$25,000 to Doheny Eye Institute, Los Angeles, CA. For general support.
$15,000 to International Center for Global Communications, New York, NY. For general support.

35
Baiardi Family Foundation, Inc.
2328 Pinecrest St.
Harbor Springs, MI 49740-9261
(231) 526-8395
County: Emmet
Contact: Chris A. Baiardi, Pres.
FAX: (231) 526-7966;
E-mail: info@baiardifoundation.org; Additional e-mail: grants@baiardifoundation.org; URL: http://www.baiardifoundation.org

Established in 1999.

Donors: Chris A. Baiardi; Cindy J. Baiardi; Angelo Baiardi†.

Grantmaker type: Independent foundation.

Financial data (yr. ended 12/31/09): Assets, $6,402,448 (M); expenditures, $146,115; total giving, $135,050; qualifying distributions, $135,296; giving activities include $135,050 for 21 grants (high: $29,500; low: $1,000).

Purpose and activities: The foundation's mission remains to support and effect positive change within several main categories of giving. Specifically, the foundation has an interest in health care, education, the arts, environmental stewardship, land use and conservation, Catholic and Judeo-Christian traditions and values, and community resources. The guiding principles of the foundation govern all grant requests and subsequent giving.

Fields of interest: Education; Hospitals (general); Health organizations; Human services; United Ways and Federated Giving Programs.

Limitations: Applications accepted. Giving primarily in MI, with concentrations in the Detroit metropolitan area community and in northwest lower Michigan, specifically Emmet County.

Application information: See foundation web site for application guidelines.
  Initial approach: Letter

Officers and Directors:* Chris A. Baiardi,* Pres.; Kristen L. Baiardi,* V.P.; Suzanne M. Baiardi,* V.P.; Cindy J. Baiardi,* Secy.-Treas.

EIN: 383430867

Selected grants: The following grants were reported in 2008.
$29,000 to Cranbrook Schools, Bloomfield Hills, MI.
$15,000 to Holy Childhood of Jesus Church, Harbor Springs, MI.
$15,000 to Saint Hugo of the Hills Church, Bloomfield Hills, MI.
$12,500 to Little Traverse Conservancy, Harbor Springs, MI.
$10,500 to Cornerstone Schools, Detroit, MI.
$9,000 to Tip of the Mitt Watershed Council, Petoskey, MI.
$5,000 to Harbor Springs Area Historical Society, Harbor Springs, MI.
$5,000 to North Central Michigan College, Petoskey, MI.
$5,000 to Tip of the Mitt Watershed Council, Petoskey, MI.

36
The Howard Baker Foundation
c/o Paul J. Gambka, C.P.A.
4057 Pioneer Dr., Ste. 500
Walled Lake, MI 48390-1363
County: Oakland
Application address: c/o Michele Baker, Exec. Dir., 12312 County Road 10, Ranburne, AL 36273, tel.: (313) 268-0636 (MI) or (256) 568-5714 (AL), e-mail: baker.michele@yahoo.com
Scholarship application address: Office of Scholarship and Financial Aid, Wayne State University, Welcome Center, 42 W. Warren, 3rd Fl., Detroit, MI 48202, tel.: (313) 577-3378

Established in 1992 in MI.

Donor: Howard Baker Trust.

Grantmaker type: Independent foundation.

Financial data (yr. ended 09/30/09): Assets, $1,568,543 (M); expenditures, $498,678; total giving, $323,183; qualifying distributions, $323,183; giving activities include $323,183 for 6 grants (high: $198,183; low: $25,000).

Purpose and activities: Giving primarily for human services, as well as to a fund that has been established to provide assistance to residents of Detroit, MI, in financing their education at Wayne State University, and to encourage continued progress towards a degree.

Fields of interest: Higher education, university; Animal welfare; Human services; Children/youth, services; African Americans/Blacks.

Type of support: General/operating support; Scholarship funds.

Limitations: Applications accepted. Giving limited to the greater Detroit, MI area. No support for political causes or candidates.

Publications: Financial statement.

Application information: Application form not required.
  Initial approach: Proposal
  Copies of proposal: 1
  Deadline(s): None
  Board meeting date(s): Dec.
  Final notification: None

Officers: Charlie J. Williams, Pres.; Ronald F. Michaels, V.P.; Dennis Gabrian, Secy.; O'Neal O. Wright, Treas.; Michelle L. Baker, Exec. Dir.

Directors: Paul J. Gambka; John J. Howe.

Number of staff: 1 full-time professional.

EIN: 383083465

Selected grants: The following grants were reported in 2007.
$160,883 to Wayne State University, Detroit, MI.
$50,000 to CANTER Michigan, East Lansing, MI.
$50,000 to Detroit Central City Community Mental Health, Detroit, MI.
$50,000 to Detroit Impact, Detroit, MI.
$50,000 to YMCA of Metropolitan Detroit, Camping Services, Detroit, MI.
$25,000 to Old Newsboys Goodfellow Fund of Detroit, Detroit, MI.
$5,000 to Capuchin Soup Kitchen, Detroit, MI.

37
Baker U.S.-Japan Study Foundation
6024 Eastman Ave.
Midland, MI 48640-2518
County: Midland
Contact: George R. Baker, Chair.
Application address: P.O. Box 1544, Midland, MI 48641-1544, tel.: (989) 832-6124

Established in 2006 in MI.

Donors: George R. Baker; Shin-Etsu, Inc.

Grantmaker type: Independent foundation.

Financial data (yr. ended 12/31/09): Assets, $254,090 (M); gifts received, $50,000; expenditures, $11,090; total giving, $10,000; qualifying distributions, $10,000; giving activities include $10,000 for grants.

Purpose and activities: Scholarship awards for students at American universities and colleges.

Fields of interest: Higher education.

Type of support: Scholarships—to individuals.

Application information: Application form required.
  Deadline(s): None

Officers: George R. Baker, Chair.; Guy Merriam, Treas.

Directors: Richard Ferrando; Chihiro Kanagawa; Dick Mason; Ramon F. Rolf, Jr.

EIN: 383630589

38
Baldwin Foundation
P.O. Box 1828
Grand Rapids, MI 49501-1828 (616) 575-5704
County: Kent
Contact: Dan Baas

Established in 1964 in MI.
Donor: Members of the Baldwin family.
Grantmaker type: Independent foundation.
Financial data (yr. ended 11/30/09): Assets,
$2,989,113 (M); expenditures, $98,419; total
giving, $73,500; qualifying distributions, $73,500;
giving activities include $73,500 for 7 grants (high:
$20,000; low: $5,000).
Fields of interest: Arts; Higher education; Hospitals
(general); Human services; Children/youth,
services; Christian agencies & churches.
Type of support: Annual campaigns; Capital
campaigns; Building/renovation; Equipment;
Professorships; Fellowships.
Limitations: Applications accepted. Giving primarily
in western MI. No grants to individuals.
Application information: Application form not
required.
  Deadline(s): None
  Board meeting date(s): July or Aug.
Officers: Dana Baldwin II, Pres.; Greg Conway, V.P.;
Lisa Laidler, Secy.-Treas.
Trustee: Founders Bank and Trust.
EIN: 386085641
Selected grants: The following grants were reported
in 2009.
$10,000 to Grand Valley State University, Allendale,
MI.
$10,000 to University of Michigan, Ann Arbor, MI.
$8,500 to Degage Ministries, Grand Rapids, MI.

39
James & Shirley Balk Foundation
1230 Monroe Ave. N.W.
Grand Rapids, MI 49505-4620
County: Kent
Contact: James H. Balk II, Tr.

Established in 1984 in MI.
Donors: James H. Balk II; Shirley Balk.
Grantmaker type: Independent foundation.
Financial data (yr. ended 12/31/09): Assets,
$3,592,710 (M); gifts received, $185,000;
expenditures, $109,650; total giving, $109,650;
qualifying distributions, $109,650; giving activities
include $109,650 for 20 grants (high: $50,000;
low: $200).
Purpose and activities: Giving primarily for Christian
education; support also for the arts, churches,
human services, and botanical gardens.
Fields of interest: Arts; Higher education;
Education; Botanical gardens; Human services;
United Ways and Federated Giving Programs;
Christian agencies & churches.
Type of support: General/operating support.
Limitations: Applications accepted. Giving primarily
in Grand Rapids, MI. No grants to individuals.
Application information:
  Initial approach: Letter on organization's
    letterhead
  Deadline(s): None
Trustees: James H. Balk; James H. Balk II; Martin
Balk; Shirley Balk; Steven Balk.
EIN: 382556356
Selected grants: The following grants were reported
in 2008.

$30,000 to American Cancer Society, Naples, FL.
$5,000 to Aquinas College, Grand Rapids, MI.

40
Edmund F. and Virginia B. Ball Foundation, Inc.
P.O. Box 1408
Muncie, IN 47308-1408
County: Delaware
Contact: Kris Gross

Established in 1994 in IN.
Donors: Edmund F. Ball‡; Virginia B. Ball‡.
Grantmaker type: Independent foundation.
Financial data (yr. ended 09/30/10): Assets,
$23,357,732 (M); expenditures, $1,332,596; total
giving, $1,227,000; qualifying distributions,
$1,227,000; giving activities include $1,227,000
for grants.
Fields of interest: Arts; Education; Health
organizations; Children/youth, services.
Limitations: Giving primarily in MI and IN. No grants
to individuals.
Application information:
  Initial approach: Proposal
  Deadline(s): None
Officers and Directors:* Frank E. Ball,* Pres.;
Robert B. Ball,* V.P.; Douglas J. Foy,* Secy.-Treas.;
Michael J. Fisher, Jr., Exec. Dir.; Douglas A. Bakken;
Nancy B. Keilty.
EIN: 351911169
Selected grants: The following grants were reported
in 2009.
$228,000 to Ball State University Foundation,
Muncie, IN.
$100,000 to Ball Memorial Hospital Foundation,
Muncie, IN.
$100,000 to Ball State University Foundation,
Muncie, IN.
$75,000 to Minnetrista Cultural Foundation,
Muncie, IN.
$60,000 to Munson Healthcare Regional
Foundation, Traverse City, MI.
$50,000 to Community Enhancement Projects,
Muncie, IN.
$37,500 to TEAMwork for Quality Living, Muncie, IN.
$32,896 to Ball State University Foundation,
Muncie, IN.
$30,000 to Inland Seas Education Association,
Suttons Bay, MI.
$25,000 to Yale University, New Haven, CT.

41
Bardsley Charities
3032 Davenport Ave.
Saginaw, MI 48602-3660
County: Saginaw

Donors: P.E. Bardsley; Ailene Bardsley.
Grantmaker type: Independent foundation.
Financial data (yr. ended 12/31/08): Assets,
$73,493 (M); expenditures, $1,491; total giving,
$0; qualifying distributions, $0.
Fields of interest: Higher education; Christian
agencies & churches.
Limitations: Giving primarily in Anderson, IN.
Application information:
  Initial approach: Letter
  Deadline(s): None
Trustees: William Bardsley; Jane Hutchins.
EIN: 356060020

42
The J. Spencer Barnes Memorial Foundation
3073 Fulton St. E.
Grand Rapids, MI 49506-1813
County: Kent
Contact: Robert C. Woodhouse, Jr., Pres.
Application address: 109 Logan St. S.W., Grand
Rapids, MI 49503-5125, tel.: (616) 949-4854

Established in 1999 in MI.
Donor: John P. Williams.
Grantmaker type: Independent foundation.
Financial data (yr. ended 06/30/10): Assets,
$63,909 (M); expenditures, $4,863; total giving,
$3,500; qualifying distributions, $3,500; giving
activities include $3,500 for grants.
Fields of interest: Diabetes; Children/youth;
Disabilities, people with.
Type of support: Program development; Income
development.
Limitations: Giving primarily in Grand Rapids, MI.
Application information:
  Initial approach: Proposal
  Deadline(s): None
Officers: Robert C. Woodhouse, Jr., Pres. and
Treas.; Stevens Wharton-Bickley, V.P.; Scott Dwyer,
Secy.
Director: Stuart Schockley.
EIN: 383499166

43
Shelley & Terry Barr Foundation
29600 Northwestern Hwy., Ste. 102
Southfield, MI 48034-1016
County: Oakland

Established in MI.
Donor: Terry A. Barr.
Grantmaker type: Independent foundation.
Financial data (yr. ended 12/31/09): Assets,
$48,218 (M); expenditures, $38; total giving, $0;
qualifying distributions, $0; giving activities include
$0 for grants to individuals.
Purpose and activities: Scholarship awards to
graduates of Grand Rapids Central High School, and
Rogers High School, Wyoming, Michigan.
Type of support: Scholarships—to individuals.
Limitations: Applications accepted. Giving limited to
residents of Grand Rapids and Wyoming, MI.
Application information: Application form required.
  Deadline(s): None
Officers and Directors:* Shelley E. Barr,* Pres.,
V.P., and Treas.; Mary C. Kravutske,* Secy.; Terry A.
Barr.
EIN: 382258156

44
The Barstow Foundation
c/o Chemical Bank & Trust Co.
235 E. Main St.
Midland, MI 48640-5137 (989) 839-5305
County: Midland
Contact: John E. Kessler, Secy.

Trust established in 1967 in MI.
Donors: Florence K. Barstow‡; Ruth M. Dixon.
Grantmaker type: Independent foundation.
Financial data (yr. ended 12/31/09): Assets,
$5,228,949 (M); expenditures, $235,114; total
giving, $210,000; qualifying distributions,

$210,000; giving activities include $210,000 for 21 grants (high: $50,000; low: $1,000).
Fields of interest: Higher education, university; Libraries (public); Environment; Food banks; Boys & girls clubs; Human services; YM/YWCAs & YM/YWHAs; Neighborhood centers; Children/youth, services; Family services, domestic violence; United Ways and Federated Giving Programs.
Type of support: General/operating support; Capital campaigns; Program development; Scholarship funds.
Limitations: Applications accepted. Giving primarily in MI; giving also in states where trustees reside, including AZ, CA, and TX. No grants to individuals, or for research, continuing support, deficit financing, scholarships, or fellowships; no loans.
Application information: Application form not required.
  Initial approach: Letter
  Copies of proposal: 2
  Deadline(s): July 31
  Board meeting date(s): Nov.
  Final notification: After annual meeting
Officers and Trustees:* David O. Barstow,* Co-Chair.; William R. Dixon,* Co-Chair.; John E. Kessler,* Secy.; John C. Barstow; Richard G. Barstow; Robert G. Barstow; Ruth M. Dixon.
EIN: 386151026
Selected grants: The following grants were reported in 2009.
$30,000 to CARE, Merrifield, VA.
$30,000 to United States Fund for UNICEF, New York, NY.
$5,000 to Easter Seals Northern California, Novato, CA.
$5,000 to Enterprise Community Partners, Columbia, MD.
$4,000 to Food Bank of Eastern Michigan, Flint, MI.
$4,000 to Greater Boston Food Bank, Boston, MA.
$4,000 to MANNA FoodBank, Asheville, NC.
$3,000 to Marin Abused Womens Services, San Rafael, CA.
$2,000 to Roots of Peace, San Rafael, CA.
$1,000 to Chattooga Conservancy, Clayton, GA.

45
Charles F. and Adeline L. Barth Charitable Foundation
3023 Davenport St.
P.O. Box 3275
Saginaw, MI 48602-3652 (989) 793-9830
County: Saginaw
Contact: David A. Beyerlein, Treas.

Established in 1989 in MI.
Donor: Adeline L. Barth†.
Grantmaker type: Independent foundation.
Financial data (yr. ended 12/31/09): Assets, $906,458 (M); expenditures, $43,747; total giving, $26,030; qualifying distributions, $27,772; giving activities include $26,030 for 10 grants (high: $10,000; low: $500).
Fields of interest: Arts; Higher education; Hospitals (general); Human services; United Ways and Federated Giving Programs.
Type of support: General/operating support; Capital campaigns; Building/renovation; Program development; Matching/challenge support.
Limitations: Applications accepted. Giving primarily in Saginaw, MI.
Application information: Application form not required.
  Initial approach: Letter

Copies of proposal: 3
Deadline(s): None
Board meeting date(s): Semiannually
Officers: Jane Barth, Pres.; Susan Langhorne, V.P.
Trustees: Dick Stringer; Judy Weldy.
Number of staff: 1 part-time professional.
EIN: 386556893

46
Bartsch Memorial Trust
(formerly Ruth Bartsch Memorial Bank Trust)
c/o JPMorgan Services Inc.
P.O. Box 6089
Newark, DE 19714-6089
County: New Castle
Application address: c/o Peggy Swarzman, V.P., JPMorgan Chase Philanthropic Svcs., 270 Park Ave., 16th Fl., New York NY 10017-2014; tel.: (212) 464-2342

Established in 1983 in NY.
Donor: Ruth Bartsch†.
Grantmaker type: Independent foundation.
Financial data (yr. ended 11/30/09): Assets, $8,339,966 (M); expenditures, $485,584; total giving, $400,000; qualifying distributions, $425,864; giving activities include $400,000 for 9 grants (high: $48,000; low: $44,000).
Purpose and activities: Giving primarily for education, and children, youth, and social services.
Fields of interest: Elementary/secondary education; Education, special; Youth development, scouting agencies (general); Human services; Blind/visually impaired; Economically disadvantaged.
Limitations: Applications accepted. Giving primarily in CT, FL, IL, MA, MI, and NY. No grants to individuals.
Application information: Application form not required.
  Initial approach: Letter
  Deadline(s): None
Trustees: Mark S. Richards; Vincent William Richards, Jr.; JPMorgan Chase Bank, N.A.
EIN: 133188775
Selected grants: The following grants were reported in 2008.
$49,500 to Coast Guard Foundation, Stonington, CT.
$49,500 to Lighthouse International, New York, NY.

47
Basch Family Foundation
7420 Hillsboro Dr.
Canton, MI 48187-2204
County: Wayne

Established in 2006.
Grantmaker type: Independent foundation.
Financial data (yr. ended 12/31/09): Assets, $1 (M); expenditures, $2,752; total giving, $1,107; qualifying distributions, $2,752; giving activities include $1,107 for 3 grants (high: $867; low: $90).
Fields of interest: Education, services; Athletics/sports, Special Olympics.
Director: Dawn Basch.
Trustee: Jeffrey Basch.
EIN: 205776797

48
Barry Bashur Foundation
3072 Newport Ct.
Troy, MI 48084-1313 (248) 649-0174
County: Oakland
Contact: Margaret Barry Bashur, Pres.

Established in 2004 in MI.
Donors: John Bashur; Margaret Barry Bashur.
Grantmaker type: Independent foundation.
Financial data (yr. ended 12/31/09): Assets, $14,936 (M); gifts received, $10,000; expenditures, $10,752; total giving, $9,950; qualifying distributions, $10,552; giving activities include $9,950 for 15 grants (high: $4,000; low: $50).
Fields of interest: Education; Animal welfare; Medical research.
Limitations: Applications accepted. Giving primarily in MI. No grants to individuals.
Application information: Application form not required.
  Initial approach: Letter
  Deadline(s): Varies
Officers: Margaret Barry Bashur, Pres.; John Bashur, V.P.
Director: John Grenke.
EIN: 201149345

49
Basilica of St. Adalbert Foundation
701 4th St., N.W.
Grand Rapids, MI 49504-5104 (616) 458-3065
County: Kent

Grantmaker type: Independent foundation.
Financial data (yr. ended 06/30/10): Assets, $352,716 (M); gifts received, $622; expenditures, $22,933; total giving, $22,913; qualifying distributions, $22,933; giving activities include $9,885 for 2 grants (high: $6,187; low: $3,698), and $13,028 for 6 grants to individuals (high: $4,080; low: $750).
Purpose and activities: Support for education through grants and educational scholarships to parishioners of Basilica of St. Adalbert for attendance at Catholic elementary or Catholic high schools.
Fields of interest: Catholic agencies & churches.
Type of support: Scholarships—to individuals.
Limitations: Applications accepted. Giving primarily in Grand Rapids, MI.
Application information:
  Initial approach: Letter
  Deadline(s): Apr. 30
Officers and Directors:* Rev. R. Louis Stasker, Pres.; Bernard Prawozik, V.P.; Daniel Davis, Secy.; Donald G. Karpinski, Treas.; Margaret Downer; Miles Schmidt.
EIN: 382685451

50
The Bates Foundation
40950 Woodward Ave., Ste. 306
Bloomfield Hills, MI 48304-5124
(248) 642-5770
County: Oakland

Established in 1997 in MI.
Donors: Gwendolyn H. Bates; Martha J. Bates.
Grantmaker type: Independent foundation.

Financial data (yr. ended 12/31/09): Assets, $46,203 (M); gifts received, $749; expenditures, $5,789; total giving, $4,975; qualifying distributions, $4,975; giving activities include $4,975 for grants.
Fields of interest: Education; Human services.
Limitations: Giving primarily in MI. No grants to individuals.
Application information:
Initial approach: Letter
Deadline(s): None
Officers: Gwendolyn H. Bates, Pres.; Martha J. Bates, V.P.; James H. LoPrete, Secy.
EIN: 383278032

51

Charles M. Bauervic Foundation, Inc.
2155 Butterfield Dr., Ste. 305A
Troy, MI 48084-3452
County: Oakland
Application address: c/o Exec. Dir., 10260 E. Hilltop Rd., Suttons Bay, MI 49682

Incorporated in 1967 in MI.
Donor: Charles M. Bauervic†.
Grantmaker type: Independent foundation.
Financial data (yr. ended 12/31/08): Assets, $2,885,537 (M); expenditures, $266,442; total giving, $110,000; qualifying distributions, $110,000; giving activities include $110,000 for grants.
Fields of interest: Performing arts; Elementary/secondary education; Higher education; Holistic medicine; Human services; Family services, counseling; Civil liberties, right to life; Christian agencies & churches.
Type of support: Building/renovation; Equipment; Program development.
Limitations: Giving primarily in MI. No support for organizations lacking 501(c)(3) status. No grants to individuals, or for scholarship funds, operating expenses, fund drives, or building campaigns.
Publications: Application guidelines.
Application information: Application form required.
Initial approach: Letter
Copies of proposal: 2
Deadline(s): Apr. 30
Board meeting date(s): June
Final notification: June 30
Officers: Patricia A. Leonard, Pres. and Secy.; Beverly D. Sewell, V.P.; Theodore Leonard, Treas.
Directors: Kathryn R. Bolton; John C. Leonard; Timothy J. Leonard.
Number of staff: 1 part-time support.
EIN: 386146352
Selected grants: The following grants were reported in 2007.
$11,000 to Hillsdale College, Hillsdale Academy, Hillsdale, MI.
$1,500 to Detroit Symphony Orchestra, Detroit, MI.
$1,000 to Madonna University, Livonia, MI.
$500 to City Opera House Heritage Association, Traverse City, MI.

52

Peggy Bauervic Foundation
(formerly Bauervic-Carroll Foundation)
3 Bluffwood Dr.
South Haven, MI 49090-1663   (269) 639-8931
County: Van Buren
Contact: Peggy L. Maitland, Pres.

Established in 1984 in MI.
Grantmaker type: Independent foundation.
Financial data (yr. ended 12/31/09): Assets, $349,568 (M); expenditures, $45,224; total giving, $33,600; qualifying distributions, $33,909; giving activities include $33,600 for 6 grants (high: $12,000; low: $200).
Fields of interest: Health care; Family services.
Limitations: Giving primarily in MI. No grants to individuals.
Application information: Application form required.
Initial approach: Letter
Copies of proposal: 1
Deadline(s): Oct. 1
Peggy L. Maitland,* Pres. and Secy.; Jane Peruyeso, V.P.; Stuart Maitland,* Treas.
Directors: Jose Peruyeso; Michael Smith; Jane Spartz.
Number of staff: 1 full-time professional.
EIN: 382494383

53

Bauervic-Paisley Foundation
501 E. Mullett Lake Rd.
Indian River, MI 49749-9123   (231) 238-7817
County: Cheboygan

Established in 1984 in MI.
Grantmaker type: Independent foundation.
Financial data (yr. ended 12/31/09): Assets, $875,414 (M); expenditures, $86,157; total giving, $4,000; qualifying distributions, $4,000; giving activities include $4,000 for grants.
Fields of interest: Higher education; Hospitals (general); Housing/shelter; Youth development; Human services; Residential/custodial care, hospices.
Type of support: General/operating support; Building/renovation; Equipment; Program development.
Limitations: Giving primarily in MI. No grants to individuals.
Application information: Application form required.
Deadline(s): Oct. 1
Officers and Directors:* Beverly Paisley,* Pres.; Martha Paisley,* V.P.; Bonnie Paisley, Secy.; Peter Paisley, Treas.; Charles Paisley; Peter Paisley, Jr.
EIN: 382494390

54

Grayce David Baxter Honorary Scholarship
9710 E. Townline Rd.
Frankenmuth, MI 48734-8500
County: Saginaw
Contact: Lyle Davis II, Tr.

Established in MI.
Donor: Maurice W. Davis.
Grantmaker type: Independent foundation.
Financial data (yr. ended 12/31/08): Assets, $0 (M); expenditures, $2,000; total giving, $2,000; qualifying distributions, $2,000; giving activities include $2,000 for grants.
Purpose and activities: Scholarship awards to students attending Bridgeport High School, Michigan, planning to attend an accredited college.
Fields of interest: Higher education, college.
Type of support: Scholarship funds.
Limitations: Applications accepted. Giving limited to residents of Bridgeport, MI.
Application information: Application form required.

Initial approach: Letter
Deadline(s): None
Trustees: Lyle Davis II; Maurice W. Davis; Jeff McNally.
EIN: 201288725

55

Bernard H. Beal Scholarship Foundation
c/o National City Bank
2322 Tittabawassee Rd.
Saginaw, MI 48604-9476
County: Saginaw
Application address: c/o Millington High School, Attn.: Dolores VanSickle, 8780 Dean Dr., Millington, MI 48746-9694, tel.: (517) 871-5220

Established in 1998 in MI.
Grantmaker type: Independent foundation.
Financial data (yr. ended 12/31/09): Assets, $523,324 (M); expenditures, $34,228; total giving, $28,025; qualifying distributions, $28,025; giving activities include $28,025 for grants to individuals.
Purpose and activities: Scholarship awards to graduates of Millington High School, Michigan.
Fields of interest: Higher education.
Type of support: Scholarships—to individuals.
Limitations: Applications accepted. Giving limited to residents of Millington, MI.
Application information: Application must include essay. Application form required.
Initial approach: Letter or telephone
Deadline(s): Jan. 31
Trustee: National City Bank.
EIN: 383381079

56

Joseph & Mari Beals Family Foundation
16824 Kercheval Pl., Ste. 202
Grosse Pointe, MI 48230-1500   (313) 886-8700
County: Wayne

Established in 1999 in MI.
Donor: Joseph M. Beals.
Grantmaker type: Independent foundation.
Financial data (yr. ended 07/31/10): Assets, $34,681 (M); expenditures, $1,700; total giving, $1,700; qualifying distributions, $1,700; giving activities include $1,700 for grants.
Fields of interest: Christian agencies & churches.
Type of support: General/operating support.
Officer: Joseph M. Beals, Pres.
EIN: 383478253

57

Joseph E. Beauchamp Charitable Trust
c/o JPMorgan Chase Bank, N.A.
P.O. Box 3038
Milwaukee, WI 53201-3038
County: Milwaukee
Contact: Michael Barry, Mgr.
Application address: c/o JPMorgan Chase Bank, N.A., Endowment and Foundation Div., 611 Woodward Ave., Detroit, MI 48226-3408, tel.: (313) 225-1249; E-mail: michael_barry@em.fcnbd.com

Established in 1976 in MI.
Grantmaker type: Independent foundation.
Financial data (yr. ended 12/31/09): Assets, $325,794 (M); expenditures, $7,183; total giving,

$2,500; qualifying distributions, $2,500; giving activities include $2,500 for grants.
Fields of interest: Performing arts; Higher education; Human services; Protestant agencies & churches.
Type of support: General/operating support; Continuing support; Annual campaigns; Equipment; Program development.
Limitations: Giving limited to MI. No grants to individuals.
Application information: Application form not required.
Initial approach: Letter or telephone
Deadline(s): None
Officer: Michael Barry, Mgr.
Trustee: JPMorgan Chase Bank, N.A.
EIN: 382119454

58
John & Nesbeth Bees School Foundation
c/o Citizens Bank, Wealth Mgmt.
328 S. Saginaw St., MC 002072
Flint, MI 48502-1923
County: Genesee
Application address: c/o Citizens Bank, N.A. Attn.: Helen James, Wealth Mgmt., 101 N. Washington Ave., Saginaw, MI 48607-1207, tel.: (989) 776-7368

Established in 1997 in MI.
Grantmaker type: Independent foundation.
Financial data (yr. ended 12/31/09): Assets, $573,666 (M); expenditures, $35,280; total giving, $21,500; qualifying distributions, $21,500; giving activities include $21,500 for grants to individuals.
Fields of interest: Higher education.
Type of support: Scholarships—to individuals.
Limitations: Giving limited to residents of Saginaw County, MI.
Application information: Application form required.
Deadline(s): May 1
Trustee: Citizens Bank.
EIN: 386601371

59
The Gloria Wille Bell and Carlos R. Bell Charitable Trust
c/o McGuire Woods, LLP
One James Center
901 E. Cary St.
Richmond, VA 23219-4030
County: Richmond City
Contact: John O'Grady
E-mail for John O'Grady: jogrady@mcguirewoods.com; URL: http://www.bellscholarship.org

Established in 2002 in VA.
Donor: Carlos R. Bell‡.
Grantmaker type: Independent foundation.
Financial data (yr. ended 06/30/10): Assets, $4,530,125 (M); expenditures, $401,499; total giving, $240,000; qualifying distributions, $240,000; giving activities include $240,000 for grants to individuals.
Purpose and activities: Funds scholarship awards to first year students attending the University of Michigan, Ann Arbor, entering the College of Engineering or the College of Literature, Science, and the Arts, who are enrolled in an undergraduate

degree program in the sciences and who meet specific geographic criteria.
Fields of interest: Higher education.
Type of support: Scholarships—to individuals; Scholarship funds.
Limitations: Applications accepted. Giving limited to benefit University of Michigan students at Ann Arbor who also meet one of the following geographic criteria: resident of the Commonwealth of VA; graduate of the Chicago, IL public, parochial, private school system, New Trier High School in Winnetka, IL, or Illinois Mathematics and Science Academy in Aurora; or resident of Allegan, Barry, Berrien, Branch, Calhoun, Cass, Eaton, Hillsdale, Ingham, Jackson, Kalamazoo, Lenawee, Livingston, Monroe, Oakland, St. Joseph, Van Buren, Washtenaw, or Wayne counties, MI.
Application information: Applications must be submitted online through Trust web site. Application form required.
Deadline(s): Feb. 1
Trustee: John B. O'Grady.
EIN: 546500526

60
Brian A. Bell Foundation
1032 Stonegate Ct.
Flint, MI 48532-2173
County: Genesee

Established in 2006 in MI.
Grantmaker type: Independent foundation.
Financial data (yr. ended 12/31/09): Assets, $1,270 (M); expenditures, $300; total giving, $0; qualifying distributions, $0.
Director: Howard Stout.
EIN: 205064269

61
Don & Iva Bellinger Scholarship Fund
c/o Citizens Bank, Wealth Mgmt.
328 S. Saginaw St., M/C 002072
Flint, MI 48502-1923 (989) 776-7368
County: Genesee
Application address: c/o Citizens Bank Wealth Mgmt., N.A., Attn.: Helen M. James, 101 N. Washington Ave., Saginaw, MI 48607-1207, tel.: (989) 776-7368

Established in 1993 in MI.
Donor: Iva Bellinger‡.
Grantmaker type: Independent foundation.
Financial data (yr. ended 12/31/09): Assets, $1,010,475 (M); expenditures, $54,916; total giving, $37,100; qualifying distributions, $48,978; giving activities include $37,100 for 32 grants to individuals (high: $1,750; low: $100).
Purpose and activities: Scholarship awards to students admitted to or already enrolled in a nursing program.
Fields of interest: Nursing school/education.
Type of support: Scholarships—to individuals.
Limitations: Giving limited to residents of MI.
Application information: Application form required.
Deadline(s): Jan. 31
Trustee: Citizens Bank.
EIN: 386615679

62
Samuel L. Bemis Scholarship Fund
c/o Fifth Third Bank
P.O. Box 3636
Grand Rapids, MI 49501-3636
County: Kent
Application address: c/o Brattleboro High School, Attn.: Guidance Counselor, 131 Fairground Rd., Brattleboro, VT 05301-6328, tel.: (802) 451-3400

Established in 1995 in IL.
Grantmaker type: Independent foundation.
Financial data (yr. ended 12/31/09): Assets, $1,162,471 (M); expenditures, $63,576; total giving, $49,733; qualifying distributions, $49,733; giving activities include $49,733 for grants to individuals.
Purpose and activities: Giving for Brattleboro Union High School, Vermont, including scholarship awards to graduating female seniors.
Fields of interest: Higher education; Women.
Type of support: General/operating support; Scholarships—to individuals.
Limitations: Giving limited to residents of Brattleboro, VT.
Application information:
Initial approach: Format provided by school
Deadline(s): May 10
Trustee: Fifth Third Bank.
EIN: 367112890

63
Alvin M. Bentley Foundation
P.O. Box 1516
Owosso, MI 48867-6516 (989) 723-7464
County: Shiawassee
Contact: Ann Marie Bentley, V.P.

Incorporated in 1961 in MI.
Donors: Alvin M. Bentley‡; Arvella D. Bentley‡.
Grantmaker type: Independent foundation.
Financial data (yr. ended 12/31/09): Assets, $2,022,252 (M); expenditures, $173,321; total giving, $148,500; qualifying distributions, $148,500; giving activities include $148,500 for 11 grants (high: $82,500; low: $500).
Purpose and activities: Giving primarily for higher education.
Fields of interest: Higher education; Human services.
Type of support: Scholarship funds.
Limitations: Applications accepted. Giving primarily in MI. No grants to individuals, or for building or endowment funds, or matching gifts.
Publications: Informational brochure.
Application information: Application form not required.
Initial approach: Letter
Deadline(s): Mar. 1
Officers: Paul Brown, Pres.; Ann Marie Bentley, V.P.; Marianne Manderfield, Secy.; Richard A. Batchelor, Treas.
Directors: Denise Bannan; Alvin M. Bentley IV; Susan Bentley; Mary Alice Campbell; Constance E. Cook; George W. Hoddy; Jan Barney Newman; David McDowell.
Number of staff: 1 part-time support.
EIN: 386076280
Selected grants: The following grants were reported in 2006.
$101,250 to University of Michigan, Ann Arbor, MI.
$1,000 to Boy Scouts of America.

64
Mary Maybury Berkery Memorial Trust
c/o Comerica Bank
P.O. Box 75000
Detroit, MI 48275-3302 (734) 930-2405
County: Wayne

Established in 1998 in MI.
Donor: Berkery Trust.
Grantmaker type: Independent foundation.
Financial data (yr. ended 08/31/10): Assets,
$246,298 (M); expenditures, $18,382; total giving,
$14,500; qualifying distributions, $14,500; giving
activities include $14,500 for grants.
Purpose and activities: Giving restricted to Roman
Catholic colleges and universities for scholarships
to women; some giving to organizations assisting
the needy.
Fields of interest: Higher education; Catholic
agencies & churches; Women; Economically
disadvantaged.
Type of support: Scholarship funds.
Limitations: Applications accepted. Giving limited to
MI. No grants to individuals.
Application information: Application form not
required.
   Initial approach: Letter
   Deadline(s): None
Trustee: Comerica Bank.
EIN: 386719148

65
Hy and Greta Berkowitz Foundation
c/o Daniels
1100 E. Paris Ave. S.E.
Grand Rapids, MI 49546-8367
County: Kent
Application address: c/o Grant Committee, 1600
Beard Dr. S.E., Grand Rapids, MI 49546-6408,
tel.: (616) 538-6000

Established in 1969 in MI.
Donors: Rogers Department Store; Hyman
Berkowitz; Greta Berkowitz.
Grantmaker type: Independent foundation.
Financial data (yr. ended 12/31/09): Assets,
$1,284,493 (M); expenditures, $36,436; total
giving, $23,119; qualifying distributions, $23,119;
giving activities include $23,119 for 7 grants (high:
$10,000; low: $300).
Fields of interest: Hospitals (specialty); Medical
research; Youth development.
Type of support: Annual campaigns.
Limitations: Applications accepted. Giving primarily
in Grand Rapids, MI and Middleton, OH. No grants
to individuals.
Application information:
   Initial approach: Letter
   Deadline(s): None
Officers: Shirley B. Hurwitz, Pres. and Secy.; Luanne
B. Thodey, V.P. and Treas.
EIN: 381907981

66
The Berry Foundation
3505 Stanton Ct.
Ann Arbor, MI 48105-3032
County: Washtenaw

Established in 1997 in OH.
Donor: Philip C. Berry.

Grantmaker type: Independent foundation.
Financial data (yr. ended 12/31/09): Assets,
$23,837 (M); gifts received, $13,112;
expenditures, $13,524; total giving, $13,500;
qualifying distributions, $13,500; giving activities
include $13,500 for grants.
Fields of interest: Higher education; Protestant
agencies & churches; Children/youth.
Limitations: Giving primarily in MI; giving also in NC.
No grants to individuals.
Trustees: Anne K. Beaubien; Philip C. Berry; Philip
K. Berry; Kathleen B. Irvin.
EIN: 311538611

67
**John W. and Margaret G. Bertsch
Charitable Foundation**
525 Buena Vista
Spring Lake, MI 49456-1736
County: Ottawa
Contact: J.R. Bertsch, Secy.-Treas.

Established in MI.
Donor: John W. Bertsch.
Grantmaker type: Independent foundation.
Financial data (yr. ended 12/31/09): Assets,
$1,350,038 (M); expenditures, $73,677; total
giving, $65,000; qualifying distributions, $65,000;
giving activities include $65,000 for grants.
Fields of interest: Elementary/secondary
education; Mental health, treatment; Recreation,
camps; Protestant agencies & churches; Physically
disabled.
Type of support: General/operating support.
Limitations: Giving primarily in Grand Rapids, MI,
and Philadelphia, PA. No grants to individuals.
Application information:
   Initial approach: Letter
   Deadline(s): None
Officer: J.R. Bertsch, Secy.-Treas.
EIN: 382772589

68
John & Melissa Besse Foundation
P.O. Box 29
Gladstone, MI 49837-0352
County: Delta
Contact: John D. Besse, Pres.

Established in 2005 in MI.
Donors: John D. Besse; Melissa Besse.
Grantmaker type: Independent foundation.
Financial data (yr. ended 12/31/09): Assets,
$2,347,585 (M); expenditures, $177,300; total
giving, $156,500; qualifying distributions,
$177,300; giving activities include $156,500 for 6
grants (high: $50,000; low: $500).
Fields of interest: Performing arts centers; Higher
education, college (community/junior); Animals/
wildlife; Boy scouts.
Type of support: General/operating support.
Limitations: Applications accepted. Giving primarily
in MI.
Application information:
   Initial approach: Letter or telephone
   Deadline(s): Varies
Officer: John D. Besse, Pres.
EIN: 203497950

69
Besser Foundation
123 N. 2nd Ave., Ste. 3
Alpena, MI 49707-2801 (989) 354-4722
County: Alpena
Contact: Gary Dawley, Secy.-Treas.
FAX: (989) 354-8099;
E-mail: besserfoundation@verizon.net

Incorporated in 1944 in MI.
Donors: J.H. Besser†; Besser Co.
Grantmaker type: Independent foundation.
Financial data (yr. ended 12/31/09): Assets,
$17,047,690 (M); expenditures, $905,196; total
giving, $766,212; qualifying distributions,
$766,212; giving activities include $766,212 for
grants.
Purpose and activities: Grants primarily to local
schools and colleges and health and social service
agencies; giving also to Africare for projects in
underdeveloped nations in Africa. In addition, the
foundation partially supports the Jesse Besser
Museum, a local historical and art museum.
Fields of interest: Museums; Arts; Education;
Human services; Children/youth, services.
Type of support: General/operating support;
Continuing support; Capital campaigns; Building/
renovation; Matching/challenge support.
Limitations: Applications accepted. Giving limited to
the Alpena, MI, area. No support for video projects.
No grants to individuals, or for endowment funds,
meeting or conference expenses, travel, or
research.
Publications: Annual report (including application
guidelines).
Application information: Applications sent via fax
accepted. Application form not required.
   Initial approach: Letter of introduction
   Copies of proposal: 1
   Deadline(s): End of 1st month in each calendar
      quarter
   Board meeting date(s): Quarterly beginning in Mar.
Officers and Trustees:* James C. Park,* Pres.;
Patricia Gardner,* V.P.; Gary C. Dawley,*
Secy.-Treas.; Christopher McCoy; J. Richard Wilson.
Number of staff: 2 part-time support.
EIN: 386071938
Selected grants: The following grants were reported
in 2007.
$35,000 to Boys and Girls Club of Alpena, Alpena,
MI.
$29,000 to Alpena Community College, Alpena, MI.
$25,000 to Shelter, Inc., Alpena, MI.
$20,000 to Thunder Bay Theater, Alpena, MI.
$15,000 to Alpena Public Schools, Alpena, MI.
$11,000 to Boys and Girls Club of Alpena, Alpena,
MI.
$7,300 to Thunder Bay Arts Council, Alpena, MI.
$5,000 to First Congregational Church, Alpena, MI.
$5,000 to Trinity Episcopal Church, Alpena, MI.
$2,500 to Michigan Freedom Foundation, Lansing,
MI.

70
Betmar Charitable Foundation, Inc.
4868 Fairway Ridge S.
West Bloomfield, MI 48323-3314
(248) 855-0606
County: Oakland
Contact: Allan Jacobs, Pres.

Established in 1999 in MI.
Donor: Howard Bayer.

Grantmaker type: Independent foundation.
Financial data (yr. ended 12/31/09): Assets, $1,478,552 (M); expenditures, $183,378; total giving, $92,221; qualifying distributions, $92,221; giving activities include $92,221 for 59 grants (high: $14,150; low: $250).
Fields of interest: Education; Health organizations, association; Human services; Jewish federated giving programs; Jewish agencies & synagogues.
Application information: Application form required.
   Initial approach: Letter
   Deadline(s): None
Officers and Directors:* Allan Jacobs,* Pres. and Secy.; Douglas Shiffman,* V.P. and Treas.; Goldie Jacobs.
EIN: 383515213

71
Duane & Dorothy Bierlein Family Foundation
c/o Zehnder & Assocs., P.C.
516 S. Main St.
Frankenmuth, MI   48734-1639
County: Saginaw
Contact: Dorothy P. Bierlein, Pres.

Established in 2001 in MI.
Donors: Duane Bierlein; Dorothy P. Bierlein.
Grantmaker type: Independent foundation.
Financial data (yr. ended 12/31/09): Assets, $332,870 (M); gifts received, $20,000; expenditures, $15,776; total giving, $14,752; qualifying distributions, $15,316; giving activities include $14,752 for 13 grants (high: $3,352; low: $400).
Fields of interest: Human services.
Limitations: Applications accepted. Giving primarily in Frankenmuth, MI.
Application information: Application form not required.
   Initial approach: Letter
   Deadline(s): None
Officers and Directors:* Dorothy P. Bierlein, Pres.; Randall D. Bierlein, V.P.; Robert A. Loesel, Secy.-Treas.; Barbara Bierlein.
EIN: 383637097

72
Shari and Bob Bilkie Family Foundation
7798 Hidden Ridge Ln.
Northville, MI   48168-9664   (248) 223-0122
County: Wayne

Established in 2007.
Donors: Robert Bilkie; Shari Bilkie.
Grantmaker type: Independent foundation.
Financial data (yr. ended 12/31/10): Assets, $0 (M); expenditures, $3,585; total giving, $3,235; qualifying distributions, $3,235; giving activities include $3,235 for grants.
Fields of interest: Hospitals (general).
Type of support: Building/renovation.
Limitations: Giving primarily in MI.
Officers: Shari Bilkie, Pres.; Robert Bilkie, Treas.
Directors: Ashley Bilkie; Megan Bilkie; Amanda Lehnert.
EIN: 208611983

73
Guido A. & Elizabeth H. Binda Foundation
15 Capital Ave. N.E., Ste. 205
Battle Creek, MI   49017-3557   (269) 968-6171
County: Calhoun
Contact: Nancy Taber, Exec. Dir.
FAX: (269) 968-5126;
E-mail: grants@bindafoundation.org; URL: http://www.bindafoundation.org

Established in 1977 in MI.
Donor: Guido A. Binda†.
Grantmaker type: Independent foundation.
Financial data (yr. ended 06/30/10): Assets, $20,233,703 (M); gifts received, $7,485,976; expenditures, $1,107,080; total giving, $935,498; qualifying distributions, $935,498; giving activities include $935,498 for grants.
Purpose and activities: Giving primarily for education and dyslexia; support also for health care, community development, and human services.
Fields of interest: Visual arts, architecture; Arts; Elementary school/education; Secondary school/education; Higher education; Adult education—literacy, basic skills & GED; Education, reading; Education; Environment; Human services.
Type of support: Curriculum development; Program development; Scholarship funds; Seed money.
Limitations: Giving limited to Battle Creek and southwestern MI. No grants to individuals, or for endowments, capital campaigns, trips, conferences or summer camps.
Publications: Application guidelines; Occasional report.
Application information: Following a review of the letter of inquiry, the foundation will forward its grant application if the grant request is within the scope of the foundation's mission. Application form required.
   Initial approach: Letter of Inquiry (via e-mail or U.S. mail)
   Copies of proposal: 11
   Deadline(s): Dec. 1 to May 1
   Board meeting date(s): Jan. and June
   Final notification: 10 days
Officers and Trustees:* Richard Tsoumas,* V.P.; Nancy Taber, Exec. Dir.; Robert Binda; LaVerne H. Boss; Norman Brown; Chris T. Christ; John Hosking; Joel Orosz; Cindy S. Ruble.
Number of staff: 1 part-time support.
EIN: 382184423
Selected grants: The following grants were reported in 2006.
$100,000 to Binder Park Zoological Society, Battle Creek, MI.
$50,000 to Planned Parenthood Northern Michigan, Traverse City, MI.
$48,060 to Binder Park Zoological Society, Battle Creek, MI.
$42,670 to Binder Park Zoological Society, Battle Creek, MI.
$30,000 to Kingman Museum, Battle Creek, MI.
$20,000 to Teen HEART, Kalamazoo, MI.
$10,000 to Olivet College, Olivet, MI.
$5,000 to Art Center of Battle Creek, Battle Creek, MI.
$2,500 to Albion College, Albion, MI.
$1,500 to Family Health Center of Battle Creek, Battle Creek, MI.

74
Natalie Binion Foundation
c/o Gerald Nelson
17695 Glenmore
Redford, MI   48240-2159
County: Wayne

Established in MI.
Grantmaker type: Independent foundation.
Financial data (yr. ended 12/31/08): Assets, $183 (M); expenditures, $0; total giving, $0; qualifying distributions, $0.
Officers: Natalie Binion, Pres.; Gerald Nelson, V.P.
EIN: 223859203

75
Birkenstock Family Foundation
32100 Telegraph Rd., Ste. 200
Bingham Farms, MI   48025-2454
(248) 642-7733
County: Oakland
Contact: Thomas W. Payne, Tr.

Established in 2001 in MI; funded in 2005.
Donor: Horace C. Birkenstock Trust.
Grantmaker type: Independent foundation.
Financial data (yr. ended 12/31/09): Assets, $92,493 (M); expenditures, $20,263; total giving, $18,418; qualifying distributions, $18,418; giving activities include $18,418 for grants to individuals.
Purpose and activities: Scholarship awards to residents of Birkenstock Farms, Hidden Ponds, and Pebble Creek Village Estates, Howell, Michigan.
Fields of interest: Higher education.
Type of support: Scholarships—to individuals.
Limitations: Applications accepted. Giving limited to residents of Howell, MI.
Application information: Application form required.
   Deadline(s): None
Trustees: Thomas W. Payne; First National Bank of Howell.
EIN: 912119072

76
F. Ross & Laura Jean Birkhill Family Foundation
c/o Comerica Bank
P.O. Box 75000, MC 3302
Detroit, MI   48275-3302
County: Wayne
Contact: William Birkhill, Pres.
Application address: 253 Marblehead Dr., Bloomfield Hills, MI 8304-3338, tel.: (248) 258-0366

Established in 2006 in MI.
Donor: Laura Jean Birkhill.
Grantmaker type: Independent foundation.
Financial data (yr. ended 12/31/09): Assets, $1,267,227 (M); expenditures, $83,594; total giving, $70,650; qualifying distributions, $70,650; giving activities include $70,650 for grants.
Fields of interest: Animal welfare; Foundations (community).
Type of support: General/operating support.
Limitations: Giving primarily in MI.
Application information:
   Initial approach: Letter
   Deadline(s): None

Officers: William Birkhill, Pres.; Frederick Birkhill, Jr., V.P.
EIN: 412184583

77
Birtwistle Family Foundation
(formerly Donald B. Birtwistle Foundation)
300 N. Rath Ave., Apt. 25
Ludington, MI   49431-3005   (616) 843-2501
County: Mason
Contact: Joclyn Birtwhistle, Pres.

Established in 1987 in MI.
Donor: Donald B. Birtwistle.
Grantmaker type: Independent foundation.
Financial data (yr. ended 12/31/09): Assets, $1,830,118 (M); expenditures, $122,805; total giving, $119,500; qualifying distributions, $119,500; giving activities include $119,500 for 20 grants (high: $58,000; low: $500).
Purpose and activities: Giving primarily for education, including scholarships to graduates of the Ludington, MI, area school district. Applicants must be in their senior year of college for scholarships.
Fields of interest: Education; Human services; Foundations (community).
Type of support: General/operating support; Scholarships—to individuals.
Limitations: Giving limited to MI, primarily in the Ludington area.
Application information: Application form required.
   Deadline(s): Apr. 1 for applicants who are in their senior year of high school
Officers: Joclyn Birtwistle, Pres.; Sarah Pelfresne, V.P.; Jeff Slaggert, Secy.; Sheryl Rice, Treas.
EIN: 382787567

78
A. G. Bishop Charitable Trust
c/o JPMorgan Chase Bank, N.A.
P.O. Box 3038
Milwaukee, WI   53201-3038
County: Milwaukee
Application address: c/o JPMorgan Chase Bank, N.A., 125 S. Main St., Ann Arbor, MI 48104-1902, tel.: (734) 995-8171

Trust established in 1944 in MI.
Donor: Arthur Giles Bishop‡.
Grantmaker type: Independent foundation.
Financial data (yr. ended 12/31/09): Assets, $10,132,041 (M); expenditures, $554,401; total giving, $478,200; qualifying distributions, $478,200; giving activities include $478,200 for grants.
Purpose and activities: Giving primarily for education, the arts, and youth and social services.
Fields of interest: Arts; Higher education; Human services; Children/youth, services; Foundations (private grantmaking); United Ways and Federated Giving Programs.
Type of support: General/operating support; Continuing support; Annual campaigns; Building/renovation; Equipment; Land acquisition; Debt reduction; Emergency funds; Seed money; Research.
Limitations: Giving limited to the Flint and Genesee County, MI, community. No grants to individuals, or for endowment funds, scholarships, fellowships, or matching gifts; no loans.

Publications: Application guidelines.
Application information: Application form not required.
   Initial approach: Letter
   Copies of proposal: 3
   Deadline(s): None
   Board meeting date(s): 2 to 3 times per year
   Final notification: 6 months
Trustees: Robert J. Bellairs, Jr.; Elizabeth B. Wentworth; JPMorgan Chase Bank, N.A.
EIN: 386040693
Selected grants: The following grants were reported in 2009.
$130,000 to United Way of Genesee County, Flint, MI.
$53,000 to Flint Cultural Center Corporation, Flint, MI.
$20,500 to Shelter of Flint, Flint, MI.
$20,000 to Crim Fitness Foundation, Flint, MI.
$20,000 to Foundation for Mott Community College, Flint, MI.
$11,000 to Big Brothers Big Sisters of Greater Flint, Flint, MI.
$10,000 to Boy Scouts of America, Flint, MI.
$10,000 to Genesee Intermediate School District, Flint, MI.
$10,000 to Habitat for Humanity, Genesee County, Flint, MI.
$10,000 to Urban League of Flint, Flint, MI.

79
BJB Charitable Trust
6115-28th St. S.E.
Grand Rapids, MI   49546
County: Kent
Contact: Daniel J. Kamphuis, Tr.
Application address: 7043 60th St., Grand Rapids, MI 49512

Established in 1995 in MI.
Donors: Daniel J. Kamphuis; Rhonda Kamphuis.
Grantmaker type: Independent foundation.
Financial data (yr. ended 12/31/09): Assets, $67,739 (M); expenditures, $42,667; total giving, $42,100; qualifying distributions, $42,100; giving activities include $42,100 for grants.
Fields of interest: Christian agencies & churches.
Limitations: Giving primarily in MI.
Application information: Application form not required.
   Deadline(s): None
Trustees: William Hitchcock; Daniel J. Kamphuis.
EIN: 383266496

80
Dorothy Blakely Foundation
6075 Browns Lake Rd.
Jackson, MI   49203
County: Jackson
Application address: c/o Charles H. Aymond, 100 S. Jackson St., Ste. 206, Jackson, MI 49201, tel.: (517) 787-5600

Donor: Dorothy M. Blakely.
Grantmaker type: Independent foundation.
Financial data (yr. ended 11/30/09): Assets, $2,233,846 (M); expenditures, $179,454; total giving, $155,000; qualifying distributions, $155,000; giving activities include $155,000 for 10 grants (high: $60,000; low: $5,000).

Fields of interest: Museums; Performing arts; Animal welfare; Family services; Aging, centers/services.
Limitations: Applications accepted. Giving primarily in the Jackson, MI, area. No grants to individuals.
Application information:
   Initial approach: Letter
   Deadline(s): Oct. 1
Officers: Douglas Burdick, Pres.; Charles H. Aymond, Secy.
Director: James A. Hildreth.
EIN: 616055236
Selected grants: The following grants were reported in 2008.
$50,000 to Jackson Symphony Orchestra Association, Jackson, MI.
$15,000 to John George Home, Jackson, MI.
$10,000 to Jackson Interfaith Shelter, Jackson, MI.
$8,000 to Family Services and Childrens Aid, Jackson, MI.
$8,000 to Jackson Friendly Home, Jackson, MI.
$5,000 to Michigan Shakespeare Festival, Jackson, MI.

81
Blaske-Hill Foundation
500 S. Main St.
Ann Arbor, MI   48104-2921   (734) 747-7055
County: Washtenaw
Contact: E. Robert Blaske, Secy.-Treas.

Established in MI.
Donors: Patricia MacLeod; Members of the Blaske Family.
Grantmaker type: Independent foundation.
Financial data (yr. ended 02/28/10): Assets, $316,041 (M); expenditures, $22,131; total giving, $20,000; qualifying distributions, $21,087; giving activities include $20,000 for 10 grants to individuals (high: $2,000; low: $2,000).
Purpose and activities: Scholarship awards to graduates of Battle Creek Central, Battle Creek St. Philip, and Niles high schools, Michigan.
Fields of interest: Higher education.
Type of support: Scholarships—to individuals.
Limitations: Giving limited to Battle Creek and Niles, MI.
Application information: Application form required.
   Initial approach: Letter
   Deadline(s): Mar. 15
Officers: Patricia MacLeod, Pres.; Thomas H. Blaske, V.P.; E. Robert Blaske, Secy.-Treas.
EIN: 382525817

82
The Blodgett Foundation
2740 Littlefield Dr. N.E.
Grand Rapids, MI   49506-1231
County: Kent
Contact: Vicki Patton

Established in 1994 in MI.
Donor: Edith I. Blodgett.
Grantmaker type: Independent foundation.
Financial data (yr. ended 12/31/09): Assets, $3,295,324 (M); expenditures, $315,676; total giving, $264,500; qualifying distributions, $265,420; giving activities include $264,500 for 31 grants (high: $50,000; low: $500).
Purpose and activities: Giving primarily for the arts, higher education, and human services.

Fields of interest: Arts; Higher education; Human services; Children/youth, services; Aging, centers/ services.

Type of support: Building/renovation; Equipment; Program development; Curriculum development; Consulting services; Program evaluation; Matching/ challenge support.

Limitations: Applications accepted. Giving primarily in Grand Rapids and the western MI, area. No support for religious groups or affiliations. No grants to individuals.

Publications: Application guidelines.

Application information: Application form required.

Initial approach: Letter
Copies of proposal: 1
Deadline(s): None
Board meeting date(s): Spring and fall

Officer: Edith I. Blodgett, Pres.

Trustee: Wendy Greeney.

Number of staff: 1 part-time support.

EIN: 383202330

Selected grants: The following grants were reported in 2008.

$50,000 to Camp Blodgett, Grand Rapids, MI.
$25,000 to Opera Grand Rapids, Grand Rapids, MI.
$10,000 to Grand Rapids Symphony, Grand Rapids, MI.
$5,000 to Blue Lake Fine Arts Camp, Twin Lake, MI.
$5,000 to Leukemia & Lymphoma Society, Madison Heights, MI.
$5,000 to Pine Mountain Music Festival, Hancock, MI.
$3,000 to Christian Counseling Center, Grand Rapids, MI.
$2,500 to Wedgwood Christian Services, Grand Rapids, MI.
$1,000 to Close Up Foundation, Alexandria, VA.
$1,000 to Interlochen Center for the Arts, Interlochen, MI.

83
The Blue Foundation, Inc.
2732 Oakmont Dr.
Bay City, MI   48706   (734) 341-9501
County: Bay
Contact: Matt Nolan, Pres.

Donor: Matthew J. Nolan.

Grantmaker type: Independent foundation.

Financial data (yr. ended 12/31/09): Assets, $13,500 (M); gifts received, $10,875; expenditures, $2,603; total giving, $2,500; qualifying distributions, $2,500; giving activities include $2,500 for 1 grant.

Limitations: Applications accepted. Giving primarily in Muskegon, MI.

Application information: Application form required.

Initial approach: Proposal
Deadline(s): Mar.

Officer and Directors:* Matt Nolan,* Pres.; Nancy J. Moody; Daniel P. Nolan.

EIN: 262931135

84
John A. & Marlene L. Boll Foundation
100 Maple Park Blvd., Ste. 118
St. Clair Shores, MI   48081-2253
(586) 777-4770
County: Macomb

Established in 1986 in MI.

Donors: John A. Boll; Marlene L. Boll.

Grantmaker type: Independent foundation.

Financial data (yr. ended 12/31/09): Assets, $4,776,888 (M); expenditures, $2,303,416; total giving, $2,184,919; qualifying distributions, $2,184,919; giving activities include $2,184,919 for 141 grants (high: $200,000; low: $42).

Purpose and activities: Giving educational scholarships to institutions with curriculum based, in part, on Judeo-Christian traditions.

Fields of interest: Arts; Higher education; Scholarships/financial aid; Health care; Human services; Christian agencies & churches.

Type of support: General/operating support.

Limitations: Giving in the U.S., with emphasis on MI. No grants to individuals.

Application information: Letters of recommendation for scholarship candidates are required for further review. Application form not required.

Initial approach: Letter or telephone
Deadline(s): None

Directors: John A. Boll; Marlene L. Boll; Kristine B. Mestdagh.

EIN: 382708121

Selected grants: The following grants were reported in 2007.

$75,000 to Vail Valley Foundation, Cornerstone Friends, Vail, CO.
$25,000 to YMCA of Metropolitan Detroit, Detroit, MI.
$22,000 to Ecumenical Theological Seminary, Detroit, MI.
$20,000 to Vail Valley Foundation, Vail, CO.
$15,000 to Michigan Opera Theater, Detroit, MI.
$15,000 to Ocean Reef Cultural Center, Key Largo, FL.
$12,000 to Immanuel Lutheran Church, Macomb, MI.
$10,000 to Ecumenical Theological Seminary, Detroit, MI.
$5,000 to Youth Foundation, Edwards, CO.
$2,000 to Michigan Opera Theater, Detroit, MI.

85
Bonisteel Foundation
P.O. Box 7348
Ann Arbor, MI   48107-7348
County: Washtenaw
Contact: Edmund J. Sikorski, Jr., Asst. Secy.

Established in 1972 in MI.

Donors: Roscoe O. Bonisteel, Sr.‡; Lillian Bonisteel‡.

Grantmaker type: Independent foundation.

Financial data (yr. ended 12/31/09): Assets, $1,044,432 (M); expenditures, $110,760; total giving, $100,000; qualifying distributions, $100,000; giving activities include $100,000 for grants.

Purpose and activities: Giving primarily for higher education and arts centers.

Fields of interest: Arts; Higher education.

Type of support: General/operating support; Capital campaigns; Building/renovation; Equipment.

Limitations: Applications accepted. Giving primarily in Washtenaw County, MI. No support for political organizations. No grants to individuals.

Application information: Application form not required.

Initial approach: Letter
Copies of proposal: 5
Deadline(s): Oct. 15

Board meeting date(s): Dec. 15
Final notification: Dec. 31

Officer and Trustees:* Jean B. Knecht,* Pres. and Secy.; Mary C. Byl; Betty B. Johnson.

Number of staff: None.

EIN: 237155774

Selected grants: The following grants were reported in 2006.

$5,000 to Boy Scouts of America, Ann Arbor, MI.
$2,500 to Saint Joseph Mercy Hospital, Ypsilanti, MI.

86
The Bonner Foundation
507 N. Barnard St.
Howell, MI   48843-1601   (517) 540-1873
County: Livingston
Contact: Christine Bonner, Pres.

Established in MI.

Donors: Asa W. Bonner, Sr.‡; A.T.&G. Co., Inc.; M.S. Fetcher Co.

Grantmaker type: Independent foundation.

Financial data (yr. ended 12/31/09): Assets, $580,803 (M); expenditures, $43,554; total giving, $32,000; qualifying distributions, $32,000; giving activities include $32,000 for grants.

Fields of interest: Higher education; Protestant agencies & churches.

Type of support: General/operating support; Scholarship funds.

Limitations: Giving primarily in AR and MI.

Application information:

Initial approach: Letter or proposal
Deadline(s): Sept. 30

Officer: Christine Bonner, Pres.

EIN: 386068648

87
Joseph Sloan Bonsall and Mary Ann Bonsall Foundation
16845 Kercheval, Ste. 5
Grosse Pointe, MI   48230-1551
County: Wayne

Established in 1997 in MI.

Grantmaker type: Independent foundation.

Financial data (yr. ended 12/31/09): Assets, $73,493 (M); gifts received, $10,300; expenditures, $1,628; total giving, $1,500; qualifying distributions, $1,500; giving activities include $1,500 for grants.

Fields of interest: Animal welfare.

Type of support: General/operating support.

Limitations: Giving primarily in Hendersonville, TN. No grants to individuals.

Application information: Application form not required.

Deadline(s): None

Officers and Trustees:* Joseph Sloan Bonsall,* Pres.; S. Gary Spicer,* Secy.; Mary Ann Bonsall,* Treas.

EIN: 383377889

88
The Borman's, Inc. Fund
(formerly The Borman Fund)
32406 Franklin Rd.
P.O. Box 250520
Franklin, MI 48025-9991 (248) 203-9333
County: Oakland
Contact: Paul Borman, Pres.

Established in 1955 in MI.
Donors: Paul Borman; Marlene Borman; Borman's, Inc.; The Great Atlantic & Pacific Tea Co., Inc.
Grantmaker type: Independent foundation.
Financial data (yr. ended 12/31/09): Assets, $21,069 (M); gifts received, $20; expenditures, $11,565; total giving, $11,545; qualifying distributions, $11,545; giving activities include $11,545 for grants.
Fields of interest: Arts; Education; Employment; Human services; Community/economic development; Jewish federated giving programs.
International interests: Israel.
Type of support: Annual campaigns; Capital campaigns.
Limitations: Giving primarily in southeastern MI. No grants to individuals.
Publications: Application guidelines.
Application information: Application form not required.
Initial approach: Letter
Deadline(s): None
Officers: Paul Borman, Pres.; Marlene Borman, V.P.; Gilbert Borman, Secy.-Treas.
Number of staff: 1 part-time support.
EIN: 386069267

89
Borovoy Family Foundation
c/o Joyce Borovoy
6529 Pleasant Lake Ct.
West Bloomfield, MI 48322-4709
County: Oakland

Established in 1995 in MI.
Donor: Mathew Borovoy.
Grantmaker type: Independent foundation.
Financial data (yr. ended 12/31/09): Assets, $491 (M); gifts received, $3,295; expenditures, $5,778; total giving, $4,885; qualifying distributions, $4,885; giving activities include $4,885 for grants.
Fields of interest: Theology; Scholarships/financial aid; Environment, natural resources; Cancer; Arthritis; Multiple sclerosis; Diabetes; American Red Cross; Jewish agencies & synagogues.
Type of support: General/operating support; Scholarship funds.
Limitations: Giving primarily in MI and NY. No grants to individuals (directly).
Application information:
Initial approach: Letter
Deadline(s): None
Officer: Joyce Borovoy, Secy.
Directors: Marc A. Borovoy; Cynthia R. Diskin; Debra L. Garemk.
EIN: 383227208

90
Steven and Elaine Bossenbroek Family Foundation
1853 Van Buren St.
Hudsonville, MI 49426-9445
County: Ottawa

Established in 2007 in MI.
Donors: Steven L. Bossenbroek; Elaine K. Bossenbroek.
Grantmaker type: Independent foundation.
Financial data (yr. ended 12/31/09): Assets, $1,244 (M); gifts received, $9,500; expenditures, $13,010; total giving, $12,707; qualifying distributions, $12,707; giving activities include $12,707 for grants.
Fields of interest: Christian agencies & churches.
Limitations: Giving primarily in MI.
Officers: Steven L. Bossenbroek, Pres. and Treas.; Elaine K. Bossenbroek, V.P. and Secy.
Directors: Geoffrey Bossenbroek; Steven L. Bossenbroek II; Ciri Mingerink.
EIN: 260761194

91
Henry Bouma, Jr. and Carolyn L. Bouma Foundation
2749 Beechtree Dr. S.W.
Byron Center, MI 49315-9475
County: Kent

Established in 1993 in MI.
Donors: Henry Bouma, Jr.; Carolyn L. Bouma.
Grantmaker type: Independent foundation.
Financial data (yr. ended 12/31/09): Assets, $187 (M); gifts received, $1,567; expenditures, $155,140; total giving, $153,500; qualifying distributions, $153,500; giving activities include $153,500 for 8 grants (high: $50,000; low: $1,500).
Purpose and activities: Giving primarily for Christian churches, ministries, and schools.
Fields of interest: Elementary/secondary education; Higher education; Human services; Youth, services; Christian agencies & churches.
Limitations: Giving primarily in Grand Rapids, MI. No grants to individuals.
Trustees: Carolyn L. Bouma; Henry Bouma, Jr.
EIN: 383106861
Selected grants: The following grants were reported in 2006.
$50,000 to Mission 21 India, Grand Rapids, MI.
$30,000 to Bethany Christian Services, Grand Rapids, MI.
$22,500 to Guiding Light Mission, Grand Rapids, MI.
$10,000 to Calvin Christian School, Wyoming, MI.
$10,000 to Potters House, Grand Rapids, MI.
$6,000 to Back to God Ministries International, Palos Heights, IL.
$2,500 to Focus on the Family, Colorado Springs, CO.
$2,500 to Insight for Living, Anaheim, CA.
$2,200 to Holland Home, Grand Rapids, MI.

92
Boutell Memorial Fund
(formerly Arnold and Gertrude Boutell Memorial Fund)
c/o Citizens Bank Wealth Mgmt., N.A.
328 S. Saginaw St., M/C 001065
Flint, MI 48502-1926
County: Genesee
Application address: c/o Helen James, Citizens Bank Wealth Mgmt., N.A., 101 N. Washington Ave., Saginaw, MI 48607, tel.: (989) 776-7368

Established in 1961 in MI.
Donors: Arnold Boutell‡; Gertrude Boutell‡.
Grantmaker type: Independent foundation.
Financial data (yr. ended 03/31/10): Assets, $10,945,607 (M); expenditures, $658,518; total giving, $543,926; qualifying distributions, $564,322; giving activities include $543,926 for 25 grants (high: $166,666; low: $2,500).
Purpose and activities: Giving primarily for human services and federated giving programs.
Fields of interest: Museums (children's); Human services; Children/youth, services; United Ways and Federated Giving Programs; Christian agencies & churches.
Type of support: Equipment; Program development.
Limitations: Giving limited to Saginaw County, MI. No grants to individuals, or for endowment funds.
Application information: Application form required.
Initial approach: Letter
Copies of proposal: 1
Deadline(s): None
Board meeting date(s): 3rd Wed. of Mar., June, Sept., and Dec.
Trustee: Citizens Bank.
EIN: 386040492
Selected grants: The following grants were reported in 2010.
$166,666 to Mid-Michigan Childrens Museum, Saginaw, MI.
$100,000 to United Way of Saginaw County, Saginaw, MI.
$100,000 to United Way of Saginaw County, Saginaw, MI.
$10,000 to East Side Soup Kitchen, Saginaw, MI.
$10,000 to Food Bank of Eastern Michigan, Flint, MI.
$10,000 to Hidden Harvest, Saginaw, MI.
$10,000 to Neighborhood House, Saginaw, MI.
$10,000 to Underground Railroad, Saginaw, MI.
$5,000 to Underground Railroad, Saginaw, MI.

93
The Brauer Foundation
16333 Heron Dr.
Spring Lake, MI 49456 (616) 846-2648
County: Ottawa
Contact: Harold C. Schmidt, Pres.

Established around 1978 in MI.
Donor: Carl A. Brauer, Jr.
Grantmaker type: Independent foundation.
Financial data (yr. ended 03/31/10): Assets, $1,038,668 (M); expenditures, $83,944; total giving, $76,500; qualifying distributions, $76,500; giving activities include $76,500 for grants.
Purpose and activities: Giving primarily to Lutheran charities.
Fields of interest: Elementary/secondary education; Higher education; Human services; Protestant agencies & churches.
Type of support: General/operating support.

Limitations: Applications accepted. Giving primarily in MI. No support for advocacy, athletic, political or veterans organizations, the United Way, or state and local government agencies. No grants to individuals, or for special events.
Application information: Application form not required.
Deadline(s): None
Officers and Trustees:* Harold C. Schmidt,* Pres.; Richard D. Brauer, V.P.; Carol D. Schmidt,* Secy.-Treas.; Janet E. Ash; Carl A. Brauer, Jr.
EIN: 382156710

94
Viola E. Bray Charitable Trust
c/o Merrill Lynch Trust Co.
580 Westlake Park Blvd., Ste. 1100
Houston, TX 77079-2669
County: Harris
Contact: Manjula Shaw, Trust Off.

Established in 1961 in MI.
Donor: Viola E. Bray‡.
Grantmaker type: Independent foundation.
Financial data (yr. ended 09/30/07): Assets, $3,763,450 (M); expenditures, $194,504; total giving, $115,669; qualifying distributions, $123,744; giving activities include $115,669 for 13 grants (high: $63,044; low: $875).
Purpose and activities: Giving primarily for women's services.
Fields of interest: Museums (art); Reproductive health, family planning; American Red Cross; YM/YWCAs & YM/YWHAs; Children/youth, services; Women, centers/services.
Type of support: Continuing support; Annual campaigns; Building/renovation; Equipment; Emergency funds; Seed money; Matching/challenge support.
Limitations: Applications accepted. Giving limited to the Flint, MI, area. No grants to individuals, research, scholarships, or fellowships; no loans.
Publications: Application guidelines; Program policy statement.
Application information: Application form not required.
Initial approach: 1-page proposal
Copies of proposal: 1
Deadline(s): Aug. 1
Board meeting date(s): Sept.
Final notification: 3 months
Trustees: James Johnson; Molly Bray McCormick; Sally Richards Ricker; William L. Ricker; Merrill Lynch Trust Co.
EIN: 386039741
Selected grants: The following grants were reported in 2005.
$63,865 to Flint Institute of Arts, Flint, MI. For general support of the Bray Gallery.
$10,780 to Every Womans Place, Muskegon, MI. For general support.
$10,000 to Kentucky Fish and Wildlife Education and Resource Foundation, Frankfort, KY. For national Archery In Schools program.
$7,500 to Junior Achievement, Greater Genesee Valley, Flint, MI. For program support.
$5,800 to Womens Resource Center of Northern Michigan, Petoskey, MI. For capital support.

95
Jonathan D. Brege Memorial Foundation
c/o JPMorgan Chase Bank, N.A.
P.O. Box 3038
Milwaukee, WI 53201-3038
County: Milwaukee
Application address: c/o Donald R. Brege, 5224 Byron Rd., Corunna, MI 48817-9742

Established in MI.
Donor: Donald R. Brege.
Grantmaker type: Independent foundation.
Financial data (yr. ended 09/30/07): Assets, $529,887 (M); expenditures, $29,925; total giving, $22,500; qualifying distributions, $24,637; giving activities include $22,500 for grants to individuals.
Purpose and activities: Scholarship awards to graduating students from Onaway High School and New Lothrop High School, Michigan.
Fields of interest: Higher education.
Type of support: Scholarships—to individuals.
Limitations: Applications accepted. Giving limited to MI.
Application information: Application form required.
Initial approach: Letter
Deadline(s): None
Trustee: JPMorgan Chase Bank, N.A.
EIN: 386477703

96
The Brennan Family Charitable Trust
123 Noren Rd.
Iron River, MI 49935-8478
County: Iron
Contact: Margaret M. Brennan, Tr.

Established in 1995 in OH.
Grantmaker type: Independent foundation.
Financial data (yr. ended 12/31/09): Assets, $134,542 (M); expenditures, $12,026; total giving, $9,040; qualifying distributions, $9,040; giving activities include $9,040 for grants.
Fields of interest: Museums; Human services; Christian agencies & churches.
Limitations: Giving primarily in Iron River, MI. No grants to individuals.
Application information:
Initial approach: Proposal
Deadline(s): Jan., Apr., July, Oct.
Trustees: James R. Brennan; Margaret M. Brennan.
EIN: 341813450

97
C. William Brenske Scholarship Fund
c/o Citizens Bank Wealth Mgmt., N.A.
328 S. Saginaw St., M/C 002072
Flint, MI 48502-1923
County: Genesee
Contact: Helen James
Application address: Helen James, c/o Citizens Bank Wealth Mgmt., NA, 101 N. Washington Ave., Saginaw, MI 48607, tel.: (989) 776-7368

Established in MI.
Grantmaker type: Independent foundation.
Financial data (yr. ended 12/31/09): Assets, $120,660 (M); expenditures, $9,741; total giving, $4,600; qualifying distributions, $7,243; giving activities include $4,600 for 11 grants to individuals (high: $500; low: $300).

Purpose and activities: Scholarships only to residents of Saginaw County, MI, attending Nouvel Catholic Central High School.
Type of support: Scholarships—to individuals.
Limitations: Applications accepted. Giving limited to residents of Saginaw County, MI.
Application information: Application form required.
Deadline(s): May 1
Trustee: Citizens Bank.
EIN: 386568888

98
Anthony Stephen & Elizabeth E. Brenske Student Loan Fund
c/o Citizens Bank Wealth Mgmt., N.A.
328 S. Saginaw St., M/C 002072
Flint, MI 48502-1923
County: Genesee
Application address: c/o Helen James, Citizens Bank Wealth Mgmt., N.A., 101 N. Washington Ave., Saginaw, MI 48607, tel.: (989) 776-7368

Established in MI.
Grantmaker type: Independent foundation.
Financial data (yr. ended 12/31/09): Assets, $228,170 (M); expenditures, $7,139; total giving, $0; qualifying distributions, $0.
Purpose and activities: Loans only to residents of Saginaw County attending a Michigan college or university.
Type of support: Student loans—to individuals.
Limitations: Giving limited to residents of Saginaw County, MI.
Application information: Application form required.
Deadline(s): May 1
Trustee: Citizens Bank.
EIN: 386568889

99
The Briggs-Fisher Foundation
46 Depetris Way
Grosse Pointe Farms, MI 48236-3701
(313) 886-9713
County: Wayne
Contact: Walter B. Fisher, Pres.

Established in 2005 in MI.
Donor: Mary Elizabeth Fisher Trust.
Grantmaker type: Independent foundation.
Financial data (yr. ended 12/31/09): Assets, $93,789 (M); gifts received, $220,000; expenditures, $291,835; total giving, $289,774; qualifying distributions, $289,774; giving activities include $289,774 for 10 grants (high: $115,000; low: $9,774).
Fields of interest: Higher education; Medical school/education; Food services; Catholic agencies & churches.
Limitations: Applications accepted. Giving primarily in MI, with emphasis on Detroit; giving also in St. Louis, MO, and in PA. No grants to individuals.
Application information:
Initial approach: Letter
Deadline(s): None
Officers: Charles T. Fisher III, Chair.; Walter B. Fisher, Pres. and Treas.; Sarah W. Fisher, Secy.
EIN: 203064253
Selected grants: The following grants were reported in 2008.
$95,000 to Society of the Sacred Heart, Saint Louis, MO.

$35,000 to Capuchin Soup Kitchen, Detroit, MI.
$25,000 to DeSales University, Center Valley, PA.
$10,000 to Madonna University, Livonia, MI.
$10,000 to Marygrove College, Detroit, MI.
$10,000 to Sacred Heart Major Seminary
Foundation, Detroit, MI.
$10,000 to Siena Heights University, Adrian, MI.
$10,000 to University of Detroit Mercy, Detroit, MI.

100
Brinkerhoff-Sample Family Foundation
1011 Lincoln Ave.
Ann Arbor, MI   48104-3526
County: Washtenaw

Established in 2004 in MI.
Donors: William F. Brinkerhoff; Kathleen Sample.
Grantmaker type: Independent foundation.
Financial data (yr. ended 12/31/09): Assets,
$155,684 (M); expenditures, $25,970; total giving,
$25,550; qualifying distributions, $25,550; giving
activities include $25,550 for grants.
Fields of interest: Protestant agencies & churches.
Type of support: General/operating support.
Limitations: Giving primarily in MI. No grants to
individuals.
Officers: William F. Brinkerhoff, Pres.; Kathleen
Sample, Secy.-Treas.
EIN: 201389996

101
Robert L. Brintnall Family Foundation
1086 Brunn Ave.
St. Joseph, MI   49085-2817   (269) 983-4891
County: Berrien
Contact: Robert L. Brintnall, Pres.

Established in 1986 in IL.
Donor: Robert L. Brintnall.
Grantmaker type: Independent foundation.
Financial data (yr. ended 12/31/09): Assets,
$46,994 (M); gifts received, $5,000; expenditures,
$2,731; total giving, $1,150; qualifying
distributions, $1,150; giving activities include
$1,150 for grants.
Fields of interest: Higher education; Human
services; United Ways and Federated Giving
Programs.
Type of support: General/operating support.
Limitations: Giving primarily in MI, with emphasis on
Kalamazoo and St. Joseph; some giving also in IL.
No grants to individuals.
Application information:
   Initial approach: Proposal
   Deadline(s): None
Officers and Directors:* Robert L. Brintnall,* Pres.
and Treas.; Helene W. Brintnall,* Secy.; James W.
Brintnall.
EIN: 363488562

102
Wallace and Irene Bronner Family Charitable Foundation
P.O. Box 264
Frankenmuth, MI   48734-0264   (989) 652-9931
County: Saginaw

Established in 1989 in MI.
Donor: Wallace and Irene Bronner Family Trust.
Grantmaker type: Independent foundation.

Financial data (yr. ended 12/31/09): Assets,
$4,019,654 (M); gifts received, $175,000;
expenditures, $308,263; total giving, $306,963;
qualifying distributions, $306,963; giving activities
include $306,963 for 189 grants (high: $183,000;
low: $50).
Purpose and activities: Giving primarily to Christian
churches and organizations; funding also for
education, health and human services.
Fields of interest: Higher education; Health
organizations, association; Cancer; Youth
development; Human services; Religious federated
giving programs; Christian agencies & churches.
Type of support: General/operating support;
Scholarship funds.
Limitations: Applications accepted. Giving primarily
in MI, with emphasis on Frankenmuth and Saginaw.
No loans or program-related investments.
Application information:
   Initial approach: Letter
   Deadline(s): None
Officers: Wayne Bronner, Pres.; Carla Bronner,
Secy.; Maria Bronner, Treas.
Directors: Irene R. Bronner; Randy Bronner.
EIN: 382834541
Selected grants: The following grants were reported
in 2006.
$167,269 to YMCA of Saginaw, Saginaw, MI.
$117,600 to Boys and Girls Club of Saginaw County,
Saginaw, MI.
$115,000 to Saginaw Community Foundation,
Saginaw, MI.
$90,742 to Saginaw Valley State University,
University Center, MI.
$46,800 to Saginaw Bay Orchestra, Saginaw, MI.
$12,794 to Frankenmuth Historical Association,
Frankenmuth, MI.
$3,500 to Girl Scouts of the U.S.A., Saginaw, MI.
$2,500 to Valley Lutheran High School, Saginaw,
MI.
$2,000 to Legacy Center for Student Success,
Midland, MI.
$2,000 to Saginaw Community Foundation,
Saginaw, MI.

103
Bennie Marie Brooks Foundation
125 W. Hamilton Ave.
Flint, MI   48503-1037
County: Genesee

Established in 2003 in MI.
Donor: Lance C. Brooks.
Grantmaker type: Independent foundation.
Financial data (yr. ended 12/31/09): Assets, $649
(M); gifts received, $4,597; expenditures, $4,164;
total giving, $1,200; qualifying distributions,
$1,200; giving activities include $1,200 for grants.
Fields of interest: Education.
Limitations: Giving primarily in Flint, MI.
Officers: Lance Brooks, Pres.; Cassie Lambert, V.P.;
Gloria McCoy-Jacobs, V.P.; Kathi Turner, Secy.;
Juanita Bryant, Treas.
EIN: 371461754

104
Gregory & Helayne Brown Charitable Foundation
3716 White Trillium Dr. E.
Saginaw, MI   48603-1948   (989) 792-6200
County: Saginaw
Contact: Gregory S. Brown, Pres.

Established in 2000 in MI.
Donor: Gregory S. Brown.
Grantmaker type: Independent foundation.
Financial data (yr. ended 12/31/09): Assets,
$193,824 (M); expenditures, $7,096; total giving,
$5,000; qualifying distributions, $5,000; giving
activities include $5,000 for grants.
Fields of interest: Higher education, university;
Human services.
Limitations: Applications accepted. Giving primarily
in Saginaw and University Center, MI.
Application information: Application form not
required.
   Initial approach: Letter
   Deadline(s): None
Officers: Gregory S. Brown, Pres. and Treas.;
Helayne Brown, V.P. and Secy.
EIN: 383507502

105
Richard H. Brown Foundation
6293 Cannon Highlands Dr. N.E.
Belmont, MI   49306-9678   (616) 874-1732
County: Kent
Contact: Richard H. Brown, Pres. and Treas.

Established in 1995 in MI.
Donors: Richard H. Brown; Geraldine C. Brown.
Grantmaker type: Independent foundation.
Financial data (yr. ended 12/31/09): Assets,
$2,326,870 (M); expenditures, $190,206; total
giving, $177,200; qualifying distributions,
$177,210; giving activities include $177,200 for 27
grants (high: $64,000; low: $500).
Fields of interest: Higher education, university;
Protestant agencies & churches.
Limitations: Applications accepted. Giving primarily
in MI.
Application information: Application form not
required.
   Deadline(s): None
Officers and Directors:* Richard H. Brown, Pres.
and Treas.; Charles C. Brown,* Secy.; Nancy Brown.
EIN: 383267368
Selected grants: The following grants were reported
in 2008.
$75,000 to Michigan State University, East Lansing,
MI.
$5,000 to Grand Valley State University, Allendale,
MI.
$4,000 to American Red Cross, Chicago, IL.
$4,000 to Guiding Light Mission, Grand Rapids, MI.
$4,000 to Mel Trotter Ministries, Grand Rapids, MI.
$2,000 to American Cancer Society, Atlanta, GA.
$1,500 to Michigan State University, East Lansing,
MI.
$1,500 to Michigan State University, East Lansing,
MI.
$1,000 to Pamplin Historical Park, Petersburg, VA.

106
Richard M. & Sharon R. Brown Foundation, Inc.
1200 Ardmoor Dr.
Bloomfield Hills, MI 48301-2158
County: Oakland

Established in MI.
Donor: Richard M. Brown.
Grantmaker type: Independent foundation.
Financial data (yr. ended 07/31/09): Assets, $1 (M); gifts received, $6,750; expenditures, $8,492; total giving, $7,481; qualifying distributions, $7,481; giving activities include $7,481 for grants.
Fields of interest: Education; Medical research; Human services; Jewish federated giving programs; Jewish agencies & synagogues.
Limitations: Giving primarily in MI. No grants to individuals.
Application information:
   Initial approach: Letter
   Deadline(s): None
Officers: Richard M. Brown, Pres.; Sharon R. Brown, Secy.-Treas.
EIN: 382266194

107
Robert W. & Lynn H. Browne Foundation
(formerly Browne Foundation)
333 Trust Bldg.
Grand Rapids, MI 49503-3028 (616) 459-2009
County: Kent
Contact: Robert W. Browne, Dir.

Established around 1983.
Donors: Robert W. Browne; Lynn H. Browne.
Grantmaker type: Independent foundation.
Financial data (yr. ended 12/31/09): Assets, $3,663,304 (M); expenditures, $30,429; total giving, $30,000; qualifying distributions, $30,000; giving activities include $30,000 for 2 grants (high: $25,000; low: $5,000).
Fields of interest: Higher education.
Limitations: Applications accepted. Giving primarily in MI.
Application information: Application form required.
   Initial approach: Letter
   Deadline(s): None
Officer: Charles M. Bloom, Secy.
Directors: Robert W. Browne; James R. Browne; James N. Deboer.
EIN: 382452645
Selected grants: The following grants were reported in 2004.
$350,000 to University of Michigan, Kellogg Eye Center, Ann Arbor, MI.

108
Laura Schaeffer Bucknell College Scholarship Trust
c/o Citizens Bank
328 S. Saginaw St., M/C 002072
Flint, MI 48502-1923 (866) 308-7878
County: Genesee
Application address: c/o Sturgis Public Schools, Attn.: High School Guidance Dept., 216 Vinewood, Sturgis, MI 49091-8426, tel.: (269) 659-1500

Established in MI.
Grantmaker type: Independent foundation.
Financial data (yr. ended 12/31/09): Assets, $31,013 (M); expenditures, $2,966; total giving, $1,000; qualifying distributions, $2,527; giving activities include $1,000 for 1 grant to an individual.
Purpose and activities: Scholarship awards to graduates of Sturgis High School, Michigan.
Fields of interest: Higher education.
Type of support: Scholarships—to individuals.
Limitations: Applications accepted. Giving limited to residents of Sturgis, MI.
Application information: Application form required.
   Deadline(s): Apr. 30
Trustee: Citizens Bank.
EIN: 316502430

109
Burch Family Foundation
29 Lumberman Way
Saginaw, MI 48603-8627
County: Saginaw
Contact: Wilbur Burch, Dir.

Established in 1997 in MI.
Donor: Wilbur Burch.
Grantmaker type: Independent foundation.
Financial data (yr. ended 12/31/07): Assets, $303,766 (M); gifts received, $1,386; expenditures, $32,242; total giving, $19,500; qualifying distributions, $19,500; giving activities include $19,500 for 1 grant.
Fields of interest: Higher education.
Limitations: Giving primarily in KS.
Application information: Application form not required.
   Initial approach: Letter
   Deadline(s): None
Directors: Michael Burch; Wilbur Burch; Anita Tribble.
EIN: 383373898

110
Burnham Family Foundation
622 Jennings Ln.
Battle Creek, MI 49015-3529 (269) 441-5035
County: Calhoun
Contact: Charles C. Burnham, Pres.

Established in 2005 in MI.
Grantmaker type: Independent foundation.
Financial data (yr. ended 06/30/08): Assets, $1,082,598 (M); expenditures, $76,747; total giving, $61,050; qualifying distributions, $62,108; giving activities include $61,050 for 21 grants (high: $20,000; low: $200).
Fields of interest: Elementary/secondary education; Health care; Boy scouts; Catholic agencies & churches.
Limitations: Applications accepted. Giving primarily in Battle Creek, MI.
Application information:
   Initial approach: Letter
   Deadline(s): None
Officers: Charles C. Burnham, Pres.; M. Anne Burnham, Secy.-Treas.
EIN: 203680686

111
Burroughs Memorial Trust
c/o Citizens Bank Wealth Management, N.A.
328 S. Saginaw St., M/C 001065
Flint, MI 48502-1923 (810) 766-6987
County: Genesee
Contact: Gwen Kelley

Established in 1966 in MI.
Grantmaker type: Independent foundation.
Financial data (yr. ended 12/31/09): Assets, $782,822 (M); expenditures, $52,455; total giving, $44,814; qualifying distributions, $46,109; giving activities include $44,814 for 9 grants (high: $18,000; low: $1,814).
Purpose and activities: Giving primarily for human services, federated giving programs, and general charitable giving.
Fields of interest: Animal welfare; Human services; Children/youth, services; United Ways and Federated Giving Programs; General charitable giving.
Type of support: Continuing support; Annual campaigns; Capital campaigns; Building/renovation; Endowments; Program development.
Application information: Application form required.
   Initial approach: Letter
   Deadline(s): None
Trustees: Jonathan E. Burroughs II; Jonathan Burroughs III; Joseph S. Burroughs; Samuel S. Stewart III; Heather Williams; Citizens Bank Wealth Management, N.A.
EIN: 386041206

112
Busch Family Foundation
148 S. Industrial Dr.
Saline, MI 48176-9493 (949) 474-7368
County: Washtenaw
Application address: c/o Clinton High School, Attn.: Tim Wilson, Principal, 341 E. Michigan Ave., Clinton, MI 49236-9593

Established in CA and MI.
Donor: Timothy R. Busch.
Grantmaker type: Independent foundation.
Financial data (yr. ended 12/31/09): Assets, $27,749 (M); expenditures, $43,473; total giving, $29,300; qualifying distributions, $41,719; giving activities include $29,300 for 15 grants to individuals (high: $3,050; low: $125).
Purpose and activities: Scholarship awards to graduates of Clinton High School, Michigan; giving also to Catholic churches and organizations.
Fields of interest: Higher education; Catholic agencies & churches.
Type of support: General/operating support; Scholarships—to individuals.
Limitations: Applications accepted. Giving limited to residents of the Clinton, MI, area for scholarships, and to CA and NY for other grants.
Application information: Application form required for scholarships.
   Deadline(s): None
Trustees: Stephan L. Busch; Timothy R. Busch.
EIN: 382671217
Selected grants: The following grants were reported in 2004.
$3,000 to New York University, New York, NY.

113
Byrne Family Foundation
P.O. Box 200
Rockford, MI 49341-0200
County: Kent
Contact: Arlene Warwick
Application address: 320 Byrne Industrial Dr.,
Rockford, MI 49341

Established in 2000 in MI.
Donors: Norman Byrne; Rosemary Byrne.
Grantmaker type: Independent foundation.
Financial data (yr. ended 12/31/09): Assets,
$53,702 (M); gifts received, $12,000;
expenditures, $8,513; total giving, $8,500;
qualifying distributions, $8,500; giving activities
include $8,500 for grants to individuals.
Purpose and activities: Scholarship awards to
seniors of Lowell High School, Michigan who
maintained at least a 2.0 GPA for the last two years
of high school, and demonstrated all around ability
through participation in school and community
activities.
Fields of interest: Higher education.
Type of support: Scholarships—to individuals.
Limitations: Applications accepted. Giving limited to
residents of Lowell, MI.
Application information: Application form required.
   Deadline(s): Apr. 1 of the year preceding the
      school year with respect to which the funds are
      to be applied.
Officers: Norman Byrne, Pres.; Rosemary Byrne,
Secy.-Treas.
EIN: 383574869

114
Caesar Puff Foundation
c/o Comerica Bank
P.O. Box 75000, MC 3302
Detroit, MI 48275-3302 (313) 222-6297
County: Wayne
Contact: Beverly Suchenek

Established in 2000 in PA.
Donor: Virginia A. Campana.
Grantmaker type: Independent foundation.
Financial data (yr. ended 03/31/10): Assets,
$56,017 (M); expenditures, $45,403; total giving,
$41,000; qualifying distributions, $41,000; giving
activities include $41,000 for grants.
Fields of interest: Media/communications; Higher
education; Libraries (public); Animal welfare; Food
banks; Residential/custodial care, hospices;
Christian agencies & churches.
Limitations: Applications accepted. Giving primarily
in OH, PA, and WV. No grants to individuals.
Application information: Application form not
required.
   Deadline(s): None
Trustees: Virginia A. Campana; Comerica Bank.
EIN: 226866488
Selected grants: The following grants were reported
in 2009.
$90,692 to Rostraver Public Library, Belle Vernon,
PA.
$4,000 to Family Hospice and Palliative Care,
Pittsburgh, PA.
$4,000 to Franciscan University of Steubenville,
Steubenville, OH.

115
Samuel Higby Camp Foundation
c/o Comerica Bank, Trust Dept.
245 W. Michigan Ave.
Jackson, MI 49201-2265
County: Jackson
Application address: c/o Judy Schneider, 1320
Seymour Ave., Jackson, MI 49202-2551, tel.: (517)
206-2178

Established in 1951 in MI.
Donor: Donna Ruth Camp‡.
Grantmaker type: Independent foundation.
Financial data (yr. ended 12/31/09): Assets,
$1,172,674 (M); expenditures, $119,118; total
giving, $102,500; qualifying distributions,
$102,500; giving activities include $102,500 for
grants.
Purpose and activities: Giving primarily for
education, including higher and business education,
community development, and cultural programs.
Fields of interest: Arts; Higher education; Business
school/education; Medical school/education;
Libraries/library science; Education; Animal welfare;
Recreation; Children/youth, services; Residential/
custodial care, hospices; Community/economic
development; Biology/life sciences; Government/
public administration.
Type of support: General/operating support; Annual
campaigns; Capital campaigns; Debt reduction;
Curriculum development.
Limitations: Giving primarily in south central MI, with
emphasis on Jackson.
Application information: Application form not
required.
   Initial approach: Letter or proposal
   Copies of proposal: 1
   Deadline(s): Aug. 15
   Board meeting date(s): As needed
   Final notification: Oct. or Nov.
Officers: Linda S. Sekerke, Vice-Chair.; Judy
Schneider, Secy.; Frederick Davies, Treas.
EIN: 381643281

116
Kenneth H. Campbell Foundation for Neurological Research
c/o Fifth Third Bank
P.O. Box 3636
Grand Rapids, MI 49501-3636
County: Kent
Contact: Laidler
Application address: c/o Lisa Laidler 111 Lyon St.
N.W., Grand Rapids, MI 49503, tel.: (888)
218-7878

Grantmaker type: Independent foundation.
Financial data (yr. ended 12/31/09): Assets,
$1,014,576 (M); expenditures, $58,647; total
giving, $50,000; qualifying distributions, $50,000;
giving activities include $50,000 for 2 grants (high:
$25,000; low: $25,000).
Purpose and activities: Grants for neurological
research.
Fields of interest: Neuroscience; Neuroscience
research.
Type of support: Research.
Limitations: Applications accepted. Giving primarily
in MI.
Application information:
   Initial approach: Letter
   Deadline(s): None

Officer: James R. Dice, Secy.-Treas.
Directors: Thomas Jones; James Van Putten.
Trustee: Fifth Third Bank.
EIN: 386049653

117
Canaan Foundation
13919 S. West Bay Shore Dr., Ste. G-1
Traverse City, MI 49684-6216
County: Grand Traverse
Contact: Keith M. Nielson, Pres.

Established in 1999 in MI.
Donor: H.I.S. Foundation.
Grantmaker type: Independent foundation.
Financial data (yr. ended 12/31/09): Assets,
$3,158,779 (M); gifts received, $234,093;
expenditures, $206,382; total giving, $204,230;
qualifying distributions, $205,280; giving activities
include $204,230 for 12 grants (high: $51,968;
low: $10).
Fields of interest: Arts; Health organizations,
association; Housing/shelter; Human services;
Residential/custodial care, hospices; Women,
centers/services; Foundations (community);
Christian agencies & churches.
Type of support: General/operating support.
Limitations: Applications accepted. Giving limited to
MI, primarily in Traverse City.
Application information:
   Initial approach: Letter
   Deadline(s): None
Officers and Directors:* Keith M. Nielson,* Pres.;
Barbara A. Nielson,* V.P. and Treas.; Dale M.
Nielson,* Secy.
EIN: 383444062
Selected grants: The following grants were reported
in 2008.
$12,000 to Father Fred Foundation, Traverse City,
MI.
$11,000 to Heritage Foundation, Washington, DC.
$2,500 to Safe Harbor, Greenville, SC.
$2,000 to First Presbyterian Church, Elk Rapids, MI.
$2,000 to Samaritans Purse, Boone, NC.
$1,700 to Bay Pointe Community Church, Traverse
City, MI.
$1,250 to American Cancer Society, Traverse City,
MI.
$1,000 to Eagle Village, Hersey, MI.
$1,000 to Focus on the Family, Colorado Springs,
CO.
$1,000 to Freedom Builders, Traverse City, MI.

118
The Carls Foundation
333 W. Fort St., Ste. 1940
Detroit, MI 48226-3162 (313) 965-0990
County: Wayne
Contact: Elizabeth A. Stieg, Exec. Dir.
FAX: (313) 965-0547; URL: http://www.carlsfdn.org

Established in 1961 in MI.
Donor: William Carls‡.
Grantmaker type: Independent foundation.
Financial data (yr. ended 12/31/09): Assets,
$103,060,613 (M); expenditures, $4,976,727;
total giving, $3,957,275; qualifying distributions,
$4,445,204; giving activities include $3,957,275
for 32 grants (high: $100,000; low: $4,100).
Purpose and activities: The principal purpose and
mission of the foundation is: 1) Children's Welfare

including: health care facilities and programs, with special emphasis on the prevention and treatment of hearing impairment, and recreational, educational, and welfare programs especially for children who are disadvantaged for economic and/or health reasons; and 2) Preservation of natural areas, open space and historic buildings and areas having special natural beauty or significance in maintaining America's heritage and historic ideals, through assistance to land trusts and land conservancies and directly related environmental educational programs.

Fields of interest: Historic preservation/historical societies; Education; Environment, natural resources; Hospitals (general); Speech/hearing centers; Health care; Recreation; Children/youth, services.

Type of support: Capital campaigns; Seed money.

Limitations: Applications accepted. Giving primarily in MI. No grants to individuals, or for publications, film, research, endowments, fellowships, travel, conferences, special event sponsorships, playground or athletic facilities, or seminars; no educational loans.

Publications: Annual report.

Application information: Letter of inquiry is not required and phone calls are welcome. Use of the CMF Common Grant Application Form is optional and acceptable. Application form not required.

   Initial approach: Proposal
   Copies of proposal: 1
   Deadline(s): Mar. 1, July 1 and Nov. 1
   Board meeting date(s): Jan., May, and Sept.
   Final notification: Notification letter sent to all
     applicants

Officers and Trustees:* Arthur B. Derisley,* Pres. and Treas.; Harold E. Stieg,* V.P. and Secy.; Elizabeth A. Stieg, Exec. Dir.; Henry Fleischer; Teresa R. Krieger.

Advisory Board: Brian A. Derisley; Dr. Homer E. Nye; Rev. Delayne H. Pauling; Robert A. Sajdak; Edward C. Stieg.

Number of staff: 1 full-time professional; 1 part-time professional; 1 full-time support.

EIN: 386099935

Selected grants: The following grants were reported in 2005.

$1,000,000 to Beaumont Foundation, Southfield, MI. For capital campaign to create children's medical/pediatric center at Royal Oak facility.

$600,000 to YMCA of Metropolitan Detroit, Detroit, MI. For capital campaign earmarked to construct a full-service facility for Huron Valley YMCA.

$500,000 to Grand Traverse Regional Land Conservancy, Traverse City, MI. For land acquisition, purchase of developmental rights, and establishment of revolving fund for future purchases.

$400,000 to Nature Conservancy, Lansing, MI. For leadership grant to preserve 390 acres in Upper Peninsula.

$150,000 to Judson Center, Royal Oak, MI. For creation of Autism Center to service children and adults with autism in Metropolitan Detroit.

$100,000 to Detroit Rescue Mission Ministries, Detroit, MI. For construction of new bath house to serve youth at Wildwood Ranch.

$100,000 to Henry Ford Health System, Detroit, MI. For establishment of Pediatric Dermatology Emergency Needs to provide care for children with chronic dermatological conditions who lack insurance or resources.

$54,515 to Guidance Center, Southgate, MI. For purchase of hearing and vision equipment as well as

supplies to provide screenings for children aged 0-5.

$25,000 to Hospice of Michigan, Detroit, MI. For funding needed for staff, supplies and medication to provide hospice services to pediatric patients.

$10,000 to Peace Neighborhood Center, Ann Arbor, MI. For summer day camp program serving economically disadvantaged children from Ann Arbor area.

119
Carmell Scholarship Trust Fund

c/o National City Bank
P.O. Box 94651
Cleveland, OH   44101-4651
County: Cuyahoga
Application address: National City Bank, Attn: Scott Campbell, 171 Monroe Ave., NW KC17-63, Grand Rapids, MI 49503-2683, tel.: (616) 771-8576

Established in 2006 in OH.

Grantmaker type: Independent foundation.

Financial data (yr. ended 12/31/09): Assets, $635,686 (M); expenditures, $48,579; total giving, $40,250; qualifying distributions, $40,250; giving activities include $40,250 for grants to individuals.

Fields of interest: Higher education.

Type of support: Scholarships—to individuals.

Limitations: Applications accepted. Giving primarily to residents of MI.

Application information:

   Initial approach: Request application and
     guidelines from school guidance office
   Deadline(s): Apr. 30

Trustee: National City Bank.

EIN: 347196952

120
Norman & Ardis Carpenter Scholarship Trust

c/o JPMorgan Chase Bank, N.A.
P.O. Box 3038
Milwaukee, WI   53201-3038
County: Milwaukee
Application address: c/o Jeff Pettinga, 7517 Noffke Dr., Caledonia, MI 49316-9303, tel.: (616) 891-9961

Established in 2004 in MI.

Donor: Ardis Carpenter‡.

Grantmaker type: Independent foundation.

Financial data (yr. ended 07/31/08): Assets, $182,967 (M); expenditures, $17,797; total giving, $10,000; qualifying distributions, $13,668; giving activities include $10,000 for 9 grants to individuals (high: $1,250; low: $1,000).

Purpose and activities: Scholarship awards to graduating seniors who are members of Caledonia Christian Reformed Church, Michigan.

Fields of interest: Higher education.

Type of support: Scholarships—to individuals.

Limitations: Applications accepted. Giving primarily to residents of Caledonia, MI.

Application information: Application form required.

   Deadline(s): None

Trustee: JPMorgan Chase Bank, N.A.

EIN: 203485260

121
James C. Cassie, Jr. Foundation

629 Byron Ct.
Rochester Hills, MI   48307-4206
County: Oakland

Established in MI.

Grantmaker type: Independent foundation.

Financial data (yr. ended 12/31/08): Assets, $450 (M); expenditures, $50; total giving, $50; qualifying distributions, $50; giving activities include $50 for grants.

Officer and Director:* James C. Cassie, Jr., Pres.

EIN: 352195948

122
C. Glen and Barbara A. Catt Foundation

P.O. Box 304
Petoskey, MI   49770-0304
County: Emmet
Contact: Thomas J. Webb, Secy.-Treas.

Established in 1995 in MI.

Donors: C. Glenn Catt; Barbara A. Catt.

Grantmaker type: Independent foundation.

Financial data (yr. ended 06/30/09): Assets, $341,615 (M); expenditures, $19,035; total giving, $15,000; qualifying distributions, $15,000; giving activities include $15,000 for grants.

Fields of interest: Hospitals (general).

Limitations: Giving primarily in Gaylord, MI. No grants to individuals.

Application information:

   Initial approach: Letter
   Deadline(s): None

Officers: Barbara A. Catt, Pres.; Russell H. VanGilder, V.P.; Thomas J. Webb, Secy.-Treas.

EIN: 383249470

123
Center for Alternative Media and Culture

c/o AGS
200 Park Ave. S., 8th Fl.
New York, NY   10003-1503   (212) 768-4500
County: New York
Contact: Frank Selvaggi

Established in MI.

Donor: Michael Moore.

Grantmaker type: Independent foundation.

Financial data (yr. ended 12/31/09): Assets, $364,626 (M); gifts received, $10,000; expenditures, $13,630; total giving, $10,438; qualifying distributions, $10,438; giving activities include $10,438 for 4 grants (high: $5,000; low: $1,000).

Fields of interest: Media/communications; Media, film/video; History/archaeology; Arts.

Type of support: Grants to individuals.

Limitations: Applications accepted. Giving primarily in CA, FL, MI, and NY.

Application information:

   Initial approach: Letter
   Deadline(s): None

Officers: Michael Moore, Pres.; Kathleen Glynn, Treas.

EIN: 382415253

124
The Chamberlain Foundation
1680 Crooks Rd.
Troy, MI 48084-5305   (248) 273-4306
County: Oakland
Contact: Calvin M. Chamberlain, Pres.

Established in 1988 in MI.
Donor: Calvin M. Chamberlain.
Grantmaker type: Independent foundation.
Financial data (yr. ended 05/31/10): Assets,
$78,355 (M); expenditures, $6,085; total giving,
$5,275; qualifying distributions, $5,935; giving
activities include $5,275 for 5 grants (high: $4,000;
low: $75).
Fields of interest: Education; Youth development;
Protestant agencies & churches.
Type of support: General/operating support;
Scholarship funds.
Limitations: Applications accepted. Giving primarily
in MI.
Application information: Application form not
required.
  Initial approach: Letter
  Deadline(s): None
Directors: Calvin M. Chamberlain*; Janet R.
Chamberlain*.
EIN: 382837915

125
Chang Foundation
807 Asa Gray Dr., Ste. 401
Ann Arbor, MI 48105-2566   (810) 238-4617
County: Washtenaw
Contact: Cheng-Yang Chang M.D., Dir.

Established in 1987 in MI.
Donors: Cheng-Yang Chang, M.D.; Shirley Chang.
Grantmaker type: Independent foundation.
Financial data (yr. ended 09/30/09): Assets,
$244,592 (M); gifts received, $2,300;
expenditures, $19,899; total giving, $13,400;
qualifying distributions, $13,400; giving activities
include $13,400 for grants.
Purpose and activities: Scholarship awards through
pre-selected universities to students who have
exhibited a potential and the talent to excel in the
field of Chinese traditional art in Taiwan.
Fields of interest: Higher education.
Type of support: Scholarship funds.
Limitations: Giving primarily in Taiwan.
Application information: Recipients are
recommended by their respective department
heads.
  Initial approach: Essay, resume and transcript of
    college grades
  Deadline(s): Varies
Director: Cheng-Yang Chang, M.D.
EIN: 382796315

126
Lawrence S. Charfoos Charitable
Foundation
1800 Penobscot Bldg.
Detroit, MI 48226
County: Wayne
Contact: Alan A. May, Secy.
Application address: 3000 Town Ctr., Southfield, MI
48075, tel.: (248) 358-3800

Grantmaker type: Independent foundation.

Financial data (yr. ended 10/31/09): Assets, $1
(M); expenditures, $300; total giving, $0; qualifying
distributions, $0.
Purpose and activities: Scholarship awards to
students living in Detroit, MI, or the surrounding
area, and enrolled in an accredited state school.
Type of support: Scholarships—to individuals.
Limitations: Giving primarily in Detroit, MI.
Application information: Application form required.
  Initial approach: Letter
  Deadline(s): May 31
Officers: Lawrence S. Charfoos, Pres.; Alan A. May,
Secy.
EIN: 237328773

127
Allen and Franka Charlupski Foundation
6230 Orchard Lake Rd., Ste. 100
West Bloomfield, MI 48322-2393
(248) 851-9700
County: Oakland
Contact: Lawrence Charlupski, Pres.

Established in 1972 in MI.
Donors: Helen Charlupski; Allen Charlupski; Franka
Charlupski.
Grantmaker type: Independent foundation.
Financial data (yr. ended 09/30/08): Assets,
$1,452,570 (M); expenditures, $77,923; total
giving, $71,626; qualifying distributions, $71,626;
giving activities include $71,626 for grants.
Purpose and activities: Giving primarily for
educational and religious institutions.
Fields of interest: Arts; Education; Hospitals
(general); Human services; Jewish federated giving
programs; Jewish agencies & synagogues.
Type of support: General/operating support.
Limitations: Giving primarily in MI. No grants to
individuals.
Application information: Application form not
required.
  Initial approach: Letter or proposal
  Deadline(s): None
Officers: Lawrence Charlupski, Pres. and Secy.;
Helen Charlupski, V.P.
EIN: 237191093

128
Lavere Leonard and Gladys Loraine Chase
Scholarship Fund
c/o Comerica Bank
P.O. Box 75000 M/C 3302
Detroit, MI 48275-3302
County: Wayne
Application address: c/o Kimberly Hill, 101 N. Main
St., Ste. 100, Ann Arbor, MI 48104-5507, tel.: (734)
930-2405

Established in 2006 in MI.
Donor: Lavere Leonard Chase‡.
Grantmaker type: Independent foundation.
Financial data (yr. ended 10/31/09): Assets,
$802,703 (M); expenditures, $64,355; total giving,
$48,475; qualifying distributions, $48,475; giving
activities include $48,475 for grants.
Purpose and activities: Scholarship awards to
graduates of Jonesville School System, who have
been residents of Jonesville county, Michigan, for a
period of 5 years.
Fields of interest: Higher education.
Type of support: Scholarships—to individuals.

Limitations: Applications accepted. Giving limited to
residents of Jonesville, MI.
Application information: Application form is
available at the Jonesville school. Application form
required.
  Deadline(s): Dec. 31
Trustee: Comerica Bank.
EIN: 206975298

129
Chelsea Kiwanis Club Foundation
P.O. Box 61
Chelsea, MI 48118-0061   (269) 968-1099
County: Washtenaw
URL: http://www.kiwanis.org

Established in MI.
Donor: Jean E. Lewis.
Grantmaker type: Independent foundation.
Financial data (yr. ended 09/30/09): Assets,
$19,001 (M); gifts received, $3,000; expenditures,
$4,040; total giving, $4,000; qualifying
distributions, $4,000; giving activities include
$4,000 for 1 grant.
Fields of interest: Elementary/secondary
education; Athletics/sports, school programs;
Youth development.
Type of support: Program development; Scholarship
funds.
Limitations: Applications accepted. Giving in MI,
primarily in Chelsea.
Application information: Application form not
required.
  Initial approach: Letter
  Deadline(s): None
Officers: John Knox, Pres.; Lucy Steiber, Pres.-Elect;
Ray Kemner, Secy.; Bob Milbrodt, Treas.
Directors: Rod Dewyer; Jack Kehoe; Tom Ritter; Judy
Szeman; Peter Wasilewski.
EIN: 383044995

130
Alan W. Chernick Foundation
5635 Ridgewood
West Bloomfield, MI 48322-1406
(248) 661-2352
County: Oakland
Contact: Alan W. Chernick, Pres.

Donor: Alan W. Chernick.
Grantmaker type: Independent foundation.
Financial data (yr. ended 12/31/09): Assets,
$31,222 (M); gifts received, $35,000;
expenditures, $3,900; total giving, $3,900;
qualifying distributions, $3,900; giving activities
include $3,900 for 1 grant.
Application information: Application form required.
  Initial approach: Letter
  Deadline(s): None
Officers: Alan W. Chernick, Pres.; Ronald H. Moss,
Secy.-Treas.
EIN: 262281806

131
Christian Missionary Scholarship Foundation

1899 Orchard Lake Rd., Ste. 203
Sylvan Lake, MI 48320-1776
County: Oakland
E-mail: info@christianmissionaryscholarship.org;
URL: http://
www.christianmissionaryscholarship.org
Scholarship application address: 3230 Lake Dr. S.E.,
Grand Rapids, MI 49546, tel.: (616) 526-7731,
fax: (616) 526-6777

Established in MI.
Donors: Stanley Van Reken; Randall S. Van Reken;
Capital Ventures of NV.
Grantmaker type: Independent foundation.
Financial data (yr. ended 12/31/09): Assets,
$7,159,776 (M); gifts received, $29,050;
expenditures, $251,783; total giving, $246,375;
qualifying distributions, $246,375; giving activities
include $246,375 for 8 grants (high: $117,625;
low: $1,000).
Purpose and activities: Giving for scholarships to
children of missionaries attending one of the
following six colleges: Calvin College, Dordt College,
Hope College, Kuyper College, Trinity Christian
College and Wheaton College.
Fields of interest: Theological school/education;
Christian agencies & churches.
Type of support: Scholarship funds.
Limitations: Applications accepted. Giving primarily
in IA, IL and MI. No grants to individuals.
Application information: See web site for complete
application policies and guidelines and for an online
application. Application form required.
Deadline(s): Feb. 15
Final notification: Apr. 1
Officers: Gaylen Byker, Co-Pres.; Stanley R. Van
Reken, Co-Pres.; Randall Van Reken, Treas.
Directors: Brett Holleman; Marge Hoogeboom;
Walter Olsson; Thomas Stuit; Calvin P. Van Reken;
Robert Weeldreyer.
EIN: 363553749
Selected grants: The following grants were reported
in 2008.
$209,200 to Calvin College, Grand Rapids, MI.
$63,000 to Wheaton College, Wheaton, IL.
$33,250 to Hope College, Holland, MI.
$19,000 to Dordt College, Sioux Center, IA.

132
The Christopher Foundation

5089 Shady Creek Dr.
Troy, MI 48085-3200 (248) 619-9925
County: Oakland
Contact: Carroll J. Christopher, Pres.

Established in 2002 in MI.
Donor: Carroll J. Christopher.
Grantmaker type: Independent foundation.
Financial data (yr. ended 12/31/09): Assets,
$102,951 (M); gifts received, $311; expenditures,
$3,864; total giving, $2,132; qualifying
distributions, $2,132; giving activities include
$2,132 for grants.
Fields of interest: Protestant agencies & churches.
Limitations: Giving primarily in MI. No grants to
individuals.
Application information: Application form not
required.
Deadline(s): None

Officers and Director:* Carroll J. Christopher,*
Pres.; Kimberly A. Christopher, Secy.-Treas.
EIN: 371422862

133
The Cipa Foundation

P.O. Box 70451
Rochester Hills, MI 48307-0010
County: Oakland
Contact: Chris A. Wilson, Pres.

Established in 1999 in MI.
Donors: Bernard J. Cipa; Scott Cipa; Drew M. Cipa;
Bernard D. Cipa.
Grantmaker type: Independent foundation.
Financial data (yr. ended 12/31/09): Assets,
$437,863 (M); expenditures, $49,879; total giving,
$28,430; qualifying distributions, $44,382; giving
activities include $28,430 for 8 grants (high:
$24,980; low: $200).
Purpose and activities: Giving primarily for
education, a Roman Catholic church, and a
community foundation.
Fields of interest: Secondary school/education;
Education; Foundations (community); Catholic
agencies & churches.
Type of support: Program development; Research.
Limitations: Applications accepted. Giving limited to
MI.
Application information: Application form not
required.
Deadline(s): Varies
Officers: Chris A. Wilson, Pres.; Lisa Cipa, V.P.;
Bernard J. Cipa, Secy.-Treas.
Directors: Bernard D. Cipa; Drew M. Cipa; Eleanor
R. Cipa; Scott Cipa.
EIN: 383506568

134
Citizens First Foundation, Inc.

(formerly Citizens First Savings Charitable
Foundation, Inc.)
c/o David Devendorf
901 Huron Ave.
Port Huron, MI 48060-3700 (810) 985-8171
County: St. Clair
Contact: Marshall J. Campbell, Pres.

Established in 1998 in MI.
Donor: Citizens First Savings Bank.
Grantmaker type: Independent foundation.
Financial data (yr. ended 12/31/09): Assets,
$1,349,374 (M); expenditures, $389,916; total
giving, $371,808; qualifying distributions,
$371,808; giving activities include $371,808 for 88
grants (high: $110,000; low: $100).
Purpose and activities: Giving primarily for
education, hospitals, children, youth and social
services, and community development.
Fields of interest: Education; Hospitals (general);
Human services; Children/youth, services;
Community/economic development; Foundations
(community); United Ways and Federated Giving
Programs.
Type of support: General/operating support;
Program development; Scholarship funds.
Limitations: Giving primarily in areas of company
operations in Huron, Lapeer, Macomb, Oakland, and
St. Clair County, MI. No grants to individuals.

Application information: Application form required.
Initial approach: Letter or telephone requesting
application form
Officers: Marshall J. Campbell, Pres.; Timothy D.
Regan, Secy.-Treas.
Directors: Ronald W. Cooley; Walid Demashkieh,
M.D.; David C. Devendorf.
EIN: 383401243
Selected grants: The following grants were reported
in 2008.
$30,000 to Downtown Detroit Partnership, Detroit,
MI.

135
CKT Foundation

c/o Merrill Lynch Bank & Trust Co.
P.O. Box 1525
Pennington, NJ 08534-1525
County: Mercer
Application address: c/o Ralph and Mary Stebbins,
3557 Kings Mill Rd., North Branch, MI 48461

Established in 2005 in MI.
Donors: Ralph S. Stebbins; Mary J. Stebbins.
Grantmaker type: Independent foundation.
Financial data (yr. ended 12/31/09): Assets,
$8,649,016 (M); expenditures, $583,197; total
giving, $390,573; qualifying distributions,
$455,981; giving activities include $390,573 for 1
grant.
Purpose and activities: Giving primarily through an
affiliated family foundation for the betterment of Port
Huron, Michigan.
Fields of interest: Housing/shelter, development;
Human services; Community/economic
development; Foundations (private independent);
United Ways and Federated Giving Programs.
Limitations: Applications accepted. Giving primarily
in the Port Huron, MI, area.
Application information:
Initial approach: Letter
Officers: Deborah Post, Pres.; Ralph S. Stebbins,
V.P.; Mary J. Stebbins, Secy.-Treas.
EIN: 203927820
Selected grants: The following grants were reported
in 2007.
$22,000 to Childrens Miracle Network, Salt Lake
City, UT.
$10,000 to United Way of Saint Clair County, Port
Huron, MI.
$6,000 to Cystic Fibrosis Foundation, Bethesda,
MD.

136
Clannad Foundation

40950 Woodward Ave., Ste. 306
Bloomfield Hills, MI 48304-5124
County: Oakland

Established in 1994 in MI.
Donors: Jeanne H. Graham; Ralph A. Graham.
Grantmaker type: Independent foundation.
Financial data (yr. ended 10/31/09): Assets,
$2,088,006 (M); gifts received, $15,255;
expenditures, $122,264; total giving, $104,500;
qualifying distributions, $104,500; giving activities
include $104,500 for grants.
Purpose and activities: Giving primarily for the
environment and youth services.
Fields of interest: Visual arts, architecture;
Humanities; Environment, natural resources; Food

services; Human services; Children/youth, services; Human services, emergency aid; Aging; Crime/abuse victims; Economically disadvantaged; Homeless.
Type of support: Land acquisition; General/operating support; Equipment; Emergency funds; Continuing support; Annual campaigns.
Limitations: Applications accepted. Giving primarily in MI and NC. No grants to individuals.
Publications: Informational brochure.
Application information: Application form not required.
>   *Initial approach:* Letter
>   *Copies of proposal:* 1
>   *Deadline(s):* None
>   *Board meeting date(s):* Quarterly

Officers: Jeanne H. Graham, Pres. and Treas.; Ralph A. Graham, Exec. V.P.; David Laughlin, V.P.; James H. LoPrete, Secy.; Annie West Graham, Recording Secy.
Director: William Graham.
Number of staff: 2 part-time support.
EIN: 383209484
Selected grants: The following grants were reported in 2007.
$5,000 to Cranbrook Academy of Art, Bloomfield Hills, MI.
$5,000 to Pisgah Legal Services, Asheville, NC.
$4,000 to Forgotten Harvest, Oak Park, MI.
$4,000 to Nature Conservancy, Tucson, AZ.
$3,000 to Lighthouse of Oakland County, Pontiac, MI.
$3,000 to Little Brothers - Friends of the Elderly, Hancock, MI.
$3,000 to Michigan Nature Association, Williamston, MI.
$2,000 to Nature Conservancy, Michigan Field Office, Lansing, MI.

137
The Clare Foundation
945 E. 93rd St.
Chicago, IL   60619-7813
County: Cook

Established in 1997 in IL.
Donor: Kenneth Enright Irrevocable Trust.
Grantmaker type: Independent foundation.
Financial data (yr. ended 12/31/09): Assets, $2,802,528 (M); expenditures, $102,558; total giving, $58,550; qualifying distributions, $58,550; giving activities include $58,550 for grants.
Fields of interest: Elementary/secondary education; Human services; Catholic agencies & churches.
Limitations: Giving primarily in Chicago, IL, with some giving in FL and MI.
Application information:
>   *Initial approach:* Letter
>   *Deadline(s):* None

Officer: Tim Enright, Pres. and Secy.
Director: Kenneth Enright.
EIN: 364134738

138
Clark Fund
606 Tanview Dr.
Oxford, MI   48371-4763
County: Oakland

Established in MI.

Donor: Walter W. Clark‡.
Grantmaker type: Independent foundation.
Financial data (yr. ended 12/31/09): Assets, $239,149 (M); gifts received, $1,000; expenditures, $22,557; total giving, $12,900; qualifying distributions, $12,900; giving activities include $12,900 for grants.
Purpose and activities: Giving primarily on youth programs to organizations serving North Oakland County, Michigan.
Fields of interest: Youth development; Human services; Children/youth, services.
Limitations: Applications accepted. Giving primarily for the benefit of North Oakland County, MI.
Application information:
>   *Initial approach:* Letter
>   *Deadline(s):* Dec. 1
>   *Board meeting date(s):* Dec. 15

Officers: Colette Chadwick, Pres.; Donald J. Chadwick, V.P. and Treas.; Elise Richey, Secy.
EIN: 386115484

139
Clinton Rotary Scholarship Foundation
13091 Bartlett Rd.
Clinton, MI   49236
County: Lenawee
Contact: James M. Rolland, Pres.
Application address: 104 W. Church St., Clinton, MI 49236, tel.: (517) 456-7691

Established in 1985.
Grantmaker type: Independent foundation.
Financial data (yr. ended 06/30/10): Assets, $147,212 (M); gifts received, $6,500; expenditures, $10,071; total giving, $10,000; qualifying distributions, $10,000; giving activities include $10,000 for grants to individuals.
Purpose and activities: Scholarship awards to graduates of Clinton High School, Michigan.
Fields of interest: Higher education.
Type of support: Scholarships—to individuals.
Limitations: Giving limited to Clinton, MI.
Application information: Application form required.
>   *Deadline(s):* May 1

Officers: James M. Rolland, Pres.; Bonnie Peters, V.P.; William Zimmerman, Secy.; Bernam G. Fraley, Treas.
Trustee: Howard Osterling.
EIN: 386150118

140
Edgar G. Cochrane M.D. and Agnes L. Cochrane Foundation
1575 Lakeview Ave.
Sylvan Lake, MI   48320-1642
County: Oakland
Contact: Gaylen Curtis, Dir.

Established in 2001 in MI.
Donor: Agnes L. Cochrane Trust.
Grantmaker type: Independent foundation.
Financial data (yr. ended 12/31/09): Assets, $1,065,890 (M); expenditures, $71,686; total giving, $60,334; qualifying distributions, $71,686; giving activities include $60,334 for 5 grants (high: $45,000; low: $284).
Fields of interest: Cancer; Human services; Children/youth, services; Human services, mind/body enrichment; Social sciences; Christian agencies & churches.

Type of support: Program development; General/operating support; Research.
Limitations: Applications accepted. Giving primarily in CA, MI, and TX, with emphasis on MI.
Application information: Application form not required.
>   *Initial approach:* Letter
>   *Deadline(s):* None

Director: Gaylen Curtis.
EIN: 383616370

141
Colina Foundation
1 Heritage Pl., Ste. 220
Southgate, MI   48195-3048   (734) 283-8847
County: Wayne
Contact: John Colina, Pres.
FAX: (734) 283-3725;
E-mail: info@colinafoundation.org; E-mail (for John Colina): johnc36034@aol.com; URL: http://www.colinafoundation.org/

Established in 1992 in MI.
Donors: John Colina; Nancy Colina.
Grantmaker type: Independent foundation.
Financial data (yr. ended 12/31/09): Assets, $2,174,506 (M); gifts received, $20,000; expenditures, $153,537; total giving, $116,227; qualifying distributions, $116,227; giving activities include $116,227 for grants.
Purpose and activities: Giving primarily for school-connected and/or community-based programs assisting children ages 18 and under.
Fields of interest: Education, early childhood education; Youth development, services; Children/youth, services; Family services, parent education.
Type of support: Program development; Conferences/seminars; Seed money; Matching/challenge support.
Limitations: Applications accepted. Giving limited to southern Wayne County, MI, and areas where trustees reside.
Publications: Application guidelines; Annual report; Annual report (including application guidelines); Grants list.
Application information: See web site for complete application policies and guidelines and for downloadable application. Application form required.
>   *Initial approach:* First submit a letter of inquiry to determine suitability
>   *Copies of proposal:* 1
>   *Deadline(s):* 30 days prior to board meeting
>   *Board meeting date(s):* Monthly
>   *Final notification:* Within 60 days

Officers: John Colina, Pres.; Nancy Colina, Secy.-Treas.
Trustees: Lori Colina-Lee; JoMarie Goerge; Michael Goerge; Simon Lee.
Number of staff: None.
EIN: 383082610
Selected grants: The following grants were reported in 2007.
$10,000 to Kalamazoo Nature Center, Kalamazoo, MI.
$9,000 to Southern Great Lakes Symphony, Riverview, MI.
$8,000 to Camp Fire USA, Wathana Council, Southfield, MI.
$5,000 to Henry Ford Academy, Dearborn, MI.
$2,500 to Generous Hands, Vicksburg, MI.
$2,500 to Starfish Family Services, Inkster, MI.
$1,500 to Crossroads Safehouse, Fort Collins, CO.

$1,000 to Cheff Therapeutic Riding Center, Augusta, MI.
$1,000 to Crossroads Safehouse, Fort Collins, CO.
$1,000 to Kalamazoo Drop-In Child Care Center, Kalamazoo, MI.

142
Coller Foundation
35 S. Elk St.
Sandusky, MI   48471-1353   (810) 648-2414
County: Sanilac
Contact: John Paterson, Pres.

Established around 1989.
Grantmaker type: Independent foundation.
Financial data (yr. ended 12/31/09): Assets, $1,621,348 (M); expenditures, $83,865; total giving, $80,000; qualifying distributions, $80,000; giving activities include $80,000 for grants to individuals.
Purpose and activities: Scholarships awards to graduates of high schools of Sanilac and Tuscola counties, Michigan.
Fields of interest: Higher education.
Type of support: Scholarships—to individuals.
Limitations: Applications accepted. Giving limited to residents of Sanilac and Tuscola counties, MI.
Application information: Application form required.
   Deadline(s): Mar. 1
Officers: John Paterson, Pres.; Gerald Hicks, Secy.
Directors: Allen Jones; Kenneth Michlash; Donald Teeple.
EIN: 382832816

143
Community Christian Ministries
P.O. Box 282
Grandville, MI   49468-0282
County: Kent
URL: http://www.ccmfoundation.org/

Established in 2002 in MI.
Grantmaker type: Independent foundation.
Financial data (yr. ended 12/31/09): Assets, $569,006 (M); expenditures, $32,768; total giving, $30,000; qualifying distributions, $30,000; giving activities include $30,000 for grants.
Purpose and activities: Giving to provide aid to the poor and needy in the greater Grand Rapids, Michigan, area.
Fields of interest: Human services; Christian agencies & churches; Economically disadvantaged.
Limitations: Applications accepted. Giving limited to the greater Grand Rapids, MI, area.
Application information: Application form available from foundation web site.
   Initial approach: Letter
   Deadline(s): None
Officers: Herm Scholten, Pres.; Jan Vander Weide, Treas.
Directors: Jim Brock; Mike DeVries; Jim Holkeboer; Marv Mingerink; Jan Van Manen; Tom Waalkes.
EIN: 381381272

144
Community Connection, Inc.
P.O. Box 141
Buchanan, MI   49107-0141
County: Berrien

Established in MI.
Grantmaker type: Independent foundation.
Financial data (yr. ended 12/31/09): Assets, $2,500 (M); gifts received, $2,500; expenditures, $200; total giving, $0; qualifying distributions, $0.
Officers: Arleuh Watts, Pres.; Lauretha Askew, V.P.; Cheri Treadwell, Secy.; Christine Watts, Treas.
EIN: 383257474

145
Nancy Malcomson Connable Fund
c/o Connable Assocs., Inc.
136 E. Michigan Ave., Ste. 1201
Kalamazoo, MI   49007-3936   (269) 382-5800
County: Kalamazoo

Established in 2007 in MI.
Donor: Nancy Connable Trust.
Grantmaker type: Independent foundation.
Financial data (yr. ended 12/31/09): Assets, $433,979 (M); expenditures, $20,169; total giving, $12,000; qualifying distributions, $12,000; giving activities include $12,000 for grants.
Fields of interest: Arts.
Limitations: Applications accepted. Giving primarily in WA. No grants to individuals.
Application information:
   Initial approach: Letter
   Deadline(s): None
Officers and Directors:* Bradley E. Weller,* Pres.; James C. Melvin,* V.P.; Loyal A. Eldridge III,* Secy.; David S. Kruis,* Treas.; James S. Hilboldt.
EIN: 260766003

146
Nadalynn Conway Charitable Trust
4080G Miller Rd.
Flint, MI   48507-1242   (810) 733-5140
County: Genesee
Contact: Dale E. McClelland, Tr.

Established in 1996 in MI.
Grantmaker type: Independent foundation.
Financial data (yr. ended 12/31/09): Assets, $670,116 (M); expenditures, $71,893; total giving, $44,000; qualifying distributions, $44,000; giving activities include $44,000 for grants.
Purpose and activities: Grant awards are given for the care and/or preservation of animals.
Fields of interest: Animals/wildlife, preservation/protection; Animals/wildlife.
Type of support: General/operating support.
Limitations: Giving in the U.S., with some emphasis on AZ, MI, MN, MT, and TN.
Application information:
   Initial approach: Letter
   Deadline(s): None
Trustee: Dale E. McClelland.
EIN: 386609288

147
Cook Family Foundation
P.O. Box 278
Owosso, MI   48867-0578   (989) 725-1621
County: Shiawassee
Contact: Thomas B. Cook, Secy.-Treas.
FAX: (989) 725-3138;
E-mail: tom@cookfamilyfoundation.org

Established in 1979 in MI.

Donors: Donald O. Cook†; Florence-Etta Cook†; Donald O. Cook Charitable Trust; Wolverine Sign Works.
Grantmaker type: Independent foundation.
Financial data (yr. ended 12/31/09): Assets, $9,422,516 (M); expenditures, $527,448; total giving, $385,480; qualifying distributions, $385,480; giving activities include $385,480 for grants.
Purpose and activities: Giving primarily for education and youth programs.
Fields of interest: Higher education; Education; Environment, natural resources; Human services; Children/youth, services; United Ways and Federated Giving Programs.
Type of support: General/operating support; Annual campaigns; Capital campaigns; Building/renovation; Program development; Internship funds; Scholarship funds.
Limitations: Giving limited to MI, with emphasis on Shiawassee County. No grants to individuals.
Publications: Annual report; Informational brochure.
Application information:
   Initial approach: Letter
   Deadline(s): None
   Board meeting date(s): Quarterly
Officers: Bruce L. Cook, Pres.; Laurie Caszatt Cook, V.P.; Thomas B. Cook, Secy.-Treas.
Trustees: Jacqueline P. Cook; Paul C. Cook; Anna E. Owens.
Number of staff: 1 part-time professional.
EIN: 382283809
Selected grants: The following grants were reported in 2008.
$74,750 to University of Michigan, Ann Arbor, MI.
$48,050 to Nature Conservancy, Lansing, MI.
$34,635 to Owosso Public Schools, Owosso, MI.
$29,085 to United Way, Shiawassee, Owosso, MI.
$22,676 to United Way, Shiawassee, Owosso, MI.
$21,000 to YMCA of Michigan, State, Central Lake, MI.
$20,000 to Bay Area Community Foundation, Bay City, MI.
$5,557 to Nature Conservancy, Lansing, MI.
$5,000 to Owosso Public Schools, Owosso, MI.
$4,927 to Owosso Public Schools, Owosso, MI.

148
Robert & Bess Cook Foundation
c/o Walnut Services, Inc.
30100 Telegraph Road, Ste. 403
Bingham Farms, MI   48025-4518
(248) 645-2300
County: Oakland
Contact: Regina Brodersen, Secy.

Established in MI.
Donor: Robert Cook Trust.
Grantmaker type: Independent foundation.
Financial data (yr. ended 12/31/09): Assets, $45,184 (M); gifts received, $50,000; expenditures, $7,834; total giving, $6,250; qualifying distributions, $6,250; giving activities include $6,250 for 7 grants (high: $5,000; low: $100).
Limitations: Applications accepted. Giving primarily in MI.
Application information: Application form required.
   Initial approach: Letter
   Deadline(s): None

Officers: Patricia Van Dommelen, V.P.; Minnette Grow, Treas.; Regina Brodersen, Secy.; Libby Graham, Pres.
EIN: 383016880

149
Joanne Cross Coon Foundation
3 Locust Ln.
Lansing, MI 48911-1153
County: Ingham
Contact: Joanne L. Coon, Pres.

Established in MI.
Grantmaker type: Independent foundation.
Financial data (yr. ended 09/30/10): Assets, $349,625 (M); expenditures, $18,000; total giving, $18,000; qualifying distributions, $18,000; giving activities include $18,000 for grants.
Purpose and activities: Giving primarily to Seventh Day Adventists organizations and activities.
Fields of interest: Christian agencies & churches.
Type of support: General/operating support.
Limitations: Applications accepted. Giving limited to MI, with emphasis on the greater Lansing area. No grants to individuals.
Application information: Application form not required.
   Initial approach: Letter
   Deadline(s): None
Officers: Joanne L. Coon, Pres.; Max A. Coon, V.P.; Patricia A. Markoff, Secy.; Jeff A. Coon, Treas.
Director: David Markoff.
EIN: 382359335

150
Allan B. Copley Charitable Foundation
1015 S. Higby St.
Jackson, MI 49203-2830   (517) 784-0610
County: Jackson
Contact: Kathleen M. O'Connell, Tr.

Established in 2003 in MI.
Donor: Allan B. Copley.
Grantmaker type: Independent foundation.
Financial data (yr. ended 12/31/09): Assets, $1,463,091 (M); gifts received, $70,500; expenditures, $100,788; total giving, $69,000; qualifying distributions, $80,712; giving activities include $69,000 for 19 grants (high: $5,500; low: $1,000).
Fields of interest: Elementary/secondary education; Human services; Christian agencies & churches.
Type of support: General/operating support; Scholarship funds.
Limitations: Applications accepted. Giving primarily in Jackson, MI. No grants to individuals.
Application information:
   Initial approach: Letter
   Deadline(s): None
Trustees: Eileen L. Idziak; Kathleen M. O'Connell.
EIN: 611458325

151
Virginia A. Cott & Richard S. Cott Charitable Trust
3957 Blue Water Rd.
Traverse City, MI 49686-8586
County: Grand Traverse
Contact: Robert Carolus, Tr.

Established in 1990 in IL.
Donor: Virginia A. Cott.
Grantmaker type: Independent foundation.
Financial data (yr. ended 12/31/09): Assets, $129,059 (M); expenditures, $42,947; total giving, $40,100; qualifying distributions, $40,100; giving activities include $40,100 for 5 grants (high: $10,000; low: $1,000).
Limitations: Applications accepted. Giving primarily in MI. No grants to individuals.
Application information: Application form not required.
   Deadline(s): None
Trustee: Robert Carolus.
EIN: 371270577

152
William Courtney Family Foundation
c/o Comerica Bank
P.O. Box 75000, M/C 3302
Detroit, MI 48275-8280
County: Wayne
Application address: c/o Paula Gralewski, 500 Woodward St., 21st Fl., Detroit, MI 48226-3420; tel.: (313) 222-5257

Established in 1999 in OH.
Donor: William F. Courtney‡.
Grantmaker type: Independent foundation.
Financial data (yr. ended 12/31/09): Assets, $1,484,993 (M); expenditures, $100,348; total giving, $65,725; qualifying distributions, $71,247; giving activities include $65,725 for 18 grants (high: $20,000; low: $200).
Fields of interest: Arts; Education; Hospitals (specialty); Human services; Christian agencies & churches.
Limitations: Applications accepted. Giving primarily in CA. No grants to individuals.
Application information: Application form required.
   Initial approach: Letter
   Deadline(s): None
Advisory Committee: Christopher Courtney; Frank Courtney.
Trustee: Comerica Bank.
EIN: 341905199
Selected grants: The following grants were reported in 2008.
$15,000 to Washington Jesuit Academy, Washington, DC.
$5,000 to Holy Trinity Church, Washington, DC.

153
Matilda & Harold Crane Foundation
c/o Bank of America, N.A.
40 Pearl St., N.W. 6th Fl.
Grand Rapids, MI 49503-3028
County: Kent
Application address: c/o Susan Gell Meyers, 111 Lyon St., NW Grand Rapids, MI 49503-2487; tel.: (616) 752-2184

Established in 1989 in MI.
Donor: Matilda M. Crane.
Grantmaker type: Independent foundation.
Financial data (yr. ended 12/31/08): Assets, $2,872,051 (M); expenditures, $1,093,935; total giving, $1,043,600; qualifying distributions, $1,076,138; giving activities include $1,043,600 for 4 grants (high: $1,000,000; low: $8,600).

Fields of interest: Museums (art); Human services; Salvation Army; Family services; Community/economic development; Foundations (community); Christian agencies & churches.
Type of support: General/operating support; Continuing support; Scholarship funds.
Limitations: Giving primarily in western MI. No grants to individuals.
Application information:
   Initial approach: Letter
   Deadline(s): None
Officers: Aldonna H. Kammeraad, Pres.; Marilyn J. Crane, V.P.; Diane Wynsma Hyland, Treas.
Directors: Harold D. Crane, Jr.; Terri J. Disselkoen; David Kammeraad; John H. Martin; Donald J. Swierenga.
EIN: 382903301
Selected grants: The following grants were reported in 2008.
$10,000 to Lake County Community Foundation, Waukegan, IL.

154
The Cresswell Family Foundation, Inc.
1968 Boulder Dr.
Ann Arbor, MI 48104-4164
County: Washtenaw
Contact: Ronald M. Cresswell, Dir.

Established in 1999 in MI.
Donor: Ronald M. Cresswell.
Grantmaker type: Independent foundation.
Financial data (yr. ended 12/31/09): Assets, $947,689 (M); expenditures, $100,029; total giving, $88,700; qualifying distributions, $88,700; giving activities include $88,700 for grants.
Purpose and activities: Giving primarily for education, health, and human services.
Fields of interest: Higher education; Education; Health care; American Red Cross; Human services.
Limitations: Applications accepted. Giving on a national basis. No support for private foundations. No grants to individuals.
Publications: Grants list.
Application information: Application form not required.
   Initial approach: Letter
   Copies of proposal: 1
   Deadline(s): None
   Board meeting date(s): Annually
   Final notification: 1 month
Directors: Susan Mary Brice; Eleanor Lynn Costin; Margaret B. Cresswell; Ronald M. Cresswell; Sheena Livingstone Cresswell; Jennifer Margaret Petrie; Katherine Ann Tisserand.
Number of staff: None.
EIN: 383483412
Selected grants: The following grants were reported in 2007.
$150,000 to University of Michigan, College of Pharmacy, Ann Arbor, MI.
$50,000 to Eisenhower Medical Center, Rancho Mirage, CA.
$10,000 to American Red Cross, Ann Arbor, MI.
$10,000 to University of Strathclyde, Usa Foundation, Glasgow, Scotland.
$5,000 to YMCA of Ann Arbor, Ann Arbor, MI.
$2,000 to Covenant House Michigan, Detroit, MI.
$1,000 to Detroit Institute for Children, Detroit, MI.
$1,000 to Gregorian University Foundation, New York, NY.
$1,000 to Youth Service League, Brooklyn, NY.

155
Cronin Foundation
203 E. Michigan Ave.
Marshall, MI   49068-1545   (269) 781-9851
County: Calhoun
Contact: Ronald J. DeGraw, Secy.-Treas.

Established in 1990 in MI.
Donors: Elizabeth Cronin†; Mary Virginia Cronin†.
Grantmaker type: Independent foundation.
Financial data (yr. ended 12/31/09): Assets,
$10,402,609 (M); gifts received, $412;
expenditures, $534,308; total giving, $511,790;
qualifying distributions, $511,790; giving activities
include $511,790 for 12 grants (high: $350,000;
low: $1,000).
Purpose and activities: Giving primarily for
educational, social, economic, civic, and cultural
needs of the community contained within the
Marshall, Michigan, school district.
Fields of interest: Education; Environment;
Hospitals (general); Medical care, rehabilitation;
Recreation, parks/playgrounds; Athletics/sports,
soccer; Youth development, centers/clubs; Human
services; Community/economic development.
Type of support: Building/renovation; Equipment;
Program development.
Limitations: Giving limited to Calhoun County, MI.
No grants to individuals.
Publications: Application guidelines.
Application information: Letter or telephone for
guidelines.
Initial approach: Proposal
Deadline(s): Mar. 1, June 1, Sept. 1, and Dec. 1
Board meeting date(s): Following application
deadlines and as needed
Final notification: Following board meeting
Officers and Directors:* Helen L. Hensick,* Pres.;
Monica Anderson,* V.P.; Ronald J. DeGraw,*
Secy.-Treas.; Dr. Randall Davis; Bruce Smith.
Number of staff: 1 part-time professional.
EIN: 382908362
Selected grants: The following grants were reported
in 2009.
$70,600 to Marshall Community Foundation,
Marshall, MI.
$20,000 to Calhoun County Agricultural and
Industrial Society, Marshall, MI.
$20,000 to Fountain Clinic, Marshall, MI.
$15,000 to Marshall Public Schools, Marshall, MI.
$10,000 to Marshall Public Schools, Marshall, MI.
$9,190 to Marshall Public Schools, Marshall, MI.
$7,316 to Marshall Public Schools, Marshall, MI.
$3,890 to Marshall Public Schools, Marshall, MI.
$3,593 to Marshall Public Schools, Marshall, MI.
$1,202 to Marshall Public Schools, Marshall, MI.

156
Culture Need & Heritage Foundation
c/o Joseph A. Delapa
2950 Valley Ln.
St. Joseph, MI   49085-3537
County: Berrien

Established in 2006 in MI.
Donor: Judith A. Delapa.
Grantmaker type: Independent foundation.
Financial data (yr. ended 12/31/09): Assets,
$316,298 (M); expenditures, $47,111; total giving,
$42,000; qualifying distributions, $42,000; giving
activities include $42,000 for grants.
Officer: Joseph A. Delapa, Pres.
EIN: 205152448

157
Peter D. & Julie F. Cummings Family Foundation
(formerly Peter & Julie Fisher Cummings Foundation)
2 Towne Sq., Ste. 900
Southfield, MI   48076-3760
County: Oakland

Established in 2005 in MI.
Donors: Julie Fisher Cummings; Peter D.
Cummings; Marjorie S. Fisher.
Grantmaker type: Independent foundation.
Financial data (yr. ended 12/31/09): Assets,
$4,515,317 (M); expenditures, $822,766; total
giving, $797,500; qualifying distributions,
$805,000; giving activities include $797,500 for 28
grants (high: $200,000; low: $1,000).
Purpose and activities: Giving primarily for the arts.
Fields of interest: Performing arts; Arts; United
Ways and Federated Giving Programs.
Type of support: General/operating support.
Limitations: Giving primarily in FL, MI, and NY.
Officers: Peter D. Cummings, Pres.; Julie Fisher
Cummings, V.P.; Keith L. Cummings, Secy.-Treas.
Directors: Anthony F. Cummings; Caroline B.
Cummings.
EIN: 300291756
Selected grants: The following grants were reported
in 2008.
$200,000 to Library of Congress, Washington, DC.
$149,000 to Jewish Federation of Metropolitan
Detroit, Bloomfield Hills, MI.
$50,000 to Library Foundation of Martin County,
Stuart, FL.
$50,000 to United States Artists, Los Angeles, CA.
$50,000 to University Cultural Center Association,
Detroit, MI.
$10,000 to Detroit Science Center, Detroit, MI.
$10,000 to Orpheus Chamber Orchestra, New York,
NY.
$5,000 to Carnegie Hall Society, New York, NY.
$1,700 to Council of Michigan Foundations, Grand
Haven, MI.
$1,000 to Society of the Four Arts, Palm Beach, FL.

158
The Louis Cunningham Scholarship Foundation
21411 Civic Center Dr., Ste. 206
Southfield, MI   48076-3950   (248) 263-7630
County: Oakland
Contact: Louis E. Cunningham, Treas.

Established in 1997 in MI.
Grantmaker type: Independent foundation.
Financial data (yr. ended 12/31/09): Assets,
$115,415 (M); gifts received, $20; expenditures,
$7,923; total giving, $4,436; qualifying
distributions, $4,436; giving activities include
$4,436 for grants to individuals.
Purpose and activities: Scholarship awards for
school expenses only.
Fields of interest: Higher education.
Type of support: Scholarships—to individuals.
Limitations: Giving primarily in MI.
Application information: Include grade transcript.
Application form required.
Deadline(s): Varies
Officers: Kenneth A. McKanders, Pres.; Walter
Watkins, V.P.; Louis E. Cunningham, Treas.
EIN: 383197360

159
The Cecelia B. and Kenneth B. Cutler Foundation
10 Westway
Bronxville, NY   10708-4311   (914) 961-7228
County: Westchester
Contact: Kenneth B. Cutler, Tr.

Established in 1986 in NY.
Donors: Cecelia B. Cutler; Kenneth B. Cutler.
Grantmaker type: Independent foundation.
Financial data (yr. ended 11/30/09): Assets,
$265,723 (M); expenditures, $14,613; total giving,
$13,300; qualifying distributions, $13,300; giving
activities include $13,300 for grants.
Fields of interest: Higher education.
Limitations: Applications accepted. Giving primarily
in NY and PA; some giving also in MI. No grants to
individuals.
Application information:
Initial approach: Letter
Deadline(s): None
Trustees: Cecelia B. Cutler; Kenneth B. Cutler.
EIN: 133316060

160
Mary Czado Catholic Education Fund
2112 Cawdor Ct.
Lansing, MI   48917-5133   (517) 321-0440
County: Eaton
Contact: Deborah J. Zale, Treas.

Established in 2002 in MI.
Grantmaker type: Independent foundation.
Financial data (yr. ended 12/31/09): Assets,
$111,369 (M); expenditures, $545; total giving, $0;
qualifying distributions, $0; giving activities include
$0 for grants to individuals.
Purpose and activities: Scholarship awards to
Christian students for higher education.
Fields of interest: Higher education; Theological
school/education.
Type of support: Scholarships—to individuals.
Application information: Application form required.
Deadline(s): None
Officers: Sheila M. Harper, Pres.; Jeanne Larvick,
Secy.; Deborah J. Zale, Treas.
EIN: 383269233

161
D.U. Memorial Foundation
2422 Foxway Dr.
Ann Arbor, MI   48105-9667   (734) 663-3877
County: Washtenaw
Contact: John Markiewicz, Pres.
Additional application address: c/o Will McGarrity,
1331 Hill St., Ann Arbor, MI 48104-3189

Grantmaker type: Independent foundation.
Financial data (yr. ended 12/31/09): Assets, $1
(M); expenditures, $1,073; total giving, $0;
qualifying distributions, $0; giving activities include
$0 for grants to individuals.
Purpose and activities: Scholarship awards to
students at the University of Michigan.
Fields of interest: Higher education, university.
Type of support: Scholarships—to individuals.
Limitations: Giving limited to students attending the
University of Michigan, Ann Arbor.
Application information:

Initial approach: Letter
Deadline(s): May 31
Officers: John Markiewicz, Pres.; Brian Gase, V.P.;
Lawrence Kolwalski, Secy.
EIN: 386157774

162
Robert & Jeanine Dagenais Foundation
2007 Lake Shore Dr.
Escanaba, MI   49829-1944
County: Delta
Contact: Robert A. Dagenais, Pres.

Established in 1994 in MI.
Donor: Robert A. Dagenais.
Grantmaker type: Independent foundation.
Financial data (yr. ended 12/31/09): Assets,
$1,440,819 (M); gifts received, $169,223;
expenditures, $66,678; total giving, $54,960;
qualifying distributions, $54,960; giving activities
include $54,960 for grants.
Fields of interest: Secondary school/education;
Youth development; Human services; Community/
economic development.
Type of support: Building/renovation; Equipment;
Program development.
Limitations: Giving primarily in the upper peninsula
of MI, with emphasis on Escanaba. No grants to
individuals.
Application information: Accepts CMF Common
Grant Application Form. Application form required.
Deadline(s): None
Final notification: Within 60 days
Officers: Robert A. Dagenais, Pres.; Jeanine K.
Dagenais, Secy.-Treas.
Trustees: Matthew A. Dagenais; Paul R. Dagenais;
Timothy R. Dagenais.
EIN: 383195426

163
Dorothy U. Dalton Foundation, Inc.
c/o Greenleaf Trust
211 S. Rose St.
Kalamazoo, MI   49007-4713   (269) 388-9800
County: Kalamazoo
Contact: Ronald N. Kilgore, Secy.-Treas.

Incorporated in 1978 in MI as successor to Dorothy
U. Dalton Foundation Trust.
Donor: Dorothy U. Dalton†.
Grantmaker type: Independent foundation.
Financial data (yr. ended 12/31/09): Assets,
$30,798,610 (M); expenditures, $1,856,165; total
giving, $1,734,500; qualifying distributions,
$1,793,701; giving activities include $1,734,500
for 59 grants (high: $200,000; low: $500).
Purpose and activities: Emphasis on higher
education, mental health, social service and youth
agencies, and cultural programs.
Fields of interest: Performing arts; Performing arts,
theater; Performing arts, music; Arts; Environment;
Hospitals (general); Mental health/crisis services;
Housing/shelter, development; Recreation, parks/
playgrounds; Human services; Youth, services;
Community/economic development.
Type of support: General/operating support;
Continuing support; Capital campaigns; Building/
renovation; Equipment; Land acquisition; Debt
reduction; Emergency funds; Program development;
Seed money; Research; Matching/challenge
support.

Limitations: Giving primarily in Kalamazoo County,
MI. No support for religious organizations. No grants
to individuals, or for annual campaigns,
scholarships, fellowships, publications, or
conferences; no loans.
Application information: Application form required.
Initial approach: Proposal
Copies of proposal: 5
Deadline(s): Submit proposal preferably in Apr.
and Oct.
Board meeting date(s): May and Nov.
Final notification: 30 days after board meetings
Officers and Directors:* Suzanne D. Parish,* Pres.;
Howard Kalleward,* V.P.; Ronald N. Kilgore,*
Secy.-Treas.; Thompson Bennett.
EIN: 382240062
Selected grants: The following grants were reported
in 2008.
$200,000 to Arts Council of Greater Kalamazoo,
Kalamazoo, MI.
$145,000 to Kalamazoo Civic Theater, Kalamazoo,
MI.
$100,000 to Borgess Foundation, Kalamazoo, MI.
$88,000 to Borgess Foundation, Kalamazoo, MI.
$70,000 to United Way, Greater Kalamazoo,
Kalamazoo, MI.
$50,000 to Senior Services, Kalamazoo, MI.
$25,000 to Housing Resources, Kalamazoo, MI.
$25,000 to Lift Foundation, Kalamazoo, MI.
$10,000 to Fontana Chamber Arts, Kalamazoo, MI.
$10,000 to United Way, Greater Kalamazoo,
Kalamazoo, MI.

164
The Dana Z Foundation
(formerly The Dana Foundation)
26300 Telegraph Rd.
Southfield, MI   48033-2436
County: Oakland

Established in 2007 in MI.
Grantmaker type: Independent foundation.
Financial data (yr. ended 12/31/09): Assets,
$120,800 (M); gifts received, $121,000;
expenditures, $35,184; total giving, $34,317;
qualifying distributions, $34,317; giving activities
include $34,317 for 9 grants (high: $11,070; low:
$140).
Limitations: Giving primarily in MI. No grants to
individuals.
Officers: Opada Alzohalli, Pres.; Hala Alkhatib, V.P.;
Siba Alzohalli, Secy.
EIN: 260887540

165
Opal Dancey Memorial Foundation
c/o Plante Moran Trust
P.O. Box 307
Southfield, MI   48037-0307
County: Oakland
E-mail: applicants@opaldanceygrants.org;
URL: http://www.opaldanceygrants.org

Established in 1976 in MI.
Donor: Russell V. Dancey†.
Grantmaker type: Independent foundation.
Financial data (yr. ended 10/31/09): Assets,
$1,862,102 (M); expenditures, $119,339; total
giving, $102,000; qualifying distributions,
$102,000; giving activities include $102,000 for
grants.

Purpose and activities: Giving grants to students
who hold an undergraduate degree from an
accredited university or college, and are a full time
student pursuing a Master of Divinity degree from an
accredited theological seminary, and who will be
serving in pulpit ministry. The seminary in which the
applicant is attending should be located within a
Great Lakes state, or, the applicant lives or has lived
in a Great Lakes state and the seminary in which the
applicant is attending is outside of the Great Lakes
region.
Fields of interest: Theological school/education.
Type of support: Scholarship funds.
Limitations: Applications accepted. Giving primarily
in the Great Lakes region, with emphasis on IL and
OH.
Application information: Application guidelines
available on foundation web site. Application form
required.
Initial approach: Complete online application. No
paper applications, except for the letters of
recommendation and the seminary statement
Deadline(s): May 1
Board meeting date(s): July
Final notification: Early July
Officers: Betty D. Godard, Chair.; Susan Dudas,
Secy.; Timothy F. Godard, Treas.
Trustees: David Dudas; Kathy Godard; Rev. Alice D.
Murphy; Rev. Jeffrey Rider.
EIN: 386361282

166
The Daoud Foundation
16010 19 Mile Rd., Ste. 102
Clinton Township, MI   48038-1141
County: Macomb

Established in 1986 in MI.
Donor: Tarik S. Daoud.
Grantmaker type: Independent foundation.
Financial data (yr. ended 12/31/09): Assets, $1
(M); expenditures, $55,915; total giving, $44,700;
qualifying distributions, $44,700; giving activities
include $44,700 for grants.
Fields of interest: Media, television; Education.
Limitations: Giving primarily in MI, with emphasis on
Detroit.
Trustees: Helen C. Daoud; Tarik S. Daoud; Michael
J. Lazzara.
EIN: 382709932
Selected grants: The following grants were reported
in 2005.
$20,000 to Michigan Opera Theater, Detroit, MI.
$10,000 to Madonna University, Livonia, MI.
$10,000 to Vista Maria, Dearborn Heights, MI.
$5,000 to City Year Detroit, Detroit, MI.
$5,000 to Saint Regis Catholic Church, Bloomfield
Hills, MI.
$2,500 to CATCH, Detroit, MI.

167
Carolyn Darch Ministries, Inc.
154 E. Lovell Dr.
Troy, MI   48098-1573
County: Oakland

Grantmaker type: Independent foundation.
Financial data (yr. ended 12/31/09): Assets, $205
(M); gifts received, $9,186; expenditures, $9,912;
total giving, $0; qualifying distributions, $0.

Limitations: Giving primarily in MI. No grants to individuals.
Officers and Directors: * Carolyn Darch,* Pres.; Dennis Darch,* Secy.-Treas.
EIN: 383130189

168
The Dart Foundation
500 Hogsback Rd.
Mason, MI   48854-9547   (517) 244-2190
County: Ingham
Contact: Claudia Deschaine, Grants Mgr.
FAX: (517) 244-2631;
E-mail: claudia_deschaine@dart.biz; URL: http://www.dartfoundation.org

Established in 1984 in MI.
Donor: William & Claire Dart Foundation.
Grantmaker type: Independent foundation.
Financial data (yr. ended 10/31/09): Assets, $722,291 (M); gifts received, $4,000,000; expenditures, $3,498,811; total giving, $3,413,428; qualifying distributions, $3,498,811; giving activities include $3,413,428 for 182 grants (high: $933,333; low: $250), and $55,657 for foundation-administered programs.
Purpose and activities: Historically, it has been the foundation's preference to make grants toward education (primarily math, science and engineering) and youth programs. Other major areas of interest have included health, disaster relief and journalism programs that focus on the accuracy of news reporting on scientific and environmental issues. Additionally, major support is given to national projects such as the Dart Center for Journalism & Trauma, a global resource for journalists who cover violence.
Fields of interest: Higher education; Education; Hospitals (general); Health organizations, association; Alzheimer's disease research; Boys & girls clubs; Human services; Children/youth, services; Engineering/technology; Public affairs; Children/youth; Economically disadvantaged.
Type of support: Scholarship funds; Equipment; Capital campaigns; Annual campaigns; General/operating support; Continuing support; Building/renovation; Program development; Publication; Curriculum development; Research; Matching/challenge support.
Limitations: Applications accepted. Giving primarily in Sarasota, FL central MI, and specific communities in the U.S. No grants to individuals.
Publications: Application guidelines; Annual report; Annual report (including application guidelines); Grants list.
Application information: Application form required.
   Initial approach: Letter, telephone or e-mail
   Copies of proposal: 1
   Deadline(s): Mar. 15, June 15, Sept. 15, Dec. 15
   Final notification: One month
Officers and Directors: * William A. Dart,* Chair.; James D. Lammers, V.P. and Secy.; Claire T. Dart; Kenneth B. Dart.
Number of staff: 1 full-time professional.
EIN: 382849841
Selected grants: The following grants were reported in 2007.
$1,100,000 to University of Washington, Dart Center for Journalism and Trauma, Seattle, WA.
$125,000 to Education Foundation of Sarasota County, Sarasota, FL.
$100,000 to Alzheimers Association National Headquarters, Chicago, IL.

$100,000 to American Red Cross, Southwest Florida Chapter, Sarasota, FL.
$66,000 to Michigan State University, East Lansing, MI. For Science Olympiad.
$50,000 to American Red Cross, Lansing, MI.
$50,000 to Volunteers of America of Greater Lansing, Lansing, MI.
$30,000 to Nature Conservancy, Arlington, VA.

169
Henry & Sidney T. Davenport Educational Family Foundation
(formerly Henry & Sidney T. Davenport Educational Fund)
c/o Comerica Bank
P.O. Box 75000, MC 3302
Detroit, MI   48275-3302   (252) 454-4017
County: Wayne
Contact: Sharon M. Stephens, Trust Off., Comerica Bank
Application address: c/o 130 S. Franklin St., Rocky Mount, NC 27804-5707, tel.: (252) 467-4743

Established in 1960 in NC.
Donors: Henry N. Davenport‡; Sidney T. Davenport.
Grantmaker type: Independent foundation.
Financial data (yr. ended 06/30/10): Assets, $752,738 (M); expenditures, $52,107; total giving, $32,000; qualifying distributions, $32,000; giving activities include $32,000 for grants to individuals.
Purpose and activities: Student loans to students residing in Nash or Edgecombe counties, North Carolina.
Fields of interest: Higher education.
Type of support: Student loans—to individuals.
Limitations: Giving limited to residents of Nash and Edgecombe counties, NC.
Application information: Application form required.
   Deadline(s): May 1
Trustee: Comerica Bank.
EIN: 237422939

170
M. E. Davenport Foundation
415 E. Fulton St.
Warren Hall, Main Fl.
Grand Rapids, MI   49503-5926   (616) 234-6280
County: Kent
Contact: Margaret E. Moceri, Pres.
FAX: (616) 732-1147;
E-mail: pmoceri@davenport.edu; URL: http://www.medavenport.org

Established in 1986 in MI.
Donors: Robert W. and Margaret D. Sneden Foundation; Margaret Moceri; Gregory Moceri; Kathleen Sneden; Mary Sneden Sullivan; Watson Pierce; Elsie Pierce; Barbara DeMoor.
Grantmaker type: Independent foundation.
Financial data (yr. ended 09/30/10): Assets, $17,029,595 (M); gifts received, $4,050; expenditures, $977,272; total giving, $701,343; qualifying distributions, $775,627; giving activities include $701,343 for 17 grants (high: $482,143; low: $200).
Purpose and activities: Support primarily for private institutions of higher education, and specific social and community needs, usually related to business education, training, employment, and community stability, such as housing.

Fields of interest: Higher education; Employment, training; Youth development, business.
Type of support: Building/renovation; Capital campaigns; Program development; Seed money; Curriculum development.
Limitations: Applications accepted. Giving primarily in western lower MI. No support for religious or political agendas. No grants to individuals, debt retirement or budget deficit remediation, and taxable organizations or activities.
Publications: Application guidelines; Annual report; Financial statement; Grants list; Occasional report.
Application information: Application form not required.
   Initial approach: Letter
   Copies of proposal: 1
   Deadline(s): June 30
   Board meeting date(s): Triennially
   Final notification: 30-45 days
Officers and Trustees: * Margaret E. Moceri,* Chair.; Gregory C. Moceri, V.P. and Treas.; Mary P. Sullivan, Secy.; Donald Maine; Marcia A. Sneden; James Setchfield, M.D.
Number of staff: 2 full-time professional.
EIN: 382646809
Selected grants: The following grants were reported in 2009.
$155,777 to Davenport University, Grand Rapids, MI.
$80,000 to Grand Rapids Community Foundation, Grand Rapids, MI.

171
The John R. & M. Margrite Davis Foundation
40950 Woodward Ave., Ste. 306
Bloomfield Hills, MI   48304-5124
County: Oakland
Application address: c/o Raymond C. Cunningham, Jr., 125 Babbs Hollow Rd., Greenville, SC, tel.: (843) 671-1108

Established in 1955 in MI.
Donors: John R. Davis‡; M. Margrite Davis.
Grantmaker type: Independent foundation.
Financial data (yr. ended 12/31/09): Assets, $9,695,549 (M); expenditures, $454,750; total giving, $409,450; qualifying distributions, $409,450; giving activities include $409,450 for 57 grants (high: $50,000; low: $250).
Fields of interest: Higher education; Hospitals (general); Medical research, institute; Human services; Children/youth, services.
Type of support: Continuing support; Annual campaigns; Capital campaigns; Building/renovation; Research.
Limitations: Giving primarily in MI and SC. No grants to individuals.
Application information:
   Initial approach: Letter
   Copies of proposal: 1
   Deadline(s): None
   Board meeting date(s): Dec.
Officers and Trustees: * Raymond C. Cunningham, Jr., Pres.; Deborah Sue Cunningham,* Secy.-Treas.; Debra Cunningham; James H. LoPrete; Mary M. Lyneis.
EIN: 386058593
Selected grants: The following grants were reported in 2008.
$20,000 to Detroit Athletic Club Foundation, Detroit, MI.

$13,000 to Henry Ford Community College, Dearborn, MI.
$10,000 to Henry Ford Hospital, Health Systems, Detroit, MI.
$10,000 to Heritage Foundation, Washington, DC.
$10,000 to Saint Charles Preparatory School, Columbus, OH.
$5,000 to Adrian Dominican Sisters, Adrian, MI.
$5,000 to Thomas More Law Center, Ann Arbor, MI.
$3,000 to Tax Foundation, Washington, DC.
$2,500 to Carolina Youth Symphony, Greenville, SC.
$1,000 to Sigma Chi Foundation, Evanston, IL.

172
Elizabeth B. Davisson & Abelina Suarez Education Trust
542 Barrington Rd.
Grosse Pointe Park, MI 48230
County: Wayne

Established in 2002 in MI.
Grantmaker type: Independent foundation.
Financial data (yr. ended 12/31/09): Assets, $17,135 (M); expenditures, $9,025; total giving, $6,500; qualifying distributions, $6,500; giving activities include $6,500 for grants.
Purpose and activities: Giving primarily for education, including college scholarships to residents of Grosse Pointe Park, Michigan.
Fields of interest: Higher education.
Type of support: Scholarships—to individuals; General/operating support.
Limitations: Giving primarily in Grosse Pointe Park, MI.
Trustee: Great Lakes Management.
EIN: 386771501

173
Joseph C. Day Foundation
P.O. Box 957
Bloomfield Hills, MI 48303-0957
(248) 646-4347
County: Oakland
Contact: Joseph C. Day, Tr.

Established in 2000 in MI.
Donor: Joseph C. Day.
Grantmaker type: Independent foundation.
Financial data (yr. ended 12/31/09): Assets, $839,171 (M); expenditures, $30,599; total giving, $22,136; qualifying distributions, $26,211; giving activities include $22,136 for 12 grants (high: $6,576; low: $100).
Fields of interest: Education; Health care; Children/youth, services; Community/economic development.
Limitations: Applications accepted. Giving primarily in MI. No grants to individuals.
Application information: Application form required.
Initial approach: Letter
Deadline(s): Dec. 31
Officer and Trustees:* Erin Day Healer,* Mgr.; Joseph C. Day; Shannon Day Drumm; Marri Fairbanks.
EIN: 383543776

174
Daystar Foundation
7210 Thornapple River Dr. S.E.
Caledonia, MI 49316-8305 (616) 554-9557
County: Kent
Contact: Douglas J. Bouma, Pres.

Established in 1999 in MI.
Donors: Douglas J. Bouma; Sherri L. Bouma.
Grantmaker type: Independent foundation.
Financial data (yr. ended 12/31/09): Assets, $10,003 (M); expenditures, $24,867; total giving, $24,073; qualifying distributions, $24,073; giving activities include $24,073 for grants.
Purpose and activities: Giving to Christian organizations and churches, and for Christian education.
Fields of interest: Education; Christian agencies & churches.
Limitations: Giving primarily in MI.
Application information:
Initial approach: Letter
Deadline(s): None
Officers: Douglas J. Bouma, Pres.; Sherri L. Bouma, Secy.-Treas.
EIN: 383486245
Selected grants: The following grants were reported in 2007.
$276,800 to Resurrection Life Full Gospel Church, Grandville, MI.
$247,500 to Tri-Unity Christian School Association, Wyoming, MI.

175
DeBower Foundation Charitable Trust
P.O. Box 479
Muskegon, MI 49443-0479
County: Muskegon
Contact: Charles E. Silky, Jr., Tr.
Application address: P.O. Box 1242, Muskegon, MI 49443-1242, tel.: (616) 726-4853

Established in MI.
Grantmaker type: Independent foundation.
Financial data (yr. ended 12/31/09): Assets, $44,388 (M); expenditures, $7,187; total giving, $3,250; qualifying distributions, $3,250; giving activities include $3,250 for grants.
Fields of interest: Higher education.
Type of support: Scholarship funds.
Limitations: Giving primarily in MI. No grants to individuals (directly).
Application information: Application form required.
Deadline(s): None
Trustees: Cathy Houseman; Christine O'Connell; Charles E. Silky, Jr.
EIN: 386475514

176
George S. and Helen G. Deffenbaugh Foundation
5842 E. Millerway Rd.
Bloomfield Hills, MI 48301-1937
County: Oakland
Application address: c/o Joellyn D. Kuhn, 30100 Telegraph Rd., Ste. 337, Bingham Farms, MI 4805-5807

Established in 1991 in MI.
Grantmaker type: Independent foundation.

Financial data (yr. ended 12/31/09): Assets, $3,092,330 (M); expenditures, $163,090; total giving, $151,090; qualifying distributions, $151,090; giving activities include $151,090 for 12 grants (high: $35,000; low: $90).
Fields of interest: Media, television; Performing arts; Hospitals (general); Cancer research; Human services; Christian agencies & churches.
Type of support: General/operating support; Building/renovation; Scholarship funds.
Limitations: Giving primarily in MI.
Application information: Application form not required.
Initial approach: Letter
Copies of proposal: 1
Deadline(s): Dec. 31
Board meeting date(s): Quarterly
Officers: Joellyn D. Kuhn, Pres. and Secy.-Treas.; John Kuhn, V.P. and Secy.; Elizabeth Kuhn, Co-Treas.
Number of staff: 3 part-time professional.
EIN: 383117862
Selected grants: The following grants were reported in 2004.
$75,000 to Detroit Rotary Foundation, Detroit, MI. For Outside Historic Lighting Project.
$37,500 to Brighton Hospital, Brighton, MI. To build serenity garden.
$28,591 to Furniture Bank of Oakland County, Pontiac, MI. To purchase truck.
$20,000 to Furniture Bank of Oakland County, Pontiac, MI. For furniture pick up program.
$5,000 to North Oakland SCAMP Funding Corporation, Clarkston, MI. For summer camps scholarships.

177
Lucille B. Deinzer Charitable Trust
c/o Monroe Bank & Trust
102 E. Front St.
Monroe, MI 48161
County: Monroe
Application address: c/o Deinzer Fund Committee, Trinity Lutheran Church, 323 Scott St., Monroe MI 48161, tel.: (734) 242-2734

Grantmaker type: Independent foundation.
Financial data (yr. ended 12/31/09): Assets, $1,662,740 (M); expenditures, $169,937; total giving, $138,381; qualifying distributions, $152,931; giving activities include $138,381 for 1 grant.
Application information: Application form required.
Initial approach: Proposal
Deadline(s): None
Trustee: Monroe Bank and Trust.
EIN: 266251718

178
DeLange Family Foundation, Inc.
(formerly CT Charitable Foundation, Inc.)
13721 S.W. 97th Ave.
Miami, FL 33176-6867
County: Miami-Dade
Contact: Daniel DeLange, Pres.
Application address: 14000 S.W. 216th St., Miami, FL 33170-2405

Established in 1985 in FL.
Grantmaker type: Independent foundation.

Financial data (yr. ended 10/31/10): Assets, $306,739 (M); expenditures, $46,379; total giving, $44,530; qualifying distributions, $44,530; giving activities include $44,530 for grants.
Fields of interest: Elementary/secondary education; Foundations (community); Christian agencies & churches.
Limitations: Applications accepted. Giving primarily in FL, with emphasis on Miami, and Grand Rapids, MI. No grants to individuals.
Application information:
  Initial approach: Letter
  Deadline(s): None
Officer: Daniel DeLange, Pres. and Treas.
EIN: 592483255

179
The Mignon Sherwood Delano Foundation
834 King Hwy., Ste. 110
Kalamazoo, MI 49001-2579 (269) 344-9236
County: Kalamazoo
URL: http://www.delanofoundation.com/

Incorporated in 1985 in MI.
Donor: Mignon Sherwood Delano‡.
Grantmaker type: Independent foundation.
Financial data (yr. ended 12/31/09): Assets, $3,956,043 (M); expenditures, $219,239; total giving, $197,997; qualifying distributions, $219,335; giving activities include $197,997 for 27 grants (high: $40,000; low: $1,882).
Purpose and activities: Giving for the furtherance of humanitarian, educational, cultural and environmental enrichment in the City of Allegan, Allegan County and southwestern Michigan.
Fields of interest: Arts; Education; Reproductive health, family planning; Health care; Health organizations; Food banks; Housing/shelter; Youth development; Human services; Residential/custodial care; Community/economic development; Catholic agencies & churches.
Type of support: General/operating support; Equipment; Program development.
Limitations: Applications accepted. Giving limited to the City of Allegan, Allegan County and southwestern MI. No grants to individuals.
Application information: See web site for application policies and application form. Application form required.
  Deadline(s): 2nd Tues. in Sept.
Officers and Direcors:* Bernard Riker,* Pres.; Ellen Altamore,* V.P.; Rebecca Burnett,* Secy.; Thomas Hunter,* Treas.; Thomas Berlin; Julie Sosnowski.
Trustee: PNC Bank, N.A.
EIN: 382557743
Selected grants: The following grants were reported in 2004.
$18,000 to Allegan County Crisis Response Services, Allegan, MI. For operating support.
$16,095 to Allegan Area Arts Council, Allegan, MI. For program support.
$10,000 to Four-H Clubs of Allegan County, Bloomingdale, MI. For program support.
$10,000 to Gildas Club Grand Rapids, Grand Rapids, MI. For program support.
$7,750 to Allegan Public Schools, Allegan, MI.
$5,000 to Kairos Dwelling, Kalamazoo, MI. For operating support.
$2,500 to Michigan Festival of Sacred Music, Kalamazoo, MI.

180
DeRoy Testamentary Foundation
26999 Central Park Blvd., Ste. 160N
Southfield, MI 48076-4174 (248) 827-0920
County: Oakland
Contact: Julie A. Rodecker Holly, V.P. and Prog. Off.
FAX: (248) 827-0922; *E-mail:* deroyfdtn@aol.com

Established in 1979 in MI.
Donor: Helen L. DeRoy‡.
Grantmaker type: Independent foundation.
Financial data (yr. ended 12/31/09): Assets, $42,513,567 (M); expenditures, $2,605,048; total giving, $1,967,816; qualifying distributions, $2,270,675; giving activities include $1,967,816 for 129 grants (high: $100,000; low: $260).
Purpose and activities: Giving primarily for youth development and services, education, human services, health care, and the arts.
Fields of interest: Museums; Performing arts; Animal welfare; Zoos/zoological societies; Health care, single organization support; Medical care, community health systems; Public health; Substance abuse, services; Mental health, counseling/support groups; Cancer; Food distribution, groceries on wheels; Youth development; Residential/custodial care, hospices.
Type of support: General/operating support; Annual campaigns; Continuing support; Building/renovation; Program development; Scholarship funds.
Limitations: Applications accepted. Giving primarily in MI. No grants to individuals.
Application information: Application form not required.
  Initial approach: Letter or telephone
  Copies of proposal: 1
  Deadline(s): None
  Board meeting date(s): Monthly
  Final notification: 1 - 3 months
Officers and Trustees:* Arthur Rodecker,* Pres.; Julie A. Rodecker Holly,* V.P. and Prog. Off.; Gregg D. Watkins,* Secy.; Marian Keidan Seltzer,* Treas.
Number of staff: 1 full-time professional; 3 part-time professional; 1 full-time support.
EIN: 382208833
Selected grants: The following grants were reported in 2009.
$100,000 to Hillsdale College, Hillsdale, MI.
$72,000 to Oakland Family Services, Pontiac, MI.
$50,000 to Barbara Ann Karmanos Cancer Institute, Detroit, MI.
$50,000 to College for Creative Studies, Detroit, MI.
$50,000 to Interlochen Center for the Arts, Interlochen, MI.
$40,000 to Jewish Federation of Metropolitan Detroit, Bloomfield Hills, MI.
$15,000 to Dominican Literacy Center, Detroit, MI.
$10,000 to HAVEN, Pontiac, MI.
$10,000 to Variety FAR Conservatory of Therapeutic and Performing Arts, Birmingham, MI.
$8,800 to Inside Out Literary Arts Project, Detroit, MI.

181
Detroit Armory Corporation
8270 Denwood Dr., Apt. 17
Sterling Heights, MI 48312-5967
County: Macomb
Contact: Edward L. Cox, Jr., Secy.-Treas.

Established in 1882 in MI.
Grantmaker type: Independent foundation.

Financial data (yr. ended 11/30/09): Assets, $1,088,021 (M); expenditures, $71,147; total giving, $45,538; qualifying distributions, $45,538; giving activities include $45,538 for grants.
Fields of interest: Education; Hospitals (specialty); Human services; Christian agencies & churches.
Type of support: General/operating support.
Limitations: Giving limited to MI, with emphasis on the metropolitan Detroit area. No support for organizations lacking 501(c)(3) status. No grants to individuals, or for scholarships, conventions, conferences, exhibits, seminars, travel, or fundraising events; no loans.
Application information: Application form not required.
  Initial approach: Letter
  Copies of proposal: 2
  Deadline(s): None
  Board meeting date(s): As required
Officers and Directors:* Lonnie G. VanNoy,* Pres.; Stanley J. Wilk,* V.P.; Edward L. Cox, Jr.,* Secy.-Treas.; George A. Bronson; James F. Clark; Sylvin J. Gaynor; Walter G. Hinckfoot, Jr.; William J. Maiorana; Ruth A. Newman; Joseph G. Saad; Clarence E. Weinand.
Number of staff: 1 part-time professional.
EIN: 386066969

182
Detroit Industrial School
28411 Northwestern Hwy., No. 800
Southfield, MI 48034-5538
County: Oakland

Established in MI in 1857.
Grantmaker type: Independent foundation.
Financial data (yr. ended 10/31/10): Assets, $1,537,077 (M); gifts received, $81,118; expenditures, $64,500; total giving, $61,375; qualifying distributions, $61,375; giving activities include $61,375 for 35 grants (high: $4,000; low: $500).
Purpose and activities: Giving primarily to the metropolitan Detroit area agencies serving children and youth services.
Fields of interest: Children/youth, services.
Limitations: Applications accepted. Giving limited to the Wayne, Macomb, and Oakland Tri-county area, MI. No grants for salaries.
Application information: Application form required.
  Initial approach: Letter
  Copies of proposal: 1
  Deadline(s): Mar. 1 and Aug. 1
Officers: Cynthia Huebner, Pres.; Polly Tech, V.P.; Lucinda Prost, Recording Secy.; Terri Brown, Corresponding Secy.; Carol Lytle, Treas.
EIN: 381360534

183
Detter Family Foundation, Inc.
371 Channelside Walk Way, Rm. 1802
Tampa, FL 33602-6766
County: Hillsborough
Contact: Iris F. Detter, Pres.

Established in 2005 in FL.
Donor: Gerald Detter.
Grantmaker type: Independent foundation.
Financial data (yr. ended 12/31/09): Assets, $3,278,200 (M); gifts received, $143; expenditures, $155,721; total giving, $110,742;

qualifying distributions, $110,742; giving activities include $110,742 for grants.
Fields of interest: Education; Health organizations; Human services.
Type of support: Scholarship funds; General/operating support.
Limitations: Giving primarily in MI, with emphasis on Ann Arbor, Saline, and Grand Rapids; giving also in Naples, FL, and New York, NY.
Application information: Application form not required.
   Initial approach: Letter
   Deadline(s): None
Officers: Iris F. Detter, Pres.; Jill Wiedmeyer, V.P.; Jodi Koerner, Secy.; Jason Detter, Treas.
EIN: 203696924

184
Deur Endowment Fund
599 W. Brooks St.
Newaygo, MI 49337
County: Newaygo

Grantmaker type: Independent foundation.
Financial data (yr. ended 06/30/09): Assets, $1,850,078 (M); expenditures, $80,533; total giving, $62,500; qualifying distributions, $67,073; giving activities include $44,800 for 7 grants (high: $19,400; low: $1,700), and $17,700 for 21 grants to individuals (high: $1,075; low: $500).
Application information: Application form required.
   Initial approach: Letter
   Deadline(s): Sep. 30
Officers: Jim Arends, Pres.; Vern Willet, V.P.; Leslie Ostyn, Secy.; Steve Jacobs, Treas.; Marilyn Vankoevering.
Board Members: Thomas Boufford; Bernie Hinkley; Jack Hoffman; Larry Maile; Marilyn Vankoevering.
EIN: 900578696

185
The DeVlieg Foundation
(formerly The Charles DeVlieg Foundation)
500 Woodward Ave., Ste. 2500
Detroit, MI 48226-5499 (313) 961-0200
County: Wayne
Contact: Curtis J. DeRoo, Secy.; Janet DeVlieg Pope, Pres.; Julia DeVlieg, V.P.

Incorporated in 1961 in MI.
Donors: Charles B. DeVlieg‡; Charles R. DeVlieg‡; Kathryn S. DeVlieg‡; DeVlieg Machine Co.
Grantmaker type: Independent foundation.
Financial data (yr. ended 12/31/09): Assets, $7,893,545 (M); expenditures, $440,950; total giving, $223,140; qualifying distributions, $300,896; giving activities include $223,140 for 29 grants (high: $20,000; low: $1,000).
Purpose and activities: Support largely for higher education, including education in engineering and technology, the environment, and wildlife; funding also for other animal and wildlife organizations, the arts and youth services.
Fields of interest: Arts; Higher education; Engineering school/education; Environment, natural resources; Animals/wildlife; Youth, services.
Type of support: General/operating support; Professorships; Scholarship funds.
Limitations: Applications accepted. Giving primarily in the ID, southeastern MI, and eastern WA, areas.

No grants to individuals, or for endowment funds; no loans.
Publications: Annual report (including application guidelines).
Application information: Application form required.
   Initial approach: Letter
   Copies of proposal: 2
   Deadline(s): None
   Board meeting date(s): Semiannually
Officers and Directors:* Janet DeVlieg Pope,* Pres.; Julia C. DeVlieg,* V.P.; Curtis J. DeRoo,* Secy.; Richard A. Jerue; Romany O'Neill; James Pope; Gary Stetler; Gerald Stetler.
Number of staff: 1 part-time professional.
EIN: 386075696
Selected grants: The following grants were reported in 2008.
$20,000 to High Rocks Academy, Hillsboro, WV.
$20,000 to Idaho State University, College of Natural Resources, Pocatello, ID.
$20,000 to Michigan Colleges Foundation, Southfield, MI.
$20,000 to Michigan Technological University, Houghton, MI.
$20,000 to University of Idaho, College of Engineering, Office of the President, Moscow, ID.
$20,000 to Washington State University, Director College Relations, College of Engineering, Pullman, WA.
$10,000 to Chief Joseph Foundation, Bonnie Ewing, Lapwai, ID.
$10,000 to Interlochen Center for the Arts, Interlochen, MI.
$10,000 to University of Idaho Foundation, Office of the Dean, College of Natural Resources, Moscow, ID.
$5,000 to Detroit Institute of Arts, Detroit, MI.

186
Daniel and Pamella DeVos Foundation
P.O. Box 230257
Grand Rapids, MI 49523-0257 (616) 643-4700
County: Kent
Contact: Ginny Vander Hart, Exec. Dir.
FAX: (616) 774-0116; E-mail: virginiav@rdvcorp.com

Established in 1992 in MI.
Donors: The Richard and Helen DeVos Foundation; Daniel DeVos; Pamella DeVos.
Grantmaker type: Independent foundation.
Financial data (yr. ended 12/31/09): Assets, $0 (M); gifts received, $6,195,000; expenditures, $6,852,758; total giving, $6,712,930; qualifying distributions, $6,852,234; giving activities include $6,712,930 for 83 grants (high: $4,031,000; low: $500).
Purpose and activities: Giving primarily for the arts, particularly an art museum and for the performing arts; funding also for higher education, health care, including a children's hospital, and for children, youth, and social services.
Fields of interest: Museums (art); Performing arts; ballet; Performing arts, orchestras; Arts; Elementary/secondary education; Higher education; Education; Hospitals (specialty); Health care; Health organizations, association; Human services; Children/youth, services; Public policy, research; Christian agencies & churches.
Type of support: General/operating support; Continuing support; Annual campaigns; Capital campaigns; Building/renovation; Program development; Seed money; Matching/challenge support.

Limitations: Applications accepted. Giving primarily in Grand Rapids, MI. No grants to individuals.
Publications: Application guidelines.
Application information: Application form not required.
   Initial approach: Letter
   Copies of proposal: 1
   Deadline(s): None
   Final notification: 3 to 5 months
Officers: Jerry L. Tubergen, C.O.O., V.P. and Secy.; Daniel G. DeVos, Pres.; Pamella DeVos, V.P.; Jeffery K. Lambert, V.P.; Robert H. Schierbeek, Treas.; Ginny Vander Hart, Exec. Dir.
EIN: 383035976
Selected grants: The following grants were reported in 2007.
$3,011,704 to Helen DeVos Childrens Hospital Foundation, Grand Rapids, MI. For general operating support.
$533,720 to Grand Rapids Art Museum, Grand Rapids, MI. For general operating support.
$342,000 to Cape Eleuthera Foundation, Lawrenceville, NJ. For general operating support.
$258,800 to Public Museum of Grand Rapids, Grand Rapids, MI. For general operating support.
$108,000 to Frederik Meijer Gardens and Sculpture Park, Grand Rapids, MI. For general operating support.
$80,000 to Grand Rapids Ballet Company, Grand Rapids, MI. For general operating support.
$65,750 to Whitney Museum of American Art, New York, NY. For general operating support.
$37,500 to Grand Rapids Civic Theater, Grand Rapids, MI. For general operating support.
$23,605 to John F. Kennedy Center for the Performing Arts, Washington, DC. For general operating support.
$10,000 to Spectrum Health Foundation, Grand Rapids, MI. For general operating support.

187
Dick & Betsy DeVos Foundation
P.O. Box 230257
Grand Rapids, MI 49523-0257 (616) 643-4700
County: Kent
Contact: Ginny Vander Hart, Exec. Dir.; Sue Volkers, Fdn. Admin.
FAX (for Ginny Vander Hart): (616) 774-0116; E-mail (for Ginny Vander Hart): virginiav@rdvcorp.com

Established in 1989 in MI.
Donors: Dick DeVos; Betsy DeVos; Prince Foundation.
Grantmaker type: Independent foundation.
Financial data (yr. ended 12/31/09): Assets, $54,829,634 (M); gifts received, $8,000,000; expenditures, $8,135,254; total giving, $7,600,422; qualifying distributions, $9,264,245; giving activities include $7,600,422 for 183 grants (high: $520,000; low: $50), and $1,300,000 for 1 loan/program-related investment.
Purpose and activities: The foundation seeks to create a legacy of caring and stewardship through its support of projects that build a strong community. To demonstrate this commitment, the foundation concentrates its funding in support of various initiatives that promote a healthier community, with a focus on the arts, health and children's causes.
Fields of interest: Arts; Education; Children/youth, services; Family services; Public policy, research; Christian agencies & churches.

Type of support: Program-related investments/ loans; General/operating support; Continuing support; Annual campaigns; Capital campaigns.
Limitations: Applications accepted. Giving primarily in west MI. No grants to individuals.
Publications: Application guidelines.
Application information: Application form not required.

Initial approach: Letter
Copies of proposal: 1
Deadline(s): 2 weeks prior to review
Board meeting date(s): Quarterly
Final notification: 4 to 5 months

Officers and Directors:* Jerry L. Tubergen,* C.O.O., V.P. and Secy.; Richard M. DeVos, Jr.,* Pres.; Elisabeth DeVos,* V.P.; Jeffrey K. Lambert, V.P.; Robert H. Schierbeek, Treas.; Ginny Vander Hart, Exec. Dir. and Fdn. Dir.
EIN: 382902412
Selected grants: The following grants were reported in 2008.
$1,000,000 to Thunderbird, The Garvin School of International Management, Glendale, AZ. For unrestricted grant to General Fund.
$500,000 to Haggai Institute for Advanced Leadership Training, Norcross, GA. For unrestricted grant to general fund.
$500,000 to Willow Creek Association, South Barrington, IL. For unrestricted grant to general fund.
$305,000 to Education Freedom Fund, Charlotte, MI. For unrestricted grant to general fund.
$257,180 to John F. Kennedy Center for the Performing Arts, Washington, DC. For unrestricted grant to general fund.
$250,000 to International Aid, Spring Lake, MI. For unrestricted grant to general fund.
$50,000 to Diocese of Grand Rapids, Grand Rapids, MI. For unrestricted grant to general fund.
$49,700 to Grand Rapids Christian School Association, Grand Rapids, MI. For unrestricted grant to general fund.
$29,750 to TEDGlobal/Sapling Foundation, New York, NY. For unrestricted grant to general fund.
$25,000 to Bridges of Understanding Foundation, Washington, DC. For unrestricted grant to general fund.

188
Douglas & Maria DeVos Foundation

P.O. Box 230257
Grand Rapids, MI   49523-0257   (616) 643-4700
County: Kent
Contact: Ginny Vander Hart, Exec. Dir.
FAX: (616) 774-0116;
E-mail: info@dmdevosfoundation.org; URL: http://www.dmdevosfoundation.org/

Established in 1992 in MI.
Donors: Douglas DeVos; Maria DeVos.
Grantmaker type: Independent foundation.
Financial data (yr. ended 12/31/09): Assets, $61,992,136 (M); gifts received, $19,000,000; expenditures, $11,627,818; total giving, $10,433,131; qualifying distributions, $11,458,562; giving activities include $10,433,131 for 129 grants (high: $2,501,000; low: $250), and $546,392 for 1 foundation-administered program.
Purpose and activities: The foundation seeks to share the importance of their Christian faith by building holistic and sustainable communities that empower youth and families to prosper physically,

intellectually, and spiritually. Foundation focus areas include youth, family and community.
Fields of interest: Health care; Human services; Family services; Community/economic development; Christian agencies & churches; Youth.
Type of support: General/operating support; Capital campaigns; Program development.
Limitations: Applications accepted. Giving primarily in western MI, with a significant focus on the Grand Rapids area. No support for non 501(c)(3) organizations, or for start-up organizations (within 18 months of incorporation), organizations working outside the United States, or for organizations that contradict the stated values of the foundation. No grants or loans to individuals, or for endowments, debt retirement, or for investment opportunities.
Publications: Application guidelines.
Application information: Very few grants are awarded to new organizations with no previous relationship with the trustees. Any grants to new organizations will rarely exceed $5,000. The foundation prefers to receive applications from organizations once every 12 months. In addition, the foundation will not consider second requests from organizations for capital projects. Application form required.

Initial approach: Submit via application form on foundation web site.
Copies of proposal: 1
Deadline(s): None
Board meeting date(s): Quarterly
Final notification: Within 3 weeks following quarterly board meetings

Officers: Douglas DeVos, Pres.; Jerry L. Tubergen, C.O.O, V.P. and Secy.; Maria DeVos, V.P.; Jeffrey K. Lambert, V.P.; Robert H. Schierbeek, Treas.; Ginny Vander Hart, Exec. Dir.
EIN: 383035972
Selected grants: The following grants were reported in 2008.
$3,001,000 to Helen DeVos Childrens Hospital Foundation, Grand Rapids, MI. For general support.
$2,107,000 to Grand Rapids Christian School Association, Grand Rapids, MI. For general support.
$579,500 to Grand Rapids Public Schools, Grand Rapids, MI. For general support.
$355,000 to Ada Christian School, Ada, MI. For general support.
$285,000 to Gospel Communications International, Muskegon, MI. For general support.
$150,000 to Bethany Christian Services, Grand Rapids, MI. For general support.
$88,359 to Michigan State University, School of Education, East Lansing, MI. For general support.
$50,000 to Diocese of Grand Rapids, Grand Rapids, MI. For general support.
$40,000 to CURE International, Lemoyne, PA. For general support.
$30,000 to Baxter Community Center, Grand Rapids, MI. For general support.

189
The Richard and Helen DeVos Foundation

P.O. Box 230257
Grand Rapids, MI   49523-0257   (616) 643-4700
County: Kent
Contact: Ginny Vander Hart, Exec. Dir.
FAX: (616) 774-0116;
E-mail: virginiav@rdvcorp.com; Application address: 126 Ottawa Ave., N.W., Ste. 500, Grand Rapids, MI 49503

Incorporated in 1969 in MI.
Donors: Richard M. DeVos; Helen J. DeVos; Alticor Inc.
Grantmaker type: Independent foundation.
Financial data (yr. ended 12/31/09): Assets, $89,446,796 (M); gifts received, $43,220,000; expenditures, $52,844,411; total giving, $46,457,200; qualifying distributions, $48,406,668; giving activities include $46,457,200 for 178 grants (high: $5,650,000; low: $500; average: $100,000–$1,000,000), and $1,639,685 for foundation-administered programs.
Purpose and activities: The foundation primarily supports the work of religious agencies, churches, and schools in ministry, outreach, and education. Its secondary focus includes social outreach, the arts, public policy, and health care. The foundation focuses its funding in the areas of western Michigan and central Florida.
Fields of interest: Arts; Health care; Social sciences; Public policy, research; Religion.
Type of support: General/operating support; Continuing support; Annual campaigns; Capital campaigns; Building/renovation; Program development; Seed money; Matching/challenge support.
Limitations: Applications accepted. Giving primarily in central FL and western MI. No grants to individuals.
Publications: Application guidelines.
Application information: Application form not required.

Initial approach: Letter
Copies of proposal: 1
Deadline(s): 2 weeks prior to review
Board meeting date(s): Every 3 months
Final notification: None

Officers: Helen J. DeVos, Pres.; Jerry L. Tubergen, V.P. and Secy.; Jeffrey K. Lambert, V.P.; Robert H. Schierbeek, Treas.; Ginny Vander Hart, Exec. Dir.
EIN: 237066873
Selected grants: The following grants were reported in 2009.
$5,650,000 to Grand Rapids Christian School Association, Grand Rapids, MI. For general support.
$2,268,200 to Grand Rapids Symphony, Grand Rapids, MI. For general support.
$2,065,000 to Calvin College, Grand Rapids, MI. For general support.
$1,278,000 to Coral Ridge Presbyterian Church, Fort Lauderdale, FL. For general support.
$1,050,000 to Holland Home, Grand Rapids, MI. For general support.
$1,000,000 to Crystal Cathedral Ministries, Garden Grove, CA. For general support.
$251,000 to Palm Beach Atlantic University, West Palm Beach, FL. For general support.
$180,000 to LaGrave Avenue Christian Reformed Church, Grand Rapids, MI. For general support.
$50,000 to Salvation Army of West Palm Beach, Palm Beach County Division, West Palm Beach, FL. For general support.
$35,000 to Music Mission Kiev, Casselberry, FL. For general support.

190
Louis M. Dexter Memorial Foundation, Inc.

1514 Wildwood Ln.
Naples, FL   34105-3207   (239) 649-6627
County: Collier
Contact: Kirk Munroe, Tr.

Established in 1998 in MI.

Grantmaker type: Independent foundation.
Financial data (yr. ended 12/31/09): Assets, $675,471 (M); expenditures, $33,669; total giving, $30,895; qualifying distributions, $30,895; giving activities include $30,895 for grants.
Fields of interest: Performing arts; Higher education; Human services; Christian agencies & churches.
Type of support: General/operating support.
Limitations: Giving primarily in MI, with emphasis on Grand Rapids.
Application information:
  Initial approach: Letter
  Deadline(s): None
Officer: Marjorie R. Wege, Pres.; Patrice Epner, V.P.; Janice Jacobson, Secy.; Kirk Munroe, Treas.; Mary Bardolph, Admin.
Trustee: Andrea Darling.
EIN: 383383892

191
Dickinson County War Veterans Scholarship Association
P.O. Box 370
Iron Mountain, MI 49801-0370
County: Dickinson
Contact: Johana Ostwald, Pres.
Application address: c/o Dickinson-Iron Intermediate School, 1074 Pyle Dr., Kingsford, MI 49802-4451, tel.: (906) 774-2690

Established in MI.
Grantmaker type: Independent foundation.
Financial data (yr. ended 12/31/09): Assets, $24,393 (M); expenditures, $770; total giving, $750; qualifying distributions, $750; giving activities include $750 for grants to individuals.
Purpose and activities: Scholarship awards to veterans or children of veterans who are graduates of Dickinson County high schools, Michigan.
Fields of interest: Higher education; Military/veterans.
Type of support: Scholarships—to individuals.
Limitations: Applications accepted. Giving limited to residents of Dickinson County, MI.
Application information: Application form required.
  Deadline(s): Varies
Officers: Johana Ostwald, Pres.; Denny Chartier, Secy.; Dan A. Peterson, Treas.
Trustee: Chris Ninomiya.
EIN: 237265519

192
Bruce & Rika Diephouse Foundation
1961 Hillsboro Ave. S.E.
Grand Rapids, MI 49546-9791
County: Kent

Established in 2003 in MI.
Donors: Bruce Diephouse; Rika Diephouse.
Grantmaker type: Independent foundation.
Financial data (yr. ended 12/31/09): Assets, $275,930 (M); gifts received, $9,000; expenditures, $8,225; total giving, $8,205; qualifying distributions, $8,205; giving activities include $8,205 for grants.
Fields of interest: Christian agencies & churches.
Limitations: Giving primarily in Grand Rapids, MI. No grants to individuals.

Officers: Bruce Diephouse, Pres.; Rika Diephouse, Treas.
EIN: 841622296

193
The Angelo & Margaret DiPonio Foundation
14800 Farmington Rd., Ste. 102
Livonia, MI 48154-5464
County: Wayne

Established in 1987 in MI.
Donor: Margaret E. DiPonio.
Grantmaker type: Independent foundation.
Financial data (yr. ended 10/31/09): Assets, $3,373,117 (M); expenditures, $35,540; total giving, $5,500; qualifying distributions, $5,500; giving activities include $5,500 for grants.
Fields of interest: Alzheimer's disease; Goodwill Industries; Human services; Residential/custodial care, hospices; Disabilities, people with.
Limitations: Giving limited to MI. No grants to individuals.
Application information: Telephone inquiries will not be accepted.
  Initial approach: Proposal
  Deadline(s): None
Directors: Charles E. Bietler; Margaret E. DiPonio; Ralph H. Houghton, Jr.
EIN: 382828486
Selected grants: The following grants were reported in 2009.
$1,000 to Leader Dogs for the Blind, Rochester, MI.

194
DJD Foundation
5326 Hunt Club Way
Sarasota, FL 34238-4010 (941) 926-8280
County: Sarasota
Contact: L. Jean Daane, Pres.

Established in 2000 in MI.
Donors: David A. Daane; L. Jean Daane.
Grantmaker type: Independent foundation.
Financial data (yr. ended 12/31/09): Assets, $941,851 (M); expenditures, $22,298; total giving, $15,500; qualifying distributions, $15,500; giving activities include $15,500 for grants.
Fields of interest: Christian agencies & churches.
Limitations: Giving primarily in Grand Rapids, MI. No grants to individuals.
Application information:
  Initial approach: Letter
  Deadline(s): None
Officers: L. Jean Daane, Pres.; David A. Daane, V.P. and Treas.; Jana Baker, Secy.
EIN: 383553476

195
The Doan Family Foundation
(formerly The Herbert & Junia Doan Foundation)
3801 Valley Dr.
Midland, MI 48640-6601
County: Midland
Contact: Anna Junia Doan, Pres.
E-mail: dffoundation@yahoo.com

Established in 1964 in MI.
Donor: Herbert D. Doan‡.
Grantmaker type: Independent foundation.

Financial data (yr. ended 12/31/09): Assets, $1,375,328 (M); expenditures, $104,878; total giving, $93,500; qualifying distributions, $93,500; giving activities include $93,500 for grants.
Fields of interest: Historic preservation/historical societies; Higher education; Environment; United Ways and Federated Giving Programs.
Type of support: Endowments; Equipment; General/operating support; Continuing support.
Limitations: Applications accepted. Giving primarily in Midland, MI. No grants to individuals.
Application information: Application form not required.
  Initial approach: Letter
  Deadline(s): May 1
Officers and Trustees:* Anna Junia Doan, Pres.; Jeffrey Doan,* V.P.; Michael Doan,* V.P.
Number of staff: 1 part-time support.
EIN: 386078714
Selected grants: The following grants were reported in 2006.
$26,000 to Michigan Molecular Institute, Fund for New Ventures, Midland, MI.
$26,000 to Midland Center for the Arts, Fund for New Ventures, Midland, MI.
$23,500 to United Way of Midland County, Midland, MI.
$15,000 to Little Forks Conservancy, Midland, MI.
$10,500 to Midland Center for the Arts, MATRIX:MIDLAND, Midland, MI.
$4,000 to Midland County Historical Society, Midland, MI.
$2,000 to North Midland Family Center, Midland, MI.
$1,000 to Boy Scouts of America.
$1,000 to Midland Center for the Arts, Theater Guild, Midland, MI.
$1,000 to Salvation Army, MI.

196
The Herbert and Junia Doan Foundation
c/o BCRS Associates, LLC
100 Wall St., 11th Fl.
New York, NY 10005-3701
County: New York
Contact: Anna Junia Doan, Pres.
E-mail: hjfoundation@yahoo.com

Established in 2003 in MI.
Donor: The Doan Family Foundation.
Grantmaker type: Independent foundation.
Financial data (yr. ended 12/31/09): Assets, $1,491,566 (M); expenditures, $93,436; total giving, $92,800; qualifying distributions, $92,883; giving activities include $92,800 for 23 grants (high: $43,750; low: $100).
Fields of interest: Arts; Education; Youth development; Human services; Biology/life sciences; Jewish agencies & synagogues.
Type of support: General/operating support.
Limitations: Applications accepted. Giving primarily in Midland, MI.
Application information:
  Initial approach: Letter
  Deadline(s): May 1
Officer: Anna Junia Doan, Pres.; Alexandra A.A. Doan, Exec. V.P.
EIN: 200048522

197
Don't Just Sit There Foundation, Inc.
3811 Wedgewood Dr.
Bloomfield Hills, MI 48301-3950
County: Oakland

Established in 2006 in MI.
Grantmaker type: Independent foundation.
Financial data (yr. ended 12/31/09): Assets, $26,818 (M); gifts received, $8,508; expenditures, $36,609; total giving, $1,000; qualifying distributions, $1,000; giving activities include $1,000 for grants.
Officer: Erica Nader, Pres.
Directors: Frederick Nader; Rita Nader.
EIN: 204448930

198
Mildred Mary Donlin Charitable Corporation
2850 Dixie Hwy.
Waterford, MI 48328-1713 (248) 674-2291
County: Oakland
Contact: Peter J. Donlin, Exec. Dir.

Grantmaker type: Independent foundation.
Financial data (yr. ended 12/31/09): Assets, $39,547 (M); gifts received, $1,000; expenditures, $965; total giving, $950; qualifying distributions, $950; giving activities include $950 for 2 grants (high: $500; low: $450).
Fields of interest: Human services; Christian agencies & churches; Economically disadvantaged.
Limitations: Applications accepted. Giving primarily in MI.
Application information: No special form required. Application form not required.
Initial approach: Letter
Deadline(s): None
Officer: Peter J. Donlin, Exec. Dir.
Trustee: Kathleen Donlin Badalament; John Badalament.
EIN: 383082159

199
Dooge Family Foundation
813 Cascade Hills E. Dr. S.E.
Grand Rapids, MI 49546-3672 (616) 957-0007
County: Kent
Contact: Lawrence E. Dooge, Jr., Pres.

Established in 2006 in MI.
Donor: Lawrence Dooge, Jr.
Grantmaker type: Independent foundation.
Financial data (yr. ended 12/31/09): Assets, $474,320 (M); expenditures, $20,122; total giving, $15,000; qualifying distributions, $15,000; giving activities include $15,000 for grants.
Fields of interest: Residential/custodial care, hospices.
Type of support: General/operating support.
Limitations: Giving primarily in Grand Junction, CO. No grants to individuals.
Application information:
Initial approach: Letter
Deadline(s): None
Officers and Directors: Lawrence E. Dooge, Jr.,* Pres. and Treas.; Carol A. Dooge,* V.P.; Janet Comerford; Sally Keevan.
EIN: 205556551

200
The Doran Foundation
1 Prestwick Ct.
Dearborn, MI 48120-1166
County: Wayne

Established in 1994 in MI.
Donor: Wayne S. Doran.
Grantmaker type: Independent foundation.
Financial data (yr. ended 11/30/09): Assets, $652,738 (M); expenditures, $124,461; total giving, $113,279; qualifying distributions, $113,279; giving activities include $113,279 for grants.
Purpose and activities: Support primarily for college scholarship funds.
Fields of interest: Higher education; Scholarships/financial aid; Human services.
Type of support: Scholarship funds.
Limitations: Giving primarily in AZ and MI. No grants to individuals.
Application information:
Initial approach: Letter
Deadline(s): None
Officers: Wayne S. Doran, Pres.; Maureen K. Doran, Secy.; Robert Bacon, Treas.
EIN: 383211447
Selected grants: The following grants were reported in 2008.
$2,000 to Crisis Nursery, Phoenix, AZ.
$2,000 to Henry Ford Health System, Detroit, MI.

201
Henry S. & Mala Dorfman Foundation
838 W. Long Lake, Ste. 205
Bloomfield Hills, MI 48302-2040
County: Oakland
Contact: Joel Dorfman, V.P.

Established in 1972 in MI.
Donors: Henry Dorfman‡; Mala Dorfman.
Grantmaker type: Independent foundation.
Financial data (yr. ended 09/30/09): Assets, $376,211 (M); expenditures, $33,763; total giving, $33,350; qualifying distributions, $33,350; giving activities include $33,350 for grants.
Fields of interest: Performing arts, dance; Jewish agencies & synagogues.
Type of support: General/operating support.
Limitations: Applications accepted. Giving limited to MI. No grants to individuals.
Application information:
Initial approach: Letter
Deadline(s): None
Officers: Mala Dorfman, Chair. and C.E.O.; Carolyn Dorfman, Pres.; Joel Dorfman, V.P. and Treas.; Gayle Dorfman, Secy.
EIN: 237191091

202
The Herbert H. and Grace A. Dow Foundation
1018 W. Main St.
Midland, MI 48640-4292 (989) 631-3699
County: Midland
Contact: Margaret Ann Riecker, Pres.
FAX: (989) 631-0675;
E-mail: info@hhdowfoundation.org; Grant application e-mail: grants@hhdowfoundation.org;
URL: http://www.hhdowfoundation.org

Established in 1936 in MI.
Donor: Grace A. Dow‡.
Grantmaker type: Independent foundation.
Financial data (yr. ended 12/31/09): Assets, $392,388,544 (M); gifts received, $3,905; expenditures, $15,055,400; total giving, $9,771,115; qualifying distributions, $11,897,461; giving activities include $9,771,115 for 157 grants (high: $500,000; low: $1,000), and $2,169,747 for 1 foundation-administered program.
Purpose and activities: Support for religious, charitable, scientific, literacy, or educational purposes for the public benefaction of the inhabitants of the city of Midland and of the people of the state of Michigan. Grants largely for education, particularly higher education, community and social services, civic improvement, conservation, scientific research, church support (only in Midland County, MI), and cultural programs; maintains Dow Gardens, a public horticultural garden.
Fields of interest: Arts; Higher education; Libraries/library science; Education; Environment, natural resources; Human services; Community/economic development; Engineering/technology; Science.
Type of support: General/operating support; Building/renovation; Equipment; Endowments; Program development; Seed money; Research; Matching/challenge support.
Limitations: Applications accepted. Giving limited to MI, with emphasis on Midland County. No support for political organizations or sectarian religious organizations or programs, other than churches in Midland County. No grants to individuals, or for travel or conferences; no loans.
Publications: Annual report (including application guidelines); Financial statement; Grants list.
Application information: Application form not required.
Initial approach: Proposal
Copies of proposal: 1
Deadline(s): None
Board meeting date(s): Bimonthly
Final notification: 2 months
Officers and Trustees: Margaret Ann Riecker,* Pres.; Michael Lloyd Dow,* V.P.; Margaret E. Thompson,* Secy.; Macauley Whiting, Jr.,* Treas.; Jenee Velasquez, Exec. Dir.; Julie Carol Arbury; Ruth Alden Doan; Diane Dow Hullet; Andrew N. Liveris; Bonnie B. Matheson; Terence F. Moore; Willard Mott; Helen Dow Whiting.
EIN: 381437485
Selected grants: The following grants were reported in 2008.
$1,400,000 to Michigan Baseball Foundation, Midland, MI. For capital support and operating support for new stadium.
$1,000,000 to Albion College, Albion, MI. For science facility renovation.
$1,000,000 to Alma College, Center for Responsible Leadership, Alma, MI. For endowment.
$1,000,000 to Northwood University, Midland, MI. For expansion of Michigan Campus.
$994,614 to Interlochen Center for the Arts, Interlochen, MI. For visual arts facility.
$600,000 to Grand Traverse Regional Land Conservancy, Traverse City, MI. For acreage.
$400,000 to Greater Midland Community Centers, Midland, MI. For George Street renovation project.
$250,000 to Detroit Area Pre-College Engineering Program, Detroit, MI. For summer program.
$100,000 to Mid-Michigan Childrens Museum, Saginaw, MI. For continued development of center.

$97,142 to Farwell Area Schools, Farwell, MI. For labs-classrooms.

203
Del & Jean Doyle Family Foundation
3230 Broadmoor Ave. S.E., Ste. C
Grand Rapids, MI 49512-8180
County: Kent

Established in 2005 in MI.
Donors: D&J Properties; Doyle & Ogden, Inc.
Grantmaker type: Independent foundation.
Financial data (yr. ended 12/31/09): Assets, $109,849 (M); gifts received, $22,525; expenditures, $10,548; total giving, $9,342; qualifying distributions, $9,342; giving activities include $9,342 for grants.
Fields of interest: Christian agencies & churches; Children/youth.
Limitations: Giving primarily in MI.
Directors: Mary Jo Carrier; Eileen M. Doyle; Jean B. Doyle; John B. Doyle; Maureen J. Doyle; Michael K. Doyle; Sarah Ann Doyle; Timothy P. Doyle; Thomas B. Doyle; William G. Doyle; Kathleen Richter; Patricia M. Szura; Sue Terreburg.
EIN: 203236955

204
Herman & Sheila Drazick Foundation
675 Brockmoor Ln.
Bloomfield Hills, MI 48304-1415
County: Oakland

Established in 2006 in MI.
Donors: Herman Drazick; Sheila Drazick.
Grantmaker type: Independent foundation.
Financial data (yr. ended 12/31/09): Assets, $1 (M); expenditures, $2,600; total giving, $2,250; qualifying distributions, $2,250; giving activities include $2,250 for grants.
Directors: Herman Drazick; Sheila Drazick.
EIN: 208057775

205
Milton H. Dresner Foundation, Inc.
28777 Northwestern Hwy., Ste. 100
Southfield, MI 48034-8321
County: Oakland

Established in 2003 in MI.
Donor: Milton H. Dresner.
Grantmaker type: Independent foundation.
Financial data (yr. ended 12/31/09): Assets, $153,662 (M); gifts received, $246,500; expenditures, $104,507; total giving, $102,255; qualifying distributions, $102,255; giving activities include $102,255 for 47 grants (high: $20,000; low: $50).
Fields of interest: Jewish agencies & synagogues.
Limitations: Giving primarily in New York, NY. No grants to individuals.
Application information: Unsolicited requests for funds not accepted.
Officer: Milton H. Dresner, Pres.
EIN: 352204352
Selected grants: The following grants were reported in 2008.
$2,500 to New Yorkers for Children, New York, NY.
$2,000 to New Yorkers for Children, New York, NY.

$1,500 to American Jewish Committee, New York, NY.
$1,500 to American Jewish Committee, New York, NY.
$1,500 to Buddy Program, Aspen, CO.
$1,000 to Madison Project Foundation, Bro, Santa Monica, CA.
$1,000 to Unicorn Childrens Foundation, Boca Raton, FL.

206
Drew & Mike Charitable Private Foundation
c/o Comerica Bank
P.O. Box 75000, MC 3302
Detroit, MI 48275-3302
County: Wayne

Established in 2002 in MI.
Donors: Lynn Marie Temby; D&M Productions.
Grantmaker type: Independent foundation.
Financial data (yr. ended 12/31/09): Assets, $103,141 (M); expenditures, $1,440; total giving, $0; qualifying distributions, $0.
Purpose and activities: Financial assistance to the families of law enforcement or armed forces from the seven counties in southeast Michigan.
Fields of interest: Human services; Military/veterans.
Type of support: Grants to individuals.
Limitations: Giving in southeastern MI.
Application information:
    Initial approach: Letter
    Deadline(s): None
Trustee: Comerica Bank.
EIN: 436874093

207
Drew Family Foundation
P.O. Box 639
Suttons Bay, MI 49682-0639 (231) 271-4127
County: Leelanau
Contact: Gary P. Drew, Pres.

Established in 1998 in MI.
Donors: Gary Drew; Sandra Drew.
Grantmaker type: Independent foundation.
Financial data (yr. ended 12/31/09): Assets, $108,661 (M); expenditures, $34,703; total giving, $33,000; qualifying distributions, $33,807; giving activities include $33,000 for 2 grants (high: $30,000; low: $3,000).
Fields of interest: Education; Environment; Agriculture.
Limitations: Applications accepted. Giving primarily in MI. No support for organizations lacking 501(c)(3) status. No grants to individuals.
Application information:
    Initial approach: Letter or telephone
    Deadline(s): None
Officers and Directors:* Gary Drew,* Pres. and Treas.; Sandra Drew,* V.P. and Secy.
EIN: 383417301

208
Driggers Foundation
89 N Baldwin
Clarkston, MI 48348-2301
County: Oakland
Contact: Joy M. Driggers, Pres.

Established in 1991 in MI and FL.
Donors: Nathan B. Driggers; Joy M. Driggers.
Grantmaker type: Independent foundation.
Financial data (yr. ended 03/31/10): Assets, $385,449 (M); expenditures, $50,869; total giving, $50,000; qualifying distributions, $50,020; giving activities include $50,000 for 1 grant (high: $50,000).
Fields of interest: Environment, volunteer services; Environment, natural resources; Environment, water resources; Environment, land resources.
Limitations: Applications accepted. Giving on a national basis, with emphasis on FL. No grants to individuals.
Application information:
    Initial approach: Letter
    Deadline(s): None
Officers and Directors:* Joy M. Driggers,* Pres. and Secy.; John S. Driggers,* Treas.; Jennifer Cecil.
EIN: 383024358

209
DSLT Foundation
(formerly The Diamond Crystal Foundation)
c/o Fifth Third Bank
200 S. Riverside Ave.
St. Clair, MI 48079-5330
County: St. Clair
Contact: Frederick S. Moore, Tr.
Application address: 970 N. Riverside Ave., St. Clair, MI 48079-4265, tel.: (810) 326-1123

Established in 1955 in MI.
Grantmaker type: Independent foundation.
Financial data (yr. ended 12/31/09): Assets, $781,574 (M); expenditures, $42,323; total giving, $34,500; qualifying distributions, $34,775; giving activities include $34,500 for 7 grants (high: $13,000; low: $500).
Fields of interest: Education; Health organizations, association; Human services; Community/economic development; United Ways and Federated Giving Programs.
Limitations: Applications accepted. Giving in MI, primarily in St. Clair and Port Huron. No grants to individuals.
Application information: Application form required.
    Initial approach: Letter
    Deadline(s): None
Trustees: Hugh McMorran; Franklin H. Moore, Jr.; Frederick S. Moore.
EIN: 386055060

210
Doris J. & Donald L. Duchene Foundation
c/o Comerica Bank
P.O. Box 75000, MC 3302
Detroit, MI 48275-3302
County: Wayne
Contact: Gary Spicer, Secy.
Application address: 16845 Kercheval Ave., Ste. 5, Grosse Pointe, MI 48230-1551, tel.: (313) 884-9700

Established in 1997 in MI.
Donor: Doris Duchene.
Grantmaker type: Independent foundation.
Financial data (yr. ended 12/31/09): Assets, $1,261,351 (M); expenditures, $85,599; total giving, $61,500; qualifying distributions, $61,500; giving activities include $61,500 for grants.

Fields of interest: Elementary/secondary education; Higher education; Catholic agencies & churches.
Limitations: Giving primarily in Detroit, MI.
Application information: Application form not required.
Deadline(s): None
Officers: Donald L. Duchene, Sr., Pres.; Gary Spicer, Secy.; David Wind, Treas.
EIN: 383312705

211
Hubert and Marie Duffy Memorial Trust
120 S. Berkshire Rd.
Bloomfield Hills, MI 48302-0410
(248) 335-1709
County: Oakland
Contact: Gerald R. Gase, Trustee

Established in 1991 in MI.
Donor: Marie Duffy‡.
Grantmaker type: Independent foundation.
Financial data (yr. ended 09/30/09): Assets, $561,471 (M); expenditures, $40,698; total giving, $37,000; qualifying distributions, $37,000; giving activities include $37,000 for grants.
Purpose and activities: To provide for food, clothing and medical expenses for the poor.
Fields of interest: Human services; Christian agencies & churches; Catholic agencies & churches.
Limitations: Applications accepted. Giving primarily in KY, LA and MI. No grants to individuals.
Application information:
Initial approach: Letter
Trustee: Gerald R. Gase.
EIN: 386559353

212
The Richard and Barbara Duncan Family Foundation
4605 Valley View Pt.
Rochester, MI 48306-1746
County: Oakland

Established in 2006 in MI.
Grantmaker type: Independent foundation.
Financial data (yr. ended 12/31/09): Assets, $1 (M); gifts received, $3,343; expenditures, $3,343; total giving, $0; qualifying distributions, $0.
Officers: Richard Duncan, Pres.; Karen Nichols, Secy.; Barbara Duncan, Treas.
EIN: 320073445

213
Margaret Dunning Foundation
994 Penniman Ave.
Plymouth, MI 48170-1624 (734) 453-7566
County: Wayne
Contact: Margaret Dunning, Pres.

Established in 1997 in MI.
Donors: Margaret Dunning; Irene Walldorf.
Grantmaker type: Independent foundation.
Financial data (yr. ended 12/31/09): Assets, $217,527 (M); expenditures, $357,217; total giving, $346,204; qualifying distributions, $346,204; giving activities include $346,204 for 2 grants (high: $336,204; low: $10,000).
Fields of interest: Historic preservation/historical societies.

Limitations: Applications accepted. Giving primarily in Plymouth, MI.
Application information:
Initial approach: Letter
Deadline(s): None
Officers: Margaret Dunning, Pres.; Robert M. Stulberg, V.P. and Secy.
Trustees: Phillip M. Appel; Robert Appel; Betty Barbour; Lloyd Leach; Lois Stulberg.
EIN: 383352930

214
Dunnings Foundation, Inc.
530 S. Pine St.
Lansing, MI 48933-2239
County: Ingham

Grantmaker type: Independent foundation.
Financial data (yr. ended 09/30/09): Assets, $180,430 (M); expenditures, $4,999; total giving, $3,349; qualifying distributions, $3,349; giving activities include $3,349 for grants.
Fields of interest: Education.
Type of support: Scholarship funds.
Limitations: Giving primarily in MI.
Officer: Stuart J. Dunnings, Jr., Pres. and Secy.-Treas.
Director: Susan Dunnings.
EIN: 382709388

215
Dyer-Ives Foundation
Waters Bldg.
161 Ottawa Ave. N.W., Ste. 501-H
Grand Rapids, MI 49503-2716 (616) 452-4502
County: Kent
Contact: Linda B. Patterson, Exec. Dir.
FAX: (616) 454-8545; E-mail: dyer_ives@msn.com;
URL: http://www.dyer-ives.org

Established in 1961 in MI.
Donor: John R. Hunting.
Grantmaker type: Independent foundation.
Financial data (yr. ended 08/31/09): Assets, $5,008,223 (M); expenditures, $456,521; total giving, $258,039; qualifying distributions, $359,597; giving activities include $258,039 for 40 grants (high: $25,000; low: $100), and $310,842 for 4 foundation-administered programs.
Purpose and activities: The foundation acts primarily as a catalyst and stimulator for small innovative projects that encourage a sense of community in educational, social, environmental or cultural fields.
Fields of interest: Humanities; Arts; Education; Environment; Employment; Housing/shelter; Youth development, services; Human services; Community development, neighborhood development.
Type of support: Program development; Publication; Seed money; Curriculum development; Technical assistance; Consulting services.
Limitations: Applications accepted. Giving limited to the central city of Grand Rapids, MI. No grants to individuals, or for building or endowment funds, operating budgets, or scholarship funds.
Publications: Biennial report (including application guidelines); Financial statement; Grants list; Informational brochure (including application guidelines); Multi-year report.

Application information: Application form not required.
Initial approach: Telephone and proposal
Copies of proposal: 1
Deadline(s): None
Board meeting date(s): Monthly
Final notification: After board meetings
Officers: John R. Hunting, Chair.; John D. Hibbard, Jr., Vice-Chair.; Jocelyn Dettloff, Pres.; Steeve O. Buckridge, V.P.; R. Malcolm Cumming, Secy.; Susan Cobb, Treas.; Linda B. Patterson, Exec. Dir.
Directors: Rosalyn Bliss; Andy Guy; Simone Jonaitis; Carl Kelly; Betty Zylstra.
Number of staff: 2 part-time professional.
EIN: 386049657
Selected grants: The following grants were reported in 2008.
$25,000 to Fair Housing Center of West Michigan, Grand Rapids, MI. For Community Foreclosure Coordinator.
$25,000 to Grand Valley State University, Community Research Institute, Grand Rapids, MI. For web-based GIS mapping system, to help citizens make data driven decisions to improve conditions in their community and specific neighborhoods.
$20,000 to Grand Rapids, City of, Grand Rapids, MI. For Green Grand Rapids Master Plan update.
$20,000 to Oakdale Neighbors, Grand Rapids, MI. For Kalamazoo Corridor Plan.
$18,000 to Local Initiatives Support Corporation, Grand Rapids, MI. For Business District Market Profiles.
$16,450 to West Michigan Environmental Action Council, Grand Rapids, MI. For Save Your Ash, collaborative work to connect citizens and communities with current information on utilizing preventative treatment to minimize the loss of ash trees due to infestation by emerald ash bores.
$15,000 to Disability Advocates of Kent County, Grand Rapids, MI. For ZeroStep Marketing, house plans, standard books, and website shopping cart marketing products.
$14,500 to United Growth for Kent County, Grand Rapids, MI. For Zoning Education Project, to support staff position to educate neighborhood residents about necessary level and quality of citizen participation.
$10,000 to Kent Intermediate School District, Grand Rapids, MI. For Kent Schools Services Network, for pilot program for delivering after school career readiness workshops to students and their parents.
$3,000 to Grandville Avenue Arts and Humanities, Grand Rapids, MI. For Development Director Training.

216
Dykstra Foundation
1173 W. Glengarry Cir.
Bloomfield Hills, MI 48301-2225
(248) 644-8264
County: Oakland
Contact: Betty Steele, Pres.

Established in MI.
Grantmaker type: Independent foundation.
Financial data (yr. ended 12/31/08): Assets, $569,178 (M); expenditures, $32,229; total giving, $30,000; qualifying distributions, $30,000; giving activities include $30,000 for grants.
Fields of interest: Hospitals (general).

Limitations: Applications accepted. Giving in the U.S., with emphasis on Detroit, MI. No grants to individuals.
Application information: Application form not required.
  Deadline(s): None
Officers: Betty Steele, Pres.; Marion Hawkins, V.P.; John O. Steele, Secy.-Treas.
EIN: 386066092

217
Earhart Foundation
2200 Green Rd., Ste. H
Ann Arbor, MI 48105-1569 (734) 761-8592
County: Washtenaw
Contact: Ingrid A. Gregg, Pres.

Incorporated in 1929 in MI.
Donor: Harry Boyd Earhart‡.
Grantmaker type: Independent foundation.
Financial data (yr. ended 12/31/09): Assets, $35,723,529 (M); expenditures, $6,154,181; total giving, $5,049,476; qualifying distributions, $6,003,897; giving activities include $3,273,906 for 123 grants (high: $150,000; low: $1,000), and $1,775,570 for 119 grants to individuals (high: $41,400; low: $1,000).
Purpose and activities: H.B. Earhart Fellowships for graduate study awarded through a special nominating process for which direct applications will not be accepted; research fellowships for individual projects in economics, history, philosophy, international affairs, and political science awarded upon direct application to faculty members; grants also to educational and research organizations legally qualified for private foundation support.
Fields of interest: History/archaeology; Philosophy/ethics; Graduate/professional education; Economics; Political science; International studies.
Type of support: Conferences/seminars; Publication; Curriculum development; Fellowships; Research; Grants to individuals; Scholarships—to individuals.
Limitations: Applications accepted. Giving on a national basis. No grants for capital, building, or endowment funds, operating budgets, continuing support, annual campaigns, seed money, emergency funds, deficit financing, or matching gifts; no loans.
Publications: Annual report (including application guidelines).
Application information: Direct applications from candidates or uninvited sponsors for H.B. Earhart Fellowships (for graduate study) are not accepted. Application form not required.
  Initial approach: Letter
  Copies of proposal: 1
  Deadline(s): Proposal should be submitted at least 4 months before beginning of project work period
  Board meeting date(s): Monthly except in Aug.
Officers and Trustees:* Dennis L. Bark,* Chair.; John H. Moore,* Vice-Chair.; Ingrid A. Gregg,* Pres.; Montgomery B. Brown, Secy. and Dir., Progs.; Kathleen B. Mason, Treas.; Peter B. Clark, Tr. Emeritus; Paul W. McCracken, Tr. Emeritus; Richard A. Ware, Tr. Emeritus; Thomas J. Bray; Kimberly O. Dennis; Earl I. Heenan III; Ann K. Irish; David B. Kennedy; Robert L. Queller.
Number of staff: 2 full-time professional; 3 full-time support.
EIN: 386008273

Selected grants: The following grants were reported in 2008.
$200,000 to Social Philosophy and Policy Foundation, Bowling Green, OH. For Visiting Scholars Program.
$118,267 to Institute of World Politics, Washington, DC. For professor.
$110,000 to Mackinac Center for Public Policy, Midland, MI. For Labor and Education project.
$100,000 to Ethics and Public Policy Center, Washington, DC. For The New Atlantis quarterly journal.
$65,000 to Russell Kirk Center for Cultural Renewal, Mecosta, MI. For library archival organization and development.
$50,000 to American Enterprise Institute for Public Policy Research, Washington, DC. For book, A History of the Federal Reserve, Volume II.
$35,000 to Atlas Economic Research Foundation, Washington, DC. For graduate fellowship at Georgetown University.
$20,480 to Duke University, Office of Research Support, Durham, NC. For post-doctoral fellowship.
$20,000 to George Mason University, Mercatus Center, Fairfax, VA. For senior research fellow.
$20,000 to Young Americas Foundation, Herndon, VA. For Cold War seminar for college students.

218
C. K. Eddy Family Memorial Fund
c/o Citizens Bank Wealth Mgmt., N.A.
328 S. Saginaw St., M/C 002072
Flint, MI 48502-1923
County: Genesee
Application address: c/o Helen James, Trust Off., Citizens Bank Wealth Mgmt., N.A., 101 N. Washington Ave., Saginaw, MI 48607-1207, tel.: (989) 776-7368

Trust established in 1925 in MI.
Donor: Arthur D. Eddy‡.
Grantmaker type: Independent foundation.
Financial data (yr. ended 06/30/10): Assets, $14,603,208 (M); expenditures, $895,127; total giving, $644,785; qualifying distributions, $1,067,795; giving activities include $644,785 for 18 grants (high: $250,000; low: $5,000), and $245,620 for 66 loans to individuals (high: $4,000; low: $2,700).
Purpose and activities: Giving primarily for student loans and community programs.
Fields of interest: Arts; Education; Zoos/zoological societies; Housing/shelter, development; Boys & girls clubs; Human services; Children/youth, services; Community/economic development; United Ways and Federated Giving Programs.
Type of support: Equipment; Program development; Student loans—to individuals.
Limitations: Giving limited to Saginaw County, MI, with some emphasis on the city of Saginaw.
Publications: Application guidelines.
Application information: Application form required.
  Deadline(s): None for grants; May 1 for student loans
  Board meeting date(s): 3rd Wed. of Mar., June, Sept., and Dec.
Trustee: Citizens Bank.
EIN: 386040506
Selected grants: The following grants were reported in 2009.
$166,667 to Mid-Michigan Childrens Museum, Saginaw, MI.

$115,000 to Saginaw Eddy Concert Band, Pinckney, MI.
$50,000 to Covenant Healthcare Foundation, Saginaw, MI.
$50,000 to Holy Cross Childrens Services, Saginaw, MI.
$30,000 to Saginaw County Youth Protection Council, Saginaw, MI.
$10,000 to Saginaw Symphony Association, Saginaw, MI.
$8,000 to East Side Soup Kitchen, Saginaw, MI.
$5,000 to YMCA of Saginaw, Saginaw, MI.

219
Dr. & Mrs. Edmund T. Bott Foundation, Inc.
1801 14th St.
Wyandotte, MI 48192-3634
County: Wayne
Application address: c/o John Clancy, 114 Chestnut St., Wyandotte, MI 48192-5123, tel.: (734) 649-2004

Established in 2006 in MI.
Donors: Dr. Edmund T. Bott; Mrs. Edmund T. Bott.
Grantmaker type: Independent foundation.
Financial data (yr. ended 12/31/09): Assets, $557,557 (M); expenditures, $133,176; total giving, $107,731; qualifying distributions, $107,731; giving activities include $107,731 for grants.
Purpose and activities: Scholarship awards to students who attend school in Michigan and maintain a G.P.A. of at least 2.0.
Fields of interest: Higher education.
Type of support: Scholarships—to individuals.
Limitations: Applications accepted. Giving primarily in MI.
Application information: Application form not required.
  Deadline(s): Apr. 30
Officers and Directors:* Edward R. Elsesser,* Pres.; Joseph Elsesser,* Secy.; George Rennie,* Treas.; Julie Poslajko; Michele Reitmeyer.
EIN: 205068278

220
R. Hugh Elliott Family Foundation
c/o R. Hugh Elliott
1882 Pond Run Rd.
Auburn Hills, MI 48326-2768
County: Oakland

Established in 2007 in MI.
Donor: R. Hugh Elliott.
Grantmaker type: Independent foundation.
Financial data (yr. ended 12/31/09): Assets, $2,113,116 (M); gifts received, $529,683; expenditures, $60,932; total giving, $43,000; qualifying distributions, $43,000; giving activities include $43,000 for grants.
Directors: Chad K. Elliott; Nancy N. Elliott; R. Hugh Elliott.
EIN: 371557038

221
Patricia and Thomas Emmenecker Charitable Foundation
101 N. Washington Ave.
Saginaw, MI 48607-1207
County: Saginaw

Established in 2007 in MI.
Grantmaker type: Independent foundation.
Financial data (yr. ended 12/31/09): Assets, $82,877 (M); expenditures, $6,451; total giving, $4,025; qualifying distributions, $4,025; giving activities include $4,025 for grants.
Trustee: Citizens Bank Wealth Management, N.A.
EIN: 260354260

222
En Gedi Foundation
P.O. Box 2172
Grand Rapids, MI 49501-2172 (616) 530-7000
County: Kent
Contact: Daniel A. Gordon, Pres.

Established in 2000 in MI.
Donors: Daniel A. Gordon; Marguerite B. Gordon.
Grantmaker type: Independent foundation.
Financial data (yr. ended 12/31/09): Assets, $513,619 (M); gifts received, $50,000; expenditures, $65,263; total giving, $60,000; qualifying distributions, $60,000; giving activities include $60,000 for grants.
Fields of interest: Recreation, camps; Youth development, religion; Christian agencies & churches.
Type of support: General/operating support.
Limitations: Giving in MI, with emphasis on Grand Rapids. No support for private foundations. No grants to individuals.
Application information:
Initial approach: Letter
Deadline(s): None
Officers: Daniel A. Gordon, Pres.; Marguerite B. Gordon, Secy.-Treas.
EIN: 383569279

223
Enterprise TFL Foundation
c/o Plains Capital Bank
3707 Camp Bowie, Ste. 220
Fort Worth, TX 76107-3330 (817) 258-3730
County: Tarrant
Contact: Edward T. Fritz, Secy.-Treas.

Established in 1997 in IL.
Grantmaker type: Independent foundation.
Financial data (yr. ended 12/31/09): Assets, $53,072 (M); gifts received, $2,150; expenditures, $7,338; total giving, $5,250; qualifying distributions, $5,250; giving activities include $5,250 for grants.
Limitations: Giving primarily in MI. No grants to individuals.
Application information:
Initial approach: Letter
Deadline(s): None
Officers: Susan M. Mullins, Pres.; Taylor M. Schaeffer, V.P.; Edward T. Fritz, Secy.-Treas.
EIN: 364128410

224
Fred A. and Barbara M. Erb Family Foundation
(doing business as Erb Family Foundation)
800 N. Old Woodward Ave., Ste. 201
Birmingham, MI 48009-3802 (248) 498-2501
County: Oakland
Contact: John M. Erb, Pres.; Jodee Fishman Raines, V.P., Progs.
FAX: (248) 644-1517;
E-mail: jraines@erbfamilyfoundation.org;
URL: http://www.erbfamilyfoundation.org/

Established in 2008 in MI.
Donors: Barbara M. Erb; Fred A. Erb.
Grantmaker type: Independent foundation.
Financial data (yr. ended 06/30/10): Assets, $97,079,085 (M); gifts received, $442; expenditures, $5,044,282; total giving, $4,511,278; qualifying distributions, $4,606,695; giving activities include $4,274,500 for 56 grants (high: $300,000; low: $10,000), and $236,778 for 38 employee matching gifts.
Purpose and activities: The mission of the foundation is to nurture environmentally healthy and culturally vibrant communities in metropolitan Detroit and support initiatives to restore the Great Lakes Basin.
Fields of interest: Arts education; Arts; Environment, pollution control; Environment, water resources; Environmental education; Environment; Alzheimer's disease research.
Type of support: Seed money; Matching/challenge support; Management development/capacity building; General/operating support; Program development.
Limitations: Applications accepted. Giving primarily in the metropolitan Detroit, MI area (Wayne, Oakland and Macomb counties) though water quality programs will be considered in the watersheds impacting Detroit and the Bayfield area of Ontario. Certain basin-wide planning efforts will also be considered as will planning efforts impacting Lake Huron. No support for religious activities. No grants to individuals, for capital projects, research (unless solicited from the foundation) fundraisers or conferences; no loans.
Application information: Letter of inquiry and application instructions and forms available on foundation web site. Application form required.
Initial approach: Letter of inquiry (via foundation web site)
Deadline(s): None
Board meeting date(s): Mar., June, Sept. and Dec.
Final notification: Following board meetings
Officers and Directors:* Ira J. Jaffe,* Chair.; John M. Erb,* Pres.; Jodee Fishman Raines, V.P., Progs.; Daryl Larsen, C.F.O.; Susan E. Cooper; Barbara M. Erb; Debbie D. Erb; Fred A. Erb; John M. Erb; Wendy Elaine Erb; Chacona W. Johnson; Leslie Erb Liedtke.
EIN: 205966333

225
The Joseph & Linda Erlich Foundation
2655 Northfield
White Lake, MI 48383-2131
County: Oakland

Established in 1998 in MI.
Donors: Joseph E. Erlich; Linda Erlich.
Grantmaker type: Independent foundation.

Financial data (yr. ended 12/31/09): Assets, $43,594 (M); expenditures, $6,116; total giving, $4,361; qualifying distributions, $4,361; giving activities include $4,361 for grants.
Fields of interest: Jewish agencies & synagogues.
Application information: Application form not required.
Deadline(s): None
Directors: Joseph E. Erlich; Linda Erlich.
EIN: 383416469

226
Robert Chase Erskine Foundation
c/o Bank of America, N.A.
P.O. Box 831041
Dallas, TX 75283-1041
County: Dallas
Application address: Leon Masse, 715 Peachtree St. N.E., Atlanta, GA 30308-1215, tel.: (877) 264-9992

Established in 1998 in WA.
Donor: R.C. Erskine Trust.
Grantmaker type: Independent foundation.
Financial data (yr. ended 07/31/09): Assets, $409,617 (M); expenditures, $29,947; total giving, $23,315; qualifying distributions, $26,396; giving activities include $23,315 for 2 grants (high: $14,846; low: $8,469).
Purpose and activities: Grants awarded to discourage, prevent and prohibit alcoholic beverages in the United States.
Fields of interest: Substance abuse, services; Alcoholism.
Limitations: Applications accepted. Giving primarily in Birmingham, AL, and Lansing, MI.
Application information: Application form not required.
Initial approach: Letter
Deadline(s): None
Trustee: Bank of America, N.A.
EIN: 916491855

227
J. F. Ervin Foundation
P.O. Box 1168
Ann Arbor, MI 48106-1168 (734) 769-4600
County: Washtenaw
Contact: John Pearson, Pres.

Established in 1953 in MI.
Donor: J.F. Ervin†.
Grantmaker type: Independent foundation.
Financial data (yr. ended 12/31/09): Assets, $2,778,586 (M); expenditures, $110,839; total giving, $110,800; qualifying distributions, $110,800; giving activities include $110,800 for grants.
Purpose and activities: Giving to assist in local needs; primary areas of interest include child welfare and development, delinquency, the elderly, and health services.
Fields of interest: Humanities; Arts; Child development, education; Hospitals (general); Health care; Substance abuse, services; Crime/violence prevention, youth; Children/youth, services; Child development, services; Aging, centers/services; Homeless, human services; Aging; Homeless.
Type of support: General/operating support; Continuing support; Annual campaigns; Emergency funds; Program development.

Limitations: Giving limited to southeastern MI. No grants to individuals, or for scholarships; no loans.
Publications: Annual report (including application guidelines).
Application information: Application form not required.
> *Initial approach:* Proposal in letter form
> *Copies of proposal:* 1
> *Deadline(s):* None

Officers and Trustees:* John E. Pearson,* Pres.; Debra A. Pearson,* V.P. and Treas.; Heidi Pearson,* Secy.; Susan R. Pearson; James T. Pearson.
Number of staff: 2 part-time support.
EIN: 386053755
Selected grants: The following grants were reported in 2007.
$7,500 to Adrian Symphony Orchestra, Adrian, MI.
$6,000 to Catholic Social Services.
$5,000 to Herrick Medical Center, Tecumseh, MI.
$5,000 to Ronald McDonald House.
$2,500 to American Heart Association, Dallas, TX.
$2,500 to YMCA of Ann Arbor, Ann Arbor, MI.

228
The Rudolf & Ruth Eschbach Family Foundation
25101 Groesbeck Hwy.
Warren, MI 48089-1970
County: Macomb

Established in 1997 in MI.
Donors: Reinhard Eschbach; Lisa Eschbach; Roland Eschbach.
Grantmaker type: Independent foundation.
Financial data (yr. ended 12/31/09): Assets, $106,552 (M); expenditures, $13,049; total giving, $12,000; qualifying distributions, $12,000; giving activities include $12,000 for 2 grants (high: $10,000; low: $2,000).
Fields of interest: Pediatrics; Children.
Limitations: Applications accepted. Giving primarily in MI.
Application information: Application form not required.
> *Initial approach:* Letter
> *Deadline(s):* None

Officers: Ruth Eschbach, Pres.; Dietmar Eschbach, V.P.; Reinhard Eschbach, V.P.; Anita Hobbs, Secy.; Monica Eschbach, Treas.
EIN: 383310055

229
Charles Robert Evenson Foundation
P.O. Box 352
Bridgewater Pl.
Grand Rapids, MI 49501-0352 (616) 336-6808
County: Kent
Contact: Fredric Sytsma, Secy.-Treas.

Established in MI.
Grantmaker type: Independent foundation.
Financial data (yr. ended 10/31/09): Assets, $230,227 (M); expenditures, $19,289; total giving, $13,000; qualifying distributions, $13,000; giving activities include $13,000 for grants.
Fields of interest: Museums; Performing arts; Environment, natural resources.
Limitations: Giving limited to Grand Rapids, MI. No grants to individuals.
Application information:

Initial approach: Letter
Deadline(s): None
Officers: Joan Newberry, Pres.; Fredric Sytsma, Secy.-Treas.
Directors: Robert Evenson, Jr.; William Newberry.
EIN: 386085626

230
Ever Young and Green Foundation Trust
P.O. Box 61
Glen Arbor, MI 49636-0061 (231) 334-3372
County: Leelanau
Contact: R. Duncan McPherson, Tr.

Donor: R. Duncan McPherson.
Grantmaker type: Independent foundation.
Financial data (yr. ended 12/31/09): Assets, $26,207 (M); gifts received, $2,000; expenditures, $4,505; total giving, $4,500; qualifying distributions, $4,500; giving activities include $4,500 for grants.
Purpose and activities: The trust supports projects promoting the welfare of children and the conservation and preservation of the northern Michigan landscape.
Fields of interest: Environment, natural resources; Children/youth, services.
Limitations: Applications accepted. Giving primarily in northern MI. No grants to individuals.
Application information:
> *Initial approach:* Letter
> *Deadline(s):* None

Trustees: Mary Ann Smith McPherson; R. Duncan McPherson; Mary Vardigan.
EIN: 383380307

231
Evereg-Fenesse Mesrobian-Roupinian Educational Society, Inc.
28302 Cypress Ct.
Farmington Hills, MI 48331-2996
(248) 553-0597
County: Oakland

Grantmaker type: Independent foundation.
Financial data (yr. ended 07/31/10): Assets, $18,518 (M); expenditures, $13,320; total giving, $11,440; qualifying distributions, $11,440; giving activities include $11,440 for 51 grants to individuals.
Purpose and activities: Scholarship awards to students attending Armenian day schools and to full-time college students attending four-year undergraduate or two-year postgraduate schools.
Fields of interest: Higher education.
Type of support: Grants to individuals; Scholarships—to individuals.
Limitations: Applications accepted. Giving limited to CA, MI, and NY.
Application information: Submit application to local chapter representative. Application form required.
> *Deadline(s):* Dec. 15

Officers and Board Members:* Vahram Fantazian,* Pres.; Mary Negosian,* V.P.; Laura Negosian Lucassian,* Secy.; Ilene Fantazian,* Treas.; Stephanie Dallakian.
EIN: 136154468

232
H. T. Ewald Foundation
15450 E. Jefferson Ave., Ste. 180
Grosse Pointe, MI 48230-2031 (313) 821-1278
County: Wayne
Contact: Shelagh K. Czuprenski, Secy.
FAX: (313) 821-3299; E-mail: ewaldfndtn@aol.com;
URL: http://www.ewaldfoundation.org

Established in 1928 in MI.
Donor: Henry T. Ewald‡.
Grantmaker type: Independent foundation.
Financial data (yr. ended 12/31/09): Assets, $2,693,618 (M); gifts received, $3,865; expenditures, $158,853; total giving, $91,690; qualifying distributions, $91,690; giving activities include $91,690 for grants.
Purpose and activities: Scholarship awards to local area high school seniors of Detroit, Michigan, for undergraduate study.
Fields of interest: Higher education; Human services.
Type of support: General/operating support; Scholarships—to individuals.
Limitations: Giving limited to the metropolitan Detroit, MI, area.
Publications: Informational brochure (including application guidelines).
Application information: See foundation web site for scholarship application guidelines. Application form required.
> *Initial approach:* Letter or telephone
> *Copies of proposal:* 1
> *Deadline(s):* Mar. 1 for scholarships
> *Final notification:* Mid-June

Officers: Kristi Petry, Co-Pres.; Judy Ewald, Co-Pres.; Holly S. Ewald, V.P.; Carolyn Ewald-Kratzet, V.P.; Shelagh K. Czuprenski, Secy.; Cliff Ewald, Treas.
Number of staff: 1 part-time support.
EIN: 386007837

233
Eyster Charitable Family Foundation
1475 Epley Rd.
Williamston, MI 48895-9473 (517) 655-3217
County: Ingham
Contact: Janet Tolson Eyster, Dir.

Established in 2000 in MI.
Donors: George E. Eyster; Janet Tolson Eyster.
Grantmaker type: Independent foundation.
Financial data (yr. ended 12/31/09): Assets, $3,040 (M); gifts received, $404; expenditures, $420; total giving, $0; qualifying distributions, $0.
Fields of interest: Higher education, college; Veterinary medicine.
Limitations: Applications accepted. Giving primarily in Lansing, MI.
Application information:
> *Initial approach:* Letter
> *Deadline(s):* None

Directors: George E. Eyster; Janet Tolson Eyster.
EIN: 383501935

234
Ida M. Faigle Charitable Foundation
24800 Denso Dr., Ste. 265
Southfield, MI 48033-7449
County: Oakland

Established in 1978 in MI.

Donor: Ida M. Faigle†.
Grantmaker type: Independent foundation.
Financial data (yr. ended 12/31/09): Assets, $450,503 (M); expenditures, $48,624; total giving, $18,750; qualifying distributions, $21,250; giving activities include $18,750 for 13 grants (high: $5,000; low: $100).
Fields of interest: Cancer; Eye diseases; Human services.
Type of support: General/operating support.
Limitations: Applications accepted. Giving primarily in MI. No grants to individuals.
Application information:
Initial approach: Letter
Deadline(s): None
Final notification: Within 4 months
Trustee: Michael M. Wild.
EIN: 237366145

235
The Falk Family Foundation
4628 E. Beltline N.E.
Grand Rapids, MI 49525-9786 (616) 361-6906
County: Kent
Contact: Daniel C. Falk, Pres.

Established in 1998 in MI.
Donors: Daniel C. Falk; Susan G. Falk.
Grantmaker type: Independent foundation.
Financial data (yr. ended 12/31/09): Assets, $41,870 (M); expenditures, $39,034; total giving, $38,150; qualifying distributions, $38,150; giving activities include $38,150 for grants.
Fields of interest: Christian agencies & churches.
Officers: Daniel C. Falk, Pres.; Matthew Falk, V.P.; Michael Falk, V.P.; Susan G. Falk, Secy.-Treas.
EIN: 383441180

236
The O. B. Falls and Elizabeth L. Falls Foundation
1515 Helmsdale Dr
Richmond, VA 23238-4721
County: Henrico
Contact: Donald L. Falls, Secy.
Application address: 600 E. Main St., Ste. 2400, Richmond, VA 23219-2437, tel.: (804) 644-1136

Established in 1999 in VA.
Grantmaker type: Independent foundation.
Financial data (yr. ended 12/31/09): Assets, $591,829 (M); expenditures, $49,360; total giving, $36,000; qualifying distributions, $36,000; giving activities include $36,000 for grants.
Fields of interest: Arts; Higher education; Animals/wildlife, special services; Health care; Independent living, disability; Blind/visually impaired.
Type of support: General/operating support.
Limitations: Giving primarily in FL and MI. No grants to individuals.
Application information:
Initial approach: Letter
Deadline(s): None
Officers and Directors:* Laird Burnett,* Pres.; Donald L. Falls, Secy.-Treas.; Harriet F. Burnett; Marti DiBianco; Susan Fegley.
EIN: 541949243

237
Callant Family Foundation
c/o Comerica Bank & Trust, N.A.
P.O. Box. 75000, MC 3302
Detroit, MI 48275-3302 (303) 294-3349
County: Wayne
Contact: Ted Stumpp

Donor: Marcel Callant Estate Trust.
Grantmaker type: Independent foundation.
Financial data (yr. ended 09/30/09): Assets, $4,312,853 (M); gifts received, $4,020,581; expenditures, $14,188; total giving, $0; qualifying distributions, $0.
Limitations: Applications accepted. Giving limited to Harlowton, MT. No grants for Harlowton, MT.
Application information: Application form required.
Initial approach: Letter
Deadline(s): None
Trustee: Comerica Bank & Trust, N.A.
Advisors: Laurence G. Callant; Mary A. Callant; Duane Kolman.
EIN: 266582447

238
The Paul Farago Foundation Trust
3508 Erie Dr.
Orchard Lake, MI 48324-1522
County: Oakland
Contact: Frank Campanale, Pres.

Established in 1998 in MI.
Grantmaker type: Independent foundation.
Financial data (yr. ended 12/31/09): Assets, $2,857,358 (M); expenditures, $255,859; total giving, $165,050; qualifying distributions, $255,859; giving activities include $165,050 for 11 grants (high: $110,000; low: $200).
Fields of interest: Education; Human services; Christian agencies & churches; Disabilities, people with.
Limitations: Applications accepted. Giving primarily in MI. No grants to individuals.
Application information:
Initial approach: Letter on organization letterhead
Deadline(s): None
Officer: Frank Campanale, Pres.
EIN: 383378111
Selected grants: The following grants were reported in 2008.
$11,000 to Detroit Zoological Society, Royal Oak, MI.

239
William and Audrey Farber Family Foundation
32640 Whatley Rd.
Franklin, MI 48025-1123 (248) 851-0747
County: Oakland
Contact: William Farber, Pres.

Established in 1993 in MI.
Donors: William Farber; Audrey Farber.
Grantmaker type: Independent foundation.
Financial data (yr. ended 12/31/08): Assets, $71,170 (M); expenditures, $47,909; total giving, $47,104; qualifying distributions, $47,104; giving activities include $47,104 for grants.
Fields of interest: Higher education; Human services; Jewish federated giving programs; Jewish agencies & synagogues.

Limitations: Applications accepted. Giving primarily in MI, with emphasis on Bloomfield and Detroit.
Application information:
Initial approach: Letter
Deadline(s): None
Officers: William Farber, Pres.; Audrey Farber, Secy.
EIN: 383159762

240
Marcus Martin Farley and Mable Stone Farley Memorial Foundation
121 Pepperidge Ln.
Battle Creek, MI 49015-3109 (269) 963-6750
County: Calhoun
Contact: Larry L. Payne, Pres.

Established in MI.
Grantmaker type: Independent foundation.
Financial data (yr. ended 12/31/09): Assets, $212,993 (M); expenditures, $14,716; total giving, $3,150; qualifying distributions, $3,150; giving activities include $3,150 for grants.
Fields of interest: Education; Health care.
Type of support: Program development; Equipment.
Limitations: Applications accepted. Giving limited to Calhoun County, MI. No grants to individuals.
Application information: Application form required.
Deadline(s): Dec. 1
Officers: Larry L. Payne, Pres.; Brenda Payne, Secy.
Trustee: Lynn Eberhard.
EIN: 383114865

241
The Farver Foundation
626 Depot St.
Blissfield, MI 49228-1399
County: Lenawee
Contact: Patrick Farver, Tr.
URL: http://www.farverfoundation.org/

Established in 1988 in MI.
Donors: Orville W. Farver†; Constance Farver; Herbert Farver.
Grantmaker type: Independent foundation.
Financial data (yr. ended 12/31/09): Assets, $3,710,831 (M); expenditures, $271,966; total giving, $252,325; qualifying distributions, $252,325; giving activities include $252,325 for 31 grants (high: $51,775; low: $250).
Fields of interest: Arts; Higher education; Education; Health organizations; Human services; Community/economic development; Foundations (private grantmaking).
Type of support: General/operating support; Continuing support; Annual campaigns; Capital campaigns; Building/renovation; Equipment; Emergency funds.
Limitations: Applications accepted. Giving primarily in Lenawee County, MI, with emphasis on the Adrian and Blissfield areas. No grants to individuals.
Application information: Application form not required.
Initial approach: Letter
Deadline(s): None
Trustees: Constance Farver; Michael Farver; Patrick Farver; Cynthia F. Galiette.
EIN: 386540398
Selected grants: The following grants were reported in 2006.
$50,000 to Adrian College, Adrian, MI.

$50,000 to Bixby Community Health Foundation, Adrian, MI.
$15,000 to Boys and Girls Club of Lenawee, Adrian, MI.
$15,000 to Share Our Strength, BROWARD TASTE OF THE NATION, Washington, DC.
$12,000 to Overlanders Association, Adrian, MI.
$10,000 to Adrian Symphony Orchestra, Adrian, MI.
$10,000 to Associated Charities of Lenawee County, Adrian, MI.
$10,000 to Gerontology Network of West Michigan, Grand Rapids, MI.
$6,000 to Kids in Distress, Fort Lauderdale, FL.
$5,000 to Siena Heights University, Adrian, MI.

242
Drusilla Farwell Foundation
3250 W. Big Beaver, Ste. 101
Troy, MI 48084-2900 (248) 649-8930
County: Oakland
Contact: Leslie Wise, Secy.

Established in 1937 in MI.
Grantmaker type: Independent foundation.
Financial data (yr. ended 08/31/09): Assets, $2,808,041 (M); expenditures, $204,154; total giving, $151,700; qualifying distributions, $163,300; giving activities include $151,700 for 111 grants (high: $5,000; low: $200).
Fields of interest: Arts; Higher education; Education; Health organizations; Human services; Children/youth, services; Christian agencies & churches.
Limitations: Giving primarily in FL and MI; funding also in New York, NY.
Application information:
 Initial approach: Proposal
 Deadline(s): None
Officers: Randolph Fields, Pres.; Leslie Wise, Secy.
Trustee: Charles Peltz.
EIN: 386082430
Selected grants: The following grants were reported in 2009.
$5,000 to Presbyterian Villages of Michigan, Southfield, MI.
$3,500 to Dartmouth College, Hanover, NH.
$3,000 to American Cancer Society, Southfield, MI.
$3,000 to Oakland University, Rochester, MI.
$3,000 to University of Michigan, Ann Arbor, MI.
$2,500 to Brighton Hospital, Brighton, MI.
$2,500 to Central Michigan University, Mount Pleasant, MI.
$2,500 to Detroit Institute of Arts, Detroit, MI.
$2,500 to Georgia Tech Foundation, Atlanta, GA.
$1,500 to Alternatives for Girls, Detroit, MI.

243
Allie & Wanda Fayz Family Foundation
P.O. Box 5326
Dearborn, MI 48128-5326
County: Wayne

Donors: Allie Fayz; Wanda Fayz.
Grantmaker type: Independent foundation.
Financial data (yr. ended 12/31/09): Assets, $14,220 (M); gifts received, $200; expenditures, $200; total giving, $0; qualifying distributions, $0.
Fields of interest: Islam.
Limitations: Giving primarily in MI.
Director: Allie Fayz.
EIN: 204193049

244
Feather Foundation
728 Indiana Woods
P.O. Box 626
Leland, MI 49654-0626 (231) 256-9125
County: Leelanau
Contact: Nancy Boynton Fisher, Secy.

Established in 2002 in MI.
Donor: Jeffrey E. Fisher.
Grantmaker type: Independent foundation.
Financial data (yr. ended 09/30/09): Assets, $374,966 (M); gifts received, $17,700; expenditures, $15,787; total giving, $9,000; qualifying distributions, $9,000; giving activities include $9,000 for grants.
Fields of interest: Historic preservation/historical societies; Environment, energy; Environmental education; Animals/wildlife, preservation/protection; Marine science.
Limitations: Giving primarily in MI. No grants to individuals.
Application information:
 Initial approach: Proposal
 Deadline(s): None
Officers: Jeffrey E. Fisher, Pres.; Nancy Boynton Fisher, Secy.; Wayne A. Pahssen, Treas.
Directors: Amy Drake; Chris Fisher.
EIN: 300141451

245
C. Scott Fedewa Foundation
298 W. Chicago St.
Coldwater, MI 49036-1895
County: Branch
Contact: C. Scott Fedewa, Pres.

Established in 1992 in CA.
Donor: C. Scott Fedewa.
Grantmaker type: Independent foundation.
Financial data (yr. ended 12/31/09): Assets, $3,914 (M); expenditures, $53; total giving, $0; qualifying distributions, $0; giving activities include $0 for grants to individuals.
Purpose and activities: Scholarship award paid directly to the college or university for graduating senior from Detroit, Michigan.
Fields of interest: Higher education.
Type of support: Scholarships—to individuals.
Limitations: Giving limited to residents of Detroit, MI.
Officers: C. Scott Fedewa, Pres. and Treas.; Constance Mettler, Secy.
Directors: Jonathan Fedewa; Philip Fedewa.
EIN: 383040444

246
The Sergei Fedorov Foundation
322 N. Old Woodward Ave.
Birmingham, MI 48009-5321 (248) 646-8292
County: Oakland
Contact: Brian D. O'Keefe, Secy.-Treas.

Established in MI.
Donor: Sergei Fedorov.
Grantmaker type: Independent foundation.
Financial data (yr. ended 12/31/09): Assets, $1,004,569 (M); expenditures, $66,707; total giving, $8,000; qualifying distributions, $8,000; giving activities include $8,000 for grants.

Purpose and activities: Giving primarily for children's services including scholarship funds for academically or athletically outstanding financially needy students generally between the ages of 10 and 14. Both U.S. residents non U.S. residents seeking to study stateside are eligible.
Fields of interest: Scholarships/financial aid; Children, services; United Ways and Federated Giving Programs.
Type of support: Sponsorships; Scholarship funds.
Limitations: Applications accepted. Giving primarily in MI.
Application information: Application form required.
 Initial approach: Letter
 Deadline(s): None
Officers: Sergei Fedorov, Pres.; Natalya Fedorov, V.P.; Victor Fedorov, V.P.; Brian D. O'Keefe, Secy.-Treas.
EIN: 383437116

247
Frank B. and Virginia V. Fehsenfeld Charitable Foundation
1107 1st Ave., Ste. 1404
Seattle, WA 98101-2947 (206) 621-7962
County: King
Contact: H. Warren Smith, Treas.

Established in 1987 in MI.
Donors: Frank Fehsenfeld; Virginia V. Fehsenfeld.
Grantmaker type: Independent foundation.
Financial data (yr. ended 12/31/09): Assets, $1,677,344 (M); expenditures, $108,783; total giving, $101,550; qualifying distributions, $101,550; giving activities include $101,550 for grants.
Fields of interest: Arts; Education; Environment, natural resources; Health care; Human services; Children/youth, services.
Type of support: Annual campaigns.
Limitations: Giving primarily in the Grand Rapids, MI, and Seattle, WA, areas. No grants to individuals.
Application information:
 Initial approach: Letter
 Deadline(s): None
Officers: William Fehsenfeld, Pres.; Thomas V. Fehsenfeld, V.P.; Nancy Fehsenfeld Smith, Secy.; H. Warren Smith, Treas.
Trustee: John A. Fehsenfeld.
EIN: 382775201

248
Ferries Family Foundation
c/o Northpoint Financial
920 E. Lincoln St.
Birmingham, MI 48009-3608
County: Oakland
Contact: John C. Ferries, Pres.
Application address: 80 Chestnut Hill Rd., Wilton, CT 06897-4605; NY tel.: (212) 468-3622

Established in 1998 in DE.
Donor: John C. Ferries.
Grantmaker type: Independent foundation.
Financial data (yr. ended 12/31/09): Assets, $32,788 (M); expenditures, $54,676; total giving, $52,903; qualifying distributions, $52,903; giving activities include $52,903 for grants.
Fields of interest: Higher education, college; Protestant agencies & churches.
Limitations: Giving primarily in CT and NH.

Application information:
Initial approach: Proposal
Deadline(s): June 30
Officers and Directors:* John C. Ferries,* Pres. and
Treas.; Donna Ferries,* V.P. and Secy.; Alexander
Ferries; Jason Ferries; Karen Ferries.
EIN: 134000700

249
John E. Fetzer Memorial Trust Fund
c/o Michael C. Gergely
P.O. Box 117
Vicksburg, MI 49097-0117   (269) 679-5334
County: Kalamazoo
URL: http://www.fetzertrust.org/

Established in 1991 in MI.
Donor: John E. Fetzer Revocable Trust.
Grantmaker type: Independent foundation.
Financial data (yr. ended 06/30/09): Assets,
$66,915,152 (M); gifts received, $80,000;
expenditures, $4,631,808; total giving, $528,999;
qualifying distributions, $1,113,496; giving
activities include $528,999 for 10 grants (high:
$149,250; low: $5,239).
Fields of interest: Higher education; Human
services, mind/body enrichment; Voluntarism
promotion; Psychology/behavioral science.
Type of support: General/operating support;
Research.
Limitations: Giving primarily to Kalamazoo, MI, also
and some giving in San Francisco, CA. No grants to
individuals.
Application information: Contributes only to
pre-selected organizations.
Officers: Robert Lehman, Pres.; Bruce Fetzer, Exec.
V.P.; Thomas Beaver, V.P.; Michael Gergely, Secy.;
Louis Leeburg, Treas.
Number of staff: 1 full-time professional.
EIN: 383010714
Selected grants: The following grants were reported
in 2008.
$5,400,000 to John E. Fetzer Institute, Kalamazoo,
MI.
$88,000 to Auburn University, Auburn, AL. For
microscope development.
$79,743 to Mayo Clinic Rochester, Rochester, MN.
For nanobacteria assay.
$70,074 to NIS Labs, Klamath Falls, OR. For blood
analysis.
$49,750 to California State University, Sacramento,
CA. For Consciousness Studies.
$38,877 to John E. Fetzer Institute, Kalamazoo, MI.
For scientific research.
$33,210 to Celio Laboratory, Asheville, NC. For
research.
$18,658 to Mayer Applied Research, Ann Arbor, MI.
For energy research.

250
Seymour S. & Diana M. Feuer Foundation
4117 Chatfield Ln.
Troy, MI 48098-4327
County: Oakland
Contact: Seymour S. Feuer, Tr.
Application address: 1141 Near Ocean Dr., Vero
Beach, FL 32963-2472

Donors: Seymour S. Feuer; Diana M. Feuer.
Grantmaker type: Independent foundation.

Financial data (yr. ended 08/31/09): Assets,
$46,129 (M); expenditures, $4,556; total giving,
$4,470; qualifying distributions, $4,470; giving
activities include $4,470 for grants.
Fields of interest: Education; Human services;
Jewish agencies & synagogues.
Application information: Application form not
required.
Deadline(s): None
Trustees: Diana M. Feuer; Seymour S. Feuer.
EIN: 382690090

251
Phillip & Elizabeth Filmer Memorial
Charitable Trust
c/o Comerica Bank
P.O. Box 75000, M.C. 3302
Detroit, MI 48275-3302
County: Wayne
Application address: c/o Scott Drogs, 101 N. Main
St., Ste. 100, Ann Arbor, MI 38104-5002, tel.: (734)
930-2416

Established in 2006 in MI.
Donor: Elizabeth Filmer Estate Trust.
Grantmaker type: Independent foundation.
Financial data (yr. ended 08/31/10): Assets,
$5,528,098 (M); expenditures, $451,398; total
giving, $400,000; qualifying distributions,
$401,464; giving activities include $400,000 for 44
grants (high: $25,000; low: $1,000).
Fields of interest: Education; Children/youth,
services; Family services; Human services;
Christian agencies & churches.
Limitations: Applications accepted. Giving limited to
Oakland County, MI.
Application information:
Initial approach: Letter
Deadline(s): None
Advisory Council: Frank Brooks; Ann Conrad; Lassie
Lewis; Joseph McGlynn.
Trustee: Comerica Bank.
EIN: 203341412
Selected grants: The following grants were reported
in 2009.
$25,000 to Lighthouse P.A.T.H., Pontiac, MI.
$20,000 to Leader Dogs for the Blind, Rochester,
MI.
$17,607 to First Presbyterian Church of
Birmingham, Birmingham, MI.
$15,000 to Catholic Social Services of Oakland
County, Royal Oak, MI.
$15,000 to Forgotten Harvest, Oak Park, MI.
$15,000 to Fresh Air Society, Bloomfield Hills, MI.
$15,000 to Loyola High School Foundation, Detroit,
MI.
$12,000 to Manresa Jesuit Retreat House,
Bloomfield Hills, MI.
$10,000 to Oak Park Business and Education
Alliance, Oak Park, MI.
$8,000 to Angels Place, Southfield, MI.

252
George R. and Elise M. Fink Foundation
377 Fisher Rd., Ste. C-5
Grosse Pointe, MI 48230-1673   (313) 886-8451
County: Wayne
Contact: Elyse F. Jones, Pres.
E-mail: finknews@aol.com

Incorporated in 1955 in MI.

Donors: George R. Fink†; Elise M. Fink†.
Grantmaker type: Independent foundation.
Financial data (yr. ended 11/30/09): Assets,
$1,902,026 (M); expenditures, $76,764; total
giving, $49,500; qualifying distributions, $49,500;
giving activities include $49,500 for grants.
Fields of interest: Education; Health care; Mental
health, treatment; Human services; Children,
services.
Type of support: General/operating support.
Limitations: Giving primarily in MI. No grants to
individuals, for scholarships or fellowships; no
loans.
Application information: Application form not
required.
Initial approach: Letter
Deadline(s): None
Officers: Elyse F. Jones, Pres.; John M. Fink, V.P.;
Lynn Carpenter, Secy.
Number of staff: 1 part-time support.
EIN: 386059952
Selected grants: The following grants were reported
in 2005.
$25,000 to Bon Secours Cottage Health Services
Foundation, Grosse Pointe, MI. For general
operating support.
$20,000 to Cradle Foundation, Evanston, IL. For
general operating support.
$20,000 to Salvation Army of Baltimore, Baltimore,
MD. For Hurricane Relief Fund.
$16,150 to Friends School in Detroit, Detroit, MI.
For general operating support.
$15,000 to Grosse Pointe Animal Adoption Society,
Grosse Pointe Farms, MI. For general operating
support.
$10,000 to American Red Cross National
Headquarters, Washington, DC. For general
operating support.
$10,000 to Save the Children Federation, Westport,
CT. For general operating support.

253
Morton M. Finkelstein Family Charitable
Foundation
18053 N. Fruitport Rd.
Spring Lake, MI 49456-1573   (616) 459-2233
County: Ottawa
Contact: Morton M. Finkelstein, Tr.

Established in 1999 in MI.
Donor: Morton M. Finkelstein.
Grantmaker type: Independent foundation.
Financial data (yr. ended 12/31/09): Assets,
$223,080 (M); gifts received, $50,000;
expenditures, $34,716; total giving, $34,500;
qualifying distributions, $34,500; giving activities
include $34,500 for grants.
Fields of interest: Jewish federated giving programs.
Limitations: Giving primarily in MI.
Application information: Application form not
required.
Initial approach: Letter
Deadline(s): None
Trustee: Morton M. Finkelstein.
EIN: 383507986

254
Harvey Firestone, Jr. Foundation
2000 Brush St., Ste. 440
Detroit, MI 48226-2251 (313) 961-0500
County: Wayne
Contact: Christine Jaggi

Established in 1983 in OH.
Grantmaker type: Independent foundation.
Financial data (yr. ended 12/31/09): Assets,
$18,452,911 (M); gifts received, $1,000;
expenditures, $1,114,234; total giving,
$1,036,000; qualifying distributions, $1,036,000;
giving activities include $1,036,000 for 106 grants
(high: $129,000; low: $500).
Fields of interest: Arts; Education; Health care;
Human services; Christian agencies & churches.
Type of support: General/operating support.
Limitations: Giving primarily in CT and MI; giving also
in Washington, DC and NY. No grants to individuals.
Application information: Application form not
required.
   Initial approach: Letter
   Deadline(s): None
Trustees: Anne F. Ball; Martha F. Ford; JPMorgan
Chase Bank, N.A.
EIN: 341388254
Selected grants: The following grants were reported
in 2008.
$100,000 to Henry Ford Health System, Detroit, MI.
$90,000 to Christ Church Grosse Pointe, Grosse
Pointe, MI.
$52,000 to Miss Porters School, Farmington, CT.
$50,000 to United Way of Greenwich, Greenwich,
CT.
$30,000 to Foxcroft School, Middleburg, VA.
$26,500 to Princeton University, Princeton, NJ.
$15,000 to Archdiocese for the Military Services
USA, Washington, DC.
$15,000 to College for Creative Studies, Detroit, MI.
$7,000 to Chapin School, Burkert, New York, NY.
$3,000 to Leelanau Township Community
Foundation, Northport, MI.

255
Fish Foundation
7500 Patterson Rd.
Caledonia, MI 49316-9319
County: Kent
Contact: David J. Smies, Pres.

Established in 1998 in MI.
Donors: David J. Smies; Deborah Smies.
Grantmaker type: Independent foundation.
Financial data (yr. ended 12/31/09): Assets,
$243,883 (M); gifts received, $10,000;
expenditures, $31,152; total giving, $19,900;
qualifying distributions, $19,900; giving activities
include $19,900 for grants.
Fields of interest: Theological school/education;
Human services; United Ways and Federated Giving
Programs; Christian agencies & churches.
Type of support: General/operating support.
Limitations: Giving primarily in Grand Rapids, MI. No
support for political parties, television or radio
ministries, non-Christian institutions or causes, or
educational facilities. No grants for building projects
or other capital expenditures, debt retirement, or
educational projects or tuition; no loans to
individuals.
Application information:
   Initial approach: Proposal

Deadline(s): Mar. or Apr. for requests of $2,500
   or more; requests of less than $2,500 can be
   made at any time
   Final notification: Generally in June
Officers: David J. Smies, Pres. and Treas.; Deborah
Smies, V.P. and Secy.
EIN: 383419231

256
Fitzgibbon Dermidoff Foundation
1776 S. Bates St.
Birmingham, MI 48009-1905 (248) 433-3527
County: Oakland
Contact: Jane Fitzgibbon, Pres.

Established in 1996 in MI.
Donor: Jane Fitzgibbon.
Grantmaker type: Independent foundation.
Financial data (yr. ended 12/31/09): Assets,
$169,608 (M); gifts received, $10,000;
expenditures, $5,066; total giving, $4,000;
qualifying distributions, $4,000; giving activities
include $4,000 for grants.
Fields of interest: Higher education.
Limitations: Giving emphasis is on MI, NY, and TX.
Application information:
   Initial approach: Letter
   Deadline(s): None
Officers: Jane Fitzgibbon, Pres.; Howard Kastner,
Secy.; Karen Dermidoff Reilly, Treas.
EIN: 383323499

257
Nora Flemington Scholarship Trust
508 E. Margaret St.
Iron Mountain, MI 49801-1844
County: Dickinson
Contact: Nancy Finch, Dir.
Application address: 115 West C St., Iron Mountain,
MI 49801

Grantmaker type: Independent foundation.
Financial data (yr. ended 12/31/09): Assets,
$35,511 (M); gifts received, $1,500; expenditures,
$1,500; total giving, $1,500; qualifying
distributions, $1,500; giving activities include
$1,500 for grants to individuals.
Purpose and activities: Scholarship awards to
full-time female students who are over the age of 22
and residents of Dickinson or Iron counties,
Michigan, or Menominee County, Wisconsin.
Fields of interest: Higher education; Women.
Type of support: Scholarships—to individuals.
Limitations: Giving limited to residents of Dickinson
and Iron counties, MI, and Menominee County, WI.
Application information:
   Initial approach: Letter
   Deadline(s): June 15
Directors: Carol Curtis; Nancy Finch; Margaret
Jones; Nancy Schaub.
EIN: 386509939

258
Foellinger Foundation, Inc.
520 E. Berry St.
Fort Wayne, IN 46802-2002 (260) 422-2900
County: Allen
Contact: Cheryl K. Taylor, C.E.O.
FAX: (260) 422-9436; E-mail: info@foellinger.org;
Additional e-mail (for Cheryl K. Taylor):

cheryl@foellinger.org; URL: http://
www.foellinger.org

Incorporated in 1958 in IN.
Donors: Esther A. Foellinger†; Helene R.
Foellinger†.
Grantmaker type: Independent foundation.
Financial data (yr. ended 08/31/09): Assets,
$142,775,705 (M); expenditures, $7,323,534;
total giving, $5,438,328; qualifying distributions,
$6,345,195; giving activities include $5,438,328
for 98 grants (high: $290,000; low: $1,500), and
$83,962 for 3 foundation-administered programs.
Purpose and activities: Giving in Allen County, IN,
for early childhood development, youth development
and family development, especially for the most in
need with the least opportunity, and organizational
effectiveness.
Fields of interest: Children/youth, services; Family
services; Children/youth; Youth; Economically
disadvantaged.
Type of support: General/operating support;
Continuing support; Program development;
Research; Technical assistance; Consulting
services; Program evaluation; Matching/challenge
support.
Limitations: Applications accepted. Giving primarily
in the Allen County, IN, area. Generally, no grants for
religious groups for religious purposes, elementary
or secondary schools independent of their school
systems, or purposes taxpayers are expected to
support. No grants to individuals, or for
endowments, deficit financing, sponsorships,
special events, conferences, commercial
advertising, group trips, capital projects, annual
campaigns or appeals, or for capital projects.
Publications: Application guidelines; Annual report;
Grants list; Occasional report.
Application information: See foundation's web site
for downloadable grant guideline packet. Not
currently accepting applications for capital support.
Only 1 application per organization per year.
Application form required.
   Initial approach: Grant application
   Copies of proposal: 1
   Deadline(s): No deadline for grants for
      Strengthening Organizations. First Mon. in Feb.
      for Family Development and Community
      Interestes; First Mon. in Aug. for Early
      Childhood Development; and First Mon. in Nov.
      for Youth Development; as invited for all other
      foundation-invited initiatives
   Board meeting date(s): Quarterly in Feb., May,
      Aug., and Nov.
   Final notification: One week after board meeting
Officers and Directors:* Carolyn R. Hughes,*
Chair.; David A. Bobilya,* Vice-Chair. and Secy.;
Cheryl K. Taylor,* C.E.O. and Pres.; Robert N. Taylor,
Treas.; Hon. Thomas J. Felts; Helen Murray; Richard
B. Pierce; Todd Rumsey.
Number of staff: 3 full-time professional; 3 full-time
support.
EIN: 356027059

259
Jeff Foran Charitable Trust
c/o Frank S. Arval, Tr.
888 W. Big Beaver Rd., Ste. 890
Troy, MI 48084-4746
County: Oakland
Contact: William R. "Bill" Nixon, Jr., Tr.

Application address: BHYSL Scholarship Committee, 3845 Woodlake Dr., Bloomfield Hills, MI 48304-3075, tel.: (248) 540-9153

Established in 2001 in MI.
Grantmaker type: Independent foundation.
Financial data (yr. ended 12/31/09): Assets, $22,042 (M); expenditures, $902; total giving, $0; qualifying distributions, $0.
Purpose and activities: Scholarship awards to students who have played soccer: 1) within the Bloomfield School District boundaries, 2) at least three years in the Bloomfield Hills Youth Soccer League, or 3) played on a high school soccer team.
Fields of interest: Athletics/sports, soccer.
Type of support: Scholarships—to individuals.
Limitations: Giving to residents of the greater Bloomfield, MI, area.
Application information: Application form required.
   Deadline(s): Aug. 15
Trustees: John F. Lecznar; Mary R. Lecznar; Barbara P. Nixon; William R. "Bill" Nixon, Jr.
EIN: 386773411

260
Ford Foundation

320 E. 43rd St.
New York, NY   10017-4801   (212) 573-5000
County: New York
Contact: Secy.
FAX: (212) 351-3677;
E-mail: office-secretary@fordfoundation.org;
URL: http://www.fordfoundation.org

Incorporated in 1936 in MI.
Donors: Henry Ford‡; Edsel Ford‡.
Grantmaker type: Independent foundation.
Financial data (yr. ended 09/30/10): Assets, $10,881,598,073 (M); expenditures, $603,589,296; total giving, $468,301,444; qualifying distributions, $611,250,946; giving activities include $466,705,410 for grants, $184,042 for grants to individuals, $1,411,992 for employee matching gifts, $4,204,348 for foundation-administered programs and $49,546,742 for loans/program-related investments.
Purpose and activities: The foundation supports visionary leaders and organizations working on the frontlines of social change worldwide. Its goals for more than half a century have been to strengthen democratic values, reduce poverty and injustice, promote international cooperation, and advance human achievement. The foundation focuses on nine issues: 1) Human Rights; 2) Democratic and Accountable Government; 3) Educational Opportunity and Scholarship; 4) Economic Fairness; 5) Metropolitan Opportunity; 6) Sustainable Development; 7) Freedom of Expression; 8) Sexuality and Reproductive Health and Rights; and 9) Social Justice Philanthropy.
Fields of interest: Media/communications; Media, film/video; Museums; Performing arts; Performing arts, dance; Performing arts, theater; Performing arts, music; Arts; Education, research; Secondary school/education; Higher education; Education; Environment, natural resources; Environment; Reproductive health; Reproductive health, sexuality education; AIDS; Crime/violence prevention, abuse prevention; Legal services; Employment; Agriculture; Housing/shelter, development; Youth development, research; Human services; Women, centers/services; Minorities/immigrants, centers/

services; International economic development; International human rights; International affairs; Civil rights, race/intergroup relations; Civil/human rights; Economic development; Urban/community development; Rural development; Community/ economic development; Philanthropy/voluntarism; Social sciences; Economics; Law/international law; Government/public administration; Public affairs, citizen participation; Leadership development; Religion, interfaith issues; Youth; Minorities; Asians/Pacific Islanders; African Americans/ Blacks; Hispanics/Latinos; Indigenous peoples; Women; AIDS, people with; LGBTQ; Immigrants/ refugees; Economically disadvantaged.
International interests: Africa; Asia; Latin America; Middle East.
Type of support: General/operating support; Continuing support; Management development/ capacity building; Endowments; Program development; Program evaluation; Program-related investments/loans; Employee matching gifts; Grants to individuals.
Limitations: Applications accepted. Giving in the United States, Africa, the Middle East, Asia, Latin America and the Caribbean, and also on a global basis, with a focus on nine core issues. No support for programs for which substantial support from government or other sources is readily available, or for religious sectarian activities. No grants for construction or maintenance of buildings, undergraduate scholarships, or for purely personal or local needs. The foundation provides a very limited number of graduate fellowship opportunities for individuals, which are generally channeled through grants to universities or other organizations.
Publications: Annual report; Informational brochure; Occasional report.
Application information: Prospective applicants are advised to carefully review the foundation's initiatives online, and to download and review the Grant Application Guide for additional details about the grant-review process at http://www.fordfoundation.org/pdfs/grants/grant-application-guide.pdf. Application form not required.
   Initial approach: After reviewing the Grant Application Guide, submit an inquiry online using the Grant Inquiry Form (http://www.fordfoundation.org/grants/select-country-or-region)
   Copies of proposal: 1
   Deadline(s): None, grants are made throughout the year
   Final notification: Initial indication as to whether proposal falls within program interests within 6 weeks
Officers and Trustees: * Irene Hirano Inouye,* Chair.; Luis A. Ubinas,* Pres.; Eric Doppstadt, V.P. and C.I.O.; Nicholas M. Gabriel, V.P., C.F.O. and Treas.; Nancy P. Feller, V.P., Secy. and Genl. Counsel; John L. Colborn, V.P., Opers.; Pablo J. Farias, V.P., Economic Opportunity and Assets; Maya L. Harris, V.P., Democracy, Rights and Justice; Marta L. Tellado, V.P., Comms.; Darren Walker, V.P., Education, Creativity, and Free Expression; Kofi Appenteng; Afsaneh M. Beschloss; Juliet V. Garcia; J. Clifford Hudson; Yolanda Kakabadse; Robert S. Kaplan; Thurgood Marshall, Jr.; N.R. Narayana Murthy; Peter A. Nadosy; Cecile Richards.
Number of staff: 254 full-time professional; 116 full-time support.
EIN: 131684331
Selected grants: The following grants were reported in 2010.

$2,554,000 to Urban Institute, Washington, DC. To plan state-level demonstration project using integrated approach to increase enrollment and retention of low-income individuals and families in income and work support programs, payable over 2.00 years.
$2,000,000 to Family Values at Work: A Multi-State Consortium, Milwaukee, WI. For grant making, technical assistance, networking and advocacy to educate public and policy makers in 14 states and nationally about need for paid sick days and paid family leave.
$1,350,000 to Greater New Orleans Foundation, New Orleans, LA. For grant making by Community Revitalization Fund and Metropolitan Innovations Programs to promote inclusive regional housing, transit and community revitalization in the greater New Orleans region.
$1,014,887 to Innovations for Poverty Action, New Haven, CT. To evaluate pilot programs that provide asset and support services to very poor people in developing countries to help them to increase incomes and gain access to microfinance programs, payable over 3.00 years.
$1,000,000 to Complete College America, Zionsville, IN. For general support to partner with state policy makers to develop and implement comprehensive strategies for increasing college completion rates, particularly for marginalized groups, payable over 2.00 years.
$1,000,000 to Focus: HOPE, Detroit, MI. For recoverable grant to provide working capital line of credit to support operations and position organization for financial sustainability, payable over 5.00 years.
$500,000 to Fund for Public Schools, New York, NY. For New York City Department of Education's Innovation Zone program to design, pilot and evaluate time and staffing innovations that increase instructional time and make instruction more effective.
$500,000 to Land of Rights, Curitiba, Brazil. For strategic litigation and advocacy on land rights in Brazil, payable over 2.00 years.
$450,000 to Project on Government Oversight, Washington, DC. For general support to investigate contracting abuses in federal government and improve oversight systems that make government accountable, payable over 2.00 years.
$350,000 to Urgent Action Fund for Womens Human Rights Africa, Nairobi, Kenya. For small grants program to promote and protect rights of women and girls and for fundraising, training, technical assistance and networking to build own capacity and that of grantees, payable over 2.00 years.

261
Geraldine C. and Emory M. Ford Foundation

P.O. Box 33
Roseville, MI   48066-0033
County: Macomb
Contact: Allen Olinger, Pres.
Application address: c/o 2338 Anza St., San Francisco, CA 94118-3533, tel.: (415) 571-8442

Established in 1994 in MI.
Donor: Geraldine C. Ford‡.
Grantmaker type: Independent foundation.
Financial data (yr. ended 06/30/10): Assets, $891,356 (M); expenditures, $58,636; total giving,

$45,950; qualifying distributions, $45,950; giving activities include $45,950 for grants.
Purpose and activities: Supports work by American composers and musicians by assisting in establishment of professional careers through programs.
Fields of interest: Performing arts; Performing arts, music; Performing arts, orchestras.
Type of support: General/operating support.
Limitations: Applications accepted. Giving primarily in CA and NJ. No grants to individuals.
Application information: Must be recommended by director of a symphony or music festival if grant is for a music-related program. Application form not required.
    Initial approach: Letter
    Copies of proposal: 1
    Board meeting date(s): As required
    Final notification: 1 month
Officers: Allen Olinger, Pres. and Treas.; Deborah Olinger, V.P.; Gregg Carpene, Secy.
EIN: 383190683

262
William & Lisa Ford Foundation
1901 Saint Antoine St., 6th Fl. at Ford Field
Detroit, MI 48226-2310
County: Wayne
Contact: David M. Hempstead, Secy.

Established in 1998 in MI.
Donors: William Clay Ford, Jr.; Lisa V. Ford.
Grantmaker type: Independent foundation.
Financial data (yr. ended 12/31/09): Assets, $10,653,149 (M); expenditures, $736,105; total giving, $665,300; qualifying distributions, $678,132; giving activities include $665,300 for 17 grants (high: $410,000; low: $3,000).
Purpose and activities: Giving primarily for children's services and higher education; funding also for human services.
Fields of interest: Museums; Higher education; Education; Environment, land resources; Health care; Human services; Children, services; United Ways and Federated Giving Programs; Buddhism.
Limitations: Giving primarily in MI and NJ. No grants to individuals.
Application information: Awards are generally limited to charitable organizations already known and of interest to the foundation.
    Initial approach: Letter
    Deadline(s): None
    Board meeting date(s): As necessary
Officers and Trustee: * William Clay Ford, Jr.,* Pres. and Dir.; Lisa V. Ford,* V.P.; David M. Hempstead, Secy.; Rodney P. Wood, Treas.; Eleanor C. Ford.
EIN: 383441138
Selected grants: The following grants were reported in 2009.
$410,000 to Princeton University, Princeton, NJ.
$20,000 to Spirit Rock Meditation Center, Woodacre, CA.
$15,000 to Huron River Watershed Council, Ann Arbor, MI.
$10,000 to Greenhills School, Ann Arbor, MI.
$10,000 to Henry Ford Health System, Detroit, MI.
$10,000 to Henry Ford Hospital, Detroit, MI.
$5,000 to Telluride Academy, Telluride, CO.
$3,000 to Michigan State University, East Lansing, MI.
$3,000 to University of Michigan, Ann Arbor, MI.

263
Benson and Edith Ford Fund
1901 Saint Antoine St., 6th Fl. at Ford Field
Detroit, MI 48226-2310   (313) 259-7777
County: Wayne
Contact: David M. Hempstead, Secy.

Incorporated in 1943 in MI as the Hotchkiss Fund.
Donor: Benson Ford‡.
Grantmaker type: Independent foundation.
Financial data (yr. ended 12/31/09): Assets, $31,043,791 (M); expenditures, $2,386,514; total giving, $2,263,238; qualifying distributions, $2,284,099; giving activities include $2,263,238 for 45 grants (high: $1,294,738; low: $500).
Purpose and activities: Support for health, human services, education, and arts and culture.
Fields of interest: Arts; Education; Hospitals (general); Youth development, services; Children/youth, services; United Ways and Federated Giving Programs; Jewish agencies & synagogues.
Limitations: Giving primarily in MI, with emphasis on Detroit. No grants to individuals.
Application information: Awards generally limited to charities already favorably known to substantial contributors of the foundation.
    Initial approach: Letter
    Deadline(s): None
    Board meeting date(s): As necessary
Officers and Trustees: * Lynn Ford Alandt,* Pres.; Benson Ford, Jr.,* V.P.; David M. Hempstead,* Secy.; Rodney P. Wood, Treas.
EIN: 386066333
Selected grants: The following grants were reported in 2009.
$1,294,738 to Henry Ford Health System, Detroit, MI.
$80,000 to College for Creative Studies, Detroit, MI.
$25,000 to Saint John Health System, Detroit, MI.
$10,000 to Detroit Institute for Children, Detroit, MI.
$10,000 to Planned Parenthood of Southeast Michigan, Detroit, MI.
$5,000 to Childrens Hospital of Michigan Foundation, Detroit, MI.
$5,000 to Masters School, Dobbs Ferry, NY.
$5,000 to Northern Michigan Hospital Foundation, Petoskey, MI.
$5,000 to Racing for Kids, Grosse Pointe Farms, MI.
$2,000 to United Negro College Fund, Fairfax, VA.

264
William and Martha Ford Fund
1901 Saint Antoine St., 6th Fl. at Ford Field
Detroit, MI 48226-2310
County: Wayne
Contact: David M. Hempstead, Secy.

Incorporated in 1953 in MI.
Donors: William Clay Ford; Martha Firestone Ford.
Grantmaker type: Independent foundation.
Financial data (yr. ended 12/31/09): Assets, $291,984 (M); expenditures, $2,798,844; total giving, $2,769,300; qualifying distributions, $2,780,355; giving activities include $2,769,300 for 60 grants (high: $1,585,000; low: $200).
Purpose and activities: The fund provides financial support to corporations, trusts, community chests, funds or foundations, organized and operated solely for religious, charitable, scientific, literary or educational purposes, or for the prevention of cruelty to children or animals.
Fields of interest: Museums; Arts; Higher education; Education; Zoos/zoological societies;

Hospitals (general); Health care; Substance abuse, services; Boys & girls clubs; Human services; Foundations (community); United Ways and Federated Giving Programs.
Limitations: Giving in the U.S., with emphasis on CT and MI. No grants to individuals.
Application information: Awards generally limited to charities already favorably known to substantial contributors of the foundation.
    Initial approach: Letter
    Deadline(s): None
    Board meeting date(s): As necessary
Officers and Trustees: * William Clay Ford,* Pres.; David M. Hempstead,* Secy.; Rodney P. Wood, Treas.; Martha F. Ford.
EIN: 386066335
Selected grants: The following grants were reported in 2009.
$1,585,000 to Hotchkiss School, Lakeville, CT.
$464,500 to Henry Ford Health System, Detroit, MI.
$250,000 to Texas Heart Institute, Houston, TX.
$20,000 to Saint Lukes Episcopal Hospital, Houston, TX.
$15,000 to East Hampton Healthcare Foundation, East Hampton, NY.
$10,000 to Detroit Institute for Children, Detroit, MI.
$5,500 to Yale University, New Haven, CT.
$5,000 to College for Creative Studies, Detroit, MI.
$5,000 to Greenhills School, Ann Arbor, MI.
$5,000 to New Canaan Country School, New Canaan, CT.

265
Edsel B. Ford II Fund
1901 Saint Antoine St., 6th Fl.
Detroit, MI 48226-2310   (313) 259-7777
County: Wayne
Contact: David M. Hempstead, Secy.

Established in 1993 in MI.
Donor: Edsel B. Ford II.
Grantmaker type: Independent foundation.
Financial data (yr. ended 12/31/09): Assets, $5,089,301 (M); gifts received, $50,000; expenditures, $388,828; total giving, $362,173; qualifying distributions, $367,941; giving activities include $362,173 for 43 grants (high: $55,000; low: $1,000).
Purpose and activities: Giving primarily for higher education, health, social services, children and youth services, particularly juvenile diabetes, federated giving programs, and a Presbyterian church.
Fields of interest: Arts; Higher education; Education; Zoos/zoological societies; Hospitals (general); Health care; Diabetes; Human services; Children/youth, services; United Ways and Federated Giving Programs; Protestant agencies & churches.
Limitations: Giving primarily in MI. No grants to individuals.
Application information: Generally grants awards to organizations already known to the donor.
    Initial approach: Letter
    Deadline(s): None
    Board meeting date(s): As needed
Officers and Director: * Edsel B. Ford II,* Pres.; David M. Hempstead, Secy.; George A. Straitor, Treas.
EIN: 383153050
Selected grants: The following grants were reported in 2008.
$50,000 to Detroit Institute for Children, Detroit, MI.

$34,376 to Babson College, Babson Park, MA.
$25,000 to Henry Ford Health System, Detroit, MI.
$10,000 to Deerfield Academy, Deerfield, MA.
$10,000 to Mosaic Youth Theater of Detroit, Detroit, MI.
$10,000 to Motown Historical Museum, Detroit, MI.
$10,000 to Rollins College, Winter Park, FL.
$10,000 to Smithsonian Institution, Washington, DC.
$5,000 to Childrens Hospital of Michigan Foundation, Detroit, MI.
$5,000 to Saint Lukes Wood River Foundation, Ketchum, ID.

266
William C. Ford, Jr. Scholarship Program
1901 Saint Antoine St., 6th Fl.
Ford Field
Detroit, MI   48226-2310
County: Wayne
Application address: c/o Scholarship America, P.O. Box 297, Saint Peter, MN 56082-0297, tel.: (800) 537-4180

Established in 2005 in MI.
Donor: William C. Ford, Jr.
Grantmaker type: Independent foundation.
Financial data (yr. ended 12/31/09): Assets, $757,967 (M); expenditures, $260,837; total giving, $249,000; qualifying distributions, $255,959; giving activities include $249,000 for 166 grants to individuals (high: $1,500; low: $1,500).
Purpose and activities: Grants scholarships to students who are a dependent of an active full-time Ford employee, not married, a U.S. citizen, under the age of 25, and enrolled to be a sophomore in the upcoming year.
Fields of interest: Higher education.
Type of support: Scholarship funds.
Limitations: Giving primarily to children of Ford company employees.
Application information: Application form required.
  Deadline(s): July 1
Officers: William C. Ford, Jr., Pres.; David M. Hempstead, Secy.; James G. Vella, Treas.
EIN: 202462203

267
Foren Family Foundation
33 Bloomfield Hills Pkwy., Ste. 260
Bloomfield Hills, MI   48304-2946
(248) 879-4636
County: Oakland
Contact: Belinda Foren, Tr.

Established in 2005 in MI.
Donor: Frazier C. Foren Irrevocable Trust.
Grantmaker type: Independent foundation.
Financial data (yr. ended 12/31/09): Assets, $5,034,160 (M); expenditures, $300,019; total giving, $250,000; qualifying distributions, $250,000; giving activities include $250,000 for 19 grants (high: $30,000; low: $2,000).
Fields of interest: Higher education; Education; Animal welfare; Cancer research; Children/youth, services; Christian agencies & churches.
Limitations: Applications accepted. Giving primarily in CA, FL, MI, and UT. No grants to individuals.
Application information: Application form not required.

Initial approach: Letter
Deadline(s): Varies
Trustees: Belinda Foren; Donald Foren; John E. Grenke; Jessica Trotter.
EIN: 202766137
Selected grants: The following grants were reported in 2008.
$96,000 to Best Friends Animal Society, Kanab, UT.
$34,000 to Marine Mammal Center, Sausalito, CA.
$20,000 to University of Michigan, Dearborn, MI.
$20,000 to Wayne State University, Detroit, MI.
$15,000 to CARE, Merrifield, VA.
$10,000 to Genesee Intermediate School District, Flint, MI.
$1,000 to Case Western Reserve University, Cleveland, OH.
$1,000 to University of Hawaii Foundation, Honolulu, HI.

268
Foster Family Foundation
P.O. Box 437
St. Clair, MI   48079-0437
County: St. Clair

Established in 2005 in MI.
Donors: Richard Foster; Virginia Foster; John Foster; Jennifer Foster; Tom Foster; Michele Foster; Marjorie Foster-Cummins.
Grantmaker type: Independent foundation.
Financial data (yr. ended 12/31/09): Assets, $275,256 (M); gifts received, $50,000; expenditures, $40,810; total giving, $38,000; qualifying distributions, $38,000; giving activities include $38,000 for grants to individuals.
Purpose and activities: Scholarship awards to graduating seniors from St. Clair, Michigan high schools.
Fields of interest: Higher education.
Type of support: Scholarships—to individuals.
Limitations: Giving primarily to residents of St. Clair, MI.
Application information: Recommendation from high school counselors.
  Deadline(s): None
Officers: Richard Foster, Pres.; Virginia Foster, Secy.-Treas.
Directors: John Foster; Tom Foster; Marjorie Foster-Cummins.
EIN: 203439954

269
Foster Foundation
(formerly Foster Welfare Foundation)
P.O. Box 3220
Grand Rapids, MI   49501-3230
County: Kent
Contact: Karley D. Johns, Exec. Dir.
Application address: 581 Alta Dale Ave. S.E., Ada, MI 49301-7818, tel.: (616) 676-5958

Established in MI.
Donor: Clara J. Foster.
Grantmaker type: Independent foundation.
Financial data (yr. ended 04/30/10): Assets, $49,833 (M); gifts received, $24,309; expenditures, $32,581; total giving, $21,000; qualifying distributions, $21,000; giving activities include $21,000 for grants to individuals.

Purpose and activities: Scholarship awards to students in Kent County, Michigan, for higher education.
Fields of interest: Education.
Type of support: Scholarships—to individuals.
Limitations: Giving limited to residents of Kent County, MI.
Application information:
  Initial approach: Letter
  Deadline(s): Feb. 1
Officers: Robert VanDongen, Pres.; Andrea K. Sugiyama, V.P.; Karley D. Johns, Exec. Dir.
Directors: Vern Boss; Gilbert Davis; Emery Freeman; Barbara Jackoboice; Vernis Schad.
EIN: 380831533

270
Foundation for Birmingham Senior Residents
2121 Midvale St.
Birmingham, MI   48009-1509   (248) 619-3400
County: Oakland

Established around 1984.
Grantmaker type: Independent foundation.
Financial data (yr. ended 12/31/09): Assets, $393,212 (M); expenditures, $31,531; total giving, $27,845; qualifying distributions, $27,845; giving activities include $27,845 for grants.
Purpose and activities: Awards granted to Birmingham Area Seniors Coordinating Council and directly to senior residents of Birmingham, MI, for minor home repairs and maintenance.
Fields of interest: Aging.
Type of support: Loans—to individuals; Building/renovation.
Limitations: Giving limited to residents of Birmingham, MI.
Application information: Grants limited to the benefit of Birmingham, MI, homeowners 60 years of age or older with financial need. Application form required.
Officers: Benedict J. Smith, Pres.; Jack Fawcett, V.P.; David E. Hershey, Treas.
Directors: Rackeline Hoff; Claudia Jackson; Robert Stevenson.
EIN: 382507882

271
Thomas F. Franke Foundation
c/o Thomas F. Franke
410 N. Eagle St.
Marshall, MI   49068-1106   (269) 781-9280
County: Calhoun

Established in 2005.
Donor: Thomas F. Franke.
Grantmaker type: Independent foundation.
Financial data (yr. ended 06/30/10): Assets, $2,740 (M); gifts received, $30,000; expenditures, $30,732; total giving, $30,700; qualifying distributions, $30,700; giving activities include $30,700 for grants (high: $25,000; low: $200).
Limitations: Giving primarily in Marshall, MI.
Officers: Thomas F. Franke, Pres.; Marsha L. Franke, V.P. and Secy.; Patricia F. Belew, V.P. and Treas.
EIN: 203947225

272
Frazier Fund, Inc.
c/o Wells Fargo Bank Michigan, N.A.
P.O. Box 580, Trust Dept.
Marquette, MI 49855-0580
County: Marquette
Contact: Mary C. Nurmi
Additional telephone: (906) 228-1386

Established in 1980 in MI.
Donor: Anne M. Frazier†.
Grantmaker type: Independent foundation.
Financial data (yr. ended 09/30/09): Assets,
$1,561,766 (M); expenditures, $92,551; total
giving, $77,900; qualifying distributions, $77,900;
giving activities include $77,900 for grants.
Purpose and activities: Giving primarily for
children's museums and youth services.
Fields of interest: Museums (children's); Housing/
shelter; Youth development; Human services; YM/
YWCAs & YM/YWHAs; United Ways and Federated
Giving Programs.
Limitations: Giving limited to Marquette, MI. No
grants to individuals.
Application information:
  Initial approach: Proposal
  Deadline(s): Apr. 30
Officers: Peter W. Frazier, Pres.; Julia Q. Frazier,
V.P.; William I. McDonald, Secy.; Robert J. Toutant,
Treas.
Director: Lincoln B. Frazier, Jr.
Trustee: Wells Fargo Bank Michigan, N.A.
EIN: 382287345

273
E. Fredericksen Scholarship Fund
P.O. Box 3636
Grand Rapids, MI 49501-3636
County: Kent
Application address: c/o Fifth Third Bank, 640
Pasquinelli Dr., Westmont, IL 60559-5568

Established in IL.
Grantmaker type: Independent foundation.
Financial data (yr. ended 12/31/09): Assets,
$734,970 (M); expenditures, $62,428; total giving,
$52,606; qualifying distributions, $52,606; giving
activities include $52,606 for grants to individuals.
Purpose and activities: Scholarship awards to
graduates of Riverside-Brookfield High School,
Illinois for technical college or trade school
education expenses.
Fields of interest: Vocational education; Higher
education.
Type of support: Scholarships—to individuals.
Limitations: Applications accepted. Giving primarily
to residents of Brookfield, IL.
Application information: Application form required.
  Initial approach: Letter
  Deadline(s): May 1
Trustee: Fifth Third Bank.
EIN: 206956670

274
The Freeman Foundation
(formerly Westran Corporation Foundation)
5588 W. 32nd St.
Fremont, MI 49412-7723 (231) 924-3058
County: Newaygo
Contact: Rebecca Llewellyn, Mgr.

Established in MI.
Grantmaker type: Independent foundation.
Financial data (yr. ended 12/31/09): Assets,
$168,473 (M); expenditures, $21,795; total giving,
$17,500; qualifying distributions, $17,500; giving
activities include $17,500 for grants.
Fields of interest: Education; Health care; Human
services.
Type of support: General/operating support.
Limitations: Giving primarily in MI, with emphasis on
Fremont; some giving also in TN and VA. No grants
to individuals.
Application information: Application form not
required.
  Initial approach: Letter
  Deadline(s): None
Officer: Rebecca Llewellyn, Mgr.
EIN: 386048805

275
Twink Frey Charitable Trust
(doing business as Nokomis Foundation)
161 Ottawa Ave., N.W., Ste. 305-C
Grand Rapids, MI 49503-2710 (616) 451-0267
County: Kent
Contact: Mary Alice Williams

Established in MI.
Grantmaker type: Independent foundation.
Financial data (yr. ended 12/31/09): Assets,
$12,145,100 (M); gifts received, $85,000;
expenditures, $938,176; total giving, $246,668;
qualifying distributions, $729,049; giving activities
include $246,668 for 67 grants (high: $100,000;
low: $75).
Limitations: Giving primarily in western MI. No
support for religious organizations for religious
purposes. No grants to individuals; no funding for
scholarships, fellowships, medical research, capital
requests, endowments or conferences.
Application information:
  Initial approach: Proposal no more than 5 pages
  in length
  Deadline(s): None
Officers and Trustees: * Mary Caroline Frey,* Chair.;
Mary Alice Williams, Pres.; Jim McKay, Treas.;
Carroll Velie.
EIN: 261131263

276
Frey Foundation
40 Pearl St. N.W., Ste. 1100
Grand Rapids, MI 49503-3028 (616) 451-0303
County: Kent
Contact: Milton W. Rohwer, Pres.
FAX: (616) 451-8481; *E-mail:* contact@freyfdn.org;
URL: http://www.freyfdn.org

Established in 1974 in MI; endowed in 1988.
Donors: Edward J. Frey, Sr.†; Frances T. Frey†.
Grantmaker type: Independent foundation.
Financial data (yr. ended 12/31/09): Assets,
$123,390,443 (M); expenditures, $5,518,694;
total giving, $3,193,712; qualifying distributions,
$6,986,080; giving activities include $3,193,712
for 173 grants (high: $1,500,000; low: $50), and
$2,686,905 for 1 loan/program-related investment.
Purpose and activities: Priorities include promoting
healthy developmental outcomes for children in their
early years (0-6 years); support for land use planning
and growth management, and protection of natural
resources; stimulating the vitality, effectiveness,
and growth of community-based arts; encouraging
civic progress and leadership; and strengthening
philanthropy.
Fields of interest: Arts, cultural/ethnic awareness;
Arts, folk arts; Arts education; Visual arts;
Museums; Museums (art); Museums (children's);
Museums (ethnic/folk arts); Museums (history);
Museums (marine/maritime); Museums (natural
history); Museums (science/technology); Museums
(specialized); Performing arts; Performing arts
centers; Performing arts, dance; Performing arts,
ballet; Performing arts, theater; Performing arts,
theater (musical); Performing arts, music;
Performing arts, orchestras; Performing arts, opera;
Performing arts, music (choral); Performing arts,
music ensembles/groups; Performing arts,
education; Historic preservation/historical
societies; Arts; Education, reform; Education, early
childhood education; Child development, education;
Libraries (public); Environment, water pollution;
Environment, natural resources; Environment, water
resources; Environment, land resources; Botanical
gardens; Environment, beautification programs;
Environment; Animals/wildlife, preservation/
protection; Animals/wildlife, fisheries; Zoos/
zoological societies; Children/youth, services;
Children, day care; Children, services; Child
development, services; Family services; Family
services, parent education; Community
development, neighborhood development;
Community development, civic centers; Community
development, public/private ventures; Urban/
community development; Foundations (community);
Philanthropy/voluntarism.
Type of support: Capital campaigns; Land
acquisition; Program development; Seed money;
Research; Technical assistance; Employee
matching gifts.
Limitations: Applications accepted. Giving primarily
in Emmet, Charlevoix, and Kent counties, MI. No
support for sectarian charitable activity. No grants
to individuals, or for endowment funds, debt
retirement, general operating expenses,
scholarships, conferences, speakers, travel, or to
cover routine, current, or emergency expenses.
Publications: Application guidelines; Annual report.
Application information: Application form required
for all requests; online application available.
Application form required.
  Initial approach: Letter of inquiry or telephone
  Copies of proposal: 1
  Deadline(s): Feb. 15, May 15, Aug. 15, and Nov.
  15
  Board meeting date(s): Feb., May, Aug., and Nov.
Officers and Trustees: * David G. Frey,* Chair.; John
M. Frey,* Vice-Chair.; Milton W. Rohwer, Pres.;
Edward J. Frey, Jr.,* Secy.-Treas.; Mary Caroline
"Twink" Frey, Tr. Emeritus.
Number of staff: 5 full-time professional; 1 full-time
support.
EIN: 237094777
Selected grants: The following grants were reported
in 2008.
$750,000 to Grand Rapids Community Foundation,
Grand Rapids, MI. For Anonymous Advised Fund.
$550,000 to Saint Marys Health Care, Grand
Rapids, MI. For construction of the Hauenstein
Center, a new medical facility dedicated to diagnosis
and treatment of neuroscience disorders in addition
to other more traditional services.
$500,000 to University of Michigan, Ann Arbor, MI.
To establish Edward J. Frey Deanship.

$425,000 to Wedgwood Christian Services, Grand Rapids, MI. For Building Hope for Children Campaign.
$346,000 to Kent County Parks Foundation, Grand Rapids, MI. For Millennium Park Connections Project.
$100,000 to Frederik Meijer Gardens and Sculpture Park, Grand Rapids, MI. For Maintaining the Masterpiece Campaign.
$100,000 to Opera Grand Rapids, Grand Rapids, MI.
$48,000 to Council of Michigan Foundations, Grand Haven, MI. For 36th Annual Conference Speaker.
$35,000 to West Michigan Environmental Action Council Education Foundation, Grand Rapids, MI. For Opening Doors to a Sustainable Future project.
$25,000 to North Central Michigan College Foundation, Petoskey, MI. For Health Education and Science Center facility.

277
The Fruehauf Foundation
c/o Sentinel Trust
2001 Kirby Dr., Ste. 1200
Houston, TX 77019-6081
County: Harris
Application address: c/o Dian Stallings, 100 Maple Park Blvd., Ste. 106, St. Clair Shores, MI 48081, tel.: (586) 774-5130

Incorporated in 1968 in MI.
Donors: Barbara F. Bristol; Angela Fruehauf; Harvey C. Fruehauf, Jr.; Susanne M. Fruehauf.
Grantmaker type: Independent foundation.
Financial data (yr. ended 12/31/09): Assets, $4,653,308 (M); expenditures, $260,783; total giving, $235,000; qualifying distributions, $247,056; giving activities include $235,000 for 74 grants (high: $28,000; low: $200).
Fields of interest: Arts; Higher education; Theological school/education; Hospitals (general); Health care; Human services; Christian agencies & churches.
Type of support: General/operating support; Endowments; Program development.
Limitations: Applications accepted. Giving primarily in states where directors reside (FL, MA, MI, and VA). No grants to individuals.
Application information:
Initial approach: Letter
Deadline(s): None; applications reviewed monthly
Board meeting date(s): As required
Officers and Directors:* Harvey C. Fruehauf, Jr.,* Pres. and Treas.; Barbara F. Bristol,* V.P.; Bartley J. Rainey, V.P.; Virginia L. Kirila, Secy.; Martha S. Fruehauf; Harvey B. Wallace II.
EIN: 237015744
Selected grants: The following grants were reported in 2008.
$20,000 to Hillsdale College, Hillsdale, MI.
$20,000 to Houston Museum of Natural Science, Houston, TX.
$8,000 to Lost Tree Chapel, North Palm Beach, FL.
$7,500 to Lost Tree Village Charitable Foundation, North Palm Beach, FL.
$7,000 to Saint Martins Episcopal Church, Houston, TX.
$6,000 to Family Research Council, Washington, DC.
$6,000 to Gordon College, Wenham, MA.
$5,000 to Mayo Clinic Rochester, Rochester, MN.
$2,500 to Peabody Essex Museum, Salem, MA.

$1,000 to Shelter for Help in Emergency, Charlottesville, VA.

278
The Albert & Dorothy Fruman Foundation
P.O. Box 250642
Franklin, MI 48025-0642
County: Oakland

Established in 1988 in MI.
Donor: Hubbell Steel.
Grantmaker type: Independent foundation.
Financial data (yr. ended 12/31/09): Assets, $279,364 (M); expenditures, $15,408; total giving, $15,037; qualifying distributions, $15,037; giving activities include $15,037 for grants.
Fields of interest: Higher education; Jewish federated giving programs; Catholic agencies & churches; Jewish agencies & synagogues.
Limitations: Giving primarily in MI.
Officers: Dorothy Fruman, Pres.; Lee Fruman, V.P. and Secy.-Treas.
EIN: 386109134

279
Fund for Cancer Research
28595 Orchard Lake Rd., Ste. 110
Farmington Hills, MI 48334-1625
(248) 443-5800
County: Oakland
Contact: Jeffrey D. Forman M.D., Pres.

Fund operates in conjunction with Harper Grace Hospital.
Grantmaker type: Independent foundation.
Financial data (yr. ended 09/30/09): Assets, $999,283 (M); gifts received, $262; expenditures, $250,253; total giving, $185,157; qualifying distributions, $225,689; giving activities include $185,157 for 3 grants (high: $150,000; low: $5,000).
Fields of interest: Higher education, university; Cancer research.
Type of support: Research.
Limitations: Applications accepted. Giving primarily in MI.
Application information:
Initial approach: Letter
Deadline(s): None
Officers and Directors:* Irving Laker,* Chair.; Jeffrey D. Forman, M.D., Pres.; Ken Honn, Ph.D., Secy.; Bruce Gershenson, Treas.; E. Jan Hartmann; Anita Mellen; Philip Minkin; Daniel Share; and 5 additional directors.
EIN: 382483703

280
G. II Charities
3333 Evergreen Dr. N.E., Ste. 201
Grand Rapids, MI 49525-9493
County: Kent
Contact: Ken Kregel

Established in MI.
Donor: Gordon Food Service Inc.
Grantmaker type: Independent foundation.
Financial data (yr. ended 12/31/09): Assets, $10,893,827 (M); gifts received, $8,000,000; expenditures, $6,198,020; total giving, $6,187,106; qualifying distributions, $6,187,106;

giving activities include $6,187,106 for 86 grants (high: $2,050,000; low: $3,000).
Fields of interest: Christian agencies & churches.
Limitations: Giving primarily in MI.
Application information:
Initial approach: Letter
Deadline(s): None
Officers: Ronald K. Williams, Pres.; James D. Gordon, V.P.; John M. Gordon, Jr., Secy.-Treas.
EIN: 900098975

281
Jon A. Gallant Foundation
3519 Wayland Dr.
P.O. Box 1675
Jackson, MI 49204-1675 (517) 784-2857
County: Jackson

Established in 1986 in MI.
Grantmaker type: Independent foundation.
Financial data (yr. ended 09/30/10): Assets, $42,488 (M); expenditures, $2,420; total giving, $2,000; qualifying distributions, $2,000; giving activities include $2,000 for 4 grants (high: $500; low: $500).
Fields of interest: Human services.
Limitations: Giving primarily in Jackson, MI.
Trustee: Thomas Gallant.
EIN: 386511184

282
The Harendra S. Gandhi Foundation
4694 Valleyview Dr.
West Bloomfield, MI 48323-3355
County: Oakland

Established in 1999 in MI.
Grantmaker type: Independent foundation.
Financial data (yr. ended 12/31/09): Assets, $13,191 (M); expenditures, $5,570; total giving, $5,470; qualifying distributions, $5,470; giving activities include $5,470 for 6 grants (high: $1,920; low: $100).
Application information: Unsolicited requests for funds not accepted.
EIN: 383502285

283
Harold & Ruth Garber Family Foundation
4402 Ramsgate Ln.
Bloomfield Hills, MI 48302-1642
County: Oakland
Contact: Stanley Garber, V.P.

Established in MI.
Donor: Ruth Garber.
Grantmaker type: Independent foundation.
Financial data (yr. ended 12/31/09): Assets, $145,584 (M); gifts received, $50,000; expenditures, $2,675; total giving, $2,500; qualifying distributions, $2,500; giving activities include $2,500 for grants.
Fields of interest: Jewish agencies & synagogues.
Limitations: Giving primarily in MI. No grants to individuals.
Application information:
Initial approach: Letter
Deadline(s): Dec. 1

Officers: Ruth Garber, Pres. and Treas.; Stanley Garber, V.P. and Secy.; Judith Freund, V.P.; Marjory Santacreu, V.P.
EIN: 383324811

284
Gardner Charitable Enterprises
7221 State Rd.
Burtchville, MI   48059-1816
County: St. Clair

Established in 2000 in MI.
Grantmaker type: Independent foundation.
Financial data (yr. ended 06/30/10): Assets, $25 (M); expenditures, $951; total giving, $500; qualifying distributions, $500; giving activities include $500 for grants.
Director: Donald Gardner.
EIN: 383441364

285
Colin Gardner Foundation
c/o KeyBank N.A.
34 N. Main St., 4th Fl.
Dayton, OH   45402-1994
County: Montgomery

Established in OH.
Grantmaker type: Independent foundation.
Financial data (yr. ended 12/31/09): Assets, $527,510 (M); expenditures, $33,057; total giving, $28,634; qualifying distributions, $28,634; giving activities include $28,634 for grants.
Fields of interest: Arts; Higher education; Education; Hospitals (general); Health care; Human services; American Red Cross; Youth, services; Christian agencies & churches.
Type of support: General/operating support.
Limitations: Applications accepted. Giving primarily in CA, CO, DE, FL, MI, NC, NH and OH. No grants to individuals.
Application information:
    Deadline(s): None
Trustees: Colin Gardner IV; Marilyn C. Gardner; Stephen V. Gardner; Elinor Lashley; Eugenie Millan; KeyBank N.A.
EIN: 316026289

286
Garland-Schut Foundation
487 W. Division St.
P.O. Box 246
Sparta, MI   49345-1046   (616) 887-7301
County: Kent
Contact: Warren H. Schut, Secy.-Treas.

Established in 1986 in MI.
Donors: Warren H. Schut; D. Maxine Schut; Dorothy Schut.
Grantmaker type: Independent foundation.
Financial data (yr. ended 12/31/08): Assets, $270,298 (M); gifts received, $10,408; expenditures, $20,720; total giving, $20,500; qualifying distributions, $20,500; giving activities include $20,500 for grants.
Fields of interest: Education; Community/economic development; Christian agencies & churches.
Limitations: Giving primarily in Sparta, MI. No grants to individuals.
Application information:

Initial approach: Letter
    Deadline(s): None
Officers: D. Maxine Schut, Pres.; Warren H. Schut, Secy.-Treas.
EIN: 382705026

287
Gary Sisters Foundation
107 W. Michigan Ave., PH
Kalamazoo, MI   49007-3970   (269) 344-6143
County: Kalamazoo
Contact: William T. Little, Tr.

Established in 1993 in MI.
Grantmaker type: Independent foundation.
Financial data (yr. ended 12/31/09): Assets, $959,982 (M); expenditures, $65,750; total giving, $56,750; qualifying distributions, $56,750; giving activities include $56,750 for grants.
Fields of interest: Higher education; Libraries (public); Education; Environment, natural resources; Human services; Children/youth, services.
Type of support: General/operating support.
Limitations: Giving primarily in Kalamazoo, MI. No grants to individuals.
Application information:
    Initial approach: Letter
    Deadline(s): None
Officers and Trustees:* George T. Schumacher,* Secy.; Shirley Palmer, Treas.; Mary Delehanty; Fran Little; William T. Little.
EIN: 383109660

288
Geiger Foundation for Cancer Research
3433 Oak Alley Ct., Ste. 103
Toledo, OH   43606-1380
County: Lucas
Contact: Mary Ellen Geiger, Tr.

Established in OH.
Grantmaker type: Independent foundation.
Financial data (yr. ended 12/31/09): Assets, $21,648 (M); gifts received, $1,190; expenditures, $3,060; total giving, $3,000; qualifying distributions, $3,000; giving activities include $3,000 for grants.
Fields of interest: Cancer research.
Type of support: General/operating support.
Limitations: Giving primarily in Ann Arbor, MI, and Toledo, OH. No grants to individuals.
Application information:
    Initial approach: Letter
    Deadline(s): None
Trustee: Mary Ellen Geiger.
EIN: 341325354

289
George Fund
P.O. Box 930408
Wixom, MI   48393-0408
County: Oakland
Contact: Janice Erichsen, Secy.
Application address: P.O. BOX 108, Birmingham, MI 48012

Established in 1965 in MI.
Donor: Henry E. George‡.
Grantmaker type: Independent foundation.

Financial data (yr. ended 12/31/09): Assets, $1,065,356 (M); expenditures, $76,494; total giving, $51,000; qualifying distributions, $51,000; giving activities include $51,000 for grants.
Fields of interest: Higher education; Environment, natural resources; Medical care, community health systems; Medical research; Family services; Residential/custodial care, hospices.
Type of support: General/operating support.
Limitations: Giving limited to MI. No grants to individuals.
Application information:
    Initial approach: Letter
    Deadline(s): Sept. 1
Officers: Richard Hinterman, Pres.; Linda L. Wroten, V.P.; Janice Erichsen, Secy.
EIN: 386115722

290
The Gerber Foundation
(formerly The Gerber Companies Foundation)
4747 W. 48th St., Ste. 153
Fremont, MI   49412-8119   (231) 924-3175
County: Newaygo
Contact: Catherine A. Obits, Prog. Mgr.
FAX: (231) 924-7906; E-mail: tgf@ncresa.org;
Additional e-mail (Catherine A. Obits): cobits@ncresa.org; URL: http:// www.gerberfoundation.org

Incorporated in 1952 in MI with funds from Gerber Products Co.
Grantmaker type: Independent foundation.
Financial data (yr. ended 12/31/10): Assets, $72,293,973 (M); expenditures, $3,882,089; total giving, $3,607,083; qualifying distributions, $3,855,710; giving activities include $3,222,133 for grants, $240,050 for grants to individuals, and $144,900 for employee matching gifts.
Purpose and activities: The foundation seeks to enhance the quality of life for infants and children by focusing on their nutrition, care, and development.
Fields of interest: Health care, infants; Pediatrics; Health organizations; Medical research, institute; Pediatrics research; Nutrition; Infants/toddlers; Children.
Type of support: Research; Scholarships—to individuals.
Limitations: Applications accepted. Giving on a national basis. No support for national child welfare or international based programs. No grants to individuals (except for scholarships), or for capital campaigns or operating support.
Publications: Application guidelines; Annual report (including application guidelines); Program policy statement.
Application information: The foundation prefers that applications be submitted only after receiving approval of a letter of inquiry. Application guidelines are available on foundation web site. All materials should be submitted on CD. Application form required.
    Initial approach: Letter of inquiry
    Copies of proposal: 7
    Deadline(s): Feb. 15 and Aug. 15; June 1 and Dec. 1 for letter of inquiry
    Board meeting date(s): Feb., May, Aug., Nov.
    Final notification: May and Nov.
Officers and Trustees:* Barbara J. Ivens,* Pres.; Fernando Flores-New,* V.P.; Tracy A. Baker,* Secy.; Stan M. VanderRoest,* Treas.; William L. Bush, M.D.; Ted C. Davis; Michael J. Ebert; Raymond J. Hutchinson, M.D.; John J. James, Esq.; Jane M.

Jeannero; David C. Joslin; Carolyn R. Morby; Nancy Nevin-Folino; Steven W. Poole.

Number of staff: 1 full-time professional; 1 part-time support.

EIN: 386068090

Selected grants: The following grants were reported in 2010.

$200,000 to Duke University, Durham, NC. For peripheral blood neutrophil gene expression during neonatal sepsis, payable over 2.00 years.

$196,630 to Helen DeVos Childrens Hospital, Grand Rapids, MI. For Benefits of Single Room Design for Neonates, payable over 2.00 years.

$192,680 to University of Colorado, Denver, CO. For use of Vitamin E to improve treatment for iron deficiency, payable over 2.00 years.

$181,685 to University of Colorado, Denver, CO. For Mannose requirements in Preterm and IUGR Neonates, payable over 2.00 years.

$148,459 to University of Miami, Miami, FL. For early detection of progressive kidney disease in preterm infants, payable over 2.00 years.

$100,000 to Indiana University, Indianapolis, IN. For lung growth after premature birth, payable over 2.00 years.

$50,000 to Friends of the Orphans, Chicago, IL. For Haiti Children's Hospital.

$20,000 to Hackley Community Care Center, Muskegon, MI. For Teen Health Center.

$12,000 to MGH Family Health Center, Muskegon Family Care, Muskegon, MI. For expanding dental clinic.

$10,536 to Baldwin Family Health Care, Baldwin, MI. For purchase of oral health kits for children.

291
The Gerberding/Fackler Family Foundation, Inc.

P.O. Box 6
Arcadia, MI 49613-0006 (231) 889-3203
County: Manistee
Contact: Miles C. Gerberding, Pres.

Established in 1999 in MI.

Donors: Miles C. Gerberding; Joan W. Gerberding.

Grantmaker type: Independent foundation.

Financial data (yr. ended 12/31/09): Assets, $214,323 (M); expenditures, $11,500; total giving, $11,500; qualifying distributions, $11,500; giving activities include $11,500 for 10 grants (high: $2,000; low: $750).

Purpose and activities: Support primarily for medical, youth, and Lutheran organizations; giving also for the arts and assistance for the abused and needy through food, shelter and counsel services.

Fields of interest: Arts; Health care; Children/youth, services; Family services, domestic violence; Protestant agencies & churches; Economically disadvantaged.

Limitations: Applications accepted. Giving primarily in MI.

Application information: Application form required.
Deadline(s): Nov. 30

Officers: Miles C. Gerberding, Pres.; Joan W. Fackler Gerberding, V.P.; Karla M. Smith, M.D., Secy.; Steven W. Fackler, Treas.

Directors: Greta I. Cowart; Brian K. Gerberding; Kent E. Gerberding; Deborah Holbrook.

EIN: 383493199

292
The Rollin M. Gerstacker Foundation

P.O. Box 1945
Midland, MI 48641-1945 (989) 631-6097
County: Midland
Contact: Ruth Wright

Incorporated in 1957 in MI.

Donors: Eda U. Gerstacker†; Carl A. Gerstacker†.

Grantmaker type: Independent foundation.

Financial data (yr. ended 12/31/09): Assets, $145,930,303 (M); expenditures, $8,627,110; total giving, $8,181,668; qualifying distributions, $8,314,028; giving activities include $8,181,668 for 302 grants (high: $300,000; low: $250).

Purpose and activities: Giving to assist community projects, with emphasis on the aged and the youth; grants also for higher education, health care, medical research, and hospitals.

Fields of interest: Higher education; Hospitals (general); Health care; Mental health/crisis services; Health organizations, association; Human services; Children/youth, services; Aging, centers/services; Government/public administration; Aging.

Type of support: General/operating support; Continuing support; Annual campaigns; Capital campaigns; Building/renovation; Equipment; Land acquisition; Endowments; Emergency funds; Seed money; Research; Matching/challenge support.

Limitations: Applications accepted. Giving primarily in Midland County, MI; giving also in OH. No grants to individuals, or for scholarships or fellowships; no loans.

Publications: Annual report.

Application information: Application form not required.
Initial approach: Letter
Copies of proposal: 1
Deadline(s): Prior to June 1 or Dec. 1
Board meeting date(s): May, Sept., and Dec.
Final notification: 1 month

Officers and Trustees:* Gail E. Lanphear,* Pres.; Lisa J. Gerstacker,* V.P. and Secy.; Alan W. Ott,* V.P. and Treas.; E.N. Brandt,* V.P.; William D. Schuette,* V.P.; Alexio R. Baum; Frank Gerace; Paula A. Liveris; Thomas L. Ludington; Paul F. Oreffice; William S. Stavropoulos.

EIN: 386060276

Selected grants: The following grants were reported in 2009.

$300,000 to Central Michigan University, Mount Pleasant, MI. For general operating support.

$300,000 to Saginaw Valley State University, University Center, MI. For general operating support.

$200,000 to Kings Daughters and Sons of Midland, Midland, MI. For general operating support.

$200,000 to Kings Daughters and Sons of Midland, Midland, MI. For general operating support.

$150,000 to Temple Theater Foundation, Saginaw, MI. For general operating support.

$97,000 to United Way of Midland County, Midland, MI. For general operating support.

$35,000 to Council on Domestic Violence and Sexual Assault, Midland, MI. For general operating support.

$30,000 to Southern University and A & M College, Baton Rouge, LA. For general operating support.

$15,000 to Midland Area Community Foundation, Midland, MI. For general operating support.

$10,000 to Midland Music Society, Midland, MI. For general operating support.

293
Herman & Irene Gertz Foundation

c/o Monroe Bank & Trust
102 E. Front St.
Monroe, MI 48161-2162 (734) 241-3431
County: Monroe

Established in 1966.

Donors: Irene Gertz†; Herman F. Gertz†.

Grantmaker type: Independent foundation.

Financial data (yr. ended 12/31/09): Assets, $1,146,367 (M); expenditures, $62,374; total giving, $51,000; qualifying distributions, $51,000; giving activities include $51,000 for grants.

Fields of interest: Historic preservation/historical societies; Higher education; Hospitals (general); Human services; Community/economic development; Christian agencies & churches.

Limitations: Giving primarily in MI; some giving also in Fort Myers, FL. No grants to individuals.

Application information: Application form not required.
Initial approach: Letter
Deadline(s): None

Officers: Alice Frank, Pres.; Marjorie Gertz, Secy.-Treas.

Trustee: Monroe Bank & Trust.

EIN: 386153472

294
Ruby L. Gibbs Charitable Trust

c/o Citizens Bank Wealth Management, N.A.
328 S. Saginaw St., M/C 001065
Flint, MI 48502-1923 (517) 797-4815
County: Genesee
Application addresses: c/o Ovid-Elsie High School, 8989 E. Colony Rd., Elsie, MI 48831, or c/o Arthur Hill High School, 3115 Mackinaw St., Saginaw, MI 49602-3221

Established in 1995 in MI.

Donor: Ruby Gibbs Trust.

Grantmaker type: Independent foundation.

Financial data (yr. ended 12/31/09): Assets, $1,143,005 (M); gifts received, $6,596; expenditures, $60,605; total giving, $45,967; qualifying distributions, $57,649; giving activities include $45,967 for 3 grants (high: $28,000; low: $8,983).

Purpose and activities: Scholarship awards to students graduating from Arthur Hill High School attending any accredited Michigan college and students graduating from Ovid-Elsie High School attending Central Michigan University; some giving to two Methodist churches.

Fields of interest: Scholarships/financial aid; Protestant agencies & churches.

Type of support: General/operating support; Scholarships—to individuals.

Limitations: Applications accepted. Giving limited to residents of MI.

Application information: Application form required.
Initial approach: Proposal
Deadline(s): May 1

Trustee: Citizens Bank Wealth Management, N.A.

EIN: 386658848

295
Kirk Gibson Foundation
15135 Charlevoix St.
Grosse Pointe Park, MI   48230-1007
County: Wayne

Donor: Kirk Gibson.
Grantmaker type: Independent foundation.
Financial data (yr. ended 12/31/08): Assets,
$17,501 (M); expenditures, $343; total giving, $0;
qualifying distributions, $0.
Fields of interest: Education.
Limitations: Giving primarily in MI.
Officers: Kirk Gibson, Pres.; JoAnn Gibson, Secy.;
Sandra Kempa, Treas.
EIN: 383353375

296
Muriel Gilbert Memorial Scholarship Fund
c/o KeyBank N.A.
4900 Tiedeman Rd., 1st Fl.
Brooklyn, OH   44144-2613
County: Cuyahoga
Application addresses: c/o Eastern Michigan Univ.,
Attn.: James Hause, Prof., Music Dept., 1215 Huron
River Dr., Ypsilanti, MI 48197-2351, or c/o Supt. of
Schools, Milan Area Schools, 920 North St., Milan,
MI 48160-1140

Established in 1988 in MI.
Grantmaker type: Independent foundation.
Financial data (yr. ended 09/30/09): Assets,
$749,493 (M); expenditures, $12,562; total giving,
$6,300; qualifying distributions, $6,300; giving
activities include $6,300 for grants to individuals.
Purpose and activities: Scholarship awards to a
full-time music major with a voice concentration at
Eastern Michigan University, and to graduating
seniors majoring in music from Milan, Michigan,
area high schools.
Fields of interest: Performing arts, music.
Type of support: Scholarship funds.
Limitations: Giving limited to the Milan, MI, area.
Application information: Application form required.
Deadline(s): Prior to end of academic year
Trustee: KeyBank N.A.
EIN: 386525706

297
Mary Williams Gillenwater Scholarship Fund
c/o JPMorgan Chase Bank, N.A.
P.O. Box 3038
Milwaukee, WI   53201-3038
County: Milwaukee
Application address: c/o Ypsilanti Schools Board of
Education, Attn.: Alan Dowdy, Deputy
Superintendent, 1885 Packard Rd., Ypsilanti, MI
48197-1846, tel.: (734) 995-8027

Established in 2007 in MI.
Donor: Mary N. Gillenwater†.
Grantmaker type: Independent foundation.
Financial data (yr. ended 10/31/09): Assets,
$741,646 (M); expenditures, $30,958; total giving,
$20,700; qualifying distributions, $20,700; giving
activities include $20,700 for grants.
Purpose and activities: Scholarship awards to
graduates of Ypsilanti Public Schools, Michigan.
Fields of interest: Higher education.
Type of support: Scholarships—to individuals.

Limitations: Applications accepted. Giving to
residents of Ypsilanti, MI.
Application information: Application form not
required.
Deadline(s): None
Trustee: JPMorgan Chase Bank, N.A.
EIN: 616335599

298
Herbert & Florence Gilles Scholarship Trust
c/o Citizens Bank
328 S. Saginaw St., M/C 002072
Flint, MI   48502-1923
County: Genesee
Application address: c/o Oscar Mendoza, Saginaw
Area Schools, 5802 Weiss, Saginaw, MI 48603,
tel.: (989) 797-6661

Established in 1999 in MI.
Donor: Herbert A. Gilles†.
Grantmaker type: Independent foundation.
Financial data (yr. ended 12/31/09): Assets,
$164,562 (M); expenditures, $12,189; total giving,
$6,100; qualifying distributions, $6,100; giving
activities include $6,100 for grants to individuals.
Purpose and activities: Scholarship awards to
students of Nouvel Catholic Central High School with
financial need.
Fields of interest: Higher education.
Type of support: Scholarships—to individuals.
Limitations: Applications accepted. Giving to
residents of Saginaw, MI.
Application information: Application form required.
Initial approach: Request application
Deadline(s): 2nd Mon. in May
Trustee: Citizens Bank, N.A.
EIN: 386738557

299
Irving S. Gilmore Foundation
136 E. Michigan Ave., Ste. 900
Kalamazoo, MI   49007-3915   (269) 342-6411
County: Kalamazoo
Contact: Richard M. Hughey, Jr., Exec. V.P. and
C.E.O.
FAX: (269) 342-6465; URL: http://
www.isgilmore.org

Established in 1972 in MI.
Donor: Irving S. Gilmore†.
Grantmaker type: Independent foundation.
Financial data (yr. ended 12/31/09): Assets,
$186,519,893 (M); expenditures, $10,415,991;
total giving, $8,437,614; qualifying distributions,
$9,357,075; giving activities include $8,397,013
for 165 grants (high: $1,000,000; low: $750;
average: $2,500–$200,000), and $40,601 for
employee matching gifts.
Purpose and activities: The mission of the
foundation is to support and enrich the cultural,
social, and economic life of the greater Kalamazoo,
MI, area. The priorities of the foundation are: 1) arts,
culture, and humanities; 2) human services; 3)
education and youth activities; 4) community
development; and 5) health and well-being.
Fields of interest: Performing arts; Arts; Education;
Health care; Youth development; Human services;
Community/economic development.
Type of support: General/operating support;
Continuing support; Annual campaigns; Capital

campaigns; Building/renovation; Equipment; Land
acquisition; Debt reduction; Emergency funds;
Program development; Conferences/seminars;
Publication; Seed money; Scholarship funds;
Technical assistance; Consulting services; Program
evaluation; Employee matching gifts; Matching/
challenge support.
Limitations: Applications accepted. Giving primarily
in the greater Kalamazoo, MI, area. No support for
political organizations. No grants to individuals.
Publications: Application guidelines; Annual report.
Application information: Organizations that are first
time foundation applicants or have not received
foundation funding since 2007 must contact the
foundation at least four weeks prior to an applicable
submission deadline. Please refer to foundation
web site for further guidelines and deadlines.
Application form not required.
Initial approach: Unbound proposal including
cover letter
Copies of proposal: 1
Deadline(s): Jan. 10, Mar. 1, May 2, July 1, Sept.
1 and Nov. 1
Board meeting date(s): Jan., Mar., May, July,
Sept., and Nov.
Final notification: Acknowledgement letter within
2 weeks
Officers and Trustees:* Richard M. Hughey, Jr.,
C.E.O. and Exec. V.P.; Floyd L. Parks,* Pres.;
Howard D. Kalleward,* 1st, V.P.; Janice C. Elliott,
V.P., Admin.; Russell L. Gabier,* Secy.; Charles D.
Wattles,* Treas.; Richard M. Hughey, Sr., Tr.
Emeritis; Judith H. Moore.
Number of staff: 3 full-time professional; 1 full-time
support; 2 part-time support.
EIN: 237236057
Selected grants: The following grants were reported
in 2008.
$1,750,000 to Irving S. Gilmore International
Keyboard Festival, Kalamazoo, MI. For operating
support.
$620,000 to Kalamazoo Regional Educational
Service Agency, Kalamazoo, MI. For operating
support.
$600,000 to Kalamazoo Public Schools,
Kalamazoo, MI. For Chenery Auditorium renovations.
$500,000 to YMCA and Outdoor Center, Sherman
Lake, Augusta, MI. For capital campaign.
$350,000 to Southwest Michigan First Corporation,
Kalamazoo, MI. For operating support.
$238,500 to Arts Council of Greater Kalamazoo,
Kalamazoo, MI. For operating support.
$50,000 to Communities in Schools Foundation,
Kalamazoo, Kalamazoo, MI. For operating support.
$30,000 to Fontana Chamber Arts, Kalamazoo, MI.
For Summer Music Festival.
$30,000 to Kalamazoo Eastside Neighborhood
Association, Kalamazoo, MI. For Through Our Eyes
program.
$20,000 to Kalamazoo Gay-Lesbian Resource
Center, Kalamazoo, MI. For operating support.

300
Norbert and Paula Gits Foundation
c/o Bessemer Trust Co., N.A.
630 5th Ave., 34th Fl.
New York, NY   10111-0100
County: New York
Contact: Philip C. Kalafatis, Trust Off., Bessemer
Trust Co., N.A.

Established in 2000 in FL.
Donors: Norbert Gits; Paula Gits.

Grantmaker type: Independent foundation.
Financial data (yr. ended 06/30/09): Assets, $468,742 (M); gifts received, $3,000; expenditures, $32,797; total giving, $26,497; qualifying distributions, $26,497; giving activities include $26,497 for grants.
Fields of interest: Education; Health care; Christian agencies & churches.
Limitations: Giving primarily in FL and MI.
Application information:
   Initial approach: Letter
   Deadline(s): None
Advisory Committee: Norbert Gits; Paula Gits.
Trustee: Bessemer Trust Co., N.A.
EIN: 527109505

301
Hal & Jean Glassen Memorial Foundation
3603 Breezy Point Dr.
Okemos, MI   48864-5923
County: Ingham

Established in 1991 in MI; funded in 1993.
Donor: Harold Glassen†.
Grantmaker type: Independent foundation.
Financial data (yr. ended 12/31/09): Assets, $4,161,334 (M); expenditures, $214,265; total giving, $120,000; qualifying distributions, $120,000; giving activities include $120,000 for grants.
Purpose and activities: Giving primarily for higher education.
Fields of interest: Elementary/secondary education; Higher education; Environmental education; Animals/wildlife, public education; Veterinary medicine.
Type of support: Building/renovation; Program development; Scholarship funds.
Limitations: Applications accepted. Giving primarily in MI, with emphasis on East Lansing. No grants to individuals.
Application information: Application form not required.
   Deadline(s): None
Officers: Neil A. McLean, Pres.; Tom Huggler, Secy.; Glen Miller, D.V.M., Treas.
Director: C. Allan Stewart.
EIN: 383012223
Selected grants: The following grants were reported in 2008.
$50,000 to Michigan State University, Fisheries and Wildlife Department, East Lansing, MI.
$50,000 to Michigan State University, East Lansing, MI.
$50,000 to Michigan State University, East Lansing, MI.
$25,000 to Humane Society, Capital Area, Lansing, MI.

302
Louis Glick Memorial & Charitable Trust
P.O. Box 1166
Jackson, MI   49204-1166   (517) 769-2529
County: Jackson

Established in 1968.
Donors: Glick Iron and Metal Co.; Alro Steel Corp.; Edith Glick†.
Grantmaker type: Independent foundation.
Financial data (yr. ended 12/31/09): Assets, $1,392,358 (M); gifts received, $12,000;

expenditures, $25,939; total giving, $19,800; qualifying distributions, $22,470; giving activities include $19,800 for 27 grants (high: $2,500; low: $50).
Purpose and activities: Grants for Jewish organizations, health, and human services. The trust also provides college loans to local high school graduates to attend a college in MI. Funding also for the arts, children, youth and social services, Jewish organizations and temples, and the United Way.
Fields of interest: Arts; Human services; Children/ youth, services; United Ways and Federated Giving Programs; Jewish federated giving programs; Jewish agencies & synagogues.
Type of support: Student loans—to individuals.
Limitations: Applications accepted. Giving primarily in Jackson County, MI.
Application information: Application form required.
   Initial approach: Proposal
   Deadline(s): May 15
Officer: Carlton L. Glick, Pres.
Trustee: Barry J. Glick.
EIN: 386156959

303
The Goad Foundation
(formerly The Louis C. Goad Foundation)
1840 Redding Rd.
Birmingham, MI   48009-1054   (248) 644-2086
County: Oakland
Contact: Thomas C. Goad, Pres.

Established in MI.
Donor: Clarissa A. Goad.
Grantmaker type: Independent foundation.
Financial data (yr. ended 12/31/09): Assets, $105,714 (M); expenditures, $11,328; total giving, $8,100; qualifying distributions, $8,100; giving activities include $8,100 for grants.
Fields of interest: Arts; Education; Health care; Protestant agencies & churches.
Limitations: Giving primarily in MI. No grants to individuals.
Application information:
   Initial approach: Letter
   Deadline(s): Varies
Officers: Thomas C. Goad, Pres.; Douglass C. Goad, V.P.; Theodore C. Goad, Secy.
Trustees: Elizabeth G. Enders; Linda C. Goad Larisch.
EIN: 381678220

304
God's Gift Foundation
P.O. Box 150467
Grand Rapids, MI   49515-0467
County: Kent
Application address: 4020 Silvergrass Dr. N.E., Grand Rapids, MI 49525-9551, tel.: (616) 308-5083

Established in 2003 in MI.
Donor: God's Gift Foundation of Ohio.
Grantmaker type: Independent foundation.
Financial data (yr. ended 12/31/09): Assets, $1,251,423 (M); gifts received, $1,500; expenditures, $48,248; total giving, $40,000; qualifying distributions, $40,500; giving activities include $40,000 for 6 grants (high: $15,000; low: $1,000).

Purpose and activities: Giving primarily to Christian churches and national Christian-focused organizations.
Fields of interest: Christian agencies & churches.
Limitations: Applications accepted. Giving primarily in MI. No grants to individuals.
Application information: Application form not required.
   Initial approach: Letter
   Deadline(s): None
Officers and Trustees:* Jeffrey W. Greene,* Pres.; Bonnie Jane Greene,* V.P.; Amanda L. Greene, Secy.-Treas.; C. Craig Covrett; Kenneth W. Greene.
EIN: 270038384

305
Harry & Bertha A. Goldman Foundation
37684 Enterprise Ct., Ste. A
Farmington Hills, MI   48331-3440
County: Oakland
Contact: Irving Goldman, Tr.
Application address: 32519 Scottsdale, Franklin, MI 48025-1755, tel.: (248) 851-2080

Established in MI.
Grantmaker type: Independent foundation.
Financial data (yr. ended 07/31/10): Assets, $21,926 (M); expenditures, $20,911; total giving, $20,000; qualifying distributions, $20,021; giving activities include $20,000 for 1 grant.
Type of support: Scholarships—to individuals.
Limitations: Applications accepted. Giving primarily in Detroit, MI.
Application information:
   Initial approach: Letter with brief resume of academic qualifications
   Deadline(s): None
Trustee: Irving Goldman.
EIN: 510147560

306
David Goodrich College Education Fund
c/o Fifth Third Bank
P.O. Box 3636
Grand Rapids, MI   49501-3636
County: Kent
Application address: c/o Elsie Area Supt. of Schools, Attn.: Wayne Petroelje, 8989 E. Colony Rd., Elsie, MI 48831-9724, tel. (989) 834-2271

Established in 1995 in MI.
Grantmaker type: Independent foundation.
Financial data (yr. ended 12/31/09): Assets, $640,837 (M); expenditures, $33,611; total giving, $27,630; qualifying distributions, $27,630; giving activities include $27,630 for grants to individuals.
Purpose and activities: Scholarship awards to needy students who have a high scholastic average and are living within a four-mile radius of Ovid, Michigan.
Fields of interest: Higher education.
Type of support: Scholarships—to individuals.
Limitations: Applications accepted. Giving limited to residents of the Ovid, MI, area.
Application information: Application form required.
   Deadline(s): May 1
Trustee: Fifth Third Bank.
EIN: 386658237

307
Gordon Christian Foundation
3333 Evergreen Dr. N.E., Ste. 201
Grand Rapids, MI 49525-9493 (616) 363-9209
County: Kent
Contact: Ken Kregel

Established in 1967 in MI.
Donors: Paul B. Gordon; Gordon Food Service, Inc.
Grantmaker type: Independent foundation.
Financial data (yr. ended 12/31/09): Assets,
$515,349 (M); expenditures, $85,935; total giving,
$85,506; qualifying distributions, $85,506; giving
activities include $85,506 for 19 grants (high:
$15,160; low: $300).
Purpose and activities: Giving for Christian
missionary support.
Fields of interest: Protestant agencies & churches.
Type of support: General/operating support.
Limitations: Giving primarily in FL, GA, MI and NY.
No grants to individuals.
Application information:
  Initial approach: Letter
  Deadline(s): None
Officers: Philip M. Gordon, Pres.; John M. Gordon,
Jr., V.P. and Treas.; Joyce G. Williams, Secy.
EIN: 386123463

308
The Frank & Doris Gordon Foundation
1917 Cross Bend St., N.E.
Grand Rapids, MI 49505-6397 (616) 361-0412
County: Kent
Contact: Doris M. Gordon, Pres.

Grantmaker type: Independent foundation.
Financial data (yr. ended 12/31/09): Assets,
$272,823 (M); expenditures, $11,803; total giving,
$10,800; qualifying distributions, $10,800; giving
activities include $10,800 for grants.
Purpose and activities: Giving primarily to
Protestant organizations, and for education.
Fields of interest: Higher education; Protestant
agencies & churches.
Limitations: Giving primarily in IL and MI. No grants
to individuals.
Application information:
  Initial approach: Letter
  Deadline(s): None
Officers: Doris M. Gordon, Pres. and Treas.; Joseph
P. Gordon, V.P.; Mary Beth DeKoning, Secy.
Directors: Gwenda Broucek; Kristina Davis.
EIN: 237068918

309
Gordy Foundation, Inc.
2656 W. Grand Blvd.
Detroit, MI 48208-1237 (313) 875-0656
County: Wayne
Contact: Robin Terry, Treas.

Established in 1967 in MI.
Donors: Berry Gordy; Jobete Music Co., Inc.
Grantmaker type: Independent foundation.
Financial data (yr. ended 06/30/09): Assets,
$2,432,337 (M); expenditures, $161,195; total
giving, $51,355; qualifying distributions, $51,355;
giving activities include $51,355 for grants.
Fields of interest: Museums (specialized);
Performing arts, music; Higher education, university;
Jewish agencies & synagogues.

Limitations: Applications accepted. Giving primarily
in Detroit, MI. No grants to individuals.
Application information: Application form not
required.
  Initial approach: Letter
  Deadline(s): None
Officers and Directors:* Esther G. Edwards,* C.E.O.
and Pres.; Robin Terry, Treas.; Berry Gordy,* Exec.
Dir.
Board Members: Robert Bullock; Elesha Cherry.
EIN: 386149511
Selected grants: The following grants were reported
in 2009.
$40,459 to Motown Historical Museum, Detroit, MI.

310
The Gornick Fund
P.O. Box 957
Bloomfield Hills, MI 48303-0957
County: Oakland
Contact: Diana Gornick Day, Pres.

Established about 1957 in MI.
Donor: Alan L. Gornick†.
Grantmaker type: Independent foundation.
Financial data (yr. ended 06/30/09): Assets,
$1,343,692 (M); expenditures, $91,593; total
giving, $69,585; qualifying distributions, $69,585;
giving activities include $69,585 for grants.
Fields of interest: Arts, cultural/ethnic awareness;
Higher education; Hospitals (general); Health
organizations, association; Human services;
Children/youth, services.
Type of support: Annual campaigns.
Limitations: Giving primarily in MI. No grants to
individuals.
Application information: Application form not
required.
  Initial approach: Letter
  Deadline(s): June 30
Officers and Trustees:* Diana Gornick Day,* Pres.;
Keith H. Gornick,* V.P. and Secy.; Margaret A.
Richard,* V.P.
EIN: 386063404
Selected grants: The following grants were reported
in 2005.
$6,875 to Community House Association,
Birmingham, MI.

311
Beatrice I. Goss Educational Testamentary Trust
c/o Fifth Third Bank
P.O. Box 3636
Grand Rapids, MI 49501-3636
County: Kent
Application address: c/o Fifth Third Bank, Cincinnati,
OH 45263, tel.: (800) 336-6782

Established around 1980 in IN.
Donor: Beatrice I. Goss†.
Grantmaker type: Independent foundation.
Financial data (yr. ended 09/30/09): Assets,
$145,303 (M); expenditures, $12,420; total giving,
$7,680; qualifying distributions, $7,680; giving
activities include $7,680 for grants to individuals.
Purpose and activities: Scholarship awards to
residents of Marshall County, Indiana.
Fields of interest: Higher education.
Type of support: Scholarships—to individuals.

Limitations: Giving limited to residents of Marshall
County, IN.
Application information: Application form required.
  Deadline(s): Mar. 15
Trustee: Fifth Third Bank.
EIN: 356361029

312
Rodger A. Graef Foundation
c/o U.S. Bank, N.A.
P.O. Box 3168
Portland, OR 97208-3168
County: Multnomah
Application address: c/o U.S. Bank, N.A.,
Attn.: Frank King, 2300 W. Sahara Ave., Las Vegas,
NV 89102

Established in NV.
Donor: Rodger Graef†.
Grantmaker type: Independent foundation.
Financial data (yr. ended 12/31/09): Assets,
$2,131,953 (M); gifts received, $37,454;
expenditures, $119,443; total giving, $78,000;
qualifying distributions, $78,000; giving activities
include $78,000 for grants.
Fields of interest: Human services; Children/youth,
services; Christian agencies & churches.
Type of support: General/operating support.
Limitations: Giving primarily in MI; some giving also
in CA. No grants to individuals.
Application information:
  Initial approach: Proposal
  Deadline(s): Contact the Foundation
Trustee: U.S. Bank, N.A.
EIN: 880485247
Selected grants: The following grants were reported
in 2007.
$20,000 to Whaley Childrens Center, Flint, MI.
$10,000 to Ann Arbor Teen Center, Ann Arbor, MI.
$10,000 to Holy Cross Childrens Services, Clinton,
MI.
$10,000 to New Urban Learning, Detroit, MI.
$10,000 to YMCA of Ann Arbor, Ann Arbor, MI.
$5,000 to Peace Neighborhood Center, Ann Arbor,
MI.

313
Granger Foundation
P.O. Box 22187
Lansing, MI 48909-7185 (517) 393-1670
County: Ingham
Contact: Eva Lee
E-mail: elee@grangerconstruction.com; URL: http://
www.grangerfoundation.org/

Established in 1978.
Donors: Granger Associates, Inc.; Granger
Construction Co.; and members of the Granger
family.
Grantmaker type: Independent foundation.
Financial data (yr. ended 12/31/09): Assets,
$9,426,284 (M); expenditures, $1,603,593; total
giving, $1,531,129; qualifying distributions,
$1,531,129; giving activities include $1,531,129
for 86 grants (high: $150,711; low: $30).
Purpose and activities: The foundation's primary
mission is to support Christ-centered activities. It
also supports efforts that enhance the lives of youth
in the community.

Fields of interest: Youth development; Human services; YM/YWCAs & YM/YWHAs; Christian agencies & churches; Youth.
Type of support: Annual campaigns; Capital campaigns.
Limitations: Applications accepted. Giving primarily in the greater Lansing and the Tri-County (Ingham, Eaton and Clinton counties), MI, areas. No grants to individuals, or for endowments, fundraising, social events, conferences, or exhibits; no grants for capital funds or improvements for churches or public schools.
Publications: Application guidelines; Annual report; Program policy statement.
Application information: Application guidelines and forms available on foundation web site. Application form required.
   Initial approach: Completed Request for Funding form
   Copies of proposal: 4
   Deadline(s): Apr. 15 and Oct. 15
   Board meeting date(s): Semiannually
Trustees: Alton L. Granger; Donna Granger; Janice Granger; Jerry P. Granger; Lynne Granger; Ronald K. Granger.
EIN: 382251879
Selected grants: The following grants were reported in 2006.
$70,000 to Volunteers of America.
$50,000 to Youth for Christ.
$20,000 to Youth for Christ.

314
Granger III Foundation, Inc.
P.O. Box 27185
Lansing, MI   48909-7185
County: Ingham
Contact: Todd J. Granger, Secy.
Application address: 16980 Wood Rd., Lansing, MI 48906-1044, tel.: (517) 372-2800

Established in 2000 in OH.
Donors: Granger Electric; Granger Energy; Granger Associates, Inc.; Granger Holdings, LLC; Granger Energy of Decatur, LLC; Granger Energy of Honeybrook, LLC; Granger Meadows, LLC.
Grantmaker type: Independent foundation.
Financial data (yr. ended 12/31/09): Assets, $2,942,633 (M); gifts received, $745,000; expenditures, $964,485; total giving, $958,200; qualifying distributions, $958,200; giving activities include $958,200 for grants.
Purpose and activities: Giving primarily for a Christian school as well as for other Christian organizations; funding also for human services, education, volunteer organizations, and YMCAs.
Fields of interest: Theological school/education; Human services; YM/YWCAs & YM/YWHAs; Philanthropy/voluntarism; Christian agencies & churches.
Limitations: Giving primarily in the Lansing, MI, area. No grants to individuals.
Application information:
   Initial approach: Letter
   Deadline(s): None
Officers and Directors:* Thomas D. Hofman,* Pres.; Ray A. Easton,* V.P.; Todd J. Granger,* Secy.; Keith L. Granger,* Treas.; Randy J. Russ; Joel M. Zylstra.
EIN: 383555568
Selected grants: The following grants were reported in 2007.
$120,147 to Lansing Christian School, Lansing, MI.

$115,000 to Calvin College, Grand Rapids, MI.
$93,000 to Schwab Charitable Fund, San Francisco, CA.
$30,000 to United Way.
$25,000 to Volunteers of America, Alexandria, VA.
$11,500 to Fellowship of Christian Athletes, Jenison, MI.
$10,000 to Second Mile, State College, PA.

315
Greater Ann Arbor Omega Foundation
P.O. Box 7421
Ann Arbor, MI   48107
County: Washtenaw
Contact: Melvin Anglin, Chair.
Application address: Melvin Anglin, 6830 Central City Pkwy., Westland, MI 48185

Donors: Dorian Moore; Sidney L. Moore†.
Grantmaker type: Independent foundation.
Financial data (yr. ended 12/31/09): Assets, $12,169 (M); gifts received, $5,000; expenditures, $1,854; total giving, $875; qualifying distributions, $1,854; giving activities include $875 for 3 grants to individuals (high: $500; low: $125).
Application information: Application form required.
   Initial approach: Proposal
   Deadline(s): None
Officers: Melvin Anglin, Chair.; Paul Ajegba, Vice-Chair.; Robert Brown, Co-Treas.; Marvin Perry, Co-Treas.
EIN: 383297827

316
Green Vision Foundation
P.O. Box 758
Saugatuck, MI   49453-0758   (616) 857-1247
County: Allegan
Contact: Suzy A. Richardson, Dir.

Established in 1997 in MI.
Donor: Phillip D. Miller.
Grantmaker type: Independent foundation.
Financial data (yr. ended 12/31/09): Assets, $82,861 (M); gifts received, $25,000; expenditures, $13,106; total giving, $12,420; qualifying distributions, $12,420; giving activities include $12,420 for grants.
Fields of interest: Performing arts, music; Environment; Human services.
Limitations: Giving primarily in MI.
Application information: Application form not required.
   Deadline(s): None
Directors: Phillip D. Miller; Suzy A. Richardson.
EIN: 411876575

317
Greene View Foundation
3662 Tartan Cir.
Portage, MI   49024-7889
County: Kalamazoo
Contact: Lois A. Stuck, Pres.

Established in 1988 in MI.
Grantmaker type: Independent foundation.
Financial data (yr. ended 12/31/09): Assets, $225,780 (M); expenditures, $11,364; total giving, $9,500; qualifying distributions, $9,500; giving activities include $9,500 for grants.

Fields of interest: Children/youth, services; Christian agencies & churches.
Type of support: General/operating support.
Limitations: Giving primarily in MI, with some emphasis on Kalamazoo.
Application information:
   Initial approach: Proposal
   Deadline(s): June 30
Officers and Director:* Lois A. Stuck,* Pres.; David T. Stuck, Secy.-Treas.
EIN: 382769679

318
Donald C. & Doris G. Griffith Foundation
1701 Clear Creek Ct. N.E.
Grand Rapids, MI   49505-7700   (616) 949-5759
County: Kent
Contact: Doris G. Griffith, Pres.

Established in 1984 in MI.
Donor: Doris G. Griffith.
Grantmaker type: Independent foundation.
Financial data (yr. ended 12/31/09): Assets, $223,782 (M); gifts received, $40,000; expenditures, $58,395; total giving, $55,225; qualifying distributions, $55,225; giving activities include $55,225 for grants.
Fields of interest: Arts; Education; Environment, natural resources; Animals/wildlife; Human services; United Ways and Federated Giving Programs; Christian agencies & churches.
Limitations: Giving primarily in MI, with some emphasis on Grand Rapids. No grants to individuals.
Application information:
   Initial approach: Letter
   Deadline(s): None
Officers and Directors:* Doris G. Griffith,* Pres.; Kay G. Hammond,* V.P.; Martha A. O'Brien,* Secy.; Kim A. Griffith,* Treas.; Douglas T. Griffith.
EIN: 382566349

319
The Grimaldi Foundation
30100 Telegraph Rd., Ste. 306
Bingham Farms, MI   48025-5804
County: Oakland

Established in 1990 in MI.
Donors: Thomas J. Grimaldi; Ruth E. Grimaldi.
Grantmaker type: Independent foundation.
Financial data (yr. ended 12/31/09): Assets, $764,050 (M); expenditures, $55,776; total giving, $46,530; qualifying distributions, $46,530; giving activities include $46,530 for grants.
Fields of interest: Secondary school/education; Theological school/education; Christian agencies & churches; Catholic agencies & churches.
Type of support: Scholarship funds; Scholarships—to individuals.
Limitations: Giving primarily to residents of Macomb, Oakland, and Wayne counties, MI.
Application information:
   Initial approach: Letter or proposal for grants; essay, copies of academic records, and references for scholarships
   Deadline(s): None
Directors: Thomas J. Grimaldi; Paul L. McCoy.
EIN: 382938393
Selected grants: The following grants were reported in 2006.
$5,000 to Kettering University, Flint, MI.

$750 to Multiple Sclerosis Society, National, Southfield, MI.
$500 to Angels Place, Southfield, MI.
$500 to Capuchin Soup Kitchen, Detroit, MI.
$500 to Salvation Army National Headquarters, Alexandria, VA.
$300 to Leukemia & Lymphoma Society, Pittsfield, MA.
$200 to American Cancer Society, Oklahoma City, OK.

320
Charles Grosberg Foundation
555 S. Federal Hwy., Ste. 250
Boca Raton, FL 33432-6033
County: Palm Beach
Contact: Merwin K. Grosberg, Pres.

Established in 1948 in MI.
Grantmaker type: Independent foundation.
Financial data (yr. ended 12/31/07): Assets, $35,525 (M); gifts received, $100; expenditures, $150,906; total giving, $148,987; qualifying distributions, $148,987; giving activities include $148,987 for 17 grants (high: $85,342; low: $100).
Purpose and activities: Giving primarily to Jewish agencies.
Fields of interest: Higher education; Jewish federated giving programs; Jewish agencies & synagogues.
Limitations: Giving primarily in MI and NY. No grants to individuals.
Application information:
  Initial approach: Letter
  Deadline(s): None
Officers: Merwin K. Grosberg, Pres.; Susan Bloom, Secy.-Treas.
EIN: 386088859
Selected grants: The following grants were reported in 2008.
$1,500 to JARC, Farmington Hills, MI.

321
The Guilliom Family Foundation
P.O. Box 5009
Waddy, KY 40076-0509 (502) 829-0778
County: Shelby
Contact: Heather Guilliom, Vice-Chair.

Established in KY.
Grantmaker type: Independent foundation.
Financial data (yr. ended 12/31/09): Assets, $73,291 (M); gifts received, $19,924; expenditures, $5,398; total giving, $5,398; qualifying distributions, $5,398; giving activities include $5,398 for grants.
Fields of interest: Children, services.
Limitations: Applications accepted. Giving primarily in CO, HI, KY and MI. No grants to individuals.
Officers: Gregory Guilliom, Chair.; Heather Guilliom, Vice-Chair.; Anthony Guilliom, Secy.
EIN: 616275892

322
Mary L. Gumaer Scholarship Foundation
c/o Fifth Third Bank
P.O. Box 3636
Grand Rapids, MI 49501-3636 (989) 862-5820
County: Kent
Application address: Supt. of Schools, 8989 Colony Rd., Elsie, MI 48831, tel.: (989) 862-5820

Established in 2000 in MI.
Donor: Mary L. Grumaer.
Grantmaker type: Independent foundation.
Financial data (yr. ended 12/31/09): Assets, $274,865 (M); expenditures, $18,366; total giving, $14,660; qualifying distributions, $14,935; giving activities include $14,660 for 27 grants to individuals (high: $550; low: $360).
Purpose and activities: Scholarships awarded to graduating seniors of Ovid-Elsie High School who are entering college as a full-time student.
Fields of interest: Higher education.
Type of support: Scholarships—to individuals.
Limitations: Applications accepted. Giving limited to residents in the Ovid-Elsie, MI, area.
Application information: Application form required.
  Deadline(s): May 1
Trustee: Fifth Third Bank.
EIN: 386751392

323
The Christopher L. & M. Susan Gust Foundation
c/o Wolverine Trading, LLC
175 W. Jackson Blvd., 2nd Fl.
Chicago, IL 60604-2615 (312) 884-3724
County: Cook
Contact: Christopher L. Gust, Dir.

Established in 2001 in IL.
Donor: Christopher L. Gust.
Grantmaker type: Independent foundation.
Financial data (yr. ended 12/31/09): Assets, $6,068,274 (M); gifts received, $15; expenditures, $569,916; total giving, $513,000; qualifying distributions, $558,406; giving activities include $513,000 for 22 grants (high: $225,000; low: $500).
Fields of interest: Elementary/secondary education; Higher education; Human services.
Type of support: Program development; General/operating support; Capital campaigns.
Limitations: Giving primarily in Chicago, IL; some funding also in Ann Arbor, MI.
Application information:
  Initial approach: Letter
  Deadline(s): None
Directors: Diane Edmundson; Christopher L. Gust; M. Susan Gust.
EIN: 611405669
Selected grants: The following grants were reported in 2009.
$225,000 to Chicago Public Schools, Chicago, IL.
$175,000 to University of Michigan, Ann Arbor, MI.
$28,500 to Sacred Heart Schools, Chicago, IL.
$2,500 to Northwestern University, Evanston, IL.

324
Ben Gutierrez and Frances Gutierrez Family Foundation
5299 E. 28th St.
Au Gres, MI 48703-9434
County: Arenac

Established in 2007 in MI.
Grantmaker type: Independent foundation.
Financial data (yr. ended 12/31/07): Assets, $674 (M); gifts received, $2,194; expenditures, $1,524; total giving, $1,500; qualifying distributions, $1,500; giving activities include $1,500 for grants to individuals.
Directors: Ben Gutierrez; Frances Gutierrez.
EIN: 352309217

325
Rita Guy Christian Music Ministry, Inc.
5338 Lawn Arbor Dr.
Houston, TX 77066-1606
County: Harris
Contact: Rev. Clara M. Lewis, Treas.

Established in 1985 in CA.
Grantmaker type: Independent foundation.
Financial data (yr. ended 12/31/09): Assets, $29,164 (M); expenditures, $891; total giving, $0; qualifying distributions, $0.
Purpose and activities: To support and promote the art form of Christian music and the related performing arts of dance and drama in the worship of God by providing education, instruction, and performance opportunities on a non-denominational basis.
Fields of interest: Performing arts, music; Christian agencies & churches.
Limitations: Giving primarily in MI; giving also in TX. No grants to individuals.
Application information: Application form required.
  Initial approach: Proposal
  Copies of proposal: 7
  Deadline(s): Varies
Officers: Gordon E. Nelson, Pres.; Harry Platt, Secy.; Rev. Clara M. Lewis, Treas.
Director: Erik Winter.
EIN: 770101026

326
Guzikowski Family Foundation
231 S. LaSalle St., IL1-231-14-19
Chicago, IL 60697-0001
County: Cook
Contact: Frank Guzikowski, Tr.
Application address: 1012 Chancery Ln. S., Nashville, TN 37205

Established in 1986 in TN.
Donors: Frank Guzikowski; Jane Guzikowski; Edward Grabowski; Marjorie Grabowski.
Grantmaker type: Independent foundation.
Financial data (yr. ended 11/30/09): Assets, $298,756 (M); gifts received, $12,000; expenditures, $62,998; total giving, $58,000; qualifying distributions, $59,970; giving activities include $58,000 for 27 grants (high: $10,000; low: $300).
Fields of interest: Higher education; Catholic federated giving programs; Catholic agencies & churches.
Type of support: General/operating support.

Limitations: Applications accepted. Giving primarily in TN, with some giving in KY and MI. No grants to individuals.
Application information: Application form required.
Initial approach: Letter
Deadline(s): None
Trustees: Frank Guzikowski; Bank of America, N.A.
EIN: 626195892

327
H.I.S. Foundation
13919 S. West Bay Shore Dr., Ste. G-1
Traverse City, MI 49684-6216
County: Grand Traverse
Contact: Dale M. Nielson, V.P.

Established in 1990 in MI.
Donors: Nielson Enterprises Corp.; Dale M. Nielson.
Grantmaker type: Independent foundation.
Financial data (yr. ended 12/31/09): Assets, $1,476 (M); gifts received, $468,019; expenditures, $7,992; total giving, $0; qualifying distributions, $0.
Purpose and activities: Giving primarily for Protestant and Roman Catholic agencies, as well as for Christian education, pro-life causes, conservative public policy, and entrepreneurship assistance.
Fields of interest: Education; Youth development, religion; Residential/custodial care, hospices; Civil liberties, right to life; Business/industry; Social sciences, public policy; Christian agencies & churches.
International interests: China; Mexico.
Type of support: Continuing support; Income development; Annual campaigns; Capital campaigns; Building/renovation; Equipment; Land acquisition; Seed money; Fellowships; Scholarship funds; Matching/challenge support.
Limitations: Applications accepted. Giving worldwide, with emphasis on Antrim, Bonzie, Crawford, Grand Traverse, Kalkaska and Leelanau counties, MI. No support for liberal public policy, or religious organizations other than faith-based Christian.
Application information: Application form not required.
Initial approach: Letter
Copies of proposal: 1
Deadline(s): None
Board meeting date(s): Dec.
Officers and Directors:* Melvin K. Nielson,* Pres.; Dale M. Nielson,* V.P.; Ruth E. Nielson,* Secy.-Treas.
EIN: 382953594
Selected grants: The following grants were reported in 2005.
$60,918 to Bay Pointe Community Church, Traverse City, MI.
$35,920 to Father Fred Foundation, Traverse City, MI.
$22,000 to Right to Life of Michigan Educational Fund, Farmington Hills, MI.
$12,333 to Goodwill Industries, Burton, MI.
$10,500 to Faith Reformed Church, Traverse City, MI.
$5,167 to Bethany Christian Services, Grand Rapids, MI.
$5,000 to Salvation Army, MI.
$5,000 to Womens Resource Center, Grand Rapids, MI.
$4,000 to Convoy of Hope, Springfield, MO.

328
H.O.N.O.R. Foundation
19428 Gill Rd.
Livonia, MI 48152-1117
County: Wayne

Established in 2003.
Grantmaker type: Independent foundation.
Financial data (yr. ended 12/31/09): Assets, $1 (M); expenditures, $20,973; total giving, $20,676; qualifying distributions, $20,676; giving activities include $20,676 for grants.
Officers: Gary R. Thomas, Pres.; Laura L. Thomas, V.P.
EIN: 320080904

329
Carroll J. Haas Foundation
27020 Simpson Rd.
P.O. Box 248
Mendon, MI 49072-0248
County: St. Joseph
Contact: Carroll J. Haas, Pres. and Treas.

Established in 1998 in MI.
Donor: Carroll J. Haas.
Grantmaker type: Independent foundation.
Financial data (yr. ended 03/31/10): Assets, $2,313,038 (M); expenditures, $44,004; total giving, $28,250; qualifying distributions, $28,250; giving activities include $28,250 for grants.
Fields of interest: Higher education, university; Animals/wildlife, preservation/protection; Agriculture; Boy scouts; Human services; Catholic agencies & churches.
Limitations: Applications accepted. Giving primarily in MI.
Application information: Application form not required.
Initial approach: Letter
Deadline(s): None
Officers: Carroll J. Haas, Pres. and Treas.; Robert G. Haas, Secy.
Directors: Kathleen A. Gray; Carroll J. Haas II; James H. Haas; Theresa Haas; Mary Jo McKee.
EIN: 383415066
Selected grants: The following grants were reported in 2009.
$51,000 to University of Michigan, Ann Arbor, MI.
$2,000 to Ministry with Community, Kalamazoo, MI.
$1,000 to Kalamazoo Nature Center, Kalamazoo, MI.

330
Clarence & Marion Wiggins Haas Scholarship Fund
c/o Citizens Bank Wealth Mgmt., N.A.
328 S. Saginaw St., MC 002072
Flint, MI 48502-1923
County: Genesee
Application address: c/o Saginaw High School, 3100 Webber St., Saginaw, MI 48601, tel.: (989) 776-0421

Established in MI.
Grantmaker type: Independent foundation.
Financial data (yr. ended 12/31/09): Assets, $77,804 (M); expenditures, $4,192; total giving, $250; qualifying distributions, $2,507; giving activities include $250 for 1 grant to an individual.

Purpose and activities: Scholarship awards to graduates of Saginaw High School, Michigan who rate the highest in academics, citizenship, and character.
Fields of interest: Higher education.
Type of support: Scholarships—to individuals.
Limitations: Applications accepted. Giving limited to Saginaw, MI.
Application information: Application form required.
Initial approach: Letter
Deadline(s): May 1
Trustee: Citizens Bank.
EIN: 386219139

331
The Antoon and Nita Haboush Foundation
c/o National City Bank
P.O. Box 94651
Cleveland, OH 44101-4651
County: Cuyahoga
Application addresses: c/o The Arab American Community Center, 2651 Saulino Ct., Dearborn, MI 48120-1556, tel.: (313) 842-7010

Established in 2001 in MI.
Donor: Antoon & Nita Haboush Charitable Trust.
Grantmaker type: Independent foundation.
Financial data (yr. ended 12/31/09): Assets, $192,369 (M); expenditures, $10,776; total giving, $5,000; qualifying distributions, $5,000; giving activities include $5,000 for grants.
Purpose and activities: Scholarships for economically needy Christian Arabic Americans, as chosen by the selected educational institutions.
Type of support: Scholarship funds.
Limitations: Applications accepted. Giving primarily in MI.
Application information: Application form required.
Initial approach: Letter or telephone
Deadline(s): None
Trustee: National City Bank.
EIN: 386773712

332
Hagen Family Foundation
2760 N.E. 16th St.
Fort Lauderdale, FL 33304-1619
County: Broward
Contact: David F. Hagen, Pres.
E-mail: webmaster@hagenfamilyfoundation.org;
URL: http://www.hagenfamilyfoundation.org

Established in 1999 in MI.
Donors: David F. Hagen; Virginia Hagen.
Grantmaker type: Independent foundation.
Financial data (yr. ended 12/31/09): Assets, $1,479,216 (M); expenditures, $140,902; total giving, $90,417; qualifying distributions, $90,417; giving activities include $90,417 for grants.
Fields of interest: Arts; Education, reading; Education; Environment; Human services; Religion.
Type of support: Program development; Conferences/seminars; Seed money; Curriculum development; Scholarship funds; Technical assistance; Matching/challenge support.
Limitations: Giving in the U.S., including but not limited to CA, CO, FL, IL and MI. No support for on-going programs. No grants to individuals, for annual drives, capital campaigns, research or scholarships.

Application information: See foundation web site for application guidelines, formats, and timeline for current grant cycle. Application form required.
Initial approach: Letter of intent
Copies of proposal: 4
Deadline(s): April for letter of intent, June for full proposal
Board meeting date(s): Aug. 10
Final notification: Aug.
Officers and Directors:* David F. Hagen,* Pres. and Treas.; Virginia Hagen,* V.P.; Patricia Born,* Secy.; Christopher Born; Rev. Dr. Andrew Hagen; Laura C. Hagen; Dr. Susan Dingle Hagen.
EIN: 383482329
Selected grants: The following grants were reported in 2008.
$20,000 to American Risk and Insurance Association, Malvern, PA.
$20,000 to Nova Southeastern University, Fort Lauderdale, FL.
$19,000 to Museum of Discovery and Science, Fort Lauderdale, FL.
$15,000 to Florida Grand Opera, Miami, FL.
$10,000 to Evangelical Lutheran Church in America, Chicago, IL.
$10,000 to University of Michigan, Ann Arbor, MI.
$7,500 to Warm Blankets Childrens Foundation, Rolling Meadows, IL.
$5,000 to Habitat for Humanity of South Palm Beach County, Delray Beach, FL.
$5,000 to Santa Monica High School, Santa Monica, CA.

333
The Haggard Foundation
P.O. Box 2256
Traverse City, MI   49685-1067
County: Grand Traverse
Contact: Ward M. Haggard, Jr., Pres.
Application address: P.O. Box 56248, Houston, TX 77256-6248

Established in 1986 in MI.
Donors: Ward M. Haggard, Jr.; Dee Bowman Haggard.
Grantmaker type: Independent foundation.
Financial data (yr. ended 12/31/09): Assets, $97,161 (M); expenditures, $4,061; total giving, $2,500; qualifying distributions, $2,500; giving activities include $2,500 for grants.
Fields of interest: Education; Protestant agencies & churches.
Type of support: General/operating support.
Application information:
Initial approach: Letter
Deadline(s): None
Officers: Ward M. Haggard, Jr., Pres.; Dee Bowman Haggard, Secy.-Treas.
EIN: 382711484

334
William and Sharon Hahn Foundation, Inc.
500 S. Opdyke Rd.
Pontiac, MI   48343-3186   (248) 332-9300
County: Oakland
Contact: Sharon Hahn, Secy.

Established in 2000 in MI.
Donors: Sharon Hahn; William Hahn.
Grantmaker type: Independent foundation.

Financial data (yr. ended 12/31/10): Assets, $1,043 (M); gifts received, $70,000; expenditures, $70,975; total giving, $70,000; qualifying distributions, $70,000; giving activities include $70,000 for 9 grants (high: $50,000; low: $1,000).
Purpose and activities: Giving primarily for family and other human services.
Fields of interest: Arts, association; Crime/violence prevention, child abuse; Human services; Children/ youth, services; Family services; Women, centers/ services; United Ways and Federated Giving Programs.
Limitations: Applications accepted. Giving primarily in MI, with emphasis on Pontiac. No grants to individuals.
Application information: Application form is currently in development.
Officers: William Hahn, Pres. and Treas.; Sharon Hahn, Secy.
EIN: 383549321
Selected grants: The following grants were reported in 2009.
$10,000 to Bound Together, Pontiac, MI.
$10,000 to Child Abuse and Neglect Council of Oakland County, Pontiac, MI.
$10,000 to Common Ground Sanctuary, Bloomfield Hills, MI.
$10,000 to Furniture Bank of Oakland County, Pontiac, MI.
$10,000 to HAVEN, Pontiac, MI.
$10,000 to Oakland Family Services, Pontiac, MI.
$10,000 to Oakland Livingston Human Service Agency, Pontiac, MI.

335
Halcyon Foundation
663 Halcyon Ct.
Ann Arbor, MI   48103-1579   (517) 782-0557
County: Washtenaw
Contact: Thomas R. Larson, Treas.

Established in 2002 in MI.
Donor: Thomas R. Larson.
Grantmaker type: Independent foundation.
Financial data (yr. ended 12/31/09): Assets, $45,879 (M); expenditures, $3,170; total giving, $2,550; qualifying distributions, $2,550; giving activities include $2,550 for grants.
Fields of interest: Education; Human services.
Limitations: Giving primarily in MI. No grants to individuals.
Application information:
Initial approach: Letter
Deadline(s): None
Officers and Directors:* Claudia K. Larson,* Pres.; Jonathan B. Larson,* V.P.; Scott T. Larson,* V.P.; Elizabeth A. Moraw,* Secy.; Thomas R. Larson,* Treas.
EIN: 300012887

336
Marcella L. Hamar Scholarship
P.O. Box 380
Dollar Bay, MI   49922-0380
County: Houghton
Application address: c/o Superintendent, 41585 U.S. Hwy. 41, Chassell, MI 49913

Reorganized as a private foundation in 2003.
Grantmaker type: Independent foundation.

Financial data (yr. ended 12/31/09): Assets, $12,203 (M); expenditures, $846; total giving, $1,800; qualifying distributions, $1,800; giving activities include $1,800 for 3 grants to individuals.
Purpose and activities: Scholarship awards to selected graduates of Chassell High School, Michigan.
Fields of interest: Higher education.
Type of support: Scholarships—to individuals.
Limitations: Applications accepted. Giving primarily to residents of Chassell, MI.
Application information: Submit application prior to graduation. Application form required.
Initial approach: Letter
Trustees: Michael Gaunt; Douglas J. Hamar; John C. Hamar; Julie A. Hamar.
EIN: 382314909

337
Hammel-Delangis Scholarship Trust
c/o Northern Michigan Bank & Trust Co.
1502 W. Washington St.
Marquette, MI   49855-3195
County: Marquette
Application address: c/o Scholarship Selection Comm., 300 West B. St., Iron Mountain, MI 49801, tel.: (906) 779-2610

Established in 1987 in MI.
Grantmaker type: Independent foundation.
Financial data (yr. ended 09/30/10): Assets, $64,996 (M); expenditures, $2,440; total giving, $1,000; qualifying distributions, $1,000; giving activities include $1,000 for 1 grant to an individual.
Purpose and activities: Scholarship awards to graduates of the Iron Mountain High School, MI, pursuing a baccalaureate degree in the health fields of optometry, medicine, or any similar course of instruction.
Fields of interest: Medical school/education.
Type of support: Scholarships—to individuals.
Limitations: Applications accepted. Giving limited to Iron Mountain, MI.
Application information: Applicant must also submit ACT score, high school transcript and 3 letters of recommendation. Application form not required.
Deadline(s): Apr. 25
Trustee: Northern Michigan Bank & Trust Co.
EIN: 386513191

338
Hampson Foundation
800 W. Long Lake Rd., Ste. 210
Bloomfield Hills, MI   48302-2058
County: Oakland
Contact: Robert J. Hampson, Pres.
Application address: P.O. Box 250614, Franklin, MI 48025-0614, tel.: (248) 626-3264

Established in MI.
Donors: Robert J. Hampson; Sadie G. Hampson.
Grantmaker type: Independent foundation.
Financial data (yr. ended 12/31/08): Assets, $5,105 (M); expenditures, $710; total giving, $0; qualifying distributions, $0.
Purpose and activities: Giving primarily for education, particularly to a women's college; funding also for health associations and human services.

Fields of interest: Higher education; Education; Health organizations, association; Human services.
Type of support: General/operating support.
Limitations: Giving primarily in MI; some funding nationally.
Application information:
Initial approach: Letter
Deadline(s): Dec. 1
Officers: Robert J. Hampson, Pres. and Treas.; Jane J. Hampson Berca, V.P.; Sadie G. Hampson, V.P.
EIN: 386066115

339
Bernard and Dorothy Hamstra Charitable Foundation
629 St. Marks Ave.
Westfield, NJ 07090-1345
County: Union
Contact: Faith H. Bennett, Tr.

Established in 1995 in NJ.
Donor: Bernard Hamstra‡.
Grantmaker type: Independent foundation.
Financial data (yr. ended 12/31/09): Assets, $2,070,662 (M); expenditures, $104,332; total giving, $74,800; qualifying distributions, $74,800; giving activities include $74,800 for grants.
Purpose and activities: Giving primarily for Christian higher education, as well as Presbyterian churches and organizations; giving also for general mission activities.
Fields of interest: Higher education; Theological school/education; Food services; Human services; Christian agencies & churches; Protestant agencies & churches.
Limitations: Applications accepted. Giving primarily in Grand Rapids, MI and NJ. No support for political organizations. No grants to individuals.
Application information: Application form required.
Initial approach: Letter requesting application form
Deadline(s): None
Trustees: Faith H. Bennett; John K. Bennett; Frances K. Hamstra.
Number of staff: None.
EIN: 223285822
Selected grants: The following grants were reported in 2007.
$28,000 to Calvin College, Grand Rapids, MI.
$16,800 to Calvin Theological Seminary, Grand Rapids, MI.
$14,500 to Presbyterian Church, Agape, Westfield, NJ.
$10,000 to Christian Reformed World Relief Committee, Grand Rapids, MI.
$10,000 to Habitat for Humanity, Greater Plainfield Area, Plainfield, NJ.
$10,000 to Zuni Christian Mission School, Zuni, NM.
$5,000 to Plainfield Community Outreach, Grace Episcopal Church, Plainfield, NJ.
$5,000 to Young Life, Colorado Springs, CO.
$2,500 to American Bible Society, New York, NY.
$2,500 to Christian Appalachian Project, Lancaster, KY.

340
The Hancock Foundation
675 Robinson Rd.
P.O. Box 449
Jackson, MI 49204-0449 (517) 841-4886
County: Jackson
Contact: James A. Hildreth, Tr.

Donor: Arline M. Hancock.
Grantmaker type: Independent foundation.
Financial data (yr. ended 11/30/09): Assets, $372,064 (M); expenditures, $15,020; total giving, $15,000; qualifying distributions, $16,057; giving activities include $15,000 for 1 grant.
Fields of interest: Visual arts; Museums; Performing arts; Arts; Elementary/secondary education; Elementary school/education; Education; Human services; Catholic federated giving programs; Catholic agencies & churches; Religion.
Type of support: Building/renovation; Program development; Seed money; Matching/challenge support.
Limitations: Applications accepted. Giving primarily in Jackson County, MI.
Application information: Application form required.
Initial approach: Letter
Deadline(s): Oct. 1
Trustees: Jack D. Bunce; James A. Hildreth; Robert H. Moore.
EIN: 386096275

341
Joseph & Sally Handleman Charitable Foundation Trust A
c/o JPMorgan Chase Bank, N.A.
P.O. Box 3038
Milwaukee, WI 53201-3038
County: Milwaukee
Application address: c/o JPMorgan Chase Bank, N.A., 3399 PGA Blvd., Ste. 100, Palm Beach Gardens, FL 33410, tel.: (561) 799-1132

Donor: Joan Sadoff.
Grantmaker type: Independent foundation.
Financial data (yr. ended 12/31/08): Assets, $6,843,741 (M); expenditures, $3,670,143; total giving, $3,593,109; qualifying distributions, $3,611,317; giving activities include $3,593,109 for 18 grants (high: $2,000,000; low: $1,000).
Purpose and activities: Giving primarily to Jewish organizations and for higher education.
Fields of interest: Arts; Higher education; Business school/education; Health sciences school/education; Education; Legal services; Housing/shelter, development; Human services; American Red Cross; Residential/custodial care, hospices; Aging, centers/services; Jewish agencies & synagogues; Women.
International interests: Israel.
Limitations: Applications accepted. Giving primarily in FL, MI, NY, and PA.
Application information: Application form not required.
Initial approach: Proposal
Deadline(s): None
Trustee: Joan Ara Sadoff.
Agent: JPMorgan Chase Bank, N.A.
EIN: 656263326
Selected grants: The following grants were reported in 2006.
$75,000 to American Jewish Joint Distribution Committee, New York, NY.

$55,000 to Womens International Zionist Organization, New York, NY.
$17,000 to Saint Jude Childrens Research Hospital, Memphis, TN.
$15,000 to Anti-Defamation League of Bnai Brith, New York, NY.
$10,000 to Southern Poverty Law Center, Montgomery, AL.
$10,000 to Theater for a New Audience, New York, NY.
$10,000 to University of Miami, Coral Gables, FL.
$10,000 to W H Y Y, Philadelphia, PA.
$6,000 to Israel Guide Dog Center for the Blind, Warrington, PA.
$3,500 to Human Rights Watch, New York, NY.

342
Harry Hannan and Eugene Kraft - Amalgamated Clothing and Textile Workers of America Educational Trust Fund
c/o ACTWU
38025 Jay Kay Dr.
Romulus, MI 48174-5083
County: Wayne

Established in MI.
Grantmaker type: Independent foundation.
Financial data (yr. ended 12/31/09): Assets, $1 (M); gifts received, $750; expenditures, $750; total giving, $750; qualifying distributions, $750; giving activities include $750 for grants to individuals.
Purpose and activities: Scholarship awards to union employees to further their education in the textile field.
Fields of interest: Education.
Type of support: Scholarships—to individuals.
Limitations: Giving primarily in the Detroit, MI, area.
Application information: Application form required.
Deadline(s): Aug. 31
Trustee: Lawrence H. "Larry" Kraft.
EIN: 237379955

343
Hannan Foundation
8383 Warwick Groves
Grand Blanc, MI 48439-7425
County: Genesee
Contact: Ahmad T. Hannan, Pres.

Established in 2002 in MI.
Donor: Ahmad Hannan.
Grantmaker type: Independent foundation.
Financial data (yr. ended 12/31/09): Assets, $19,889 (M); expenditures, $25,000; total giving, $25,000; qualifying distributions, $25,000; giving activities include $25,000 for grants.
Fields of interest: Islam.
Limitations: Applications accepted. Giving primarily in MI.
Application information:
Deadline(s): None
Officers: Ahmad Hannan, Pres. and Treas.; Samir Rifai, V.P. and Secy.
EIN: 383544600

344
Jens and Maureen Hansen Charitable Foundation
1230 Monroe Ave. N.W.
Grand Rapids, MI 49505-4620 (616) 458-1414
County: Kent
Contact: Shirley Balk, Pres.

Donors: Jens Hansen Residuary Trust; Jens Hansen Marital Trust; M. Hansen Qualified Domestic Trust; Margaret M. Hansen Trust.
Grantmaker type: Independent foundation.
Financial data (yr. ended 12/31/09): Assets, $744,760 (M); expenditures, $103,425; total giving, $103,035; qualifying distributions, $103,035; giving activities include $103,035 for grants.
Fields of interest: Museums; Higher education, college; Education; Botanical gardens; United Ways and Federated Giving Programs; Protestant agencies & churches.
Limitations: Giving primarily in Grand Rapids, MI.
Application information:
Initial approach: Letter on organization's letterhead
Deadline(s): None
Officers: Shirley Balk, Pres.; Steven Balk, Secy.-Treas.
Directors: James H. Balk; James H. Balk II; Martin Balk.
EIN: 383220087
Selected grants: The following grants were reported in 2008.
$5,000 to Camp Blodgett, Grand Rapids, MI.
$5,000 to Words of Hope, Grand Rapids, MI.
$1,500 to Guiding Light Mission, Grand Rapids, MI.

345
Harbor Beach Student Loan Fund Association
8118 Section Line Rd.
Harbor Beach, MI 48441-9436
County: Huron
Contact: Marilyn Ritchie, Treas.

Established in 1997 in MI.
Grantmaker type: Independent foundation.
Financial data (yr. ended 06/30/09): Assets, $52,120 (M); gifts received, $20; expenditures, $193; total giving, $0; qualifying distributions, $0.
Purpose and activities: Student loans to graduates of Harbor Beach High School, Michigan.
Fields of interest: Higher education.
Type of support: Student loans—to individuals.
Limitations: Giving limited to residents of the Harbor Beach, MI, area.
Application information: Application form required.
Deadline(s): None
Officers: Beth Bowen, Pres.; Vickie Erdman, Secy.; Marilyn Ritchie, Treas.
EIN: 386091395

346
Charles Stewart Harding Foundation
111 E. Court St., Ste. 3D
Flint, MI 48502-1649 (810) 767-0136
County: Genesee
Contact: Frederick S. Kirkpatrick

Established in 1963 in MI.

Donors: C.S. Harding Mott†; C.S. Harding Mott II†; Claire Mott White.
Grantmaker type: Independent foundation.
Financial data (yr. ended 06/30/10): Assets, $10,636,728 (M); expenditures, $544,145; total giving, $485,161; qualifying distributions, $485,161; giving activities include $485,161 for grants.
Purpose and activities: Giving primarily for the arts.
Fields of interest: Media, television; Performing arts, music; Performing arts, orchestras; Arts; Human services.
Type of support: General/operating support; Continuing support; Annual campaigns; Scholarship funds.
Limitations: Applications accepted. Giving primarily in Flint, MI. No grants to individuals.
Application information: Application form not required.
Initial approach: Letter
Copies of proposal: 1
Deadline(s): Feb. 15
Board meeting date(s): Usually Apr.
Final notification: June
Officers and Trustees:* Claire Mott White,* Pres.; Paula M. Turrentine,* V.P.; C. Edward White, Jr., Secy.; William S. White,* Treas.; Tiffany W. Lovett; Ridgway H. White.
Number of staff: None.
EIN: 386081208
Selected grants: The following grants were reported in 2009.
$196,265 to Flint Institute of Arts, Flint, MI.
$50,000 to Crystal Lake Camps, Hughesville, PA.
$50,000 to Flint Cultural Center Corporation, Flint, MI.
$50,000 to Flint Institute of Music, Flint, MI.
$11,000 to YWCA of Greater Flint, Flint, MI.
$5,000 to Community Foundation of Greater Flint, Flint, MI.
$5,000 to Flint Youth Theater, Flint, MI.
$5,000 to Greater Flint Arts Council, Flint, MI.
$1,000 to Whaley Childrens Center, Flint, MI.

347
Jennifer Howell Harding Foundation
2601 John R Rd.
Troy, MI 48083-2365
County: Oakland
Contact: Jennifer Harding, Tr.

Established in 1999 in MI.
Donor: Don N. Howell.
Grantmaker type: Independent foundation.
Financial data (yr. ended 12/31/09): Assets, $185,467 (M); gifts received, $30,830; expenditures, $8,453; total giving, $7,800; qualifying distributions, $7,800; giving activities include $7,800 for grants.
Fields of interest: Protestant agencies & churches.
Type of support: Building/renovation; Scholarship funds; General/operating support.
Limitations: Giving in the U.S., with some emphasis on MI. No grants to individuals.
Application information: Application form not required.
Initial approach: Letter
Deadline(s): None
Trustees: Jennifer Harding; Michael Harding.
EIN: 586396643

348
The George Harding Scholarship Fund
c/o Bodman LLP
229 Court St.
P.O. Box 405
Cheboygan, MI 49721-1907 (231) 627-8000
County: Cheboygan
Contact: Lloyd C. Fell, Tr.

Grantmaker type: Independent foundation.
Financial data (yr. ended 12/31/09): Assets, $54,085 (M); gifts received, $7,500; expenditures, $12,452; total giving, $8,000; qualifying distributions, $8,000; giving activities include $8,000 for grants to individuals.
Purpose and activities: Scholarship awards to Michigan residents who are full time students, enrolled in a four-year Michigan college or university pursuing a finance-related degree. Scholarships are only available for the student's senior year of college, or first year of graduate school.
Fields of interest: Business school/education; Economics.
Type of support: Scholarships—to individuals.
Limitations: Giving limited to residents of MI.
Application information: Application form required.
Deadline(s): None
Trustees: Lloyd C. Fell; Gregory J. Hofbauer; Donald B. Jeffery, Jr.; Gerald A. Johnson; James C. Kurt; Mary D. Naz; Lawrence J. Sauter.
EIN: 382527040

349
Harlan Foundation
660 Woodward Ave.
2290 First National Bldg.
Detroit, MI 48226-3506
County: Wayne
Contact: John M. Harlan, Chair.; Glenn Lowenstein, Secy.-Treas.

Grantmaker type: Independent foundation.
Financial data (yr. ended 12/31/08): Assets, $933,860 (M); expenditures, $73,625; total giving, $66,000; qualifying distributions, $66,000; giving activities include $66,000 for grants.
Purpose and activities: Giving primarily for education.
Fields of interest: Arts; Higher education; Education; Zoos/zoological societies; Boy scouts; Youth development, business; Community/ economic development.
Limitations: Applications accepted. Giving primarily in MI; some giving also in PA and WV. No grants to individuals.
Application information: Application form not required.
Initial approach: Letter
Deadline(s): None
Officers and Trustees:* John M. Harlan,* Chair. and Pres.; William R. Patterson,* V.P.; Glenn Lowenstein,* Secy.-Treas.
EIN: 386041516

350
Lewis G. Harmon Foundation
300 Park St., Ste. 285
Birmingham, MI 48009-3413
County: Oakland

Established in 1998 in MI.

Donor: Lewis G. Harmon.
Grantmaker type: Independent foundation.
Financial data (yr. ended 12/31/09): Assets, $2,927 (M); gifts received, $1,250; expenditures, $2,357; total giving, $500; qualifying distributions, $500; giving activities include $500 for grants.
Limitations: Giving primarily in Detroit, MI.
Officers and Directors:* Lewis G. Harmon,* Pres.; Charles J. Carson,* V.P. and Secy.; James C. Carson,* V.P.; Gary C. Holvick,* Treas.
EIN: 383416481

351
Rodney C. and Karen S. Harris Foundation
50499 Laurel Ridge Ct.
Northville, MI 48168-8811
County: Wayne

Established in 2006 in MI.
Donors: Rodney C. Harris; Karen S. Harris.
Grantmaker type: Independent foundation.
Financial data (yr. ended 12/31/09): Assets, $3,500 (M); expenditures, $500; total giving, $500; qualifying distributions, $500; giving activities include $500 for grants.
Fields of interest: Education.
Limitations: Giving primarily in OH.
Directors: Karen S. Harris; Rodney C. Harris.
EIN: 208021077

352
Alice Kales Hartwick Foundation
c/o Comerica Bank
P.O. Box 75000, MC 3302
Detroit, MI 48275-3302
County: Wayne
Application address: c/o Peter A. Dow, 191 Ridge Rd., Grosse Pointe Farms, MI 48236, tel.: (305) 664-9093

Donor: Alice Kales Hartwick Unitrust.
Grantmaker type: Independent foundation.
Financial data (yr. ended 12/31/09): Assets, $1,311,484 (M); gifts received, $87,529; expenditures, $205,240; total giving, $190,000; qualifying distributions, $190,698; giving activities include $190,000 for 27 grants (high: $20,000; low: $1,000).
Fields of interest: Arts, association; Visual arts, ceramic arts; Performing arts; Performing arts, orchestras; Arts; Libraries (public); Education; Zoos/zoological societies; Human services; Community/economic development; United Ways and Federated Giving Programs.
Limitations: Giving primarily in Detroit and Grosse Pointe, MI.
Application information: Application form not required.
Initial approach: Proposal
Deadline(s): None
Officers and Trustees:* Carl Eckert,* Chair.; John O'Brien,* V.P.; Peter A. Dow, Secy.-Treas.
EIN: 382248118
Selected grants: The following grants were reported in 2009.
$20,000 to Detroit Institute of Arts, Detroit, MI.
$10,000 to College for Creative Studies, Detroit, MI.
$10,000 to Crossroads of Michigan, Detroit, MI.
$10,000 to Detroit Zoological Society, Royal Oak, MI.
$10,000 to Neighborhood Club, Grosse Pointe, MI.

$10,000 to Pewabic Pottery, Detroit, MI.
$5,000 to Detroit Historical Society, Detroit, MI.
$5,000 to Detroit Science Center, Detroit, MI.
$5,000 to Purple Rose Theater Company, Chelsea, MI.
$5,000 to Services for Older Citizens, Grosse Pointe, MI.

353
The Harvest Foundation
900 Fifth Third Ctr.
111 Lyon St. N.
Grand Rapids, MI 49503-2487
County: Kent
Contact: Geraldine L. Anderson, Pres.
Application address: 3278 Roosevelt Rd., Muskegon, MI 49441-6223

Established in 1985 in MI.
Donor: Thomas Seyferth†.
Grantmaker type: Independent foundation.
Financial data (yr. ended 12/31/09): Assets, $198,842 (M); expenditures, $16,582; total giving, $9,350; qualifying distributions, $9,350; giving activities include $9,350 for grants.
Fields of interest: Foundations (community).
Limitations: Giving primarily in MI. No grants to individuals.
Application information:
Initial approach: Letter
Deadline(s): None
Officers: Geraldine L. Anderson, Pres.; Roger H. Oetting, Secy.-Treas.
EIN: 382642065

354
Harvey Memorial Foundation
300 St. Andrews Rd.
Saginaw, MI 48603-5977 (989) 790-3908
County: Saginaw
Contact: Albert S. Harvey, Pres.

Established in MI.
Grantmaker type: Independent foundation.
Financial data (yr. ended 12/31/09): Assets, $214,445 (M); expenditures, $15,406; total giving, $10,250; qualifying distributions, $10,250; giving activities include $10,250 for 16 grants (high: $1,000; low: $100).
Fields of interest: Family services; Human services.
Limitations: Applications accepted. Giving primarily in Saginaw, MI.
Application information: Application form not required.
Initial approach: Letter
Deadline(s): None
Officers: Albert S. Harvey, Pres. and Treas.; Katherine Almirall, V.P. and Secy.
Directors: Thomas C. Harvey, Jr.; William L. Harvey.
EIN: 386072427

355
The Ernie Harwell Foundation
16845 Kercheval Ave., Ste. 5
Grosse Pointe, MI 48230-1551
County: Wayne

Established in 2007 in MI.
Grantmaker type: Independent foundation.

Financial data (yr. ended 12/31/07): Assets, $21,537 (M); gifts received, $23,500; expenditures, $2,000; total giving, $0; qualifying distributions, $0.
Officers and Trustees:* Ernie Harwell,* Pres.; S. Gary Spicer,* Secy.; Duane L. Tarnecki; David Wind.
EIN: 382987354

356
Hasey Foundation, Inc.
262 Commercial Blvd.
Lauderdale By The Sea, FL 33308-4439
County: Broward
Application address: c/o Robert J. Fredrikson, 1877 S. Federal Hwy., Ste. 202, Boca Raton, FL 33432-7467

Established in 1998 in FL.
Grantmaker type: Independent foundation.
Financial data (yr. ended 12/31/09): Assets, $905,113 (M); expenditures, $47,658; total giving, $46,700; qualifying distributions, $46,700; giving activities include $46,700 for grants.
Fields of interest: Education; Medical research; Christian agencies & churches; Catholic agencies & churches.
Type of support: General/operating support.
Limitations: Giving primarily in FL; some giving also in MI and NY. No grants to individuals.
Application information:
Initial approach: Typewritten letter
Deadline(s): None
Officers and Directors:* Regina M. Hasey,* Pres.; Catherine Seydel,* V.P.; Martin J. Hasey,* Secy.
EIN: 591851950

357
James & Catherine Haveman Family Foundation
(also known as Haveman Family Foundation, Inc.)
12471 Jansma Dr.
Grand Haven, MI 49417-9379
County: Ottawa
Contact: James Haveman, Dir.

Established in 1998 in MI.
Donor: Catherine Haveman†.
Grantmaker type: Independent foundation.
Financial data (yr. ended 12/31/09): Assets, $10,000 (M); expenditures, $445,927; total giving, $439,613; qualifying distributions, $439,613; giving activities include $439,613 for 1 grant.
Fields of interest: Foundations (community).
Limitations: Giving primarily in MI.
Application information:
Initial approach: Letter or proposal
Deadline(s): Aug. 31
Officers: James Haveman, Pres.; Barbara Haveman Powazek, V.P. and Secy.; Kathryn Haveman Schauer, Treas.
EIN: 383419761

358
Heart of Gold Charity, Inc.
509 Torrey Pines Dr.
Twin Lakes, WI 53181-9530 (815) 790-1299
County: Kenosha
E-mail: heartofgoldcharity@yahoo.com; *URL:* http://heartofgoldcharity.org

Established in 2007 in WI.
Grantmaker type: Independent foundation.
Financial data (yr. ended 12/31/09): Assets, $40,221 (M); gifts received, $49,192; expenditures, $33,179; total giving, $16,500; qualifying distributions, $16,500; giving activities include $16,500 for grants.
Purpose and activities: The organization's mission is to provide resources for families dealing with the effects of congenital heart defects and hypoplastic left heart syndrome (HLHS); scholarship awards to graduates of Harvard High School, Johnsburg High School, Richmond-Burton High School, Richmond, Illinois, Munising High School, Michigan, Badger High School, Lake Geneva, and Wilmot High School, Wisconsin, for medical and nursing education.
Fields of interest: Medical school/education; Nursing school/education; Heart & circulatory diseases.
Type of support: Scholarships—to individuals.
Limitations: Applications accepted. Giving limited to residents of Harvard, Johnsburg, and Richmond, IL, Munising, MI, and Lake Geneva and Wilmot, WI.
Application information: Application form and guidelines available on foundation web site. Application form required.
   Deadline(s): Apr. 1
Officer: Lois Petska, Secy.
Directors: Richard Petska; Stephanie Petska.
Board Members: Lisa Eisele; Tim Hiller; Jeff Roach; Mariene Stevens; Andy Youra.
EIN: 205680190

359
Hebert Memorial Scholarship Fund
c/o Kim M. Gardey
100 Harrow Ln.
Saginaw, MI 48638-6095 (989) 755-0545
County: Saginaw
URL: http://www.saginawfoundation.org/

Grantmaker type: Independent foundation.
Financial data (yr. ended 12/31/09): Assets, $2,071,227 (M); expenditures, $25,573; total giving, $0; qualifying distributions, $47,487.
Application information: Application form required.
   Initial approach: See website for application form
   Deadline(s): Feb. 1
Trustee: Kim M. Gardey.
EIN: 262764191

360
The Hees Family Foundation
P.O. Box 127
Belleville, MI 48112-0127 (734) 461-1878
County: Wayne
Contact: Ronald D. Hees, Pres.

Established in 1997 in MI.
Donor: Ronald D. Hees.
Grantmaker type: Independent foundation.
Financial data (yr. ended 08/31/09): Assets, $470,900 (M); expenditures, $23,087; total giving, $20,000; qualifying distributions, $20,000; giving activities include $20,000 for grants.
Fields of interest: Housing/shelter; Human services.
Type of support: General/operating support.
Limitations: Giving primarily in MI, with emphasis on Gaylord. No grants to individuals.
Application information:

Initial approach: Letter
   Deadline(s): Aug. 31
Officers: Ronald D. Hees, Pres.; David G. Hees, V.P.; Mildred M. McGuire, Secy.-Treas.
Directors: Daniel A. Hees; Michael D. Hees.
EIN: 383368989

361
Helppie Family Charitable Foundation
P.O. Box 607
Bloomfield Hills, MI 48303-0607
(248) 386-8300
County: Oakland
Contact: Richard D. Helppie, Jr., Pres.

Established in 1997 in MI.
Donors: Richard Helppie; Richard D. Helppie Trust.
Grantmaker type: Independent foundation.
Financial data (yr. ended 12/31/09): Assets, $3,774,138 (M); expenditures, $567,260; total giving, $552,550; qualifying distributions, $553,800; giving activities include $552,550 for 45 grants (high: $250,000; low: $100).
Purpose and activities: Giving for organizations involved with the disadvantaged, medically impaired children, community improvement, and education.
Fields of interest: Elementary/secondary education; Hospitals (specialty); Health organizations; Human services; Children, services; Community/economic development; Protestant agencies & churches; Economically disadvantaged.
Limitations: Giving limited to MI. No support for private foundations. No grants to individuals.
Application information:
   Initial approach: Letter
   Deadline(s): None
Officers and Directors: * Richard D. Helppie, Jr.,* Pres.; Leslie S. Helppie,* V.P.; Susan M. Synor,* Secy.-Treas.
EIN: 383374687
Selected grants: The following grants were reported in 2008.
$30,000 to Childrens Hospital of Michigan, Detroit, MI.
$20,072 to Lutheran Church of the Redeemer, Birmingham, MI.
$9,000 to Wayne-Westland Community Schools, Westland, MI.
$1,000 to Lighthouse of Oakland County, Pontiac, MI.

362
Hennessey Family Foundation
c/o Comerica Bank
P.O. Box 75000, MC 3302
Detroit, MI 48275-3302
County: Wayne
Application address: 265 Winter St., Ste. 401, Waltham, MA 02451-8714

Established in 2005 in MI.
Donor: Frank Michael Hennessey.
Grantmaker type: Independent foundation.
Financial data (yr. ended 06/30/09): Assets, $1,004,017 (M); gifts received, $69,545; expenditures, $58,429; total giving, $41,001; qualifying distributions, $41,001; giving activities include $41,001 for grants.
Fields of interest: Cancer.
Type of support: General/operating support.
Application information:

Initial approach: Letter
   Deadline(s): None
Officers: Frank Michael Hennessey, Pres.; Michael I. Hennessey, Secy.; Kaitlin Hennessey Wolf, Treas.
EIN: 010825321

363
Paul B. Henry Foundation
16 Campau Cir. N.W.
Grand Rapids, MI 49501-0352 (616) 774-2863
County: Kent
Contact: Karen Henry Stokes, Pres.

Established in 1994 in MI.
Grantmaker type: Independent foundation.
Financial data (yr. ended 12/31/09): Assets, $168,069 (M); gifts received, $250; expenditures, $17,377; total giving, $14,300; qualifying distributions, $14,300; giving activities include $14,300 for grants.
Fields of interest: Performing arts; Higher education; Human services.
Type of support: Continuing support; Endowments; Internship funds; Scholarship funds.
Limitations: Giving primarily in Grand Rapids, MI. No grants to individuals.
Application information: Application form not required.
   Initial approach: Letter
   Deadline(s): June 30
   Board meeting date(s): Fall
Officers and Directors: * Karen Henry Stokes,* Pres.; Jordan Henry, V.P.; Megan Henry, Secy.; Kara Henry,* Treas.; Hilary Snell.
EIN: 383158473

364
Elizabeth A. Herdegen Trust
c/o Comerica Bank
P.O. Box 75000
Detroit, MI 48275-0001 (313) 222-9067
County: Wayne
Application address: c/o Taylor Statten Camps, 28 Longwood, Don Mills, Ontario, Canada M4S 2X5, tel.: (416) 486-6959

Established in MI.
Grantmaker type: Independent foundation.
Financial data (yr. ended 12/31/09): Assets, $131,619 (M); expenditures, $10,021; total giving, $7,000; qualifying distributions, $7,000; giving activities include $7,000 for grants to individuals.
Purpose and activities: Grant to financially needy Canadian campers between the ages of 7 and 17.
Fields of interest: Recreation, camps.
Type of support: Grants to individuals.
Limitations: Applications accepted. Giving limited to residents of Canada.
Application information: Application form required.
   Initial approach: Request application from Statten Camps
   Deadline(s): Feb. 15
Trustee: Comerica Bank.
EIN: 386461176

365
Here to Help Foundation

P.O. Box 480
Royal Oak, MI   48068-0480   (248) 330-0723
County: Oakland
FAX: (248) 534-1490;
E-mail: info@heretohelpfoundation.org; URL: http://www.heretohelpfoundation.com

Established in 2007 in MI.
Donors: Ilene Schwartz; Leonard Schwartz.
Grantmaker type: Independent foundation.
Financial data (yr. ended 12/31/09): Assets, $2,657,941 (M); gifts received, $21,000; expenditures, $254,161; total giving, $199,039; qualifying distributions, $239,653; giving activities include $199,039 for 259 grants to individuals (high: $3,600; low: $40).
Purpose and activities: Grant awards are based on a one-time basis to individuals who have encountered a crisis and need assistance in moving forward and being independent.
Fields of interest: Disasters, preparedness/services; Economically disadvantaged.
Type of support: Grants to individuals.
Limitations: Applications accepted. Giving to benefit residents of southeastern MI, specifically the counties of Wayne and Oakland. No grants for scholarships or tuition, student loans, summer camps, property tax bills, funeral expenses, medical and dental expenses, wheelchair-associated expenses and wheelchair ramps, driver responsibility fees, or for major home repairs.
Publications: Application guidelines.
Application information: See foundation web site for full application guidelines and requirements. Application form required.
Initial approach: Completion of online application form from a qualified advocate, including social workers, employees at charitable organizations, members of the clergy, or DHS, JET and Michigan Works employees
Deadline(s): None
Officers: Robert Schwartz, C.E.O. and Secy.; Robin Schwartz, Pres.; Adam Schwartz, V.P.; Ilene Schwartz, Treas.; Citibank, N.A.
EIN: 208057969

366
The F. B. Heron Foundation

100 Broadway, 17th Fl.
New York, NY   10005-4506
County: New York
Contact: Clara Miller, Pres.
E-mail: info@fbheron.org; URL: http://www.fbheron.org/

Established in 1992 in DE.
Grantmaker type: Independent foundation.
Financial data (yr. ended 12/31/09): Assets, $240,876,761 (M); expenditures, $14,820,116; total giving, $10,957,050; qualifying distributions, $18,379,334; giving activities include $10,957,050 for 246 grants (high: $500,000; low: $25), $72,776 for foundation-administered programs and $4,794,273 for loans/program-related investments.
Purpose and activities: To advance its mission, the foundation supports organizations that help low-income people to create and preserve wealth to help them take control of their lives and make decisions for themselves and their families. The foundation makes grants to and investments in entities that are engaged in one or more of the following wealth-creation strategies-including emerging opportunities to incorporate sustainable practices within the context of healthy environments-that benefit low- and moderate-income families and communities. The specific wealth-creation and preservation strategies are: 1) Advancing home ownership; 2) Supporting enterprise development; and 3) Increasing access to capital and preserving assets. The foundation will also support research and policy efforts that advance these wealth creation strategies. The foundation makes grants and investments, and commits other foundation resources, to efforts that: 1) Encourage effective practices in philanthropy, specifically to expand social impact through mission-related investing, as well as to promote core support funding, practical means of assessing impact, and high quality customer service to partner grantees and investees. 2) Develop systems and approaches for reliable, credible data, research and technology systems that inform and expand practice and policy in wealth creation. 3) Provide financial or technical assistance to community-based development organizations or coordinate practitioner networks to exchange lessons learned.
Fields of interest: Housing/shelter, home owners; Community development, neighborhood development; Economic development; Foundations (private grantmaking); Financial services.
Type of support: General/operating support; Continuing support; Program development; Technical assistance; Program evaluation; Program-related investments/loans; Employee matching gifts; Matching/challenge support.
Limitations: Applications accepted. Giving primarily in New York City, NY, MI, TX, Appalachia and the Mid-South Delta region; some giving also in South Africa. No grants to individuals, or for endowments or capital campaigns.
Publications: Application guidelines; Annual report (including application guidelines); Grants list; Occasional report.
Application information: The foundation will likely not fund new organizations it currently does not support. Information available on the foundation's web site. Videotapes, CDs, DVDs, etc. will not be accepted. Applications not accepted for South Africa grantmaking. Application form not required.
Initial approach: Letter of inquiry (2 - 3 pages)
Copies of proposal: 1
Deadline(s): None
Board meeting date(s): Quarterly
Final notification: 1 week to initial letter of inquiry; 4 weeks max to full proposal, if requested
Officers and Directors:* Buzz Schmidt,* Chair.; Clara Miller, Pres.; Luther M. Ragin, Jr., V.P., Investments; Kathleen Starr; William F. McCalpin; William M. Dietel; Amb. James A. Joseph; John Otterlei.
Number of staff: 6 full-time professional; 1 part-time professional; 3 full-time support; 1 part-time support.
EIN: 133647019
Selected grants: The following grants were reported in 2009.
$500,000 to Community Reinvestment Fund, USA, Minneapolis, MN. For project support, payable over 2.00 years.
$300,000 to Kuyasa Fund, Cape Town, South Africa. For project support, payable over 2.00 years.
$300,000 to National Community Reinvestment Coalition, Washington, DC. For general support, payable over 2.00 years.
$300,000 to Neighborhood Reinvestment Corporation, NeighborWorks America, Washington, DC. For general support, payable over 2.00 years.
$250,000 to Housing Assistance Council, Washington, DC. For general support, payable over 2.00 years.
$250,000 to Shorebank Corporation, Chicago, IL.
$150,000 to Brookings Institution, Washington, DC. For project support, payable over 2.00 years.
$100,000 to Center for Responsible Lending, Durham, NC. For general support, payable over 2.00 years.
$100,000 to Housing Partnership Network, Boston, MA. For general support.
$100,000 to Native American Community Development Corporation, Browning, MT. For general support, payable over 2.00 years.

367
Herrick Foundation

First National Bldg.
660 Woodward Ave., Ste. 2290
Detroit, MI   48226-3506   (313) 465-7733
County: Wayne
Contact: Todd W. Herrick, Pres.

Incorporated in 1949 in MI.
Donors: Ray W. Herrick‡; Hazel M. Herrick‡.
Grantmaker type: Independent foundation.
Financial data (yr. ended 09/30/09): Assets, $134,750,486 (M); expenditures, $10,517,997; total giving, $7,227,673; qualifying distributions, $8,381,196; giving activities include $7,227,673 for 34 grants (high: $1,000,000; low: $1,100; average: $15,000–$1,000,000).
Purpose and activities: Emphasis on higher education, including research grants, scholarship programs (made through college and postgraduate educational institutions, not individual scholarships), and capital funding; grants also for church support, youth, health and welfare agencies, hospitals, and libraries.
Fields of interest: Secondary school/education; Higher education; Hospitals (general); Health care; Cancer; Human services; Children/youth, services.
Type of support: General/operating support; Continuing support; Annual campaigns; Capital campaigns; Building/renovation; Equipment; Land acquisition; Endowments; Emergency funds; Program development; Professorships; Curriculum development; Scholarship funds; Research; Matching/challenge support.
Limitations: Applications accepted. Giving primarily in MI. No support for international organizations, or for domestic organizations for international programs. No grants to individuals.
Publications: Application guidelines.
Application information: Application form not required.
Initial approach: 1- to -3 page grant proposal letter
Copies of proposal: 1
Deadline(s): None
Board meeting date(s): Monthly
Final notification: By letter
Officers and Trustees:* Todd W. Herrick,* Chair., Pres. and Treas.; Kent B. Herrick,* V.P. and Exec. Dir.; Michael A. Indenbaum,* Secy.
Number of staff: 1 part-time support.
EIN: 386041517
Selected grants: The following grants were reported in 2009.

$1,000,000 to AOPA Air Safety Foundation, Frederick, MD. For image transformation, public relations, and education campaign.

$1,000,000 to Barbara Ann Karmanos Cancer Institute, Detroit, MI. For $300,000 for National Oncogenomics and Molecular Imaging Center, $239,115 for new Imaging Technologies for Cancer Detection and Treatment, $150,000 for pediatric leukemia, $169,885 for lung cancer research, and $141,000 for prostate cancer research.

$1,000,000 to Heritage Foundation, Washington, DC. For renovation of House Annex Building.

$1,000,000 to Northern Michigan Hospital Foundation, Petoskey, MI. For Wellness Pavilion for outpatient therapy services.

$500,000 to Nature Conservancy, Michigan Field Office, Lansing, MI. For Great Lakes Fund for Partnership in Conservation Science and Economics program.

$250,000 to AOPA Air Safety Foundation, Frederick, MD. For image transformation, public relations and education campaign.

$174,064 to Howe Military School, Howe, IN. For general support.

$150,000 to Mackinac Center for Public Policy, Midland, MI. For Energize Michigan project.

$118,557 to Saint Francis of Assisi School, Ann Arbor, MI. For general, charitable, and educational purposes of Saint Francis of Assisi Catholic School.

$15,659 to Purdue University, West Lafayette, IN. For research in clean energy in field of electro hydrodynamic energy conversion devices.

368
Myrtle E. & William G. Hess Charitable Trust

c/o JPMorgan Chase Bank, N.A.
P.O. Box 3038
Milwaukee, WI   53201-3038
County: Milwaukee
E-mail: matthew.h.wasmund@jpmorgan.com;
Application address: c/o JPMorgan Chase Bank, N.A., 611 Woodward Ave., Ste. MI1-8113, Detroit, MI 48226-3408, tel.: (313) 225-3454, fax: (313) 225-3516

Established in 1984 in MI.
Donor: Myrtle E. Hess‡.
Grantmaker type: Independent foundation.
Financial data (yr. ended 09/30/09): Assets, $6,570,852 (M); expenditures, $436,617; total giving, $360,000; qualifying distributions, $378,437; giving activities include $360,000 for 29 grants (high: $100,000; low: $5,000).
Purpose and activities: Giving only to Roman Catholic institutions and agencies located in Oakland County, MI, including Roman Catholic hospitals and schools, or to those institutions that received grants during the donor's lifetime or that were designated for support in the donor's will.
Fields of interest: Elementary/secondary education; Child development, education; Education; Hospitals (general); Alcoholism; Recreation; Human services; Child development, services; Catholic federated giving programs; Catholic agencies & churches; Religion.
Type of support: General/operating support; Annual campaigns; Building/renovation; Endowments; Program development; Scholarship funds.
Limitations: Applications accepted. Giving limited to Oakland County, MI.
Application information: Application form not required.

Initial approach: Proposal
Copies of proposal: 2
Deadline(s): Mar. 1
Board meeting date(s): Mar.
Trustees: Thomas W. Payne; JPMorgan Chase Bank, N.A.
EIN: 382617770
Selected grants: The following grants were reported in 2009.
$100,000 to Saint Patrick Church, White Lake, MI.
$10,000 to Guest House, Lake Orion, MI.
$10,000 to Manresa Jesuit Retreat House, Bloomfield Hills, MI.
$5,000 to American Diabetes Association, Camp Midicha, Bingham Farms, MI.
$5,000 to Brother Rice High School, Bloomfield Hills, MI.
$5,000 to Educational Center for Life, Troy, MI.
$5,000 to Holy Cross Childrens Services, Clinton, MI.
$5,000 to Marian High School, Bloomfield Hills, MI.
$5,000 to Mercy High School, Farmington Hills, MI.
$5,000 to Open Door Outreach Center, Waterford, MI.

369
William G. and Myrtle E. Hess Charitable Trust

c/o JPMorgan Chase Bank, N.A.
P.O. Box 3038
Milwaukee, WI   53201-3038
County: Milwaukee
Application address: c/o JP Morgan Chase Bank, N.A. 200 Ottawa Ave., NW, Grand Rapids, MI 49503-2405; tel.: (616) 771-7613; e-mail: matthew.h.wasmund@jpmorgan.com

Established in 1969 in MI.
Donors: William Hess‡; Myrtle Hess‡.
Grantmaker type: Independent foundation.
Financial data (yr. ended 12/31/09): Assets, $3,398,523 (M); expenditures, $200,590; total giving, $182,500; qualifying distributions, $187,592; giving activities include $182,500 for 28 grants (high: $20,000; low: $1,000).
Fields of interest: Arts; Health care; Health organizations; Youth development; Youth, services.
Limitations: Applications accepted. Giving limited to Oakland County, MI. No support for religious or political organizations. No grants to individuals.
Application information: Application form not required.
Initial approach: Proposal
Copies of proposal: 1
Deadline(s): None
Trustee: JPMorgan Chase Bank, N.A.
EIN: 386166831
Selected grants: The following grants were reported in 2008.
$15,000 to American Red Cross, Southeastern Michigan Chapter, Detroit, MI.
$12,500 to National Bone Marrow Transplant Link, Southfield, MI.
$10,000 to Angels Place, Southfield, MI.
$10,000 to Childrens Leukemia Foundation of Michigan, Southfield, MI.
$10,000 to Hospice of Michigan, Detroit, MI.
$10,000 to Saint Joseph Mercy Oakland, Pontiac, MI.
$8,000 to North Oakland SCAMP Funding Corporation, Clarkston, MI.
$5,000 to Camp Fire USA, Wathana Council, Southfield, MI.

$5,000 to March of Dimes Birth Defects Foundation, Southfield, MI.
$5,000 to Open Door Outreach Center, Waterford, MI.

370
Frances Hess Scholarship Fund

c/o Fifth Third Bank
P.O. Box 3636
Grand Rapids, MI   49501-3636
County: Kent
Application address: c/o Fifth Third Bank, 38 Fountain Sq. Plz., Cincinnati, OH 45263-3102, tel.: (800) 795-4115

Established in 1995 in IL.
Donor: Frances P. Hess‡.
Grantmaker type: Independent foundation.
Financial data (yr. ended 12/31/09): Assets, $331,767 (M); expenditures, $6,506; total giving, $0; qualifying distributions, $0; giving activities include $0 for grants to individuals.
Purpose and activities: Scholarship awards to graduating high school students, residents of Champaign, Illinois and will attend a four year college or university.
Fields of interest: Higher education.
Type of support: Scholarships—to individuals.
Limitations: Giving primarily in IL.
Application information:
Initial approach: Proposal
Deadline(s): May 1
Trustee: Fifth Third Bank.
EIN: 364006773

371
The Stephen L. Hickman Family Foundation

2711 E. Maumee St.
Adrian, MI   49221-3534   (517) 263-5055
County: Lenawee
Contact: Sally D. Hickman, V.P. and Treas.

Established in 1997 in MI.
Donors: Sally D. Hickman; Stephen L. Hickman.
Grantmaker type: Independent foundation.
Financial data (yr. ended 12/31/09): Assets, $4,009,827 (M); expenditures, $183,496; total giving, $143,502; qualifying distributions, $143,502; giving activities include $143,502 for 14 grants (high: $50,000; low: $1,000).
Purpose and activities: Giving primarily for youth services, education and for health and human services.
Fields of interest: Arts; Education; Environment; Hospitals (general); Health care; Cancer research; Boys & girls clubs; Human services; YM/YWCAs & YM/YWHAs; Children/youth, services.
Type of support: Capital campaigns; Endowments; Scholarship funds.
Limitations: Applications accepted. Giving primarily in Adrian and Lenawee County, MI. No grants to individuals.
Application information:
Initial approach: Letter
Deadline(s): Oct. 1
Officers: Tracy L. Hickman, Pres.; Sally D. Hickman, V.P. and Treas.; Stephanie L. Hickman-Boyse, Secy.
Trustee: Stephen L. Hickman.
EIN: 383349206

Selected grants: The following grants were reported in 2008.
$25,000 to Adrian Schools Educational Foundation, Adrian, MI.
$16,000 to Siena Heights University, Adrian, MI.
$15,000 to Boys and Girls Club of Lenawee, Adrian, MI.
$15,000 to Lincoln Park Zoo, Chicago, IL.
$15,000 to Saint Joseph Academy, Adrian, MI.
$11,000 to United Way, Lenawee, Adrian, MI.
$10,000 to Bixby Medical Center, Adrian, MI.
$5,000 to METROsquash, Chicago, IL.
$1,000 to Frist Center for the Visual Arts, Nashville, TN.

372
Lisa Higgins-Hussman Foundation, Inc.
10215 Tarpley Ct.
Ellicott City, MD 21042-1681
County: Howard
Contact: Lisa Marie Higgins, Pres.

Established in 2006 in MD.
Donor: John P. Hussman, Ph.D.
Grantmaker type: Independent foundation.
Financial data (yr. ended 06/30/10): Assets, $2,302,689 (M); gifts received, $300,000; expenditures, $214,312; total giving, $210,400; qualifying distributions, $210,400; giving activities include $210,400 for grants.
Purpose and activities: Giving primarily for 1) medical research, particularly efforts to improve scientific knowledge of, and to develop therapies and find cures for conditions such as autism, addiction, alcoholism and neurological disorders, 2) therapeutic care, particularly for hospice care and therapeutic intervention for individuals with debilitating health or neurological disorders, and 3) issues relating to women's health.
Fields of interest: Substance abuse, services; Health organizations; Human services; Children/youth, services; Residential/custodial care, hospices; Mentally disabled; Women.
Limitations: Applications accepted. Giving primarily in MD and MI.
Officers and Directors:* Lisa Marie Higgins,* Pres.; Stacy Loiacono,* V.P. and Treas.; Joseph Loiacono,* Secy.
EIN: 203409415
Selected grants: The following grants were reported in 2009.
$40,250 to Angels Place, Southfield, MI.
$10,500 to ARC of Howard County, Ellicott City, MD.
$10,500 to Nova Southeastern University, Fort Lauderdale, FL.
$10,250 to Ulman Cancer Fund for Young Adults, Columbia, MD.
$3,000 to CollegeBound Foundation, Baltimore, MD.
$1,000 to Kennedy Krieger Institute, Baltimore, MD.
$1,000 to Maryland Food Bank, Baltimore, MD.
$1,000 to Maryland School for the Deaf, Frederick, MD.

373
Hildreth Foundation, Inc.
41 S. High St.
Columbus, OH 43215-3406
County: Franklin
Contact: Mark Merkle, V.P.

Established in 1949 in OH.
Donor: Helen R. Davies.
Grantmaker type: Independent foundation.
Financial data (yr. ended 12/31/09): Assets, $1,021,865 (M); expenditures, $70,234; total giving, $50,500; qualifying distributions, $50,500; giving activities include $50,500 for grants.
Fields of interest: Arts; Elementary/secondary education; Higher education; Environment, natural resources; Medical care, rehabilitation; Human services.
Type of support: Scholarship funds; General/operating support; Annual campaigns.
Limitations: Giving primarily in Columbus, OH, and MI. No grants to individuals.
Officers: Louis H. Sanford, Pres.; Louis Hildreth II, V.P. and Secy.; Mark Merkle, V.P. and Treas.
EIN: 316026444

374
Robert D. Hill Foundation
10539 Whispering Brook N.W.
Grand Rapids, MI 49544-9535
County: Kent

Grantmaker type: Independent foundation.
Financial data (yr. ended 12/31/09): Assets, $52,530 (M); expenditures, $14,624; total giving, $14,000; qualifying distributions, $14,000; giving activities include $14,000 for 4 grants (high: $7,500; low: $500).
Fields of interest: Elementary/secondary education; Reproductive health, family planning; Cerebral palsy; United Ways and Federated Giving Programs.
Limitations: Applications accepted. Giving primarily in Coopersville, MI. No grants to individuals.
Application information: Application form required.
Initial approach: Letter
Deadline(s): Oct. 31
Trustees: Priscilla Hill Gregels; Barbara Hill Newby.
EIN: 386071614

375
Clarence and Jack Himmel Foundation
2000 Town Ctr., Ste. 1780
Southfield, MI 48075-1313
County: Oakland

Established in 1975 in MI.
Donor: Clarence Himmel†.
Grantmaker type: Independent foundation.
Financial data (yr. ended 10/31/10): Assets, $1,860,840 (M); expenditures, $119,635; total giving, $70,500; qualifying distributions, $70,500; giving activities include $70,500 for 18 grants (high: $10,000; low: $3,000).
Fields of interest: Arts; Education; Health care; Health organizations, association; Human services; Children/youth, services; Jewish agencies & synagogues.
Limitations: Applications accepted. Giving primarily in MI, with emphasis on the greater Detroit metropolitan area. No grants to individuals.
Application information: Application form not required.
Initial approach: Letter
Deadline(s): None
Officers: Robert A. Karbel, Pres. and Secy.; David Wallace, V.P.; Ronald A. Rothstein, Treas.
EIN: 510140773

376
The Hire Family Foundation
c/o Red Diamond, Ltd.
26 E. Main St., Ste. 2
Lexington, OH 44904-1223 (419) 884-3522
County: Richland
Contact: Janis Williams

Established in 2003 in OH.
Donor: Phyllis F. Hire.
Grantmaker type: Independent foundation.
Financial data (yr. ended 12/31/09): Assets, $1,221 (M); gifts received, $245,000; expenditures, $252,504; total giving, $252,503; qualifying distributions, $252,503; giving activities include $252,503 for 16 grants (high: $100,000; low: $500).
Fields of interest: Performing arts, ballet; Health care; Salvation Army; Residential/custodial care, hospices.
Limitations: Applications accepted. Giving primarily in Garfield and Pitkin counties, CO, Charlotte County, FL, Inverness Township, MI and Richland County, OH. No grants to individuals, or for operating expenses, debt reduction, capital campaigns, or endowments.
Application information: Application form required.
Initial approach: Letter
Deadline(s): July 31
Final notification: Dec. 31
Officers and Directors:* Phyllis F. Hire,* Pres.; John S. Hire,* Secy.; Lawrence M. Wolf,* Treas.
EIN: 770590536
Selected grants: The following grants were reported in 2008.
$50,000 to Humane Society of Richland County, Mansfield, OH.
$38,376 to Friendly House, Mansfield, OH.
$37,500 to Ohio Bird Sanctuary, Mansfield, OH.
$20,000 to Mansfield Christian School, Mansfield, OH.
$15,000 to MedCentral College of Nursing, Mansfield, OH.
$12,000 to North Central State College, Mansfield, OH.
$10,000 to Discovery School, Mansfield, OH.
$1,000 to Indiana Wesleyan University, Marion, IN.

377
Ray & Peg Hirvonen Charitable Foundation
451 Lakewood Ln.
Marquette, MI 49855-9513 (906) 249-1578
County: Marquette
Contact: Mark Hirvonen, Secy.

Established in 1993.
Donors: Ray Hirvonen; Peg Hirvonen.
Grantmaker type: Independent foundation.
Financial data (yr. ended 12/31/09): Assets, $1,930,391 (M); expenditures, $94,642; total giving, $92,347; qualifying distributions, $92,347; giving activities include $92,347 for grants.
Fields of interest: Museums; Historic preservation/historical societies; Higher education; Health care; Human services; Protestant agencies & churches.
Type of support: Program development; Debt reduction; Capital campaigns.
Limitations: Giving primarily in MI, with emphasis on Marquette. No grants to individuals.
Application information: Application form required.
Initial approach: Letter
Deadline(s): None

Officers: Linda Hirvonen, Pres.; Matt Hirvonen, V.P.; Mark Hirvonen, Secy.; Ray Hirvonen, Treas.
Director: Rachel S. Hetico.
EIN: 311388018
Selected grants: The following grants were reported in 2007.
$110,000 to Finlandia University, Hancock, MI.

378
His Work Private Foundation
2221 Health Dr. S.W., Ste. 2200
Wyoming, MI 49519-9650 (616) 248-3566
County: Kent
Contact: Gary Granger, Pres.

Established in 1998 in MI.
Donor: Gary Granger.
Grantmaker type: Independent foundation.
Financial data (yr. ended 11/30/09): Assets, $88,094 (M); gifts received, $610; expenditures, $4,862; total giving, $3,100; qualifying distributions, $3,100; giving activities include $3,100 for grants.
Fields of interest: International development; Christian agencies & churches.
Type of support: Building/renovation; General/operating support.
Limitations: Giving primarily in MI.
Officer: Gary Granger, Pres.
EIN: 383444500

379
Helmut and Ellen Hof Charitable Foundation
3452 Charlevoix Dr. S.E.
Grand Rapids, MI 49546-7054
County: Kent
Contact: Helmut Hof, Pres.

Established in 1989 in MI.
Grantmaker type: Independent foundation.
Financial data (yr. ended 12/31/09): Assets, $28,326 (M); expenditures, $1,928; total giving, $1,490; qualifying distributions, $1,490; giving activities include $1,490 for grants.
Limitations: Giving primarily in MI; some giving also in AZ.
Application information:
Initial approach: Letter or proposal
Deadline(s): None
Officers: Helmut Hof, Pres. and Treas.; Ellen Hof, Secy.
EIN: 382920772

380
Leonard and Ethel Hoffman Scholarship Trust
P.O. Box 3636
Grand Rapids, MI 49501-3636 (630) 468-8946
County: Kent

Grantmaker type: Independent foundation.
Financial data (yr. ended 12/31/09): Assets, $423,201 (M); expenditures, $23,614; total giving, $18,034; qualifying distributions, $18,259; giving activities include $18,034 for 38 grants (high: $500; low: $454).
Limitations: Applications accepted. Giving primarily in Culver, IN.
Application information: Application form required.

Initial approach: Letter
Deadline(s): Mar. 15
Trustee: Fifth Third Bank.
EIN: 386813892

381
James and Lynelle Holden Fund
802 E. Big Beaver Rd.
Troy, MI 48083-1404 (248) 689-5252
County: Oakland
Contact: Donald J. Miller, Pres.
FAX: (313) 962-5792;
E-mail: hmmlaw@sbcglobal.net; Additional address: 615 Griswold, No. 600, Detroit, MI 48226-3904, tel.: (313) 962-8710

Incorporated in 1941 in MI.
Donors: James S. Holden†; Lynelle A. Holden†.
Grantmaker type: Independent foundation.
Financial data (yr. ended 10/31/10): Assets, $2,276,529 (M); expenditures, $276,326; total giving, $153,000; qualifying distributions, $189,990; giving activities include $153,000 for 35 grants (high: $50,000; low: $1,000).
Purpose and activities: Support for medical research, including medical schools and children's hospitals, youth agencies, minority and underprivileged children, higher education, and cultural programs.
Fields of interest: Arts; Higher education; Hospitals (specialty); Medical research, institute; Children/youth, services; Children/youth; Children; Girls; Boys.
Type of support: General/operating support; Continuing support; Building/renovation; Equipment; Publication; Scholarship funds; Research; Matching/challenge support.
Limitations: Applications accepted. Giving primarily in Macomb, Oakland, Washtenaw, and Wayne counties, MI; giving to colleges and universities throughout MI. No support for religious or ethnic organizations, or for disease-specific organizations. No grants to individuals, or for endowment funds; no loans.
Application information: Application form not required.
Initial approach: Letter or proposal
Copies of proposal: 1
Deadline(s): None
Board meeting date(s): Feb., May, Aug., and Nov.
Final notification: Several weeks, or until the next board meeting
Officers and Trustees:* Donald J. Miller,* Pres.; Herbert E. Weston,* V.P. and Treas.; Ingrid O. Vernier, Secy.; Daniel T. Lis.
Number of staff: 3 part-time professional; 1 part-time support.
EIN: 386052154
Selected grants: The following grants were reported in 2009.
$25,000 to Detroit Zoological Society, Royal Oak, MI.
$20,000 to University of Detroit Mercy, Detroit, MI.
$3,000 to Gleaners Community Food Bank, Detroit, MI.
$2,500 to Detroit Historical Society, Detroit, MI.
$2,500 to Detroit Symphony Orchestra, Max M Fisher Music Center, Detroit, MI.
$2,500 to Michigan Opera Theater, Detroit, MI.
$1,500 to American Red Cross, Southeastern Michigan Chapter, Detroit, MI.
$1,500 to Capuchin Soup Kitchen, Detroit, MI.
$1,500 to Forgotten Harvest, Oak Park, MI.

$1,500 to Penrickton Center for Blind Children, Taylor, MI.

382
The Laura Ludington Hollenbeck Foundation
c/o Deloitte & Touche, LLP
3320 Ridgecrest Dr., Ste. 400
Midland, MI 48642-5864 (989) 631-2370
County: Midland
Contact: Laura L. Hollenbeck, Pres.

Established in 1996 in MI.
Donor: John S. Ludington.
Grantmaker type: Independent foundation.
Financial data (yr. ended 12/31/09): Assets, $558,045 (M); gifts received, $48,847; expenditures, $28,918; total giving, $24,750; qualifying distributions, $24,750; giving activities include $24,750 for grants.
Purpose and activities: Giving primarily to a community foundation, and for health and human services.
Fields of interest: Health care; Human services; Foundations (community); Protestant agencies & churches.
Limitations: Giving primarily in MI.
Application information:
Initial approach: Letter
Deadline(s): None
Officers: Laura L. Hollenbeck, Pres.; Martyn T. Hollenbeck, V.P.; John S. Ludington, Treas.
EIN: 383323698

383
The Holley Foundation
c/o Private Bank of Bloomfield Hills
38505 Woodward Ave., Ste. 1300
Bloomfield Hills, MI 48304
County: Oakland
E-mail: grants@theholleyfoundation.org; Application address: c/o Rev. George M. Holley III, 1846 Heydon Ct., Henderson, NV 89014; URL: http://www.theholleyfoundation.org

Established in 1944 in MI.
Donor: George M. Holley†.
Grantmaker type: Independent foundation.
Financial data (yr. ended 12/31/09): Assets, $2,649,205 (M); gifts received, $1,230; expenditures, $186,014; total giving, $145,600; qualifying distributions, $163,200; giving activities include $145,600 for 10 grants (high: $48,000; low: $1,000).
Purpose and activities: Supports education and various other programs for young people, primarily in southeastern MI. The foundation is interested in programs, other than bricks and mortar, which are imaginative and well-articulated and that can enable, enhance, or heal.
Fields of interest: Arts; Education; Human services; Children/youth, services.
Type of support: Endowments; Program development; Seed money.
Limitations: Applications accepted. Giving primarily in southeastern MI.
Publications: Application guidelines.
Application information: Application form may be obtained from the foundation by e-mail. Application form required.
Initial approach: E-mail using required form

Copies of proposal: 1
Deadline(s): Apr. 1
Board meeting date(s): May and Nov.
Final notification: About 2 months
Officers and Trustees: Gregg Kuehn, Jr.,* Pres.;
Rev. George M. Holley III,* V.P. and Progs. Comm.
Chair.; Margaret E. Holley,* Secy.; John C. Holley,
Jr., Treas. and Chair., Fin Comm.; Ben deVries;
Daane deVries; Barbara K. Frank; Stephen Holley;
Charlie Kuehn; Lynn Krugman; Margery H. Uihlein.
EIN: 386055168
Selected grants: The following grants were reported
in 2009.
$30,000 to Jefferson Avenue Presbyterian Tutoring
Tree, Detroit, MI.
$28,000 to Project SEED, Detroit, MI.
$26,000 to Student Mentor Partners, Saint Clair
Shores, MI.
$15,000 to Insideout Literacy Arts Project, Detroit,
MI. For Writer-in-Residence at Southeastern High
School.
$10,000 to Adult Well-Being Services, Detroit, MI.
$10,000 to Gleaners Community Food Bank,
Detroit, MI. For KidSnack Program in Southeastern
Village Schools.

384
Home & Building Association Foundation
(also known as HBA Foundation)
(formerly Greater Grand Rapids Home Builders
Association Foundation)
c/o Housing Center of West Michigan
1633 E. Beltline Ave. N.E.
Grand Rapids, MI   49525-4509   (616) 447-7262
County: Kent
Contact: Marci Muller, Fdn. Dir.
FAX: (616) 281-6002; Toll-free tel.: (800) 305-2021,
ext. 256

Established in 1988 in MI.
Donor: Samuel I. Newhouse Foundation, Inc.
Grantmaker type: Independent foundation.
Financial data (yr. ended 12/31/09): Assets,
$235,095 (M); gifts received, $1,100;
expenditures, $23,026; total giving, $5,000;
qualifying distributions, $5,000; giving activities
include $5,000 for grants.
Purpose and activities: Giving to provide
opportunities to support the community by providing
community service grants focusing on special needs
housing and to provide scholarships for students
pursuing a career related to the building industry.
Fields of interest: Housing/shelter, development;
Housing/shelter, rehabilitation; Housing/shelter,
temporary shelter; Housing/shelter, homeless;
Housing/shelter, repairs; Community development,
business promotion; Economically disadvantaged;
Homeless.
Type of support: Building/renovation; Program
development; Scholarships—to individuals.
Limitations: Applications accepted. Giving limited to
Kent, Ionia, Montcalm, and eastern Ottawa
counties, MI.
Publications: Application guidelines; Annual report;
Newsletter.
Application information: Foundation Grants and
Community Projects Committee reviews all
requests. See foundation web site for full
application guidelines and requirements, including
downloadable application forms for grants and
scholarships. Application form required.
    Deadline(s): 2nd Fri. in Feb. for grants; 2nd Fri. in
       Mar. for scholarships

Officers and Directors: Judy Barnes,* C.E.O. and
Exec. V.P.; Daniel N. Grzywacz,* Pres.; Brian
Bosgraaf,* V.P.; Jan Lehman,* Secy.; Benham R.
Wrigley,* Treas.; Marci Muller, Fdn. Dir.; Sarah Baar;
Ben Brinks, Jr.; Duane Gunnink; Nick Nicola; Tim
Rottschafer; Brad Uhl; Ken Van Haaften; Bonnie
Zaskowski.
EIN: 382836920

385
The Honholt Family Foundation
3025 Wood Duck Ln.
Ada, MI   49301-8353
County: Kent

Established in 2006 in MI.
Donors: Douglas P. Honholt; Karen L. Honholt;
Universal Forest Products, Inc.
Grantmaker type: Independent foundation.
Financial data (yr. ended 12/31/09): Assets,
$1,146 (M); gifts received, $22,013; expenditures,
$25,268; total giving, $25,256; qualifying
distributions, $25,256; giving activities include
$25,256 for grants.
Fields of interest: Theological school/education;
Health care; Christian agencies & churches.
Limitations: Giving primarily in MI. No grants for
individuals.
Director: Douglas P. Honholt.
EIN: 204999271

386
The Joseph W. Hood Foundation
11636 Highland Rd., Ste. 104
Hartland, MI   48353-2728
County: Livingston
Contact: Joseph W. Hood, Pres.
Application address: 5161 Harp Dr., Linden, MI
48451-9060

Established in 2001 in MI.
Donors: Joseph Chevrolet, Inc.; Joseph Pontiac, Inc.
Grantmaker type: Independent foundation.
Financial data (yr. ended 12/31/08): Assets, $1
(M); gifts received, $1,500; expenditures, $156;
total giving, $0; qualifying distributions, $0.
Purpose and activities: Giving primarily for St. Judes
Hospital, Detroit, Michigan.
Fields of interest: Hospitals (specialty).
Limitations: Giving primarily in Detroit, MI. No grants
to individuals.
Application information:
    Initial approach: Letter
    Deadline(s) None
Officers and Directors: Joseph W. Hood,* Pres.;
Cheryl Luttman,* V.P.; Kevin Hood; Nancy Hood.
EIN: 383564128

387
Charles & Alda Horgan Charitable Trust
c/o Citizens Bank, N.A.
328 S. Saginaw St., MC 002072
Flint, MI   48502-1923
County: Genesee
Application address: c/o Citizens Bank, N.A., Wealth
Mgmt., Attn.: Helen James, Trust Off., 101 N.
Washington St., Saginaw, MI 48607-1207,
tel.: (989) 776-7368

Established in 1996 in MI.

Grantmaker type: Independent foundation.
Financial data (yr. ended 09/30/10): Assets,
$1,040,556 (M); expenditures, $60,800; total
giving, $43,760; qualifying distributions, $43,760;
giving activities include $43,760 for grants.
Purpose and activities: Giving to the Saginaw,
Michigan community through annual grants to ten
organizations specified in the trust agreement, and
through scholarship awards to its residents with a
minimum 2.5 GPA.
Fields of interest: Museums (art); Performing arts,
orchestras; Historic preservation/historical
societies; Education; Zoos/zoological societies;
Cancer; Human services; United Ways and
Federated Giving Programs; Christian agencies &
churches.
Type of support: General/operating support;
Scholarships—to individuals.
Limitations: Giving limited to Saginaw, MI.
Application information: Application form required.
    Initial approach: Letter requesting application
    Deadline(s): July 1
Trustee: Citizens Bank.
EIN: 386661683

388
Leon & Audrey Hovarter Scholarship Fund
Trust
P.O. Box 247
Marcellus, MI   49067-0247   (269) 646-5345
County: Cass
Contact: Donald R. France, Tr.

Established in 2004 in MI.
Grantmaker type: Independent foundation.
Financial data (yr. ended 12/31/09): Assets,
$410,688 (M); expenditures, $32,486; total giving,
$25,000; qualifying distributions, $25,000; giving
activities include $25,000 for grants to individuals.
Purpose and activities: Scholarship awards to
graduating seniors from Marcellus High School,
Michigan, and must attend full-time in the State of
Michigan, any accredited community college or
university.
Fields of interest: Higher education.
Type of support: Scholarships—to individuals.
Limitations: Applications accepted. Giving to
residents of MI.
Application information:
    Initial approach: Letter
    Deadline(s): Apr. 15
Trustee: Donald R. France.
EIN: 616309487

389
John C. and Mary Jane Howard Foundation
180 S. Union St.
Battle Creek, MI   49014-4918   (269) 209-1651
County: Calhoun
Contact: Winship C. Howard, Pres. and Treas.

Established in 1999 in MI.
Donor: Mary Jane Howard.
Grantmaker type: Independent foundation.
Financial data (yr. ended 12/31/09): Assets,
$1,525,251 (M); expenditures, $103,336; total
giving, $86,100; qualifying distributions, $89,957;
giving activities include $86,100 for 43 grants (high:
$8,000; low: $300).
Fields of interest: Education; Health organizations;
Human services; American Red Cross; United Ways

and Federated Giving Programs; Christian agencies & churches; Protestant agencies & churches.
Type of support: General/operating support.
Limitations: Applications accepted. Giving primarily in MI and NY. No grants to individuals; no loans.
Application information: Application form required.
Initial approach: Proposal
Deadline(s): None
Officers and Directors: * Winship C. Howard,* Pres. and Treas.; Ann E. Howard,* Secy.; Andrew T. Howard; Michael J. Howard; Mary E. Keyser.
EIN: 383452536

390
Marjorie W. Howe & Howard C. Howe Scholarship Trust
(also known as M. & H. Howe Scholarship Trust)
c/o Fifth Third Bank
111 Lyon St. N.W.
P.O. Box 3636
Grand Rapids, MI 49503-2406
County: Kent
Application address: c/o Fifth Third Bank, 1701 Golf Rd., MD GRLM8C, Rolling Meadows, IL 60008-4227

Established in 1995 in IL.
Grantmaker type: Independent foundation.
Financial data (yr. ended 12/31/09): Assets, $781,263 (M); expenditures, $22,069; total giving, $7,133; qualifying distributions, $7,133; giving activities include $7,133 for grants to individuals.
Purpose and activities: Scholarship awards to residents of Waukegan, Illinois, who are graduates of Waukegan High School.
Fields of interest: Higher education.
Type of support: Scholarships—to individuals.
Limitations: Giving limited to residents of Waukegan, IL.
Application information: Application form required.
Deadline(s): Apr. 1
Trustees: Robert Bollman; Fifth Third Bank.
EIN: 364005689

391
Robert P. & Ella B. Hudson Foundation, Inc.
P.O. Box 699
Sault Sainte Marie, MI 49783-0699
County: Chippewa
Application address: c/o Gillett, Halvorsen & Leonhardt, PC, 478 W. Spruce St., Sault Sainte Marie, MI 49783-1848, tel.: (906 635-1589

Established in 1948 in MI.
Grantmaker type: Independent foundation.
Financial data (yr. ended 12/31/09): Assets, $1,445,586 (M); expenditures, $76,727; total giving, $48,079; qualifying distributions, $48,079; giving activities include $48,079 for grants.
Purpose and activities: Giving primarily for education.
Fields of interest: Education; Health care; Recreation, camps; Human services; Community/ economic development.
Type of support: General/operating support; Capital campaigns; Building/renovation; Program development; Scholarship funds.
Limitations: Giving limited to Chippewa County, MI, with emphasis on Sault Sainte Marie.
Publications: Annual report.

Application information: Application form not required.
Initial approach: Proposal
Copies of proposal: 1
Deadline(s): None
Board meeting date(s): 3rd Thurs. of each month
Officer: Don Wilson, Pres.
Directors: Robert Arfstrom; James Halvorsen; William Oberman; Roger L. Paris.
Number of staff: 1 part-time support.
EIN: 386057714

392
Hudson-Webber Foundation
333 W. Fort St., Ste. 1310
Detroit, MI 48226-3149 (313) 963-7777
County: Wayne
Contact: David O. Egner, C.E.O. and Pres.
FAX: (313) 963-2818;
E-mail: info@hudson-webber.org; *URL:* http://www.hudson-webber.org

Incorporated in 1943 in MI; on Jan. 1, 1984 absorbed the Richard H. and Eloise Jenks Webber Charitable Fund, Inc., and the Eloise and Richard Webber Foundation.
Donors: Eloise Webber‡; Richard Webber‡; The J.L. Hudson Co.; Mary Webber Parker; and members of the Webber family.
Grantmaker type: Independent foundation.
Financial data (yr. ended 12/31/09): Assets, $150,553,592 (M); gifts received, $450,190; expenditures, $7,644,215; total giving, $5,823,313; qualifying distributions, $6,972,782; giving activities include $5,337,500 for 71 grants (high: $1,000,000; low: $100), $478,450 for 133 employee matching gifts, and $7,363 for foundation-administered programs.
Purpose and activities: The foundation concentrates efforts and resources in support of projects with four missions: 1) physical revitalization of the central city; 2) economic development of southeastern Michigan; 3) enhancement of major art and cultural institutions in Detroit; and 4) safe communities in Detroit.
Fields of interest: Arts; Crime/violence prevention; Urban/community development.
Type of support: General/operating support; Continuing support; Annual campaigns; Capital campaigns; Building/renovation; Program development; Seed money; Consulting services; Program evaluation; Employee matching gifts; Matching/challenge support.
Limitations: Applications accepted. Giving primarily in the city of Detroit, and the tri-county Wayne, Oakland, and Macomb area of southeastern MI. No support for educational institutions or neighborhood organizations (except for projects that fall within current program missions). No grants to individuals (except for J.L. Hudson Co. employees and their families), or for emergency funds, deficit financing, endowment funds, scholarships, fellowships, publications, conferences, fundraising, social events, or exhibits; no loans.
Publications: Application guidelines; Biennial report (including application guidelines); Financial statement; Grants list.
Application information: Accepts CMF Common Grant Application Form. Application form not required.
Initial approach: Letter of request or proposal
Copies of proposal: 1

Deadline(s): Apr. 15, Aug. 15 (for July and Dec. meetings), and Dec. 15 (for meeting in Apr. of following year)
Board meeting date(s): Apr., July, and Dec.
Final notification: 1 week after board decision
Officers and Trustees: * Jennifer Hudson Parke,* Chair.; David O. Egner,* C.E.O. and Pres.; Katy Locker, V.P., Progs.; Amanda Van Dusen,* Secy.; David E. Meador, Treas.; Matthew P. Cullen; Stephen R. D'Arcy; Anthony F. Earley; W. Frank Fountain; Gilbert Hudson; Joseph L. Hudson, Jr.; Joseph L. Hudson IV; Reginald M. Turner, Jr.; Jean Hudson Witmer.
Number of staff: 3 full-time professional; 2 part-time support.
EIN: 386052131
Selected grants: The following grants were reported in 2008.
$1,000,000 to Community Foundation for Southeast Michigan, Detroit, MI. For New Economy Initiative for Southeast Michigan.
$1,000,000 to Detroit Renaissance Foundation, Detroit, MI. For East Riverfront Development/Lower Woodward Gap Financing.
$500,000 to Local Initiatives Support Corporation, Detroit, MI. For Sustainable Communities.
$250,000 to Detroit Symphony Orchestra, Detroit, MI. For general operating support.
$225,000 to University Cultural Center Association, Detroit, MI. For Facade Improvement Program.
$200,000 to Detroit Institute of Arts, Detroit, MI. For Great Art New Start Campaign.
$150,000 to Detroit Science Center, Detroit, MI. For Engineering the Future Campaign.
$75,000 to Downtown Detroit Partnership, Detroit, MI. For Eastern Market Corporation.
$60,000 to Detroit Chamber Winds, Southfield, MI. For collaborative shared-services program.
$20,000 to Detroit Symphony Orchestra, Detroit, MI. For general program needs.

393
Carrie & Luther Huffines Educational Fund
c/o Comerica Bank
P.O. Box 75000, MC 3302
Detroit, MI 48275-3302
County: Wayne
Application address: c/o Sharon Stephens, 130 S. Franklin, Rocky Mount, NC 27804-5707

Established in 1955 in NC.
Donor: Robert L. Huffines, Jr.
Grantmaker type: Independent foundation.
Financial data (yr. ended 06/30/10): Assets, $106,232 (M); expenditures, $9,053; total giving, $5,000; qualifying distributions, $5,900; giving activities include $5,000 for 1 loan to an individual.
Purpose and activities: Loans to students residing in Edgecombe and Nash counties, NC.
Fields of interest: Higher education.
Type of support: Student loans—to individuals.
Limitations: Applications accepted. Giving limited to Edgecombe and Nash counties, NC.
Application information: Application form required.
Deadline(s): June 1
Trustee: Comerica Bank.
EIN: 566046187

394
Huizenga Family Foundation
P.O. Box 159
Niles, MI   49120-0159
County: Berrien

Established in 2006 in MI.
Donor: Charles B. Huizenga.
Grantmaker type: Independent foundation.
Financial data (yr. ended 12/31/09): Assets,
$2,014,739 (M); gifts received, $35; expenditures,
$78,544; total giving, $70,000; qualifying
distributions, $70,000; giving activities include
$70,000 for grants.
Fields of interest: Elementary/secondary
education.
Officers: Charles B. Huizenga, Pres.; Douglas L.
Huizenga, V.P.; William R. Landgraf, Secy.; James F.
Scarpone, Treas.
EIN: 205350762

395
Humane Society of Macomb Foundation, Inc.
11350 22 Mile Rd.
Utica, MI   48317-2604   (586) 731-9210
County: Macomb
Contact: Shirley Burgess, Dir.

Established in 1994 in MI.
Grantmaker type: Independent foundation.
Financial data (yr. ended 12/31/09): Assets,
$1,252,575 (M); expenditures, $71,192; total
giving, $68,134; qualifying distributions, $68,134;
giving activities include $68,134 for grants.
Purpose and activities: Giving for animal welfare
organizations. Some giving for scholarship awards
to veterinary students.
Fields of interest: Graduate/professional
education; Animal welfare; Veterinary medicine.
Type of support: Scholarships—to individuals.
Limitations: Giving primarily in MI.
Application information: Application form not
required.
    Deadline(s): None
Officers: Erich Puff, Pres.; Phil Boos, V.P.; Robert
Weidenbach, Secy.
Director: Shirley Burgess.
EIN: 383183238

396
Paul A. Humbert Scholarship Trust
c/o Fifth Third Bank
P.O. Box 3636
Grand Rapids, MI   49501-3636
County: Kent
Application address: c/o Culver Community High
School, Attn.: Guidance Office, 701 N. School St.,
Culver, IN 46511-1099, tel.: (219) 842-3391

Established in 1988 in IN.
Donor: Ines M. Humbert.
Grantmaker type: Independent foundation.
Financial data (yr. ended 06/30/10): Assets,
$497,891 (M); expenditures, $34,558; total giving,
$28,855; qualifying distributions, $28,855; giving
activities include $28,855 for grants to individuals.
Purpose and activities: Scholarship awards to
graduates of Culver Community High School,
Indiana.
Fields of interest: Higher education.

Type of support: Scholarships—to individuals.
Limitations: Giving limited to residents of the
Culver, IN area.
Application information: Application form required.
    Deadline(s): Apr. 15
Scholarship Committee: Don Adams; M. Karen
Mendenhall; Brenda Sheldon; Barbara Winters.
Trustee: Fifth Third Bank.
EIN: 356505726

397
Edward and Irma Hunter Foundation
423 Sycamore St., Ste. 101
Niles, MI   49120-0960   (269) 684-3248
County: Berrien
Contact: James F. Keenan, Pres.

Established in 1968 in MI.
Donors: Edward Hunter†; Irma Hunter†.
Grantmaker type: Independent foundation.
Financial data (yr. ended 12/31/09): Assets,
$4,525,811 (M); expenditures, $225,563; total
giving, $107,500; qualifying distributions,
$107,500; giving activities include $107,500 for
grants.
Fields of interest: Education; Employment; Human
services; YM/YWCAs & YM/YWHAs; Community/
economic development; Government/public
administration.
Type of support: Annual campaigns; Building/
renovation; Equipment; Land acquisition;
Emergency funds; Matching/challenge support.
Limitations: Applications accepted. Giving limited to
the Buchanan and Niles, MI, area. No grants to
individuals, or for operating budgets, continuing
support, seed money, deficit financing, endowment
funds, scholarships, fellowships, program support,
research, demonstration projects, publications, or
conferences; no loans.
Publications: Informational brochure (including
application guidelines).
Application information: Application form not
required.
    Initial approach: Letter
    Copies of proposal: 7
    Deadline(s): 2nd week of Feb., May, Aug., and
    Nov.
    Board meeting date(s): 4th Mon. of Feb., May,
    Aug., and Nov.
    Final notification: 1 week
Officer: James F. Keenan, Pres.
Trustees: Jerry E. French; Gerald H. Frieling, Jr.;
William D. Haslett; David L. Lawrence; William
Racine; Donald F. Walter.
EIN: 237065471

398
The Hurst Foundation
675 Robinson Rd.
Jackson, MI   49203-1155   (517) 841-4886
County: Jackson

Trust established in 1955 in MI.
Donors: Peter F. Hurst†; Elizabeth S. Hurst†.
Grantmaker type: Independent foundation.
Financial data (yr. ended 12/31/09): Assets,
$9,280,601 (M); expenditures, $537,294; total
giving, $519,333; qualifying distributions,
$519,333; giving activities include $519,333 for
grants.

Fields of interest: Arts; Secondary school/
education; Higher education; Human services;
Youth, services; Community/economic
development; Protestant agencies & churches.
Type of support: General/operating support;
Building/renovation; Equipment; Program
development; Seed money.
Limitations: Giving primarily in Jackson County, MI.
No grants to individuals, or for endowment funds,
scholarships, fellowships, or matching gifts; no
loans.
Application information: Application form not
required.
    Initial approach: Letter
    Copies of proposal: 2
    Deadline(s): Oct. 1
    Board meeting date(s): Dec. and as necessary
    Final notification: Within 60 days for favorable
    decisions
Officer: Anthony P. Hurst, Pres.
EIN: 386089457
Selected grants: The following grants were reported
in 2008.
$25,000 to Dahlem Conservancy, Jackson, MI.
$20,000 to John George Home, Jackson, MI.
$12,500 to Shop Rat Foundation, Pleasant Lake,
MI.
$12,000 to Saint Lukes Clinic, Jackson, MI.
$9,000 to Hanover-Horton Schools, Hanover, MI.
$7,500 to buildOn, Stamford, CT.
$7,500 to First Presbyterian Church, Jackson, MI.
$7,500 to Junior Achievement of the Michigan Edge,
Jackson, MI.
$5,000 to Center for Family Health, Jackson, MI.
$5,000 to Jackson Nonprofit Support Center,
Jackson, MI.

399
Theodore Huss, Sr. and Elsie Endert Huss Memorial Fund
c/o Citizens Bank Wealth Mgmt., N.A.
328 S. Saginaw St., M/C 001065
Flint, MI   48502-1923
County: Genesee
Application address: c/o Helen James, Citizens
Bank, N.A., Wealth Mgmt., 101 N. Washington Ave.,
Saginaw, MI 48607, tel.: (989) 776-7368

Established in 1985 in MI.
Grantmaker type: Independent foundation.
Financial data (yr. ended 12/31/09): Assets,
$338,451 (M); expenditures, $21,541; total giving,
$12,500; qualifying distributions, $12,500; giving
activities include $12,500 for 25 grants to
individuals (high: $500; low: $500).
Purpose and activities: Scholarships awards to full
time undergraduate students from Saginaw County,
Michigan.
Fields of interest: Higher education.
Type of support: Scholarships—to individuals.
Limitations: Giving limited to residents of Saginaw
County, MI.
Application information: Application form required.
    Deadline(s): June 1
Trustee: Citizens Bank.
EIN: 386476850

400

I Have a Dream Foundation - Port Huron

5538 Lakeshore Rd.
Fort Gratiot, MI 48059-2813 (810) 385-3315
County: St. Clair
Contact: Chris M. Kurzweil, Pres.

Established in 1994 in MI.
Donor: Chris M. Kurzweil.
Grantmaker type: Independent foundation.
Financial data (yr. ended 06/30/10): Assets,
$2,465 (M); gifts received, $61,000; expenditures,
$77,929; total giving, $72,773; qualifying
distributions, $72,773; giving activities include
$72,773 for grants to individuals.
Purpose and activities: Giving primarily to provide
comprehensive educational support and guidance to
selected disadvantaged elementary school children.
Fields of interest: Education; Minorities;
Economically disadvantaged.
Type of support: Grants to individuals; Scholarships
—to individuals.
Limitations: Giving primarily in Port Huron, MI.
Officers: Chris M. Kurzweil, Pres.; Joanne Kurzweil,
Secy.; Richard F. Dufner, Treas.
Number of staff: 1 full-time professional.
EIN: 383193498

401

Julie A. Ibbetson Memorial Scholarship

3455 Lincoln St.
Dearborn, MI 48124-3561
County: Wayne

Grantmaker type: Independent foundation.
Financial data (yr. ended 12/31/09): Assets, $1
(M); gifts received, $1,000; expenditures, $1,000;
total giving, $1,000; qualifying distributions,
$1,000; giving activities include $1,000 for grants.
Officer: Steve Phelps, Pres.
EIN: 300204194

402

Bill and Bea Idema Foundation

(formerly Wren Foundation)
c/o Fifth Third Bank
111 Lyon St. N.W. - RMNR5B
Grand Rapids, MI 49503-2406
County: Kent
Contact: Joyce Versluis, V.P.

Established in 1986 in MI.
Donors: Beatrice A. Idema; William W. Idema†.
Grantmaker type: Independent foundation.
Financial data (yr. ended 06/30/10): Assets,
$3,474,463 (M); expenditures, $175,149; total
giving, $135,000; qualifying distributions,
$135,000; giving activities include $135,000 for
grants.
Purpose and activities: The Bill and Bea Idema
Foundation focuses its grants primarily on funding
special projects or programs in the Grand Rapids,
Michigan area that are consistent with its mission:
The Bill and Bea Idema Foundation exists to give
expression to our traditional Christian values by
supporting schools, organizations and community
programs that help children and families.
Fields of interest: Performing arts; Secondary
school/education; Higher education; Education;
Health care, blood supply; Cancer; Girl scouts;
Human services; YM/YWCAs & YM/YWHAs;

Children/youth, services; Christian agencies &
churches; Blind/visually impaired.
Type of support: General/operating support; Capital
campaigns; Building/renovation; Program
development; Seed money; Scholarship funds.
Limitations: Applications accepted. Giving primarily
in the Grand Rapids, MI, area.
Application information:
Initial approach: Letter
Copies of proposal: 1
Deadline(s): June 15 and Nov. 15
Board meeting date(s): July and Dec.
Officers: Beatrice A. Idema, Pres.; Joyce Versluis,
V.P.; Jeff Power, Secy.; Paul Ryan, Treas.
Trustees: Chad Versluis; Peter Versluis; Susan
Vogel-Vanderson; Tonya Williamson.
Manager: Fifth Third Bank.
EIN: 382653272
Selected grants: The following grants were reported
in 2009.
$15,000 to Michigan Colleges Foundation,
Southfield, MI.
$15,000 to West Side Christian School, Grand
Rapids, MI.
$5,000 to Kids Food Basket, Grand Rapids, MI.

403

John & Ella Imerman Foundation

1501 E. 11 Mile Rd.
Royal Oak, MI 48067-2027
County: Oakland
Contact: Joan Jampel, Pres.

Established in MI.
Grantmaker type: Independent foundation.
Financial data (yr. ended 12/31/09): Assets,
$335,830 (M); expenditures, $19,423; total giving,
$18,000; qualifying distributions, $18,000; giving
activities include $18,000 for grants.
Fields of interest: Jewish agencies & synagogues.
Limitations: Giving in MI, primarily in Bloomfield
Hills and West Bloomfield.
Application information:
Initial approach: Letter
Deadline(s): None
Officers: Joan Jampel, Pres. and Secy.; Dr. Robert
Jampel, Treas.
EIN: 386088885

404

Frances B. Imoberstag Charitable Foundation

c/o Rennie & Assenmacher, PC
22211 W. Warren St.
Dearborn Heights, MI 48127-2531
County: Wayne
Contact: Margaret Campbell, Pres.

Established in 1994 in MI.
Donor: Frances B. Imoberstag†.
Grantmaker type: Independent foundation.
Financial data (yr. ended 12/31/09): Assets,
$215,779 (M); expenditures, $21,160; total giving,
$20,600; qualifying distributions, $20,600; giving
activities include $20,600 for 2 grants (high:
$15,000; low: $5,600).
Fields of interest: Higher education, university.
Limitations: Giving primarily in Dearborn, MI. No
grants to individuals.
Application information:

Initial approach: Letter
Deadline(s): None
Officer: Margaret Campbell, Pres.; Sallie F. Snyder,
V.P.; Mary E. Biddinger, Secy.; Frances A. Knoop,
Treas.
EIN: 383172291

405

Inbounds, Inc.

3463 Autumn Ln.
Ann Arbor, MI 48105-9746
County: Washtenaw

Grantmaker type: Independent foundation.
Financial data (yr. ended 12/31/09): Assets,
$2,365 (M); expenditures, $10,224; total giving,
$0; qualifying distributions, $0.
Officers and Director:* Donald L. Simons,* Pres.;
Donna Rice, Secy.; Alena Cowsette, Exec. Dir.
EIN: 382949412

406

India Foundation

3505 Coolidge Rd.
East Lansing, MI 48823-6377
County: Ingham
Contact: Shrikumar Poddar, Pres.

Established in 1970 in MI.
Donors: Shrikumar Poddar; Mayurika Poddar;
Devesh Darshan Poddar.
Grantmaker type: Independent foundation.
Financial data (yr. ended 12/31/09): Assets,
$2,157,501 (M); gifts received, $21,849;
expenditures, $154,469; total giving, $62,831;
qualifying distributions, $62,831; giving activities
include $62,831 for grants.
Purpose and activities: Giving primarily for East
Indian religious and charitable organizations.
Fields of interest: Education; Hinduism; Religion,
interfaith issues.
Type of support: Conferences/seminars; Seed
money; Technical assistance; In-kind gifts;
Matching/challenge support.
Limitations: Giving primarily in MI. No grants to
individuals.
Application information: Application form not
required.
Copies of proposal: 1
Deadline(s): Apr. 30 and Aug. 31
Board meeting date(s): Semiannually in June and
Sept.
Officers: Shrikumar Poddar, Pres. and Treas.;
Mayurika Poddar, V.P.; Daniel J. Warmels, Secy.
Director: Ted Simmons.
EIN: 237300230

407

The Barton J. & Gail G. Ingraham Foundation

10203 E. Shady Ln.
Suttons Bay, MI 49682-9452
County: Leelanau

Established in 2000 in MI.
Grantmaker type: Independent foundation.
Financial data (yr. ended 12/31/09): Assets,
$1,813 (M); gifts received, $8; expenditures, $119;
total giving, $110; qualifying distributions, $110;
giving activities include $110 for grants.

Limitations: Giving primarily in MI.
Trustees: Barton Ingraham; Gail Ingraham.
EIN: 383597295

408
The Irwin Foundation
50 Crocker Blvd., Ste. 100
Mount Clemens, MI 48043-2580
(586) 469-5050
County: Macomb
Contact: Sharon L. Potter, Secy.-Treas.
FAX: (586) 469-0018;
E-mail: inquiries@irwinfoundation.com; Additional
email: spotter@irwinfoundation.com; URL: http://
www.irwinfoundation.com/

Established in 1996 in MI.
Donors: Claire Irwin†; James Irwin†.
Grantmaker type: Independent foundation.
Financial data (yr. ended 12/31/09): Assets,
$235,218 (M); expenditures, $55,671; total giving,
$10,000; qualifying distributions, $10,000; giving
activities include $10,000 for grants.
Purpose and activities: Giving for the promotion of
veterinary education, including the funding of
student scholarships in schools, departments, or
units accredited in veterinary medicine or veterinary
technology, within a major university. Other support
includes use of foundation mobile veterinary facility
for remote medical programs and various
veterinary-related activities and events.
Fields of interest: Medical school/education;
Education; Veterinary medicine.
Type of support: Building/renovation; Equipment;
Fellowships; Scholarship funds.
Limitations: Giving in the U.S., with emphasis on
East Lansing, MI. No grants to individuals.
Application information:
  Initial approach: Letter
  Deadline(s): None
Officers and Directors:* William J. Cari,* Pres.;
Sharon L. Potter,* Secy.-Treas.; Sean P. Kelly.
EIN: 383262167

409
The Isabel Foundation
111 E. Court St., Ste. 3D
Flint, MI 48502-1649   (810) 767-0136
County: Genesee
Contact: Frederick S. Kirkpatrick
FAX: (810) 767-1207; URL: http://www.isabel.org

Established in 1988 in MI.
Grantmaker type: Independent foundation.
Financial data (yr. ended 06/30/09): Assets,
$47,373,286 (M); gifts received, $80,314;
expenditures, $3,665,618; total giving,
$3,205,148; qualifying distributions, $3,319,633;
giving activities include $3,205,148 for 90 grants
(high: $300,000; low: $120), and $211,970 for
foundation-administered programs.
Purpose and activities: Funding primarily for
churches and other religious organizations
dedicated to supporting or contributing to the cause
of Christian Science; support also for the arts,
education, and convalescent facilities.
Fields of interest: Arts; Higher education; Nursing
home/convalescent facility; Recreation, camps;
Christian agencies & churches.
Type of support: Program development; Capital
campaigns; General/operating support; Continuing

support; Annual campaigns; Building/renovation;
Equipment.
Limitations: Applications accepted. Giving in the
U.S., including but not limited to CA, CO, FL, MA, ME,
MI, MO, NY, OH, PA, TX, and WA. No grants to
individuals.
Application information: Application guidelines
available on foundation web site. Application form
not required.
  Initial approach: Letter
  Copies of proposal: 1
  Deadline(s): Mar. 1
  Final notification: Grants are primarily made in
  June
Officers and Trustees:* Claire Mott White,* Chair.
and Treas.; William S. White,* Pres. and Secy.;
Tiffany W. Lovett; Ridgeway H. White.
Number of staff: 2 part-time professional.
EIN: 382853004
Selected grants: The following grants were reported
in 2007.
$300,000 to Adventure Unlimited, Greenwood
Village, CO.
$200,000 to Broadview, Los Angeles, CA.
$200,000 to Flint Institute of Arts, Flint, MI.
$200,000 to Principia College, Saint Louis, MO.
$145,000 to First Church of Christ Scientist, Flint,
MI.
$85,000 to Twelveacres, Campbell, CA.
$64,000 to High Ridge House, Riverdale, NY.
$50,000 to Crystal Lake Camps, Hughesville, PA.
$10,000 to Metropolitan Opera Association, New
York, NY.
$10,000 to Smith College, Northampton, MA.

410
Keith A. Iverson Foundation
300 E. Huron St.
Milford, MI 48381-2349
County: Oakland

Established in 1998 in MI.
Donor: Keith A. Iverson.
Grantmaker type: Independent foundation.
Financial data (yr. ended 12/31/09): Assets, $568
(M); expenditures, $20; total giving, $0; qualifying
distributions, $0.
Limitations: Giving limited to MI.
Officers: Keith A. Iverson, Pres. and Treas.; Mark D.
Hamlin, Secy.
Directors: John M. Foster; Amy M. Iverson; Clifford
T. Iverson; Michael H. Russell.
EIN: 383378231

411
Corwill and Margie Jackson Foundation
c/o Comerica Bank
P.O. Box 75000, MC 3302
Detroit, MI 48275-3302
County: Wayne
Contact: David J. Hall, Pres.
Application address: 6954 W. Jackson Rd.,
Ludington, MI 49431-9428

Established in MI.
Donors: Corwill Jackson†; Margie Jackson†.
Grantmaker type: Independent foundation.
Financial data (yr. ended 12/31/09): Assets,
$2,132,344 (M); expenditures, $133,647; total
giving, $110,000; qualifying distributions,

$111,533; giving activities include $110,000 for 51
grants to individuals (high: $6,000; low: $500).
Purpose and activities: Scholarship awards to
graduating high school seniors in Mason County,
Michigan, starting their first year of college.
Fields of interest: Higher education.
Type of support: Scholarships—to individuals.
Limitations: Applications accepted. Giving limited to
residents of Mason County, MI.
Application information: Application form required.
  Deadline(s): May 1
Officers: David J. Hall, Pres.; Margie N. Bach, Secy.;
Thomas Hall, Treas.
Trustees: Jens Bach; Diane Graham-Henry; Chrissie
Hall; Susan Meyers.
EIN: 386064502

412
The Jerome Jacobson Foundation, Inc.
6931 Arlington Rd., Ste. 300
Bethesda, MD 20814-5231
County: Montgomery
Contact: Jerome Jacobson, Pres.
Application address: 4200 Massachusetts Ave.
N.W., Washington, DC 20016-4744

Established in 1990 in FL.
Donor: Jerome Jacobson.
Grantmaker type: Independent foundation.
Financial data (yr. ended 12/31/09): Assets,
$1,432,644 (M); gifts received, $26,060;
expenditures, $40,472; total giving, $35,000;
qualifying distributions, $35,000; giving activities
include $35,000 for grants.
Fields of interest: Higher education; Hospitals
(specialty); Eye research; Jewish federated giving
programs.
Limitations: Giving primarily in Ann Arbor, MI, and
New York, NY. No grants to individuals.
Application information:
  Initial approach: Letter
  Deadline(s): None
Officers and Director:* Jerome Jacobson,* Pres.;
Joshua Jacobson, Secy.-Treas.
EIN: 650167227

413
The Jafari Foundation
1338 Highland Meadows
Flint, MI 48532-2062
County: Genesee

Established in 2007 in MI.
Donor: Jehad Jafari.
Grantmaker type: Independent foundation.
Financial data (yr. ended 12/31/09): Assets,
$108,400 (M); gifts received, $50,000;
expenditures, $12,600; total giving, $12,600;
qualifying distributions, $12,600; giving activities
include $12,600 for grants.
Fields of interest: Islam.
Limitations: Giving primarily in Swartz Creek, MI. No
grants to individuals.
Officers: Jehad Jafari, Pres.; Tharaa Chanda Jafari,
V.P.
EIN: 261647284

414

Fredrica, Neva & Abraham Jaffe Scholarship Fund f/b/o Colon High School

(formerly Jaffe Charitable Trust f/b/o Colon High School)
c/o Citizens Bank Wealth Mgmt., N.A.
328 S. Saginaw St., M/C 001065
Flint, MI 48502-2401   (866) 308-7878
County: Genesee
Application address: c/o Lloyd Kirby, Superintendent, Colon Community Schools, 400 Dallas St., Colon, MI 49040-9318, tel.: (269) 432-3231

Established in 1992 in MI.
Grantmaker type: Independent foundation.
Financial data (yr. ended 12/31/09): Assets, $174,408 (M); expenditures, $12,344; total giving, $9,000; qualifying distributions, $11,065; giving activities include $9,000 for 4 grants to individuals (high: $3,000; low: $1,500).
Purpose and activities: Scholarships awarded to graduates of Colon High School, Michigan, pursuing a medical degree.
Fields of interest: Medical school/education; Nursing school/education.
Type of support: Scholarship funds; Scholarships—to individuals.
Limitations: Applications accepted. Giving limited to residents of the Colon, MI, area.
Application information: Application form required.
   Deadline(s): May 1
Trustee: Citizens Bank.
EIN: 316447467

415

Karen Sokolof Javitch Charitable Foundation

c/o Comerica Bank
P.O. Box 75000, MC 3302
Detroit, MI 48275-3302
County: Wayne
Application address: c/o Comerica Bank, Attn: Ted Stumpp, P.O. Box 75000, MC 5124, Detroit, MI 48275-5124, Colorado tel.: (303) 294-3349

Established in 2004 in NE.
Donor: Phil Sokolof†.
Grantmaker type: Independent foundation.
Financial data (yr. ended 12/31/09): Assets, $1,337,231 (M); expenditures, $111,996; total giving, $97,078; qualifying distributions, $97,078; giving activities include $97,078 for grants.
Fields of interest: Jewish agencies & synagogues; Children/youth; Blind/visually impaired.
Limitations: Applications accepted. Giving primarily in Omaha, NE. No support for organizations lacking 501(c)(3) status. No grants to individuals.
Application information: Application form not required.
   Deadline(s): None
Trustee: Comerica Bank.
EIN: 746536463
Selected grants: The following grants were reported in 2005.
$5,000 to Jewish Federation of Omaha, Omaha, NE.
$1,000 to Cystic Fibrosis Foundation, Omaha, NE.
$500 to Omaha Community Playhouse, Omaha, NE.
$125 to Omaha Symphony, Omaha, NE.

416

Michael Jeffers Memorial Education Fund

c/o Citizens Bank Wealth Mgmt., N.A.
328 S. Saginaw St., M/C 001065
Flint, MI 48502-1923   (989) 776-7368
County: Genesee
Application address: c/o Helen James, Citizens Bank, N.A., Wealth Mgmt., 101 N. Washington Ave., Saginaw, MI 48607, tel.: (989) 776-7368

Established in 1999 in MI.
Donor: Michael Jeffers Memorial Fund.
Grantmaker type: Independent foundation.
Financial data (yr. ended 12/31/09): Assets, $6,845,831 (M); expenditures, $98,330; total giving, $0; qualifying distributions, $310,461.
Purpose and activities: Student loans to residents of Saginaw, MI, ages 16 to 19, with a need for economic aid.
Fields of interest: Higher education.
Type of support: Student loans—to individuals.
Limitations: Giving primarily to residents of Saginaw, MI.
Application information: Application form required.
   Deadline(s): June 1 for renewals, June 15 for new loans
Trustee: Citizens Bank.
EIN: 383431990

417

John Michael Jeffers Memorial Fund

c/o Citizens Bank Wealth Mgmt., N.A.
325 S. Saginaw St., M/C 002072
Flint, MI 48502-1908
County: Genesee
Application address: c/o Citizens Bank Wealth Mgmt., N.A., Attn.: Helen James, 101 N. Washington Ave., Saginaw, MI 48607-1207, tel.: (989) 776-7368

Established in 1994 in MI.
Grantmaker type: Independent foundation.
Financial data (yr. ended 04/30/10): Assets, $2,541,720 (M); expenditures, $141,191; total giving, $114,000; qualifying distributions, $117,784; giving activities include $114,000 for 9 grants (high: $30,000; low: $2,000).
Fields of interest: Human services; Children/youth, services; Community/economic development; Foundations (community).
Limitations: Applications accepted. Giving limited to Saginaw County, MI. No grants to individuals.
Application information:
   Initial approach: Letter or telephone requesting application guidelines
   Deadline(s): None
Trustee: Citizens Bank Wealth Management, N.A.
EIN: 237425043
Selected grants: The following grants were reported in 2010.
$20,000 to United Way of Saginaw County, Saginaw, MI.
$17,500 to Delta College Foundation, University Center, MI.
$13,000 to Emmaus House of Saginaw, Saginaw, MI.
$10,000 to Covenant Healthcare Foundation, Saginaw, MI.
$9,000 to Teen Challenge of Saginaw, Saginaw, MI.

418

Jennings Memorial Foundation

c/o Citizens Bank Wealth Mgmt., N.A.
328 S. Saginaw St., Ste. 001051
Flint, MI 48502-1923
County: Genesee
Contact: Donald A. Snide, Dir.

Established in 1997 in MI.
Donors: Edith Jennings Trust; Wyman Jennings Trust.
Grantmaker type: Independent foundation.
Financial data (yr. ended 12/31/09): Assets, $3,773,858 (M); expenditures, $319,020; total giving, $219,304; qualifying distributions, $274,094; giving activities include $219,304 for 26 grants (high: $53,500; low: $100).
Purpose and activities: The foundation supports charities in the area of Montrose, Michigan, with emphasis on public education, Protestant churches, and municipal agencies.
Fields of interest: Elementary/secondary education; Disasters, fire prevention/control; Human services; Government/public administration; Protestant agencies & churches.
Type of support: General/operating support; Equipment.
Limitations: Applications accepted. Giving primarily in Montrose, MI, and surrounding areas. No support for political organizations.
Publications: Application guidelines.
Application information: Grant suggestions are made by the Board of Directors. Application form not required.
   Copies of proposal: 1
   Deadline(s): None
   Board meeting date(s): 3rd Thurs. in Feb., Apr., June, Oct., and Dec.
Directors: James McCartney; Donald A. Snide; Donald W. Snide; John C. Wendling.
Trustee: Citizens Bank.
EIN: 386684041
Selected grants: The following grants were reported in 2008.
$34,000 to Montrose Community Schools, Montrose, MI.
$8,500 to Shelter of Flint, Flint, MI.
$5,000 to Genesee Intermediate School District, Flint, MI.
$4,000 to Carriage Town Ministries, Flint, MI.
$3,000 to Christian Faith Church, Montrose, MI.
$3,000 to Montrose Baptist Church, Montrose, MI.
$2,000 to Montrose Community Schools, Montrose, MI.

419

Jensen Foundation

1702 Hill St.
Ann Arbor, MI 48104-2641   (734) 995-0694
County: Washtenaw
Contact: James Jensen, Pres.

Established in MI.
Donors: Keith D. Jensen; A. Paul Jensen.
Grantmaker type: Independent foundation.
Financial data (yr. ended 12/31/09): Assets, $171,025 (M); expenditures, $703; total giving, $0; qualifying distributions, $288.
Purpose and activities: Giving primarily to support disadvantaged youth.
Fields of interest: Hospitals (specialty); Health care, clinics/centers.

Limitations: Giving primarily in MI. No support for operating budgets or building funds. No grants to individuals.
Application information: Application form not required.
Initial approach: Proposal
Deadline(s): None
Officers: James Jensen, Pres.; Keith C. Jensen, V.P.; Patricia Verhage, Secy.; Thomas Jensen, Treas.
EIN: 386082462

420
Alan & Jeanette Jenuwine Family Foundation
15028 Hough Rd.
Allenton, MI 48002-3623
County: St. Clair

Established in 2005 in MI.
Donors: Dr. William F. Nill; Mabel E. Nill.
Grantmaker type: Independent foundation.
Financial data (yr. ended 12/31/09): Assets, $28,495 (M); gifts received, $6,180; expenditures, $2,745; total giving, $1,000; qualifying distributions, $1,000; giving activities include $1,000 for grants.
Trustee: Alan Jenuwine.
EIN: 203605564

421
JMJ Foundation
c/o Edwardine A. Muraski
51 Peartree Ln. N.E.
Grand Rapids, MI 49546-1462
County: Kent

Established in 2007 in MI.
Donors: Edwardine A. Muraski; Kenneth J. Muraski.
Grantmaker type: Independent foundation.
Financial data (yr. ended 12/31/08): Assets, $786,535 (M); expenditures, $38,076; total giving, $10,000; qualifying distributions, $10,000; giving activities include $10,000 for grants.
Officers and Trustees:* Edwardine A. Muraski,* Co-Pres.; Kenneth J. Muraski,* Co-Pres.
EIN: 260702760

422
Conrad & Caroline Jobst Foundation
c/o KeyBank N.A.
P.O. Box 10099
Toledo, OH 43699-0099 (419) 259-8655
County: Lucas
Contact: Diane Ohns, V.P., KeyBank N.A.

Established in 1986 in OH.
Grantmaker type: Independent foundation.
Financial data (yr. ended 12/31/09): Assets, $10,796,906 (M); expenditures, $652,012; total giving, $555,000; qualifying distributions, $555,000; giving activities include $555,000 for grants.
Purpose and activities: Giving primarily for health associations and medical education; funding also for an Episcopal church, and the symphony.
Fields of interest: Performing arts, orchestras; Higher education; Medical research, institute; Protestant agencies & churches.

Limitations: Giving primarily in Toledo, OH; funding also in Ann Arbor, MI. No grants to individuals.
Application information:
Initial approach: Letter
Deadline(s): July 31
Trustees: John M. Curphey, Esq.; Douglas Metz, Esq.; Orval Seydlitz; KeyBank N.A.
EIN: 346872214
Selected grants: The following grants were reported in 2008.
$210,000 to University of Michigan, 2101 Taubman Center, Ann Arbor, MI.
$65,000 to Toledo Symphony, Toledo, OH.
$65,000 to Trinity Episcopal Church, Toledo, OH.

423
The Paul T. and Frances B. Johnson Foundation
787 Michigan Ave.
P.O. Box 203
Benzonia, MI 49616-0203 (231) 882-4681
County: Benzie
Contact: Jon M. Haugen, Chair.

Established in 1997.
Donors: Paul Johnson; Frances Johnson.
Grantmaker type: Independent foundation.
Financial data (yr. ended 06/30/09): Assets, $3,216,554 (M); expenditures, $203,512; total giving, $187,100; qualifying distributions, $187,100; giving activities include $20,000 for grants, and $167,100 for 94 grants to individuals.
Purpose and activities: Giving primarily for college scholarships; some giving also for human services and community services.
Fields of interest: Education; Human services; Community/economic development.
Type of support: General/operating support; Scholarships—to individuals.
Limitations: Applications accepted. Giving limited to residents of Benzie, Grand Traverse, and Leelanau counties, MI.
Application information:
Initial approach: Application form required for scholarships
Deadline(s): May 1 for scholarships and honoraria
Final notification: No later than July 30 for scholarships and honoraria
Officers and Directors:* Jon M. Haugen,* Chair. and Treas.; Lawrence I. McKay III,* Secy.; Ingrid K. Brey; James Kaiser; Dale A. Penny.
EIN: 383382755

424
Sherrie L. Jones Foundation
254 Charlevoix Ave.
Grosse Pointe, MI 48236-3359
County: Wayne
Contact: Sherrie L. Jones, Pres.

Established in 1998 in MI.
Donor: Sherrie L. Jones.
Grantmaker type: Independent foundation.
Financial data (yr. ended 12/31/09): Assets, $1,257 (M); expenditures, $1,487; total giving, $1,000; qualifying distributions, $1,000; giving activities include $1,000 for grants.
Fields of interest: Higher education.
Type of support: General/operating support.
Limitations: Giving primarily in MI. No grants to individuals.

Application information: Application form not required.
Deadline(s): None
Officers and Trustees:* Sherrie L. Jones,* Pres.; Jennifer Shapiro,* Secy.
EIN: 383407495

425
Marjorie and Maxwell Jospey Foundation
1 Towne Sq., Ste. 600
Southfield, MI 48076-3710 (248) 368-8816
County: Oakland
Contact: Maxwell Jospey, Pres.; Marjorie R. Jospey, V.P.

Established in 1948 in MI.
Donor: Maxwell Jospey.
Grantmaker type: Independent foundation.
Financial data (yr. ended 11/30/09): Assets, $2,707 (M); expenditures, $21; total giving, $0; qualifying distributions, $0.
Fields of interest: Performing arts; Animals/wildlife, special services; United Ways and Federated Giving Programs; Jewish federated giving programs; Blind/visually impaired.
Limitations: Applications accepted. Giving primarily in MI. No grants to individuals.
Application information:
Initial approach: Proposal
Deadline(s): None
Officers: Maxwell Jospey, Pres.; Marjorie R. Jospey, V.P.
EIN: 386061846

426
Joy Foundation
350 24th St.
Hudsonville, MI 49426-8673
County: Ottawa
Contact: Steven C. Windemuller, Dir.

Donors: Steven C. Windemuller; Debra Windemuller.
Grantmaker type: Independent foundation.
Financial data (yr. ended 12/31/09): Assets, $6 (M); gifts received, $1,500; expenditures, $101,061; total giving, $100,500; qualifying distributions, $100,500; giving activities include $100,500 for grants.
Fields of interest: Christian agencies & churches.
Type of support: General/operating support.
Limitations: Giving primarily in MI. No grants to individuals.
Application information:
Initial approach: Letter
Deadline(s): None
Directors: Debra Windemuller; Steven C. Windemuller.
EIN: 382898700

427
The Joyce Foundation
70 W. Madison St., Ste. 2750
Chicago, IL 60602-4344 (312) 782-2464
County: Cook
Contact: Prog. Staff
FAX: (312) 782-4160; E-mail: info@joycefdn.org;
URL: http://www.joycefdn.org

Incorporated in 1948 in IL.

Donor: Beatrice Joyce Kean†.
Grantmaker type: Independent foundation.
Financial data (yr. ended 12/31/09): Assets, $773,231,000 (M); expenditures, $42,096,443; total giving, $36,046,443; qualifying distributions, $36,046,443; giving activities include $36,046,443 for grants.
Purpose and activities: The foundation supports efforts to protect the natural environment of the Great Lakes, to reduce poverty and violence in the region, and to ensure that its people have access to good schools, decent jobs, and a diverse and thriving culture. It is especially interested in improving public policies, because public systems such as education and welfare directly affect the lives of so many people, and because public policies help shape private sector decisions about jobs, the environment, and the health of our communities. To ensure that public policies truly reflect public rather than private interests, the foundation supports efforts to reform the system of financing election campaigns.
Fields of interest: Arts; Education; Environment; Crime/violence prevention; Crime/violence prevention, gun control; Employment; Public affairs, finance; Public affairs, political organizations.
Type of support: General/operating support; Continuing support; Program development; Conferences/seminars; Research; Program evaluation; Employee matching gifts.
Limitations: Applications accepted. Giving primarily in the Great Lakes region, including IL, IN, MI, MN, OH, and WI; limited number of environment grants made in Canada; culture grants are primarily restricted to the metropolitan Chicago, IL, area. No support for religious activities, or for political organizations. No grants for endowment campaigns, scholarships, direct service programs, or capital proposals.
Publications: Annual report (including application guidelines); Financial statement; Newsletter; Occasional report.
Application information: Program policy and grant proposal guidelines reviewed annually in Dec. Proposals in all program areas will be considered at each board meeting. Applicants are encouraged to submit their proposals for the Apr. or July meeting, since most grant funds will be distributed at those times. Proposal cover sheet available on foundation Web site. Online proposals will not be considered. Application form required.
  Initial approach: Contact foundation for application guidelines prior to submitting 2- to 3-page letter of inquiry
  Copies of proposal: 1
  Deadline(s): Letter of inquiry required at least 6 to 8 weeks before proposal deadlines. For formal proposals: Dec. 11 (for Apr. meeting); Apr. 16 (for July meeting); Aug. 15 (for Dec. meeting)
  Board meeting date(s): Apr., July, and Dec.
  Final notification: 2 weeks after meeting
Officers and Directors:* John T. Anderson,* Chair.; Ellen S. Alberding,* Pres.; Deborah Gillespie, V.P., Finance and Admin. and Treas.; Gretchen Crosby Sims, V.P., Progs.; Jane R. Patterson, C.I.O.; Gil M. Sarmiento, Cont.; Jose B. Alvarez; Robert G. Bottoms; Charles U. Daly; Anthony S. Earl; Roger R. Fross; Carlton L. Guthrie; Daniel P. Kearney; Tracey L. Meares; Margot M. Rogers; Paula Wolff.
Number of staff: 14 full-time professional; 1 part-time professional; 9 full-time support.
EIN: 366079185
Selected grants: The following grants were reported in 2009.

$600,500 to Wisconsin Department of Workforce Development, Madison, WI. For continuation of RISE Initiative, state policy reform effort to create career pathways for low-skilled adults that will lead to employment in high-demand jobs, payable over 2.00 years.
$585,000 to Violence Policy Center, Washington, DC. To continue research, public education, communications, advocacy and coalition efforts in support of effective gun violence prevention policies.
$300,000 to Chicago Theater Group, Chicago, IL. To increase minority audience, staff and board participation at Goodman Theater, payable over 2.00 years.
$200,000 to Enterprise Community Partners, Columbia, MD. To launch Emerald Cities Collaborative, multi-city energy efficiency and green jobs initiative in the Midwest.
$85,274 to Educational Fund to Stop Gun Violence, Washington, DC. To work at state and federal levels to close secondary gun markets and to work with District of Columbia on constitutionally permissible gun law after Heller decision, legal case in which the Supreme Court of the United States held that the Second Amendment to the U.S. Constitution protects an individual's right to possess a firearm for private use in federal enclaves.
$60,000 to Goodwill Industries Easter Seal Society of Minnesota, Saint Paul, MN. To disseminate Transitional Jobs Reentry Demonstration research findings in Minnesota. Demonstration is initiative to help former prisoners find and keep jobs and stay out of prison.

428
George W. & Sadie Marie Juhl Scholarship Fund
c/o Southern Michigan Bank & Trust
51 W. Pearl St.
Coldwater, MI 49036-0309
County: Branch
Contact: Mary Guthrie, Trust Off., Southern Michigan Bank

Established in 1983 in MI.
Grantmaker type: Independent foundation.
Financial data (yr. ended 03/31/10): Assets, $2,582,244 (M); expenditures, $156,553; total giving, $138,000; qualifying distributions, $138,000; giving activities include $138,000 for 70 grants to individuals (high: $2,000; low: $1,000).
Purpose and activities: Scholarship awards for Branch County, Michigan, students to attend a local institution of higher education.
Fields of interest: Higher education.
Type of support: Scholarships—to individuals.
Limitations: Giving limited to residents of Branch County, MI.
Application information: Applications available through Branch County High School counseling offices. Application form required.
  Initial approach: Contact local high school
  Deadline(s): None
Trustee: Southern Michigan Bank & Trust.
EIN: 386372257

429
Leo A. Kahan and Emelie O. Kahan Charitable Foundation
300 St. Andrews Rd., No. 402
Saginaw, MI 48638-5977 (989) 791-2110
County: Saginaw
Contact: Bill J. Thomas C.P.A., Dir.

Established in 1997 in MI.
Donors: Emelie O. Kahan†; Leo A. Kahan†.
Grantmaker type: Independent foundation.
Financial data (yr. ended 12/31/09): Assets, $0 (M); expenditures, $6,773; total giving, $5,000; qualifying distributions, $5,000; giving activities include $5,000 for grants.
Fields of interest: Higher education; Human services.
Limitations: Giving primarily in MI, with emphasis on Saginaw.
Officer: Bill J. Thomas, Pres.
Director: Janet Kabobel.
EIN: 383341030

430
Kahn Sovel Mertz Fund
3405 Pine Estates Dr.
Orchard Lake, MI 48323-1956 (248) 682-1172
County: Oakland
Contact: Susan Sovel, Secy.-Treas.

Established in 2000 in MI.
Donor: Kopel I. Kahn.
Grantmaker type: Independent foundation.
Financial data (yr. ended 12/31/09): Assets, $218,809 (M); expenditures, $54,194; total giving, $49,889; qualifying distributions, $49,889; giving activities include $49,889 for 41 grants (high: $15,000; low: $25).
Fields of interest: Jewish federated giving programs; Jewish agencies & synagogues.
Type of support: General/operating support.
Limitations: Applications accepted. Giving in the U.S., primarily in MI and IN. No grants to individuals.
Application information: Application form not required.
  Initial approach: Letter
  Deadline(s): None
Officers: Kopel I. Kahn, Pres.; Alyssa Mertz, V.P.; Susan Sovel, Secy.-Treas.
EIN: 383570641

431
Terrence S. Kaiser and Barbara A. Kaiser Foundation
4922 Barnes Rd.
Millington, MI 48746-9043 (989) 921-0010
County: Tuscola
E-mail: tbkaiserfoundation@gmail.com

Donors: Terrence S. Kaiser; Barbara A. Kaiser.
Grantmaker type: Independent foundation.
Financial data (yr. ended 12/31/09): Assets, $1,041,622 (M); expenditures, $55,040; total giving, $44,470; qualifying distributions, $52,597; giving activities include $44,470 for 12 grants (high: $12,000; low: $1,000).
Limitations: Applications accepted. Giving primarily in Millington, MI.
Application information: Application form required.
  Initial approach: Proposal
  Deadline(s): None

Officers and Trustees: * Terrence S. Kaiser,* Pres.
and Treas.; Barbara A. Kaiser, Secy.; Erik M. Kaiser;
Stephanie A. Kaiser-Winslow.
EIN: 262534235

432
Kakarala Foundation
2808 Mayfair Dr.
Troy, MI 48084-2668
County: Oakland
Contact: Ramani Kakarala, Pres.

Established in 1986 in MI.
Donors: Sriman N. Kakarala; Bhavani P. Garapati;
Dr. Chandrasekhara Rao Kakarala.
Grantmaker type: Independent foundation.
Financial data (yr. ended 12/31/09): Assets,
$141,581 (M); gifts received, $14,990;
expenditures, $12,261; total giving, $12,200;
qualifying distributions, $12,200; giving activities
include $12,200 for grants.
Fields of interest: Optometry/vision screening;
Hinduism; Blind/visually impaired.
International interests: India.
Type of support: General/operating support;
Building/renovation.
Limitations: Giving primarily in Detroit, MI, and in
India. No grants to individuals.
Application information:
Initial approach: Proposal
Deadline(s): None
Officers: Ramani Kakarala, Pres.; Vijaya Kakarala,
Secy.
Trustees: Raghuram Kakarala; Ramesh Kakarala.
EIN: 382703534

433
Kalt Family Foundation
595 Longwood Ave.
Glencoe, IL 60022-1736   (847) 242-0905
County: Cook
Contact: Susan Kalt, Dir.

Established in 2006 in IL.
Donor: David S. Kalt.
Grantmaker type: Independent foundation.
Financial data (yr. ended 12/31/09): Assets,
$1,016,207 (M); expenditures, $201,162; total
giving, $189,362; qualifying distributions,
$189,362; giving activities include $189,362 for 39
grants (high: $36,764; low: $75).
Fields of interest: Performing arts, education;
Education, early childhood education; Higher
education; Jewish agencies & synagogues.
Type of support: General/operating support; Annual
campaigns; Capital campaigns; Building/
renovation; Program development; Scholarship
funds.
Limitations: Applications accepted. Giving primarily
in Chicago, IL and MI.
Application information:
Initial approach: Letter
Deadline(s): None
Directors: David S. Kalt; Mark Kalt; Susan Kalt.
EIN: 010852305
Selected grants: The following grants were reported
in 2008.
$70,000 to University of Michigan, Ann Arbor, MI.
$25,000 to Merit School of Music, Chicago, IL.
$25,000 to Merit School of Music, Chicago, IL.
$22,500 to DePaul University, Chicago, IL.

$15,000 to Steppenwolf Theater Company,
Chicago, IL.
$5,000 to JARC, Farmington Hills, MI.
$1,000 to Greater Chicago Food Depository,
Chicago, IL.
$1,000 to Leukemia & Lymphoma Society, White
Plains, NY.
$1,000 to University of Chicago, Chicago, IL.

434
The Kantzler Foundation
919 Boutell Pl., Ste. 200
Bay City, MI 48708-5994   (989) 893-4438
County: Bay
Contact: Kathleen Czerwinski; Dominic Monastiere,
Pres.
FAX: (989) 893-4448;
E-mail: kathyc@bayfoundation.org

Incorporated in 1974 in MI.
Donor: Leopold J. Kantzler‡.
Grantmaker type: Independent foundation.
Financial data (yr. ended 12/31/09): Assets,
$5,081,429 (M); expenditures, $260,399; total
giving, $232,501; qualifying distributions,
$239,183; giving activities include $232,501 for 6
grants (high: $100,000; low: $5,000).
Purpose and activities: To support projects and
capital improvements of charitable, artistic,
educational, and cultural organizations in the
greater metropolitan Bay City, MI, area.
Fields of interest: Media, television; Performing
arts, theater; Historical activities; Arts; Libraries
(public); Education; Environment, natural resources;
Housing/shelter, homeless; Human services;
Community/economic development; Foundations
(community).
Type of support: Capital campaigns; Building/
renovation; Equipment; Land acquisition; Program
development; Seed money; Scholarship funds;
Matching/challenge support.
Limitations: Applications accepted. Giving limited to
the greater Bay City, MI, area. No grants to
individuals, or for operating budgets, continuing
support, annual campaigns, special projects,
publications, conferences, emergency funds, deficit
financing, research, scholarships, or fellowships; no
loans.
Publications: Financial statement; Informational
brochure (including application guidelines).
Application information: Application form not
required.
Initial approach: Proposal
Copies of proposal: 11
Deadline(s): 2 weeks before board meeting
Board meeting date(s): Approximately 3 times per
year
Final notification: 2 months
Officers: Dominic Monastiere, Pres.; Robert D.
Sarow, Secy.
Trustees: Linda R. Heemstra; Andrea Hales; Ruth M.
Jaffe; D. Brian Law; Valerie Roof; Clifford C. Van
Dyke; Jerome L. Yantz.
EIN: 237422733
Selected grants: The following grants were reported
in 2007.
$60,000 to Great Lakes Center Foundation, Bay
City, MI. Toward restoration of former Pere
Marquette Railroad depot in downtown Bay Area for
use as Bay Area Community Foundation's office
facility.

$40,000 to Mid-Michigan Childrens Museum,
Saginaw, MI. For development of children's
museum.
$33,333 to Bay Health Foundation, Bay City, MI. For
Nickless Volunteer Clinic.
$33,333 to Boy Scouts of America, Lake Huron Area
Council, Auburn, MI. Toward costs of renovation and
expansion of Camp Rotary and The Paul Bunyan
Scout Reserve.
$30,000 to Bay Area Community Foundation, Bay
City, MI. For Bay Commitment project which will
provide counseling and financial assistance for Bay
County high school students who plan to attend
Delta College or Saginaw Valley State University.
$30,000 to Saginaw Basin Land Conservancy, Bay
City, MI. For permanent endowment to provide funds
for monitoring and enforcing land protection
agreements in Saginaw Bay watershed.
$20,000 to City Rescue Mission of Saginaw,
Saginaw, MI. Toward costs of renovating Good
Samaritan Rescue Mission facility.
$20,000 to Do-All, Inc., Bay City, MI. To provide
funds for Do-All to set up and operate a coffee shop
in downtown Bay City.
$20,000 to Saginaw Valley State University
Foundation, University Center, MI. For Leadership
Fellows Program, to provide consultants and
volunteers to promote and conduct community
improvement projects in Bay County.
$16,667 to Delta College, University Center, MI. For
Peter Boyse Endowment Fund to support
recruitment of minority instructors.
$15,000 to Bay City Garden Club, Bay City, MI.
Toward costs of improved landscaping around
Veterans Memorial and Vietnam Memorial in
Veterans Park in Bay City.
$10,000 to State Theater of Bay City, Bay County,
Bay City, MI. Toward cost of new marquee.
$500 to Great Lakes Center Foundation, Bay City,
MI.

435
Stanley J. Kasiewicz Foundation
c/o Stanley J. Kasiewicz
1807 Harvest Ln.
Bloomfield Hills, MI 48302-1227
County: Oakland

Established in 2007 in MI.
Donor: Stanley J. Kasiewicz.
Grantmaker type: Independent foundation.
Financial data (yr. ended 07/31/09): Assets,
$728,255 (M); expenditures, $47,073; total giving,
$40,566; qualifying distributions, $40,566; giving
activities include $40,566 for grants.
Fields of interest: Animal welfare; Veterinary
medicine, hospital.
Limitations: Giving primarily in MI, with some giving
also in OK.
Officers: Stanley J. Kasiewicz, Pres.; Andrea M.
Kasiewicz, V.P.; Sandra M. Kasiewicz, V.P.
EIN: 611543491

436
The Katz Family Foundation, Inc.
P.O. Box 40857
Indianapolis, IN 46240-0857
County: Marion
Application address: c/o Irwin Katz, 8648 N. Cricket
Tree Ln., Indianapolis, IN 46260, tel.: (317)
580-2000

Established in 1997 in IN.
Donors: Irwin Katz; Ann Katz; Donald Katz; Nancy Katz; Ann Katz Family Charitable Trust.
Grantmaker type: Independent foundation.
Financial data (yr. ended 06/30/10): Assets, $435,445 (M); gifts received, $125,000; expenditures, $132,787; total giving, $132,268; qualifying distributions, $132,268; giving activities include $132,268 for grants.
Fields of interest: Museums; Education; Genetic diseases and disorders; Human services; Civil liberties, advocacy; Jewish federated giving programs; Jewish agencies & synagogues; LGBTQ.
Type of support: General/operating support.
Limitations: Applications accepted. Giving primarily in IN, MI, NY, and WI. No grants to individuals.
Application information:
Initial approach: Letter
Deadline(s): None
Directors: Donald Katz; Irwin Katz; Nancy Katz.
EIN: 352028874
Selected grants: The following grants were reported in 2009.
$50,000 to Jewish Funds for Justice, New York, NY.
$12,500 to Community Foundation for Southeast Michigan, Detroit, MI.
$3,000 to Threshold Foundation, San Francisco, CA.
$1,500 to Washtenaw Community College Foundation, Ann Arbor, MI.
$1,000 to Indiana University, Borns Jewish Studies Program, Bloomington, IN.
$1,000 to WISDOM, Cudahy, WI.

437
Barney Katzman Foundation
5655 Wing Lake Rd.
Bloomfield Hills, MI 48301-1252
(248) 641-8400
County: Oakland
Contact: Barney Katzman, Pres.

Established in MI.
Grantmaker type: Independent foundation.
Financial data (yr. ended 12/31/08): Assets, $93,333 (M); expenditures, $5,451; total giving, $4,720; qualifying distributions, $4,720; giving activities include $4,720 for grants.
Fields of interest: Performing arts; Higher education; Medical research, institute; United Ways and Federated Giving Programs; Jewish agencies & synagogues.
Type of support: General/operating support.
Limitations: Giving primarily in MI.
Application information:
Initial approach: Proposal
Deadline(s): None
Officers and Directors: Barney Katzman,* Pres. and Treas.; Jeanette Katzman,* V.P.; Richard Katzman,* Secy.; Jane Glass.
EIN: 386064688

438
Sidney and Robert Katzman Foundation
(formerly Sidney Katzman Foundation)
30100 Telegraph Rd., Ste. 366
Bingham Farms, MI 48025-5800
(248) 641-8400
County: Oakland
Contact: Robert Katzman, Pres.

Established in MI.

Donor: Betty Katzman.
Grantmaker type: Independent foundation.
Financial data (yr. ended 12/31/09): Assets, $349,470 (M); expenditures, $24,692; total giving, $22,930; qualifying distributions, $22,930; giving activities include $22,930 for grants.
Fields of interest: Arts; Higher education; Athletics/sports, winter sports; Jewish federated giving programs; Jewish agencies & synagogues.
Limitations: Giving in the U.S., primarily in MI. No grants to individuals.
Application information:
Initial approach: Proposal
Deadline(s): None
Officers: Robert Katzman, Pres.; Betty Katzman, V.P.; Martin Stoneman, Secy.-Treas.
EIN: 386064687

439
Louis G. Kaufman Endowment Fund
c/o Wells Fargo Bank, N.A.
1919 Douglas St., 2nd Fl.
Omaha, NE 68102-1310
County: Douglas
Application address: c/o Wells Fargo Bank, N.A., Attn.: Michael Kolasa, 101 W. Washington, Marquette, MI 49855, tel.: (906) 228-1464

Established in 1927 in MI.
Donor: L.G. Kaufman Trust.
Grantmaker type: Independent foundation.
Financial data (yr. ended 12/31/09): Assets, $3,055,614 (M); expenditures, $285,364; total giving, $250,603; qualifying distributions, $250,603; giving activities include $250,603 for 20 grants (high: $60,000; low: $500).
Purpose and activities: Grants are limited to the advancement of the moral, physical, and mental development of the youth of the City of Marquette, Michigan.
Fields of interest: Secondary school/education; Education; Recreation; Youth development; Human services; Children/youth, services; Family services; Community/economic development; Children/youth.
Type of support: General/operating support; Annual campaigns; Program development; Scholarship funds.
Limitations: Giving primarily in Marquette, MI. No grants to individuals, or for continuing support, deficit financing, land acquisition, endowment funds, matching gifts, research, publications, or conferences; no loans.
Publications: Application guidelines.
Application information: Application form required.
Initial approach: Letter
Copies of proposal: 7
Deadline(s): Apr. 30
Board meeting date(s): As required
Officer and Fund Committee: Harild N. Herlich,* Secy.; Henry Bothwell; Ann Kaufman Jordan; Audrey Kaufman; Stephen Mattson; Peter Kaufman; Kenneth Seavoy; and five additional Fund Committee members.
Trustee: Wells Fargo Bank, N.A.
EIN: 386048505
Selected grants: The following grants were reported in 2004.
$50,000 to Marquette Area Public Schools, Marquette, MI. For high school scholarship program.
$15,000 to Marquette Area Public Schools, Marquette, MI. For middle school scholarship program.

$10,000 to Marquette Junior Hockey, Marquette, MI. For youth scholarship program.
$8,000 to Bay Cliff Health Camp, Big Bay, MI. For scholarships for Marquette youth.
$5,000 to YMCA of Marquette County, Marquette, MI. For shiras pool and strong kids campaign.
$4,000 to Upper Peninsula Childrens Museum, Marquette, MI. For good lung/bad lung and supplies.
$1,900 to Pine Mountain Music Festival, Hancock, MI. For childrens symphony concert.
$1,500 to Father Marquette Catholic Central Schools System, Marquette, MI. For scholarship program.
$1,000 to Father Marquette Catholic Central Schools System, Marquette, MI. For scholarship program.
$1,000 to Liberty Childrens Art Project, Big Bay, MI. For City of Marquette youth scholarships.

440
Kaufman Foundation
4927 Stariha Dr., Ste. A
Muskegon, MI 49441 (231) 798-7500
County: Muskegon
Contact: Richard F. Kaufman, Tr.; Sylvia C. Kaufman, Tr.

Established in 1959 in MI.
Grantmaker type: Independent foundation.
Financial data (yr. ended 12/31/09): Assets, $1,886,210 (M); expenditures, $169,325; total giving, $157,815; qualifying distributions, $157,815; giving activities include $157,815 for 32 grants (high: $80,250; low: $35).
Purpose and activities: Giving primarily to museums, the arts, and Jewish agencies.
Fields of interest: Museums; Arts; Jewish federated giving programs; Jewish agencies & synagogues.
Limitations: Giving primarily in MI.
Application information:
Initial approach: Letter
Deadline(s): None
Trustees: Richard F. Kaufman; Sylvia C. Kaufman.
EIN: 386091556

441
The Chaim, Fanny, Louis, Benjamin and Anne Florence Kaufman Memorial Trust
c/o JPMorgan Chase Bank, N.A.
P.O. Box 3038
Milwaukee, WI 53201-3038
County: Milwaukee
Application address: c/o JPMorgan Chase Bank, N.A., Trust Dept., Attn.: Kimberly Kalmar, 685 St. Clair Ave., Grosse Pointe, MI 48230, tel.: (313) 343-8540

Established in 1986 in MI.
Donor: Anne F. Kaufman‡.
Grantmaker type: Independent foundation.
Financial data (yr. ended 05/31/10): Assets, $2,339,530 (M); expenditures, $172,035; total giving, $145,333; qualifying distributions, $145,333; giving activities include $145,333 for grants.
Fields of interest: Museums; Performing arts; Education; Reproductive health, family planning; Health care; Human services; Jewish federated giving programs.

Type of support: General/operating support; Building/renovation; Program development; Seed money; Research.
Limitations: Applications accepted. Giving primarily in southeastern MI, with emphasis on Detroit. No grants to individuals.
Application information: Application form not required.
Initial approach: Letter
Copies of proposal: 1
Deadline(s): None
Trustee: JPMorgan Chase Bank, N.A.
EIN: 386504432

442
Helen L. Kay Charitable Trust
(formerly Helen L. Kay Foundation)
c/o Comerica Bank
P.O. Box 75000 M.C. 3302
Detroit, MI 48275-3302 (877) 405-1091
County: Wayne
Contact: Scott Drogs, V.P., Comerica Charitable Services Group

Established in 2000 in MI.
Grantmaker type: Independent foundation.
Financial data (yr. ended 12/31/09): Assets, $7,197,851 (M); expenditures, $553,685; total giving, $492,544; qualifying distributions, $502,506; giving activities include $492,544 for 37 grants (high: $50,000; low: $1,000).
Purpose and activities: Giving primarily for human services and hospitals.
Fields of interest: Elementary/secondary education; Hospitals (general); Health care; Cancer; Goodwill Industries; Human services; Salvation Army; Children/youth, services; Protestant agencies & churches.
Limitations: Giving primarily in MI and PA. No grants to individuals.
Application information: Application form not required.
Initial approach: Letter
Deadline(s): None
Trustee: Comerica Bank.
EIN: 383047073
Selected grants: The following grants were reported in 2009.
$40,000 to Goodwill Industries of Greater Detroit, Detroit, MI.
$38,544 to University of Michigan, Ann Arbor, MI.
$30,000 to First Presbyterian Church, East Brady, PA.
$30,000 to Starr Commonwealth, Albion, MI.
$20,000 to Leader Dogs for the Blind, Rochester, MI.
$15,000 to Forgotten Harvest, Oak Park, MI.
$15,000 to Henry Ford Health System, Detroit, MI.
$10,000 to Barbara Ann Karmanos Cancer Institute, Detroit, MI.
$10,000 to El Camino Hospital Foundation, Mountain View, CA.
$10,000 to University of Michigan Health System, Ann Arbor, MI.

443
Ryan Michael Kay Scholarship Foundation
4820 Leonard Ct.
West Bloomfield, MI 48322-2207
County: Oakland
Application address: c/o West Bloomfield High School, Attn.: Karen Brody, 4925 Orchard Lake Rd., West Bloomfield, MI 48323, tel.: (248) 865-6720

Established in 2004 in MI.
Donors: Kay Family; Harriet Dryburgh; Mandel Stanley; Iola Stanley; Marion Moorehead; Gwen Leach.
Grantmaker type: Independent foundation.
Financial data (yr. ended 12/31/09): Assets, $64,173 (M); expenditures, $10,217; total giving, $10,000; qualifying distributions, $10,000; giving activities include $10,000 for 2 grants to individuals (high: $5,000; low: $5,000).
Purpose and activities: Scholarships to graduates of West Bloomfield High School, Michigan for post-secondary education.
Type of support: Scholarships—to individuals.
Limitations: Applications accepted. Giving limited to residents of MI.
Application information: Application form provided by West Bloomfield High School. Application form required.
Deadline(s): May 10
Officers: Christine Kay, Pres. and Secy.; Neil Kay, V.P. and Treas.
EIN: 320102123

444
Kazrus Foundation
c/o Plante Moran Trust
P.O. Box 307
Southfield, MI 48037-0307 (248) 352-2500
County: Oakland
Contact: S. Campbell

Established in 2004 in OH.
Donors: Susan Dudas; David Dudas.
Grantmaker type: Independent foundation.
Financial data (yr. ended 12/31/08): Assets, $1,816,662 (M); expenditures, $117,653; total giving, $98,060; qualifying distributions, $98,060; giving activities include $98,060 for grants.
Fields of interest: Human services; Christian agencies & churches.
Limitations: Giving primarily in CA and OH.
Officers and Director:* Susan Dudas,* Pres.; David Dudas, Secy.-Treas.
EIN: 201762096

445
Kebok Foundation
c/o Soon K. Kim
6500 W. 6 Mile Rd.
Northville, MI 48168-9452
County: Wayne

Established in 2002 in MI.
Grantmaker type: Independent foundation.
Financial data (yr. ended 12/31/09): Assets, $927,273 (M); gifts received, $500,000; expenditures, $52,050; total giving, $48,950; qualifying distributions, $48,950; giving activities include $48,950 for grants.
Fields of interest: Media, radio; Cancer, leukemia.
Limitations: Giving primarily in San Francisco, CA.

Application information:
Initial approach: Letter
Deadline(s): None
Final notification: Within 2 months
Officer: Bouh H. Kim, Pres.
EIN: 300106301

446
The Keeler Foundation
(formerly The Miner S. & Mary Ann Keeler Fund)
200 Monroe Ave. N.W., Ste. 240
Grand Rapids, MI 49503-2213 (616) 774-0422
County: Kent
Contact: Rita Miller, Secy.-Treas.

Incorporated in 1985 in MI as successor to the First Keeler Fund established in 1953, which transferred its assets to the new Keeler Fund in 1986.
Donors: Mary Ann Keeler; Miner S. Keeler II†; The Keeler Fund.
Grantmaker type: Independent foundation.
Financial data (yr. ended 07/31/09): Assets, $1,091,418 (M); expenditures, $125,773; total giving, $120,327; qualifying distributions, $120,327; giving activities include $120,327 for grants.
Purpose and activities: Giving primarily to organizations that are artistic or scholastic in nature.
Fields of interest: Museums (art); Performing arts; Arts; Secondary school/education; Higher education; Libraries (public); Environment; Hospitals (general); Health organizations, association; Human services; United Ways and Federated Giving Programs; Christian agencies & churches.
Limitations: Applications accepted. Giving primarily in MI, with emphasis on Grand Rapids; some giving in NY. No grants to individuals.
Application information:
Initial approach: Letter
Deadline(s): None
Officers: Mary Ann Keeler, Pres.; Isaac S. Keeler, V.P.; Rita L. Miller, Secy.-Treas.
Director: Donald Johnson.
EIN: 382625402
Selected grants: The following grants were reported in 2007.
$25,000 to Frederik Meijer Gardens and Sculpture Park, Grand Rapids, MI.
$16,000 to Grand Rapids Symphony, Grand Rapids, MI.
$13,250 to Education Freedom Fund, Charlotte, MI.
$10,100 to Grand Rapids Art Museum, Grand Rapids, MI.
$10,000 to Grand Horizons Foundation, Jenison, MI.
$10,000 to Opera Grand Rapids, Grand Rapids, MI.
$8,055 to Kennedy Center, Trumbull, CT.
$5,000 to Aquinas College, Grand Rapids, MI.
$5,000 to Arts Council of Greater Grand Rapids, Grand Rapids, MI.
$2,000 to YMCA of Greater Grand Rapids, Grand Rapids, MI.

447
Hattie Hannah Keeney Trust
c/o JPMorgan Chase Bank, N.A.
P.O. Box 3038
Milwaukee, WI 53201-3038
County: Milwaukee
Application address: c/o JPMorgan Chase Bank,
N.A., 21805 Field Pkwy., 1st Fl., Deer Park, IL
60010, tel.: (847) 726-3619

Established in 1950 in IL.
Donor: Hattie Hannah Keeney†.
Grantmaker type: Independent foundation.
Financial data (yr. ended 12/31/09): Assets,
$4,420,177 (M); expenditures, $188,658; total
giving, $155,620; qualifying distributions,
$164,510; giving activities include $155,620 for 4
grants (high: $75,000; low: $5,000).
Fields of interest: Hospitals (general); Children/
youth, services; Disabilities, people with.
Type of support: General/operating support.
Limitations: Applications accepted. Giving primarily
in the Traverse City, MI, area. No grants to
individuals.
Application information:
  Deadline(s): None
Trustee: JPMorgan Chase Bank, N.A.
EIN: 366016171
Selected grants: The following grants were reported
in 2008.
$100,000 to Munson Medical Center, Traverse City,
MI.

448
Keller Foundation
c/o Northern Trust Bank FSB
P.O. Box 803878
Chicago, IL 60680-3878 (616) 949-5138
County: Cook
Contact: Zelene Wilkins, Exec. Dir.
E-mail for Zelene Wilkins:
zelene@kellerfoundation.org; URL: http://
www.kellerfoundation.org

Established around 1980 in MI.
Donor: Paragon Die & Engineering Co.
Grantmaker type: Independent foundation.
Financial data (yr. ended 06/30/10): Assets,
$4,722,627 (M); expenditures, $242,024; total
giving, $199,200; qualifying distributions,
$199,200; giving activities include $199,200 for
grants.
Purpose and activities: Giving to support innovative
programs for city youth in Grand Rapids, Michigan,
that foster nurturing environments, spark curiosity,
enhance opportunities for self-sufficiency, and
inspire high aspirations.
Fields of interest: Museums (art); Performing arts;
Education; Botanical/horticulture/landscape
services; Zoos/zoological societies; Health care;
Human services; Children/youth, services.
Type of support: General/operating support;
Continuing support; Capital campaigns; Building/
renovation; Program development; Seed money;
Curriculum development; Scholarship funds;
Matching/challenge support.
Limitations: Applications accepted. Giving primarily
in the Grand Rapids, MI, area. No support for
political organizations. No grants to individuals.
Publications: Application guidelines.
Application information: Application form available
on foundation web site. Application form required.
  Initial approach: Letter of request

Copies of proposal: 1
Deadline(s): None
Board meeting date(s): Nov., Mar., and June
Officers and Directors: Kathleen K. Muir,* Chair.;
Lorissa K. MacAllister,* Vice-Chair.; William M.
Muir,* Secy.; David F. Muir,* Treas.; Zelene Wilkins,
Exec. Dir.; Bernadine J. Keller; Christina L. Keller;
Frederick P. Keller; Linn Maxwell Keller; Wes
MacAllister; Cathy Muir; Elizabeth M. Muir; William
W. Muir, Jr.; Lars Whitman; Susan T.K. Whitman.
Number of staff: 1 part-time professional.
EIN: 382331693
Selected grants: The following grants were reported
in 2005.
$10,000 to Garrett-Evangelical Theological
Seminary, Evanston, IL. For general support.
$10,000 to Spectrum Health System, Grand
Rapids, MI. For general support.
$6,585 to First United Methodist Church, Grand
Rapids, MI.
$5,000 to Camp Henry, Newaygo, MI.
$5,000 to In the Image, Grand Rapids, MI.
$4,000 to Christian Camps for Inner-City Youth,
Camp Tall Turf, Grand Rapids, MI.
$4,000 to Grand Rapids Childrens Museum, Grand
Rapids, MI.

449
Edward and June Kellogg Foundation, Inc.
1250 Byron Rd.
Howell, MI 48843-1007 (517) 546-3330
County: Livingston

Established in 2001 in MI.
Donor: June Kellogg.
Grantmaker type: Independent foundation.
Financial data (yr. ended 06/30/09): Assets,
$4,079,038 (M); expenditures, $336,968; total
giving, $259,246; qualifying distributions,
$262,751; giving activities include $259,246 for 28
grants (high: $49,270; low: $64).
Purpose and activities: Giving primarily in the areas
of improving education and creating opportunities
for careers in dentistry; advancing the dental health
and well-being of youth in local communities as well
as those underserved in other parts of the world;
providing spiritual support in the process of these
endeavors; supporting the humane treatment of
animals; and promoting community stewardship.
Fields of interest: Elementary/secondary
education; Dental school/education; Animal
welfare; Dental care; Boy scouts; Human services;
Youth, services; Community/economic
development; Christian agencies & churches.
Type of support: General/operating support; Capital
campaigns; Equipment; Program development;
Scholarship funds.
Limitations: Applications accepted. Giving primarily
in MI.
Application information:
  Initial approach: Letter
  Deadline(s): None
Officer: Thomas A. Kellogg, Pres.
Directors: Ryan Kellogg; Sarah Tottingham.
EIN: 300057241
Selected grants: The following grants were reported
in 2009.
$33,000 to Boy Scouts of America, Ann Arbor, MI.
$25,000 to Boy Scouts of America, Traverse City,
MI.
$20,000 to Shared Hope International, Vancouver,
WA.

$10,000 to Boy Scouts of America, Traverse City,
MI.
$7,500 to Boy Scouts of America, Traverse City, MI.
$6,000 to Ball State University, Muncie, IN.
$5,000 to Boy Scouts of America, Saint Charles, IL.
$2,790 to Family Impact Center, Fowlerville, MI.
$1,000 to Boy Scouts of America, Traverse City, MI.

450
W. K. Kellogg Foundation
1 Michigan Ave. E.
Battle Creek, MI 49017-4005 (269) 968-1611
County: Calhoun
URL: http://www.wkkf.org

Incorporated in 1930 in MI.
Donors: W.K. Kellogg†; W.K. Kellogg Foundation
Trust; Carrie Staines Kellogg Trust.
Grantmaker type: Independent foundation.
Financial data (yr. ended 08/31/10): Assets,
$7,238,160,845 (M); expenditures,
$358,022,541; total giving, $270,011,667;
qualifying distributions, $336,126,232; giving
activities include $266,431,866 for grants,
$3,579,801 for employee matching gifts, and
$1,142,320 for foundation-administered programs.
Purpose and activities: The Kellogg Foundation
makes grants to organizations that embrace a
similar mission of creating communities, systems,
and nations in which all children have an equitable
and promising future - one in which all children
thrive. Grants fund programs and projects that
support children, families, and communities as they
strengthen and create conditions that propel
children to achieve success as individuals and as
contributors to the larger community and society.
Fields of interest: Education, early childhood
education; Elementary school/education;
Secondary school/education; Education; Health
care, reform; Health care; Health organizations,
association; Agriculture; Agriculture/food; Youth
development, services; Youth, services; Minorities/
immigrants, centers/services; Community
development, neighborhood development; Rural
development; Community/economic development;
Voluntarism promotion; Leadership development;
Infants/toddlers; Children/youth; Children; Youth;
Minorities; Asians/Pacific Islanders; African
Americans/Blacks; Hispanics/Latinos; Native
Americans/American Indians; Indigenous peoples;
Single parents; Immigrants/refugees; Economically
disadvantaged.
International interests: Brazil; Haiti; Latin America;
Mexico.
Type of support: Program development; Seed
money; Program evaluation; Employee matching
gifts; Matching/challenge support.
Limitations: Applications accepted. Giving primarily
in the U.S., with emphases on MI, MS, and NM,
funding also for programs focused in Southern
Mexico, Haiti, and northeast Brazil. No support for
religious purposes or for capital facilities. No grants
to individuals, or for scholarships, endowment
funds, development campaigns, films, equipment,
publications, conferences, or radio and television
programs unless they are an integral part of a project
already being funded; no grants for operating
budgets.
Publications: Annual report; Financial statement;
Grants list; Occasional report; Program policy
statement.
Application information: The foundation requires all
proposals to be submitted via an initial process

online at www.wkkf.org. Please contact the Proposal Processing office for assistance if you are having difficulty submitting your request online or don't have internet access. Please note only nonprofit organizations are eligible for funding from the foundation and grants are currently limited to programs focused in southern Mexico, Haiti, northeast Brazil, and the United States. While the foundation funds nationally in the United States, it prioritize funding in Michigan, Mississippi, and New Mexico. (While the foundation remains committed to the southern African region, it is not currently accepting proposal submissions.)Should you have additional questions, please contact the Central Proposal Processing office at (269) 969-2329. Application form required.

Initial approach: Online submission is required. Contact the Central Proposal Processing office at (269) 969-2329 for instructions if unable to submit online
Copies of proposal: 1
Deadline(s): None
Board meeting date(s): Monthly
Final notification: 45 days

Officers and Trustees:* Sterling K. Speirn,* C.E.O. and Pres.; La June Montgomery-Tabron, C.O.O. and Treas.; James E. McHale, Chief of Staff; Gail C. Christopher, V.P., Prog. Strategy; Joel R. Wittenberg, V.P. and C.I.O.; Joanne K. Krell, V.P., Comms.; Gregory B. Taylor, V.P., Prog. Strategy; Susan Katz Froning, Corp. Secy. and General Counsel; Roderick D. Gillum; Dorothy A. Johnson; Fred P. Keller; Hanmin Liu; Cynthia H. Milligan; Wenda Weekes Moore; Bobby Moser; Ramon Murguia; Joseph M. Stewart; Richard M. Tsoumas.
Number of staff: 102 full-time professional; 44 full-time support.
EIN: 381359264
Selected grants: The following grants were reported in 2009.
$25,000,000 to Fundacao de Desenvolvimento da Pesquisa, Belo Horizonte, Brazil. To sustain cause of racial equity and social inclusion in northeast Brazil by providing endowment funds to charitable organization, payable over 5.00 years.
$2,017,000 to Institute for Agriculture and Trade Policy, Minneapolis, MN. To impact policy through communications efforts by providing fellowships to professionals from across U.S., payable over 2.25 years.
$300,000 to Angela Borba Fund-A Resource for Women, Rio de Janeiro, Brazil. To promote culture of giving in Brazil through support of projects promoting women's rights and reducing racial discrimination in northeast region.
$200,000 to New Mexico Indian Affairs Department, Santa Fe, NM. To improve health and economic outcomes for Native American children and families by collaborating with other state government entities, tribal governments, businesses, and nonprofit organizations, payable over 1.25 years.

451
C. L. Kelly Charitable Trust
c/o Comerica Bank
P.O. Box 75000, MC 3302
Detroit, MI 48275-3302
County: Wayne
Application address: c/o Sharon Stephens, 130 S. Franklin, Rocky Mount, NC 27802-5707, tel.: (252) 467-4743

Established in 1980 in NC.

Donor: C.L. Kelly, Sr.†.
Grantmaker type: Independent foundation.
Financial data (yr. ended 01/31/10): Assets, $1,637,516 (M); expenditures, $137,573; total giving, $102,200; qualifying distributions, $102,200; giving activities include $102,200 for grants.
Purpose and activities: Giving to Methodist and Baptist churches; Also, student loans for higher education to members, of said faith-based churches, and are residents of Brinkleyville, Butterwood, or Faucette townships in Halifax County, North Carolina.
Fields of interest: Higher education; Protestant agencies & churches.
Type of support: General/operating support; Student loans—to individuals.
Limitations: Giving limited to NC.
Application information: Application form required.
Deadline(s): June 15
Board meeting date(s): June
Loan Committee Members: Sharon Arrington; V. Vaughn Holland; Charles R. Swindell.
Trustee: Comerica Bank.
EIN: 566218777

452
The W. J. and Lillian Kemler Foundation
39300 W. 12 Mile Rd., Ste. 100
Farmington Hills, MI 48331-2989
County: Oakland
Contact: Margaret Savage, Pres.
Application address: 5328 Mirror Lake Ct., West Bloomfield, MI 48323-1582

Established in 1997 in MI.

Donor: Lillian Kemler.
Grantmaker type: Independent foundation.
Financial data (yr. ended 11/30/09): Assets, $1,137,248 (M); expenditures, $119,520; total giving, $74,751; qualifying distributions, $74,751; giving activities include $74,751 for 12 grants (high: $10,225; low: $859).
Fields of interest: Higher education; Human services; Community/economic development; Jewish agencies & synagogues.
Type of support: General/operating support.
Limitations: Applications accepted. Giving primarily in MI.
Application information: Application form not required.
Initial approach: Letter
Deadline(s): None
Officer: Margaret Savage, Pres.
Directors: Carolyn McCarren; James Savage.
EIN: 383384888

453
Kent Charitable Trust
c/o Fifth Third Bank
P.O. Box 3636
Grand Rapids, MI 49501-3636
County: Kent
Application address: c/o Brian Deuby, 111 Lyon St., Grand Rapids, MI 49504-2406, tel.: (616) 771-5627

Established in MI.

Grantmaker type: Independent foundation.
Financial data (yr. ended 11/30/10): Assets, $337,824 (M); expenditures, $21,338; total giving,

$16,734; qualifying distributions, $17,009; giving activities include $16,734 for grants.
Fields of interest: Foundations (community); United Ways and Federated Giving Programs.
Limitations: Applications accepted. Giving limited to the Grand Rapids, MI, area. No grants to individuals.
Application information:
Initial approach: Letter
Deadline(s): None
Trustee: Fifth Third Bank.
EIN: 386050486

454
Kent Medical Foundation
c/o William McClimans
234 Division Ave. N., Ste. 300
Grand Rapids, MI 49503-2532 (616) 458-4157
County: Kent

Established in 1961 in MI.

Donors: Matilda Crane; Kent County Medical Society.
Grantmaker type: Independent foundation.
Financial data (yr. ended 12/31/09): Assets, $415,305 (M); gifts received, $9,870; expenditures, $18,088; total giving, $0; qualifying distributions, $0; giving activities include $0 for grants to individuals.
Purpose and activities: The foundation provides loans to medical students who have resided in Kent County and adjoining counties. The foundation also provides tuition grants to nurses attending the three local nursing schools, and achievement awards to graduating seniors, from the five local colleges and university, pursuing careers in the allied health sciences.
Fields of interest: Medical school/education; Nursing school/education; Health sciences school/education.
Type of support: Scholarships—to individuals; Student loans—to individuals.
Limitations: Giving limited to Kent, MI, and its bordering counties.
Officers and Trustees:* Jay LaBine,* Chair.; Patrick Miles, Jr.,* Vice-Chair.; William McClimans, Pres.; Anita Avery, Secy.-Treas.; Michael J. DeJong, M.D.; Judith Hiemenga; William R. Jewell; Thomas Petersen; Jack L. Romence, M.D.; Willard S. Stawski, M.D.
EIN: 386089794

455
Kentwood Foundation
(formerly Stauffer Kentwood Foundation)
c/o Clark Hill
200 Ottawa Dr. N.W., Ste. 500
Grand Rapids, MI 49503-2426 (616) 608-1100
County: Kent
Contact: John P. Schneider, Secy.-Treas.

Established around 1978 in MI.

Grantmaker type: Independent foundation.
Financial data (yr. ended 12/31/09): Assets, $406,885 (M); gifts received, $57,000; expenditures, $4,490; total giving, $0; qualifying distributions, $0.
Fields of interest: Community development, public/private ventures.
Type of support: General/operating support.
Limitations: Giving limited to Kentwood, MI.
Application information:

Initial approach: Letter
Deadline(s): None
Officers and Directors:* David C. Bottrall,* Pres.;
Hon. William G. Kelly,* V.P.; John P. Schneider,*
Secy.-Treas.; Mayor Richard Root.
EIN: 386378785

456
Kerkstra Family Charitable Foundation
8609 Cedar Lake Dr.
Jenison, MI   49428-9559   (616) 895-6126
County: Ottawa
Contact: Lawrence Kerkstra, Pres.

Established in 1999 in MI.
Donors: Lawrence Kerkstra; Virginia Kerkstra.
Grantmaker type: Independent foundation.
Financial data (yr. ended 12/31/09): Assets,
$248,451 (M); expenditures, $55,859; total giving,
$52,750; qualifying distributions, $52,750; giving
activities include $52,750 for 32 grants (high:
$4,000; low: $500).
Fields of interest: Theological school/education;
Family services; Christian agencies & churches.
Type of support: General/operating support.
Limitations: Applications accepted. Giving primarily
in MI. No grants to individuals.
Application information:
   Initial approach: Proposal
   Deadline(s): Sept. 30
Officers: Lawrence Kerkstra, Pres.; Virginia
Kerkstra, Secy.-Treas.
EIN: 383502922

457
The Worth M. & Madeline C. Key
Scholarship Trust
P.O. Box 75000, MC 3302
Detroit, MI   48275-3302   (252) 467-4741
County: Wayne
Contact: J. Lloyd Strickland
Application addresses: c/o Altavista High School,
904 Bedford Ave., Altavista, VA 24517-1915; and
c/o Gretna Senior High School, 100 Gretna Hawk
Cir., Gretna, VA 24557

Established in 2007 in VA.
Donor: Medline C. Key.
Grantmaker type: Independent foundation.
Financial data (yr. ended 12/31/09): Assets,
$294,183 (M); expenditures, $20,261; total giving,
$14,000; qualifying distributions, $14,000; giving
activities include $14,000 for grants.
Purpose and activities: Scholarship awards to
graduates of John L. Hurt Elementary School,
Virginia.
Fields of interest: Higher education.
Type of support: Scholarships—to individuals.
Limitations: Applications accepted. Giving limited to
residents of VA.
Application information: Application form required.
   Initial approach: Letter or telephone
   Deadline(s): June 30
Trustee: Comerica Bank & Trust, N.A.
EIN: 386847320

458
John E. Klobucar and Joseph D. Klobucher
Foundation
P.O. Box 404
Frankenmuth, MI   48734-0404   (989) 798-1882
County: Saginaw
Contact: Joseph D. Klobucher, Pres.

Established in 2002.
Donors: John E. Klobucar; Joseph D. Klobucher.
Grantmaker type: Independent foundation.
Financial data (yr. ended 12/31/09): Assets,
$293,376 (M); gifts received, $25,000;
expenditures, $43,333; total giving, $42,500;
qualifying distributions, $42,500; giving activities
include $42,500 for 14 grants (high: $7,000; low:
$1,000).
Fields of interest: Children/youth, services; United
Ways and Federated Giving Programs; Christian
agencies & churches.
Application information: Application form not
required.
   Initial approach: Letter
   Deadline(s): None
Officers: Joseph D. Klobucher, Pres.; Wayne
Stewart, Secy.; John E. Klobucar, Treas.
EIN: 383605623

459
Edward M. and Henrietta M. Knabusch
Charitable Trust No. 2
c/o Monroe Bank & Trust
102 E. Front St.
Monroe, MI   48161-2162   (734) 242-2068
County: Monroe
Contact: Andrew M. Weisenburger

Established in 1995 in MI.
Donor: Edward M. Knabusch Marital Trust.
Grantmaker type: Independent foundation.
Financial data (yr. ended 12/31/09): Assets,
$5,203,178 (M); expenditures, $431,581; total
giving, $414,000; qualifying distributions,
$422,791; giving activities include $414,000 for 23
grants (high: $100,000; low: $2,000).
Fields of interest: Health care; Human services.
Limitations: Applications accepted. Giving primarily
in Monroe, MI. No grants to individuals.
Application information: Application form not
required.
   Deadline(s): None
Trustees: Charles T. Knabusch, Jr.; John F. Weaver;
Gregory D. White.
EIN: 386643328
Selected grants: The following grants were reported
in 2009.
$100,000 to Mercy Memorial Hospital, Monroe, MI.
$20,000 to Grace Lutheran Church, Monroe, MI.
$20,000 to Philadelphia House, Monroe, MI.
$20,000 to Trinity Lutheran Church, Monroe, MI.
$20,000 to Trinity Lutheran School, Monroe, MI.
$12,000 to Humane Society of Monroe, Monroe, MI.

460
Edward M. and Henrietta M. Knabusch
Scholarship Foundation
c/o Monroe Bank & Trust
102 E. Front St.
Monroe, MI   48161-2162
County: Monroe
Contact: Paul J. Wannemacher

E-mail: paul.wannemacher@mbandt.com

Established in 1998 in MI.
Donors: La-Z-Boy Foundation; Edward M. &
Henrietta M. Knabusch Charitable Trust No. 2.
Grantmaker type: Independent foundation.
Financial data (yr. ended 12/31/09): Assets,
$1,811,505 (M); expenditures, $58,920; total
giving, $39,814; qualifying distributions, $39,814;
giving activities include $39,814 for grants to
individuals.
Purpose and activities: Scholarships awarded to
high school seniors who are children of La-Z-Boy,
Inc., employees.
Fields of interest: Education.
Type of support: Scholarships—to individuals.
Limitations: Giving limited to children of La-Z-Boy,
Inc., employees in the following locations: Siloam
Springs, AR, Redlands, CA, Monroe, MI, Neosho,
MO, Leland and Newton, MS, Hudson, Lenoir, and
Lincolnton, NC, Florence, SC, Dayton and New
Tazewell, TN, Tremonton, UT, Bedford, VA, and
Waterloo, Ontario, Canada.
Publications: Annual report.
Application information: Applications are only
accepted from children of La-Z-Boy, Inc., employees
(or affiliated companies). Application form required.
   Deadline(s): Aug. 1
   Board meeting date(s): July 1
   Final notification: Aug. 30
Trustees: John F. Weaver; Betty Lou White; Greg
White.
EIN: 383450698

461
James A. and Faith Knight Foundation
180 Little Lake Dr., Ste. 6B
Ann Arbor, MI   48103-6219   (734) 769-5653
County: Washtenaw
Contact: Margaret A. Talburtt Ph.D., Exec. Dir.
FAX: (734) 769-8383;
E-mail: info@knightfoundationmi.org; *URL:* http://
www.knightfoundationmi.org

Established in 1999 in MI.
Donor: James A. Knight Trust.
Grantmaker type: Independent foundation.
Financial data (yr. ended 12/31/09): Assets,
$14,358,500 (M); expenditures, $813,243; total
giving, $636,588; qualifying distributions,
$707,513; giving activities include $636,588 for 61
grants (high: $30,000; low: $1,200).
Purpose and activities: Primarily serving Jackson
and Washtenaw counties, Michigan, the foundation
is dedicated to improving communities by providing
grant support to qualified nonprofit organizations
including, but not limited to, those that address the
needs of women and girls, animals and the natural
world, and internal capacity. Giving primarily for
human services, including a neighborhood center,
women's organizations, and family services;
support also for nonprofit management, the United
Way, housing, the arts, education, and
environmental conservation.
Fields of interest: Arts; Adult education—literacy,
basic skills & GED; Environment, natural resources;
Housing/shelter, development; Human services;
Family services; Women, centers/services;
Nonprofit management; Women; Girls; Young
adults, female.
Type of support: Building/renovation; Capital
campaigns; Debt reduction; General/operating

support; Management development/capacity building; Program development.

Limitations: Applications accepted. Giving limited to MI, with emphasis on Jackson and Washtenaw counties. No support for religious or political organizations. No grants to individuals, or for conferences or special events, or for annual campaigns.

Publications: Application guidelines; Grants list; Occasional report; Program policy statement.

Application information: All applicants are expected to submit applications online using the Community Grants online system at http://www.communitygrants.org. Application form required.

    Initial approach: 2-page concept letter
    Copies of proposal: 3
    Deadline(s): Early Jan. and early Sept.
    Board meeting date(s): 10 times per year
    Final notification: Approximately 90 days

Officers: Carol Knight-Drain, Pres. and Treas.; Margaret A. Talburtt, Secy.

Directors: Christopher Ballard; Scott Drain.

Number of staff: 1 part-time professional; 1 part-time support.

EIN: 383465904

Selected grants: The following grants were reported in 2007.

$30,000 to Ann Arbor Teen Center, Ann Arbor, MI. For purchase and renovation of new building.

$30,000 to SOS Community Services, Ypsilanti, MI. To promote economic self-sufficiency of homeless women and children through rapid placement into permanent housing, tenant-based rental assistance, and supportive services that will improve homeless women's opportunities for employment, education, and independence.

$25,000 to Planned Parenthood of Mid-Michigan, Ann Arbor, MI. For capital funds to open second health center and to help establish an endowment fund to train new physicians in reproductive health care.

$17,500 to Leslie Science and Nature Center, Ann Arbor, MI. For operational and governance support due to transition to independent nonprofit status in 2007.

$15,000 to Wild Swan Theater, Ann Arbor, MI. For Hawk, I'm Your Brother, play integrating science and language arts to further environmental education for young people.

$10,000 to Jackson Nonprofit Support Center, Jackson, MI. To build capacity among Jackson's nonprofits by offering value added consulting and training programs.

$6,700 to Washtenaw Literacy, Ypsilanti, MI. For Women Only English as second language (ESL) tutoring groups.

$6,000 to Community Action Network, Ann Arbor, MI. To allow children living at low income housing sites to observe and interact with dogs, teaching them empathy and proper pet care; to help children analyze animal and their own behaviors and to implement a fun and nonjudgmental, low stress summer reading program.

$6,000 to Friends in Deed Washtenaw Area Social Ministries Network, Ypsilanti, MI. To enable more women to work towards or maintain self sufficiency by providing transportation-related assistance for employment purposes.

$6,000 to Girls Group, Ann Arbor, MI. For program for young women in 8th through 10th grades from low-income homes designed to help them develop into healthy, self-confident, articulate women.

462
John S. and James L. Knight Foundation

(formerly Knight Foundation)
Wachovia Financial Ctr., Ste. 3300
200 S. Biscayne Blvd.
Miami, FL 33131-2349 (305) 908-2600
County: Miami-Dade
Contact: Grant Admin.
FAX: (305) 908-2698; Additional tel. for publication requests: (305) 908-2629; E-mail: publications@knightfoundation.org, or web@knightfoundation.org; URL: http://www.knightfoundation.org

Incorporated in 1950 in OH.

Donors: John S. Knight‡; James L. Knight‡; and their families.

Grantmaker type: Independent foundation.

Financial data (yr. ended 12/31/09): Assets, $2,079,000,000 (M); expenditures, $126,590,102; total giving, $105,887,097; qualifying distributions, $105,887,097; giving activities include $101,719,474 for grants, $240,011 for 165 employee matching gifts, $3,094,279 for foundation-administered programs and $833,333 for 1 loan/program-related investment.

Purpose and activities: The foundation advances journalism in the digital age and invests in the vitality of communities where the Knight brothers owned newspapers. The foundation focuses on projects that promote informed, engaged communities and that lead to transformational change. The foundation promotes these goals through its journalism, communities and national programs.

Fields of interest: Media, print publishing; Arts; Education; Children, services; Family services; Civil rights, race/intergroup relations; Community development, neighborhood development; Economic development; Public affairs, citizen participation.

Type of support: General/operating support; Management development/capacity building; Capital campaigns; Building/renovation; Endowments; Emergency funds; Program development; Seed money; Curriculum development; Fellowships; Technical assistance; Program evaluation; Program-related investments/loans; Employee matching gifts.

Limitations: Applications accepted. Giving limited to projects serving the 26 communities where the Knight brothers published newspapers for communities and local grants: Long Beach and San Jose, CA, Boulder, CO, Bradenton, Miami, Palm Beach County, and Tallahassee, FL, Columbus, Macon, and Milledgeville, GA, Fort Wayne and Gary, IN, Wichita, KS, Lexington, KY, Detroit, MI, Duluth and St. Paul, MN, Biloxi, MS, Charlotte, NC, Grand Forks, ND, Akron, OH, Philadelphia and State College, PA, Columbia and Myrtle Beach, SC, and Aberdeen, SD; international for Journalism. No support for organizations whose mission is to prevent, eradicate and/or alleviate the effects of a specific disease; hospitals, unless for community-wide capital campaigns; activities to propagate a religious faith or restricted to one religion or denomination; political candidates; international programs, except U.S.-based organizations supporting free press around the world; charities operated by service clubs; or activities that are the responsibility of government (the foundation will in selective cases, join with units of government in supporting special projects). No grants to individuals, or for fundraising events;

second requests for previously funded capital campaigns; operating deficits; general operating support; films, videos, or television programs; honoraria for distinguished guests-except in initiatives of the foundation in all three cases; group travel; memorials; medical research; or conferences.

Publications: Annual report; Grants list.

Application information: Please do not submit a proposal until you have been invited to do so by the Grants Admin. or a Prog. Off. Application form required.

    Initial approach: Online inquiry
    Copies of proposal: 2
    Deadline(s): None, except for special initiatives (approximately 6-month grant cycle)
    Board meeting date(s): Mar., June, Sept., and Dec.
    Final notification: 2 weeks after meeting dates

Officers and Trustees: * Robert W. Briggs,* Chair.; Alberto Ibarguen,* C.E.O. and Pres.; Paula Ellis, V.P., National and New Initiatives; Belinda Turner Lawrence, V.P., Secy. and C.A.O.; Juan J. Martinez, V.P., C.F.O. and Treas.; Marc Fest, V.P., Comms.; Michael Maness, V.P., Journalism Prog.; Mayur Patel, V.P., Strategy and Assessment; Dennis Scholl, V.P., Arts and Prog. Dir., Miami; Trabian Shorters,* V.P., Communities Prog.; Jonathan Sotsky, Off., Strategic Assessment; Cesar L. Alvarez; Mary Sue Coleman; Marjorie Knight Crane; James N. Crutchfield; Paul S. Grogan; Rolfe Neill; Mariam C. Noland; Beverly Knight Olson; Earl W. Powell; Ray Rodriguez; John W. Rogers, Jr.; E. Roe Stamps IV; Paul Steiger.

Number of staff: 44 full-time professional; 1 part-time professional.

EIN: 650464177

Selected grants: The following grants were reported in 2009.

$6,000,000 to International Center for Journalists, Washington, DC. For general support for effort to lead new group of high-impact projects advancing news in the public interest through Knight International Journalism Fellowships, payable over 3.00 years.

$6,000,000 to Teach for America, New York, NY. For operating support for work to close achievement gap of 25,000 students in Miami-Dade public school system by providing support for Teach For America Miami-Dade to grow from 95 teachers to 350 teachers per year, while placing the teachers in a feeder pattern, payable over 5.00 years.

$3,300,000 to OneCommunity, Cleveland, OH. For operations for Knight Center of Digital Excellence, which was created to provide universal digital access in 26 Knight communities within 5 years.

$1,080,000 to Cranbrook Educational Community, Bloomfield Hills, MI. For general support for work to establish Cranbrook as new cultural and education partner in Detroit's Creative Corridor while developing a long-term, integrated partnership with Arts League of Michigan, payable over 3.00 years.

$1,010,000 to Pro Publica, New York, NY. To create sustainable business model for ProPublica, payable over 3.00 years.

$900,000 to Miami City Ballet, Miami Beach, FL. For operating support for efforts to showcase ballet, and regions cultural significance, by providing orchestral accompaniment during 2011-13 repertory seasons, payable over 4.00 years.

$719,500 to Pro Publica, New York, NY. To create public, easily searchable index of original source documents on the Web, payable over 2.25 years.

$388,615 to Mississippi Center for Nonprofits, Jackson, MS. For general support for work to raise bar on professionalism for Biloxi's 400 nonprofits through core competencies certification program, payable over 2.75 years.

$250,000 to University of Southern California, Los Angeles, CA. To expand Spot.us, project that publicly finances local investigative reporting, to Los Angeles in partnership with Annenberg School of Communication, payable over 1.75 years.

$150,000 to United Way of Miami-Dade, Miami, FL. For general program support.

463
Robert & Margaret Koch Bomarko Founders Scholarship Fund

c/o Fifth Third Bank
P.O. Box 3636
Grand Rapids, MI   49501-3636
County: Kent

Established in 1989 in IN.
Donors: Robert Koch; Margaret Koch.
Grantmaker type: Independent foundation.
Financial data (yr. ended 09/30/09): Assets, $94,129 (M); expenditures, $6,665; total giving, $3,700; qualifying distributions, $3,700; giving activities include $3,700 for grants.
Purpose and activities: Scholarship awards to students or graduates of the Argos, Bremen, Culver, LaVille, Plymouth or Triton schools. Scholarship awards provided for employees of Bomarko, Plymouth high, who will attend Ancilla College, Donaldson, Indiana.
Fields of interest: Higher education.
Type of support: Scholarships—to individuals.
Limitations: Giving limited to residents of IN.
Application information: Application form required.
Deadline(s): Apr. 15
Trustee: Fifth Third Bank.
EIN: 351781577

464
John and Ann L. Koester Charitable Trust

P.O. Box 180
Frankenmuth, MI   48734-0180   (989) 652-6207
County: Saginaw

Established in 1994 in MI.
Donors: John C. Koester; Ann Leone Koester.
Grantmaker type: Independent foundation.
Financial data (yr. ended 12/31/09): Assets, $117,674 (M); expenditures, $24,599; total giving, $22,800; qualifying distributions, $22,800; giving activities include $22,800 for grants.
Purpose and activities: Giving primarily to Evangelical Lutheran churches and schools.
Fields of interest: Elementary/secondary education; Theological school/education; Protestant agencies & churches.
Limitations: Giving primarily in MI; giving also in WI.
Application information:
Initial approach: Letter
Deadline(s): None
Trustees: Ann Leone Koester; John C. Koester.
EIN: 383150475

465
The Kohn-Bancroft Family Foundation

c/o Robert A. Kohn
3389 Linco Rd.
Stevensville, MI   49127-9725   (269) 465-5757
County: Berrien

Established in 2000 in MI.
Donors: Robert A. Kohn; Elizabeth J. Kohn.
Grantmaker type: Independent foundation.
Financial data (yr. ended 12/31/09): Assets, $108,616 (M); expenditures, $29,065; total giving, $28,295; qualifying distributions, $28,295; giving activities include $28,295 for grants.
Purpose and activities: Scholarship awards to employees of Supreme Casting, Inc., Stevensville, Michigan, and their dependents.
Fields of interest: Higher education; Education.
Type of support: Employee-related scholarships.
Limitations: Giving primarily in MI.
Application information: Application form required.
Deadline(s): May 1 and Oct. 1
Officers: Robert A. Kohn, Pres.; Robert W. Bancroft, V.P.; William R. Bancroft, Jr., V.P.; Elizabeth J. Kohn, Secy.-Treas.
EIN: 383537827

466
Christian W. Konstanzer Endowment Fund

(also known as Christian W. Konstanzer Endowment Fund of the Kiwanis Club of Mt. Clemens)
50025 Magdalina Dr.
Macomb, MI   48044-6310
County: Macomb
Contact: Gregory Dudek, Tr.
Application address: 207 Moross St., Mount Clemens, MI 48043-2227

Established in 2002.
Grantmaker type: Independent foundation.
Financial data (yr. ended 09/30/09): Assets, $189,536 (M); gifts received, $246; expenditures, $2,666; total giving, $2,494; qualifying distributions, $2,494; giving activities include $2,494 for grants.
Purpose and activities: Giving to assist indigent and low income hearing-impaired individuals in Mount Clemens and Clinton Township, Michigan, providing devices to improve their abilities to hear; also some giving to Kiwanis Club of Mount Clemens.
Fields of interest: Human services; Deaf/hearing impaired; Economically disadvantaged.
Type of support: Program development; Grants to individuals.
Limitations: Giving limited to Mount Clemens and Clinton Township, MI.
Application information: Application form required.
Deadline(s): Sept. 30
Trustees: Gordon Brown; Gregory Dudek; Jill Johnson.
EIN: 412046188

467
Donald & Mary Kosch Foundation

(formerly Donald F. Kosch Foundation)
9 West Ln.
Dearborn, MI   48124-1193
County: Wayne
Application address: c/o Donald F. Kosch, 2450 Wyoming St., Dearborn, MI 48126-1518, tel.: (313) 842-2375

Established in 1994 in MI.
Donor: Donald F. Kosch.
Grantmaker type: Independent foundation.
Financial data (yr. ended 12/31/09): Assets, $1,433,275 (M); gifts received, $299,528; expenditures, $180,104; total giving, $164,000; qualifying distributions, $172,051; giving activities include $164,000 for 8 grants (high: $100,000; low: $1,000).
Fields of interest: Museums; Arts; Hospitals (general); Recreation, parks/playgrounds; Christian agencies & churches.
Type of support: General/operating support.
Limitations: Applications accepted. Giving primarily in MI, with emphasis on Ann Arbor, Dearborn, and Detroit.
Application information:
Initial approach: Letter
Deadline(s): None
Officers and Directors:* Donald F. Kosch,* Pres. and Treas.; Mary T. Kosch,* Secy.; Susan L. Kosch-Meier.
EIN: 383147426
Selected grants: The following grants were reported in 2008.
$125,000 to Oakwood Hospital Medical Center, Dearborn, MI.
$15,000 to Childrens Hospital of Michigan, Detroit, MI.
$10,000 to Eton Academy, Birmingham, MI.
$1,000 to Henry Ford Community College, Dearborn, MI.

468
Daniel J. & Ardith A. Koster Foundation

2015 8th Ave.
Byron Center, MI   49315-8926   (616) 878-5554
County: Kent
Contact: Greg Koster, Exec. Dir.

Established in 1992 in MI.
Donors: Daniel J. Koster‡; Ardith A. Koster.
Grantmaker type: Independent foundation.
Financial data (yr. ended 12/31/09): Assets, $48,734 (M); gifts received, $117,728; expenditures, $138,480; total giving, $132,960; qualifying distributions, $138,480; giving activities include $132,960 for 31 grants (high: $18,060; low: $500).
Purpose and activities: Giving primarily to Christian organizations; giving also for scholarships to full-time students who are engaged in substantial Christian service and who will attend a qualified Christian educational institution.
Fields of interest: Education; Christian agencies & churches.
Limitations: Applications accepted. Giving primarily in MI. No grants to individuals.
Application information: Application form required.
Initial approach: Letter
Deadline(s): None
Board meeting date(s): Jan. and June
Officers: Ardith A. Stephenson, Pres.; Greg Koster, Exec. Dir.
Board Members: Cheryl Koster; Kurt Koster; Linda Koster; Rick Koster; Susan Koster.
EIN: 383067600
Selected grants: The following grants were reported in 2008.
$25,100 to Camp Ao-Wa-Kiya, Shelby, MI.
$10,200 to Closed Door Ministries, Grand Rapids, MI.
$7,800 to SEND International, Farmington, MI.

$7,500 to Grace Ministries, Moundsville, WV.
$7,200 to Transformation Life Center, West Park, NY.
$6,600 to New Tribes Mission, Sanford, FL.
$2,300 to Freedom Baptist Schools, Hudsonville, MI.
$2,000 to Frontier School of the Bible, Lagrange, WY.
$1,600 to NorthPointe Christian Schools, Grand Rapids, MI.
$1,000 to Calvary Baptist Church, Grand Rapids, MI.

469
Cmdr. and Mrs. Robert Krause Foundation
132 State St.
Harbor Beach, MI   48441-1203
County: Huron
Application address: c/o Harbor Beach Community School, 402 S. 5th St., Harbor Beach, MI 48441-1309, tel.: (989) 479-3261

Established in 2003 in MI.
Grantmaker type: Independent foundation.
Financial data (yr. ended 12/31/09): Assets, $668,910 (M); expenditures, $52,450; total giving, $35,825; qualifying distributions, $35,825; giving activities include $35,825 for grants to individuals.
Purpose and activities: Scholarship awards to graduates of Harbor Beach Community School, Michigan, for post-secondary education.
Fields of interest: Higher education.
Type of support: Scholarships—to individuals.
Limitations: Applications accepted. Giving limited to residents of Harbor Beach, MI.
Application information: Application form required.
   Deadline(s): Fourth Friday in Apr.
Trustee: Marilyn S. Townley.
EIN: 527317516

470
R. & W. Krause Foundation, Inc.
140 Krause St.
Rockford, MI   49341-1214   (616) 866-0515
County: Kent
Contact: Barbara K. Bunbury, Pres.

Established in MI.
Grantmaker type: Independent foundation.
Financial data (yr. ended 10/31/09): Assets, $196,482 (M); gifts received, $70,968; expenditures, $31,849; total giving, $30,865; qualifying distributions, $30,865; giving activities include $30,865 for 4 grants (high: $25,000; low: $100).
Fields of interest: Education; Protestant agencies & churches.
Type of support: General/operating support.
Limitations: Applications accepted. Giving primarily in MI. No grants to individuals.
Application information: Application form not required.
   Initial approach: Letter
   Deadline(s): None
Officers: Barbara K. Bunbury, Pres.; John D. Bunbury, V.P.
EIN: 386111582

471
The Kresge Foundation
3215 W. Big Beaver Rd.
Troy, MI   48084-2818   (248) 643-9630
County: Oakland
Contact: Rip Rapson, C.E.O. and Pres.
FAX: (248) 643-0588; E-mail: info@kresge.org;
URL: http://www.kresge.org

Incorporated in 1924 in MI.
Donor: Sebastian S. Kresge†.
Grantmaker type: Independent foundation.
Financial data (yr. ended 12/31/09): Assets, $3,130,801,054 (M); expenditures, $233,234,142; total giving, $200,616,569; qualifying distributions, $277,920,647; giving activities include $199,342,308 for grants, $1,274,261 for employee matching gifts, and $10,920,000 for 5 loans/program-related investments (high: $4,750,000; low: $760,000).
Purpose and activities: The foundation seeks to strengthen nonprofit organizations by catalyzing their growth, connecting them to their stake holders, and challenging greater support through grants. The foundation believes that strong, sustainable, high capacity organizations are positioned to achieve their missions and strengthen communities. Grants are awarded to nonprofit organizations operating in the fields of education, health and long-term care, human services, arts and humanities, public affairs, and science, nature, and the environment.
Fields of interest: Humanities; Arts, artist's services; Arts; Higher education; Environment, alliance/advocacy; Environment, public policy; Environment, reform; Environment, government agencies; Environment, natural resources; Environment, energy; Environment; Health care; Human services; Science; Public affairs.
Type of support: Capital campaigns; Building/renovation; Equipment; Land acquisition; Employee matching gifts; Matching/challenge support.
Limitations: Applications accepted. Giving on a national basis with emphasis on Detroit, MI, as well as some international funding. No support for religious organizations, (unless applicant is operated by a religious organization and it serves secular needs and has financial and governing autonomy separate from the parent organization with space formally dedicated to its programs) private foundations, or elementary and secondary schools (unless they predominantly serve individuals with physical and/or developmental disabilities). No grants to individuals, or for debt retirement, projects that are already substantially completed, minor equipment purchases, or for constructing buildings for worship services.
Publications: Application guidelines; Annual report.
Application information: Green Building Initiative has been retired. See foundation web site for more application information. Application procedures vary for each foundation program area. See foundation web site for information on Community Relief Loans. Until Sept., 2011 the foundation will only make grants to human services organizations on an invitation-only basis. Application form required.
   Initial approach: Letter or proposal
   Copies of proposal: 1
   Deadline(s): None
   Board meeting date(s): Mar., June, Sept., and Dec.
   Final notification: Generally within 4 to 6 months; decisions announced after each board meeting, applicants notified in writing

Officers and Trustees:* Elaine D. Rosen,* Chair.; Rip Rapson,* C.E.O. and Pres.; Amy B. Coleman, V.P., Finance and Treas.; Robert J. Manilla, V.P. and C.I.O.; Richard K. Rappleye, V.P., Admin.; Sheryl Madden, Cont.; James L. Bildner; Lee C. Bollinger; Phillip L. Clay; Jane L. Delgado, Ph.D.; Susan K. Drewes; Steven K. Hamp; Paul C. Hillegonds; Irene Y. Hirano; David W. Horvitz; Nancy M. Schlichting.
Number of staff: 23 full-time professional.
EIN: 381359217
Selected grants: The following grants were reported in 2010.
$4,298,701 to National Alliance for Hispanic Health, Washington, DC. To augment leadership and management development in human services area, payable over 3.00 years.
$3,000,000 to Living Cities: The National Community Development Initiative, New York, NY. For General Operating Support for 2010-2013 Funding Round, payable over 3.00 years.
$2,500,000 to Haven for Hope of Bexar County, San Antonio, TX. To provide housing and supportive services.
$2,000,000 to Carnegie Foundation for the Advancement of Teaching, Stanford, CA. For Statway and Mathway, programs providing alternative mathematical pathways for community college students, payable over 2.00 years.
$1,502,940 to College for Creative Studies, Detroit, MI. For Kresge Arts in Detroit: Eminent Artist Award and Artist Fellowships. Eminent Artist Award recognizes an exceptional artist for his or her professional achievements and contributions to the cultural community and encourages that individual's pursuit of a chosen art form as well as an ongoing commitment to metropolitan Detroit and Fellowships seek to advance the art forms and professional careers of artists from the visual, performing and literary arts as well as elevate the profile of the artistic community and encourage creative expression in the region, payable over 2.25 years.
$1,500,000 to Energy Foundation, San Francisco, CA. For program to promote energy efficiency in the Southeast.
$780,000 to Project HOPE - The People-to-People Health Foundation, Millwood, VA. To publish special issue of Health Affairs entitled, Environmental Health and to hold briefing on the subject, payable over 2.00 years.
$500,000 to University of Pennsylvania, Graduate School of Education, Philadelphia, PA. For Models of Success at Minority Serving Institutions, payable over 3.00 years.
$250,000 to First Nations Development Institute, Longmont, CO. For Native Agriculture and Food Systems Initiative.
$75,000 to Detroit Science Center, Detroit, MI. For Detroit Children's Museum.

472
Krishnamurti Rajghat Foundation, Inc.
5549 Blue Spruce Ln.
Kalamazoo, MI   49009-4568
County: Kalamazoo
Contact: Krishna M. Jain, Pres.

Established in 1989 in MI.
Donors: Suresh Bazaj; Alka Bazaj.
Grantmaker type: Independent foundation.
Financial data (yr. ended 01/31/10): Assets, $7,055 (M); gifts received, $23,819; expenditures, $24,124; total giving, $22,700; qualifying

distributions, $22,700; giving activities include $22,700 for 2 grants (high: $21,600; low: $1,100).
Fields of interest: Education.
Limitations: Giving primarily in India.
Application information:
 Initial approach: Letter
 Deadline(s): None
Officers and Director:* Krishna M. Jain,* Pres.; Armand M. Clark, Treas.
EIN: 382799825

473
Kronlund Foundation Charitable Trust
c/o JPMorgan Chase Bank, N.A.
P.O. Box 3038
Milwaukee, WI 53201-3038
County: Milwaukee
Application address: c/o JPMorgan Chase Bank, N.A., Attn.: M. Wasmund, 611 Woodward Ave., Ste. MI18038, Detroit, MI 48226-3408, tel.: (313) 225-3454

Established in MI.
Donor: Louise B. Kronlund‡.
Grantmaker type: Independent foundation.
Financial data (yr. ended 12/31/09): Assets, $650,120 (M); expenditures, $1,527; total giving, $0; qualifying distributions, $0.
Purpose and activities: Giving primarily to Lutheran and Episcopal churches.
Fields of interest: Human services; Protestant agencies & churches.
Limitations: Giving primarily in MI. No grants to individuals.
Application information: Application form not required.
 Deadline(s): None
Trustees: Thomas W. Payne; JPMorgan Chase Bank, N.A.
EIN: 382117538

474
Marie Lafler Foundation
1823 W. Kirby Rd.
Battle Creek, MI 49017-9014
County: Calhoun

Established in 2006 in MI.
Grantmaker type: Independent foundation.
Financial data (yr. ended 12/31/09): Assets, $301,253 (M); expenditures, $15,934; total giving, $4,000; qualifying distributions, $4,000; giving activities include $4,000 for grants.
Limitations: Giving primarily in Battle Creek, MI.
Officers: Patricia A. McCulley, Pres. and Treas.; Anna West, V.P.; Barbara J. Butcher, Secy.
Director: Dorothy Thomas.
EIN: 300309136

475
William T. Laflin Scholarship Fund, Inc.
c/o Trustees
3226 Arthur Rd.
Remus, MI 49340-9541 (989) 967-2100
County: Mecosta

Established in MI.
Grantmaker type: Independent foundation.
Financial data (yr. ended 12/31/09): Assets, $80,736 (M); expenditures, $2,966; total giving,

$2,500; qualifying distributions, $2,500; giving activities include $2,500 for grants to individuals.
Purpose and activities: Scholarship awards to high school graduates and residents of the Chippewa Hills School District, MI.
Fields of interest: Higher education.
Type of support: Scholarships—to individuals.
Limitations: Giving limited to MI.
Application information: Application form required.
 Deadline(s): None
Officers: Shirley Howard, Pres.; Bob Thompson, V.P.; Kathy Gaffner, Secy.; John Ruddell, Treas.
EIN: 381579001

476
Lahti Family Foundation
c/o Comerica Bank
P.O. Box 75000, MC 3302
Detroit, MI 48275-3302
County: Wayne
Application address: Brenda Pearson, 60 S. 6th St., Minneapolis, MN 55402, tel.: (612) 215-3603

Established in 2004 in MI.
Donor: Martha Lahti.
Grantmaker type: Independent foundation.
Financial data (yr. ended 12/31/09): Assets, $1,934,315 (M); expenditures, $135,374; total giving, $103,000; qualifying distributions, $103,000; giving activities include $103,000 for grants.
Fields of interest: Arts; Youth development; Human services; YM/YWCAs & YM/YWHAs; Children/youth, services.
Limitations: Giving primarily in Duluth, MN. No grants to individuals.
Application information: Application form not required.
 Deadline(s): None
Trustee: Comerica Bank.
EIN: 202988335
Selected grants: The following grants were reported in 2006.
$15,000 to Life House, Duluth, MN.
$13,000 to Boys and Girls Club of Duluth, Duluth, MN.
$10,000 to Second Harvest Northern Lakes Food Bank, Duluth, MN.
$5,000 to Duluth Childrens Museum, Duluth, MN.
$5,000 to Union Gospel Mission, Duluth, MN.

477
Maxine Sprague Lahti Foundation for the Performing Arts
c/o National City Bank
P.O. Box 94651
Cleveland, OH 44101-4651
County: Cuyahoga
Application address: c/o Laura Bozell, 1900 E. 9th St., LOC 01-2111, Cleveland, OH 44114-3404, tel.: (216) 222-2799

Established in 1987 in MI.
Grantmaker type: Independent foundation.
Financial data (yr. ended 12/31/09): Assets, $109,427 (M); expenditures, $6,272; total giving, $4,500; qualifying distributions, $4,500; giving activities include $4,500 for grants.
Fields of interest: Performing arts; Performing arts, theater; Performing arts, music; Libraries/library science.

Type of support: General/operating support.
Limitations: Giving limited to the Monroe, MI, area. No grants to individuals.
Application information: Application form required.
 Initial approach: Letter or telephone
 Deadline(s): Oct. 31
Trustee: National City Bank.
EIN: 382720188

478
The Helen Laidlaw Foundation
314 Newman St.
East Tawas, MI 48730-1214 (989) 362-4491
County: Iosco

Established in 1989 in MI.
Grantmaker type: Independent foundation.
Financial data (yr. ended 12/31/09): Assets, $422,584 (M); expenditures, $30,416; total giving, $17,000; qualifying distributions, $17,000; giving activities include $17,000 for grants.
Purpose and activities: Scholarship awards limited to those pursuing an education in the health care field.
Fields of interest: Medical school/education; Nursing school/education; Public health school/education; Health sciences school/education.
Type of support: Scholarships—to individuals.
Limitations: Applications accepted. Giving limited to northeast MI.
Application information: Application form required.
 Deadline(s): Mar. 1
Officers and Directors:* James C. Laidlaw,* Pres.; Nancy E. Huck,* V.P.; Brenda Redding,* Secy.; W. William Laidlaw,* Treas.; Thomas B. Huck; Barbara G. Laidlaw.
EIN: 382901107

479
Frank and Mary Lamberson Foundation
c/o JPMorgan Chase Bank, N.A.
P.O. Box 3038
Milwaukee, WI 53201-3038
County: Milwaukee
Application address: c/o JPMorgan Chase Bank, N.A., 2385 Executive Center Dr., Boca Raton, FL 33431-8579, tel.: (561) 995-5052

Established in 1997 in FL.
Grantmaker type: Independent foundation.
Financial data (yr. ended 12/31/09): Assets, $1,202,502 (M); expenditures, $68,438; total giving, $59,000; qualifying distributions, $59,000; giving activities include $59,000 for grants.
Fields of interest: Museums; Higher education; Environment; Zoos/zoological societies.
Limitations: Applications accepted. Giving primarily in FL, MI, Asheville, NC, and Poughkeepsie, NY. No grants to individuals.
Application information: Application form required.
 Initial approach: Letter
 Deadline(s): None
Trustees: Frank A. Lamberson; Mary T. Lamberson; JPMorgan Chase Bank, N.A.
EIN: 597096409

480
Patricia A. & William E. LaMothe Foundation
620 Jennings Ln.
Battle Creek, MI   49015-3529
County: Calhoun
Contact: Patricia A. LaMothe, Pres.

Established in 1986 in MI.
Donors: Patricia A. LaMothe; William E. LaMothe; Sydney McManus.
Grantmaker type: Independent foundation.
Financial data (yr. ended 12/31/09): Assets, $5,014,326 (M); expenditures, $285,127; total giving, $277,411; qualifying distributions, $280,348; giving activities include $277,411 for 88 grants (high: $27,000; low: $100).
Purpose and activities: Giving primarily for higher education, Roman Catholic organizations, and conservation.
Fields of interest: Education; Environment, natural resources; Health organizations, association; Human services; Catholic agencies & churches.
Limitations: Applications accepted. Giving primarily in Battle Creek and Kalamazoo, MI.
Application information:
   Initial approach: Letter
   Deadline(s): None
Officers and Trustees:* Patricia A. LaMothe,* Pres.; Alexis LaMothe,* V.P.; Sydney McManus,* Secy.; William E. LaMothe,* Treas.
EIN: 386517929
Selected grants: The following grants were reported in 2008.
$50,000 to University of Texas Foundation, Md Anderson Cancer Center, Houston, TX.
$26,000 to Saint Meinrad Archabbey, Saint Meinrad, IN.
$10,000 to Hillsdale College, Hillsdale, MI.
$10,000 to Saint Aloysius School, New York, NY.
$3,000 to Heritage Foundation, Washington, DC.
$3,000 to Xavier High School, New York, NY.
$2,000 to Judicial Watch, Washington, DC.
$1,500 to Tax Foundation, Washington, DC.
$1,045 to Kalamazoo College, Kalamazoo, MI.
$1,044 to Rosemont College, Rosemont, PA.

481
Arnold G. & Martha M. Langbo Foundation
20137 Evans Ct.
Beverly Hills, MI   48025-3845   (239) 395-1688
County: Oakland
Application address: c/o Martha M. Langbo, 5606 Baltusrol Ct., Sanibel Island, FL 33957

Established in 1991 in MI.
Donors: Arnold G. Langbo; Martha M. Langbo.
Grantmaker type: Independent foundation.
Financial data (yr. ended 12/31/09): Assets, $731,446 (M); gifts received, $52,098; expenditures, $119,374; total giving, $116,404; qualifying distributions, $118,024; giving activities include $116,404 for 10 grants (high: $80,654; low: $600).
Purpose and activities: Giving for education, human services, and Roman Catholic churches and schools.
Fields of interest: Higher education; Human services; United Ways and Federated Giving Programs; Catholic agencies & churches.
Limitations: Applications accepted. Giving limited to MI. No grants to individuals.
Application information:

Initial approach: Letter
Deadline(s): None
Officers: Martha M. Langbo, Pres. and Secy.-Treas.; Arnold G. Langbo, V.P.
Directors: Sharon A. Bateman; Maureen Langbo; Susan C. Maks; Keith Langbo.
EIN: 383026270
Selected grants: The following grants were reported in 2007.
$35,000 to Our Lady of the Mississippi Abbey, Dubuque, IA.
$10,300 to Blessed Sacrament Church, Stowe, VT.
$2,100 to Diocese of Burlington, Bishops Fund, Burlington, VT.
$1,000 to Autism Speaks, Port Chester, NY.

482
Ann H. and Robert C. Lange Foundation
514 N. Elmwood Ave.
Traverse City, MI   49684-1454
County: Grand Traverse

Established in 2004 in MI.
Grantmaker type: Independent foundation.
Financial data (yr. ended 12/31/08): Assets, $63 (M); expenditures, $0; total giving, $0; qualifying distributions, $0.
Fields of interest: Human services.
Limitations: Giving primarily in Traverse City, MI. No grants to individuals.
Officers: Robert Lange, Pres. and Treas.; Ann H. Lange, Secy.
EIN: 201804898

483
Matt Langley Foundation, Inc.
4233 Delemere Blvd.
Royal Oak, MI   48073-1804   (248) 549-9200
County: Oakland
Contact: Charles Clay Langley, Pres.

Established in 2007 in MI.
Grantmaker type: Independent foundation.
Financial data (yr. ended 12/31/09): Assets, $29,249 (M); expenditures, $13,086; total giving, $2,000; qualifying distributions, $2,000; giving activities include $2,000 for 2 grants to individuals (high: $1,000; low: $1,000).
Purpose and activities: Scholarship awards to residents of Royal Oak, Michigan.
Fields of interest: Higher education.
Type of support: Scholarships—to individuals.
Limitations: Applications accepted. Giving primarily to residents of Royal Oak, MI.
Application information: Application form required.
   Deadline(s): None
Officers: Charles Clay Langley, Pres. and Treas.; Charles O. Langley, Secy.
EIN: 550886985

484
The Greater Lansing Foundation
c/o National City Bank
120 N. Washington Sq., Ste. 650
Lansing, MI   48933-1619   (517) 334-5299
County: Ingham
Contact: Steven J. Peters

Established as a community foundation in 1947 in MI; status changed in 1980 to independent foundation.
Donor: Ardis Denise Trust.
Grantmaker type: Independent foundation.
Financial data (yr. ended 12/31/09): Assets, $12,141,391 (M); gifts received, $6,259; expenditures, $614,567; total giving, $482,051; qualifying distributions, $495,148; giving activities include $482,051 for 57 grants (high: $119,500; low: $114).
Purpose and activities: Support for charitable, public, or educational institutions, including support for health and the handicapped.
Fields of interest: Arts; Education; Health care; Health organizations, association; Disabilities, people with; Economically disadvantaged.
Type of support: Annual campaigns; Capital campaigns; Building/renovation; Equipment; Emergency funds; Program development; Conferences/seminars; Publication; Seed money; Scholarship funds; Research; Consulting services; Matching/challenge support.
Limitations: Applications accepted. Giving limited to Ingham, Clinton, and Eaton counties, MI. No grants to individuals, or for operating budgets, endowment funds, continuing support, deficit financing, land acquisition, or technical assistance; no loans.
Application information:
   Initial approach: Letter
   Deadline(s): Apr. 1
   Board meeting date(s): May and Nov.
Directors: Richard O. Berndt; Charles E. Bunch; Paul W. Chellgren; Robert N. Clay; Kay Coles James; Richard B. Kelson; Bruce C. Lindsay; Anthony A. Massaro; Jane G. Pepper; James E. Rohr; Donald J. Shepard; Lorene K. Steffes; Dennis P. Strigl; Stephen G. Thieke; Thomas J. Usher; George H. Walls, Jr.; Helge H. Wehmeier.
Trustee Bank: PNC Bank, N.A.
EIN: 386057513
Selected grants: The following grants were reported in 2007.
$284,500 to Woldumar Nature Center, Lansing, MI.
$50,000 to Hospice of Palm Beach County, West Palm Beach, FL.
$40,000 to Stetson University, DeLand, FL.
$30,740 to Humane Society, Capital Area, Lansing, MI.
$30,000 to Jupiter Medical Center, Jupiter, FL.
$25,000 to Eles Place, Lansing, MI.
$25,000 to Interlochen Center for the Arts, Interlochen, MI.
$25,000 to R. E. Olds Transportation Museum Association, Lansing, MI.
$14,071 to Volunteers of America.
$13,072 to National Anti-Vivisection Society, Chicago, IL.

485
The Larson Family Fund
(formerly The Larson Family Foundation)
91 W. Long Lake Rd.
Bloomfield Hills, MI   48304-2747
(248) 593-0710
County: Oakland
Contact: Robert C. Larson, Chair.

Established in 1987 in MI.
Donor: Robert C. Larson.
Grantmaker type: Independent foundation.

Financial data (yr. ended 12/31/09): Assets, $1,063 (M); gifts received, $178; expenditures, $548; total giving, $0; qualifying distributions, $0.
Fields of interest: Health care; Human services.
Application information: Application form not required.
Initial approach: Letter
Deadline(s): None
Officers: Robert C. Larson, Chair.; Elizabeth L. Willoughby, Pres.; Eric B. Larson, V.P. and Secy.; Kathryn W. Larson, V.P. and Treas.
EIN: 382711975

486
Larson Land Foundation
c/o Comerica Bank
P.O. Box 75000
Detroit, MI 48275-8280
County: Wayne
Application address: c/o Kim Fulgenzi, 500 Woodward Ave., 21st Fl., Detroit, MI 48226-3416, tel.: (313) 222-9457

Established in 2001 in MI.
Donor: Ruth L. Chartier†.
Grantmaker type: Independent foundation.
Financial data (yr. ended 12/31/09): Assets, $1,945,674 (M); gifts received, $507; expenditures, $136,039; total giving, $115,000; qualifying distributions, $115,000; giving activities include $115,000 for grants.
Purpose and activities: Giving to programs that protect and preserve land.
Fields of interest: Environment, natural resources; Environment, land resources.
Type of support: General/operating support.
Limitations: Giving primarily in NJ. No grants to individuals.
Application information:
Initial approach: Letter
Deadline(s): None
Advisory Committee: Edith Hillman; Wade Martin; Robert Sajdak.
Trustee: Comerica Bank.
EIN: 386776837
Selected grants: The following grants were reported in 2005.
$65,000 to D and R Greenway Land Trust, Princeton, NJ.
$20,000 to Land Conservancy of New Jersey, Boonton, NJ.
$15,000 to Land Trust Alliance, Saratoga Springs, NY.
$5,000 to Monmouth Conservation Foundation, Middletown, NJ.
$5,000 to Nature Conservancy, Arlington, VA.

487
Henry E. & Annabel Larzelere Foundation
1944 Winchester Dr.
East Lansing, MI 48823-1355
County: Ingham

Established in 2000 in MI.
Grantmaker type: Independent foundation.
Financial data (yr. ended 12/31/09): Assets, $2,835 (M); gifts received, $150; expenditures, $65; total giving, $65; qualifying distributions, $65; giving activities include $65 for 1 grant.
Limitations: Giving primarily in MI. No grants to individuals.

Directors: Martha Larzelere Campbell; G. Paul Dygert; Mary Larzelere Dygert; Annabel S. Larzelere; John H. Larzelere.
EIN: 383530833

488
John C. Lasko Foundation
P.O. Box 1525
Pennington, NJ 08534-1525
County: Mercer
Contact: Clint Blair
Application address: P.O. Box 339 Belleville, MI 48111; tel.: (734) 699-3400

Established in 1998 MI. Reincorporated in 2010 under a new IRS EI number.
Donors: John C. Lasko; Republic Die & Tool Co.
Grantmaker type: Independent foundation.
Fields of interest: Elementary/secondary education; Higher education.
Type of support: Scholarships—to individuals.
Limitations: Applications accepted. Giving primarily in MI.
Application information:
Initial approach: Letter
Deadline(s): None
Officers: John C. Lasko, Pres.; Barbara T. Huston, Secy.; Charles Zimmerman, Treas.
EIN: 276173297

489
Daisy Harder LaVictoire Memorial Scholarship
c/o John Schaefer
7254 Michigan Ave.
Pigeon, MI 48755-5145 (989) 453-2097
County: Huron
Contact: Robert Smith, Tr.

Established in 1993.
Donor: Daisy Harder Lavictoire Trust.
Grantmaker type: Independent foundation.
Financial data (yr. ended 03/31/10): Assets, $223,798 (M); expenditures, $5,842; total giving, $3,350; qualifying distributions, $3,350; giving activities include $3,350 for grants to individuals.
Purpose and activities: Scholarship awards to students of Laker High School, Pigeon, Michigan.
Fields of interest: Higher education.
Type of support: Scholarships—to individuals.
Limitations: Giving limited to residents of MI.
Application information: Recipient submission by area high schools. Application form required.
Deadline(s): Mar. 31
Trustees: Paul Clabuesch; Dwight Gascho; Robert Smith.
EIN: 386629469

490
Richard Barton Law Memorial Trust
227 Lagoon Beach Dr.
Bay City, MI 48706-1436
County: Bay

Established in MI.
Grantmaker type: Independent foundation.
Financial data (yr. ended 12/31/09): Assets, $600,093 (M); gifts received, $3,000; expenditures, $32,075; total giving, $26,500;

qualifying distributions, $26,500; giving activities include $26,500 for grants.
Purpose and activities: The trust makes awards for the benefit of Bay County, Michigan for medical research, health care, youth, and community development, and state-wide for higher education.
Fields of interest: Higher education; Health care; Medical research; Youth development; Community/economic development.
Type of support: Endowments; General/operating support.
Limitations: Giving limited to MI.
Application information:
Initial approach: Proposal
Deadline(s): Nov. 15
Trustees: Bruce Law; Jacquelyn D. Law.
EIN: 386081726

491
Joachim Lay Charitable Private Foundation
c/o Comerica Bank
P.O. Box 75000, MC 3302
Detroit, MI 48275-3302
County: Wayne
Application address: c/o Scott Drogs, 101 N. Main St., Ste. 100, Ann Arbor, MI 48104, tel.: (734) 930-2416

Established in 2007 in MI.
Grantmaker type: Independent foundation.
Financial data (yr. ended 10/31/09): Assets, $1,969,644 (M); gifts received, $200,000; expenditures, $201,927; total giving, $161,158; qualifying distributions, $175,008; giving activities include $161,158 for 7 grants (high: $95,000; low: $750).
Fields of interest: Youth development; Residential/custodial care, senior continuing care; Aging, centers/services.
Type of support: General/operating support.
Limitations: Applications accepted. Giving in MI, with emphasis on Alma.
Application information:
Initial approach: Letter
Deadline(s): None
Trustees: Janet Haering; Comerica Bank.
EIN: 206996945
Selected grants: The following grants were reported in 2009.
$95,000 to Michigan Masonic Home, Alma, MI.
$3,500 to Lions of Michigan Service Foundation, Lansing, MI.

492
Whilma B. Lee Scholarship Trust Fund
P.O. Box 247
Marcellus, MI 49067-0247 (269) 646-5345
County: Cass
Contact: Donald R. France, Tr.

Established in 1988 in MI.
Donor: Whilma B. Lee†.
Grantmaker type: Independent foundation.
Financial data (yr. ended 12/31/09): Assets, $88,956 (M); expenditures, $13,853; total giving, $10,250; qualifying distributions, $12,368; giving activities include $10,250 for 17 grants to individuals (high: $1,000; low: $250).
Purpose and activities: Scholarship awards to graduating seniors at public or private high schools

in Van Buren, Cass, Kalamazoo, and St. Joseph counties, MI, primarily for training in the ministry or for nursing education.
Fields of interest: Nursing school/education; Theological school/education.
Type of support: Scholarships—to individuals.
Limitations: Giving limited to residents of Cass, Kalamazoo, St. Joseph and Van Buren counties, MI.
Application information: Application form required.
Deadline(s): Apr. 15
Final notification: Approximately 3 to 4 weeks following deadline
Trustee: Donald R. France.
EIN: 386547465

493

E.C. Lefevre Scholarship Fund
c/o Citizens Bank Wealth Management, N.A.
328 S. Saginaw St.
Flint, MI   48502   (517) 797-6605
County: Genesee

Grantmaker type: Independent foundation.
Financial data (yr. ended 08/31/10): Assets, $1 (M); expenditures, $49,002; total giving, $44,041; qualifying distributions, $44,041; giving activities include $44,041 for grants.
Limitations: Applications accepted. Giving primarily in Saginaw, MI.
Application information: Application form required.
Initial approach: Proposal
Deadline(s): None
Trustee: Citizens Bank Wealth Management, N.A.
EIN: 386160874

494

The Legion Foundation
1750 S. Telegraph Rd., Ste. 301
Bloomfield Hills, MI   48302-0179
(248) 253-1100
County: Oakland
Contact: James E. Mulvoy Esq., Pres.

Established in 1997 in MI.
Donors: The Thewes Trust; The TT Trust; The Thewes Charitable Annuity Lead Trust.
Grantmaker type: Independent foundation.
Financial data (yr. ended 12/31/09): Assets, $9,854,745 (M); expenditures, $648,058; total giving, $506,823; qualifying distributions, $554,347; giving activities include $89,500 for 4 grants (high: $32,000; low: $15,500), and $417,323 for 42 grants to individuals (high: $45,127; low: $869).
Purpose and activities: The foundation awards scholarships to individuals and grant awards to facilitate and encourage the study and maintenance of their Christian faith.
Fields of interest: Education; Christian agencies & churches.
Type of support: General/operating support; Scholarships—to individuals.
Limitations: Giving in the U.S., with emphasis on FL, MI, and NC.
Application information: Application form required.
Deadline(s): None
Officers: James E. Mulvoy, Esq., Pres.; Maree R. Mulvoy, V.P.; William C. Hanson, Secy.
EIN: 383330588
Selected grants: The following grants were reported in 2008.

$56,268 to University of Miami, Miami, FL.
$32,630 to Bullis School, Potomac, MD.
$18,839 to Grand Valley State University, Allendale, MI.
$18,404 to Towson University, Towson, MD.
$18,000 to University of New Hampshire, Durham, NH.
$16,270 to Hillsdale College, Hillsdale, MI.
$6,625 to Western Michigan University, Kalamazoo, MI.
$5,000 to Grove City College, Grove City, PA.
$4,622 to Aquinas College, Jeffrey Wierzbicki, Grand Rapids, MI.
$3,657 to Towson University, Towson, MD.

495

Leighton-Oare Foundation, Inc.
1999 Morris Ave.
Niles, MI   49120-8620
County: Berrien
Contact: Nancy O. Butler, Pres.

Incorporated in 1955 in IN.
Donors: Mary Morris Leighton; Judd C. Leighton.
Grantmaker type: Independent foundation.
Financial data (yr. ended 12/31/09): Assets, $19,705,878 (M); expenditures, $1,295,823; total giving, $1,114,400; qualifying distributions, $1,114,400; giving activities include $1,114,400 for 73 grants (high: $420,000; low: $100).
Fields of interest: Performing arts; Historic preservation/historical societies; Arts; Higher education; Law school/education; Health care, fund raising/fund distribution; Health care, clinics/centers; Goodwill Industries; Athletics/sports; equestrianism.
Type of support: Matching/challenge support; Annual campaigns; General/operating support; Continuing support; Building/renovation; Endowments.
Limitations: Applications accepted. Giving primarily in IN and MI; selected interest in FL and VA. No grants to individuals.
Application information: Application form not required.
Initial approach: Letter
Copies of proposal: 1
Deadline(s): None
Board meeting date(s): Feb., May, Aug., and Nov.
Final notification: 90 to 120 days
Officers and Directors:* Nancy O. Butler,* Pres.; Ernest M. Oare,* V.P.; Carol F. Oare,* Secy.; Kevin J. Butler,* Treas.; Joseph E. Kernan.
EIN: 356034243
Selected grants: The following grants were reported in 2007.
$600,000 to University of Notre Dame, Notre Dame, IN.
$100,000 to Goodwill Industries of Michiana, South Bend, IN.
$69,000 to YMCA of Michiana, South Bend, IN.
$65,000 to Logan Community Resources, South Bend, IN.
$40,000 to Logan Community Resources, South Bend, IN.
$15,000 to Metropolitan Ministries, Tampa, FL.
$10,000 to Educational Foundation, Chapel Hill, NC.
$10,000 to Stanley Clark School, South Bend, IN.
$10,000 to YMCA of Niles Michigan, Niles, MI.
$5,000 to Lake Michigan College Foundation, Benton Harbor, MI.

496

Wayne E. Lemmen, Helene Lemmen & B. J. Lemmen Foundation
(formerly The Bernie J. Lemmen Foundation)
633 Center St.
Coopersville, MI   49404-1041
County: Ottawa
Contact: Wayne E. Lemmen, Treas.

Established in MI.
Grantmaker type: Independent foundation.
Financial data (yr. ended 03/31/10): Assets, $492,185 (M); expenditures, $26,107; total giving, $25,000; qualifying distributions, $25,020; giving activities include $25,000 for 3 grants (high: $18,000; low: $2,000).
Purpose and activities: Giving primarily to Christian schools and churches.
Fields of interest: Elementary/secondary education; Christian agencies & churches.
Limitations: Applications accepted. Giving limited to MI, primarily in Coopersville and Allendale. No grants to individuals.
Application information: Application form not required.
Initial approach: Letter
Deadline(s): None
Officers: Helene Lemmen, Pres.; Wayne E. Lemmen, Treas.
EIN: 386069061

497

Dorothy Below Lesher Scholarship Trust
c/o Central District Dental Hygienists
1121 N. Waverly Rd.
Lansing, MI   48917-2270   (517) 614-2035
County: Eaton

Established in MI.
Grantmaker type: Independent foundation.
Financial data (yr. ended 12/31/09): Assets, $24,537 (M); gifts received, $1,774; expenditures, $2,187; total giving, $1,500; qualifying distributions, $1,500; giving activities include $1,500 for grants to individuals.
Purpose and activities: Scholarship awards to students enrolled in the Dental Hygiene Program at Lansing Community College, Michigan.
Fields of interest: Dental school/education.
Type of support: Scholarships—to individuals.
Limitations: Applications accepted. Giving limited to residents of Lansing, MI.
Application information: Application form required.
Initial approach: Letter or telephone
Deadline(s): Dec. 1
Officers: Mary Ellen Sickles, Pres.; Pam Manning, Treas.
Board Members: Paula Bates; Eve Easter; Chris Farrell; Sue Garbarini; Rosalyn Routson; Renie Russo; Judy Sibal.
EIN: 020664210

498

The Myron P. Leven Foundation
25899 W. 12 Mile Rd., Ste. 350
Southfield, MI   48034-8315
County: Oakland

Established in 1998 in MI.
Donor: Myron P. Leven†.
Grantmaker type: Independent foundation.

Financial data (yr. ended 12/31/09): Assets, $3,739,699 (M); gifts received, $205,000; expenditures, $366,379; total giving, $132,550; qualifying distributions, $232,940; giving activities include $132,550 for 13+ grants (high: $31,450).
Fields of interest: Performing arts; Arts; Higher education; Minorities/immigrants, centers/services; Economic development; Jewish federated giving programs.
Type of support: Program development; Scholarship funds.
Limitations: Giving primarily in MI, with some emphasis on Detroit. No grants to individuals.
Officers: Aram Vosgerchian, Pres.; Arnold P. Garber, Secy.
EIN: 383443921
Selected grants: The following grants were reported in 2008.
$29,000 to Detroit Symphony Orchestra, Detroit, MI.
$20,500 to University of Michigan, Ann Arbor and Dearborn, Ann Arbor, MI.
$18,000 to University of Detroit Mercy, Detroit, MI.
$10,000 to Michigan State University, East Lansing, MI.
$10,000 to Wayne State University, Detroit, MI.
$6,000 to Oakland University, Rochester, MI.
$2,000 to Detroit Historical Society, Detroit, MI.

499
The William R. and Susan K. Lewis Charitable Foundation

1144 Idema Dr. S.E.
Grand Rapids, MI 49506-3167
County: Kent

Established in 2006.
Grantmaker type: Independent foundation.
Financial data (yr. ended 12/31/09): Assets, $205,127 (M); gifts received, $50,000; expenditures, $90,843; total giving, $90,221; qualifying distributions, $90,221; giving activities include $90,221 for grants.
Trustees: Susan K. Lewis; William R. Lewis.
EIN: 204821581

500
Pam Lewis Foundation

c/o S. Gary Spicer
16845 Kercheval St., Ste. 5
Grosse Pointe, MI 48230-1551
County: Wayne

Established in 1997 in MI.
Donor: Pam Lewis.
Grantmaker type: Independent foundation.
Financial data (yr. ended 12/31/09): Assets, $37,914 (M); expenditures, $45,664; total giving, $38,280; qualifying distributions, $38,280; giving activities include $38,280 for 52 grants (high: $3,750; low: $50).
Purpose and activities: Giving primarily for the arts, health and human services, the environment, and animal welfare.
Fields of interest: Arts; Education; Environment; Animals/wildlife; Human services; Children/youth, services.
Type of support: General/operating support.
Limitations: Applications accepted. Giving primarily in Nashville, TN. No grants to individuals.

Application information: Contact foundation for application guidelines.
Deadline(s): None
Officers and Trustees:* Pam Lewis,* Pres.; S. Gary Spicer, Sr., Secy.; John Lewis,* Treas.
EIN: 383278908

501
Lileikis Family Foundation

3417 Roger B. Chaffee Memorial Dr. S.E.
Wyoming, MI 49548-2323 (616) 243-2661
County: Kent
Contact: Frank Lileikis, Pres.

Grantmaker type: Independent foundation.
Financial data (yr. ended 12/31/09): Assets, $127,152 (M); expenditures, $7,779; total giving, $7,250; qualifying distributions, $7,250; giving activities include $7,250 for grants.
Fields of interest: Health care; Human services.
Limitations: Giving primarily in Grand Rapids, MI. No grants to individuals.
Application information: Application form not required.
Deadline(s): None
Officers: Frank Lileikis, Pres. and Treas.; Thomas Lileikis, V.P. and Secy.
Directors: Christine Erskine; Katherine Lileikis.
EIN: 383390415

502
August Lilja Family Memorial Fund

c/o Northern Michigan Bank & Trust Co.
1502 W. Washington St.
Marquette, MI 49855-3118
County: Marquette
Application address: c/o Judge Thomas Slagle, Probate/Juvenile Court Div., P.O. Box 609, Iron Mountain, MI 49801, tel.: (906) 774-1555

Grantmaker type: Independent foundation.
Financial data (yr. ended 12/31/09): Assets, $499,888 (M); expenditures, $54,208; total giving, $42,863; qualifying distributions, $42,863; giving activities include $42,863 for grants.
Fields of interest: Environment, beautification programs; Recreation, parks/playgrounds.
Limitations: Giving primarily in Iron Mountain, MI. No grants to individuals.
Application information:
Initial approach: Letter
Deadline(s): None
Trustee: Northern Michigan Bank & Trust Co.
EIN: 386648816

503
J. Stewart Linden Foundation

33776 Old Timber Rd.
Farmington Hills, MI 48331-1526
County: Oakland
Contact: Sanford J. Linden, Secy.-Treas.

Established in MI.
Donor: J. Stewart Linden†.
Grantmaker type: Independent foundation.
Financial data (yr. ended 12/31/09): Assets, $248,203 (M); expenditures, $14,545; total giving, $14,125; qualifying distributions, $14,125; giving activities include $14,125 for grants.

Fields of interest: Higher education; Human services; Jewish agencies & synagogues.
Type of support: Research; Building/renovation; General/operating support.
Limitations: Giving primarily in MI. No grants to individuals.
Application information:
Initial approach: Letter
Deadline(s): None
Officers and Trustees:* Hanna Linden,* Pres.; Allan J. Linden,* V.P.; Sanford J. Linden,* Secy.-Treas.
EIN: 386109122

504
William Tedrow Little Foundation

107 W. Michigan Ave., Penthouse
Kalamazoo, MI 49007-3970 (269) 344-6143
County: Kalamazoo
Contact: William Tedrow Little, Pres. and Treas.

Established in 1998 in MI.
Donor: William Tedrow Little.
Grantmaker type: Independent foundation.
Financial data (yr. ended 12/31/08): Assets, $115,852 (M); gifts received, $92,095; expenditures, $999; total giving, $0; qualifying distributions, $499.
Fields of interest: Cancer; Muscular dystrophy; Big Brothers/Big Sisters; Residential/custodial care, hospices.
Type of support: General/operating support.
Application information: Application form required.
Initial approach: Proposal
Deadline(s): None
Officers and Trustees:* William Tedrow Little,* Pres. and Treas; Virginia S. Little,* V.P.; Frances A. Little,* Secy.; James M. Elsworth.
EIN: 383443723

505
The Earle and Elsie Little Scholarship Trust

c/o Monroe Bank & Trust
102 E. Front St.
Monroe, MI 48161-2162
County: Monroe

Established in 1998 in MI.
Donor: Elsie Little.
Grantmaker type: Independent foundation.
Financial data (yr. ended 12/31/09): Assets, $338,992 (M); expenditures, $6,610; total giving, $3,400; qualifying distributions, $3,400; giving activities include $3,400 for grants to individuals.
Purpose and activities: Scholarship awards to U.S. citizens for undergraduate studies in an accredited Michigan college or university.
Fields of interest: Higher education.
Type of support: Scholarships—to individuals.
Limitations: Giving limited to U.S. citizens, with preference to residents of MI.
Application information: Request application guidelines. Application form required.
Deadline(s): Varies
Trustee: Monroe Bank & Trust.
EIN: 386729055

506

Stella & Frederick Loeb Charitable Trust

c/o Citizens Bank
328 S. Saginaw St., MC 001061
Flint, MI 48502-1926 (810) 766-7826
County: Genesee
Contact: Dawn Bentley, Trust Off.

Established in 1990 in MI.
Donor: Frederick Loeb‡.
Grantmaker type: Independent foundation.
Financial data (yr. ended 08/31/10): Assets,
$4,657,191 (M); gifts received, $6,719;
expenditures, $350,401; total giving, $289,340;
qualifying distributions, $340,697; giving activities
include $289,340 for 46 grants (high: $20,000;
low: $1,000).
Fields of interest: Performing arts; Arts; Education;
Youth development; Human services; Children/
youth, services; United Ways and Federated Giving
Programs.
Limitations: Applications accepted. Giving primarily
in Flint, MI.
Publications: Application guidelines.
Application information: Application form required.
Initial approach: Letter
Deadline(s): None
Trustee: Citizens Bank.
EIN: 386571896
Selected grants: The following grants were reported
in 2009.
$10,000 to Hurley Foundation, Flint, MI.
$7,500 to Genesee County Free Medical Clinic,
Flint, MI.
$7,500 to Priority Children, Flint, MI.
$7,500 to Priority Children, Flint, MI.
$5,000 to American Red Cross, Flint, MI.
$5,000 to Flint Cultural Center Corporation, Flint,
MI.
$5,000 to Flint Institute of Arts, Flint, MI.
$5,000 to Girl Scouts of the U.S.A., Flint, MI.
$5,000 to University of Michigan, Flint, MI.
$3,000 to Genesee Intermediate School District,
Flint, MI.

507

The Loutit Foundation

c/o Bank of America, N.A.
231 S. LaSalle St., IL1-231-14-19
Chicago, IL 60604-1426
County: Cook
Application address: c/o Jon Eshleman, One S.
Harbor Dr., Grand Haven, MI 49417

Incorporated in 1957 in MI.
Donors: William R. Loutit‡; William Loutit Memorial
Trust.
Grantmaker type: Independent foundation.
Financial data (yr. ended 06/30/09): Assets,
$691,327 (M); gifts received, $186,424;
expenditures, $271,114; total giving, $252,650;
qualifying distributions, $260,601; giving activities
include $252,650 for 36 grants (high: $100,000;
low: $100).
Fields of interest: Arts; Higher education; Libraries
(public); Human services; Community/economic
development; United Ways and Federated Giving
Programs; Christian agencies & churches.
Limitations: Applications accepted. Giving limited to
western MI, with emphasis on Ottawa and Kent
County. No grants to individuals or for research; no
loans.
Publications: Biennial report.

Application information: Application form not
required.
Initial approach: Letter
Deadline(s): None
Officers and Trustees:* Jon W. Eshleman,* Pres.;
Thomas M. Boven,* V.P.; Diane Wynsma Hyland,
Secy.-Treas.; Kennard Creason; Bari Johnson; Bank
of America, N.A.
EIN: 386053445
Selected grants: The following grants were reported
in 2009.
$100,000 to Loutit District Library, Grand Haven,
MI.
$25,000 to Michigan Colleges Foundation,
Southfield, MI.
$12,500 to Grand Valley State University, Allendale,
MI.
$10,300 to Habitat for Humanity, Tri-Cities Area,
Grand Haven, MI.
$10,000 to Opera Grand Rapids, Grand Rapids, MI.
$10,000 to Van Buren United Civic Organization,
Covert, MI.
$5,000 to Albion College, Albion, MI.
$5,000 to Alma College, Alma, MI.
$5,000 to Hillsdale College, Hillsdale, MI.
$1,000 to Grand Rapids Symphony, Grand Rapids,
MI.

508

Lovelight Foundation

2531 Jackson Rd., Ste. 168
Ann Arbor, MI 48103-3818
County: Washtenaw
Contact: Julie F. Cummings, Pres.
E-mail: ptalburtt@lovelightfoundation.org;
URL: http://www.lovelightfoundation.org/

Incorporated in 1992 in MI.
Grantmaker type: Independent foundation.
Financial data (yr. ended 12/31/09): Assets,
$963,435 (M); expenditures, $71,330; total giving,
$51,000; qualifying distributions, $51,000; giving
activities include $51,000 for grants.
Purpose and activities: The foundation provides
grants to other charitable organizations within the
metropolitan Detroit area that provide support to
impoverished women and children through programs
focusing on health, nutrition, and education.
Fields of interest: Children/youth, services;
Women, centers/services; Economically
disadvantaged.
Limitations: Giving primarily in the metropolitan
Detroit, MI area. No grants to individuals.
Officers and Director:* Julie F. Cummings,* Pres.;
Caroline Cummings, Secy.; Dina Cummings,*
Treas.; Peg Talburtt, C.E.O.; Peter D. Cummings.
Number of staff: 1 full-time professional.
EIN: 383092224

509

Lubin, Schwartz & Goldman Foundation

2369 Franklin Rd.
Bloomfield Hills, MI 48302-0333
(248) 332-3100
County: Oakland

Established in 1996 in MI.
Donors: Sheldon Goldman; Joel Lubin; Robert
Schwartz; Jay Schreibman; Mark Fisher.
Grantmaker type: Independent foundation.

Financial data (yr. ended 03/31/10): Assets,
$5,422 (M); gifts received, $129,075;
expenditures, $128,935; total giving, $128,802;
qualifying distributions, $128,802; giving activities
include $128,802 for grants.
Purpose and activities: Giving primarily for hospitals
and Jewish federated giving programs.
Fields of interest: Hospitals (general); Disasters,
Hurricane Katrina; Human services; American Red
Cross; Jewish federated giving programs; Jewish
agencies & synagogues.
Limitations: Giving primarily in MI. No grants to
individuals.
Application information: Application form not
required.
Deadline(s): None
Directors: David Colburn; Robert Colburn; Mark
Fisher; Sheldon Goldman; Jay Schreibman; Robert
Schwartz.
EIN: 382777749
Selected grants: The following grants were reported
in 2009.
$5,555 to Congregation Shaarey Zedek, Southfield,
MI.
$3,311 to Temple Israel, West Bloomfield, MI.
$2,500 to Capuchin Soup Kitchen, Detroit, MI.
$1,775 to Leukemia & Lymphoma Society, Madison
Heights, MI.
$1,500 to American Jewish Committee, Bloomfield
Hills, MI.
$1,386 to ORT America, Bloomfield Hills, MI.
$1,250 to Alzheimers Association, Southfield, MI.
$1,000 to University of Michigan, Cancer Center,
Ann Arbor, MI.

510

The Thomas L. Ludington Foundation

c/o Deloitte & Touche, LLP
3320 Ridgecrest Dr.
Midland, MI 48642-5859 (989) 631-2370
County: Midland
Contact: Thomas L. Ludington, Pres.

Established in 1996 in MI.
Donor: John S. Ludington.
Grantmaker type: Independent foundation.
Financial data (yr. ended 12/31/09): Assets,
$586,721 (M); gifts received, $48,929;
expenditures, $28,545; total giving, $24,350;
qualifying distributions, $26,148; giving activities
include $24,350 for 40 grants (high: $4,100; low:
$100).
Fields of interest: Education; Human services;
Christian agencies & churches.
Limitations: Applications accepted. Giving primarily
in MI. No grants to individuals.
Application information:
Initial approach: Letter
Deadline(s): None
Officers: Thomas L. Ludington, Pres.; Katrina K.
Ludington, V.P.; John S. Ludington, Treas.
EIN: 383323700

511

Lugers Family Foundation

288 McVea Rd.
Douglas, MI 49406
County: Allegan
Contact: Janet Lugers, Dir.
Application address: P.O. Box 820, Douglas, MI
49406-0820, tel.: (269) 857-4042

Established in 1999 in MI.
Grantmaker type: Independent foundation.
Financial data (yr. ended 12/31/09): Assets, $460,486 (M); expenditures, $29,232; total giving, $24,465; qualifying distributions, $24,465; giving activities include $24,465 for grants.
Fields of interest: Education; Environment; Animal welfare; Human services; Children/youth, services; Residential/custodial care, hospices; Community/economic development.
Type of support: General/operating support.
Limitations: Applications accepted. Giving limited to Holland, MI, and its surrounding areas. No grants to individuals.
Application information:
   Initial approach: Letter or telephone
   Deadline(s): None
Directors: Marilyn Hoffer; Janet Lugers; Beth Post.
EIN: 383369937

512
Lukens Family Foundation
c/o Brad Solomon, C.P.A.
2035 28th St. S.E., Ste. U
Grand Rapids, MI 49508-1535 (616) 855-4384
County: Kent
Application address: c/o Brad Solomon, C.P.A., 2524 Woodmeadow Dr. S.E., Ste. A, Grand Rapids, MI 49546-8051, tel.: (616) 855-4384

Established in 1997 in MI.
Donors: Jack G. Lukens; Katherine Lukens.
Grantmaker type: Independent foundation.
Financial data (yr. ended 12/31/09): Assets, $973,240 (M); gifts received, $444,012; expenditures, $36,927; total giving, $30,100; qualifying distributions, $30,100; giving activities include $30,100 for grants.
Fields of interest: Human services; United Ways and Federated Giving Programs.
Type of support: General/operating support.
Limitations: Giving primarily in Grand Rapids, MI. No grants to individuals.
Application information:
   Initial approach: Letter
   Deadline(s): None
Officers: Jack G. Lukens, Pres.; Janet L. Dietsch, Secy.
EIN: 593486468

513
Luneack Family Foundation
308 Gratiot Ave.
Alma, MI 48801-1809
County: Gratiot
Contact: Doug Hoard

Established in 2005 in MI.
Donor: Ken Luneack.
Grantmaker type: Independent foundation.
Financial data (yr. ended 12/31/09): Assets, $106,692 (M); expenditures, $3,660; total giving, $0; qualifying distributions, $6,880.
Application information:
   Initial approach: by letter
   Deadline(s): none
Officers: Ken Luneack, Pres.; Paul Luneack, V.P.; Charles Fortino, Secy.; Doug Hoard, Treas.
Director: Richard Prestage.
EIN: 202784486

514
Ray J. & Leila M. Lynch Charitable Trust
15 Windemere Pl.
Grosse Pointe Farms, MI 48236-9080
County: Wayne

Established in 1985 in MI.
Donors: Ray J. Lynch; Leila M. Lynch.
Grantmaker type: Independent foundation.
Financial data (yr. ended 12/31/09): Assets, $331,497 (M); expenditures, $32,493; total giving, $29,855; qualifying distributions, $29,855; giving activities include $29,855 for grants.
Fields of interest: Human services; Children/youth, services; Catholic agencies & churches.
Limitations: Giving primarily in the Detroit and southeastern MI, area. No grants to individuals.
Application information:
   Initial approach: Proposal
   Deadline(s): Dec. 31
Trustees: Leila M. Lynch; Ray J. Lynch; Tim J. Lynch; Richard E. Rassel.
EIN: 382637861

515
Lyon Foundation, Inc.
1592 Redding Rd.
Birmingham, MI 48009-1029
County: Oakland
Contact: Albert Randolph Judd, Pres.

Incorporated in 1951 in MI.
Donor: G. Albert Lyon, Sr.
Grantmaker type: Independent foundation.
Financial data (yr. ended 12/31/08): Assets, $2,189,922 (M); expenditures, $173,311; total giving, $145,100; qualifying distributions, $155,405; giving activities include $145,100 for 36 grants (high: $25,000; low: $500).
Purpose and activities: Support primarily for the Community Foundation for Southeast Michigan.
Fields of interest: Media/communications; Education; Environment; Human services; Foundations (community).
Limitations: Applications accepted. Giving limited to southeastern MI. No grants to individuals.
Application information:
   Deadline(s): None
Officers: Albert Randolph Judd, Pres. and Secy.; Winn Lyon Moore, V.P.; John Terrill Judd, Treas.
Number of staff: 1 full-time support.
EIN: 386121075
Selected grants: The following grants were reported in 2006.
$25,000 to Tilton School, Tilton, NH.
$20,000 to Presbyterian Hemby Childrens Hospital, Charlotte, NC.
$10,000 to Oakland University, Rochester, MI.
$8,000 to Make-A-Wish Foundation of South Carolina, Greenville, SC.
$6,000 to Generation of Promise Program, Detroit, MI.
$5,000 to Chatham Hall, Chatham, VA.
$5,000 to Hospice of Michigan, Detroit, MI.
$5,000 to Pats Place Child Advocacy Center, Charlotte, NC.
$3,000 to Wayne State University, Detroit, MI.
$2,000 to Franklin-Wright Settlements, Detroit, MI.

516
Bob and Jan Lyons Foundation
3549 W. Pineview Dr.
Dexter, MI 48130-9710
County: Washtenaw
Contact: Mike Cicchella

Established in 1999 in MI.
Grantmaker type: Independent foundation.
Financial data (yr. ended 12/31/09): Assets, $1,144,304 (M); expenditures, $77,280; total giving, $58,000; qualifying distributions, $58,000; giving activities include $58,000 for grants.
Fields of interest: Museums; Historic preservation/historical societies; Higher education; Hospitals (general); Health care; Human services; Protestant agencies & churches.
Type of support: General/operating support; Income development; Capital campaigns; Building/renovation; Program development.
Limitations: Applications accepted. Giving primarily in MI, with some emphasis on Ann Arbor and Dexter. No grants to individuals.
Application information:
   Initial approach: Letter
   Deadline(s): Nov. 1
Officers: Jan Lyons, Pres.; Robert C. Lyons, Secy.-Treas.
Directors: Suezahn Lyons Simmons; Ronald Tupper.
EIN: 383423247

517
Edward E. MacCrone Trust
c/o Comerica Bank
P.O. Box 75000, MC 3302
Detroit, MI 48275-3302 (313) 222-3304
County: Wayne
Application address: c/o Comerica Bank, N.A., Attn.: Scott Drogs, 101 N. Main St., Ste. 100, Ann Arbor, MI 48104-5515, tel.: (734) 930-2416

Established in 1959 in MI.
Donor: Edward E. MacCrone†.
Grantmaker type: Independent foundation.
Financial data (yr. ended 12/31/09): Assets, $1,518,342 (M); expenditures, $99,449; total giving, $80,000; qualifying distributions, $81,945; giving activities include $80,000 for 9 grants (high: $16,000; low: $8,000).
Fields of interest: Museums (art); Performing arts, orchestras; Higher education; Libraries (public); Hospitals (specialty); Mental health, residential care; Boy scouts; Children/youth.
Limitations: Applications accepted. Giving primarily in MI and WI; giving also in Washington, DC, MA, and NJ. No grants to individuals.
Application information:
   Initial approach: Letter
   Deadline(s): None
Trustee: Comerica Bank.
EIN: 386043730

518
George R. and Doris Engblom MacDonald Scholarship Trust
c/o Northern Michigan Bank & Trust Co.
1502 W. Washington St.
Marquette, MI 49855-3195
County: Marquette
Application address: c/o The Scholarship Selection Committee, 300 W. B. St., Iron Mountain, MI 49801-3300

Established in 1987 in MI.
Grantmaker type: Independent foundation.
Financial data (yr. ended 09/30/09): Assets, $15,170 (M); expenditures, $1,352; total giving, $500; qualifying distributions, $500; giving activities include $500 for grants to individuals.
Purpose and activities: Scholarship awards to graduates of Iron Mountain High School to pursue an education in the field of social studies and to graduates of Norway-Vulcan High School for higher education.
Fields of interest: Higher education.
Type of support: Scholarships—to individuals.
Limitations: Giving limited to Iron Mountain and Norway, MI.
Application information: Application should include ACT score, high school transcript and one letter of recommendation. Application form required.
Deadline(s): Apr. 24
Trustee: Northern Michigan Bank & Trust Co.
EIN: 386462968

519
Anna M. MacRae Scholarship Trust
c/o National City Bank
171 Monroe Ave., N.W.
Grand Rapids, MI 49503-2634
County: Kent

Established in 2000 in MI.
Grantmaker type: Independent foundation.
Financial data (yr. ended 12/31/09): Assets, $181,324 (M); expenditures, $11,485; total giving, $8,000; qualifying distributions, $8,945; giving activities include $8,000 for 11 grants to individuals (high: $1,000; low: $500).
Purpose and activities: Scholarship awards to graduates of Cass City High School or from the surrounding area within 20 miles of Cass City, Michigan, for the nursing profession or a related medical field.
Fields of interest: Nursing school/education.
Type of support: Scholarships—to individuals.
Limitations: Applications accepted. Giving limited to Cass City, MI, area.
Application information: Application form required.
Deadline(s): Apr. 15
Trustee: National City Bank.
EIN: 386706105

520
Mahogany Foundation
3757 Woodside Dr.
Traverse City, MI 49684-7170 (231) 932-7142
County: Grand Traverse
Contact: Meridith I. Falconer, V.P.

Established in 2003 in MI.
Donors: Daniel P. Falconer; Erik J. Falconer.
Grantmaker type: Independent foundation.

Financial data (yr. ended 12/31/09): Assets, $1,446,618 (M); expenditures, $84,389; total giving, $74,780; qualifying distributions, $74,780; giving activities include $74,780 for grants.
Purpose and activities: Giving primarily for environmental conservation and preservation.
Fields of interest: Media, film/video; Environment, natural resources.
Limitations: Giving primarily in MI, with emphasis on Traverse City. No grants to individuals, for annual campaigns or endowments.
Application information:
Initial approach: Proposal
Deadline(s): June 1 and Nov. 1
Officers and Trustees: * Daniel P. Falconer,* Pres. and Treas.; Meridith I. Falconer,* V.P. and Secy.
EIN: 200126179
Selected grants: The following grants were reported in 2004.
$25,000 to Natural Resources Defense Council, New York, NY.

521
The Mall Family Foundation
P.O. Box 667
Greenville, MI 48838-0667 (616) 754-5024
County: Montcalm
Contact: Thomas H. Mall, Pres.

Established in 2006 in MI.
Donors: Thomas H. Mall; Catherine S. Mall.
Grantmaker type: Independent foundation.
Financial data (yr. ended 12/31/09): Assets, $464,469 (M); gifts received, $50,000; expenditures, $27,380; total giving, $20,000; qualifying distributions, $20,000; giving activities include $20,000 for grants.
Fields of interest: Higher education; Autism; Christian agencies & churches.
Type of support: Scholarship funds.
Limitations: Giving in MI. No grants to individuals.
Officers: Thomas H. Mall, Pres. and Treas.; Catherine S. Mall, V.P. and Secy.
EIN: 208058288

522
Chester F. and Laura L. Mally Foundation
97 N. Cass Ave.
Pontiac, MI 48342-2003
County: Oakland
Contact: C. Lane Mally, Pres.

Established in 1986 in MI.
Grantmaker type: Independent foundation.
Financial data (yr. ended 08/31/09): Assets, $294,308 (M); expenditures, $15,898; total giving, $15,048; qualifying distributions, $15,048; giving activities include $15,048 for grants.
Fields of interest: Human services.
Limitations: Giving limited to MI, with emphasis on Pontiac.
Application information:
Initial approach: Letter
Deadline(s): None
Officer: C. Lane Mally, Pres.
Trustees: Steven Jones; Mark A. Kaminski.
EIN: 382709513

523
C. Malovey Educational Scholarship Fund
c/o Century Bank and Trust
100 W. Chicago St.
Coldwater, MI 49036-1899 (517) 279-7311
County: Branch
Contact: Dylan Foster, Trust Off.

Established in 2009 in MI.
Donor: Clement Malovey†.
Grantmaker type: Independent foundation.
Financial data (yr. ended 12/31/09): Assets, $1,807,489 (M); gifts received, $1,867,444; expenditures, $4,390; total giving, $0; qualifying distributions, $1,399.
Purpose and activities: Scholarship awards to high school graduates of Branch County, Michigan.
Fields of interest: Higher education.
Type of support: Scholarships—to individuals.
Limitations: Applications accepted. Giving primarily to residents of Branch County, MI.
Application information: Application form required.
Initial approach: Proposal
Deadline(s): Apr. 1
Trustee: Century Bank and Trust.
EIN: 383804156

524
Oliver Dewey Marcks Foundation
645 Griswold St., Ste. 3180
Detroit, MI 48226-4250
County: Wayne
Contact: John M. Chase, Jr., Pres.

Established in 1960.
Donors: Eula D. Marcks†; Oliver Dewey Marcks†.
Grantmaker type: Independent foundation.
Financial data (yr. ended 12/31/09): Assets, $12,694,508 (M); expenditures, $767,238; total giving, $622,500; qualifying distributions, $660,101; giving activities include $622,500 for 41 grants (high: $70,000; low: $5,000).
Fields of interest: Arts; Education; Environment, natural resources; Animal welfare; Human services.
Type of support: General/operating support; Program development.
Limitations: Giving limited to Detroit, MI, and surrounding communities. No grants to individuals.
Publications: Application guidelines.
Application information: Application form required.
Initial approach: Letter, including a 1-page summary
Copies of proposal: 4
Board meeting date(s): May, July and Oct.
Officers and Board Members: * John M. Chase, Jr.,* Pres.; Marion Valentine,* Secy.; Michael J. Predhomme,* Treas.
EIN: 386081311
Selected grants: The following grants were reported in 2009.
$37,500 to Old Newsboys Goodfellow Fund of Detroit, Detroit, MI.
$25,000 to Michigan Opera Theater, Detroit, MI.
$25,000 to Parade Company, Detroit, MI.
$20,000 to Capuchin Soup Kitchen, Detroit, MI.
$20,000 to Detroit Central City Community Mental Health, Detroit, MI.
$20,000 to Detroit Symphony Orchestra, Detroit, MI.
$20,000 to Wayne State University, Detroit, MI.
$15,000 to Focus: HOPE, Detroit, MI.
$15,000 to University of Michigan, Ann Arbor, MI.

$10,000 to Barbara Ann Karmanos Cancer Institute, Detroit, MI.

525
Edward & Helen Mardigian Foundation
c/o Comerica Bank
P.O. Box 75000, MC 3318
Detroit, MI 48275-3318
County: Wayne
Application address: c/o Edward Mardigian, Jr., 39400 Woodward Ave., Ste. 225, Bloomfield Hills, MI 48304, tel.: (248) 647-0077

Incorporated in 1955 in MI.
Donors: Edward S. Mardigian†; Helen Mardigian; Arman Mardigian†.
Grantmaker type: Independent foundation.
Financial data (yr. ended 12/31/09): Assets, $20,213,777 (M); gifts received, $250,000; expenditures, $907,662; total giving, $859,860; qualifying distributions, $909,239; giving activities include $859,860 for 43 grants (high: $200,000; low: $250).
Purpose and activities: Giving primarily for Armenian organizations and churches in the U.S.; funding also for children, youth and social services, and health associations.
Fields of interest: Arts; Higher education; Zoos/zoological societies; Health organizations, association; Human services; Children/youth, services; Christian agencies & churches.
Limitations: Applications accepted. Giving primarily in MI; some funding nationally. No grants to individuals.
Application information: Application form not required.
Initial approach: Letter
Deadline(s): None
Officers: Helen Mardigian, Pres. and Secy.; Edward S. Mardigian, V.P. and Treas.
Director: Robert D. Mardigian.
EIN: 386048886
Selected grants: The following grants were reported in 2007.
$200,000 to Fund for Armenian Relief, New York, NY.
$165,000 to Beaumont Foundation, Southfield, MI.
$150,000 to University of Michigan, Ann Arbor, MI.
$130,000 to Diocese of the Armenian Church of America, New York, NY.
$100,000 to Detroit Symphony Orchestra, Detroit, MI.
$63,000 to Armenian Apostolic Society, Southfield, MI.
$50,000 to Detroit Zoological Society, Royal Oak, MI.
$26,940 to Saint Johns Armenian Church, Southfield, MI.
$5,000 to Childrens Hospital of Michigan, Detroit, MI.
$4,000 to Project Discovery, Salem, VA.

526
Marshall Rotary Foundation, Inc.
311 E. Mansion St.
Marshall, MI 49068
County: Calhoun

Grantmaker type: Independent foundation.
Financial data (yr. ended 06/30/10): Assets, $448,949 (M); gifts received, $24,196;

expenditures, $15,543; total giving, $14,900; qualifying distributions, $14,900; giving activities include $14,900 for grants.
Fields of interest: Arts; Elementary/secondary education; Libraries (public); Health care, clinics/centers; Youth development; Human services; Community/economic development; Christian agencies & churches.
Type of support: General/operating support; Building/renovation; Equipment; Program development.
Limitations: Applications accepted. Giving limited to Marshall, MI.
Application information: Application form required.
Deadline(s): None
Officer: Doug Jackson, Treas.
EIN: 382463694

527
The W.E. Martin Foundation
207 N. Franklin
Mount Pleasant, MI 48858 (989) 773-4931
County: Isabella
Contact: William L. Martin, Pres.

Established in 2007 in MI.
Donors: William L. Martin; Eleanor Martin; Alice L. Martin Trust; 205 SHS, PepsiCo; 1,155 SHS, PepsiCo; 700 SHS, Takeda Pharmaceuticals Co.
Grantmaker type: Independent foundation.
Financial data (yr. ended 12/31/09): Assets, $2,412,301 (M); gifts received, $2,050,041; expenditures, $11,159; total giving, $3,850; qualifying distributions, $3,850; giving activities include $3,850 for grants.
Application information: Application form not required.
Initial approach: Proposal
Deadline(s): None
Officers: William L. Martin, Pres.; John Martin, V.P.; Michael Martin, V.P.; Eleanor Martin, Secy.-Treas.
EIN: 261192966

528
Ludgardis S. Marxer College Educational Trust
c/o Comerica Bank
P.O. Box 75000, MC 3302
Detroit, MI 48275-3302
County: Wayne
Application address: c/o Brenda Pearson, 60 S. 6th St., Minneapolis, MN 55402-4400, tel.: (612) 215-3603

Established in 2005 in MN.
Donor: Marxer Ludgardis S. Trust.
Grantmaker type: Independent foundation.
Financial data (yr. ended 12/31/08): Assets, $405,731 (M); expenditures, $39,819; total giving, $28,500; qualifying distributions, $28,500; giving activities include $28,500 for grants.
Fields of interest: Higher education, university.
Type of support: Scholarship funds.
Limitations: Giving primarily in IL, MO, and WI.
Application information: Application form not required.
Deadline(s): None
Trustees: John E. Marxer; Comerica Bank.
EIN: 597243596

529
The Marzke Family Foundation
1207 Broad St.
St. Joseph, MI 49085-1258 (269) 983-7314
County: Berrien
Contact: L. Richard Marzke, Pres.

Established in 2001 in MI.
Donors: Nancy Ann Marzke; L. Richard Marzke; Christopher J. Marzke; Craig S. Marzke; Kurt R. Marzke; Kevin W. Marzke; Lynn Ann Marzke-Schmidt.
Grantmaker type: Independent foundation.
Financial data (yr. ended 12/31/09): Assets, $584,712 (M); gifts received, $296,010; expenditures, $35,449; total giving, $34,150; qualifying distributions, $34,150; giving activities include $34,150 for grants.
Purpose and activities: Giving primarily for Catholic schools and other organizations.
Fields of interest: Education; Health care; Human services; Catholic agencies & churches.
Type of support: General/operating support; Fellowships; Scholarship funds.
Limitations: Applications accepted. Giving primarily in the greater St. Joseph/Benton Harbor, MI, area.
Application information:
Initial approach: Letter
Deadline(s): None
Officers: L. Richard Marzke, Pres.; Christopher J. Marzke, V.P.; Craig S. Marzke, V.P.; Kevin W. Marzke, V.P.; Kurt R. Marzke, V.P.; Lynn Ann Marzke-Fletcher, V.P.; Nancy Ann Marzke, Secy.-Treas.
EIN: 383584852

530
Lorraine D. Matson Trust
c/o Comerica Bank
P.O. Box 75000
Detroit, MI 48275-0001
County: Wayne
Application addresses: c/o Avondale High School, Attn.: Principal, 2800 Waukegan St., Auburn Hills, MI 48326, or c/o Auburn Hills Presbyterian Church, Pastor, 3456 Primary St., Auburn Hills, MI 48236

Established in MI.
Grantmaker type: Independent foundation.
Financial data (yr. ended 11/30/09): Assets, $195,233 (M); expenditures, $13,914; total giving, $9,300; qualifying distributions, $9,300; giving activities include $9,300 for grants.
Purpose and activities: Scholarships awards paid directly to the college or university for graduates of Avondale High School or members of the Auburn Hills Presbyterian Church, MI.
Fields of interest: Higher education.
Type of support: Scholarships—to individuals.
Limitations: Giving limited to residents of Auburn Hills, MI.
Application information: Application form required.
Deadline(s): Jan. 1 to Apr. 1
Trustee: Comerica Bank.
EIN: 386523330

531
Matthaei Foundation
P.O. Box 2480
Birmingham, MI 48012-2480 (248) 647-4810
County: Oakland
Contact: Frederick C. Matthaei, Jr., Secy.-Treas.

Established in MI.
Grantmaker type: Independent foundation.
Financial data (yr. ended 12/31/09): Assets, $11,607 (M); expenditures, $10,920; total giving, $10,119; qualifying distributions, $10,119; giving activities include $10,119 for 1 grant.
Fields of interest: Education; Youth development; Urban/community development.
Limitations: Applications accepted. Giving primarily in MI. No grants to individuals.
Application information: Application form not required.
Deadline(s): None
Officers: Mary K. Matthaei, Pres.; Morgan Crowther, V.P.; Frederick C. Matthaei, Jr., Secy.-Treas.
Trustees: Amy F. Matthaei; Julie A. Matthaei; Konrad H. Matthaei.
EIN: 386041527

532
Mauser Harmony with Nature Foundation, Inc.
9911 Fairfield St.
Livonia, MI 48150-2707 (734) 261-9393
County: Wayne
Contact: William T. Cook, Pres.

Established in 1999 in MI.
Grantmaker type: Independent foundation.
Financial data (yr. ended 12/31/09): Assets, $763,924 (M); expenditures, $57,060; total giving, $7,320; qualifying distributions, $31,619; giving activities include $7,320 for 3 grants.
Fields of interest: Higher education; Animals/wildlife; Public affairs.
Limitations: Applications accepted. Giving primarily in Detroit, MI.
Application information: Application form not required.
Initial approach: Proposal
Deadline(s): None
Officers: William T. Cook, Pres.; Rose M. Cook, Secy.
Trustees: Christopher W. Cook; Heather M. Cook.
EIN: 383408710

533
The Edwin J. May Foundation
615 Abbey St.
Birmingham, MI 48009-5620
County: Oakland
Contact: Brian S. May, Tr.

Established in 1994 in FL.
Donors: Daniel May; Dianne L. May.
Grantmaker type: Independent foundation.
Financial data (yr. ended 12/31/09): Assets, $1,925,502 (M); gifts received, $147,835; expenditures, $8,192; total giving, $0; qualifying distributions, $0.
Fields of interest: American Red Cross; International relief; Christian agencies & churches.
International interests: Haiti.

Limitations: Applications accepted. Giving primarily in FL and NC. No grants to individuals.
Application information:
Initial approach: Letter
Trustees: Brian S. May; Daniel May; Dianne L. May; Wachovia Bank, N.A.
EIN: 650501566
Selected grants: The following grants were reported in 2005.
$100,000 to Hope for Haiti, Naples, FL.

534
Doeren Mayhew Foundation
755 W. Big Beaver Rd., Ste. 2300
Troy, MI 48084-0231
County: Oakland
Contact: Joseph C. DeGennaro, V.P.

Established in MI.
Grantmaker type: Independent foundation.
Financial data (yr. ended 12/31/09): Assets, $16,217 (M); gifts received, $1,000; expenditures, $1,874; total giving, $1,850; qualifying distributions, $1,850; giving activities include $1,850 for grants to individuals.
Type of support: Scholarships—to individuals.
Limitations: Giving primarily to residents of MI.
Application information: Application form not required.
Deadline(s): None
Officers: Mark Crawford, Pres.; Joseph C. DeGennaro, V.P.; Michael J. Berry, Secy.-Treas.
EIN: 386147314

535
Robert J. McBain Foundation
1240 Woodcliff Dr. S.E.
Grand Rapids, MI 49506-4243 (616) 458-4218
County: Kent
Contact: Robert P. McBain, Pres.

Established in MI.
Donor: Robert J. McBain‡.
Grantmaker type: Independent foundation.
Financial data (yr. ended 12/31/08): Assets, $0 (M); expenditures, $19,520; total giving, $14,883; qualifying distributions, $14,883; giving activities include $14,883 for 6 grants (high: $5,000; low: $500).
Fields of interest: Education; Human services.
Limitations: Giving primarily in Grand Rapids, MI.
Application information: Application form not required.
Initial approach: Proposal
Deadline(s): None
Officer and Trustee:* Gwendolyn McBain,* Pres.
EIN: 237114594

536
Donald C. and Helene Marienthal McCabe Charitable Foundation
c/o National City Bank
171 Monroe Ave. N.W.
Grand Rapids, MI 49503-2634
County: Kent

Established in 1994 in MI.
Grantmaker type: Independent foundation.
Financial data (yr. ended 12/31/08): Assets, $715,740 (M); expenditures, $52,523; total giving,

$43,406; qualifying distributions, $43,406; giving activities include $43,406 for grants.
Purpose and activities: Scholarship awards to students of Delta Community College, Saginaw Valley State University, MI, with preference to needy Jewish and Presbyterian students in Bay, Saginaw, and Midland counties, Michigan. Annual support also for a public library system.
Fields of interest: Libraries (public); Protestant agencies & churches; Jewish agencies & synagogues.
Type of support: Scholarships—to individuals.
Limitations: Giving for the benefit of MI organizations and residents, with emphasis on Bay, Saginaw, and Midland counties.
Application information: Application form required.
Deadline(s): Apr. 30
Trustee: National City Bank.
EIN: 383184550

537
Helen McCalla Foundation
c/o KeyBank N.A.
4900 Tiedeman Rd., OH-01-49-0150
Brooklyn, OH 44144-2302
County: Cuyahoga
Application address: c/o Key Bank N.A., Attn.: Caroline Chipman, Admin., 100 S. Main St., P.O. Box 8612, Ann Arbor, MI 48104-1944, tel.: (737) 747-7992

Established in 1995 in MI.
Donor: Helen McCalla‡.
Grantmaker type: Independent foundation.
Financial data (yr. ended 12/31/09): Assets, $1,986,813 (M); expenditures, $136,923; total giving, $107,342; qualifying distributions, $107,342; giving activities include $107,342 for grants.
Purpose and activities: Giving to organizations that provide assistance to the elderly or handicapped children.
Fields of interest: Hospitals (general); Aging, centers/services; Children; Disabilities, people with.
Limitations: Giving limited to the Washtenaw County, MI, area. No grants to individuals.
Application information:
Initial approach: Letter
Deadline(s): Mar. 31
Trustee: KeyBank N.A.
EIN: 383195451

538
The W. B. McCardell Family Foundation
165 Township Line Rd., Ste. 3000
Jenkintown, PA 19046-3509
County: Montgomery
Contact: Bradley W. McCardell, Pres.

Established in 1994 in MI.
Donor: Willard B. McCardell, Jr.
Grantmaker type: Independent foundation.
Financial data (yr. ended 12/31/09): Assets, $156,411 (M); expenditures, $76,538; total giving, $63,000; qualifying distributions, $63,000; giving activities include $63,000 for grants.
Purpose and activities: Giving in areas that promote spiritual values and support family independence.
Fields of interest: Physical therapy; Athletics/sports, equestrianism; Disabilities, people with.

Type of support: General/operating support; Endowments.
Limitations: Giving primarily in MI.
Application information: Accepts CMF Common Grant Application Form. Application form required.
Initial approach: Letter
Deadline(s): Oct. 1
Officers: Willard B. McCardell, Jr., Chair.; Sheran M. McCardell, Vice-Chair.; Bradley W. McCardell, Pres.; Michael D. Mulcahy, Secy.; Tracy L. McCardell, Treas.
Trustees: Scott I. Andrews; Tina M. Andrews; Ann-Marie McCardell; Kenneth W. McCardell; Steven R. McCardell.
EIN: 383211106
Selected grants: The following grants were reported in 2008.
$6,500 to Academy of the New Church, Bryn Athyn, PA.

539
McClendon Family Foundation
2 Chestnut St.
South Haven, MI 49090-1258
County: Van Buren
Contact: Joanne McClendon, Pres.; Robert McClendon, Dir.

Established in 1997 in MI.
Donors: Robert "Bob" McClendon; Joanne McClendon.
Grantmaker type: Independent foundation.
Financial data (yr. ended 12/31/09): Assets, $190,942 (M); expenditures, $127,075; total giving, $124,000; qualifying distributions, $124,000; giving activities include $124,000 for grants.
Fields of interest: Human services; Community development, neighborhood development.
Limitations: Giving primarily in South Haven, MI. No grants to individuals.
Application information:
Initial approach: Letter
Deadline(s): None
Officers: Joanne McClendon, Pres.; G. Philip Dietrich, Secy.-Treas.
Directors: Margaret McClendon; Mark McClendon.
EIN: 383403655

540
Theo & Mable McClendon Scholarship Foundation
(formerly Theo and Mable McClendon Scholarship Fund)
c/o Sherry M. Pickett
P.O. Box 2623
Southfield, MI 48037-2623
County: Oakland

Grantmaker type: Independent foundation.
Financial data (yr. ended 03/31/08): Assets, $1,133 (M); gifts received, $65; expenditures, $68; total giving, $0; qualifying distributions, $0.
Officers: Sherry Pickett, Pres.; Kiatra M. Pickett, Secy.; Jason A. Pickett, Treas.
EIN: 383174912

541
McCurdy Memorial Scholarship Foundation
c/o Comerica Bank
49 W. Michigan Ave.
Battle Creek, MI 49017-3603
County: Calhoun
Application address: c/o Michael C. Jordon, 2 W. Michigan Ave., Ste. 301, Battle Creek, MI 49017; tel.: (269) 962-9591

Established in 1961 in MI.
Grantmaker type: Independent foundation.
Financial data (yr. ended 12/31/09): Assets, $560,543 (M); expenditures, $47,022; total giving, $40,500; qualifying distributions, $40,500; giving activities include $40,500 for grants to individuals.
Purpose and activities: Scholarship awards to high school graduates from Calhoun County, Michigan, for post-secondary education, for a period of not more than four years.
Fields of interest: Higher education.
Type of support: Scholarships—to individuals.
Limitations: Applications accepted. Giving limited to residents of Calhoun County, MI.
Application information: Application form required.
Deadline(s): Apr. 1
Officers: Sandra Morgan, Pres.; Karen Reeves, V.P.; Edward Tersteeg, Secy.; Lori Hill, Treas.
Trustees: Dave Dillman; Joan Dillman; Sonja Dotson; Louis H. Ryason.
Corporate Trustee: Comerica Bank.
EIN: 381687120

542
McGregor Fund
333 W. Fort St., Ste. 2090
Detroit, MI 48226-3134 (313) 963-3495
County: Wayne
Contact: C. David Campbell, Pres.
FAX: (313) 963-3512;
E-mail: info@mcgregorfund.org; *URL:* http://www.mcgregorfund.org

Incorporated in 1925 in MI.
Donors: Tracy W. McGregor‡; Katherine W. McGregor‡.
Grantmaker type: Independent foundation.
Financial data (yr. ended 06/30/09): Assets, $140,703,167 (M); expenditures, $7,404,528; total giving, $5,924,974; qualifying distributions, $6,690,943; giving activities include $5,771,050 for 59 grants, and $153,924 for employee matching gifts.
Purpose and activities: A private foundation organized to relieve misfortune and improve the well-being of people. The foundation provides grants to support activities in human services, education, health care, arts and culture, and public benefit.
Fields of interest: Arts; Higher education; Education; Medical care, in-patient care; Health organizations, association; Human services; Youth, services; Homeless.
Type of support: General/operating support; Continuing support; Capital campaigns; Building/renovation; Equipment; Program development; Seed money; Employee matching gifts.
Limitations: Applications accepted. Giving primarily in the metropolitan Detroit, MI, area, including Wayne, Oakland, and Macomb counties. No support for disease-specific organizations (or their local affiliates). No grants to individuals, or for

scholarships directly, fellowships, travel, workshops, seminars, special events, film or video projects, or conferences; no loans.
Publications: Application guidelines; Annual report (including application guidelines); Grants list.
Application information: Grantmaking guidelines and application procedures are available on the foundation's Web site. Potential applicants are encouraged to contact the foundation to discuss proposed projects before submitting a proposal. Organizations are limited to submitting one grant application per year. Application form not required.
Initial approach: Cover letter and proposal
Copies of proposal: 1
Deadline(s): Applicants are encouraged to submit proposals at least 3 months in advance of board meetings
Board meeting date(s): Mar., June, Sept., and Dec.
Final notification: 90 to 120 days
Officers and Trustees:* James B. Nicholson,* Chair.; Ruth R. Glancy,* Vice-Chair.; C. David Campbell,* Pres. and Secy.; William W. Shelden, Jr.,* Treas.; Dave Bing, Tr. Emeritus; Eugene A. Miller, Tr. Emeritus; Bruce W. Steinhauer, M.D.*, Tr. Emeritus; Gerard M. Anderson; Cynthia N. Ford; Ira J. Jaffe; Denise J. Lewis; Susan Schooley, M.D.
Number of staff: 4 full-time professional; 1 full-time support.
EIN: 380808800
Selected grants: The following grants were reported in 2009.
$2,000,000 to Detroit Institute of Arts, Detroit, MI. For Great Art-New Start, campaign to complete structural renovation, reinstall art and carry on daily operation of museum, payable over 5.00 years.
$1,500,000 to Community Foundation for Southeast Michigan, Detroit, MI. For New Economy Initiative for Southeast Michigan, collaboration of local and national foundations to foster economic growth and speed transition of southeast Michigan to knowledge-based economy, payable over 3.00 years.
$1,500,000 to Local Initiatives Support Corporation, New York, NY. For Detroit LISC's Sustainable Communities work plan for five investment areas, payable over 3.00 years.
$600,000 to Detroit Science Center, Detroit, MI. For general operations and to upgrade planetarium to full-dome video, as part of Engineering the Future Campaign, payable over 3.00 years.
$500,000 to Wayne State University, Detroit, MI. For expansion of Center for Community-Based Education, as part of new Honors College that is being established, payable over 2.00 years.
$360,000 to Alternatives for Girls, Detroit, MI. For Emergency Shelter/Transition to Independent Living and Street Outreach programs for girls and young women ages 13-21, payable over 2.00 years.
$240,000 to City Connect Detroit, Detroit, MI. For general operations to increase collaboration among nonprofits, funders, government, businesses and others, payable over 3.00 years.
$150,000 to Michigan Opera Theater, Detroit, MI. For general operating support.
$117,000 to Friends School in Detroit, Detroit, MI. For Curriculum Alignment Program, payable over 2.00 years.
$100,000 to Boys Hope Girls Hope, Detroit, MI. For re-opening of second home for academically capable and motivated boys who would benefit from a more supportive living environment, payable over 3.00 years.

543
B. D. and Jane E. McIntyre Foundation
c/o JPMorgan Chase Bank, N.A.
P.O. Box 3038
Milwaukee, WI 53201-1308
County: Milwaukee
Application address: c/o JPMorgan Chase Bank, N.A., Attn.: Cleveland Thurber, III, 685 St. Clair Ave., Grosse Point, MI 48230, tel.: (313) 225-3523

Trust established in 1961 in MI.
Donor: Members of the McIntyre family.
Grantmaker type: Independent foundation.
Financial data (yr. ended 11/30/09): Assets, $4,283,936 (M); expenditures, $340,010; total giving, $320,600; qualifying distributions, $325,071; giving activities include $320,600 for 25 grants (high: $100,000; low: $1,000).
Purpose and activities: Giving primarily for higher education and to Episcopal and other churches; support also for the arts and health organizations.
Fields of interest: Arts; Higher education; Education; Health organizations; Medical research; Christian agencies & churches.
Type of support: Continuing support; Scholarship funds.
Limitations: Giving primarily in MI, with some emphasis on Monroe and Midland; some giving also in FL. No grants to individuals.
Application information: Application form not required.
Initial approach: Proposal
Copies of proposal: 1
Deadline(s): None
Board meeting date(s): As required
Trustee and Advisory Committee: Rocque L. Lipford; C.S. McIntyre III; JPMorgan Chase Bank, N.A.
EIN: 386046718
Selected grants: The following grants were reported in 2008.
$25,000 to Hillsdale College, Hillsdale, MI.
$25,000 to Northwood University, Midland, MI.
$25,000 to Trinity Episcopal Church, Monroe, MI.
$15,000 to River Raisin Center for the Arts, Monroe, MI.
$10,000 to Automotive Hall of Fame, Dearborn, MI.
$5,000 to Historical Society of Martin County, Stuart, FL.
$5,000 to United Way of Monroe County, Monroe, MI.
$2,500 to Community Foundation of Monroe County, Monroe, MI.
$2,000 to New Convictions Outreach, Wetumpka, AL.
$1,000 to Salvation Army of Monroe, Monroe, MI.

544
C. S. and Marion F. McIntyre Foundation
c/o JPMorgan Chase Bank, N.A.
P.O. Box 3038
Milwaukee, WI 53201-3038
County: Milwaukee
Application address: c/o JPMorgan Chase Bank, N.A., Attn.: Cleveland Thurber III, 611 Woodward Ave., Detroit, MI 48226, tel.: (313) 225-3523

Trust established in 1961 in MI.
Donor: Members of the McIntyre family.
Grantmaker type: Independent foundation.
Financial data (yr. ended 11/30/09): Assets, $2,665,633 (M); expenditures, $186,052; total giving, $171,500; qualifying distributions,

$175,757; giving activities include $171,500 for 8 grants (high: $100,000; low: $500).
Purpose and activities: Support primarily for a college and other education.
Fields of interest: Arts; Higher education, college; Education; Hospitals (general); Housing/shelter, development; Human services; Christian agencies & churches.
Limitations: Applications accepted. Giving primarily in MI, with emphasis on the Monroe area. No grants to individuals.
Application information: Application form not required.
Initial approach: Letter
Copies of proposal: 1
Deadline(s): None
Board meeting date(s): As required
Final notification: Oct. 31
Advisory Committee: Rocque L. Lipford; David L. McIntyre; James T. McIntyre.
Trustee: JPMorgan Chase Bank, N.A.
EIN: 386046733
Selected grants: The following grants were reported in 2008.
$50,000 to Alma College, Alma, MI.
$20,000 to First Presbyterian Church of Monroe, Monroe, MI.
$15,000 to Habitat for Humanity of Monroe County, Monroe, MI.
$5,000 to Florida Atlantic University Foundation, Boca Raton, FL.
$2,000 to Variety FAR Conservatory of Therapeutic and Performing Arts, Birmingham, MI.

545
W. D. & Prudence McIntyre Foundation
c/o JPMorgan Chase Bank, N.A.
P.O. Box 3038
Milwaukee, WI 53201-1308
County: Milwaukee
Application address: c/o JPMorgan Chase Bank, N.A., Attn.: Cleveland Thurber III, 611 Woodward Ave., Detroit, MI 48226, tel.: (313) 225-3523

Established in 1960 in MI.
Grantmaker type: Independent foundation.
Financial data (yr. ended 11/30/09): Assets, $1,073,833 (M); expenditures, $108,637; total giving, $102,000; qualifying distributions, $102,000; giving activities include $102,000 for grants.
Fields of interest: Hospitals (general); Human services; Catholic agencies & churches.
Type of support: General/operating support.
Limitations: Applications accepted. Giving primarily in MI, with emphasis on Monroe. No grants to individuals.
Application information: Application form required.
Initial approach: Letter
Deadline(s): None
Advisory Committee: Rocque E. Lipford; William D. McIntyre, Jr.
Trustee: JPMorgan Chase Bank, N.A.
EIN: 386046659

546
The McKeen Foundation
c/o Comerica Bank
P.O. Box 75000, MC 3302
Detroit, MI 48275-3302   (313) 222-5576
County: Wayne
Application address: c/o David C. Wind, 500 Woodward Ave., 22nd Fl., Detroit, MI, 48226-5415, tel.: (313) 222-5576

Established in 2001 in MI.
Grantmaker type: Independent foundation.
Financial data (yr. ended 12/31/09): Assets, $901,032 (M); expenditures, $52,705; total giving, $46,300; qualifying distributions, $46,300; giving activities include $46,300 for grants.
Fields of interest: Arts; Higher education; Environment, climate change/global warming; Children/youth, services; Protestant agencies & churches.
Limitations: Giving primarily in MI. No grants to individuals.
Application information: Application form not required.
Initial approach: Letter
Deadline(s): None
Advisory Committee: Alexander McKeen; Evelyn McKeen.
Trustee: Comerica Bank.
EIN: 912119007

547
Verna McKibben Memorial Foundation
c/o Comerica Bank
P.O. Box 75000, MC 3302
Detroit, MI 48275-3302
County: Wayne
Contact: Joel R. Aberth, Tr.
Application address: 3296 W. Market St., Akron, OH 44333-3355, tel.: (330) 865-7722

Established in 1999 in OH.
Donor: Verna McKibben†.
Grantmaker type: Independent foundation.
Financial data (yr. ended 04/30/10): Assets, $403,643 (M); expenditures, $11,096; total giving, $0; qualifying distributions, $0.
Fields of interest: Arts; Health organizations, association; Human services.
Limitations: Giving primarily in OH.
Application information:
Initial approach: Letter
Deadline(s): None
Trustees: Joel R. Aberth; Comerica Bank.
EIN: 316608261

548
Mary I. McLeod Foundation
16845 Kercheval St., Ste. 5
Grosse Pointe, MI 48230-1551
County: Wayne
Contact: Mary I. McLeod, Pres.

Established in 1998 in MI.
Donor: Mary I. McLeod.
Grantmaker type: Independent foundation.
Financial data (yr. ended 12/31/09): Assets, $125,969 (M); expenditures, $11,800; total giving, $10,350; qualifying distributions, $10,350; giving activities include $10,350 for grants.

Fields of interest: Higher education; Animals/wildlife, special services; Protestant agencies & churches.
Type of support: General/operating support.
Limitations: Giving primarily in MI. No grants to individuals.
Application information: Application form required.
   Deadline(s): None
Officers and Trustees:* Mary I. McLeod,* Pres.; S. Gary Spicer,* Secy.
EIN: 383407098

549
William F. McNally Family Foundation
(formerly William F. and Marjorie A. McNally Memorial Foundation)
4493 Warren St.
Bridgeport, MI 48722-5112
County: Saginaw
Contact: William F. McNally, Pres.

Established in 1982 in MI.
Donor: William F. McNally.
Grantmaker type: Independent foundation.
Financial data (yr. ended 12/31/09): Assets, $4,635,690 (M); gifts received, $543,000; expenditures, $156,200; total giving, $153,600; qualifying distributions, $153,600; giving activities include $153,600 for 24 grants (high: $100,000; low: $100).
Fields of interest: Museums (art); Higher education; Theological school/education; Hospitals (general); Human services; Protestant agencies & churches.
Limitations: Applications accepted. Giving primarily in MI.
Application information: Application form not required.
   Initial approach: Letter
   Deadline(s): None
Officer: William F. McNally, Pres. and Treas.
Trustees: Brian McNally; Dwight McNally.
EIN: 382429175
Selected grants: The following grants were reported in 2008.
$100,000 to Covenant Healthcare Foundation, Saginaw, MI.
$10,000 to Boy Scouts of America, Lake Huron Area Council, Auburn, MI.
$5,000 to Alma College, Alma, MI.
$5,000 to University of Michigan, Ann Arbor, MI.
$3,500 to Saginaw Community Foundation, Saginaw, MI.
$3,000 to Delta College, University Center, MI.
$2,000 to Pheasants Forever, Saint Paul, MN.
$2,000 to Underground Railroad, Saginaw, MI.
$1,000 to American Red Cross, Saginaw County Chapter, Saginaw, MI.
$1,000 to Saginaw Valley State University, University Center, MI.

550
Margaret McNally Memorial Fund
c/o Citizens Bank Wealth Mgmt., N.A.
328 S. Saginaw St., M/C 002072
Flint, MI 48502-1923
County: Genesee
Application address: c/o Wealth Mgmt., Citizens Bank, N.A., Attn.: Helen James, 101 N. Washington Ave., Saginaw, MI 48607-1207, tel.: (989) 776-7638

Established in 1985 in MI.
Grantmaker type: Independent foundation.
Financial data (yr. ended 12/31/09): Assets, $94,828 (M); expenditures, $6,683; total giving, $3,500; qualifying distributions, $3,500; giving activities include $3,500 for grants.
Purpose and activities: Giving to organizations to provide assistance to blind residents of Saginaw County, Michigan.
Fields of interest: Blind/visually impaired.
Type of support: General/operating support; Equipment.
Limitations: Giving limited to Saginaw County, MI. No grants to individuals.
Application information: Application form required.
   Initial approach: Letter or telephone
   Deadline(s): None
Trustee: Citizens Bank Wealth Management, N.A.
EIN: 386234122

551
McNish Family Foundation
26622 Woodward Ave., Ste. 200
Royal Oak, MI 48067-0956   (248) 544-4800
County: Oakland
Contact: Carol A. McNish, Pres.
E-mail: christinemcnish@sbcglobal.net

Established in 2003 in MI.
Donors: W.J. McNish; C.A. McNish.
Grantmaker type: Independent foundation.
Financial data (yr. ended 12/31/09): Assets, $122,833 (M); gifts received, $45,112; expenditures, $47,312; total giving, $47,254; qualifying distributions, $47,312; giving activities include $47,254 for 7 grants (high: $18,000; low: $1,500).
Fields of interest: Elementary/secondary education; Athletics/sports, training; Youth development; Catholic agencies & churches.
Type of support: Scholarship funds.
Limitations: Applications accepted. Giving primarily in MI. No grants to individuals.
Application information: Application form required.
   Initial approach: Letter
   Deadline(s): None
Officers and Directors:* Carol A. McNish,* Pres.; Christine McNish,* V.P.; Elizabeth McNish,* Secy.; Suzanne McNish Moceri,* Treas.; Megan Curoe.
EIN: 300184715

552
McShane Family Foundation
3521 Madison St.
Oak Brook, IL 60523-2759   (630) 654-0216
County: Dupage
Contact: Stephen J. McShane, Pres.

Established in 2006 in IL.
Donor: Stephen J. McShane.
Grantmaker type: Independent foundation.
Financial data (yr. ended 12/31/09): Assets, $229,691 (M); gifts received, $50,000; expenditures, $31,211; total giving, $30,990; qualifying distributions, $30,990; giving activities include $30,990 for grants.
Fields of interest: Performing arts, education; Education, reading; Health organizations; Human services; Catholic agencies & churches.
Limitations: Applications accepted. Giving primarily in IL and MI.

Application information:
   Initial approach: Letterhead
   Deadline(s): None
Officers and Directors:* Stephen J. McShane,* Pres. and Treas.; Kathleen McShane,* Secy.; Erin McShane.
EIN: 203967708

553
Madeline Sweeney Meeks Foundation
2443 Warrenville Rd., Ste. 610
Lisle, IL 60532-4357
County: Dupage
Contact: Robert Meeks, Dir.

Established in 1998 in IL.
Donors: Robert Meeks; Debra Meeks.
Grantmaker type: Independent foundation.
Financial data (yr. ended 12/31/09): Assets, $51,928 (M); expenditures, $7,985; total giving, $7,400; qualifying distributions, $7,400; giving activities include $7,400 for grants.
Fields of interest: Education; Food services.
Type of support: General/operating support; Scholarships—to individuals.
Limitations: Giving primarily in IL and MI.
Application information: Application form not required.
   Initial approach: Letter
   Deadline(s): None
Directors: Andrew Meeks; Debra Meeks; Jenny Lynn Meeks; Robert Meeks.
EIN: 364258774

554
Richard D. & Lynette S. Merillat Private Foundation
c/o Merrill Lynch Trust Co.
P.O. Box 1525
Pennington, NJ 08534-0686
County: Mercer
Application address: c/o Richard D. Merillat, Pres., 2600 Gordon Dr., Naples, FL 34102

Established in 1993 in MI.
Donors: Richard D. Merillat; Lynette S. Merillat.
Grantmaker type: Independent foundation.
Financial data (yr. ended 06/30/09): Assets, $15,205,235 (M); expenditures, $1,002,711; total giving, $849,000; qualifying distributions, $865,191; giving activities include $849,000 for 29 grants (high: $365,000; low: $2,000).
Purpose and activities: Grants primarily to organizations promoting Christian values.
Fields of interest: Higher education; Human services; Family services; Christian agencies & churches.
Limitations: Giving primarily in Adrian MI, and the surrounding communities. No grants to individuals.
Application information:
   Initial approach: Letter
   Deadline(s): None
Officers and Trustees:* Richard D. Merillat,* Pres.; Lynette S. Merillat,* Secy.; John Thurman.
EIN: 383148627
Selected grants: The following grants were reported in 2009.
$365,000 to Huntington University, Huntington, IN.
$60,000 to Huntington University, Huntington, IN.
$50,000 to Focus on the Family, Colorado Springs, CO.

$30,000 to CEO Forum, Colorado Springs, CO.
$30,000 to World Sports, Bonita Springs, FL.
$15,000 to Boys and Girls Club of Collier County, Naples, FL.
$5,000 to RBC Ministries, Grand Rapids, MI.
$5,000 to Salvation Army of Naples, Naples, FL.

555
Merkley Charitable Trust
c/o Citizens Bank
328 S. Saginaw St., M/C 001065
Flint, MI 48502-1923 (810) 766-7826
County: Genesee
Contact: Dawn Bentley, Trust Off., Citizens Bank

Established in 1986.
Donor: Martha K. Merkley‡.
Grantmaker type: Independent foundation.
Financial data (yr. ended 11/30/10): Assets, $4,235,502 (M); expenditures, $238,316; total giving, $195,798; qualifying distributions, $233,196; giving activities include $195,798 for 11 grants (high: $106,023; low: $1,200).
Purpose and activities: Giving primarily to benefit youth and the elderly.
Fields of interest: Education; Recreation, parks/playgrounds; Human services; Youth, services; Christian agencies & churches; Aging.
Type of support: Continuing support; Program development.
Limitations: Applications accepted. Giving limited to Genesee County, MI. No grants to individuals.
Publications: Application guidelines.
Application information: Application form not required.
  Initial approach: Letter
  Copies of proposal: 1
  Deadline(s): None
  Board meeting date(s): Quarterly
Trustee: Citizens Bank.
EIN: 386528749
Selected grants: The following grants were reported in 2009.
$28,034 to Humane Society of Genesee County, Burton, MI.
$15,000 to Hurley Foundation, Flint, MI.
$10,000 to Food Bank of Eastern Michigan, Flint, MI.
$3,500 to Mott Community College, Flint, MI.
$2,500 to Flint Community Schools, Flint, MI.
$2,000 to Muscular Dystrophy Association, Tucson, AZ.

556
Metro Health Foundation
333 W. Fort St., Ste. 1370
Detroit, MI 48226-3134 (313) 965-4220
County: Wayne
Contact: Theresa L. Sondys, Sr. Prog. Off.
FAX: (313) 965-3626;
E-mail: metrohealthfdn@aol.com; Additional e-mail: theresasondys@aol.com

Incorporated in 1986 in MI; converted from Group Health Plan of Southeast Michigan.
Grantmaker type: Independent foundation.
Financial data (yr. ended 12/31/09): Assets, $6,592,149 (M); expenditures, $581,690; total giving, $178,595; qualifying distributions, $366,456; giving activities include $178,595 for 18 grants (high: $30,000; low: $2,500).

Purpose and activities: Dedicated to helping metropolitan Detroit organizations meet the community's health care needs. Grants support a wide variety of health-related services for people of all ages. Collaborative programs which make comprehensive, primary health care accessible to at-risk urban groups are a priority. Areas of primary interest include: teenage pregnancy crisis; health care transportation for the elderly and homeless; in-home healthcare assistance; medically-related assistance to the homeless; healthcare equipment and medical supplies in limited amounts, preferably for underfunded organizations; medical education in special situations in the tri-county Detroit, Michigan, area; and start-up and support money for projects such as AIDS, epilepsy, cancer, heart disease, leukemia, and other major ills of substantial public concern. Support given to all medically indigent people.
Fields of interest: Nursing school/education; Health care; Health organizations, association; AIDS; Children/youth, services; Aging, centers/services; Homeless, human services; Infants/toddlers; Children/youth; Children; Youth; Adults; Aging; Young adults; Disabilities, people with; Blind/visually impaired; Deaf/hearing impaired; Mentally disabled; Minorities; African Americans/Blacks; Women; Girls; Adults, women; Young adults, female; Men; Boys; Adults, men; Young adults, male; AIDS, people with; LGBTQ; Immigrants/refugees; Economically disadvantaged; Homeless.
Type of support: General/operating support; Management development/capacity building; Equipment; Program development; Scholarship funds; Matching/challenge support.
Limitations: Giving limited to Macomb, Oakland and Wayne counties, MI, with primary emphasis on the city of Detroit. No support for religious organizations or government agencies (except by specific Board action), or for organizations which discriminate because of age, race, ethnic origin, religion, sexual orientation, handicap or sex. No grants to individuals, or for building campaigns, conferences or seminars, or for research projects; no loans.
Publications: Application guidelines; Grants list; Program policy statement (including application guidelines).
Application information: Common Grant Application of Council of Michigan Foundations accepted. Application form required.
  Initial approach: Telephone for application and to discuss proposal idea
  Copies of proposal: 6
  Deadline(s): Aug. 1 and Feb. 1
  Board meeting date(s): Oct. and Apr.
  Final notification: Within 90 days
Officers and Trustees:* Lillie M. Tabor,* Pres.; Cheryl Chandler,* V.P.; Raymond Cochran,* Treas.; Randy Walainis,* Exec. Dir.; Glenn F. Kossick, Pres. Emeritus; Judith Bean, Ph.D.; Valerie Herod Belay; Laura Champagne; Robert Doll; Doris M. Fell; Barbara Justice; Gloria Robinson.
Number of staff: 1 full-time professional; 1 part-time professional; 1 part-time support.
EIN: 382100939
Selected grants: The following grants were reported in 2009.
$30,000 to Community Health and Social Services Center, Detroit, MI. To furnish four procedure rooms in planned new facility, and purchase new equipment for preventive treatment screenings for cervical and colon cancer so that testing may take place in familiar setting, and in timely and culturally competent manner.

$30,000 to Covenant Community Care, Detroit, MI. To pilot centralized pharmacy program to provide prescription medication assistance not only for patients but collaboration with service agencies who serve the poor and homeless in Detroit.
$22,242 to Hope Medical Clinic, Ypsilanti, MI. For part-time Medical Clinic Coordinator to expand services provided at Hope-Wayne Medical Clinic new facility.
$20,000 to Optometric Institute and Clinic of Detroit, Detroit, MI. To pay for retinal surgery for Clinic's low-income, uninsured clients, who have no other way to obtain/pay for the procedure.
$12,000 to Joy-Southfield Community Development Corporation, Detroit, MI. To improve quality of care provided to patients with hypertension through aggressive medication management, increased blood pressure screening, reducing barriers to care by providing transportation vouchers, increased use of lab testing and EKGs, and partnering with Optometric Institute of Detroit for eye exams.
$10,000 to Beaumont Cancer Institute, Royal Oak, MI. For continuing support and enhancement of Minority Outreach Program focusing on culturally competent education and cancer screening for minority populations (African-American, Arab American/Chaldean, Hispanic/Latino, Native American, Asian) in southeastern Michigan Wayne, Oakland and Macomb Counties.
$10,000 to Macomb Community College Foundation, Warren, MI. For scholarships for students in MCC nursing program.
$10,000 to Michigan AIDS Coalition, Ferndale, MI. For 7-member AmeriCorps Team, which will be trained to serve as HIV/AIDS prevention educators, testers, and counselors, providing direct client services, leveraging over $225,000 in human resources to agencies serving persons infected/affected by HIV/AIDS.
$10,000 to National Kidney Foundation of Michigan, Ann Arbor, MI. For community-based program (Healthy Families Start With You) that works with Wayne County Head Start to provide pre-school-aged children and their families with tools and techniques to adopt healthy lifestyles and personal motivation to embrace and implement positive health practices, reducing risk for several chronic conditions, and help people living with these diseases to manage them more effectively.
$10,000 to World Medical Relief, Detroit, MI. For Prescription Assistance Program through purchase of medications not available by donation of good-dated samples.

557
Allen H. and Nydia Meyers Foundation
(formerly Allen H. Meyers Foundation)
P.O. Box 100
Tecumseh, MI 49286-0100 (517) 423-8086
County: Lenawee
URL: http://www.meyersfoundation.org/
Application address: c/o Lenawee County Education Foundation, 4107 N. Adrian Hwy., Adrian, MI 49221-8813

Established in 1966 in MI.
Donor: Nydia Meyers‡.
Grantmaker type: Independent foundation.
Financial data (yr. ended 04/30/10): Assets, $606,761 (M); expenditures, $21,717; total giving, $18,031; qualifying distributions, $18,031; giving activities include $18,031 for grants to individuals.

Purpose and activities: Scholarship awards to graduating seniors from the Lenawee County, Michigan School District for college studies in aeronautics, science and allied fields.
Fields of interest: Medical school/education; Engineering school/education; Physical/earth sciences; Space/aviation; Chemistry.
Type of support: Scholarships—to individuals.
Limitations: Applications accepted. Giving limited to residents of Lenawee County, MI.
Application information: See foundation web site for full application requirements and guidelines, including downloadable application form. Application form required.
Deadline(s): Applications accepted between Jan. 1 and Mar. 1 annually
Officers and Directors:* Timothy Husband,* Pres.; Jerry Nelson,* V.P. and Treas.; Ann Hinsdale-Knisel,* Secy.; Michael Beil; Dianne Froelich; Kim Koch; Lloyd Miller; Sr. Sharon Weber; Pareese Young.
Trustee: Sarah White*.
EIN: 386143278

558
Michigan Agri-Business Association Educational Trust Fund
(also known as Michigan Agri-Dealers Educational Trust)
1501 Northshore Dr., Ste. A
East Lansing, MI 48823-7622 (517) 336-0223
County: Ingham
Contact: James E. Byrum, Pres.

Established in MI.
Grantmaker type: Independent foundation.
Financial data (yr. ended 12/31/09): Assets, $438,106 (M); gifts received, $14,705; expenditures, $21,675; total giving, $20,400; qualifying distributions, $20,400; giving activities include $20,400 for 31 grants to individuals (high: $1,150; low: $250).
Purpose and activities: Scholarship awards to students enrolled in grain elevator management and related courses.
Fields of interest: Higher education.
Type of support: Scholarships—to individuals.
Limitations: Applications accepted. Giving limited to MI.
Application information: Application form required.
Initial approach: Letter
Deadline(s): None
Officers: James R. Suchodolski, Chair.; James E. Byrum, Pres.
Trustees: Bill Drushel; John Christian; Ward Forquer; Phil Schmiege.
EIN: 382086180

559
Michigan Elks Association Charitable Grant Fund
150 Woodrow Ave. S.
Battle Creek, MI 49015-3044
County: Calhoun
Application address: c/o Michigan Elks Lodge, P.O. Box 2006, 1200 Harmonia Rd., Battle Creek, MI 49015. tel.: (616) 962-8593

Donor: Michigan Elks Assn.
Grantmaker type: Independent foundation.

Financial data (yr. ended 03/31/10): Assets, $93,810 (M); gifts received, $25,000; expenditures, $78,435; total giving, $72,000; qualifying distributions, $72,000; giving activities include $72,000 for grants to individuals.
Purpose and activities: Scholarship awards to disabled college students who are residents of Michigan and members of an Elk's Lodge.
Fields of interest: Higher education.
Type of support: Scholarships—to individuals.
Limitations: Applications accepted. Giving limited to residents of MI.
Application information: Application form required.
Initial approach: Applications are made to members of Elks Lodges
Deadline(s): Jan. 31
Officers: Dale O. Orchard, Chair.; Kevin M. Quinn, Vice-Chair.; Al Spear, Secy.
EIN: 382599208

560
Joseph & Lottie Michner Educational Foundation
P.O. Box 274
Jackson, MI 49204-0274
County: Jackson
Contact: Julius J. Hoffman, Dir.

Established in MI.
Grantmaker type: Independent foundation.
Financial data (yr. ended 12/31/09): Assets, $343,353 (M); expenditures, $1,264; total giving, $0; qualifying distributions, $0; giving activities include $0 for grants to individuals.
Purpose and activities: Scholarship awards to students who attend Lumen Christi High School, Jackson, Michigan.
Fields of interest: Higher education.
Type of support: Scholarships—to individuals.
Limitations: Applications accepted. Giving limited to residents of Jackson, MI.
Application information: Application form required.
Initial approach: Letter requesting application form
Deadline(s): Apr. 30
Directors: Camilla A. Cavanaugh; Julius J. Hoffman; Walter J. Michner.
EIN: 382346759

561
Claud "Bud" Mick, Jr. Education Scholarship Foundation
6775 Carpenter Rd.
Ypsilanti, MI 48197-8844
County: Washtenaw
Application address: c/o Kanawha Alumni Assn., P.O. Box 324, Burnsville, WV 26335-0324

Established in 2007 in MI.
Donor: Debra J. Mick.
Grantmaker type: Independent foundation.
Financial data (yr. ended 04/30/10): Assets, $97,869 (M); expenditures, $12,543; total giving, $7,000; qualifying distributions, $7,000; giving activities include $7,000 for grants.
Purpose and activities: Scholarship awards to high school graduates of the Burnsville school district, West Virginia, to attend college or trade school.
Fields of interest: Higher education.
Type of support: Scholarships—to individuals.

Limitations: Applications accepted. Giving limited to residents of Burnsville, WV.
Application information: Application form required.
Initial approach: Letter
Deadline(s): None
Officers: Debra J. Mick, Pres. and Treas.; David Palmer, Secy.
Directors: Shirley Lloyd; Paul Peck; Cherry Ramsey; Ann Willey; Larry Wine.
EIN: 208953474

562
C. E. Miller Family Foundation
(formerly Clyde & Betty Miller Charitable Foundation)
P.O. Box 348
Traverse City, MI 49685-0348
County: Grand Traverse
Contact: Kelly E. Miller, Dir.

Established in 1985 in MI.
Donors: C.E. Miller; Betty E. Miller.
Grantmaker type: Independent foundation.
Financial data (yr. ended 09/30/08): Assets, $45,773 (M); expenditures, $73,253; total giving, $70,000; qualifying distributions, $70,000; giving activities include $70,000 for grants.
Purpose and activities: Giving primarily for higher education, as well as for Christian elementary and secondary education.
Fields of interest: Elementary/secondary education; Higher education, college; Health care; Christian agencies & churches.
Type of support: General/operating support; Capital campaigns; Building/renovation; Scholarship funds.
Limitations: Applications accepted. Giving primarily in MI; some giving also in OH.
Application information: Application form not required.
Initial approach: Letter
Deadline(s): None
Officers: Clyde E. Miller, Pres.; Betty E. Miller, V.P.
Directors: Sue E. Bell; Daniel R. Miller; David A. Miller; Kelly E. Miller.
EIN: 382620981
Selected grants: The following grants were reported in 2007.
$80,000 to Traverse City Christian School, Traverse City, MI.
$30,000 to Cornerstone University, Grand Rapids, MI.

563
J. William & Lorraine M. Miller Family Foundation
2814 Canterbury Dr.
Midland, MI 48642-6611
County: Midland

Established in 1992 in MI.
Donors: J. William Miller; Lorraine M. Miller.
Grantmaker type: Independent foundation.
Financial data (yr. ended 12/31/09): Assets, $654,412 (M); gifts received, $577; expenditures, $28,081; total giving, $27,500; qualifying distributions, $27,500; giving activities include $27,500 for grants to individuals.
Purpose and activities: Scholarship awards to high school graduates from Saginaw, Bay, and Midland counties, Michigan.
Fields of interest: Higher education.
Type of support: Scholarships—to individuals.

Limitations: Giving limited to residents of Saginaw, Bay, and Midland counties, MI.
Application information: Application form required.
Initial approach: Application with high school transcript
Deadline(s): Apr. 10
Officers and Directors:* Jan E. Brauer,* Pres.; L.A. Preston,* Secy.; Virginia Morrison.
EIN: 383009465

564
Gordon and Gayle Miller Foundation
3099 Main St.
P.O. Box 188
Marlette, MI 48453-1243
County: Sanilac
Contact: W. Gordon Miller, Tr.

Established in 2005 in MI.
Donor: W. Gordon Miller.
Grantmaker type: Independent foundation.
Financial data (yr. ended 12/31/09): Assets, $612,370 (M); gifts received, $100,000; expenditures, $27,400; total giving, $27,250; qualifying distributions, $27,250; giving activities include $27,250 for 5 grants (high: $20,000; low: $250).
Fields of interest: Higher education; Hospitals (general).
Limitations: Applications accepted. Giving primarily in MI and MN. No grants to individuals.
Application information: Application form not required.
Deadline(s): None
Officers: W. Gordon Miller, Pres.; David Miller, V.P.; Peggy Macumber, Secy.; Deborah Langolf, Treas.
EIN: 203929241

565
The Miller Foundation
310 WahWahTaySee Way
Battle Creek, MI 49015-4065 (269) 964-3542
County: Calhoun
Contact: Diane Thompson, Exec. Dir.
FAX: (269) 964-8455;
E-mail: dthompson@millerfdn.org; URL: http://www.themillerfoundation.org/

Incorporated in 1963 in MI.
Donors: Louise B. Miller‡; Robert B. Miller‡.
Grantmaker type: Independent foundation.
Financial data (yr. ended 12/31/09): Assets, $25,274,336 (M); expenditures, $1,015,444; total giving, $616,822; qualifying distributions, $616,822; giving activities include $616,822 for 39 grants (high: $451,000; low: $100).
Purpose and activities: Giving mainly to improve the quality of life in the Battle Creek, MI, community area by supporting local organizations and government agencies that provide for economic development, neighborhood improvement, improving educational outcomes for youth, and eliminating barriers to employment for all in Battle Creek, MI, and the surrounding area.
Fields of interest: Adult/continuing education; Human services; Children/youth, services; Community development, neighborhood development; Economic development.
Type of support: Scholarship funds; Management development/capacity building; Employee matching gifts; General/operating support; Annual

campaigns; Capital campaigns; Building/renovation; Equipment; Emergency funds; Program development; Seed money; Consulting services; Program-related investments/loans; Matching/challenge support.
Limitations: Applications accepted. Giving limited to the greater Battle Creek, MI, area. No support for religious or political organizations. No grants to individuals, or for endowments.
Publications: Application guidelines; Annual report; Annual report (including application guidelines).
Application information: Application guidelines available on foundation web site. Application form required.
Initial approach: Initial letter
Copies of proposal: 11
Deadline(s): Jan. 1, Mar. 1, May 1, July 1, Sept. 1, and Nov. 1
Board meeting date(s): Jan., Mar., May, July, Sept., and Nov.
Final notification: 2 months
Officers and Trustees:* Barbara L. Comai,* Chair.; Greg D. Dotson,* Vice-Chair.; Rance L. Leaders,* Secy.; John J. Gallagher,* Treas.; Arthur W. Angood; Allen B. Miller; Paul R. Ohm; Gloria J. Robertson.
Number of staff: 1 full-time professional; 1 part-time support.
EIN: 386064925
Selected grants: The following grants were reported in 2009.
$451,000 to Robert B. Miller College, Battle Creek, MI. For operating support.
$25,000 to Community Inclusive Recreation, Battle Creek, MI. For arts studio.
$25,000 to Neighborhoods, Inc. of Battle Creek, Battle Creek, MI.
$25,000 to United Way of Greater Battle Creek, Battle Creek, MI. For community solutions.
$24,590 to Seconds New Vision and Outreach Ministries, Battle Creek, MI. For reading program.
$15,000 to Music Center of South Central Michigan, Battle Creek, MI. For IMPACT Program.
$10,000 to Alano Club of Battle Creek, Battle Creek, MI. For Community Recovery Center.
$6,000 to Kingman Museum, Battle Creek, MI. For archives project.
$5,000 to Calhoun Health Plan, Battle Creek, MI. For operating support.
$5,000 to Community Action Agency of South Central Michigan, Battle Creek, MI. For VITA program.

566
Louise Tuller Miller Trust
c/o JPMorgan Chase Bank, N.A.
611 Woodward Ave. MI1-8088
Detroit, MI 48226-3408 (313) 226-0882
County: Wayne
Contact: Tammie D. Poplar, Fiduciary Client Svc. Assoc.

Established in 1961 in MI.
Donor: Louise Tuller Miller‡.
Grantmaker type: Independent foundation.
Financial data (yr. ended 06/30/10): Assets, $1,303,863 (M); expenditures, $30,322; total giving, $20,000; qualifying distributions, $24,527; giving activities include $20,000 for 1 grant.
Fields of interest: Education; Mental health, treatment; Human services; Children/youth, services; Civil/human rights.
Type of support: General/operating support; Continuing support; Annual campaigns; Capital

campaigns; Endowments; Program development; Curriculum development; Scholarship funds.
Limitations: Applications accepted. Giving limited to MI, with emphasis on Detroit and southeastern MI. No grants for individuals.
Publications: Application guidelines.
Application information: Application form not required.
Initial approach: Letter
Copies of proposal: 2
Deadline(s): None
Board meeting date(s): Varies
Trustees: Harry S. Stark; JPMorgan Chase Bank, N.A.
EIN: 386046007

567
Frances Goll Mills Fund
c/o Citizens Bank, N.A.
328 S. Saginaw St., MC 002072
Flint, MI 48502-1923
County: Genesee
Application address: c/o Citizens Bank, N.A., Attn.: Helen James, 101 N. Washington Ave., Saginaw, MI 48607-1207, tel.: (989) 776-7368

Established in 1982 in MI.
Donor: Frances Goll Mills‡.
Grantmaker type: Independent foundation.
Financial data (yr. ended 09/30/10): Assets, $5,046,392 (M); expenditures, $224,532; total giving, $165,397; qualifying distributions, $195,356; giving activities include $165,397 for 12 grants (high: $50,000; low: $4,000).
Fields of interest: Elementary/secondary education; Higher education; Environmental education; Health care, cost containment; Health care; Employment, vocational rehabilitation; Youth development; Human services; YM/YWCAs & YM/YWHAs; Protestant agencies & churches.
Type of support: General/operating support; Scholarship funds.
Limitations: Applications accepted. Giving limited to MI, with emphasis on Bay City, Midland, and Saginaw. No grants to individuals; no loans.
Publications: Application guidelines.
Application information: Application form required.
Initial approach: Letter or proposal requesting application guidelines
Copies of proposal: 1
Deadline(s): None
Board meeting date(s): 3rd Thurs. of Mar., June, Sept., and Dec.
Trustee: Citizens Bank.
EIN: 382434002
Selected grants: The following grants were reported in 2009.
$50,000 to First Congregational Church, Saginaw, MI.
$40,000 to Delta College Foundation, University Center, MI.
$40,000 to First Congregational Church, Saginaw, MI.
$40,000 to YMCA, Bay Area Family, Bay City, MI.
$20,000 to New Dimensions, Bay City, MI.
$15,000 to YMCA, Bay Area Family, Bay City, MI.
$6,666 to Saginaw Community Foundation, Saginaw, MI.
$5,000 to First Congregational Church, Saginaw, MI.
$5,000 to Little Forks Conservancy, Midland, MI.
$4,000 to Delta College, University Center, MI.

568
Allan C. Mims & Margaret L. Mims Charitable Trust
c/o Comerica Bank
P.O. Box 75000, MC 3302
Detroit, MI 48275-3302
County: Wayne
Application address: Sharon Stephens, 130 S.
Franklin Rd., Rocky Mount, NC 27802-5707,
tel.: (252) 467-4743

Established in 2000 in NC.
Grantmaker type: Independent foundation.
Financial data (yr. ended 12/31/09): Assets,
$1,103,023 (M); expenditures, $90,685; total
giving, $58,000; qualifying distributions, $58,000;
giving activities include $58,000 for grants.
Fields of interest: Arts; Higher education; YM/
YWCAs & YM/YWHAs.
Type of support: Scholarship funds.
Limitations: Applications accepted. Giving limited to
the eastern portion of NC, primarily in Rocky Mount.
No grants to individuals.
Application information: Application form required.
Initial approach: Letter
Deadline(s): None
Trustees: Thomas A. Betts, Jr.; Lou Uzzle Blackman;
G. Allen Ives III; William R. Johnston, Jr.; Comerica
Bank.
EIN: 566207750

569
Katharine B. Miner Charitable
c/o JPMorgan Chase Bank, N.A.
P.O. Box 3038
Milwaukee, WI 53201-3038
County: Milwaukee
Application address: c/o JPMorgan Chase Bank,
N.A., Attn.: Steven Christiansen, Trust Off., 125 S.
Main St., Ann Arbor, MI 48104-1902, tel.: (734)
995-8027

Established in MI.
Grantmaker type: Independent foundation.
Financial data (yr. ended 10/31/09): Assets,
$647,786 (M); expenditures, $45,532; total giving,
$37,171; qualifying distributions, $37,171; giving
activities include $37,171 for grants.
Fields of interest: Arts; Housing/shelter; United
Ways and Federated Giving Programs; Protestant
agencies & churches.
Limitations: Giving limited to MI, with emphasis on
Flint. No grants to individuals.
Application information:
Initial approach: Letter
Deadline(s): None
Trustee: JPMorgan Chase Bank, N.A.
EIN: 386419379

570
Helen Lancaster Minton Educational Trust
c/o Comerica Bank
P.O. Box 75000, MC 3302
Detroit, MI 48275-3302 (252) 467-4743
County: Wayne
Application address: c/o Sharon Stephens, 130 S.
Franklin St., Rocky Mount, NC 27804-5707

Donor: Helen Lancaster Minton.
Grantmaker type: Independent foundation.

Financial data (yr. ended 03/31/10): Assets,
$609,108 (M); expenditures, $48,615; total giving,
$4,000; qualifying distributions, $4,000; giving
activities include $4,000 for grants to individuals.
Purpose and activities: Grant awards to North
Carolina Wesleyan College, Rocky Mount, for high
school graduates from Edgecombe and Nash
counties pursuing a college degree.
Fields of interest: Higher education.
Type of support: Scholarship funds.
Limitations: Giving limited to residents of
Edgecombe and Nash counties, NC.
Application information: Application form required.
Deadline(s): May 1
Trustee: Comerica Bank.
EIN: 566180453

571
The Mistele Foundation, Inc.
(formerly Christian Advancement, Inc.)
100 W. Big Beaver Rd., Ste. 385
Troy, MI 48084-5283
County: Oakland

Established in MI.
Donors: Harold E. Mistele; Henry E. Mistele;
Elisabeth M. Mistele.
Grantmaker type: Independent foundation.
Financial data (yr. ended 12/31/09): Assets,
$46,521 (M); gifts received, $5,000; expenditures,
$1,599; total giving, $1,000; qualifying
distributions, $1,000; giving activities include
$1,000 for grants.
Officers: Henry E. Mistele, Pres.; Elisabeth M.
Mistele, Secy.-Treas.
EIN: 386089267

572
Mitchell Foundation
P.O. Box 1592
Owosso, MI 48867-6592 (989) 725-2172
County: Shiawassee
Contact: Lara Bramer, Tr.

Established in 1962 in MI.
Grantmaker type: Independent foundation.
Financial data (yr. ended 12/31/09): Assets,
$103,493 (M); expenditures, $6,058; total giving,
$5,400; qualifying distributions, $5,400; giving
activities include $5,400 for grants.
Fields of interest: Animal welfare; Children/youth,
services; Foundations (community).
Type of support: Program development.
Limitations: Giving primarily in MI. No grants to
individuals.
Application information: Application form not
required.
Initial approach: Letter
Deadline(s): None
Trustees: Lara Bramer; Christine L. Mitchell; William
F. Mitchell.
EIN: 386091190

573
The Larry & Celia Moh Foundation
(formerly The Celia Moh Foundation)
404B E. Main St.
Charlottesville, VA 22902-5236
County: Charlottesville City

Established in 2002 in NC.
Donors: Sorgente No. 3 Trust; Sorgente
Investments LLC.
Grantmaker type: Independent foundation.
Financial data (yr. ended 12/31/09): Assets,
$18,699,597 (M); expenditures, $698,136; total
giving, $606,510; qualifying distributions,
$606,510; giving activities include $606,510 for
grants.
Purpose and activities: Scholarship funds for
students provided through the qualified institutions.
Fields of interest: Higher education; Scholarships/
financial aid.
Type of support: Scholarship funds.
Limitations: Giving primarily in CA, MI, and NC.
Officer: Joe Carroll, Pres.
Directors: Celia Moh; Michael Moh; R. Ted
Weschler.
EIN: 680492736
Selected grants: The following grants were reported
in 2009.
$96,846 to High Point University, High Point, NC.
$39,541 to East Carolina University, Greenville, NC.
$20,502 to Appalachian State University, Boone,
NC.
$13,493 to North Carolina State University, Raleigh,
NC.

574
Mojo Foundation
5940 Tahoe Dr. S.E.
Grand Rapids, MI 49546-7121 (616) 455-0200
County: Kent
Contact: Michael A. McGraw, Pres.

Established in 1996 in MI.
Donor: Michael A. McGraw.
Grantmaker type: Independent foundation.
Financial data (yr. ended 12/31/09): Assets,
$4,747,195 (M); gifts received, $1,500;
expenditures, $292,152; total giving, $244,000;
qualifying distributions, $244,020; giving activities
include $244,000 for 19 grants (high: $100,000;
low: $250).
Fields of interest: Human services; Children,
services; Family services; Christian agencies &
churches.
Limitations: Applications accepted. Giving primarily
in Grand Rapids, MI. No grants to individuals.
Application information:
Initial approach: Letter
Deadline(s): None
Officers: Michael A. McGraw, Pres.; Michael R.
McGraw, V.P. and Secy.; Joshua D. McGraw, V.P.
EIN: 383325750
Selected grants: The following grants were reported
in 2007.
$16,000 to Church of the Nazarene, Global Treasury
Services, Kansas City, MO.
$10,000 to Home Repair Services of Kent County,
Grand Rapids, MI.
$10,000 to Inner City Christian Federation, Grand
Rapids, MI.
$10,000 to Saint Johns Home, Grand Rapids, MI.
$5,000 to Pregnancy Resource Center, Grand
Rapids, MI.
$3,500 to Fair Housing Center of West Michigan,
Grand Rapids, MI.
$1,000 to Family Life, Little Rock, AR.
$1,000 to Focus on the Family, Colorado Springs,
CO.
$1,000 to Interact Ministries, Boring, OR.

$1,000 to International Justice Mission, Washington, DC.

575
Molinello Family Foundation

P.O. Box 721067
Berkley, MI 48072-0067 (248) 544-2775
County: Oakland
Contact: Earl C. Bossenberry, Pres.

Established in 2000 in MI.
Donors: Richard Molinello Revocable Trust; John Molinello Revocable Trust.
Grantmaker type: Independent foundation.
Financial data (yr. ended 12/31/09): Assets, $15,425,415 (M); expenditures, $854,263; total giving, $850,000; qualifying distributions, $854,263; giving activities include $850,000 for 25 grants (high: $58,000; low: $2,000).
Fields of interest: Health care; Medical research, institute; Human services; Christian agencies & churches; Blind/visually impaired; Economically disadvantaged.
Limitations: Giving primarily in MI.
Application information:
Initial approach: Letter
Deadline(s): None
Officers: Earl C. Bossenberry, Pres.; Rita Morelli, V.P.
EIN: 383494266
Selected grants: The following grants were reported in 2005.
$47,130 to American Red Cross, Bay City, MI.
$47,130 to Capuchin Soup Kitchen, Detroit, MI.
$47,130 to Guest House, Lake Orion, MI.
$47,130 to Leader Dogs for the Blind, Rochester, MI.
$47,130 to Little Sisters of the Poor, Milwaukee, WI.
$47,130 to Salvation Army, MI.
$4,000 to Furniture Bank of Oakland County, Pontiac, MI.
$3,000 to Angels Place, Southfield, MI.
$2,000 to Gildas Club Metro Detroit, Royal Oak, MI.

576
Molloy Foundation, Inc.

2651 Hawthorne Rd.
Ann Arbor, MI 48104-4033 (248) 720-2669
County: Washtenaw

Established in 1962 in MI.
Donor: Brian J. Molloy‡.
Grantmaker type: Independent foundation.
Financial data (yr. ended 01/31/10): Assets, $1,222,653 (M); expenditures, $95,018; total giving, $44,500; qualifying distributions, $53,697; giving activities include $44,500 for 17 grants (high: $5,000; low: $500).
Fields of interest: Education; Human services; Catholic agencies & churches.
Type of support: General/operating support; Continuing support.
Limitations: Applications accepted. Giving primarily in MI, with some emphasis on Ann Arbor and Detroit. No grants to individuals.
Application information: Application form not required.
Initial approach: Letter
Deadline(s): None
Officers: Constance M. Kinnear, Pres.-Treas.; Catherine B. Molloy, V.P.; Stephen P. Molloy, Secy.

Directors: Mary Alice Molloy; Thomas C. Molloy.
EIN: 386061859

577
Monroe-Brown Foundation

7950 Moorsbridge Rd., Rm. 300
Portage, MI 49024-4420 (269) 324-5586
County: Kalamazoo
Contact: Jane Baker, Dir.
FAX: (269) 324-0686;
E-mail: jbaker@monroebrown.org; *URL:* http://www.monroebrown.org

Incorporated in 1983 in MI.
Donors: Albertine M. Brown‡; Robert J. Brown‡; Robert M. Brown; Gail B. Kasdorf; Jane B. Todd; Robert J. Brown Charitable Lead Trust.
Grantmaker type: Independent foundation.
Financial data (yr. ended 12/31/09): Assets, $13,536,183 (M); gifts received, $25,196; expenditures, $754,656; total giving, $599,106; qualifying distributions, $665,226; giving activities include $599,106 for 30 grants (high: $271,457; low: $100).
Purpose and activities: The mission of the foundation is twofold: to provide support for higher education in the State of Michigan, and to advance economic development in the Kalamazoo community through programs designed to encourage the retention and employment of local scholars.
Fields of interest: Arts; Higher education; Education; Human services; Urban/community development; Foundations (community).
Type of support: Annual campaigns; Capital campaigns; Building/renovation; Program development; Matching/challenge support.
Limitations: Giving primarily in the Kalamazoo, MI area. No grants to individuals.
Publications: Application guidelines.
Application information: Application guidelines and form available on foundation Web site. Application form required.
Initial approach: Letter
Copies of proposal: 7
Deadline(s): Mar. 31, June 30, Sept. 30, and Nov. 20
Board meeting date(s): Apr., July, Oct. and Dec.
Officers and Trustees:* Robert M. Brown,* Pres.; Gail B. Kasdorf,* V.P.; Jane B. Todd,* Treas.; Frederick O. Brown; Robert M. Brown, Jr.; A. John Todd; John C. Wattles.
Director: Jane Baker.
Number of staff: 1 full-time professional.
EIN: 382513263
Selected grants: The following grants were reported in 2006.
$180,000 to University of Michigan, Ann Arbor, MI.
$87,067 to Western Michigan University Foundation, Kalamazoo, MI.
$62,000 to Kalamazoo Community Foundation, Kalamazoo, MI.
$54,014 to Kalamazoo College, Kalamazoo, MI.
$40,000 to Western Michigan University Foundation, Kalamazoo, MI.
$17,247 to Kalamazoo Valley Community College, Kalamazoo, MI.
$10,000 to Communities in Schools Foundation, Kalamazoo, Kalamazoo, MI.
$6,000 to University of Michigan, Ann Arbor, MI.
$2,905 to University of Michigan, Ann Arbor, MI.
$2,500 to University of Michigan, Ann Arbor, MI.

578
Frederick S. & Lezlynne P. Moore Family Foundation

1362 N River Rd
St. Clair, MI 48079-4265 (810) 326-1123
County: St. Clair
Contact: Frederick S. Moore, Pres.

Established in 1998 in MI.
Donors: Lezlynne P. Moore; Frederick S. Moore.
Grantmaker type: Independent foundation.
Financial data (yr. ended 12/31/09): Assets, $803,769 (M); expenditures, $41,029; total giving, $37,300; qualifying distributions, $37,300; giving activities include $37,300 for 5 grants (high: $30,000; low: $400).
Fields of interest: Human services; United Ways and Federated Giving Programs; Protestant agencies & churches.
Type of support: General/operating support; Continuing support; Annual campaigns; Capital campaigns; Building/renovation; Equipment; Land acquisition; Emergency funds; Program-related investments/loans; Matching/challenge support.
Limitations: Applications accepted. Giving primarily in St. Clair County, MI. No grants to individuals.
Application information: Application form not required.
Initial approach: Letter
Copies of proposal: 1
Officers: Frederick S. Moore, Pres.; Lezlynne P. Moore, Secy.; Franklin H. Moore, Treas.
EIN: 383440665

579
Mary Moore Foundation

c/o Fifth Third Bank
P.O. Box 3636
Grand Rapids, MI 49501-3636
County: Kent
Contact: Franklin H. Moore, Jr., Pres.
Application address: c/o Fifth Third Bank, 200 S. Riverside, St. Clair, MI 48079, tel.: (810) 326-1123

Established in 1950 in MI.
Grantmaker type: Independent foundation.
Financial data (yr. ended 12/31/09): Assets, $896,369 (M); expenditures, $49,851; total giving, $41,000; qualifying distributions, $41,275; giving activities include $41,000 for 11 grants (high: $13,000; low: $1,000).
Purpose and activities: Giving primarily to Christian organizations and churches and for health and human services.
Fields of interest: Health care; Human services; YM/YWCAs & YM/YWHAs; Children/youth, services; Community/economic development; United Ways and Federated Giving Programs; Christian agencies & churches.
Type of support: General/operating support; Program development.
Limitations: Giving primarily in St. Clair, MI. No grants to individuals.
Application information:
Initial approach: Letter
Deadline(s): None
Officers: Franklin H. Moore, Jr., Pres.; Frederick S. Moore, V.P.; Charles W. Staiger, Secy.-Treas.
Trustee: Fifth Third Bank.
EIN: 386097348

580
Joan I. & John R. Moore III Foundation
c/o Comerica Bank
P.O. Box 75000, MC 3300
Detroit, MI 48275-3300 (313) 222-5257
County: Wayne
Contact: Paula Gralewski, Trust Off., Comerica Bank

Established in 2000 in OH.
Grantmaker type: Independent foundation.
Financial data (yr. ended 12/31/09): Assets,
$197,063 (M); expenditures, $15,721; total giving,
$11,970; qualifying distributions, $12,970; giving
activities include $11,970 for 6 grants (high:
$3,000; low: $100).
Fields of interest: Catholic agencies & churches.
Limitations: Applications accepted. Giving primarily
in OH. No scholarships.
Application information:
  Initial approach: Letter
  Deadline(s): None
Trustee: Comerica Bank.
EIN: 386752915

581
Carl & Irene Morath Foundation, Inc.
747 Ballantyne Rd.
Grosse Pointe Shores, MI 48236-1568
(586) 415-0995
County: Wayne
Contact: Carl Morath, Pres.

Established in MI.
Donors: Carl Morath; Irene Morath.
Grantmaker type: Independent foundation.
Financial data (yr. ended 12/31/09): Assets,
$2,400,373 (M); expenditures, $101,047; total
giving, $97,000; qualifying distributions, $97,000;
giving activities include $97,000 for 21 grants (high:
$15,000; low: $1,000).
Purpose and activities: Giving primarily for Roman
Catholic missionary work.
Fields of interest: Higher education; Food banks;
Human services; Religious federated giving
programs; Catholic agencies & churches.
International interests: Mexico.
Limitations: Applications accepted. Giving primarily
in MI. No grants to individuals.
Application information: Application form not
required.
  Initial approach: Letter
  Deadline(s): None
Officers: Paul Morath, Pres.; Lawrence Morath, V.P.;
Frederick Morath, Secy.-Treas.
EIN: 382421500

582
The Morey Foundation
P.O. Box 374
Winn, MI 48896-0374
County: Isabella
Application address: c/o Lon Morey, Pres., P.O. Box
1000, Winn, MI 48896-1000, tel.: (989) 866-2381

Established in 1990 in MI.
Donor: Norval Morey.
Grantmaker type: Independent foundation.
Financial data (yr. ended 12/31/09): Assets,
$33,432,030 (M); expenditures, $1,996,142; total
giving, $1,541,715; qualifying distributions,

$1,598,117; giving activities include $1,541,715
for 44 grants (high: $300,000; low: $50).
Purpose and activities: Scholarships are limited to
students of Central Michigan University.
Fields of interest: Higher education; Education;
Hospitals (general); Human services; Public policy,
research.
Type of support: Scholarship funds.
Limitations: Giving primarily in MI, with emphasis on
Mount Pleasant. No grants to individuals directly.
Application information: Application form required
for scholarship requests.
  Initial approach: Letter
  Deadline(s): Mar. 15 for scholarships; none for
  grants
Officers and Trustees:* Lon Morey,* Pres.; Krista
Morey,* V.P.; Terra Lynn Boone,* V.P.; Hugo E.
Braun, Jr., Secy.; Larry H. Noch, Treas.
EIN: 382965346
Selected grants: The following grants were reported
in 2009.
$200,000 to Central Michigan University, Mount
Pleasant, MI.
$35,000 to Central Michigan University, Mount
Pleasant, MI.
$10,000 to Shepherd Public Schools, Shepherd, MI.
$5,000 to Central Michigan University, Mount
Pleasant, MI.
$5,000 to Mount Pleasant High School, Mount
Pleasant, MI.
$2,050 to Mount Pleasant High School, Mount
Pleasant, MI.

583
Barbara Morgan Memorial Trust
c/o Citizens Bank Wealth Mgmt., N.A.
328 S. Saginaw St., M/C 001065
Flint, MI 48502-1923 (989) 776-7368
County: Genesee
Application address: c/o Helen James, Citizens Bank
Wealth Mgmt., N.A., 101 N. Washington Ave.,
Saginaw, MI 48607, tel.: (989) 776-7368

Established in 1998 in MI.
Donor: Barbara Morgan Trust.
Grantmaker type: Independent foundation.
Financial data (yr. ended 12/31/09): Assets,
$112,391 (M); expenditures, $6,760; total giving,
$2,325; qualifying distributions, $4,782; giving
activities include $2,325 for 2 grants (high: $1,325;
low: $1,000).
Purpose and activities: Grants awarded to Michigan
schools in order to bring professional musicians,
storytellers, dancers, and artists to appear in
programs or conduct workshops.
Fields of interest: Arts education; Elementary/
secondary education; Community/economic
development, public education.
Type of support: General/operating support.
Limitations: Applications accepted. Giving limited to
MI, primarily in Saginaw. No grants to individuals.
Application information: Application form required.
  Deadline(s): None
Trustee: Citizens Bank.
EIN: 383413062

584
Morley Foundation
(formerly Morley Brothers Foundation)
P.O. Box 2485
Saginaw, MI 48605-2485 (989) 753-3438
County: Saginaw
URL: http://www.morleyfdn.org/

Incorporated in 1948 in MI.
Donors: Ralph Chase Morley, Sr.‡; Mrs. Ralph
Chase Morley, Sr.‡.
Grantmaker type: Independent foundation.
Financial data (yr. ended 12/31/09): Assets,
$4,014,813 (M); expenditures, $243,798; total
giving, $164,340; qualifying distributions,
$175,593; giving activities include $164,340 for 72
grants (high: $20,000; low: $50).
Purpose and activities: Giving primarily in the areas
of welfare, health, education, civic improvement,
and the humanities in Michigan, with major
emphasis on Saginaw County.
Fields of interest: Museums; Performing arts; Arts;
Elementary school/education; Secondary school/
education; Higher education; Business school/
education; Education; Hospitals (general); Health
care; Health organizations, association; Human
services; Children/youth, services; Community/
economic development.
Type of support: General/operating support;
Continuing support; Annual campaigns; Capital
campaigns; Building/renovation; Equipment;
Emergency funds; Program development; Seed
money; Research; Employee matching gifts;
Matching/challenge support.
Limitations: Giving primarily in the greater Saginaw
County, MI, area. No grants to individuals, or for
endowment funds, deficit financing, land
acquisition, renovation projects, publications, or
conferences; no loans.
Publications: Application guidelines; Informational
brochure.
Application information: Application guidelines
available on foundation web site. Application form
required.
  Initial approach: Letter
  Copies of proposal: 1
  Board meeting date(s): Feb., May, Aug., and Nov.
  Final notification: 3 months
Officers and Trustees:* David H. Morley,* V.P.; Lois
K. Guttowsky,* Secy.; Carol Morley Beck,* Treas.;
Chase Brand; Michael Morley Brand; Sara Morley
LaCroix; Burrows Morley, Jr.; Burrows Morley III;
Christopher Morley; George B. Morley, Jr.; Katharyn
Morley; Peter Morley; Peter Morley, Jr.; Lucy
Thomson; Richard B. Thomson, Jr.
Number of staff: 1 part-time professional.
EIN: 386055569
Selected grants: The following grants were reported
in 2008.
$25,000 to Mid-Michigan Childrens Museum,
Saginaw, MI.
$10,000 to Habitat for Humanity, Saginaw,
Saginaw, MI.
$10,000 to Saginaw Art Museum, Saginaw, MI.
$5,000 to Holy Cross Childrens Services, Saginaw,
MI.
$5,000 to United Way of Saginaw County, Saginaw,
MI.
$3,000 to Junior Achievement of Northeast
Michigan, Saginaw, MI.
$3,000 to Saginaw Choral Society, Saginaw, MI.
$1,000 to American Red Cross, Saginaw, MI.
$1,000 to Saginaw County Vision 2020, Saginaw,
MI.

585
James K. Morrill Scholarship Fund
c/o Fifth Third Bank
P.O. Box 3636
Grand Rapids, MI   49501-3636   (413) 534-2020
County: Kent
Application address: c/o Holyoke High School, Attn.: Guidance Counselor, 500 Beech St., Holyoke, MA 01040-2202, tel.: (413) 534-2020

Established in 1995 in IL.
Grantmaker type: Independent foundation.
Financial data (yr. ended 12/31/09): Assets, $1,217,865 (M); expenditures, $58,639; total giving, $39,498; qualifying distributions, $39,513; giving activities include $39,498 for 7 grants to individuals (high: $5,962; low: $5,454).
Purpose and activities: Scholarship awards to female graduates from Holyoke High School, Massachusetts.
Fields of interest: Higher education.
Type of support: Scholarships—to individuals.
Limitations: Applications accepted. Giving limited to residents of Holyoke, MA.
Application information: Application form required.
   Initial approach: Letter or telephone
   Deadline(s): May 10
Trustee: Fifth Third Bank.
EIN: 367112892

586
Arno & Caroline Mossner Memorial Foundation
515 S. Main St.
Frankenmuth, MI   48734-1617
County: Saginaw
Contact: William A. Mossner, Tr.

Established in MI.
Donor: Caroline Mossner.
Grantmaker type: Independent foundation.
Financial data (yr. ended 12/31/09): Assets, $294,750 (M); expenditures, $10,692; total giving, $9,200; qualifying distributions, $9,200; giving activities include $9,200 for 16 grants (high: $2,700; low: $300).
Fields of interest: Higher education; Human services; Protestant agencies & churches.
Limitations: Applications accepted. Giving primarily in MI, with some emphasis on Frankenmuth. No grants to individuals.
Application information: Application form not required.
   Initial approach: Letter
   Deadline(s): None
Trustees: Caroline Mossner; William A. Mossner; David Beyerlein.
EIN: 237444484

587
Charles Stewart Mott Foundation
Mott Foundation Bldg.
503 S. Saginaw St., Ste. 1200
Flint, MI   48502-1851   (810) 238-5651
County: Genesee
FAX: (810) 766-1753; E-mail: info@mott.org;
URL: http://www.mott.org/

Incorporated in 1926 in MI.
Donors: Charles Stewart Mott‡; and members of the Mott family.
Grantmaker type: Independent foundation.
Financial data (yr. ended 12/31/09): Assets, $2,080,000,000 (M); expenditures, $141,190,677; total giving, $112,542,064; qualifying distributions, $127,968,394; giving activities include $110,320,830 for 432 grants (high: $20,000,000; low: $5,000), $1,342,911 for 646 employee matching gifts, and $878,323 for 16 foundation-administered programs.
Purpose and activities: To support efforts that promote a just, equitable and sustainable society with the primary focus on civil society, the environment, the area of Flint, MI and poverty. The foundation makes grants for a variety of purposes within these program areas including: philanthropy and voluntarism; assisting emerging civil societies in Central/Eastern Europe, Russia and South Africa; conservation of fresh water ecosystems in North America; reform of international finance and trade; improving the outcomes for children, youth and families at risk of persistent poverty; education and neighborhood and economic development. The foundation also makes grants to strengthen the capacity of local institutions in its home community of Flint, MI.
Fields of interest: Education; Environment, pollution control; Environment, natural resources; Employment, services; Human services; Children, services; Child development, services; Family services, parent education; Civil rights, race/intergroup relations; Economic development; Urban/community development; Rural development; Community/economic development; Voluntarism promotion; Leadership development; Children/youth; Young adults; Minorities; Economically disadvantaged.
International interests: Eastern & Central Europe; Latin America; Russia; South Africa; Ukraine.
Type of support: General/operating support; Continuing support; Management development/capacity building; Program development; Conferences/seminars; Seed money; Technical assistance; Program evaluation; Program-related investments/loans; Employee matching gifts; Matching/challenge support.
Limitations: Applications accepted. Giving nationally and to emerging countries in Central and Eastern Europe, Russia, and South Africa. No support for religious organizations for religious purposes. No grants to individuals, or for building or endowment funds in general or for research, film or video projects, books, scholarships, or fellowships.
Publications: Annual report (including application guidelines); Financial statement; Occasional report.
Application information: Applicants strongly encouraged to submit proposals during first quarter of the year. Letter of inquiry form available online. Application form not required.
   Initial approach: Letter of inquiry or proposal
   Copies of proposal: 1
   Deadline(s): None; grants are determined by Aug. 31 of any given year
   Board meeting date(s): Mar., June, Sept., and Dec.
   Final notification: 60 to 90 days
Officers and Trustees:* William S. White,* Chair., C.E.O. and Pres.; Frederick S. Kirkpatrick,* Vice-Chair.; Maureen H. Smyth, Sr. V.P., Progs. and Comms.; Phillip H. Peters, V.P., Admin. Group and Secy.-Treas.; Michael J. Smith, V.P., Investments and C.I.O.; Gavin T. Clabaugh, V.P., Inf. Svcs.; Neal R. Hegarty, V.P. and Assoc. Dir., Progs.; Carol D. Rugg, V.P., Comms.; Ridgway H. White, V.P., Special Projects; A. Marshall Acuff, Jr.; Rushworth M.

Kidder; Tiffany W. Lovett; Webb F. Martin; Olivia P. Maynard; John Morning; Maryanne Mott; Charlie Nelms; Douglas X. Patino; William H. Piper; John W. Porter; Marise M.M. Stewart; Claire M. White.
Number of staff: 57 full-time professional; 25 full-time support.
EIN: 381211227
Selected grants: The following grants were reported in 2010.
$7,000,000 to Foundation for the Uptown Reinvestment Corporation, Flint, MI. For repayable grant increase for work to expand Riverfront Residence Hall project, increasing number of available beds from 243 to 541 for the 2010 academic year. Building originally constructed as the Hyatt Regency Hotel, has been converted into state-of-the-art residence hall for local universities. Grantee will provide grant funds to supported organization, Uptown Reinvestment Corporation, which intends to use funds to invest in the project, payable over 8.00 years.
$3,100,000 to Genesee Area Focus Fund, Flint, MI. For operating support for YouthQuest After School Initiative, formerly known as the Bridges to the Future Afterschool Program. Mission of YouthQuest is to provide children with opportunities to grow through safe, engaging and exciting afterschool learning experience, surrounded with caring, responsible adults and sustained by involved, contributing community.
$2,626,390 to Community Foundation of Greater Flint, Flint, MI. To add to endowment funds established for the benefit of the Foundation, the Flint Cultural Center Corporation, the Flint Institute of Arts, and the Flint Institute of Music. Endowments will provide general operating support to these community institutions.
$1,000,000 to Afterschool Alliance, Washington, DC. For general support to continue to support vision that all children and youth, particularly those in underserved populations, will have access to quality, affordable afterschool programs.
$500,000 to Great Lakes Commission, Ann Arbor, MI. To bring together decisionmakers and stakeholders from across the Great Lakes to identify how to restore the natural division between the Mississippi and the Great Lakes as a way to halt Asian Carp movement while providing economic, social, and environmental benefits to the region. Asian Carp is an invasive species poised to enter and disrupt the Great Lakes ecosystem thorugh connections to the Mississippi River, payable over 1.50 years.
$420,000 to National Employment Law Project, New York, NY. For technical assistance initiative to bolster Michigan's and Flint's knowledge of how to piece together a rapid and effective response to severe job loss and economic dislocation. Initiative promotes battery of better practices that have proven more effective in getting workers to participate in retraining and take fuller advantage of range of dislocated worker programs. In Flint, grantee will continue to deploy dislocated worker facilitator, payable over 2.00 years.
$300,000 to State Environmental Leadership Program, Madison, WI. To engage state and local environmental groups in broad-based efforts to inform policymakers, media and public about the federal deficit and implications of various proposals to reduce the budget deficit and/or reform budget processes. Goal of efforts is to ensure that sufficient federal resources will be available in short and long term to address key social priorities in our country. Grantee will support communications

activities and technical assistance and provide small grants to select number of member organizations, payable over 2.00 years.
$150,000 to Foundation Center, New York, NY. To continue to support efforts to provide education funders with the most up-to-date, relevant, and in-depth information about education reform to help drive strategy development. Specifically, the Center will: 1) reorganize the content of the Web-based portal and add other relevant features to the site; 2) launch Philanthropy In/Sight - Education Edition, a custom-designed data visualization tool to help education grantmakers assess areas where funding investments might have the greatest impact; 3) issue research briefs, shifting the focus of the e-newsletter to include more state information and update the research area of the Web-based portal; 4) support the Moving Forward conference by providing statistical information on education-related funding; and 5) hold a monthly series of teleconferences and webinars during the coming year that will focus on issues of most concern to education grantmakers working on long-term reform efforts.
$120,000 to Ikhala Trust, Port Elizabeth, South Africa. For general operating support, payable over 1.75 years.
$90,000 to Bulgarian Donors Forum, Sofia, Bulgaria. For general suppor toward consolidating and strengthening the philanthropic community in Bulgaria, payable over 3.00 years.

588
Ruth Mott Foundation
111 E. Court St., Ste. 3C
Flint, MI   48502-1649   (810) 233-0170
County: Genesee
Contact: Joy Murray, Fdn. Secy.
FAX: (810) 233-7022; E-mail: rmf@rmfdn.org; E-mail (for Joy Murray): jmurray@rmfdn.org; URL: http://www.ruthmottfoundation.org

Established in 1989 in MI.
Donor: Ruth R. Mott†.
Grantmaker type: Independent foundation.
Financial data (yr. ended 12/31/09): Assets, $198,621,065 (M); gifts received, $2,500; expenditures, $11,487,136; total giving, $8,642,088; qualifying distributions, $10,397,171; giving activities include $6,798,247 for 140 grants (high: $1,161,489; low: $45), and $1,843,841 for 4 foundation-administered programs.
Purpose and activities: Giving primarily for community arts, community health promotion, and community beautification.
Fields of interest: Arts, cultural/ethnic awareness; Arts; Higher education; Libraries (public); Education; Health care; Youth development; Human services; Children/youth, services; Community/economic development; Foundations (community); United Ways and Federated Giving Programs; Protestant agencies & churches.
Type of support: General/operating support; Continuing support; Management development/ capacity building; Program development; Scholarship funds; Technical assistance; Program evaluation; Matching/challenge support.
Limitations: Applications accepted. Giving primarily in Genesee County and Flint, MI. No grants to individual scholarships or fellowships, or for capital projects, major equipment, land purchases, deficit financing, endowments, or renovations; no loans.

Publications: Annual report; Annual report (including application guidelines); Grants list; Informational brochure (including application guidelines); Multi-year report; Newsletter; Program policy statement.
Application information: Application form not required.
  Initial approach: Letter (2 - 3 pages)
  Copies of proposal: 2
  Deadline(s): Jan. 15, Apr. 15, and Sept. 15
  Board meeting date(s): Mar., June, and Nov.
  Final notification: 1 month
Officers and Trustees:* Maryanne T. Mott,* Pres.; Dolores Ennis, Secy.; Joseph R. Robinson, Treas.; Maria Jordan, Cont.; Steven M. Wilson, Exec. Dir.; Gloria Coles; Harriet Kenworthy; Lawrence E. Moon; Melissa Patterson; Robert Pestronk.
Number of staff: 15 full-time professional; 9 full-time support; 2 part-time support.
EIN: 382876435
Selected grants: The following grants were reported in 2009.
$350,000 to Marin Community Foundation, Novato, CA. For RMF Donor Advised Fund.
$272,238 to United Way of Genesee County, Flint, MI. For BEST Non-Profit Capacity Building Collaborative Supplement - Third Cohort, payable over 3.25 years.
$206,728 to Foundation for Mott Community College, Flint, MI. For Beecher Scholarship Incentive Program (BSIP).
$200,000 to Priority Children, Flint, MI. For training and technical assistance to replicate Flint Carrera, project which provides pregnancy prevention education and activities for 11-12 year olds that will continue through graduation from high school, payable over 2.00 years.
$150,000 to Flint Institute of Music, Flint, MI. For outreach programs, payable over 1.50 years.
$142,000 to Crim Fitness Foundation, Flint, MI. For Safe and Active Genesee for Everyone (SAGE), payable over 2.00 years.
$83,650 to Genesee Intermediate School District, Flint, MI. For Comprehensive Sexuality - Train the Trainer Program, payable over 2.00 years.
$55,000 to Christ Enrichment Center, Flint, MI. For Arts R 4 U Program.
$50,000 to Urban League of Flint, Flint, MI. For general operating support.
$16,750 to Flint, City of, Flint, MI. For Neighborhood Action - Community Forums.

589
Mt. Zion Lutheran Church Foundation
42681 Jason Ct.
Sterling Heights, MI   48313-2632
(586) 739-9219
County: Macomb
Contact: Robert Hughes, V.P.

Established in 1997 in MI.
Grantmaker type: Independent foundation.
Financial data (yr. ended 09/30/09): Assets, $425,716 (M); gifts received, $3,540; expenditures, $26,426; total giving, $22,459; qualifying distributions, $22,459; giving activities include $22,459 for grants.
Purpose and activities: Giving primarily for Lutheran churches and selected Michigan support communities programs.
Fields of interest: Protestant agencies & churches.
Type of support: Building/renovation; Program development; Publication; Seed money.

Limitations: Applications accepted. Giving primarily in Macomb, Oakland and Wayne counties, MI. No grants to individuals.
Publications: Annual report; Financial statement; Grants list; Newsletter.
Application information: Application form required.
  Deadline(s): Mar. 15
Officers: David Fox, Pres.; Diane Rotha, V.P.; Robert Hughes, V.P.; Arlene Kangas, Secy.; Evelyne Russell, Treas.
Directors: Gustav Jensen; Nancy Kaminski; Norman Rotha; Harold Schlachtenhaufen; Kari Schlachtenhaufen; Madeline Smith; Stanley Smith.
EIN: 383364539

590
Chuck Muer and Chef Larry Memorial Scholarship Fund
21 Beacon Hill Rd.
Grosse Pointe Farms, MI   48236-3001
County: Wayne
Contact: Leo J. Beil, Pres.

Established in MI.
Grantmaker type: Independent foundation.
Financial data (yr. ended 12/31/09): Assets, $23,508 (M); expenditures, $7,001; total giving, $5,000; qualifying distributions, $5,000; giving activities include $5,000 for grants.
Purpose and activities: Funding for training at culinary institutes.
Fields of interest: Vocational education.
Application information:
  Initial approach: Letter
  Deadline(s): None
Officers: Leo J. Beil, Pres.; Greg Ochoa, V.P.
EIN: 382508826

591
Mukkamala Family Foundation
4545 Warwick Cir.
Grand Blanc, MI   48439-8031   (810) 257-9828
County: Genesee
Contact: Apparao Mukkamala, Pres.

Established in 1995 in MI.
Donors: Apparao Mukkamala; Sumathi Mukkamala.
Grantmaker type: Independent foundation.
Financial data (yr. ended 12/31/09): Assets, $55,921 (M); gifts received, $34,573; expenditures, $21,936; total giving, $21,101; qualifying distributions, $21,101; giving activities include $21,101 for grants.
Fields of interest: Medical school/education; Hospitals (general); Rural development; Hinduism; Spirituality.
International interests: India.
Type of support: General/operating support.
Limitations: Applications accepted. Giving primarily in MI; giving also in India.
Application information:
  Initial approach: Letter
  Deadline(s): None
Officer: Apparao Mukkamala, Pres.
Directors: Aparna Mukkamala; Srinivas Mukkamala; Sumathi Mukkamala.
EIN: 383224822

592

Wanda Muntwyler Foundation For Animals
P.O. Box 3636
Grand Rapids, MI 49501-3636
County: Kent
Application address: c/o Fifth Third Bank, 640
Pasquinelli Dr., Westmont, IL 60559, tel.: (630)
468-8933; URL: http://muntwylerfoundation.org/

Established in 1996 in IL.
Donor: Wanda Muntwyler‡.
Grantmaker type: Independent foundation.
Financial data (yr. ended 12/31/09): Assets,
$1,609,298 (M); expenditures, $133,804; total
giving, $110,700; qualifying distributions,
$110,700; giving activities include $110,700 for
grants.
Purpose and activities: Giving for the prevention of
cruelty to animals and to strengthen the
human-animal bond.
Fields of interest: Higher education; Animal welfare;
Veterinary medicine.
Type of support: General/operating support;
Scholarship funds.
Limitations: Applications accepted. Giving limited to
IL. No grants to individuals.
Application information: Projects submitted for
consideration should be limited to a budget of
$5,000 or less. See web site for additional
application information.
　Initial approach: Proposal
　Deadline(s): July 31
Directors: Lyle Brumley; Enid Kempe.
Trustee: Fifth Third Bank.
EIN: 367155124
Selected grants: The following grants were reported
in 2008.
$7,500 to Humane Society, Naperville, Naperville,
IL.
$6,500 to Humane Society of Hinsdale, Hinsdale,
IL.
$6,000 to Humane Society of Quincy, Quincy, IL.
$4,000 to Humane Society of Peoria, Peoria, IL.
$2,696 to Anderson Animal Shelter, South Elgin, IL.
$2,500 to Joliet Junior College, Joliet, IL.

593

Munuscong River Watershed Association
20275 S. Riverside Dr.
Pickford, MI 49774-9222
County: Chippewa

Established in MI.
Grantmaker type: Independent foundation.
Financial data (yr. ended 10/01/09): Assets,
$2,420 (L); gifts received, $100; expenditures,
$79; total giving, $0; qualifying distributions, $79.
Officers: Terri Tavenner, Chair.; Gerald Garrow,
Treas.
EIN: 383439483

594

The Laura Jane Musser Fund
(formerly The Musser Fund)
318 W. 48th St.
Minneapolis, MN 55419-5418 (612) 825-2024
County: Hennepin
Contact: Mary Karen Lynn-Klimenko, Grants Program
Mgr.
E-mail: ljmusserfund@earthlink.net; URL: http://
www.musserfund.org/

Established in 1990 in MN.
Donor: Laura J. Musser‡.
Grantmaker type: Independent foundation.
Financial data (yr. ended 12/31/09): Assets,
$16,486,968 (M); expenditures, $777,335; total
giving, $493,447; qualifying distributions,
$493,447; giving activities include $493,447 for
grants.
Purpose and activities: Primary areas of interest
include community-based approaches to solving
environmental problems, smaller participatory arts
programs, securing intercultural harmony and
developing leadership in rural communities.
Fields of interest: Arts; Environment; Civil rights,
race/intergroup relations; Rural development.
Type of support: Program development; Seed
money.
Limitations: Applications accepted. Giving primarily
in CO, HI, MI, MN, NY, OH and WY. No grants for
general operating support, or for ongoing programs,
or for capital projects.
Publications: Application guidelines; Grants list;
Program policy statement.
Application information: No additional giving for the
Environmental Initiative until Spring, 2011.
Application guidelines and procedures, and
application form available on foundation web site.
Application form required.
　Initial approach: Proposal
　Copies of proposal: 1
　Deadline(s): Application deadlines available on
　　foundation web site.
　Board meeting date(s): Biannually
　Final notification: 4 months
Officer and Directors:* Joseph S. Micallef,* Pres.;
Lisa Duke; Tom Drean; Robert Strasburg; Jane
Taylor; Drew Walker; Meg Walker; Tim Walker.
Trustee: U.S. Bank, N.A.
Number of staff: None.
EIN: 416334475
Selected grants: The following grants were reported
in 2007.
$35,000 to Port Orford Ocean Resource Team, Port
Orford, OR.
$30,000 to White Earth Land Recovery Project,
Callaway, MN.
$25,000 to Mountain Studies Institute, Silverton,
CO.
$20,000 to TVbyGIRLS, Minneapolis, MN.
$15,000 to Boys and Girls Clubs of Central
Wyoming, Casper, WY.
$10,000 to Saint Francis Music Center, Little Falls,
MN.
$7,500 to Thomas-Dale District 7 Planning Council,
Saint Paul, MN.
$5,000 to Community Programs in the Arts and
Sciences, Saint Paul, MN.
$5,000 to Telluride Foundation, Telluride, CO.
$2,000 to Lets Go Fishing of Minnesota, Willmar,
MN.

595

Myers Church Scholarship
c/o Fifth Third Bank
P.O. Box 630858
Cincinnati, OH 45263-0858
County: Hamilton
Application address: c/o Rev. William Collins, 6108
Barnhart Rd., Ludington, MI 49431-8625, tel.: (616)
843-9275

Established in 1995 in MI.
Donor: Keith T. Myers.

Grantmaker type: Independent foundation.
Financial data (yr. ended 12/31/07): Assets,
$208,537 (M); expenditures, $10,935; total giving,
$7,160; qualifying distributions, $7,435; giving
activities include $7,160 for 6 grants to individuals
(high: $1,110; low: $610).
Purpose and activities: Scholarship awards to high
school graduates residing in or whose parents
reside in Mason County, Michigan.
Fields of interest: Higher education.
Type of support: Scholarships—to individuals.
Limitations: Giving limited to residents of Mason
County, MI.
Application information: Application form required.
　Deadline(s): Apr. 20
Scholarship Committee: Sally Barbo; Richard
Loerup; John Pavlick; Dick Powell; Scott Sitler; Jeff
Wooster.
Trustee: Fifth Third Bank.
EIN: 383288570

596

Frank & Irene Myers Foundation
P.O. Box 4418
Jackson, MI 49204-4418 (517) 563-2773
County: Jackson

Established in 2005 in MI.
Donor: Irene Myers.
Grantmaker type: Independent foundation.
Financial data (yr. ended 12/31/09): Assets,
$204,505 (M); gifts received, $80,000;
expenditures, $6,837; total giving, $6,791;
qualifying distributions, $6,791; giving activities
include $6,791 for grants.
Fields of interest: Elementary/secondary
education; Catholic agencies & churches.
Limitations: Applications accepted. Giving limited to
Jackson county, MI. No grants to individuals.
Application information:
　Initial approach: Letter
　Deadline(s): None
Officers: Irene Myers, Pres.; Nathan Myers, V.P.;
Martha Myers, Secy.; Margaret Myers, Treas.
EIN: 300281873

597

National Healthcare Scholars Foundation
(formerly United American Healthcare Foundation)
300 River Pl., Rm. 4700
Detroit, MI 48207-5069 (313) 393-4549
County: Wayne
Contact: J.V. Combs, M.D., Pres.
FAX: (313) 393-3394; E-mail: info@nhsfonline.org
Additional tel.: (313) 393-7944

Established in 1987 in MI.
Donors: United American Healthcare Corp.; Julius
V. Combs, M.D.; OmniCare Health Plan; Ford Motor
Co.; Chrysler Motor Co.; General Motors Corp.; MGM
Grand Casino; Atwater Entertainment; Greektown
Casino; Comerica Bank; Standard Federal Bank N.A.
Grantmaker type: Independent foundation.
Financial data (yr. ended 09/30/08): Assets,
$84,953 (M); expenditures, $83,086; total giving,
$78,500; qualifying distributions, $78,500; giving
activities include $78,500 for grants.
Purpose and activities: To serve the community by
providing financial assistance to educate minority
health care professionals through scholarships and
to support those institutions and organizations

dedicated to enriching the community through programs and education. Scholarships assist qualified African-American, Asian, Hispanic, and Native American students in the fields of medicine, nursing, pharmacy, and allied health professions.

Fields of interest: Medical school/education; Nursing school/education; Pharmacy/prescriptions; Minorities; Asians/Pacific Islanders; African Americans/Blacks; Hispanics/Latinos; Native Americans/American Indians.

Type of support: Annual campaigns; General/operating support; Scholarships—to individuals.

Limitations: Giving on a national basis.

Publications: Biennial report (including application guidelines); Grants list; Informational brochure.

Application information: See foundation Web site for list of participating educational institutions. Application form not required.

  Deadline(s): None

  Board meeting date(s): Feb., June, and Sept.

Officers and Directors:* Julius V. Combs, M.D.*, Chair. and Pres.; Milton H. Watson,* Vice-Chair. and V.P.; Ronald R. Dobbins,* Secy.-Treas.; Monica Y. Allen; Hon. Norma Y. Dotson; Marie Draper Dykes; Henry W. Foster, M.D.; Lorna L. Thomas, M.D.

Advisory Board: Alice G. Combs; Tonya Corbin; Tonya M. Corbitt; Sharon Simpson; Kimberly Combs Voss; and 9 additional advisory members.

Number of staff: 1 part-time support.

EIN: 382894517

598
Neal Sisters Foundation

c/o JPMorgan Chase Bank, N.A.
P.O. Box 3038
Milwaukee, WI 53201-3038
County: Milwaukee

Contact: Carl Holmes, Treas.

Application address: 1080 W. Northwood Dr., Caro, MI 48723-1117, tel.: (989) 673-3543

Established in 1991 in MI.

Donor: Eleanor Neal.

Grantmaker type: Independent foundation.

Financial data (yr. ended 12/31/09): Assets, $1,379,445 (M); expenditures, $70,071; total giving, $63,000; qualifying distributions, $63,000; giving activities include $63,000 for grants.

Purpose and activities: Giving primarily for higher education and human services, including an adult care center and an assault crisis center. Preference given to qualified charities in the education field in the Caro, Michigan, area.

Fields of interest: Higher education; Libraries/library science; Human services; Residential/custodial care, special day care.

Limitations: Applications accepted. Giving primarily in the Caro, MI, area. No grants to individuals.

Application information:

  Initial approach: Letter

  Copies of proposal: 2

  Deadline(s): None

Officers: Steve Fillion, Pres.; Martha Thurston, Secy.; Carl Holmes, Treas.

Trustees: Dolores Rock Hutchinson; JPMorgan Chase Bank, N.A.

EIN: 382942765

599
J. N. Nelson Family Foundation

9095 S. Saginaw Rd., Unit 13
Grand Blanc, MI 48439-9579 (810) 767-7800
County: Genesee

Contact: Jay N. Nelson, Pres.

Established in 1997 in MI.

Donors: Jay N. Nelson; Marilyn S. Nelson.

Grantmaker type: Independent foundation.

Financial data (yr. ended 12/31/09): Assets, $580,665 (M); gifts received, $27,776; expenditures, $10,280; total giving, $3,000; qualifying distributions, $3,634; giving activities include $3,000 for 1 grant.

Fields of interest: Arts; Education.

Type of support: Grants to individuals; Scholarship funds; Capital campaigns.

Limitations: Giving primarily in MI.

Application information: Application form required.

  Deadline(s): None

Officers: Jay N. Nelson, Pres. and Treas.; Marilyn S. Nelson, V.P. and Secy.

Directors: Bonnie S. Nelson; David N. Nelson; Robin N. Nelson.

EIN: 383342652

600
Donald E. and Margaret L. Nelson Scholarship Fund

W9473 H. Lucas Dr.
Iron Mountain, MI 49801-9409
County: Dickinson

Application address: c/o North Dickinson County School, Attn.: Daniel J. Nurmi, Principal, W6588 M-69, Felch, MI 49831-8890, tel.: (906) 542-9281

Established in 1987 in MI.

Donors: Allen J. Nelson; Irving T. Nelson; Merlin A. Nelson.

Grantmaker type: Independent foundation.

Financial data (yr. ended 12/31/09): Assets, $131,354 (M); gifts received, $3,847; expenditures, $7,495; total giving, $7,375; qualifying distributions, $7,375; giving activities include $7,375 for grants to individuals.

Purpose and activities: Scholarship awards to residents of Felch, MI, who are graduates of North Dickinson County School.

Fields of interest: Higher education.

Type of support: Scholarships—to individuals.

Limitations: Applications accepted. Giving limited to Felch, MI.

Application information: Application form required.

  Deadline(s): Apr. 1

Officers and Directors:* Alice M. Brown,* Chair.; Merlin A. Nelson,* Admin.; Shirley A. Nelson, Secy.; Allen J. Nelson; Donald J. Nelson; Irving T. Nelson; Patricia A. Nolf; Mavis C. Powell; Norma T. Scolatti; Carol R. Trautner.

EIN: 382731508

601
Newaygo Public Schools Educational Advancement Foundation

c/o Selection Comm.
360 S. Mill St.
Newaygo, MI 49337-8545
County: Newaygo

Established in 1990 in MI.

Grantmaker type: Independent foundation.

Financial data (yr. ended 06/30/09): Assets, $290,629 (M); gifts received, $2,200; expenditures, $14,756; total giving, $13,066; qualifying distributions, $13,066; giving activities include $13,066 for grants.

Purpose and activities: Scholarship awards to graduating seniors of Newaygo, Michigan, for higher education; some grants for teachers of the Newaygo school system for higher education.

Fields of interest: Higher education.

Type of support: Grants to individuals; Scholarships—to individuals.

Limitations: Applications accepted. Giving primarily in Newaygo, MI.

Application information: Application form required.

  Deadline(s): Apr. 1

Officers: Larry J. Lethorn, Pres.; Mary Reese-Pumford, V.P.; Ralph Burde, Secy.; Paul Eno, Treas.

Trustees: James Badgero; Jelanie Bush; Edward Grodus.

EIN: 382989275

602
The Newman Family Foundation

5455 Corporate Dr., Ste. 300
Troy, MI 48098-2620 (248) 641-8400
County: Oakland

Contact: Craig S. Skulsky, Treas.

Established in 1990 in MI.

Donors: Max K. Newman; Donald L. Newman, M.D.; Steven E. Newman, M.D.

Grantmaker type: Independent foundation.

Financial data (yr. ended 12/31/09): Assets, $1,990,438 (M); expenditures, $119,219; total giving, $116,118; qualifying distributions, $116,118; giving activities include $116,118 for grants.

Limitations: Giving primarily in MI.

Application information:

  Initial approach: Letter

  Deadline(s): None

Officers: Steven E. Newman, M.D., Pres. and Secy.; Donald L. Newman, M.D., V.P.; Craig S. Skulsky, Treas.

EIN: 382986180

603
The Nickless Family Charitable Foundation

2121 University Park Dr.
Okemos, MI 48602-5325
County: Saginaw

Application address: c/o James E. McCartney, P.O. Box 23127, Lansing, MI 48909-3125, tel.: (517) 347-5000

Established in 2000 in MI.

Grantmaker type: Independent foundation.

Financial data (yr. ended 12/31/09): Assets, $2,132,947 (M); expenditures, $106,143; total giving, $80,000; qualifying distributions, $80,000; giving activities include $80,000 for grants.

Fields of interest: Medical care, community health systems; Health organizations, association.

Limitations: Applications accepted. Giving primarily in the Sun City West, AZ, and Bay City, MI, areas. No grants to individuals.

Application information: Application form not required.

Deadline(s): None

Officers: Arthur H. Nickless, Pres.; Judy N. Graham, V.P.; Joan N. Tankersley, V.P.; James E. McCartney, Secy.; Janet Royce, Treas.

EIN: 383501091

Selected grants: The following grants were reported in 2006.

$50,000 to Sun City Area Interfaith Services, Surprise, AZ.

604
Allen E. & Marie A. Nickless Memorial Foundation

3023 Davenport Ave.
Saginaw, MI 48602-3652
County: Saginaw
Application address: c/o B.J. Humphries, 5090 State St., Building A, Ste. 1, Saginaw, MI 48603, tel.: (989) 792-2552

Established about 1971.

Donors: Marie A. Nickless; Allen E. Nickless†.

Grantmaker type: Independent foundation.

Financial data (yr. ended 12/31/09): Assets, $4,786,958 (M); gifts received, $136,000; expenditures, $199,810; total giving, $160,530; qualifying distributions, $176,276; giving activities include $160,530 for 37 grants (high: $13,700; low: $500).

Fields of interest: Arts; Education; Foundations (community); Christian agencies & churches.

Type of support: General/operating support.

Limitations: Giving primarily in Saginaw County, MI. No loans or program-related investments.

Application information: Application form not required.

Initial approach: Letter

Deadline(s): None

Officers: Charles Nickless, Pres.; Darcy Nickless, V.P.; B.J. Humphreys, Secy.; David A. Beyerlein, Treas.

Trustees: John Humphreys; John Kunitzer.

EIN: 237011258

605
Ernest L. Nicolay Family Foundation

c/o Comerica Bank
P.O. Box 75000, MC 3302
Detroit, MI 48275-0001
County: Wayne
Application address: c/o Ernest L. Nicolay III, 866 Westchester Way, Birmingham, MI 48009-2918, tel.: (313) 222-5576

Established in 1962 in MI.

Grantmaker type: Independent foundation.

Financial data (yr. ended 12/31/09): Assets, $482,030 (M); expenditures, $82,951; total giving, $75,000; qualifying distributions, $75,900; giving activities include $75,000 for 1 grant.

Fields of interest: Higher education; Human services; Salvation Army.

Type of support: General/operating support.

Limitations: Applications accepted. Giving primarily in MI.

Application information: Application form not required.

Initial approach: Letter

Deadline(s): None

Board meeting date(s): Dec.

Trustees: Ernest L. Nicolay, Jr.; Ernest L. Nicolay III; JoAnn Nicolay; Keith Shreve; Chuck Wood; Comerica Bank.

EIN: 386096839

Selected grants: The following grants were reported in 2008.

$75,000 to Adrian College, Adrian, MI.

606
Joanne Nicolay Foundation

c/o S. Gary Spicer
16845 Kercheval St., Ste. 5
Grosse Pointe Park, MI 48230-1551
(313) 884-9700
County: Wayne

Established in 1997 in MI.

Donor: Joanne Nicolay.

Grantmaker type: Independent foundation.

Financial data (yr. ended 12/31/09): Assets, $695,662 (M); gifts received, $327,371; expenditures, $48,694; total giving, $30,450; qualifying distributions, $30,450; giving activities include $30,450 for 11 grants (high: $18,000; low: $200).

Purpose and activities: Support primarily for an affiliated foundation.

Fields of interest: Historical activities; Education; Residential/custodial care; Foundations (private independent).

Type of support: General/operating support.

Limitations: Applications accepted. Giving primarily in MI. No grants to individuals.

Application information:

Initial approach: Proposal

Deadline(s): None

Final notification: 3 months

Officers and Trustees:* S. Gary Spicer, Sr.,* Pres.; Mary Lynn Martin,* Secy.; Edward Zionkowski,* Treas.

EIN: 383302112

607
Dr. William F. and Mabel E. Nill Foundation, Inc.

39288 Dodge Park Rd.
Sterling Heights, MI 48313-5047
County: Macomb
Contact: Wayne Stewart, Dir.
Application address: 41700 Hayes Rd., Ste. A, Clinton Township, MI 48038-5823

Established in 2003 in MI.

Donor: Mabel E. Nill Trust.

Grantmaker type: Independent foundation.

Financial data (yr. ended 12/31/09): Assets, $1,021,079 (M); expenditures, $67,429; total giving, $6,917; qualifying distributions, $6,917; giving activities include $6,917 for grants.

Purpose and activities: Giving primarily for medical research and scholarships for medical school.

Fields of interest: Medical school/education; Cancer research; Brain research.

Type of support: Scholarships—to individuals; Research.

Limitations: Applications accepted. Giving primarily in MI.

Application information: Application form not required.

Deadline(s): None

Directors: Jean Chapaton; Oscar Chapaton; Wayne Stewart.

EIN: 383546563

608
Amos Nordman Foundation Charitable Trust

(also known as Amos Nordman Charitable Trust)
P.O. Box 1242
Muskegon, MI 49443-1242
County: Muskegon
Contact: Charles E. Silky, Jr., Tr.

Established in 1973 in MI.

Grantmaker type: Independent foundation.

Financial data (yr. ended 12/31/09): Assets, $361,737 (M); expenditures, $43,150; total giving, $2,808; qualifying distributions, $2,808; giving activities include $2,808 for grants.

Purpose and activities: Scholarship awards to residents of Muskegon, Michigan, for higher education.

Fields of interest: Higher education.

Type of support: Scholarship funds; Scholarships—to individuals.

Limitations: Giving limited to MI.

Application information: Application form required.

Deadline(s): None

Trustees: Richard C. Gillard; Cathy Houseman; Charles E. Silky, Jr.

EIN: 237251583

609
The Northwind Foundation

c/o AFR Mostafa, CPA
26300 Telegraph Rd.
Southfield, MI 48033-2436
County: Oakland

Established in 2007 in MI.

Grantmaker type: Independent foundation.

Financial data (yr. ended 12/31/09): Assets, $69,946 (M); gifts received, $15,000; expenditures, $3,095; total giving, $2,400; qualifying distributions, $2,400; giving activities include $2,400 for grants.

Fields of interest: Islam.

Limitations: Giving primarily in MI.

Officer: Sarih Dalati, Pres.

EIN: 260165399

610
Nowak Family Foundation

4213 Crayton Rd.
Naples, FL 34103-8524 (616) 834-8717
County: Collier
Contact: John M. Nowak, Pres.

Established in 2001 in OH.

Donor: John M. Nowak.

Grantmaker type: Independent foundation.

Financial data (yr. ended 12/31/09): Assets, $1,038,725 (M); gifts received, $150,000; expenditures, $103,583; total giving, $98,500; qualifying distributions, $98,500; giving activities include $98,500 for grants.

Fields of interest: Higher education; Hospitals (specialty); Human services; Catholic agencies & churches.
Type of support: General/operating support.
Limitations: Giving primarily in MI, with emphasis on Grand Rapids. No grants to individuals.
Application information:
   Initial approach: Letter
   Deadline(s): None
Officers: John M. Nowak, Pres. and Treas.; Maureen K. Nowak, V.P. and Secy.
EIN: 311813059

611
Nusbaum Family Foundation
26575 Willowgreen Dr.
Franklin, MI   48025-1337   (248) 473-7570
County: Oakland
Contact: Irving Nusbaum, Pres.

Established in 1990 in MI.
Donors: Irving Nusbaum; Barbara Nusbaum.
Grantmaker type: Independent foundation.
Financial data (yr. ended 12/31/09): Assets, $1,065,680 (M); gifts received, $1,009,000; expenditures, $147,280; total giving, $134,239; qualifying distributions, $138,032; giving activities include $134,239 for 45 grants (high: $35,000; low: $18).
Fields of interest: Child development, education; Residential/custodial care, hospices; Jewish federated giving programs; Jewish agencies & synagogues.
Limitations: Applications accepted. Giving primarily in MI.
Application information:
   Initial approach: Letter
   Deadline(s): None
Officers: Irving Nusbaum, Pres.; Barbara Nusbaum, Secy.
Directors: Michael Roth; Bruce H. Seyburn.
EIN: 382917028
Selected grants: The following grants were reported in 2005.
$25,000 to Cleveland Clinic Foundation, Cleveland, OH.
$10,536 to Congregation Beth Ahm, West Bloomfield, MI.
$10,000 to Congregation Beth Ahm, West Bloomfield, MI.
$5,000 to Congregation Beth Ahm, West Bloomfield, MI.
$5,000 to JARC, Farmington Hills, MI.

612
Nuveen Benevolent Trust
333 W. Wacker Dr., Ste 2000
Chicago, IL   60606-7413   (312) 236-6700
County: Cook
Contact: Charles Michod, Jr., Tr.

Trust established in 1936 in IL.
Donor: John Nuveen†.
Grantmaker type: Independent foundation.
Financial data (yr. ended 12/31/09): Assets, $2,215,285 (M); expenditures, $167,319; total giving, $138,950; qualifying distributions, $153,328; giving activities include $138,950 for 23 grants (high: $53,000; low: $100).
Fields of interest: Arts; Higher education; Human services.

Type of support: General/operating support; Continuing support.
Limitations: Applications accepted. Giving in the U.S., primarily in IL and MI. No grants to individuals.
Application information:
   Initial approach: Letter
   Deadline(s): None
   Board meeting date(s): As required
Trustees: Charles L. Michod, Jr.; John S. Nuveen; Thomas Reynolds; JPMorgan Chase Bank, N.A.
EIN: 366069509
Selected grants: The following grants were reported in 2008.
$5,000 to United Negro College Fund, Chicago, IL.
$4,000 to American Farm School, New York, NY.
$4,000 to Rhode Island School of Design, Providence, RI.
$3,000 to Vermont Law School, South Royalton, VT.
$2,100 to Ramapo for Children, Rhinebeck, NY.
$1,000 to Saint Pauls School, Concord, NH.
$1,000 to Williams College, Williamstown, MA.

613
The O'Brien-VRBA Scholarship Trust
c/o PNC Bank, N.A.
P.O. Box 94651
Cleveland, OH   44101-4651
County: Cuyahoga
Application address: c/o PNC Bank, N.A., Attn.: Jo Ann Harlan, P.O. Box 749, Peoria, IL 61652-0749, tel.: (309) 655-5000

Established in 1991 in IL.
Grantmaker type: Independent foundation.
Financial data (yr. ended 12/31/09): Assets, $3,077,868 (M); expenditures, $121,558; total giving, $108,000; qualifying distributions, $108,000; giving activities include $10,000 for 4 grants (high: $2,500; low: $2,500), and $98,000 for 37 grants to individuals (high: $3,000; low: $2,000).
Purpose and activities: Giving for higher education, primarily to individuals of Roman Catholic faith.
Fields of interest: Higher education; Catholic agencies & churches.
Type of support: Scholarship funds; Scholarships—to individuals.
Limitations: Applications accepted. Giving primarily to residents of IA, IL, IN, MI, and WI.
Application information: Application form required for scholarship program. Application form required.
   Initial approach: Letter for grants
   Deadline(s): Apr. 1 for scholarship
Directors: John Bass; Rev. Thomas C. Brady; James R. Doyle; Ann Hupert; Harvey Share.
Trustee: National City Bank.
EIN: 376277500
Selected grants: The following grants were reported in 2008.
$1,500 to Benedictine University, Kendra Black, Lisle, IL.
$1,500 to DePaul University, Ana Grahovac, Chicago, IL.
$1,500 to DePaul University, John Grogan, Chicago, IL.
$1,500 to DePaul University, Lauran Kolack, Chicago, IL.
$1,500 to DePaul University, Joseph Kepecky, Chicago, IL.
$1,500 to DePaul University, Mary Jane Schlitz, Chicago, IL.
$1,500 to Indiana University, Stephanie Kuzydym, Bloomington, IN.

$1,500 to Indiana University, Stephanie Kuzydym, Bloomington, IN.
$1,500 to Northern Illinois University, Christine Pugh, DeKalb, IL.
$1,000 to DePaul University, Mariola Zoltowski, Chicago, IL.

614
Leo A. Obloy and Bernice Obloy Foundation
2161 Clinton View Cir.
Rochester Hills, MI   48309-2984
(248) 588-5333
County: Oakland
Contact: Michael H. Obloy, Pres.

Established in 1987 in MI.
Donors: Leo A. Obloy; Bernice Obloy.
Grantmaker type: Independent foundation.
Financial data (yr. ended 12/31/09): Assets, $15,192 (M); expenditures, $891; total giving, $800; qualifying distributions, $800; giving activities include $800 for grants.
Fields of interest: Higher education; Health care; Catholic agencies & churches.
Type of support: General/operating support.
Limitations: Applications accepted. Giving primarily in MI. No grants to individuals.
Application information:
   Initial approach: Letter
   Deadline(s): None
Officers: Michael H. Obloy, Pres.; Phillis Hudsek, V.P.
EIN: 382805957

615
Marvin and Rosalie Okun Foundation
527 S. Rose St.
Kalamazoo, MI   49007-5243   (269) 349-9603
County: Kalamazoo
Contact: Marvin Okun, Pres.

Donors: Marvin Okun; Rosalie Okun.
Grantmaker type: Independent foundation.
Financial data (yr. ended 12/31/09): Assets, $135,886 (M); gifts received, $10,000; expenditures, $7,721; total giving, $6,500; qualifying distributions, $6,500; giving activities include $6,500 for grants.
Fields of interest: Jewish agencies & synagogues.
Type of support: General/operating support.
Limitations: Applications accepted. Giving primarily in Kalamazoo, MI.
Application information: Application form not required.
   Initial approach: Letter or telephone
   Deadline(s): Nov. 15
Officers: Marvin Okun, Pres.; Rosalie Okun, Secy.-Treas.
EIN: 383323820

616
R. E. Olds Foundation
(formerly Ransom Fidelity Company)
P.O. Box 4900
East Lansing, MI   48826-4900
County: Ingham
Contact: Doris B. Anderson, Pres.

Incorporated in 1915 in MI.

Donor: Ransom E. Olds‡.
Grantmaker type: Independent foundation.
Financial data (yr. ended 12/31/09): Assets, $3,156,369 (M); expenditures, $165,082; total giving, $137,000; qualifying distributions, $137,000; giving activities include $137,000 for grants.
Purpose and activities: Giving to community-based education programs focusing on youth, access to health care, animal welfare and environmental issues, greater Lansing Tri-County, Michigan.
Fields of interest: Education; Environment; Animals/wildlife; Health care; Youth development.
Type of support: Annual campaigns; Capital campaigns; Equipment; Emergency funds; Program development; Conferences/seminars; Seed money; Matching/challenge support.
Limitations: Applications accepted. Giving in the U.S., with emphasis on Lansing and the Tri-County, MI, area. No support for religious organizations. No grants to individuals.
Application information: Application form not required.
　Initial approach: Letter of proposal
　Copies of proposal: 1
　Board meeting date(s): Quarterly
　Final notification: Up to 3 months
Officer: Doris B. Anderson, Pres.
Directors: Ron Beckwith; Ed McKree; Deborah Stephens; Diane Anderson Tarpoff.
Number of staff: 2 full-time professional.
EIN: 381485403
Selected grants: The following grants were reported in 2006.
$16,500 to Woldumar Nature Center, Lansing, MI.
$5,000 to American Red Cross, Adrian, MI.
$5,000 to Highfields, Onondaga, MI.
$5,000 to YMCA of Lansing, Lansing, MI.
$4,000 to Eles Place, Lansing, MI.
$1,000 to Arts Council of Greater Lansing, Lansing, MI.
$1,000 to Boarshead Theater, Lansing, MI.
$500 to Humane Society, Capital Area, Lansing, MI.
$300 to Tip of the Mitt Watershed Council, Petoskey, MI.

617
Oleson Foundation
P.O. Box 904
Traverse City, MI　49685-0904
County: Grand Traverse
Contact: Kathryn L. Huschke, Exec. Dir.
E-mail: kathy@olesonfoundation.org; *URL:* http://www.olesonfoundation.org

Established in 1959 in MI.
Donors: Don Oleson; Gerald Oleson; Gerald W. Oleson‡; Frances M. Oleson‡.
Grantmaker type: Independent foundation.
Financial data (yr. ended 12/31/09): Assets, $18,863,854 (M); gifts received, $3,600; expenditures, $1,453,351; total giving, $988,382; qualifying distributions, $1,026,809; giving activities include $988,382 for 96 grants.
Purpose and activities: The foundation's mission is to help people help themselves achieve the greatest good for the greatest number efficiently over a broad range of social and environmental interests.
Fields of interest: Historic preservation/historical societies; Elementary/secondary education; Higher education; Environment; Health care; Youth development, centers/clubs; Human services;

United Ways and Federated Giving Programs; Christian agencies & churches.
Type of support: General/operating support; Continuing support; Annual campaigns; Capital campaigns; Building/renovation; Equipment; Land acquisition; Curriculum development; Technical assistance; Matching/challenge support.
Limitations: Applications accepted. Giving limited to the Lower Peninsula region in northwestern MI. No grants to individuals, or for endowments.
Application information: Application information available on foundation web site. Application form required.
　Initial approach: Contact foundation for application cover and budget sheets
　Copies of proposal: 1
　Deadline(s): Apr. 1
　Board meeting date(s): June
　Final notification: Usually in late June
Officers and Directors:* Donald W. Oleson,* Pres.; Gerald E. Oleson,* V.P.; Richard Ford,* Secy.-Treas.; Kathryn L. Huschke, Exec. Dir.; John Tobin.
Number of staff: 1 part-time professional.
EIN: 386083080
Selected grants: The following grants were reported in 2004.
$75,000 to Goodwill Industries of Northern Michigan, Traverse City, MI.
$35,000 to Grand Traverse Regional Land Conservancy, Traverse City, MI.
$21,250 to Saint Marys School, Lake Leelanau, MI.
$20,000 to Michigan Community Blood Centers Foundation, Grand Rapids, MI.

618
Olson-Kulka Foundation
(formerly Robert G. & Celia S. Olson Foundation)
2000 Town Ctr., Ste. 1500
Southfield, MI　48075-1195
County: Oakland
Contact: Barry R. Bess, Secy.

Grantmaker type: Independent foundation.
Financial data (yr. ended 12/31/09): Assets, $612,419 (M); expenditures, $30,364; total giving, $25,200; qualifying distributions, $25,200; giving activities include $25,200 for grants.
Fields of interest: Education; Health care; Human services; Christian agencies & churches.
Limitations: Giving primarily in MI. No grants to individuals.
Application information:
　Initial approach: Proposal
　Deadline(s): None
Officers and Trustees:* Justine Olson Kulka,* Pres. and Treas.; Robert Kulka,* V.P.; Barry R. Bess,* Secy.
EIN: 386074650

619
Oshlag Stuckey Foundation
c/o Comerica Bank & Trust, N.A.
P.O. Box 75000
Detroit, MI　48275-3302　(561) 961-6627
County: Wayne
Contact: Peter Steib

Donor: Oshlag Stuckey Charitable Remainder Unitrust.
Grantmaker type: Independent foundation.

Financial data (yr. ended 12/31/09): Assets, $844,318 (M); gifts received, $492,746; expenditures, $898; total giving, $0; qualifying distributions, $35.
Application information: Application form not required.
　Initial approach: Proposal
　Deadline(s): None
Trustee: Comerica Bank & Trust, N.A.
EIN: 276410285

620
Annette L. Ott Scholarship Fund
18620 Fort St.
Riverview, MI　48192-7443
County: Wayne

Established in 2004 in MI.
Grantmaker type: Independent foundation.
Financial data (yr. ended 12/31/09): Assets, $2,825 (M); expenditures, $0; total giving, $0; qualifying distributions, $0.
Officers: Richard E. Ott, Chair.; Alise Welsh, Pres. and Treas.; Richard E. Ott, Jr., V.P. and Secy.
EIN: 201978806

621
Owen Scholarship Trust
c/o Fifth Third Bank
P.O. Box 3636
Grand Rapids, MI　49501-3636
County: Kent
Contact: Eve Phillips
Application address: c/o Plano High School, 704 W. Abe St., Plano, IL 60545, tel.: (630) 552-3178

Established in MI.
Grantmaker type: Independent foundation.
Financial data (yr. ended 12/31/09): Assets, $27,994 (M); expenditures, $4,393; total giving, $1,400; qualifying distributions, $1,400; giving activities include $1,400 for 6 grants to individuals (high: $250; low: $150).
Purpose and activities: Scholarship awards to graduates of Plano High School, IL.
Type of support: Scholarships—to individuals.
Limitations: Applications accepted. Giving limited to Plano, IL.
Application information: Application form required.
　Initial approach: Letter or telephone
　Deadline(s): Apr. 15
Scholarship Committee: Becky Cooper; Cara Cooper; Jeff Cooper; Fran Sauer.
Trustee: Fifth Third Bank.
EIN: 386080449

622
The OYK Foundation
3660 Valleyview Ln.
West Bloomfield, MI　48323-3362
County: Oakland

Established in 2007 in MI.
Grantmaker type: Independent foundation.
Financial data (yr. ended 12/31/09): Assets, $101,764 (M); expenditures, $9,275; total giving, $8,599; qualifying distributions, $8,599; giving activities include $8,599 for grants.
Officer: Fayiz Hadid, Pres.
EIN: 260879024

623
Lawrence C. Page, Sr. Family Charitable Foundation
62157 Wolcott Rd.
Ray Township, MI 48096-3015
County: Macomb

Established in 2007 in MI.
Donor: Lawrence C. Page, Sr.
Grantmaker type: Independent foundation.
Financial data (yr. ended 12/31/09): Assets, $283,811 (M); gifts received, $69,536; expenditures, $65,780; total giving, $50,500; qualifying distributions, $50,500; giving activities include $50,500 for grants.
Officer: Lawrence C. Page, Sr., Pres.
Directors: Michael N. Rice; David Stone.
EIN: 260367507

624
Paine Family Foundation
c/o Northwest Investment and Trust
P.O. Box 1380
Traverse City, MI 49685-1380
County: Grand Traverse
Application address: c/o Carol Paine-McGovern, 625 S. Garfield Ave., Traverse City, MI 49686, tel.: (616) 285-0409

Established in 1991 in MI.
Donors: Martha L. Paine; G. William Paine; Carol Paine-McGovern.
Grantmaker type: Independent foundation.
Financial data (yr. ended 12/31/09): Assets, $5,733,399 (M); gifts received, $515,000; expenditures, $3,213,156; total giving, $3,164,775; qualifying distributions, $3,178,124; giving activities include $3,164,775 for 24 grants (high: $3,004,415; low: $500).
Fields of interest: Historic preservation/historical societies; Higher education; Education; Health care; Human services; United Ways and Federated Giving Programs.
Type of support: General/operating support; Endowments; Scholarship funds.
Limitations: Applications accepted. Giving primarily in MI, with emphasis on Manistee, Ludington, Scottville, and Traverse City; giving also in Boulder, CO.
Application information: Application form not required.
Deadline(s): None
Officers: Carol Paine-McGovern, Pres.; G. William Paine, V.P.; Martha L. Paine, Secy.-Treas.
EIN: 382996404
Selected grants: The following grants were reported in 2009.
$3,004,415 to Manistee Area Public Schools, Manistee, MI.
$25,745 to United Way of Mason County, Ludington, MI.
$12,050 to West Shore Community College, Scottville, MI.
$10,000 to Munson Healthcare Regional Foundation, Traverse City, MI.
$10,000 to University of Colorado Foundation, Boulder, CO.
$3,000 to Salvation Army of Grand Rapids, Grand Rapids, MI.
$2,500 to Kids Food Basket, Grand Rapids, MI.

625
Walter E. and Maria F. Palmer Foundation
P.O. Box 312
Frankenmuth, MI 48734-0312 (989) 652-6648
County: Saginaw
Contact: Maria F. Palmer, Pres.

Established in 1990 in MI.
Donors: Walter E. Palmer; Maria F. Palmer.
Grantmaker type: Independent foundation.
Financial data (yr. ended 12/31/09): Assets, $0; expenditures, $2,236,501; total giving, $2,227,540; qualifying distributions, $2,230,815; giving activities include $2,227,540 for 3 grants (high: $2,135,061; low: $10,000).
Fields of interest: Performing arts, music; Secondary school/education; Youth development; Foundations (community); Government/public administration.
Type of support: Endowments; Program development.
Limitations: Applications accepted. Giving primarily in Frankenmuth, MI. No grants to individuals.
Application information:
Initial approach: Letter
Deadline(s): None
Officer: Maria F. Palmer, Pres.
Directors: Thomas A. Jaffke; Franklin Rittmueller; W. Don Zehnder.
EIN: 382962926

626
Pappas Foundation, Inc.
30301 Northwestern Hwy., Ste. 200
Farmington Hills, MI 48334-3278
County: Oakland

Established in 1997 in MI.
Donor: Norman A. Pappas.
Grantmaker type: Independent foundation.
Financial data (yr. ended 12/31/09): Assets, $1,564,224 (M); gifts received, $237,750; expenditures, $71,725; total giving, $70,847; qualifying distributions, $70,847; giving activities include $70,847 for grants.
Fields of interest: Jewish agencies & synagogues.
Limitations: Giving primarily in MI.
Directors: Charles N. Pappas; Norman A. Pappas; Susan L. Pappas.
EIN: 383386198

627
Parchment Community Tennis Association
222 Glendale Blvd.
Kalamazoo, MI 49004-1320
County: Kalamazoo

Established in 2007 in MI.
Grantmaker type: Independent foundation.
Financial data (yr. ended 12/31/08): Assets, $5 (M); gifts received, $1,795; expenditures, $4,291; total giving, $165; qualifying distributions, $165; giving activities include $165 for grants.
Officers: Bill Luke, Pres.; Mike Conklin, V.P.; Michael Koehler, Secy.; Bryan Zocher, Treas.
EIN: 300349775

628
Elsa U. Pardee Foundation
P.O. Box 2767
Midland, MI 48641-2767
County: Midland
Contact: James A. Kendall, Secy.
E-mail: dougherty@pardeefoundation.org;
URL: http://www.pardeefoundation.org

Incorporated in 1944 in MI.
Donor: Elsa U. Pardee†.
Grantmaker type: Independent foundation.
Financial data (yr. ended 12/31/09): Assets, $75,426,678 (M); expenditures, $4,493,641; total giving, $4,256,864; qualifying distributions, $4,322,589; giving activities include $4,256,864 for 35 grants (high: $300,000; low: $6,000).
Purpose and activities: Giving primarily to support: 1) research programs directed toward discovering new approaches for cancer treatment and cure; and 2) financial support for cancer treatment.
Fields of interest: Cancer; Medical research, institute; Cancer research.
Type of support: Research.
Limitations: Applications accepted. Giving on a national basis. No grants to individuals, or for capital campaigns, building, or endowment funds, equipment (except when used in a specific project), scholarships, fellowships, general purposes, matching gifts, or fundraising campaigns; no loans.
Publications: Application guidelines; Annual report.
Application information: See web site for application guidelines. Application form not required.
Initial approach: Online Application
Deadline(s): None
Board meeting date(s): 3 times per year
Final notification: 4 to 6 months
Officers and Trustees:* Gail E. Lanphear,* Pres.; Lisa J. Gerstacker,* V.P.; James A. Kendall,* Secy.; Alan W. Ott,* Treas.; W. James Allen; Laurie G. Bouwman; Mary M. Neely; William D. Schuette; Michael Woolhiser.
Number of staff: 1 part-time support.
EIN: 386065799
Selected grants: The following grants were reported in 2007.
$500,000 to Pardee Cancer Treatment Fund of Midland/Gladwin, Midland, MI. For program support.
$225,000 to Pardee Cancer Treatment Fund of Gratiot County, Alma, MI. For program support.
$225,000 to Pardee Cancer Treatment Fund of Isabella County, Mount Pleasant, MI. For program support.
$200,000 to Pardee Cancer Treatment Fund of Clare County, Clare, MI. For program support.
$187,500 to Mount Sinai School of Medicine of New York University, New York, NY. For study of epigenetic factors that contribute to B-ALL.
$150,000 to Vanderbilt University Medical Center, Nashville, TN. For study of cPLA2-dependent signaling in irradiated endothelium.
$142,567 to Thomas Jefferson University, Philadelphia, PA. For study of CAV1 in breast cancer pathogenesis.
$135,000 to Pardee Cancer Treatment Fund of Bay County, Bay City, MI. For program support.
$134,000 to University of Texas Health Science Center, Dallas, TX. For study of interplay between JNK activity and microRNA-155 expression in lymphomas.
$116,242 to State University of New York at Buffalo, Buffalo, NY. For study of vitamin E derivatives as

selective and anti-cancer agents: structure, activity, relationship, and mechanism.

629
Donald and Ann Parfet Family Foundation
350 E. Michigan Ave., Ste. 500
Kalamazoo, MI   49007-3856   (269) 349-8483
County: Kalamazoo
Contact: Wendy Van Peenan, Compt.
FAX: (269) 349-8993;
E-mail: daparfetfoundation@ameritech.net

Established in 1996 in MI.
Donors: Donald R. Parfet; Ann V. Parfet.
Grantmaker type: Independent foundation.
Financial data (yr. ended 12/31/09): Assets, $658,139 (M); expenditures, $346,718; total giving, $325,822; qualifying distributions, $345,490; giving activities include $325,822 for 114 grants (high: $50,200; low: $25).
Purpose and activities: Giving primarily for health, quality of life, the arts, and educational organizations.
Fields of interest: Arts; Education; Health care; Human services; Community/economic development.
Type of support: Equipment; General/operating support; Continuing support; Annual campaigns; Capital campaigns; Building/renovation; Endowments; Emergency funds; Program development; Seed money; Scholarship funds.
Limitations: Applications accepted. Giving primarily in Kalamazoo, MI, and surrounding communities. No support for political organizations. No grants to individuals.
Application information: The foundation prefers letter and attachments in PDF or electronic files when possible. Submit 7 copies of anything that cannot be sent electronically. Application form not required.
  Initial approach: Letter with accompanying information.
  Copies of proposal: 7
  Deadline(s): 3 weeks prior to board meetings
  Board meeting date(s): Feb. 5, Apr. 23, Sept. 10, Nov. 12 and Dec. 16
  Final notification: 2 weeks after a board meeting
Officers and Trustees:* Ann V. Parfet,* Pres.; Andrew Worgess,* V.P.; Rachel E. Worgess,* V.P.; Sydney E. Waldorf,* Secy.; Donald R. Parfet,* Co-Treas.; C. MacKenzie Waldorf,* Co-Treas.
Number of staff: 1 part-time professional.
EIN: 383326370
Selected grants: The following grants were reported in 2009.
$3,500 to Specialized Language Development Center, Kalamazoo, MI. For annual grant.
$1,000 to Michigan Womens Foundation, Grosse Pointe Farms, MI. For annual support.
$600 to Housing Resources, Kalamazoo, MI. For walk for the homeless.
$500 to InterAct of Michigan, Kalamazoo, MI. For capital and relocation.
$500 to WMUK, Kalamazoo, MI. For annual support.
$500 to YWCA of Kalamazoo, Kalamazoo, MI. For Mentoring Program.
$300 to Gull Lake Area Community Volunteers, Richland, MI. For Bright Holiday Program.
$300 to Kalamazoo Nature Center, Kalamazoo, MI. For camp scholarships.

630
Suzanne Upjohn Delano Parish Foundation
(formerly Suzanne D. Parish Foundation)
211 S. Rose St.
Kalamazoo, MI   49007-4713   (269) 388-9800
County: Kalamazoo
Contact: Ronald N. Kilgore, V.P.

Established in MI.
Donor: Suzanne U.D. Parish.
Grantmaker type: Independent foundation.
Financial data (yr. ended 12/31/09): Assets, $6,659,889 (M); expenditures, $522,901; total giving, $500,000; qualifying distributions, $509,401; giving activities include $500,000 for 1 grant.
Purpose and activities: Support primarily to an aviation history museum.
Fields of interest: Museums (history); Space/aviation.
Type of support: General/operating support.
Limitations: Giving primarily in Kalamazoo, MI. No grants to individuals; no loans.
Application information:
  Initial approach: Letter
  Deadline(s): None
Officers and Directors:* Suzanne U.D. Parish,* Pres. and Secy.; Ronald N. Kilgore,* V.P. and Treas.; Katharine P. Miller; Preston L. Parish.
EIN: 382484268

631
Park Family Foundation
801 Johnson St.
Alpena, MI   49707-1870
County: Alpena

Established in 2007 in MI.
Donors: Kimberly A. Park; Philip Scott Park; Community Foundation of Northeast Michigan.
Grantmaker type: Independent foundation.
Financial data (yr. ended 12/31/09): Assets, $1,326,782 (M); gifts received, $383,337; expenditures, $234,489; total giving, $60,000; qualifying distributions, $60,000; giving activities include $60,000 for grants.
Fields of interest: Recreation, centers.
Limitations: Giving primarily in Alpena, MI.
Officers: James C. Park, Pres. and Secy.; Philip Scott Park, V.P.
Director: Kimberly A. Park.
EIN: 202210340

632
The Liz Parks-Novitsky Memorial Scholarship Fund
3585 Tripp Rd.
Woodside, CA   94062-3635
County: San Mateo

Established in CA.
Donors: John Novitsky; Liz Parks.
Grantmaker type: Independent foundation.
Financial data (yr. ended 06/30/09): Assets, $4,292 (M); gifts received, $5,000; expenditures, $3,500; total giving, $3,500; qualifying distributions, $3,500; giving activities include $3,500 for grants to individuals.
Type of support: Scholarships—to individuals.

Limitations: Giving to residents of MI, with emphasis on Berkeley, Huntington Woods, and Oak Park.
Officer: John F. Novitsky, C.E.O.
EIN: 943372742

633
Stan and Jean Parrish Family Foundation
5104 Old Maumee Rd.
Fort Wayne, IN   46803-1723
County: Allen

Established in 2002 in IN.
Donors: Jean Parrish; Stan Parrish.
Grantmaker type: Independent foundation.
Financial data (yr. ended 12/31/09): Assets, $165,228 (M); expenditures, $11,660; total giving, $11,315; qualifying distributions, $11,315; giving activities include $11,315 for grants.
Fields of interest: Christian agencies & churches.
Limitations: Giving primarily in MI, with some giving in Fort Wayne, IN.
Officers: Stan Parrish, Pres.; Jean Parrish, V.P.
EIN: 300060142

634
Raji Pati Foundation
68 Portuguese Bend Rd.
Rolling Hills, CA   90274-5070
County: Los Angeles
Contact: Damoder Reddy, Pres.

Established in 2004 in CA.
Donor: Damoder Reddy.
Grantmaker type: Independent foundation.
Financial data (yr. ended 12/31/09): Assets, $1 (M); gifts received, $10,000; expenditures, $9,861; total giving, $9,861; qualifying distributions, $9,861; giving activities include $9,861 for grants.
Fields of interest: Higher education; Human services; Public affairs.
Type of support: General/operating support.
Limitations: Applications accepted. Giving primarily in CA, IL, and MI.
Application information:
  Initial approach: Letter
  Deadline(s): None
Officer: Damoder Reddy, Pres.
EIN: 200359534

635
Beatrice & Reymont Paul Foundation
5912 Shillingham Dr.
West Bloomfield, MI   48322-1557
County: Oakland

Established in 2004 in MI.
Donor: Beatrice Paul.
Grantmaker type: Independent foundation.
Financial data (yr. ended 12/31/09): Assets, $1 (M); expenditures, $78,899; total giving, $55,100; qualifying distributions, $55,100; giving activities include $55,100 for grants.
Officers: Beatrice Paul, Chair.; Susan H. Garin, Pres.
EIN: 201279991

636
Paulsen Trust
5230 Village Dr. S.W.
Wyoming, MI 49509-5147
County: Kent
Contact: Nelson R. Allen, Tr.
Application address: 2121 Pantano Rd., No. 267,
Tucson, AZ 85710-6119, tel.: (520) 751-7897

Established in 1988 in MI.
Grantmaker type: Independent foundation.
Financial data (yr. ended 12/31/09): Assets,
$192,358 (M); expenditures, $7,525; total giving,
$6,600; qualifying distributions, $6,600; giving
activities include $6,600 for grants to individuals.
Purpose and activities: The trust awards
scholarships to graduating Michigan high school
seniors who wish to pursue their studies at any
accredited Michigan Institution that provides
programs for post high school learning skills, trade,
career opportunities and/or updates, business,
non-degree programs, associate degrees and/or
advanced college work.
Fields of interest: Higher education.
Type of support: Scholarships—to individuals.
Limitations: Giving limited to residents of MI.
Application information: Application form required.
Deadline(s): May 1
Trustees: Nelson R. Allen; John Barnett; Agnes
Karas.
EIN: 386537948

637
J. Red Peach Foundation
1999 Morris Dr.
Niles, MI 49120-8620 (269) 687-6290
County: Berrien
Contact: Robin Oare Brown, Pres.

Established in 2003 in MI.
Donor: Nancy Oare Butler.
Grantmaker type: Independent foundation.
Financial data (yr. ended 12/31/09): Assets,
$79,098 (M); gifts received, $10,000;
expenditures, $9,733; total giving, $8,823;
qualifying distributions, $9,278; giving activities
include $8,823 for 2 grants (high: $7,823; low:
$1,000).
Fields of interest: Homeless, human services.
Limitations: Giving primarily in South Bend, IN. No
grants to individuals.
Application information:
Initial approach: Letter
Deadline(s): None
Officers and Directors:* Robin Oare Brown,* Pres.;
James H. Brown,* V.P.; Donald E. Hill, Jr.,* V.P.;
Ericka L. Benson,* Secy.-Treas.
EIN: 200530854

638
Pellerito, Manzella, Certa & Cusmano
Family Foundation
30295 Embassy St.
Beverly Hills, MI 48025-5021
County: Oakland
Contact: Frank A. Pellerito, Tr.

Established in 1988 in MI.
Grantmaker type: Independent foundation.
Financial data (yr. ended 12/31/09): Assets,
$314,270 (M); expenditures, $15,684; total giving,

$15,080; qualifying distributions, $15,080; giving
activities include $15,080 for grants.
Fields of interest: Education; Human services;
Children/youth, services; Catholic agencies &
churches.
Type of support: General/operating support;
Equipment; Emergency funds; Seed money;
Research; Matching/challenge support.
Limitations: Giving primarily in MI.
Application information:
Initial approach: Letter or in person
Deadline(s): None
Board meeting date(s): Annually
Final notification: 60 days
Trustees: Coleen O. Pellerito; Frank A. Pellerito.
EIN: 382776130

639
The Peninsula Foundation
c/o Scholarship Comm.
1512 Pacheco St., Ste. D-203
Santa Fe, NM 87505-5111 (505) 986-6874
County: Santa Fe

Established in TX.
Donors: Ame Vennema‡; Catherine S. Vennema.
Grantmaker type: Independent foundation.
Financial data (yr. ended 12/31/09): Assets,
$6,527 (M); gifts received, $5,000; expenditures,
$10,775; total giving, $10,000; qualifying
distributions, $10,000; giving activities include
$10,000 for 4 grants to individuals (high: $2,500;
low: $2,500).
Purpose and activities: Scholarship awards to
graduating seniors from Menominee High School,
Michigan.
Fields of interest: Higher education.
Type of support: Scholarships—to individuals.
Limitations: Giving limited to Menominee, MI.
Application information: Application form can be
obtained from Menominee High, MI School
Guidance Dept. Application form required.
Deadline(s): Feb. 1
Trustees: Margaret K. Lemen; John Vennema; Peter
A. Vennema; Linda V. White.
EIN: 742028228

640
Penner Foundation
10133 Diamond Park Rd.
Interlochen, MI 49643-9513
County: Grand Traverse
Contact: Ruth M. Penner, Dir.

Established in 1991.
Donor: Leroy King.
Grantmaker type: Independent foundation.
Financial data (yr. ended 12/31/09): Assets,
$47,149 (M); expenditures, $10,653; total giving,
$7,679; qualifying distributions, $10,653; giving
activities include $7,679 for 1 grant.
Fields of interest: Higher education; Christian
agencies & churches.
Limitations: Applications accepted. Giving primarily
in MI. No grants to individuals.
Application information: Application form required.
Initial approach: Letter
Deadline(s): None
Officers: Robert Raese, Chair.; Linda Samelson,
Pres.; Kristine Engel, Secy.; Susan Bowen, Treas.

Directors: Jonathon Penner; Ruth Penner; Michael
Usey.
EIN: 382974470

641
Joe D. Pentecost Foundation
1515 Turf Ln., Ste. 300
East Lansing, MI 48823-6393 (517) 336-5000
County: Ingham
Contact: Rita F. Stoskopf, Pres.
FAX: (517) 336-5882;
E-mail: rita@jdpfoundation.org; URL: http://
jdpfoundation.org

Established in 2002 in MI.
Donor: Joe D. Pentecost‡.
Grantmaker type: Independent foundation.
Financial data (yr. ended 12/31/09): Assets,
$12,882,972 (M); gifts received, $5,303,523;
expenditures, $415,113; total giving, $240,000;
qualifying distributions, $382,916; giving activities
include $240,000 for 5 grants (high: $185,000;
low: $2,000).
Purpose and activities: The foundation focuses on
youth and education.
Fields of interest: Higher education; Higher
education, university; Protestant agencies &
churches; Children/youth; Children; Substance
abusers.
Type of support: Annual campaigns; Program
development; Building/renovation; Endowments.
Limitations: Applications accepted. Giving primarily
in Ingham, Eaton and Clinton counties, MI. No
support for political organizations. No grants to
individuals.
Application information: Application form available
on foundation web site. Application form required.
Initial approach: Letter
Copies of proposal: 3
Deadline(s): Oct. 15
Board meeting date(s): Varies
Final notification: 90 days
Officers and Directors:* Rita F. Stoskopf,* Pres.;
Robert J. Phipps,* Secy.-Treas.; Calvin C. Lutz.
EIN: 352178154
Selected grants: The following grants were reported
in 2008.
$228,500 to Michigan State University, East
Lansing, MI.

642
Perrone Charitable Foundation, Inc.
38570 Northfarm Dr.
Northville, MI 48167-9037
County: Wayne
Contact: Christine Bartlett, Pres.

Established in 1997 in MI.
Donor: John Perrone.
Grantmaker type: Independent foundation.
Financial data (yr. ended 12/31/09): Assets,
$48,892 (M); expenditures, $2,056; total giving,
$0; qualifying distributions, $0.
Limitations: Applications accepted. Giving primarily
in MI.
Application information:
Initial approach: Letter
Deadline(s): None
Officers: Christine Bartlett, Pres. and Treas.; Dianne
C. Perrone, Secy.
EIN: 383378779

643
Perry-Morrice-Shaftsburg Emergency Relief Council
P.O. Box 783
Perry, MI 48872-0783
County: Shiawassee

Grantmaker type: Independent foundation.
Financial data (yr. ended 12/31/09): Assets, $30,677 (M); gifts received, $31,967; expenditures, $30,339; total giving, $0; qualifying distributions, $0.
Purpose and activities: Provides emergency assistance, including cash and food, to residents of Shiawassee County, Michigan.
Fields of interest: Human services; Economically disadvantaged.
Type of support: Emergency funds; In-kind gifts.
Limitations: Giving primarily in the Morrice and Perry, MI, areas.
Officers: Sharon Ledy, Pres.; Shirley Shaw, V.P.; Alilah Smith, Secy.; David Robertson, Treas.
EIN: 382417568

644
The Herman & Katherine Peters Foundation Corp.
351 W. Glade Rd.
Palatine, IL 60067-6831
County: Cook
Contact: Scot A. Leonard, Pres.
E-mail: sleonard@petersfoundation.org

Established in 1998 in IL.
Donors: Katherine Peters†; Katherine Peters Trust.
Grantmaker type: Independent foundation.
Financial data (yr. ended 12/31/09): Assets, $9,508,597 (M); expenditures, $556,415; total giving, $408,000; qualifying distributions, $494,626; giving activities include $290,500 for 31 grants (high: $40,000; low: $500), and $117,500 for 19 grants to individuals (high: $15,000; low: $2,500).
Purpose and activities: Scholarship awards to financially needy students pursuing studies relating to environmental concerns or Christian-based religious instruction. Some giving for educational field trips for underprivileged children to heighten their awareness about the importance of conservation.
Fields of interest: Higher education; Environmental education; Christian agencies & churches.
Type of support: Scholarships—to individuals.
Limitations: Applications accepted. Giving primarily in AZ, CO, IL, MI, and WI.
Application information: Application form required.
Initial approach: E-mail
Deadline(s): None
Officers and Directors:* Scot A. Leonard,* Pres.; James P. Devine, Jr.,* V.P.; Jeanine Holtsford,* Secy.-Treas.; George Carroll; Cyndy Hass.
Number of staff: 1 full-time professional.
EIN: 364180010
Selected grants: The following grants were reported in 2007.
$40,000 to Chicago Coalition for the Homeless, Chicago, IL.
$40,000 to Lydia Home Association, Chicago, IL.
$35,000 to American Red Cross.
$35,000 to Salvation Army.
$1,000 to Girl Scouts of the U.S.A., Chicago, IL.

645
Peterson Family Foundation
c/o McDonnell, Conley, Arslanian & Neveux, LLP
74 E. Long Lake Rd., Ste. 100
Bloomfield, MI 48304-2397 (248) 540-7500
County: Oakland
Contact: Paul Arslanian, Dir.

Established in 1999 in MI.
Donor: Robert Peterson†.
Grantmaker type: Independent foundation.
Financial data (yr. ended 12/31/09): Assets, $2,176,500 (M); expenditures, $126,381; total giving, $81,500; qualifying distributions, $81,500; giving activities include $81,500 for grants.
Fields of interest: Foundations (community); Protestant agencies & churches.
Limitations: Applications accepted. Giving limited to MI.
Application information:
Initial approach: Letter
Deadline(s): None
Directors: Paul Arslanian; Mark R. Peterson.
EIN: 383457564

646
W. H. Pettibone & Associates Foundation, Inc.
4260 N. Atlantic Blvd.
Auburn Hills, MI 48326-1578
County: Oakland

Established in MI.
Grantmaker type: Independent foundation.
Financial data (yr. ended 12/31/09): Assets, $326,549 (M); expenditures, $2,144; total giving, $0; qualifying distributions, $0.
Fields of interest: Education; Youth, services; Foundations (community).
Type of support: Scholarship funds.
Limitations: Giving primarily in MI.
Officer: Stephen Fragnoli, Mgr.
Trustees: Michael Pettibone; William Pettibone, Jr.
EIN: 386107400

647
Physicians' Organization of Western Michigan Foundation, Inc.
(also known as POWM Foundation)
c/o David Silliven
233 E. Fulton, Ste. 101
Grand Rapids, MI 49503-3200 (616) 458-7324
County: Kent

Established in 2000 in MI.
Donor: Physicians' Organization of Western Michigan.
Grantmaker type: Independent foundation.
Financial data (yr. ended 12/31/09): Assets, $18,170 (M); expenditures, $9,000; total giving, $9,000; qualifying distributions, $9,000; giving activities include $9,000 for grants.
Purpose and activities: Giving primarily to improve patient care and to support health-related charitable activities.
Fields of interest: Health care; Human services.
Limitations: Applications accepted. Giving primarily in Grand Rapids, MI.
Application information: Application form not required.
Deadline(s): None

Officers: Peter A. Kuhl, M.D., Pres.; Andrew M. Welch, M.D., V.P.; Alan Siegel, M.D., Secy.-Treas.
Directors: Randall Clark, M.D.; Steven Crane, M.D.; Vincent A. Dubravec, M.D.; Kenneth Dudley, M.D.; Roger Edvenson, M.D.; Mark A. Frederickson, M.D.; David D. Hamm, M.D.; Gregory Johnson, M.D.; John Keller, M.D.; David E. Langholz, M.D.; Charles Lawrence, M.D.; David F. McCorry, D.O.; Henry J. Mulder; Khan J. Nedd, M.D.; Kenneth Nelson, M.D.; David Thompson, M.D.; Douglas Vandrie, M.D.; Darryl J. Varda; Philip J. Weighner, M.D.; Jeffrey A. Wolfson, M.D.; Terrence P. Wright, M.D.; Ivars Zadvinskis, M.D.
EIN: 383522988

648
The Pietrasiuk Family Foundation
2395 S. Huron Pkwy., Ste. 100
Ann Arbor, MI 48104-5129 (734) 971-8088
County: Washtenaw
Contact: Catherine M. Miller, Pres.

Established in MI.
Donor: Catherine M. Miller.
Grantmaker type: Independent foundation.
Financial data (yr. ended 12/31/08): Assets, $84,218 (M); gifts received, $12,000; expenditures, $37,158; total giving, $35,225; qualifying distributions, $35,225; giving activities include $35,225 for grants.
Purpose and activities: Giving primarily to organizations that care for disabled, handicapped, unprivileged and at-risk people, and other organizations that provide the opportunity for children and adults to develop mentally and physically through academic, religious and physical development programs. The foundation also provides funds for scholarships and fellowships to colleges and universities and to national organizations that are involved in research and development that lead to disease prevention and cure.
Fields of interest: Secondary school/education; Higher education; Health care; Medical research; Human services; Religion; Disabilities, people with.
Type of support: General/operating support.
Limitations: Giving limited to southeastern MI.
Application information:
Initial approach: Letter
Deadline(s): None
Officers and Directors:* Catherine M. Miller,* Pres.; Patrick D. Miller,* V.P.
EIN: 383348405

649
Plym Foundation
P.O. Box 906
Niles, MI 49120-0906
County: Berrien
Application address: c/o James Keenan, 423 Sycamore St., Ste. 101, Niles, MI 49120, tel.: (269) 684-3248

Incorporated in 1952 in MI.
Donor: Mrs. Francis J. Plym†.
Grantmaker type: Independent foundation.
Financial data (yr. ended 12/31/09): Assets, $5,906,241 (M); expenditures, $278,521; total giving, $184,000; qualifying distributions, $218,800; giving activities include $184,000 for 12 grants (high: $30,000; low: $5,000).

Purpose and activities: Giving primarily for higher education and human services.

Fields of interest: Higher education; Education; Human services; YM/YWCAs & YM/YWHAs; Community/economic development; United Ways and Federated Giving Programs; Public affairs.

Type of support: Building/renovation; Program development; Matching/challenge support.

Limitations: Applications accepted. Giving primarily in MI; giving also in FL, IN, and NY. No grants to individuals.

Application information: Application form not required.

  Initial approach: Letter or telephone
  Copies of proposal: 1
  Deadline(s): None
  Board meeting date(s): May

Officers: J. Eric Plym, Pres.; Donald F. Walter, V.P. and Treas.; James F. Keenan, Secy.

Trustees: John M. Campbell; John E. Plym, Jr.; Nancy S. Plym.

EIN: 386069680

650
John Polakovic Charitable Trust

32100 Telegraph Rd., Ste. 200
Bingham Farms, MI 48025-2454
County: Oakland
Contact: James B. Tintera, Tr.
Application address: 117 Scissortail Trail, Georgetown, TX 78628-4811, tel.: (517) 930-1732

Established in MI.

Grantmaker type: Independent foundation.

Financial data (yr. ended 12/31/09): Assets, $90,066 (M); expenditures, $8,533; total giving, $7,500; qualifying distributions, $8,533; giving activities include $7,500 for 5 grants to individuals (high: $1,500; low: $1,500).

Purpose and activities: Scholarship awards to graduating seniors at J. Sterling Morton High School, Illinois.

Fields of interest: Scholarships/financial aid.

Type of support: Scholarships—to individuals.

Limitations: Applications accepted. Giving primarily to residents of IL.

Application information:

  Initial approach: Letter
  Deadline(s): None

Trustees: Evelyn Tintera; James B. Tintera.

EIN: 386390004

651
Jennifer Gordon Polan Foundation

27340 Willowgreen Ct.
Franklin, MI 48025-1787   (248) 626-2231
County: Oakland
Contact: Jesse N. Polan, Tr.

Established in MI.

Donors: Alfred Berkowitz Foundation; Jesse N. Polan.

Grantmaker type: Independent foundation.

Financial data (yr. ended 12/31/09): Assets, $22,369 (M); gifts received, $47; expenditures, $4,647; total giving, $4,000; qualifying distributions, $4,000; giving activities include $4,000 for 4 grants to individuals (high: $1,000; low: $1,000).

Fields of interest: Higher education.

Type of support: Scholarships—to individuals.

Limitations: Giving primarily in MI.

Application information: Application form required.

  Initial approach: Letter
  Deadline(s): May 1

Trustee: Jesse N. Polan.

EIN: 383540779

652
Sara Pollack Educational Trust

345 Sumac Ln.
Ann Arbor, MI 48105-3012   (734) 663-9151
County: Washtenaw
Contact: Margaret Guire
Application address: c/o Margaret Guire, 2108 Shadford Rd., Ann Arbor, MI 48104-4552, tel.: (734) 662-2040

Established in MI.

Grantmaker type: Independent foundation.

Financial data (yr. ended 12/31/09): Assets, $50,596 (M); gifts received, $950; expenditures, $2,800; total giving, $2,800; qualifying distributions, $2,800; giving activities include $2,800 for 1 grant.

Purpose and activities: Grants are primarily awarded to public elementary and high school students in southeast Michigan for music education or other educational purposes.

Fields of interest: Arts education; Performing arts, music.

Type of support: Grants to individuals.

Limitations: Applications accepted. Giving primarily to residents and organizations in Ann Arbor and southeast MI.

Application information:

  Initial approach: Proposal
  Deadline(s): None
  Final notification: Within 3 months

Trustees: Henry N. Pollack; Lana B. Pollack.

EIN: 386424735

653
Herbert and Elsa Ponting Foundation

535 Griswold St., Ste. 1900
Detroit, MI 48226-3679   (313) 496-1200
County: Wayne
Contact: John L. King, Pres.
FAX: (313) 496-1300;
E-mail: jking@berrymoorman.com

Established in 1987 in MI.

Donor: The William Fitzherbert Ponting Trust.

Grantmaker type: Independent foundation.

Financial data (yr. ended 12/31/09): Assets, $1,864,451 (M); expenditures, $216,695; total giving, $161,000; qualifying distributions, $161,000; giving activities include $161,000 for 34 grants (high: $10,000; low: $1,000).

Purpose and activities: Giving primarily for academic scholarships, educational equipment, and specific educational programs for the staff of agencies that have been in existence for at least five years, within the state of Michigan.

Fields of interest: Elementary school/education; Secondary school/education; Higher education; Business school/education; Law school/education; Education.

Type of support: General/operating support; Equipment; Program development; Scholarship funds.

Limitations: Applications accepted. Giving primarily in MI. No grants to individuals.

Publications: Application guidelines; Informational brochure (including application guidelines).

Application information: Application form not required.

  Initial approach: Letter
  Copies of proposal: 1
  Deadline(s): Mar. 1 and Oct. 1
  Board meeting date(s): May and Nov.

Officers and Directors:* John L. King,* Pres.; Sheila P. Geier,* V.P.; Dennis M. Mitzel,* Secy.-Treas.

Number of staff: 1 part-time professional.

EIN: 386058868

Selected grants: The following grants were reported in 2006.

$10,000 to Cornerstone Schools, Detroit, MI.
$10,000 to Detroit Science Center, Detroit, MI.
$10,000 to Detroit Zoological Society, Royal Oak, MI.
$5,000 to Battle Creek Academy, Battle Creek, MI.
$5,000 to Byron Center Christian School, Byron Center, MI.
$5,000 to Friends School in Detroit, Detroit, MI.
$5,000 to Walsh University, North Canton, OH.
$4,000 to Boys and Girls Club.
$4,000 to Interlochen Center for the Arts, Interlochen, MI.

654
The Popeye Animal Cancer Foundation

1776 Latham St.
Birmingham, MI 48009-3043
County: Oakland

Established in 2005 in MI.

Grantmaker type: Independent foundation.

Financial data (yr. ended 12/31/09): Assets, $3,646 (M); gifts received, $4,152; expenditures, $6,227; total giving, $5,477; qualifying distributions, $5,477; giving activities include $5,477 for grants.

Officers: Ann O. Calvert, Pres.; Kenneth A. Calvert, V.P.

EIN: 203184631

655
Porter Foundation

P.O. Box 6484
Grand Rapids, MI 49516-6484   (616) 459-9531
County: Kent
Contact: Margaret Beusse, Pres. and Secy.

Established in 1966.

Donors: Burke E. Porter Machinery Co.; Burke Porter Trust.

Grantmaker type: Independent foundation.

Financial data (yr. ended 06/30/09): Assets, $1,782,823 (M); gifts received, $25,000; expenditures, $109,280; total giving, $91,200; qualifying distributions, $91,200; giving activities include $91,200 for grants.

Fields of interest: Museums (art); Performing arts, theater; Performing arts, orchestras; Arts; Higher education; Higher education, college; Education; Human services.

Type of support: General/operating support; Matching/challenge support.

Limitations: Applications accepted. Giving primarily in Grand Rapids, MI. Generally prefers programs with no religious affiliation.

Application information:
Initial approach: Letter, including letter from school counselor
Deadline(s): None
Officers and Director:* Margaret Beusse,* Pres. and Secy.; Heather Beusse, V.P.; Blake Beusse, Treas.
EIN: 386118663
Selected grants: The following grants were reported in 2007.
$20,000 to Grand Rapids Ballet Company, Grand Rapids, MI.
$15,000 to Grand Rapids Art Museum, Grand Rapids, MI.
$15,000 to Grand Rapids Civic Theater, Grand Rapids, MI.
$15,000 to Grand Rapids Symphony, Grand Rapids, MI.
$15,000 to Kalamazoo College, Kalamazoo, MI.
$6,000 to GLOBIO, Portland, OR.
$5,000 to Arts Council of Greater Grand Rapids, Grand Rapids, MI.
$5,000 to Flagstaff Symphony Association, Flagstaff, AZ.
$5,000 to Planned Parenthood, Fayetteville, AR.
$4,000 to Sedona Arts Center, Sedona, AZ.

656
The Irwin Andrew Porter Foundation
3325 W. 34 1/2 St.
Minneapolis, MN   55416-4652
County: Hennepin
URL: http://www.iapfoundation.org

Established in 1996 in MN.
Donor: Amy L. Hubbard.
Grantmaker type: Independent foundation.
Financial data (yr. ended 08/31/09): Assets, $2,884,185 (M); expenditures, $354,356; total giving, $312,483; qualifying distributions, $312,483; giving activities include $312,483 for 27 grants (high: $58,000; low: $200).
Purpose and activities: The mission of the foundation is to fund innovative projects that foster connections between individuals, communities, the environment and the world at large.
Fields of interest: Museums (art); Arts; Education; Environment, water resources; Environment; Health care; Human services; YM/YWCAs & YM/YWHAs; International economic development.
Type of support: Matching/challenge support.
Limitations: Applications accepted. Giving primarily in the U.S., with focus on IA, IL, MI, MN, ND, SD, and WI; also giving on an international basis to projects located outside the U.S. unrestricted by country or region. No support for political organizations or religious programs. No grants to individuals, or for operating expenses, capital campaigns, or endowments.
Application information: Complete application guidelines available on foundation web site.
Copies of proposal: 1
Board meeting date(s): Quarterly
Officer and Directors:* Amy L. Hubbard,* Pres.; Arta Cheney; Scott Elkins; Gleason Glover; Jay Goldberg; Gloria Perez Jordan; Geoffrey Kehoe; Dipankar Mukherjee.
EIN: 411852392
Selected grants: The following grants were reported in 2006.
$20,000 to Mano a Mano Medical Resources, Mendota Heights, MN.
$8,000 to Dakota Rural Action, Brookings, SD.

$8,000 to YWCA of Minneapolis, Minneapolis, MN.
$7,200 to Tubman, Minneapolis, MN.
$5,600 to Forecast Public Artworks, Saint Paul, MN.
$5,600 to Ten Thousand Things, Minneapolis, MN.
$4,000 to Kulture Klub Collaborative, Minneapolis, MN.
$4,000 to Metropolitan Family Services, Chicago, IL.
$2,800 to YouthCARE, Minneapolis, MN.
$1,648 to Center for Victims of Torture, Minneapolis, MN.

657
The Meyer and Anna Prentis Family Foundation, Inc.
P.O. Box 7055
Huntington Woods, MI   48070-7055
County: Oakland
Application address: c/o Robert M. Justin, 1142 N. Main St., Rochester, MI 48307-1114, tel.: (248) 652-9000

Incorporated in 1955 in MI.
Donor: Members of the Prentis family.
Grantmaker type: Independent foundation.
Financial data (yr. ended 12/31/09): Assets, $3,127,572 (M); expenditures, $180,777; total giving, $143,336; qualifying distributions, $174,532; giving activities include $143,336 for 71 grants (high: $17,500; low: $50).
Purpose and activities: Giving primarily for Jewish organizations, as well as for the performing arts, education, hospitals and health care, and human services.
Fields of interest: Performing arts; Historic preservation/historical societies; Arts; Education, early childhood education; Elementary school/education; Higher education; Education; Hospitals (general); Health care; Human services; Residential/custodial care, senior continuing care; Jewish federated giving programs; Jewish agencies & synagogues.
Limitations: Applications accepted. Giving primarily in FL and MI. No grants to individuals, or for endowment funds, scholarships, fellowships, or matching gifts; no loans.
Application information:
Initial approach: Letter
Copies of proposal: 1
Deadline(s): None
Board meeting date(s): July and Dec.
Officers: Ronald E.P. Frenkel, M.D., Pres.; Denise L. Brown, V.P.; Marvin A. Frenkel, Secy.-Treas.
Trustees: Cindy P. Frenkel; Dale P. Frenkel; Nelson P. Lande; Ricki Farber Zitner.
EIN: 386090332
Selected grants: The following grants were reported in 2008.
$35,000 to Allied Jewish Campaign, Detroit, MI.
$10,000 to Vassar College, Poughkeepsie, NY.
$5,000 to Maimonides School, Brookline, MA.
$5,000 to Massachusetts General Hospital, Boston, MA.
$5,000 to Pine Street Inn, Boston, MA.
$4,500 to Michigan Opera Theater, Detroit, MI.
$4,500 to Music Hall Center for the Performing Arts, Detroit, MI.
$3,000 to Detroit Historical Society, Detroit, MI.
$1,600 to Oakland University, Meadowbrook Theater, Rochester, MI.
$1,100 to Council of Michigan Foundations, Grand Haven, MI.

658
Dan R. and Pamela M. Prevo Foundation
374 Autumn Ridge
Traverse City, MI   49686-1993   (231) 223-4669
County: Grand Traverse
Contact: Dan R. Prevo, Pres.

Established in 1999 in MI.
Donor: Prevo's Family Markets, Inc.
Grantmaker type: Independent foundation.
Financial data (yr. ended 11/30/09): Assets, $278,472 (M); expenditures, $39,222; total giving, $10,250; qualifying distributions, $10,250; giving activities include $10,250 for grants.
Fields of interest: Education; Human services; Women.
Limitations: Giving limited to MI. No grants to individuals.
Application information: Application form required.
Deadline(s): None
Final notification: Within 2 months
Officers: Dan R. Prevo, Pres.; Pamela M. Prevo, V.P.; Aaron P. Prevo, Treas.
EIN: 383454586

659
Maxwell Pribil Memorial Trust
c/o Citizens Bank Wealth Mgmt., N.A.
328 S. Saginaw St., M/C 002072
Flint, MI   48502-1923
County: Genesee
Application Address: c/o Citizens Bank Wealth Mgmt., N.A., Attn.: Helen James, 101 N. Washington Ave., Saginaw, MI 48607, tel.: (989) 776-7368

Established in 1998 in MI.
Grantmaker type: Independent foundation.
Financial data (yr. ended 12/31/09): Assets, $2,949,250 (M); expenditures, $131,167; total giving, $101,000; qualifying distributions, $101,000; giving activities include $101,000 for grants.
Fields of interest: Arts; Education.
Limitations: Applications accepted. Giving primarily in Bay City and Saginaw, MI.
Application information: Grants must be for cultural or artistic purposes. Application form required.
Deadline(s): None
Trustee: Citizens Bank Wealth Management, N.A.
EIN: 386723513
Selected grants: The following grants were reported in 2008.
$40,000 to Saginaw Art Museum, Saginaw, MI.
$35,700 to Midland Center for the Arts, Midland, MI.
$20,000 to Saginaw Choral Society, Saginaw, MI.
$15,000 to Pit and Balcony, Saginaw, MI.
$5,200 to Pit and Balcony, Saginaw, MI.

660
The Robert E. Price Foundation, Inc.
P.O. Box 605
Adrian, MI   49221-0605   (517) 265-6160
County: Lenawee
Contact: Robert E. Price, Pres.

Established in 1995 in MI.
Donor: Robert E. Price.
Grantmaker type: Independent foundation.
Financial data (yr. ended 12/31/09): Assets, $1,840,453 (M); expenditures, $120,295; total

giving, $118,000; qualifying distributions, $118,000; giving activities include $118,000 for grants.

Purpose and activities: Giving primarily for education.

Fields of interest: Performing arts, orchestras; Elementary/secondary education; Higher education; Cancer; Youth development.

Limitations: Applications accepted. Giving primarily in Adrian, MI. No grants to individuals.

Application information:

Initial approach: Letter

Deadline(s): None

Officers: Robert E. Price, Pres.; Henry E. Mistele, Secy.-Treas.

EIN: 383247629

Selected grants: The following grants were reported in 2008.

$25,000 to Adrian College, Adrian, MI.

$25,000 to Adrian Schools Educational Foundation, Adrian, MI.

$5,000 to Lenawee Intermediate School District, Adrian, MI.

661

The Pryor Foundation

29 Fernbrook

West Hartford, CT 06107-1613

County: Hartford

Contact: Esther A. Pryor, Tr.

E-mail: fpryor1@swarthmore.edu

Established in 1947 in MI.

Donors: Mary S. Pryor†; Millard H. Pryor†; Corey Kienholz; Millard H. Pryor, Jr.; Daniel A. Pryor.

Grantmaker type: Independent foundation.

Financial data (yr. ended 12/31/09): Assets, $3,330,519 (M); expenditures, $383,490; total giving, $352,000; qualifying distributions, $363,495; giving activities include $352,000 for 19 grants (high: $50,000; low: $1,500).

Purpose and activities: Giving to the arts, culture and education.

Fields of interest: Arts; Higher education; Human services; United Ways and Federated Giving Programs.

Type of support: Annual campaigns; Capital campaigns; Emergency funds; Consulting services.

Limitations: Giving primarily in Hartford, CT, Ann Arbor, MI, MS, Mansfield, OH, and PA. No support for religious or political organizations. No grants for building funds or land acquisition.

Application information:

Initial approach: Letter

Deadline(s): None

Board meeting date(s): Nov.

Officer and Trustees: * F. Loyal Bemiller, Secy.; H. Elizabeth Bradley; Daniel A. Pryor; Esther A. Pryor; Frederic L. Pryor.

Number of staff: None.

EIN: 386056108

Selected grants: The following grants were reported in 2008.

$95,000 to Tougaloo College, Tougaloo, MS.

$75,000 to Hartford Symphony Orchestra, Hartford, CT.

$25,000 to Peace Neighborhood Center, Ann Arbor, MI.

$16,000 to University of Hartford, West Hartford, CT.

$5,000 to Georgetown University, Georgetown Library Recovery, Washington, DC.

$4,000 to Grace Episcopal Church, Mansfield, OH.

$3,000 to Chester Childrens Chorus, Department of Music and Dance, Swarthmore College, Swarthmore, PA.

662

George Puschelberg Foundation

10000 Harbor Place Dr.

St. Clair Shores, MI 48080-1518

(586) 779-8252

County: Macomb

Contact: Allan Neef, Tr.

Established in MI.

Grantmaker type: Independent foundation.

Financial data (yr. ended 04/30/10): Assets, $264,405 (M); expenditures, $25,707; total giving, $15,000; qualifying distributions, $15,000; giving activities include $15,000 for grants.

Fields of interest: Medical school/education; Animals/wildlife, special services; Cancer research; Independent living, disability.

Limitations: Giving primarily in MI. No grants to individuals.

Application information: Application form not required.

Initial approach: Letter

Deadline(s): None

Trustees: Allan Neef; Jack Porter.

EIN: 382319247

663

R.J. Ministries

P.O. Box 44

Trenton, MI 48183   (734) 282-8235

County: Wayne

Contact: John Russell, Pres.

URL: http://www.rjministries.com/

Grantmaker type: Independent foundation.

Financial data (yr. ended 12/31/09): Assets, $3,118 (M); expenditures, $20; total giving, $0; qualifying distributions, $0.

Application information: Application form not required.

Initial approach: Letter

Deadline(s): None

Officers: John Russell, Pres.; Ronda Russell, V.P.

Director: Janice Jakaus.

EIN: 203706613

664

Rainbow Foundation

5131 Rosabelle Beach Ave.

Holland, MI 49424-1034   (616) 786-0548

County: Ottawa

Contact: Marjorie G. Hoogeboom, Secy.-Treas.

Established in 1990 in MI.

Donors: Thomas J. Hoogeboom; Marjorie G. Hoogeboom.

Grantmaker type: Independent foundation.

Financial data (yr. ended 12/31/09): Assets, $797,894 (M); expenditures, $39,906; total giving, $38,250; qualifying distributions, $38,250; giving activities include $38,250 for 3 grants (high: $15,000; low: $11,250).

Purpose and activities: Giving primarily to Christian organizations and schools.

Fields of interest: Higher education; Education; Christian agencies & churches.

Limitations: Applications accepted. Giving primarily in the western MI area, with emphasis on Grand Rapids.

Application information: Application form not required.

Initial approach: Letter or proposal

Deadline(s): None

Final notification: Within 3 months

Officers: Thomas J. Hoogeboom, Pres.; Cheryl L. Hoogewind, V.P.; Karen J. Vanderlaan, V.P.; Marjorie G. Hoogeboom, Secy.-Treas.

Director: Robert P. Egly, Jr.

EIN: 382939744

665

Dominic J. Raiola Foundation

48035 Bellagio Ct.

Northville, MI 48167-9808

County: Wayne

Established in HI.

Grantmaker type: Independent foundation.

Financial data (yr. ended 12/31/09): Assets, $47,954 (M); expenditures, $19,815; total giving, $19,200; qualifying distributions, $19,200; giving activities include $19,200 for grants.

Fields of interest: Cystic fibrosis research.

Officers: Dominic J. Raiola, Pres.; Anthony J. Raiola, V.P. and Treas.; Yvonne Raiola, V.P.; Wendy S. Raiola, Secy.

EIN: 203730021

666

Ramser-Morgan Foundation

c/o Comerica Bank

P.O. Box 75000, MC 3300

Detroit, MI 48275-0001   (313) 222-6105

County: Wayne

Contact: Robert Sajdak, Pres.

Established in 1991 in MI.

Donor: M. Louise Morgan.

Grantmaker type: Independent foundation.

Financial data (yr. ended 12/31/09): Assets, $995,007 (M); expenditures, $59,510; total giving, $47,250; qualifying distributions, $47,250; giving activities include $47,250 for grants.

Fields of interest: Higher education; Hospitals (general); Cancer; Human services; Salvation Army; Foundations (community); United Ways and Federated Giving Programs.

Limitations: Applications accepted. Giving in MI, primarily in Detroit.

Application information: Application form not required.

Deadline(s): None

Officers: Robert Sajdak, Pres.; Steve Milbeck, V.P. and Treas.; Thomas W. Payne, Secy.

EIN: 383003280

667

The Mamie and Harold K. Randall Charitable Trust

2035 Hamburg Tpke., Ste. E

Wayne, NJ 07470-6251   (973) 831-8700

County: Passaic

Contact: Brian W. Hanse, Tr.

Established in 1998 in NJ.

Donor: Harold K. Randall†.

Grantmaker type: Independent foundation.
Financial data (yr. ended 12/31/09): Assets, $2,358,909 (M); expenditures, $151,489; total giving, $113,000; qualifying distributions, $113,000; giving activities include $113,000 for grants.
Purpose and activities: Giving primarily to Christian churches and organizations to promote religious teaching.
Fields of interest: Education; Boys & girls clubs; Human services; Christian agencies & churches.
Limitations: Giving primarily in AR, MI, NJ, and WI. No grants to individuals.
Application information: Application form not required.
  Initial approach: Proposal
  Copies of proposal: 1
  Deadline(s): None
  Final notification: Within 3 months of receipt
Trustees: Brian W. Hanse; William C. Hanse.
Number of staff: 1 part-time support.
EIN: 311612173
Selected grants: The following grants were reported in 2007.
$37,500 to Ron Hutchcraft Ministries, Harrison, AR.
$25,000 to Chilton Memorial Hospital Foundation, Pompton Plains, NJ.
$20,000 to Grace United Presbyterian Church, Wayne, NJ.
$15,000 to New Jersey Family Policy Council, Parsippany, NJ.
$10,000 to Bethany Christian Services, Grand Rapids, MI.
$10,000 to Chicago Hope Academy, Chicago, IL.
$10,000 to Christian Union, Princeton, NJ.
$5,000 to Kensington Community Church, Troy, MI.
$5,000 to Kings College, New York, NY.

668
Milton M. Ratner Foundation
P.O. Box 250628
Franklin, MI 48025-0628
County: Oakland
Contact: Therese M. Thorn, Treas.
E-mail: ratner_foundation@sbcglobal.net

Incorporated in 1968 in MI.
Donor: Milton M. Ratner‡.
Grantmaker type: Independent foundation.
Financial data (yr. ended 08/31/10): Assets, $6,317,666 (M); expenditures, $468,929; total giving, $348,000; qualifying distributions, $419,234; giving activities include $348,000 for 46 grants (high: $20,000; low: $1,000).
Purpose and activities: Giving primarily for higher education, and health and human services for children, families, and the elderly. Giving also for research to fight heart disease, for aid and training for the blind, and to aid physically handicapped children.
Fields of interest: Higher education; Scholarships/financial aid; Hospitals (general); Health organizations, association; Medical research, institute; Heart & circulatory research; Blind/visually impaired.
Type of support: General/operating support; Continuing support; Building/renovation; Equipment; Endowments; Program development; Scholarship funds; Research; Matching/challenge support.
Limitations: Applications accepted. Giving primarily in GA and MI. No grants to individuals.
Publications: Application guidelines; Grants list.

Application information: Council of Michigan Foundations Common Grant Application Form accepted. Application form not required.
  Initial approach: Letter no more than 3 pages
  Copies of proposal: 1
  Deadline(s): Aug. 31
  Board meeting date(s): Oct.
  Final notification: Dec. 31
Officers and Trustees: * Mary Jo Rossen,* Pres.; Charles R. McDonald,* V.P. and Secy.; Therese M. Thorn,* Treas.
Agent: Meadowbrook Investment Advisors.
Number of staff: None.
EIN: 386160330
Selected grants: The following grants were reported in 2007.
$20,000 to Calhoun Gordon Arts Council, Calhoun, GA. For capital campaign.
$20,000 to Calhouns GEM Theater, Friends of, Calhoun, GA. For capital campaign.
$20,000 to Gordon Hospital Foundation, Calhoun, GA. For capital campaign.
$10,000 to Alzheimers Association.
$10,000 to Child Abuse and Neglect Council of Oakland County, Pontiac, MI. For general operating support.
$10,000 to Childrens Tumor Foundation, New York, NY.
$10,000 to United Way for Southeastern Michigan, Detroit, MI.
$10,000 to United Way of Gordon County, Calhoun, GA. For general operating support.
$10,000 to University of Georgia Foundation, Athens, GA.
$5,000 to Shepherd Center, Atlanta, GA.

669
The Raval Education Foundation, Inc.
1004 Browns Lake Rd.
Jackson, MI 49203-5669 (517) 414-3400
County: Jackson
Contact: Harish Rawal, Pres.

Established in 2001 in MI.
Donor: Harish Rawal.
Grantmaker type: Independent foundation.
Financial data (yr. ended 12/31/09): Assets, $18,013 (M); gifts received, $1,700; expenditures, $13,281; total giving, $13,000; qualifying distributions, $13,000; giving activities include $13,000 for 7 grants to individuals (high: $4,000; low: $1,000).
Purpose and activities: Scholarship awards to graduates of Jackson High School, Michigan.
Fields of interest: Higher education.
Type of support: Scholarships—to individuals.
Limitations: Giving primarily in Jackson, MI.
Application information:
  Initial approach: Letter
  Deadline(s): None
Officers: Harish Rawal, Pres.; Tejas H. Raval, V.P.; Sudha Raval, Secy.-Treas.
EIN: 383624064

670
Rawson Foundation, Inc.
4717 Hospital Dr.
Cass City, MI 48726-1097
County: Tuscola
Contact: Daniel Derfiny, Secy.-Treas.

Grantmaker type: Independent foundation.
Financial data (yr. ended 12/31/08): Assets, $309,683 (M); expenditures, $10,872; total giving, $10,462; qualifying distributions, $10,462; giving activities include $10,462 for grants.
Purpose and activities: Support for Christian organizations for education through scholarships primarily to graduates of Cass City High School for attendance at Central Michigan University.
Fields of interest: Higher education; Children/youth, services; Protestant agencies & churches.
Type of support: Building/renovation; Scholarship funds.
Limitations: Giving primarily in MI; some giving also in VA.
Application information: Application form not required.
  Deadline(s): None
Officers: Robert Green, Pres.; Robert L. Tuckey, V.P.; Daniel Derfiny, Secy.-Treas.
Director: Mary Jane VanVliet.
EIN: 386060361

671
Recreational Boating Industries Educational Foundation
32398 Five Mile Rd.
Livonia, MI 48154-6109 (734) 261-0123
County: Wayne
Contact: Van W. Snider, Jr., Dir.

Established in MI.
Donor: Michigan Boating Industries Assn.
Grantmaker type: Independent foundation.
Financial data (yr. ended 12/31/09): Assets, $81,807 (M); expenditures, $21,007; total giving, $10,000; qualifying distributions, $10,000; giving activities include $10,000 for 14 grants to individuals (high: $1,000; low: $500).
Purpose and activities: Scholarship awards to permanent residents of Michigan who would not be able to attend college without the financial assistance.
Fields of interest: Higher education; Economically disadvantaged.
Type of support: Scholarships—to individuals.
Limitations: Giving limited to MI.
Application information:
  Initial approach: Letter
  Deadline(s): Apr. 20
Officers: John Hatfield, Pres.; Robert G. Liggett, Jr., V.P.; Gregory Krueger, Secy.; Horst Sherriff, Treas.
Directors: James A. Coburn; Theodore Sampanes; Van W. Snider, Jr.; Ray L. Underwood.
EIN: 382704909

672
C. M. & A. A. Reid Educational Trust
c/o Citizens Bank
328 S. Saginaw St., M/C 002072
Flint, MI 48502-1923
County: Genesee
Application address: c/o Citizens Bank Wealth Mgmt., N.A., Attn.: Helen James, 101 N. Washington Ave., Saginaw, MI 48607-1207, tel.: (989) 776-7368

Established in 1976 in MI.
Donor: Alex Reid‡.
Grantmaker type: Independent foundation.

Financial data (yr. ended 08/31/10): Assets, $687,957 (M); gifts received, $22,110; expenditures, $15,532; total giving, $0; qualifying distributions, $0.
Purpose and activities: Student loans to Saginaw County, Michigan, residents, between the ages of 15-30 for higher education.
Fields of interest: Higher education.
Type of support: Student loans—to individuals.
Limitations: Giving limited to residents of Saginaw County, MI.
Application information: Application form required.
  Deadline(s): June 1
Trustee: Citizens Bank.
Number of staff: 2 full-time support.
EIN: 386347006

673
The Joseph D. and Jerry L. Reid Foundation
222 N. Washington Sq., Ste. 210
Lansing, MI   48933-1800   (517) 371-5540
County: Ingham
Contact: Colleen Reid, Pres.

Established in 1996 in MI.
Donors: Joseph D. Reid; Jerry Reid.
Grantmaker type: Independent foundation.
Financial data (yr. ended 12/31/09): Assets, $222,377 (M); expenditures, $110,785; total giving, $94,200; qualifying distributions, $94,200; giving activities include $94,200 for 12 grants (high: $35,000; low: $100).
Fields of interest: Libraries (public); Education; United Ways and Federated Giving Programs; Catholic agencies & churches.
Type of support: General/operating support.
Limitations: Applications accepted. Giving primarily in Lansing, MI. No grants to individuals.
Application information: Application form required.
  Initial approach: Letter
  Deadline(s): Sept. 30
Officers: Jerry Reid, C.E.O.; Colleen Reid, Pres.
Directors: Brian English; Cristin Reid; Joseph D. Reid; Joseph D. Reid III.
EIN: 383327108
Selected grants: The following grants were reported in 2005.
$100,000 to Saint Vincent Catholic Charities, Lansing, MI.
$75,000 to United Way.
$5,000 to Lansing Community College, Lansing, MI.
$5,000 to Our Lady of the Snows.
$5,000 to Our Lady of the Snows.
$5,000 to Saint Marys Catholic Church.

674
Reimer Family Charitable Trust
6221 Indian Garden Rd.
Petoskey, MI   49770-9244
County: Emmet

Established in 1999 in FL.
Grantmaker type: Independent foundation.
Financial data (yr. ended 12/31/07): Assets, $113 (M); expenditures, $10; total giving, $10; qualifying distributions, $10; giving activities include $10 for grants.
Fields of interest: Cancer.
Type of support: General/operating support.
Limitations: Giving primarily in Tampa, FL. No grants to individuals.

Trustees: Borge R. Reimer; Hennie Reimer.
EIN: 367279828

675
Reimer Family Charitable Trust
4049 Cedar Bluff Rd.
Petoskey, MI   49770-8697
County: Emmet

Established in 1999.
Grantmaker type: Independent foundation.
Financial data (yr. ended 12/31/07): Assets, $113 (M); expenditures, $10; total giving, $10; qualifying distributions, $10; giving activities include $10 for grants.
Limitations: Giving primarily in Petoskey, MI.
Trustees: Borge R. Reimer; Hennie Reimer.
EIN: 367279827

676
Robert C. Reinhardt Trust
5915 Eastman Ave., Ste. 1000
Midland, MI   48640
County: Midland

Grantmaker type: Independent foundation.
Financial data (yr. ended 12/31/08): Assets, $1,172,685 (M); gifts received, $1,688,586; expenditures, $12,652; total giving, $0; qualifying distributions, $12,652.
EIN: 266594353

677
Florence M. Rennie Scholarship Trust
c/o Fifth Third Bank
P.O. Box 3636
Grand Rapids, MI   49501-3636
County: Kent
Application address: c/o Douglas Fletcher, 2248 LSA Bldg, 500 S. State St., Ann Arbor, MI 48109

Grantmaker type: Independent foundation.
Financial data (yr. ended 12/31/09): Assets, $270,788 (M); expenditures, $3,751; total giving, $0; qualifying distributions, $0.
Purpose and activities: Scholarship awards to students of the University of Michigan.
Fields of interest: Scholarships/financial aid.
Type of support: Scholarship funds.
Limitations: Giving limited to Ann Arbor, MI.
Application information: Application form required.
  Initial approach: Applications will be provided by the University of Michigan
  Deadline(s): Jan. and Feb.
Officers: Kirsten Willis, Chair.; Harry Marsden, Admin.
Trustee: Fifth Third Bank.
EIN: 386111647

678
Resnal Foundation
7010 76th St. S.E.
Caledonia, MI   49316-8213   (616) 891-1072
County: Kent
Contact: Peter L. Lanser, Pres.

Established in 2000 in MI.
Donors: Peter L. Lanser; Janet L. Lanser.
Grantmaker type: Independent foundation.

Financial data (yr. ended 12/31/09): Assets, $199,382 (M); expenditures, $17,700; total giving, $17,700; qualifying distributions, $17,700; giving activities include $17,700 for grants.
Fields of interest: Christian agencies & churches.
Limitations: Giving primarily in MI.
Application information: Application form not required.
  Initial approach: Letter
  Deadline(s): None
Officers: Peter L. Lanser, Pres.; Janet L. Lanser, Secy.-Treas.
EIN: 383533081

679
Loraine & Melinese Reuter Foundation
c/o Comerica Bank
P.O. Box 75000, MC 3302
Detroit, MI   48275-3302
County: Wayne

Established in 2003 in MI.
Donor: Loraine Reuter Estate Trust.
Grantmaker type: Independent foundation.
Financial data (yr. ended 08/31/10): Assets, $642,010 (M); expenditures, $41,018; total giving, $31,000; qualifying distributions, $31,000; giving activities include $31,000 for grants.
Fields of interest: Arts education; Performing arts, music.
Type of support: Scholarship funds.
Application information:
  Initial approach: Letter
  Deadline(s): None
Trustee: Comerica Bank.
EIN: 201535256

680
Roy and Beverly Rewold Foundation
333 E. 2nd St.
Rochester, MI   48307-2005
County: Oakland
Contact: Craig Wolanin

Established in 2005 in MI.
Donor: Roy E. Rewold.
Grantmaker type: Independent foundation.
Financial data (yr. ended 12/31/09): Assets, $3,794 (M); gifts received, $5,000; expenditures, $2,620; total giving, $2,600; qualifying distributions, $2,600; giving activities include $2,600 for grants.
Limitations: Giving primarily in MI.
Officers: Roy E. Rewold, Pres.; Beverly J. Rewold, V.P.; Christy Weisenbach, Treas.
EIN: 201768196

681
Phyllis and Max Reynolds Foundation
c/o Wells Fargo Bank Michigan, N.A.
P.O. Box 580
Marquette, MI   49855-0580   (906) 228-1244
County: Marquette
Contact: Mary Nurmi

Established in 1997 in MI.
Donor: Phyllis M. Reynolds.
Grantmaker type: Independent foundation.
Financial data (yr. ended 12/31/09): Assets, $1,312,934 (M); expenditures, $78,519; total

giving, $65,300; qualifying distributions, $65,300; giving activities include $65,300 for grants.
Fields of interest: Arts; Elementary/secondary education; Athletics/sports, training; Recreation; Youth development, centers/clubs; Human services; Children/youth, services.
Type of support: Capital campaigns; Building/renovation; Equipment; Program development.
Limitations: Giving primarily in MI, with emphasis on the greater Marquette area.
Application information: Application form required.
Deadline(s): None
Officers and Directors:* Joan R. Miller,* Chair.; Robert J. Toutant,* Treas.; John F. Marshall; William I. McDonald; Patricia L. Micklow; Katherine R. Muller; Alice M. Reynolds; Frances Reynolds; Phyllis M. Reynolds.
EIN: 383354883

682
Chi Sun Rhee Foundation
811 N. Macomb St.
Monroe, MI 48162-3078 (313) 242-5659
County: Monroe
Contact: Sung Hi Rhee, Secy.-Treas.

Established in 1984 in MI.
Donors: Chi Sun Rhee; Sung Hi Rhee.
Grantmaker type: Independent foundation.
Financial data (yr. ended 09/30/09): Assets, $76,591 (M); gifts received, $20,000; expenditures, $1,519; total giving, $600; qualifying distributions, $600; giving activities include $600 for grants.
Purpose and activities: Support for innovation in the sciences.
Fields of interest: Science.
Application information: Application form not required.
Deadline(s): None
Officers: Chi Sun Rhee, Pres.; Hyun A. Rhee Steward, V.P.; Sung Hi Rhee, Secy.-Treas.
Directors: Stephan Reed; Robert Rhee.
EIN: 382485264

683
Francis P. and Nell A. Rhoades Memorial Foundation
(formerly Francis P. Rhoades Memorial Foundation)
2250 Butterfield Dr., Ste. 220
Troy, MI 48084-3412
County: Oakland
Application address: c/o Wayne County Medical Society, 3031 W. Grand Blvd., Ste. 645, Detroit, MI 48202-5002, tel.: (313) 874-1360

Established in MI.
Grantmaker type: Independent foundation.
Financial data (yr. ended 12/31/09): Assets, $508,194 (M); expenditures, $30,921; total giving, $21,000; qualifying distributions, $22,194; giving activities include $21,000 for 4 grants (high: $8,000; low: $1,000).
Fields of interest: AIDS research; Medical research; Homeless, human services.
Limitations: Applications accepted. Giving primarily in Wayne County, MI. No grants to individuals.
Application information: Application form not required.
Initial approach: Letter
Deadline(s): Nov. 15

Officers: Gilbert B. Bluhm, Pres.; Joseph Beals, Secy.
Trustees: Howard O. Emory; Melvin Hollowell; Charlotte Neuhauser; Nell Rhoades; Dennis Rahaley; Fred Whitehouse; L. James Wilson.
EIN: 386108728

684
R. Gene and Nancy D. Richter Foundation, Inc.
48741 Wildrose Dr.
Canton, MI 48187-5641
County: Wayne

Established in 2003 in MI.
Donor: Nancy D. Richter.
Grantmaker type: Independent foundation.
Financial data (yr. ended 12/31/08): Assets, $428,860 (M); gifts received, $141,065; expenditures, $146,685; total giving, $129,200; qualifying distributions, $129,200; giving activities include $129,200 for grants.
Purpose and activities: Grant awards of up to $5,000 per year to individuals seeking education and training in the area of Supply Chain Management.
Fields of interest: Business school/education.
Type of support: Scholarships—to individuals.
Application information: Application form required.
Deadline(s): Feb. 15
Officer and Director:* Nancy D. Richter,* Pres. and Secy.
EIN: 161679880

685
The Riley Foundation
c/o Comerica Bank
P.O Box 75000, MC 3302
Detroit, MI 48275-3302
County: Wayne
Application address: c/o Comerica Charitable Svcs. Group , P.O. Box 75000, Detroit, MI 48275-9413; tel.: (734) 930-2416

Established in 1998 in MI.
Donors: George Riley; Dolores Riley.
Grantmaker type: Independent foundation.
Financial data (yr. ended 09/30/10): Assets, $3,484,115 (M); gifts received, $7,654; expenditures, $875,917; total giving, $802,874; qualifying distributions, $845,134; giving activities include $802,874 for 25 grants (high: $510,000; low: $1,000).
Purpose and activities: Giving primarily to a public television station, as well as for education, and human services.
Fields of interest: Media, television; Higher education; Human services; Pregnancy centers; Community/economic development; Public affairs; Catholic agencies & churches.
Limitations: Giving primarily in MI, with emphasis on Detroit and Farmington Hills. No grants or loans to individuals.
Application information: Application form not required.
Deadline(s): None
Board of Managers: Cheryl Lutz; Daniel G. Riley; George K. Riley; William D. Riley.
Trustees: Kimberly A. Fouts; Comerica Bank.
EIN: 383439851

Selected grants: The following grants were reported in 2009.
$100,000 to Madonna University, Livonia, MI.
$5,000 to First Baptist Church of Naples, Naples, FL.
$5,000 to Lance Armstrong Foundation, Austin, TX.

686
Eunice & Milton H. Ring Charitable Foundation
(formerly Harry B. & Anna Korman Foundation)
25665 River
Franklin, MI 48025-1727 (248) 626-7699
County: Oakland
Contact: Eunice Ring, V.P.

Established in 1956 in MI.
Donor: Harry B. Korman.
Grantmaker type: Independent foundation.
Financial data (yr. ended 12/31/09): Assets, $852,556 (M); expenditures, $58,119; total giving, $41,192; qualifying distributions, $41,192; giving activities include $41,192 for 13 grants (high: $10,000; low: $500).
Fields of interest: Jewish federated giving programs; Jewish agencies & synagogues.
Limitations: Giving primarily in Boca Raton, FL, and MI. No grants to individuals.
Application information:
Initial approach: Letter
Deadline(s): None
Officers and Directors:* Milton Ring,* Pres.; Eunice Ring,* V.P. and Secy.-Treas.; Marianne Caplan; Elizabeth Fellows; Karen Weiss.
EIN: 386078083
Selected grants: The following grants were reported in 2007.
$1,151,666 to Jewish Federation of South Palm Beach County, Boca Raton, FL.
$33,911 to Temple Israel, West Bloomfield, MI.
$27,504 to Barbara Ann Karmanos Cancer Institute, Detroit, MI.
$23,500 to Jewish Federation of Metropolitan Detroit, Bloomfield Hills, MI.
$17,800 to American Society for Technion-Israel Institute of Technology, New York, NY.
$1,500 to Alzheimers Association, Southfield, MI.
$1,000 to Bar-Ilan University in Israel, New York, NY.
$1,000 to Congregation Shaarey Zedek, Southfield, MI.
$1,000 to JARC, Farmington Hills, MI.
$1,000 to Michigan AIDS Coalition, Ferndale, MI.

687
Sigurd & Jarmila Rislov Foundation
206 S. Main St., Ste. 218
Ann Arbor, MI 48103-5408
County: Washtenaw
Contact: Sue Ann Savas, Secy.
URL: http://www.rislovfoundation.org

Established in 1998 in MI.
Grantmaker type: Independent foundation.
Financial data (yr. ended 12/31/09): Assets, $1,034,096 (M); expenditures, $55,082; total giving, $40,000; qualifying distributions, $41,350; giving activities include $32,000 for 3 grants (high: $25,000; low: $2,000), and $8,000 for 4 grants to individuals (high: $2,000; low: $2,000).

Purpose and activities: Scholarship awards to qualified music students; giving to organizations for classical music education.
Fields of interest: Performing arts, music composition; Performing arts, education.
Type of support: General/operating support; Scholarships—to individuals.
Limitations: Applications accepted. Giving primarily in MI and OR.
Application information: See foundation web site for application information. Application form not required.
> *Deadline(s):* None
> *Board meeting date(s):* Mar., June, Sept., and Dec.
Officers: Zachary Savas, Pres.; Sue Ann Savas, Secy.; Martha Post, Treas.
EIN: 931247286

688
Frank E. Robbins Memorial Scholarship Fund
c/o Bank of America, N.A.
P.O. Box 1802
Providence, RI 02940-1802
County: Providence
Application address: c/o Augusta Haydock, Bank of America, N.A., 100 Federal St., Boston, MA 02110

Established in MA.
Donor: Edith M. Robbins.
Grantmaker type: Independent foundation.
Financial data (yr. ended 12/31/07): Assets, $995,605 (M); expenditures, $66,570; total giving, $55,785; qualifying distributions, $61,008; giving activities include $55,785 for grants.
Purpose and activities: Scholarship funds to the University of Michigan, Ann Arbor, Michigan.
Fields of interest: Higher education.
Type of support: Scholarship funds.
Limitations: Giving limited to Ann Arbor, MI.
Application information:
> *Initial approach:* Letter
> *Deadline(s):* None
Trustee: Bank of America, N.A.
EIN: 046072097

689
Robertson Family Foundation
3555 Pierce Rd.
Saginaw, MI 48604-9246
County: Saginaw
Contact: Joel C. Robertson, Pres.

Established in 2007.
Donors: Joel C. Robertson; Vickie L. Robertson; Robertson Institute, Ltd.
Grantmaker type: Independent foundation.
Financial data (yr. ended 12/31/09): Assets, $180 (M); gifts received, $7,587; expenditures, $8,839; total giving, $6,175; qualifying distributions, $6,175; giving activities include $6,175 for grants.
Fields of interest: Secondary school/education; Human services; Christian agencies & churches.
Limitations: Applications accepted. Giving primarily in MI, with emphasis on Saginaw.
Application information: Application form not required.
> *Initial approach:* Letter
> *Deadline(s):* None

Officers: Joel C. Robertson, Pres.; Vickie L. Robertson, Secy.-Treas.
Directors: Nicole L. Decker; Brooke J. Robertson; Heidi L. Robertson.
EIN: 204587472

690
Harold & Carolyn Robison Foundation
500 Woodward Ave.
Detroit, MI 48226-3407
County: Wayne
Contact: Norma Kumbier, Pres.
Application address: 2110 Silver Maples Dr., Chelsea, MI 48118-1189

Established in 1966 in MI.
Donor: Harold Robison†.
Grantmaker type: Independent foundation.
Financial data (yr. ended 06/30/10): Assets, $1,212,197 (M); expenditures, $97,209; total giving, $80,000; qualifying distributions, $80,000; giving activities include $80,000 for grants.
Fields of interest: Education; Hospitals (general); Food services; Human services.
Type of support: General/operating support; Continuing support; Capital campaigns; Building/renovation; Equipment; Scholarship funds; Research.
Limitations: Giving primarily in Detroit, MI. No grants to individuals.
Application information: Application form not required.
> *Initial approach:* Letter
> *Deadline(s):* None
> *Board meeting date(s):* Spring and Fall
Officers and Trustees:* Norma Kumbier,* Pres. and Treas.; Daniel Gwinn, Secy.; George Carter; Laura Mastracci; Martin C. Oetting; Marcy Carolyn Seymour.
EIN: 386105557

691
Rock Charitable Foundation
(formerly Rock Foundation)
13919 S.W. Bayshore Dr., Ste. G01
Traverse City, MI 49684-6216
County: Grand Traverse
Contact: Cori E. Nielson, Tr.

Established in 2001 in MI.
Donors: His Foundation; Canaan Foundation.
Grantmaker type: Independent foundation.
Financial data (yr. ended 12/31/09): Assets, $3,158,801 (M); gifts received, $230,693; expenditures, $207,471; total giving, $204,687; qualifying distributions, $206,080; giving activities include $204,687 for 15 grants (high: $45,794; low: $150).
Purpose and activities: Giving primarily to Christian churches and institutions.
Fields of interest: Education; Health organizations, association; Human services; Christian agencies & churches.
Limitations: Applications accepted. Giving primarily in MI.
Application information:
> *Initial approach:* Letter
> *Deadline(s):* None
Trustees: Dana A. Crosby; Jonathan E. Crosby; Cori E. Nielson.
EIN: 916526685

Selected grants: The following grants were reported in 2008.
$51,250 to Father Fred Foundation, Traverse City, MI.
$10,668 to Right to Life of Michigan, Grand Rapids, MI.
$5,000 to Charlevoix County Community Foundation, East Jordan, MI.
$2,500 to First Presbyterian Church, Elk Rapids, MI.
$2,000 to Eternal Word Television Network, Irondale, AL.
$1,000 to American Center for Law and Justice, Virginia Beach, VA.

692
The Rodney Fund
19100 W. 8 Mile Rd.
Southfield, MI 48075-5726
County: Oakland
Contact: James M. Rodney, Pres.

Established in 1992 in MI.
Donor: James M. Rodney.
Grantmaker type: Independent foundation.
Financial data (yr. ended 12/31/09): Assets, $10,261,947 (M); gifts received, $119,017; expenditures, $1,137,228; total giving, $1,112,750; qualifying distributions, $1,112,750; giving activities include $1,112,750 for 40 grants (high: $325,000; low: $1,000).
Purpose and activities: Giving primarily for public affairs institutes and centers. The fund supports libertarian principles: limited government, private property, free markets, individual liberty, free trade, and rule by law, as established by the U.S. Constitution.
Fields of interest: Education, research; Higher education; Education; Employment, public policy; Human services; United Ways and Federated Giving Programs; Social sciences; Public affairs.
Limitations: Giving on a national basis.
Application information:
> *Initial approach:* Letter
> *Deadline(s):* None
Officer and Directors:* James M. Rodney,* Pres.; Lawrence Reed; Leigh Rodney.
EIN: 383030437
Selected grants: The following grants were reported in 2009.
$12,000 to Institute for Justice, Arlington, VA.
$1,000 to Multiple Sclerosis Society, National, New York, NY.

693
Otto & Helen Roethke Scholarship Fund
c/o Citizens Bank, Wealth Mgmt.
328 S. Saginaw St., MC 002072
Flint, MI 48502-1923
County: Genesee
Application address: c/o Mercedes Perez, Selection Comm., 3115 Mackinaw St., Saginaw, MI 48602-3221, tel.: (517) 797-4815

Established in 1999 in MI.
Donor: Otto Roethke†.
Grantmaker type: Independent foundation.
Financial data (yr. ended 07/31/10): Assets, $111,476 (M); expenditures, $5,921; total giving, $0; qualifying distributions, $0.
Purpose and activities: Scholarship awards to Arthur Hill High School, Saginaw, Michigan, students

attending the University of Michigan; preference given to students majoring in English.
Fields of interest: Higher education.
Type of support: Scholarships—to individuals.
Limitations: Giving limited to residents of Saginaw, MI.
Application information: Application form required.
Deadline(s): May 1
Trustee: Citizens Bank.
EIN: 386720940

694
Rolka Scholarship Foundation
c/o James L. Rolka
1619 Van Geisen Rd.
Caro, MI 48723-1344
County: Tuscola

Established in 1999 in MI.
Donor: James Rolka.
Grantmaker type: Independent foundation.
Financial data (yr. ended 12/31/08): Assets, $276,027 (M); gifts received, $1,618; expenditures, $24,300; total giving, $24,000; qualifying distributions, $24,000; giving activities include $24,000 for grants.
Fields of interest: Higher education.
Type of support: Scholarships—to individuals.
Limitations: Giving primarily to residents of Caro, MI.
Officers: James L. Rolka, Pres.; Paul Langlois, V.P.; Cindie Dubs, Secy.-Treas.
Directors: Gary R. Anderson; Gary J. Crews.
EIN: 383448069

695
Pierson J. Roon Family Foundation
11355 Ripple Dr.
P.O. Box 86
Allendale, MI 49401-8769
County: Ottawa
Contact: Pierson J. Roon, Dir.

Established in 2000 in MI.
Donors: Idamarie Roon; Pierson J. Roon.
Grantmaker type: Independent foundation.
Financial data (yr. ended 10/31/09): Assets, $490,286 (M); expenditures, $21,086; total giving, $21,000; qualifying distributions, $21,020; giving activities include $21,000 for 18 grants (high: $2,800; low: $500).
Purpose and activities: Giving primarily to Christ-centered organizations, including educational institutions.
Fields of interest: Elementary/secondary education; Christian agencies & churches.
Limitations: Giving primarily in western MI, with emphasis on Allendale, Grand Rapids, and Hudsonville.
Application information:
Initial approach: Letter
Deadline(s): None
Officer: Ruth Washburn, Treas.
Directors: Idamarie Roon; Pierson J. Roon.
EIN: 383628676

696
Roscommon Area Historical Society
P.O. Box 916
Roscommon, MI 48653-0916
County: Roscommon

Grantmaker type: Independent foundation.
Financial data (yr. ended 12/31/09): Assets, $39,805 (M); gifts received, $6,049; expenditures, $10,866; total giving, $1,165; qualifying distributions, $1,165; giving activities include $1,165 for grants.
Officers: Ronald Swain, Pres.; Pat Murray, V.P.; Margaret Karinen, Secy.; Gerry Toeman, Treas.
EIN: 382767399

697
Carl F. and Donna M. Rose Family Foundation
1976 S. Telegraph Rd.
Bloomfield Hills, MI 48302-0245
County: Oakland

Established in 2001 in MI.
Donors: Carl F. Rose; Donna M. Rose.
Grantmaker type: Independent foundation.
Financial data (yr. ended 12/31/09): Assets, $107,796 (M); expenditures, $15,144; total giving, $14,074; qualifying distributions, $14,074; giving activities include $14,074 for grants.
Fields of interest: Protestant agencies & churches.
Limitations: Giving primarily in FL and MI. No grants to individuals.
Officers: Carl F. Rose, Pres.; Donna M. Rose, V.P.
EIN: 383547473

698
May Mitchell Royal Foundation
c/o Comerica Bank
P.O. Box 75000, MC 3302
Detroit, MI 48275-0001
County: Wayne
Application address: c/o Susan Hartley, 45 W. 74th St., New York, NY 10023-4725, tel.: (917) 612-2756

Established in 1981 in MI.
Donor: May Mitchell Royal Trust.
Grantmaker type: Independent foundation.
Financial data (yr. ended 09/30/09): Assets, $2,344,163 (M); expenditures, $188,374; total giving, $140,325; qualifying distributions, $157,585; giving activities include $140,325 for 10 grants (high: $45,000; low: $2,500).
Purpose and activities: Giving for the research and treatment of cancer, vision, and heart disease; support also for hospital equipment and nursing training.
Fields of interest: Higher education, university; Medical school/education; Hospitals (general); Cancer; Eye diseases; Heart & circulatory diseases; Eye research.
Type of support: General/operating support; Equipment; Scholarship funds; Research.
Limitations: Applications accepted. Giving limited to FL, HI, and MI. No grants to individuals.
Application information: Application form required.
Initial approach: Letter
Deadline(s): May 30

Officer and Committee Members: Susan J. Hartley,* Chair.; Michael Kennerly; Ross Kennerly; Ruth Lishman.
Trustee: Comerica Bank.
EIN: 382387140

699
Rudlaff Family Foundation
12701 Mastique Beach Blvd.
Ft. Myers, FL 33908-7010
County: Lee
Contact: F. Richard Rudlaff

Established in 1997 in MI.
Donor: F. Richard Rudlaff III.
Grantmaker type: Independent foundation.
Financial data (yr. ended 12/31/10): Assets, $15,183 (M); expenditures, $18,434; total giving, $16,440; qualifying distributions, $16,440; giving activities include $16,440 for 6 grants (high: $11,440; low: $1,000).
Fields of interest: Human services; Children/youth; Disabilities, people with.
Limitations: Giving in the U.S., with some emphasis on MI. No grants to individuals.
Application information:
Initial approach: Letter
Deadline(s): None
Trustee: F. Richard Rudlaff III.
EIN: 383391369

700
Lillian & Harold Rudy Scholarship Fund
(also known as Rudy Scholarship)
c/o Fifth Third Bank
P.O. Box 3636
Grand Rapids, MI 49501-3636
County: Kent
Application address: c/o Wauconda School District, Attn.: Daniel Cole, Supt., 555 N. Main St., Wauconda, IL 60084-1299, tel.: (847) 526-6611

Established in 1997 in IL.
Grantmaker type: Independent foundation.
Financial data (yr. ended 12/31/09): Assets, $502,421 (M); expenditures, $30,296; total giving, $24,000; qualifying distributions, $24,000; giving activities include $24,000 for grants to individuals.
Purpose and activities: Scholarship awards to students from Wauconda High School, Illinois.
Fields of interest: Higher education.
Type of support: Scholarships—to individuals.
Limitations: Giving primarily in Wauconda, IL.
Application information: Application form required.
Deadline(s): Apr. 1
Trustees: Amanda Caskey-Kostecki; Daniel Cole; Salvatore Saccomanno; Fifth Third Bank.
EIN: 367168424

701
Clara A. Ruf Scholarship Trust
207 S. Saginaw St.
St. Charles, MI 48655-1428   (989) 652-9945
County: Saginaw
Contact: Robert F. Loomis, Chair.

Established in 1985 in MI.
Grantmaker type: Independent foundation.
Financial data (yr. ended 12/31/09): Assets, $88,279 (M); expenditures, $2,523; total giving,

$2,000; qualifying distributions, $2,000; giving activities include $2,000 for 2 grants to individuals (high: $1,000; low: $1,000).

Purpose and activities: Scholarship awards to graduates of St. Charles High School, Michigan.

Fields of interest: Higher education.

Type of support: Scholarships—to individuals.

Limitations: Applications accepted. Giving limited to the St. Charles, MI, area.

Application information: Application form not required.

   Initial approach: Letter

   Deadline(s): Varies

Officers: Robert F. Loomis, Chair.; Anna Marie Loubert, Vice-Chair.; Patricia Sands, Secy.; Kathy Borough, Treas.

Trustees: Heather Ballien; Michael Olson.

EIN: 382587560

702
Nelson D. Rupp Foundation

P.O. Box 771
Marquette, MI 49855-0771
County: Marquette

Established in 2000 in MI.

Grantmaker type: Independent foundation.

Financial data (yr. ended 12/31/09): Assets, $114,677 (M); expenditures, $2,496; total giving, $0; qualifying distributions, $0.

Officer: Nelson D. Rupp, Pres.

Directors: Timothy Desrochers; Jed Patrick; Thomas Poisson.

EIN: 383563211

703
The John Rusch Family Scholarship

164 W. Chicago Rd.
Sturgis, MI 49091-1708 (269) 651-7861
County: St. Joseph
Contact: Donald S. Eaton, Tr.

Established in 1994 in MI.

Grantmaker type: Independent foundation.

Financial data (yr. ended 04/30/10): Assets, $1,625 (M); expenditures, $4,220; total giving, $3,500; qualifying distributions, $3,500; giving activities include $3,500 for grants.

Purpose and activities: Scholarship awards annually to graduates of Mason High School, Mason, Michigan.

Fields of interest: Higher education.

Type of support: Scholarships—to individuals.

Limitations: Giving limited to residents in Mason, MI.

Application information:

   Initial approach: Letter

   Deadline(s): May

Trustee: Donald S. Eaton.

EIN: 386635264

704
Herman Russell Foundation

c/o Comerica Bank
P.O. Box 75000, MC 3302
Detroit, MI 48275-3302
County: Wayne
Application address: c/o Herman Russell, 504 Fair St. S.W., Atlanta, GA 30313-1206, tel.: (404) 231-2474

Established in GA.

Donor: Herman Russell.

Grantmaker type: Independent foundation.

Financial data (yr. ended 12/31/09): Assets, $94,027 (M); gifts received, $265,000; expenditures, $221,655; total giving, $218,000; qualifying distributions, $218,900; giving activities include $218,000 for 11 grants (high: $100,000; low: $3,000).

Fields of interest: Museums; Elementary/secondary education; Hospitals (general); Health care; Kidney diseases.

Type of support: Scholarship funds; General/operating support.

Limitations: Giving in the U.S., primarily in Los Angeles, CA, Atlanta, GA, and MD.

Application information:

   Initial approach: Letter

   Deadline(s): None

Trustee: Herman Russell.

EIN: 586343476

Selected grants: The following grants were reported in 2009.

$100,000 to Childrens Healthcare of Atlanta, Atlanta, GA.

$25,000 to BeltLine Partnership, Atlanta, GA.

$10,000 to Westminster Schools, Atlanta, GA.

$5,000 to Paideia School, Atlanta, GA.

$5,000 to Whitefoord Community Program, Atlanta, GA.

705
Ryals Foundation

2018 Caniff St.
Flint, MI 48504-5414
County: Genesee

Established in 2002 in MI.

Grantmaker type: Independent foundation.

Financial data (yr. ended 12/31/09): Assets, $2,234 (M); expenditures, $145; total giving, $25; qualifying distributions, $25; giving activities include $25 for grants.

Fields of interest: Protestant agencies & churches.

Trustees: Kassondra Ryals; Marqueretta Ryals; Patrick L. Ryals, Sr.

EIN: 383639184

706
Edward J. Sackerson Charitable Foundation

P.O. Box 716
Escanaba, MI 49829-0716 (906) 786-0220
County: Delta
Contact: Matt N. Smith, Jr., Tr.

Established in 1997 in MI.

Donor: Edward J. Sackerson.

Grantmaker type: Independent foundation.

Financial data (yr. ended 12/31/09): Assets, $4,380,592 (M); expenditures, $248,038; total giving, $226,462; qualifying distributions, $226,462; giving activities include $226,462 for 32 grants (high: $124,554; low: $1,000).

Fields of interest: Elementary/secondary education; Youth development; Human services; Community/economic development; Christian agencies & churches.

Limitations: Applications accepted. Giving primarily in Escanaba, MI. No grants to individuals.

Application information:

   Initial approach: Letter

   Deadline(s): None

Trustees: Paul Kangas; Gary Olsen; Helen A. Sackerson; Matt N. Smith, Jr.

EIN: 383351811

Selected grants: The following grants were reported in 2008.

$154,109 to Holy Name School, Escanaba, MI.

$7,000 to Salvation Army, Escanaba, MI.

$3,079 to Lions Club, Escanaba, MI.

$1,000 to YMCA of Delta County, Escanaba, MI.

707
Sacred Family Causes Foundation

110 Merriweather Rd.
Grosse Pointe, MI 48236-3623 (313) 882-8266
County: Wayne
Contact: Daniel Goodnow, Chair.

Established in 1999 in MI.

Grantmaker type: Independent foundation.

Financial data (yr. ended 12/31/09): Assets, $650,638 (M); expenditures, $36,302; total giving, $28,305; qualifying distributions, $28,305; giving activities include $28,305 for grants.

Fields of interest: Human services; Christian agencies & churches.

Limitations: Giving primarily in MI.

Application information:

   Initial approach: Letter

   Deadline(s): None

Officers and Trustees:* Daniel Goodnow,* Chair.; Susan Goodnow,* Secy.

EIN: 383417814

708
Sage Foundation

P.O. Box 1919
Brighton, MI 48116-5719
County: Livingston
Contact: Melissa Sage Fadim, Chair.

Incorporated in 1954 in MI.

Donors: Charles F. Sage†; Effa L. Sage†.

Grantmaker type: Independent foundation.

Financial data (yr. ended 12/31/09): Assets, $50,055,133 (M); expenditures, $3,001,364; total giving, $2,462,700; qualifying distributions, $2,670,526; giving activities include $2,462,700 for 127 grants (high: $475,000; low: $1,000).

Purpose and activities: Giving primarily for the arts, education, health organizations, social services, and Roman Catholic churches and agencies.

Fields of interest: Arts; Higher education; Education; Health organizations, association; Human services; Catholic agencies & churches.

Type of support: General/operating support; Continuing support; Annual campaigns; Capital campaigns; Building/renovation; Equipment; Endowments; Program development; Scholarship funds; Research; Matching/challenge support.

Limitations: Applications accepted. Giving primarily in IL and MI.

Application information: Application form not required.

   Initial approach: Letter

   Copies of proposal: 1

   Deadline(s): None

   Board meeting date(s): Quarterly

   Final notification: 12 weeks

Officers and Trustees:* Melissa Sage Fadim,* Chair., Pres., and Treas.; John J. Ayaub,* V.P. and Secy.; Anne Sage Price; James E. Van Doren.
Number of staff: 1 part-time professional.
EIN: 386041518
Selected grants: The following grants were reported in 2008.
$200,000 to Art Institute of Chicago, Chicago, IL.
$150,000 to American Symphony Orchestra League, New York, NY.
$125,000 to Herrick Medical Center Foundation, Tecumseh, MI.
$125,000 to Herrick Medical Center Foundation, Tecumseh, MI.
$100,000 to Big Shoulders Fund, Chicago, IL.
$30,000 to Catholic Social Services of Lenawee County, Adrian, MI.
$20,000 to Michigan Opera Theater, Detroit, MI.
$15,000 to Herrick Medical Center Foundation, Tecumseh, MI.
$10,000 to Saint Ignatius College Prep, Chicago, IL.
$6,600 to Adrian Community Nursery Corporation, Adrian, MI.

709
Dr. Shanti Swarup & Mrs. Chawli Devi Saini Memorial Foundation

4337 Bender Ct.
Troy, MI 48098-4475 (248) 641-1822
County: Oakland
Contact: Inder Jit Saini M.D., Pres.

Established in 1998 in MI.
Donor: Inder Jit Saini, M.D.
Grantmaker type: Independent foundation.
Financial data (yr. ended 09/30/09): Assets, $64,421 (M); gifts received, $50; expenditures, $4,215; total giving, $3,790; qualifying distributions, $3,790; giving activities include $3,790 for grants.
Fields of interest: Higher education.
Type of support: Scholarship funds.
Limitations: Giving primarily in MI.
Application information: Application form required.
Deadline(s): None
Officers: Inder Jit Saini, M.D., Pres.; Mrs. Inder Saini, V.P.; Robert Saini, Secy.; Rashmi Saini, Treas.
Director: Krishan Saini.
EIN: 383408285

710
The Salahi Foundation

26300 Telegraph Rd., 2nd Fl.
Southfield, MI 48033-2436
County: Oakland

Established in MI.
Grantmaker type: Independent foundation.
Financial data (yr. ended 12/31/08): Assets, $76 (M); expenditures, $1,800; total giving, $1,130; qualifying distributions, $1,130; giving activities include $1,130 for grants.
Limitations: Giving primarily in MI.
Officer: Farouk Salahi, Pres.
EIN: 383452435

711
Burl E. Salisbury Memorial Scholarship Fund

c/o Southern Michigan Bank & Trust
P.O. Box 309
Coldwater, MI 49036-0309
County: Branch
Contact: Mary Guthrie, Trust Off., Southern Michigan Bank & Trust

Established in MI.
Grantmaker type: Independent foundation.
Financial data (yr. ended 04/30/10): Assets, $290,726 (M); expenditures, $46,137; total giving, $32,500; qualifying distributions, $32,500; giving activities include $32,500 for 33 loans to individuals (high: $1,000; low: $500).
Purpose and activities: Student loans to graduating students of Bronson High School, Michigan.
Fields of interest: Higher education.
Type of support: Student loans—to individuals.
Limitations: Giving limited to residents of Bronson, MI.
Application information: Application form required.
Deadline(s): May 1
Trustee: Southern Michigan Bank & Trust.
EIN: 386429664

712
Fritchof T. Sallness and Marian M. Sallness Memorial Scholarship Fund

c/o Citizens Bank
328 S. Saginaw St., M/C 002072
Saginaw, MI 48602
County: Saginaw
Application address: Helen James, 101 N. Washington Ave., Saginaw, MI 48607-1206, tel.: (989) 776-7368

Established in 1990 in MI.
Grantmaker type: Independent foundation.
Financial data (yr. ended 12/31/09): Assets, $226,576 (M); expenditures, $9,038; total giving, $1,000; qualifying distributions, $1,000; giving activities include $1,000 for grants to individuals.
Purpose and activities: Scholarships and student loans awarded to graduates of Two Harbors High School, Minnesota, with remaining income loaned to Saginaw County residents attending a Michigan public college or university.
Fields of interest: Education.
Type of support: Scholarships—to individuals; Student loans—to individuals.
Limitations: Giving limited to residents of Saginaw County, MI, and Two Harbors, MN.
Application information:
Initial approach: Letter
Deadline(s): May 1
Trustee: Citizens Bank.
EIN: 386565588

713
Salpietra Family Charitable Foundation

2693 Heights View Ct.
Oakland Township, MI 48306-4947
County: Oakland

Established in 2007 in MI.
Donor: John M. Salpietra.
Grantmaker type: Independent foundation.

Financial data (yr. ended 12/31/09): Assets, $24,897 (M); gifts received, $20,796; expenditures, $22,103; total giving, $21,000; qualifying distributions, $21,000; giving activities include $21,000 for grants.
Officers: John M. Salpietra, Pres.; Mary Salpietra, V.P.; Andrea Salpietra, Secy.
Directors: John M. Salpietra, Jr.; Ronald J. Zadora.
EIN: 261321797

714
Sankrithi Foundation

1437 Sodon Lake Dr.
Bloomfield Hills, MI 48302-2356
County: Oakland

Established in 2002 in MI.
Donors: Mahalakshmi Honasoge; Nataraj Honasoge.
Grantmaker type: Independent foundation.
Financial data (yr. ended 12/31/09): Assets, $61,155 (M); gifts received, $3,000; expenditures, $2,532; total giving, $2,500; qualifying distributions, $2,500; giving activities include $2,500 for grants.
Fields of interest: Human services.
International interests: India.
Limitations: Giving primarily in India.
Officers: Nataraj Honasoge, Pres.; Mahalakshmi Honasoge, Secy.
EIN: 522380135

715
The A. Paul and Carol C. Schaap Foundation

c/o Comerica Bank
500 Woodward Ave., 21st Fl.
Detroit, MI 48226-3416 (313) 222-3304
County: Wayne

Established in MI.
Donors: A. Paul Schaap; Carol C. Schaap.
Grantmaker type: Independent foundation.
Financial data (yr. ended 12/31/09): Assets, $6,574,423 (M); expenditures, $297,246; total giving, $242,500; qualifying distributions, $243,373; giving activities include $220,000 for 12 grants (high: $60,000; low: $10,000), and $22,500 for 6 grants to individuals (high: $3,750; low: $3,750).
Purpose and activities: Giving primarily for higher education, including a Presbyterian seminary.
Fields of interest: Media, radio; Higher education; Theological school/education.
Limitations: Applications accepted. Giving primarily in Louisville, KY, and MI.
Application information: Application form not required.
Initial approach: Letter
Deadline(s): None
Trustee: Comerica Bank.
EIN: 207097647
Selected grants: The following grants were reported in 2008.
$30,000 to University Liggett School, Grosse Pointe, MI.
$10,000 to Hope College, Holland, MI.
$10,000 to Hope College, Holland, MI.

716
The Schalon Foundation
4418 Tanglewood Trail
St. Joseph, MI   49085-9686
County: Berrien
Application address: c/o Jon F. Sleder, 2265
Shiawasee Ln., Stevensville, MI 49127, tel.: (269)
429-5667

Established in 1997 in MI.
Donors: Edward I. Schalon†; Marcella J. Schalon.
Grantmaker type: Independent foundation.
Financial data (yr. ended 12/31/09): Assets,
$4,707,926 (M); gifts received, $425,000;
expenditures, $744,992; total giving, $730,880;
qualifying distributions, $730,880; giving activities
include $730,880 for grants.
Fields of interest: Performing arts, orchestras;
Performing arts, opera; Arts; Education; Housing/
shelter, development; Recreation, community;
Human services; Christian agencies & churches.
Type of support: Building/renovation.
Limitations: Applications accepted. Giving primarily
in St. Joseph, MI. No grants to individuals.
Application information:
   Initial approach: Letter
   Deadline(s): None
   Final notification: Dec. 1
Officers and Directors:* Marcella J. Schalon,* V.P.;
Susan K. Schalon,* Secy.; Scott Schalon,* Treas.
EIN: 383341098
Selected grants: The following grants were reported
in 2008.
$30,000 to Curious Kids Museum, Saint Joseph,
MI.
$30,000 to Lake Michigan College, Benton Harbor,
MI.
$21,380 to Opera Grand Rapids, Grand Rapids, MI.
$5,000 to Silver Beach Carousel Society, Saint
Joseph, MI.
$2,500 to Taylor University, Upland, IN.

717
Maude Ripley Schemm Scholarship Trust
c/o Citizens Bank Wealth Mgmt., N.A.
328 S. Saginaw St., M/C 002072
Flint, MI   48502-1923   (989) 776-7368
County: Genesee
Application address: c/o Arthur Hill High School,
3115 Mackinaw St., Saginaw, MI 48602-3221,
tel.: (989) 797-4815

Established in MI.
Grantmaker type: Independent foundation.
Financial data (yr. ended 12/31/09): Assets,
$182,836 (M); expenditures, $10,376; total giving,
$4,650; qualifying distributions, $8,301; giving
activities include $4,650 for 9 grants to individuals
(high: $2,000; low: $250).
Purpose and activities: Scholarship awards to
graduates of Arthur Hill High School, Saginaw, MI.
Fields of interest: Higher education.
Type of support: Scholarships—to individuals.
Limitations: Applications accepted. Giving limited to
residents of Saginaw, MI.
Application information: Application form required.
   Deadline(s): May 1
Trustee: Citizens Bank.
EIN: 386095919

718
Leslie & Regene Schmier Foundation
c/o Walnut Svcs., Inc.
30100 Telegraph Rd., No. 403
Bingham Farms, MI   48025-4518
County: Oakland
Contact: Regene Schmier, Pres.

Established in 1953 in MI.
Donor: Regene Schmier.
Grantmaker type: Independent foundation.
Financial data (yr. ended 12/31/09): Assets,
$233,546 (M); gifts received, $20,000;
expenditures, $26,919; total giving, $20,064;
qualifying distributions, $20,064; giving activities
include $20,064 for grants.
Fields of interest: Health organizations; Human
services; Jewish agencies & synagogues.
Type of support: General/operating support.
Limitations: Giving primarily in MI.
Application information:
   Initial approach: Proposal
   Deadline(s): None
Officers: Regene Schmier, Pres.; Martin Stoneman,
V.P.; Gary Vandeputte, Secy.-Treas.
EIN: 386064686

719
The Art and Mary Schmuckal Family Foundation
4249 U.S. 31 S.
Traverse City, MI   49684-7996   (231) 943-8544
County: Grand Traverse
Contact: Arthur M. Schmuckal, Pres.

Established in 1999 in MI.
Donors: Arthur M. Schmuckal; Schmuckal Land Co.
Grantmaker type: Independent foundation.
Financial data (yr. ended 06/30/10): Assets,
$4,233,760 (M); expenditures, $264,897; total
giving, $211,180; qualifying distributions,
$216,606; giving activities include $211,180 for 27
grants (high: $50,000; low: $1,000).
Purpose and activities: Giving primarily to enhance
the well-being of children, to strengthen the
residents economically, and for community
development.
Fields of interest: Theological school/education;
Medical care, community health systems; Human
services; YM/YWCAs & YM/YWHAs; Residential/
custodial care, hospices; Community/economic
development; Foundations (community); Children.
Type of support: Annual campaigns; Capital
campaigns; Program development; Scholarship
funds.
Limitations: Applications accepted. Giving primarily
in Traverse City, MI.
Application information:
   Initial approach: Letter
   Deadline(s): None
Officers: Arthur M. Schmuckal, Pres.; Barbara F.
Benson, V.P.; Donald A. Schmuckal, V.P.; Evelyn K.
Richardson, Secy.; Paul M. Schmuckal, Treas.
EIN: 383498264
Selected grants: The following grants were reported
in 2005.
$50,000 to Munson Healthcare Regional
Foundation, Traverse City, MI. For building
construction.
$33,750 to Grand Traverse Pavilions Foundation,
Traverse City, MI.

$22,000 to Area Agency on Aging, Grand Rapids, MI.
For computer purchases.
$5,000 to Community Health Clinic.
$5,000 to Great Lakes Childrens Museum, Traverse
City, MI.
$5,000 to House of Hope, Northwest Michigan,
Traverse City, MI.
$5,000 to Womens Resource Center.

720
Schoonbeck Family Foundation
705 Kent Hills Rd. N.E.
Grand Rapids, MI   49505-5112
County: Kent
Contact: Katherine S. Miller, Secy.
Application address: 310 Riders Trail, N.E., Ada, MI
49301-9554

Established in 1997 in MI.
Grantmaker type: Independent foundation.
Financial data (yr. ended 12/31/09): Assets,
$944,701 (M); expenditures, $78,169; total giving,
$72,500; qualifying distributions, $72,500; giving
activities include $72,500 for grants.
Fields of interest: Housing/shelter, development;
Human services.
Limitations: Giving limited to western MI.
Application information:
   Initial approach: Letter
   Deadline(s): None
Officers and Directors:* Caroline P. Schoonbeck,*
Pres.; Katherine S. Miller,* Secy.; Fredrick
Schoonbeck,* Treas.
EIN: 383382133

721
Fred D. & Evelyn A. Schroeder Foundation
146 Flag Point Dr.
Roscommon, MI   48653-8963   (989) 821-6684
County: Roscommon
Contact: Bobbe Morley, Pres.

Established in MI.
Donors: Fred D. Schroeder; Bobbe Dale Morley.
Grantmaker type: Independent foundation.
Financial data (yr. ended 09/30/09): Assets,
$368,172 (M); expenditures, $19,576; total giving,
$15,800; qualifying distributions, $15,800; giving
activities include $15,800 for grants.
Fields of interest: Human services; Economically
disadvantaged.
Type of support: General/operating support.
Limitations: Applications accepted. Giving limited to
MI, primarily in Roscommon. No grants to
individuals.
Application information:
   Deadline(s): Sept. 1
Officer: Bobbe Dale Morley, Pres.
EIN: 382558752

722
Elizabeth Schultheiss Memorial Scholarship Fund, Inc.
4121 Okemos Rd., Ste. 10
Okemos, MI   48864   (517) 381-2663
County: Ingham
Contact: Paul T. Joseph, Tr.

Grantmaker type: Independent foundation.

Financial data (yr. ended 12/31/09): Assets, $1,089 (M); gifts received, $9,050; expenditures, $9,651; total giving, $9,574; qualifying distributions, $9,574; giving activities include $9,574 for grants.
Application information: Application form required.
  Initial approach: Letter
  Deadline(s): None
Trustees: Harry Guenther; Paul T. Joseph; Mik Worthy.
EIN: 205894065

723
Carrie E. Smith Schuyler Estate Trust
10000 Harbor Place Dr.
St. Clair Shores, MI   48080-1518
(586) 779-8252
County: Macomb
Contact: Allan Neef, Tr.

Grantmaker type: Independent foundation.
Financial data (yr. ended 12/31/09): Assets, $319,842 (M); expenditures, $21,594; total giving, $18,000; qualifying distributions, $19,675; giving activities include $18,000 for 4 grants (high: $4,500; low: $4,500).
Purpose and activities: Scholarship awards for needy girls pursuing an education in music, dance, or business.
Fields of interest: Performing arts, dance; Performing arts, music; Business school/education; Girls.
Type of support: Scholarship funds.
Limitations: Applications accepted. Giving limited to MI. No grants to individuals.
Application information: Application form not required.
  Initial approach: Letter
  Deadline(s): None
Trustees: Allan Neef; Katherine W. Remsen; Gladys M. Young.
EIN: 386093210

724
Schwartz Family Foundation
2290 First National Bldg.
Detroit, MI   48226-3506   (313) 465-7700
County: Wayne
Contact: Alan E. Schwartz, Pres.

Established in 1959 in MI.
Grantmaker type: Independent foundation.
Financial data (yr. ended 12/31/09): Assets, $281,016 (M); gifts received, $98,500; expenditures, $182,384; total giving, $178,959; qualifying distributions, $180,658; giving activities include $178,959 for 65 grants (high: $48,620; low: $36).
Fields of interest: Performing arts, orchestras; Arts; Higher education; Education; Health care; Health organizations, association; Cancer; Human services; Community/economic development; United Ways and Federated Giving Programs; Jewish agencies & synagogues.
Limitations: Giving primarily in MI. No loans, program-related investments or direct charitable giving.
Application information: Application form not required.
  Initial approach: Letter
  Deadline(s): None

Officers and Directors: * Alan E. Schwartz,* Pres. and Treas.; Marianne S. Schwartz,* V.P.; Marc A. Schwartz,* Secy.
EIN: 386059415

725
Emily Scofield Trust
2 Michigan Ave. W., Ste. 301
Battle Creek, MI   49017-7002   (269) 962-9591
County: Calhoun
Contact: Michael C. Jordan, Tr.

Donor: Emily Scofield‡.
Grantmaker type: Independent foundation.
Financial data (yr. ended 12/31/07): Assets, $197,515 (M); expenditures, $9,377; total giving, $5,600; qualifying distributions, $9,377; giving activities include $5,600 for 8 grants to individuals (high: $700; low: $700).
Purpose and activities: Scholarship awards to graduates of Calhoun County High School, Michigan.
Fields of interest: Higher education.
Type of support: Scholarships—to individuals.
Limitations: Applications accepted. Giving primarily to residents of Calhoun County, MI.
Application information: Application form not required.
  Initial approach: Letter
  Deadline(s): None
Trustee: Michael C. Jordan.
EIN: 386087167

726
John Scully Foundation
c/o Comerica Bank
P.O. Box 75000, M/C 3302
Detroit, MI   48275-3302
County: Wayne
Application address: c/o Brenda Pearson, 60 S. 6th St., Ste. 2550, Minneapolis, MN 55402-4406, tel.: (612) 215-3603

Established in 2002 in SD.
Donor: John Scully.
Grantmaker type: Independent foundation.
Financial data (yr. ended 12/31/09): Assets, $345,370 (M); expenditures, $41,775; total giving, $30,000; qualifying distributions, $30,900; giving activities include $30,000 for 2 grants (high: $20,000; low: $10,000).
Fields of interest: Higher education, college; Theological school/education.
Type of support: General/operating support.
Limitations: Giving in the U.S., with some preference in SD. No grants to individuals.
Application information: Application form required.
  Initial approach: Letter
  Deadline(s): None
Trustee: Comerica Bank.
EIN: 266003516

727
The Seabury Foundation
1111 N. Wells St., Ste. 503
Chicago, IL   60610-7633
County: Cook
Contact: Boyd McDowell III
FAX: (312) 587-7332;
E-mail: seabury@seaburyfoundation.org;
URL: http://www.seaburyfoundation.org

Trust established in 1947 in IL.
Donors: Charles Ward Seabury‡; Louise Lovett Seabury‡.
Grantmaker type: Independent foundation.
Financial data (yr. ended 12/31/09): Assets, $21,375,685 (M); expenditures, $1,235,525; total giving, $805,050; qualifying distributions, $1,189,237; giving activities include $805,050 for 74 grants (high: $32,000; low: $1,500).
Purpose and activities: Giving primarily for community and social services.
Fields of interest: Performing arts, theater; Arts; Secondary school/education; Higher education; Education; Environment; Health care; Employment, training; Human services; Children/youth, services; Family services; Community/economic development.
Type of support: Seed money; Matching/challenge support; Equipment; General/operating support; Program development; Scholarship funds; Technical assistance.
Limitations: Applications accepted. Giving primarily in Chicago, IL; giving also in MI. No grants to individuals, or for benefits; no loans.
Publications: Application guidelines; Program policy statement; Program policy statement (including application guidelines).
Application information: All submissions must be made to The Seabury Foundation office by e-mail and one mailed hard copy of the LOI or proposal, and both must be received by the close of business (4:30 p.m., Central Time) on the due dates. The hard copy should be addressed to the Foundation Director, with the e-mail copy being sent to lstigsen@seaburyfoundation.org. Full proposals accepted by invitation only following letter of inquiry. See foundation web site for details. Application form not required.
  Initial approach: 1-2-page letter of inquiry at least 30 days in advance of deadlines
  Copies of proposal: 1
  Deadline(s): For letters of inquiry: Sept. 15, Jan. 15 and June 15; for proposals: Nov. 1, Mar. 1, and Aug. 1
  Board meeting date(s): Feb., May, and Oct.
  Final notification: Feb. 28, May 31, and Oct. 31
Officers and Trustees: * Deborah Seabury Holloway,* Exec. Secy.; Fanny Boone Zeddies, Exec. Dir.; Emily Boone; Robert S. Boone; Shannon Fisk; Stephen G. Fisk; Seabury J. Hibben; The Northern Trust Co.
Director: Boyd McDowell III.
Number of staff: 2 full-time professional.
EIN: 366027398
Selected grants: The following grants were reported in 2006.
$30,000 to Family Matters, Chicago, IL.
$30,000 to Habitat for Humanity, Morgan County, Madison, GA.
$27,000 to Friends of the Orphans, Tempe, AZ.
$20,000 to Catholic Relief Services, Chicago, IL.
$20,000 to Family Matters, Chicago, IL.
$15,000 to Garfield Park Conservatory Alliance, Chicago, IL.
$15,000 to Grand Traverse Regional Land Conservancy, Traverse City, MI.
$12,500 to Architecture, Construction and Engineering Technical Charter High School, Chicago, IL.
$10,000 to Good News Community Kitchen, Chicago, IL.
$4,000 to Berea College, Berea, KY.

728
Sebastian Foundation
c/o Linda Jones
3333 Evergreen Dr. N.E., Ste. 110
Grand Rapids, MI   49525-9756
County: Kent
Contact: David S. Sebastian, Exec. Dir.

Established in 1980 in MI.
Donors: Audrey M. Sebastian; James R. Sebastian.
Grantmaker type: Independent foundation.
Financial data (yr. ended 08/31/09): Assets, $13,656,183 (M); expenditures, $1,550,135; total giving, $1,277,518; qualifying distributions, $1,402,026; giving activities include $1,277,518 for 65 grants (high: $150,000; low: $500).
Purpose and activities: Supports human services and public benefit organizations, education, and the arts.
Fields of interest: Arts; Education; Human services.
Limitations: Applications accepted. Giving primarily in the Grand Rapids, MI, area. No support for religious programs. No grants to individuals.
Application information: Application form not required.
   Initial approach: Proposal
   Copies of proposal: 1
   Deadline(s): None
Officer: David S. Sebastian, Exec. Dir.
Trustees: Audrey M. Sebastian; John Sebastian.
Number of staff: 2 full-time support.
EIN: 382340219
Selected grants: The following grants were reported in 2009.
$65,000 to Inner City Christian Federation, Grand Rapids, MI.
$53,300 to First United Methodist Church, Grand Rapids, MI.
$51,000 to Grand Rapids Community Foundation, Grand Rapids, MI.
$50,000 to Camp Blodgett, Grand Rapids, MI.
$50,000 to Grand Rapids Childrens Museum, Grand Rapids, MI.
$50,000 to United Way, Heart of West Michigan, Grand Rapids, MI.
$33,000 to Kent Intermediate School District, Grand Rapids, MI.
$25,000 to Aquinas College, Association for the Blind and Visually Impaired, Grand Rapids, MI.
$25,000 to Porter Hills Foundation, Grand Rapids, MI.
$12,700 to Grand Rapids Art Museum, Grand Rapids, MI.

729
Seidman Family Foundation
(formerly The Thomas Erler Seidman Foundation)
28451 County Rd. 49
Kiowa, CO   80117
County: Elbert
Contact: Robin Volock

Trust established in 1950 in MI.
Donors: Frank E. Seidman†; Esther L. Seidman†.
Grantmaker type: Independent foundation.
Financial data (yr. ended 12/31/09): Assets, $5,225,265 (M); expenditures, $315,682; total giving, $283,184; qualifying distributions, $283,184; giving activities include $283,184 for 150 grants (high: $25,000; low: $500).
Fields of interest: Arts; Higher education; Environment, natural resources; Hospitals (general); Health organizations; Food banks; Athletics/sports,

winter sports; Human services; Christian agencies & churches.
Type of support: General/operating support.
Limitations: Applications accepted. Giving primarily in CA, MA, MI, MT, NH, NM, and VT. No grants to individuals.
Application information:
   Deadline(s): None
   Board meeting date(s): Dec.
Officers: Sarah M. Seidman, Chair.; Tracy S. Hephner, Vice-Chair.; Nancy C. Seidman, Secy.; Margaret Williams, Treas.
Trustees: B. Thomas Seidman; Jane R. Volock.
Number of staff: 1 part-time professional.
EIN: 136098204
Selected grants: The following grants were reported in 2008.
$5,000 to Grand Valley State University, Grand Rapids, MI.
$5,000 to Keshet Dance Company, Albuquerque, NM.
$4,000 to Inner-City Filmmakers, Santa Monica, CA.
$3,700 to Cibola High School, Albuquerque, NM.
$2,600 to Cibola High School, Albuquerque, NM.
$2,500 to Food Depot, Santa Fe, NM.
$2,500 to Roadrunner Food Bank, Albuquerque, NM.
$2,000 to Leukemia & Lymphoma Society, White Plains, NY.
$2,000 to Vermont Studio Center, Johnson, VT.
$2,000 to Woodbury College, Montpelier, VT.

730
The George & Elizabeth Seifert Foundation
1300 Mead Rd.
Rochester, MI   48306-3524
County: Oakland
Contact: George H. Seifert, Pres.

Established in 1996 in MI.
Donors: Elizabeth J. Seifert; George H. Seifert; Sid Mitra.
Grantmaker type: Independent foundation.
Financial data (yr. ended 12/31/09): Assets, $229,665 (M); gifts received, $85,000; expenditures, $79,760; total giving, $65,125; qualifying distributions, $65,125; giving activities include $65,125 for grants.
Fields of interest: Arts; Education; Community/economic development.
Limitations: Applications accepted. Giving primarily in MI. No grants to individuals.
Application information: Application form not required.
   Board meeting date(s): Oct.
Officers and Directors: * George H. Seifert,* Pres. and Treas.; Elizabeth J. Seifert,* Secy.; Elizabeth L. Calcei; George K. Seifert; Gail J. Strunk.
EIN: 383313644

731
Thomas E. Sequin, Jr. Family Foundation
3375 Anna Dr.
Bay City, MI   48706-2001   (989) 684-0087
County: Bay
Contact: Thomas E. Sequin, Jr., Pres.

Established in 1990 in MI.
Donors: Thomas E. Sequin, Jr.; Sequin Lumber Corp.
Grantmaker type: Independent foundation.

Financial data (yr. ended 12/31/09): Assets, $466,102 (M); gifts received, $52,500; expenditures, $56,978; total giving, $50,250; qualifying distributions, $50,250; giving activities include $50,250 for grants.
Fields of interest: Catholic agencies & churches.
Limitations: Giving in the U.S., with emphasis on MI. No grants to individuals.
Application information:
   Initial approach: Proposal
   Deadline(s): None
Officers: Thomas E. Sequin, Jr., Pres.; Denise A. Sequin, Secy.-Treas.
EIN: 382931537

732
Serra Family Foundation
5644 N. Rainbow Ln.
Waterford, MI   48329-1557
County: Oakland
Application Address: c/o Lynne Parker, 3118 E. Hill Rd., Grand Blanc, MI 48439, tel.: (810) 694-1720

Established in 1997 in MI.
Donors: Albert Serra; Lois Serra.
Grantmaker type: Independent foundation.
Financial data (yr. ended 12/31/09): Assets, $3,926,779 (M); expenditures, $150,690; total giving, $141,900; qualifying distributions, $141,900; giving activities include $141,900 for 19 grants (high: $30,000; low: $1,000).
Fields of interest: Higher education; Environment, natural resources; Health care; Christian agencies & churches.
Type of support: General/operating support.
Limitations: Applications accepted. Giving primarily in MI.
Application information:
   Initial approach: Letter
   Deadline(s): None
Officers and Directors: * Amy Albright,* V.P.; Ann Lowney,* V.P.; Mary McMahon,* V.P.; Alice Serra Reid,* V.P.; Lynne Parker, Treas.
EIN: 383352324
Selected grants: The following grants were reported in 2004.
$30,000 to Duke Center for Living, Durham, NC.
$21,100 to Lourdes, Inc., Waterford, MI.
$20,000 to Albion College, Albion, MI.
$20,000 to Genesys Health Foundation, Grand Blanc, MI.
$20,000 to Genesys Health System, Grand Blanc, MI.
$17,000 to Northwood University, Midland, MI.
$10,000 to Conservation Resource Alliance, Traverse City, MI.
$5,000 to Grand Traverse Regional Land Conservancy, Traverse City, MI.

733
Paul & Marlene Serwinek Foundation
2385 Learmonth Ln.
Milford, MI   48381-1301   (248) 685-1299
County: Oakland
Contact: Paul Serwinek, Pres.

Established in 2005 in MI.
Donors: Marlene Serwinek; Paul Serwinek.
Grantmaker type: Independent foundation.
Financial data (yr. ended 12/31/09): Assets, $66,108 (M); expenditures, $3,087; total giving,

$2,560; qualifying distributions, $2,560; giving activities include $2,560 for grants.
Fields of interest: Higher education.
Type of support: Scholarship funds.
Limitations: Applications accepted. Giving primarily in MI.
Application information:
Initial approach: Letter
Deadline(s): None
Officers: Paul Serwinek, Pres.; Marlene Serwinek, Secy.-Treas.
EIN: 201384407

734
The Sharing of Blessings Foundation
13425 Windcrest Ln.
Grand Haven, MI   49417-9495
County: Ottawa

Established in MI.
Donor: Judith Van Kampen.
Grantmaker type: Independent foundation.
Financial data (yr. ended 12/31/09): Assets, $627,241 (M); expenditures, $41,851; total giving, $40,460; qualifying distributions, $40,460; giving activities include $40,460 for grants.
Fields of interest: Human services; Christian agencies & churches.
Limitations: Giving primarily in IL, IA, and MI.
Directors: Diane M. Tannel; Jerald A. Tannel.
EIN: 201864617

735
Shelby Family Foundation
559 Oak St.
Winnetka, IL   60093-2649   (847) 784-1812
County: Cook
Contact: Carole Shelby, Pres.

Established in 1995 in IL.
Donors: David T. Shelby; Carole Shelby.
Grantmaker type: Independent foundation.
Financial data (yr. ended 11/30/09): Assets, $802,280 (M); expenditures, $49,136; total giving, $42,490; qualifying distributions, $42,490; giving activities include $42,490 for grants.
Fields of interest: Arts; Education; Environment, natural resources; Human services; Science; Christian agencies & churches.
Limitations: Giving primarily in IL and MI. No grants to individuals.
Application information:
Initial approach: Letter
Deadline(s): None
Officers: Carole Shelby, Pres.; Kaylynn Shelby, V.P.; Sarah Shelby, V.P.; David Shelby, Secy.-Treas.
Directors: Christian Shelby; Justin Shelby; Paige Shelby.
EIN: 364055432

736
Elizabeth, Allan and Warren Shelden Fund
17152 Kercheval St.
Grosse Pointe Farms, MI   48230-1661
County: Wayne
Contact: William W. Shelden, Jr., Pres.

Incorporated in 1937 in MI.
Donors: Elizabeth Warren Shelden†; Allan Shelden III†; W. Warren Shelden†.

Grantmaker type: Independent foundation.
Financial data (yr. ended 12/31/09): Assets, $31,574,954 (M); expenditures, $1,743,652; total giving, $1,659,480; qualifying distributions, $1,660,700; giving activities include $1,659,480 for 51 grants (high: $250,000; low: $5,000).
Purpose and activities: Giving primarily for the arts, education, and health care.
Fields of interest: Arts; Education; Environment, natural resources; Hospitals (general); Health care; Human services; United Ways and Federated Giving Programs.
Type of support: General/operating support; Continuing support; Annual campaigns; Capital campaigns; Building/renovation; Equipment; Endowments; Research.
Limitations: Giving primarily in the metropolitan Detroit, MI, area. No grants to individuals, or for scholarships, fellowships, or matching gifts; no loans.
Publications: Annual report.
Application information: Application form not required.
Initial approach: Proposal
Copies of proposal: 1
Deadline(s): Submit proposal preferably in Nov.; no set deadline
Board meeting date(s): Nov. or Dec.
Final notification: Positive replies only
Officers and Trustees:* William W. Shelden, Jr.,* Pres. and Treas.; David M. Hempstead,* Secy.; Sally S. Sheldon.
Number of staff: 1 part-time professional; 1 part-time support.
EIN: 386052198
Selected grants: The following grants were reported in 2008.
$250,000 to Henry Ford Health System, Detroit, MI.
$200,000 to Detroit Riverfront Conservancy, Detroit, MI.
$150,000 to University Liggett School, Grosse Pointe, MI.
$75,000 to Detroit Institute of Arts, Detroit, MI.
$60,000 to Coalition on Temporary Shelter, Detroit, MI.
$50,000 to College for Creative Studies, Detroit, MI.
$35,000 to American Red Cross, Detroit, MI.
$25,000 to Detroit Institute for Children, Detroit, MI.
$10,000 to Michigan Opera Theater, Detroit, MI.
$10,000 to Nature Conservancy, Lansing, MI.

737
Leon and Josephine Wade Shepard Scholarship Fund Foundation, Inc.
c/o National City Bank
171 Monroe Ave. N.W., KC17063
Grand Rapids, MI   49503-2634
County: Kent
Application address: c/o Alan Hogenmiller, 4 Memorial Dr., Fennville, MI 49408-9370

Established in MI.
Grantmaker type: Independent foundation.
Financial data (yr. ended 03/31/09): Assets, $586,763 (M); expenditures, $52,404; total giving, $42,000; qualifying distributions, $42,000; giving activities include $42,000 for grants to individuals.
Purpose and activities: Scholarship awards to needy and qualified graduates of Fennville High School for full-time study at an institution of higher education in Michigan.
Fields of interest: Higher education.
Type of support: Scholarships—to individuals.

Limitations: Giving limited to residents of Fennville, MI.
Application information: Application form required.
Initial approach: Letter
Deadline(s): Between late Feb. and early Mar.
Officers: Scott Campbell, Pres.; Steven Peters, V.P.; Donna Bruner, Secy.-Treas.
Trustee: National City Bank.
EIN: 386101349

738
The Shepherd Foundation
2967 Lakeshore Dr.
Holland, MI   49424-6023
County: Ottawa
Application address: c/o Max O. DePree, 145 Columbia Ave., No. 539, Holland, MI 49423

Established in 1992 in MI.
Donors: Barbara DePree; Esther DePree; Kris DePree; Max O. DePree.
Grantmaker type: Independent foundation.
Financial data (yr. ended 12/31/09): Assets, $55,732 (M); expenditures, $1,884; total giving, $0; qualifying distributions, $0.
Purpose and activities: Giving primarily to Christian programs, including theological education and Christian youth groups.
Fields of interest: Theological school/education; Hospitals (general); Housing/shelter, services; Youth development; Human services; Christian agencies & churches.
Type of support: General/operating support; Capital campaigns.
Limitations: Applications accepted. Giving primarily in MI.
Application information:
Initial approach: Letter
Deadline(s): None
Officers: Max O. DePree, Pres. and Secy.; Jody VanDerwel, Treas.
Directors: Esther DePree; Kris DePree.
EIN: 383046929
Selected grants: The following grants were reported in 2008.
$124,644 to Hope College, World Christian Lecture, Holland, MI.
$50,000 to Jubilee Ministries, Lebanon, PA.
$22,500 to Young Life, Colorado Springs, CO.
$20,000 to Words of Hope, Grand Rapids, MI.
$10,000 to Seattle Pacific University, Seattle, WA.
$3,500 to Western Theological Seminary, Holland, MI.
$1,000 to Hope College, Holland, MI.

739
The Shiffman Foundation
18135 Hamilton Rd.
Detroit, MI   48203-4036   (313) 345-1225
County: Wayne
Contact: Richard H. Levey, Pres.
FAX: (313) 345-1930; *E-mail:* ShiffmanFd@aol.com

Incorporated in 1948 in MI.
Donors: Abraham Shiffman†; Richard H. Levey.
Grantmaker type: Independent foundation.
Financial data (yr. ended 09/30/09): Assets, $137,615 (M); expenditures, $24,890; total giving, $12,065; qualifying distributions, $12,065; giving activities include $12,065 for grants.

Purpose and activities: Giving to program-related investments for community development and economic justice through the Episcopal Diocese of Michigan and other suitable institutions.
Fields of interest: Arts; Higher education; Education; International human rights; Civil rights, race/intergroup relations; Urban/community development; Community/economic development; Minorities; Economically disadvantaged.
Type of support: General/operating support; Continuing support; Building/renovation; Conferences/seminars; Seed money; Technical assistance; Program-related investments/loans; In-kind gifts.
Limitations: Applications accepted. Giving primarily in MI. No grants to individuals.
Publications: Occasional report.
Application information: Application form not required.
  Initial approach: 1 to 2-page letter outlining purpose of request
  Copies of proposal: 1
  Deadline(s): None
  Board meeting date(s): Annually and as needed
Officer: Richard H. Levey, Pres.
EIN: 381396850

740
Shin Foundation for Medical Research and Betterment of Mankind
c/o Dong H. Shin
3350 Sutton Ln.
Commerce Township, MI   48390-1219
(248) 242-6150
County: Oakland
Contact: Chae S. Shin, Pres.

Established in 1998 in MI.
Grantmaker type: Independent foundation.
Financial data (yr. ended 12/31/09): Assets, $523,557 (M); expenditures, $1,943; total giving, $1,000; qualifying distributions, $1,000; giving activities include $1,000 for grants.
Purpose and activities: Support for medical research, medical and Christian missionary service, worthy social causes, and the improvement of individuals' skills and preparedness for scientific research and the betterment of mankind.
Fields of interest: Medical research; Christian agencies & churches.
Type of support: Internship funds.
Limitations: Giving in MI, primarily in Detroit.
Application information: Application form not required.
  Initial approach: Resume and proposal
  Deadline(s): None
  Final notification: Within 2 months
Officer: Chae S. Shin, Pres. and Secy.-Treas.
EIN: 383267984
Selected grants: The following grants were reported in 2005.
$40,000 to New Life Fellowship, Corona, NY.

741
Edwin J. & Ruth M. Shoemaker Foundation
840 W. Long Lake Rd., Ste. 200
Troy, MI   48098-6358
County: Oakland
Application address: c/o Robert L. Shoemaker, Pres., 9130 Hunter Ln., Traverse City, MI 49684, tel.: (231) 943-4717

Established in 1998 in MI.
Donors: Edwin J. Shoemaker‡; Dale Shoemaker.
Grantmaker type: Independent foundation.
Financial data (yr. ended 12/31/09): Assets, $15,542,013 (M); expenditures, $839,867; total giving, $754,500; qualifying distributions, $795,183; giving activities include $754,500 for 22 grants (high: $150,000; low: $2,000).
Purpose and activities: The foundation supports organizations that pursue and further the tenets of the Christian faith.
Fields of interest: Civil liberties, right to life; Christian agencies & churches.
Limitations: Applications accepted. Giving in the U.S. primarily in MI; some emphasis also in Washington, DC and North TX. No grants to individuals.
Application information:
  Initial approach: Letter
  Final notification: None
Officers and Directors:* Robert L. Shoemaker,* Pres.; Dale A. Shoemaker,* V.P.; Mary Kaye Johnston,* Secy.-Treas.; David S. Johnston; Rocque E. Lipford; Erich C. Shoemaker.
EIN: 383137832
Selected grants: The following grants were reported in 2009.
$75,000 to Ekklesia Society, Carrollton, TX.
$40,000 to Lutheran Special Education Ministries, Detroit, MI.
$12,000 to Mercy Memorial Hospital, Monroe, MI.
$10,000 to Focus on the Family, Colorado Springs, CO.
$10,000 to Salvation Army of Monroe, Monroe, MI.
$2,500 to Saint Marys School, Lake Leelanau, MI.

742
William Shoer and Jennie Smidt Shoer Educational Trust
1 Greenleaf Woods Dr., Unit 301
Portsmouth, NH   03801-5437
County: Rockingham

Established in 2005 in MA.
Donor: Jennie Shoer.
Grantmaker type: Independent foundation.
Financial data (yr. ended 12/31/09): Assets, $471,221 (M); expenditures, $22,811; total giving, $19,000; qualifying distributions, $19,000; giving activities include $19,000 for grants.
Fields of interest: Jewish agencies & synagogues.
Type of support: General/operating support.
Limitations: Giving primarily in MA and MI.
Trustees: Justin A. Remis; Martin J. Shoer; Stephen Smidt.
EIN: 202886204

743
Shubeck Monsour Foundation
1500 Long Rd.
Kalamazoo, MI   49008-1322   (269) 343-1452
County: Kalamazoo
Contact: Michael B. Shubeck, Dir.

Established in 1994 in MI.
Donors: Michael B. Shubeck; Nancy A. Monsour.
Grantmaker type: Independent foundation.
Financial data (yr. ended 12/31/09): Assets, $367,382 (M); gifts received, $5,000; expenditures, $24,396; total giving, $23,100;

qualifying distributions, $23,100; giving activities include $23,100 for grants.
Fields of interest: Arts; Education; Human services.
Type of support: General/operating support.
Limitations: Giving primarily in western MI, with emphasis on Kalamazoo.
Application information:
  Initial approach: Letter
  Deadline(s): None
Directors: Emily Shubeck; Nancy A. Monsour; Michael B. Shubeck.
EIN: 383211370

744
Siebenthaler Foundation
225 N.W. Torch Lake Dr.
Kewadin, MI   49648-9251   (231) 883-4715
County: Antrim
Contact: Jessica E. Thompson, V.P.

Established in 2002 in MI.
Donor: William A. Siebenthaler.
Grantmaker type: Independent foundation.
Financial data (yr. ended 12/31/09): Assets, $479,784 (M); expenditures, $65,673; total giving, $35,681; qualifying distributions, $35,681; giving activities include $35,681 for grants.
Fields of interest: Health care; Human services; Christian agencies & churches.
Limitations: Giving in the U.S., with emphasis on MI.
Application information: Application form not required.
  Deadline(s): None
Officers: William A. Siebenthaler, Pres.; Jessica E. Thompson, V.P. and Secy.; Jeffrey D. Terrell, V.P.; Elizabeth C. Siebenthaler, Treas.
EIN: 043662001

745
Bill & Vi Sigmund Foundation
P.O. Box 1128
Jackson, MI   49204-1128   (517) 784-5464
County: Jackson
Contact: Carolyn M. Pratt, Secy.
E-mail: sigmundfoundation@sbcglobal.net;
URL: http://www.sigmundfoundation.org/

Established in 2002 in MI.
Donors: William A. Sigmund‡; Violet S. Sigmund Trust; W.A. Sigmund Trust.
Grantmaker type: Independent foundation.
Financial data (yr. ended 12/31/09): Assets, $9,870,175 (M); gifts received, $1,918; expenditures, $619,826; total giving, $563,972; qualifying distributions, $563,972; giving activities include $563,972 for grants.
Purpose and activities: The mission of the foundation is to assist citizens of Jackson and Lenewee counties, Michigan in improving the quality of their lives, including scholarships to indivduals, with some preference given to students majoring in the medical and aviation fields.
Fields of interest: Education; Youth development; Human services.
Type of support: Scholarships—to individuals; General/operating support.
Limitations: Giving limited to Jackson and Lenawee counties, MI.
Application information: See foundation web site for full application requirements and guidelines, including downloadable grant letter of intent and

scholarship application form. Application form required.

Initial approach: Letter of intent for grants, completed application form for scholarships

Deadline(s): Apr. 15 for scholarships

Final notification: 8 to 12 weeks for following submission of invited proposal

Officers and Directors:* Charles C. McClafferty,* Pres. and Treas.; Ralph L. Bodman,* V.P.; Carolyn M. Pratt, Secy.; Kenneth A. Dillon; John Macchia; Kent Mauer.

EIN: 380002491

Selected grants: The following grants were reported in 2007.

$20,000 to Salvation Army of Jackson, Jackson, MI.

$10,000 to Community Respite Center, Jackson, MI.

$10,000 to Jackson Interfaith Shelter, Jackson, MI.

$10,000 to United Way of Jackson County, Jackson, MI.

$7,500 to Catholic Charities of Jackson, Jackson, MI.

$7,500 to Saint Lukes Clinic, Jackson, MI.

$2,500 to Goodwill Industries of Central Michigan, Jackson, MI.

$2,000 to Food Bank of South Central Michigan, Battle Creek, MI.

746
Bill and Vi Sigmund Foundation
P.O. Box 1128
Jackson, MI   49204-1128   (517) 784-5464
County: Jackson
Contact: Carolyn M. Pratt, Secy.
E-mail: sigmundfoundation@sbcglobal.net;
URL: http://www.sigmundfoundation.org

Grantmaker type: Independent foundation.

Financial data (yr. ended 12/31/09): Assets, $9,870,175 (M); gifts received, $1,918; expenditures, $619,826; total giving, $563,972; qualifying distributions, $567,610; giving activities include $180,447 for 23 grants (high: $15,000; low: $500), and $383,525 for 163 grants to individuals (high: $20,377; low: $8).

Purpose and activities: Scholarships primarily awarded to students majoring in the medical and aviation fields who are residents of Jackson or Lenawee County, Michigan; have been acceptance to an accredited college or university; have proof of financial need; have a cumulative grade point average of 2.5 or higher; and who have completed the Free Application for Federal Student Aid (FAFSA).

Fields of interest: Salvation Army; United Ways and Federated Giving Programs.

Type of support: Scholarships—to individuals.

Limitations: Applications accepted. Giving primarily limited to Jackson and Lewanee Counties, MI.

Application information: If applicant has been selected for a formal grant review, the foundation will send an application with complete instructions.

Initial approach: Letter of intent, no more than 2 pages in length

Deadline(s): Apr. 15

Final notification: Usually between 8 and 12 weeks

Officers: Charles C. McClafferty, Pres. and Treas.; Ralph I. Bodman, V.P.; Carolyn M. Pratt, Secy.

Directors: Kenneth A. Dillon; John Macchia; Kent Mauer.

EIN: 300002491

747
Silverwing Foundation
2905 Lucerne Dr., Ste. 230
Grand Rapids, MI   49546-7160
County: Kent
Contact: James Rosloniec, Treas.

Established in CA and MI.

Donors: Jay and Betty Van Andel Foundation; Jay Van Andel Trust; RDV Foundation.

Grantmaker type: Independent foundation.

Financial data (yr. ended 12/31/09): Assets, $45,085,727 (M); expenditures, $4,024,570; total giving, $3,187,262; qualifying distributions, $3,187,262; giving activities include $3,187,262 for 49 grants (high: $1,000,000; low: $2,000).

Fields of interest: Human services; Christian agencies & churches.

Type of support: General/operating support; Capital campaigns; Seed money.

Limitations: Giving in the U.S., with emphasis on MI, particularly Grand Rapids, as well as CA and TX.

Application information:

Initial approach: Letter of reference

Deadline(s): None

Officers: Nan Van Andel, Pres.; James Rosloniec, Treas.

EIN: 202110480

Selected grants: The following grants were reported in 2007.

$370,000 to LIFE International, Grand Rapids, MI.

$162,000 to Bible League, Chicago, IL.

$95,000 to Luke Society, Sioux Falls, SD.

$40,000 to Christian Camps for Inner-City Youth, Camp Tall Turf, Grand Rapids, MI.

$10,000 to Baptist International Evangelistic Ministries, Danville, IN.

$3,000 to Cary Christian Center, Cary, MS.

748
Simmons Foundation
3390 Travis Pointe Rd., Ste. B
Ann Arbor, MI   48108-9620   (734) 996-0900
County: Washtenaw
Contact: David T. Simmons, Pres. and Treas.

Established in 1961 in MI.

Grantmaker type: Independent foundation.

Financial data (yr. ended 12/31/09): Assets, $993,731 (M); expenditures, $74,156; total giving, $49,715; qualifying distributions, $52,290; giving activities include $49,715 for 17 grants (high: $13,400; low: $500).

Fields of interest: Higher education.

Type of support: General/operating support; Equipment; Scholarship funds.

Limitations: Applications accepted. Giving primarily in MI, with emphasis on Ann Arbor. No grants to individuals.

Application information: Application form required.

Initial approach: Letter

Deadline(s): None

Officers: David T. Simmons, Pres. and Treas.; Clifford Simmons, V.P.; Christine R. West, Secy.

EIN: 386075922

749
Donald R. and Esther Simon Foundation
6318 Ramwyck Ct.
West Bloomfield, MI   48322-2251
County: Oakland

Established in 2005 in MI.

Donors: Donald R. Simon; Esther Simon.

Grantmaker type: Independent foundation.

Financial data (yr. ended 12/31/09): Assets, $675,725 (M); expenditures, $61,150; total giving, $60,130; qualifying distributions, $60,130; giving activities include $60,130 for 51 grants (high: $19,450; low: $25).

Fields of interest: Education; Human services; Religion.

Limitations: Giving primarily in MI. No grants to individuals.

Application information: Unsolicited requests for funds not accepted.

Initial approach: Letter of request

Deadline(s): None

Officers: Donald R. Simon, Pres.; Esther Simon, V.P.; Scott Pietras, Secy.-Treas.

EIN: 203651333

750
Eleanor R. Simonis Educational Fund "D"
c/o Fifth Third Bank
P.O. Box 3636
Grand Rapids, MI   49501-3636
County: Kent

Established in NC.

Grantmaker type: Independent foundation.

Financial data (yr. ended 12/31/08): Assets, $136,170 (M); expenditures, $4,135; total giving, $0; qualifying distributions, $9,800; giving activities include $9,600 for loans to individuals.

Purpose and activities: Student loans to residents of Cabarrus County, North Carolina.

Fields of interest: Higher education.

Type of support: Student loans—to individuals.

Limitations: Applications accepted. Giving primarily to residents of Cabarrus County, NC.

Application information: Minimum age of applicant is 18, maximum amount per semester is $2,500, maximum combined loan amount per student (all funds) is $10,000. Application form required.

Deadline(s): None

Trustee: Fifth Third Bank.

EIN: 626336489

751
Sinai Medical Staff Foundation
3000 Town Ctr., Ste. 2150
Southfield, MI   48075-1313   (248) 353-0150
County: Oakland

Established in 2000 in MI.

Grantmaker type: Independent foundation.

Financial data (yr. ended 06/30/09): Assets, $2,565,513 (M); expenditures, $196,524; total giving, $129,793; qualifying distributions, $129,793; giving activities include $129,793 for grants.

Purpose and activities: Support for medical research and dissemination of medical information in Michigan.

Fields of interest: Education; Hospitals (general); Health care; Muscular dystrophy; Alzheimer's disease; Medical research, institute.

Limitations: Applications accepted. Giving limited to MI.

Application information: Application form not required.

Initial approach: Letter
Deadline(s): None
Officers: Robert S. Michaels, Pres.; Hugh Beckman, V.P.; Gaylord D. Alexander, Secy.-Treas.; Rothstein & Karbel, P.C., Mgr.
EIN: 237078893
Selected grants: The following grants were reported in 2008.
$20,000 to Henry Ford Health System, Senior Development Officer, Detroit, MI.
$11,000 to Wayne State University, School of Medicine Office of Development and Alumni Affairs, Detroit, MI.
$1,000 to AIDS Partnership Michigan, Detroit, MI.

752
Harry A. Sisson Charitable Trust
c/o Comerica Bank, Trust Tax Div.
P.O. Box 75000, MC 3462
Detroit, MI   48275-3462   (313) 222-7859
County: Wayne
Contact: Sharon Vitale

Established in 1952.
Donor: Harry A. Sisson†.
Grantmaker type: Independent foundation.
Financial data (yr. ended 12/31/09): Assets, $679,184 (M); expenditures, $36,375; total giving, $30,000; qualifying distributions, $30,600; giving activities include $30,000 for 18 grants (high: $10,000; low: $500).
Fields of interest: Museums; Arts; Education; Community/economic development.
Limitations: Giving primarily in Birmingham and Grand Rapids, MI. No grants to individuals.
Application information: Application form not required.
Deadline(s): None
Trustee: Comerica Bank.
EIN: 386043587

753
Skandalaris Family Foundation
c/o Robert J. Skandalaris
1030 Doris Rd.
Auburn Hills, MI   48326-2613   (248) 292-5678
County: Oakland
FAX: (248) 648-8889;
E-mail: info@skandalaris.com; URL: http://www.skandalaris.com
College Scholarship tel.: (248) 220-2004, fax: (248) 220-2038

Established in 1997 in MI.
Grantmaker type: Independent foundation.
Financial data (yr. ended 12/31/09): Assets, $270,068 (M); gifts received, $246,514; expenditures, $301,986; total giving, $259,656; qualifying distributions, $259,656; giving activities include $259,656 for 117 grants to individuals (high: $15,000; low: $1,000).
Purpose and activities: Scholarship awards to a group of students, characterized by their special talents, leadership skills, unselfish ways, strong values and commitment to excellence. Applicants must be high school seniors or undergraduate college students and U.S. citizens.
Fields of interest: Higher education.
Type of support: Scholarships—to individuals.

Limitations: Applications accepted. Giving primarily to residents of MI. No support for candidates attending trade or foreign schools.
Application information: Application guidelines available on foundation web site. Application form required.
Deadline(s): College scholarships: Previous scholarship recipients: Apr. 15; current college students who are first time applicants and current high school students: May 1. Future Leaders Merit Scholarship: May 31
Officers: Robert J. Skandalaris, Pres.; Julie A. Skandalaris, V.P.; Kristin M. Puro, Secy.
EIN: 383394567

754
The Skiles Foundation
c/o Comerica Bank
P.O. Box 75000, MC 3302
Detroit, MI   48275-3302
County: Wayne
Application address: c/o Ann Skiles McGinty, 1640 Harvard St., Houston, TX 77008, tel.: (713) 862-8408

Established in 1999 in TX.
Donor: Elwin L. Skiles, Jr.
Grantmaker type: Independent foundation.
Financial data (yr. ended 12/31/09): Assets, $3,591,752 (M); expenditures, $218,144; total giving, $200,000; qualifying distributions, $200,570; giving activities include $200,000 for 1 grant.
Fields of interest: Arts; Libraries (public); Education; Environment, natural resources.
Limitations: Applications accepted. Giving limited to TX. No grants to individuals.
Application information:
Initial approach: Letter
Officers and Trustees:* Ann Skiles McGinty,* Pres. and Treas.; Sarah Skiles Zachry,* V.P. and Secy.
EIN: 752845190
Selected grants: The following grants were reported in 2006.
$100,000 to Nature Conservancy of Texas, San Antonio, TX.
$25,000 to Hardin-Simmons University, Abilene, TX.

755
The Skillman Foundation
100 Talon Centre Dr., Ste. 100
Detroit, MI   48207-4266   (313) 393-1185
County: Wayne
Contact: Prog. Off.
FAX: (313) 393-1187; E-mail: mailbox@skillman.org;
URL: http://www.skillman.org

Incorporated in 1960 in MI.
Donor: Rose P. Skillman†.
Grantmaker type: Independent foundation.
Financial data (yr. ended 12/31/09): Assets, $457,235,000 (M); expenditures, $26,225,000; total giving, $21,123,000; qualifying distributions, $21,123,000; giving activities include $21,123,000 for grants.
Purpose and activities: The foundation is a resource for improving the lives of children in metropolitan Detroit, MI. Children in disadvantaged situations are of special concern. The foundation applies its resources to foster positive relationships between children and adults, support high quality learning

opportunities and strengthen healthy, safe and supportive homes and communities.
Fields of interest: Visual arts; Performing arts; Arts; Education, early childhood education; Child development, education; Education, reading; Education; Health care; Substance abuse, services; Crime/violence prevention, youth; Food services; Recreation; Human services; Children/youth, services; Child development, services; Family services; Homeless, human services; Children/youth; Children; Youth; Economically disadvantaged; Homeless.
Type of support: Continuing support; General/operating support; Program development; Program-related investments/loans; Employee matching gifts.
Limitations: Applications accepted. Giving primarily in metropolitan Detroit, with emphasis on six neighborhoods in the city of Detroit. No support for long-term projects not being aided by other sources, sectarian religious activities, political lobbying or legislative activities, or new organizations which do not have an operational and financial history. The foundation does not make grants to organizations that had public support and revenues of less than $100,000 for the preceding year. No grants to individuals, or for endowment funds, annual campaigns, purchase, construct or renovate facilities, basic research or deficit financing.
Publications: Application guidelines; Annual report; Informational brochure (including application guidelines); Newsletter; Occasional report; Program policy statement.
Application information: The foundation accepts grant applications online. Application form required.
Initial approach: Letter of intent
Copies of proposal: 1
Deadline(s): None
Board meeting date(s): Mid-March, June, Sept. and Nov.
Final notification: 6 weeks after board meeting
Officers and Trustees:* David Baker Lewis,* Chair.; Lizabeth Ardisana, Vice-Chair.; Carol A. Goss,* C.E.O. and Pres.; Tonya Allen, C.O.O. and V.P., Prog.; Alan Harris, V.P. and C.I.O.; Danielle Olekszyk, C.F.O. and Treas.; Lillian Bauder; William M. Brodhead; Stephen E. Ewing; Edsel B. Ford II; Herman B. Gray, M.D.; Denise Ilitch; Mary L. Kramer; Amyre Makupson; Eddie R. Munson; Jerry Norcia; Robert S. Taubman.
Number of staff: 20 full-time professional; 5 full-time support.
EIN: 381675780
Selected grants: The following grants were reported in 2010.
$1,500,000 to Teach for America, New York, NY. To establish Teach for America in Detroit, bringing 100 outstanding college graduates annually to teach in public and charter schools. It will recruit Teach for America alumni to become school leaders in new and existing schools, payable over 3.00 years.
$800,000 to University of Michigan, Ann Arbor, MI. To continue to support technical assistance to effectively implement the Foundation's Good Neighborhoods work in targeted communities of Detroit, payable over 2.00 years.
$400,000 to City Connect Detroit, Detroit, MI. To expand summer youth employment jobs in six targeted Good Neighborhoods.
$300,000 to Don Bosco Hall, Detroit, MI. To support planning and development of coordinated youth development program delivery system in Cody Rouge and Brightmoor neighborhoods.

$275,000 to Wayne County Regional Educational Service Agency, Wayne, MI. To continue to build capacity and improve quality of child-care in Skillman-targeted neighborhoods and throughout Detroit through Quality Rating and Improvement System (QRIS) for day care centers and homes.
$185,000 to Detroit Hispanic Development Corporation, Detroit, MI. To strengthen the collaboration of Latino-led organizations through the development of a Latino Agenda for Southwest Detroit children, youth and families.
$175,000 to Prevailing Community Development Corporation, Detroit, MI. To support expansion of successful youth employment program in Chadsey Condon neighborhood.
$144,500 to United Way for Southeastern Michigan, Detroit, MI. For consultant support needed to develop the implementation work plan for Excellent Schools Detroit.
$115,000 to Alternatives for Girls, Detroit, MI. To support youth-leadership development program in Chadsey Condon neighborhood that grows and nurtures cadre of young people to participate in community service, leadership training and civic engagement.
$110,000 to Clark Park Coalition, Detroit, MI. For the Clark Park Youth Employment, Recreation and Development Program to improve and expand existing youth programs, and develop new youth employment opportunities at Clark Park in Southwest Detroit.

756
The D. Jerome and Margery C. Slack Foundation
3687 Courtney Pl.
Traverse City, MI 49684-8810
County: Grand Traverse
Contact: D. Jerome Slack, Pres.

Established in 1995 in MI.
Donor: D. Jerome Slack.
Grantmaker type: Independent foundation.
Financial data (yr. ended 12/31/09): Assets, $413,169 (M); expenditures, $22,597; total giving, $19,000; qualifying distributions, $19,000; giving activities include $19,000 for grants.
Fields of interest: Higher education; Christian agencies & churches.
Type of support: Scholarship funds.
Limitations: Giving primarily in MI.
Officers: D. Jerome Slack, Pres.; Margery C. Slack, V.P.
EIN: 383265519

757
Suzanne Sloat and Ray Okonski Foundation
25050 Skye Dr.
Farmington Hills, MI 48336-1670
(248) 476-5050
County: Oakland
Contact: Raymond N. Okonski, Chair.

Established in 1997 in MI.
Donors: Raymond N. Okonski; Suzanne M. Sloat.
Grantmaker type: Independent foundation.
Financial data (yr. ended 04/30/10): Assets, $220,932 (M); gifts received, $8,973; expenditures, $19,238; total giving, $14,995;

qualifying distributions, $14,995; giving activities include $14,995 for grants.
Fields of interest: Arts; Higher education; Education; Youth development; Human services; Christian agencies & churches.
Limitations: Applications accepted. Giving primarily in MI. No grants to individuals.
Application information:
Initial approach: Letter
Deadline(s): None
Officers: Raymond N. Okonski, Chair., V.P. and Treas.; Suzanne M. Sloat, Pres. and Secy.
Director: Timothy C. Yoe.
EIN: 383352871

758
Arthur L. & Carra J. Smith Family Foundation
428 Yale Ave.
Alma, MI 48801-1426 (989) 463-3779
County: Gratiot
Contact: Karen L. Smith

Established in 2002 in MI.
Donors: Arthur L. Smith; Carra J. Smith.
Grantmaker type: Independent foundation.
Financial data (yr. ended 12/31/09): Assets, $2,015,132 (M); expenditures, $203,585; total giving, $143,698; qualifying distributions, $143,698; giving activities include $143,698 for 5 grants (high: $50,000; low: $8,698).
Fields of interest: Higher education, college; American Red Cross; Salvation Army; Protestant agencies & churches.
Type of support: Capital campaigns; Program development.
Limitations: Applications accepted. Giving in MI.
Application information:
Initial approach: Letter
Deadline(s): None
Officers: Richard D. Froh, Pres.; Tracy N. Froh, V.P.; Karen L. Smith, Secy.-Treas.
EIN: 371451908
Selected grants: The following grants were reported in 2008.
$123,947 to Alma College, Alma, MI.

759
Jeff & Patrice Smith Family Foundation, Inc.
1217 Briarcrest Dr.
Wooster, OH 44691-2484 (330) 262-1460
County: Wayne
Contact: Jeff Smith, Dir.; Patrice Smith, Dir.

Established in 1999 in FL.
Grantmaker type: Independent foundation.
Financial data (yr. ended 12/31/09): Assets, $5,584 (M); gifts received, $316; expenditures, $562; total giving, $0; qualifying distributions, $0.
Purpose and activities: Giving primarily for medical research, particularly for paralysis.
Fields of interest: Spine disorders research.
Limitations: Giving primarily in MI.
Application information:
Initial approach: Letter
Deadline(s): None
Directors: E.A. Smith; Jeffrey Smith; Patrice Smith.
EIN: 593575843

760
Jean M. R. Smith Foundation
c/o Robert A. Sajdak
P.O. Box 42
Bad Axe, MI 48413-0042
County: Huron
Contact: Edward J. Moore, Treas.
Application address: 64 Westland Dr., Bad Axe, MI 48413-7741, tel.: (989) 269-9909

Established in 1997 in MI.
Donor: Jean M.R. Smith.
Grantmaker type: Independent foundation.
Financial data (yr. ended 12/31/09): Assets, $1,559,011 (M); gifts received, $348,736; expenditures, $126,535; total giving, $100,184; qualifying distributions, $100,184; giving activities include $100,184 for 24 grants to individuals (high: $7,517; low: $1,914).
Purpose and activities: Scholarships awards for residents of Huron County, Michigan.
Fields of interest: Higher education; Athletics/sports, winter sports.
Type of support: Scholarships—to individuals.
Limitations: Giving primarily to residents of Huron County, MI.
Application information: Individual applicants should submit academic records and 2 letters of reference.
Deadline(s): Senior year of high school
Officers: Robert Sajdak, Chair.; John Schwedler, Secy.; Edward J. Moore, Treas.; Rosemary Esch, Vice-Chair.
Director: Richard M. Mieitinen.
EIN: 383323030

761
Snyder Christian Environmental Preservation Foundation
1171 Doerr Rd., Ste. B
Mancelona, MI 49659-8641
County: Antrim

Donor: Harold Z. Snyder.
Grantmaker type: Independent foundation.
Financial data (yr. ended 04/30/09): Assets, $92,948 (M); gifts received, $4,000; expenditures, $72,064; total giving, $0; qualifying distributions, $0.
Limitations: Giving primarily in Spring Arbor, MI. No grants to individuals.
Officers: Rev. Mark Willey, Pres.; James A. Snyder, V.P.; Steve Snyder, Secy.; Charles Stankey, Treas.
Trustee: Rick Duerksen.
EIN: 382385269

762
The Snyder Foundation, Inc.
c/o David White
40900 N. Woodward Ave.
Bloomfield Hills, MI 48304-5115
(517) 750-2778
County: Oakland
Contact: Snyder

Established in 1944 in MI.
Donors: Clarence A. Snyder†; Mrs. Clarence A. Snyder†.
Grantmaker type: Independent foundation.
Financial data (yr. ended 12/31/09): Assets, $191,085 (M); gifts received, $16,000;

expenditures, $44,348; total giving, $40,000; qualifying distributions, $40,000; giving activities include $40,000 for 1 grant.

Purpose and activities: Giving to the Free Methodist Missions in Africa. Giving includes scholarship programs for worthy national students in Rwanda, Africa, for advanced training based on a selection process and criteria established at Mission Hospital in Kibogora, Africa.

Fields of interest: Medical school/education; Education; Hospitals (general); Health care; Human services; Religious federated giving programs; Christian agencies & churches; Religion.

International interests: Africa.

Type of support: General/operating support; Scholarship funds.

Limitations: Applications accepted. Giving primarily in Africa. No grants to individuals.

Application information: Application form not required.

   Initial approach: Letter

   Deadline(s): None

Officers: Arthur H. Snyder, Pres.; Thomas Synder, V.P.; James Snyder, Secy.; David White, Treas.

Directors: Ruth E. White; Harold Snyder; Glenn White.

EIN: 381710360

763
The Sonneveldt Foundation

18042 Wildwood Springs Pkwy.
Spring Lake, MI 49456-9048   (616) 847-0801
County: Ottawa
Contact: Carol A. Sonneveldt, Pres.

Established in 1988 in MI.

Grantmaker type: Independent foundation.

Financial data (yr. ended 12/31/09): Assets, $602,380 (M); gifts received, $7,900; expenditures, $80,423; total giving, $47,250; qualifying distributions, $63,754; giving activities include $47,250 for 14 grants (high: $12,500; low: $1,000).

Purpose and activities: Scholarship awards paid directly to the college or university for persons or children of persons who have been involved in substantial Christian service.

Fields of interest: Higher education; Theological school/education.

Type of support: Scholarship funds.

Limitations: Applications accepted. Giving primarily in CO and MI.

Application information: Include three recommendation letters as well as transcripts from all secondary schools and colleges attended. Application form required.

   Initial approach: Letter

   Deadline(s): None

Officers and Directors:* Carol A. Sonneveldt,* Pres. and Treas.; Robyn J. Brodie; Sharon S. Everest; Lance C. Sonneveldt.

EIN: 382835613

764
Souder Family Foundation

c/o The Northern Trust Bank of FL
P.O. Box 803878
Chicago, IL 60680-3878
County: Cook

Established in 1986 in FL.

Donors: Susanna J. Souder; William F. Souder, Jr. Charitable Lead Trust; Susanna Souder Charitable Lead Trust.

Grantmaker type: Independent foundation.

Financial data (yr. ended 12/31/09): Assets, $14,698,752 (M); gifts received, $398,363; expenditures, $889,399; total giving, $750,437; qualifying distributions, $750,437; giving activities include $750,437 for grants.

Fields of interest: Museums (children's); Historic preservation/historical societies; Education; Zoos/zoological societies; Aquariums; Hospitals (general); Human services; Protestant agencies & churches.

Type of support: General/operating support; Annual campaigns; Building/renovation.

Limitations: Giving primarily in FL, IL, MI, and WI. No grants to individuals.

Application information: Application form not required.

   Deadline(s): None

Directors: Scott Harlow; Susanna J. Souder; William F. Souder, Jr.

EIN: 391560019

Selected grants: The following grants were reported in 2008.

$20,000 to Little Traverse Conservancy, Harbor Springs, MI.

$10,000 to Harbor Springs Area Historical Society, Harbor Springs, MI.

$7,800 to Medical College of Wisconsin, Delwin C Jacobus Internship/Scholarship, Milwaukee, WI.

$6,650 to Mount Mary College, Delwin C Jacobus Internship/Scholarship, Milwaukee, WI.

$4,000 to Daniel Murphy Scholarship Foundation, Chicago, IL.

$3,000 to Harbor Hall Foundation, Petoskey, MI.

$3,000 to Petoskey-Harbor Springs Area Community Foundation, Petoskey, MI.

$1,000 to CircEsteem, Chicago, IL.

$1,000 to CRC Recovery Foundation, Delray Beach, FL.

$1,000 to W P B T Channel 2, Miami, FL.

765
Southeastern Michigan Chapter NECA Educational and Research Foundation

25180 Lahser Rd.
Southfield, MI 48037-5866   (248) 355-3500
County: Oakland
Application address: c/o Scholarship Committee, P.O. Box 385, Southfield, MI 48037-0385

Established in 2003 in MI.

Donor: Electrical Industry Educational Fund.

Grantmaker type: Independent foundation.

Financial data (yr. ended 12/31/09): Assets, $522,538 (M); expenditures, $53,618; total giving, $42,721; qualifying distributions, $42,721; giving activities include $42,721 for 22 grants to individuals (high: $3,300; low: $197).

Purpose and activities: Scholarship awards paid directly to college or university for employees of SMC/NECA and their relatives.

Fields of interest: Higher education.

Type of support: Scholarship funds.

Limitations: Applications accepted. Giving primarily in areas of company operations.

Application information: Application form required.

   Deadline(s): Apr. 15

Directors: Art Ashley; John Colley; John Munro; Tim Shaw; Daniel T. Tripp.

EIN: 300134735

766
The Southeastern Michigan Tarbut Foundation

1301 W. Long Lake Rd., Ste. 200
Troy, MI 48098-6348
County: Oakland
Contact: Joel M. Nass, Pres.

Established in 1998 in MI.

Grantmaker type: Independent foundation.

Financial data (yr. ended 12/31/09): Assets, $19,089 (M); gifts received, $664; expenditures, $664; total giving, $0; qualifying distributions, $0.

Purpose and activities: Support for organizations which promote an appreciation for either Israeli or Jewish art and/or culture.

Fields of interest: Arts, cultural/ethnic awareness; Jewish agencies & synagogues.

Limitations: Giving primarily in IL and MI. No grants to individuals.

Application information:

   Initial approach: Letter

   Deadline(s): None

Officer: Joel M. Nass, Pres.

Directors: Hugh Parks; Rabbi Norman T. Roman.

EIN: 383360386

767
Southwest Michigan Rehab Foundation

3 Heritage Oak Lake
Battle Creek, MI 49015-4262
County: Calhoun
Contact: Cheryl Humbarger, Grant Coord.
Application address: 100 Peets Cove, Battle Creek, MI 49015; tel.:(269) 969-0974

Established in 1991 in MI.

Donor: Southwest Regional Rehabilitation Center.

Grantmaker type: Independent foundation.

Financial data (yr. ended 12/31/09): Assets, $1,677,092 (M); expenditures, $76,069; total giving, $60,359; qualifying distributions, $60,359; giving activities include $10,000 for grants, and $50,359 for grants to individuals.

Purpose and activities: Giving primarily to people with temporary or permanent conditions related to handicap, including prosthetics and equipment for home enablement.

Fields of interest: Physical therapy; Disabilities, people with.

Type of support: Equipment.

Limitations: Applications accepted. Giving limited to residents of southwestern MI, with emphasis on the Battle Creek area, including Calhoun County.

Publications: Informational brochure.

Application information: Application form required.

   Initial approach: Request application form

   Copies of proposal: 1

   Deadline(s): Fri. prior to board meetings

   Board meeting date(s): 3rd Thurs. of each month

   Final notification: Friday prior to monthly meeting

Officers and Directors:* Carl F. Greene,* Pres.; Richard Allen, M.D.*, V.P.; Robert Humbarger,* Secy.; William Comai, M.D.*, Treas.; Roger Mattens; Marilyn Sharp; Jan Smith.

Number of staff: 1 part-time support.

EIN: 382939930

Selected grants: The following grants were reported in 2005.

$2,651 to Binder Park Zoological Society, Battle Creek, MI.

768
Speckhard-Knight Charitable Foundation
771 Bogey Ct.
Ann Arbor, MI 48103-8844 (734) 761-8752
County: Washtenaw
Contact: Gerald Knight
FAX: (734) 827-0091; E-mail: zmjk@comcast.net

Established in 1999 in MI.
Donors: Gerald Knight; Maureen Knight.
Grantmaker type: Independent foundation.
Financial data (yr. ended 12/31/09): Assets,
$4,660,378 (M); gifts received, $65,059;
expenditures, $258,243; total giving, $177,000;
qualifying distributions, $185,638; giving activities
include $177,000 for 17 grants (high: $30,000;
low: $1,000).
Purpose and activities: The foundation is dedicated
to improving the quality of life in Jackson and
Washtenaw counties in MI, and aiding
environmental efforts in the third world. The
foundation strives to assist nonprofit organizations
that work in the important areas of adoption, foster
care, at risk families and the environment.
Fields of interest: Environment; Human services;
Children, adoption; Children, foster care.
Type of support: General/operating support; Land
acquisition; Program development.
Limitations: Applications accepted. Giving primarily
in MI.
Application information:
  Initial approach: E-mail
  Copies of proposal: 1
  Board meeting date(s): Mar., July, and Nov.
  Final notification: 1-2 weeks
Directors: Gerald Knight; Maureen Knight.
EIN: 383466344
Selected grants: The following grants were reported
in 2006.
$60,000 to University of Michigan Health System,
Ann Arbor, MI.
$22,970 to Wildlife Conservation Society, Bronx,
NY.
$20,000 to Center for Family Health, Jackson, MI.
$12,050 to Catholic Social Services of Washtenaw
County, Ann Arbor, MI.
$10,000 to Amazon Watch, San Francisco, CA.
$10,000 to Lily Missions Center, Jackson, MI.
$10,000 to Michigan Stewardship Network, Ann
Arbor, MI.
$10,000 to POWER, Inc., Ann Arbor, MI.
$7,000 to Washtenaw Land Trust, Ann Arbor, MI.
$5,000 to Bethany Christian Services, Grand
Rapids, MI.

769
The Alvin B. Spector Foundation for the Arts
(formerly Lois & Alvin Spector Foundation for the
Arts)
148 Chesterfield Rd.
Bloomfield Hills, MI 48304-3518
(248) 644-7387
County: Oakland
Contact: Lois Spector Freeman, Pres.

Established in MI.
Grantmaker type: Independent foundation.
Financial data (yr. ended 12/31/09): Assets,
$12,702 (M); gifts received, $775; expenditures,
$1,925; total giving, $1,000; qualifying
distributions, $1,000; giving activities include
$1,000 for grants.

Fields of interest: Arts.
Type of support: General/operating support.
Limitations: Giving primarily in MI. No grants to
individuals.
Application information: Application form not
required.
  Initial approach: Project description
  Deadline(s): None
Officers: Lois Spector Freeman, Pres. and Treas.;
Neal J. Spector, Secy.
EIN: 382283492

770
Peter and Evelyn Speerstra Scholarship Fund Trust
c/o Fifth Third Bank
P.O. Box 3636
Grand Rapids, MI 49501-3636
County: Kent
Application address: c/o Lowell High School,
Attn: Barbara Pierce, 750 Foreman St., Lowell, MI
49331-1028, tel.: (616) 897-4125

Established in 1985 in MI.
Grantmaker type: Independent foundation.
Financial data (yr. ended 02/28/10): Assets,
$211,795 (M); expenditures, $11,901; total giving,
$8,200; qualifying distributions, $8,200; giving
activities include $8,200 for grants to individuals.
Purpose and activities: Scholarship awards to high
school graduates from the Lowell, Michigan, public
school district.
Fields of interest: Higher education.
Type of support: Scholarships—to individuals.
Limitations: Applications accepted. Giving limited to
the Lowell, MI, area.
Application information: Application form required.
  Deadline(s): Apr. 1
Scholarship Committee: William Christensen;
Barbara Pierce; Errolyn Weeks.
Trustee: Fifth Third Bank.
EIN: 386480250

771
Spencer Family Foundation
909 Cascade Hills Dr. S.E.
Grand Rapids, MI 49546-3678 (616) 942-4743
County: Kent
Contact: Kenneth Spencer, Pres.

Established in 1993 in MI.
Grantmaker type: Independent foundation.
Financial data (yr. ended 12/31/07): Assets,
$5,540 (M); gifts received, $35,000; expenditures,
$31,501; total giving, $30,950; qualifying
distributions, $30,950; giving activities include
$30,950 for grants.
Fields of interest: Education; Christian agencies &
churches.
Limitations: Giving primarily in MI.
Application information: Application form not
required.
  Deadline(s): None
Officers: Kenneth Spencer, Pres.; Carol Spencer,
Secy.-Treas.
EIN: 383076355

772
S. Gary Spicer, Sr. Foundation
16845 Kercheval St., Ste. 5
Grosse Pointe, MI 48230-1551
County: Wayne

Established in 1997 in MI.
Donor: S. Gary Spicer.
Grantmaker type: Independent foundation.
Financial data (yr. ended 12/31/09): Assets,
$1,084,080 (M); gifts received, $166,293;
expenditures, $85,312; total giving, $66,405;
qualifying distributions, $66,405; giving activities
include $66,405 for 23 grants (high: $24,000; low:
$25).
Fields of interest: Historical activities; Higher
education; Environment; Health organizations;
Protestant agencies & churches.
Type of support: General/operating support.
Limitations: Applications accepted. Giving primarily
in MI. No grants to individuals.
Application information: Contact foundation for
application guidelines.
  Deadline(s): None
Officers and Trustee:* S. Gary Spicer,* Pres.; Ed
Zionkowski, Secy.
EIN: 383341391

773
Springview Foundation
1 Haworth Ctr.
Holland, MI 49423-9570
County: Ottawa
Contact: Richard G. Haworth, Tr.

Established in 1998 in MI.
Donors: Ethelyn L. Haworth; Richard G. Haworth;
Richard and Ethelyn Haworth Foundation; Anna
Haworth.
Grantmaker type: Independent foundation.
Financial data (yr. ended 12/31/09): Assets,
$3,757,661 (M); gifts received, $25,000;
expenditures, $197,810; total giving, $181,100;
qualifying distributions, $196,518; giving activities
include $181,100 for 12 grants (high: $55,000;
low: $2,450).
Fields of interest: Theological school/education;
Human services; Children/youth, services; Family
services; Christian agencies & churches; Protestant
agencies & churches.
Limitations: Applications accepted. Giving primarily
in Grand Rapids and Holland, MI.
Application information: Application form required.
  Initial approach: Letter
  Copies of proposal: 6
  Deadline(s): Sept. 1
  Board meeting date(s): 1st half of Nov.
  Final notification: Mid-Dec.
Trustees: Sara E. Dykema; Timothy J. Dykema; Anna
C. Haworth; Ethelyn L. Haworth; Jennifer L. Haworth;
Matthew R. Haworth; Richard G. Haworth.
Number of staff: None.
EIN: 383422204
Selected grants: The following grants were reported
in 2008.
$38,000 to Helen DeVos Childrens Hospital
Foundation, Spectrum Health, Grand Rapids, MI.
$30,502 to Holland Rescue Mission, Holland, MI.
$10,000 to Campus Crusade for Christ
International, Orlando, FL.
$9,360 to Outdoor Discovery Center of Wildlife
Unlimited, Holland, MI.

$3,500 to Lakeshore Ethnic Diversity Alliance, Holland, MI.

$2,500 to Hospice of Holland, Holland, MI.

774
St. Clair Foundation
c/o Fifth Third Bank
P.O. Box 3636
Grand Rapids, MI 49501-3636
County: Kent
Application address: c/o Franklin H. Moore, Jr., Fifth Third Bank, 200 S. Riverside Ave., St. Clair, MI 48079, tel.: (810) 326-1123

Established in 1956 in MI.
Donors: Alice W. Moore; John Emig Trust A; John Emig Trust B.
Grantmaker type: Independent foundation.
Financial data (yr. ended 12/31/09): Assets, $2,659,559 (M); expenditures, $148,315; total giving, $123,300; qualifying distributions, $123,300; giving activities include $123,300 for grants.
Fields of interest: Elementary school/education; Secondary school/education; Libraries (public); Hospitals (general); Youth development; Human services; Community/economic development; Foundations (community); Government/public administration.
Type of support: Program development; Annual campaigns; Equipment; Scholarship funds.
Limitations: Applications accepted. Giving limited to the city of St. Clair, MI, and its immediate vicinity. No grants to individuals.
Application information:
Initial approach: Letter
Deadline(s): None
Trustees: William Cedar; Gerald M. Emig; James Fredericks; Bernard Kuhn; Franklin H. Moore, Jr.
EIN: 386064622
Selected grants: The following grants were reported in 2008.
$25,500 to Saint Clair, City of, Saint Clair, MI.
$25,000 to Saint Clair High School, Senior Scholarships, Saint Clair, MI.
$20,000 to Saint Clair High School, Graduate Scholarships, Saint Clair, MI.
$10,000 to River District Hospital, Digital Mammorgraphy Equip, Saint Clair, MI.
$5,500 to Saint Clair High School, Program Support, Saint Clair, MI.
$3,500 to Saint Clair Art Association, Saint Clair, MI.

775
St. Joseph Kiwanis Foundation
414 Main St.
St. Joseph, MI 49085-1235 (269) 983-0531
County: Berrien
Contact: Jonathan B. Sauer, Treas.
E-mail: emeny@parrett.net; *URL:* http://sjkiwanis.org/programs_events.htm
Application address: 2975 McLin Rd., St. Joseph, MI 49085-3536, tel.: (616) 429-2025

Established in 1965 in MI.
Grantmaker type: Independent foundation.
Financial data (yr. ended 12/31/09): Assets, $497,192 (M); expenditures, $24,768; total giving, $18,750; qualifying distributions, $18,750; giving activities include $18,750 for grants to individuals.

Purpose and activities: The foundation provides financial aid to local students who are, or will be, pursuing undergraduate college or university degrees. Applications are accepted seniors or recent graduates from the following high schools: from St. Joseph, Lake Michigan Catholic, Lakeshore, and Michigan Lutheran.
Fields of interest: Higher education.
Type of support: Scholarships—to individuals.
Limitations: Applications accepted. Giving limited to residents of the St. Joseph, MI, area.
Application information: See foundation web site for application form. Application form required.
Officers: Edward E. Meny, Pres.; Louis A. Pinderski, Secy.; Jonathan B. Sauer, Treas.
Directors: John Festa; Daryl Godke; John Helsley; Clare Musgrove; Garry Sisson.
EIN: 386117678

776
The Stanton Foundation
714 W. Michigan Ave.
Jackson, MI 49201-1909
County: Jackson

Established in 1999 in MI.
Donor: David J. Stanton.
Grantmaker type: Independent foundation.
Financial data (yr. ended 06/30/09): Assets, $641,042 (M); gifts received, $449,463; expenditures, $70,531; total giving, $28,500; qualifying distributions, $28,500; giving activities include $28,500 for grants.
Fields of interest: Catholic agencies & churches.
Limitations: Giving primarily in MI. No grants to individuals.
Officers: David J. Stanton, Pres.; Laura M. Stanton, Secy.
EIN: 383448185

777
The Starfish Alliance, Inc.
9880 Musch Rd.
Brighton, MI 48116-8215
County: Livingston

Established in 2007 in MI.
Grantmaker type: Independent foundation.
Financial data (yr. ended 12/31/09): Assets, $1 (M); gifts received, $2,550; expenditures, $2,550; total giving, $2,550; qualifying distributions, $2,550; giving activities include $2,550 for grants.
Officers: Colleen M. Falcone, Pres.; Joseph Falcone, V.P.
EIN: 200237763

778
Richard A. and Donna L. Sterban Foundation
16845 Kercheval St., Ste. 5
Grosse Pointe, MI 48230-1551
County: Wayne

Established in 1997 in MI.
Donors: Donna L. Sterban; Richard A. Sterban.
Grantmaker type: Independent foundation.
Financial data (yr. ended 12/31/09): Assets, $226,085 (M); gifts received, $10,500; expenditures, $9,962; total giving, $9,000; qualifying distributions, $9,962; giving activities

include $9,000 for 2 grants (high: $5,000; low: $4,000).
Fields of interest: Education; Protestant agencies & churches.
Limitations: Applications accepted. Giving primarily in TN. No grants to individuals.
Application information: Contact foundation for application guidelines.
Officers and Trustees: * Richard A. Sterban,* Pres.; S. Gary Spicer,* Secy.; Donna L. Sterban,* Treas.
EIN: 383383414

779
The Sterken Family Foundation
6177 Windmill Ct.
Saline, MI 48176-9101 (734) 316-2701
County: Washtenaw
Contact: James J. Sterken, Dir.

Established in 2005 in MI.
Donors: James Sterken; Gwynn Sterken.
Grantmaker type: Independent foundation.
Financial data (yr. ended 12/31/09): Assets, $209,161 (M); expenditures, $75,860; total giving, $74,260; qualifying distributions, $74,260; giving activities include $74,260 for grants.
Fields of interest: Health care; Human services; Protestant agencies & churches; Catholic agencies & churches.
Application information: Application form not required.
Deadline(s): None
Directors: James J. Sterken; Gwynn E. Sterken.
EIN: 203966962
Selected grants: The following grants were reported in 2008.
$1,000 to Purple Rose Theater Company, Chelsea, MI.

780
Stewart Management Group Charitable Foundation
31850 Ford Rd.
Garden City, MI 48135-1506
County: Wayne
Contact: Gordon L. Stewart, Pres.

Established in 1994 in MI.
Grantmaker type: Independent foundation.
Financial data (yr. ended 11/30/09): Assets, $172,723 (M); gifts received, $9,000; expenditures, $6,249; total giving, $5,450; qualifying distributions, $5,810; giving activities include $5,450 for 11 grants to individuals (high: $500; low: $450).
Purpose and activities: Scholarship awards to local area residents who are students of the Westland and Garden City, Michigan.
Fields of interest: Higher education.
Type of support: Scholarships—to individuals.
Limitations: Applications accepted. Giving limited to residents of Garden City and Westland, MI.
Application information: Selection based on recommendations of the committee at each school. Application form required.
Deadline(s): None
Officers: Gordon L. Stewart, Pres.; Linda A. Stewart, Secy.; Craig M. Hale, Treas.
EIN: 383189964

781
Stockbridge Foundation
3717 Wards Pt.
Orchard Lake, MI 48324-1662
County: Oakland
Contact: Mahmoud Alhadidi, Pres.

Established in 2003 in MI.
Donors: Mahmoud Alhadidi, M.D.; Stockbridge Enterprise Inc.
Grantmaker type: Independent foundation.
Financial data (yr. ended 12/31/09): Assets, $30,565 (M); gifts received, $30,000; expenditures, $28,018; total giving, $26,935; qualifying distributions, $26,935; giving activities include $26,935 for grants.
Fields of interest: Education; Islam.
Limitations: Giving limited to MI.
Application information:
   Initial approach: Letter
   Deadline(s): 60 days prior to the fiscal year end
Officer: Mahmoud Alhadidi, M.D., Pres. and Treas.
EIN: 352191395

782
North J. and Florence Stockton Charitable Foundation
c/o JPMorgan Chase Bank, N.A.
P.O. Box 3038
Milwaukee, WI 53201-3038
County: Milwaukee
Application address: c/o JPMorgan Chase Bank, N.A., 2385 Executive Center Dr., Boca Raton, FL 33431-8579, tel.: (561) 995-5052

Established in 1995 in FL.
Donor: Florence Stockton.
Grantmaker type: Independent foundation.
Financial data (yr. ended 12/31/09): Assets, $1,142,633 (M); expenditures, $72,577; total giving, $56,340; qualifying distributions, $56,340; giving activities include $56,340 for grants.
Fields of interest: Eye diseases; Alzheimer's disease; Food services; Catholic agencies & churches.
Type of support: General/operating support.
Limitations: Applications accepted. Giving limited to Broward County, FL, and Wayne County, MI.
Application information: Application form not required.
   Initial approach: Letter
   Deadline(s): None
Trustees: Judy K. Nowak; JPMorgan Chase Bank, N.A.
EIN: 386662894

783
Alice A. Stoddard Trust
c/o Monroe Bank & Trust
102 E. Front St.
Monroe, MI 48161-2162 (734) 384-8114
County: Monroe
Application address: c/o University of Michigan, Medical Research Program, Attn.: Medical Admin., P.O. Box 0624, Ann Arbor, MI 48109-0624, tel.: (734) 763-9600

Established in MI.
Donor: Alice A. Stoddard‡.
Grantmaker type: Independent foundation.

Financial data (yr. ended 06/30/09): Assets, $157,474 (M); expenditures, $12,624; total giving, $8,597; qualifying distributions, $10,480; giving activities include $8,597 for 1 grant.
Purpose and activities: Giving to the University of Michigan for research on lymph gland diseases.
Fields of interest: Medical school/education; Medical specialties research.
Type of support: Fellowships; Research; Scholarship funds.
Limitations: Applications accepted. Giving limited to Ann Arbor, MI. No grants to individuals (directly).
Application information: Individuals must be selected by the University of Michigan for Lymph Gland Research. Application form required.
   Initial approach: Proposal
   Deadline(s): Feb. 1
Trustee: Monroe Bank & Trust.
EIN: 386052244

784
Margaret Jane Stoker Charitable Trust
c/o Citizens Bank Wealth Management, N.A.
328 S. Saginaw St., M/C 001065
Flint, MI 48502-1923 (989) 776-1416
County: Genesee
Contact: Karen McNish
Application address: c/o Citizens Bank Wealth Mgmt., N.A., 101 N. Washington Ave., Saginaw, MI 48607, tel.: (989) 776-1416

Established in 2001 in MI.
Grantmaker type: Independent foundation.
Financial data (yr. ended 09/30/10): Assets, $2,611,519 (M); expenditures, $120,576; total giving, $87,895; qualifying distributions, $101,286; giving activities include $87,895 for 7 grants (high: $35,000; low: $3,000).
Fields of interest: Higher education; Human services; Children/youth, services.
Limitations: Applications accepted. Giving primarily in the Saginaw County, MI, area.
Application information: Application form required.
   Initial approach: Applications available through Citizens Bank
   Deadline(s): None
Trustee: Citizens Bank Wealth Management, N.A.
EIN: 320000318
Selected grants: The following grants were reported in 2007.
$25,000 to YMCA of Saginaw, Saginaw, MI.
$20,000 to United Way of Saginaw County, Saginaw, MI.
$18,000 to First Ward Community Service, Saginaw, MI.
$7,816 to Underground Railroad, Saginaw, MI.
$3,795 to Read Association of Saginaw County, Saginaw, MI.

785
Olive A. Stokes Scholarship Trust
c/o Comerica Bank
P.O. Box 75000, MC 3302
Detroit, MI 48275-3302
County: Wayne
Application address: c/o Sharon Stephens, 1305 S. Franklin, Rocky Mount, NC 27804, tel.: (252) 467-4743

Established in 2001 in NC.
Grantmaker type: Independent foundation.

Financial data (yr. ended 09/30/09): Assets, $452,849 (M); expenditures, $38,906; total giving, $30,000; qualifying distributions, $30,000; giving activities include $30,000 for grants to individuals.
Purpose and activities: Scholarship awards to U.S. citizens who are residents of Nash or Edgecombe counties, North Carolina, with a GAP of C plus or better.
Fields of interest: Higher education.
Type of support: Scholarships—to individuals.
Limitations: Giving primarily in Nash and Edgecombe Counties, NC.
Application information: Application form not required.
   Deadline(s): June 1
Trustee: Comerica Bank.
EIN: 316646001

786
The Wally and Jo Strobel Foundation
c/o Susan Waters
2228 Chestnut Crescent
Saline, MI 48176-1667
County: Washtenaw
Contact: Josephine Strobel, V.P.
Application address: 1301 N. Tamiami Trail, Sarasota, FL 34236-2402, tel.: (941) 366-6335

Established in 2004 in MI.
Donor: Josephine Strobel.
Grantmaker type: Independent foundation.
Financial data (yr. ended 12/31/09): Assets, $1 (M); gifts received, $4,547; expenditures, $23,031; total giving, $20,850; qualifying distributions, $20,850; giving activities include $20,850 for grants.
Fields of interest: Arts; Animals/wildlife; Health care; Human services; Military/veterans; Economically disadvantaged.
Limitations: Applications accepted. Giving primarily in FL and MI.
Application information:
   Initial approach: Letter
   Deadline(s): None
Officers: Susan Waters, Pres.; Josephine Strobel, V.P.; Sarah King, Secy.-Treas.
EIN: 201570905

787
The Charles J. Strosacker Foundation
812 W. Main St.
P.O. Box 471
Midland, MI 48640-0471 (989) 832-0066
County: Midland
Contact: Marian L. Cimbalik, Tr.

Incorporated in 1957 in MI.
Donors: Charles J. Strosacker‡; Ula G. Shaffer Administration Trust.
Grantmaker type: Independent foundation.
Financial data (yr. ended 12/31/09): Assets, $49,996,011 (M); expenditures, $2,793,012; total giving, $2,711,549; qualifying distributions, $2,711,549; giving activities include $2,711,549 for 85 grants (high: $500,000; low: $250).
Purpose and activities: Giving to assist and benefit political subdivisions of the state of Michigan, educational organizations, and social services.
Fields of interest: Higher education; Human services; Community/economic development; United Ways and Federated Giving Programs.

Type of support: Continuing support; Building/renovation; Equipment; Endowments; Program development; Seed money; Research.
Limitations: Applications accepted. Giving primarily in MI, with emphasis on Midland County. No grants to individuals, or for matching gifts; no loans.
Publications: Annual report (including application guidelines).
Application information: Application form not required.
Initial approach: Letter
Copies of proposal: 1
Deadline(s): None
Board meeting date(s): May, Aug., and Nov.
Officers and Trustees: David J. Arnold,* Chair.; Bobbie N. Arnold, C.E.O. and Pres.; Richard M. Reynolds, Exec. V.P.; Donna T. Morris,* Secy.; James L. Borin, Treas.; Lawrence Burks, Tr. Emeritus; Ralph A. Cole, Tr. Emeritus; Richard Hazleton, Tr. Emeritus; Kimberlee K. Baczewski; John N. Bartos; Stephanie A. Burns; David H. Dunn; Carolyn Thrune Durand; John S. Ludington; Charles J. Thrune; Carolyn Thrune-Durand; Charlie C. Thrune-Lundquist.
Number of staff: 1 part-time support.
EIN: 386062787
Selected grants: The following grants were reported in 2005.
$225,000 to Midland Public Schools, Midland, MI.
$164,845 to Eagle Village, Hersey, MI.
$125,000 to Kalamazoo College, Kalamazoo, MI.
$110,000 to Cleveland Manor, Midland, MI.
$100,000 to Boy Scouts of America, Auburn, MI.
$75,000 to Delta College Foundation, University Center, MI.
$50,000 to Gratiot Health System, Alma, MI.
$43,000 to Cleveland Manor, Midland, MI.
$15,000 to Midland Area Homes, Midland, MI.
$8,000 to Meharry Medical College, Nashville, TN.

788
The Ronda E. Stryker and William D. Johnston Foundation
211 S. Rose St.
Kalamazoo, MI 49007-4713 (269) 388-9800
County: Kalamazoo
Contact: William D. Johnston, Secy.-Treas.

Established in 1995 in MI.
Donors: Ronda E. Stryker; William Johnston.
Grantmaker type: Independent foundation.
Financial data (yr. ended 12/31/09): Assets, $11,672,633 (M); gifts received, $2,738,722; expenditures, $4,464,438; total giving, $4,368,188; qualifying distributions, $4,392,614; giving activities include $4,638,188 for grants (high: $2,750,000; low: $550).
Purpose and activities: Giving primarily for the arts, higher education and human services.
Fields of interest: Arts; Higher education; Education; Human services; YM/YWCAs & YM/YWHAs; Community/economic development; Foundations (community).
Limitations: Applications accepted. Giving primarily in Kalamazoo, MI. No grants to individuals.
Application information: Application form not required.
Initial approach: Letter
Officers and Trustees: Ronda E. Stryker,* Pres.; William D. Johnston,* Secy.-Treas.; Lisa Thomas;

Anne E. Johnston; Megan M. Johnston; Michael B. Johnston.
EIN: 383224966
Selected grants: The following grants were reported in 2005.
$700,000 to Western Michigan University Foundation, Kalamazoo, MI. For Partnering for Success: The Centennial Campaign for Western Michigan University.
$430,000 to Southwest Michigan First Corporation, Kalamazoo, MI. For general support.
$392,000 to Kalamazoo Institute of Arts, Kalamazoo, MI. For general support.
$200,000 to Kalamazoo College, Kalamazoo, MI. For Mary Jane Underwood Stryker Institute for Service Learning.
$110,000 to Kalamazoo Community Foundation, Kalamazoo, MI. For Community Redevelopment Fund.
$102,500 to Starr Commonwealth, Albion, MI. For general support.
$100,000 to American Red Cross Greater Kalamazoo Area, Kalamazoo, MI. For general support.
$100,000 to Western Michigan University Foundation, Kalamazoo, MI. For general support.

789
Maurice & Dorothy Stubnitz Foundation
153 E. Maumee St.
Adrian, MI 49221-2703
County: Lenawee
Contact: Charles E. Gross, Pres.

Established in 1981 in MI.
Grantmaker type: Independent foundation.
Financial data (yr. ended 09/30/10): Assets, $5,925,778 (M); expenditures, $353,855; total giving, $295,933; qualifying distributions, $295,933; giving activities include $295,933 for 18 grants (high: $48,620; low: $1,600).
Purpose and activities: Giving primarily for higher education and human services.
Fields of interest: Performing arts, orchestras; Higher education; Housing/shelter, development; Human services; Community/economic development.
Type of support: Building/renovation; Equipment; Land acquisition; Emergency funds; Program development; Seed money; Scholarship funds.
Limitations: Applications accepted. Giving primarily in Adrian, MI. No grants to individuals.
Publications: Application guidelines; Informational brochure.
Application information: Application form not required.
Copies of proposal: 5
Deadline(s): Apr. 30
Board meeting date(s): Semiannually
Final notification: 4-6 weeks for positive responses
Officers: Charles E. Gross, Pres. and Treas.; Betty Gross, V.P.; William Benz, Secy.
Directors: James L. Feeney; Hildreth Spencer.
EIN: 382392373
Selected grants: The following grants were reported in 2007.
$50,000 to Adrian Schools Educational Foundation, Adrian, MI.
$37,200 to YMCA of Lenawee County, Adrian, MI.
$35,000 to Croswell Opera House and Fine Arts Association, Adrian, MI.
$25,000 to Adrian College, Adrian, MI.

$25,000 to Adrian Symphony Orchestra, Adrian, MI.
$24,500 to Goodwill Industries, Burton, MI.
$24,395 to Adrian, City of, Adrian, MI.
$20,000 to Bixby Medical Center, Adrian, MI.
$18,195 to Lenawee Intermediate School District, Stubnitz Environmental Education Center, Adrian, MI.
$16,041 to Siena Heights University, Adrian, MI.
$6,607 to Hope Community Center, Adrian, MI.
$4,885 to Habitat for Humanity of Lenawee County, Adrian, MI.

790
David & Lois Stulberg Foundation
655 Longboat Club Rd., Apt. 16A
Longboat Key, FL 34228-3859
County: Manatee
Contact: Lois Stulberg, Pres.
Tel. for Lois Stulberg: (248) 334-5353

Established in 1984 in MI.
Donors: Margaret Dunning; David A. Stulberg; Lois Stulberg.
Grantmaker type: Independent foundation.
Financial data (yr. ended 12/31/09): Assets, $2,928,693 (M); expenditures, $213,132; total giving, $201,500; qualifying distributions, $201,500; giving activities include $201,500 for grants.
Fields of interest: Arts; Higher education; Health care; Cancer; Jewish federated giving programs; Jewish agencies & synagogues; Women.
Limitations: Giving primarily in FL, MI and MN.
Application information:
Initial approach: Letter
Deadline(s): None
Officers: Lois Stulberg, Pres. and Treas.; Robert M. Stulberg, Secy.
Trustees: Robert Appel; Susan A. Rosenstein.
EIN: 382575785
Selected grants: The following grants were reported in 2008.
$3,000 to American Red Magen David for Israel, Southfield, MI.

791
Anup and Parul Sud Family Foundation
1126 Millcreek Rd.
Flint, MI 48532-2347
County: Genesee
Contact: Anup Sud, Pres.

Established in 1995 in MI.
Donors: Anup Sud; Parul Sud.
Grantmaker type: Independent foundation.
Financial data (yr. ended 12/31/09): Assets, $235,631 (M); expenditures, $6,298; total giving, $3,700; qualifying distributions, $3,700; giving activities include $3,700 for grants.
Limitations: Giving primarily in Flint, MI.
Application information:
Initial approach: Letter
Deadline(s): None
Officers: Anup Sud, Pres.; Parul Sud, V.P.
EIN: 383206403

792
The Ann Ludington Sullivan Foundation
c/o DeLoitte Tax Srvs., LLP
3320 Ridgecrest Dr., Ste. 400
Midland, MI 48642-5864   (989) 631-2370
County: Midland
Contact: Ann L. Sullivan, Pres.

Established in 1996 in MI.
Donor: John S. Ludington.
Grantmaker type: Independent foundation.
Financial data (yr. ended 12/31/09): Assets, $557,195 (M); gifts received, $48,929; expenditures, $25,017; total giving, $24,500; qualifying distributions, $24,500; giving activities include $24,500 for grants.
Fields of interest: Higher education; Substance abuse, services; Food banks; Human services; Christian agencies & churches.
Limitations: Applications accepted. Giving primarily in MI and NC.
Application information: Application form required.
Initial approach: Letter
Deadline(s): None
Officers: Ann L. Sullivan,* Pres.; Patrick M. Sullivan,* V.P.; John S. Ludington, Treas.
EIN: 383323702

793
Robert and Timothy Sullivan Scholarship Fund Trust
(formerly Sullivan Scholarship Fund Trust)
2745 DeHoop Ave. S.W.
Wyoming, MI 49509-1867   (616) 538-6380
County: Kent
Contact: Dana L. Snoap, Tr.

Established in MI.
Donors: Robert Sullivan; B&B Beer Distributing Co.
Grantmaker type: Independent foundation.
Financial data (yr. ended 09/30/10): Assets, $74,102 (M); gifts received, $7,000; expenditures, $16,754; total giving, $16,000; qualifying distributions, $16,373; giving activities include $16,000 for 6 grants (high: $5,000; low: $2,000).
Purpose and activities: Scholarship awards through Calvin College, Davenport College, Aquinas College, Grand Rapids Community College, and Grand Valley State University in Michigan.
Fields of interest: Scholarships/financial aid.
Type of support: Scholarship funds.
Limitations: Giving limited to the metropolitan Grand Rapids, MI, area.
Application information:
Initial approach: Letter
Deadline(s): May 1
Trustee: Dana L. Snoap.
EIN: 382448544

794
Sunrise Community Foundation
8546 Eastbeach Trail
Traverse City, MI 49686-1674
County: Grand Traverse
Contact: Ronald R. Pohl, Dir.

Established in 2004 in MI.
Donors: Ronald R. Pohl; Judy C. Pohl.
Grantmaker type: Independent foundation.
Financial data (yr. ended 12/31/09): Assets, $101,467 (M); expenditures, $43,780; total giving, $42,000; qualifying distributions, $42,000; giving activities include $42,000 for grants.
Fields of interest: Education; Housing/shelter; Human services; Christian agencies & churches.
Limitations: Applications accepted. Giving primarily in Traverse City, MI.
Application information:
Initial approach: Letter
Deadline(s): None
Directors: Judy C. Pohl; Ronald R. Pohl.
EIN: 202005328

795
Sutar-Sutaruk-Meyer Foundation
2301 W. Big Beaver, Ste. 777
Troy, MI 48084   (248) 649-1900
County: Oakland
Contact: Stuart Lee Sherman

Donor: William Sutar†.
Grantmaker type: Independent foundation.
Financial data (yr. ended 12/31/09): Assets, $860,527 (M); gifts received, $835,571; expenditures, $70,000; total giving, $40,000; qualifying distributions, $70,000; giving activities include $40,000 for 2 grants (high: $38,000; low: $2,000).
Application information: Application form required.
Initial approach: Proposal
Deadline(s): None
Directors: Jonathon Meyer; Kathleen Meyer; Thomas Meyer; Olga Sutar-meyer.
EIN: 262377296

796
The Richard J. and Frances B. Swiat Foundation
1615 W. Centre Ave.
Portage, MI 49024-5379
County: Kalamazoo
Contact: Richard G. Swiat, Pres. and Treas.

Established in 1987 in MI.
Donor: Richard J. Swiat.
Grantmaker type: Independent foundation.
Financial data (yr. ended 12/31/09): Assets, $3,041,390 (M); expenditures, $304,924; total giving, $223,500; qualifying distributions, $265,920; giving activities include $223,500 for 8 grants (high: $65,000; low: $5,000).
Purpose and activities: Giving primarily to organizations that will aid mentally-impaired individuals in the states of Illinois, Michigan, and Wisconsin.
Fields of interest: Mental health, disorders; Mentally disabled.
Type of support: General/operating support.
Limitations: Applications accepted. Giving primarily in IL, MI, and WI. No grants to individuals.
Application information:
Initial approach: Letter
Deadline(s): None
Officers: Richard G. Swiat, Pres. and Treas.; Shelly Swiat, V.P. and Secy.
Trustees: Sally J. Hanley; James R. Swiat.
EIN: 382813470
Selected grants: The following grants were reported in 2008.
$60,000 to Saint Louis Center, Chelsea, MI.
$55,000 to Shalom, Philadelphia, PA.
$5,000 to Residential Opportunities, Kalamazoo, MI.

797
Sylvia Weider-Amber Family Foundation
5455 Corporate Dr., Ste. 300
Troy, MI 48098-2620
County: Oakland

Established in 2006 in MI.
Grantmaker type: Independent foundation.
Financial data (yr. ended 12/31/09): Assets, $894,765 (M); gifts received, $4,035; expenditures, $56,131; total giving, $46,312; qualifying distributions, $46,312; giving activities include $46,312 for grants.
Fields of interest: Arts; Education; Health care; Human services; Jewish agencies & synagogues.
Limitations: Giving primarily in San Diego, CA, Washington, DC, MI, and New York, NY. No support for organizations lacking 501(c)(3) status. No grants to individuals.
Application information: Application form not required.
Initial approach: Letter
Deadline(s): None
Officers: Sylvia W. Amber, Pres.; Rhonda J. Amber, V.P.; Betty Amber, Secy.; Craig Skulsky, Treas.
EIN: 203939647

798
Tassell-Wisner-Bottrall Foundation
(formerly The Leslie E. Tassell Foundation)
c/o Fifth Third Bank
111 Lyon St. N.W.
Grand Rapids, MI 49501-3636
County: Kent
Application address: c/o Joyce Wisner, 3439 Quiggle Ave. S.E., Ada, MI 49301-9237

Established in 1994 in MI.
Donors: Leslie E. Tassell†; The Leslie Metal Arts Co., Inc.
Grantmaker type: Independent foundation.
Financial data (yr. ended 12/31/09): Assets, $7,302,676 (M); expenditures, $355,460; total giving, $286,054; qualifying distributions, $305,824; giving activities include $231,760 for 5 grants (high: $100,000; low: $2,500), and $54,294 for 33 grants to individuals (high: $3,000; low: $294).
Purpose and activities: Giving primarily for higher education, including scholarships to individuals; giving also for health care.
Fields of interest: Higher education; Health care.
Type of support: General/operating support; Scholarships—to individuals.
Limitations: Applications accepted. Giving primarily in Grand Rapids, MI.
Application information: Application form required.
Initial approach: Write for application form
Deadline(s): None
Trustees: David C. Bottrall; Michael R. Julien; Hilary F. Snell; Donald Wisner; Joyce S. Wisner; Leslie Wisner.
EIN: 383186818
Selected grants: The following grants were reported in 2006.
$50,000 to Alano Club of Kent County, Grand Rapids, MI.
$25,000 to Aquinas College, Grand Rapids, MI.

$15,000 to Habitat for Humanity of Kent County, Grand Rapids, MI.
$10,000 to West Michigan Trails and Greenways Coalition, Comstock Park, MI.
$4,000 to Forest Hills Educational Foundation, Grand Rapids, MI.

799
Brent Taylor Perpetual Charitable Trust
c/o Mercantile Bank
200 N. 33rd St.
P.O. Box 3455
Quincy, IL 62305-3714
County: Adams
Application address: c/o Titan International, Attn.: Courtney Leeser, 2701 Spruce St., Quincy, IL 62301-3473, tel.: (217) 221-4489

Established in IL.
Donors: Maurice Taylor; Michelle Taylor.
Grantmaker type: Independent foundation.
Financial data (yr. ended 12/31/09): Assets, $75,252 (M); gifts received, $290,795; expenditures, $256,096; total giving, $253,909; qualifying distributions, $254,452; giving activities include $253,909 for 180 grants to individuals (high: $14,748; low: $1,000).
Purpose and activities: Scholarship awards paid directly to the college or university for persons who are enrolled in a qualified educational institution on a full-time basis for the succeeding semester or quarter, and are either qualified employees or children of qualified employees of Titan International, Inc., or any of its subsidiaries, OTR Wheel, Inc., or any of its subsidiaries or affiliates, or residents of Quincy, Illinois, Ellsworth, Michigan, or Saltville, Virginia.
Fields of interest: Higher education.
Type of support: Employee-related scholarships; Scholarships—to individuals.
Limitations: Applications accepted. Giving primarily to benefit of residents of Quincy, IL, Ellsworth, MI, or Saltville, VA.
Application information: Application form required.
Initial approach: Letter requesting application form
Deadline(s): None
Trustee: Mercantile Bank.
EIN: 376353965

800
P. & H. Taylor Scholarship Trust
c/o Century Bank and Trust
100 W. Chicago St.
Coldwater, MI 49036-1807
County: Branch
Contact: Alicia Cole, Trust Off.

Established in 2004 in MI.
Donors: Helen Taylor Irrevocable Trust; Percy Taylor Unitrust.
Grantmaker type: Independent foundation.
Financial data (yr. ended 12/31/09): Assets, $2,391,949 (M); expenditures, $109,541; total giving, $93,500; qualifying distributions, $93,500; giving activities include $93,500 for grants.
Purpose and activities: Scholarship awards to graduates of Branch County schools in MI.
Fields of interest: Higher education; Children/youth.
Type of support: Scholarships—to individuals.

Limitations: Applications accepted. Giving limited to residents of Branch County, MI.
Application information: Application form required.
Initial approach: Letter
Deadline(s): 1st Fri. in Mar.
Trustee: Century Bank and Trust.
EIN: 326030259

801
Team Michigan, Inc.
440 Lake Park Dr.
Birmingham, MI 48009-4604
County: Oakland

Established in 2001 in MI.
Grantmaker type: Independent foundation.
Financial data (yr. ended 12/31/09): Assets, $2,076 (M); expenditures, $20; total giving, $0; qualifying distributions, $0.
Officer and Director:* Frederick A. Lavery, Jr.,* Pres.
EIN: 383303712

802
Temple-Krick YFU Scholarship Fund, Inc.
2345 Delaware Dr.
Ann Arbor, MI 48103-6170 (734) 663-6472
County: Washtenaw
Contact: Barbara T. Krick, Pres.

Established in 1988 in MI.
Donor: Barbara T. Krick.
Grantmaker type: Independent foundation.
Financial data (yr. ended 03/31/10): Assets, $5,148 (M); gifts received, $4,000; expenditures, $9,918; total giving, $9,895; qualifying distributions, $9,895; giving activities include $9,895 for grants to individuals.
Purpose and activities: Scholarship awards to individuals to participate in the Youth for Understanding Cultural Exchange program.
Fields of interest: International exchange, students.
Type of support: Scholarships—to individuals.
Limitations: Applications accepted. Giving limited to residents of MI.
Application information: Application form not required.
Deadline(s): None
Officer and Directors:* Barbara T. Krick,* Pres.; Mary Alvery; Ken Clover; Deborah T. Curtis; James H. Krick; Rebecca Krick.
EIN: 382808315

803
The Tepper Family Foundation
111 Great Neck Rd., Ste. 408
Great Neck, NY 11021-5404 (516) 773-3800
County: Nassau
Contact: Marvin B. Tepper, Pres.

Established in 2000 in NY.
Donors: Marvin B. Tepper; Elise C. Tepper.
Grantmaker type: Independent foundation.
Financial data (yr. ended 12/31/09): Assets, $55,897 (M); gifts received, $1,000; expenditures, $1,050; total giving, $1,000; qualifying distributions, $1,000; giving include $1,000 for grants.
Fields of interest: Arts; Higher education; Hospitals (general); Jewish agencies & synagogues.

Limitations: Giving primarily in NY, with emphasis on New York and Long Island, and in MI. No grants to individuals.
Application information:
Initial approach: Letter
Deadline(s): None
Officers: Marvin B. Tepper, Pres.; Elise C. Tepper, V.P. and Secy.-Treas.; Edward M. Tepper, V.P.; Jacqueline G. Tepper, V.P.
EIN: 113563659
Selected grants: The following grants were reported in 2008.
$10,000 to Cleveland Clinic, Cleveland, OH.
$7,500 to Metropolitan Opera, New York, NY.

804
The Howard and Margery Ternes Foundation, Ltd.
c/o Plante Moran Trust
27400 Northwestern Hwy.
Southfield, MI 48037-4724 (248) 223-3507
County: Oakland

Established in 2007 in MI.
Donors: Howard Ternes; Margery Ternes.
Grantmaker type: Independent foundation.
Financial data (yr. ended 12/31/09): Assets, $833,768 (M); expenditures, $46,421; total giving, $36,000; qualifying distributions, $36,000; giving activities include $36,000 for grants.
Application information:
Initial approach: Letter or telephone
Deadline(s): None
Officers and Directors:* Howard Ternes,* Pres. and Secy.; Margery Ternes,* V.P.; Charles Ross,* Treas.
EIN: 562629502

805
Bhagwani Thawani Foundation
6145 Brookstone Ln.
Grand Blanc, MI 48439-9433
County: Genesee
Contact: Hemant Thawani, Pres.

Established in 2002 in MI.
Donor: Hermant Thawani.
Grantmaker type: Independent foundation.
Financial data (yr. ended 12/31/09): Assets, $28,302 (M); expenditures, $4,581; total giving, $3,750; qualifying distributions, $3,750; giving activities include $3,750 for grants.
Fields of interest: Human services, mind/body enrichment; Hinduism.
Limitations: Giving primarily in Flint, MI and in India.
Application information:
Initial approach: Letter
Deadline(s): None
Officer: Hermant Thawani, Pres. and Secy.-Treas.
EIN: 320057659

806
Jean and Stewart Thiemkey Scholarship Foundation
c/o Jean Thiemkey
44 Hunting Lodge Dr.
Black Mountain, NC 28711-9799
County: Buncombe

Established in 1999 in MI.
Donors: William Thiemkey; Roberta Thiemkey.

Grantmaker type: Independent foundation.
Financial data (yr. ended 12/31/09): Assets, $65,848 (M); gifts received, $7,393; expenditures, $2,556; total giving, $2,100; qualifying distributions, $2,100; giving activities include $2,100 for grants to individuals.
Purpose and activities: Scholarship awards to graduates of Lapeer West High School, with an interest in pursuing teaching as a career. Preference given to those attending Eastern Michigan University, the University of Michigan, or Alma College, Michigan.
Fields of interest: Higher education.
Type of support: Scholarships—to individuals.
Limitations: Applications accepted. Giving limited to residents of Lapeer, MI.
Application information: Application form not required.
  Initial approach: Letter
  Deadline(s): None
Officers: Richard Thiemkey, Pres.; William Thiemkey, Secy.-Treas.
EIN: 383461005

807
W. B. & Candace Thoman Foundation
222 N. Washington Sq., Ste. 400
Lansing, MI 48933-1800
County: Ingham
Contact: Benjamin O. Schwendener, Jr., Pres.

Established in 1968 in MI.
Donors: W.B. Thoman†; Candace Thoman†.
Grantmaker type: Independent foundation.
Financial data (yr. ended 12/31/09): Assets, $2,720,215 (M); expenditures, $314,761; total giving, $283,425; qualifying distributions, $283,425; giving activities include $283,425 for 8 grants (high: $110,000; low: $8,000).
Purpose and activities: Giving primarily for education, orphans and the economically disadvantaged.
Fields of interest: Performing arts, education; Education, special; Higher education; Adult education—literacy, basic skills & GED; Education, reading; Education; Recreation, camps; Human services; Economically disadvantaged.
Type of support: General/operating support; Program development.
Limitations: Giving primarily in Ingham County, MI, with some emphasis on the Lansing area. No support for political organizations, churches, or religious organizations or programs. No grants to individuals.
Publications: Application guidelines; Program policy statement.
Application information:
  Initial approach: Letter requesting guidelines
  Copies of proposal: 6
  Deadline(s): 2 weeks prior to board meetings
  Board meeting date(s): Quarterly
Officers and Trustees:* Benjamin O. Schwendener, Jr.,* Pres. and Secy.; Louis E. Legg,* V.P.; Dorothy Silk,* Treas.; Frederick M. Baker; Helen Pratt Mickens; Dr. Harvey Sparks.
Number of staff: 1 part-time support.
EIN: 237029842
Selected grants: The following grants were reported in 2006.
$55,000 to Literacy Volunteers of America/Capitol Area Literacy Coalition, Lansing, MI.
$30,000 to Boarshead Theater, Lansing, MI.

$28,000 to Michigan State University, Michigan State University Gifted And Talented Program Division of Honors College, East Lansing, MI.
$22,000 to Ingham Intermediate School District, Mason, MI.
$4,000 to Happendance School, Okemos, MI.

808
The Thomas Foundation
201 W. Big Beaver Rd., Ste. 600
Troy, MI 48084-4161
County: Oakland

Established in 1984 in MI.
Donor: Harriet Kay Thomas Revocable Trust.
Grantmaker type: Independent foundation.
Financial data (yr. ended 03/31/10): Assets, $2,899,345 (M); expenditures, $116,407; total giving, $70,000; qualifying distributions, $70,000; giving activities include $70,000 for grants.
Purpose and activities: Giving primarily for medical research, particularly a juvenile diabetes foundation, and a medical school; funding also for children, youth, and social services.
Fields of interest: Higher education; Medical school/education; Health organizations; Medical research, institute; Diabetes research; Boys & girls clubs; Human services; Children/youth, services.
Limitations: Applications accepted. Giving primarily in southeast MI.
Application information:
  Initial approach: Letter
  Deadline(s): None
  Final notification: Within 60 days
Directors: Jay Howard Brody; Chester L. Uncapher.
EIN: 382510591
Selected grants: The following grants were reported in 2009.
$22,217 to Wayne State University, School of Medicine, Detroit, MI.
$5,000 to Detroit Institute for Children, Detroit, MI.
$3,000 to United Negro College Fund, Detroit, MI.
$2,500 to Gleaners Community Food Bank, Detroit, MI.
$2,500 to Yad Ezra, Berkley, MI.
$1,000 to Boys and Girls Club of South Oakland County, Royal Oak, MI.
$1,000 to Boys Hope Girls Hope, Detroit, MI.
$1,000 to Saint Peters Home for Boys, Detroit, MI.
$1,000 to Saint Vincent and Sarah Fisher Center, Farmington Hills, MI.

809
Russ Thomas Scholarship Fund
3707 W. Maple St., Ste. 13
Bloomfield Hills, MI 48301-3212
(313) 216-4050
County: Oakland
Contact: Dorothy S. Thomas, Tr.

Established in 1991 in MI.
Donors: Dorothy S. Thomas; John R. Thomas; James E. Thomas.
Grantmaker type: Independent foundation.
Financial data (yr. ended 11/30/10): Assets, $896,524 (M); gifts received, $34,665; expenditures, $80,909; total giving, $72,750; qualifying distributions, $72,750; giving activities include $72,750 for 26 grants to individuals (high: $5,500; low: $1,000).

Purpose and activities: Scholarship awards to graduates of Bloomfield, Michigan, high schools.
Fields of interest: Higher education.
Type of support: Scholarships—to individuals.
Limitations: Giving limited to the greater Detroit, MI, area.
Application information: Application form required.
  Initial approach: Letter
  Deadline(s): None
Trustees: Dorothy S. Thomas; James E. Thomas; John Thomas, Jr.
EIN: 382984958

810
Edward N. & Della L. Thome Memorial Foundation
c/o Bank of America, N.A.
100 Federal St., MA5-100-16-01
Boston, MA 02110-1802
County: Suffolk
Contact: George Thorn, V.P.
URL: http://www.bankofamerica.com/grantmaking

Established in 2003 in MD.
Donor: Robert P. Thome.
Grantmaker type: Independent foundation.
Financial data (yr. ended 12/31/08): Assets, $78,159,130 (M); gifts received, $99,245,999; expenditures, $448,131; total giving, $81,400; qualifying distributions, $294,896; giving activities include $81,400 for grants.
Purpose and activities: The foundation supports dignified treatment of older adults as well as medical research on diseases affecting older adults.
Fields of interest: Nursing care; Geriatrics; Human services; Aging.
Type of support: General/operating support.
Limitations: Giving on a national basis, with emphasis on MD and MI. No grants to individuals.
Application information:
  Initial approach: Letterhead
  Deadline(s): None
Trustee: Bank of America, N.A.
EIN: 597241019
Selected grants: The following grants were reported in 2009.
$250,000 to California Institute of Technology, Pasadena, CA. For research on novel diagnostics for Age-Related Macular Degeneration (AMD).
$250,000 to Harvard University, Cambridge, MA. For research on the promotion of photoreceptor survival using HDACs and gluconeogenic genes.
$250,000 to Johns Hopkins University, Baltimore, MD. For Cigarette smoking and Early Age-Related Macular Degeneration, research on how cigarette smoking induces oxidative damage and enhanced innate immune response during early Age-related Macular Degeneration.
$250,000 to Johns Hopkins University, Baltimore, MD. For Age-Related Macular Degeneration (AMD) Research on sustained delivery of antiangiogenic peptides for neovascular AMD.
$250,000 to Massachusetts Eye and Ear Infirmary, Boston, MA. For Identifying underlying mechanisms of Age-Related Macular Degeneration (AMD), research on identifying underlying mechanisms of AMD for the development of appropriate preventive and therapeutic interventions.
$200,000 to Easter Seals Greater Washington-Baltimore Region, Silver Spring, MD. For general operating funds to support the Center for

Excellence in Adult Day Services at Easter Seals' Inter-Generational Center in Silver Spring, MD. $150,000 to Area Agency on Aging, Region 3B, Battle Creek, MI. For general operating support to expand and increase the agency's capacity to serve older adults through home and community-based services that promote health, independence and choice.
$125,000 to Area Agency on Aging 1-B, Southfield, MI. For safe and independent living support for older adults program to continue providing essential services which support the dignity and independence of older adults while building the infrastructure necessary to continue serving older adults.
$100,000 to Gerontology Network Resources, Grand Rapids, MI. For general operating funds to support expansion of existing operations and provide additional adult day service.
$75,000 to Jewish Family Services of Washtenaw County, Ann Arbor, MI. For Enhancing the Lives of Low-Income Older Adults to provide comprehensive, client-centered services for low income older adults in Washtenaw in three main areas: case management, coordination of geriatric volunteer services, transportation.

811
Mary Thompson Foundation
c/o Comerica Bank
P.O. Box 75000, MC 3302
Detroit, MI 48275-0001
County: Wayne
Application address: c/o Mrs. Douglas F. Roby, Jr.,
P.O. Box 568, St. Clair Shores, MI 48080-0568,
tel.: (313) 886-2471

Established in 1979.
Donor: Mary Thompson†.
Grantmaker type: Independent foundation.
Financial data (yr. ended 12/31/09): Assets, $2,839,701 (M); expenditures, $141,416; total giving, $113,900; qualifying distributions, $113,900; giving activities include $113,900 for grants.
Purpose and activities: Giving primarily to assist the frail and elderly.
Fields of interest: Nursing home/convalescent facility; Geriatrics; Aging, centers/services; Aging.
Type of support: General/operating support; Continuing support; Equipment; Program development; Conferences/seminars.
Limitations: Applications accepted. Giving limited to MI, with emphasis on Oakland and Wayne counties.
Publications: Application guidelines.
Application information: Application form required.
Initial approach: Letter
Copies of proposal: 1
Deadline(s): None
Board meeting date(s): Spring and fall
Final notification: 1 month from receipt
Officers: Mrs. Douglas F. Roby, Jr., Chair.; Mrs. William D. Dahling, Pres.; Mrs. E. L. Book,* V.P.; Mrs. John Snyder,* Secy.; Mrs. Lynn Cameron, Treas.
EIN: 381359097
Selected grants: The following grants were reported in 2008.
$35,000 to Services for Older Citizens, Grosse Pointe, MI.
$25,000 to Wayne State University, Institute of Gerontology, Detroit, MI.
$20,000 to Adult Well-Being Services, Detroit, MI.

$17,500 to Accounting Aid Society, Detroit, MI.
$12,000 to Michigan Opera Theater, Detroit, MI.
$12,000 to Saint Joseph Mercy Health System, Ann Arbor, MI.
$10,000 to Detroit Symphony Orchestra, Detroit, MI.
$10,000 to Oakland Livingston Human Service Agency, Pontiac, MI.
$10,000 to Project Compassion Ministries, Detroit, MI.
$5,000 to Saint Joseph Mercy Oakland, Pontiac, MI.

812
Thorrez Foundation
126 Hanover St.
P.O. Box 307
Concord, MI 49237-0307 (517) 750-3160
County: Jackson
Contact: Camiel E. Thorrez, Pres.

Donors: Camiel E. Thorrez; C. Thorrez Industries, Inc.
Grantmaker type: Independent foundation.
Financial data (yr. ended 06/30/09): Assets, $125,564 (M); expenditures, $125; total giving, $0; qualifying distributions, $0.
Fields of interest: Community/economic development.
Limitations: Giving primarily in MI.
Application information: Application form not required.
Deadline(s): None
Officers: Camiel E. Thorrez, Pres.; Theresa J. Stevens, V.P.; Phyllis J. Thorrez, Secy.-Treas.
Trustees: Jeoffrey A. Thorrez; Mary C. Thorrez-Wheeler.
EIN: 237231150

813
Three Sisters Foundation
(formerly Karen L. Gilhooly & Rowan Gilhooly Sanford Educational Foundation)
100 Park St.
Traverse City, MI 49684-5700 (231) 946-2843
County: Grand Traverse
Contact: Kurt Sanford, Pres.
Application address: 9295 Majestic Ridge, Traverse City, MI 49684-7427

Established in 2004 in MI.
Donors: David Handleman; Charlene Handleman; Kurt Sanford.
Grantmaker type: Independent foundation.
Financial data (yr. ended 12/31/09): Assets, $793 (M); gifts received, $39,000; expenditures, $68,916; total giving, $68,847; qualifying distributions, $68,847; giving activities include $68,847 for 10 grants.
Fields of interest: Education; Human services.
Limitations: Applications accepted. Giving primarily in MI.
Application information: Application form not required.
Initial approach: Letter
Deadline(s): None
Officers: Kurt Sanford, Pres.; Todd Sanford, Treas.
EIN: 201848629

814
The Tiscornia Foundation
1010 Main St., Ste. A
St. Joseph, MI 49085-1462 (269) 983-4711
County: Berrien
Contact: James W. Tiscornia, Pres.

Incorporated in 1942 in MI.
Donors: James W. Tiscornia†; Waldo V. Tiscornia†; Auto Specialties Manufacturing Co.; Lambert Brake Corp.
Grantmaker type: Independent foundation.
Financial data (yr. ended 12/31/09): Assets, $2,901,905 (M); expenditures, $205,656; total giving, $114,300; qualifying distributions, $114,300; giving activities include $114,300 for grants.
Fields of interest: Arts; Higher education; Health care; Health organizations; Human services; Youth, services; Physically disabled.
Type of support: Continuing support; Capital campaigns; Building/renovation; Equipment; Emergency funds; Seed money; Scholarship funds; Scholarships—to individuals.
Publications: Annual report (including application guidelines).
Application information: Scholarships only for northern Berrien County high school seniors at the following schools: St. Joseph, Benton Harbor, Coloma, Watervliet, Lake Shore, Lake Michigan Catholic, and Lake Michigan Lutheran. Application form not required.
Initial approach: Letter or proposal
Copies of proposal: 1
Deadline(s): Apr. 1 for scholarships; Jan. 31 for grants
Board meeting date(s): Jan.
Officers and Trustees:* James W. Tiscornia,* Pres.; Edward C. Tiscornia,* V.P. and Treas.; James Winston Tiscornia,* Secy.; Christopher Tiscornia; Jeanne Tiscornia; Joanne Tiscornia.
Number of staff: 1 part-time professional; 1 part-time support.
EIN: 381777343
Selected grants: The following grants were reported in 2008.
$30,000 to Ecumenical Faith in Action, Abingdon, VA.
$11,000 to Michigan State University, East Lansing, MI.
$7,500 to Michigan Colleges Foundation, Southfield, MI.
$1,000 to Denison University, Granville, OH.
$1,000 to Lake Michigan College, Benton Harbor, MI.

815
Torgow Family Foundation
P.O. Box 310737
Detroit, MI 48231-0737
County: Wayne

Established in 2000 in MI.
Donors: Gary Torgow; Malka Torgow.
Grantmaker type: Independent foundation.
Financial data (yr. ended 12/31/09): Assets, $52,136 (M); gifts received, $80,000; expenditures, $238,266; total giving, $229,517; qualifying distributions, $229,517; giving activities include $229,517 for 100 grants (high: $23,800; low: $25).
Purpose and activities: Giving primarily for Yeshivas.

Fields of interest: Jewish federated giving programs; Jewish agencies & synagogues.
Type of support: General/operating support.
Limitations: Applications accepted. Giving primarily in NY and MI. No grants to individuals.
Application information:
Initial approach: Letter
Deadline(s): None
Officers and Trustees:* Gary Torgow,* Pres.; Malka Torgow, Secy.; Eliezer Torgow; Yonah Torgow.
EIN: 383560590
Selected grants: The following grants were reported in 2008.
$5,000 to V Hechzakta Bo, Detroit, MI.
$3,600 to Yad Yisroel, Brooklyn, NY.
$1,800 to Talmudical Yeshiva of Philadelphia, Philadelphia, PA.
$1,000 to Bonei Olam, Brooklyn, NY.
$1,000 to Yad Lachim, New York, NY.

816
The Harry A. and Margaret D. Towsley Foundation
240 W. Main St., Ste. 2400
P.O. Box 349
Midland, MI   48640-5191   (989) 837-1100
County: Midland
Contact: Lynn T. White, Pres.
FAX: (989) 837-3240;
E-mail: chatland@towsleyfoundation.org

Incorporated in 1959 in MI.
Donor: Margaret D. Towsley‡.
Grantmaker type: Independent foundation.
Financial data (yr. ended 12/31/09): Assets, $41,879,640 (M); expenditures, $2,503,064; total giving, $2,410,100; qualifying distributions, $2,491,953; giving activities include $2,410,100 for 27 grants (high: $304,000; low: $4,700).
Purpose and activities: Support for medical and preschool education, social services, and continuing education and research in the health sciences.
Fields of interest: Arts; Education, early childhood education; Higher education; Medical school/education; Education; Medical research, institute; Human services.
Type of support: General/operating support; Continuing support; Annual campaigns; Capital campaigns; Building/renovation; Endowments; Program development; Professorships; Seed money; Research; Employee matching gifts; Matching/challenge support.
Limitations: Applications accepted. Giving primarily in MI. No grants to individuals, or for travel, scholarships, fellowships, conferences, books, publications, films, tapes, audio-visual, or other communication media; no loans.
Publications: Annual report (including application guidelines).
Application information: Environmental Impact Statement is required for all capital projects. Application form not required.
Initial approach: Letter and proposal
Copies of proposal: 2
Deadline(s): Mar. 31
Board meeting date(s): Apr., July, Sept., and Dec.
Final notification: 60 to 90 days
Officers and Trustees:* Margaret Ann Riecker,* Chair.; Lynn T. White,* Pres.; Judith D. Rumelhart,* V.P.; Wendell Dunbar,* Treas.; David Inglish;

Douglas Inglish; Jennifer R. Poteat-Flores; Steven Towsley Riecker; Margaret E. Thompson, M.D.
Number of staff: 1 part-time support.
EIN: 386091798
Selected grants: The following grants were reported in 2008.
$650,000 to Friends of the Claude Moore Colonial Farm at Turkey Run, McLean, VA.
$575,000 to Washington Theater Awards Society, Washington, DC.
$300,000 to Young Adults Health Center, Corner Health Center, Ypsilanti, MI.
$125,000 to Greenhills School, Ann Arbor, MI.
$100,000 to Munson Healthcare Regional Foundation, Traverse City, MI.
$100,000 to West Midland Family Center, Shepherd, MI.
$100,000 to YMCA of Grand Traverse Bay, Traverse City, MI.
$25,000 to Therapeutic Riding, Ann Arbor, MI.

817
Tremble Foundation, Inc.
(also known as St. Deny's Foundation, Inc.)
c/o Comerica Bank
99 Monroe Ave. N.W., Ste. 550
Grand Rapids, MI   49503-6211   (616) 752-4705
County: Kent
Contact: Kelly Deridder, Trust. Off., Comerica Bank
URL: http://www.stdenys.org/

Established in 1988 in MI.
Donor: Helen R. Tremble‡.
Grantmaker type: Independent foundation.
Financial data (yr. ended 12/31/09): Assets, $5,316,212 (M); expenditures, $474,564; total giving, $362,646; qualifying distributions, $362,646; giving activities include $362,646 for 61 grants (high: $40,000; low: $500).
Purpose and activities: Giving primarily for higher education, arts and art education programs, Christian agencies and health and hospice programs.
Fields of interest: Arts; Secondary school/education; Higher education; Education; Environment; Animals/wildlife; Hospitals (general); Human services; Christian agencies & churches.
Type of support: General/operating support; Program development; Scholarship funds.
Limitations: Applications accepted. Giving primarily in MI, with emphasis on the Dowagiac area.
Application information: Application form not required.
Initial approach: Proposal
Copies of proposal: 1
Deadline(s): None
Board meeting date(s): Spring and fall
Final notification: 6 months
Officers: Thomas Dalton, Pres.; Lynn Dalton, V.P.; Cara Dalton, Secy.
Directors: Dillon Dalton; Dustin Dalton; Jim McWilliams.
Trustee: Comerica Bank.
EIN: 382869889
Selected grants: The following grants were reported in 2009.
$15,000 to Southwestern Michigan College, Dowagiac, MI.
$15,000 to Southwestern Michigan College, Dowagiac, MI.
$6,000 to Indiana University, Bloomington, IN.
$5,000 to Grand Valley State University, Allendale, MI.

$2,500 to Southwestern Michigan College, Dowagiac, MI.
$2,500 to Southwestern Michigan College, Dowagiac, MI.
$1,000 to Southwestern Michigan College, Dowagiac, MI.

818
Otto Trinklein Educational Trust
c/o Citizens Bank Wealth Mgmt., N.A.
328 S. Saginaw St., M/C 002072
Flint, MI   48502-1923   (989) 776-7368
County: Genesee
Contact: Donald J. Zoeller
Application address: Attn: Donald J. Zoeller, c/o Frankenmuth High School, 525 E. Genesee Street, Frankenmuth, MI 48734, tel: (989) 652-5955
Application address: c/o Frankenmuth High School, Attn.: Donald J. Zoeller, 525 E. Genesee St., Frankenmuth, MI 48734-1139, tel.: (989) 652-9955

Established in MI.
Grantmaker type: Independent foundation.
Financial data (yr. ended 12/31/09): Assets, $141,702 (M); expenditures, $10,329; total giving, $5,200; qualifying distributions, $8,508; giving activities include $5,200 for 4 grants to individuals (high: $1,300; low: $1,300).
Purpose and activities: Scholarship awards to graduates of Frankenmuth, Michigan, public schools.
Fields of interest: Higher education.
Type of support: Scholarships—to individuals.
Limitations: Applications accepted. Giving limited to residents of Frankenmuth, MI.
Application information: Available only to graduates of Frankenmuth Public Schools. Application form required.
Deadline(s): May 1
Trustee: Citizens Bank.
EIN: 386040607

819
Trixie Puff Foundation
c/o Comerica Bank
P.O. Box 75000, MC 3302
Detroit, MI   48275-0001   (313) 222-6297
County: Wayne
Contact: Beverly Suchenek

Established in 2000 in PA.
Donor: Mary Lou Campana.
Grantmaker type: Independent foundation.
Financial data (yr. ended 03/31/10): Assets, $2,464,589 (M); gifts received, $1,903,321; expenditures, $258,297; total giving, $234,000; qualifying distributions, $234,900; giving activities include $234,000 for 11 grants (high: $200,000; low: $3,000).
Purpose and activities: Giving primarily for higher education and animal welfare.
Fields of interest: Higher education, university; Animal welfare; Christian agencies & churches.
Limitations: Applications accepted. Giving primarily in PA, with emphasis on Greensburg; giving also in Washington, DC. No grants to individuals.
Application information: Application form not required.
Deadline(s): None

Trustee: Comerica Bank.
EIN: 226866487
Selected grants: The following grants were reported in 2009.
$4,000 to American Anti-Vivisection Society, Jenkintown, PA.
$4,000 to Animal Friends, Pittsburgh, PA.
$4,000 to Doris Day Animal League, Washington, DC.
$4,000 to Greenpeace, Washington, DC.
$4,000 to People for the Ethical Treatment of Animals, Norfolk, VA.

820
Blanche Barr Trone Scholarship Trust
20152 East Ave. N.
Battle Creek, MI 49017-9707 (269) 964-7348
County: Calhoun
Contact: Stig Renstrom, Tr.

Established in MI.
Grantmaker type: Independent foundation.
Financial data (yr. ended 12/31/09): Assets, $426,330 (M); expenditures, $20,480; total giving, $14,000; qualifying distributions, $14,000; giving activities include $14,000 for grants to individuals.
Purpose and activities: Scholarship awards to residents of the Battle Creek, Michigan, area.
Fields of interest: Higher education.
Type of support: Scholarships—to individuals.
Limitations: Giving limited to residents of Battle Creek, MI, area.
Application information: Application form required.
Deadline(s): June
Trustee: Stig Renstrom.
EIN: 386500164

821
Trudell Scholarship Trust
c/o First National Bank & Trust Co.
233 S. Stephenson Ave.
Iron Mountain, MI 49801-2921 (906) 779-2259
County: Dickinson

Established in 2004 in MI.
Grantmaker type: Independent foundation.
Financial data (yr. ended 12/31/09): Assets, $119,717 (M); gifts received, $695; expenditures, $6,355; total giving, $5,200; qualifying distributions, $5,200; giving activities include $5,200 for 7 grants to individuals (high: $1,094; low: $400).
Purpose and activities: Scholarship awards to students at Bay de Noc Community College, Escanaba, Michigan who are residents of Dickinson, Iron or Menominee counties, Michigan, or Florence, Marinette or Forest counties, Wisconsin.
Fields of interest: Higher education.
Type of support: Scholarships—to individuals.
Limitations: Applications accepted. Giving limited to U.S. citizens with a minimum one-year residency in Dickinson, Iron or Menominee counties, MI, or Florence, Marinette or Forest counties, WI.
Application information: Application form required.
Initial approach: Letter or telephone
Deadline(s): Varies
Trustee: First National Bank & Trust Co.
EIN: 726230453

822
Trumley Family Foundation
c/o Lowe Law Firm, PC
2375 Woodlake Dr., Ste. 380
Okemos, MI 48864-6021 (517) 908-0909
County: Ingham
Contact: Richard C. Lowe, Asst. Secy.

Donor: ICAT Investments, LLC.
Grantmaker type: Independent foundation.
Financial data (yr. ended 12/31/09): Assets, $820,898 (M); expenditures, $125,735; total giving, $124,450; qualifying distributions, $125,450; giving activities include $124,450 for 10 grants (high: $65,000; low: $100).
Fields of interest: Health care, clinics/centers; Cemeteries/burial services, burial association.
Limitations: Giving primarily in MI.
Application information: Application form not required.
Deadline(s): None
Officers: Richard L. Trumley, Pres.; Stephen R. Trumley, Secy.; Beverly R. Trumley, Treas.
EIN: 203400591
Selected grants: The following grants were reported in 2008.
$1,000 to American Diabetes Association, Alexandria, VA.
$1,000 to SIREN/Eaton Shelter, Charlotte, MI.

823
R. Gerstell Trust f/b/o Datrmouth Et al.
c/o BNY Mellon, N.A.
P.O. Box 185
Pittsburgh, PA 15230-0815
County: Allegheny

Established in 2007 in PA.
Donor: Richard Gerstell Trust.
Grantmaker type: Independent foundation.
Financial data (yr. ended 12/31/09): Assets, $1,612,530 (M); expenditures, $41,549; total giving, $28,331; qualifying distributions, $28,331; giving activities include $28,331 for grants.
Fields of interest: Higher education, university.
Type of support: General/operating support.
Limitations: Giving primarily in Hanover, NH; some giving also in Ann Arbor, MI.
Trustee: BNY Mellon, N.A.
EIN: 206931792

824
Tuesdays with Mitch Charitable Foundation
c/o Morgensten & Assoc.
767 E. Route 70, Ste. B100
Marlton, NJ 08053-2345
County: Burlington
Contact: Mitchell Albom, Tr.

Established in 1999 in PA.
Donor: Mitchel Albom.
Grantmaker type: Independent foundation.
Financial data (yr. ended 12/31/09): Assets, $211 (M); gifts received, $3,410; expenditures, $4,271; total giving, $4,240; qualifying distributions, $4,240; giving activities include $4,240 for grants.
Fields of interest: Human services.
Limitations: Giving primarily in MI.
Application information:

Initial approach: Letter
Deadline(s): None
Trustee: Mitchell Albom.
EIN: 226827705

825
The Doris Tuinstra Foundation
3737 Wentworth Dr. S.W.
Wyoming, MI 49509-3142
County: Kent
Contact: Kenneth Vander Molen, Dir.

Established in 2003.
Grantmaker type: Independent foundation.
Financial data (yr. ended 12/31/09): Assets, $10,024 (M); gifts received, $2,195; expenditures, $942; total giving, $450; qualifying distributions, $450; giving activities include $450 for 1 grant.
Fields of interest: Christian agencies & churches.
Type of support: General/operating support.
Limitations: Applications accepted. Giving primarily in MI. No grants to individuals.
Application information:
Initial approach: Letter
Deadline(s): None
Officers: Kenneth Vander Molen, Pres.; Jamison Worst, Secy.; Jacob Tuinstra, Treas.
EIN: 043670914

826
Tuktawa Foundation
4812 Willow Ln.
Orchard Lake, MI 48324-3073
County: Oakland
Contact: Charles J. Andrews, Pres.

Established in 1998 in MI.
Donor: Delphine J. Andrews.
Grantmaker type: Independent foundation.
Financial data (yr. ended 12/31/09): Assets, $7,515,155 (M); expenditures, $403,201; total giving, $349,240; qualifying distributions, $349,240; giving activities include $349,240 for 45 grants (high: $50,000; low: $970).
Fields of interest: Historic preservation/historical societies; Higher education; Animals/wildlife; Hospitals (general); Youth development; Human services.
Type of support: General/operating support.
Limitations: Giving in the U.S., primarily in MI.
Application information: Application form not required.
Deadline(s): None
Officers: Charles J. Andrews, Pres.; Adelaide Ford, Secy.-Treas.
Directors: Christopher C. Andrews; Tracey Andrews; Carolyn Ford Kowles; Jennifer Andrews Moilanen; Joanna Ford Virgne.
EIN: 383393453
Selected grants: The following grants were reported in 2008.
$10,000 to Boy Scouts of America, Detroit, MI.

827
Tummala Charitable Foundation
1240 Woodkrest Dr.
Flint, MI 48532-2249 (810) 733-8673
County: Genesee
Contact: Madhusudana Rao Tummala, Pres.

Established in 2007 in MI.
Donor: Madhusudana Rao Tummala.
Grantmaker type: Independent foundation.
Financial data (yr. ended 12/31/09): Assets, $718,458 (M); gifts received, $200,000; expenditures, $37,801; total giving, $35,363; qualifying distributions, $36,500; giving activities include $35,363 for 19 grants (high: $12,000; low: $30).
Fields of interest: Higher education; Food services; Jewish agencies & synagogues.
Limitations: Applications accepted. Giving primarily in Flint, MI. No grants to individuals.
Application information:
> *Initial approach:* Letter
> *Deadline(s):* None
Officers: Madhusudana Rao Tummala, Pres. and Treas.; Sabita Tummala, Secy.
Directors: Pradyumna E. Tummala; Pratyusha Tummala-Narra.
EIN: 208021751

828
Alexander Alan Turfe Family Foundation
45697 Southwyck Dr.
Canton, MI 48188-6231   (360) 566-7649
County: Wayne
Contact: Alexander Alan Turfe, Pres.

Established in 2007 in MI.
Donor: Alexander Alan Turfe.
Grantmaker type: Independent foundation.
Financial data (yr. ended 12/31/09): Assets, $172,356 (M); expenditures, $10,022; total giving, $9,100; qualifying distributions, $9,100; giving activities include $9,100 for grants.
Application information:
> *Initial approach:* Proposal
> *Deadline(s):* None
Officers and Trustees:* Alexander Alan Turfe,* Pres.; Lenda Turfe,* Secy.-Treas.
EIN: 261543968

829
Alice E. Turner Memorial Trust
5090 State St., Bldg. A , Ste. 1
Saginaw, MI 48603-7705
County: Saginaw
Contact: B.J. Humphreys, Pres.

Established in 1996 in MI.
Donor: Alice E. Turner†.
Grantmaker type: Independent foundation.
Financial data (yr. ended 12/31/09): Assets, $1,039,371 (M); expenditures, $62,930; total giving, $54,998; qualifying distributions, $54,998; giving activities include $54,998 for 22 grants (high: $9,000; low: $200).
Purpose and activities: Giving for Lutheran organizations, health and medical services, education, youth groups, human services, and community improvement.
Fields of interest: Education; Health care; Youth development; Human services; Community/ economic development; Protestant agencies & churches.
Limitations: Applications accepted. Giving primarily in Saginaw, MI.
Application information:
> *Initial approach:* Letter
> *Deadline(s):* None

Officer: B.J. Humphreys, Pres.
Trustees: John Humphreys; Michael Tribble.
EIN: 386501366

830
The Turtle Lake Wildlife Foundation
P.O. Box 99027
Troy, MI 48099-9027
County: Oakland

Established in 2003 in MI.
Grantmaker type: Independent foundation.
Financial data (yr. ended 12/31/09): Assets, $245,801 (M); gifts received, $190,000; expenditures, $340,736; total giving, $0; qualifying distributions, $0.
Limitations: Giving primarily in Turtle Lake, MI.
Officers: Arvin F. Mueller, Pres.; Arthur Ronan, Secy.; J. Michael Campbell, Treas.
EIN: 743070493

831
University of Michigan Scholarship Fund of Bay City
(also known as U of M Scholarship Fund of Bay City)
900 Center Ave.
Bay City, MI 48708-6118   (989) 892-0591
County: Bay
Contact: D. Keith Birchler, Secy.

Grantmaker type: Independent foundation.
Financial data (yr. ended 12/31/09): Assets, $8,438 (M); gifts received, $2,045; expenditures, $1,500; total giving, $1,500; qualifying distributions, $1,500; giving activities include $1,500 for grants to individuals.
Purpose and activities: Scholarship awards limited to residents of Bay County, Michigan, enrolling at the University of Michigan, Ann Arbor campus.
Fields of interest: Higher education.
Type of support: Scholarships—to individuals.
Limitations: Giving limited to residents of Bay City, MI.
Application information: Application form required.
> *Deadline(s):* Apr. 15
Officers: Marge Marchlewicz, Pres.; Vaughn Begick, V.P.; D. Keith Birchler, Secy.; David Huiskens, Treas.
EIN: 386118064

832
Harold and Grace Upjohn Foundation
136 E. Michigan Ave., Ste. 9B
Kalamazoo, MI 49007-3947   (269) 344-2818
County: Kalamazoo
Contact: Floyd L. Parks, Secy.-Treas.

Incorporated in 1958 in MI.
Donors: Grace G. Upjohn†; Edwin Meader†; Mary Meader.
Grantmaker type: Independent foundation.
Financial data (yr. ended 10/31/09): Assets, $10,283,382 (M); gifts received, $500,000; expenditures, $555,579; total giving, $470,000; qualifying distributions, $485,186; giving activities include $470,000 for 49 grants (high: $30,000; low: $1,000).
Purpose and activities: Grants primarily to promote scientific research for the alleviation of human suffering; to care for the sick, aged, and helpless whose private resources are inadequate; to conduct

research for and otherwise assist in the improvement of living, moral and working conditions; to promote the spread of education and to provide scholarships for deserving young men and women; to promote and aid in the mental, moral, intellectual and physical improvement, assistance and relief of the poor, indigent or deserving inhabitants of the U.S., regardless of race, color or creed.
Fields of interest: Arts; Higher education; Environment; Family services; Aging, centers/ services; Community development, neighborhood development; Christian agencies & churches.
Type of support: Program development; Seed money; Scholarship funds; Research.
Limitations: Giving limited to greater Kalamazoo, MI. No grants to individuals, or for operating budgets or annual campaigns.
Publications: Application guidelines; Annual report.
Application information: Application packages should be no more than 12 pages. Application form required.
> *Initial approach:* Call or write for application form and instructions
> *Copies of proposal:* 6
> *Deadline(s):* Apr. 1 and Sept. 1
> *Board meeting date(s):* Spring and fall
> *Final notification:* 30 days after board meeting
Officers and Trustees:* Janet J. Deal-Koestner,* Pres.; Timothy Light,* V.P.; Floyd L. Parks,* Secy.-Treas.; Randall W. Eberts; Janet M. Karpus; Florence Upjohn Orosz.
EIN: 386052963
Selected grants: The following grants were reported in 2005.
$40,000 to Ministry with Community, Kalamazoo, MI.
$30,000 to Housing Resources, Kalamazoo, MI.
$25,000 to Goodwill Industries of Southwestern Michigan, Kalamazoo, MI.
$25,000 to Kalamazoo Civic Theater, Kalamazoo, MI.
$25,000 to Mount Zion Safe House, Kalamazoo, MI.
$25,000 to United Way, Greater Kalamazoo, Kalamazoo, MI.
$20,000 to W. E. Upjohn Unemployment Trustee Corporation, Kalamazoo, MI.

833
Frederick S. Upton Foundation
100 Ridgeway St.
St. Joseph, MI 49085-1047   (269) 982-1905
County: Berrien
Contact: Stephen E. Upton, Chair.
FAX: (269) 982-0323;
E-mail: uptonfoundation@comcast.net

Trust established in 1954 in IL.
Donor: Frederick S. Upton†.
Grantmaker type: Independent foundation.
Financial data (yr. ended 12/31/09): Assets, $14,558,430 (M); expenditures, $1,022,249; total giving, $856,653; qualifying distributions, $895,501; giving activities include $856,653 for grants.
Type of support: General/operating support; Management development/capacity building; Annual campaigns; Capital campaigns; Building/ renovation; Equipment; Program development; Seed money; Research.
Limitations: Applications accepted. Giving primarily in MI and SC.
Publications: Application guidelines.
Application information: Application form required.

Initial approach: Letter or telephone
Copies of proposal: 5
Deadline(s): Mar. 15, June 15, and Oct. 15
Board meeting date(s): Varies
Final notification: All applicants will be notified
Officers and Trustees:* Stephen E. Upton,* Chair.;
Sylvia Upton Wood,* Secy.; Priscilla Upton Byrns;
Matt Fowler; Betsy Stover; Ben Upton; Fred Upton;
Carrie Vill; JPMorgan Chase Bank, N.A.
Number of staff: 1 part-time professional.
EIN: 366013317
Selected grants: The following grants were reported
in 2005.
$74,000 to Salvation Army.
$5,000 to Womens Community Association,
Albuquerque, NM.
$3,000 to Lawrence University, Appleton, WI.

834
V Care Jainism & Jivdaya Foundation
27208 Hampstead Blvd.
Farmington Hills, MI   48331-3678
County: Oakland
Contact: Mahesh H. Vora, Tr.
E-mail: mhvora@yahoo.com

Established in 2004 in MI.
Donors: Kirti M. Vora; Mahesh H. Vora; Sejal Parag
Vora; Ami Anand Vora; Kalpanaben Ashokbhai
Choksi; Koradia Chetan Anantbhai.
Grantmaker type: Independent foundation.
Financial data (yr. ended 12/31/09): Assets,
$216,309 (M); gifts received, $30,101;
expenditures, $20,324; total giving, $20,251;
qualifying distributions, $20,251; giving activities
include $20,251 for grants.
Purpose and activities: Grants to organizations and
for projects that supports the principles of Jainism.
Fields of interest: Human services; Religion.
Limitations: Applications accepted. Giving primarily
in India.
Application information: Application form not
required.
Initial approach: Letter
Deadline(s): None
Officer and Trustees:* Mahesh H. Vora,* Mgr.; Kirti
M. Vora.
EIN: 030544707

835
David and Carol Van Andel Foundation
3133 Orchard Vista Dr. S.E.
Grand Rapids, MI   49546-7033
County: Kent
Contact: Mark J. Bugge, Secy.

Established in 2005 in MI.
Donors: Jay and Betty Van Andel Foundation; Jay
Van Andel Trust.
Grantmaker type: Independent foundation.
Financial data (yr. ended 12/31/09): Assets,
$45,034,514 (M); expenditures, $3,239,777; total
giving, $1,869,395; qualifying distributions,
$2,152,661; giving activities include $1,869,395
for 63 grants (high: $920,000; low: $250).
Purpose and activities: Giving primarily for Christian
religious activities, including higher and secondary
education; support also for museums and
performing arts groups.

Fields of interest: Museums; Performing arts;
Secondary school/education; Higher education;
Christian agencies & churches.
Type of support: General/operating support.
Limitations: Applications accepted. Giving primarily
in Grand Rapids, MI.
Application information:
Initial approach: Letter
Deadline(s): None
Officer: Mark J. Bugge, Secy.
Trustee: David Van Andel.
Number of staff: 1 full-time professional; 1 full-time
support.
EIN: 202110420
Selected grants: The following grants were reported
in 2008.
$320,000 to Hope College, Holland, MI.
$50,000 to Inner City Christian Federation, Grand
Rapids, MI.
$35,000 to Pine Rest Christian Mental Health
Services, Grand Rapids, MI.
$25,000 to Calvin Theological Seminary, Grand
Rapids, MI.
$25,000 to Western Theological Seminary, Holland,
MI.
$25,000 to Words of Hope, Grand Rapids, MI.
$20,000 to Dwelling Place of Grand Rapids, Grand
Rapids, MI.
$10,000 to Mel Trotter Ministries, Grand Rapids,
MI.
$8,000 to Potters House, Grand Rapids, MI.
$1,750 to Pine Rest Foundation, Grand Rapids, MI.

836
Steve & Cindy Van Andel Foundation
P.O. Box 172
Ada, MI   49301-0172   (616) 787-6554
County: Kent
Contact: Deb Rushlo

Established in 2005 in MI.
Donor: Jay and Betty Van Andel Foundation.
Grantmaker type: Independent foundation.
Financial data (yr. ended 12/31/09): Assets,
$46,882,242 (M); expenditures, $2,804,307; total
giving, $625,062; qualifying distributions,
$625,062; giving activities include $625,062 for 56
grants (high: $166,667; low: $25).
Fields of interest: Hospitals (general); Youth
development; Human services; Children/youth,
services; Community/economic development;
Public policy, research; Children/youth; Aging;
Adults, women; Economically disadvantaged;
Homeless.
Type of support: General/operating support; Annual
campaigns; Capital campaigns; Program
development; Scholarship funds.
Limitations: Applications accepted. Giving primarily
in MI, with some emphasis on Grand Rapids.
Application information:
Initial approach: Letter of request
Deadline(s): None
Officer: Cynthia Van Andel, C.E.O.
Number of staff: 2
EIN: 202110604
Selected grants: The following grants were reported
in 2008.
$25,000 to Mel Trotter Ministries, Grand Rapids,
MI.
$15,000 to Baxter Community Center, Grand
Rapids, MI.
$15,000 to Pine Rest Foundation, Grand Rapids,
MI.

$12,500 to Potters House, Grand Rapids, MI.
$10,000 to CASA of Kent County, Grand Rapids, MI.
$10,000 to Saint Johns Home, Grand Rapids, MI.
$10,000 to Van Andel Institute, Grand Rapids, MI.
$5,000 to Guiding Light Mission, Grand Rapids, MI.
$5,000 to Hillsdale College, Hillsdale, MI.
$2,500 to Heartside Ministry, Grand Rapids, MI.

837
Van Andel Fund, Inc.
3133 Orchard Vista Dr. S.E.
Grand Rapids, MI   49546-7033
County: Kent
Contact: Mark J. Bugge, Secy.-Treas.

Established in 2007 in MI.
Donor: Jan & Betty Van Andel Foundation.
Grantmaker type: Independent foundation.
Financial data (yr. ended 12/31/09): Assets,
$211,173,677 (M); gifts received, $1,200,000;
expenditures, $3,388,698; total giving,
$2,402,500; qualifying distributions, $2,419,847;
giving activities include $2,402,500 for 1 grant.
Fields of interest: Museums (specialized).
Limitations: Giving primarily in Grand Rapids, MI.
Application information:
Initial approach: Letter of reference
Deadline(s): None
Officers: David Van Andel, Pres.; Mark Bugge,
Secy.-Treas.
Director: Steve Van Andel.
EIN: 208446997
Selected grants: The following grants were reported
in 2007.
$4,000,000 to Public Museum of Grand Rapids,
Grand Rapids, MI.

838
William and Anna Van Den Bosch Gospel
Foundation
111 Lyon St. N.W., Ste. 900
Grand Rapids, MI   49503-2487
County: Kent
Contact: William Van Den Bosch, Jr., Pres.
Application address: 1000 Hancock St. S.E., Grand
Rapids, MI 49507

Established in 2000 in MI.
Donors: William Van Den Bosch, Sr.‡; Anna Van
Den Bosch.
Grantmaker type: Independent foundation.
Financial data (yr. ended 12/31/09): Assets,
$1,721,442 (M); gifts received, $6,166;
expenditures, $110,487; total giving, $91,041;
qualifying distributions, $91,041; giving activities
include $91,041 for grants.
Purpose and activities: The foundation's mission is
to provide funds and encouragement of Bible-based
Christian organizations for projects that promote the
spread of the Gospel of Jesus Christ.
Fields of interest: Christian agencies & churches.
Type of support: Scholarship funds; Building/
renovation; Equipment; Program development.
Limitations: Applications accepted. Giving primarily
in MI.
Application information:
Initial approach: Letter
Deadline(s): Nov. 15
Officers and Directors:* William Van Den Bosch,
Jr.,* Pres.; Mark Van Den Bosch,* V.P.; Michael
Veenstra,* Secy.; Janice Veenstra, Treas.; Sarah

Hoogeboom; Kristen Van Andel; Joel Veenstra; Timothy W. Veenstra.
EIN: 383509996

839
Homer J. Van Hollenbeck Foundation

13231 23 Mile Rd.
Shelby Township, MI   48315-2713
County: Macomb

Established in 1992 in MI.
Donor: Homer J. Van Hollenbeck.
Grantmaker type: Independent foundation.
Financial data (yr. ended 12/31/09): Assets, $1,095,469 (M); expenditures, $36,836; total giving, $32,000; qualifying distributions, $32,000; giving activities include $32,000 for grants to individuals.
Purpose and activities: Scholarship awards to graduates of Macomb County, Michigan, high schools.
Fields of interest: Higher education.
Type of support: Scholarships—to individuals.
Limitations: Giving limited to residents of Macomb County, MI.
Officers: Stefan Wanczyk, Pres.; Michael G. Cumming, Secy.; Paul F. Rhoders, Treas.
EIN: 383085929

840
Van Kampen Boyer Molinari Charitable Foundation

13285 Southfields Rd.
Wellington, FL   33414-7308
County: Palm Beach
Contact: Kimberly Van Kampen Boyer, Pres.

Donor: Kimberly Van Kampen Boyer.
Grantmaker type: Independent foundation.
Financial data (yr. ended 12/31/07): Assets, $491,722 (M); expenditures, $150,329; total giving, $146,414; qualifying distributions, $146,414; giving activities include $146,414 for 11 grants (high: $50,000; low: $1,000).
Fields of interest: Arts; Education; Hospitals (specialty); Cancer; Health organizations; Athletics/ sports, equestrianism; Human services; Children/ youth, services; Children/youth.
Limitations: Applications accepted. Giving primarily in IL and MI; giving also in CA, NJ, and NY.
Application information: Application form required.
Deadline(s): None
Officers and Directors:* Kimberly Van Kampen Boyer,* Pres.; Frederic Jacques Boyer,* Secy.; Michael William Molinari.
EIN: 201190854
Selected grants: The following grants were reported in 2008.
$45,000 to Muskegon Museum of Art, Muskegon, MI.
$20,000 to La Rabida Childrens Hospital, Chicago, IL.
$10,000 to American Cancer Society, Oklahoma City, OK.
$1,000 to Kentucky Horse Park Foundation, Lexington, KY.
$1,000 to National Kidney Foundation, New York, NY.

841
Richard D. Van Lunen Charitable Foundation

c/o Peacock, Condron, Anderson & Co.
6851 Oak Hall Ln., Ste. 300
Columbia, MD   21045-5868   (410) 720-5220
County: Howard
Contact: David Condron

Established in 1985 in DE and MD.
Donor: Richard D. Van Lunen†.
Grantmaker type: Independent foundation.
Financial data (yr. ended 12/31/09): Assets, $84,613,647 (M); gifts received, $641,000; expenditures, $5,979,088; total giving, $4,497,393; qualifying distributions, $4,775,106; giving activities include $4,497,393 for 16 grants (high: $890,000; low: $20,000).
Purpose and activities: Giving primarily for Christian churches and education.
Fields of interest: Higher education; Christian agencies & churches.
Limitations: Giving primarily in IL, KY, MD, MI, and NM. No grants to individuals.
Application information:
Initial approach: Letter
Deadline(s): None
Officer and Trustees:* James Achterhof,* Exec. Dir.; James Ellis; Gordon Van Der Brug.
EIN: 521419025
Selected grants: The following grants were reported in 2006.
$3,895,000 to Lexington Christian Academy, Lexington, MA.
$619,100 to Calvin College, Grand Rapids, MI.
$285,000 to Campbellsville University, Campbellsville, KY.
$231,000 to Gardner-Webb University, Boiling Springs, NC.
$202,500 to Trinity Christian College, Palos Heights, IL.
$150,000 to Spruce Hill Christian Academy, Philadelphia, PA.
$35,000 to Roseland Christian School, Chicago, IL.
$20,000 to Zuni Christian Mission School, Zuni, NM.
$5,500 to Lexington Christian Academy, Lexington, MA.

842
Van Wormer Family Foundation

311 River Dr.
Bay City, MI   48706-1447   (989) 686-8151
County: Bay
Contact: Norman C. Van Wormer, Pres.

Established in 2002 in MI.
Donors: Norman C. Van Wormer; Melissa Van Wormer; Globe Technologies, Inc.; Bay Fire Protection, Inc.
Grantmaker type: Independent foundation.
Financial data (yr. ended 12/31/09): Assets, $1,195 (M); gifts received, $2,000; expenditures, $1,620; total giving, $0; qualifying distributions, $0.
Fields of interest: Christian agencies & churches.
Application information:
Initial approach: Letter
Deadline(s): None
Officers: Norman C. Van Wormer, Pres.; Jason S. Van Wormer, Secy.
EIN: 300048447

843
James and Almeda Vanderwaals Foundation

c/o Fifth Third Bank
P.O. Box 3636
Grand Rapids, MI   49501-3636   (888) 218-7878
County: Kent

Established in 1986 in MI.
Grantmaker type: Independent foundation.
Financial data (yr. ended 12/31/09): Assets, $750,621 (M); expenditures, $42,998; total giving, $42,998; qualifying distributions, $42,998; giving activities include $42,998 for grants.
Fields of interest: Museums; Youth development; Human services; Salvation Army; Children/youth, services; Foundations (community).
Type of support: General/operating support; Building/renovation.
Limitations: Giving limited to the greater Grand Rapids, MI, area.
Application information: Application form not required.
Initial approach: Letter
Deadline(s): None
Officers and Trustees:* David N. Keyser,* Pres.; Margaret S. Bradshaw,* V.P.; Conrad A. Bradshaw,* Secy.-Treas.
EIN: 382683671

844
VanderWeide Family Foundation

(formerly Robert & Cheri VanderWeide Foundation)
P.O. Box 230257
Grand Rapids, MI   49523-0257   (616) 643-4700
County: Kent
Contact: Ginny Vander Hart, Exec. Dir.; Sue Volkers, Fdn. Admin.
FAX: (616) 774-0116;
E-mail: info@vw-foundation.org; E-mail: virginiav@rdvcorp.com (for G. Vander Hart) or SueV@rdvcorp.com (for S. Volkers); URL: http:// www.vw-foundation.org

Established in 1992 in MI.
Donor: Suzanne DeVos Vanderweide.
Grantmaker type: Independent foundation.
Financial data (yr. ended 12/31/09): Assets, $24,323,098 (M); gifts received, $9,500,000; expenditures, $10,678,640; total giving, $10,278,375; qualifying distributions, $10,622,588; giving activities include $10,278,375 for 99 grants (high: $2,501,000; low: $250).
Purpose and activities: The foundation seeks to create a legacy of caring and stewardship through their support of projects that build community and improve the quality of people's lives. To carry out this commitment, it focuses on organizations, projects, or programs that demonstrate Christian charity to meet both the spiritual and physical needs of people, which strengthen the bond of families and communities, and bring opportunity to disadvantaged persons. Giving primarily for Christian churches; giving also for education and human services.
Fields of interest: Education; Medical specialties; Human services; Youth, services; Family services; Community/economic development; United Ways and Federated Giving Programs; Christian agencies & churches; Protestant agencies & churches.

Type of support: General/operating support; Continuing support; Annual campaigns; Capital campaigns; Building/renovation; Program development; Matching/challenge support.
Limitations: Applications accepted. Giving primarily in west MI and central FL. No grants to individuals.
Publications: Application guidelines.
Application information: Tapes, DVD's CD's, brochures or bound proposals are not accepted. Application form not required.
   Initial approach: On-line application
   Copies of proposal: 1
   Deadline(s): 3 weeks prior to review
   Board meeting date(s): 3 times annually
   Final notification: 3 to 5 months
Officers: Suzanne C. Vanderweide, Pres.; Jerry L. Tubergen, C.O.O., V.P., and Secy.; Robert A. Vanderweide, V.P.; Robert H. Schierbeek, Treas.
Number of staff: 3 full-time professional.
EIN: 383035978
Selected grants: The following grants were reported in 2008.
$3,008,500 to Helen DeVos Childrens Hospital Foundation, Grand Rapids, MI. For general support.
$2,594,720 to Grand Rapids Christian School Association, Grand Rapids, MI. For general support.
$450,000 to Boys and Girls Clubs of Grand Rapids Youth Commonwealth, Grand Rapids, MI. For general support.
$256,205 to Ada Christian School, Ada, MI. For general support.
$100,000 to Boys and Girls Clubs of Central Florida, Orlando, FL. For general support.
$75,000 to Rehoboth Christian School, Rehoboth, NM. For general support.
$50,500 to Hope College, Holland, MI. For general support.
$50,000 to Boys and Girls Club of Greater Holland, Holland, MI. For general support.
$32,000 to Potters House, Grand Rapids, MI. For general support.
$30,500 to Young Life in Grand Rapids, Grand Rapids, MI. For general support.

845
Vogt Foundation
c/o JPMorgan Chase Bank, N.A.
P.O. Box 3038
Milwaukee, WI 53201-3038
County: Milwaukee
Contact: James B. Vogt, Pres.
Application address: c/o Vogt Industries, 4542 Roger B. Chaffee Blvd. S.E., Grand Rapids, MI 49548-7522

Established in MI.
Grantmaker type: Independent foundation.
Financial data (yr. ended 12/31/09): Assets, $564,340 (M); expenditures, $31,083; total giving, $23,500; qualifying distributions, $23,500; giving activities include $23,500 for grants.
Fields of interest: Performing arts, orchestras; Higher education; Human services; United Ways and Federated Giving Programs; Christian agencies & churches.
Limitations: Giving primarily in Grand Rapids, MI. No grants to individuals.
Application information:
   Initial approach: Letter
   Deadline(s): None

Officers: James B. Vogt, Pres.; Frederick J. Vogt, Jr., V.P.; Hillary F. Snell, Secy.; Joseph McCormick, Treas.
EIN: 386083816

846
Frederick A. Vollbrecht Foundation
31700 Telegraph Rd., Ste. 220
Bingham Farms, MI 48025-3466
(248) 646-0627
County: Oakland
Contact: Richard E. Mida, Pres.

Incorporated in 1959 in MI.
Donor: Frederick A. Vollbrecht†.
Grantmaker type: Independent foundation.
Financial data (yr. ended 12/31/09): Assets, $1,507,469 (M); expenditures, $134,967; total giving, $110,500; qualifying distributions, $110,500; giving activities include $110,500 for 7 grants (high: $38,500; low: $3,000).
Purpose and activities: Giving primarily for the disabled and children in need.
Fields of interest: Child development, education; Education, special; Art & music therapy; Crime/violence prevention, child abuse; Youth development; Human services; Neighborhood centers; Children/youth, services; Family services; Disabilities, people with; Economically disadvantaged.
Type of support: Equipment; General/operating support; Continuing support.
Limitations: Applications accepted. Giving limited to MI. No grants to individuals.
Publications: Annual report.
Application information: Application form not required.
   Initial approach: Proposal
   Copies of proposal: 1
   Deadline(s): None
   Board meeting date(s): June
Officers: Richard E. Mida, Pres. and Treas.; Kenneth J. Klebba, Secy.
EIN: 386056173
Selected grants: The following grants were reported in 2008.
$35,000 to Child Abuse and Neglect Council of Oakland County, Pontiac, MI.
$18,000 to Community House Association, Birmingham, MI.
$3,900 to Rochester Hills, City of, Rochester Hills, MI.

847
The Vomberg Foundation
c/o Olivet College
320 S. Main St.
Olivet, MI 49076-9406   (269) 749-9364
County: Eaton
Contact: Christina M. Heisler, Secy.

Established in MI.
Grantmaker type: Independent foundation.
Financial data (yr. ended 12/31/09): Assets, $553,803 (M); expenditures, $32,050; total giving, $26,500; qualifying distributions, $26,500; giving activities include $26,500 for grants to individuals.
Purpose and activities: Scholarship awards to students in Eaton County, Michigan, in good academic standing, and who can demonstrate financial need.

Fields of interest: Higher education.
Type of support: Scholarships—to individuals.
Limitations: Applications accepted. Giving limited to residents of Eaton County, MI, area.
Application information: Application form required.
   Initial approach: Letter or telephone
   Deadline(s): Dec. 1 of senior year in high school
Officers: Richard L. Trumley, Pres.; Christina M. Heisler, Secy.-Treas.
Trustees: Thomas C. Blesch; Christi Dutcher; Gary Rogers; Anthony G. Sommer; Thomas R. Winquist.
EIN: 386072845

848
Richard T. and Marianne H. Walsh Charitable Trust
5039 Van Ness Dr.
Bloomfield Hills, MI 48302-2661
(248) 626-9610
County: Oakland
Contact: Marianne H. Walsh, Tr.

Established in 1997 in MI.
Donors: Marianne H. Walsh; Richard T. Walsh.
Grantmaker type: Independent foundation.
Financial data (yr. ended 04/30/10): Assets, $50,975 (M); expenditures, $13,295; total giving, $13,283; qualifying distributions, $13,283; giving activities include $13,283 for grants.
Fields of interest: Higher education; Catholic agencies & churches.
Type of support: General/operating support.
Limitations: Giving primarily in MI. No grants to individuals.
Application information: Application form not required.
   Initial approach: Letter
   Deadline(s): None
Trustees: Marianne H. Walsh; Richard T. Walsh.
EIN: 386692940

849
Jane and Frank Warchol Foundation
43033 W. Kirkwood Dr.
Clinton Township, MI 48038-1220
County: Macomb
Contact: Frank L. Warchol, Pres.
FAX: (586) 286-7926; E-mail: puttygut1@aol.com

Established in 1993 in MI.
Donors: Frank L. Warchol; Virginia J. Warchol.
Grantmaker type: Independent foundation.
Financial data (yr. ended 12/31/09): Assets, $576,306 (M); expenditures, $76,785; total giving, $70,230; qualifying distributions, $70,230; giving activities include $70,230 for 26 grants (high: $15,000; low: $100).
Purpose and activities: Giving for scholarship funds and education, human services, women, religion, and arts and culture.
Fields of interest: Historic preservation/historical societies; Higher education; Zoos/zoological societies; Human services; Science; Christian agencies & churches.
Type of support: General/operating support; Continuing support; Annual campaigns; Building/renovation; Emergency funds; Curriculum development; Scholarship funds; Exchange programs; In-kind gifts; Matching/challenge support.

Limitations: Applications accepted. Giving primarily in southeastern MI. No support for political organizations. No grants to individuals.
Publications: Grants list; Informational brochure (including application guidelines).
Application information: Application form not required.
  Initial approach: Letter
  Copies of proposal: 1
  Deadline(s): None
  Board meeting date(s): Varies
Officers: Frank L. Warchol, Pres.; Jane Warchol, Secy.
Director: Karen Wudcoski.
Number of staff: None.
EIN: 383148034
Selected grants: The following grants were reported in 2007.
$60,000 to Wayne State University, Detroit, MI.
$11,000 to Detroit Zoological Society, Royal Oak, MI.

850
John W. and Rose E. Watson Foundation
c/o Citizens Bank Wealth Mgmt., N.A.
328 S. Saginaw St., MC 002072
Flint, MI 48502-1923
County: Genesee
Application address: c/o Jean Seman, 5800 Weiss St., Saginaw, MI 48602, tel.: (989) 792-2011

Established about 1959 in MI.
Grantmaker type: Independent foundation.
Financial data (yr. ended 12/31/09): Assets, $6,790,370 (M); gifts received, $841; expenditures, $317,402; total giving, $255,500; qualifying distributions, $307,126; giving activities include $13,500 for 8 grants (high: $10,000; low: $500), and $242,000 for 121 grants to individuals (high: $2,000; low: $2,000).
Purpose and activities: Support primarily for Roman Catholic organizations; scholarship awards limited to Saginaw, MI, residents graduating from local Roman Catholic high schools.
Fields of interest: Education; Human services; Children/youth, services; Catholic agencies & churches.
Type of support: General/operating support; Scholarships—to individuals.
Limitations: Applications accepted. Giving primarily in Saginaw, MI; scholarships limited to residents of Saginaw, MI.
Application information: Application form required.
  Deadline(s): 1 month prior to academic year
Officers: William L. Ruger, Pres.; Anne Hamilton, V.P.; Don Popielarz, Secy.; Jean Seman, Treas.
Trustee: Citizens Bank.
EIN: 386091611
Selected grants: The following grants were reported in 2009.
$2,000 to Central Michigan University, Mount Pleasant, MI.
$2,000 to Central Michigan University, Mount Pleasant, MI.
$2,000 to Central Michigan University, Mount Pleasant, MI.
$2,000 to Central Michigan University, Mount Pleasant, MI.

851
Raymond E. & Evona Watson Foundation
c/o Comerica Bank, Tr.
P.O. Box 75000, M/C 3302
Detroit, MI 48275-3302 (888) 446-9489
County: Wayne
Application address: c/o Colorado School of Mines, Attn.: Financial Aid Office, 1500 Illinois St., Golden, CO 80401-1887, tel.: (800) 446-9488

Established in 1999 in OH.
Grantmaker type: Independent foundation.
Financial data (yr. ended 12/31/09): Assets, $154,843 (M); expenditures, $5,875; total giving, $1,075; qualifying distributions, $1,832; giving activities include $1,075 for 1 grant.
Purpose and activities: Scholarship awards paid directly to the Colorado School of Mines, for students who will be attending after graduating from high school.
Fields of interest: Higher education.
Type of support: Scholarships—to individuals.
Limitations: Applications accepted. Giving limited to CO.
Application information: Application form required.
  Initial approach: Proposal
  Deadline(s): None
Officer: Evona Watson, Mgr.
Trustee: Comerica Bank.
EIN: 383493259

852
Weatherwax Foundation
P.O. Box 1111
Jackson, MI 49204-1111 (517) 787-2117
County: Jackson
Contact: Maria M. Dotterweich, Exec. Dir.
E-mail: wwfnd@sbcglobal.net

Established in 1981 in MI.
Donor: K.A. Weatherwax Trust I†.
Grantmaker type: Independent foundation.
Financial data (yr. ended 09/30/09): Assets, $13,981,685 (M); expenditures, $1,394,473; total giving, $1,116,848; qualifying distributions, $1,279,677; giving activities include $1,116,848 for 37 grants (high: $162,965; low: $600).
Purpose and activities: Support primarily for arts and culture, classical education, and civic and social programs.
Fields of interest: Arts education; Performing arts; Arts.
Type of support: General/operating support; Annual campaigns; Capital campaigns; Building/renovation; Equipment; Emergency funds; Conferences/seminars; Curriculum development; Technical assistance; Consulting services; Program evaluation; Matching/challenge support.
Limitations: Giving limited to Hillsdale, Lenawee, and Jackson counties, MI. No grants to individuals, or for computer purchases.
Publications: Application guidelines; Grants list.
Application information: Application form required.
  Initial approach: Proposal (not to exceed 2 pages)
  Copies of proposal: 3
  Deadline(s): None
  Board meeting date(s): Monthly
  Final notification: Acknowledgement within 60 days
Officer: Maria Miceli Dotterweich, Exec. Dir.
Trustees: Lawrence Bullen; Comerica Bank.

Number of staff: 1 part-time professional.
EIN: 386439807
Selected grants: The following grants were reported in 2009.
$150,000 to University of Michigan, Ann Arbor, MI.
$100,000 to John George Home, Jackson, MI.
$62,820 to Community Action Agency, Jackson, MI.
$50,000 to Shop Rat Foundation, Pleasant Lake, MI.
$34,248 to Dahlem Conservancy, Jackson, MI.
$24,600 to Saint Lukes Clinic, Jackson, MI.
$20,000 to Adrian Symphony Orchestra, Adrian, MI.
$15,000 to American Red Cross, Jackson, MI.
$12,500 to Cornerstone Schools Association, Detroit, MI.
$5,000 to Blue Lake Fine Arts Camp, Twin Lake, MI.

853
Webster Family Foundation
(also known as Frank and Sara Webster Family Foundation, Inc.)
1535 Lincolnshire Dr.
Lapeer, MI 48446-3147
County: Lapeer
Contact: Sarah Webster, Tr.
Application address: c/o Freedman & Goldberg, C.P.A., 2444 E. Hill Rd., Grand Blanc, MI 48439-5098, tel.: (810) 694-0336

Established in 1998 in MI.
Donor: Sarah Webster.
Grantmaker type: Independent foundation.
Financial data (yr. ended 12/31/09): Assets, $15,389 (M); expenditures, $4,914; total giving, $4,200; qualifying distributions, $4,200; giving activities include $4,200 for grants.
Fields of interest: Catholic agencies & churches.
Limitations: Giving primarily in Lapeer, MI.
Application information:
  Initial approach: Proposal
  Deadline(s): None
Trustee: Sarah Webster.
EIN: 383416886

854
Arthur H. Webster, Jr. Endowment Fund
c/o Citizens Bank Wealth Management, N.A.
328 S. Saginaw St., M/C 001065
Flint, MI 48502-1923
County: Genesee
Application address: c/o Citizens Bank Wealth Mgmt., N.A., Attn.: Helen James, 101 N. Washington Ave., Saginaw, MI 48607-1207, tel.: (989) 776-7368

Established in 2004 in MI.
Donor: Lorraine Webster Residual Trust.
Grantmaker type: Independent foundation.
Financial data (yr. ended 08/31/09): Assets, $1,372,922 (M); expenditures, $81,527; total giving, $61,943; qualifying distributions, $73,558; giving activities include $61,943 for 6 grants (high: $20,000; low: $2,500).
Purpose and activities: Giving primarily to the Saginaw Community Foundation.
Fields of interest: Children/youth, services; Family services; Foundations (community).
Type of support: General/operating support.
Limitations: Applications accepted. Giving primarily in Saginaw, MI.

Application information: Application form required.
Deadline(s): None
Trustee: Citizens Bank.
EIN: 386635520

855
Irene M. & Milton R. Weed Foundation
1009 Audubon Rd.
Grosse Pointe Park, MI 48230-1406
(586) 773-7720
County: Wayne
Contact: Bruno F. Domzalski, Dir.

Established in 2004 in MI.
Grantmaker type: Independent foundation.
Financial data (yr. ended 12/31/09): Assets,
$1,560,215 (M); expenditures, $116,553; total
giving, $79,600; qualifying distributions, $79,600;
giving activities include $79,600 for grants.
Fields of interest: Elementary/secondary
education; Medical school/education; Human
services; Christian agencies & churches; Children/
youth; Economically disadvantaged.
Type of support: Program development; Equipment;
Scholarship funds.
Limitations: Applications accepted. Giving primarily
in MI; giving also in IL.
Application information: Application form not
required.
Initial approach: Letterhead
Deadline(s): None
Director: Bruno F. Domzalski.
EIN: 300241901

856
Wege Foundation
P.O. Box 6388
Grand Rapids, MI 49516-6388 (616) 957-0480
County: Kent
Contact: Ellen Satterlee, C.E.O. and Treas.
URL: http://wegefoundation.org/index.html

Established on July 13, 1967 in MI.
Donor: Peter M. Wege.
Grantmaker type: Independent foundation.
Financial data (yr. ended 12/31/09): Assets,
$100,866,387 (M); expenditures, $16,114,510;
total giving, $13,822,485; qualifying distributions,
$14,728,842; giving activities include
$13,822,485 for 53 grants (high: $1,530,000; low:
$594).
Purpose and activities: Giving primarily to the
environment, education, arts and culture,
community service and health care.
Fields of interest: Museums; Performing arts;
Elementary/secondary education; Higher education;
Environment, natural resources; Hospitals (general);
Human services; Children/youth, services;
Community/economic development.
Type of support: Scholarship funds; General/
operating support; Annual campaigns; Capital
campaigns; Building/renovation; Equipment;
Endowments; Program development; Curriculum
development; Matching/challenge support.
Limitations: Applications accepted. Giving primarily
in greater Kent County, MI, with emphasis on the
Grand Rapids area. No grants to individuals.
Publications: Application guidelines; Annual report.
Application information: See foundation's web site
for online grant application. Application form
required.

Initial approach: Online grant application
Copies of proposal: 1
Deadline(s): Spring and Fall. Check web site for
dates
Board meeting date(s): Apr. 15
Officers and Directors:* Peter M. Wege,* Chair;
Ellen Satterlee, C.E.O. and Treas.; Peter M. Wege
II,* Pres.; Terri McCarthy, V.P., Progs; Jonathan C.
Wege,* V.P.; W. Michael Van Haren,* Secy.; Jody
Price, C.F.O.; Mary Goodwillie Nelson; Christopher
Wege; Diana Wege.
Number of staff: 3 full-time professional.
EIN: 386124363
Selected grants: The following grants were reported
in 2007.
$20,321,793 to Healing our Waters Great Lakes
Coalition, Washington, DC.

857
Barbara J. Weidemann Foundation, Inc.
41700 Hayes Rd., Ste. A
Clinton Twp, MI 48038-5823
County: Macomb

Established in 2007 in MI.
Donor: Barbara J. Weidemann.
Grantmaker type: Independent foundation.
Financial data (yr. ended 12/31/09): Assets,
$362,809 (M); expenditures, $77,304; total giving,
$21,617; qualifying distributions, $21,617; giving
activities include $21,617 for grants.
Fields of interest: Health organizations.
Limitations: Giving primarily in MI and TN.
Application information:
Initial approach: Letter
Deadline(s): Varies
Final notification: 2 months after request
Officer: Wayne Stewart, Pres.
EIN: 383732911

858
Weigel Family Foundation
c/o Whitney National Bank
1370 E. Venice Ave., Ste. 104
Venice, FL 34285-9083 (941) 794-6969
County: Sarasota

Established in 1997 in FL.
Donors: Raymond A. Weigel, Jr.; Wavelet M. Weigel.
Grantmaker type: Independent foundation.
Financial data (yr. ended 12/31/09): Assets,
$513,026 (M); expenditures, $32,795; total giving,
$28,500; qualifying distributions, $28,500; giving
activities include $28,500 for grants.
Fields of interest: Education; Christian agencies &
churches.
Limitations: Giving primarily in FL and MI. No grants
to individuals.
Application information:
Initial approach: Proposal
Deadline(s): None
Trustee: Wavelet M. Weigel.
EIN: 650741135

859
Weikart Family Foundation
P.O. Box 622
Clinton, MI 49236-0622
County: Lenawee
Contact: Phyllis S. Weikart, Pres.

Established in 2004 in MI.
Donor: David Weikart‡.
Grantmaker type: Independent foundation.
Financial data (yr. ended 12/31/09): Assets,
$1,891,920 (M); expenditures, $82,900; total
giving, $50,000; qualifying distributions, $69,272;
giving activities include $50,000 for 2 grants (high:
$25,000; low: $25,000).
Fields of interest: Education; Children/youth,
services.
Type of support: Research.
Application information: Application form required.
Initial approach: Letter
Deadline(s): Mar. 31
Officers: Phyllis S. Weikart, Pres.; Jennifer D. Danko,
V.P.; Catherine L. Yeckel, Secy.; Cynthia W. Embry,
Treas.
EIN: 200456632
Selected grants: The following grants were reported
in 2006.
$60,000 to Columbia University, Saltzman Inst of
War & Peace Studies, New York, NY.

860
Weiner Family Foundation
P.O. Box 604
Walled Lake, MI 48390-3005
County: Oakland

Established in 1999 in MI.
Donor: Josephine S. Weiner.
Grantmaker type: Independent foundation.
Financial data (yr. ended 12/31/09): Assets,
$206,572 (M); gifts received, $44; expenditures,
$16,747; total giving, $13,500; qualifying
distributions, $13,500; giving activities include
$13,500 for grants.
Fields of interest: Arts; Education, early childhood
education; Human services; Family services.
Type of support: Program development.
Limitations: Giving primarily in the greater
metropolitan Detroit, MI, and Chicago, IL, areas. No
grants to individuals or generally for ongoing
expenses.
Application information:
Initial approach: Letter
Deadline(s): None
Officers: Laura Keidan Martin, Pres.; Marian Keidan
Seltzer, Secy.-Treas.
EIN: 383449750

861
**Weinlander, Fitzhugh & Schairer
Foundation, Inc.**
P.O. Box 775
Bay City, MI 48707-0775
County: Bay
Contact: David D. Quimby, Secy.

Established in 1997 in MI.
Grantmaker type: Independent foundation.
Financial data (yr. ended 09/30/10): Assets,
$18,521 (M); gifts received, $14,250;
expenditures, $15,870; total giving, $15,848;
qualifying distributions, $15,848; giving activities
include $15,848 for grants.
Fields of interest: Human services; Community/
economic development.
Limitations: Giving primarily in Bay City, MI.
Application information:

Initial approach: Letter
Deadline(s): None
Officers: Michael L. Hanisko, Pres.; David D. Quimby, Secy.
EIN: 383383676

862
Bernard and Helen Weisberg Family Foundation
2075 E. 14 Mile Rd.
Birmingham, MI 48009-7279 (248) 647-4333
County: Oakland

Established in 1985 in MI.
Donors: Bernard Weisberg; Helen Weisberg.
Grantmaker type: Independent foundation.
Financial data (yr. ended 10/31/09): Assets, $158,741 (M); expenditures, $13,709; total giving, $12,870; qualifying distributions, $12,870; giving activities include $12,870 for grants.
Fields of interest: Jewish federated giving programs; Jewish agencies & synagogues.
Application information:
Initial approach: Letter
Deadline(s): None
Officers: Bernard Weisberg, Pres.; Helen Weisberg, V.P.
EIN: 382639090

863
The Weisblat Foundation, Inc.
c/o Michele C. Marquardt
211 E. Water St., Ste. 401
Kalamazoo, MI 49007-5806 (269) 344-9236
County: Kalamazoo

Established in 1991 in MI.
Donor: Christine Weisblat.
Grantmaker type: Independent foundation.
Financial data (yr. ended 12/31/09): Assets, $699,767 (M); expenditures, $39,515; total giving, $21,400; qualifying distributions, $21,400; giving activities include $21,400 for grants.
Fields of interest: Arts; Education; Environment; Health care; Safety/disasters; Children/youth, services.
Type of support: General/operating support.
Limitations: Applications accepted. Giving primarily in MI.
Application information: Application form not required.
Initial approach: Letter
Deadline(s): Oct. 31
Officers: Sara L. Schastok, Pres. and Treas.; David A. Weisblat, V.P.; Ann M. Ford, Secy.
EIN: 383014535

864
Weiss Family Foundation
2290 1st National Bldg.
Detroit, MI 48226-3506 (313) 465-7596
County: Wayne
Contact: Robert B. Weiss, Pres.

Donors: Robert Weiss; Susan Weiss.
Grantmaker type: Independent foundation.
Financial data (yr. ended 11/30/09): Assets, $112,307 (M); gifts received, $106,912; expenditures, $40,974; total giving, $40,200; qualifying distributions, $40,200; giving activities include $40,200 for grants.
Application information:
Initial approach: Proposal
Deadline(s): None
Officers: Robert B. Weiss, Pres.; Shira Weiss, Secy.; Susan Weiss, Treas.
EIN: 263073419

865
James D. Weiss, Sr. Foundation
1509 E. Chicago Rd.
Sturgis, MI 49091-1991 (269) 651-1080
County: St. Joseph
Contact: James D. Weiss Sr., Tr.

Established in MI.
Grantmaker type: Independent foundation.
Financial data (yr. ended 12/31/09): Assets, $1,384 (M); expenditures, $300; total giving, $0; qualifying distributions, $0.
Fields of interest: Animal welfare; Animals/wildlife, preservation/protection; Veterinary medicine.
Type of support: General/operating support.
Limitations: Giving primarily in MI. No grants to individuals.
Application information: Within 6 months.
Initial approach: Proposal
Deadline(s): None
Trustees: Nancy A. Phillips; James D. Weiss, Sr.
EIN: 383726370

866
Evelyn & Fredrick Weissman Education and Charitable Foundation
30238 Spring River Dr.
Southfield, MI 48076-1047 (248) 203-9270
County: Oakland
Contact: Rebecca Weissman, Dir.

Established in 1994 in MI.
Donor: Fredrick & Evelyn Weissman Charitable Lead Trust.
Grantmaker type: Independent foundation.
Financial data (yr. ended 12/31/08): Assets, $29,583 (M); expenditures, $9,336; total giving, $8,300; qualifying distributions, $8,300; giving activities include $8,300 for grants.
Fields of interest: Performing arts, dance; Arts; Education.
Type of support: Program development; Scholarships—to individuals.
Limitations: Giving primarily in CO and MI.
Application information: Application form required.
Deadline(s): None
Directors: Margaret Weissman; Patricia Weissman; Rebecca Weissman.
EIN: 383196147

867
Weitzenhoffer-Seminole Foundation
(formerly Seminole Foundation)
P.O. Box 1366
Columbus, MS 39703-1366 (662) 329-0037
County: Lowndes
Contact: Marjorie Robertson, Secy.

Established in 1985 in MS.
Grantmaker type: Independent foundation.

Financial data (yr. ended 12/31/09): Assets, $960,017 (M); expenditures, $80,491; total giving, $74,825; qualifying distributions, $74,825; giving activities include $74,825 for grants.
Fields of interest: Higher education; Education; Environment; Boy scouts; Children/youth, services; United Ways and Federated Giving Programs.
Type of support: General/operating support.
Limitations: Giving primarily in Kalamazoo, MI, and Columbus, MS.
Application information:
Initial approach: Letter
Deadline(s): Oct. 30
Officers: Max Weitzenhoffer, Pres.; William J. Threadgill, V.P.; Marjorie Robertson, Secy.
EIN: 640711566

868
James A. Welch Foundation
5206 Gateway Ctr., Ste. 100
Flint, MI 48507-3917 (810) 238-4617
County: Genesee
Contact: Eugene Grice, Pres.

Established in 1960 in MI.
Grantmaker type: Independent foundation.
Financial data (yr. ended 06/30/10): Assets, $1,802,214 (M); expenditures, $93,445; total giving, $72,319; qualifying distributions, $72,319; giving activities include $72,319 for 11 grants (high: $17,500; low: $2,134).
Purpose and activities: Giving to organizations providing educational guidance and counseling for local gifted students, including museums, educational institutions, and performing arts groups.
Fields of interest: Performing arts, theater; Performing arts, music; Secondary school/education; Education; Recreation, camps; YM/YWCAs & YM/YWHAs; Children/youth, services; Science.
Type of support: General/operating support.
Limitations: Applications accepted. Giving limited to Genesee County, MI. No grants to individuals.
Application information: Application form required.
Initial approach: Proposal
Copies of proposal: 8
Deadline(s): Feb. 20, May 20, Aug. 20, and Nov. 20
Board meeting date(s): Jan., Mar., June, and Sept.
Officers: Eugene Grice, Pres.; James Kettler, V.P.; John C. Briggs, Secy.-Treas.
Directors: Gail Ganakas; Patricia Gruener; Dennis Haley; Stephen Schlott.
EIN: 381690381

869
Leon Wells Trust
c/o Monroe Bank & Trust
102 E. Front St.
Monroe, MI 48161-2162 (734) 242-2734
County: Monroe

Established in MI.
Donor: Leon Wells†.
Grantmaker type: Independent foundation.
Financial data (yr. ended 05/31/10): Assets, $268,932 (M); expenditures, $11,749; total giving, $8,000; qualifying distributions, $9,748; giving activities include $8,000 for 23 grants to individuals (high: $500; low: $200).

Purpose and activities: Scholarship awards to graduates of Dundee Community and Summerfield Community high schools, Michigan.
Fields of interest: Higher education.
Type of support: Scholarships—to individuals.
Limitations: Giving limited to residents of Dundee and Summerfield, MI.
Application information: Application form required.
Deadline(s): May 1
Trustee: Monroe Bank & Trust.
EIN: 386146348

870
Wellspring of Hope Foundation, Inc.
P.O. Box 250703
Franklin, MI 48025-0703 (248) 672-9292
County: Oakland
Contact: Sue Simmers, Secy.
E-mail: Cameroonkids@aol.com; E-mail for Susan Simmers: sues@wellspringofhope.net; URL: http://wellspringofhope.net/

Established in 2006 in MI.
Donors: Michael Simmers; Sue Simmers; Ulrich Herter; Martha Condit; David Dowler; Marie Dowler; Bill Molnar; Marie Molnar.
Grantmaker type: Independent foundation.
Financial data (yr. ended 12/31/09): Assets, $6,827 (M); gifts received, $41,938; expenditures, $55,233; total giving, $27,945; qualifying distributions, $27,945; giving activities include $27,945 for grants.
Purpose and activities: The foundation strives to make a positive difference in the lives of underprivileged children in Cameroon, Africa and beyond through education, financial support and spiritual partnership.
Fields of interest: International relief; Children; Economically disadvantaged.
International interests: Cameroon.
Limitations: Giving primarily in Cameroon.
Officers and Board Members:* John Lane,* Pres.; Susan Simmers,* Secy.; William Barnes, C.P.A.; Kimber Bishop-Yanke; Marie Molnar; Emily Vancleff.
EIN: 412202580

871
Thomas Welsh Foundation
P.O. Box 290
St. Clair Shores, MI 48080-0290
County: Macomb
Application address: c/o Macomb Community College, Office of Resource Devel. or Office of Financial Aid, 14500 E. 12 Mile Rd., Warren, MI 48093-3896, tel.: (586) 445-7302

Established in MI.
Grantmaker type: Independent foundation.
Financial data (yr. ended 11/30/08): Assets, $165,422 (M); gifts received, $500; expenditures, $16,286; total giving, $10,783; qualifying distributions, $10,783; giving activities include $10,783 for grants.
Fields of interest: Christian agencies & churches.
Type of support: Scholarship funds.
Limitations: Giving limited to Warren, MI.
Officers and Directors:* Lorie Jo Welsh, Pres.; Thomas S. Welsh III,* Secy.; Michael D. Murray.
EIN: 383111330

872
Samuel L. Westerman Foundation
40950 Woodward Ave., Ste. 306
Bloomfield Hills, MI 48304-5124
County: Oakland
Contact: Ruth R. LoPrete, Grant Off.
Application address: 2861 Masefield Dr., Bloomfield Hills, MI 48304-1949, tel.: (248) 203-9343

Established in 1971 in MI.
Donor: Samuel L. Westerman‡.
Grantmaker type: Independent foundation.
Financial data (yr. ended 12/31/09): Assets, $7,643,192 (M); gifts received, $114; expenditures, $507,923; total giving, $464,500; qualifying distributions, $464,500; giving activities include $464,500 for 139 grants (high: $25,000; low: $50).
Purpose and activities: Giving primarily for education, youth services and religious programs.
Fields of interest: Performing arts, music; Arts; Higher education; Education; Hospitals (general); Health care; Health organizations, association; Human services; Children/youth, services; Religion.
Type of support: General/operating support; Continuing support; Endowments; Program development; Scholarship funds; Research.
Limitations: Applications accepted. Giving primarily in MI. No grants to individuals.
Publications: Grants list.
Application information: Very limited funds available for new grants. Application form not required.
Initial approach: Letter
Copies of proposal: 1
Deadline(s): None
Board meeting date(s): Quarterly
Final notification: Via letter
Officers and Trustees:* James H. LoPrete,* Pres.; Cameron K. Muir,* V.P. and Treas.; Ruth LoPrete, V.P. and Grant Off.; Kent G. LoPrete,* V.P., Investment Comm.; Gordon J. Muir, V.P., Investment Comm.; Martha M. Muir,* V.P.; Mary M. Lyneus, Secy.
EIN: 237108795
Selected grants: The following grants were reported in 2009.
$100,000 to Culver Educational Foundation, Culver, IN.
$80,000 to Culver Educational Foundation, Culver, IN.
$75,000 to University of Notre Dame, Notre Dame, IN.
$70,000 to Detroit Zoological Society, Royal Oak, MI.
$60,000 to Cedarville University, Cedarville, OH.
$60,000 to Spring Arbor University, Spring Arbor, MI.
$40,000 to Grand Rapids Christian Schools, Grand Rapids, MI.
$30,000 to Helen DeVos Childrens Hospital, Grand Rapids, MI.
$25,000 to Henry Ford Health System, Detroit, MI.
$5,000 to DePauw University, Greencastle, IN.

873
Western Michigan Society of Professional Engineers Scholarship Fund
1201 Glenaire Dr. N.W.
Grand Rapids, MI 49544-1725
County: Kent
Contact: Alan Pennington, Dir.

Application address: 2678 Cascade Springs Dr. S.E., Grand Rapids MI 49546, tel: (616) 363-9801

Established in MI.
Grantmaker type: Independent foundation.
Financial data (yr. ended 12/31/09): Assets, $34,514 (M); gifts received, $9,000; expenditures, $1,525; total giving, $1,500; qualifying distributions, $1,500; giving activities include $1,500 for grants to individuals.
Purpose and activities: Scholarship awards to study engineering for high school seniors who are U.S. citizens and living in Michigan.
Fields of interest: Engineering school/education; Engineering.
Type of support: Scholarships—to individuals.
Limitations: Giving limited to residents of MI.
Application information: Application form required.
Deadline(s): Jan. 31
Officers: Matt Tipping, Chair.; Tom Byle, Treas.
Directors: Christopher Cruickshank; Alan Pennington.
EIN: 382277658

874
Robert B. Westfall Foundation
906 James St.
Adrian, MI 49221-3914
County: Lenawee
Contact: Jamie Hill, Mgr.
Application address: 6795 S.E. Tuscany Ct., Milwaukee, OR 97267-1950, tel.: (503) 334-5038

Established in 1986 in MI.
Donor: Ruthmary Westfall.
Grantmaker type: Independent foundation.
Financial data (yr. ended 09/30/08): Assets, $1,390,038 (M); expenditures, $77,947; total giving, $52,360; qualifying distributions, $52,360; giving activities include $52,360 for grants.
Fields of interest: Secondary school/education; Higher education.
Type of support: Scholarships—to individuals; Scholarship funds.
Limitations: Applications accepted. Giving primarily in Ann Arbor and Hillsdale, MI.
Application information:
Initial approach: Request application guidelines
Deadline(s): None
Officers: Ruthmary Westfall,* Pres.; Harley J. Westfall,* Secy.; Jamie Hill, Mgr.
Director: Charles D. Dunham.
EIN: 382711284

875
Louis F. and Florence H. Weyand 1977 Charitable Trust
c/o Trust Tax Services
P.O. Box 64713
St. Paul, MN 55164-0713
County: Ramsey
Application address: 800 Nicollet Mall, Minneapolis, MN 55402-7000, tel.: (651) 303-3813

Established in 1977 in CA and MN.
Donors: Louis F. Weyand‡; Florence H. Weyand.
Grantmaker type: Independent foundation.
Financial data (yr. ended 09/30/09): Assets, $2,939,132 (M); expenditures, $215,398; total giving, $167,200; qualifying distributions,

$167,200; giving activities include $167,200 for grants.
Fields of interest: Arts; Education; Health care; Youth development; Human services; Christian agencies & churches.
Type of support: General/operating support.
Limitations: Applications accepted. Giving limited to CA, FL, and MI. No grants to individuals.
Application information:
   Initial approach: Proposal
   Deadline(s): None
Trustees: Lois V. Bachman; Carolyn Yorston; U.S. Bank, N.A.
EIN: 942473421
Selected grants: The following grants were reported in 2008.
$8,620 to Athenaeum Music and Arts Library, La Jolla, CA.
$8,000 to Petaluma Educational Foundation, Petaluma, CA.
$6,599 to La Jolla Music Society, La Jolla, CA.
$6,000 to Lost Tree Chapel, North Palm Beach, FL.
$3,000 to Boys and Girls Club of Petaluma, Petaluma, CA.
$3,000 to Carousel Fund, Petaluma, CA.
$3,000 to Hospice of Palm Beach County, West Palm Beach, FL.
$3,000 to Petaluma Valley Hospital, Petaluma, CA.
$1,265 to Bishops School, La Jolla, CA.
$1,225 to Patrons of the Prado, San Diego, CA.

876
Weyerhaeuser/Day Foundation
30 E. 7th St., Ste. 2000
St. Paul, MN   55101-4930   (651) 228-0935
County: Ramsey
Contact: Vivian W. Day, Pres.

Established in 1995 in MN.
Donors: Lynn Weyerhaeuser Day‡; Stanley R. Day.
Grantmaker type: Independent foundation.
Financial data (yr. ended 12/31/09): Assets, $8,758,928 (M); gifts received, $239,844; expenditures, $475,872; total giving, $424,492; qualifying distributions, $447,694; giving activities include $424,492 for 9 grants (high: $301,992; low: $5,000).
Fields of interest: Elementary/secondary education; Environment, natural resources; Transportation.
Type of support: General/operating support; Annual campaigns; Endowments.
Limitations: Applications accepted. Giving primarily in Chicago, IL, and MI, with some emphasis on Detroit.
Application information: Application form not required.
   Initial approach: Proposal
   Deadline(s): None
Officers and Directors: Vivian W. Day,* Pres.; Lincoln W. Day,* V.P.; Stanley R. Day, Jr.,* Secy.; Frederick K.W. Day,* Treas.
EIN: 411815686
Selected grants: The following grants were reported in 2006.
$300,000 to World Vision, Federal Way, WA.
$10,000 to Bon Secours Cottage Health Services Foundation, Grosse Pointe, MI.
$10,000 to Forest History Society, Durham, NC.
$10,000 to Miss Porters School, Farmington, CT.
$5,000 to Detroit Institute for Children, Detroit, MI.
$5,000 to Detroit Institute of Arts, Detroit, MI.
$5,000 to Nature Conservancy, Lansing, MI.

877
Albert A. White Foundation
c/o Raymond H. Lemmen
3511 Coolidge Rd., Ste. 100
East Lansing, MI   48823-6390   (517) 351-6836
County: Ingham
Application address: c/o Gilbert M. White, P.O. Box 477, Haslett, MI 48840

Grantmaker type: Independent foundation.
Financial data (yr. ended 12/31/09): Assets, $0 (M); expenditures, $210,039; total giving, $200,235; qualifying distributions, $204,787; giving activities include $200,235 for 1 grant.
Fields of interest: Recreation, parks/playgrounds; Community/economic development.
Limitations: Giving primarily in East Lansing, MI.
Officers and Directors: Gilbert M. White,* Pres.; Douglas Austin,* Secy.; Ray Lemmen,* Treas.
EIN: 352170141

878
The John and Elizabeth Whiteley Foundation
c/o Hubbard Law Firm
5801 W. Michigan Ave.
Lansing, MI   48908-0857   (517) 886-7176
County: Eaton
Contact: Donald B. Lawrence, Jr., Secy.-Treas.
Application address: P.O. Box 80502, Lansing, MI 48908-0502

Incorporated in 1955 in MI.
Donor: Nellie M. Zimmerman‡.
Grantmaker type: Independent foundation.
Financial data (yr. ended 12/31/09): Assets, $1,584,616 (M); expenditures, $80,680; total giving, $45,000; qualifying distributions, $45,000; giving activities include $45,000 for grants.
Purpose and activities: Giving primarily for human services and education, including education scholarship awards to students in Ingham, Eaton or Clinton counties, Michigan.
Fields of interest: Higher education; Salvation Army; Protestant agencies & churches.
Type of support: General/operating support; Scholarships—to individuals.
Limitations: Applications accepted. Giving primarily in Ingham, Eaton and Clinton counties, MI.
Application information: Application form required.
   Deadline(s): May 1 for scholarships
Officers: Romayne E. Hicks, Pres.; John Smythe, V.P.; Donald B. Lawrence, Jr., Secy.-Treas.
Directors: George J. Petroff; Stephen D. Plumb.
Trustee: Richard F. Burmeister.
EIN: 381558108

879
The Whitfield Fund, Inc.
c/o Leon Whitfield
1515 Woodslea Dr.
Flint, MI   48507-1846
County: Genesee

Established in 2006 in MI and TX.
Donors: Leon Whitfield; Rebekkah Serra; Jesakkah Serra.
Grantmaker type: Independent foundation.
Financial data (yr. ended 12/31/09): Assets, $2,483 (M); gifts received, $1,508; expenditures, $711; total giving, $0; qualifying distributions, $0.

Fields of interest: Higher education; Athletics/sports, soccer; Protestant agencies & churches.
Type of support: Scholarships—to individuals.
Limitations: Giving primarily in MI and TX.
Application information: Application form not required.
   Initial approach: Letter
   Deadline(s): None
Officer and Director: Leon Whitfield,* C.E.O.
EIN: 680624077

880
The Whiting Foundation
718 Harrison St.
Flint, MI   48502-1614   (810) 767-3600
County: Genesee
Contact: Donald E. Johnson, Jr., Pres.

Incorporated in 1940 in MI.
Donor: Members of the Johnson family.
Grantmaker type: Independent foundation.
Financial data (yr. ended 06/30/10): Assets, $7,818,477 (M); expenditures, $494,099; total giving, $411,000; qualifying distributions, $454,868; giving activities include $411,000 for 50 grants (high: $50,000; low: $1,000).
Purpose and activities: Giving primarily for cultural activities, and for basic needs for people who are underprivileged.
Fields of interest: Historic preservation/historical societies; Arts; Education; Cancer; Medical research, institute; Housing/shelter, development; Children/youth, services; Community/economic development; United Ways and Federated Giving Programs.
Type of support: General/operating support; Program development.
Limitations: Giving primarily in the Genesee County, MI, area, including the city of Flint.
Application information: Application form not required.
   Initial approach: Concise proposal
   Copies of proposal: 1
   Deadline(s): Apr. 30
Officers: Donald E. Johnson, Jr., Pres.; John T. Lindholm, Secy.-Treas.; Marsha A. Kump, Exec. Dir.
Trustees: Mary Alice J. Heaton; Linda J. LeMieux.
EIN: 386056693
Selected grants: The following grants were reported in 2009.
$50,000 to Flint Cultural Center Corporation, Flint, MI.
$50,000 to Flint Institute of Arts, Flint, MI.
$27,500 to United Way of Genesee County, Flint, MI.
$20,000 to American Red Cross, Flint, MI.
$20,000 to Flint Community Players, Flint, MI.
$17,500 to New McCree Theater, Flint, MI.
$15,000 to Cancer Research Institute, New York, NY.
$5,000 to Lifeline, Peoria, IL.
$5,000 to Memorial Sloan-Kettering Cancer Center, New York, NY.
$2,500 to National Foundation for Cancer Research, Bethesda, MD.

THE MICHIGAN FOUNDATION DIRECTORY   153

881
Henry and Harriet Whiting Memorial Foundation

c/o Fifth Third Bank
P.O. Box 3636
Grand Rapids, MI   49501-3636
County: Kent
Application address: c/o Franklin H. Moore Jr., 200 S. Riverside Ave., St. Clair, MI 48079-5330; tel.: (810) 326-1123

Established in 1950 in MI.
Donor: Harriet Clark Whiting†.
Grantmaker type: Independent foundation.
Financial data (yr. ended 12/31/09): Assets, $2,323,307 (M); expenditures, $128,312; total giving, $106,000; qualifying distributions, $106,000; giving activities include $106,000 for grants.
Purpose and activities: Giving for community foundations, health, religion, youth groups, community services, and federated giving programs.
Fields of interest: Health care; Health organizations, association; Recreation, parks/playgrounds; Youth development; Human services; YM/YWCAs & YM/YWHAs; Children/youth, services; Community/economic development; Foundations (community); United Ways and Federated Giving Programs; Christian agencies & churches.
Type of support: General/operating support; Building/renovation; Equipment; Endowments; Emergency funds.
Limitations: Giving primarily in St. Clair and Port Huron, MI. No grants to individuals.
Application information:
  Initial approach: Letter
  Deadline(s): None
Officers: Franklin H. Moore, Jr., Pres. and Treas.; Charles Staiger, Secy.
Trustee: Frederick S. Moore.
EIN: 386091633
Selected grants: The following grants were reported in 2008.
$10,000 to Mental Health Association in Michigan, Southfield, MI.
$5,000 to Bridge Builders Counseling, Port Huron, MI.
$5,000 to Safe Horizons, Port Huron, MI.
$5,000 to Saint Pauls Episcopal Church, Saint Clair, MI.
$5,000 to Salvation Army, Port Huron, MI.

882
Harvey Randall Wickes Foundation

Plaza N., Ste. 472
4800 Fashion Sq. Blvd.
Saginaw, MI   48604-2677   (989) 799-1850
County: Saginaw
Contact: Hugo E. Braun, Jr., Pres.
FAX: (989) 799-3327; E-mail: hrwickes@att.net

Incorporated in 1945 in MI.
Donors: Harvey Randall Wickes†; members of the Wickes family.
Grantmaker type: Independent foundation.
Financial data (yr. ended 12/31/09): Assets, $35,177,457 (M); expenditures, $2,031,364; total giving, $1,768,248; qualifying distributions, $1,860,162; giving activities include $1,768,248 for 55 grants (high: $757,619; low: $1,000).
Purpose and activities: Giving primarily for civic affairs groups, parks and recreation agencies; support also for a library, youth and social services, hospitals, and cultural programs, for the betterment of Saginaw County, MI.
Fields of interest: Arts; Libraries/library science; Education; Hospitals (general); Recreation; Human services; Children/youth, services.
Type of support: Annual campaigns; Building/renovation; Equipment; Seed money.
Limitations: Applications accepted. Giving limited to the Saginaw, MI, area. No support for government where support is forth coming from tax dollars. No grants to individuals, or for endowments, travel, conferences, or film or video projects; no loans.
Publications: Application guidelines; Financial statement.
Application information: Application form not required.
  Initial approach: Letter followed by proposal
  Copies of proposal: 1
  Deadline(s): Submit proposal 2 weeks prior to meeting
  Board meeting date(s): Mar., June, Sept. and Dec.
  Final notification: 2 weeks following board meeting
Officers and Trustees:* Hugo E. Braun, Jr.,* Pres.; Craig W. Horn,* V.P.; Michele Pavlicek, Secy.; Wlliam A. Hendrick,* Treas.; Mary Lou Case; Ellen Crane; Peter Ewend; William A. Hendrick; Richard Heuschele; Richard Katz.
Number of staff: 1 part-time professional; 1 part-time support.
EIN: 386061470
Selected grants: The following grants were reported in 2007.
$60,000 to Boys and Girls Club of Saginaw County, Saginaw, MI.
$60,000 to Underground Railroad, Saginaw, MI. For parking lot.
$20,000 to Pit and Balcony, Saginaw, MI. For renovations.
$18,000 to First Ward Community Service, Saginaw, MI. For renovations.
$13,000 to Junior Achievement of Northeast Michigan, Saginaw, MI.
$5,000 to City Rescue Mission of Saginaw, Saginaw, MI. For food and consumables.

883
Wickson-Link Memorial Foundation

3023 Davenport St.
P.O. Box 3275
Saginaw, MI   48602-3652
County: Saginaw

Established in 1973 in MI.
Donors: James Wickson†; Meta Wickson†.
Grantmaker type: Independent foundation.
Financial data (yr. ended 12/31/09): Assets, $4,585,354 (M); expenditures, $228,341; total giving, $189,362; qualifying distributions, $206,264; giving activities include $189,362 for 34 grants (high: $16,666; low: $500).
Purpose and activities: Support for community funds, social services and programs for the disadvantaged, youth and child welfare, cultural organizations, health, education, and libraries.
Fields of interest: Arts; Education, early childhood education; Higher education; Business school/education; Libraries/library science; Health care; Health organizations, association; Human services; Children/youth, services; Children/youth; Children; Youth; Minorities; Economically disadvantaged.
Type of support: General/operating support; Continuing support; Management development/capacity building; Capital campaigns; Building/renovation; Equipment; Program development; Matching/challenge support.
Limitations: Applications accepted. Giving primarily in Saginaw County, MI. No support for churches for building or operations. No grants to individuals.
Application information: Application form not required.
  Initial approach: Letter
  Copies of proposal: 7
  Deadline(s): Apr. 1, July 1, Sept. 1, and Dec. 1
  Board meeting date(s): Quarterly
  Final notification: 60 days
Officers: B.J. Humphreys, Pres.; John Humphreys, Secy.; David Beyerlein, Treas.
Directors: Louis Hanisho; Charles Nickless; Susan Piesko.
Number of staff: None.
EIN: 386083931
Selected grants: The following grants were reported in 2008.
$41,667 to Mid-Michigan Childrens Museum, Saginaw, MI. For general support.
$36,867 to Boys and Girls Club of Saginaw County, Saginaw, MI. For general support.
$20,850 to YMCA of Saginaw, Saginaw, MI. For building renovations.
$15,000 to Saginaw School District, Saginaw, MI. For early education and care.
$13,000 to Underground Railroad, Saginaw, MI. For general support.
$11,000 to Delta College Foundation, University Center, MI. For general support.
$10,500 to Saginaw Valley State University Foundation, University Center, MI. For general support.
$7,667 to Old Town Christian Outreach Center, Saginaw, MI. For Soup Kitchen.
$6,000 to Saginaw Art Museum, Saginaw, MI. For general support.
$4,500 to United Way of Saginaw County, Saginaw, MI. For program support.

884
The Wierenga Family Foundation, Inc.

18608 Via Catania
Rancho Santa Fe, CA   92091-0292
(858) 756-2045
County: San Diego
Contact: Wendell Wierenga, Pres.

Established in 2000 in MI.
Donor: Wendell Wierenga.
Grantmaker type: Independent foundation.
Financial data (yr. ended 12/31/09): Assets, $886,707 (M); gifts received, $50; expenditures, $59,057; total giving, $52,000; qualifying distributions, $52,000; giving activities include $52,000 for grants.
Fields of interest: Christian agencies & churches.
Limitations: Giving primarily in MI.
Application information:
  Initial approach: Letter
  Deadline(s): None
Officer: Wendell Wierenga, Pres.
Directors: Melissa Bok; Janelle Wierenga; Pamela Wierenga.
EIN: 943374775

885
Wigginton Educational Foundation

c/o Fifth Third Bank
233 Washington Ave.
Grand Haven, MI 49417-1374
County: Ottawa
Contact: Lisa Danicek, Treas.
Application address: 1415 S. Beachtree St., Grand Haven, MI 49417-2843, tel.: (616) 842-6760

Donor: Ruth Wigginton†.
Grantmaker type: Independent foundation.
Financial data (yr. ended 12/31/09): Assets, $380,096 (M); gifts received, $31; expenditures, $23,053; total giving, $18,178; qualifying distributions, $18,786; giving activities include $18,178 for 90 grants to individuals (high: $1,025; low: $13).
Purpose and activities: Scholarship awards to residents of Grand Haven, or the counties of Ottawa and Muskegon, Michigan.
Fields of interest: Higher education.
Type of support: Scholarships—to individuals.
Limitations: Applications accepted. Giving limited to residents of the City of Grand Haven and Muskegon and Ottawa counties, MI.
Application information: Application form required.
  Deadline(s): 5 days prior to board meeting
  Board meeting date(s): 1st Wed. in Feb., Apr., June, Sept., Oct., and Dec.
Officers: Tracy Wilson, Pres.; Anne Runschke, V.P.; Lisa Danicek, Secy.-Treas.
Trustees: Paul Kunde; Mike Shelton; Sandra Teeple; Sue Mueller; Julia Houle.
EIN: 382388277

886
Wilcox Family Foundation

6377 Cardeno Dr.
La Jolla, CA 92037-6955
County: San Diego
Application address: c/o Win Schrader, 6260 Tower Rd., Plymouth, MI 48170, tel.: (734) 455-6222; URL: http://wilcoxfoundation.org/
Scholarship address: Win Schrader, c/o Plymouth Salem High School, 45181 Joy Rd., Canton, MI 48187

Established in 2002 in MI.
Donor: Daniel Herriman.
Grantmaker type: Independent foundation.
Financial data (yr. ended 12/31/09): Assets, $3,035,348 (M); gifts received, $1,250; expenditures, $166,055; total giving, $99,370; qualifying distributions, $99,370; giving activities include $99,370 for grants.
Purpose and activities: Scholarship awards to high school seniors residing in the Plymouth/Canton school district; grant awards to organizations that improve the quality of life for residents of Plymouth, Michigan.
Fields of interest: Higher education; Human services.
Type of support: General/operating support; Building/renovation; Program development; Scholarships—to individuals.
Limitations: Giving primarily in Plymouth, MI.
Application information: Scholarship applicants must submit an essay or research paper based on the history of one or more of Plymouth, Michigan's longtime businesses or business districts. Application form required.

Initial approach: Completed application form for grants; completed application for scholarships
Deadline(s): Apr. 1 and Oct. 1 for grants; Mar. 22 for scholarships
Officers: Scott Dodge, Pres. and Treas.; Win Schrader, V.P. and Secy.; Dan Herriman, V.P.
EIN: 311804402
Selected grants: The following grants were reported in 2005.
$16,500 to University of Michigan, Ann Arbor, MI.
$16,000 to Salvation Army, Plymouth, MI.
$10,000 to Plymouth, City of, Plymouth, MI.
$3,700 to Plymouth Community Arts Council, Plymouth, MI.
$3,000 to Brigham Young University, Provo, UT.
$3,000 to Cornerstone University, Grand Rapids, MI.
$3,000 to Grand Valley State University, Allendale, MI.
$2,000 to Massachusetts Institute of Technology, Cambridge, MA.
$2,000 to Michigan State University, East Lansing, MI.
$1,500 to DePaul University, Chicago, IL.

887
Ronald A. & Patricia M. Williams Charitable Foundation

1535 44th St. S.W., Ste. 400
Wyoming, MI 49509-4481 (616) 261-2800
County: Kent
Contact: Ronald A. Williams, Pres.

Established in 1997 in MI.
Donor: Ronald A. Williams.
Grantmaker type: Independent foundation.
Financial data (yr. ended 12/31/09): Assets, $1,149,115 (M); expenditures, $87,929; total giving, $81,000; qualifying distributions, $82,215; giving activities include $81,000 for 6 grants (high: $55,000; low: $1,000).
Purpose and activities: Giving primarily for Catholic institutions.
Fields of interest: Children, services; Catholic agencies & churches.
Limitations: Applications accepted. Giving primarily in MI. No grants to individuals.
Application information: Application form not required.
  Initial approach: Proposal
  Deadline(s): None
Officers: Ronald A. Williams, Pres.; Patricia M. Williams, Secy.-Treas.
EIN: 383382931

888
The Jamison Williams Foundation

380 N. Old Woodward Ave., Ste. 300
Birmingham, MI 48009-5322 (248) 642-0333
County: Oakland
Contact: R. Jamison Williams, Jr., Pres.

Established in 1988 in MI.
Donors: R. Jamison Williams; Betty J. Williams.
Grantmaker type: Independent foundation.
Financial data (yr. ended 12/31/09): Assets, $4,547,508 (M); expenditures, $324,929; total giving, $290,000; qualifying distributions, $290,000; giving activities include $290,000 for 21 grants (high: $42,500; low: $1,000).
Purpose and activities: Giving primarily for the arts.

Fields of interest: Museums; Performing arts; Performing arts, orchestras; Performing arts, opera; Arts; Education.
Type of support: General/operating support.
Limitations: Applications accepted. Giving primarily in MI and NY. No grants to individuals.
Application information:
  Initial approach: Proposal
  Deadline(s): None
  Final notification: Within 2 months
Officer and Directors:* R. Jamison Williams, Jr.,* Pres.; Wendy J. Lynch.
EIN: 382837463
Selected grants: The following grants were reported in 2008.
$100,000 to Michigan Opera Theater, Detroit, MI.
$25,000 to American Academy in Rome, New York, NY.
$25,000 to Public Art Fund, New York, NY.
$15,000 to Grass River Natural Area, Bellaire, MI.
$5,000 to Hospice of Michigan, Detroit, MI.
$1,500 to Trisha Brown Dance Company, New York, NY.

889
Elizabeth Ruthruff Wilson Foundation

P.O. Box 1525
Pennington, NJ 08534-1525 (609) 274-6968
County: Mercer
Contact: Theresa Powers
Application address: P.O. Box 27, Tecumseh, MI 49286, tel.: (517) 423-4148
Application address for scholarships: Ms. Janet McDowell, Lenawee Intermediate School District, 4107 North Adrian Hwy., Adrian, MI 49221, tel.: (517) 265-1626

Established in 1997 in Tecumseh, MI.
Donor: Mary Elizabeth Wilson†.
Grantmaker type: Independent foundation.
Financial data (yr. ended 12/31/09): Assets, $3,420,841 (M); expenditures, $231,086; total giving, $164,664; qualifying distributions, $192,767; giving activities include $164,664 for 13 grants (high: $40,000; low: $1,200).
Purpose and activities: Giving for the promotion of music and the performing arts in Lenawee County, Michigan.
Fields of interest: Performing arts, music.
Type of support: Program development; Scholarship funds; Scholarships—to individuals; Matching/challenge support.
Limitations: Applications accepted. Giving primarily in Lenawee County, MI. No support for political or religious organizations, or athletic and recreational facilities. No grants for endowments, salaries, travel expenses, loans or debt retirement, or emergency funding.
Publications: Application guidelines.
Application information: Application form required.
  Initial approach: Letter
  Copies of proposal: 1
  Deadline(s): Dec. and June
  Board meeting date(s): 2nd Tues. in Jan., Apr., July, and Oct.
  Final notification: Jan. and July
Officers: Theresa Powers, Pres. and Treas.; John Waltman, V.P.; Sheri Powers, Secy.
Trustee: Marilyn Mason.
Number of staff: 1 part-time support.
EIN: 383372941
Selected grants: The following grants were reported in 2007.

$40,000 to Lenawee Community Foundation, Tecumseh, MI. For Friends of the Tecumseh Schools Orchestra.
$10,000 to Tecumseh Center for the Arts, Tecumseh, MI.
$7,000 to Adrian Symphony Orchestra, Adrian, MI.
$5,000 to Croswell Opera House and Fine Arts Association, Adrian, MI.
$4,200 to Britton Macon Area School, Britton, MI.
$4,200 to Deerfield Public Schools, Deerfield, MI.

890
Karen Colina Wilson Foundation

1 Heritage Pl., Ste. 261
Southgate, MI 48195-2574 (734) 324-0966
County: Wayne
Contact: Karen M. Wilson, Pres.
FAX: (734) 324-0977; E-mail: tmcquiston@kcwf.org; URL: http://www.kcwf.org/

Donor: Karen M. Wilson.
Grantmaker type: Independent foundation.
Financial data (yr. ended 12/31/09): Assets, $699,123 (M); expenditures, $103,273; total giving, $54,227; qualifying distributions, $54,227; giving activities include $54,227 for grants.
Purpose and activities: Giving primarily to enhance the health, safety, and well being of children, youth, and women, and to develop opportunities in the areas of education, art, literature, and music.
Fields of interest: Performing arts, music; Literature; Arts; Education; Children/youth; Women.
Limitations: Applications accepted. Giving primarily in the southern and western Wayne County, MI, area, with additional support in communities where trustees live. No support for camps that are not locally located. No grants for buildings, construction, capital expenditures, sports activity booster funds, or on-going operational support.
Application information: See foundation web site for guidelines and application form. Application form required.
  Initial approach: Completed application
  Deadline(s): None
Officer: Karen M. Wilson, Pres.
Trustees: Richard Lyons; Trudee (Gertrude) Lyons; Kristi Partain; Robert Partain.
EIN: 205336111

891
Matilda R. Wilson Fund

1901 Saint Antoine St., 6th Fl. (Ford Field)
Detroit, MI 48226-2310
County: Wayne
Contact: David P. Larsen, Secy.
FAX: (313) 393-7579;
E-mail: roosterveen@bodmanlaw.com

Incorporated in 1944 in MI.
Donors: Matilda R. Wilson†; Alfred G. Wilson†.
Grantmaker type: Independent foundation.
Financial data (yr. ended 12/31/09): Assets, $26,349,914 (M); expenditures, $3,736,026; total giving, $3,423,605; qualifying distributions, $3,657,130; giving activities include $3,423,605 for 37 grants (high: $500,000; low: $3,000).
Purpose and activities: Support for the arts, youth agencies, higher education, and social services.
Fields of interest: Arts; Higher education; Hospitals (general); Human services; Youth, services.

Type of support: General/operating support; Building/renovation; Equipment; Endowments; Program development; Scholarship funds; Research; Matching/challenge support.
Limitations: Applications accepted. Giving primarily in southeast MI. No grants to individuals; no loans.
Application information: Application form not required.
  Initial approach: Letter
  Copies of proposal: 1
  Deadline(s): None
  Board meeting date(s): Jan., Apr., and Sept.
  Final notification: At the Jan., Apr., and Sept. board meetings
Officers and Trustees:* David M. Hempstead,* Pres.; David P. Larsen,* Secy.; David B. Stephens,* Treas.
EIN: 386087665
Selected grants: The following grants were reported in 2006.
$3,597,103 to Oakland University, Rochester, MI. For capital support for Meadowbrook Hall.
$500,000 to Michigan State University, East Lansing, MI. For capital support for critical care center.
$105,000 to Chamber Music Society of Detroit, Farmington Hills, MI. For general operating support.
$100,000 to College for Creative Studies, Detroit, MI. For general operating support.
$100,000 to Detroit Symphony Orchestra, Detroit, MI. For capital support.
$62,500 to Bon Secours Cottage Health Services, Grosse Pointe, MI. For capital support for emergency center.
$50,000 to Alma College, Alma, MI. For general operating support.
$50,000 to Beloit College, Beloit, WI. For general operating support.
$50,000 to Friends School in Detroit, Detroit, MI. For general operating support.
$50,000 to Michigan Opera Theater, Detroit, MI. For general operating support.

892
Wilson Scholarship Fund

(formerly Rodney B. Wilson Scholarship Fund)
c/o Citizens Bank Wealth Management, N.A.
328 S. Saginaw St., M/C 002072
Flint, MI 48502-1923
County: Genesee
Application address: c/o St. John's Public High School, Attn.: Janet Thelen, P.O. Box 230, St. Johns, MI 48879-0230, tel.: (989) 227-4023

Established in 2004 in MI.
Donor: Rodney B. Wilson.
Grantmaker type: Independent foundation.
Financial data (yr. ended 12/31/09): Assets, $345,274 (M); expenditures, $45,635; total giving, $40,000; qualifying distributions, $40,000; giving activities include $40,000 for grants to individuals.
Purpose and activities: Scholarship awards to graduating seniors at St. John's Public High School, Michigan, who are in the upper one-third of their class.
Fields of interest: Higher education.
Type of support: Scholarships—to individuals.
Limitations: Applications accepted. Giving limited to residents of St. John's, MI.
Application information: Application form required.
  Deadline(s): Apr. 1 and Aug. 1
Trustee: Citizens Bank.
EIN: 386619088

893
Lula C. Wilson Trust

c/o JPMorgan Chase Bank, N.A.
1116 W. Long Lake, 2nd Fl.
Bloomfield Hills, MI 48302-1963
(248) 645-7308
County: Oakland
FAX: (248) 645-5742;
E-mail: nayda.schwartz@jpmorgan.com

Trust established in 1963 in MI.
Donor: Lula C. Wilson†.
Grantmaker type: Independent foundation.
Financial data (yr. ended 12/31/09): Assets, $2,526,227 (M); expenditures, $169,523; total giving, $148,700; qualifying distributions, $154,368; giving activities include $148,700 for 37 grants (high: $7,500; low: $1,250).
Purpose and activities: Giving primarily for community development; also for family and social services, youth and child welfare, women, the handicapped, hospices, performing arts groups and other cultural programs, and higher and secondary education.
Fields of interest: Performing arts; Performing arts, theater; Arts; Child development, education; Secondary school/education; Higher education; Reproductive health, family planning; Substance abuse, services; Human services; Children/youth, services; Child development, services; Family services; Residential/custodial care, hospices; Women, centers/services; Community/economic development; Disabilities, people with; Women; Economically disadvantaged.
Type of support: General/operating support; Continuing support; Annual campaigns; Capital campaigns; Building/renovation; Equipment; Emergency funds; Seed money; Program-related investments/loans; Matching/challenge support.
Limitations: Applications accepted. Giving limited to Pontiac and Oakland County, MI. No grants to individuals, or for endowment funds, research, deficit financing, land acquisition, special projects, publications, conferences, scholarships, or fellowships.
Application information: Application form not required.
  Initial approach: Letter
  Copies of proposal: 1
  Deadline(s): None
  Board meeting date(s): As required
  Final notification: 1 month
Trustee: JPMorgan Chase Bank, N.A.
EIN: 386058895
Selected grants: The following grants were reported in 2008.
$10,000 to Judson Center, Royal Oak, MI.
$10,000 to March of Dimes Birth Defects Foundation, Southfield, MI.
$10,000 to On My Own of Michigan, Troy, MI.
$10,000 to Saint Joseph Mercy Oakland, Pontiac, MI.
$7,500 to Lighthouse Emergency Services, Pontiac, MI.
$7,500 to Open Door Outreach Center, Waterford, MI.
$7,301 to Special Olympics Michigan, Central Michigan University, Mount Pleasant, MI.
$4,000 to Childrens Leukemia Foundation of Michigan, Southfield, MI.
$3,250 to Oakland County Pioneer and Historical Society, Pontiac, MI.
$2,500 to Eisenhower Dance Ensemble, Southfield, MI.

894
Charles Stanley Wilson, Jr. Foundation, Inc.
19440 Bretton Dr.
Detroit, MI 48223-1271
County: Wayne

Established in 2007 in MI.
Donors: Carol Ann Wilson Allen; Chris Allen.
Grantmaker type: Independent foundation.
Financial data (yr. ended 12/31/09): Assets, $2,836 (M); gifts received, $2,600; expenditures, $5,778; total giving, $2,500; qualifying distributions, $2,500; giving activities include $2,500 for grants.
Fields of interest: United Ways and Federated Giving Programs.
Limitations: Giving primarily in GA.
Officers: Carol Jean Wilson Allen, Chair.; Candice A. Mullings, Secy.; Poppy Marable, Treas.
Board Member: Lawrence Denson.
EIN: 431833000

895
Winans Foundation Trust
P.O. Box 47650
Oak Park, MI 48237-5350
County: Oakland

Donor: Michael L. Winans.
Grantmaker type: Independent foundation.
Financial data (yr. ended 12/31/08): Assets, $6,990 (M); gifts received, $5,667,024; expenditures, $5,913,553; total giving, $5,547,713; qualifying distributions, $5,547,713; giving activities include $5,547,713 for grants.
Trustee: Michael Winans, Jr.
EIN: 616333623

896
The Irving Winer Foundation
(formerly Irving Winer Charitable Trust)
P.O. Box 75000
Detroit, MI 48275-3302
County: Wayne
Contact: Donald Winer, Tr.

Grantmaker type: Independent foundation.
Financial data (yr. ended 12/31/08): Assets, $192,727 (M); gifts received, $1,900; expenditures, $11,776; total giving, $9,090; qualifying distributions, $9,090; giving activities include $9,090 for grants.
Fields of interest: Arts; Education.
Limitations: Giving primarily in FL.
Application information: Application form not required.
Deadline(s): None
Trustees: Margaret Winer Sherin; Peter M. Sherin; Donald Winer.
EIN: 596210819

897
John J. Winkler Memorial Trust
c/o University of Michigan, English Dept.
3187 Angell Hall
435 S. State St.
Ann Arbor, MI 48109-1003 (734) 647-5884
County: Washtenaw

Established in 1990 in CA.
Grantmaker type: Independent foundation.
Financial data (yr. ended 05/31/10): Assets, $27,057 (M); gifts received, $527; expenditures, $2,894; total giving, $2,000; qualifying distributions, $2,000; giving activities include $2,000 for 2 grants to individuals (high: $1,000; low: $1,000).
Purpose and activities: Grant awards for written work to students in the classics awarding the Winkler Prize to winners.
Fields of interest: Journalism school/education.
Type of support: Grants to individuals.
Application information: Application form not required.
Initial approach: Essay on neglected or marginal topics in classical studies
Deadline(s): Apr. 1
Trustees: David M. Halperin; David A. Braaten; Lesley Dean-Jones; Kirk Ormand; Daniel L. Selden; Froma I. Zeitlin.
EIN: 776062330

898
Bill and June Winn Foundation
9450 Cottage Pointe Dr.
Charlevoix, MI 49720-2041
County: Charlevoix
Contact: William H. Winn, Sr., Pres.
Application Address: P.O. Box 4219, Traverse City, MI 49685-4219, tel.: (231) 922-7777

Established in 1988 in MI.
Donors: William H. Winn, Sr.; June C. Winn.
Grantmaker type: Independent foundation.
Financial data (yr. ended 12/31/09): Assets, $56,242 (M); expenditures, $32,310; total giving, $29,149; qualifying distributions, $29,149; giving activities include $29,149 for grants.
Fields of interest: Arts; Higher education; Human services.
Type of support: General/operating support.
Limitations: Giving primarily in FL and the Washington, DC area, including VA. No grants to individuals.
Application information: Application form not required.
Initial approach: Letter or telephone
Deadline(s): None
Officers: William H. Winn, Sr., Pres.; June C. Winn, Secy.-Treas.
EIN: 382786283

899
John and Zita Winn Foundation
(formerly John and Mary Jo Winn Foundation)
125 Belvedere Ave.
Charlevoix, MI 49720-1410
County: Charlevoix
Contact: John A. Winn, Pres.

Established in 1988 in MI.
Donors: John A. Winn; Mary Jo Winn.
Grantmaker type: Independent foundation.
Financial data (yr. ended 12/31/09): Assets, $11,413 (M); expenditures, $181; total giving, $0; qualifying distributions, $0.
Fields of interest: Environmental education; Athletics/sports, training; Foundations (community).
Type of support: General/operating support.

Limitations: Applications accepted. Giving primarily in MI.
Application information: Application form not required.
Initial approach: Letter
Deadline(s): None
Officer: John A. Winn, Pres. and Secy.-Treas.
Trustee: Dorenda R. Buisch.
EIN: 382792625

900
Winship Memorial Scholarship Foundation
c/o Comerica Bank, Trust Div.
49 W. Michigan Ave.
Battle Creek, MI 49017-3603 (269) 966-6344
County: Calhoun

Established in 1961 in MI.
Donor: Virginia Winship†.
Grantmaker type: Independent foundation.
Financial data (yr. ended 12/31/09): Assets, $3,239,706 (M); expenditures, $235,234; total giving, $165,600; qualifying distributions, $207,561; giving activities include $165,600 for 87 grants to individuals (high: $3,150; low: $800).
Purpose and activities: Scholarships only for graduates of Battle Creek, Michigan, area public high schools.
Fields of interest: Education.
Type of support: Scholarships—to individuals.
Limitations: Applications accepted. Giving limited to residents of the Battle Creek, MI, area.
Publications: Application guidelines; Annual report; Informational brochure.
Application information: Application form required.
Copies of proposal: 1
Deadline(s): Nov. 15th
Board meeting date(s): 3rd Wed. in Apr.
Officers and Trustees:* David P. Lucas,* Pres.; Kathy Shaw,* V.P.; Lori A. Hill, Secy.; Michael J. Evans, Exec. Dir.; Bruce Barney; Kim Brubaker; Marilyn Burtrum; Donna Gray; Pat Howard; Terrance Lunger; John Stetler; Erick Stewart; William S. Ticknor.
Corporate Trustee: Comerica Bank.
EIN: 386092543

901
Evelyn and Ronald Wirick Foundation
504 Maple Dr.
Morenci, MI 49256-1222 (517) 458-7189
County: Lenawee
Contact: Ralph R. Ferris, Pres.

Established in 1987 in MI.
Grantmaker type: Independent foundation.
Financial data (yr. ended 12/31/09): Assets, $1,097,746 (M); expenditures, $50,703; total giving, $28,800; qualifying distributions, $28,800; giving activities include $28,800 for grants to individuals.
Purpose and activities: Scholarship awards to the graduates of the Morenci Public School District, Michigan.
Fields of interest: Higher education.
Type of support: Scholarships—to individuals.
Limitations: Applications accepted. Giving limited to residents of Morenci, MI.
Application information:
Initial approach: Letter
Deadline(s): None

Officers: Ralph R. Ferris, Pres.; Margaret Porter, V.P.; Judy J. Randall, Secy.; Mary E. Ferris, Treas. **Trustees:** Russell Beaverson; Dale Stormer.
EIN: 382700421

902
John W. and Wanda A. Wirtz Charitable Foundation
c/o John W. Wirtz
P.O. Box 610037
Port Huron, MI 48061-0037
County: St. Clair

Established in 2001 in MI.
Donors: John W. Wirtz; Wanda A. Wirtz.
Grantmaker type: Independent foundation.
Financial data (yr. ended 12/31/09): Assets, $44,181 (M); gifts received, $40; expenditures, $14,415; total giving, $13,625; qualifying distributions, $13,625; giving activities include $13,625 for 20 grants (high: $5,000; low: $75).
Fields of interest: Education; End of life care; YM/YWCAs & YM/YWHAs; Religion.
Type of support: General/operating support.
Application information: Application form not required.
  Initial approach: Letter
  Deadline(s): None
Trustee: John W. Wirtz.
EIN: 383640193

903
Wirtz Family Foundation
1105 24th St.
P.O. Box 5006
Port Huron, MI 48061-5006
County: St. Clair

Established in 2000 in MI.
Grantmaker type: Independent foundation.
Financial data (yr. ended 12/31/09): Assets, $33,280 (M); gifts received, $1,240; expenditures, $12,532; total giving, $11,100; qualifying distributions, $11,100; giving activities include $11,100 for 4 grants (high: $9,000; low: $100).
Fields of interest: Higher education.
Limitations: Giving primarily in MI. No grants to individuals.
Application information: Application form not required.
  Initial approach: Letter
  Deadline(s): None
Officers: John O. Wirtz, Pres.; Jason T. Wirtz, V.P.; John W. Wirtz II, Secy.
EIN: 383572595

904
Wise Fund
2026 Devonshire Rd.
Ann Arbor, MI 48104-4058
County: Washtenaw

Established in MI.
Donor: Manfred Kochen‡.
Grantmaker type: Independent foundation.
Financial data (yr. ended 12/31/09): Assets, $136 (M); expenditures, $55; total giving, $25; qualifying distributions, $25; giving activities include $25 for grants.

Officer: Paula Kochen, Pres.
EIN: 382441115

905
WMY Fund
(formerly William R. & Madeleine Couzens Yaw Foundation)
c/o Miller, Canfield, Paddock & Stone
840 W. Long Lake Rd., Ste. 200
Troy, MI 48098-6358 (248) 879-2000
County: Oakland
Contact: Dawn Schluter Esq.

Established in 1987 in MI.
Donor: William Rumer Yaw‡.
Grantmaker type: Independent foundation.
Financial data (yr. ended 12/31/09): Assets, $625,408 (M); expenditures, $53,804; total giving, $40,000; qualifying distributions, $46,901; giving activities include $40,000 for 44 grants (high: $3,300; low: $200).
Fields of interest: Arts; Higher education; Health care; Human services; Children/youth, services; Christian agencies & churches.
Type of support: General/operating support.
Limitations: Applications accepted. Giving primarily in Washington, DC, MD, MI, and VA. No grants to individuals.
Application information: Application form not required.
  Initial approach: Letter
  Deadline(s): None
Officers: Margot Y. Burgwyn, Pres.; James J. Yaw, V.P. and Treas.; Madeleine Yaw Kirk, V.P.; Carol K. Yaw, Secy.
EIN: 382364686

906
Wolfe Family Foundation
(formerly Howard H. & Joan M. Wolfe Family Foundation)
909 Willow St.
Ann Arbor, MI 48103-3741
County: Washtenaw
Contact: Howard H. Wolfe, Pres.

Established in 1984 in MI.
Donor: Howard H. Wolfe.
Grantmaker type: Independent foundation.
Financial data (yr. ended 04/30/10): Assets, $324,561 (M); expenditures, $32,343; total giving, $31,500; qualifying distributions, $31,500; giving activities include $31,500 for grants.
Fields of interest: Higher education; Protestant agencies & churches.
Limitations: Giving primarily in FL, VA, and WV. No grants to individuals.
Application information:
  Initial approach: Letter
  Deadline(s): None
Officers and Directors:* Howard H. Wolfe,* Pres.; C. Christopher Wolfe,* V.P.; Ann H. Doerfler; Victoria R. Mueller.
EIN: 382532527

907
Jean & Lewis Wolff Family Foundation
c/o Comerica Bank
P.O. Box 75000, MC 3302
Detroit, MI 48275-3302
County: Wayne
Application address: c/o Keith Wolff, 11828 La Grange Ave., Ste. 200, Los Angeles, CA 90025-5200, tel.: (650) 462-6016

Established in 1998 in CA.
Donors: Jean Wolff; Lewis Wolff.
Grantmaker type: Independent foundation.
Financial data (yr. ended 05/31/10): Assets, $1,109,166 (M); expenditures, $129,256; total giving, $115,100; qualifying distributions, $115,100; giving activities include $115,100 for grants.
Fields of interest: Museums (art); Education; Reproductive health, family planning; Health organizations, association; Human services; Children/youth, services; Jewish agencies & synagogues.
Limitations: Applications accepted. Giving primarily in CA. No grants to individuals.
Application information: Application form not required.
  Initial approach: Letter
  Deadline(s): None
Officers: Lewis Wolff, Pres.; Jean Wolff, V.P.; Kevin Wolff, V.P.; Kari Wolff Goldstein, Secy.; Keith Wolff, Treas.
EIN: 954679221
Selected grants: The following grants were reported in 2009.
$10,000 to Child Advocates of Silicon Valley, Milpitas, CA.
$5,000 to Planned Parenthood Los Angeles, Los Angeles, CA.
$5,000 to Rush University Medical Center, Chicago, IL.
$2,500 to Alliance for School Choice, Washington, DC.

908
Kate & Richard Wolters Foundation
2260 Cascade Springs Dr. S.E.
Grand Rapids, MI 49546-7410 (616) 956-9030
County: Kent
Contact: Kate P. Wolters, Pres.

Established in 1997 in MI.
Donors: Kate Pew Wolters; Richard Wolters‡; Robert C. Pew.
Grantmaker type: Independent foundation.
Financial data (yr. ended 12/31/09): Assets, $6,390,827 (M); gifts received, $200,000; expenditures, $1,561,489; total giving, $1,519,000; qualifying distributions, $1,522,330; giving activities include $1,519,000 for 26 grants (high: $500,000; low: $1,000).
Purpose and activities: Giving primarily for arts and culture, higher education, health organizations, and human services.
Fields of interest: Museums (art); Performing arts, orchestras; Arts; Higher education; Health organizations; Human services; United Ways and Federated Giving Programs; Religious federated giving programs; Disabilities, people with.
Type of support: Endowments; General/operating support; Capital campaigns; Program development.
Limitations: Applications accepted. Giving primarily in Grand Rapids, MI.

Application information:
Initial approach: Letter
Deadline(s): None
Officer and Trustee: Kate Pew Wolters,* Pres. and
Secy.-Treas.
EIN: 383384598
Selected grants: The following grants were reported
in 2009.
$500,000 to Michigan State University, East
Lansing, MI.
$250,000 to Mayo Foundation, Jacksonville, FL.
$160,000 to Urban Institute for Contemporary Arts,
Grand Rapids, MI.
$120,000 to Grand Rapids Art Museum, Grand
Rapids, MI.
$100,000 to Grand Rapids Art Museum, Grand
Rapids, MI.
$25,000 to Aquinas College, Grand Rapids, MI.
$25,000 to Aquinas College, Grand Rapids, MI.
$15,000 to Aquinas College, Grand Rapids, MI.
$15,000 to Saint Cecilia Music Society, Grand
Rapids, MI.

909
The Lawrence and Sylvia Wong Foundation

6378 Hart Dr.
Kalamazoo, MI   49009-6805
County: Kalamazoo
Application address: c/o James Vanderroest, 834
King Hwy., Ste. 110, Kalamazoo, MI 49001-2579,
tel.: (269) 344-9236

Established in 1995 in MI.
Donors: Lawrence Wong; Sylvia Wong.
Grantmaker type: Independent foundation.
Financial data (yr. ended 12/31/09): Assets,
$1,130,266 (M); expenditures, $84,463; total
giving, $72,500; qualifying distributions, $72,500;
giving activities include $72,500 for grants.
Purpose and activities: Giving to organizations
which benefit southwestern Michigan children,
including through the visual and performing arts;
giving also for education about and the preservation
of endangered species of plants and animals,
medical research for the understanding of Sjogren's
Syndrome and related diseases and their treatment,
and the conservation of areas of significant
biodiversity.
Fields of interest: Environment, natural resources;
Animals/wildlife, endangered species; Health
organizations; Youth development.
Limitations: Applications accepted. Giving primarily
in southwestern MI.
Application information: Application form not
required.
Deadline(s): Sept. 30
Officers and Directors: Sylvia Wong,* Pres.;
Michael Wong,* V.P. and Treas.; James
Vanderroest, Secy.; Laura Wong.
EIN: 383244488
Selected grants: The following grants were reported
in 2008.
$10,000 to Kalamazoo Nature Center, Kalamazoo,
MI.
$8,000 to Nature Conservancy, Arlington, VA.
$8,000 to Southwest Michigan Land Conservancy,
Portage, MI.
$5,000 to Food Bank of South Central Michigan,
Battle Creek, MI.
$5,000 to Fred Hutchinson Cancer Research
Center, Seattle, WA.
$5,000 to Kalamazoo Institute of Arts, Kalamazoo,
MI.

$4,000 to Bat Conservation International, Austin,
TX.
$4,000 to Kalamazoo Valley Community College
Foundation, Kalamazoo, MI.
$4,000 to Sjogrens Syndrome Foundation,
Bethesda, MD.
$4,000 to United Way of Saint Joseph County, South
Bend, IN.

910
The Workers Foundation

567 Purdy St.
Birmingham, MI   48009-1736   (248) 642-0910
County: Oakland
Contact: Edward F. Andrews, Jr., Pres.

Established in 1993 in MI.
Donor: General Motors Corp.
Grantmaker type: Independent foundation.
Financial data (yr. ended 12/31/09): Assets,
$351,923 (M); expenditures, $8,246; total giving,
$8,000; qualifying distributions, $8,000; giving
activities include $8,000 for grants.
Fields of interest: Elementary/secondary school
reform; Employment, services; Food services;
Housing/shelter, temporary shelter.
Limitations: Giving limited to MI, with emphasis on
Detroit.
Application information:
Initial approach: Letter
Deadline(s): None
Final notification: Within 2 months
Officers: Edward F. Andrews, Jr., Pres. and Treas.;
Robert C. Seger, V.P. and Secy.
EIN: 383112401

911
World Heritage Foundation

2675 W. Jefferson Ave.
Trenton, MI   48183-3284
County: Wayne
Contact: Waltraud Prechter, Chair.

Established in 1985 in MI.
Donors: Heinz C. Prechter‡; Thomas Denomme;
Waltraud E. Prechter; Heinz C. Prechter Charitable
Lead Trust.
Grantmaker type: Independent foundation.
Financial data (yr. ended 12/31/09): Assets,
$9,429,868 (M); gifts received, $1,092,316;
expenditures, $565,277; total giving, $460,030;
qualifying distributions, $478,050; giving activities
include $460,030 for 82 grants (high: $100,000;
low: $100).
Purpose and activities: Giving primarily for
education and medical research; funding also for the
arts, social services, and children's services,
including a children's hospital.
Fields of interest: Arts; Higher education; Hospitals
(specialty); Health care; Health organizations,
association; Medical research, institute; Human
services; Children/youth, services.
Type of support: General/operating support; Capital
campaigns; Program development; Professorships.
Limitations: Giving primarily in MI; some giving also
in Washington, DC. No grants to individuals.
Publications: Informational brochure (including
application guidelines).
Application information: Application form required.
Initial approach: Letter
Deadline(s): None

Officers: Waltraud Prechter, Chair. and Pres.; Paul
Prechter, V.P.; Stephanie Prechter, Treas.
Director: J. Patrick Howe.
EIN: 382640416
Selected grants: The following grants were reported
in 2008.
$100,000 to Georgetown University, Washington,
DC.
$12,500 to Covenant House Michigan, Detroit, MI.
$10,000 to College for Creative Studies, Detroit, MI.
$10,000 to College for Creative Studies, Detroit, MI.
$10,000 to University of Detroit Mercy, Detroit, MI.
$5,000 to Henry Ford Health System, Detroit, MI.
$5,000 to Oakwood Healthcare System Foundation,
Dearborn, MI.
$1,000 to Henry Ford Health System, Detroit, MI.
$1,000 to Hospice of Michigan, Detroit, MI.
$1,000 to Soldiers Angels, Pasadena, CA.

912
The Worsham Family Foundation

7465 Sweetbriar
West Bloomfield, MI   48324-2555
County: Oakland

Established in 2006 in MI.
Donor: Richard B. Worsham.
Grantmaker type: Independent foundation.
Financial data (yr. ended 12/31/09): Assets,
$236,429 (M); gifts received, $15,000;
expenditures, $14,123; total giving, $12,000;
qualifying distributions, $12,000; giving activities
include $12,000 for grants.
Fields of interest: Animal welfare; Children,
services.
Director: Richard B. Worsham.
EIN: 205698279

913
V. Ennis Wright Trust

c/o Citizens Bank, Wealth Mgmt.
328 Saginaw St., MC 002072
Flint, MI   48502-1923
County: Genesee
Contact: Richard D. Fauble
Application address: c/o Litchfield Community
Schools, 210 Williams St., Litchfield, MI 49252,
tel.: (517) 542-2388

Established in 1998 in MI.
Donor: V. Ennis Wright‡.
Grantmaker type: Independent foundation.
Financial data (yr. ended 12/31/09): Assets,
$492,292 (M); expenditures, $6,575; total giving,
$0; qualifying distributions, $1,179.
Purpose and activities: Scholarships awarded to
graduates of Litchfield Community High School.
Fields of interest: Education.
Type of support: Scholarships—to individuals.
Limitations: Giving limited to residents of Litchfield,
MI.
Application information: Application available in the
Litchfield Counseling Office. Application form
required.
Deadline(s): May 15
Trustee: Citizens Bank, N.A.
EIN: 386115132

914
Robert & Patricia Wynalda Foundation
3395 Valley View
Rockford, MI   49341-8032   (616) 866-1561
County: Kent
Contact: Robert Wynalda

Established in 1989 in MI.
Donors: Wynalda Litho, Inc.; Robert Wynalda;
Patricia Wynalda.
Grantmaker type: Independent foundation.
Financial data (yr. ended 12/31/09): Assets,
$4,969 (M); expenditures, $585; total giving, $0;
qualifying distributions, $0.
Purpose and activities: Giving primarily to missions.
Fields of interest: Christian agencies & churches;
Religion.
Type of support: General/operating support;
Continuing support; Building/renovation; Land
acquisition; Debt reduction; Emergency funds.
Limitations: Giving primarily in MI and PA. No grants
to individuals.
Application information: Application form not
required.
  Initial approach: Letter
  Copies of proposal: 3
  Deadline(s): None
Officers: Robert Wynalda, Pres. and Treas.; Patricia
Wynalda, V.P. and Secy.
Director: Robert Wynalda, Jr.
EIN: 382851989
Selected grants: The following grants were reported
in 2005.
$10,000 to Bibles International, Grand Rapids, MI.

915
Frederick and Katherine Yaffe Foundation
(formerly Frederick S. Yaffe Foundation)
2000 Tiverton Rd.
Bloomfield Hills, MI   48304-2392
County: Oakland
Contact: Frederick Yaffe, Chair.
Application address: 26913 Northwestern Hwy., Ste.
500, Southfield, MI 48034-4715

Established in 1995 in MI.
Donors: Frederick Yaffe; Katherine Yaffe; The Fung
Foundation.
Grantmaker type: Independent foundation.
Financial data (yr. ended 12/31/09): Assets,
$10,523 (M); gifts received, $10,000;
expenditures, $10,361; total giving, $0; qualifying
distributions, $0.
Fields of interest: Higher education; Human
services; Jewish agencies & synagogues.
Limitations: Applications accepted. Giving primarily
in MI.
Application information: Application form not
required.
  Deadline(s): None
Officers and Directors:* Frederick Yaffe,* Chair.;
Katherine Yaffe,* Secy.; John Cassidy, Treas.
EIN: 383232086

916
Yankama Feed the Children Charitable Foundation
601 S. Shore Dr.
Battle Creek, MI   49014-5440   (269) 962-2055
County: Calhoun

Established in 1994 in MI.
Donor: Andrew S. Yankama.
Grantmaker type: Independent foundation.
Financial data (yr. ended 12/31/09): Assets,
$4,351 (M); gifts received, $39,164; expenditures,
$38,704; total giving, $36,814; qualifying
distributions, $38,704; giving activities include
$36,814 for 6 grants to individuals (high: $18,500;
low: $100).
Fields of interest: Food services; Christian agencies
& churches; Children/youth; Economically
disadvantaged.
Type of support: General/operating support; Grants
to individuals.
Limitations: Giving in the U.S., primarily in Battle
Creek, MI; giving also in Canada and Guyana.
Officers: Andrew S. Yankama, Pres.; Rachel D.
Yankama, Treas.
EIN: 383219667

917
The Thomas and Maria Yeager Family Foundation
544 Ridgeway St.
St. Joseph, MI   49085-1033
County: Berrien
Contact: Thomas C. Yeager, Pres.

Established in 2007 in MI.
Donor: Printek, Inc.
Grantmaker type: Independent foundation.
Financial data (yr. ended 12/31/09): Assets,
$581,682 (M); expenditures, $12,645; total giving,
$8,600; qualifying distributions, $10,622; giving
activities include $8,600 for 3 grants (high: $5,000;
low: $1,000).
Fields of interest: Crime/law enforcement, police
agencies.
Limitations: Giving primarily in Benton Harbor, MI.
No grants to individuals.
Application information:
  Initial approach: Letter
  Deadline(s): None
Officers: Thomas C. Yeager, Pres.; Julie Kay
Payovich, V.P.; T.J. Passaro, Secy.; David
Vanderploeg, Treas.
EIN: 261141395

918
Charles F. Yeager Foundation, Inc.
3155 W. Big Beaver Rd., Ste. 103
Troy, MI   48084-3006   (248) 643-4965
County: Oakland
Contact: Mark Zurek, Pres.

Established in 2001 in MI.
Donor: Charles F. Yeager Trust.
Grantmaker type: Independent foundation.
Financial data (yr. ended 12/31/09): Assets,
$219,814 (M); expenditures, $49,211; total giving,
$11,325; qualifying distributions, $11,325; giving
activities include $11,325 for grants.
Fields of interest: Hospitals (specialty); Pediatrics
research; Medical research; Human services;
Children/youth, services.
Type of support: General/operating support.
Limitations: Giving primarily in MI and Memphis, TN.
Application information:
  Initial approach: Letter
  Deadline(s): None
  Final notification: 2 months

Officers: Mark Zurek, Pres.; Wayne Stewart,
Secy.-Treas.
EIN: 383530854

919
Yeo Family Foundation
1169 Glendale St.
Saginaw, MI   48603-4722   (989) 792-7151
County: Saginaw
Contact: Judith N. Yeo, Pres.

Established in 1994 in MI.
Donors: Judith N. Yeo; Lloyd J. Yeo‡.
Grantmaker type: Independent foundation.
Financial data (yr. ended 12/31/09): Assets,
$224,908 (M); gifts received, $88,861;
expenditures, $39,570; total giving, $39,275;
qualifying distributions, $39,275; giving activities
include $39,275 for 13 grants (high: $12,000; low:
$100).
Fields of interest: Human services; Community/
economic development.
Limitations: Applications accepted. Giving primarily
in Saginaw, MI. No grants to individuals.
Application information: Application form not
required.
  Initial approach: Letter
  Deadline(s): None
Officers: Judith N. Yeo, Pres.; William E. Yeo, V.P.;
Barbara Haines, Secy.
EIN: 382426134

920
Jerome B. & Eilene M. York Foundation
950 Lake George Rd.
Oakland, MI   48363-1118
County: Oakland
Application address: c/o Jerome B. York, 3700
Tremonte Cir. S., Rochester, MI 48306

Established in 1997 in MI.
Donors: Eilene M. York; Jerome B. York.
Grantmaker type: Independent foundation.
Financial data (yr. ended 12/31/09): Assets,
$18,899 (M); gifts received, $2,485; expenditures,
$11,485; total giving, $9,000; qualifying
distributions, $11,470; giving activities include
$9,000 for 3 grants (high: $5,000; low: $2,000).
Fields of interest: Elementary school/education;
Protestant agencies & churches.
Type of support: General/operating support.
Limitations: Applications accepted. Giving primarily
in MI.
Application information: Application form not
required.
  Initial approach: Letter of inquiry
  Deadline(s): None
Trustees: Eilene M. York; Jerome B. York; Lisa
Shelton.
EIN: 383353431

921
Young Foundation
6372 Muirfield Ct.
Bloomfield Hills, MI   48301-1503
County: Oakland
Contact: Donna H. Young, Secy.-Treas.

Established in 1994 in MI.
Donor: Walter R. Young, Jr.
Grantmaker type: Independent foundation.

Financial data (yr. ended 12/31/09): Assets, $2,656,252 (M); expenditures, $136,721; total giving, $133,100; qualifying distributions, $135,370; giving activities include $133,100 for 18 grants (high: $30,000; low: $600).
Purpose and activities: Giving primarily for innovative, quality projects that will benefit at-risk children and families.
Fields of interest: Humanities; Education; Human services; Children, services; Family services.
Type of support: General/operating support; Program development.
Limitations: Applications accepted. Giving primarily in Oakland County, MI. No support for political organizations. No grants to individuals (including scholarships), or for endowments.
Application information: Application form required.
  Initial approach: Letter
  Copies of proposal: 1
  Deadline(s): Nov. 1
Officers: Walter R. Young, Jr., Pres.; Donna H. Young, Secy.-Treas.
Directors: Mark Young; Michelle Young-Bueltel.
Number of staff: None.
EIN: 383193515

922
Young Woman's Home Association
(formerly Young Woman's Home Association of Detroit)
c/o Grant Chair
17150 Waterloo
Grosse Pointe, MI 48230-1201
County: Wayne
E-mail: ywha@inbox.com

Established in 1877 in MI.
Donor: Jessie Castle Roberts†.
Grantmaker type: Independent foundation.
Financial data (yr. ended 04/30/10): Assets, $2,040,842 (M); gifts received, $6,394; expenditures, $113,814; total giving, $102,150; qualifying distributions, $102,150; giving activities include $102,150 for grants.
Purpose and activities: Grants made to non-profit organizations that provide basic needs and educational programs for disadvantaged women and children in the Detroit, Michigan, metropolitan area.
Fields of interest: Child development, education; Children/youth, services; Disabilities, people with; Women; Economically disadvantaged.
Type of support: Continuing support; Equipment; Emergency funds; Program development; Curriculum development.
Limitations: Applications accepted. Giving in the Detroit, MI, metropolitan area. No grants for general operating budgets, capital campaigns, salaries, start-up programs, or scholarships.
Application information: Application form required.
  Initial approach: Letter or e-mail requesting application
  Copies of proposal: 1
  Deadline(s): Sept. 1 for fall grants and Mar. 1 for spring grants
  Board meeting date(s): 3rd Tues. of Jan., Mar., Apr., Sept., Oct., and Dec.
  Final notification: Apr. or Oct.
Officers and Trustees:* Susan Durant, Pres.; Patricia Colett,* V.P.; Susan Heinen,* Recording Secy.; Kathy Forster, Corresponding Secy.; Ann Nicholson,* Treas.; and 14 additional trustees.
EIN: 381360595

Selected grants: The following grants were reported in 2007.
$5,000 to Assistance League of Southeastern Michigan, Rochester Hills, MI. For Operation School Bell.
$4,500 to Fowler Center, Mayville, MI. For camperships.
$4,000 to City Mission, Detroit, MI. For computers.

923
The Youth Foundation of America
P.O. Box 2068
Petoskey, MI 49770-2068   (906) 847-3351
County: Emmet
Contact: Paul W. Brown, Tr.

Incorporated in 1947 in MI.
Donor: Franklin C. Browne Trust.
Grantmaker type: Independent foundation.
Financial data (yr. ended 12/31/09): Assets, $18,251 (M); gifts received, $58,176; expenditures, $66,218; total giving, $4,000; qualifying distributions, $4,000; giving activities include $4,000 for grants.
Purpose and activities: Grants to Michigan organizations that provide outdoor, overnight camping experience for Michigan youth.
Fields of interest: Recreation, camps; Youth development, scouting agencies (general); YM/YWCAs & YM/YWHAs.
Type of support: General/operating support.
Limitations: Giving limited to MI. No grants to individuals.
Application information: Application form not required.
  Initial approach: Letter
  Copies of proposal: 1
  Deadline(s): None
  Board meeting date(s): Annually
Trustees: Robert Bales, Jr.; Paul W. Brown; Kimberly Hines; Pamela Siena.
EIN: 386090960

924
The T. K. Zampetis Family Foundation
125 Wakefield Run Blvd.
Hinckley, OH 44233-9224   (330) 659-3076
County: Medina
Contact: Theodore K. Zampetis, Pres.

Established in 2004 in OH.
Donor: Theodore K. Zampetis.
Grantmaker type: Independent foundation.
Financial data (yr. ended 12/31/09): Assets, $1,238,504 (M); expenditures, $60,422; total giving, $53,500; qualifying distributions, $53,500; giving activities include $53,500 for grants.
Fields of interest: Orthodox agencies & churches.
Limitations: Applications accepted. Giving primarily in NY and OH; some giving also in MI and PA.
Application information:
  Initial approach: Letter
  Deadline(s): None
Officers: Theodore K. Zampetis, Pres.; Constantine T. Zampetis, V.P.; Callie A. Zampetis, Secy.; Ann J. Zampetis, Treas.
EIN: 202057665

925
Beverly A. Zelt Foundation
10153 E. Munro Lake Dr.
Levering, MI 49755-8507
County: Emmet
Contact: Beverly A. Zelt, Pres.

Established in 2002 in MI.
Grantmaker type: Independent foundation.
Financial data (yr. ended 12/31/09): Assets, $4,840 (M); expenditures, $847; total giving, $800; qualifying distributions, $800; giving activities include $800 for grants.
Fields of interest: Protestant agencies & churches.
Limitations: Giving primarily in CA.
Application information:
  Initial approach: Letter
  Deadline(s): None
Officer: Beverly A. Zelt, Pres. and Secy.-Treas.
EIN: 371423013

926
Zemke Scholarship Fund
4396 Coats Grove Rd.
Hastings, MI 49058-8425
County: Barry
Application address: c/o Maple Valley Schools, Attn.: Dawn Yager, Guidance Dept., 11090 Nashville Hwy., Vermontville, MI 49096-8578

Donor: Martha Zemke.
Grantmaker type: Independent foundation.
Financial data (yr. ended 12/31/09): Assets, $14,135 (M); gifts received, $73; expenditures, $513; total giving, $500; qualifying distributions, $500; giving activities include $500 for grants.
Purpose and activities: Scholarship awards for one year to graduating seniors at Maple Valley High School, Michigan, intending to study agriculture, health, education, mathematics or science.
Fields of interest: Higher education.
Type of support: Scholarships—to individuals.
Limitations: Giving limited to the residents of Vermontville, MI, area.
Application information: Application form required.
  Deadline(s): Apr. 1
Trustees: Durwood Bocher; Jeanne Bocher; Margaret Cook; Edith Grashuis; Mary Zemke.
EIN: 386515402

927
Zimmerman-Wolff Family Foundation
c/o Comerica Bank
P.O. Box 75000, MC 3302
Detroit, MI 48275-3302
County: Wayne
Contact: Amy Zimmerman Wolff, Pres.
Application address: 11828 La Grange Ave., Ste. 200, Los Angeles, CA 90025-5212, tel.: (310) 966-2373

Established in CA.
Donors: Keith Wolff; Amy Zimmerman Wolff.
Grantmaker type: Independent foundation.
Financial data (yr. ended 12/31/09): Assets, $77,476 (M); expenditures, $6,456; total giving, $6,250; qualifying distributions, $6,250; giving activities include $6,250 for grants.
Fields of interest: Education; Human services; Christian agencies & churches.
Type of support: General/operating support.

Limitations: Giving primarily in CA. No grants to individuals.
Application information: Application form not required.
   Initial approach: Letter
   Deadline(s): None
Officers: Amy Zimmerman Wolff, Pres.; Keith Wolff, Secy.-Treas.
EIN: 954718221

928
The Zionist Cultural Committee
6735 Telegraph Rd., Ste. 350
Bloomfield Hills, MI   48301-3173
County: Oakland
Contact: Dr. Lester Zeff, V.P.
Application address: 4318 Bristol Dr., Troy, MI 48098-4866

Established in 1999 in MI.
Donor: Jewish Welfare Federation Metro Detroit.
Grantmaker type: Independent foundation.
Financial data (yr. ended 06/30/09): Assets, $216,683 (M); expenditures, $15,602; total giving, $12,000; qualifying distributions, $12,000; giving activities include $12,000 for grants.
Fields of interest: Jewish agencies & synagogues.
Type of support: General/operating support.
Limitations: Giving primarily in Bloomfield Hills, MI. No grants to individuals.
Application information:
   Initial approach: Letter
   Deadline(s): None
Officers: George P. Mann, Pres.; Beverly Baker, V.P. and Secy.; Ann Gonte-Silver, V.P.; Dr. Lester Zeff, V.P.; Sidney Silverman, Treas.
EIN: 383473208

929
Zoller Family Foundation
26235 Pembroke Rd.
Huntington Woods, MI   48070-1624
County: Oakland
Contact: Howard L. Zoller, Treas.
Application address: 25800 Northwestern Hwy., Ste. 950, Southfield, MI 48075-6116, tel.: (248) 353-5559

Established in 1990; funded in 1991.
Grantmaker type: Independent foundation.
Financial data (yr. ended 12/31/09): Assets, $41,960 (M); gifts received, $2,000; expenditures, $2,650; total giving, $2,500; qualifying distributions, $2,500; giving activities include $2,500 for grants.
Purpose and activities: Scholarship awards paid through the University of Florida, College of Design,

Construction and Planning for students who are residents.
Fields of interest: Higher education.
Type of support: Scholarship funds.
Limitations: Giving primarily in Gainesville, FL. No grants to individuals.
Application information:
   Initial approach: Letter
   Deadline(s): None
Officers: Lawrence C. Zoller, Pres.; Walter F. Zoller, Secy.; Howard L. Zoller, Treas.
EIN: 382948781

930
P. J. and Mary Zondervan Foundation
(also known as Zondervan Foundation)
2955 Shady Oaks Dr. S.W.
Grandville, MI   49418-2049
County: Kent
Application address: c/o Mary Beth Schouten, 752 Bragg Hill, Norwich, VT 05055-9596

Established in 1981 in MI.
Donors: Peter J. Zondervan†; Mary Zondervan.
Grantmaker type: Independent foundation.
Financial data (yr. ended 12/31/09): Assets, $3,006,324 (M); gifts received, $1,010,353; expenditures, $149,863; total giving, $114,700; qualifying distributions, $114,700; giving activities include $114,700 for grants.
Purpose and activities: To spread the gospel of Jesus Christ.
Fields of interest: Theological school/education; Christian agencies & churches.
Type of support: Professorships; Equipment; Program development; Conferences/seminars; Curriculum development; Scholarship funds; Research.
Limitations: Applications accepted. Giving primarily in MI. No grants to individuals.
Application information: Application form required.
   Initial approach: Letter
   Deadline(s): None; requests are reviewed in Apr. and Sept.
   Final notification: Within 12 months
Officers and Directors: * Robert Lee Zondervan, M.D.*, Pres.; Mary Beth Schouten,* Secy.; Tom Kladder,* Treas.; Norman Pylman.
EIN: 382411884
Selected grants: The following grants were reported in 2007.
$101,700 to Calvin Theological Seminary, Grand Rapids, MI.
$4,573 to Potters House, Grand Rapids, MI.
$2,500 to House of Hope, Northwest Michigan, Traverse City, MI.
$2,500 to Volunteers in Service, Grand Rapids, MI.

$2,000 to Calvin Christian School Association, Grandville, MI.
$2,000 to Foothill Country Day School, Claremont, CA.
$2,000 to Forgotten Man Ministries, Grand Rapids, MI.
$2,000 to Gideons International, Nashville, TN.
$2,000 to Guiding Light Mission, Grand Rapids, MI.
$2,000 to Samaritan Counseling Center, Upland, CA.

931
Zonta Club of Muskegon Area Foundation
2340 Glade Rd.
Muskegon, MI   49444-1317
County: Muskegon

Established in 2006 in MI.
Donor: Zonta Club of Muskegon.
Grantmaker type: Independent foundation.
Financial data (yr. ended 05/31/07): Assets, $11,944 (M); gifts received, $15,627; expenditures, $7,170; total giving, $6,182; qualifying distributions, $9,577; giving activities include $6,182 for grants, and $3,395 for foundation-administered programs.
Limitations: Giving primarily in Muskegon, MI.
Officers: Mary Wolfinger, Pres.; Linda Walker, V.P.; Lynda Varin, Secy.; JoAnne Hoekenga, Treas.
Directors: Dolores Brondyke; Susan Schecter.
EIN: 261208329

932
W. Tom Zurschmiede, Sr. Foundation
10 Stratton Pl.
Grosse Pointe Shores, MI   48236-1755
County: Wayne
Contact: Kathryn Groesbeck
Application address: 9512 Peninsula Dr., Traverse City, MI 49686, tel.: (231) 929-7417

Donors: W. Thomas Zurschmiede; W. Thomas Zurschmiede, Jr.
Grantmaker type: Independent foundation.
Financial data (yr. ended 12/31/09): Assets, $21,796 (M); gifts received, $1,000; expenditures, $1,664; total giving, $700; qualifying distributions, $700; giving activities include $700 for grants.
Fields of interest: Arts; Education; Health care; Human services.
Limitations: Giving primarily in MI. No grants to individuals.
Application information:
   Initial approach: Letter
   Deadline(s): None
Officer: W. Thomas Zurschmiede, Jr., Chair.
EIN: 237423944

CORPORATE FUNDERS

933
Abbott Fund
(formerly Abbott Laboratories Fund)
100 Abbott Park Rd., D379/AP6D
Abbott Park, IL 60064-3500 (847) 937-7075
County: Lake
Contact: Cindy Schwab, V.P.
URL: http://www.abbottfund.org

Incorporated in 1951 in IL.
Donor: Abbott Laboratories.
Grantmaker type: Company-sponsored foundation.
Financial data (yr. ended 12/31/09): Assets,
$171,252,256 (M); gifts received, $901,667;
expenditures, $43,707,701; total giving,
$34,202,053; qualifying distributions,
$43,580,165; giving activities include
$34,202,053 for grants.
Purpose and activities: The fund supports
organizations involved with arts and culture,
education, health, mental health, oncology,
cardiovascular health, HIV/AIDS, diabetes, career
development, nutrition, human services, community
development, science, civic affairs, children,
minorities, and economically disadvantaged people.
Fields of interest: Arts; Elementary/secondary
education; Higher education; Education; Health
care, infants; Reproductive health, OBGYN/Birthing
centers; Health care; Mental health/crisis services;
Cancer; Heart & circulatory diseases; AIDS;
Diabetes; Employment, training; Nutrition; Family
services; Human services; Community/economic
development; United Ways and Federated Giving
Programs; Science, formal/general education;
Science; Public affairs; Children; Minorities;
Economically disadvantaged.
Type of support: General/operating support;
Continuing support; Fellowships; Scholarship funds;
Research; Employee matching gifts.
Limitations: Applications accepted. Giving on a
national and international basis in areas of company
operations, with emphasis on Casa Grande, AZ,
Alameda, Fairfield, Redwood City, and Santa Clara,
CA, Abbott Park, Des Plaines, and North Chicago, IL,
Worcester, MA, Sturgis, MI, Columbus, OH, Irving,
TX, Barceloneta and Jayuya, PR, Altavista, VA, Rio
de Janeiro, Brazil, Brockville and Kanata, Canada,
Abingdon and Queensborough, England,
Delkenheim and Ludwigshafen, Germany, Clonmel,
Cootehill, and Sligo, Ireland, Campoverde, Italy,
Katsuyama, Japan, and Zwolle, Netherlands. No
support for social organizations, political parties or
candidates, sectarian religious organizations, or
trade or business associations. No grants to
individuals, or for scholarships, advertising journals
or booklets, capital campaigns, congresses,
symposiums, or meetings, medical research that
supports Abbott products, political activities,
fundraising events, ticket purchases, sporting
events, travel, trips, tours, or cultural exchange
programs; no employee volunteer services.
Publications: Application guidelines; Program policy
statement.
Application information: Eligibility test must be
completed and passed to get access to on-line
application. Requests for funding to the United Way

and its agencies will be considered on an exception
basis only. Unsolicited applications for Global AIDS
Care are not accepted. Grant requests should not
exceed $100,000. Grants in excess of $100,000
will be considered only by invitation. Application form
not required.
   Initial approach: Complete online application
   Deadline(s): Jan. to Oct.
   Board meeting date(s): Ongoing
   Final notification: 6 to 8 weeks
Officers and Directors:* Catherine V. Babington,*
Pres.; Cindy Schwab, V.P.; Brian J. Smith, Secy.;
Carol Sebesta, Treas.; Thomas M. Wascoe; Miles D.
White.
Number of staff: 1 full-time professional; 1 part-time
professional; 1 full-time support; 1 part-time
support.
EIN: 366069793
Selected grants: The following grants were reported
in 2007.
$4,767,133 to Baylor College of Medicine
International Pediatric AIDS Initiative, Houston, TX.
$3,205,627 to Axios Foundation, Cleveland, OH. For
work in Tanzania.
$2,606,212 to JK Group, Plainsboro, NJ.
$1,218,554 to International HIV/AIDS Alliance,
Brighton, England.
$1,098,617 to Family Health International,
Washington Office, Arlington, VA.
$900,000 to Project HOPE - The People-to-People
Health Foundation, Millwood, VA.
$254,652 to United Way of the Inland Valleys,
Riverside, CA.
$50,000 to American College of Medical Genetics
Foundation, Bethesda, MD.
$50,000 to TOUCH Foundation, New York, NY.
$20,000 to Redwood City Education Foundation,
Redwood City, CA.

934
AEP Corporate Giving Program
1 Riverside Plz.
Columbus, OH 43215-2355
County: Franklin
Contact: Mary K. Walsh, Community Rels. Mgr.
E-mail: mkwalsh@aep.com; E-mail:
rody_woischke@aep.com; URL: http://
www.aep.com/citizenship/community/

Grantmaker type: Corporate giving program.
Financial data (yr. ended 12/31/08): Total giving,
$11,945,314, including $11,945,314 for grants.
Purpose and activities: AEP makes charitable
contributions to nonprofit organizations involved
with K-12 education. Support is given primarily in
areas of company operations.
Fields of interest: Elementary/secondary
education.
Type of support: General/operating support;
Sponsorships; Employee matching gifts.
Limitations: Giving primarily in areas of company
operations in AR, IN, KY, LA, MI, OH, OK, TN, TX, VA,
and WV.
Application information: Application form not
required.

Initial approach: Proposal to headquarters
Deadline(s): None
Final notification: Varies

935
The Allstate Foundation
2775 Sanders Rd., Ste. F4
Northbrook, IL 60062-6127 (847) 402-5502
County: Cook
Contact: Jan Epstein, Exec. Dir.
FAX: (847) 326-7517; E-mail: Grants@Allstate.com;
Additional Tel.: (847) 402-2794; E-mail for Keep the
Drive High School Journalism Awards:
KeeptheDrive@allstate.com; URL: http://
www.allstate.com/citizenship/
Allstate-foundation.aspx

Incorporated in 1952 in IL.
Donors: The Allstate Corp.; Allstate Insurance Co.
Grantmaker type: Company-sponsored foundation.
Financial data (yr. ended 12/31/09): Assets,
$31,544,604 (M); gifts received, $16,699,793;
expenditures, $18,671,058; total giving,
$18,344,750; qualifying distributions,
$18,641,831; giving activities include
$18,344,750 for 2,753 grants (high: $1,025,000;
low: $25).
Purpose and activities: The foundation supports
organizations involved with education, youth
anti-violence, employment, disaster relief,
automotive safety, domestic violence, financial and
economic literacy, diversity, neighborhood
development, and economic development.
Fields of interest: Education; Crime/violence
prevention, youth; Employment, services;
Employment, training; Employment; Disasters,
preparedness/services; Safety, automotive safety;
Safety/disasters; Family services, domestic
violence; Human services, financial counseling;
Civil/human rights, equal rights; Civil rights, race/
intergroup relations; Community development,
neighborhood development; Economic
development.
Type of support: General/operating support;
Management development/capacity building;
Program development; Conferences/seminars;
Film/video/radio; Publication; Curriculum
development; Employee volunteer services;
Employee matching gifts; Employee-related
scholarships.
Limitations: Applications accepted. Giving in areas
of company operations, in AK, AL, AR, AZ, CA, CO,
CT, DC, DE, FL, GA, HI, IA, ID, IL, IN, KS, KY, LA, MD,
ME, MI, MN, MO, MS, MT, NC, ND, NE, NH, NJ, NM,
NV, NY, OH, OK, OR, PA, RI, SC, SD, TN, TX, UT, VA,
VT, WA, WI, WV, and WY; giving also to regional and
national organizations. No support for athletic
teams, bands or choirs, religious organizations not
of direct benefit to the entire community,
pass-through organizations, scouting groups, or
private elementary or secondary schools. No grants
to individuals (except for employee-related
scholarships), or for fundraising events or
sponsorships, capital campaigns or endowments,
equipment not part of a community outreach

program, athletic events, memorials, travel, audio, film, or video production, or continuing support.

Publications: Application guidelines; Grants list; Informational brochure (including application guidelines); Program policy statement.

Application information: Application form required.

Initial approach: Complete online eligibility quiz and application; complete online application for Keep the Drive High School Journalism Awards and Act Out Loud

Deadline(s): Varies for Teen Safe Driving, Domestic Violence, Safe and Vital Communities, Economic Empowerment, and Tolerance, Inclusion, and Diversity; None; Oct. 1 to Mar. 1 for Keep the Drive High School Journalism Awards; Sept. 30 to Apr. 11 for Act Out Loud

Board meeting date(s): Mar., June, Sept., and Dec.

Officers and Trustees:* Thomas J. Wilson,* Pres.; Joan H. Walker,* V.P. and Secy.; Judith P. Greffin,* V.P. and C.I.O; Victoria A. Dinges, V.P.; San L. Macrie, V.P.; Steven C. Verney, Treas.; Jan Epstein,* Exec. Dir.; Don Civgin; Joseph P. Lacher, Jr.; Michele Coleman Mayes; Mathew E. Winter.

Number of staff: 2 full-time professional.

EIN: 366116535

Selected grants: The following grants were reported in 2009.

$1,025,000 to Museum of Science and Industry, Chicago, IL. For Safe and Vital Communities programs.

$500,000 to Boys and Girls Clubs of America, National Headquarters, Atlanta, GA. For Tolerance and Inclusion programs.

$500,000 to Channel One Network, New York, NY. For Safe and Vital Communities programs.

$400,000 to Junior Achievement Worldwide, Colorado Springs, CO. For Economic Empowerment programs.

$300,000 to National Network to End Domestic Violence, Washington, DC. For Economic Empowerment programs.

$25,000 to Boys and Girls Club of Lake County, North Chicago, IL. For Tolerance and Inclusion programs.

$25,000 to Brees Dream Foundation, Alpine, CA. For Safe and Vital Communities programs.

$10,000 to Gabriels Angels, Mesa, AZ. For operating support.

$10,000 to Junior Achievement of Alaska, Anchorage, AK. For Economic Empowerment programs.

$6,345 to Shepardson Stern and Kaminsky, New York, NY. For Safe and Vital Communities programs.

936
American Axle & Manufacturing Holdings, Inc. Corporate Giving Program

1 Dauch Dr.
Detroit, MI   48211-1198   (313) 758-4884
County: Wayne
Contact: Dawn Uranis, Mgr., Corp. Rels.
FAX: (313) 974-3442; E-mail: uranisd@aam.com

Grantmaker type: Corporate giving program.
Purpose and activities: American Axle & Manufacturing makes charitable contributions to nonprofit organizations involved with education and youth development. Support is given primarily in areas of company operations.
Fields of interest: Education; Youth development.

Type of support: Employee volunteer services; Sponsorships.
Limitations: Giving primarily in areas of company operations.

937
American Electric Power Foundation

c/o AEP Tax Dept.
P.O. Box 16428
Columbus, OH   43216-6428   (614) 716-1000
County: Franklin
Application address: Lynette Cregge, c/o AEP Ohio, 850 Tech Center Dr., Gahanna, OH 43230, E-mail: llcregge@aep.com; URL: http://www.aep.com/citizenship/aepfoundation/

Established in 2005 in OH.
Donor: American Electric Power Service Corp.
Grantmaker type: Company-sponsored foundation.
Financial data (yr. ended 12/31/09): Assets, $65,849,585 (M); expenditures, $11,659,089; total giving, $11,629,202; qualifying distributions, $11,629,202; giving activities include $11,629,202 for 22+ grants (high: $1,363,750).
Purpose and activities: The foundation supports programs designed to improve lives through education from early childhood through higher education; protect the environment; provide basic human services in the areas of hunger, housing, health, and safety; and enrich the quality of life of communities through art, music, and cultural heritage.
Fields of interest: Arts; Elementary/secondary education; Education, early childhood education; Higher education; Education; Environment; Hospitals (general); Health care; Food services; Food banks; Housing/shelter; Safety/disasters; Human services.
Type of support: Scholarship funds; Capital campaigns; Endowments; Building/renovation; Program development; General/operating support; Continuing support.
Limitations: Applications accepted. Giving primarily in areas of company operations in AR, IN, KY, LA, MI, OK, TN, TX, VA, and WV, with an emphasis on OH. No support for religious, fraternal, athletic or veterans' organizations. No grants to individuals.
Publications: Application guidelines; Annual report; IRS Form 990 or 990-PF printed copy available upon request.
Application information: Proposals should be submitted using organization letterhead. Application form not required.

Initial approach: Proposal to nearest company facility
Deadline(s): None

Trustees: Nicholas K. Akins; Carl L. English; Teresa L. McWain; Michael G. Morris; Robert M. Powers; Brian X. Tierney; Susan Tomasky; Dennis E. Welch.
EIN: 203886453

938
Amerisure Mutual Insurance Company Contributions Program

c/o Corp. Contribs.
26777 Halsted Rd.
Farmington Hills, MI   48331-3586
(800) 257-1900
County: Oakland
URL: http://www.amerisure.com/Community_Service.asp

Grantmaker type: Corporate giving program.
Purpose and activities: As a complement to its foundation, Amerisure also makes charitable contributions to organizations directly. Special emphasis is directed toward programs designed to promote children and youth development. Support is given primarily in areas of company operations in Arizona, Florida, Georgia, Illinois, Indiana, Minnesota, Missouri, North Carolina, Tennessee, and Texas, with emphasis on Michigan.
Fields of interest: Arts; Education, association; Education, reform; Education; Health care, patient services; Health care; Genetic diseases and disorders; Heart & circulatory diseases; Neuroscience; Breast cancer research; Athletics/sports, Special Olympics; Boys & girls clubs; Youth development, business; Salvation Army; Children/youth, services; Economics.
Type of support: General/operating support; Employee volunteer services; Sponsorships; Employee matching gifts.
Limitations: Giving primarily in areas of company operations in AZ, FL, GA, IL, IN, MN, MO, NC, TN, and TX, with emphasis on MI; giving also to national organizations.
Number of staff: 5 full-time professional.

939
Amway Corporation Contributions Program

5101 Spaulding Plz. S.E.
Ada, MI   49355-0001
County: Kent
E-mail: contributions@amway.com; URL: http://www.amwayonebyone.com

Grantmaker type: Corporate giving program.
Purpose and activities: Amway makes charitable contributions to nonprofit organizations involved with at-risk children. Support is given primarily in areas of company operations in Buena Park, California, Lakeview, California, Norcross, Georgia, Honolulu, Hawaii, Arlington, Texas, and Kent, Washington, with emphasis on the greater Grand Rapids, Michigan, area, and in Africa, Asia, Australia, Europe, and Latin America.
Fields of interest: Arts; Health care; Nutrition; Disasters, preparedness/services; Boys & girls clubs; Children, services; Developmentally disabled, centers & services; Children.
International interests: Africa; Asia; Australia; Europe; Latin America.
Type of support: General/operating support; Employee volunteer services; In-kind gifts.
Limitations: Applications accepted. Giving primarily in areas of company operations in Buena Park and Lakeview, CA, Norcross, GA, Honolulu, HI, Arlington, TX, and Kent, WA, with emphasis on the greater Grand Rapids, MI, area, and in Africa, Asia, Australia, Europe, and Latin America. No support for fraternal organizations or school athletic teams, bands, or choirs, political, legislative, or lobbying organizations. No grants to individuals, or for travel, scholarships, religious projects, sports or fundraising events, movie, film, or television documentaries, general awareness campaigns, marketing sponsorships, cause-related marketing, or advertising projects; no in-kind gifts for conferences or conventions, personal use, distribution at an expo, fair, or event, family reunions, or sports fundraising events.
Publications: Application guidelines.

Application information: Videos, reports, publications, and other unsolicited materials are not encouraged. In-kind donation values do not exceed $250. Application form required.

> *Initial approach:* Complete online application form
> *Deadline(s):* None
> *Final notification:* 2 months

940
Barton-Malow Company Foundation
c/o Barton-Malow Co.
26500 American Dr.
Southfield, MI 48034-2252
County: Oakland

Established in 1954 in MI.
Donors: Barton-Malow Enterprises, Inc.; Cloverdale Equipment Co.
Grantmaker type: Company-sponsored foundation.
Financial data (yr. ended 03/31/10): Assets, $344,539 (M); gifts received, $300,000; expenditures, $200,171; total giving, $193,551; qualifying distributions, $193,551; giving activities include $193,551 for grants.
Purpose and activities: The foundation supports community foundations and organizations involved with higher education, health, and community development.
Fields of interest: Higher education; Hospitals (general); Health care; Boy scouts; YM/YWCAs & YM/YWHAs; Community/economic development; Foundations (community); United Ways and Federated Giving Programs.
Type of support: General/operating support; Scholarship funds.
Limitations: Applications accepted. Giving primarily in MI. No grants to individuals.
Application information: Application form not required.

> *Initial approach:* Letter of inquiry
> *Deadline(s):* None

Trustee: Douglas Maibach.
EIN: 386088176
Selected grants: The following grants were reported in 2009.
$50,000 to University of Michigan, Office of Medical Development and Alumni Relations, Ann Arbor, MI.
$35,000 to University of Michigan, Office of Medical Development and Alumni Relations, Ann Arbor, MI.
$25,000 to Detroit Renaissance, Detroit, MI.
$15,000 to Habitat for Humanity of Oakland County, Pontiac, MI.
$10,000 to Pennsylvania State University, University Park, PA.
$6,000 to Metropolitan Affairs Coalition, Detroit, MI.
$5,000 to American Cancer Society, Southfield, MI.
$5,000 to American Heart Association, Southfield, MI.
$5,000 to New Detroit, Detroit, MI.
$3,000 to Purdue University, West Lafayette, IN.

941
The Batts Foundation
3855 Sparks Dr. S.E., Ste. 222
Grand Rapids, MI 49546-2427   (616) 956-3053
County: Kent
E-mail: jsand@battsgroup.com

Established in 1988 in MI.
Donor: The Batts Group, Ltd.
Grantmaker type: Company-sponsored foundation.

Financial data (yr. ended 12/31/09): Assets, $1,945,153 (M); expenditures, $66,385; total giving, $49,650; qualifying distributions, $53,040; giving activities include $49,650 for 22 grants (high: $11,000; low: $100).
Purpose and activities: The foundation supports organizations involved with arts and culture, K-12 and higher education, disease, and human services.
Fields of interest: Arts; Elementary/secondary education; Higher education; Health organizations; Children/youth, services; Human services.
Type of support: General/operating support; Continuing support; Annual campaigns; Capital campaigns; Building/renovation; Endowments; Program development; Scholarship funds; Matching/challenge support.
Limitations: Applications accepted. Giving primarily in Holland, Zeeland, and the Grand Rapids, MI, area. No grants to individuals.
Application information: Application form not required.

> *Initial approach:* Proposal
> *Copies of proposal:* 1
> *Deadline(s):* None

Officer and Directors:* John H. Batts,* Pres.; James L. Batts; John T. Batts; Michael A. Batts; Robert H. Batts.
Number of staff: 1 part-time support.
EIN: 382782168

942
Blue Cross Blue Shield of Michigan Corporate Giving Program
c/o Corp. Contribs.
600 E. Lafayette Blvd., M.C. 1808
Detroit, MI 48226-2927   (313) 225-0539
County: Wayne
FAX: (313) 225-9693;
E-mail: volunteer@bcbsm.com; URL: http://www.bcbsm.com/home/commitment/community_support.shtml

Grantmaker type: Corporate giving program.
Purpose and activities: As a complement to its foundation, Blue Cross Blue Shield of Michigan also makes charitable contributions to nonprofit organizations directly. Support is limited to Michigan.
Fields of interest: Public health; Public health, physical fitness; Health care; Nutrition; Youth; Aging.
Type of support: General/operating support; Employee volunteer services.
Limitations: Applications accepted. Giving limited to areas of company operations in MI. No support for political organizations or candidates or alumni associations. No grants to individuals, or for political campaigns, extracurricular school activities, endowments, scholarships, research, multi-year pledges, general operating expenses, group travel, or capital campaigns.
Publications: Application guidelines.
Application information: Application form required.

> *Initial approach:* Download application form and mail with proposal to headquarters
> *Deadline(s):* None
> *Final notification:* 15 days

Number of staff: 2 part-time professional; 2 part-time support.

943
Bodman LLP
(formerly Bodman, Longley & Dahling LLP)
1901 St. Antoine St., 6th Fl., Ford Field
Detroit, MI 48226   (313) 259-7777
County: Wayne
Contact: Christopher J. Dine, Partner
FAX: (313) 393-7579; E-mail: cdine@bodmanllp.com; URL: http://www.bodmanllp.com/givingback.php

Grantmaker type: Corporate giving program.
Purpose and activities: Bodman attorneys have a long tradition of supporting worthy organizations through donations, volunteerism and pro bono legal services to charitable and community-based organizations. Its public service commitment extends to universities, professional associations and governmental agencies.
Fields of interest: Legal services; Philanthropy/voluntarism.
Limitations: Giving primarily in MI.

944
Borders Group, Inc. Corporate Giving Program
100 Phoenix Dr.
Ann Arbor, MI 48108-2202
County: Washtenaw
URL: http://www.borders.com/online/store/BGIView_community

Grantmaker type: Corporate giving program.
Purpose and activities: As a complement to its foundation, Borders also makes charitable contributions to organizations directly. Support is given primarily in areas of company operations, with some emphasis on Ann Arbor, Michigan.
Fields of interest: Visual arts; Performing arts; Literature; Education, reading; Education.
Type of support: General/operating support; In-kind gifts.
Limitations: Giving primarily in areas of company operations, with some emphasis on Ann Arbor, MI; giving also to national organizations.
Administrators: Sherry Pringle, Admin., Corp. Affairs; Anne Roman, Dir., Public Affairs.

945
BorgWarner Inc. Corporate Giving Program
3850 Hamlin Rd.
Auburn Hills, MI 48326-2872   (248) 754-9200
County: Oakland
URL: http://www.borgwarner.com/en/Company/SocialResponsibility/default.aspx

Grantmaker type: Corporate giving program.
Purpose and activities: Borg Warner makes charitable contributions to nonprofit organizations involved with children, education, and the environment. Support is given primarily in areas of company operations in Illinois, Michigan, Mississippi, New York, North Carolina, South Carolina, and Texas, and in Brazil, China, France, Germany, Hungary, India, Ireland, Italy, Japan, Mexico, Monaco, Poland, Portugal, South Korea, Spain, and the United Kingdom.
Fields of interest: Education; Environment, energy; Environment; Health care, patient services; Health care; Disasters, preparedness/services; Children,

services; Science; Engineering/technology; General charitable giving; Children.

International interests: Brazil; China; France; Germany; Hungary; India; Ireland; Italy; Japan; Mexico; Monaco; Poland; Portugal; South Korea; Spain; United Kingdom.

Type of support: General/operating support; Employee volunteer services; Employee matching gifts.

Limitations: Giving primarily in areas of company operations in IL, MI, MS, NC, NY, SC, and TX, and in Brazil, China, France, Germany, Hungary, India, Ireland, Italy, Japan, Mexico, Monaco, Poland, Portugal, South Korea, Spain, and the United Kingdom.

946
Butzel Long Charitable Trust
(formerly The Butzel Long Gust & Van Zile Charitable Trust)
150 W. Jefferson Ave., Ste. 100
Detroit, MI 48226-4450 (313) 225-7000
County: Wayne
Contact: Richard E. Rassel, Tr.

Established in 1983 in MI.
Donor: Butzel Long.
Grantmaker type: Company-sponsored foundation.
Financial data (yr. ended 12/31/09): Assets, $5,147 (M); gifts received, $8,242; expenditures, $9,972; total giving, $9,725; qualifying distributions, $9,725; giving activities include $9,725 for grants.
Purpose and activities: The foundation supports organizations involved with education, hunger, and human services. Special emphasis is directed toward legal institutions and Bar related activities.
Fields of interest: Education; Legal services; Food services; YM/YWCAs & YM/YWHAs; Children/youth; Human services; Economically disadvantaged.
Type of support: General/operating support; Annual campaigns; Scholarship funds; Sponsorships.
Limitations: Applications accepted. Giving primarily in MI.
Application information: Application form not required.
   Initial approach: Proposal
   Deadline(s): Dec. 31
Trustees: Keefe Brooks; Phillip Kessler; Joe Melnick; Richard E. Rassel.
EIN: 382384883

947
Cabot Corporation Foundation, Inc.
2 Seaport Ln., Ste. 1300
Boston, MA 02210-2058 (617) 345-0100
County: Suffolk
Contact: Jane A. Bell, Exec. Dir.
E-mail: jane_bell@cabot-corp.com; Additional tel.: (617) 342-6221; Additional Contact: Cynthia L. Gullotii, E-mail: Cynthia_Gullotti@cabot-corp.com; URL: http://www.cabot-corp.com/About-Cabot/Corporate-Giving

Incorporated in 1953 in MA.
Donor: Cabot Corp.
Grantmaker type: Company-sponsored foundation.
Financial data (yr. ended 09/30/09): Assets, $409,959 (M); gifts received, $1,000,000; expenditures, $623,200; total giving, $622,735;

qualifying distributions, $622,735; giving activities include $622,735 for grants.

Purpose and activities: The foundation supports organizations involved with education, the environment, health, safety, human services, community development, and science and technology.

Fields of interest: Elementary/secondary education; Education, early childhood education; Higher education; Education; Environment; Hospitals (general); Health care; Disasters, fire prevention/control; Safety/disasters; Residential/custodial care, hospices; Human services; Community/economic development; United Ways and Federated Giving Programs; Chemistry; Mathematics; Engineering/technology; Computer science; Biology/life sciences; Science.

Type of support: General/operating support; Annual campaigns; Capital campaigns; Building/renovation; Equipment; Program development; Seed money; Scholarship funds; Technical assistance; Employee volunteer services; Employee matching gifts; In-kind gifts; Matching/challenge support.

Limitations: Applications accepted. Giving primarily in areas of company operations in Support is given primarily in areas of company operations in Alpharetta, GA, Tuscola, Il, Franklin and Ville Platte, LA, Billerica, Boston, and Haverhill, MA, Midland, MI, Boyertown, PA, Pampa and The Woodlands, TX, and in Argentina, Belgium, Brazil, Canada, China, Columbia, Czech Republic, Dubai, France, Germany, India, Indonesia, Italy, Japan, Malaysia, Mexico, Netherlands, Norway, Spain, Switzerland, Venezuela, and Wales. No support for religious organizations not of direct benefit to the entire community or political or fraternal organizations. No grants to individuals, or for capital campaigns or endowments, advertising, or dinners.

Publications: Annual report (including application guidelines); Occasional report.

Application information: Organizations receiving support are asked to submit periodic progress reports. Application form required.
   Initial approach: Download application form and email proposal and application form to foundation
   Copies of proposal: 1
   Deadline(s): 1 month prior to board meetings
   Board meeting date(s): Jan., Apr., July, and Oct.
   Final notification: 3 months
Officers and Directors:* Patrick Prevost,* Pres.; Jane A. Bell, Exec. Dir.; John J. Lawler,* Treas.; Christina Bramante; Christopher Cornille; Robby D. Sisco.
EIN: 046035227
Selected grants: The following grants were reported in 2005.
$100,000 to People to People Aid in Support of Nurani Dunia, Athens, OH.
$25,000 to Boston Athenaeum, Boston, MA.
$25,000 to Boyertown Area Multi-Service, Boyertown, PA.

948
Cadillac Products Inc. Foundation
5800 Crooks Rd.
Troy, MI 48098-2830 (248) 879-5000
County: Oakland
Contact: Roger K. Williams, Treas.

Established in 1985 in MI.
Donors: Cadillac Products Inc.; Robert J. Williams, Sr.

Grantmaker type: Company-sponsored foundation.
Financial data (yr. ended 07/31/08): Assets, $776,454 (M); expenditures, $7,014; total giving, $6,000; qualifying distributions, $6,000; giving activities include $6,000 for grants.
Purpose and activities: The foundation supports organizations involved with education, children and youth, human services, and Catholicism.
Fields of interest: Education, fund raising/fund distribution; Higher education; Education; Children/youth, services; Residential/custodial care; Human services; Catholic agencies & churches.
Type of support: General/operating support.
Limitations: Applications accepted. Giving primarily in Phoenix, AZ, and MI.
Application information: Application form not required.
   Initial approach: Letter of inquiry
   Deadline(s): None
Officers: Robert J. Williams, Sr., Pres.; Michael P. Williams II, V.P.; Robert J. Williams, Jr., Secy.; Roger K. Williams, Treas.
EIN: 382636705

949
Campbell Soup Foundation
(formerly Campbell Soup Fund)
1 Campbell Pl.
Camden, NJ 08103-1799 (856) 342-4800
County: Camden
Contact: Jerry S. Buckley, Chair.
E-mail: community_relations@campbellsoup.com; URL: http://www.campbellsoupcompany.com/community_center.asp

Incorporated in 1953 in NJ.
Donor: Campbell Soup Co.
Grantmaker type: Company-sponsored foundation.
Financial data (yr. ended 06/30/09): Assets, $14,821,402 (M); gifts received, $2,250,000; expenditures, $1,600,087; total giving, $1,505,748; qualifying distributions, $1,505,748; giving activities include $1,371,285 for 99 grants (high: $200,000; low: $70), and $134,463 for 137 employee matching gifts.
Purpose and activities: The foundation supports programs designed to promote hunger relief; wellness; education; and community revitalization.
Fields of interest: Performing arts; Higher education; Education; Health care; Food services; Nutrition; Recreation, camps; Recreation; Children/youth, services; Human services; Economic development; Community/economic development; United Ways and Federated Giving Programs.
Type of support: General/operating support; Building/renovation; Equipment; Program development; Employee volunteer services; Employee matching gifts; Employee-related scholarships; Matching/challenge support.
Limitations: Applications accepted. Giving primarily in areas of company operations in Davis, Sacramento, and Stockton, CA, Bloomfield and Norwalk, CT, Lakeland, FL, Downers Grove, IL, Marshall, MI, Maxton, NC, South Plainfield, NJ, Napoleon, Wauseon, and Willard, OH, Denver and Downingtown, PA, Aiken, SC, Paris, TX, Richmond, UT, Everett, WA, and Milwaukee, WI, with emphasis on Camden, NJ. No support for religious organizations not of direct benefit to the entire community, political organizations, or units of government. No grants to individuals (except for employee-related scholarships), or for events or sponsorships.

Publications: Application guidelines.
Application information: Support is limited to 1 contribution per organization during any given year. Application form not required.

> *Initial approach:* E-mail proposal to foundation
> *Copies of proposal:* 1
> *Deadline(s):* None
> *Board meeting date(s):* As required
> *Final notification:* Up to 3 months

Officers and Trustees:* Jerry S. Buckley,* Chair.; Carlos M. Del Sol,* Vice-Chair.; Wendy A. Milanese, Secy.; Ashok Madhaven, Treas.; Anthony P. DiSilvestro, Cont.; Michael Dunn; Karen J. Lewis; Maureen Linder; Steve White.
Number of staff: 1 part-time professional; 1 part-time support.
EIN: 216019196
Selected grants: The following grants were reported in 2008.
$25,000 to Zoological Society of Philadelphia, Philadelphia, PA.
$2,478 to United Way of New York City, New York, NY.
$2,000 to Philadelphia Childrens Alliance, Philadelphia, PA.

950
Charter One Bank Foundation

1215 Superior Ave.
Cleveland, OH   44114   (216) 566-5300
County: Cuyahoga
URL: http://www.charterone.com/community/

Grantmaker type: Corporate giving program.
Purpose and activities: Charter One makes charitable contributions to nonprofit organizations that promote affordable housing, encourage the development of innovative responses to basic human needs, encourage community-based services targeted to low - and moderate-income families and individuals, support community development initiatives that are catalysts for economically distressed areas, and promote new ways to address issues of economic self-sufficiency. Support is given primarily in areas of company operations.
Fields of interest: Housing/shelter; Human services, financial counseling; Human services; Community/economic development; Economically disadvantaged.
Type of support: Annual campaigns; Capital campaigns; Donated products; Employee matching gifts; Employee volunteer services; Program development; Sponsorships; Use of facilities.
Limitations: Applications accepted. Giving primarily in areas of company operations in IL, MI, and OH. No support for religious, political, labor, fraternal, veterans, governmental, quasi-governmental, research, or discriminatory organizations, foundations, or public or private educational institutions. No grants to individuals, or for annual appeals, operating deficits, endowments, conferences and seminars, trips and tours, historic preservation, or payment on bank loans (including loans from Charter One).
Publications: Application guidelines.
Application information: Multiyear grants are generally for a capital campaign and are paid over a three-year period. Application form required.

> *Initial approach:* Complete online application
> *Deadline(s):* None
> *Final notification:* Up to 8 weeks

951
Chemical Financial Corporation Contributions Program

333 E. Main St.
P.O. Box 569
Midland, MI   48640-6511   (800) 567-9757
County: Midland
URL: http://www.chemicalbankmi.com/cb/About_Chemical.htm

Grantmaker type: Corporate giving program.
Purpose and activities: Chemical Financial Corporation makes charitable contributions to nonprofit organizations involved with cancer research, housing, youth development, and community development. Support is given primarily in areas of company operations in Michigan.
Fields of interest: Cancer research; Housing/shelter; Youth development, business; Youth development; Community/economic development; United Ways and Federated Giving Programs.
Type of support: General/operating support; Employee volunteer services.
Limitations: Giving primarily in areas of company operations in MI.

952
CHS Foundation

5500 Cenex Dr.
Inver Grove Heights, MN   55077-1733
(800) 814-0506
County: Dakota
Contact: William J. Nelson, Pres.
FAX: (651) 355-5073;
E-mail: info@chsfoundation.org; URL: http://www.chsfoundation.org
Contact for scholarships: Jennifer Thatcher, Mgr., tel.: (800) 814-0506 ext. 3

Trust established in 1947 in MN.
Donors: Farmers Union Central Exchange, Inc.; CENEX, Inc.; Cenex Harvest States Cooperatives; CHS Inc.
Grantmaker type: Company-sponsored foundation.
Financial data (yr. ended 12/31/09): Assets, $26,510,360 (M); gifts received, $1,250,000; expenditures, $2,367,036; total giving, $1,902,673; qualifying distributions, $2,328,704; giving activities include $1,643,469 for 177 grants (high: $170,000; low: $100), and $259,204 for 69 grants to individuals (high: $12,000; low: $1,000).
Purpose and activities: The foundation supports organizations involved with education, agriculture, safety, youth development, rural development, and leadership development. Special emphasis is directed toward programs that invest in the future of rural America, agriculture, and cooperative business.
Fields of interest: Higher education; Education, community/cooperative; Education; Agriculture; Disasters, preparedness/services; Youth development, agriculture; Youth development; American Red Cross; Rural development; Leadership development; Children/youth; Youth; Adults; Young adults.
Type of support: General/operating support; Annual campaigns; Program development; Conferences/seminars; Seed money; Curriculum development; Scholarship funds; Research; Use of facilities; Sponsorships; Program evaluation; Scholarships—to individuals.
Limitations: Applications accepted. Giving on a national basis, primarily in areas of company

operations in CO, IA, ID, IL, IN, KS, MI, MN, MO, MT, NE, ND, OH, OK, OR, SD, TX, UT, WA, WI, and WY. No support for religious or political organizations. No grants for building projects, debt reduction, community development, or program related loans.
Publications: Application guidelines; Grants list; Informational brochure; Program policy statement.
Application information: Application form required.

> *Initial approach:* Complete online application form
> *Deadline(s):* None; May 1 for High School Scholarships and Two-Year Scholarships; Sept. 30 for Cooperative Education Grants Program
> *Board meeting date(s):* Monthly
> *Final notification:* 30 to 90 days; Dec. for Cooperative Education Grants Program

Officer and Trustees:* Michael Toelle,* Chair.; Robert Bass,* Vice-Chair.; William J. Nelson, Pres.; Bruce Anderson,* Secy.-Treas.; Donald Anthony; Dennis Carlson; Curt Eischens; Steve Fritel; Jerry Hasnedl; David Kayser; James Kile; Randy Knecht; Greg Krueger; Michael Mulcahey; Richard Owen; Steve Riegel; Dan Schurr; Duane Stenzel.
Number of staff: 1 part-time professional; 2 part-time support.
EIN: 416025858
Selected grants: The following grants were reported in 2008.
$114,200 to Future Farmers of America Foundation, National, Indianapolis, IN. For general programming.
$65,000 to Ogallala Commons, Nazareth, TX. For support of youth leadership and internships.
$50,000 to Agriculture Future of America, Kansas City, MO. For support of leadership development and scholarships at annual conference.
$30,000 to Agricultural and Food Sciences Academy, Vadnais Heights, MN. For general programming.
$25,000 to Agrisafe Network, Spencer, IA. For the Live Stronger, Farm Longer program.
$25,000 to Junior Achievement of the Upper Midwest, Maplewood, MN. For Titan Challenge.
$15,000 to Marketplace of Ideas/Marketplace for Kids, Bismarck, ND. For Marketplace for Entrepreneurs program.
$10,000 to Wisconsin Academy of Sciences, Arts and Letters, Council of Rural Initiatives, Madison, WI. For Building Sustainable Communities Through Economic, Organizational and Leadership Development.
$5,000 to Cooperative Network, Madison, WI. For the Big Mac youth cooperative leadership conference.
$5,000 to United States Department of Agriculture, Washington, DC. For Outlook Diversity program.

953
The Circle K Corporation Contributions Program

c/o Comms. Dept.
P.O. Box 52085
Phoenix, AZ   85072-2085
County: Maricopa
Application addresses: FL: 12911 N. Telecom Pkwy., Temple Terrace, FL 33637; AL, AR, Panhandle, FL, LA, MS, and TN: 25 W. Cedar St., Ste. 100, Pensacola, FL 32502; GA, NC, and SC: 2440 Whitehall Dr., Ste. 800, Charlotte, NC 28273; CA, OR, and WA: 495 E. Rincon Ste., 1150, Corona, CA 91709; NM, CO, OK, and TX: 3001 Gateway Dr. Ste. 130, Irving, TX 75063; IA, IL, IN, and KY: P.O. Box 347, Columbus, IN 47201; and MI, OH, and PA: 935

E. Talmadge Ave., Akron, OH 44310; URL: http://www.circlek.com/CircleK/AboutUs/CommunityService.htm

Grantmaker type: Corporate giving program.
Purpose and activities: Circle K makes charitable contributions to nonprofit organizations involved with education, cerebral palsy, hunger, and at-risk youth. Support is given primarily in areas of company operations.
Fields of interest: Education; Cerebral palsy; Agriculture/food; Youth.
Type of support: General/operating support; Program development; Employee volunteer services; Sponsorships; In-kind gifts.
Limitations: Applications accepted. Giving primarily in areas of company operations in AL, AR, AZ, CA, CO, FL, GA, IA, IL, IN, KY, LA, MI, MS, NC, NM, NV, OH, OK, OR, PA, SC, TN, and TX.
Publications: Application guidelines.
Application information: The Communications Department handles giving. Application form not required.

> *Initial approach:* Proposal to nearest application address
> *Copies of proposal:* 1
> *Deadline(s):* None
> *Committee meeting date(s):* Jan. and Feb.
> *Final notification:* 4 to 6 weeks

954
The Cliffs Foundation

(formerly The Cleveland-Cliffs Foundation)
1100 Superior Ave., Ste. 1500
Cleveland, OH 44114-2544
County: Cuyahoga
Contact: Dana W. Byrne, V.P. and Asst. Treas.
URL: http://www.cliffsnaturalresources.com/Development/CommunityRelations/Pages/Cleveland-CliffsFoundation.aspx

Established in 1962 in OH.
Donors: Cleveland-Cliffs Inc.; Tilden Mining Co.; Empire Iron Mining Partnership; Hibbing Taconite Co.; Northshore Mining Co.; Cliffs Natural Resources.
Grantmaker type: Company-sponsored foundation.
Financial data (yr. ended 12/31/09): Assets, $3,432,104 (M); gifts received, $3,000,000; expenditures, $1,786,266; total giving, $1,785,968; qualifying distributions, $1,786,266; giving activities include $1,741,325 for 135 grants (high: $900,000; low: $300), and $44,643 for 34 employee matching gifts.
Purpose and activities: The foundation supports organizations involved with arts and culture, health, human services, and civic affairs. Special emphasis is directed toward education.
Fields of interest: Museums; Performing arts, theater; Performing arts, orchestras; Arts; Higher education; Education; Hospitals (general); Health care; Children/youth, services; Human services; United Ways and Federated Giving Programs; Public affairs.
Type of support: Annual campaigns; Building/renovation; Capital campaigns; Employee matching gifts; General/operating support; Scholarship funds.
Limitations: Applications accepted. Giving primarily in areas of company operations, with emphasis on northwest AL, the upper MI peninsula, northeastern MN, Cleveland, OH, and southern WV. No grants to individuals; no loans.

Publications: Application guidelines.
Application information: Support is limited to 1 contribution per organization during any given year. Application form not required.

> *Initial approach:* Proposal
> *Copies of proposal:* 1
> *Deadline(s):* None

Officers and Trustees:* Joseph A. Carrabba,* Pres.; Donald J. Gallagher,* V.P. and Treas.; Dana W. Byrne, V.P.; George W. Hawk, Jr., Secy.; Laurie Brlas; William R. Calfee.
EIN: 346525124
Selected grants: The following grants were reported in 2009.
$400,000 to Bell Memorial Hospital, Ishpeming, MI.
$10,000 to University of Saint Thomas, Saint Paul, MN.
$6,000 to Negaunee High School, Negaunee, MI.
$5,000 to Kent State University, Kent, OH.
$2,500 to Itasca Community College, Grand Rapids, MN.
$2,000 to Ohio Foundation of Independent Colleges, Columbus, OH.

955
CMS Energy Foundation

c/o Consumers Energy, Tax Dept.
1 Energy Plz., EP 8-210
Jackson, MI 49201-2276   (517) 788-0432
County: Jackson
Contact: Carolyn A. Bloodworth, Secy.-Treas.

Established in 2001 in MI.
Donor: CMS Energy Corp.
Grantmaker type: Company-sponsored foundation.
Financial data (yr. ended 12/31/09): Assets, $98,360 (M); expenditures, $12,420; total giving, $12,400; qualifying distributions, $12,420; giving activities include $12,400 for 5 grants (high: $4,400; low: $1,000).
Purpose and activities: The foundation supports organizations involved with arts and culture, higher education, the environment, human services, community economic development, and civic affairs. Special emphasis is directed toward programs that reach underserved populations and communities.
Fields of interest: Arts; Higher education; Environment; Children/youth, services; Family services; Human services; Economic development; Community/economic development; United Ways and Federated Giving Programs.
Type of support: General/operating support; Capital campaigns; Building/renovation; Equipment.
Limitations: Applications accepted. Giving primarily in areas of company operations, with some emphasis on MI. No support for discriminatory organizations, United Way-supported organizations, political organizations, religious organizations not of direct benefit to the entire community, or labor, veterans', fraternal, or social organizations. No grants to individuals, or for fundraising, debt reduction, sports tournaments, talent or beauty contests, or political campaigns; no loans for small business.
Application information: Proposals should be no longer than 2 pages in length. Additional information may be requested at a later date. Application form not required.

> *Initial approach:* Proposal
> *Deadline(s):* None

Officers and Directors:* David G. Mengebier, Pres.; Carolyn A. Bloodworth, Secy.-Treas.; James E.

Brunner; John M. Butler; David W. Joos; Philip G. Polyak; Thomas J. Webb.
EIN: 383575175

956
Comerica Charitable Foundation

c/o Corporate Contributions
P.O. Box 75000, M.C. 3390
Detroit, MI 48275-3390
County: Wayne
Contact: Caroline E. Chambers, Pres.
FAX: (313) 222-5555; Application addresses: Florida: Corp. Contribs. Mgr., M.C. 5172, 1675 N. Military Trail, Ste. 600, Boca Raton, FL 33486, Michigan: Corp. Contribs. Mgr., M.C. 3390, P.O. Box 75000, Detroit, MI 48275-3390, Texas: Corp. Contribs. Mgr., M.C. 6503, P.O. Box 650282, Dallas, TX 75265-0282, Western Market: Corp. Contribs. Mgr., M.C. 4805, 333 W. Santa Clara St., San Jose, CA 95113; Tel. for Caroline E. Chambers: (313) 222-3571; URL: http://www.comerica.com/vgn-ext-templating/v/index.jsp?vgnextoid=374970d75d994010VgnVCM1000004502a8c0RCRD

Established in 1997 in MI.
Donors: Comerica Bank; Comerica Inc.
Grantmaker type: Company-sponsored foundation.
Financial data (yr. ended 12/31/09): Assets, $479,715 (M); gifts received, $1,900,000; expenditures, $5,937,048; total giving, $5,937,048; qualifying distributions, $5,937,048; giving activities include $5,937,048 for 562 grants (high: $830,000; low: $100).
Purpose and activities: The foundation supports organizations involved with education, health, employment, housing, financial literacy, community development, and economically disadvantaged people, and programs designed to promote diversity and inclusion.
Fields of interest: Elementary/secondary education; Business school/education; Adult/continuing education; Education; Health care; Employment, training; Employment; Housing/shelter; Human services, financial counseling; Civil/human rights, equal rights; Business/industry; Community development, small businesses; Community/economic development; Economically disadvantaged.
Type of support: General/operating support; Capital campaigns; Program development; Scholarship funds.
Limitations: Applications accepted. Giving primarily in areas of company operations in AZ, CA, FL, MI, and TX.
Publications: Application guidelines; Program policy statement.
Application information: Application form not required.

> *Initial approach:* Proposal to application address
> *Deadline(s):* Mar. 15, June 15, Sept 15, and Nov. 15
> *Final notification:* Apr. 15, July 15, Oct. 15, and Dec. 15

Officers and Directors:* Linda D. Forte,* Chair.; Caroline E. Chambers, Pres.; Nicole V. Gersch, Secy.; Paul Burdiss, Treas.; Jon W. Bilstrom.
EIN: 383373052
Selected grants: The following grants were reported in 2008.
$923,000 to United Way for Southeastern Michigan, Detroit, MI.

$137,500 to Womens Initiative for Self Employment, San Francisco, CA.
$100,000 to American Red Cross National Headquarters, Washington, DC.
$100,000 to Detroit Symphony Orchestra, Detroit Symphony Orchestra Hall, Detroit, MI.
$100,000 to Wayne State University, Detroit, MI.
$25,000 to Jewish Federation of Metropolitan Detroit, Bloomfield Hills, MI.
$25,000 to Neighborhood Recovery Community Development Corporation, Houston, TX.
$20,000 to Cranbrook Schools, Bloomfield Hills, MI.
$20,000 to Detroit Historical Society, Detroit, MI.
$15,000 to YMCA, Valley of the Sun, Phoenix, AZ.

957
Comerica Incorporated Corporate Giving Program

c/o Corp. Contribs. Mgr.
MC 3390, P.O. Box 75000
Detroit, MI 48275-3390
County: Wayne
Florida application address: MC 5172, 1675 N. Military Trail, Ste. 600, Boca Raton, FL 33486; Michigan application address: MC 3390, P.O. Box 75000, Detroit, MI 48275; Texas application address: MC 6503, P.O. Box 650282, Dallas, TX 75265; Western application address: MC 4805, 333 West Santa Clara St., San Jose, CA 95113; URL: http://www.comerica.com/vgn-ext-templating/v/index.jsp?vgnextoid=25fa788635bd2010VgnVCM1000004302a8c0RCRD

Grantmaker type: Corporate giving program.
Purpose and activities: As a complement to its foundation, Comerica also makes charitable contributions to nonprofit organizations directly. Support is limited to Arizona, California, Florida, Michigan, and Texas.
Fields of interest: Education; Business/industry; Community development, small businesses; Community/economic development; Economics; Public affairs, finance; Minorities; Adults, women.
Type of support: Equipment; General/operating support; Employee volunteer services; Sponsorships.
Limitations: Applications accepted. Giving limited to AZ, CA, FL, MI, and TX. No grants for capital funding or program development.
Publications: Application guidelines.
Application information: Application form not required.
Initial approach: Mail proposal to nearest application address

958
Con-way Inc. Corporate Giving Program
(formerly CNF Inc. Corporate Giving Program)
2211 Old Earhart Rd., Ste. 100
Ann Arbor, MI 48105-2751 (734) 757-1444
County: Washtenaw
URL: http://www.con-way.com/en/about_con_way/corporate_social_responsibility/

Grantmaker type: Corporate giving program.
Purpose and activities: Con-way makes charitable contributions to nonprofit organizations involved with children, education, health, and motor vehicle safety. Support is given primarily in areas of company operations.

Fields of interest: Education; Health care; Safety, automotive safety; Children, services.
Type of support: General/operating support; Employee volunteer services; Employee-related scholarships.
Limitations: Applications accepted. Giving primarily in areas of company operations.
Application information:
Initial approach: Complete online application

959
ConAgra Foods Foundation
(formerly The ConAgra Foundation, Inc.)
1 ConAgra Dr.
Omaha, NE 68102-5001
County: Douglas
Contact: Candy Becker, Fdn. Coord.
FAX: (402) 595-4595;
E-mail: foundation@conagrafoods.com; URL: http://www.nourishkidstoday.org

Established in 1977.
Donors: ConAgra, Inc.; ConAgra Foods, Inc.; Barbara Rodkin; Gary M. Rodkin.
Grantmaker type: Company-sponsored foundation.
Financial data (yr. ended 05/30/10): Assets, $8,284,780 (M); gifts received, $199,867; expenditures, $4,201,754; total giving, $4,017,824; qualifying distributions, $4,201,754; giving activities include $4,017,824 for 78 grants (high: $1,000,000; low: $250).
Purpose and activities: The foundation supports programs designed to provide solutions for child hunger and nutrition education. Special emphasis is directed toward programs designed to help children in need.
Fields of interest: Public health, physical fitness; Health organizations, research; Health organizations, public education; Agriculture/food, public policy; Agriculture/food, public education; Food services; Food banks; Food services, congregate meals; Nutrition; Agriculture/food; Youth development, agriculture; Children.
Type of support: Management development/capacity building; Program development; Research; Employee matching gifts; Employee-related scholarships; Donated products; In-kind gifts.
Limitations: Applications accepted. Giving on a national basis in areas of company operations, with emphasis on AR, AZ, CA, CO, Washington, DC, FL, GA, ID, IL, IN, LA, MA, MI, MS, NC, NE, NM, OH, OR, PA, SC, TN, TX, WA, and WI. No support for religious organizations not of direct benefit to the entire community, fraternal, social, labor, veteran, or alumni organizations, exclusive membership clubs, professional or amateur sports organizations or teams, political organizations, terrorist organizations or those not compliant with the USA Patriot Act, or elementary or secondary schools. No grants to individuals (except for scholarships), or for fundraising or testimonial events or dinners, travel or tours, advertising, endowments, capital campaigns (unless solicited at the funders discretion), conferences, seminars, workshops, symposia, or publication of proceedings, radio or television programming underwriting, emergency needs, or athletic events.
Publications: Application guidelines; Program policy statement.
Application information: A full proposal may be requested at a later date for Community Impact Grants. Organizations receiving support are asked to

submit interim reports and a final report. Application form required.
Initial approach: Complete online eligibility survey and letter of intent for Community Impact Grants
Deadline(s): Jan. 3 to Jan 19 for Community Impact Grants
Officers: Christopher P. Kircher, Chair.; Kori E. Reed, Pres.; Colleen Batcheler, Secy.; Robert G. Wise, Treas.
Number of staff: 2 full-time professional.
EIN: 362899320
Selected grants: The following grants were reported in 2009.
$715,000 to Creighton University, Omaha, NE.
$500,000 to American Red Cross National Headquarters, Washington, DC. For disaster relief.
$301,903 to Scholarship America, Saint Peter, MN.
$248,500 to United Way of the Midlands, Omaha, NE.
$203,000 to Strategic Air and Space Museum, Ashland, NE.
$88,669 to JK Group, Plainsboro, NJ.
$81,350 to Common Threads, Chicago, IL.
$33,250 to Omaha Theater Company for Young People, Omaha, NE.
$25,000 to Assistance League of Boise, Boise, ID.
$15,000 to United Way of Metropolitan Chicago, Chicago, IL.

960
Consumers Energy Company Contributions Program
(formerly Consumers Power Company Contributions Program)
1 Energy Plz., EP8-210
Jackson, MI 49201-2276
County: Jackson
URL: http://www.consumersenergy.com/content.aspx?id=3221

Grantmaker type: Corporate giving program.
Purpose and activities: As a complement to its foundation, Consumers Energy also makes charitable contributions to nonprofit organizations directly. Support is given primarily in Michigan, with emphasis on the Lower Peninsula.
Fields of interest: Human services; Salvation Army; United Ways and Federated Giving Programs; Utilities; General charitable giving.
Type of support: Equipment; In-kind gifts; General/operating support; Program development; Donated products.
Limitations: Applications accepted. Giving primarily in MI, with emphasis on the Lower Peninsula. No grants to individuals.
Publications: Application guidelines.
Application information: Telephone calls, faxes, and e-mails are not encouraged. Video and computer disk submissions are not accepted. Application form required.
Initial approach: Download application form and mail to headquarters; mail letter of inquiry to headquarters for product donations
Copies of proposal: 1
Deadline(s): None
Committee meeting date(s): Quarterly
Final notification: 6 to 8 weeks
Number of staff: 1 full-time professional; 1 full-time support.

961
Consumers Energy Foundation
(formerly Consumers Power Foundation)
1 Energy Plz., Rm. EP8-210
Jackson, MI 49201-2276 (517) 788-0432
County: Jackson
Contact: Carolyn A. Bloodworth, Secy.-Treas.
FAX: (517) 788-2281;
E-mail: foundation@consumersenergy.com;
Additional tel.: (877) 501-4952; URL: http://
www.consumersenergy.com/foundation

Established in 1990 in MI.
Donors: Consumers Power Co.; Consumers Energy Co.
Grantmaker type: Company-sponsored foundation.
Financial data (yr. ended 12/31/09): Assets, $3,839,173 (M); expenditures, $998,637; total giving, $998,617; qualifying distributions, $998,637; giving activities include $882,935 for 500 grants (high: $100,000; low: $125), and $115,682 for 108 employee matching gifts.
Purpose and activities: The foundation supports programs designed to promote social welfare; Michigan growth and environmental enhancement; education; community and civic development; and culture and the arts.
Fields of interest: Performing arts; Arts; Education, early childhood education; Higher education; Business school/education; Libraries (public); Education; Environment, natural resources; Environment, water resources; Environment, land resources; Environment, energy; Environmental education; Environment; Zoos/zoological societies; Food services; Food banks; Recreation, parks/playgrounds; Boys & girls clubs; Salvation Army; Family services; Family services, domestic violence; Developmentally disabled, centers & services; Homeless, human services; Human services; Community development, neighborhood development; Community development, civic centers; Community/economic development; Foundations (community); United Ways and Federated Giving Programs; Mathematics; Engineering/technology; Science; Economics; Political science; Leadership development.
Type of support: General/operating support; Continuing support; Capital campaigns; Building/renovation; Equipment; Curriculum development; Scholarship funds; Employee volunteer services; Employee matching gifts.
Limitations: Applications accepted. Giving primarily in areas of company operations in MI. No support for discriminatory organizations, United Way supported organizations, political, labor, or veterans' organizations, religious organizations not of direct benefit to the entire community, fraternal orders, or social clubs. No grants to individuals, or for fundraising, endowments, political campaigns, sports tournaments, talent or beauty contests, or debt reduction; no loans for small businesses.
Publications: Annual report; Annual report (including application guidelines); Program policy statement.
Application information: The CMF Common Grant Application Form is required. Video and audio submissions are not accepted. Telephone, e-mail, or faxed requests are not accepted. Additional information may be requested at a later date. Application form required.
   Initial approach: Download application form and mail proposal and application form to foundation
   Copies of proposal: 1
   Deadline(s): None

Board meeting date(s): Quarterly
Final notification: 6 to 8 weeks
Officers and Directors:* David W. Joos, Chair.; David G. Mengebier,* Pres.; Carolyn A. Bloodworth, Secy.-Treas.; James E. Brunner; John M. Butler; Debra A. Harmon; Nancy A. Popa; Thomas J. Webb; Leeroy Wells, Jr.
Number of staff: 2 full-time professional; 2 full-time support.
EIN: 382935534
Selected grants: The following grants were reported in 2006.
$50,000 to Western Michigan University, Kalamazoo, MI.
$45,000 to Detroit Renaissance Foundation, Detroit, MI.
$40,000 to Nature Conservancy, Lansing, MI.
$20,000 to YMCA of Saginaw, Saginaw, MI.
$10,000 to Great Lakes Naval Memorial and Museum, Muskegon, MI.
$5,000 to Frederik Meijer Gardens and Sculpture Park, Grand Rapids, MI.
$2,000 to Boys and Girls Club of Lenawee, Adrian, MI.
$1,000 to Lily Missions Center, Jackson, MI.
$950 to Saint Louis Public Schools, Saint Louis, MI.
$500 to Rotary Foundation of Rotary International, Evanston, IL.

962
CSX Corporation Contributions Program
500 Water St.
Jacksonville, FL 32202-4423
County: Duval
E-mail: corporatecontributions@csx.com;
URL: http://www.csx.com/?
fuseaction=corporategiving.main

Grantmaker type: Corporate giving program.
Financial data (yr. ended 12/31/09): Total giving, $6,000,000, including $6,000,000 for grants.
Purpose and activities: CSX makes charitable contributions to nonprofit organizations involved with arts and culture, education, and health and human services. Support is given on a national basis in areas of company operations.
Fields of interest: Arts; Education; Health care; Children, services; Family services; Human services.
Type of support: General/operating support; Employee volunteer services; In-kind gifts.
Limitations: Applications accepted. Giving primarily in areas of company operations, including Auburn, AL, Jacksonville, FL, Atlanta and Waycross, GA, Chicago, IL, Louisville, KY, New Orleans, LA, Baltimore, MD, Detroit, MI, Albany, Rochester, and Selkirk, NY, Raleigh, NC, Cincinnati, Toledo, and Walbridge, OH, Philadelphia, PA, Columbia, SC, and Richmond, VA. Giving also to national organizations. No support for religious organizations.
Application information: The Corporate Communications Department handles giving. A contributions committee reviews all requests. Application form required.
   Initial approach: Complete online application form
   Copies of proposal: 1
   Deadline(s): 6 weeks prior to need
   Committee meeting date(s): Weekly
   Final notification: Following review

963
Dana Corporation Foundation
c/o One Village Center Drive
Van Buren Township, MI 48111 (419) 535-4500
County: Wayne
Contact: Joe Stancati

Incorporated in 1956 in OH.
Donor: Dana Corporation.
Grantmaker type: Company-sponsored foundation.
Financial data (yr. ended 03/31/10): Assets, $629,700 (M); gifts received, $522,500; expenditures, $383,505; total giving, $382,320; qualifying distributions, $382,320; giving activities include $330,249 for 56 grants (high: $100,000; low: $250), and $52,071 for employee matching gifts.
Purpose and activities: The foundation supports organizations involved with arts and culture, education, health, human services, community development, international law, and government and public administration.
Fields of interest: Arts; Higher education; Education; Health care; American Red Cross; Children/youth, services; Human services; Community/economic development; United Ways and Federated Giving Programs; Law/international law; Government/public administration.
Type of support: General/operating support; Continuing support; Annual campaigns; Capital campaigns; Building/renovation; Equipment; Land acquisition; Emergency funds; Employee matching gifts; Scholarships—to individuals.
Limitations: Applications accepted. Giving primarily in areas of company operations. No grants to individuals (except for the Driveshaft Scholarship Fund), or for fellowships; no loans.
Application information: Application form not required.
   Initial approach: Proposal
   Copies of proposal: 1
   Deadline(s): None
   Board meeting date(s): Apr., Aug., and Dec. or May, Sept., and Jan.
Officers and Directors:* Robert Marcin,* Pres.; Anne Marie Riley,* V.P.; Joe Stancati,* Secy.; Cindy Simon, Treas.; Bob Fesenmyer.
Number of staff: 1 part-time professional.
EIN: 346544909
Selected grants: The following grants were reported in 2006.
$115,234 to American Red Cross, Greater Toledo Chapter, Toledo, OH.
$32,000 to United Way of the Lakeshore, Muskegon, MI.
$25,000 to Junior Achievement of Northwestern Ohio, Toledo, OH.
$25,000 to Public Broadcasting Foundation of Northwest Ohio, Toledo, OH.
$21,950 to United Way of Allen County, Fort Wayne, IN.
$15,500 to United Way of Grant County, Marion, IN.
$13,000 to United Way of Greater Longview, Longview, TX.
$10,798 to American Cancer Society, Mid-South Division, Jackson, TN.
$10,000 to Hardin County Schools, Performing Arts Center, Elizabethtown, KY.
$10,000 to United Way of Henderson County, Henderson, KY.

964
The Dart Energy Foundation, Inc.
600 Dart Rd.
Mason, MI 48854-1077 (517) 676-2900
County: Ingham
Contact: Joanne Wiliams, Secy.
URL: http://www.dartenergyfoundation.org/

Established in 2006 in MI.
Grantmaker type: Company-sponsored foundation.
Financial data (yr. ended 12/31/09): Assets,
$1,578,215 (M); expenditures, $89,062; total
giving, $0.
Purpose and activities: The foundation supports
organizations involved with education, employment
training, housing development, sports, and human
services.
Fields of interest: Higher education; Education;
Employment, training; Housing/shelter,
development; Athletics/sports, amateur leagues;
Children/youth, services; Human services.
Type of support: General/operating support;
Scholarship funds; Employee-related scholarships.
Limitations: Applications accepted. Giving primarily
in KS, MI, TX, and WY.
Publications: Application guidelines.
Application information: Application form not
required.
  Initial approach: Proposal
  Deadline(s): None
Officers and Directors:* Justin N. Dart,* Pres.;
Joanne Williams, Secy.; Phillip Leece, Treas.; Alexis
A. Learmond.
EIN: 204580958

965
Dearborn Cable Communications Fund
22211 W. Warren St.
Dearborn Heights, MI 48127-2531
(313) 277-5800
County: Wayne
Contact: Michael F. Katona, V.P.

Established in 1984 in MI.
Donors: Group W Cable, Inc.; Cablevision of
Michigan, Inc.
Grantmaker type: Company-sponsored foundation.
Financial data (yr. ended 12/31/09): Assets,
$767,208 (M); expenditures, $125,502; total
giving, $96,145; qualifying distributions, $96,145;
giving activities include $96,145 for grants.
Purpose and activities: The foundation supports
programs designed to provide cable television
programming of interest to the general community.
Fields of interest: Media/communications.
Type of support: Conferences/seminars; General/
operating support; Equipment; Technical
assistance.
Limitations: Applications accepted. Giving primarily
in the Dearborn, MI, area.
Application information: Additional information may
be requested at a later date. Application form not
required.
  Initial approach: Proposal
  Deadline(s): None
  Board meeting date(s): Bimonthly
  Final notification: 60 days
Officers and Directors: Andy Fradkin, Pres.; Michael
F. Katona, V.P.; Barbara Parker, Secy.; Mark
Campbell, Treas.; Nancy Daher; Said Deep; Kurt
Doelle; Russ Gibb.
EIN: 382571195

966
Delphi Corporation Contributions Program
(formerly Delphi Automotive Systems Corporation
Contributions Program)
c/o Community Rels.
5725 Delphi Dr.
Troy, MI 48098-2815
County: Oakland
URL: http://delphi.com/about/social

Grantmaker type: Corporate giving program.
Purpose and activities: As a complement to its
foundation, Delphi also makes charitable
contributions to nonprofit organizations directly.
Support is given on a national and international
basis in areas of company operations.
Fields of interest: Education; Disasters,
preparedness/services; American Red Cross;
United Ways and Federated Giving Programs;
Science; Engineering/technology; General
charitable giving.
Type of support: General/operating support;
Employee volunteer services.
Limitations: Giving on a national and international
basis in areas of company operations.
Number of staff: 4 part-time professional; 1
part-time support.

967
DENSO International America, Inc.
Corporate Giving Program
24777 Denso Dr.
P.O. Box 5133, M.C. 4610
Southfield, MI 48086-5047 (248) 350-7500
County: Oakland
URL: http://www.densocorp-na.com/corporate/
community.html

Grantmaker type: Corporate giving program.
Purpose and activities: As a complement to its
foundation, DENSO International also makes
charitable contributions to nonprofit organizations
directly. Support is given primarily in areas of
company operations in California, Iowa, and Ohio,
with emphasis on southeast Michigan.
Fields of interest: Arts; Higher education;
Environment, air pollution; Environment, water
pollution; Environment, land resources;
Environment; Human services; Science;
Engineering.
Type of support: Employee volunteer services;
General/operating support.
Limitations: Applications accepted. Giving primarily
in areas of company operations in CA, IA, and OH,
with emphasis on southeast MI. No support for
discriminatory organizations, religious, political,
veterans', or labor organizations, or social clubs. No
grants to individuals, or for endowments, dinners or
fundraisers, political campaigns, capital campaigns,
conferences, trips, or similar events, or advertising.
Publications: Application guidelines.
Application information: Application form required.
  Initial approach: Complete online application form
Contributions Committee: William Steffan, Chair.;
Barbara Wertheimer, Prog. Coord.
Number of staff: 1 part-time professional.
Selected grants: The following grants were reported
in 2006.
$60,000 to Charles H. Wright Museum of African
American History, Detroit, MI. For exhibit
development.

$40,000 to Focus: HOPE, Machinist Training
Institute, Detroit, MI. For urban development
education.
$40,000 to Society of Automotive Engineers
Foundation, Warrendale, PA. For A World in Motion,
K-12 math and science support.
$30,000 to Greening of Detroit, Detroit, MI. For
urban park development.
$25,000 to Lawrence Technological University,
Southfield, MI. For LTU team, U.S. Department of
Energy's Solar Decathlon.
$20,000 to Detroit Area Pre-College Engineering
Program, Detroit, MI. For program support.
$12,500 to University of Michigan, Ann Arbor, MI.
For UM solar car team, American Solar Challenge.
$11,500 to Friends of the Rouge, Dearborn, MI. For
Rouge Education Program.
$10,000 to Oakland Land Conservancy, Rochester,
MI. For Riparian Homeowners education.
$5,000 to Detroit Chamber Winds, Southfield, MI.
For residency program in Southfield Schools.

968
DENSO North America Foundation
24777 DENSO Dr., MC 4610
Southfield, MI 48086-5047 (248) 372-8225
County: Oakland
FAX: (248) 213-2551;
E-mail: densofoundation@denso-diam.com;
Additional tel.: (248) 372-8250; URL: http://
www.densofoundation.org

Established in 2001 in MI.
Donor: DENSO International America, Inc.
Grantmaker type: Company-sponsored foundation.
Financial data (yr. ended 12/31/09): Assets,
$9,770,667 (M); expenditures, $446,346; total
giving, $437,400; qualifying distributions,
$438,225; giving activities include $437,400 for 12
grants (high: $50,000; low: $7,400).
Purpose and activities: The foundation supports
organizations involved with engineering education
and related business areas. Special emphasis is
directed toward programs designed to demonstrate
technological innovation and automotive
engineering.
Fields of interest: Business school/education;
Engineering school/education; Engineering/
technology.
International interests: Canada; Mexico.
Type of support: Capital campaigns; Building/
renovation; Equipment; Program development.
Limitations: Applications accepted. Giving primarily
in CA, MI, MS, OH, and TN, and in Canada and
Mexico. No grants to individuals, or for
administrative costs, stipends, trips, conferences,
or travel expenses.
Publications: Application guidelines; Grants list.
Application information: The foundation considers
proposals on an invitation and request basis. If
applicants are approved, they will be asked to
submit a 1 page concept paper. Application form not
required.
  Initial approach: Telephone foundation to discuss
    possible funding
  Deadline(s): None
  Board meeting date(s): May and Oct.
Officers and Directors: Dennis Dawson,* Pres.;
Robert Townsend, V.P.; Sharon Brosch, Secy.; Kim
Madaj, Treas.; Hugh Cantrell; David Cole; Karen
Cooper-Boyer; Douglas Patton; Richard Shiozaki.
Agent: JPMorgan Chase Bank, N.A.

Number of staff: 1 full-time professional.
EIN: 383547055
Selected grants: The following grants were reported in 2005.
$50,000 to Pellissippi State Technical Community College, Knoxville, TN. For equipment.
$50,000 to Robert B. Miller College, Battle Creek, MI. For equipment.
$50,000 to University of Michigan, Dearborn, MI. For building improvement.
$45,000 to Lawrence Technological University, Southfield, MI. For building improvement.
$41,000 to California State University, Long Beach, CA. For equipment.
$37,500 to Tennessee Technological University, Cookeville, TN. For building improvement.
$30,000 to Michigan Technological University, Houghton, MI. For program support.
$25,000 to American Red Cross National Headquarters, Washington, DC. For disaster relief for Hurricane Katrina.
$25,000 to University of Tennessee, Knoxville, TN. For equipment.
$20,000 to Kettering University, Flint, MI. For building improvement.

969

The Detroit Lions, Inc. Corporate Giving Program

222 Republic Dr.
Allen Park, MI 48101-3650
County: Wayne
URL: http://www.detroitlions.com/community/index.html

Grantmaker type: Corporate giving program.
Purpose and activities: The Detroit Lions make charitable contributions of memorabilia to nonprofit organizations on a case by case basis. Support is given primarily in areas of company operations in Michigan.
Fields of interest: General charitable giving.
Type of support: Loaned talent; In-kind gifts.
Limitations: Applications accepted. Giving primarily in areas of company operations in MI. No game ticket donations.
Publications: Application guidelines.
Application information: Proposals should be submitted using organization letterhead. Telephone calls, faxes, mail, and e-mail messages are not encouraged. Application form required.
> *Initial approach:* Complete online application form and upload proposal
> *Deadline(s):* 6 weeks prior to need

970

Detroit Pistons Basketball Company Contributions Program

c/o Community Rels.
6 Championship Dr.
Auburn Hills, MI 48326-9906 (248) 377-8637
County: Oakland
FAX: (248) 377-0309; URL: http://www.nba.com/pistons/community/

Grantmaker type: Corporate giving program.
Purpose and activities: The Detroit Pistons make charitable contributions of game tickets and memorabilia to nonprofit organizations involved with youth development, and on a case by case basis. Support is limited to Michigan.

Fields of interest: Education; Tropical diseases; Breast cancer research; Autism research; Food services; Boys & girls clubs; Youth development; Children/youth, services; General charitable giving; Military/veterans; Economically disadvantaged.
Type of support: Income development; Building/renovation; Scholarship funds; In-kind gifts.
Limitations: Applications accepted. Giving limited to MI. No support for political organizations or candidates. No grants to individuals, or for general operating support, political campaigns, trips or tours, or seminars; no in-kind gifts for prizes, recognition gifts, or giveaways.
Publications: Application guidelines; Corporate giving report; Newsletter.
Application information: Proposals should be submitted using organization letterhead, and be brief. Support is limited to 1 contribution per organization during any given year. The Community Relations Department handles giving. Application form required.
> *Initial approach:* Proposal to headquarters or complete online form for product and ticket donations; fax letter of inquiry for Player Ticket Sections
> *Deadline(s):* 6 weeks prior to need; none for Player Ticket Sections
> *Final notification:* 1 to 2 weeks prior to need

971

Detroit Red Wings, Inc. Corporate Giving Program

19 Steve Yzerman Dr.
Detroit, MI 48226-4428 (313) 396-7524
County: Wayne
FAX: (313) 567-0296; URL: http://redwings.nhl.com/club/page.htm?bcid=com_default

Grantmaker type: Corporate giving program.
Purpose and activities: The Detroit Red Wings make charitable contributions of memorabilia to nonprofit organizations on a case by case basis. Support is given primarily in Michigan.
Fields of interest: General charitable giving.
Type of support: Loaned talent; In-kind gifts.
Limitations: Applications accepted. Giving primarily in MI. No game ticket donations.
Publications: Application guidelines.
Application information: Proposals should be submitted using organization letterhead. Support is limited to 1 contribution per organization during any given year. Application form not required.
> *Initial approach:* Download application form and mail or fax with proposal to headquarters
> *Deadline(s):* 4 weeks prior to need

972

Domino's Pizza, Inc. Corporate Giving Program

c/o Community Rels.
30 Frank Lloyd Wright Dr.
P.O. Box 997
Ann Arbor, MI 48106-0997 (734) 930-3030
County: Washtenaw
FAX: (734) 930-4346;
E-mail: communitygiving@dominos.com;
URL: http://www.dominosbiz.com/Public-EN/Site+Content/Secondary/Inside+Dominos/Domino's+Cares/

Grantmaker type: Corporate giving program.
Purpose and activities: Domino's makes charitable contributions of pizza to nonprofit organizations on a case by case basis. Support is given primarily in areas of company operations, with emphasis on southeastern Michigan.
Fields of interest: General charitable giving.
Type of support: Donated products.
Limitations: Applications accepted. Giving primarily in areas of company operations, with emphasis on southeastern MI.
Application information: Application form not required.
> *Initial approach:* Mail proposal to nearest company store; for organizations located in the southeastern MI area, e-mail or fax proposal to headquarters
> *Deadline(s):* 1 month prior to event
> *Final notification:* 2 weeks

973

The Dow Chemical Company Foundation

2030 Dow Ctr.
Midland, MI 48674-0001
County: Midland
Contact: R.N. "Bo" Miller, Pres. and Exec. Dir.
FAX: (989) 636-3518; E-mail: bomiller@dow.com;
URL: http://www.dow.com/commitments/corp_cit.htm

Established in 1979 in MI.
Donor: The Dow Chemical Co.
Grantmaker type: Company-sponsored foundation.
Financial data (yr. ended 12/31/09): Assets, $20,253,635 (M); expenditures, $20,145,179; total giving, $20,145,179; qualifying distributions, $20,145,179; giving activities include $20,145,179 for 1,183 grants (high: $1,000,000; low: $35).
Purpose and activities: The foundation supports organizations involved with K-12 education, the environment, community development, and chemical research.
Fields of interest: Elementary/secondary education; Environment; Community/economic development; United Ways and Federated Giving Programs; Chemistry.
Type of support: Equipment; Program development; Seed money; Employee matching gifts; Donated products; In-kind gifts.
Limitations: Applications accepted. Giving on a national and international basis primarily in areas of company operations. No support for political or religious organizations. No grants for travel or administrative costs.
Application information: Application form not required.
> *Initial approach:* Letter of inquiry
> *Copies of proposal:* 1
> *Deadline(s):* None
> *Board meeting date(s):* 4 times per year
> *Final notification:* 2 to 3 months

Officers and Trustees:* Dave E. Kepler, Chair.; R.N. "Bo" Miller,* Pres. and Exec. Dir.; Nancy Logan, Secy.; Colleen W. Kay, Treas.; Bill Banholzer; Gregory M. Freiwald; Geoffery E. Merszei; William H. Weideman.
Number of staff: 1 full-time professional; 7 part-time professional.
EIN: 382314603
Selected grants: The following grants were reported in 2009.

$1,000,000 to University of California, Haas School of Business, Berkeley, CA. For Center for Responsible Business.
$1,000,000 to YMCA, Bay Area Family, Bay City, MI.
$776,000 to United Way of Midland County, Midland, MI.
$700,000 to John F. Kennedy Center for the Performing Arts, Washington, DC.
$540,000 to King Baudouin Foundation United States, New York, NY.
$500,000 to Nature Conservancy, Arlington, VA.
$300,000 to Chemical Heritage Foundation, Philadelphia, PA.
$12,500 to United Way of Licking County, Newark, OH.
$3,750 to Rice University, Department of Chemical Engineering, Houston, TX.
$1,000 to Faith in Action of Brazosport, Lake Jackson, TX.

974
Dow Corning Corporation Contributions Program

P.O. Box 994
Midland, MI 48686-0994   (989) 496-4400
County: Midland
E-mail: community@dowcorning.com; URL: http://www.dowcorning.com/content/about/aboutcomm/?e=About+Dow+Corning

Grantmaker type: Corporate giving program.
Purpose and activities: As a complement to its foundation, Dow Corning also makes charitable contributions to nonprofit organizations directly. Support is given primarily in Seneffe, Belgium, Campinas, Brazil, Songjiang, China, Saint-Laurent-du-Pont, France, Wiesbaden, Germany, Fukui and Yamakita, Japan, Jincheon, South Korea, and Barry, Wales.
Fields of interest: Community/economic development; Mathematics; Science.
International interests: Belgium; Brazil; China; France; Germany; Japan; South Korea; Wales.
Type of support: General/operating support; Employee matching gifts; Donated equipment; Donated products.
Limitations: Applications accepted. Giving primarily in Seneffe, Belgium, Campinas, Brazil, Songjiang, China, Saint-Laurent-du-Pont, France, Wiesbaden, Germany, Fukui and Yamakita, Japan, Jincheon, South Korea, and Barry, Wales. No support for political, veterans', religious, or government-funded organizations. No grants to individuals, or for fundraising, collegiate athletic activities, scholarships, conferences, or travel.
Publications: Application guidelines.
Application information: Organizations receiving support are asked to provide a final report. Application form not required.
   Initial approach: E-mail letter of inquiry to headquarters

975
Dow Corning Foundation

2200 W. Salzburg Rd., Mail No. C01316
Midland, MI 48686-0994   (989) 496-5883
County: Midland
Contact: Kimberly Houston-Philpot, Pres.
E-mail: community@dowcorning.com; URL: http://www.dowcorning.com/content/about/aboutcomm/aboutcomm_globalgivingstrategy1.asp

Established in 1982 in MI.
Donors: Dow Corning Corp.; Hemlock Semiconductor Corp.
Grantmaker type: Company-sponsored foundation.
Financial data (yr. ended 12/31/09): Assets, $23,198,941 (M); gifts received, $2,750,000; expenditures, $867,950; total giving, $849,775; qualifying distributions, $865,450; giving activities include $849,775 for 31+ grants (high: $100,000).
Purpose and activities: The foundation supports organizations involved with K-12 education and community vitality. Special emphasis is directed toward programs designed to increase access to math, science, and technology education.
Fields of interest: Elementary/secondary education; Higher education; Community/economic development; Science, formal/general education; Mathematics; Engineering/technology.
Type of support: Continuing support; Capital campaigns; Building/renovation; Equipment; Program development; Seed money; Curriculum development; Scholarship funds; Employee matching gifts.
Limitations: Applications accepted. Giving in areas of company operations, with emphasis on Kendallville, IN, Carrollton and Elizabethtown, KY, Bay, Midland, and Saginaw counties, MI, and Greensboro, NC. No support for veterans', political, or religious groups. No grants to individuals, or for scholarships, conferences, travel costs of groups, dinners, fundraising events, or public advertisements; no research grants or funding for building or maintenance of university infrastructures.
Publications: Application guidelines.
Application information: An application form will be sent following a telephone or personal interview. Organizations receiving support are asked to submit annual progress reports and a final report. Application form required.
   Initial approach: E-mail foundation
   Deadline(s): None
   Board meeting date(s): Quarterly
Officers and Trustees:* Mary Lou Benecke,* Chair.; Kimberly R. Houston-Philpot,* Pres.; Jeanne D. Dodd,* Secy.; Ronald G. Thompson,* Treas.; Robert L. Kain; Thomas H. Lane; Christopher C. Shirk; Christian A. Velasquez.
Number of staff: 1 part-time professional; 1 part-time support.
EIN: 382376485
Selected grants: The following grants were reported in 2006.
$125,000 to Junior Achievement of Central Michigan, Midland, MI.
$100,000 to Delta College, University Center, MI.
$100,000 to Midland Public Schools, Midland, MI.
$50,000 to YMCA of Saginaw, Saginaw, MI.
$45,700 to American Chemical Society, Washington, DC.
$35,000 to National Inventors Hall of Fame, Akron, OH.
$22,500 to Legacy Center for Student Success, Midland, MI.
$15,000 to American Chemical Society, Washington, DC.
$5,000 to Michigan Technological University, Houghton, MI.

976
DTE Energy Company Contributions Program

1 Energy Plz.
Detroit, MI 48226-1221
County: Wayne
URL: http://www.dteenergy.com/dteEnergyCompany/community/

Grantmaker type: Corporate giving program.
Purpose and activities: As a complement to its foundation, DTE also makes charitable contributions to nonprofit organizations directly. Support is given primarily in Michigan.
Fields of interest: Education; Environment; Animals/wildlife; Public health; Food banks; Food distribution, meals on wheels; Nutrition; Safety/disasters, public education; Aging, centers/services; Homeless, human services; Human services; Civil/human rights, equal rights.
Type of support: Employee volunteer services; Sponsorships; In-kind gifts.
Limitations: Giving primarily in Michigan.
Number of staff: 3 full-time professional; 2 full-time support.

977
DTE Energy Foundation

(formerly Detroit Edison Foundation)
1 Energy Plaza, 1046 WCB
Detroit, MI 48226-1279   (313) 235-9271
County: Wayne
Contact: Karla Hall, V.P. and Secy.
E-mail: foundation@dteenergy.com; Additional tel.: (313) 235-9416; URL: http://www.dteenergy.com/dteEnergyCompany/community/

Established in 1986 in MI.
Donors: The Detroit Edison Co.; DTE Energy Ventures, Inc.
Grantmaker type: Company-sponsored foundation.
Financial data (yr. ended 12/31/09): Assets, $31,125,813 (M); gifts received, $17,074,232; expenditures, $7,951,660; total giving, $7,733,278; qualifying distributions, $7,873,804; giving activities include $7,733,278 for 555 grants (high: $572,475; low: $50).
Purpose and activities: The foundation supports programs designed to promote LEAD initiatives including, leadership, education, environment, achievement, development, and diversity in DTE Energy service territories.
Fields of interest: Arts, cultural/ethnic awareness; Performing arts; Arts; Elementary/secondary education; Higher education; Business school/education; Engineering school/education; Education, services; Education; Environment, natural resources; Environment, energy; Environment, forests; Environmental education; Environment; Employment; Food distribution, meals on wheels; Youth development; American Red Cross; Human services; Civil/human rights, equal rights; Community development, neighborhood development; Urban/community development; Business/industry; Community/economic development; Mathematics; Engineering/technology; Science; Leadership development; Minorities; Women.
Type of support: General/operating support; Continuing support; Capital campaigns; Program development; Curriculum development; Employee volunteer services; Sponsorships; Employee matching gifts.

Limitations: Applications accepted. Giving primarily in areas of company operations in MI. No support for political parties or organizations, religious organizations not of direct benefit to the entire community, discriminatory organizations, national or international organizations (unless they provide benefits directly to DTE Energy service areas), single purpose health organizations, or hospitals for building or equipment needs. No grants to individuals, or for political activities, student group trips, conferences, or building or equipment needs for hospitals.

Publications: Application guidelines; Program policy statement.

Application information: Telephone calls and video submissions are not encouraged. Organizations receiving support are asked to provide a final report. Application form required.

Initial approach: Download application form and E-mail proposal and application form to foundation

Copies of proposal: 1

Deadline(s): Jan. 3 to Mar. 4; Apr. 11 to May 13; July 11 to Aug. 12; and Oct. 10 to Nov. 11

Board meeting date(s): Quarterly

Final notification: Apr. 15, July 15, Oct. 14, and Dec. 30

Officers and Directors:* Frederick E. Shell, Pres.; Karla D. Hall,* V.P. and Secy.; Naif A. Khouri,* Treas.; J. Christopher Brown; Robert J. Buckler; Lynne Ellyn; Stephen E. Ewing; Joyce V. Hayes-Giles; Paul C. Hillegonds; Bruce D. Peterson; Michael C. Porter; Larry E. Steward.

Number of staff: 1 full-time professional; 2 full-time support.

EIN: 382708636

Selected grants: The following grants were reported in 2008.

$1,500,000 to University of Michigan, College of Engineering, Ann Arbor, MI. To establish DTE Energy Professorship of Advanced Energy Research.

$600,000 to Cranbrook Institute of Science, Bloomfield Hills, MI. To establish DTE Energy Watershed and Great Lakes Education program.

$481,622 to United Way for Southeastern Michigan, Detroit, MI.

$289,270 to University of Michigan, Office of the President, Ann Arbor, MI.

$261,377 to Detroit Symphony Orchestra, Detroit, MI.

$250,000 to Detroit Renaissance Foundation, Detroit, MI.

$71,500 to Community Foundation of Monroe County, Monroe, MI.

$40,000 to Detroit Economic Growth Foundation, Detroit, MI.

$37,000 to Oakland Schools Education Foundation, Waterford, MI.

$25,000 to Michigan Aerospace Foundation, Ann Arbor, MI.

978
The Engle Foundation

3850 Munson Hwy.
Hudson, MI   49247-9800   (517) 448-8921
County: Lenawee
Contact: Edward J. Engle, Jr., Pres. and Treas.

Established in 1988 in MI.

Donors: The Rima Manufacturing Co.; Edward J. Engle, Jr.

Grantmaker type: Company-sponsored foundation.

Financial data (yr. ended 08/31/09): Assets, $74,530 (M); gifts received, $4,779; expenditures, $4,395; total giving, $1,426; qualifying distributions, $1,426; giving activities include $1,426 for 3 grants (high: $831; low: $295).

Purpose and activities: The foundation supports organizations involved with K-12 and higher education and Catholicism.

Fields of interest: Museums; Elementary/secondary education; Libraries (public); United Ways and Federated Giving Programs; Military/veterans' organizations.

Type of support: General/operating support.

Limitations: Applications accepted. Giving primarily in Hudson, MI. No grants to individuals.

Application information: Application form not required.

Initial approach: Proposal

Deadline(s): None

Officers: Edward J. Engle, Jr., Pres. and Treas.; Jennifer Engle, Secy.

Director: Edward Engle II.

EIN: 382826866

979
Entergy Corporation Contributions Program

639 Loyola Ave.
New Orleans, LA   70161-1000   (504) 576-6980
County: Orleans
Contact: Patty Riddlebarger, Dir., Corp. Social Responsibility
URL: http://www.entergy.com/our_community

Grantmaker type: Corporate giving program.

Financial data (yr. ended 12/31/09): Total giving, $12,200,000, including $11,632,996 for 1,956+ grants, $190,000 for 38 grants to individuals, and $377,004 for 683 employee matching gifts.

Purpose and activities: As a complement to its foundation, Entergy also makes charitable contributions to nonprofit organizations directly. Support is given primarily in areas of company operations.

Fields of interest: Arts, cultural/ethnic awareness; Performing arts; Arts; Education, reading; Education; Environment; Housing/shelter; Disasters, preparedness/services; Children, services; Family services; Human services; Community development, neighborhood development; Economic development; United Ways and Federated Giving Programs; Economically disadvantaged.

Type of support: Annual campaigns; Emergency funds; Program development; Scholarship funds; Employee volunteer services; Use of facilities; Employee matching gifts; Employee-related scholarships; Donated equipment; In-kind gifts.

Limitations: Applications accepted. Giving primarily in areas of company operations in AR, LA, MA, MI, MS, NH, NY, TX, and VT. No support for political organizations, or candidates or sectarian religious organizations, organizations owned or operated by an employee of Entergy, or amateur sports teams. No grants to individuals, or for general operating support, consultant fees, administrative expenses, capital campaigns, or purchase of uniforms or trips for school-related organizations.

Publications: Application guidelines; Corporate report.

Application information: Complete online application at least 3 months before funding is needed. The Corporate Contributions Department handles giving. The company has a staff that only handles contributions. A contributions committee reviews all requests. Support is limited to 1 contribution per organization during any given year. Application form required.

Initial approach: Complete online application form

Deadline(s): None for Open Grants and Micro Grants; Jan to Apr. for Community Partnership Grants

Committee meeting date(s): Quarterly

Final notification: 6 to 8 weeks

Number of staff: 3 full-time professional; 1 full-time support.

980
Fabri-Kal Foundation

600 Plastics Pl.
Kalamazoo, MI   49001-4882   (269) 385-5050
County: Kalamazoo
Contact: Robert P. Kittredge, Pres.
URL: http://www.f-k.com/our-company/foundation-50-43.html

Established in 1969 in MI.

Donor: Fabri-Kal Corp.

Grantmaker type: Company-sponsored foundation.

Financial data (yr. ended 12/31/09): Assets, $48 (M); gifts received, $677,242; expenditures, $677,242; total giving, $677,222; qualifying distributions, $677,242; giving activities include $159,527 for 18 grants (high: $37,789; low: $2,000), and $517,695 for 71 grants to individuals (high: $22,416; low: $111).

Purpose and activities: The foundation supports health clinics and organizations involved with trailways, family planning, human services, and neighborhood development. Special emphasis is directed toward cultural and educational causes.

Fields of interest: Performing arts, theater; Arts; Higher education; Education; Environment, land resources; Health care, clinics/centers; Reproductive health, family planning; Goodwill Industries; Girl scouts; YM/YWCAs & YM/YWHAs; Aging, centers/services; Human services; Community development, neighborhood development; United Ways and Federated Giving Programs.

Type of support: Capital campaigns; Building/renovation; Equipment; Employee-related scholarships.

Limitations: Applications accepted. Giving limited to areas of company operations in Kalamazoo, MI, Hazleton, PA, and Greenville, SC.

Publications: Application guidelines; Grants list.

Application information: Application form not required.

Initial approach: Proposal

Deadline(s): None

Board meeting date(s): May

Officers: Robert P. Kittredge, Pres.; Gary C. Galia, Exec. V.P., Finance; Bob Weyhing, Secy.

EIN: 237003366

Selected grants: The following grants were reported in 2009.

$37,789 to United Way of Greater Hazleton, Hazleton, PA.

$30,608 to United Way of Greenville County, Greenville, SC.

$11,130 to United Way, Greater Kalamazoo, Kalamazoo, MI.

$10,000 to YMCA of Kalamazoo, Kalamazoo, MI.

$5,000 to Edison Neighborhood Association, Kalamazoo, MI.

$5,000 to Kalamazoo Civic Theater, Kalamazoo, MI.
$4,000 to Kalamazoo Regional Chamber Foundation, Kalamazoo, MI.
$4,000 to Senior Services, Kalamazoo, MI.
$2,500 to Fontana Chamber Arts, Kalamazoo, MI.
$2,500 to YMCA and Outdoor Center, Sherman Lake, Augusta, MI.

981
Federal Screw Works Foundation, Inc.
20229 Nine Mile Rd.
St. Clair Shores, MI 48080-1775
(586) 443-4200
County: Macomb
Contact: W. Thomas Zurschmiede, Jr., Tr.

Established in 1953 in MI.
Donor: Federal Screw Works.
Grantmaker type: Company-sponsored foundation.
Financial data (yr. ended 06/30/10): Assets, $67,981 (M); expenditures, $3,407; total giving, $2,900; qualifying distributions, $2,900; giving activities include $2,900 for grants.
Purpose and activities: The foundation supports organizations involved with opera, higher education, health, cancer, hunger, children and youth, and economic development.
Fields of interest: Performing arts, opera; Higher education; Health care; Cancer; Food services; American Red Cross; Children/youth, services; Economic development.
Type of support: General/operating support.
Limitations: Applications accepted. Giving primarily in Detroit, MI. No grants to individuals.
Application information: Application form not required.
  Initial approach: Letter
  Copies of proposal: 1
  Deadline(s): None
Officer and Trustees:* David C. Swerc,* Treas.; Wade C. Plaskey; W. Thomas Zurschmiede, Jr.; Thomas Zurschmiede.
EIN: 386088208

982
Fibre Converters Foundation, Inc.
1 Industrial Dr.
P.O. Box 248
Constantine, MI 49042-0248   (269) 279-1700
County: St. Joseph
Contact: David T. Stuck, Dir.

Incorporated in 1957 in MI.
Donor: Fibre Converters, Inc.
Grantmaker type: Company-sponsored foundation.
Financial data (yr. ended 03/31/10): Assets, $984,231 (M); expenditures, $96,860; total giving, $83,000; qualifying distributions, $85,331; giving activities include $83,000 for 16 grants (high: $30,000; low: $250).
Purpose and activities: The foundation supports organizations involved with education, health, and Christianity.
Fields of interest: Education; Health care; Health organizations, association; Christian agencies & churches; Disabilities, people with.
Type of support: General/operating support.
Application information: Application form required.
  Initial approach: Proposal
  Deadline(s): None

Directors: David T. Stuck; James D. Stuck.
EIN: 386081026

983
Fifth Third Bank Corporate Giving Program
c/o Community Affairs
Fifth Third Ctr., M.D. 10AT92
Cincinnati, OH 45263-0001   (513) 534-8697
County: Hamilton
URL: http://www.53.com/wcm/connect/FifthThirdSite/About+53/In+the+Community/

Grantmaker type: Corporate giving program.
Purpose and activities: As a complement to its foundation, Fifth Third also makes charitable contributions to nonprofit organizations directly. Support is given primarily in areas of company operations.
Fields of interest: Housing/shelter; Human services, financial counseling; Community/economic development.
Type of support: Program development; Employee volunteer services; Sponsorships.
Limitations: Giving primarily in areas of company operations in central, Naples, and Tampa Bay, FL, Chicago, IL, Evansville and Indianapolis, IN, Florence, Lexington, and Louisville, KY, Detroit, Grand Rapids, and Traverse City, MI, Cincinnati, Cleveland, Columbus, Dayton, and Toledo, OH, Nashville, TN, and Huntington, WV.
Publications: Corporate giving report.
Application information: The Community Affairs Department handles giving.

984
The Fifth Third Foundation
Fifth Third Ctr., M.D. 1090CA
Cincinnati, OH 45263-0001   (513) 534-4397
County: Hamilton
Contact: Heidi B. Jark, Mgr.
FAX: (513) 534-0960; Additional tel.: (513) 5340-7001; URL: https://www.53.com/wps/portal/av/?New_WCM_Context=/wps/wcm/connect/FifthThirdSite/About+53/In+the+Community

Trust established in 1948 in OH.
Donor: Fifth Third Bank.
Grantmaker type: Company-sponsored foundation.
Financial data (yr. ended 09/30/09): Assets, $6,464,436 (M); gifts received, $2,110,200; expenditures, $4,066,500; total giving, $4,014,053; qualifying distributions, $4,030,077; giving activities include $4,014,053 for 576 grants (high: $450,000; low: $25).
Purpose and activities: The foundation supports organizations involved with arts and culture, education, health, human services, and community development.
Fields of interest: Arts; Education; Health care; Human services; Community/economic development.
Type of support: Annual campaigns; Continuing support; Capital campaigns; Building/renovation; Equipment; Employee-related scholarships.
Limitations: Applications accepted. Giving primarily in areas of company operations in FL, Chicago, IL, IN, KY, MI, St. Louis, MO, OH, and Nashville, TN. No support for publicly-supported organizations or government agencies; generally, no support for elementary schools. No grants to individuals (except

for employee-related scholarships), or for capital campaigns for individual churches.
Publications: Application guidelines; Corporate giving report.
Application information: Visit Web site for nearest company facility address. A full proposal may be requested. A site visit may be requested. Support is limited to 1 contribution per organization during any given year. Support is limited to 1 contribution per organization during any given three-year period for grants of over $10,000. Support is limited to 3 years for multi-year grants. Organizations receiving support are asked to provide a final report. Application form not required.
  Initial approach: Letter of inquiry to nearest company facility; contact foundation for major campaign requests
  Copies of proposal: 1
  Deadline(s): None
  Board meeting date(s): Jan., Mar., June, and Sept.
Trustee: Fifth Third Bank.
EIN: 316024135
Selected grants: The following grants were reported in 2006.
$375,000 to University of Cincinnati Foundation, Cincinnati, OH. For capital support.
$325,000 to United Way of Greater Cincinnati, Cincinnati, OH. For annual fund.
$200,000 to Cincinnati, City of, Cincinnati, OH. For capital support.
$200,000 to Greater Cincinnati Arts and Education Center, Cincinnati, OH. For capital support.
$150,000 to Grand Action Foundation, Grand Rapids, MI. For capital support.
$50,000 to Akron Community Service Center and Urban League, Akron, OH. For capital support.
$28,000 to Elgin Academy, Elgin, IL. For program support.
$25,000 to Florida West Coast Symphony, Sarasota Orchestra, Sarasota, FL. For program support.
$25,000 to Ohio CDC Association, Columbus, OH. For program support.
$22,000 to United Way of Greater Cincinnati-Northern Kentucky, Florence, KY. For annual fund.

985
Ford Motor Company Contributions Program
P.O. Box 1899
Dearborn, MI 48121-1899   (888) 313-0102
County: Wayne
URL: http://www.ford.com/our-values/ford-fund-community-service

Grantmaker type: Corporate giving program.
Purpose and activities: As a complement to its foundation, Ford also makes charitable contributions to nonprofit organizations directly. Support is given on a national and international basis in areas of company operations.
Fields of interest: Education; Breast cancer research; Diabetes research; Agriculture; Disasters, preparedness/services; Safety, automotive safety; Youth development; United Ways and Federated Giving Programs; Physically disabled; Military/veterans.
Type of support: General/operating support; Employee volunteer services; Sponsorships; In-kind gifts.
Limitations: Giving on a national and international basis in areas of company operations.
Publications: Corporate giving report.

Number of staff: 9 full-time professional; 7 full-time support.

986
Ford Motor Company Fund

1 American Rd.
P.O. Box 1899
Dearborn, MI 48126-2798 (313) 248-4745
County: Wayne
FAX: (313) 594-7001; E-mail: fordfund@ford.com; Additional tel.: (888) 313-0102; Contact for Ford Driving Dreams through Education: David Perez, Devel. Dir., LULAC, tel.: (202) 833-6130 ext. 12, E-mail: DPerez@LULAC.org; E-mail for Capital Grants: fcapfund@ford.com; E-mail for Belt It Out Contest: FordDSFL@ford.com; URL: http://corporate.ford.com/about-ford/community

Incorporated in 1949 in MI.
Donors: Ford Motor Co.; Ford Motor Credit Co.
Grantmaker type: Company-sponsored foundation.
Financial data (yr. ended 12/31/09): Assets, $39,855,247 (M); gifts received, $10,101,614; expenditures, $21,774,573; total giving, $19,952,391; qualifying distributions, $21,932,571; giving activities include $19,952,391 for 246 grants (high: $2,000,000; low: $1,000).
Purpose and activities: The fund supports programs designed to promote innovation and education; community development and American heritage and diversity; and auto-related safety education.
Fields of interest: Museums; Performing arts; Performing arts, music; Performing arts, orchestras; Arts; Elementary/secondary education; Charter schools; Higher education; Engineering school/education; Scholarships/financial aid; Education, drop-out prevention; Education; Food services; Food banks; Safety, automotive safety; Civil/human rights, equal rights; Community/economic development; United Ways and Federated Giving Programs; Minorities; African Americans/Blacks; Hispanics/Latinos.
Type of support: Continuing support; Annual campaigns; Capital campaigns; Building/renovation; Equipment; Emergency funds; Program development; Publication; Curriculum development; Internship funds; Scholarship funds; Employee volunteer services; Sponsorships; Employee matching gifts; Employee-related scholarships; Grants to individuals.
Limitations: Applications accepted. Giving primarily in areas of company operations, with emphasis on southeastern MI; giving also in Phoenix, AZ, San Diego, CA, Miami, FL, Chicago, IL, Detroit, MI, Nashville, TN, and San Antonio, TX. No support for animal-rights organizations, lobbying organizations, fraternal organizations, labor groups, political organizations, private K-12 schools, profit-making enterprises, religious organizations not of direct benefit to the entire community, species-specific organizations, or sports teams. No grants to individuals (except for scholarships), or for advocacy-directed programs, beauty or talent contests, general operating support, debt reduction, endowments, or sponsorships related to fundraising activities; no loans for small businesses or program-related investments; no vehicle donations.
Publications: Application guidelines; Annual report; Corporate giving report; Informational brochure; Newsletter.
Application information: Requests for capital grants should include a 2 page narrative. Applicants for

capital grants may be invited to make a short presentation. Application form required.
  Initial approach: Complete online application
  Deadline(s): None; Jan. 17 to Apr. 1 for capital grants; May 1 for Belt it Out Contest; visit Website for scholarship programs
  Board meeting date(s): Apr. and Oct.
  Final notification: Within 8 weeks; May 15 for capital grants
Officers and Trustees:* James G. Vella,* Chair. and Pres.; Neil M. Schloss, V.P.; Peter J. Sherry, Jr., Secy.; Susan M. Cischke; Alfred B. Ford; Sheila Ford Hamp; David G. Leitch; Martin J. Mulloy; Ziad S. Ojakli.
Number of staff: 11 full-time professional; 10 full-time support.
EIN: 381459376
Selected grants: The following grants were reported in 2009.
$2,000,000 to Henry Ford Learning Institute, Dearborn, MI. For Henry Ford Academies.
$1,740,587 to Governors Highway Safety Association, Washington, DC. For Driving Skills for Life Program.
$1,450,000 to Edison Institute, The Henry Ford, Dearborn, MI. For The Inspiration Project and renovation of Auto History Exhibit.
$1,250,000 to United Way for Southeastern Michigan, Detroit, MI. For Torch Drive.
$1,197,998 to Education Development Center, Newton, MA. For Ford Partnership for Advanced Studies.
$250,000 to Michigan Opera Theater, Detroit, MI. For Crowning Achievement Campaign Pledge for Ford Center for Arts and Learning.
$75,000 to Mosaic Youth Theater of Detroit, Detroit, MI. For Mosaic Singers.
$35,000 to Jewish Federation of Washtenaw County, Ann Arbor, MI. For main event sponsorship.
$25,000 to Vanderbilt University, Monroe Carell Junior Children's Hospital, Nashville, TN. For Safe Escape Program at Children's Hospital.
$25,000 to Wayne County Regional Educational Service Agency, Wayne, MI. For educational leadership and professional development.

987
Foremost Insurance Company Grand Rapids, Michigan Corporate Giving Program

c/o Corp. Contribs.
5600 Beech Tree Ln.
Caledonia, MI 49316-9587 (616) 942-3000
County: Kent
URL: http://www.foremost.com/about-foremost/community.htm

Grantmaker type: Corporate giving program.
Purpose and activities: Foremost makes charitable contributions to nonprofit organizations involved education, birth defects, breast cancer research, diabetes research, and youth development in business. Support is given primarily in Michigan.
Fields of interest: Museums (children's); Education, reading; Education; Genetic diseases and disorders; Breast cancer research; Diabetes research; Youth development, business; United Ways and Federated Giving Programs.
Type of support: General/operating support; Employee volunteer services; Sponsorships; In-kind gifts.

Limitations: Giving primarily in MI; giving also to national organizations.

988
Gannett Foundation, Inc.

7950 Jones Branch Dr.
McLean, VA 22107-0001 (703) 854-6000
County: Fairfax
Contact: Pat Lyle, Mgr.
FAX: (703) 854-2167;
E-mail: foundation@gannett.com; URL: http://www.gannettfoundation.org

Established in 1991 in VA.
Donor: Gannett Co., Inc.
Grantmaker type: Company-sponsored foundation.
Financial data (yr. ended 12/31/09): Assets, $15,547,586 (M); expenditures, $4,240,103; total giving, $4,119,946; qualifying distributions, $4,193,623; giving activities include $2,725,750 for 69 grants (high: $1,500,000; low: $250), and $1,394,196 for 4,118 employee matching gifts.
Purpose and activities: The foundation supports organizations involved with arts and culture, media and journalism, education, conservation, health, youth development, human services, diversity, community development, minorities, women, and economically disadvantaged people.
Fields of interest: Arts, cultural/ethnic awareness; Media/communications; Media, print publishing; Arts; Journalism school/education; Education; Environment, natural resources; Health care; Youth development; Human services; Civil/human rights, equal rights; Civil liberties, first amendment; Community development, neighborhood development; Economic development; Community/economic development; Minorities; Women; Economically disadvantaged.
International interests: United Kingdom.
Type of support: Capital campaigns; Conferences/seminars; Employee matching gifts; Equipment; Program development; Scholarship funds.
Limitations: Applications accepted. Giving on a national and international basis in areas of company operations, with emphasis on AZ, Washington DC, FL, IN, MI, NY, OH, VA and the United Kingdom. No support for private foundations, regional or national organizations not addressing local needs, elementary or secondary schools (except for special initiatives not provided by regular school budgets), political action or legislative advocacy groups, medical or research organizations, fraternal groups, athletic teams, bands, veterans' organizations, or volunteer firefighters. No grants to individuals (except for employee-related scholarships), or for religious programs or initiatives, endowments, or multi-year pledge campaigns.
Publications: Application guidelines; Annual report; Informational brochure; IRS Form 990 or 990-PF printed copy available upon request; Program policy statement.
Application information: Proposals should be no longer than 5 pages. Telephone calls during the application process are not encouraged. Visit website to confirm application deadline for specific areas. Application form required.
  Initial approach: Download application form and mail proposal and application form to nearest company daily newspaper or broadcast station
  Copies of proposal: 1
  Deadline(s): Feb. 16 and Aug. 17; Mar. 15, July 15, and Nov. 15 for Media Grants; Autumn for Newsquest Grants

Board meeting date(s): 3 times per year from Feb. to Oct.

Final notification: 90 to 120 days

Officers and Director:* Craig A. Dubow,* Chair. and Pres.; Daniel S. Ehrman, V.P.; Gracia C. Martore,* V.P.; Todd A. Mayman, Secy.; Michael A. Hart, Treas.; Robin Pence, Exec. Dir.

Number of staff: 1 full-time professional; 1 full-time support.

EIN: 541568843

Selected grants: The following grants were reported in 2010.

$640,000 to Quartet Community Foundation, Bristol, England.

$302,000 to Arizona Community Foundation, Phoenix, AZ. To match donations from readers of The Republic's annual Season for Sharing campaign that benefits local nonprofit agencies.

$62,532 to American Press Institute, Reston, VA. For general support.

$30,000 to Greater Phoenix Economic Council, Phoenix, AZ. To support economic development strategies in the Phoenix Metro area.

$25,000 to Des Moines Public Library Foundation, Des Moines, IA. For Final phase of campaign to fund the building of a new central library and the renovation and/or expansion of all five branch libraries.

$5,000 to Coleman A. Young Foundation, Detroit, MI. For REAL Skills Program, a year-round drop-out prevention program focusing on life skills for Detroit middle and high school students, now serving 120.

$5,000 to Wildlife Experience, Parker, CO. For Education Outreach Program serves low income children by providing compelling, accurate environmental science instruction.

$4,000 to United Way of Greater Portland, Portland, ME. For general support.

$3,000 to Heritage University, Toppenish, WA. For general support.

$2,500 to Companion Day Services, Marshfield, WI. To support programs for adult day care and respite care for elderly/special needs individuals in the community.

989
General Dynamics Corporation Contributions Program

2941 Fairview Park Dr., Ste. 100
Falls Church, VA 22042-4523 (703) 876-3305
County: Fairfax
Contact: Arlene Nestel, Mgr., Community Rels.
FAX: (703) 876-3125; URL: http://www.generaldynamics.com/

Grantmaker type: Corporate giving program.

Purpose and activities: General Dynamics makes charitable contributions to nonprofit organizations on a case by case basis. Support is given on a national basis.

Fields of interest: General charitable giving.

Type of support: Employee volunteer services; General/operating support; Scholarship funds; Sponsorships.

Limitations: Applications accepted. Giving in areas of company operations on a national and international basis. No grants to individuals.

Application information: Application form not required.

Initial approach: Proposal to headquarters
Copies of proposal: 1
Deadline(s): None
Final notification: 3 months

990
General Motors Foundation, Inc.

(also known as GM Foundation)
300 Renaissance Ctr., M.C. 482-C27-D76
Detroit, MI 48265-3000
County: Wayne
Contact: Ann Kihn
E-mail: ann.kihn@gm.com; URL: http://www.gm.com/corporate/responsibility/community

Incorporated in 1976 in MI.

Donor: General Motors Corp.

Grantmaker type: Company-sponsored foundation.

Financial data (yr. ended 12/31/09): Assets, $157,666,694 (M); expenditures, $9,011,341; total giving, $7,985,218; qualifying distributions, $8,197,667; giving activities include $7,985,218 for 104 grants (high: $917,387; low: $100).

Purpose and activities: The foundation supports programs designed to promote education; health and human services; environment and energy; and community development.

Fields of interest: Business school/education; Engineering school/education; Education; Environment, natural resources; Environment, energy; Environment; Animal welfare; Public health; Health care; Cancer research; Heart & circulatory research; Diabetes research; Medical research; Disasters, preparedness/services; Safety, automotive safety; American Red Cross; Human services; Business/industry; Community/economic development; United Ways and Federated Giving Programs; Science, formal/general education.

Type of support: General/operating support; Continuing support; Annual campaigns; Equipment; Emergency funds; Program development; Scholarship funds; Research; Employee volunteer services; Employee matching gifts; Matching/challenge support.

Limitations: Applications accepted. Giving primarily in areas of company operations, with emphasis on MI. No support for discriminatory organizations, religious organizations, or political parties or candidates. No grants to individuals (except for the Buick Scholarship Program), or for capital campaigns, endowments, general operating support for U.S. hospitals or health care institutions, conferences, workshops, or seminars not directly related to GM's business interests.

Publications: Application guidelines; Annual report (including application guidelines); Corporate giving report; Informational brochure; Program policy statement.

Application information: Multi-year requests are not encouraged. Additional information may be requested at a later date. Application form required.

Initial approach: Complete online eligibility quiz and application form; complete online application for Buick Scholarship Program
Deadline(s): None; Mar. 31 for Buick Scholarship Program
Board meeting date(s): Quarterly
Final notification: 4 to 8 weeks

Officers and Directors:* Robert Ferguson, Chair.; Deborah I. Dingell,* Vice-Chair.; Vivian Pickard, Pres.; Kimberly K. Hudolin, Secy.; Tom P. Gaff, C.F.O.; Mary Williams, Treas.; Kevin W. Cobb, Tax Off.; Kenneth W. Cole; Susan E. Docherty; Mark R. Laneve; Timothy E. Lee; Kathryn M. McBride; Mark L. Reuss; John F. Smith; Edd G. Snyder; Diane D. Tremblay; Janice K. Uhlig; Edward T. Welburn, Jr.

Number of staff: 3 full-time professional; 2 full-time support.

EIN: 382132136

Selected grants: The following grants were reported in 2008.

$3,648,000 to Safe Kids Worldwide, Washington, DC.

$714,290 to Smithsonian Institution, Washington, DC.

$630,000 to Focus: HOPE, Detroit, MI.

$502,290 to United Way for Southeastern Michigan, Detroit, MI.

$480,000 to United Negro College Fund, Fairfax, VA.

$414,043 to United Way International, Alexandria, VA.

$200,000 to Detroit Renaissance Foundation, Detroit, MI.

$50,550 to Lehigh University, Bethlehem, PA.

$40,000 to Mosaic Youth Theater of Detroit, Detroit, MI.

$33,000 to United Way of Greater Cleveland, Cleveland, OH.

991
Generations Foundation

c/o Trustees
13919 S.W. Bay Shore Dr., Ste. G-01
Traverse City, MI 49684
County: Grand Traverse

Established in 2003 in MI.

Donors: Generations Management LLC; HIS Foundation; Canaan Foundation; Rock Charitable Foundation; Melvin K. Nielson.

Grantmaker type: Company-sponsored foundation.

Financial data (yr. ended 12/31/09): Assets, $109 (M); gifts received, $10,250; expenditures, $10,070; total giving, $9,450; qualifying distributions, $9,450; giving activities include $9,450 for 4 grants (high: $7,000; low: $150).

Purpose and activities: The foundation supports festivals and organizations involved with land conservation and youth development.

Fields of interest: Environment, land resources; Recreation, fairs/festivals; Boy scouts; Girl scouts.

Type of support: General/operating support.

Limitations: Applications accepted. Giving primarily in MI. No grants to individuals.

Application information:

Initial approach: Proposal
Deadline(s): None

Trustees: Jonathan Crosby; Cori Nielson; Keith Nielson.

EIN: 746524789

992
Georgia-Pacific Foundation, Inc.

133 Peachtree St. N.E., 39th Fl
Atlanta, GA 30303-1808 (404) 652-4581
County: Fulton
Contact: Curley M. Dossman, Jr., Chair. and Pres.
FAX: (404) 749-2754; Additional contact: Charmaine Ward, Dir., Community Affairs, tel.: (404) 652-5302; URL: http://www.gp.com/gpfoundation/index.html

Incorporated in 1958 in OR.

Donor: Georgia-Pacific Corp.

Grantmaker type: Company-sponsored foundation.

Financial data (yr. ended 12/31/09): Assets, $478,326 (M); gifts received, $2,612,740; expenditures, $2,596,095; total giving, $2,596,064; qualifying distributions, $2,596,095;

giving activities include $2,596,064 for 328 grants (high: $384,211; low: $100).

Purpose and activities: The foundation supports programs designed to promote education; environment; community enrichment; and entrepreneurship.

Fields of interest: Historic preservation/historical societies; Arts; Elementary/secondary education; Higher education; Education, reading; Education; Environment, air pollution; Environment, recycling; Environment, natural resources; Environment, land resources; Environmental education; Environment; Employment, training; Employment; Housing/shelter, development; Housing/shelter; Disasters, preparedness/services; Disasters, fire prevention/control; Safety/disasters; Youth development, business; Youth development; Social entrepreneurship; Community development, small businesses; Community/economic development; United Ways and Federated Giving Programs; Youth; Minorities; Women.

Type of support: General/operating support; Continuing support; Annual campaigns; Capital campaigns; Building/renovation; Equipment; Program development; Conferences/seminars; Scholarship funds; Employee volunteer services; Sponsorships; Employee-related scholarships; Scholarships—to individuals; In-kind gifts.

Limitations: Applications accepted. Giving limited to areas of company operations in AL, AR, AZ, CA, Washington, DC, DE, FL, GA, IA, IL, IN, KS, KY, LA, MA, MI, MN, MO, MS, NH, NJ, NM, NV, NY, NC, OH, OK, OR, PA, SC, TN, VA, WA, WI, WV, WY, and Africa, Asia, Europe, and South America. No support for discriminatory organizations, political candidates, churches or religious denominations, religious or theological schools, social, labor, veterans', alumni, or fraternal organizations not of direct benefit to the entire community, athletic associations, national organizations with local chapters already receiving support, medical or nursing schools, or pass-through organizations. No grants to individuals (except for scholarships), or for emergency needs for general operating support, political causes, legislative lobbying, or advocacy efforts, goodwill advertising, sporting events, general operating support for United Way member agencies, tickets or tables for testimonials or similar benefit events, named academic chairs, social sciences or health science programs, fundraising events, or trips or tours.

Publications: Application guidelines; Program policy statement.

Application information: Extraneous proposal materials are not encouraged. Electronic or faxed proposals are not accepted. Application form not required.

   Initial approach: Proposal; contact nearest facility for Georgia-Pacific Bucket Brigade
   Copies of proposal: 1
   Deadline(s): Between Jan. 1 and Oct. 31; Aug. 12 for Georgia-Pacific Bucket Brigade
   Board meeting date(s): As required
   Final notification: Within 60 days

Officers: Curley M. Dossman, Jr.,* Chair. and Pres.; Tye Darland, V.P. and Secy.; Tyler Woolson, C.F.O.; Marty Agard, Treas.

Number of staff: 5 full-time professional; 1 full-time support.

EIN: 936023726

Selected grants: The following grants were reported in 2005.

$372,020 to National Merit Scholarship Corporation, Evanston, IL.

$100,000 to International Corrugated Packaging Foundation, Alexandria, VA.

$75,000 to Marcus Institute for Development and Learning, Atlanta, GA.

$67,680 to United Fund, Crossett Area, Crossett, AR.

$60,000 to Rebuilding Together, Washington, DC.

$50,000 to Robert W. Woodruff Arts Center, Atlanta, GA.

$25,000 to United Way.

$20,000 to Lawrence County Civic Center, Monticello, MS.

$16,667 to Atlanta Historical Society, Atlanta, GA.

$15,000 to Southeastern Regional Office National Scholarship Service and Fund for Negro Students, Atlanta, GA.

993

Gleaner Life Insurance Society Corporate Giving Program

5200 W. U.S. Hwy. 223
Adrian, MI   49221-9461
County: Lenawee
URL: http://www.gleanerlife.org/Home.aspx?aud=Member

Grantmaker type: Corporate giving program.

Purpose and activities: As a complement to its foundation, Gleaner Life Insurance Society also makes charitable contributions to nonprofit organizations directly. Support is given primarily in areas of company operations in Arizona, Florida, Iowa, Illinois, Indiana, Kansas, Kentucky, Michigan, Missouri, Nebraska, Ohio, Tennessee, and Virginia.

Fields of interest: Youth development; Human services, emergency aid; Human services.

Type of support: Employee volunteer services.

Limitations: Giving primarily in areas of company operations in AZ, FL, IA, IL, IN, KS, KY, MI, MO, NE, OH, TN, and VA.

994

GM Corporate Giving Program

300 Renaissance Ctr.
Detroit, MI   48265-3000   (313) 556-5000
County: Wayne
URL: http://www.gm.com/corporate/responsibility/community

Grantmaker type: Corporate giving program.

Purpose and activities: As a complement to its foundation, GM also makes charitable contributions to nonprofit organizations directly. Support is given primarily in areas of company operations.

Fields of interest: Vocational education; Education; Heart & circulatory diseases; Disasters, preparedness/services; Safety, automotive safety.

Type of support: General/operating support; Employee volunteer services; Donated products; In-kind gifts.

Limitations: Giving primarily in areas of company operations.

Number of staff: 3 full-time professional; 3 full-time support.

995

Gordon Food Service, Inc. Corporate Giving Program

c/o Donation Comm.
P.O. Box 1787
Grand Rapids, MI   49501-1787
County: Kent
URL: http://www.gfs.com/en/about-us/donations.page?

Grantmaker type: Corporate giving program.

Purpose and activities: Gordon Food Service makes charitable contributions to nonprofit organizations on a case by case basis. Support is given primarily in areas of company operations, with emphasis on Michigan.

Fields of interest: General charitable giving.

Type of support: Sponsorships; Donated products.

Limitations: Applications accepted. Giving primarily in areas of company operations, with emphasis on MI.

Application information: Proposals should be submitted using organization letterhead. Faxes and e-mail messages are not encouraged. Application form not required.

   Initial approach: Proposal to headquarters
   Copies of proposal: 1
   Deadline(s): None
   Final notification: 3 weeks

996

Great Lakes Castings Corporation Foundation

800 N. Washington Ave.
Ludington, MI   49431-2724   (231) 843-2501
County: Mason
Contact: Carol Henke, Tr.

Donor: Great Lakes Castings Corp.

Grantmaker type: Company-sponsored foundation.

Financial data (yr. ended 12/31/09): Assets, $831,166 (M); gifts received, $1,446; expenditures, $29,596; total giving, $19,777; qualifying distributions, $19,777; giving activities include $8,527 for 7 grants (high: $6,092; low: $100), and $11,250 for 9 grants to individuals (high: $1,250; low: $1,250).

Purpose and activities: The foundation supports organizations involved with higher education and awards college scholarships to high school students in Ludington, Michigan, area school districts.

Fields of interest: Higher education.

Type of support: General/operating support; Scholarships—to individuals.

Limitations: Applications accepted. Giving limited to the Ludington, MI, area.

Application information:

   Initial approach: Contact foundation for application information
   Deadline(s): Apr. 1 of applicant's senior year of high school or college for scholarships

Trustees: Tim Fischer; Carol Henke; Rob Killips; Steve Stemper.

EIN: 382250546

997
Green Bay Packers, Inc. Corporate Giving Program

c/o Donations
P.O. Box 10628
Green Bay, WI 54307-0628 (920) 569-7500
County: Brown
FAX: (920) 569-7302;
E-mail: IGAMDonations@packers.com; URL: http://www.packers.com/community/index.html

Grantmaker type: Corporate giving program.
Purpose and activities: As a complement to its foundation, Green Bay Packers also makes charitable contributions of memorabilia to nonprofit organizations directly. Support is limited to upper Michigan and Wisconsin.
Fields of interest: General charitable giving.
Type of support: Loaned talent; General/operating support; In-kind gifts.
Limitations: Applications accepted. Giving limited to upper MI and WI. No game ticket donations.
Publications: Corporate giving report.
Application information: Application form required.
   Initial approach: Complete online application form
   Deadline(s): 6 to 8 weeks prior to need
   Final notification: Following review
Administrators: Julie Broeckel, Community Rels. Asst.; Cathy A. Dworak, Mgr., Community Rels.; Bobbi Jo Eisenreich, Coord., Corp. Donations; Sue Zernicke, Community Rels. Asst.
Number of staff: 1 full-time professional; 1 full-time support; 2 part-time support.

998
The Hammond Foundation

c/o Hammond Machinery, Inc.
1600 Douglas Ave.
Kalamazoo, MI 49007-1630 (269) 345-7151
County: Kalamazoo
Contact: Christine A. Hammond, Pres. and Treas.

Established in 1952 in MI.
Donor: Hammond Machinery, Inc.
Grantmaker type: Company-sponsored foundation.
Financial data (yr. ended 12/31/09): Assets, $823,875 (M); expenditures, $46,902; total giving, $39,600; qualifying distributions, $43,948; giving activities include $39,600 for 44 grants (high: $5,000; low: $100).
Purpose and activities: The foundation supports camps and organizations involved with arts and culture, education, the environment, and human services.
Fields of interest: Arts councils; Arts; Higher education; Education; Environment; Recreation, camps; Children/youth, services; Aging, centers/services; Homeless, human services; Human services; United Ways and Federated Giving Programs.
Type of support: General/operating support; Program development.
Limitations: Applications accepted. Giving primarily in Kalamazoo, MI. No grants to individuals; no loans.
Application information: Application form not required.
   Initial approach: Letter of inquiry
   Deadline(s): None
Officers and Trustee: Christine A. Hammond, Pres. and Treas.; Jeremy Hammond, Secy.; Robert E. Hammond.
EIN: 386061610

999
The Hanover Insurance Group Foundation, Inc.

(formerly Allmerica Financial Charitable Foundation, Inc.)
440 Lincoln St., N100
Worcester, MA 01653-0002 (508) 855-2608
County: Worcester
Contact: Linda M. McGowan, Pres.
E-mail: foundation@hanover.com; Michigan application address: Becky E. Best, Mgr., Corp. Community Relations, 808 Highlander Way, HWC340, Howell, MI 48843, tel.: (517) 540-4290, E-mail: bbest@hanover.com; URL: http://www.hanover.com/thg/about/community/grant.htm

Established in 1990 in MA.
Donors: First Allmerica Financial Life Insurance Co.; The Hanover Insurance Co.
Grantmaker type: Company-sponsored foundation.
Financial data (yr. ended 12/31/09): Assets, $6,640,466 (M); gifts received, $1,505,487; expenditures, $1,268,157; total giving, $1,248,843; qualifying distributions, $1,259,783; giving activities include $1,248,843 for 222 grants (high: $55,000; low: $50).
Purpose and activities: The foundation supports organizations involved with arts and culture, health, medical research, hunger, housing, human services, and community development. Special emphasis is directed toward programs designed to build world class public education systems; and inspire and empower youth to achieve their full potential.
Fields of interest: Visual arts; Performing arts; Arts; Higher education; Education; Health care; Medical research; Food services; Housing/shelter; Youth development; Aging, centers/services; Homeless, human services; Human services; Community/economic development; Youth.
Type of support: Employee-related scholarships; Scholarships—to individuals; Building/renovation; Employee volunteer services; General/operating support; Program development; Scholarship funds.
Limitations: Applications accepted. Giving primarily in areas of company operations in the greater Worcester County, MA, area and the Howell and Livingston County, MI, area. No support for private schools, amateur or professional sporting groups, or religious, political, professional, fraternal, or labor organizations. No grants to individuals (except for scholarships), or for national fundraising drives, capital campaigns, or beauty or talent contests.
Publications: Application guidelines; Corporate giving report; Program policy statement.
Application information: Support is limited to 1 contribution per organization during any given year. Organizations receiving support are asked to provide a final report. Application form required.
   Initial approach: Download application form and mail to application address
   Deadline(s): Jan. 15, Apr. 15, July 15, and Sept. 15
   Board meeting date(s): Mar., June, Sept., and Nov.
Officers and Directors:* Linda M. McGowan,* Pres.; Charles F. Cronin, Clerk; Ann K. Tripp, Investment Off.; Bryan D. Allen; Frederick H. Eppinger.
EIN: 043105650
Selected grants: The following grants were reported in 2009.
$60,000 to Reading Matters, Boston, MA.

$55,000 to United Way, Livingston County, Brighton, MI.
$25,000 to Student Leadership Services, Waterford, MI.
$25,000 to Worcester Community Action Council, Worcester, MA.
$25,000 to YMCA of Central Massachusetts, Worcester, MA.
$24,500 to Scholarship America, Saint Peter, MN.
$15,000 to Old Sturbridge Village, Sturbridge, MA.
$7,150 to EcoTarium, Worcester, MA.
$5,000 to Henry Lee Willis Community Center, Worcester, MA.
$5,000 to Pinckney Community Schools, Pinckney, MI.

1000
Hastings Mutual Insurance Company Charitable Foundation

404 E. Woodlawn Ave.
Hastings, MI 49058-1005
County: Barry
Contact: Cindy Beckwith
FAX: (877) 714-9574;
E-mail: foundation@hastingsmutual.com

Established in 2004 in MI.
Donor: Hastings Mutual Insurance Co.
Grantmaker type: Company-sponsored foundation.
Financial data (yr. ended 12/31/09): Assets, $2,609,969 (M); expenditures, $115,390; total giving, $112,227; qualifying distributions, $112,227; giving activities include $112,227 for 38 grants (high: $30,413; low: $250).
Purpose and activities: The foundation supports programs designed to provide essential needs of the living, including food, clothing, and medical services to at-risk youth and financially challenged families; and programs designed promote general welfare and betterment of the community.
Fields of interest: Health care; Food banks; Family services; Human services; Community/economic development; Youth; Economically disadvantaged.
Type of support: Building/renovation; Matching/challenge support; General/operating support; Equipment; Program development.
Limitations: Applications accepted. Giving limited to IL, IN, MI, OH, and WI. No grants to individuals.
Publications: Informational brochure.
Application information: Organizations receiving support are asked to submit a final report. Application form required.
   Initial approach: Contact foundation for application form
   Deadline(s): Mar. 31, June 30, Sept. 30, and Dec. 31
   Final notification: 45 days
Officers and Directors: William H. Wallace, Pres.; Michael W. Puerner, Secy.; Michael T. Kinnary, Treas.; Sue Ann Burns; Mark A. Kolanowski; Bruce J. Osterink; James Toburen; James Wiswell.
EIN: 202031029

1001
Haworth Inc. Corporate Giving Program

1 Haworth Ctr.
Holland, MI 49423-9570 (616) 393-3000
County: Ottawa
URL: http://www.haworth.com/en-us/About-Us/Sustainability/Social-Responsibility/Pages/Social-Responsibility.aspx

Grantmaker type: Corporate giving program.
Purpose and activities: Haworth makes charitable contributions to nonprofit organizations involved with the sciences, arts, medicine, and environmental preservation. Special emphasis is directed towards education. Support is given on a national and international basis in areas of company operations.
Fields of interest: Arts; Education; Environment; Science; General charitable giving.
Type of support: Employee-related scholarships; General/operating support; Employee volunteer services; Donated products.
Limitations: Giving on a national and international basis in areas of company operations.

1002

HCR ManorCare Foundation, Inc.
(formerly Manor Care Foundation, Inc.)
333 N. Summit St.
P.O. Box 10086
Toledo, OH 43699-0086 (419) 252-5989
County: Lucas
Contact: Jennifer Steiner, Exec. Dir.
FAX: (419) 754-2290;
E-mail: foundation@hcr-manorcare.com;
URL: http://www.hcr-manorcare.org/

Established in 1997 in MD.
Donors: Manor Care, Inc.; HCR Manor Care, Inc.; Virginia Hill Trust; Anna Mae Lee; Mary Louise and Marjori Lord Trust Fund; Elizabeth O'Brien.
Grantmaker type: Company-sponsored foundation.
Financial data (yr. ended 05/31/09): Assets, $2,321,690 (M); gifts received, $1,150,911; expenditures, $1,676,166; total giving, $148,817; qualifying distributions, $1,640,208; giving activities include $148,817 for 88 grants (high: $59,317; low: $500), and $1,027,375 for 4 foundation-administered programs.
Purpose and activities: The foundation supports organizations involved with Alzheimer's disease, geriatrics, hospice and palliative care, post-acute services, and senior citizens.
Fields of interest: Palliative care; Alzheimer's disease; Geriatrics; Geriatrics research; Residential/custodial care, hospices; Residential/custodial care, senior continuing care; Aging, centers/services; Aging.
Type of support: General/operating support; Program development; Seed money; Curriculum development; Research; Employee volunteer services; Employee matching gifts; Matching/challenge support.
Limitations: Giving on a national basis in areas of company operations in AR, CA, CO, CT, DE, FL, GA, IA, IL, IN, KS, KY, MD, MI, MN, MO, NC, ND, NV, NJ, NM, OH, OK, PA, SC, SD, TN, TX, UT, VA, WA, WI, and WV. No grants to individuals, or for building or capital campaigns, endowments, fundraising events, overhead fees, advertising, political purposes, or continuing support.
Publications: Application guidelines.
Application information: Unsolicited applications are currently not accepted for the General Grant Program.
Board meeting date(s): June and Dec.
Officers and Directors:* Rick Rump,* Pres.; Matt Kang,* Treas.; Jennifer Steiner, Exec. Dir.; Deborah Arrendale; Lynn Hood; Carla Hughes; Beth Kaczor; Jason Perry.

Number of staff: 3 full-time professional; 2 full-time support.
EIN: 522031975
Selected grants: The following grants were reported in 2006.
$50,000 to American Medical Student Association Foundation, Chicago, IL. For End-of-Life Initiative.
$29,167 to University of Colorado Health Sciences Center, Denver, CO. For clinical implementation and testing of Alzheimer's-Hospice Placement Evaluation Scale (AHOPE).
$24,000 to Menorah Park Center for Senior Living, Beachwood, OH. For Better Visits: Improving Family Visits for Persons with Dementia and Their Families.
$15,000 to Bernal Heights Neighborhood Center, San Francisco, CA. For Neighborhood Elder Support Team (NEST) program.
$14,000 to Community Hospice of Northeast Florida, Jacksonville, FL. For Camp healing Powers.
$10,304 to Family Service: Prevention, Education and Counseling, Highland Park, IL. For Elder Mental health Serviecs program.
$10,000 to East Liberty Family Health Care Center, Pittsburgh, PA. For Homebound Elderly Outreach Program.
$5,000 to ARK, Adult Respite Care, Summerville, SC. For A Friend Project.
$5,000 to Family Eldercare, Austin, TX. For In-Home Care and Respite Services.
$5,000 to Jewish Vocational Service and Community Workshop, Southfield, MI. For Caring Partners Project (CPP).

1003

The Humana Foundation, Inc.
500 W. Main St., Ste. 208
Louisville, KY 40202-2946 (502) 580-4140
County: Jefferson
Contact: Barbara Wright; Virginia K. Judd, Exec. Dir.
FAX: (502) 580-1256;
E-mail: bwright@humana.com; Additional E-mail: HumanaFoundation@humana.com; URL: http://www.humanafoundation.org
Address for scholarships: Scholarship Mgmt. Svcs., Scholarship America, One Scholarship Way, P.O. Box 297, St. Peter, MN 56082, tel.: (507) 931-1682, (800) 537-4180

Incorporated in 1981 in KY.
Donor: Humana Inc.
Grantmaker type: Company-sponsored foundation.
Financial data (yr. ended 12/31/09): Assets, $53,531,847 (M); expenditures, $4,231,093; total giving, $4,203,985; qualifying distributions, $4,203,985; giving activities include $4,203,985 for 68 grants (high: $675,000; low: $2,500).
Purpose and activities: The foundation supports programs designed to promote healthy lives and healthy communities, with a focus on the needs of children, families, and seniors. Special emphasis is directed toward programs designed to promote health and fitness that lead to better decisions and lifestyles; promote literacy to improve health experiences; and develop the technology, tools, and resources that lead to healthy communities.
Fields of interest: Education; Health care; Children, services; Family services; Human services; Aging.
Type of support: General/operating support; Continuing support; Annual campaigns; Capital campaigns; Building/renovation; Program development; Professorships; Curriculum development; Scholarship funds; Employee

volunteer services; Employee-related scholarships; Matching/challenge support.
Limitations: Applications accepted. Giving primarily in areas of company operations in Phoenix, AZ, Denver, CO, Jacksonville, Miramar, and Tampa, FL, Atlanta, GA, Chicago, IL, Indianapolis, IN, Kansas City, KS, Louisville, KY, Metairie, LA, Detroit, MI, Cincinnati, OH, San Juan, PR, Memphis, TN, Austin, Corpus Christi, Dallas, Houston, and San Antonio, TX, Salt Lake City, UT, and Green Bay and Milwaukee, WI. No support for social, labor, political, veterans', or fraternal organizations, lobbying efforts, or mission-focused activities. No grants for start up needs or seed money, salary expenses or other administrative costs, general operating support for religious organizations, or for construction or renovation of sanctuaries.
Publications: Application guidelines; Grants list; Informational brochure; Newsletter.
Application information: Support is limited to 1 contribution per organization during any given year. Application form required.
Initial approach: Complete online application form
Copies of proposal: 1
Deadline(s): Nov. 1 through Jan. 15 for organizations located in Louisville, KY; Nov. 1 through June 15 for organizations located outside of Louisville, KY
Board meeting date(s): Every 2 months
Final notification: Generally, 6 weeks to 2 months
Officers and Directors:* Michael B. McCallister,* Chair., C.E.O. and Pres.; James H. Bloem, Sr. V.P., C.F.O., and Treas.; George G. Bauernfeind, V.P.; Joan O. Lenahan, Secy.; Virginia K. Judd, Exec. Dir.; David A. Jones; David A. Jones, Jr.
EIN: 611004763
Selected grants: The following grants were reported in 2009.
$733,935 to Scholarship America, Saint Peter, MN. For scholarships for children of Humana employees.
$675,000 to Actors Theater of Louisville, Louisville, KY. For Humana Festival of New American Plays.
$510,000 to United Way, Metro, Louisville, KY. For annual support.
$320,000 to Fund for the Arts, Louisville, KY. For campaign.
$177,500 to National Center for Family Literacy, Louisville, KY. For Health Literacy Project WellZone.
$100,000 to Kentucky Country Day School, Louisville, KY. For scholarship endowment.
$100,000 to Louisville Free Public Library Foundation, Louisville, KY. For Newburg Project.
$50,000 to Louisiana Tech Foundation, Ruston, LA. For business school challenge grant.

1004

Huntington Bancshares Incorporated Contributions Program
Huntington Ctr.
41 S. High St.
Columbus, OH 43287 (614) 480-8300
County: Franklin
URL: https://www.huntington.com/regions/

Grantmaker type: Corporate giving program.
Purpose and activities: As a complement to its foundation, Huntington Bancshares makes charitable contributions to nonprofit organizations directly. Support is given primarily in areas of company operations in Indiana, Kentucky, Michigan, Ohio, Pennsylvania, and West Virginia.
Limitations: Giving primarily in areas of company operations in IN, KY, MI, OH, PA, and WV.

1005
IMRA America, Inc. Contributions Program
1044 Woodridge Ave.
Ann Arbor, MI   48105-9748   (734) 930-2560
County: Washtenaw
URL: http://www.imra.com/

Grantmaker type: Corporate giving program.
Purpose and activities: IMRA America makes charitable contributions to nonprofit organizations on a case by case basis. Support is given on a national and international basis.
Fields of interest: General charitable giving.
Type of support: General/operating support.
Limitations: Giving on a national and international basis.

1006
Isabella Bank and Trust Foundation
200 E. Broadway
P.O. Box 100
Mount Pleasant, MI   48804-0100
County: Isabella

Established in 1997 in MI.
Donor: Isabella Bank and Trust.
Grantmaker type: Company-sponsored foundation.
Financial data (yr. ended 12/31/09): Assets, $845,071 (M); expenditures, $110,093; total giving, $106,234; qualifying distributions, $106,234; giving activities include $106,234 for grants.
Purpose and activities: The foundation supports hospitals and community foundations and organizations involved with arts and culture, higher education, and human services.
Fields of interest: Arts; Higher education; Hospitals (general); American Red Cross; Residential/custodial care, hospices; Human services; Foundations (community); United Ways and Federated Giving Programs.
Type of support: General/operating support; Sponsorships.
Limitations: Applications accepted. Giving primarily in Isabella County, MI, with emphasis on the Mt. Pleasant area. No grants to individuals.
Application information: Application form not required.
   Initial approach: Proposal
   Deadline(s): None
Officers and Directors:* William J. Strickler,* Chair.; Richard J. Barz,* Pres.; Roxanne Schultz,* Secy.; Steven D. Pung,* Treas.; Dennis P. Angner.
EIN: 383348258
Selected grants: The following grants were reported in 2006.
$20,000 to Central Michigan University, Mount Pleasant, MI.
$7,500 to American Red Cross.
$7,500 to United Way of Isabella County, Mount Pleasant, MI.
$7,000 to Farwell Area Schools, Farwell, MI.
$5,000 to Faith Action for Community Equity, Honolulu, HI.
$5,000 to Garfield Memorial Library, Clare, MI.
$3,100 to Central Michigan University, Mount Pleasant, MI.
$2,630 to United Way of Isabella County, Mount Pleasant, MI.
$2,500 to United Way of Clare County, Clare, MI.
$1,000 to American Red Cross.

1007
Jackson National Community Fund
1 Corporate Way
Lansing, MI   48951-0001
County: Ingham
E-mail: jncf@jackson.com; *URL:* https://www.jackson.com/about/Community.jsp?

Grantmaker type: Corporate giving program.
Purpose and activities: The Jackson National Community Fund makes charitable contributions to educational institutions and nonprofit organizations involved with community enrichment. Special emphasis is directed towards programs designed to enhance the lives of children and the elderly. Support is limited to Denver, Colorado, Chicago, Illinois, Lansing, Michigan, and Nashville, Tennessee.
Fields of interest: Higher education; Children, services; Aging, centers/services; Community/economic development; Children; Aging.
Type of support: Program development; General/operating support; Employee volunteer services; Sponsorships; Employee matching gifts; In-kind gifts.
Limitations: Applications accepted. Giving limited to Denver, CO, Chicago, IL, Lansing, MI, and Nashville, TN. No support for private foundations, health clinics, treatment centers or hospitals, political parties or candidates, religious organizations not of benefit to the entire community, elementary or secondary schools, industry or professional organizations, service organizations, or fraternal, labor, or veterans' organizations. No grants to individuals.
Publications: Application guidelines; Corporate giving report.
Application information: A contributions committee reviews all requests. DVDs, CDs, and other unsolicited materials are not encouraged. Application form required.
   Initial approach: Complete online application form
   Copies of proposal: 1
   Deadline(s): Nov. 11, Feb. 10, May 26, and Aug. 11
   Committee meeting date(s): Quarterly
   Final notification: Jan 21, March 25, July 8, and Sept. 30
Administrator: Danielle Weller, Corp. Responsibility Specialist.
Number of staff: 1 full-time professional.

1008
JPMorgan Chase Bank, N.A. Corporate Giving Program
(formerly The Chase Manhattan Bank Corporate Social Responsibility Program)
1111 Polaris Pkwy.
Columbus, OH   43240-7001
County: Delaware
Contact: Steven W. Gelston, V.P.
E-mail: corporate.secretary@jpmchase.com;
URL: http://www.jpmorganchase.com/corporate/Corporate-Responsibility/corporate-responsibility.htm

Grantmaker type: Corporate giving program.
Purpose and activities: As a complement to its foundation, JPMorgan Chase also makes charitable contributions to nonprofit organizations directly. Special emphasis is directed toward organizations involved with community asset development, community life, and youth education.

Fields of interest: Media, film/video; Visual arts; Performing arts; Performing arts, dance; Performing arts, theater; Performing arts, music; Arts; Education, reform; Elementary/secondary education; Education; Employment, training; Employment; Housing/shelter; Human services; Civil rights, race/intergroup relations; Economic development; Nonprofit management; Community/economic development; Public policy, research; Public affairs; Minorities; Economically disadvantaged.
Type of support: General/operating support; Continuing support; Equipment; Program development; Technical assistance; Employee volunteer services; Sponsorships; Employee matching gifts; Donated equipment; In-kind gifts.
Limitations: Applications accepted. Giving primarily in the CT, NJ, and NY tri-state area, AZ, CA, CO, DE, FL, IL, IN, KY, LA, MI, OH, OK, TX, UT, WV, WI, and on an international basis in areas of company operations; giving also to national organizations and U.S.-based international organizations. No support for religious, fraternal, or veterans' organizations, or United Way member organizations. No grants to individuals, or for medical research, fundraising events, debt reduction, deficit financing, capital endowments, scholarships, or tuition; generally no grants for health issues or higher education.
Publications: Application guidelines.
Application information: Visit corporate Web site for details. The company has a staff that only handles contributions. A contributions committee at each company location reviews all requests originating from that particular area. Application form required.
   Initial approach: Complete online eligibility quiz
   Copies of proposal: 1
   Deadline(s): Various
   Final notification: Following review

1009
JPMorgan Chase Philanthropy - Michigan
611 Woodward Ave., MI1-8038
Detroit, MI   48226-3408   (313) 225-2125
County: Wayne
Contact: Christine Kageff, V.P., Philanthropy and Community Relations
FAX: (313) 225-3333;
E-mail: christine.kageff@chase.com; *URL:* http://www.jpmorganchase.com/giving

Donor: JPMorgan Chase & Co.
Grantmaker type: Company-sponsored foundation.
Purpose and activities: JPMorgan Chase provides support to Michigan not-for-profit organizations through grants and sponsorships whose missions are in alignment with its three focus areas of philanthropic giving: community asset development - to encourage, sustain and develop economic self-reliance through affordable housing, quality jobs, and business opportunities; youth education - to help young people succeed in life and in work through strong public schools, programs that support and enable educational excellence, and educational opportunities for all; and community life - to enrich communities with sponsorships and events focused on arts and culture, including quality of life through arts and culture, arts and civic programming that celebrates diversity, programs that help build arts and cultural capacity and sustainability, and environmental awareness.
Fields of interest: Arts, cultural/ethnic awareness; Arts education; Visual arts; Performing arts; Arts; Employment, training; Housing/shelter,

development; Community development, neighborhood development; Economic development; Community development, small businesses; Community/economic development; Economically disadvantaged.

Type of support: Program development; Technical assistance; Sponsorships.

Limitations: Applications accepted. Giving limited to areas of company operations in MI. No support for fraternal organizations, athletic teams or social groups, public agencies, private schools, public schools (unless in partnership with a qualified not-for-profit organization), parent-teacher associations, volunteer-operated organizations, programs designed to promote religious or political doctrines, higher education (unless program is specifically within guidelines), health- or medical-related organizations (unless program fits within stated giving guidelines), or organizations that discriminate on the basis of race, sex, sexual orientation, age or religion. No grants to individuals, or for funds to pay down operating deficits, fundraising events, advertising (including ads in event, performance or athletic programs), scholarships or tuition assistance; generally no grants for endowments or capital campaigns (exceptions are made by invitation only).

Application information: The company has a staff that only handles contributions.

Initial approach: Submit completed online application form

Deadline(s): Generally application should be made in first quarter for payment during calendar year

Final notification: By Nov. 1

Number of staff: 2 full-time professional.

1010
JSJ Foundation

700 Robbins Rd.
Grand Haven, MI 49417-2603
County: Ottawa
Contact: Dana Plowman
FAX: (616) 847-3112;
E-mail: plowmand@jsjcorp.com; URL: http://www.jsjcorp.com/community/philanthropy/

Established in 1983 in MI.
Donor: JSJ Corp.
Grantmaker type: Company-sponsored foundation.
Financial data (yr. ended 12/31/09): Assets, $416,532 (M); gifts received, $150,000; expenditures, $198,380; total giving, $196,372; qualifying distributions, $196,372; giving activities include $196,372 for 35 grants (high: $24,404; low: $500).
Purpose and activities: The foundation supports organizations involved with arts and culture, education, health, human services, and civic affairs.
Fields of interest: Performing arts, orchestras; Humanities; Arts; Higher education; Libraries (public); Education; Health care; Children/youth, services; Residential/custodial care; Human services; United Ways and Federated Giving Programs; Public affairs.
Type of support: General/operating support; Continuing support; Annual campaigns; Capital campaigns; Building/renovation; Endowments; Program development; Scholarship funds.
Limitations: Applications accepted. Giving primarily in areas of company operations in Florence, AL, Ormond Beach, FL, Middleburg, IN, Grand Haven and Grand Rapids, MI, and La Crosse, WI. No support for

political organizations or specific disease-related organizations. No grants to individuals, or for exchange programs, fellowships, internships, lectureships, or professorships, or golf outings; no loans.

Publications: Application guidelines.
Application information: Application form not required.

Initial approach: Mail or E-mail proposal to foundation

Copies of proposal: 1

Deadline(s): Nov. 1

Board meeting date(s): Nov.

Final notification: 30 days following board meeting

Officers and Trustees:* Lynne Sherwood,* Chair.; Erick P. Johnson,* Secy.-Treas.; Nelson C. Jacobson; Bari S. Johnson; Melinda E. Johnson; Robert J. Mesereau; Mark F. Sherwood.
Number of staff: None.
EIN: 382421508
Selected grants: The following grants were reported in 2009.
$24,400 to United Way, Greater Ottawa County, Holland, MI. For program support.
$16,700 to Loutit District Library, Grand Haven, MI. For new library.
$10,000 to Grand Haven Schools Foundation, Grand Haven, MI. For endowment.
$10,000 to Grand Rapids Symphony, Grand Rapids, MI. For operating support.
$10,000 to Hospice of North Ottawa Community, Spring Lake, MI.
$10,000 to Kandu, Inc., Holland, MI. For capital campaign.
$10,000 to Love INC of the Tri-Cities, Grand Haven, MI.
$10,000 to Tri-Cities Ministries, Grand Haven, MI.
$6,000 to West Michigan Symphony Orchestra, Muskegon, MI.

1011
Kadant Johnson, Inc. Scholarship Foundation

(formerly Johnson Corporation Scholarship Foundation)
805 Wood St.
Three Rivers, MI 49093-1053
County: St. Joseph
Application address: Three Rivers High School Guidance Office, 700 Sixth Ave., Three Rivers, MI 49093

Donors: The Johnson Corp.; Kadant Johnson; Kadant Johnson, Inc.
Grantmaker type: Company-sponsored foundation.
Financial data (yr. ended 06/30/10): Assets, $204 (M); gifts received, $10,800; expenditures, $10,800; total giving, $10,800; qualifying distributions, $10,800; giving activities include $10,800 for 12 grants to individuals (high: $1,800; low: $1,800).
Purpose and activities: The foundation awards college scholarships to graduates of Three Rivers High School in Michigan planning to attend a Michigan institution to pursue studies in engineering, dentistry, nursing, medicine, teaching, or science.
Fields of interest: Dental school/education; Medical school/education; Nursing school/education; Teacher school/education; Engineering school/education.
Type of support: Scholarships—to individuals.

Limitations: Applications accepted. Giving limited to Three Rivers, MI.
Application information: Application form required.

Initial approach: Proposal

Deadline(s): Apr. 17

Officer: Greg Wedel, Chair.
EIN: 386098327

1012
Kawasaki Good Times Foundation

P.O. Box 81469
Lincoln, NE 68501-1469 (402) 476-6600
County: Lancaster
Contact: Rob Fairchild

Established in 1993 in NE.
Donors: Kawasaki Motors Manufacturing Corp., U.S.A.; Kawasaki Heavy Industries (USA), Inc.; Kawasaki Motors Corp., U.S.A.; Kawasaki Rail Car, Inc.; Kawasaki Robotics (USA) Inc.
Grantmaker type: Company-sponsored foundation.
Financial data (yr. ended 12/31/09): Assets, $2,791,085 (M); gifts received, $14,113; expenditures, $301,098; total giving, $280,500; qualifying distributions, $281,125; giving activities include $280,500 for 6 grants (high: $100,000; low: $5,500).
Purpose and activities: The foundation supports museums and organizations involved with Japanese culture, music, and higher education.
Fields of interest: Arts, cultural/ethnic awareness; Museums (art); Museums (specialized); Performing arts, music; Higher education; United Ways and Federated Giving Programs; Asians/Pacific Islanders.
Type of support: General/operating support.
Limitations: Applications accepted. Giving primarily in NE; some giving also MI and NY.
Application information: Application form not required.

Initial approach: Proposal

Deadline(s): None

Officers and Directors:* Kazushi Hattori,* Pres.; Toshio Kuwata, V.P.; Kazuhiro Kobayashi, Secy.-Treas.; Matsuhiro Asand; Takeshi Teranishi.
EIN: 363879896
Selected grants: The following grants were reported in 2008.
$100,000 to University of Nebraska Foundation, Lincoln, NE.
$40,000 to Metropolitan Museum of Art, New York, NY.
$30,000 to University of Nebraska Foundation, Lincoln, NE.

1013
Kellogg Company 25-Year Employees Fund, Inc.

c/o Kellogg Co.
1 Kellogg Sq.
P.O. Box 3599
Battle Creek, MI 49016-3599 (269) 961-2000
County: Calhoun
Contact: Timothy S. Knowlton, Pres.

Established in 1944 in MI.
Donor: W.K. Kellogg‡.
Grantmaker type: Company-sponsored foundation.
Financial data (yr. ended 12/31/09): Assets, $63,547,168 (M); expenditures, $3,120,556; total giving, $2,588,658; qualifying distributions,

$2,814,108; giving activities include $1,380,000 for 4 grants (high: $600,000; low: $80,000), and $1,208,658 for 168 grants to individuals (high: $41,615; low: $200).

Purpose and activities: The fund supports retiree associations and awards grants for living and medical expenses to current and former 25-year employees and the dependents of 25-year employees of Kellogg.

Fields of interest: Zoos/zoological societies; Food banks; Community/economic development; United Ways and Federated Giving Programs.

International interests: Canada; Mexico; South Africa; United Kingdom.

Type of support: Grants to individuals; Emergency funds.

Limitations: Applications accepted. Giving primarily in areas of company operations, with emphasis on Battle Creek, MI; giving also in Canada, England, the United Kingdom, Mexico, and South Africa. No grants to individuals (except for employee-related fund).

Application information: Must be employees or dependents of employees employed by Kellogg or a Kellogg subsidiary for at least 25 years. Application form not required.

Initial approach: Proposal

Board meeting date(s): Jan., Apr., July, and Oct.

Officers and Directors:* Timothy S. Knowlton,* Pres.; Mike L. Bivens, V.P.; Joel Vanderkooi, Co-Treas.; Joel Wittenberg, Co-Treas.; Margaret Bath; Celeste A. Clark; Ron Dissinger; Ed Rector.

Number of staff: 1 full-time support.

EIN: 386039770

Selected grants: The following grants were reported in 2006.

$3,500,000 to Battle Creek Public Schools, Battle Creek, MI.

$200,000 to YMCA and Outdoor Center, Sherman Lake, Augusta, MI.

1014
Kellogg Company Contributions Program

1 Kellogg Sq.
P.O. Box 3599
Battle Creek, MI   49016-3599   (269) 961-2000
County: Calhoun
URL: http://www.kelloggcompany.com/corporateresponsibility.aspx

Grantmaker type: Corporate giving program.

Purpose and activities: As a complement to its foundation, Kellogg also makes charitable contributions to nonprofit organizations directly. Special emphasis is directed towards programs that educate children and parents about nutrition and fitness. Support is given on a national and international basis in areas of company operations.

Fields of interest: Elementary/secondary education; Public health; Public health, physical fitness; Food banks; Nutrition; Disasters, Hurricane Katrina; Youth development, services; Civil/human rights, equal rights; United Ways and Federated Giving Programs; Children/youth.

Type of support: General/operating support; Employee volunteer services; Sponsorships; Employee matching gifts; Donated products.

Limitations: Giving on a national and international basis in areas of company operations; giving also to national organizations.

1015
Kellogg's Corporate Citizenship Fund

1 Kellogg Sq.
Battle Creek, MI   49016-3599   (269) 961-2867
County: Calhoun
Contact: Linda Fields
E-mail: linda.fields@kelloggs.com; URL: http://www.kelloggcompany.com/corporateresponsibility.aspx?id=659

Established in 1994 in MI.

Donor: Kellogg Co.

Grantmaker type: Company-sponsored foundation.

Financial data (yr. ended 12/31/09): Assets, $39,303,021 (M); gifts received, $20,000,000; expenditures, $8,756,433; total giving, $8,351,486; qualifying distributions, $8,734,164; giving activities include $8,351,486 for 488 grants (high: $1,000,000; low: $25).

Purpose and activities: The fund supports food banks and organizations involved with arts and culture, education, fitness and health, hunger, nutrition, swimming, and human services.

Fields of interest: Arts; Elementary/secondary education; Higher education; Education; Public health, obesity; Public health, physical fitness; Health care; Food services; Food banks; Nutrition; Athletics/sports, water sports; American Red Cross; YM/YWCAs & YM/YWHAs; Children/youth, services; Human services; United Ways and Federated Giving Programs.

Type of support: General/operating support; Building/renovation; Program development; Scholarship funds; Research; Technical assistance; Employee volunteer services; Employee matching gifts.

Limitations: Applications accepted. Giving primarily in areas of company operations in CA, Washington, DC, IL, and TX, with emphasis on Battle Creek, MI; some giving also in Australia and the United Kingdom.

Application information: Application form not required.

Initial approach: Letter of inquiry

Deadline(s): None

Officers and Directors:* Celeste A. Clark,* Pres.; Gary H. Pilnick, V.P.; Janice L. Perkins,* Treas.; Timothy S. Knowlton,* Exec. Dir.; George Ball; Paul Norman; Mark Wagner; Kathleen Wilson-Thompson.

EIN: 383167772

Selected grants: The following grants were reported in 2008.

$1,435,119 to United Way of Greater Battle Creek, Battle Creek, MI.

$1,200,000 to Community Foundation for Greater Manchester, Manchester, England.

$527,500 to Action for Healthy Kids, Skokie, IL.

$520,000 to Resource Foundation, Larchmont, NY.

$250,000 to Feeding America, Chicago, IL.

$250,000 to Global FoodBanking Network, Chicago, IL.

$150,000 to Baylor College of Medicine, Houston, TX. For USDA-ARS Children's Nutrition Research Center.

$131,390 to Battle Creek Area Catholic Schools Foundation, Battle Creek, MI.

$34,751 to United Way of Rome and Floyd County, Rome, GA.

$15,364 to Kellogg Community College Foundation, Battle Creek, MI.

1016
The Kelly Services, Inc. Foundation

999 W. Big Beaver Rd.
Troy, MI   48084-4716
County: Oakland
Contact: Kirk Hanna, Dir., Govt. Affairs
FAX: (248) 244-5497;
E-mail: hannaki@kellyservices.com; Additional tel.: (248) 244-5370

Established in 1994 in MI.

Donor: Kelly Services, Inc.

Grantmaker type: Company-sponsored foundation.

Financial data (yr. ended 01/03/10): Assets, $1,583 (M); gifts received, $158,750; expenditures, $148,592; total giving, $147,400; qualifying distributions, $148,592; giving activities include $147,400 for 22 grants (high: $33,000; low: $1,000).

Purpose and activities: The foundation supports organizations involved with historical societies, education, health, heart disease, the automotive industry, community economic development, and African-Americans.

Fields of interest: Historic preservation/historical societies; Elementary/secondary education; Higher education; Nursing school/education; Education; Health care; Heart & circulatory diseases; Business/industry; Community/economic development; United Ways and Federated Giving Programs; African Americans/Blacks.

Type of support: Scholarship funds; Sponsorships; General/operating support; Program development.

Limitations: Applications accepted. Giving primarily in southeast MI, with emphasis on Detroit. No grants to individuals.

Application information: Application form not required.

Initial approach: Proposal

Copies of proposal: 1

Deadline(s): None

Board meeting date(s): Semiannually

Final notification: Within 1 month

Officers and Directors:* Carl T. Camden,* Pres. and C.E.O.; Patricia A. Little, Exec. V.P. and C.F.O.; Michael L. Durik,* Exec. V.P. and C.A.O.; Daniel T. Lis,* Sr. V.P. and Secy.; Michael E. Debs, Sr. V.P. and C.A.O.; Michael F. Orsini, V.P., Tax; Thomas L. Totte, V.P.; Joel D. Starr, Treas.

EIN: 383207679

Selected grants: The following grants were reported in 2010.

$33,000 to Concours d Elegance of America, Troy, MI.

$12,500 to National Academy Foundation, New York, NY.

$10,000 to American Heart Association, Southfield, MI.

$10,000 to Cornerstone Schools, Detroit, MI.

$10,000 to Detroit Economics Club, Detroit, MI.

$10,000 to Executive Leadership Foundation, Alexandria, VA.

$10,000 to Oakland University, Rochester, MI.

$5,000 to HAVEN, Pontiac, MI.

$5,000 to United Way for Southeastern Michigan, Detroit, MI.

$2,500 to Case Western Reserve University, Cleveland, OH.

1017
Kemp Klein Foundation
(formerly Kemp, Klein, Umphrey, Endelman & May Foundation)
201 W. Big Beaver Rd., Ste. 600
Troy, MI 48084-4161 (248) 528-1111
County: Oakland
Contact: Ralph A. Castelli, Jr., Pres.
URL: http://www.kkue.com/kemp-klein-charitable-foundation.php

Established in 1994 in MI.
Donors: Kemp, Klein, Umphrey, Endelman & May, PC; Turner & Turner, P.C.
Grantmaker type: Company-sponsored foundation.
Financial data (yr. ended 12/31/09): Assets, $13,516 (M); gifts received, $11,649; expenditures, $11,220; total giving, $11,138; qualifying distributions, $11,138; giving activities include $11,138 for 30 grants (high: $6,463; low: $50).
Purpose and activities: The foundation supports food banks and organizations involved with education, animal welfare, health, legal aid, human services, and voluntarism promotion.
Fields of interest: Higher education; Law school/education; Education, reading; Education; Animal welfare; Animals/wildlife, special services; Health care; Legal services; Food banks; Children/youth, services; Residential/custodial care, hospices; Human services; Voluntarism promotion.
Type of support: General/operating support; Program development; Curriculum development.
Limitations: Applications accepted. Giving primarily in MI. No grants to individuals.
Application information: Application form not required.
Initial approach: Proposal
Deadline(s): None
Officers: Ralph A. Castelli, Jr., Pres. and Treas.; Thomas J. O'Connor, Secy.
Directors: Irwin M. Alterman; Thomas L. Boyer; Marie B. Goedtel; Susan M. Halligan; Margaret A. Sagese; Shannon Scheloski; Diane Szalkiewicz.
EIN: 383169464

1018
KeyBank Foundation
(formerly Key Foundation)
800 Superior Ave., 1st Fl.
M.C. OH-01-02-0126
Cleveland, OH 44114-2601 (216) 828-7349
County: Cuyahoga
Contact: Valerie Raines, Sr. Prog. Off.
FAX: (216) 828-7845;
E-mail: KeyBank_Foundation@keybank.com;
URL: http://www.key.com/html/A-12.html

Established about 1969 in OH.
Donors: Society Corp.; Society Capital Corp.; KeyBank N.A.; KeyCorp.
Grantmaker type: Company-sponsored foundation.
Financial data (yr. ended 12/31/08): Assets, $29,936,600 (M); gifts received, $12,000,000; expenditures, $12,582,207; total giving, $12,449,003; qualifying distributions, $12,449,003; giving activities include $11,474,645 for 1,840 grants (high: $1,150,000; low: $250), and $974,358 for 1,785 employee matching gifts.
Purpose and activities: The foundation supports organizations involved with arts and culture, health, employment, financial education, human services,

and diversity. Special emphasis is directed toward programs designed to promote economic self sufficiency.
Fields of interest: Arts; Health care; Employment, training; Employment; Human services, financial counseling; Human services; Civil/human rights, equal rights; Physically disabled; Minorities; Asians/Pacific Islanders; African Americans/Blacks; Hispanics/Latinos; Native Americans/American Indians; Indigenous peoples; LGBTQ; Economically disadvantaged.
Type of support: Annual campaigns; Capital campaigns; Continuing support; Curriculum development; Employee matching gifts; Employee volunteer services; General/operating support; Matching/challenge support; Professorships; Program development.
Limitations: Applications accepted. Giving primarily in areas of company operations in AK, CO, ID, IN, KY, ME, MI, NY, OH, OR, UT, VT, and WA. No support for lobbying or political organizations, veterans' or fraternal organizations, discriminatory organizations, professional organizations, or athletic teams. No grants to individuals.
Publications: Application guidelines; Annual report.
Application information: Proposals should be concise. Visit Web site for nearest company district office. Organizations receiving support are asked to provide a final report. Application form not required.
Initial approach: Letter of inquiry or telephone
Copies of proposal: 1
Deadline(s): None
Board meeting date(s): Quarterly
Final notification: Within 3 months
Officers and Trustees:* Margot James Copeland,* Chair.; Christopher Gorman, Pres.; James Hoffman, V.P.; Paul Harris, Secy.; Mark Whitham, Treas.; Cindy P. Crotty; Karen R. Haefling; Thomas E. Helfrich; Bruce D. Murphy; Elizabeth J. Oliver.
Number of staff: 4 full-time professional.
EIN: 237036607
Selected grants: The following grants were reported in 2008.
$1,150,000 to United Way of Greater Cleveland, Cleveland, OH. For operating support.
$325,500 to University Hospitals Health System, Cleveland, OH. For program support.
$250,000 to Cuyahoga Community College Foundation, Cleveland, OH. For program support.
$250,000 to Musical Arts Association, Cleveland, OH. For program support.
$200,000 to Economic Growth Foundation, Cleveland, OH. For program support.
$76,667 to Enterprise Community Partners, Cleveland, OH. For program support.
$59,500 to Urban League of Dayton, Dayton, OH. For program support.
$50,000 to Boys and Girls Clubs of South Puget Sound, Tacoma, WA. For program support.
$5,000 to Center for Community Service Fund, Seattle, WA. For program support.
$5,000 to Youth Force, Seattle, WA. For program support.

1019
Kowalski Sausage Company Charitable Trust
c/o JPMorgan Chase Bank, N.A.
P.O. Box 3038
Milwaukee, WI 53201-3038
County: Milwaukee
Application address: JPMorgan Chase Bank, N.A., 611 Woodward Ave., Detroit, MI 48226, tel.: (313) 225-3454

Established in 1951 in MI.
Donor: Kowalski Sausage Co.
Grantmaker type: Company-sponsored foundation.
Financial data (yr. ended 12/31/09): Assets, $987,046 (M); expenditures, $60,961; total giving, $60,000; qualifying distributions, $60,000; giving activities include $60,000 for grants.
Purpose and activities: The trust supports organizations involved with cancer, school athletics, children and youth services, and residential care.
Fields of interest: Cancer; Athletics/sports, school programs; Children/youth, services; Residential/custodial care.
Type of support: Program development.
Limitations: Applications accepted. Giving primarily in FL and MI. No grants to individuals.
Application information: Application form required.
Initial approach: Contact foundation for application form
Copies of proposal: 1
Deadline(s): None
Board meeting date(s): Varies
Officers and Trustees:* Stephen Kowalski,* Chair.; Donald Kowalski, Pres.; Agnes Kowalski; Kenneth Kowalski; JPMorgan Chase Bank, N.A.
EIN: 386046508

1020
The Kroger Co. Contributions Program
c/o Community Rels. Dept.
1014 Vine St.
Cincinnati, OH 45202-1100 (513) 762-4000
County: Hamilton
URL: http://www.thekrogerco.com/corpnews/corpnewsinfo_charitablegiving.htm

Grantmaker type: Corporate giving program.
Purpose and activities: As a complement to its foundation, Kroger also makes charitable contributions to nonprofit organizations directly. Special emphasis is directed towards programs designed to promote the advancement of women and minorities. Support is limited to areas of company operations in Alabama, Arizona, Arkansas, California, Colorado, Georgia, Illinois, Indiana, Kansas, Kentucky, Michigan, Mississippi, Nevada, North Carolina, Ohio, Oregon, Tennessee, Texas, Utah, Virginia, and Washington.
Fields of interest: Elementary/secondary education; Health care; Breast cancer research; Food services; Disasters, preparedness/services; Human services; American Red Cross; Salvation Army; Minorities; Women.
Type of support: General/operating support; Employee volunteer services; Donated products.
Limitations: Applications accepted. Giving limited to areas of company relations in AL, AR, AZ, CA, CO, GA, IL, IN, KS, KY, MI, MS, NC, NV, OH, OR, TN, TX, UT, VA, and WA.

Application information:
Initial approach: Contact Community Relations Department at nearest company retail division for application information

1021
The Kroger Co. Foundation
1014 Vine St.
Cincinnati, OH   45202-1148   (513) 762-4449
County: Hamilton
Contact: Lynn Marmer, Pres.
FAX: (513) 762-1295; Additional tel.: (513) 452-4441; URL: http://www.thekrogerco.com/corpnews/corpnewsinfo_charitablegiving_foundation.htm

Established in 1987 in OH.
Donor: The Kroger Co.
Grantmaker type: Company-sponsored foundation.
Financial data (yr. ended 01/31/10): Assets, $35,695,395 (M); gifts received, $4,069,163; expenditures, $5,892,121; total giving, $5,782,780; qualifying distributions, $5,782,780; giving activities include $5,782,780 for 1,397 grants (high: $312,000; low: $8).
Purpose and activities: The foundation supports organizations involved with education, women's health, breast cancer, hunger, minorities, and women.
Fields of interest: Elementary/secondary education; Education; Health care; Breast cancer; Food services; United Ways and Federated Giving Programs; Minorities; Women.
Type of support: Program development; Capital campaigns; Seed money; Employee volunteer services.
Limitations: Applications accepted. Giving primarily in areas of company operations in AL, AR, AZ, CA, CO, GA, IL, IN, KS, KY, MI, MS, NV, OH, OR, TN, TX, UT, VA, WA, and WV. No support for national or international organizations, non-educational foundations, medical research organizations, or religious organizations or institutions not of direct benefit to the entire community. No grants to individuals, or for conventions or conferences, dinners or luncheons, endowments, general operating support, sports event sponsorships, program advertisements, or membership dues.
Publications: Application guidelines.
Application information: Visit Web site for company division addresses. Application form not required.
Initial approach: Proposal to nearest company division
Deadline(s): None
Officers and Trustees: Lynn Marmer, Pres.; Paul W. Heldman, Secy.; Scott M. Henderson, Treas.; David B. Dillon; Dennis Hackett; Marnette Perry; Pete Williams.
Number of staff: 1 part-time professional.
EIN: 311192929
Selected grants: The following grants were reported in 2007.
$120,000 to United Way of Central Ohio, Columbus, OH.
$15,000 to Teachers Treasures, Indianapolis, IN.
$14,603 to South Valley Sanctuary, West Jordan, UT.
$7,500 to Girl Scouts of the U.S.A., Denver, CO.
$1,500 to Boys and Girls Club of Hutchinson, Hutchinson, KS.
$1,500 to Fulcrum Foundation, Seattle, WA.
$1,500 to Mobile Meals of Tucson, Tucson, AZ.

$1,000 to United Way, Livingston County, Brighton, MI.
$1,000 to Your Community in Unity, Brigham City, UT.

1022
La-Z-Boy Foundation
(formerly La-Z-Boy Chair Foundation)
1284 N. Telegraph Rd.
Monroe, MI   48162-3390   (734) 242-1444
County: Monroe
Contact: Donald E. Blohm, Admin.

Incorporated in 1953 in MI.
Donors: La-Z-Boy Chair Co.; La-Z-Boy Inc.; E. M. Knabusch†; Edwin J. Shoemaker†; H. F. Gertz†.
Grantmaker type: Company-sponsored foundation.
Financial data (yr. ended 12/31/09): Assets, $18,661,198 (M); expenditures, $1,021,467; total giving, $918,800; qualifying distributions, $918,800; giving activities include $918,800 for 85 grants.
Purpose and activities: The foundation supports organizations involved with education, health, human services, and government and public administration. Support is primarily in areas of company operations.
Fields of interest: Education; Health care; Human services; United Ways and Federated Giving Programs; Government/public administration.
Type of support: General/operating support; Building/renovation.
Limitations: Applications accepted. Giving primarily in areas of company operations in Siloam Springs, AR, Redlands, CA, Monroe, MI, Newton and Saltillo, MS, Neosho, MO, Hudson, Lenoir, and Taylorsville, NC, Dayton and New Tazewell, TN. No support for religious or political organizations. No grants to individuals, or for travel or conferences or start-up needs; no loans.
Publications: Application guidelines; Annual report (including application guidelines).
Application information: Proposals should be brief. Additional information may be requested at a later date. Application form not required.
Initial approach: Proposal
Copies of proposal: 1
Deadline(s): Mar. 1, June 1, Sept. 1, and Dec. 1
Board meeting date(s): Mar., June, Sept., and Dec.
Final notification: 3 months
Officer and Directors:* James W. Johnston, Chair.; June E. Knabush-Taylor,* Pres.; Marvin J. Bauman,* Secy.; Donald E. Blohm,* Treas.; Kurt L. Darrow; John H. Foss; Richard M. Gabrys; Janet Gurwitch; David. K. Hehl; Edwin Holman; Janet Kerr; H. George Levy; W. Alan McCollough; Nido R. Qubein.
Number of staff: 1 part-time support.
EIN: 386087673
Selected grants: The following grants were reported in 2009.
$47,000 to United Way of Monroe County, Monroe, MI.
$40,000 to United Way of Rhea County, Dayton, TN.
$30,000 to Neosho United Fund, Neosho, MO.
$25,000 to Newton United Fixers Fund, Newton, MS.
$15,000 to Salvation Army of Monroe, Monroe, MI.
$10,000 to American Red Cross, Monroe, MI.

1023
Life Time Fitness Foundation
c/o Life Time Fitness, Inc.
2902 Corp. Pl.
Chanhassen, MN   55317   (952) 947-0000
County: Carver
FAX: (952) 947-0099;
E-mail: foundation@lifetimefitness.com; Additional address: 6442 City West Pkwy., Eden Prairie, MN 55344; URL: http://lifetimefitness.mylt.com/community/ltf-foundation

Established in 2005 in MN.
Grantmaker type: Company-sponsored foundation.
Financial data (yr. ended 12/31/09): Assets, $120,192 (M); gifts received, $585,877; expenditures, $621,987; total giving, $605,560; qualifying distributions, $605,560; giving activities include $605,560 for grants.
Purpose and activities: The foundation supports organizations involved with education, health, athletics, children and youth, and family services. Special emphasis is directed toward programs designed to help young people maximize their potential.
Fields of interest: Secondary school/education; Education; Health care; Athletics/sports, school programs; Athletics/sports, amateur leagues; Athletics/sports, Special Olympics; Boys & girls clubs; Children/youth, services; Family services; Human services; Economically disadvantaged.
Type of support: Donated products; Equipment; Program development; In-kind gifts.
Limitations: Applications accepted. Giving limited to areas of company operations in Phoenix, AZ, Denver, CO, Washington, DC, Bacon Raton, FL, Atlanta, GA, Chicago, IL, Indianapolis, IN, Kansas City, KS, Columbia, MD, Detroit, MI, Minneapolis and St. Paul, MN, St. Louis, MO, Newark, NJ, Cary, NC, Memphis, TN, Austin, Dallas, Houston, and San Antonio, TX, and Salt Lake City, UT. No support for religious organizations, political or lobbying organizations, or for industry, trade or professional organizations. No grants to individuals, or for fundraising, endowments, capital campaigns, or general operating support; generally no loans or investments.
Publications: Application guidelines; Corporate giving report.
Application information: Applicant organizations are encouraged to use the Minnesota Common Grant Application Form. Application form required.
Initial approach: Download application form and mail, e-mail, or fax to foundation
Deadline(s): None
Board meeting date(s): Monthly
Final notification: 60 days
Officers and Directors:* Michael Gerend, Pres.; Eric Buss, V.P.; Brian Senger, Secy.; Michael Robinson, Treas.; Jason Thunstrom.
EIN: 030533192
Selected grants: The following grants were reported in 2008.
$5,000 to Boys and Girls Clubs of Greater Houston, Houston, TX.
$2,500 to Mental Health America of Greater Dallas, Dallas, TX.
$1,600 to Minneapolis Police Department, Minneapolis, MN.
$1,200 to Detroit Public Schools, Detroit, MI.
$1,200 to Detroit Public Schools, Detroit, MI.
$1,000 to Detroit Public Schools, Detroit, MI.

1024
MAC Valves Foundation
P.O. Box 111
Wixom, MI   48393-0679   (248) 624-7770
County: Oakland
Contact: Martha Welch

Grantmaker type: Company-sponsored foundation.
Financial data (yr. ended 11/30/09): Assets,
$1,153,674 (M); expenditures, $77,017; total
giving, $75,500; qualifying distributions, $76,175;
giving activities include $75,500 for 9 grants (high:
$30,000; low: $500).
Purpose and activities: The foundation supports
organizations involved with education, sleep
disorders, and children services.
Fields of interest: Higher education; Education;
Health organizations; Boy scouts; Children,
services.
Type of support: General/operating support.
Limitations: Applications accepted. Giving primarily
in Detroit, MI.
Application information: Application form not
required.
   Initial approach: Letter
   Deadline(s): None
Directors: Robert Neff; Ken Sorensen.
EIN: 382440953

1025
Masco Corporation Contributions Program
21001 Van Born Rd.
Taylor, MI   48180-1340   (313) 274-7400
County: Wayne
URL: http://www.masco.com/
corporate_information/citizenship/index.html

Grantmaker type: Corporate giving program.
Financial data (yr. ended 12/31/08): Total giving,
$4,371,218, including $3,046,855 for grants (high:
$100,000; low: $100), $238,502 for employee
matching gifts, and $1,085,860 for in-kind gifts.
Purpose and activities: As a complement to its
foundation, Masco also makes charitable
contributions to nonprofit organizations directly.
Special emphasis is directed toward programs
designed to provide affordable housing for
low-income families. Support is given primarily in
areas of company operations.
Fields of interest: Environment; Housing/shelter;
Human services; Economically disadvantaged.
Type of support: General/operating support;
Employee matching gifts; Donated products; In-kind
gifts.
Limitations: Giving primarily in areas of company
operations.
Number of staff: 1 part-time professional; 1
part-time support.

1026
Masco Corporation Foundation
(formerly Masco Corporation Charitable Trust)
c/o Corp. Affairs
21001 Van Born Rd.
Taylor, MI   48180-1340   (313) 274-7400
County: Wayne
Contact: Melonie B. Colaianne, Pres.
FAX: (313) 792-6262; *URL:* http://
www.masco.com/corporate_information/
citizenship/foundation/index.html

Trust established in 1952 in MI.
Donor: Masco Corp.
Grantmaker type: Company-sponsored foundation.
Financial data (yr. ended 12/31/09): Assets,
$15,361,941 (M); expenditures, $4,327,297; total
giving, $4,049,833; qualifying distributions,
$4,120,387; giving activities include $4,049,833
for 127 grants (high: $250,000; low: $300).
Purpose and activities: The foundation supports
organizations involved with arts and culture outreach
for disadvantaged youth, human services,
community development, and civic affairs. Special
emphasis is directed toward programs designed to
promote decent housing environments for
disadvantaged, low-income families.
Fields of interest: Performing arts; Historical
activities; Arts; Housing/shelter, development;
Housing/shelter; Human services; Community/
economic development; Public affairs; Youth;
Economically disadvantaged.
Type of support: General/operating support; Annual
campaigns; Capital campaigns; Building/
renovation; Employee matching gifts.
Limitations: Applications accepted. Giving primarily
in areas of company operations, with emphasis on
the greater Detroit, MI, area. No support for
discriminatory organizations, political organizations
or candidates or lobbying organizations, athletic
clubs, religious organizations not of direct benefit to
the entire community, or organizations benefiting
few people. No grants to individuals, or for debt
reduction, endowments, sports programs or events
or school extracurricular activities, or conferences,
travel, seminars, or film or video projects; no loans.
Publications: Application guidelines; Occasional
report.
Application information: A full proposal may be
requested after inquiry. The Council of Michigan
Foundations Common Grant Application form is also
accepted. Application form not required.
   Initial approach: Letter of inquiry or telephone
   Copies of proposal: 1
   Deadline(s): None
   Board meeting date(s): Spring and fall
   Final notification: Within 6 weeks following receipt
      of proposal
Officers and Directors: Sharon Rothwell,* Chair.;
Melonie B. Colaianne, Pres.; Eugene A. Gargaro, Jr.,
Secy.; Richard A. Manoogian; Timothy J. Wadhams.
Trustee: Comerica Bank.
Number of staff: 2 part-time professional; 2
part-time support.
EIN: 386043605
Selected grants: The following grants were reported
in 2006.
$515,000 to Detroit Institute of Arts, Detroit, MI.
$283,000 to Detroit Symphony Orchestra, Detroit,
MI.
$265,000 to Henry Ford Community College,
Dearborn, MI.
$250,000 to Habitat for Humanity International,
Americus, GA.
$235,000 to University Cultural Center Association,
Detroit, MI.
$200,000 to Detroit Renaissance Foundation,
Detroit, MI.
$50,000 to Arts League of Michigan, Detroit, MI.
$20,000 to Greater Corktown Development
Corporation, Detroit, MI.
$20,000 to Northwest Detroit Neighborhood
Development, Detroit, MI.
$20,000 to Savannah College of Art and Design,
Savannah, GA.

1027
Mason State Bank Centennial Fund, Inc.
344 S. Jefferson
Mason, MI   48854-1652   (517) 676-4253
County: Ingham
Contact: Daniel Schlattman, Treas.

Donor: Mason State Bank.
Grantmaker type: Company-sponsored foundation.
Financial data (yr. ended 12/31/09): Assets,
$43,256 (M); expenditures, $65; total giving, $0;
qualifying distributions, $45.
Purpose and activities: The foundation supports
organizations involved with education and
community development.
Fields of interest: Elementary/secondary
education; Education; Community/economic
development.
Type of support: Equipment.
Limitations: Giving limited to Alaiedon, Aurelius,
Ingham, and Vevay townships and Mason, MI. No
grants to individuals.
Officers and Directors:* Larry Silsby,* Pres.; Susan
Kosier,* Secy.; Daniel Schlattman,* Treas.; Sandra
Russell.
EIN: 382772901

1028
MEEMIC Foundation for the Future of
Education
1685 N. Opdyke Rd.
Auburn Hills, MI   48326-2656
County: Oakland
FAX: (248) 375-7549;
E-mail: foundation@meemic.com

Established in 1992 in MI.
Donors: Michigan Educational Employees Mutual
Insurance Co.; MEEMIC Insurance Co.
Grantmaker type: Company-sponsored foundation.
Financial data (yr. ended 12/31/09): Assets,
$1,630,914 (M); expenditures, $50,683; total
giving, $37,472; qualifying distributions, $40,552;
giving activities include $37,472 for 38 grants to
individuals (high: $2,000; low: $127).
Purpose and activities: The foundation awards
grants to educators at public, private, charter, and
parochial schools in Michigan for programs
designed to incorporate technology, science,
literacy, mentoring, and the arts.
Fields of interest: Arts education; Education,
reading; Education; Science.
Type of support: Grants to individuals.
Limitations: Applications accepted. Giving limited to
MI. No grants for school supplies or equipment.
Publications: Application guidelines; Grants list;
Informational brochure.
Application information: Application form required.
   Initial approach: Proposal
   Copies of proposal: 1
   Deadline(s): Apr. 30
   Final notification: The end of May
Officers: Donald Weatherspoon,* Pres.; Richard
White, Sr. V.P.; Sean Maloney,* V.P.
Number of staff: 1 full-time professional; 1 part-time
professional.
EIN: 383048526

1029

Meijer, Inc. Corporate Giving Program

2929 Walker Ave. N.W.
Grand Rapids, MI   49544-6402
County: Kent
URL: http://www.meijer.com/content/content.jsp?
pageName=meijer_75th_anniversary_community

Grantmaker type: Corporate giving program.
Purpose and activities: Meijer makes charitable
contributions to nonprofit organizations involved
with food services. Support is given primarily in
areas of company operations in Illinois, Indiana,
Kentucky, Michigan, and Ohio.
Fields of interest: Food banks; General charitable
giving.
Type of support: General/operating support;
Donated products; In-kind gifts.
Limitations: Giving primarily in areas of company
operations in IL, IN, KY, MI, and OH.

1030

Meritor Charitable Trust Fund

(formerly ArvinMeritor, Inc. Trust)
c/o Community Rels.
2135 W. Maple Rd.
Troy, MI   48084-7186   (248) 435-1913
County: Oakland
Contact: Julie Garrisi, Comms. Specialist, Govt. &
Community Rels.
FAX: (248) 435-1031;
E-mail: julie.garrisi@arvinmeritor.com; Additional
contact: Jerry Rush, Sr. Dir., Govt. & Community
Rels., e-mail: jerry.rush@arvinmeritor.com;
URL: http://www.meritor.com/ourcompany/
communities/responsibility/default.aspx

Established in 1997 in MI.
Donors: Meritor Automotive, Inc.; ArvinMeritor, Inc.
Grantmaker type: Company-sponsored foundation.
Financial data (yr. ended 09/30/09): Assets,
$250,965 (M); gifts received, $326,388;
expenditures, $320,888; total giving, $320,888;
qualifying distributions, $320,888; giving activities
include $320,888 for 81 grants (high: $76,388;
low: $500).
Purpose and activities: The foundation supports
organizations involved with arts and culture,
education, health, hunger, human services,
community development, and civic affairs. Special
emphasis is directed toward engineering, science,
and technology education.
Fields of interest: Performing arts, theater;
Performing arts, orchestras; Performing arts, opera;
Arts; Secondary school/education; Higher
education; Engineering school/education;
Education; Health care; Food services; Boys & girls
clubs; Youth development, business; Human
services; Business/industry; Community/economic
development; United Ways and Federated Giving
Programs; Science, formal/general education;
Engineering/technology; Public affairs.
Type of support: Program development; Employee
volunteer services; Employee matching gifts.
Limitations: Applications accepted. Giving primarily
in areas of company operations, with emphasis on
MI. No support for discriminatory organizations,
religious or sectarian organizations not of direct
benefit to the entire community, labor, political, or
veterans' organizations, or fraternal, athletic, or
social clubs. No grants to individuals, or for general
operating support for local United Way agencies,
sponsorship of fundraising activities for individuals,

debt reduction, or seminars, conferences, trips, or
tours; no loans.
Publications: Application guidelines.
Application information: Application form not
required.
Initial approach: Proposal
Deadline(s): Aug.
Officers: Charles G. "Chip" McClure, Chair. and
C.E.O.; Vernon G. Baker II, Sr. V.P. and Genl.
Counsel; Carsten J. Reinhardt, Sr. V.P. and C.O.O.;
Jeffrey A. Craig, Sr. V.P. and C.F.O.; Linda M.
Cummins, Sr. V.P., Comms.; Mary Lehmann, Sr. V.P.
and Treas.; Barbara Griffin Novak, V.P. and Secy.
EIN: 522089611
Selected grants: The following grants were reported
in 2008.
$200,000 to Detroit Renaissance Foundation,
Detroit, MI.
$15,000 to Detroit Symphony Orchestra, Detroit,
MI.
$10,000 to Detroit Institute of Arts, Detroit, MI.
$1,200 to Urban League of Greater Cincinnati,
Cincinnati, OH.
$1,000 to Detroit, City of, Detroit, MI.

1031

MGM Mirage Corporate Giving Program

3260 Industrial Rd.
Las Vegas, NV   89109-1132   (702) 650-7429
County: Clark
Contact: Jocelyn Bluitt-Fisher, Dir., Community
Affairs
FAX: (702) 650-7401;
E-mail: philanthropy@mgmmirage.com; URL: http://
www.mgmmiragevoice.com/pages/cg_giving.asp

Grantmaker type: Corporate giving program.
Purpose and activities: MGM Mirage makes
charitable contributions to nonprofit organizations
involved with childhood development, education,
youth development, diversity, and community
development. Special emphasis is directed toward
programs that target the needs of specific groups,
socially or economically disadvantaged populations,
and projects which are the direct result of
community collaborations. Support is given primarily
in Michigan, Mississippi, and Nevada.
Fields of interest: Education, public education;
Elementary/secondary education; Child
development, education; Youth development;
Community/economic development; Economically
disadvantaged.
Type of support: Employee volunteer services;
General/operating support.
Limitations: Giving limited to areas of company
operations in MI, MS, and NV. No support for
discriminatory organizations. No grants to
individuals, or for athletic sponsorships; no gaming
or casino items for children.
Publications: Application guidelines.
Application information: Application form not
required.
Initial approach: Mail or fax proposal to
headquarters
Copies of proposal: 1
Deadline(s): Sept. 1

1032

Michigan Automotive Compressor, Inc. Corporate Giving Program

2400 N. Dearing Rd.
Parma, MI   49269-9415
County: Jackson
URL: http://www.michauto.com/MACI/
community_page.htm

Grantmaker type: Corporate giving program.
Purpose and activities: Michigan Automotive
compressor makes charitable contributions to
nonprofit organizations involved with education and
the environment. Support is given primarily in
Jackson County, Michigan.
Fields of interest: Education; Environmental
education; Environment; United Ways and Federated
Giving Programs.
Type of support: Employee-related scholarships;
General/operating support; Scholarship funds;
In-kind gifts.
Limitations: Giving primarily in Jackson County, MI.
No grants to individuals.

1033

Michigan Cardivascular Institute Foundation

(also known as MCVI Foundation)
1015 S. Washington Ave.
Saginaw, MI   48601-2556
County: Saginaw
Contact: Diane M. Fong, Exec. Dir.
FAX: (989) 754-3365; E-mail: dfong@mcvi.com;
URL: http://www.mcvi.com/index.cfm/fuseaction/
site.content/type/43732/custom/1.cfm

Established in MI.
Donor: Michigan Cardiovascular Institute PC.
Grantmaker type: Company-sponsored foundation.
Financial data (yr. ended 12/31/09): Assets,
$566,209 (M); gifts received, $6,224;
expenditures, $161,063; total giving, $16,245;
qualifying distributions, $61,820; giving activities
include $16,245 for 3 grants (high: $10,000; low:
$875).
Purpose and activities: The foundation supports
programs designed to empower people of all ages
to live and lead healthy lives. Special emphasis is
directed toward education, prevention, and
treatment of cardiac-related diseases.
Fields of interest: Museums (specialized); Public
health, physical fitness; Health care; Heart &
circulatory diseases; Heart & circulatory research;
Nutrition.
Type of support: General/operating support;
Scholarship funds; Donated products.
Limitations: Applications accepted. Giving primarily
in areas of company operations in MI, with emphasis
on the Great Lakes Bay region and Arenac, Bay,
Clare, Gladwin, Gratiot, Huron, Iosco, Isabella,
Lapeer, Midland, Ogemaw, Roscommon, Saginaw,
Sanilac, and Tuscola counties. No support for
political, lobbying, or religious organizations. No
grants to individuals, or for annual campaigns,
endowments, fundraising or special events, deficit
or debt reduction, advertising, team sponsorships,
or travel; no loans.
Publications: Application guidelines; Occasional
report.
Application information: Applying organizations are
encouraged to telephone the foundation to discuss
projects prior to submitting a proposal. Proposals

should be no longer than 5 pages. Grants range from $2,000 to $3,000. Support is limited to 1 contribution per organization during any given year. Organizations receiving support are asked to submit an evaluation report.
Initial approach: Proposal; download application form and mail to foundation for AEFD Grants
Copies of proposal: 2
Deadline(s): None, but applications are only reviewed at year-end; Mar. 1 to Mar. 31 for AED Grants
Officers and Directors: * Peter Fatal, M.D.*, Pres.; John F. Collins, M.D., V.P.; Clarence M. Rivette, Secy.-Treas.; Diane M. Fong, Exec. Dir.; Christopher Genco, M.D.; Rao V.C. Gudipati, M.D.; Sharon Miller.
EIN: 383146518

1034
Herman Miller, Inc. Corporate Giving Program
855 E. Main Ave.
P.O. Box 302
Zeeland, MI   49464-0302
County: Ottawa
URL: http://www.hermanmiller.com/About-Us/A-Better-World-Report/Community-Service

Grantmaker type: Corporate giving program.
Purpose and activities: Herman Miller makes charitable contributions to nonprofit organizations on a case by case basis. Support is given on a national and international basis in areas of company operations.
Fields of interest: General charitable giving.
Type of support: Employee volunteer services.
Limitations: Giving on a national and international basis in areas of company operations.

1035
Mitsubishi International Corporation Contributions Program
655 3rd Ave.
New York, NY   10017-5617   (212) 605-2000
County: New York
URL: http://www.mitsubishicorp-us.com/corporatecitizenship_socialresponsibility.shtml

Grantmaker type: Corporate giving program.
Purpose and activities: As a complement to its foundation, Mitsubishi International also makes charitable contributions to nonprofit organizations directly. Support is given on a national basis.
Fields of interest: Arts; Education; Environment; Health care; Human services; International affairs; Civil/human rights; Public affairs, alliance/advocacy; Public affairs.
Type of support: General/operating support; Continuing support; Capital campaigns; Program development; Conferences/seminars; Seed money; Fellowships; Scholarship funds; Employee volunteer services; Sponsorships; Employee matching gifts; Employee-related scholarships; Donated equipment; In-kind gifts.
Limitations: Applications accepted. Giving on a national basis in areas of company operations, particularly in Los Angeles, and San Francisco, CA, Washington, DC, Chicago, IL, Boston, MA, Detroit, MI, New York, NY, Pittsburgh, PA, Dallas and Houston, TX, and Seattle, WA. No support for religious organizations.

Publications: Corporate report.
Application information: The Corporate Communications Department handles giving. Application form required.
Initial approach: Letter of inquiry
Copies of proposal: 1
Deadline(s): None
Number of staff: 3 part-time professional; 1 part-time support.

1036
Monroe Auto Equipment Company Foundation
c/o Comerica Bank, Tr.
P.O. Box 75000, M.C. 3462
Detroit, MI   48275-3462   (313) 222-4085
County: Wayne

Trust established in 1958 in MI; currently registered in OH.
Donors: Monroe Auto Equipment Co.; Tenneco Automotive Inc.; Tenneco Inc.; C.S. McIntyre†.
Grantmaker type: Company-sponsored foundation.
Financial data (yr. ended 12/31/08): Assets, $1 (M); expenditures, $71,583; total giving, $67,643; qualifying distributions, $67,643; giving activities include $67,643 for grants.
Purpose and activities: The foundation supports organizations involved with education and human services.
Fields of interest: Literature; Higher education; Education; Human services; Community/economic development; United Ways and Federated Giving Programs.
Type of support: General/operating support.
Limitations: Giving primarily in Detroit, MI.
Application information: Application form not required.
Initial approach: Letter of inquiry
Copies of proposal: 1
Deadline(s): None
Board meeting date(s): Quarterly
Trustees: Timothy R. Donovan; Mark P. Frissora; Cathy G. Garcia; Jane Ostrander; Kenneth Trammell; Comerica Bank.
Number of staff: 5
EIN: 346518867

1037
Nash Finch Company Contributions Program
P.O. Box 355
Minneapolis, MN   55440-0355
County: Hennepin
Application address for Labels for Learning: 7600 France Ave. South, Edina, MIN, 55435; Contact for Labels for Learning: Judy Welter, tel.: (952) 8440-1168; URL: http://www.nashfinch.com/about_lflprogram.html

Grantmaker type: Corporate giving program.
Purpose and activities: Nash Finch makes charitable contributions to nonprofit organizations involved with education. Support is limited to areas of store operations.
Fields of interest: Elementary/secondary education; Education.
Type of support: General/operating support.
Limitations: Applications accepted. Giving primarily in areas of store operations in CO, GA, IL, IN, KS, KY, MI, MN, MT, NC, ND, NE, OH, PA, VA, and WY.

Publications: Application guidelines.
Application information: Application form required.
Initial approach: Download registration form for Labels for Learning Program and mail to application address
Deadline(s): None

1038
New York Life Foundation
51 Madison Ave.
New York, NY   10010-1655   (212) 576-7341
County: New York
Contact: Christine Park, Pres.
E-mail: NYLFoundation@newyorklife.com;
URL: http://www.newyorklife.com/foundation

Established in 1979 in NY.
Donor: New York Life Insurance Co.
Grantmaker type: Company-sponsored foundation.
Financial data (yr. ended 12/31/09): Assets, $80,582,452 (M); gifts received, $115,000; expenditures, $10,646,086; total giving, $10,601,446; qualifying distributions, $10,610,436; giving activities include $9,627,544 for 463 grants (high: $1,000,000; low: $500), and $973,902 for 985 employee matching gifts.
Purpose and activities: The foundation supports organizations and programs that benefit young people, particularly in the areas of mentoring, safe places to learn and grow, educational enhancement opportunities and childhood bereavement.
Fields of interest: Elementary/secondary education; Child development, education; Education, reading; Education; Mental health, grief/bereavement counseling; Youth development, adult & child programs; Youth development, citizenship; Youth development; Children/youth; Children.
International interests: Mexico.
Type of support: Curriculum development; General/operating support; Continuing support; Program development; Employee volunteer services; Employee matching gifts; Employee-related scholarships.
Limitations: Applications accepted. Giving primarily in New York and Westchester County, NY; giving also to national organizations serving two or more of the following cities and regions: Phoenix, AZ, Los Angeles, Sacramento, San Francisco, and San Ramon, CA, Denver, CO, Washington, DC, Fort Lauderdale, Miami, and Tampa, FL, Atlanta, GA, Chicago, IL, Kansas City, KS, Boston and Westwood, MA, Detroit, MI, Minneapolis, MN, Clinton, Hunterdon, and Morris counties, and Edison, and Parsippany, NJ, Cleveland, OH, Philadelphia, PA, Austin, Dallas, and Houston, TX, Salt Lake City, UT, Richmond, VA, Seattle, WA, and Mexico. No support for religious or sectarian organizations not of direct benefit to the entire community, fraternal, social, professional, veterans', or athletic organizations, or discriminatory organizations. No grants for seminars, conferences, or trips, endowments, memorials, or capital campaigns, fundraising events, telethons, races, or other benefits, goodwill advertising, or basic or applied research.
Publications: Application guidelines; Annual report; Grants list; Informational brochure (including application guidelines).
Application information: Community Impact Grants must be initiated by a New York Life employee. A full proposal may be requested at a later date. Interviews and site visits may be requested.

Organizations receiving support are asked to submit progress reports. Application form required.

Initial approach: Complete online application form
Deadline(s): None; Oct. 1 to Dec. 15 for New York Life Foundation Awards Program
Board meeting date(s): Apr. and Nov.
Final notification: 2 to 3 months for regular grants
Officers and Directors:* Theodore A. Mathas, Chair.; Christine Park,* Pres.; Steven Rautenberg, Sr. V.P., Corp. Comms.; Lance LaVergne, V.P. and Chief Diversity Off.; Catherine Mamon, Secy.; Kenneth Roman, Treas.; Cynthia Bolker; Sheila K. Davidson.
Number of staff: 5 full-time professional; 1 full-time support.
EIN: 132989476
Selected grants: The following grants were reported in 2009.
$1,000,000 to Comfort Zone Camp, Richmond, VA.
$790,000 to Developmental Studies Center, Oakland, CA.
$650,000 to United Ways of the Greater New York, New Jersey and Connecticut Tri-State Area, New York, NY.
$542,500 to Four-H Council, National, Chevy Chase, MD.
$225,000 to Childrens Aid Society, New York, NY.
$106,000 to City Year New York, New York, NY.
$100,000 to Fundacion Educa Mexico, Mexico City, Mexico.
$47,900 to United Activities Unlimited, Staten Island, NY.
$25,000 to Center for Grieving Children, Portland, ME.
$16,300 to United Way of Tampa Bay, Tampa, FL.

1039
The Newsweek/Daily Beast Company LLC Contributions Program
(formerly Newsweek, Inc. Corporate Giving Program)
7 Hanover Sq.
New York, NY 10004
County: New York
Contact: Tricia Luh, Sr. V.P. and C.F.O.

Grantmaker type: Corporate giving program.
Purpose and activities: Newsweek makes charitable contributions to nonprofit organizations involved with publishing, education, and to museums. Support is given primarily in areas of company operations.
Fields of interest: Media, print publishing; Museums; Education.
Type of support: General/operating support; Scholarship funds; Employee volunteer services; Sponsorships; Employee matching gifts; In-kind gifts.
Limitations: Applications accepted. Giving primarily in areas of company operations, with emphasis on Los Angeles and San Francisco, CA, Chicago, IL, Boston, MA, Detroit, MI, New York, NY, Dallas, TX, and in FL.
Application information: Application form not required.
Initial approach: Proposal to headquarters
Deadline(s): None
Final notification: Following review

1040
The Nissan Foundation
P.O. Box 685001, M.S. B5B
Franklin, TN 37068-5001 (615) 725-1501
County: Williamson
E-mail: nissanfoundation@nissan-usa.com;
URL: http://www.nissanusa.com/about/corporate-info/community-relations.html

Established in 1993 in CA.

Donors: Nissan Motor Corp. U.S.A.; Nissan North America, Inc.
Grantmaker type: Company-sponsored foundation.
Financial data (yr. ended 06/30/10): Assets, $11,211,218 (M); expenditures, $597,024; total giving, $578,500; qualifying distributions, $578,500; giving activities include $578,500 for 28 grants (high: $60,000; low: $10,000).
Purpose and activities: The foundation supports educational programs designed to promote diverse cultural heritage.
Fields of interest: Arts, cultural/ethnic awareness; Education.
Type of support: General/operating support; Program development.
Limitations: Applications accepted. Giving limited to areas of company operations in southern CA, the Atlanta, GA, metropolitan area, Detroit, MI, south central MS, the New York, NY, metropolitan area, middle TN, and Dallas and Forth Worth, TX. No support for disease advocacy, research, or religious organizations. No grants to individuals, or for fundraising events, sponsorships, or political activities or capital campaigns.
Publications: Application guidelines; Grants list; Informational brochure (including application guidelines).
Application information: A full proposal may be requested at a later date. Support is limited to 1 contribution per organization during any given year. Application form not required.
Initial approach: Complete online letter of intent
Deadline(s): Nov. 20.
Final notification: June
Officers and Directors:* Scott Becker, Pres.; John M. Dab, Secy.; William H. Scott, Jr., Treas.; Alfonso Albaisa; Holly Braco; Alan Buddendeck; Albert Castignetti; Brian Fallon; Scott Fessenden; Gary Frigo; Rita Ghosn; Tony Lucente; Mark Perry; Brad Thacker; George Vazquez; Jeffrey Webster.
EIN: 954413799
Selected grants: The following grants were reported in 2007.
$30,000 to Accelerated School, Los Angeles, CA.
$30,000 to Nashville State Community College Foundation, Nashville, TN.
$25,000 to Nashville Public Television, Nashville, TN.
$25,000 to University of Michigan, College of Engineering, Ann Arbor, MI.
$20,000 to 100 Black Men of Jackson, Jackson, MS.
$20,000 to Discovery Center, Murfreesboro, TN.
$20,000 to Global Education Center, Nashville, TN.
$18,000 to Cerritos College Foundation, Norwalk, CA.
$15,000 to Boys and Girls Club of Middle Tennessee, Nashville, TN.
$10,000 to Los Angeles Opera Company, Los Angeles, CA.

1041
Nissan North America, Inc. Corporate Giving Program
c/o Nissan Neighbors
P.O. Box 685001, MS B-5-B
Franklin, TN 37068-5001 (310) 771-5594
County: Williamson
FAX: (310) 516-7967; URL: http://www.nissanusa.com/about/corporate-info/community-relations.html

Grantmaker type: Corporate giving program.
Purpose and activities: As a complement to its foundation, Nissan also makes charitable contributions to nonprofit organizations directly. Support is given primarily in areas of company operations.
Fields of interest: Education; Environment; Youth development.
Type of support: General/operating support; Employee volunteer services; Employee matching gifts; In-kind gifts.
Limitations: Applications accepted. Giving primarily in southern CA, metropolitan Detroit, MI, south central MS, middle TN, and Dallas and Fort Worth, TX.
Application information: Application form required.
Initial approach: Complete online application form
Copies of proposal: 1
Deadline(s): None
Final notification: 4 to 6 weeks

1042
Northwest Airlines, Inc. Corporate Giving Program
2700 Lone Oak Pkwy., Dept A1300
Eagan, MN 55121-1546 (612) 727-2111
County: Dakota
Contact: Carol Hollen, Community Rels.
FAX: (612) 727-7795; URL: http://www.nwa.com/corpinfo/aircares/giving.html

Grantmaker type: Corporate giving program.
Purpose and activities: Northwest makes charitable contributions to nonprofit organizations on a case by case basis. Support is given on a national basis in areas of company operations, with emphasis on Detroit, Michigan, Minneapolis/St. Paul, Minnesota, and Memphis, Tennessee.
Fields of interest: Arts, cultural/ethnic awareness; Child development, education; Public health; Disasters, preparedness/services; Human services, travelers' aid.
Type of support: General/operating support; In-kind gifts; Sponsorships.
Limitations: Giving on a national basis in areas of company operations, with emphasis on Detroit, MI, Minneapolis/St. Paul, MN, and Memphis, TN. No support for political, religious, fraternal, alumni, trade, professional, social, athletic, discriminatory or parent/teacher organizations, or K-12 schools or school associations. No grants to individuals, or for endowments, capital or annual operating fund drives, memorials, beauty pageants or talent contests, fundraising events, athletic events, social functions or advertising in commemorative journals, yearbooks or special event publications, basic academic or scientific research, or conference or seminars.
Application information:
Initial approach: Complete online application
Deadline(s): None

Committee meeting date(s): As needed
Final notification: Following review; 6 to 12 months prior to event for sponsorships

1043
Pamida Foundation

8800 F. St.
Omaha, NE 68127-1507 (402) 339-2400
County: Douglas
URL: http://www.pamida.com/foundation/
foundation.asp

Established in 1983 in NE.
Donor: Pamida, Inc.
Grantmaker type: Company-sponsored foundation.
Financial data (yr. ended 01/31/10): Assets,
$1,074,804 (M); gifts received, $37,584;
expenditures, $1,427,742; total giving,
$1,052,166; qualifying distributions, $1,052,166;
giving activities include $1,052,166 for 1,296
grants (high: $2,000; low: $100).
Purpose and activities: The foundation supports
programs designed to encourage and educate
youth; help families in need; and enhance quality of
life for senior citizens.
Fields of interest: Education; Health care; Food
banks; Family services; Aging, centers/services;
Youth; Aging; Economically disadvantaged.
Type of support: General/operating support;
Program development; Sponsorships; Matching/
challenge support.
Limitations: Applications accepted. Giving limited to
areas of company operations in IA, IL, IN, KS, KY,
MI, MN, MO, MT, ND, NE, OH, SD, TN, WI, and WY.
No support for religious organizations, for-profit
businesses, school cubs, athletic teams, political,
labor, or fraternal organizations, or discriminatory
organizations. No grants to individuals, or for sports
events, advertising in event programs or yearbooks,
or mass solicitations by national or international
organizations.
Publications: Application guidelines.
Application information: Proposals should be
submitted using organization letterhead. Additional
information may be requested at a later date.
Support is limited to 1 contribution per organization
during any given year. Application form required.
Initial approach: Download application form and
mail proposal and application form to
foundation
Copies of proposal: 1
Deadline(s): 60 days prior to need
Board meeting date(s): Bi-monthly
Final notification: 30 days
Officers: Laurie Wharton, Pres.; Paul Rothmal,*
V.P.; Dean Williamson, Secy.; David Enholm, Treas.
EIN: 470656225
Selected grants: The following grants were reported
in 2009.
$1,000 to United Way of Greater Cincinnati,
Cincinnati, OH.

1044
Parsons Corporation Contributions
Program

c/o Contribs. Comm.
100 W. Walnut St.
Pasadena, CA 91124-0001 (626) 440-2000
County: Los Angeles

Grantmaker type: Corporate giving program.

Purpose and activities: Parsons makes charitable
contributions to nonprofit organizations involved
with arts and culture, higher education, and human
services. Support is given on a national and
international basis in areas of company operations.
Fields of interest: Arts; Higher education; Human
services.
Type of support: General/operating support.
Limitations: Applications accepted. Giving on a
national and international basis in areas of company
operations, with emphasis on AK, AL, AZ, CA, CO,
Washington, DC, FL, GA, GU, HI, IL, IN, KS, KY, MA,
MD, MI, MN, MO, NC, NH, NJ, NV, NY, OH, OK, OR,
PA, PR, SC, TN, TX, VA, VT, WA, and WV, and in
Bahrain, Canada, England, Greece, Ireland, Italy,
Kuwait, Oman, Qatar, Romania, Russia, Saudi
Arabia, South Korea, Taiwan, Thailand, and United
Arab Emirates.
Application information: Telephone calls are not
encouraged. A contributions committee reviews all
requests. Application form not required.
Initial approach: Proposal to headquarters
Deadline(s): None
Committee meeting date(s): Bi-weekly
Final notification: 2 weeks

1045
Perrigo Company Charitable Foundation

515 Eastern Ave.
Allegan, MI 49010-9070 (269) 673-8451
County: Allegan
Contact: Michael R. Stewart, Dir.

Established in 2000 in MI.
Donor: L. Perrigo Co.
Grantmaker type: Company-sponsored foundation.
Financial data (yr. ended 06/30/09): Assets,
$689,148 (M); gifts received, $1,193,056;
expenditures, $849,143; total giving, $839,110;
qualifying distributions, $839,110; giving activities
include $263,127 for 67 grants (high: $40,000;
low: $100).
Purpose and activities: The foundation supports
organizations involved with arts and culture,
education, health, substance abuse prevention,
cancer, and human services.
Fields of interest: Arts; Higher education;
Education; Hospitals (general); Health care;
Substance abuse, prevention; Cancer; Boy scouts;
Girl scouts; American Red Cross; Developmentally
disabled, centers & services; Homeless, human
services; Human services; United Ways and
Federated Giving Programs.
Type of support: Scholarship funds; General/
operating support; Building/renovation; Program
development.
Limitations: Applications accepted. Giving primarily
in areas of company in MI. No grants to individuals.
Application information:
Initial approach: Proposal
Deadline(s): None
Officers and Director: Joseph C. Papa, Pres.; Judy
L. Brown, Exec. V.P. and C.F.O.; John T.
Hendrickson, Exec. V.P.; Todd W. Kingma, Secy.;
Ronald L. Winowiecki, Treas.; Michael R. Stewart.
EIN: 383553518
Selected grants: The following grants were reported
in 2009.
$33,900 to Seeds of Grace, Allegan, MI.
$10,000 to Safeway Foundation, Pleasanton, CA.
$5,000 to American Cancer Society, Grand Rapids,
MI.

$5,000 to American Heart Association, Grand
Rapids, MI.
$5,000 to Boy Scouts of America, Grand Rapids, MI.
$5,000 to Center for Women in Transition, Holland,
MI.
$5,000 to Girl Scouts of the U.S.A., Kalamazoo, MI.
$3,000 to Bronx High School of Science, Bronx, NY.
$3,000 to Sylvias Place, Allegan, MI.
$2,500 to Leukemia & Lymphoma Society, Grand
Rapids, MI.

1046
The Pistons-Palace Foundation

5 Championship Dr.
Auburn Hills, MI 48326-1753 (248) 377-0100
County: Oakland
Contact: Dennis Sampier
FAX: (248) 377-0309; *URL:* http://www.nba.com/
pistons/community/

Established in 1989 in MI.
Donors: Detroit Pistons Basketball Co.; The Palace
of Auburn Hills; Guardian Industries Corp.; Bank
One, N.A.; Palace Sports & Entertainment, Inc.;
Ticketmaster Group, Inc.; Belle Tire; National
Basketball Association; Pricewaterhouse Coopers
LLP; Quicken Loans; Morgan Bradley LLC.
Grantmaker type: Company-sponsored foundation.
Financial data (yr. ended 02/28/10): Assets,
$762,867 (M); gifts received, $72,406;
expenditures, $83,331; total giving, $68,814;
qualifying distributions, $75,874; giving activities
include $53,064 for grants (high: $19,634; low:
$200), and $5,750 for 5 grants to individuals (high:
$2,500; low: $500).
Purpose and activities: The foundation supports
programs designed to promote education,
recreation, and healthy lifestyles. Special emphasis
is directed toward programs serving youth and
adults.
Fields of interest: Education, reading; Education;
Hospitals (general); Cancer; Athletics/sports,
amateur leagues; Recreation; Youth development;
Children/youth, services; Human services;
Economically disadvantaged.
Type of support: General/operating support; Annual
campaigns; Building/renovation; Program
development; Scholarship funds; Sponsorships;
Scholarships—to individuals; In-kind gifts.
Limitations: Applications accepted. Giving primarily
in areas of company operations in the tri-county
metropolitan Detroit area and southeastern MI. No
grants to individuals (except for scholarships).
Publications: Application guidelines; Annual report;
Newsletter.
Application information: Application form required.
Initial approach: Contact foundation for
application form; complete online forms for
scholarship contests when available
Copies of proposal: 1
Deadline(s): Aug. 1; Feb. for Know Your Black
History
Officers and Trustees: Ralph J. Gerson, V.P.;
Thomas S. Wilson, V.P.; Ann Newman, Secy.; Ethan
Davidson; Marla Davidson-Karimipour; Byron
Gerson; Dorothy Gerson; Dan Hauser.
Number of staff: 3 full-time professional.
EIN: 382858649
Selected grants: The following grants were reported
in 2007.
$25,100 to Beaumont Foundation, Southfield, MI.
$7,000 to Cornerstone Schools, Detroit, MI.
$3,100 to Salvation Army, Alpena, MI.

$3,000 to Life Directions, Detroit, MI.
$2,000 to Catholic Social Services, Grand Rapids, MI.
$2,000 to Michigan Youth Appreciation Foundation, Detroit, MI.
$1,875 to American Red Cross, Detroit, MI.
$1,250 to CATCH, Detroit, MI.
$1,000 to Grand Rapids Public Library, Grand Rapids, MI.

1047
The PNC Foundation
(formerly PNC Bank Foundation)
1 PNC Plz.
249 5th Ave., P1-POPP-20-1
Pittsburgh, PA   15222   (412) 762-2748
County: Allegheny
Contact: Eva Tansky Blum, Chair. and Pres.
FAX: (412) 705-3584; E-mail: eva.blum@pnc.com; URL: http://www.pnccommunityinvolvement.com/PNCFoundation.htm

Established in 1970 in PA.
Donors: PNC Bank, N.A.; The PNC Financial Services Group, Inc.
Grantmaker type: Company-sponsored foundation.
Financial data (yr. ended 12/31/09): Assets, $183,609,085 (M); gifts received, $120,000,000; expenditures, $31,040,110; total giving, $29,694,921; qualifying distributions, $30,632,837; giving activities include $28,246,667 for 1,580 grants (high: $1,000,000; low: $100), $948,254 for 1,699 employee matching gifts, and $500,000 for loans/program-related investments.
Purpose and activities: The foundation supports programs designed to enhance educational opportunities for children, with emphasis on underserved pre-K children; and promote the growth of targeted communities through economic development initiatives.
Fields of interest: Arts education; Arts; Elementary/secondary education; Education, early childhood education; Child development, education; Teacher school/education; Human services; Economic development; Community/economic development; Economically disadvantaged.
Type of support: General/operating support; Continuing support; Capital campaigns; Building/renovation; Program development; Curriculum development; Program-related investments/loans; Employee matching gifts; Matching/challenge support.
Limitations: Applications accepted. Giving primarily in areas of company operations in Washington, DC, DE, FL, IL, IN, KY, MD, MI, MO, NJ, OH, TN, VA, and WI, with emphasis on PA. No support for discriminatory organizations, churches, religious organizations, advocacy groups, private foundations. No grants to individuals, or for endowments, conferences, seminars, tickets, or advertising, or annual campaigns for hospitals, colleges, or universities; no loans (except for program-related investments).
Publications: Application guidelines.
Application information: An interview may be requested. Proposals may be submitted using the Delaware Valley Grantmakers, Greater Cincinnati Foundation, or Grantmakers of Western Pennsylvania Common Grant Application. Application form not required.
   Initial approach: Proposal to nearest local representative

Copies of proposal: 1
Deadline(s): None
Board meeting date(s): Quarterly
Final notification: Approximately 6 weeks
Officers and Trustees: * Eva T. Blum,* Chair. and Pres.; George P. Long III, Secy. and Counsel; Samuel R. Patterson, Treas.; Joseph C. Guyaux; Joan L. Gulley; Peter K. Classen; Neil Hall; Roberta London-Wilson; Donna C. Peterman; James E. Rohr; PNC Bank, N.A.
EIN: 251202255
Selected grants: The following grants were reported in 2009.
$1,000,000 to Sesame Workshop, New York, NY. For general support and Math Is Everywhere.
$590,000 to United Way of Allegheny County, Pittsburgh, PA. For general support.
$480,000 to YMCA of Pittsburgh, Pittsburgh, PA. For general support.
$220,200 to Pennsylvania State University, University Park, PA. For general support.
$200,000 to Delaware Business Roundtable Education Committee, Wilmington, DE. For general support.
$11,000 to Lexington Arts and Cultural Council, Lexington, KY. For general support.
$10,000 to Pennsylvania Downtown Center, Harrisburg, PA. For general support.
$10,000 to Wilmington College, New Castle, DE. For general support.
$7,500 to Community Foundation of Central Illinois, Peoria, IL. For general support.
$5,000 to American Red Cross, Summit County Chapter, Akron, OH. For general support and processing employee matching.

1048
The Pokagon Fund, Inc.
821 E. Buffalo St.
New Buffalo, MI   49117-1522   (269) 469-9322
County: Berrien
Contact: Mary L. Dunbar, Exec. Dir.
E-mail: info@pokagonfund.org; E-mail address for applications: grants@pokagonfund.org; URL: http://www.pokagonfund.org/
E-mail address for scholarships: scholarships@pokagonfund.org

Established in 2007 in MI.
Donor: Four Winds Casino Resort.
Grantmaker type: Company-sponsored foundation.
Financial data (yr. ended 06/30/10): Assets, $9,857,943 (M); gifts received, $3,517,145; expenditures, $1,038,124; total giving, $804,070; qualifying distributions, $962,186; giving activities include $804,070 for 63 grants (high: $187,500; low: $200).
Purpose and activities: The fund supports programs designed to enhance the lives of residents in the New Buffalo, Michigan, region and the communities where the Pokagon Band of Potawatomi Indians own land. Special emphasis is directed toward arts and culture, education, the environment, health, recreation, and human services.
Fields of interest: Performing arts; Arts; Libraries (public); Education, reading; Education; Environment, recycling; Environment, land resources; Environment; Health care; Recreation, parks/playgrounds; Recreation, fairs/festivals; Recreation; Residential/custodial care, hospices; Human services; Community/economic development; Native Americans/American Indians.

Type of support: General/operating support; Continuing support; Management development/capacity building; Building/renovation; Equipment; Program development; Conferences/seminars; Seed money; Scholarship funds; Sponsorships; Scholarships—to individuals.
Limitations: Applications accepted. Giving in primarily in New Buffalo, MI, region, including the townships of Chikaming, Grand Beach, Michiana, and Three Oaks; some giving also in South Bend, IN, and Dowagia and Hartford MI. No support for political candidates, political advocacy, or religious organizations not of direct benefit to the entire community. No grants to individuals (except for scholarships).
Publications: Application guidelines; Annual report (including application guidelines).
Application information: The foundation supports municipalities, nonprofits, charities, areas where the Pokagon Band of Potawatomi Indians, and other organizations. An application form is available for each type of organization. Application form required.
   Initial approach: Download application form and e-mail to foundation
   Deadline(s): 90 days prior to need; Mar. 15 for scholarships
   Final notification: Within 90 days; May for scholarships
Officers and Directors: * Rosann Dudiak,* Chair.; Vickie Wagner,* Secy.; Mary L. Dunbar, Exec. Dir.; Rob Carpenter; Viki Gudas; Michaelina Magnuson; Margaret Murray; Alice Overly.
EIN: 300130499

1049
R. L. Polk & Co. Contributions Program
26533 Evergreen Rd., Ste. 900
Southfield, MI   48076-4249
County: Oakland
URL: https://www.polk.com/company/commitment

Grantmaker type: Corporate giving program.
Purpose and activities: R. L. Polk makes charitable contributions to nonprofit organizations on a case by case basis. Support is given primarily in areas of company operations, with emphasis on Michigan.
Fields of interest: General charitable giving.
Type of support: General/operating support; Sponsorships; In-kind gifts.
Limitations: Giving primarily in areas of company operations, with emphasis on MI.

1050
Pulte Homes, Inc. Corporate Giving Program
(formerly Pulte Corporation Contributions Program)
100 Bloomfield Hills Pkwy.
Bloomfield Hills, MI   48304-2950
(248) 647-2750
County: Oakland
FAX: (248) 433-4598; URL: http://phx.corporate-ir.net/phoenix.zhtml?c=147717&p=irol-social

Grantmaker type: Corporate giving program.
Purpose and activities: Pulte Homes makes charitable contributions to nonprofit organizations involved with higher education, the environment, health and human services, and housing. Support is given primarily in areas of company operations in Arizona, California, Colorado, Florida, Georgia,

Illinois, Indiana, Minnesota, Missouri, Nevada, New Jersey, New Mexico, North Carolina, Ohio, South Carolina, Tennessee, Texas, Virginia, and Washington, with emphasis on Michigan.
Fields of interest: Education; Environment; Health care; Housing/shelter; Human services.
Type of support: Capital campaigns; Program development; Employee volunteer services; Scholarships—to individuals.
Limitations: Applications accepted. Giving primarily in areas of company operations in AZ, CA, CO, FL, GA, IL, IN, MN, MO, NC, NJ, NM, NV, OH, SC, TN, TX, VA, and WA, with emphasis on MI. No support for discriminatory organizations, religious, fraternal, or veterans' organizations not of direct benefit to the entire community, or pass-through organizations. No grants to individuals (except for scholarships), or for general operating support.
Application information: A contributions committee reviews all requests. Application form not required.
> *Initial approach:* Proposal to headquarters for organizations located in southeastern MI; for programs outside southeastern MI, contact nearest market office
> *Copies of proposal:* 1
> *Deadline(s):* None

1051
Quicksilver Resources Inc. Corporate Giving Program
777 W. Rosedale St., Ste. 300
Fort Worth, TX 76104-4638 (817) 665-5000
County: Tarrant
FAX: (817) 665-5004;
E-mail: rbuterbaugh@qrinc.com; *URL:* http://www.qrinc.com/about/community_involvement/

Grantmaker type: Corporate giving program.
Purpose and activities: Quicksilver makes charitable contributions to hospitals and to nonprofit organizations involved with children services, arts, education, items of historical significance, and health services. Support is given primarily in Corydon, IN, Gaylord, MI, Cut Bank, MT, and Fort Worth and Granbury, TX.
Fields of interest: Historic preservation/historical societies; Arts; Education; Hospitals (general); Health care; Children, services.
Type of support: General/operating support; Employee volunteer services; Use of facilities; Sponsorships.
Limitations: Applications accepted. Giving primarily in Corydon, IN, Gaylord, MI, Cut Bank, MT, and Fort Worth and Granbury, TX.
Application information: Application form not required.
> *Initial approach:* Proposal to headquarters
> *Copies of proposal:* 1
> *Final notification:* Following review

1052
Edward F. Redies Foundation, Inc.
P.O. Box 411
Saline, MI 48176-0411 (734) 429-9421
County: Washtenaw
Application address: c/o R&B Machine Tool Co., 118 E. Michigan Ave., Saline, MI 48176

Incorporated in 1981 in MI.
Donor: R&B Machine Tool Co.
Grantmaker type: Company-sponsored foundation.

Financial data (yr. ended 12/31/09): Assets, $4,028,253 (M); expenditures, $239,293; total giving, $200,000; qualifying distributions, $200,000; giving activities include $200,000 for grants.
Purpose and activities: The foundation supports hospitals, parks and playgrounds, and organizations involved with education, child welfare, and human services.
Fields of interest: Higher education; Scholarships/financial aid; Education; Hospitals (general); Crime/violence prevention, child abuse; Recreation, parks/playgrounds; Youth, services; Residential/custodial care; Aging, centers/services; Human services.
Type of support: Capital campaigns; Building/renovation; Equipment; Scholarship funds.
Limitations: Applications accepted. Giving primarily in the greater Washtenaw County, MI, area. No grants to individuals.
Publications: Application guidelines.
Application information: Application form not required.
> *Initial approach:* Proposal
> *Copies of proposal:* 1
> *Deadline(s):* Mar. 31
Officers and Directors: R. Edward Redies, Pres.; Robert D. Redies, V.P.; Karen Redies, Secy.-Treas.; Paul Bunten; Elizabeth J. Redies; Thomas D. Redies; William D. Redies; Milton Stemen; Dennis Valenti.
EIN: 382391326
Selected grants: The following grants were reported in 2008.
$10,000 to Eastern Michigan University, Ypsilanti, MI.
$5,000 to Ozone House, Ann Arbor, MI.
$3,000 to Saint Louis Center, Chelsea, MI.
$3,000 to Saline Fiddlers, Saline, MI.
$3,000 to Special Olympics Michigan, Mount Pleasant, MI.
$1,000 to Family Learning Institute, Ann Arbor, MI.
$1,000 to Young Adults Health Center, Ypsilanti, MI.

1053
Frank Rewold & Son Foundation
333 E. Second St.
Rochester, MI 48307-2005 (248) 651-7242
County: Oakland
Contact: Bill Moesta

Established in 2005 in MI.
Donor: Frank Rewold and Son, Inc.
Grantmaker type: Company-sponsored foundation.
Financial data (yr. ended 12/31/09): Assets, $20,263 (M); expenditures, $7,170; total giving, $5,950; qualifying distributions, $5,950; giving activities include $5,950 for 6 grants (high: $2,500; low: $200).
Fields of interest: Higher education; Animals/wildlife, special services; Health care; Human services; Independent living, disability.
Limitations: Applications accepted. Giving in MI, with some emphasis on Rochester.
Application information: Application form not required.
> *Initial approach:* Proposal
> *Deadline(s):* None
Officers and Directors:* Frank H. Rewold,* Pres.; Paul Weisenbach,* V.P.; Craig Wolanin,* Secy.-Treas.
EIN: 202376123

1054
SANYO North America Corporation Contributions Program
2055 Sanyo Ave.
San Diego, CA 92154-6229
County: San Diego
URL: http://us.sanyo.com/Social-Responsibility

Grantmaker type: Corporate giving program.
Purpose and activities: SANYO North America makes charitable contributions to nonprofit organizations involved with music, education, sustainable energy, the environment, and youth development. Support is given primarily in areas of company operations in Arkansas, Georgia, Illinois, Michigan, Missouri, New Jersey, Oregon, and Texas, with emphasis on California.
Fields of interest: Performing arts, music; Education; Environment, energy; Environment; Youth development.
Type of support: Program development; Employee volunteer services; In-kind gifts.
Limitations: Giving primarily in areas of company operations in AR, GA, IL, MI, MO, NJ, OR, and TX, with emphasis on CA.

1055
ShopKo Stores, Inc. Corporate Giving Program
P.O. Box 19060
Green Bay, WI 54307-9060 (920) 429-2211
County: Brown
URL: http://www.shopko.com/company/community-giving

Grantmaker type: Corporate giving program.
Purpose and activities: As a complement to its foundation, ShopKo also makes charitable contributions to nonprofit organizations directly. Support is given primarily in areas of company operations in California, Idaho, Illinois, Iowa, Michigan, Minnesota, Montana, Nebraska, Oregon, South Dakota, Utah, Washington, and Wisconsin.
Fields of interest: Optometry/vision screening; Salvation Army; Children, services; United Ways and Federated Giving Programs.
Type of support: General/operating support; Employee volunteer services; In-kind gifts.
Limitations: Giving primarily in areas of company operations in CA, IA, ID, IL, MI, MN, MT, NE, OR, SD, UT, WA, and WI.

1056
Spark Energy, L.P., Corporate Giving Program
2501 Citywest Blvd., Ste. # 100
Houston, TX 77042-3019 (713) 977-5634
County: Harris
URL: https://www.sparkenergy.com/Community-Involvement

Grantmaker type: Corporate giving program.
Purpose and activities: Spark Energy, L.P. makes charitable contributions to nonprofits involved with children, military personnel, the mentally disabled, and homeless families. Support is given primarily in areas of company operations in Arizona, California, Colorado, Connecticut, Florida, Illinois, Indiana, Maryland, Massachusetts, Michigan, Nevada, New Mexico, New York, Ohio, Pennsylvania, and Texas; giving also to national organizations.

Fields of interest: Children, services; Family services; Homeless, human services; International relief; Children's rights; Children; Mentally disabled; Military/veterans; Homeless.
Type of support: General/operating support.
Limitations: Giving primarily in areas of company operations in AZ, CA, CO, CT, FL, IL, IN, MA, MD,MI, NM, NV, NY, OH, PA, and TX.
Officer: Frode Helgerud, C.E.O.

1057
The Spartan Motors Private Foundation
1000 Reynolds Rd.
Charlotte, MI 48813-2018 (514) 543-6400
County: Eaton
Contact: Stacy Guy

Established in 1995 in MI.
Donor: Spartan Motors, Inc.
Grantmaker type: Company-sponsored foundation.
Financial data (yr. ended 12/31/09): Assets, $35,959 (M); expenditures, $1,985; total giving, $0.
Purpose and activities: The foundation supports general charitable giving and other areas.
Fields of interest: General charitable giving.
Type of support: General/operating support.
Limitations: Applications accepted. Giving limited to organizations that benefit Charlotte, MI and the surrounding area.
Application information: Application form not required.
Initial approach: Letter of inquiry
Deadline(s): None
Officers: John E. Sztykiel, Pres.; Janine L. Nierenberger, Secy.; Lori Wade, Treas.
Directors: James Knapp; Jim Logan.
EIN: 383212131
Selected grants: The following grants were reported in 2008.
$76,452 to United Way, Eaton County, Charlotte, MI.
$12,000 to Boys and Girls Club of Lansing, Lansing, MI.
$3,500 to Partnership for Learning, Lansing, MI.
$2,500 to American Cancer Society, East Lansing, MI.
$2,500 to Boarshead Theater, Lansing, MI.
$1,500 to Potter Park Zoological Society, Lansing, MI.
$1,000 to Capital Area Community Services, Lansing, MI.
$1,000 to Pray America, Lansing, MI.

1058
Steelcase Foundation
P.O. Box 1967, GH-4E
Grand Rapids, MI 49501-1967
County: Kent
Contact: Susan Broman, Pres.
FAX: (616) 475-2200;
E-mail: sbroman@steelcase.com; Additional Contact: Phyllis Gebben, Coordinator of Donations, E-mail: pgebben@steelcase.com; URL: http://www.steelcase.com/en/company/who/steelcase-foundation/pages/steelcasefoundation.aspx

Established in 1951 in MI.
Donor: Steelcase Inc.
Grantmaker type: Company-sponsored foundation.

Financial data (yr. ended 11/30/09): Assets, $82,069,885 (M); expenditures, $5,233,695; total giving, $4,395,581; qualifying distributions, $4,415,581; giving activities include $3,963,016 for 63 grants (high: $533,005; low: $4,000), and $432,565 for 930 employee matching gifts.
Purpose and activities: The foundation supports organizations involved with arts and culture, education, the environment, health, human services, and community development. Special emphasis is directed toward programs designed to assist youth, the elderly, disabled people, and economically disadvantaged people.
Fields of interest: Arts; Education, early childhood education; Education; Environment; Health care; Homeless, human services; Human services; Economic development; Community/economic development; Youth; Aging; Disabilities, people with; Economically disadvantaged.
International interests: Canada.
Type of support: General/operating support; Management development/capacity building; Capital campaigns; Building/renovation; Equipment; Land acquisition; Program development; Seed money; Scholarship funds; Employee matching gifts; Employee-related scholarships; Matching/challenge support.
Limitations: Applications accepted. Giving limited to areas of company operations, with emphasis on Athens, AL, City of Industry, CA, Grand Rapids, MI, and Markham, Canada. No support for churches or religious organizations not of direct benefit to the entire community or discriminatory organizations. No grants to individuals (except for employee-related scholarships), or for endowments or conferences or seminars.
Publications: Application guidelines; Annual report; Grants list.
Application information: Letters of inquiry should be submitted using organization letterhead. A full proposal may be requested at a later date. Support is limited to 1 contribution per organization during any given year. Application form required.
Initial approach: Letter of inquiry for application form
Copies of proposal: 1
Deadline(s): Quarterly
Board meeting date(s): Quarterly
Final notification: At least 90 days
Officers and Trustees:* Kate Pew Wolters,* Chair.; Susan K. Broman, Pres.; James P. Hackett; Earl D. Holton; Mary Anne Hunting; Elizabeth Welch Lykins; Mary Goodwillie Nelson; Robert C. Pew III.
Number of staff: 1 full-time professional; 1 full-time support.
EIN: 386050470
Selected grants: The following grants were reported in 2008.
$750,000 to United Way, Heart of West Michigan, Grand Rapids, MI. For campaign.
$250,000 to Grand Rapids Community College Foundation, Grand Rapids, MI. For Green Roof for Applied Technology Center.
$250,000 to Wedgwood Christian Services, Grand Rapids, MI. For Building Hope for Children capital campaign for Lighthouse Academy.
$200,000 to Aquinas College, Grand Rapids, MI. For Mind, Body, Spirit capital campaign.
$200,000 to Genesis Non-Profit Housing Corporation, Grand Rapids, MI. For Heron Manor enhanced supportive housing for seniors.
$100,000 to Nature Conservancy, Michigan Field Office, Lansing, MI. For Saving the Last Great Places in Michigan - A Campaign for Conservation.

$100,000 to Opera Grand Rapids, Grand Rapids, MI. For Betty Van Andel Opera Center capital campaign.
$27,500 to Michigan Colleges Foundation, Southfield, MI. For scholarships for private colleges in Michigan.
$25,000 to Safe Haven Ministries, Grand Rapids, MI. For Saving Lives, Building Hope campaign.
$15,000 to Grand Rapids Community Foundation, Grand Rapids, MI. For Nonprofit Technical Assistance Fund.

1059
Steelcase Inc. Corporate Giving Program
c/o Community Rels.
901 44th St., SE
Grand Rapids, MI 49508-7575
County: Kent
E-mail: cr@steelcase.com; URL: http://www.steelcase.com/na/in_the_community_ourcompany.aspx?f=18478

Grantmaker type: Corporate giving program.
Purpose and activities: As a complement to its foundation, Steelcase also makes charitable contributions to nonprofit organizations directly. Support is given on a national and international basis in areas of company operations.
Fields of interest: Arts; Education; Environment; Community/economic development; Minorities.
Type of support: General/operating support; Employee volunteer services; Donated products; In-kind gifts.
Limitations: Applications accepted. Giving on a national and international basis in areas of company operations.
Application information:
Initial approach: E-mail headquarters for application information
Deadline(s): None
Final notification: 3 weeks
Number of staff: 1 full-time professional.

1060
Taubman Centers, Inc. Corporate Giving Program
200 E. Long Lake Rd., Ste. 300
Bloomfield Hills, MI 48303-0200
(248) 258-6800
County: Oakland
Contact: Karen McDonald

Grantmaker type: Corporate giving program.
Purpose and activities: Taubman Centers makes charitable contributions to nonprofit organizations on a case by case basis. Support is given primarily in Detroit, Michigan.
Fields of interest: General charitable giving.
Type of support: Employee volunteer services; General/operating support.
Limitations: Giving primarily in Detroit, MI.
Application information: Application form not required.
Initial approach: Proposal to headquarters
Copies of proposal: 1
Deadline(s): None

1061
TCF Foundation
200 Lake St. E., EXO-01-C
Wayzata, MN 55391-1693
County: Hennepin
Contact: Denise Peterson, Community Affairs Off.
FAX: (952) 745-2775; E-mail: dpete@tcfbank.com;
Additional application addresses: CO: TCF Bank,
CRA Off., 6400 S. Fiddler's Green Circle, Ste. 800,
Greenwood Village, CO 80111, tel.: (720)
200-2415; IL, IN, and WI: TCF Bank, Office of
Community Affairs, 800 Burr Ridge Pkwy., Burr
Ridge, IL 60527, tel.: (630) 986-4920; MI: TCF
Bank, Dir., Community Affairs, 17440 College
Pkwy., M.C. 604-03-E, Livonia, MI 48152, tel.: (734)
542-2900; URL: http://www.tcfbank.com/About/
about_community_relations.jsp

Established in 1989 in MN.
Donors: TCF National Bank Minnesota; TCF National
Bank; TCF Financial Corp.
Grantmaker type: Company-sponsored foundation.
Financial data (yr. ended 12/31/09): Assets,
$299,361 (M); gifts received, $2,533,552;
expenditures, $2,393,301; total giving,
$2,393,301; qualifying distributions, $2,393,301;
giving activities include $2,123,252 for 569 grants
(high: $50,000; low: $25), and $270,049 for 480
employee matching gifts.
Purpose and activities: The foundation supports
organizations involved with education, human
services, community development, and the arts; and
programs designed to improve the economic and
social well-being of the community. Support is
limited to areas of company operations and only to
non-profit organizations where there are TCF
employees actively involved.
Fields of interest: Arts; Education; Housing/shelter,
rehabilitation; Housing/shelter; Youth development;
Human services, financial counseling; Human
services; Community/economic development;
Financial services; Economically disadvantaged.
Type of support: Annual campaigns; Capital
campaigns; Continuing support; Employee matching
gifts; Employee volunteer services;
Employee-related scholarships; General/operating
support; Loaned talent; Program development;
Scholarship funds.
Limitations: Applications accepted. Giving limited to
areas of company operations in CO, MI, and MN, the
greater Chicago, IL, area, northwest IN, and
southeastern WI, including Kenosha, the greater
Milwaukee area, and Racine. No support for political
parties or candidates, churches, religious
organizations not of direct benefit to the entire
community, lobbying organizations, or social
organizations. No grants to individuals (except for
employee-related scholarships), or for social events,
fundraising activities, or advertising or publications.
Publications: Application guidelines; Corporate
report.
Application information: The Foundation accepts
full proposals by invitation only. Only non-profit
organizations where there are TCF employees
actively involved are considered.
Initial approach: Letter of inquiry
Copies of proposal: 1
Deadline(s): None
Board meeting date(s): Quarterly
Officers and Directors:* William A. Cooper,* Chair.;
Jason E. Korstange,* Vice-Chair.; Gregory J. Pulles,*
Secy.; Thomas F. Jasper, Treas.; Mark L. Jeter.
Number of staff: 1 full-time professional.
EIN: 411659826

Selected grants: The following grants were reported
in 2008.
$50,000 to University of Illinois at Chicago,
Chicago, IL.
$20,000 to Minnesota Orchestral Association,
Minnesota Orchestra, Minneapolis, MN.
$10,000 to Boys and Girls Club.
$10,000 to Northern Michigan University
Foundation, Marquette, MI.
$7,500 to Teen Challenge of Minnesota,
Minneapolis, MN.
$5,000 to Community Housing Association of
Dupage, Villa Park, IL.
$5,000 to Community Neighborhood Housing
Services, Saint Paul, MN.
$5,000 to Michigan Theater Foundation, Ann Arbor,
MI.
$5,000 to Public Education and Business Coalition,
Denver, CO.
$2,500 to Rocky Mountain Cancer Centers
Foundation, Greenwood Village, CO.

1062
Tigers Care Program
Comerica Park
2100 Woodward
Detroit, MI 48201-3470
County: Wayne
URL: http://detroit.tigers.mlb.com/det/
community/index.jsp

Grantmaker type: Corporate giving program.
Purpose and activities: As a complement to its
foundation, the Detroit Tigers also make charitable
contributions to nonprofit organizations directly.
Special emphasis is directed towards youth sports
and recreation. Support is given primarily in
Michigan.
Fields of interest: Education; Athletics/sports,
baseball; Recreation; Youth development.
Type of support: General/operating support;
Equipment; Scholarship funds; Loaned talent;
Donated equipment; In-kind gifts.
Limitations: Giving primarily in MI.
Publications: Corporate giving report.

1063
Tim Hortons Inc., Corporate Giving Program
4150 Tuller Rd., Unit 236
Dublin, OH 43017 (614) 791-4200
County: Franklin
E-mail: donations@timhortons.com; URL: http://
www.timhortons.com/us/en/difference/
donation.html

Grantmaker type: Corporate giving program.
Purpose and activities: Tim Hortons makes product
donations to, and supports fundraising events for,
nonprofit organizations in areas of company
operations. Special emphasis is directed toward
programs that help children.
Fields of interest: Children.
Type of support: Sponsorships; Donated products;
In-kind gifts.
Limitations: Applications accepted. Giving primarily
in areas of company operations in CT, KY, ME, MA,
MI, NY, OH, PA, RI, and WV. No support for political
or religious organizations. No grants to individuals.
Publications: Application guidelines.

Application information: The company does not
provide cash donations. Application form required.
Initial approach: Complete online application
Deadline(s): 10 weeks prior to need for product
donations; 12 weeks prior to event for
sponsorships

1064
A. M. Todd Company Foundation
c/o Fifth Third Bank
P.O. Box 3636
Grand Rapids, MI 49501-3636
County: Kent
Contact: Linda Hoeg
Application address: 136 E. Michigan Ave.,
Kalamazoo, MI 49007, tel.: (269) 567-7881

Established in 1962 in MI.
Donors: A.M. Todd Co.; Zink & Triest Co.
Grantmaker type: Company-sponsored foundation.
Financial data (yr. ended 12/31/09): Assets,
$104,209 (M); expenditures, $63,360; total giving,
$60,000; qualifying distributions, $60,000; giving
activities include $60,000 for grants.
Purpose and activities: The foundation supports
organizations involved with arts and culture,
education, the environment, health, human
services, community development, and Christianity.
Fields of interest: Arts; Education; Environment;
Hospitals (general); Health care; Human services;
Community/economic development; United Ways
and Federated Giving Programs; Christian agencies
& churches.
Type of support: Continuing support; Annual
campaigns; Capital campaigns; Building/
renovation.
Limitations: Applications accepted. Giving limited to
Kalamazoo County, MI. No grants to individuals.
Application information: Application form not
required.
Initial approach: Proposal
Deadline(s): None
Trustees: Ian D. Blair; A.J. Todd III; Fifth Third Bank.
EIN: 386055829
Selected grants: The following grants were reported
in 2005.
$10,000 to Doylestown Hospital, Doylestown, PA.
$5,000 to Kalamazoo Regional Chamber
Foundation, Kalamazoo, MI.
$5,000 to Lift Foundation, Kalamazoo, MI.
$5,000 to United Way, Greater Kalamazoo,
Kalamazoo, MI.
$2,500 to Kalamazoo College, Kalamazoo, MI.
$2,000 to American Red Cross Greater Kalamazoo
Area, Kalamazoo, MI.
$1,250 to Junior League of Kalamazoo, Kalamazoo,
MI.
$1,000 to Kairos Dwelling, Kalamazoo, MI.
$1,000 to Michigan Festival, East Lansing, MI.
$1,000 to Ministry with Community, Kalamazoo, MI.

1065
Toll Brothers, Inc. Corporate Giving Program
c/o Advertising and Marketing Dept.
250 Gibraltar Rd.
Horsham, PA 19044 (215) 938-8000
County: Montgomery
FAX: (215) 938-8010; URL: http://
www.tollbrothers.com/homesearch/servlet/
HomeSearch?app=aboutcharity_home

Grantmaker type: Corporate giving program.
Purpose and activities: Toll Brothers makes charitable contributions to nonprofit organizations in areas of company operations; giving also to national organizations.
Fields of interest: General charitable giving.
Type of support: Sponsorships; General/operating support; Employee volunteer services.
Limitations: Giving primarily in areas of company operations in AZ, CA, CO, CT, DE, FL, GA, IL, MD, MA, MI, MN, NC, NJ, NV, NY, PA, RI, SC, TX, VA, and WV.
Application information:
Initial approach: Mail proposal to headquarters
Deadline(s): None

1066
Toyota Motor Sales, U.S.A., Inc. Corporate Giving Program
c/o Corp. Contribs. Comm.
19001 S. Western Ave., M.S. A404
Torrance, CA   90509-2991   (310) 468-5249
County: Los Angeles
URL: http://www.toyota.com/about/community

Grantmaker type: Corporate giving program.
Purpose and activities: Toyota Motor Sales makes charitable contributions to nonprofit organizations involved with arts and culture, education, the environment, community development, and civic affairs. Support is given on a national basis.
Fields of interest: Arts; Elementary/secondary education; Education; Environment; Community/economic development; Public affairs.
Type of support: General/operating support; Continuing support; Program development; In-kind gifts.
Limitations: Applications accepted. Giving primarily in areas of major company operations in AL, CA, IN, KY, MI, NY, TX and WV; giving also to national organizations. No support for discriminatory organizations, fraternal, labor, religious, or similar organizations, or political parties or candidates. No grants to individuals, or for publications, lobbying activities, advertising, capital campaigns, or endowments.
Publications: Application guidelines.
Application information: Contributions generally do not exceed $5,000. An application form is required for organizations located in the greater Los Angeles, CA, area. Multi-year funding is not automatic.
Initial approach: Download application form and mail proposal and application form to headquarters for organizations located in the greater Los Angeles, CA, area; proposal to headquarters for organizations located outside the greater Los Angeles, CA, area
Deadline(s): None
Final notification: 3 months

1067
Universal Forest Products Education Foundation
(formerly Universal Companies, Inc. Education Foundation)
2801 E. Beltline Ave. N.E.
Grand Rapids, MI   49525-9680
County: Kent
Contact: Nancy DeGood, Dir.

Established in 1990 in MI.

Donor: Universal Forest Products, Inc.
Grantmaker type: Company-sponsored foundation.
Financial data (yr. ended 12/31/09): Assets, $603,025 (M); expenditures, $26,731; total giving, $26,440; qualifying distributions, $26,440; giving activities include $26,440 for 42 grants to individuals (high: $1,260; low: $400).
Purpose and activities: The foundation awards college scholarships to children and adopted children of full-time employees of Universal Forest Products.
Fields of interest: Higher education.
Type of support: Employee-related scholarships.
Application information: Application form required.
Initial approach: Letter
Deadline(s): None
Officer and Directors:* Michael R. Cole,* Pres.; Nancy DeGood; Glenda Glenn; Ronald J. Schollaart.
EIN: 382945715

1068
Valassis Communications, Inc. Corporate Giving Program
c/o Valassis Giving Comm.
19975 Victor Pkwy.
Livonia, MI   48152-7001   (734) 591-3000
County: Wayne
URL: http://www.valassis.com/1024/Company/citizen.aspx

Grantmaker type: Corporate giving program.
Purpose and activities: Valassis makes charitable contributions to nonprofit organizations involved with education, animal welfare, food services, human services, and abducted children. Support is given primarily in areas of company operations.
Fields of interest: Education; Animal welfare; Health care; Food banks; Food distribution, meals on wheels; Children, services; Human services; General charitable giving; Military/veterans.
Type of support: General/operating support; Employee volunteer services.
Limitations: Applications accepted. Giving primarily in areas of company operations.
Application information: Application form not required.
Initial approach: Proposal to headquarters
Deadline(s): None
Final notification: Following review

1069
Varnum, Riddering, Schmidt & Howlett LLP Corporate Giving Program
Bridgewater Pl.
P.O. Box 352
Grand Rapids, MI   49501-0352   (616) 336-6000
County: Kent
URL: http://www.varnumlaw.com/About-Us/Commitment-to-Community

Grantmaker type: Corporate giving program.
Purpose and activities: Varnum makes charitable contributions to nonprofit organizations involved with art and culture, education, and community and economic development. Support is given primarily in areas of company operations in Michigan.
Fields of interest: Arts; Education; Human services; Community/economic development; Economically disadvantaged.

Type of support: General/operating support; Employee volunteer services; Pro bono services - strategic management.
Limitations: Giving primarily in areas of company operations in MI.
Contributions Committee: Larry J. Titley, Chair.; Randy Boileau; Dirk Hoffius; Pete Livingston; Kent Vana.

1070
Venturedyne, Ltd. Foundation
(formerly Wehr Corporation Foundation)
600 College Ave.
Pewaukee, WI   53072-3572
County: Waukesha
Contact: Brian L. Nahey, Pres. and Treas.

Donor: Venturedyne, Ltd.
Grantmaker type: Company-sponsored foundation.
Financial data (yr. ended 12/31/09): Assets, $82,896 (M); expenditures, $5,600; total giving, $5,600; qualifying distributions, $5,600; giving activities include $5,600 for 2 grants (high: $3,000; low: $2,600).
Purpose and activities: The foundation supports hospices and organizations involved with higher education, cancer, children and youth services, and Christianity.
Fields of interest: Higher education; Cancer; Children/youth, services; Residential/custodial care, hospices; Christian agencies & churches.
Type of support: General/operating support; Scholarship funds.
Limitations: Applications accepted. Giving primarily in MI and WI. No grants to individuals.
Application information: Application form not required.
Initial approach: Proposal
Deadline(s): None
Officers and Directors:* Brian L. Nahey,* Pres. and Treas.; Nicole J. Daniels, V.P.; Nancy L. Johnson, Secy.
EIN: 396096050

1071
The H. O. West Foundation
(also known as The Herman O. West Foundation)
101 Gordon Dr.
Lionville, PA   19341   (610) 594-2945
County: Chester
Contact: Richard D. Luzzi, Tr.; Maureen B. Goebel, Admin.
FAX: (610) 594-3011; *URL:* http://www.westpharma.com/na/en/about/Pages/CharitableGiving.aspx

Established in 1972 in PA.
Donors: The West Co., Inc.; West Pharmaceutical Services, Inc.
Grantmaker type: Company-sponsored foundation.
Financial data (yr. ended 12/31/10): Assets, $2,076,522 (M); gifts received, $600,000; expenditures, $669,426; total giving, $669,351; qualifying distributions, $669,426; giving activities include $592,904 for 39 grants (high: $101,848; low: $500), $59,167 for 47 grants to individuals (high: $2,500; low: $833), and $17,280 for 52 employee matching gifts.
Purpose and activities: The foundation supports organizations involved with arts and culture, education, health, human services, community

development, and science and technology. Support is given primarily in areas of company operations in Arizona, Florida, Michigan, North Carolina, Nebraska, and Pennsylvania.

Fields of interest: Arts; Education, fund raising/fund distribution; Higher education; Education; Hospitals (general); Health care; Human services; Community/economic development; United Ways and Federated Giving Programs; Engineering/technology; Science.

Type of support: Annual campaigns; Building/renovation; Capital campaigns; Continuing support; Emergency funds; Employee matching gifts; Employee-related scholarships; General/operating support; Matching/challenge support; Research; Scholarships—to individuals.

Limitations: Applications accepted. Giving primarily in areas of company operations in AZ, FL, MI, NC, NE, and PA.

Publications: Application guidelines.

Application information: Application form not required.

> *Initial approach:* Proposal or letter
> *Copies of proposal:* 1
> *Deadline(s):* 1 week prior to board meetings
> *Board meeting date(s):* Spring and fall
> *Final notification:* Varies

Officer and Trustees:* George R. Bennyhoff, Chair.; Paula A. Johnson, M.D.; Richard D. Luzzi.

Number of staff: None.

EIN: 383674460

1072
Whirlpool Foundation

2000 N. M-63, MD 3106
Benton Harbor, MI 49022 (269) 923-5580
County: Berrien
Contact: Candice Garman, Coord.
FAX: (269) 925-0154;
E-mail: whirlpool_foundation@whirlpool.com; Tel. for Candice Garman: (269) 923-5583; URL: http://www.whirlpoolcorp.com/responsibility/building_communities/whirlpool_foundation.aspx

Incorporated in 1951 in MI.
Donor: Whirlpool Corp.
Grantmaker type: Company-sponsored foundation.
Financial data (yr. ended 12/31/09): Assets, $2,822,763 (M); gifts received, $7,075,000; expenditures, $10,148,447; total giving, $9,847,102; qualifying distributions, $9,966,595; giving activities include $9,394,412 for 86 grants (high: $3,300,000; low: $50), and $452,690 for 91 grants to individuals (high: $23,500; low: $650).
Purpose and activities: The foundation supports organizations involved with arts and culture, education, housing development, human services, and community development. Special emphasis is directed toward programs designed to promote lifelong learning, quality family life, and cultural diversity.
Fields of interest: Arts, cultural/ethnic awareness; Arts; Elementary/secondary education; Higher education; Business school/education; Education; Housing/shelter, development; Boys & girls clubs; Youth development, business; American Red Cross; YM/YWCAs & YM/YWHAs; Human services; Community/economic development; United Ways and Federated Giving Programs.
Type of support: General/operating support; Continuing support; Program development; Scholarship funds; Research; Employee volunteer services; Employee matching gifts;

Employee-related scholarships; Matching/challenge support.
Limitations: Applications accepted. Giving primarily in areas of company operations, with emphasis on Benton Harbor, MI. No support for social, labor, veterans', alumni, or fraternal organizations, athletic associations, or national groups whose local chapters have already received funding. No grants to individuals (except for employee-related scholarships), or for conferences or seminars, political causes, capital campaigns or endowments, sporting events, goodwill advertisements for fundraising benefits or program books, tickets for testimonials or similar benefit events, or general operating support for United Way agencies.
Publications: Application guidelines; Annual report (including application guidelines).
Application information: Support is limited to 1 contribution per organization during any given year. Application form required.

> *Initial approach:* Contact foundation for application form
> *Copies of proposal:* 1
> *Deadline(s):* Jan. 1, Apr. 1, July 1, and Oct. 1
> *Board meeting date(s):* Quarterly
> *Final notification:* 2 months

Officers and Trustees:* D. Jeffrey Noel,* Chair. and Pres.; John Geddes, Secy.-Treas.; David Binkley; Alan Holaday; Robert LaForest; Tim Reynolds.

Number of staff: 1 full-time professional; 1 full-time support.

EIN: 386077342

Selected grants: The following grants were reported in 2006.

$2,000,000 to Harbor Shores Community Redevelopment, Benton Harbor, MI. For Quality Family Life Program.

$1,000,000 to Harbor Shores Community Redevelopment, Benton Harbor, MI. For Quality Family Life Program.

$330,000 to Habitat for Humanity International, Americus, GA. For program support.

$292,631 to Cornerstone Alliance, Benton Harbor, MI.

$200,000 to Lake Michigan College Foundation, Benton Harbor, MI. For program support.

$199,809 to American Red Cross National Headquarters, Disaster Relief Fund, Washington, DC. For Disaster Relief Initiative.

$150,000 to University of Notre Dame, Notre Dame, IN. For Masters of Business Administration program support.

$25,470 to Habitat for Humanity, Harbor, Benton Harbor, MI. For program support.

$10,000 to Brookview School, Brookview School, Benton Harbor, MI. For program support.

$7,782 to American Red Cross, Evansville, IN. For Disaster relief initiative.

1073
Whole Foods Market, Inc. Corporate Giving Program

550 Bowie St.
Austin, TX 78703-4644 (512) 477-4455
County: Travis
URL: http://www.wholefoodsmarket.com/company/giving.php

Grantmaker type: Corporate giving program.
Purpose and activities: As a complement to its foundation, Whole Foods makes charitable contributions via various company locations that determine local charitable guidelines. Support is

limited to areas of company operations in Alabama, Arizona, Arkansas, California, Colorado, Connecticut, District of Columbia, Florida, Georgia, Hawaii, Illinois, Indiana, Kansas, Kentucky, Louisiana, Maine, Maryland, Massachusetts, Michigan, Minnesota, Missouri, Nebraska, Nevada, New Jersey, New Mexico, New York, North Carolina, Ohio, Oklahoma, Oregon, Pennsylvania, Rhode Island, South Carolina, Tennessee, Texas, Utah, Virginia, Washington, and Wisconsin, and in Canada and the UK.

Fields of interest: Food services; Food banks; General charitable giving.
Type of support: General/operating support; Employee volunteer services; Sponsorships; Donated products.
Limitations: Applications accepted. Giving limited to areas of company operations in AK, AL, AZ, CA, CO, CT, DC, FL, GA, HI, IL, IN, KS, KY, LA, MA, MD, ME, MI, MN, MO, NC, NJ, NM, NR, NV, NY, OH, OK, OR, PA, RI, SC, TN, TX, UT, VA, WA, and WI, and in Canada and the UK.
Application information:

> *Initial approach:* Contact Marketing Director at nearest company store or visit web site for application information

---

1074
Wisconsin Energy Corporation Foundation, Inc.

(formerly Wisconsin Electric System Foundation, Inc.)
231 W. Michigan St., Rm. P423
Milwaukee, WI 53203-0001 (414) 221-2107
County: Milwaukee
Contact: Patricia L. McNew, Admin.
FAX: (414) 221-2412;
E-mail: patti.mcnew@we-energies.com; URL: http://www.wec-foundation.com/

Incorporated in 1982 in WI.
Donor: Wisconsin Energy Corp.
Grantmaker type: Company-sponsored foundation.
Financial data (yr. ended 12/31/09): Assets, $35,379,531 (M); gifts received, $10,000,000; expenditures, $6,423,709; total giving, $6,204,461; qualifying distributions, $6,804,846; giving activities include $6,204,461 for 1,193 grants (high: $485,000; low: $25), and $478,500 for loans/program-related investments.
Purpose and activities: The foundation supports organizations involved with arts and culture, education, the environment, emergency services, and human services.
Fields of interest: Arts; Education; Environment, natural resources; Environmental education; Environment; Disasters, preparedness/services; Human services; United Ways and Federated Giving Programs.
Type of support: General/operating support; Capital campaigns; Equipment; Endowments; Scholarship funds; Sponsorships; Employee matching gifts; In-kind gifts.
Limitations: Applications accepted. Giving limited to areas of company operations in the Upper Peninsula, MI, area and WI. No support for political action or legislative advocacy organizations or veterans' or fraternal organizations. No grants to individuals, or for trips, tours, pageants, team or extra-curricular school events, or student exchange programs, programs whose primary purpose is the promotion of religious doctrine or tenets, or programs whose purpose is solely athletic in nature.

Publications: Application guidelines; Program policy statement.
Application information: Additional information may be requested at a later date. A site visit may be requested. Application form required.
Initial approach: Complete online application form or download application form and mail to foundation
Copies of proposal: 1
Deadline(s): Jan. 31, Apr. 30, July 31, and Oct. 31
Board meeting date(s): Quarterly
Final notification: 90 days
Officers and Directors:* Gale E. Klappa,* Pres.; Kristine A. Rappe,* V.P.; Keith H. Ecke, Secy.; Jeffrey P. West, Treas.; Charles R. Cole; Frederick D. Kuester; Allen L. Leverett; Thelma A. Sias.
EIN: 391433726
Selected grants: The following grants were reported in 2009.
$710,000 to Medical College of Wisconsin, Milwaukee, WI. For Reach Out and Read and Research Opportunity for Academic Development in Science program support.
$485,000 to United Performing Arts Fund, Milwaukee, WI.
$250,235 to United Way of Greater Milwaukee, Milwaukee, WI.
$250,000 to Discovery World, Milwaukee, WI. For Energy and Ingenuity Exhibit.
$200,000 to Boys and Girls Clubs of Greater Milwaukee, Milwaukee, WI. For Decade of Hope initiative.
$50,000 to United Way in Waukesha County, Waukesha, WI.
$33,000 to Boys and Girls Clubs of Greater Milwaukee, Milwaukee, WI. For Solar Thermo Heating Project.
$15,000 to Gathering Waters Conservancy, Madison, WI. For corporate sponsorship program.
$11,448 to UWM Foundation, Milwaukee, WI.
$10,175 to Fox Cities Performing Arts Center, Appleton, WI. For arts.

1075
Wisconsin Public Service Foundation, Inc.

(formerly WPS Foundation, Inc.)
700 N. Adams St.
P.O. Box 19001
Green Bay, WI 54307-9001 (920) 433-1433
County: Brown
Contact: Karmen Lemke, Mgr., Community Relations
E-mail: kmlemke@wisconsinpublicservice.com;
URL: http://www.wisconsinpublicservice.com/company/foundation.aspx

Incorporated in 1964 in WI.
Donor: Wisconsin Public Service Corp.
Grantmaker type: Company-sponsored foundation.
Financial data (yr. ended 12/31/09): Assets, $17,619,373 (M); expenditures, $991,899; total giving, $991,899; qualifying distributions, $1,004,769; giving activities include $886,727 for 841 grants (high: $100,000; low: $50), and $105,172 for grants to individuals.
Purpose and activities: The foundation supports programs designed to promote arts and culture; education; the environment; human services and health; community and neighborhood; and awards college scholarships.
Fields of interest: Arts, cultural/ethnic awareness; Museums; Performing arts; Arts; Higher education; Education; Environment, natural resources; Environment, energy; Environment; Animals/

wildlife; Hospitals (general); Health care; Mental health/crisis services; Employment; Youth development, adult & child programs; Aging, centers/services; Developmentally disabled, centers & services; Human services; Community/economic development; Minorities; Women.
Type of support: General/operating support; Continuing support; Annual campaigns; Capital campaigns; Building/renovation; Equipment; Program development; Scholarship funds; Research; Employee volunteer services; Employee matching gifts; Employee-related scholarships; Scholarships—to individuals.
Limitations: Applications accepted. Giving generally limited to areas of company operations in upper MI and northeastern WI. No support for churches and other religious organizations, political organizations, discriminatory organizations, or public or private K-12 schools. No grants to individuals (except for scholarships), or for natural gas or electric service, moving of poles, or utility construction.
Publications: Application guidelines; Grants list; Informational brochure.
Application information: Application form required.
Initial approach: Complete online application form
Copies of proposal: 1
Deadline(s): None; Nov. 1 for Innovative Educator Grant; Nov. 15 for Adult Student Technical College Scholarships; Mar. 1 for Business and Technology Scholarships and UW-Marinette Grant for Returning Adults; and May 1 for Minority and/or Female Northeast Wisconsin Technical College Grant and Tim Howard Memorial Scholarship
Board meeting date(s): May and as required
Final notification: 4 months; 6 weeks for Innovative Educator Grant
Officers: Thomas P. Meinz, Pres.; Charles A. Schrock, V.P.; Barth J. Wolf, Secy.; Joseph P. O'Leary, Treas.
EIN: 396075016
Selected grants: The following grants were reported in 2009.
$100,000 to United Way of Brown County, Green Bay, WI.
$25,000 to Grand Rapids Christian Schools, Grand Rapids, MI.
$20,000 to Bellin Foundation, Green Bay, WI.
$20,000 to Saint Vincent Hospital, Green Bay, WI.
$10,000 to Bellin College of Nursing, Green Bay, WI.
$9,000 to United Way of Marathon County, Wausau, WI.
$7,500 to United Way of Monroe County, Monroe, MI.
$5,000 to Bellin Foundation, Green Bay, WI.
$3,500 to United Way of Portage County, Stevens Point, WI.
$3,000 to Bellin College of Nursing, Green Bay, WI.

1076
Wolverine World Wide Foundation

c/o Wolverine World Wide, Inc.
9341 Courtland Dr. N.E.
Rockford, MI 49351-0001 (616) 866-5500
County: Kent
Contact: Christi Cowdin, V.P.
URL: http://www.wolverineworldwide.com/about-us/causes/

Established in MI.
Donor: Wolverine World Wide.
Grantmaker type: Company-sponsored foundation.

Financial data (yr. ended 12/31/09): Assets, $3,235,238 (M); gifts received, $588,727; expenditures, $642,776; total giving, $619,081; qualifying distributions, $619,081; giving activities include $618,606 for 81 grants (high: $200,000; low: $50), and $475 for 2 employee matching gifts.
Purpose and activities: The foundation supports organizations involved with arts and culture, education, the environment, cancer, muscular dystrophy, diabetes, housing development, youth and family services, and urban development.
Fields of interest: Museums; Performing arts, orchestras; Arts; Higher education; Medical school/education; Education; Environment, natural resources; Environment, land resources; Environment; Cancer; Muscular dystrophy; Diabetes; Housing/shelter, development; Youth development, business; YM/YWCAs & YM/YWHAs; Children/youth, services; Family services; Urban/community development; United Ways and Federated Giving Programs.
Type of support: General/operating support; Scholarship funds; Employee matching gifts.
Limitations: Applications accepted. Giving primarily in areas of company operations in MI.
Application information: Application form not required.
Initial approach: Proposal
Deadline(s): None
Officers and Trustees:* Blake W. Krueger,* Pres.; Christi L. Cowdin, V.P.; Kenneth A. Grady,* Secy.; Donald T. Grimes,* Treas.; James D. Zwiers.
EIN: 320140361

1077
Xcel Energy Foundation

414 Nicollet Mall
Minneapolis, MN 55401-1927 (612) 215-5317
County: Hennepin
Contact: Monique Lovato, Dir., Corp. Philanthropy
FAX: (612) 215-4522;
E-mail: foundation@xcelenergy.com; Additional Contacts: Jeanne Fox, Michigan and Wisconsin, E-mail: jean.fox@xcelenergy.com; James R. Garness, Sr. Fdn. Rep., Minnesota, E-mail: james.r.garness@xcelenergy.com; Judy Paukert, North and South Dakota, E-mail: judith.n.paukert@xcelenergy.com; Terry Price, Sr. Fdn. Rep., New Mexico and Texas, E-mail: terry.price@xcelenergy.com; Shanda Vangas, Sr. Fdn. Rep., Colorado, E-mail: Shanda.L.Vangas@excelenergy.com; URL: http://www.xcelenergy.com/Minnesota/Company/Community/Xcel%20Energy%20Foundation/Pages/Xcel_Energy_Foundation.aspx

Established in 2001.
Donor: Xcel Energy Inc.
Grantmaker type: Company-sponsored foundation.
Financial data (yr. ended 12/31/09): Assets, $3,042,840 (M); gifts received, $7,384,035; expenditures, $7,150,058; total giving, $7,014,692; qualifying distributions, $7,147,615; giving activities include $7,014,692 for 796 grants (high: $201,891; low: $15).
Purpose and activities: The foundation supports organizations involved with arts and culture, education, the environment, animals and wildlife, employment, and economic sustainability.
Fields of interest: Arts, equal rights; Arts education; Arts; Elementary/secondary education; Business school/education; Scholarships/financial aid; Education; Environment, alliance/advocacy;

Environment, public education; Environment, water resources; Environment, land resources; Environment, energy; Environment, beautification programs; Environmental education; Environment; Animals/wildlife, alliance/advocacy; Animals/ wildlife, public education; Animals/wildlife, preservation/protection; Employment, training; Employment, retraining; Employment; Boy scouts; Economic development; Business/industry; Community/economic development; United Ways and Federated Giving Programs; Science, formal/ general education; Mathematics; Economically disadvantaged.

Type of support: General/operating support; Program development; Employee volunteer services; Employee matching gifts.

Limitations: Applications accepted. Giving limited to areas of company operations in CO, MI, MN, ND, NM, SD, TX, and WI. No support for national organizations, government agencies, religious, political, veterans', or fraternal organizations not of direct benefit to the entire community or

disease-specific organizations. No grants to individuals, or for research programs, endowments, athletic or scholarship competitions, benefits or fundraising activities, sports or athletic programs, or capital campaigns.

Publications: Application guidelines; Grants list; Informational brochure; Program policy statement.

Application information: Applicants may be invited to submit a full proposal. Organizations receiving support are asked to submit a final report. Application form required.

Initial approach: Complete online letter of intent form

Deadline(s): Dec. 15 to Jan. 21 for Education and Environment; Apr. 25 to May 13 for Arts & Culture and Economic Sustainability

Final notification: Within 3 weeks following deadlines

Officers and Directors:* Richard C. Kelly,* Chair.; Elizabeth A. Willis, Secy.; Geroge Tyson, Treas.; David Eves; Cathy J. Hart; Judy Poferl.

EIN: 412007734

Selected grants: The following grants were reported in 2008.

$300,000 to Colorado School of Mines Foundation, Golden, CO.

$148,689 to United Way, Greater Twin Cities, Minneapolis, MN. For United Way Matching Grant.

$125,000 to Salvation Army, Northern Division, Roseville, MN.

$33,498 to United Way, Wright County, Monticello, MN. For United Way Matching Grant.

$30,000 to Science Museum of Minnesota, Saint Paul, MN.

$25,000 to Great River Greening, Saint Paul, MN.

$15,000 to Colorado Council on Economic Education, Denver, CO.

$15,000 to Minnesota Landscape Arboretum, Chaska, MN.

$10,400 to Salvation Army of Sioux Falls, Sioux Falls Corps, Sioux Falls, SD.

$10,000 to Georgetown Energy Museum, Georgetown, CO.

COMMUNITY FOUNDATIONS

1078
Albion Community Foundation
(formerly Albion Civic Foundation)
203 S. Superior St.
P.O. Box 156
Albion, MI 49224 (517) 629-3349
County: Calhoun
Contact: Elizabeth N. Schultheiss, Exec. Dir.
FAX: (517) 629-8027;
E-mail: foundation@albionfoundation.org;
URL: http://www.albionfoundation.org

Established in 1968 in MI.
Donor: Thomas T. Lloyd‡.
Grantmaker type: Community foundation.
Financial data (yr. ended 12/31/08): Assets,
$3,616,266 (M); gifts received, $133,165;
expenditures, $379,011; total giving, $208,881;
giving activities include $208,881 for 69 grants.
Purpose and activities: The mission of the
foundation is to strengthen the greater Albion area
by cultivating community assets to enhance the
community's quality of life.
Fields of interest: Arts; Education; Environment;
Children/youth, services; Economic development;
Community/economic development.
Type of support: Building/renovation; Curriculum
development; Equipment; Management
development/capacity building; Matching/
challenge support; Program development;
Publication; Scholarship funds; Seed money;
Technical assistance.
Limitations: Applications accepted. Giving limited to
greater Albion, MI. No support for religious,
fraternal, or service organizations (except for
proposed grants that meet a general community
need in a non-sectarian, non-exclusive manner). No
grants to individuals, or for general operating
support, endowments, or annual fundraising
campaigns.
Publications: Application guidelines; Annual report;
Annual report (including application guidelines);
Grants list; Informational brochure; Informational
brochure (including application guidelines);
Newsletter.
Application information: Visit foundation Web site
for application form and guidelines. Application form
required.
  Initial approach: Contact foundation
  Copies of proposal: 10
  Deadline(s): Varies
  Board meeting date(s): 12 times per year
  Final notification: Within 90 days
Officers and Trustees:* Joyce Spicer,* Pres.; Bernie
Konkle, Jr.,* V.P.; Karen Yankie,* Secy.; Tom Pitt,*
Treas.; Elizabeth N. Schultheiss, Exec. Dir.; Ken
Blight; Mandy Dubiel; Marilyn Hennon; Andrew Kooi;
Dan Ohmer; John Shedd; Peggy Sindt.
Number of staff: 1 full-time professional.
EIN: 237019029

1079
The Alger Regional Community Foundation, Inc.
100 West Munising Ave.
Munising, MI 49862-1116 (906) 387-3900
County: Alger
Contact: Janis Taylor, Exec. Dir.
FAX: (906) 387-2988;
E-mail: foundation@algercounty.com; Application
address.: P.O. Box 39, Munising, MI 49862;
URL: http://www.algercounty.com/
communityfoundation

Established in 1992 in MI; in 2003 became a
geographic affiliate of the Community Foundation of
the Upper Peninsula.
Grantmaker type: Community foundation.
Purpose and activities: The purpose of the
foundation is to enhance the quality of life in Alger
County, Michigan, in the areas of education, culture,
environment, youth, health, social welfare, and
recreation.
Fields of interest: Arts; Education; Environment;
Health care; Recreation; Youth development;
Human services.
Limitations: Giving limited to Alger County, MI. No
support for sectarian religious purposes. No grants
to individuals (except for scholarships), or for capital
campaigns, fundraising events, budget deficits,
routine operating expenses, or endowments.
Application information: ARCF grant application
form available on foundation's web site. Grants are
generally given 1-time only for specific purposes.
Application form required.
  Initial approach: Maximum 5 typed pages
  Copies of proposal: 5
  Deadline(s): Apr. 1 and Oct. 1
  Board meeting date(s): Quarterly
  Final notification: Within 1 week following board
    of directors' meeting
Officers and Directors:* Thomas Luckey,* Pres.;
Mary Bowerman, Treas.; Janis Taylor, Exec. Dir.;
Margi Beauchine; Liana Graves; Pete Kelto; Kris
Madigan; Kim Moote; Martha Vebrigge.
EIN: 383056051

1080
Allegan County Community Foundation
(formerly Allegan County Foundation)
524 Marshall St.
Allegan, MI 49010-1632 (269) 673-8344
County: Allegan
Contact: Theresa Bray, C.E.O.
FAX: (269) 673-8745;
E-mail: info@alleganfoundation.org; Additional
E-mail: theresa@gmail.com; URL: http://
www.alleganfoundation.org

Established in 1965 in MI.
Donors: Earl Delano‡; Chester Ray‡; Ethol Stone‡.
Grantmaker type: Community foundation.
Financial data (yr. ended 12/31/09): Assets,
$11,838,171 (M); gifts received, $1,058,184;
expenditures, $526,722; total giving, $246,250;
giving activities include $246,250 for 15 grants
(high: $47,086).
Purpose and activities: The foundation seeks to
provide the means for donors to make a lasting
impact on Allegan County through the establishment
and growth of endowed funds. Giving primarily for
education, health and human services.
Fields of interest: Arts; Education; Health care;
Recreation; Children/youth, services; Human
services; Community development, neighborhood
development.
Type of support: Continuing support; Building/
renovation; Equipment; Emergency funds; Program
development; Curriculum development; Matching/
challenge support.
Limitations: Applications accepted. Giving in
Allegan County, MI, only. No grants to individuals.
Publications: Annual report; Financial statement;
Grants list.
Application information: Visit foundation Web site
for application information. Application form
required.
  Initial approach: Meeting with foundation staff;
    application available at that time
  Copies of proposal: 1
  Deadline(s): 1st Fri. in Nov. for TAG grants; 2nd
    Fri. in Dec. for Legacy grants
  Board meeting date(s): Bi-monthly
  Final notification: Apr.
Officers and Trustees:* Theresa Bray, C.E.O. and
Exec. Dir.; Paula Baker,* Pres.; John Mahan,*
Secy.; Rob Marciniak,* V.P.; Steve Angle, Treas.;
David Balas; Mark Dobias; Lynn Etheridge; Nancy
Fifelski; Brian Marr; Jodi White.
Number of staff: 1 full-time professional; 1 full-time
support; 1 part-time support.
EIN: 386189947

1081
Allendale Community Foundation
P.O. Box 365
Allendale, MI 49401-0365 (616) 895-4777
County: Ottawa
Contact: Patricia Stephenson, Chair.
Email: stephepa@gvsu.edu (Patricia Stephenson);
URL: http://www.allendalecf.org/

Established in 2001 in MI as an affiliate of Grand
Haven Area Community Foundation.
Grantmaker type: Community foundation.
Purpose and activities: The foundation serves as a
catalyst and resource for philanthropy in Allendale,
leveraging resources to meet the community's
needs, and providing a cost effective way for donors
to give back to their community. Areas of priority
include youth and recreation, arts and culture, start
up projects, matching grants, heath and human
services, and problem prevention.
Fields of interest: Arts; Health care; Recreation;
Youth development; Human services.
Type of support: Matching/challenge support; Seed
money.
Limitations: Applications accepted. Giving limited to
the Allendale Charter Township area in northeast
Ottawa County, MI. No support for religious

programs or for-profit organizations. No grants to individuals, or for general operating expenses, debt reduction, or fundraising events.

Application information: See foundation web site for application form. Application form required.

Initial approach: Email 1-page summary of grant proposal to P. Stephenson

Copies of proposal: 11

Deadline(s): Mar. 1 and Sept. 1

Final notification: Grants are reviewed in Apr. and Oct.

Officers and Trustees:* Patricia Stevenson,* Chair.; Carl Piersma,* Vice-Chair.; Ruth Tanis,* Secy.; Carl Jesser,* Treas.; Chad Ayers; Robert Bosch; Pam DeJong; Roger Feenstra; Candy Kraker; Lee Scholma; Jim VanderVeen.

1082
Anchor Bay Community Foundation

51015 Washington St.

P.O. Box 88

New Baltimore, MI   48047-0088

(586) 949-5316

County: Macomb

Contact: For grants: Max J. Plante, Secy.

E-mail: abcfoundation@comcast.net; URL: http://www.abcommunityfoundation.org

Established in 1997 in MI.

Grantmaker type: Community foundation.

Financial data (yr. ended 12/31/09): Assets, $348,244 (M); gifts received, $37,037; expenditures, $36,726; total giving, $25,105; giving activities include $9,130 for grants, and $15,975 for grants to individuals.

Purpose and activities: The foundation has been organized to: 1) raise and distribute financial and other resources; 2) promote lifelong learning for children and families; and 3) enhance and strengthen cultural, social and educational opportunities for the Anchor Bay community, including the greater New Baltimore and Chesterfield, MI areas.

Fields of interest: Arts; Education; Environment; Health care; Recreation; Youth, services; Human services; Community/economic development.

Type of support: General/operating support; Scholarship funds.

Limitations: Applications accepted. Giving primarily in greater New Baltimore and Chesterfield, MI.

Application information: Visit foundation web site for application form for grants up to $500. The foundation's Board meets monthly to review applications. Application form required.

Initial approach: Submit application form

Copies of proposal: 1

Deadline(s): None

Board meeting date(s): Monthly

Officers and Directors:* Joseph D. Stabile,* Chair.; Mary R. Socia,* Vice-Chair.; Max J. Plante,* Secy.; Lois Pierson,* Treas.; Roger Facione, Dir. Emeritus; Robert Miller III, Dir. Emeritus; Mary Ann Bayer; Patricia L. Gendernalik; Marion Ashen Lusardi; Charlene McEachin; Denise Mello; Lynne Hoover Musilli; Barbara Richards; Oscar F. Socia; Juliana Texley, Ph.D.; Steven B. Whittlesey; Leonard Woodside.

EIN: 383255728

1083
Ann Arbor Area Community Foundation

(formerly Ann Arbor Area Foundation)

301 N. Main St., Ste. 300

Ann Arbor, MI   48104-1133   (734) 663-0401

County: Washtenaw

Contact: For grants: Neel Hajra, C.O.O.

FAX: (734) 663-3514; E-mail: info@aaacf.org; Grant inquiry e-mail: nhajra@aaacf.org; URL: http://www.aaacf.org

Incorporated in 1963 in MI.

Grantmaker type: Community foundation.

Financial data (yr. ended 12/31/08): Assets, $39,737,991 (M); gifts received, $4,273,079; expenditures, $3,400,822; total giving, $2,284,402; giving activities include $2,182,182 for 368 grants (high: $50,000; low: $50), and $102,220 for 121 grants to individuals (high: $5,000; low: $250).

Purpose and activities: The mission of the foundation is to enrich the quality of life in the greater Ann Arbor, MI area through building a permanent endowment, providing a flexible vehicle for donors, and acting as a leader for the philanthropic community.

Fields of interest: Visual arts; Performing arts; Performing arts, theater; Arts; Higher education; Education; Environment, natural resources; Health care; Health organizations, association; Crime/violence prevention, domestic violence; Safety/disasters; Children/youth, services; Family services; Aging, centers/services; Homeless, human services; Human services; Economic development; Community/economic development; Aging; Homeless.

Type of support: Income development; Management development/capacity building; Emergency funds; Program development; Conferences/seminars; Publication; Seed money; Scholarship funds; Research; Matching/challenge support.

Limitations: Applications accepted. Giving limited to Washtenaw County, MI. No support for religious or sectarian purposes. No grants to individuals (except for scholarships), or for construction projects (new building or routine maintenance), re-granting, annual giving campaigns, fundraising events, or computer hardware equipment; no loans.

Publications: Application guidelines; Annual report (including application guidelines); Newsletter; Program policy statement.

Application information: Visit foundation web site for application guidelines. Applicants must log on to http://www.communitygrants.org to create an online agency profile and complete the Short Community Grants Application. Application form required.

Initial approach: Create an online agency profile

Deadline(s): Feb. 2 and Oct. 5

Board meeting date(s): Jan., Mar., May, June, July, Sept., Oct., and Nov.

Officers and Trustees:* Hugh Morgan,* Chair.; Martha Darling,* Vice-Chair.; Cheryl W. Elliott, C.E.O. and Pres.; Martha L. Bloom, V.P.; Neel Hajra, C.O.O. and V.P., Community Investment; Bhushan Kulkarni,* Secy.; Doug Weber, C.F.O.; David Sarns,* Treas.; Marsha Penner, Cont.; Rebecca Boylan; Brian Campbell; Cynthia L. Cattran; Ann S. Davis; Michael Finney; Jay Hack; Fred McDonald, II; Jennifer Poteat; Molly Resnik; Paul Schutt; Dr. Levi Thompson.

Number of staff: 6 full-time professional; 4 part-time professional; 1 full-time support.

EIN: 386087967

1084
Baraga County Community Foundation

P.O. Box 338

L'Anse, MI   49946-0338   (906) 353-7898

County: Baraga

Contact: Gordette Cote-Luetz, Exec. Dir.

FAX: (906) 353-7896; E-mail: baragacf@up.net

Established in 1995 in MI.

Grantmaker type: Community foundation.

Financial data (yr. ended 12/31/08): Assets, $753,331 (M); gifts received, $28,658; expenditures, $71,550; total giving, $6,925; giving activities include $6,925 for 11 grants (high: $1,408; low: $92).

Purpose and activities: The foundation seeks to enhance the quality of life in the Baraga County area by improving the educational, cultural, recreational, environmental, and social welfare resources of the area and developing youth for community leadership.

Fields of interest: Arts; Education; Environment; Health care; Children/youth, services; Human services; Community/economic development.

Limitations: Applications accepted. Giving limited to Baraga County, MI. No support for sectarian religious purposes. No grants for endowments, or for budget deficits, or routine operating expenses of existing organizations.

Application information: Visit foundation Web site for grant application and guidelines. Application form required.

Initial approach: Submit application cover sheet and attachments

Copies of proposal: 11

Deadline(s): Apr. for spring/summer cycle, Oct. for fall/winter cycle

Officers and Trustees:* Norm McKindles III,* Pres.; Tim Luoma,* V.P.; Rob Willman,* Secy.; Joseph O'Leary,* Treas.; Gordette Leutz, Exec. Dir.; Susan LaFernier; Carol LaPointe; JoAnn Mleko; Debra Parrish.

EIN: 383198122

1085
Barry Community Foundation

231 S. Broadway St.

Hastings, MI   49058-1835   (269) 945-0526

County: Barry

Contact: Bonnie Hildreth, Pres.

FAX: (269) 945-0826; E-mail: info@barrycf.org; Additional E-mails: bonnie@barrycf.org and grants@barrycf.org; URL: http://www.barrycf.org

Established in 1996 in MI.

Grantmaker type: Community foundation.

Financial data (yr. ended 06/30/09): Assets, $15,047,917 (M); gifts received, $782,551; expenditures, $959,343; total giving, $638,988; giving activities include $548,893 for grants, and $90,095 for 53 grants to individuals.

Purpose and activities: The mission of the foundation is to develop and manage endowed funds for helping and involving the people of Barry County, MI, to make a positive difference in their lives.

Fields of interest: Arts; Education; Environment, natural resources; Health care; Children/youth, services; Human services; Community development, neighborhood development; Community/economic development.

Type of support: General/operating support; Annual campaigns; Capital campaigns; Building/

renovation; Equipment; Endowments; Program development; Conferences/seminars; Seed money; Curriculum development; Scholarship funds; Research; Technical assistance; Consulting services; Program evaluation; Matching/challenge support.

Limitations: Applications accepted. Giving limited to Barry County, MI. No support for private organizations, including churches. No grants to individuals (except for scholarships), or for operating expenses or regularly upgrading equipment.

Publications: Application guidelines; Annual report; Informational brochure; Newsletter.

Application information: The foundation is currently accepting applications for Healthy Communities Grantmaking Program; visit foundation web site for application form and guidelines. Application form required.

> *Initial approach:* Submit application and attachment
> *Deadline(s):* Apr. 15 and Oct. 15
> *Board meeting date(s):* 3rd Thurs. monthly
> *Final notification:* Within 8 weeks

Officers and Directors:* Kimberly M. Norris, M.D.*, Chair.; Bonnie Hildreth,* Pres.; Jennifer Richards,* V.P.; Bob Byington; Dave Hatfield; Jennifer Haywood; Karen Heath; Deb McKeown; Robert Perino; Rex Schad; Jon Simpson; Dave Solmes; Shauna Swantek; Jim Toburen.

Number of staff: 1 full-time professional; 2 full-time support; 1 part-time support.

EIN: 383246131

Selected grants: The following grants were reported in 2008.

$207,000 to Green Gables Haven, Hastings, MI. For operating support.

$24,000 to Heartland Center for Leadership Development, Lincoln, NE. For HTC (Home Town Competitiveness) Academy in Battle Creek.

$10,000 to McFall Elementary School, Middleville, MI. For playground equipment for Thronapple-Kellogg.

1086
Battle Creek Community Foundation
(formerly Greater Battle Creek Foundation)
1 Riverwalk Ctr.
34 W. Jackson St.
Battle Creek, MI 49017-3505 (269) 962-2181
County: Calhoun
Contact: Brenda L. Hunt, C.E.O.; For grants: Annette Chapman, Dir., Grantmaking
FAX: (269) 962-2182;
E-mail: bccf@bccfoundation.org; Grant inquiry E-mail: annette@bccfoundation.org; URL: http://www.bccfoundation.org/

Established in 1974 in MI.

Grantmaker type: Community foundation.

Financial data (yr. ended 03/31/09): Assets, $73,299,916 (M); gifts received, $4,496,607; expenditures, $9,728,383; total giving, $7,843,180; giving activities include $7,843,180 for grants.

Purpose and activities: The foundation seeks to promote giving, build endowment, and provide leadership to improve quality of life. Grantmaking for programming in the Battle Creek, MI, area serves the citizens of the community through education, health, human services, arts, public affairs, and community development; scholarships are also available to students residing in the greater Battle Creek area.

Fields of interest: Arts; Child development, education; Adult education—literacy, basic skills & GED; Education, reading; Education; Animal welfare; Hospitals (general); Health care; Health organizations, association; Children/youth, services; Child development, services; Minorities/immigrants, centers/services; Human services; Community/economic development; Public affairs; Youth; Minorities.

Type of support: Research; Film/video/radio; Building/renovation; Equipment; Land acquisition; Emergency funds; Program development; Conferences/seminars; Publication; Seed money; Curriculum development; Scholarship funds; Technical assistance; Program evaluation; Program-related investments/loans; Scholarships—to individuals; Matching/challenge support.

Limitations: Applications accepted. Giving limited to the greater Battle Creek, MI, area. No grants for operating budgets, deficit financing, endowments, or research; no loans (except for program-related investments).

Publications: Application guidelines; Annual report; Biennial report (including application guidelines); Financial statement; Grants list; Informational brochure; Newsletter; Program policy statement.

Application information: Visit foundation web site for grant application packets, guidelines per grant type, and specific deadlines. Contact high school counselors for scholarship applications and guidelines. Application form required.

> *Initial approach:* Letter or telephone
> *Copies of proposal:* 20
> *Deadline(s):* Varies
> *Board meeting date(s):* Monthly
> *Final notification:* Within 2 months

Officers and Trustees:* Ursula Case,* Chair.; Judith Cole Williamson,* Vice-Chair.; Robert A. DeVries,* 2nd Vice-Chair.; Brenda L. Hunt, C.E.O. and Pres.; Shelly Miller, Sr. V.P., Opers.; Kelly Boles Chapman, V.P., Progs.; Linda Patenaude,* Secy.; William W. Simonds,* Treas.; Susan Baldwin; Rick Baron; Carolyn Brown; Dwight M. Carattini; Sonja F. Dotson; Deonna F. Estes; James Garay; Marcus E. Glass; Dr. Michael R. Loudon, D.D.S.* Benda Minter; Benjamin Roosevelt; Shanay A. Settles; T.R. Shaw, Jr.; James K. Sholl.

Number of staff: 15 full-time professional; 2 part-time professional; 3 full-time support.

EIN: 382045459

Selected grants: The following grants were reported in 2009.

$275,000 to Battle Creek Area Catholic Schools, Battle Creek, MI. For tuition and scholarship support.

$132,137 to Family Health Center of Battle Creek, Battle Creek, MI. For Primary Care and Dental Safety Net Expansion.

$75,000 to Binder Park Zoological Society, Battle Creek, MI. For Operating Support.

$50,000 to Art Center of Battle Creek, Battle Creek, MI. For Operating Support.

$50,000 to Starr Commonwealth, Albion, MI. For Ubuntu Fund.

$10,000 to Homer Community School, Homer, MI. For School Wellness Program of Homer Community Schools.

$5,000 to All Species Kinship, Munith, MI. To be used for general programming support.

$5,000 to Brass Band of Battle Creek, Battle Creek, MI. For NPA Capacity Bldg.-organizational assessment.

$2,700 to Urban League, Southwestern Michigan, Battle Creek, MI. For the Black Arts Festival.

$2,000 to Lakeview High School, Battle Creek, MI. For 2009 Gateway Competition Award.

1087
Bay Area Community Foundation
Pere Marquette Depot
1000 Adams St., Ste. 200
Bay City, MI 48708-5994 (989) 893-4438
County: Bay
Contact: Eileen A. Curtis, C.E.O. and Pres.
FAX: (989) 893-4448;
E-mail: bacfnd@bayfoundation.org; Additional tel.: (800) 926-3217; URL: http://www.bayfoundation.org

Established in 1982 in MI.

Grantmaker type: Community foundation.

Financial data (yr. ended 12/31/09): Assets, $32,105,535 (M); gifts received, $1,289,979; expenditures, $1,824,124; total giving, $955,590; giving activities include $955,590 for grants.

Purpose and activities: The foundation seeks to fulfill a wide array of donors' charitable wishes by building permanent endowment funds and serving as a leader for community improvement through effective grantmaking and collaboration. Priority will be given to projects that focus on charitable, cultural, educational, and environmental areas for Michigan's Bay and Arenac counties.

Fields of interest: Visual arts; Performing arts; Arts; Education; Environment, energy; Environment; Health care; Housing/shelter; Recreation; Human services; Community/economic development; Science; Youth.

Type of support: General/operating support; Equipment; Emergency funds; Capital campaigns; Building/renovation; Program development; Seed money; Curriculum development; Internship funds; Scholarship funds; Research; Technical assistance; Matching/challenge support.

Limitations: Applications accepted. Giving limited to Bay and Arenac counties, MI. No grants to individuals (excluding scholarships), or for existing obligations, endowments, or fundraising events.

Publications: Annual report; Financial statement; Grants list; Informational brochure; Newsletter.

Application information: Visit foundation web site for application form and guidelines. Applications sent by fax will not be accepted. Application form required.

> *Initial approach:* Telephone
> *Deadline(s):* Varies
> *Board meeting date(s):* Quarterly
> *Final notification:* Varies

Officers and Trustees:* Debra Lutz,* Chair.; Bill Bowen,* Vice-Chair.; Eileen A. Curtis, C.E.O. and Pres.; Michael Stoner,* Secy.; William Mulders,* Treas.; Kay Burks; Mike Dewey; Beth Elliott; Karolyn Goslin; Robert Hetzler; Mike Kelly; Jeffrey Martin; Richard Milster; Amy Rodriguez; Abel Torres; Anne Trahan; Cathy Washabaugh; Carolyn Wierda; Jeff Yantz.

Number of staff: 3 full-time professional; 3 full-time support.

EIN: 382418086

Selected grants: The following grants were reported in 2008.

$20,000 to Golden Horizons Adult Day Care, Alzheimer's Fund, Bay City, MI. For Dementia Training Project.

$12,500 to American Chemical Society, Midland Section - Youth Initiative Endowment Fund, Midland,

MI. To offer science and chemistry to at-risk alternative high school students in Bay County. $10,000 to Vision Tricounty, Community Initiative Fund and Vision for Education, Midland, MI. For program development.

$7,000 to Bay Arts Council, Community Initiative Fund, Bay City, MI. To collaboratively develop comprehensive communication plan and tools to promote partnerships between arts, culture and business community.

$4,000 to Habitat for Humanity, Bay County, Youth Initiative Endowment Fund, Bay City, MI. To assist in qualifying their new builds in Bay County as environmentally-friendly builds.

$3,528 to Pinconning Area School District, Pinconning Area High School, Pinconning, MI. To update the library media center computers.

$3,300 to Saginaw County Parks, Environmental Endowment Fund, Saginaw, MI. For Great Lakes Bay Regional Path Study - two-phase project providing outline for connecting existing multi-paths in Saginaw, Midland and Bay Counties, creating Great Lakes Bay Region multi-use pathway.

$1,000 to Friends of the Bay City State Recreation Area, Civic League of Bay County Advisory Endowment Fund, Bay City, MI. For Message from the Marsh cultural performing arts series.

$1,000 to Michigan State University Extension-Arenac County, Health Initiative Non-Endowed Fund, Standish, MI. To allow low-income seniors to buy fresh Michigan produce from June 1, 2009 through October 31, 2009.

$1,000 to Nate and Mary Ida Doan Santa House, Bay City, MI. For operating support.

1088
The Bay Harbor Foundation
750 Bay Harbor Dr.
Bay Harbor, MI   49770-8056   (231) 439-2700
County: Emmet
Contact: Candace Fitzsimons, Exec. Dir.
FAX: (231) 439-2701;
E-mail: info@bayharborfoundation.org; URL: http://www.bayharborfoundation.org

Established in 2004 in MI.
Grantmaker type: Community foundation.
Financial data (yr. ended 12/31/09): Assets, $399,174 (M); gifts received, $271,725; expenditures, $285,169; total giving, $170,384; giving activities include $104,656 for 7+ grants (high: $12,500), and $65,728 for 28 grants to individuals.
Purpose and activities: The foundation is a charitable, nonprofit organization established to provide a structure for receiving donations and distributing grants in northern, lower Michigan for programs in the arts, education, the environment, and health and human services.
Fields of interest: Arts; Education; Environment; Health care; Human services.
Limitations: Applications accepted. Giving in northern lower MI.
Application information: Visit foundation web site for application information. The foundation will invite selected organizations to submit a full grant application based on letters of intent. Application form required.
Initial approach: Submit letter of intent
Deadline(s): June 1 for letter of intent; Sept. 10 for full grant application
Final notification: Aug. 5 for grant application invitation; Dec. 19 for grants

Officers and Directors:* Clayton Waldorf,* Chair.; William Cobb,* Vice-Chair.; Catherine Musto,* Secy.; William U. Parfet,* Treas.; Candace Fitzsimons, Exec. Dir.; Sen. Jason Allen, Honorary Dir.; Kim Aikens, M.D.; Tracy Bacigalupi; Sally Cannon; William Conner; Margaret Emley; Christine Etienne; Tina Frescoln; Heather Frick; Debi Goodman; Gwen Haggerty; David V. Johnson; Paul Keiswetter; Paul Knapp; Linda Lyon; Susan Marriott; John McFarland; David Moore; Scot Morrison; Judy Phillips; Rodney Phillips; James T. Ramer; Robert Roskam; Joe Sproles; Kathryn Wisne.
EIN: 371491024

1089
Bedford Community Foundation
(formerly Bedford Foundation)
P.O. Box 54
Lambertville, MI   48144   (734) 854-1722
County: Monroe
Contact: Walt Wilburn, Pres.
FAX: (734) 854-1722;
E-mail: info@bedfordcommunityfoundation.com; URL: http://www.bedfordcommunityfoundation.com

Established in MI as an affiliate of the Community Foundation of Monroe County; became an independent community foundation in 2004.
Grantmaker type: Community foundation.
Financial data (yr. ended 03/31/10): Assets, $743,021 (M); gifts received, $151,449; expenditures, $35,772; total giving, $22,516; giving activities include $14,586 for 41 grants (high: $1,500; low: $30), and $7,930 for 26 grants to individuals.
Purpose and activities: The foundation administers funds from donors to build permanent endowments for the charitable needs of Bedford Township in the areas of health, the arts, the environment, education, and youth activities.
Fields of interest: Arts; Education; Environment; Health care; Youth development; Community/economic development.
Limitations: Applications accepted. Giving limited to Bedford Township, MI.
Application information: Application form required.
Board meeting date(s): 3rd Wed. of each month
Officers and Trustees:* Walt Wilburn,* Pres.; Margaret "Meg" Smith,* V.P.; LaMar Frederick,* Secy.; Paul Bourque,* Treas.; Norbert C. Abel; Laura Collins; John Decker, Jr.; W. Thomas Graham; Gail Hauser-Hurley; Dr. Ted Magrum; Les Marsh; Mary Ann McBee; Sharon Throm; Dr. Robert Tuefel; Arlene Toyne.
EIN: 383544941

1090
Berrien Community Foundation, Inc.
2900 S. State St., Ste. 2E
St. Joseph, MI   49085-2467   (269) 983-3304
County: Berrien
Contact: Nanette Keiser Ed.D., Pres.
FAX: (269) 983-4939;
E-mail: NanetteKeiser@BerrienCommunity.org; Additional E-mail: annemccausland@BerrienCommunity.org; URL: http://www.BerrienCommunity.org

Incorporated in 1952 in MI.
Grantmaker type: Community foundation.

Financial data (yr. ended 12/31/09): Assets, $20,751,881 (M); gifts received, $2,182,444; expenditures, $2,228,388; total giving, $1,925,280; giving activities include $1,806,530 for 500 grants (high: $150,000; low: $100), and $118,750 for 100 grants to individuals (high: $5,000; low: $250).
Purpose and activities: The mission of the foundation is to promote philanthropy, to build a spirit of community, and to enhance the quality of life in Berrien County through its stewardship of permanently endowed and other funds. The foundation shall accomplish this mission by: 1) building permanent endowments and other funds, and providing a broad range of flexible and cost-effective donor services; 2) investing and managing funds prudently and professionally; 3) making grants to support a broad range of projects and programs that address community needs, with a focus on building a spirit of community/arts and culture, nurturing children, and youth leadership and development; and 4) serving as a facilitative leader, catalyst, and resource for local communities.
Fields of interest: Arts; Education; Health care; Substance abuse, prevention; Housing/shelter; Youth development; Children, day care; Youth, pregnancy prevention; Family services; Human services; Community/economic development; Children/youth; Youth; Adults; Aging.
Type of support: Program development; Seed money.
Limitations: Applications accepted. Giving primarily in Berrien County, MI for Undesignated and Field-of-Interest funds; giving in the U.S. for Advised and others funds. No support for sectarian religious purposes. No grants to individuals (except for scholarships), or for ongoing operating funds, deficit financing, national fundraising efforts, annual fund drives, or program-related investments.
Publications: Financial statement; Informational brochure (including application guidelines); Occasional report.
Application information: Visit foundation Web site for application information; guidelines and forms are available on request. 20 copies of application required for youth-oriented projects only. Application form required.
Initial approach: Telephone (ext. 2) or e-mail
Copies of proposal: 15
Deadline(s): Sept. 1 (unless specified differently on Web site)
Board meeting date(s): Oct.
Final notification: 10 to 14 weeks
Officers and Trustees:* Sharon Vargo,* Chair.; Tim Passaro,* Vice-Chair. and Treas.; Nanette Keiser, Ed.D., Pres.; Hillary Bubb,* Secy.; Lois Ashbrook; Patricia Forbes; Sam Harris; Brenda Layne; Anson Lovellette; Jane Marohn; Larry Schuler; Joanne Sims; Gregory C. Vaughn.
Number of staff: 2 full-time professional; 1 part-time support.
EIN: 386057160

1091
Branch County Community Foundation
2 W. Chicago St., Ste. E-1
Coldwater, MI   49036-1602   (517) 278-4517
County: Branch
Contact: Colleen Knight, Exec. Dir.
FAX: (517) 279-2319;
E-mail: info@brcofoundation.org; Additional E-mail: colleen@brcofoundation.org; Grant inquiry E-mail:

grants@brcofoundation.org; URL: http://www.brcofoundation.org

Established in 1991 in MI.
Grantmaker type: Community foundation.
Financial data (yr. ended 09/30/09): Assets, $4,206,109 (M); gifts received, $300,650; expenditures, $472,620; total giving, $347,345; giving activities include $347,345 for grants.
Purpose and activities: The foundation seeks to build a permanent endowment by attracting funds from and providing services to a wide range of donors, and to grant the income from those funds to serve the community.
Fields of interest: Humanities; Arts; Education; Environment; Health care; Housing/shelter, homeless; Human services; Community/economic development.
Type of support: General/operating support; Equipment; Endowments; Conferences/seminars; Scholarship funds; Technical assistance; In-kind gifts; Matching/challenge support.
Limitations: Applications accepted. Giving limited to Branch County and Bronson, Coldwater, Colon, Quincy, and Union City, MI. No support for sectarian religious programs. No grants to individuals (except for scholarships); no loans or program-related investments.
Publications: Application guidelines; Annual report; Financial statement; Informational brochure; Newsletter; Occasional report.
Application information: Visit foundation Web site for grant application guidelines. Applicants are strongly encouraged to meet with the foundation's staff prior to submitting an application. Application form required.
  Initial approach: E-mail foundation
  Deadline(s): Mar. 1
  Board meeting date(s): Monthly
  Final notification: 2 months
Officers and Directors:* Hillary Eley,* Pres.; Mary Jo Kranz,* V.P.; Ted Gordon,* Secy.; Dave Wright,* Treas.; Colleen Knight, Exec. Dir.; Susan Sparrow, Cont.; Bob Mayer, Dir. Emeritus; Patricia Shoemaker, Dir. Emeritus; Bruce Bloom; Jay Carlson; Paul Creal; Sandra Davis; Rachel Hard; Sandra Jackson; Kim Morgan; Dale Norton; Wayne Reese; Remus Rigg; Ron Rose.
Number of staff: 1 full-time professional; 1 full-time support.
EIN: 383021071

1092
Cadillac Area Community Foundation
201 N. Mitchell St., Ste. 101
Cadillac, MI 49601-1859 (231) 775-9911
County: Wexford
Contact: Linda L. Kimbel, Exec. Dir.
FAX: (231) 775-8126;
E-mail: cacf@cadillacfoundation.org; URL: http://www.cadillacfoundation.org

Established in 1988 in MI.
Grantmaker type: Community foundation.
Financial data (yr. ended 12/31/09): Assets, $5,419,051 (M); gifts received, $196,827; expenditures, $595,616; total giving, $451,840; giving activities include $444,840 for grants, and $7,000 for 4 grants to individuals.
Purpose and activities: The foundation seeks to develop a community-wide vehicle for permanent endowments to enhance the quality of life in the

area and to establish and manage worthwhile endowed funds for the betterment of the community.
Fields of interest: Arts; Education, early childhood education; Elementary school/education; Education; Environment, natural resources; Environment; Reproductive health, OBGYN/Birthing centers; Health care; Substance abuse, services; Mental health, smoking; Health organizations, association; Recreation; Youth development; Youth, services; Residential/custodial care, hospices; Aging, centers/services; Homeless, human services; Human services; Economic development; Community/economic development; United Ways and Federated Giving Programs; Economics; Aging; Homeless.
Type of support: Loans—to individuals; Income development; Building/renovation; Equipment; Emergency funds; Program development; Conferences/seminars; Publication; Seed money; Curriculum development; Research; Technical assistance; Program evaluation; Scholarships—to individuals; Matching/challenge support; Student loans—to individuals.
Limitations: Applications accepted. Giving limited to the greater Cadillac, MI, area as defined by the Wexford-Missaukee ISD, or CAPS (depends on specific grant program limitations). No support for sectarian programs. No grants to individuals (except as allowed by specific law or funds so designated), or for general operating support, endowments, fundraising campaigns, or conferences.
Publications: Application guidelines; Annual report; Annual report (including application guidelines); Financial statement; Grants list; Informational brochure; Occasional report; Occasional report (including application guidelines); Program policy statement.
Application information: Visit foundation web site for application forms and specific guidelines per grant type. Application form required.
  Initial approach: Telephone, letter, or e-mail
  Copies of proposal: 12
  Deadline(s): Feb. 28, June 30, and Oct. 31 for trustee grant program (unrestricted grants); varies for others
  Board meeting date(s): Monthly
  Final notification: Within 3 months for trustee grant program; varies for others
Officers and Trustees:* Lee J. Brown,* Pres.; Frederick O. Sprague,* V.P.; Dr. Robert J. Van Dellen,* V.P.; Scott Hunter,* Treas.; Linda L. Kimbel, Exec. Dir.; John Bishop; Barbara Darrigan; Richard Heydenberk; Chris Huckle; Dr. Michael S. Lueder; David McCurdy; Laurie Melstrom; David R. Peterson; Dr. Stephen Reznick.
Number of staff: 1 part-time professional; 1 full-time support.
EIN: 382848513

1093
Canton Community Foundation
50430 School House Rd., Ste. 200
Canton, MI 48187-5910 (734) 495-1200
County: Wayne
Contact: Joan Noricks, Pres.
FAX: (734) 495-1212;
E-mail: info@cantonfoundation.org; Additional E-mail: jnoricks@cantonfoundation.org; URL: http://www.cantonfoundation.org

Established in 1990 in MI.
Grantmaker type: Community foundation.

Financial data (yr. ended 06/30/09): Assets, $1,396,996 (M); gifts received, $159,293; expenditures, $245,712; total giving, $36,763; giving activities include $36,763 for grants to individuals, and $113,776 for 2 foundation-administered programs.
Purpose and activities: The foundation's mission is to enhance the quality of life in Canton, MI and surrounding areas by identifying and directing resources that address current and evolving community needs through grants from permanent endowments entrusted to the foundation for the common good.
Fields of interest: Visual arts, sculpture; Performing arts; Student services/organizations; Education; Environment; Health care; Human services; Community/economic development.
Type of support: Seed money; Scholarship funds; Publication; Equipment; General/operating support; Program development; Scholarships—to individuals.
Limitations: Applications accepted. Giving limited to the greater Canton, MI, area. No support for religious organizations for religious purposes. No grants to individuals (except for scholarships), or for routine operating expenses, endowment campaigns, special fundraising events and sponsorships, existing obligations, debts or liabilities, conference speakers, construction, travel, tours or trips, publications, videos, films, television, or radio programs.
Publications: Annual report; Financial statement; Grants list; Informational brochure (including application guidelines); Newsletter.
Application information: Visit foundation Web site for grant and scholarship information. Application form required.
  Initial approach: Letter
  Copies of proposal: 5
Officers and Directors:* Elizabeth Bland,* Chair.; Jerry Grady,* Vice-Chair.; Joan Noricks, Pres.; Barbara M. Rodenberg,* Secy.; Daniel G. Durack,* Treas.; Jack Demmer; Paul Denski, Jr.; James Fausone; Nancy Hillegonds; Radha Nath; Lisa Rozum; Gregory A. Schupra; Syed Taj, M.D.; Becky Widlak.
Number of staff: 1 full-time professional; 1 part-time professional; 2 part-time support.
EIN: 382898615

1094
Capital Region Community Foundation
6035 Executive Dr., Ste. 104
Lansing, MI 48911-5338 (517) 272-2870
County: Ingham
Contact: Dennis W. Fliehman, C.E.O.
FAX: (517) 272-2871;
E-mail: dfliehman@crcfoundation.org; URL: http://www.crcfoundation.org

Established in 1987 in MI.
Grantmaker type: Community foundation.
Financial data (yr. ended 12/31/08): Assets, $49,812,103 (M); gifts received, $3,719,230; expenditures, $3,983,738; total giving, $2,879,556; giving activities include $2,879,556 for grants.
Purpose and activities: The purpose of the foundation is to build the number and size of permanent endowment funds, income from which is used for grants that meet the charitable needs of Clinton, Eaton, and Ingham counties, MI. The foundation provides support for humanities,

education, environment, health care, human services, and public benefit.

Fields of interest: Humanities; Education; Environment; Health care; Children/youth, services; Human services; Community/economic development; Public affairs.

Type of support: Management development/capacity building; General/operating support; Capital campaigns; Building/renovation; Equipment; Program development; Seed money; Technical assistance; Matching/challenge support.

Limitations: Applications accepted. Giving limited to Clinton, Eaton, and Ingham counties, MI. No support for international organizations, religious programs, or sectarian purposes. No grants to individuals (except for scholarships), or for endowment funds, administrative costs of fundraising campaigns, annual meetings, routine operating expenses, or for existing obligations, debts, or liabilities.

Publications: Application guidelines; Annual report; Financial statement; Newsletter.

Application information: To apply for any CRCF grant applicants must use the foundation's online system; visit foundation web site for online application and guidelines. Application form required.

   Initial approach: Telephone

   Deadline(s): Apr. 1 for grants; Jan. 31 for Youth Fund

   Board meeting date(s): Bimonthly

   Final notification: Oct. 1 for grants

Officers and Trustees:* Douglas A. Mielock,* Chair.; Sam L. Davis,* Chair.-Elect; Dennis W. Fliehman,* C.E.O. and Pres.; Richard Comstock, V.P., Finance; Brad Patterson, V.P., Prog.; Michael Nobach,* Secy.; Denise Schroeder,* Treas.; John Abbott; Diana Rodriguez Algra; Mark E. Alley; Charles Blockett, Jr.; Kira Carter-Robinson; David J. Donovan; Nancy A. Elwood; Vincent J. Ferris; Bo Garcia; Pat Gillespie; Andy Hopping; Joan Jackson Johnson; Robert Kolt; Nancy L. Little; Dorothy E. Maxwell; Helen Pratt Mickens; Brian Priester; Mitchell Tomlinson; Carmen Turner; Steven Webster; Ryan M. Wilson.

Number of staff: 4 full-time professional; 1 full-time support.

EIN: 382776652

Selected grants: The following grants were reported in 2007.

$960,000 to ConnectMichigan Alliance, Lansing, MI.

$290,000 to Saint Joseph Catholic Church, Kalamazoo, MI. For Saint Joseph Catholic Church Orphanage Project.

$102,064 to United Way, Capital Area, East Lansing, MI. For endowment.

$35,000 to Lansing Economic Area Partnership Foundation, Lansing, MI. For LEAP annual dues.

$25,000 to Salvation Army of Lansing, Lansing, MI. For general support.

$17,964 to Saint Vincent Catholic Charities, Lansing, MI. For general support.

$10,000 to Lansing Christian School, Lansing, MI. For Hidden Treasures Pilgrim Thrift Store operating support.

$10,000 to Saint Vincent Catholic Charities, Lansing, MI. For Guardian Society Support.

$10,000 to United Way, Heart of West Michigan, Grand Rapids, MI. For Alexis de Tocqueville Society.

1095
Central Montcalm Community Foundation
P.O. Box 128
Stanton, MI   48888   (989) 289-2312
County: Montcalm
URL: http://www.cmcommunityfoundation.org

Established in 1999 in MI.

Grantmaker type: Community foundation.

Financial data (yr. ended 12/31/08): Assets, $547,799 (M); gifts received, $101,210; expenditures, $40,453; total giving, $23,620; giving activities include $17,220 for 13 grants (high: $4,000; low: $250), and $6,400 for 12 grants to individuals (high: $1,000; low: $300).

Purpose and activities: The foundation seeks to promote, encourage, aid, and supplement funds for educational and community oriented projects in the Central Montcalm area (defined as those townships wholly or partly served by the Central Montcalm School District).

Fields of interest: Education; Health care; Children/youth, services; Aging, centers/services; Community/economic development; Children/youth; Economically disadvantaged.

Type of support: Endowments; Curriculum development; Scholarships—to individuals.

Limitations: Applications accepted. Giving limited to the townships served by the Central Montcalm School District, MI.

Publications: Annual report; Informational brochure.

Application information: Visit foundation Web site for application form. Application form required.

   Initial approach: Letter or telephone

   Copies of proposal: 2

   Deadline(s): Aug. 31 for community and tobacco grants; Oct. 1 for education grants

   Board meeting date(s): Monthly

   Final notification: 60 days

Officers and Directors:* Connie McKeown,* Pres.; Franz Mogdis,* V.P.; Mary Miel,* Secy.; Vicki Korson,* Treas.; Bill Bode; Sharon Bowers; Steve Dawdy; Larry Deuel; Ginger Gurecki; Lisa Lund; Thomas Mall; Gale Parr; Hon. Charles Simon; Steve Swiecicki; Kris Thwaites.

Number of staff: 1 part-time professional.

EIN: 383068773

1096
Charlevoix County Community Foundation
507 Water St.
P.O. Box 718
East Jordan, MI   49727-9476   (231) 536-2440
County: Charlevoix
Contact: Robert A. Hansen, Pres.
FAX: (231) 536-2640; *E-mail:* info@c3f.org;
URL: http://www.c3f.org

Established in 1992 in MI.

Grantmaker type: Community foundation.

Financial data (yr. ended 12/31/09): Assets, $20,256,212 (M); gifts received, $1,053,198; expenditures, $1,401,786; total giving, $1,051,580; giving activities include $1,051,580 for grants.

Purpose and activities: The foundation seeks to enhance the quality of life in Charlevoix County, MI, now and for generations to come, by building a permanent charitable endowment from a wide range of donors, addressing needs through grantmaking, and providing leadership on matters of community concern.

Fields of interest: Arts; Higher education; Education; Environment; Health care; Recreation; Children/youth, services; Human services; Economic development; Community/economic development; Government/public administration.

Type of support: Endowments; Emergency funds; Program development; Seed money; Scholarship funds; Technical assistance; Consulting services; Scholarships—to individuals.

Limitations: Applications accepted. Giving limited to Charlevoix County, MI. No support for sectarian purposes. No grants to individuals (except for scholarships), or for ongoing organizational operating expenses, office equipment, deficit spending, or fundraising projects; no loans.

Publications: Annual report (including application guidelines).

Application information: Visit foundation web site for grant application cover sheet and guidelines. Application form required.

   Initial approach: Telephone

   Deadline(s): Mar. 1 and Oct. 1

   Board meeting date(s): 4th Tues. of the month, 5 times per year

   Final notification: May and Dec.

Officers and Trustees:* Chip Hansen,* Pres.; Bill Aten; Hugh Conklin; Bruce Herbert; Mike Hinkle; Jim Howell; Fay Keane; John Kempton; Linda Mueller; Pat O'Brien; Jeff Rogers; Valerie Snyder; Don Spencer; Rachel Swiss; Connie Wojan.

Number of staff: 3 full-time professional; 1 part-time professional.

EIN: 383033739

Selected grants: The following grants were reported in 2008.

$51,000 to Crooked Tree Arts Council, Petoskey, MI. For general operations.

$37,221 to Charlevoix, City of, Charlevoix, MI. To purchase and install a clock in East Park.

$25,000 to Icebreaker Mackinaw Maritime Museum, Mackinaw City, MI. For general operations.

$20,000 to Crooked Tree Arts Council, Petoskey, MI. To purchase a butterfly sculpture for the Charlevoix Public Library.

$20,000 to East Jordan School District, East Jordan, MI. For pool operations.

$16,000 to Michigan Land Use Institute, Traverse City, MI. For general operations.

$15,000 to University of Michigan, Dana School of Natural Resources, Ann Arbor, MI. For general operations.

$12,000 to Good Samaritan Family Services, Ellsworth, MI. For baby equipment and emergency fuel program.

$11,000 to Nature Conservancy, Lansing, MI. For general operations.

$10,000 to Charlevoix Childrens House, Charlevoix, MI. For general operations.

1097
Chippewa County Community Foundation
(formerly Sault Area Community Foundation)
511 Ashmun St., Ste. 200
P.O. Box 1979
Sault Sainte Marie, MI   49783-7979
(906) 635-1046
County: Chippewa
Contact: Ms. Sue Atkins-Wagner, Exec. Dir.
FAX: (775) 417-7368; *E-mail:* cccf@lighthouse.net;
URL: http://www.cccf4good4ever.org/

Established in MI; rejoined the Community Foundation of the Upper Peninsula as a geographic affiliate in 2005.

Grantmaker type: Community foundation.

Purpose and activities: The mission of the Chippewa County Community Foundation is to be a vehicle for receiving monies from a variety of sources to establish permanent endowment funds for charitable, educational, cultural, recreational, environmental, and social welfare purposes in a manner which promotes the spirit of philanthropy, utilizes the abilities of its youth, and meets the needs of the citizens of Chippewa County.

Fields of interest: Environment; Health care; Recreation; Youth development.

Type of support: Endowments; Program development; Scholarship funds.

Limitations: Giving limited to Chippewa County, MI, except Whitefish Township: this includes, but is not limited to Bay Mills, Brimley, Barbeau, Dafter, DeTour, Kinross, Pickford, Raber, Rudyard, Trout Lake, and Sault Ste Marie. No grants to individuals.

Application information: Application form required.

   Initial approach: Telephone or e-mail

   Copies of proposal: 11

   Deadline(s): Jan. 15, Apr. 15, July 15, and Oct. 15

   Final notification: Within 2 months

Officers and Trustees:* Kristi Little,* Chair.; Kerry O'Connor,* Vice-Chair.; Kathy Albrough,* Secy.; Julia Gervasio,* Treas.; Sue Atkins-Wagner, Exec. Dir.; Rick Barck; Jenna Belevender; Sue Clow; Orv Kabat; Margaret LaPonsie; Bud Mansfield; Desiree McCurley; Keith Neve; Walter North; Catherine Worden.

Number of staff: 1 part-time professional.

1098
Clare County Community Foundation

c/o Midland Area Community Foundation
109 E. Main St.
Midland, MI 48640-5153 (800) 906-9661
County: Midland
Contact: Janet M. McGuire, Pres. and C.E.O.
E-mail: jmcguire@midlandfoundation.org;
URL: http://www.midlandfoundation.org/clare.htm

Established in 1997 in MI; a geographic affiliate of Midland Area Community Foundation.

Grantmaker type: Community foundation.

Purpose and activities: The foundation promotes and enables philanthropic giving to enrich and improve the lives of people in our county through a wide variety of community programs, such as arts and culture, civic improvement, education, environment, health, human services, recreation and youth.

Fields of interest: Arts; Education; Environment; Health care; Recreation; Youth development; Human services; Community/economic development.

Type of support: Scholarships—to individuals; Scholarship funds.

Limitations: Applications accepted. Giving limited to benefit Clare County, MI. No support for sectarian religious programs. No grants for operating budgets, basic governmental services of educational functions, annual fund raising, normal office equipment, endowment campaigns, debt reduction, or travel.

Publications: Application guidelines; Annual report; Financial statement; Grants list; Informational brochure; Newsletter.

Application information: See foundation web site for full application guidelines and requirements. Application form required.

   Initial approach: Telephone

   Copies of proposal: 3

   Deadline(s): Jan. 15, Apr. 15, July 15, and Oct. 15

   Board meeting date(s): 3rd Wed. of every month

   Final notification: Within 2 months

Officers and Trustees:* Carol Santini,* Chair.; Harold Walls,* Vice-Chair.; Janet M. McGuire, Pres. and C.E.O.; Colleen Bremer,* Secy.; Daniel J. Timmins,* Treas.; Lawrence Barco; Jery Brandt; Bret Cook; Jim Doherty; Michael Jenkins; Michelle Neff; Carl Schwind; Anne Smith; Amy Stark.

1099
Clio Area Community Fund

c/o Community Foundation of Greater Flint
500 S. Saginaw St.
Flint, MI 48502-1811
County: Genesee
URL: http://www.cfgf.org/page10004440.cfm

Established in 1991 in MI as a geographic component fund of Community Foundation of Greater Flint.

Grantmaker type: Community foundation.

Purpose and activities: The fund is an endowment created to enhance the quality of life in the Clio area by awarding grants to eligible tax exempt organizations to benefit its residents in the areas of education, arts and recreation, community development, and health.

Fields of interest: Arts; Education; Health care; Recreation; Community/economic development.

Limitations: Giving limited to the Clio, MI, area.

Advisory Committee: Doug Vance, Chair.; Bernard Borden; Joel Clappe; John Engelhart; Fay Latture; Eileen Kerr; Judy Lee; Leesa Lee; Matthew McMichael; Ned Lockwood; William Morgan; Christina Wiskur.

1100
Community Foundation for Delta County, Michigan, Inc.

2500 7th Ave. S., Ste. 103
Escanaba, MI 49829-1176 (906) 786-6654
County: Delta
Contact: Gary LaPlant, Exec. Dir.
FAX: (906) 786-9124; *E-mail:* glaplant@cffdc.org;
URL: http://cfup.org/community_foundation/about_us/index.html

Established in 1989 in MI; a geographic affiliate of the Community Foundation of the Upper Peninsula.

Grantmaker type: Community foundation.

Purpose and activities: The foundation seeks to enhance the quality of life in the Delta County, Michigan, area by improving the educational, cultural, recreational, environmental and social welfare resources of the area, and developing youth for community leadership.

Fields of interest: Performing arts; Environment; Health care; Health organizations; Recreation; Human services; Family services; Residential/custodial care, hospices; Voluntarism promotion; Government/public administration.

Type of support: General/operating support; Emergency funds; Seed money; Scholarship funds; In-kind gifts; Matching/challenge support.

Limitations: Applications accepted. Giving limited to Delta County, MI. No grants to individuals, or for operating expenses.

Publications: Application guidelines; Annual report; Informational brochure.

Application information: See foundation web site for full guidelines and requirements, including downloadable application form. Application form required.

   Copies of proposal: 12

   Deadline(s): Jan. 1, Apr. 1, July 1 and Oct.. 1

   Board meeting date(s): Monthly

   Final notification: Jan. 31, Apr. 30, July 31, and Oct. 31

Officer: Gary LaPlant, Exec. Dir.

Trustees: John Beaumier, M.D.; Charles Becker; Lauren Belanger; Sally Bittner; James Boes, D.O.; Alice Butch; Willard Carne, Sr.; Peggy Erickson; Vicky Giguere; Dennis Harrison; Carol Kolinski, M.D.; William W. Lake, Jr.; William A. LeMire III, M.D.; Brian Pahnke; Matt Smith, Jr.; Bonnie Wenick-Kutz; John Whitman; David Williams.

EIN: 382907795

1101
Community Foundation for Livingston County

P.O. Box 200
Brighton, MI 48116-0200 (810) 229-2550
County: Livingston
Contact: Colleen Peters, Philanthropic Svcs. Dir., CFSEM
URL: http://cfsem.org/about-us/affiliates/community-foundation-livingston-county

Established in 1991 in MI as a geographic affiliate of the Community Foundation for Southeast Michigan.

Grantmaker type: Community foundation.

Purpose and activities: To support and improve the public well-being and quality of life in Livingston County, Michigan. Areas of interest include but are not limited to arts and culture, civic affairs, education, environment and land use, health, human services, neighborhood and regional economic development, and workforce development.

Fields of interest: Arts; Education; Environment, land resources; Environment; Health care; Employment, services; Human services; Community development, neighborhood development; Economic development; Government/public administration.

Limitations: Applications accepted. Giving limited for the benefit of residents of Livingston County, MI. No support for organizations lacking 501(c)(3) status or for sectarian religious programs. No grants to individuals, or for buildings or equipment, general operating support, endowments, fundraising campaigns, conferences and annual meetings, or computers or computer systems.

Application information: Application form not required.

   Initial approach: The foundation strongly encourages potential applicants to telephone prior to preparing a full grant proposal

   Deadline(s): Feb. 15, May 15, Aug. 15, and Nov. 15

   Final notification: Generally 4 months after deadline: June, Sept., Dec. and June

1102
Community Foundation for Mason County
P.O. Box 10
Ludington, MI   49431-0010   (231) 845-0326
County: Mason
Contact: Michael Oakes, Exec. Dir.
E-mail: moakes001@yahoo.com; URL: http://
www.mason-foundation.org

Established in 1988 in MI as the Ludington Area
Foundation; in 1996 became an affiliate of
Community Foundation for Muskegon County.
Donors: West Shore Family YMCA; Mason County
Central Senior Center; City of Scottville.
Grantmaker type: Community foundation.
Purpose and activities: The foundation was
established to promote philanthropy in Mason
County, and to serve as a grantmaker to the region's
nonprofit community organizations. The foundation
administers donor-advised, scholarship, field of
interest, and organization endowment funds. During
2007 $427,979 in grants and scholarships were
awarded for the benefit of Mason County.
Fields of interest: Community/economic
development; Philanthropy/voluntarism.
Type of support: Capital campaigns; Building/
renovation; Equipment; Program development.
Limitations: Applications accepted. Giving limited to
Mason County, MI.
Publications: Application guidelines; Annual report;
Grants list; Informational brochure; Occasional
report; Quarterly report.
Application information: The foundation shares an
online grant application process available on the
web site of the Community Foundation for Muskegon
County.
  Initial approach: Telephone
  Deadline(s): Mar. 30 and Sept. 30
  Board meeting date(s): Jan., Mar., May, July,
    Sept., and Nov.
  Final notification: 2 months
Officers and Trustees:* Dave Gibbs,* Chair.;
Michael Oakes,* Exec. Dir.; Carl Anderson; Wayne
Buskirk; Dr. Paul Drewry; Pete Heyse; Bill Kratz; Sue
Lindsay; Sid McKnight; Alberta Muzzin; Tom Paine;
Budde Reed; Janet Sanders.

1103
Community Foundation for Muskegon County
(formerly Muskegon County Community Foundation,
Inc.)
425 W. Western Ave., Ste. 200
Muskegon, MI   49440-1101   (231) 722-4538
County: Muskegon
Contact: Chris Ann McGuigan, C.E.O.
FAX: (231) 722-4616; E-mail: grants@cffmc.org;
URL: http://www.cffmc.org

Incorporated in 1961 in MI.
Donors: Alta Daetz‡; Harold Frauenthal‡; Charles
Goodnow‡; George Hilt; Jack Hilt; John Hilt; Paul C.
Johnson‡; Henry Klooster‡; Ernest Settle‡.
Grantmaker type: Community foundation.
Financial data (yr. ended 12/31/08): Assets,
$88,425,309 (M); gifts received, $4,289,206;
expenditures, $5,743,732; total giving,
$3,245,846; giving activities include $3,245,846
for grants.
Purpose and activities: The foundation seeks to
build community endowment, effect positive change
through grantmaking, and provide leadership on key

community issues, all to serve donor's desires to
enhance the quality of life for the people of
Muskegon County, MI. The foundation presently
supports efforts in the areas of arts, education,
environment, community development, health and
human services as well as youth development
issues.
Fields of interest: Arts education; Performing arts,
theater; Arts; Scholarships/financial aid; Education;
Environment, air pollution; Environment, water
pollution; Environment, land resources;
Environment; Health organizations, association;
Youth development; Human services; Economic
development; Urban/community development;
Community/economic development; Infants/
toddlers; Children.
Type of support: Management development/
capacity building; Building/renovation; Emergency
funds; Program development; Seed money;
Scholarship funds; Research; Consulting services;
Program-related investments/loans; Exchange
programs; Matching/challenge support.
Limitations: Applications accepted. Giving limited to
Muskegon County, MI. No support for sectarian
religious programs, or individual schools or districts.
No grants to individuals (except for scholarships), or
for deficit financing, routine operating expenses,
capital equipment, endowment campaigns, special
fundraising events, conferences, camps,
publications, videos, films, television or radio
programs, or for advertising.
Publications: Application guidelines; Annual report
(including application guidelines); Financial
statement; Grants list; Informational brochure
(including application guidelines); Newsletter.
Application information: Visit foundation Web site
for grant information; call the foundation for
proposal guidelines and specific deadlines.
  Initial approach: Telephone
  Deadline(s): Varies
  Board meeting date(s): Feb., Apr., June, Aug.,
    Oct., and Dec.
  Final notification: 3 months
Officers and Trustees:* Barbara L. DeBruyn,*
Chair.; Nancy L. Crandall,* Vice-Chair.; Chris Ann
McGuigan,* C.E.O., Pres., and Secy.; Robert
Chapla, V.P., Devel.; Ann Van Tassel, V.P., Finance;
John W. Swanson II,* Treas.; Tim Achterhoff; Wes
Eklund; Michael D. Gluhanich; Holly J. Hughes;
Susan Meston, Ph.D.; Dr. John L. Mixer, D.D.S.;
Stephen G. Olsen; Kay Olthoff; Michael A. Pepper;
Richard W. Peters, M.D.; Rev. Charles W. Poole;
Gary Post; Arthur V. Scott; Asaline Scott; Michael S.
Soimar; Roger Spoelman; Bernice L. Sydnor; Peter
M. Turner.
Trustee Banks: Comerica Bank; Fifth Third Bank;
The Huntington National Bank; National City Bank.
Number of staff: 7 full-time professional; 5 full-time
support.
EIN: 386114135
Selected grants: The following grants were reported
in 2006.
$110,000 to Frauenthal Center for the Performing
Arts, Muskegon, MI. For annual theater subsidy as
service for community.
$55,000 to Timberland Resource Conservation and
Development Area Council, Grand Rapids, MI. For
downtown Muskegon beautification and community
involvement project.
$50,000 to Muskegon Area First, Muskegon, MI. For
downtown Muskegon-rebuilding economic stability
program.

$30,000 to Downtown Muskegon Development
Corporation, Muskegon, MI. For infrastructure for
former downtown mall site.
$30,000 to Great Lakes Naval Memorial and
Museum, Muskegon, MI. For building project.
$30,000 to Muskegon, County of, Muskegon, MI.
For county-wide juvenile justice needs assessment.
$20,000 to YMCA, Muskegon Family, Muskegon,
MI. For environmental site assessment.
$16,305 to Hume Home of Muskegon, Muskegon,
MI. For capital campaign.
$15,000 to Sacred Suds, Muskegon, MI. For
Healthy Neighborhood program in McLaughlin
Neighborhood.
$10,000 to United Way of the Lakeshore,
Muskegon, MI. For Lights On Afterschool program.

1104
Community Foundation for Northeast Michigan
(formerly Northeast Michigan Community
Foundation)
111 Water St.
P.O. Box 495
Alpena, MI   49707-2838   (989) 354-6881
County: Alpena
Contact: Barbara A. Willyard, Exec. Dir.
FAX: (989) 356-3319; E-mail: bwillyard@cfnem.org;
Additional tel.: (877) 354-6881; URL: http://
www.cfnem.org

Incorporated in 1974 in MI.
Grantmaker type: Community foundation.
Financial data (yr. ended 09/30/10): Assets,
$20,861,768 (M); gifts received, $970,874;
expenditures, $1,357,955; total giving,
$1,049,983; giving activities include $809,425 for
597 grants (high: $60,000; low: $25), and
$240,558 for 184 grants to individuals (high:
$8,000; low: $100).
Purpose and activities: The foundation seeks to
serve the community and to preserve the charitable
goals of a wide range of donors now and for
generations to come.
Fields of interest: Humanities; Arts; Libraries/
library science; Education; Environment; Health
care; Health organizations, association; Children/
youth, services; Human services; Government/
public administration.
Type of support: Scholarships—to individuals;
Building/renovation; Equipment; Program
development; Conferences/seminars; Seed money;
Scholarship funds; Technical assistance.
Limitations: Applications accepted. Giving limited to
Alcona, Alpena, Montmorency, and Presque Isle
counties, MI and through affiliates: Crawford,
Cheboygan, Iosco, Ogemaw, and Oscoda counties,
MI. No support for religious purposes. No grants to
individuals (except for scholarships), or for annual
giving campaigns or capital campaigns, normal
operating expenses, or multi-year or sustained
funding; no loans.
Publications: Application guidelines; Annual report;
Financial statement; Grants list; Informational
brochure; Newsletter; Program policy statement.
Application information: Visit foundation web site
for application forms, guidelines, and deadlines. For
grants of $300 or less, organizations should use the
2-page mini-grant application and follow its specific
guidelines. Application form required.
  Initial approach: Submit application forms and
    attachments
  Copies of proposal: 1

Deadline(s): Generally Feb. 1, Aug. 1, and Nov. 1
Board meeting date(s): 2nd Tues. in Mar., June, Sept., and Dec.
Final notification: Within 6 weeks
Officers and Trustees:* Ann Burton,* Pres.; Sue Keller,* V.P.; Chuck Manning,* Secy.; Esther Ableidinger,* Treas.; Barbara A. Willyard, Exec. Dir.; Marcia Aten; Benjamin Bolser; Chad Brandt; Carolyn Brummund; Larry Bruski; Nancy Coombs; Sue Fitzpatrick; Jerry Gosnell; Georgene Hildebrand; Jennie Kerr; Steve Lappan; Jennifer Lee; Bill Morford; Dave Post; Terri Rondeau; Tom Sobeck; Bill Speer.
Number of staff: 4 full-time support.
EIN: 237384822
Selected grants: The following grants were reported in 2007.
$585,515 to Alpena Tennis Association, Presque Isle, MI. For new tennis courts and donor recognition plaques, and Ready, Set, Serve! program.
$170,277 to Alpena Regional Medical Center, Alpena, MI. For hyperbaric chamber and accessories, annual Steele Fund distribution, Tar Wars Program, Smoke Free Kids Project, probe covers for hearing screening tests, Choices tobacco cessation program for teens, and general support.
$160,680 to Multi-purpose Arena Coalition, Alpena, MI. For Northern Lights Arena, zamboni, and fundraising.
$41,380 to University of Michigan, Ann Arbor, MI. For scholarships.
$14,581 to Alpena Public Schools, Alpena, MI. For Alpena High School Band, Lincoln School Playground Project, High School KAPUT Senior Lock-in and After Prom Party, suicide prevention program, and various other projects.
$14,217 to Alcona Community Schools, Lincoln, MI. For general operating support and for track equipment at Alcona High School, increasing use of technology in math class, field improvements to softball complex, yearbook publishing, Physical/Cardiovascular Endurance program, library books for Alcona Elementary, and other projects.
$14,195 to Michigan Technological University, Houghton, MI. For scholarships.
$12,285 to Michigan State University, East Lansing, MI. For scholarships.
$12,220 to Saginaw Valley State University, University Center, MI. For scholarships.
$10,448 to Alpena Community College, Volunteer Center, Alpena, MI. For operating support.

1105
Community Foundation for Oceana County
242 N. Michigan Ave.
P.O. Box 367
Shelby, MI 49455-1078   (231) 861-8335
County: Oceana
Contact: Tammy Carey, Exec. Dir.
FAX: (231) 861-6396; E-mail: tcarey@cffmc.org;
URL: http://www.oceana-foundation.org

Established in 1989 in MI as an affiliate of Community Foundation for Muskegon County.
Grantmaker type: Community foundation.
Purpose and activities: The Community Foundation for Oceana County was the first affiliate in the state of Michigan. In 2007 it distributed $381,962 in grants to local communities.
Fields of interest: Community/economic development.
Limitations: Giving limited to Oceana County, MI.

Officers and Trustees:* Jay Bryan,* Chair. and Pres.; Dana McGrew,* V.P.; Scott Meyers,* Secy.; Tammy Carey,* Exec. Dir.; Bill Bluhm; Bill Bobier; Richard Carnes; Tina Collier; Mishelle Comstock; Todd Comstock; and 14 additional trustees.

1106
Community Foundation for Southeast Michigan
(formerly Community Foundation for Southeastern Michigan)
333 W. Fort St., Ste. 2010
Detroit, MI 48226-3134   (313) 961-6675
County: Wayne
Contact: Mariam C. Noland, Pres.
FAX: (313) 961-2886; E-mail: cfsem@cfsem.org;
URL: http://www.cfsem.org

Established in 1984 in MI.
Grantmaker type: Community foundation.
Financial data (yr. ended 12/31/09): Assets, $571,969,510 (M); gifts received, $32,537,062; expenditures, $71,893,574; total giving, $67,259,122; giving activities include $67,259,122 for grants.
Purpose and activities: The foundation strengthens the region's quality of life by: 1) building "community capital"; 2) enhancing the region's quality of life; 3) engaging people and organizations in philanthropy; 4) convening, planning, and working for positive change; and 5) supporting and launching new initiatives. Supports projects in the areas of civic affairs, social services, arts and culture, health, education, environment and land use, neighborhood and regional economic development and workforce development.
Fields of interest: Arts; Education; Environment; Health care; Health organizations, association; Youth development, services; Youth, services; Human services; Civil rights, race/intergroup relations; Economic development; Community/economic development; Government/public administration; Leadership development; Public affairs; Economically disadvantaged.
Type of support: Program development; Seed money; Scholarship funds; Technical assistance; Scholarships—to individuals.
Limitations: Applications accepted. Giving limited to Livingston, Macomb, Monroe, Oakland, St. Clair, Washtenaw, and Wayne counties, MI. No support for sectarian religious programs. No grants to individuals (from unrestricted funds), or for capital projects, endowments, annual campaigns, general operating support, conferences, computers and computer systems, fundraising, annual meetings, buildings, or equipment.
Publications: Application guidelines; Annual report (including application guidelines); Grants list; Informational brochure (including application guidelines); Newsletter.
Application information: There may be separate grantmaking guidelines for targeted grantmaking projects. These guidelines and special application forms are available by contacting the foundation or consulting the foundation's Guidelines for Grantmaking. Visit foundation web site for general grant application guidelines. Application form not required.
Initial approach: Complete online pre-application questionnaire
Copies of proposal: 2
Deadline(s): Recommended dates of Feb. 15, May 15, Aug. 15, and Nov. 15

Board meeting date(s): Mar., June, Sept., and Dec.
Final notification: 3 months after submission of proposal
Officers and Trustees:* Allan D. Gilmour,* Chair.; Alfred R. Glancy III,* Vice-Chair.; Alan E. Schwartz,* Vice-Chair.; Barbara C. Van Dusen,* Vice-Chair.; Mariam C. Noland, Pres.; Robin D. Ferriby, V.P., Philanthropic Svcs.; Karen L. Leppanen, V.P., Finance and Admin.; Elizabeth C. Sullivan, V.P., Community Investment; W. Frank Fountain,* Secy.; Michael T. Monahan,* Treas.; Vivian Day Stroh,* Chair., Prog. and Distrib. Comm.; Diane M. Kresnak, Cont.; Frederick M. Adams, Jr.; Terence E. Adderley; Margaret Acheson Allesee; Barbara E. Allushuski; Albert M. Berriz; Penny B. Blumenstein; Thomas C. Buhl; Andrew L. Camden; Ahmad Chebbani; Matthew P. Cullen; Paul R. Dimond; Deborah I. Dingell; Anthony F. Earley, Jr.; Irma B. Elder; John M. Erb; James D. Farley; David T. Fischer; Phillip W. Fisher; Steven K. Hamp; David M. Hempstead; William M. Hermann; George G. Johnson; Eric B. Larson; David Baker Lewis; John D. Lewis; Henry W. Lim; Dana M. Locniskar; Florine Mark; Jack Martin; Edward J. Miller; Eugene A. Miller; James B. Nicholson; Bruce E. Nyberg; David K. Page; Cynthia J. Pasky; William F. Pickard; Dr. Glenda D. Price; John Rakolta, Jr.; Jack A. Robinson; Pamela Rodgers; William W. Shelden, Jr.; Gary Torgow; Reginald M. Turner; Dale L. Watchowsky; Sean K. Werdlow; Ken Whipple.
Number of staff: 18 full-time professional; 1 part-time professional; 10 full-time support.
EIN: 382530980
Selected grants: The following grants were reported in 2008.
$1,500,000 to New Urban Learning, Detroit, MI. For the renovation of existing building for University Prep Science and Math High School.
$1,000,000 to Detroit Youth Foundation, Detroit, MI. For general operations.
$950,000 to Bizdom U, Detroit, MI. For entrepreneur training program.
$750,000 to Ann Arbor Spark Foundation, Ann Arbor, MI. For life sciences incubator.
$500,000 to Detroit Riverfront Conservancy, Detroit, MI. To create a sustainable programming unit within the Conservancy.
$280,000 to Detroit, City of, Economic Development Corporation, Detroit, MI. For construction and amenities of Dequindre Cut.
$150,000 to Arab-American and Chaldean Council, Lathrup Village, MI. For refugee acculturation outreach services.
$115,000 to Jefferson East Business Association, Detroit, MI. For business organizing and outreach along East Jefferson Avenue.
$100,000 to Music Hall Center for the Performing Arts, Detroit, MI. For Anita Baker Jazz Vocal Education Program for youth.
$40,000 to Volunteers in Prevention, Probation and Prisons, Detroit, MI. To expand a school-based mentoring program in Detroit.

1107
Community Foundation of Greater Flint
500 S. Saginaw St.
Flint, MI 48502   (810) 767-8270
County: Genesee
Contact: Kathi Horton, Pres.
FAX: (810) 767-0496; E-mail: info@cfgf.org;
Additional e-mail: khorton@cfgf.org; URL: http://www.cfgf.org

Established in 1988 in MI.
Grantmaker type: Community foundation.
Financial data (yr. ended 12/31/09): Assets, $127,186,236 (M); gifts received, $4,885,950; expenditures, $6,246,920; total giving, $4,527,084; giving activities include $4,361,426 for grants, and $165,658 for grants to individuals.
Purpose and activities: The foundation serves the common good in Genesee County - building a strong community by engaging people in philanthropy and developing the community's permanent endowment - now and for generations to come. The foundation seeks to respond to current or emerging needs in the local area in conservation and the environment, arts and humanities, education, health and human services, and leadership development.
Fields of interest: Humanities; Arts; Education; Environment, natural resources; Environment; Health care; Youth development, services; Children/youth, services; Human services; Leadership development; Children/youth; Economically disadvantaged.
Type of support: General/operating support; Management development/capacity building; Program development; Seed money; Scholarship funds; Technical assistance; Program evaluation; Matching/challenge support.
Limitations: Applications accepted. Giving primarily in Genesee County, MI. No support for sectarian religious purposes. No grants to individuals (except for scholarships), or for deficit reduction or routine operating expenses of existing organizations.
Publications: Application guidelines; Annual report; Financial statement; Grants list; Informational brochure; Occasional report; Program policy statement.
Application information: Visit foundation web site for application forms and guidelines per grant type (separate application form for grant requests under $25,000). Application form required.
 Initial approach: Telephone or personal contact
 Copies of proposal: 3
 Deadline(s): None. Once an application is received, the contact person listed on the application Cover Sheet will be contacted by a Program Officer to discuss a decision-making timeline
 Board meeting date(s): Feb., Apr., June, Oct., and Dec.
Officers and Trustees: Sherri E. Stephens,* Chair.; Timothy H. Knecht,* Vice-Chair.; Kathi Horton, Pres.; Mary Ittigson, V.P., Finance and Admin.; Patrick Naswell, V.P., Community Impact; AnnMarie VanDuyne, V.P., Philanthropic Svcs.; Shannon M. Easter White,* Secy.; Daniel Coffield,* Treas.; Julie Ebert, Cont.; Stephen Arellano; Samuel J. Cox; F. James Cummins; Troy Farah; Janice Gensel; Nancy Hanflik; Wanda D. Harden; Stanley Liberty; David E. Lossing; Lawrence E. Moon; Dr. Bobby Mukkamala; Ira A. Rutherford; T. Ardele Shaltz; Lori Tallman; Susan Tippett; Douglas B. Vance; Karen Williams Weaver.
Number of staff: 11 full-time professional; 3 full-time support.
EIN: 382190667
Selected grants: The following grants were reported in 2008.
$308,441 to Flint Institute of Music, Flint, MI. For grant made through Flint Cultural Center Foundation.
$106,436 to Easter Seal Society of Southeastern Michigan, Waterford, MI.
$85,199 to American Red Cross, Flint, MI.

$80,000 to United Way of Genesee County, Flint, MI. For Best Project Assessment Phase of Third Cohort.
$76,500 to Flint Cultural Center Corporation, Flint, MI.
$71,171 to United Way of Genesee County, Flint, MI.
$67,377 to Genesee County Health Department, Flint, MI. For Creating Community Change: Organizing for Community Led, Fundamental Health Improvement.
$42,390 to Whaley Childrens Center, Flint, MI.
$30,000 to Hurley Foundation, Flint, MI. For Patient-Centered Approach to Patient Satisfaction.
$24,000 to Genesee County Land Bank Authority, Flint, MI. For Durant Hotel Project.

1108
Community Foundation of Greater Rochester

(formerly Greater Rochester Area Community Foundation)
P.O. Box 80431
Rochester, MI   48308-0431   (248) 608-2804
County: Oakland
Contact: Peggy Hamilton, Exec. Dir.
FAX: (248) 608-2826; E-mail: cfound@cfound.org; URL: http://www.cfound.org
Scholarship application address for hand delivery: Community Fdn. Office, 127 W. University Dr., Rochester, MI 48307

Incorporated in 1983 in MI.
Grantmaker type: Community foundation.
Financial data (yr. ended 12/31/09): Assets, $6,346,009 (M); gifts received, $785,491; expenditures, $718,248; total giving, $346,548; giving activities include $268,123 for 6 grants (high: $110,000), and $78,425 for 71 grants to individuals.
Purpose and activities: The foundation seeks to enhance the quality of life for community residents within the following funding categories: arts and culture, education, youth, civic beautification, health, recreation, human services, and community development.
Fields of interest: Museums; Performing arts; Performing arts, music; Arts; Elementary school/education; Education; Environment, natural resources; Environment; Health care; Recreation; Youth, services; Family services; Human services; Economic development; Community/economic development; Youth; Disabilities, people with.
Type of support: General/operating support; Annual campaigns; Building/renovation; Equipment; Endowments; Emergency funds; Seed money; Scholarship funds; Scholarships—to individuals; Matching/challenge support.
Limitations: Applications accepted. Giving limited to the greater Rochester, MI, area. No grants to individuals (except for designated scholarship funds), or for operating budgets.
Publications: Annual report (including application guidelines); Financial statement; Informational brochure; Newsletter.
Application information: Visit the foundation web site for application forms and specific guidelines per grant type. A foundation staff member will contact applicants who have submitted a letter of intent to discuss their submitted proposal and funding opportunities available. Application form required.
 Initial approach: Letter of Intent
 Copies of proposal: 7

Deadline(s): Mar. 31 and Sept. 30 for grant application forms; Mar. 4 for scholarships
Board meeting date(s): Quarterly
Officers and Trustees: David de Steiger,* Chair.; Tim Anderson,* Vice-Chair., Investments; Brian Hunter,* Vice-Chair., Devel.; George Seifert,* Vice-Chair., Pro Tem; Patricia Botkin,* Secy.; Shirley Gofrank,* Treas.; Peggy Hamilton, Exec. Dir.; Ken Bilodeau; Jack DiFranco; Michael Glass; Edward A. Golick; Robert Justin; Sal LaMendola; Tom Mines; Vern Pixley; John Schultz.
Members: Barbara Andruccidi; Brian Barnett; Ken Bilodeau; Corey Bordine; Frank Cardimen; Gerald Carvey; Joe Champagne; Jerry Collins; Penny Crissman; Kathy Dziurman; Tom Finnerty; Chuck Hoover; Bruce Kresge; Karen Lewis; Deborah McDowell; Patrick McKay; Ed McKibbon; Sid Mittra; Pamela Mitzelfeld; John Modetz; Joe Mooney; Don Pixley; Katy Plummer; Linda Preede; Glenda Byers Raye; John Savio; Russ Shelton; Marty Sibert; Jennifer Sicora; Mary Beth Snyder; Lawrence Ternan; Brad Upton.
Number of staff: 1 full-time professional; 1 part-time support.
EIN: 382476777

1109
Community Foundation of Monroe County

28 S. Macomb St.
P.O. Box 627
Monroe, MI   48161-2137   (734) 242-1976
County: Monroe
Contact: Kathleen Russeau, Exec. Dir.
FAX: (734) 242-1234; E-mail: info@cfmonroe.org; URL: http://www.cfmonroe.org

Established in 1978 in MI.
Grantmaker type: Community foundation.
Financial data (yr. ended 03/31/09): Assets, $3,778,021 (M); gifts received, $660,303; expenditures, $824,347; total giving, $222,528; giving activities include $117,186 for grants, and $105,342 for 106 grants to individuals.
Purpose and activities: The foundation's mission is to encourage and facilitate philanthropy in Monroe County, MI.
Fields of interest: Performing arts; Performing arts, theater; Performing arts, music; History/archaeology; Historic preservation/historical societies; Arts; Elementary school/education; Higher education; Adult education—literacy, basic skills & GED; Education, reading; Education; Environment, natural resources; Environment; Health care; Substance abuse, services; Health organizations, association; Food services; Housing/shelter, development; Children/youth, services; Aging, centers/services; Minorities/immigrants, centers/services; Homeless, human services; Human services; Community/economic development; Voluntarism promotion; Public affairs; Aging; Disabilities, people with; Minorities; Economically disadvantaged.
Type of support: Capital campaigns; Building/renovation; Equipment; Program development; Seed money; Curriculum development; Scholarship funds; Research; Technical assistance; Scholarships—to individuals; Exchange programs; In-kind gifts; Matching/challenge support.
Limitations: Applications accepted. Giving limited to Monroe County, MI. No support for sectarian religious purposes. No grants to individuals (except through designated scholarship funds), or for annual fundraising drives, endowment campaigns,

operational phases of established programs, conferences, travel, scholarly research, or for multi-year grant commitments; no loans.
Publications: Application guidelines; Annual report; Financial statement; Grants list; Informational brochure; Newsletter.
Application information: Visit foundation Web site for application information. Foundation prefers electronic submission of application. Application form required.
   Initial approach: Telephone, letter or e-mail
   Copies of proposal: 12
   Deadline(s): Jan. 15, Apr. 15, July 15, and Oct. 15
   Board meeting date(s): 4th Wed. of each month, except Dec.
   Final notification: One month
Officers and Trustees:* Paul Wannemacher,* Pres.; Chris Knabusch,* Secy.; Dustin Leach,* Treas.; Kathleen Russeau, Exec. Dir.; Paul Braunlich; Dale Brunt; Dr. Stephen Grider; Beverly Hammerstrom; Barbara Harrington; John Kauffman, Jr.; Merel Keck; Bob Knabusch; Molly Lumpart; Shirley Massingill; Isabelle Schultz.
Number of staff: 1 full-time professional; 1 full-time support.
EIN: 382236628

1110
Community Foundation of St. Clair County
516 McMorran Blvd.
Port Huron, MI 48060-3826 (810) 984-4761
County: St. Clair
Contact: Randy D. Maiers, C.E.O.
FAX: (810) 984-3394;
E-mail: info@stclairfoundation.org; URL: http://www.stclairfoundation.org

Established in 1944 in MI.
Grantmaker type: Community foundation.
Financial data (yr. ended 12/31/08): Assets, $26,448,298 (M); gifts received, $1,477,761; expenditures, $2,665,918; total giving, $1,659,698; giving activities include $1,499,023 for grants, and $160,675 for 100 grants to individuals.
Purpose and activities: The foundation seeks to serve the charitable needs and enhance the quality of life of the community by: 1) providing a flexible and convenient vehicle for donors having a variety of charitable goals and needs; 2) receiving and investing contributions to build permanent endowments; 3) responding to changing and emerging community needs; 4) serving as a steward for individuals, families, foundations, and organizations entrusting assets to its care; and 5) providing grants to philanthropic organizations, social services, civic concerns, education, arts and culture, recreation and youth.
Fields of interest: Arts; Education; Recreation; Family services; Human services; Economic development; Community/economic development; Youth; Aging.
Type of support: Emergency funds; Management development/capacity building; Building/renovation; Equipment; Program development; Publication; Seed money; Scholarship funds; Technical assistance; Program-related investments/loans; Scholarships—to individuals; Matching/challenge support.
Limitations: Applications accepted. Giving limited to St. Clair County, MI. No support for religious activities. No grants to individuals directly, or for endowments, equipment, annual meetings,

conferences, travel expenses, venture capital funds, or film, video, or TV projects, deficit reduction, annual fundraising, capital campaigns, marketing or public relations, general operating expenses, or land use.
Publications: Application guidelines; Annual report; Financial statement; Grants list; Informational brochure; Newsletter.
Application information: Visit foundation Web site for application form and guidelines. Application form required.
   Initial approach: Contact foundation
   Copies of proposal: 1
   Deadline(s): Jan. 1, Apr. 1, July 1, and Oct. 1
   Board meeting date(s): Quarterly
   Final notification: Mar., June, Sept., and Dec.
Officers and Board Members:* Don C. Fletcher,* Chair.; Donna M. Niester,* Vice-Chair.; Randy D. Maiers, C.E.O. and Pres.; Lynn Borg, V.P.; Douglas S. Touma,* Secy.; Roy W. Klecha, Jr.,* Treas.; Douglas R. Austin; Beth A. Belanger; Heather Bokram; Marshall J. Campbell; Don C. Fletcher; Lee C. Hanson; Steve L. Hill; Thomas A. Hunter; Charles G. Kelly; Gerald J. Kramer; Phyllis Ledyard; Dan Lockwood; Michael McCartan; Hon. John R. Monaghan; Franklin H. Moore; Frederick S. Moore, Jr.; Dr. Bassam G. Nasr; David P. O'Connor; Will G. Oldford, Jr.; Dr. Sushma Reddy; Chuck Wanninger; Martin E. Weiss; Cathy Wilkinson.
Number of staff: 6 full-time professional.
EIN: 381872132

1111
The Community Foundation of the Holland/Zeeland Area
(formerly Holland Community Foundation, Inc.)
70 W. 8th St., Ste. 100
Holland, MI 49423-3166 (616) 396-6590
County: Ottawa
Contact: Janet DeYoung, Exec. Dir.
FAX: (616) 396-3573; E-mail: info@cfhz.org;
Additional E-mail: janet@cfhz.org; URL: http://www.cfhz.org

Incorporated in 1951 in MI.
Grantmaker type: Community foundation.
Financial data (yr. ended 12/31/08): Assets, $31,700,171 (M); gifts received, $7,564,929; expenditures, $2,683,811; total giving, $2,195,111; giving activities include $2,195,111 for grants.
Purpose and activities: The foundation seeks to make the greater Holland/Zeeland area a better place in which to live and work by enhancing the quality of life for all its citizens through the use of permanent endowments built from a wide variety of donors.
Fields of interest: Visual arts, art conservation; Historic preservation/historical societies; Arts; Education; Environment; Health care; Housing/shelter; Recreation; Children/youth, services; Human services; Community/economic development; Aging.
Type of support: Capital campaigns; Building/renovation; Equipment; Program development; Seed money; Curriculum development; Scholarship funds; Technical assistance; Program evaluation; Employee-related scholarships; In-kind gifts.
Limitations: Applications accepted. Giving limited to the Holland/Zeeland, MI, area and surrounding townships. No support for sectarian religious programs. No grants for endowment funds, operating budgets, expenses for established

programs, fundraising drives, capital equipment, conference attendance, salaries, stipends, sabbatical leaves, debt reduction, research, fellowships, matching gifts, travel, or computers, video equipment, or vehicles; no loans.
Publications: Application guidelines; Annual report; Financial statement; Informational brochure; Newsletter; IRS Form 990 or 990-PF printed copy available upon request.
Application information: Visit foundation web site for current application form, guidelines and copies required. Application form required.
   Initial approach: Telephone Prog. Dir. before preparing and submitting proposal
   Copies of proposal: 11
   Deadline(s): Jan. 17, June 6, and Sept. 19
   Board meeting date(s): Feb., Apr., June, Aug., and Nov.
   Final notification: Within 5 weeks of deadline
Officers and Trustees:* Matthew Lepard,* Pres.; Ann Query,* 1st V.P.; Susan Den Herder,* 2nd V.P.; Juanita Bocanegra,* Secy.; Randy Thelan,* Treas.; Janet DeYoung, Exec. Dir.; Taiyoh Afrik; Char Amante; Lori Bush; Thun Champassak; John Donnelly, Jr.; Eleanor Lopez; John R. Marquis; Ritu Mathur; Hannes Meyers, Jr.; Deb Clark Miller; Nancy Miller; P. Haans Mulder; Thor Nelson; Peter Neydon; Judith Smith; Scott Alan Spoelhof; Daniel Zwier.
Number of staff: 5 full-time professional; 1 part-time professional.
EIN: 386095283
Selected grants: The following grants were reported in 2007.
$30,000 to Jubilee Ministries, Holland, MI. For Liberty Village: To help fund local collaborative project to have 24 large, high quality apartments in former E.E. Fell building for low to moderate income senior citizens.
$30,000 to Kandu, Inc., Holland, MI. For capital campaign for various employment projects.
$30,000 to Ottagan Addictions Recovery, Holland, MI. For Community Outreach Family Treatment Project.
$25,000 to Core City Christian Community Development Association, Holland, MI. For after-school academic program to 8 and 8.5 grade level students identified as failing academically.
$25,000 to LULAC - Latin Americans United for Progress, Holland, MI. For Steps to Success Program: collaborative program to service at-risk population with skills that will make them successful in today's job market.
$21,000 to Young Life, Holland, MI. For program for grades 7-12 teaming mature Christian women with teen girls in crisis providing timely encouragement, guidance and on-going support.
$20,000 to Lakeshore Ethnic Diversity Alliance, Holland, MI. For Calling All Colors Program - High School: Geared towards 9th-12th grades to encourage leadership with skills to live harmoniously with wide variety of races, cultures and ethnic backgrounds.
$15,752 to Zeeland Library and Community Center, Zeeland, MI. For Digital Zeeland Record. To complete project (Phase 2) to bring digital collection current.
$14,300 to Resthaven Patrons, Holland, MI. For Overhead Lifting System.
$12,000 to Boys and Girls Club of Greater Holland, Holland, MI. For Volunteer Outreach Initiative to develop consistent and effective recruiting program to increase number and longevity of present volunteer base.

1112
Community Foundation of the Upper Peninsula

(formerly Upper Peninsula Community Foundation Alliance)
2500 7th Ave. S., Ste. 103
Escanaba, MI   49829-1176   (906) 789-5972
County: Delta
Contact: Gary LaPlant, Exec. Dir.
FAX: (906) 786-9124; E-mail: glaplant@cfup.org;
URL: http://www.cfup.org

Established in 1994 in MI.
Grantmaker type: Community foundation.
Financial data (yr. ended 12/31/08): Assets,
$17,379,338 (M); gifts received, $1,283,642;
expenditures, $1,580,010; total giving,
$1,074,216; giving activities include $946,326 for
grants, and $127,890 for grants to individuals.
Purpose and activities: The foundation seeks to
enhance the quality of life in the Upper Peninsula of
MI. The foundation will provide its own U.P.-wide
philanthropy and that of its geographic affiliate
members through growth of permanent endowment
funds from a wide range of donors, grants, and
leadership activities. The CFUP also provides
financial, administrative, communication, and other
support services to its affiliate members and to
other U.P. community foundations.
Fields of interest: Historic preservation/historical
societies; Environment; Health care; Human
services; Economic development; Youth.
Type of support: Capital campaigns; Scholarship
funds; Technical assistance; Scholarships—to
individuals.
Limitations: Applications accepted. Giving limited to
the Upper Peninsula, MI, area, including Chippewa
County, Gogebic County, Schoolcraft County, and
Alger, Cedarville, Delta, Ontonagon, Paradise, St.
Ignace and Watersmeet county areas. No support
for religious or sectarian purposes. No grants to
individuals (except for scholarships), or for
memberships, memorials, endowments,
fundraising, social events, exhibits, or deficits in
operating budgets or normal operating expenses,
construction of buildings, or maintenance.
Publications: Application guidelines; Annual report;
Financial statement; Informational brochure;
Informational brochure (including application
guidelines).
Application information: Visit foundation Web site
for application form and guidelines. Application form
required.
  Initial approach: Submit Cover Sheet and
    attachments
  Copies of proposal: 8
  Deadline(s): Spring
  Board meeting date(s): Feb., Apr., July, and Oct.
  Final notification: By mail
Officers and Trustees:* Tom Luckey,* Co-Chair.;
Bonnie Wenick-Kutz,* Co-Chair.; Mary Bowerman,*
Vice-Chair.; Matt Smith, Jr.,* Vice-Chair.; William
LeMire III, M.D.*, Secy.; Dr. K. Gerald Marsden,*
Treas.; Gary LaPlant, Exec. Dir.; Dr. Kenneth Drenth;
Chari Fischer; Bill Inman; William W. Lake; Margaret
LaPonsie; Todd Lysinger; Jim North; Francis E. Paoli;
Dean Wood.
Number of staff: 2 full-time professional; 2 part-time
professional; 1 part-time support.
EIN: 383227080

1113
Community Foundation of Troy

(formerly Troy Community Foundation)
1120 E. Long Lake Rd., Ste. 205
Troy, MI   48085-4960   (248) 740-7600
County: Oakland
Contact: For grants: Jim Cyrulewski, Secy.; Denise
Rondo, Exec. Dir.
E-mail: jcyrulewski@itctransco.org; Additional E-mail:
drondo@communityfoundationoftroy.org; Grant
inquiry tel.: (248) 374-7130; URL: http://
www.communityfoundationoftroy.org

Established in 1998 in MI.
Grantmaker type: Community foundation.
Financial data (yr. ended 12/31/09): Assets,
$242,706 (M); gifts received, $182,076;
expenditures, $171,856; total giving, $134,935;
giving activities include $134,935 for grants.
Purpose and activities: The foundation is a
philanthropic organization dedicated to investing in
and enhancing the quality of life in Troy and the
surrounding communities by awarding grants to
support outstanding organizations and projects.
Giving primarily in the areas of the arts, education
at all levels, human services, including senior
self-sufficiency skills building, family counseling
programs, transportation programs and parenting
skills building, and economic vitality of the
community, including economic development,
business retention, technology innovation
programs, environmental programs and crime
prevention, with an emphasis on education and
business partnerships.
Fields of interest: Museums; Performing arts; Arts;
Higher education; Libraries (public); Education;
Environment, public education; Environment; Dental
care; Public health; Health care; Substance abuse,
services; Mental health, smoking; Crime/violence
prevention; Recreation; Family services; Aging,
centers/services; Human services; Economic
development; Community development, business
promotion; Youth; Aging.
Limitations: Applications accepted. Giving limited to
the greater Troy, MI, area. No support for religious
organizations for religious (denominational)
purposes, or for single purpose health
organizations, or national or international
organizations, unless they are providing benefits
directly in service-area residents. No grants to
individuals, or for general operating support, student
group trips, conferences, or hospitals (for building or
equipment needs).
Application information: Visit foundation Web site
for application Cover Sheet and guidelines.
Requests initiated by telephone will not be acted
upon until a written request is received; requests
initiated by fax are discouraged. Application form
required.
  Initial approach: Submit application Cover Sheet
    and attachments
  Copies of proposal: 4
  Deadline(s): Mar. 31, June 30, Sept. 30, and Dec.
    31
  Board meeting date(s): Quarterly
Officers and Directors:* Gregory Merritt,* Chair.;
Thomas Kaszubski,* Pres.; Cheryl A. Whitton,* V.P.;
Jim Cyrulewski,* Secy.; Anthony Iaquinto,* Treas.;
Denise Rondo, Exec. Dir.; Alex Ballios; Vickie
Bellinger; Ren J. Carlton; Chuck Church; Jeffrey
Coval; Eric Dietz; Cele Dilley; Tom Duszynski; John
"Bruce" Gates; Bill Hall; David Hanley; Marc
Kaszubski; Michael A. Kaszubski; Kenneth
Lesperance; Joseph Semany; Tim Watts.

Number of staff: 1 full-time professional.
EIN: 383390605

1114
Constantine Area Community Foundation

67094 Blue School Rd.
Constantine, MI   49042-9713   (269) 455-7737
County: St. Joseph
Contact: Michael Freude, Pres. and Tr.
FAX: (269) 651-3262; Application address: c/o
Sturgis Area Community Foundation, 310 N. Franks
Ave., Sturgis, MI 49091; URL: http://
www.sturgisfoundation.org/
affiliate_constantine.php

Established in MI as an affiliate of Sturgis Area
Community Foundation.
Grantmaker type: Community foundation.
Purpose and activities: The foundation is
committed to serving its greater community, thereby
enhancing the quality of life for all people in the
Constantine area. Priorities include: the
improvement of living and working conditions for the
citizens of the Constantine area; youth and
recreation; public, educational, charitable or
benevolent purposes; and care of the sick or aged.
Fields of interest: Education; Health care;
Recreation; Youth development; Human services;
Aging, centers/services; Community/economic
development.
Type of support: Program development; Seed
money.
Limitations: Applications accepted. Giving limited to
the Constantine, MI, area. No support for religious
programs that appear to serve a specific religious
denomination, or organizations lacking 501(c)(3)
status. No grants to individuals, or for existing
obligations or debts, or fundraising events.
Application information: See foundation web site
for full application guidelines and requirements.
  Copies of proposal: 8
  Deadline(s): Fall and spring; contact foundation
    for specific dates
Officer: Michael Freude, Pres.
Directors: Mary Dresser; John Wiedlea.

1115
Coopersville Area Community Foundation

P.O. Box 205
Coopersville, MI   49404-0205
County: Ottawa
URL: http://www.ghacf.org/affiliates/
coopersville.htm

Established in 1993 in MI as an affiliate of Grand
Haven Area Community Foundation.
Grantmaker type: Community foundation.
Type of support: Matching/challenge support; Seed
money; Program development.
Limitations: Applications accepted. Giving limited
for the benefit the northeast Ottawa County region
of Coopersville and Polkton, Wright, Tallmadge, and
Chester townships, MI. No support for religious
programs that serve, or appear to serve, specific
religious programs or faiths. No grants to
individuals, or for general operating expenses,
fundraising events, or to eliminate existing financial
obligations, debts, or liabilities.
Publications: Occasional report.

Application information: See foundation web site for application guidelines and downloadable application forms. Application form required.

Copies of proposal: 6

Deadline(s): Mar. 1 and Oct. 1 for grants; Feb. 6 for youth grants

Board meeting date(s): Monthly

Officers and Trustees:* Ron Veldman,* Chair.; Lori Lieffers,* Vice-Chair.; Denise Busman,* Secy.; Paul Spoelman,* Treas.; William Adema; Norman LeMieux; Karen Lemmen; Carol Pfahler; Robert TerAvest; Barbara Throop.

1116
Crystal Falls Area Community Foundation
(formerly Crystal Falls/Forest Park Area Community Fund)
P.O. Box 299
Crystal Falls, MI 49920-0299
County: Iron
URL: http://
www.dickinsonareacommunityfoundation.org/
page3.asp

Established in MI; in 2001 became an affiliate of Dickinson Area Community Foundation.
Grantmaker type: Community foundation.
Fields of interest: Arts; Education; Environment; Health care; Human services; Economic development; Community/economic development.
Limitations: Giving for the benefit of the Crystal Falls/Forest Park, MI, area.
Officers: Gene Dziubinski, Pres.; Roger Stoor, Treas.
Trustees: Charlene Anderson; Susan Flood-Dziubinski; Frank Groeneveld; Patricia Kosiba; Harold Payne; Pearl Ross; Don Schmidt; Doug Wagner; Beverly Wilcox.

1117
Davison Community Fund
c/o Community Foundation of Greater Flint
500 S. Saginaw St.
Flint, MI 48502-1811 (810) 767-8270
County: Genesee
Contact: Bev Tippett, Prog. Off, CM of Greater Flint
URL: http://www.cfgf.org/page10004441.cfm

Established in MI; an affiliate of the Community Foundation of Greater Flint.
Grantmaker type: Community foundation.
Purpose and activities: Support for the arts, culture and humanities, including the performing arts, historical societies, museums, programs and activities related to arts and culture; community improvement and capacity building, including community service clubs, business services and promotion, community and neighborhood development; and environmental quality, protection and beautification, including conservation and environmental education.
Fields of interest: Performing arts; Humanities; Historic preservation/historical societies; Arts; Environment, natural resources; Environment, beautification programs; Environmental education; Community development; Community development, neighborhood development; Community development, small businesses; Community development, service clubs; Community/economic development.
Limitations: Giving limited to the City of Davison, Davison Township, and Richfield Township, MI. No

support for organizations lacking 501(c)(3) status. No grants to individuals.
Advisory Committee: Timothy Elkins, Chair.; Eric Allen; Connie Elkins; Dan Fulcher; Chris Kautz; R. Clay Perkins; Susan R. Slater; Kurt Sloper; Lori A. Tallman.

1118
Dickinson Area Community Foundation
(formerly Dickinson County Area Community Foundation)
333 S. Stephenson Ave., Ste. 204
Iron Mountain, MI 49801-2942 (906) 774-3131
County: Dickinson
Contact: Debra J. Flannery, Exec. Dir.
FAX: (906) 774-7640; E-mail: dcacf@uplogon.com;
URL: http://
www.dickinsonareacommunityfoundation.org

Established in 1995 in MI.
Grantmaker type: Community foundation.
Financial data (yr. ended 04/30/08): Assets, $5,967,895 (M); gifts received, $358,769; expenditures, $306,633; total giving, $178,362; giving activities include $78,139 for 64 grants (high: $5,457; low: $187), and $100,223 for 111 grants to individuals (high: $1,500; low: $80).
Purpose and activities: The foundation seeks to enhance the quality of life in local communities by meeting the changing needs with endowments for good and forever. To that end, the foundation makes grants in broad program areas of education, health and human services, arts and culture, environment, community and economic development.
Fields of interest: Arts; Education; Environment; Health care; Recreation; Children, services; Human services; Economic development; Community/economic development; Social sciences; Children/youth; Aging.
Type of support: Seed money.
Limitations: Applications accepted. Giving limited to the Dickinson County, MI, area and surrounding MI and WI communities, including Crystal Falls and Forest Park, MI, and Florence and Niagara, WI. No support for religious or sectarian purposes, or fraternal organizations serving a limited constituency. No grants to individuals (except for scholarships), or for endowments, fundraising, travel, deficit reduction, capital expenditures, memberships, or memorials.
Publications: Application guidelines; Annual report; Financial statement; Grants list.
Application information: Visit foundation Web site for grant application form. Application form required.
Initial approach: Telephone
Deadline(s): Mid-Sept.
Board meeting date(s): 1st Tues. of Jan., Mar., Aug., Oct., and Dec.
Final notification: Nov.
Officers and Trustees:* Gene Dziubinski,* Pres.; Karen Thekan,* V.P.; Richard J. Debelak,* Secy.; Patti Petschar,* Treas.; Debra J. Flannery, Exec. Dir.; Grant Carlson; Tom Clarke; David Kashian; Bill Miller; Jay Olivares; David Ostwald; Cal Soderberg; William Trudell.
Number of staff: 1 part-time professional; 1 part-time support.
EIN: 383218990

1119
The Eaton County Community Foundation
c/o Capital Region Community Foundation
6035 Executive Dr., Ste. 104
Lansing, MI 48911-5338
County: Ingham
Contact: Dennis W. Fliehman, Pres.
FAX: (517) 272-2871;
E-mail: dfliehman@crcfoundation.org; URL: http://
crcfoundation.org/content/
eaton-county-community-foundation

Established in 1996 in MI as an affiliate of Capital Region Community Foundation.
Grantmaker type: Community foundation.
Purpose and activities: The foundation grants funds to benefit youth, family service, education, community welfare, art and culture throughout Eaton County.
Fields of interest: Arts; Education; Youth development; Family services; Community/economic development.
Limitations: Applications accepted. Giving limited to Eaton County, MI.
Application information: See foundation web site for application requirements and guidelines. Application form required.
Initial approach: Submit completed application form online
Copies of proposal: 18
Deadline(s): Mar. 1
Advisory Board: Vince Ferris, Chair.; Susan Steiner Bolhouse; Peter Dunlap; Hon. Thomas S. Eveland; Richard Lorencen; Olivia Lowe; Joe E. Pray; Dan Templin; Gary Wichman.

1120
Fenton Community Fund
c/o Community Foundation of Greater Flint
500 S. Saginaw St.
Flint, MI 48502-1811 (810) 767-8270
County: Genesee
Contact: Kathi Horton, C.E.O.
FAX: (810) 767-0496; E-mail: khorton@cfgf.org

Established in 1991 in MI as an affiliate of the Community Foundation of Greater Flint.
Grantmaker type: Community foundation.
Purpose and activities: To support community projects and non-profit organizations that exclusively benefit the Fenton, Lake Fenton, Linden and Southern Lakes communities and enhance quality of life for area residents.
Fields of interest: Community/economic development.
Limitations: Giving limited to Fenton, MI.
Advisory Committee: Betty Carlson, Chair.; Robert Cole; Joan Garfield; Jon Gerych; Linda Hathaway; Tracy Justice; E. Doran Kasper; Timothy H. Knecht; Dennis Leyder; Patricia Lockwood; David Lossing; Patric Parker; Brian Petty; Jeff Phillips; Judith Pieczynski; Rick Selley; Roger Sharp; Terry Tibbotts; Paul Van Gilder; Kim Virkler.
EIN: 382260852

1121
Flushing Community Fund

c/o Community Foundation of Greater Flint
500 S. Saginaw St.
Flint, MI 48502-1811
County: Genesee
URL: http://www.cfgf.org/page10004443.cfm

Established in 1997 in MI; an affiliate of the
Community Foundation of Greater Flint.
Grantmaker type: Community foundation.
Fields of interest: Historic preservation/historical
societies; Education; Community/economic
development.
Limitations: Giving limited to the Flushing, MI, area.
Advisory Committee: Timothy Purman, Chair.;
Melinda Ball; John Boerger; Dennis Bow; Virginia
Bueche; John Chahbazi; Cindy Gansen; Janice
Gensel; Barbara Goebel; Patrick O'Callaghan; Henry
Thoma; Lynne Whitmire.

1122
Four County Community Foundation

(formerly Four County Foundation)
231 E. Saint Clair St.
P.O. Box 539
Almont, MI 48003-0539 (810) 798-0909
County: Lapeer
Contact: Janet Bauer, C.E.O.
FAX: (810) 798-0908; E-mail: info@4ccf.org;
Additional E-mail: janet@4ccf.org; URL: http://www.
4ccf.org

Established in 1987 in MI; originally converted from
Community Hospital Foundation and sold to Saint
Joseph Mercy of Macomb North.
Grantmaker type: Community foundation.
Financial data (yr. ended 12/31/09): Assets,
$8,385,458 (M); gifts received, $242,834;
expenditures, $486,544; total giving, $291,060;
giving activities include $291,060 for 19+ grants.
Purpose and activities: The foundation is dedicated
to bringing together human and financial resources
to support progressive ideas in education, health,
community, youth and aging programs.
Fields of interest: Education; Environment; Health
care; Health organizations, association; Recreation;
Children/youth, services; Community/economic
development.
Type of support: Scholarship funds; Program
evaluation; Grants to individuals; Program
development; General/operating support.
Limitations: Applications accepted. Giving limited to
northeast Oakland, northwest Macomb, southeast
Lapeer, and southwest St. Clair counties, MI. No
support for sectarian religious programs. No grants
for operating expenses or basic educational or
municipal functions (generally).
Publications: Application guidelines; Annual report;
Informational brochure; Newsletter.
Application information: Visit foundation web site
for application forms and additional guidelines per
grant type. Faxed applications are not accepted.
Application form required.
  Initial approach: Submit application form
  Copies of proposal: 9
  Deadline(s): Jan. 1, Apr. 1, July 1, and Oct. 1
  Board meeting date(s): 6 meetings per year
  Final notification: Within 1 month
Officers and Trustees: * Barbara Quain,* Chair.; Al
Verlinde,* Vice-Chair.; Janet Bauer, C.E.O. and
Pres.; Jennifer Parker-Moore,* Secy.; Gary
Richards,* Treas.; John Brzozowski; Andrew Hunter;

Kim M. Jorgensen; Denis McCarthy; Dina Miramonti;
Hank Nichols; Sean O'Bryan; Nancy Parmenter;
Laura Schapman; Daniel Scheer; Gregory Tarr; Joe
Worden.
Number of staff: 1 full-time professional; 2 part-time
support.
EIN: 382736601

1123
Frankenmuth Community Foundation

(formerly Greater Frankenmuth Area Community
Foundation)
P.O. Box 386
Frankenmuth, MI 48734-0386 (989) 652-8074
County: Saginaw
Contact: Karen Zehnder, Chair.; Scott Zimmer
E-mail: szimmer@zimco.net; E-mail:
ronaldbell6497@sbcglobal.net; URL: http://
www.frankenmuthfoundation.org

Established in 1977 in MI.
Grantmaker type: Community foundation.
Financial data (yr. ended 12/31/09): Assets,
$4,453,583 (M); gifts received, $2,309,331;
expenditures, $281,145; total giving, $253,917;
giving activities include $232,567 for grants (high:
$135,263), and $21,350 for 25 grants to
individuals.
Purpose and activities: The foundation seeks to
support the public, educational, recreational,
charitable, and benevolent organizations of the
greater Frankenmuth, MI, community.
Fields of interest: Community/economic
development; United Ways and Federated Giving
Programs.
Type of support: Building/renovation; Emergency
funds; Program development; Scholarship funds;
Scholarships—to individuals.
Limitations: Applications accepted. Giving limited to
the Frankenmuth, MI, area.
Application information: Visit foundation web site
for application form and guidelines. Application form
required.
  Initial approach: Submit application
  Deadline(s): Jan. 10, Feb. 7, Apr. 4, June 6, July
    5, Sept. 5, Oct. 10 and Dec. 5
  Board meeting date(s): Jan., Feb., Apr., June, July,
    Sept., Oct. and Dec.
  Final notification: After Board Meetings
Officers and Board Members: * Karen Zehnder,*
Pres.; Scott Zimmer,* Treas.; Nancy Haskin; Tom
Hildner; Alan Knoll; Dennis Krafft; Jon Webb; W. Don
Zehnder.
Trustee: National City Bank of the Midwest.
EIN: 382140032

1124
Fremont Area Community Foundation

(formerly The Fremont Area Foundation)
4424 W. 48th St.
P.O. Box B
Fremont, MI 49412-8721 (231) 924-5350
County: Newaygo
Contact: Carla Roberts, C.E.O.
FAX: (231) 924-5391; E-mail: info@tfacf.org;
Additional fax: (231) 924-7637; Additional e-mails:
croberts@tfacf.org and kpope@tfacf.org;
URL: http://www.tfacf.org

Incorporated in 1951 in MI.
Grantmaker type: Community foundation.

Financial data (yr. ended 12/31/10): Assets,
$178,178,821 (M); gifts received, $1,789,215;
expenditures, $8,756,558; total giving,
$7,057,861; giving activities include $6,759,880
for 300 grants (high: $293,000; low: $200), and
$297,981 for 73 grants to individuals.
Purpose and activities: The foundation has
established six broad funding categories: 1)
TrueNorth: to sustain operations of this autonomous
agency established for the delivery of general social
welfare services and educational programs; 2)
Community Development: to strengthen the
municipal activities of villages, cities, governmental
units, and other related organizations; 3) Education:
to augment and promote the special projects of
schools, libraries, and other organizations for
instruction and training, and for scholarships to
promote higher education and learning in
specialized programs; 4) Arts and Culture: to
support activities that promote appreciation of and
participation in artistic expression such as music,
theater, dance, sculpture, and painting; 5) Human
Services: to foster the delivery of services and the
operation of programs to help meet basic human
needs and to support the provision of rehabilitative
services; and 6) Health Care: made to health care
providers and other related organizations for
activities designed to promote optimal well-being
and to provide health-related education. The
foundation is also interested in supporting programs
that address the particular needs of youth and older
(aged) adults.
Fields of interest: Visual arts; Performing arts; Arts;
Libraries/library science; Education; Environment;
Medical care, rehabilitation; Health care; Substance
abuse, services; Health organizations, association;
Recreation; Children/youth, services; Family
services; Aging, centers/services; Human services;
Community/economic development; Government/
public administration; Children/youth; Youth;
Adults; Aging; Disabilities, people with; Physically
disabled; Deaf/hearing impaired; Mentally disabled;
Women; Girls; Economically disadvantaged.
Type of support: General/operating support;
Continuing support; Management development/
capacity building; Capital campaigns; Building/
renovation; Equipment; Endowments; Emergency
funds; Program development; Conferences/
seminars; Seed money; Curriculum development;
Scholarship funds; Technical assistance;
Consulting services; Program evaluation;
Program-related investments/loans; Employee
matching gifts; Scholarships—to individuals;
Matching/challenge support.
Limitations: Applications accepted. Giving primarily
in Newaygo County, MI. No support for religious
organizations for religious purposes. No grants to
individuals (except for scholarships), or for
contingencies, reserves, services which are
considered general government or school
obligations, or deficit financing.
Publications: Application guidelines; Annual report;
Financial statement; Grants list; Informational
brochure; Newsletter.
Application information: Visit foundation Web site
for application Cover Sheet and guidelines.
Application form required.
  Initial approach: Letter or telephone to arrange
    interview
  Copies of proposal: 1
  Deadline(s): Feb. 15, May 15, and Sept. 15 for
    grants; Mar. 15 for scholarships
  Board meeting date(s): Bi-monthly
  Final notification: Within 3 months

Officers and Trustees:* Danielle Merrill,* Chair.; Robert Wood,* Vice-Chair.; Carla Roberts, C.E.O., Pres. and Secy.; Robert Jordan, V.P., Philanthropic Svcs.; Kathy Pope, V.P., Finance; Robert Zeldenrust,* Treas.; Robert Clouse; Richard Dunning; Peggy Gunnell; Bill Johnson; Hendrick Jones; Sheryl Meyer; Lynne Robinson; Terry Sharp; Dale Twing; Kirk Wyers.
Number of staff: 3 full-time professional; 1 part-time professional; 6 full-time support; 1 part-time support.
EIN: 381443367
Selected grants: The following grants were reported in 2009.
$500,000 to Newaygo County Community Services, Fremont, MI. For program support.
$300,000 to Baldwin Family Health Care, Baldwin, MI. For equipment for new health center in White Cloud.
$289,000 to Arts Center for Newaygo County, Fremont, MI. For general operating and program support for the Dogwood Center for the Performing Arts.
$179,950 to Hesperia, Village of, Hesperia, MI. For Webster Park improvements.
$110,000 to Grant Public Schools, Grant, MI. For after-school program.
$25,532 to Fremont, City of, Fremont, MI. For park maintenance.
$12,536 to Hospice of Michigan, Big Rapids, MI. For Open Access Project in Newaygo County.
$7,758 to Lionheart Productions, Grant, MI. For AcTeen youth theater production.
$6,900 to Gerber Memorial Hospital, Fremont, MI. For Camp Tamarac: Healthy Kids - Healthy Bodies.
$6,182 to Fremont Area District Library, Fremont, MI. For Community Match Day.

1125
Grand Blanc Community Fund
c/o Community Foundation of Greater Flint
500 S. Saginaw St.
Flint, MI 48502-1811 (810) 767-8270
County: Genesee
Contact: Kathi Horton, C.E.O.
FAX: (810) 767-0496; E-mail: khorton@cfgf.org

Established in MI as an affiliate of Community Foundation of Greater Flint.
Grantmaker type: Community foundation.
Fields of interest: Historic preservation/historical societies; Arts; Education; Recreation, parks/playgrounds; Community/economic development.
Type of support: Scholarship funds; Program development; Equipment; Building/renovation.
Limitations: Giving limited to the geographic area defined by the Grand Blanc Community School District, MI.
Advisory Committee: Stacey Alarie-Tyckoski, Chair.; Andria Aucker-Tykocki; Timothy Beers; Daniel Conquest; Sam Cox; James Evans; Kamal Gupta; James Harmes; Sandy Jones; Lilian Mason; Linda Morris-Belford; Scott Sobol; Kathie Wind.
EIN: 386139854

1126
Grand Haven Area Community Foundation, Inc.
1 S. Harbor Dr.
Grand Haven, MI 49417-1385 (616) 842-6378
County: Ottawa
Contact: Ann Irish Tabor, Pres.; For grants: Carol Bedient, Dir., Grants and Progs.
FAX: (616) 842-9518; E-mail: info@ghacf.org; Grant application E-mail: cbedient@ghacf.org;
URL: http://www.ghacf.org

Incorporated in 1971 in MI.
Grantmaker type: Community foundation.
Financial data (yr. ended 12/31/09): Assets, $37,853,369 (M); gifts received, $4,607,864; expenditures, $3,230,697; total giving, $2,659,511; giving activities include $2,659,511 for grants.
Purpose and activities: The foundation seeks to improve and enhance the quality of life in the Tri-Cities area by: 1) serving as a leader, catalyst and resource for philanthropy; 2) building and holding a permanent and growing endowment for the community's changing needs and opportunities; 3) striving for community improvement through strategic grantmaking in such fields as the arts, education, health, the environment, youth, social services and other human needs; and 4) providing a flexible and cost-effective way for donors to improve their community now and in the future.
Fields of interest: Vocational education, post-secondary; Business school/education; Environment; Health care; Crime/law enforcement; Community/economic development; Mathematics.
Type of support: Capital campaigns; Equipment; Land acquisition; Program development; Seed money; Scholarship funds; Scholarships—to individuals; Matching/challenge support.
Limitations: Applications accepted. Giving primarily in the MI Tri-Cities area. No support for profit-making organizations or religious programs that serve, or appear to serve, specific religious denominations. No grants to individuals (except for scholarships), or for annual campaigns, emergency or deficit financing, operating costs or ongoing operating support, fundraising events, or endowments.
Publications: Application guidelines; Annual report (including application guidelines); Financial statement; Informational brochure (including application guidelines); Newsletter; Program policy statement.
Application information: Nonprofit agencies that apply for and/or receive a Families in Crisis grant may also be eligible for other grant awards through the foundation's competitive grant programs in the same year; visit foundation Web site for application form and guidelines. Application form required.
Initial approach: Contact foundation
Copies of proposal: 12
Deadline(s): Jan. 7, June 26, and Oct. 10 for competitive and Families in Crisis grants; Mar. 13 for youth grants
Board meeting date(s): Distribution committee meets quarterly: Jan., Apr., July, and Oct.; board meetings are usually 2 weeks following the distribution committee meeting
Final notification: 1 week after board meeting
Officers and Trustees:* Melinda Brink,* Chair.; Mike McKeough,* Vice-Chair.; Ann Irish Tabor,* Pres.; Shirley Poulton,* Secy.; Jeffrey Beswick,* Treas.; Hon. Calvin Bosman; Thomas Creswell; Lana Jacobson; Timothy Parker; Sheila Steffel; Bonnie Suchecki; L.J. Verplank.

Number of staff: 4 full-time professional.
EIN: 237108776
Selected grants: The following grants were reported in 2008.
$235,483 to Christian Haven Home, Grand Haven, MI. For capital improvements for new resident beauty shop.
$157,275 to Love INC of the Tri-Cities, Grand Haven, MI. For program support.
$156,588 to First Presbyterian Church of Grand Haven, Grand Haven, MI. For program support.
$127,000 to Ottawa, County of, West Olive, MI. For Ottawa County Parks Nature Education Center.
$102,950 to Community Foundation for Muskegon County, Muskegon, MI. For West Michigan Student Showcase.
$92,271 to Grand Haven Schools Foundation, Grand Haven, MI.
$66,050 to United Way, Greater Ottawa County, Holland, MI. For Ottawa County Community Assessment.
$21,150 to Little Red House, Spring Lake, MI. For program support.
$20,000 to Stanford University, Stanford, CA. For program support.
$13,773 to Spring Lake Presbyterian Church, Spring Lake, MI. For program support.

1127
Grand Rapids Community Foundation
(formerly The Grand Rapids Foundation)
185 Oakes St., S.W.
Grand Rapids, MI 49503-4219 (616) 454-1751
County: Kent
Contact: Diana R. Sieger, Pres.; For grant inquiries: Ann Puckett, Grants Admin.
FAX: (616) 454-6455;
E-mail: apuckett@grfoundation.org; Grant inquiry tel.: (616) 454-1751, ext. 123; URL: http://www.grfoundation.org
Scholarship contact: Ruth Bishop, tel.: (616) 454-1751, ext. 103,
e-mail: rbishop@grfoundation.org

Established in 1922 in MI by resolution and declaration of trust; Incorporated 1989.
Grantmaker type: Community foundation.
Financial data (yr. ended 06/30/09): Assets, $183,524,161 (M); gifts received, $8,286,813; expenditures, $13,230,263; total giving, $8,961,846; giving activities include $8,398,996 for 300+ grants, and $562,850 for 512 grants to individuals.
Purpose and activities: The foundation seeks to build and manage the community's permanent endowment and lead the community to strengthen the lives of its people. Grants are awarded to expand impact in Grand Rapids and surrounding communities. Leadership goals areas are academic achievement, economic prosperity, healthy ecosystems, healthy people, social enrichment and vibrant neighborhoods.
Fields of interest: Museums; Performing arts; Performing arts, theater; Humanities; Arts; Higher education; Education, reading; Education; Environment; Health organizations, association; AIDS; Alcoholism; Employment; Nutrition; Housing/shelter, development; Recreation; Youth development, services; Children/youth, services; Family services; Aging, centers/services; Women, centers/services; Minorities/immigrants, centers/services; Human services; Civil/human rights, immigrants; Civil/human rights, minorities; Civil/

human rights, disabled; Civil/human rights, women; Civil/human rights, aging; Civil/human rights, LGBTQ; Civil rights, race/intergroup relations; Civil liberties, reproductive rights; Community development, neighborhood development; Community/economic development; Voluntarism promotion; Leadership development; Infants/toddlers; Children/youth; Children; Youth; Adults; Aging; Young adults; Disabilities, people with; Blind/visually impaired; Deaf/hearing impaired; Mentally disabled; Minorities; Asians/Pacific Islanders; African Americans/Blacks; Hispanics/Latinos; Native Americans/American Indians; Women; Girls; Men; Boys; Single parents; Crime/abuse victims; LGBTQ; Immigrants/refugees; Economically disadvantaged; Homeless.

Type of support: Technical assistance; Capital campaigns; Building/renovation; Land acquisition; Program development; Seed money; Scholarship funds; Program-related investments/loans; Employee matching gifts; Employee-related scholarships; Scholarships—to individuals; Matching/challenge support.

Limitations: Applications accepted. Giving limited to Kent County, MI. No support for religious programs, hospitals, child care centers, or nursing homes/retirement facilities. No grants to individuals (except for scholarships), or for continued operating support, annual campaigns, travel expenses, medical or scholarly research, deficit financing, endowment funds, computers, vehicles, films, videos, or conferences; no student loans; no venture capital for competitive profit-making activities.

Publications: Annual report; Informational brochure; Newsletter.

Application information: Visit foundation Web site for online applications and guidelines per grant type. The foundation will request a full proposal based on the pre-application for the Fund for Community Good. Application form required.

> *Initial approach:* Submit online pre-application (reviewed every 2 weeks) for Fund for Community Good
> *Board meeting date(s):* 6 times a year (bimonthly)

Officers and Trustees:* Cecile C. Fehsenfeld,* Chair.; Bonnie K. Miller,* Vice-Chair.; Diana R. Sieger, Pres.; Lynne Black, V.P., Finance and Admin.; Roberta F. King, V.P., Public Rels. and Mktg.; Marcia Rapp, V.P., Progs.; Marilyn Zack, V.P., Devel.; Kevin Harmelink, Cont.; Wayman P. Britt; Eva Aguirre Cooper; Paul Doyle; Thomas R. Hilliker; Michael S. Hoffman; Carol J. Karr; Robert T. Roth.

Number of staff: 14 full-time professional; 9 full-time support.

EIN: 382877959

Selected grants: The following grants were reported in 2010.

$375,000 to Grand Rapids Community College Foundation, Grand Rapids, MI. For GRCC Capital Campaign/Health Careers Facility.

$350,000 to Grand Valley State University, Grand Rapids, MI. For Community Research Institute.

$300,000 to Kent, County of, Grand Rapids, MI. For Preserving Kent County's Prime Farmland.

$250,000 to First Steps Kent, Grand Rapids, MI. For Children's Healthcare Access Program Expansion.

$200,000 to Community Rebuilders, Grand Rapids, MI. For Housing Services Center.

$50,000 to Local Initiatives Support Corporation, Grand Rapids, MI. For rehabilitation of commercial businesses.

$7,500 to Dwelling Place of Grand Rapids, Grand Rapids, MI. For general operating support.

$2,500 to Other Way Ministries, Grand Rapids, MI. For Youth Employment Service (Y.E.S.).

$1,000 to Western Michigan University, Kalamazoo, MI. For scholarship.

1128
Grand Traverse Regional Community Foundation

250 E. Front St., Ste. 310
Traverse City, MI 49684-2552 (231) 935-4066
County: Grand Traverse
Contact: Jeanne Snow, Exec. Dir.
FAX: (231) 941-0021; E-mail: info@gtrcf.org;
URL: http://www.gtrcf.org

Established in 1992 in MI.
Grantmaker type: Community foundation.
Financial data (yr. ended 12/31/09): Assets, $39,417,056 (M); gifts received, $2,589,333; expenditures, $1,841,231; total giving, $1,298,823; giving activities include $1,148,086 for grants, and $150,737 for grants to individuals.
Purpose and activities: The foundation seeks to enhance the quality of life and facilitate philanthropy in Antrim, Benzie, Grand Traverse, Kalkaska, and Leelanau counties, MI.
Fields of interest: Arts; Education; Environment; Community/economic development; Youth.
Type of support: Building/renovation; Equipment; Endowments; Program development; Seed money; Curriculum development; Scholarship funds; Technical assistance; Scholarships—to individuals; Matching/challenge support.
Limitations: Applications accepted. Giving limited to the counties of Antrim, Benzie, Grand Traverse, Kalkaska, and Leelanau, MI. No grants for routine training or professional conferences, annual events, budget shortfalls, or payroll or other general operating expenses.
Publications: Annual report; Informational brochure; Newsletter.
Application information: Visit foundation Web site for application information. Application form required.

> *Initial approach:* Letter or telephone
> *Copies of proposal:* 1
> *Deadline(s):* Apr. 15 and Nov. 1
> *Board meeting date(s):* Quarterly

Officers and Directors:* Phil Ellis, Exec. Dir.; Truman Bicum; Noreen Broering; Blake Brooks; Lawrence Burks; Bud Cline; Susan Cogswell; Gail Dall'Olmo; Gary Drew; Dick Garcia; Penny Hill; John Hoagland; Gary Hoensheid; Wesley Jacobs; Robert Joyce; Carol Karas; Dick Kennedy; Teresa Mensching; Larry Miller; Jim Modrall; Virginia Mouch; Joseph Muha; David O'Neill; Clarine Olson; Al Potts; Pam Prairie; Bob Robbins; Louis H. Sanford; Ken Waichunas; Tom Wiltse; John Yeager.
Number of staff: 4 full-time professional; 1 part-time support.
EIN: 383056434
Selected grants: The following grants were reported in 2008.

$200,107 to Traverse City Area Public Schools, Traverse City, MI. For construction work completed at Thirlby Field.

$192,790 to Traverse City Area Public Schools, Traverse City, MI. For construction work completed at Thirlby Field.

$169,803 to Traverse City, City of, Traverse City, MI. For Lakewood construction work for Boathouse at Hull Park.

$127,964 to Grand Traverse Soil and Water Conservation District, Traverse City, MI. For capital campaign.

$98,000 to Grand Traverse Soil and Water Conservation District, Traverse City, MI. For capital campaign.

$70,000 to Central Lake Public Schools, Central Lake, MI. For Early Childhood Center.

$60,673 to Traverse City, City of, Traverse City, MI. For construction work for Boathouse at Hull Park.

$40,916 to Mills Community House, Benzonia, MI. For renovation.

$21,080 to Rotary Camps and Services of Traverse City, Traverse City, MI. For capacity building.

$18,000 to Grand Traverse Pavilions Foundation, Traverse City, MI. To offset sliding scale fee for Cottage tenants.

1129
Gratiot County Community Foundation

1131 E. Center St.
P.O. Box 310
Ithaca, MI 48847-0310 (989) 875-4222
County: Gratiot
Contact: Tina M. Travis, Exec. Dir.
FAX: (989) 875-2858; E-mail: gccf@edzone.net;
Additional tel.: (989) 875-5101, ext. 248;
URL: http://www.gratiotfoundation.org

Incorporated in 1992 in MI; operations began in late 1994.
Grantmaker type: Community foundation.
Financial data (yr. ended 09/30/09): Assets, $7,183,564 (M); gifts received, $2,649,955; expenditures, $240,516; total giving, $122,412; giving activities include $122,412 for 8+ grants (high: $9,870).
Purpose and activities: The foundation seeks to enhance the lives of Gratiot County citizens by identifying and addressing needs within the county, by building permanent endowments, and distributing grants in the fields of the arts, education, environment, health, youth development, human services and community development.
Fields of interest: Arts; Education; Environment; Health care; Youth development; Human services; Community/economic development.
Type of support: Building/renovation; Conferences/seminars; Curriculum development; Emergency funds; General/operating support; Internship funds; Program development; Scholarship funds; Seed money.
Limitations: Applications accepted. Giving limited to Gratiot County, MI.
Publications: Application guidelines; Annual report; Informational brochure; Newsletter.
Application information: Visit foundation web site for application form and guidelines. Application form required.

> *Initial approach:* Submit application
> *Deadline(s):* Mar. 1 and Nov. 1
> *Board meeting date(s):* 1st Tues. of each month

Officers and Directors:* Craig Zeese,* Chair.; David McMacken,* Secy.; Tim Miller,* Treas.; Tina M. Travis, Exec. Dir.; Vicki Chessin; Kevin Collison; Robert Crist; David Crumbaugh; Penny Daniels; Charles Fortino; Chesley Foster; Janet Hunter; Roger Keck; Barbara McKenzie; Rich Rice; Becky Roslund; Dan Rossman; Sheila Rummer; Dr. James Seals; Heidi Sitts; Keith Wing.
Number of staff: 2 full-time professional.
EIN: 383087756

1130
Greenville Area Community Foundation

(formerly Greenville Area Foundation)
101 N. Lafayette St.
Greenville, MI 48838-1853 (616) 754-2640
County: Montcalm
Contact: Alison Barberi, C.E.O.
FAX: (616) 754-3174; E-mail: alison@gacfmi.org;
Additional E-mail: grants@gacf.org; URL: http://
www.gacfmi.org

Established in 1989 in MI.
Grantmaker type: Community foundation.
Financial data (yr. ended 12/31/09): Assets,
$13,844,185 (M); gifts received, $1,772,646;
expenditures, $812,585; total giving, $523,961;
giving activities include $289,566 for 12 grants
(high: $94,936), and $234,395 for grants to
individuals.
Purpose and activities: The foundation seeks to
enhance the quality of life in the Greenville area.
Giving for education, health, the arts, the
environment, recreation, youth services, and
community development.
Fields of interest: Arts; Adult education—literacy,
basic skills & GED; Education; Environment; Health
care; Recreation; Children/youth, services;
Community/economic development; Government/
public administration.
Type of support: Program evaluation; Management
development/capacity building; General/operating
support; Endowments; Emergency funds;
Curriculum development; Capital campaigns;
Building/renovation; Equipment; Program
development; Publication; Seed money; Scholarship
funds; Matching/challenge support.
Limitations: Applications accepted. Giving limited to
Montcalm County, MI. No support for sectarian
religious programs. No grants for general operating
support, annual fundraising, or endowments
(outside the foundation).
Publications: Application guidelines; Annual report;
Financial statement; Grants list; Informational
brochure; Informational brochure (including
application guidelines); Newsletter.
Application information: Visit foundation web site
for grant information. The Spring Grant Cycle is for
programs and projects with a strong educational
component only and the grant if awarded is payable
over the next school year. The Fall Grant Cycle
includes general programs and projects and also a
health related focus area. Application form required.
  Initial approach: Telephone
  Copies of proposal: 16
  Deadline(s): Spring and Fall
  Board meeting date(s): Jan., Apr., June, Sept.,
    Oct., and Nov.
  Final notification: Dec. and Apr.
Officers and Directors:* Dr. Peter Blinkilde,* Chair.;
Charlotte Lothian,* Vice-Chair.; Alison Barberi,
C.E.O. and Pres.; Eric Januzelli,* Secy.-Treas.; Byron
Cook,* Chair. Emeritus; Lemont Renterghem,*
Chair. Emeritus; Susan Ayres; Keane Blazcrynski;
Bill Braman; Richard Ellafrits; Bill Ham; Doug
Hinken; Dr. Charles McNinch; John O'Donald,
D.D.S.; Fran Schuleit; Corey Smith; Phil Tower.
Number of staff: 1 full-time professional; 2 part-time
professional.
EIN: 382899657
Selected grants: The following grants were reported
in 2007.
$200,000 to Montcalm Community College, Sidney,
MI. For capital campaign to help increase capacity
for increased enrollment.

$22,944 to Feeding America West Michigan,
Comstock Park, MI. Toward cost of bringing food
truck to food banks in Montcalm County.
$15,000 to Montcalm Adult Reading Council,
Greenville, MI. For literacy program.
$14,398 to Community Hope Christian Counseling
Center, Greenville, MI. For counseling services.
$10,000 to Montcalm Community College, Sidney,
MI. For small business consultant to help local
unemployed learn about starting own business.
$10,000 to Montcalm County Sheriffs Department,
Stanton, MI. For purchase of dog, material, and
training for K-9 unit.
$5,690 to United Lifestyles, Greenville, MI. For
health screenings.

1131
Hillsdale County Community Foundation

2 S. Howell St.
P.O. Box 276
Hillsdale, MI 49242-0276 (517) 439-5101
County: Hillsdale
Contact: Sharon E. Bisher, Exec. Dir.
FAX: (517) 439-5109; E-mail: info@abouthccf.org;
URL: http://www.abouthccf.org

Established in 1991 in MI.
Grantmaker type: Community foundation.
Financial data (yr. ended 09/30/09): Assets,
$9,622,042 (M); gifts received, $555,212;
expenditures, $648,033; total giving, $311,426;
giving activities include $166,776 for grants, and
$144,650 for 128 grants to individuals.
Purpose and activities: The foundation receives and
administers funds for artistic, charitable,
educational, and scientific purposes in a manner
that both promotes the spirit of philanthropy and
meets the needs of the people of Hillsdale County,
MI.
Fields of interest: Visual arts; Performing arts;
Performing arts, theater; Arts; Education,
association; Education, early childhood education;
Child development, education; Elementary school/
education; Higher education; Libraries/library
science; Education; Environment, natural resources;
Environment; Animal welfare; Hospitals (general);
Health care; Health organizations, association;
Crime/violence prevention, youth; Crime/law
enforcement; Employment; Food services;
Recreation; Youth development, services; Children/
youth, services; Child development, services; Family
services; Residential/custodial care, hospices;
Aging, centers/services; Human services;
Community/economic development; Voluntarism
promotion; Biology/life sciences; Economics;
Leadership development; Public affairs; Aging;
Economically disadvantaged.
Type of support: Scholarships—to individuals;
Conferences/seminars; Publication; Seed money;
Scholarship funds; In-kind gifts; Matching/challenge
support.
Limitations: Applications accepted. Giving limited to
Hillsdale County, MI. No support for religious or
sectarian purposes. No grants to individuals (except
for scholarships), or for new building campaigns,
routine maintenance, remodeling, or capital
campaigns; no loans.
Publications: Application guidelines; Annual report;
Financial statement; Informational brochure
(including application guidelines); Newsletter.
Application information: Visit foundation web site
for application form and guidelines. Application form
required.

Initial approach: Telephone or in person
Copies of proposal: 1
Deadline(s): May 1 and Nov. 1 for general grants;
  May 1 and Nov. 1 for Kellogg YOUTH grants;
  and Apr. 1 for scholarships
Board meeting date(s): 1st Tues. of the month
Final notification: Within 2 months
Officers and Trustees:* David Pope,* Pres.; Harold
March,* V.P.; Diane Clow,* Secy.; Bambi
Somerlott,* Treas.; Sharon E. Bisher, Exec. Dir.;
Clint Barrett; John Barrett; Michelle Bianchi; Pat
Dillon; Jeremiah Hodshire; Les Hutchinson; Jeff
Lantis; Tim Raker; Don Sanderson; Shawn Vondra.
Number of staff: 1 full-time professional; 2 part-time
professional.
EIN: 383001297

1132
Homer Area Community Foundation

104 S. Hillsdale St.
P.O. Box 201
Homer, MI 49245-0201
County: Calhoun
Contact: Ms. Carol Petredean-DiSalvio, Pres.
URL: http://www.homeracf.org/

Established in 1994 in MI as an affiliate of Battle
Creek Community Foundation.
Grantmaker type: Community foundation.
Purpose and activities: The mission of the
foundation is to promote philanthropy within its
community, and to enhance and improve the quality
of life in the Homer area through the establishment
and maintenance of a collection of permanently
endowed funds.
Fields of interest: Community/economic
development; Voluntarism promotion; Youth.
Type of support: Scholarships—to individuals;
Program development.
Limitations: Applications accepted. Giving limited to
the Homer, MI, area.
Publications: Annual report.
Application information: See foundation web site
for full application guidelines and requirements,
including forms. Application form required.
  Initial approach: Completed proposal, not
    exceeding 8 pages (including supporting
    materials). Proposals for mini-grants should
    not exceed 2 pages.
  Copies of proposal: 10
  Deadline(s): Contact foundation for current
    deadline dates
Officers and Trustees:* Carol Petredean-Di Salvio,*
Pres.; Rachel Maksimchuk,* V.P.; Holly Blashfield,
Secy.; Richard Folk,* Treas.; Roxanne Barton;
Jeanne George; Jill Grant; Cindy Kirkbride; Joe Miller;
Rob Ridgeway; Gary Tompkins.

1133
Huron County Community Foundation

1160 S. Van Dyke Rd.
P.O. Box 56
Bad Axe, MI 48413 (989) 269-2850
County: Huron
FAX: (989) 269-8209;
E-mail: hccf@huroncounty.com; URL: http://
www.huroncounty.com/foundation

Established in 1996 in MI.
Grantmaker type: Community foundation.

Financial data (yr. ended 09/30/09): Assets, $1,854,041 (M); gifts received, $384,138; expenditures, $105,317; total giving, $47,450; giving activities include $15,000 for grants, and $32,450 for 38 grants to individuals.

Purpose and activities: The mission of the foundation is to support the public well-being and to improve the quality of life in Huron County, MI.

Fields of interest: Arts; Education; Health care; Recreation; Youth development, centers/clubs; Children/youth, services; Human services; Community/economic development.

Limitations: Applications accepted. Giving limited to Huron County, MI.

Publications: Annual report.

Application information: Visit foundation Web site for application form and guidelines. Application form required.

> *Initial approach:* Letter or telephone
> *Deadline(s):* End of Apr.
> *Final notification:* June

Officer and Trustees:* Karl E. Kraus,* Exec. Dir.; Christopher Bachman; Christopher Boyle; Clark Brock; Jeanette Hagen; Marvin Kociba; Tom Kreh; Dr. Nancy Krohn; Jane Mayes; Lowell McDonald; Sue Meyersieck; John Moore; Allan Nietzke; Debbie Oglenski; Brent Wehner.

EIN: 383160009

1134

Ionia County Community Foundation

c/o Grand Rapids Community Foundation
161 Ottawa Ave., N.W., Ste. 209-C
Grand Rapids, MI   49503-2721   (616) 522-1860
County: Kent
Contact: Brian Talbot, Grant Comm. Chair.
E-mail: brtalbot@ibcp.com; URL: http://www.grfoundation.org/ionia

Established in 1995 in MI as a regional affiliate of Grand Rapids Community Foundation.

Grantmaker type: Community foundation.

Purpose and activities: The foundation gives priority to projects that address the areas of art and culture, community development, education, environment, health, or social needs.

Fields of interest: Arts; Education; Environment; Health care; Youth development; Human services; Community/economic development; Aging.

Type of support: Capital campaigns; Building/renovation; Equipment.

Limitations: Applications accepted. Giving limited for the benefit of Ionia County, MI. No support for organizations lacking 501(c)(3) status, or for religious organizations for religious purposes. No grants to individuals, or for annual fundraising drives, ongoing operating expenses of established institutions, endowments or debt reduction, conferences, medical research, venture capital for competitive profit-making activities, sabbatical leaves, scholarly research, travel, tours or trips, or for films, videos or television projects.

Publications: Newsletter.

Application information: See foundation web site for complete guidelines and requirements. Application form required.

> *Initial approach:* Completion of online application
> *Deadline(s):* Dec. 30
> *Final notification:* Mar. 31

1135

Iosco County Community Foundation

c/o Community Foundation for Northeast Michigan
P.O. Box 495
Alpena, MI   49707-0495   (877) 354-6881
County: Alpena
Contact: Christine Hitch
FAX: (989) 356-3319; E-mail: chitch@cfnem.org; URL: http://www.iccf-online.org/

Established in 2000 in MI as an affiliate of the Community Foundation for Northeast Michigan.

Grantmaker type: Community foundation.

Purpose and activities: The foundation seeks to serve Iosco County and to preserve the charitable goals of a wide range of donors now and for generations to come by supporting 501(c)(3) organizations, churches for non-religious purposes, and government agencies.

Fields of interest: Community/economic development.

Type of support: Research; Program evaluation; Management development/capacity building; Film/video/radio; Curriculum development; Consulting services; Building/renovation; Equipment; Program development; Conferences/seminars; Publication; Seed money; Technical assistance; Scholarships—to individuals.

Limitations: Applications accepted. Giving limited to Iosco County, MI. No support for political campaigns or programs with religious overtones. No grants to individuals (except for scholarships), or for routine operating needs or budget deficits.

Publications: Application guidelines; Annual report; Financial statement; Grants list; Informational brochure; Newsletter.

Application information: See foundation web site for Common Grant Application Form and requirements. Application form required.

> *Copies of proposal:* 1
> *Deadline(s):* June 30 for Common Grants, Feb. 28 for YAC Grants
> *Board meeting date(s):* 3rd Thurs. of Feb., Apr., June, Aug., Oct., and Dec.
> *Final notification:* Within 6 weeks of deadline dates

Officers and Trustees:* Carl Huebner,* Chair.; Jane Peters,* Vice-Chair.; Sue Alexander; Libby Blatch; Chad Brandt; Shelley Buresh; Valerie Cryderman; Pauline Ferns; Stephanie Mallak Olson.

Selected grants: The following grants were reported in 2009.

$2,500 to Whittemore-Prescott Area Schools, Whittemore, MI. For public safety appreciation and community involvement.

$1,528 to Huron Hockey and Skating Association, Tawas City, MI. For On-Ice Track System Harness.

$1,000 to Alabaster, Township of, Tawas City, MI. For signage for native plants on Alabaster Bike Path.

$1,000 to American Red Cross National Headquarters, Washington, DC. For National CPR/AED Awareness Week.

$1,000 to FISH Inc., Oscoda, Oscoda, MI. For Christmas Gift House.

$1,000 to Oscoda Area First Responders, Oscoda, MI. For equipment.

$1,000 to Special Olympics Michigan, Area 31, Mount Pleasant, MI. For Bowling.

$700 to Whittemore-Prescott Area Schools, Whittemore, MI. For Student Mentor Program.

1136

Greater Ishpeming Area Community Fund

c/o Marquette Community Foundation
401 E. Fair Ave.
P.O. Box 37
Ishpeming, MI   49849-2018   (906) 226-7666
County: Marquette
Contact: Jim Steward, Chair.
E-mail: jsteward@stewardsheridan.com; URL: http://www.marquettecountycommunityfoundation.org/GIACF.html

Established in 1994 in MI with matching funds from the Kellogg Foundation as an affiliate of the Marquette Community Foundation.

Grantmaker type: Community foundation.

Purpose and activities: The fund's mission is to enhance the quality of life by attempting to meet the charitable, educational, cultural, recreational, environmental, and social welfare needs of people of the greater Ishpeming, Michigan, area.

Fields of interest: Arts; Education; Environment; Youth development; Human services; Community/economic development.

Limitations: Applications accepted. Giving limited to western Marquette County, MI, including the City of Ishpeming, Ishpeming Township, Ely Township, Tilden Township, Champion, Michigamme and Republic. No grants to individuals (except for scholarships), or generally for operating expenses or travel.

Application information: See fund web site for application guidelines and downloadable application form. Application form required.

> *Deadline(s):* Spring and fall

Officers and Board Members:* Jim Steward,* Chair.; Terri Smith,* Vice-Chair.; Glenn Adams; Marilyn Andrew; Shannon Edmark; Anne Giroux; Vicki Kulju; James T. Prophet.

1137

Jackson Community Foundation

(formerly The Jackson County Community Foundation)
1 Jackson Sq.
100 East Michigan Ave., Ste. 308
Jackson, MI   49201-1406   (517) 787-1321
County: Jackson
FAX: (517) 787-4333; E-mail: jcf@jacksoncf.org; URL: http://www.jacksoncf.org/

Incorporated in 1948 in MI.

Grantmaker type: Community foundation.

Financial data (yr. ended 12/31/09): Assets, $17,991,604 (M); gifts received, $679,168; expenditures, $2,003,601; total giving, $1,272,985; giving activities include $1,121,320 for 38+ grants (high: $283,330), and $151,665 for 75 grants to individuals.

Purpose and activities: The foundation seeks to improve the quality of life for the residents of Jackson County, MI.

Fields of interest: Humanities; Historic preservation/historical societies; Arts; Adult education—literacy, basic skills & GED; Education, reading; Education; Environment; Health care; Substance abuse, services; Recreation; Children/youth, services; Human services; Economic development; Community/economic development.

Type of support: General/operating support; Capital campaigns; Building/renovation; Equipment; Land acquisition; Program development; Seed money;

Technical assistance; Consulting services; Program evaluation; Program-related investments/loans; Scholarships—to individuals; Matching/challenge support.

Limitations: Applications accepted. Giving limited to Jackson County, MI. No support for religious purposes. No grants to individuals (except for scholarships), or for endowment funds, debt retirement, fellowships, publications, or conferences.

Publications: Application guidelines; Annual report (including application guidelines); Newsletter.

Application information: Visit foundation web site for application forms, guidelines, and specific deadlines. Grants over $5,000 require an approval based on letter of intent prior to full application submission. Application form required.

> *Initial approach:* Submit Community Partner grant application for grants less than $5,000; Letter of Intent for grants over $5,000
> *Copies of proposal:* 15
> *Deadline(s):* Varies
> *Board meeting date(s):* Jan., Mar., May, July, Sept., and Nov.
> *Final notification:* Within 14 days for Letter of Intent; 10 days after board meeting for grant determination

Officers and Trustees:* Anne E. Campau,* Chair.; Monica M. Moser, C.E.O. and Pres.; Karen A. Chaprnka; Deborah Ann Craft; Rick Davies; Edwina Divins; Travis Fojtasek; H. Ronald Griffith; Bruce A. Inosencio; Milton "Mick" Lutz; Katherine Patrick; Dr. Daniel J. Phelan; Jon Robinson; Hendrik Schuur; Ric Walton; Carlene Walz-Lefere.

Number of staff: 2 full-time professional; 1 full-time support; 2 part-time support.

EIN: 386070739

Selected grants: The following grants were reported in 2008.
$50,000 to Legal Services of South Central Michigan, Ann Arbor, MI. For operating support.
$40,000 to Jackson Nonprofit Support Center, Jackson, MI. For general support.
$35,000 to Jackson Symphony Orchestra Association, Jackson, MI. For Supporting a Sound Vision campaign.
$30,000 to Lily Missions Center, Jackson, MI. For capacity building.
$25,000 to Ducks Unlimited, Ann Arbor, MI. For phase II of Jackson County Wetland Conservation Program.
$25,000 to Hospice of Jackson, Jackson, MI. For Hospice Home.
$24,000 to Big Brothers Big Sisters of Jackson County, Jackson, MI. For capacity building position.
$18,000 to Jackson School of the Arts Association, Jackson, MI. For general support.
$15,000 to Dahlem Conservancy, Jackson, MI. For strategic funding plan.
$15,000 to Food Bank of South Central Michigan, Battle Creek, MI. For Critical Crossroads/Bridge to the Future, strategic plan for food bank.

1138
Kalamazoo Community Foundation
(formerly Kalamazoo Foundation)
151 S. Rose St., Ste. 332
Kalamazoo, MI 49007-4775 (269) 381-4416
County: Kalamazoo
FAX: (269) 381-3146; E-mail: info@kalfound.org;
URL: http://www.kalfound.org

Established in 1925; incorporated in 1930 in MI.

Grantmaker type: Community foundation.

Financial data (yr. ended 12/31/09): Assets, $266,354,216 (M); gifts received, $9,393,360; expenditures, $14,545,272; total giving, $11,337,891; giving activities include $10,166,055 for 1,683 grants, $1,171,836 for 471 grants to individuals (high: $7,500; low: $100), and $1,307,568 for 2 loans/program-related investments.

Purpose and activities: The foundation is dedicated to enhancing the spirit of the community and quality of life in the greater Kalamazoo area through its stewardship of permanently endowed funds. Primary areas of giving include: 1) economic development; 2) early childhood learning and school readiness; 3) youth development; and 4) individuals and families. Grants largely for capital purposes and innovative programs.

Fields of interest: Education; Environment; Health care; Housing/shelter, development; Youth development; Family services; Economic development; Community/economic development.

Type of support: General/operating support; Equipment; Emergency funds; Program development; Seed money; Scholarship funds; Technical assistance; Program-related investments/loans; Employee matching gifts; Scholarships—to individuals; Matching/challenge support.

Limitations: Applications accepted. Giving generally limited to Kalamazoo County, MI. No grants to individuals (except for scholarships), or for endowment funds.

Publications: Application guidelines; Annual report; Financial statement; Informational brochure; Informational brochure (including application guidelines); Newsletter; Quarterly report.

Application information: Visit foundation web site for more information and online application. Application form required.

> *Initial approach:* E-mail or telephone to schedule pre-application conversation
> *Copies of proposal:* 1
> *Deadline(s):* Jan. and July for Individuals and Families, and Economic Community Development; Apr. and Oct. for Early Childhood Learning and School Readiness, and Youth Development
> *Board meeting date(s):* Jan., Mar., May, June, July, Sept., Nov., and Dec.
> *Final notification:* 10 weeks

Officers and Trustees:* Barbara L. James,* Chair.; Ronda E. Stryker,* Vice-Chair.; Juan Olivarez, Ph.D., C.E.O. and Pres.; Ann Fergemann, V.P., Donor Rels.; Carrie Pickett-Erway, V.P., Community Investment; Susan Springgate, V.P., Finance and Admin.; Karen Racette, Cont.; Si Johnson; Frank Sardone; Donald J. Vander Kooy; Hon. Carolyn H. Williams; Dr. Eileen B. Wilson-Oyelaran.

Custodian Bank: PNC Bank.

Number of staff: 17 full-time professional; 3 part-time professional; 3 full-time support; 3 part-time support.

EIN: 383333202

Selected grants: The following grants were reported in 2009.
$300,000 to Local Initiatives Support Corporation, Kalamazoo, MI. For Connect the Dots and foreclosure prevention pilot.
$225,000 to Housing Resources, Kalamazoo, MI. For Rickman House Redevelopment.
$160,000 to YWCA of Kalamazoo, Kalamazoo, MI. For child care and education for homeless.

$150,000 to MRC Industries, Kalamazoo, MI. For capital campaign.
$110,000 to Kalamazoo Institute of Arts, Kalamazoo, MI. For Permanent Collection.
$70,000 to Girls on the Run, Greater Kalamazoo, Kalamazoo, MI. For operating support.
$70,000 to Neighborhood Housing Services of Kalamazoo, Kalamazoo, MI. For foreclosure counseling and rescue funds.
$64,680 to United Way, Heart of Illinois, Peoria, IL. For Royal Oak Office campaign.
$62,900 to Professional Development and Training Center of Southwest Michigan, Kalamazoo, MI. For relocation and growth.
$60,000 to United Way, Greater Kalamazoo, Kalamazoo, MI. For Education Income Health.
$57,500 to Family and Childrens Services, Kalamazoo, MI. For foster care and adoption staffing capacity.
$48,000 to W. E. Upjohn Institute for Employment Research, Kalamazoo, MI. For summer youth work experience.
$45,000 to Communities in Schools Foundation, Kalamazoo, Kalamazoo, MI. For Children's Defense Fund Freedom School.
$41,642 to Kalamazoo Public Library, Kalamazoo, MI. For Kid Builder Books.
$35,000 to Big Brothers Big Sisters of Greater Kalamazoo, Kalamazoo, MI. For churches and community joining forces.
$30,000 to Comstock Community Center, Comstock, MI. For Kids Korner North Preschool scholarship program.
$30,000 to Summit on Racism. For events and coordination.
$25,000 to Kalamazoo Eastside Neighborhood Association, Kalamazoo, MI. For community youth center planning.
$10,000 to Constructive Community Builders, Kalamazoo, MI. For 1713 Edwards Rehabilitation.
$7,500 to Northside Association for Community Development, Kalamazoo, MI. For grocery store planning.
$2,500 to Covenant Senior Day Program, Portage, MI. To improve the quality of care for dementia and Alzheimer's patients within our organization and community.
$2,000 to University of Michigan, Ann Arbor, MI.

1139
Keweenaw Community Foundation
236 Quincy St.
Hancock, MI 49930-1817 (906) 482-9673
County: Houghton
Contact: Barbara Rose, Exec. Dir.
FAX: (906) 482-9679; E-mail: mail@k-c-f.org;
URL: http://
www.keweenaw-community-foundation.org
Alternate URL: http://www.k-c-f.org

Established in 1994 in MI.

Grantmaker type: Community foundation.

Financial data (yr. ended 03/31/09): Assets, $3,462,112 (M); gifts received, $431,234; expenditures, $163,910; total giving, $42,180; giving activities include $42,180 for 10 grants.

Purpose and activities: The foundation is committed to serving the residents of Houghton and Keweenaw counties, MI, by: 1) developing a permanent endowment to provide stable local funding sources for grants to vital local programs; 2) increasing charitable giving to a broad range of nonprofit organizations; 3) providing a flexible

philanthropic vehicle capable of adapting to changing community needs; and 4) serving as a catalyst to nurture community leadership.
Fields of interest: Arts; Education; Environment; Health care; Athletics/sports, winter sports; Human services; Community/economic development.
Type of support: Program development; Scholarship funds; Matching/challenge support.
Limitations: Applications accepted. Giving primarily in Houghton and Keweenaw counties, MI. No grants for membership drives, fundraising events, multi-year funding, construction projects, or normal operating expenses.
Publications: Annual report; Informational brochure; Occasional report.
Application information: Visit foundation Web site for application form and guidelines. Proposals submitted by fax not accepted. Application form required.
  Initial approach: Telephone
  Copies of proposal: 1
  Deadline(s): Varies
  Board meeting date(s): 4th Wed., bimonthly beginning in Jan.
  Final notification: Varies
Officers and Trustees:* Steve Zutter,* Chair.; Tim Baroni,* Vice-Chair.; Phyllis Clevenger,* Secy.; Joseph Daavettila,* Treas.; Barbara Rose, Exec. Dir.; Linda Belote; Les Cook; Lucinda Enderby; Joseph Evans; Paul Freshwater; Mike Hauswirth; Martha Janners; James Lowrie; Stephan Olsson; Brent Peterson; Douglas Stuart; Karin VanDyke.
Number of staff: 3 part-time professional; 1 part-time support.
EIN: 383223079
Selected grants: The following grants were reported in 2006.
$11,621 to Bootjack Fire and Rescue Foundation, Lake Linden, MI. For Houghton and Keweenaw County recovery ATV and Victim Rescue Sled.
$3,000 to Western Upper Peninsula District Health Department, Hancock, MI. For Eat, Think, and Be Active, part of Media-Smart Youth Initiative.
$2,500 to Stanton Township Volunteer Fire Department, Houghton, MI. For automated electronic defibrillator for first responders.
$1,000 to Keweenaw Family Resource Center, Houghton, MI. For Healthy Times Family Education Program and Playtime.
$1,000 to Keweenaw Memorial Medical Center, Laurium, MI. For Gentle Exercises for Seniors.
$500 to Copper Country Intermediate School District, Career Tech Center, Hancock, MI. For Health Occupation Students of America.
$250 to Copper Island Cross Country Ski Club, Calumet, MI. For 2006 trail improvements.
$250 to Michigan Technological University, Nordic Ski Club, Houghton, MI. For new and beginner adult ski lessons.
$213 to Keweenaw Nordic Ski Club, Hancock, MI. For Project Tool Crib.

1140
Lake County Community Foundation
P.O. Box 995
Baldwin, MI 49304-0995   (231) 745-4601
County: Lake
Contact: Robert Fisher, Pres.
E-mail: info@lccfmichigan.org; E-mail: rfisher@losb.com; URL: http://lccfmichigan.org/

Established in 1992 in MI as an affiliate of Fremont Area Community Foundation.

Grantmaker type: Community foundation.
Purpose and activities: Grants for projects that have a lasting effect on the Lake County community and fulfill the purpose of the foundation to enhance the quality of life for Lake County citizens and visitors.
Fields of interest: Arts; Education; Environment; Human services; Community/economic development.
Type of support: General/operating support; Continuing support; Building/renovation; Program development; Scholarship funds.
Limitations: Applications accepted. Giving limited to the Lake County, MI, area. No grants for general operating support, endowments, contingencies, reserves or deficit financing; generally no grants for building campaigns.
Publications: Application guidelines; Annual report; Informational brochure; Newsletter.
Application information: See foundation web site for application guidelines and requirements, including downloadable application form. Application form required.
  Copies of proposal: 16
  Deadline(s): Contact foundation for current deadline dates
  Final notification: 90 days
Officers and Trustees:* Robert Fisher,* Pres.; Vedra Grant,* V.P.; Jane Allison,* Secy.; Ellen Kerans,* Treas.; Mary Anderson; Paul Bigford; Joseph Brooks, Jr.; Larry Doorn; John Drake; Randall Howes; Kenneth Moore; David Randall; Cinda Rock; Linda Rubin; Connie Theunick-Perley; Shawn Washington.
Number of staff: None.

1141
Lapeer County Community Foundation
(formerly Lapeer County Community Fund)
264 Cedar St.
Lapeer, MI 48446
County: Lapeer
Contact: Janet Manning, Exec. Dir.
E-mail: awhite@lapeercountycommunityfoundation.org; Tel./fax: (810) 664-0691; URL: http://www.lapeercountycommunityfoundation.org/

Established in 1996 in MI as an affiliate of the Community Foundation of Greater Flint; became an independent community foundation in 2005.
Grantmaker type: Community foundation.
Financial data (yr. ended 12/31/09): Assets, $7,522,423 (M); gifts received, $172,330; expenditures, $291,497; total giving, $133,080; giving activities include $71,566 for 4+ grants (high: $11,396), and $61,514 for 44 grants to individuals (high: $2,500; low: $914).
Purpose and activities: The foundation builds and manages permanent endowment funds from a wide variety of donors to provide grants that enhance the quality of life in Lapeer County, now and for future generations. Grants from unrestricted funds are made in the areas of education, arts and culture, the environment, health care, human services, recreation and other project topics.
Fields of interest: Arts; Education; Environment; Health care; Recreation; Human services.
Type of support: Annual campaigns; Endowments; Scholarship funds; In-kind gifts; Matching/challenge support.
Limitations: Applications accepted. Giving limited to Lapeer County, MI. No support for religious or sectarian purposes, or for legislative or political

purposes. No grants to individuals (except for scholarships).
Publications: Application guidelines; Annual report; Grants list; Informational brochure; Newsletter; Program policy statement.
Application information: The foundation encourages contacting the executive director to discuss the proposal prior to submitting an application. Full application guidelines and requirements are available at foundation web site, including downloadable application forms. Application form required.
  Initial approach: Letter, telephone, e-mail or office visit
  Copies of proposal: 4
  Deadline(s): Final business day of each month
  Board meeting date(s): 2nd Wed. of each month
  Final notification: 8 weeks
Officers and Trustees:* Nick O. Holowka,* Chair.; Janet L. Watz,* Vice-Chair.; Gaye Butterfield,* Secy.; Kim R. Brown,* Treas.; Ashley White, Exec. Dir.; Michael Blazo; Paul Bowman; Rick Burrough; Curt Carter; Timothy Denney; Ralph Deshetsky; Della Hammond; Andrew Harrington; Kathryn L. Lawter; Dahna Loeding; Charlie Mann; Thomas Neuhard.
Number of staff: 1 part-time professional.
EIN: 201271563

1142
Leelanau Township Community Foundation, Inc.
104 Wing St.
P.O. Box 818
Northport, MI 49670-0818   (231) 386-9000
County: Leelanau
Contact: Joan Moore, Admin. Dir.
FAX: (231) 386-7909;
E-mail: director@leelanaufoundation.org;
URL: http://www.leelanaufoundation.org

Incorporated in 1945 in MI.
Donor: F.H. Haserot†.
Grantmaker type: Community foundation.
Financial data (yr. ended 12/31/08): Assets, $1,868,111 (M); gifts received, $121,064; expenditures, $306,261; total giving, $233,562; giving activities include $233,562 for grants.
Purpose and activities: The foundation supports public charities in Leelanau Township, MI area.
Fields of interest: Arts; Education, early childhood education; Education; Environment, natural resources; Hospitals (general); Health care; Recreation.
Type of support: Capital campaigns; Building/renovation; Equipment; Endowments; Seed money; Scholarships—to individuals.
Limitations: Applications accepted. Giving limited to Leelanau Township, MI. No support for religious programs that serve specific religious denominations. No grants to individuals (except for scholarships), or for operating expenses, or elimination of existing financial obligations, debts, or liabilities.
Publications: Annual report; Newsletter.
Application information: Visit foundation Web site for application form and guidelines. Application form required.
  Initial approach: Telephone
  Copies of proposal: 2
  Deadline(s): 1st Monday of Jan., May, and Sept.
  Board meeting date(s): Quarterly

Officers and Trustees:* Joan Kalchik-Tenbrock,* Chair.; Basil Antenucci; Colleen Cooper, Ph.D.; Dave Johnson; Thea Kellogg; Richard L. Lang; Ann Marie Mitchell; Robert S. Walker; Ruth Steele Walker; Eugene Scott von Holt.

Number of staff: 2 part-time professional; 2 part-time support.

EIN: 386060138

Selected grants: The following grants were reported in 2005.

$16,200 to Northport Community Arts Center, Northport, MI. For operating support.

$10,660 to Leelanau Childrens Center, Family Support Program, Leland, MI. For Northport Parenting Communities.

$6,000 to Northport Community Arts Center, Northport, MI. For performances.

$4,300 to Leelanau Township Library, Northport, MI. For books.

$3,205 to Leelanau Township Community Foundation, Community Visioning Committee, Northport, MI. For New Horizons Publication.

$3,000 to Northport Community Arts Center, Northport, MI. For performances.

$2,500 to Leelanau County Department of Human Services, Family Independence Agency, Traverse City, MI. For Voices and Choices Program.

$1,500 to Leelanau County Department of Human Services, Family Independence Agency, Traverse City, MI. For Voices and Choices Program.

$1,264 to Leelanau Township Community Foundation, Community Visioning Committee, Northport, MI. For municipal sewer project.

$1,000 to Music in the Park, Northport, MI. For Chamber of Commerce.

$1,000 to Northport Public School, Northport, MI. For Camp Leelanau.

$900 to Grand Traverse Lighthouse Museum, Northport, MI. For youth program.

$800 to Northport Public School, Northport, MI. For arts enrichment - Krueger drums.

$500 to Northport Public School, Northport, MI. For Practical Technology curriculum.

$300 to Northport Public School, Northport, MI. For garden program.

1143
Lenawee Community Foundation

(formerly Tecumseh Community Fund Foundation)
603 N. Evans St.
P.O. Box 142
Tecumseh, MI   49286-1166   (517) 423-1729
County: Lenawee
Contact: Suann D. Hammersmith, C.E.O.
FAX: (517) 424-6579;
E-mail: shammersmith@ubat.com; URL: http://www.lenaweecf.com
URL: http://www.lisd.us (for scholarship application information)

Established in 1961 in MI.

Grantmaker type: Community foundation.

Financial data (yr. ended 09/30/09): Assets, $12,817,000 (M); gifts received, $781,668; expenditures, $1,518,494; total giving, $1,286,959; giving activities include $1,121,705 for grants, and $165,254 for 167 grants to individuals.

Purpose and activities: The mission of the foundation is to enhance the quality of life of the citizens of Lenawee County, Michigan by: 1) identifying and addressing current and anticipated community needs; and 2) raising, managing, and

distributing funds for charitable purposes in the areas of civic, cultural, health, education, and social services with an emphasis on permanent endowments.

Fields of interest: Arts; Education; Health organizations, association; Human services; Community/economic development; Youth.

Type of support: Program development; General/operating support; Capital campaigns; Building/renovation; Management development/capacity building; Equipment; Endowments; Conferences/seminars; Scholarship funds; Employee-related scholarships.

Limitations: Applications accepted. Giving limited for the benefit of Lenawee County, MI. No support for religious purposes. No grants to individuals (except for scholarships), or for fundraising.

Publications: Application guidelines; Annual report (including application guidelines); Grants list; Informational brochure; Newsletter.

Application information: Visit foundation web site for application guidelines. Application form required.

Initial approach: Inquiry by telephone or e-mail
Copies of proposal: 1
Deadline(s): Varies
Board meeting date(s): Bimonthly, 4th Thurs. of the month
Final notification: Varies

Officers and Directors:* David S. Hickman,* Chair. and Treas.; Charles H. Gross,* Vice-Chair.; Suann D. Hammersmith,* C.E.O. and Pres.; Scott Hill,* Secy.; Merlyn H. Downing, Dir. Emeritus; David E. Maxwell, Dir. Emeritus; Dr. Carlton Cook; Frank Dick; Eli Francoeur; Sue Goldsen; Ernie Groeb; Jim Kapnick; Breinne Reeder; Sheila D. Schwartz; Bob Vogel.

Number of staff: 2 full-time professional; 2 part-time professional.

EIN: 386095474

Selected grants: The following grants were reported in 2007.

$10,000 to Catholic Social Services of Lenawee County, Adrian, MI. For Roadmap to Graduation.

$10,000 to Communities in Schools of Lenawee County, Adrian, MI. For Youth Asset Training the Trainers.

$10,000 to Herrick Medical Center, Tecumseh, MI. For renovation.

$9,600 to Catholic Social Services of Lenawee County, Adrian, MI. For twelve-step support group for teens.

$7,500 to Habitat for Humanity of Lenawee County, Adrian, MI. For house project.

$5,000 to River Raisin Greenways Project, Tecumseh, MI.

$2,500 to Chamber of Commerce, Lenawee County, Adrian, MI. For technology.

$1,000 to Lenawee Human Services Council, Adrian, MI. For Bridges Out of Poverty Workshop.

$500 to Food Bank of South Central Michigan, Battle Creek, MI.

1144
Livonia Community Foundation, Inc.

33300 Five Mile Rd., Ste. 105
Livonia, MI   48154-3074   (734) 421-5055
County: Wayne
Contact: Brian Meakin, Pres.
FAX: (734) 421-5591;
E-mail: foundation@livoniacommunityfoundation.org
; URL: http://livoniacommunityfoundation.org

Established in 1994 in MI.

Grantmaker type: Community foundation.

Financial data (yr. ended 12/31/08): Assets, $701,445 (M); gifts received, $79,105; expenditures, $41,273; total giving, $18,700; giving activities include $18,700 for grants.

Purpose and activities: The foundation supports the promotion and development of community resources including historic edifices, public interest and support in the arts and culture, and charitable programs for the welfare of the community.

Fields of interest: Visual arts; Performing arts, theater; Performing arts, music; Historic preservation/historical societies; Arts; Education; Human services; Children/youth; Children; Adults; Aging; Physically disabled; Mentally disabled.

Limitations: Applications accepted. Giving limited to Livonia, MI. No support for religious organizations or purposes. No grants to individuals (except for donor-advised scholarship funds).

Publications: Application guidelines; Annual report; Financial statement; Grants list; Informational brochure; Occasional report.

Application information: Visit foundation Web site for application form and guidelines. Application form required.

Initial approach: Submit application form and attachments
Copies of proposal: 2
Deadline(s): Nov. 30
Board meeting date(s): 2nd Thurs., bi-monthly
Final notification: 30-60 days

Officers and Directors:* Brian Meakin,* Pres.; Nicholas Bonn,* V.P., Investments; Dan Putman,* Secy.; William C. Fried,* Treas.; Kimberly Lubig, Compt.; Hon. Robert Bennett; Hon. Jack R. Engebretson; John Hiltz; Henry D. "Bud" Kimpel; Hon. Jack Kirksey; Thomas J. Martin; Betsy McCue; Cindi Quinn; Dan West.

Number of staff: 1 part-time support.

EIN: 383104141

1145
M & M Area Community Foundation

1101 11th Ave., Ste. 2
P.O. Box 846
Menominee, MI   49858-0846   (906) 864-3599
County: Menominee
Contact: Richard O'Farrell, Exec. Dir.
FAX: (906) 864-3657;
E-mail: mmfoundation@czwireless.net; Additional E-mail: ricko@menominee.net; URL: http://www.mmcommunityfoundation.org

Established in 1994 in MI.

Grantmaker type: Community foundation.

Financial data (yr. ended 12/31/08): Assets, $4,210,606 (M); gifts received, $369,141; expenditures, $470,906; total giving, $200,904; giving activities include $189,744 for grants, and $11,160 for 14 grants to individuals.

Purpose and activities: The foundation's mission is to receive and administer funds and property in the form of permanent endowments from a wide range of donors for educational, environmental, cultural, recreational, and charitable purposes in a manner that promotes the spirit of philanthropy and meets the needs of the people of Menominee County, MI and Marinette County, WI.

Fields of interest: Arts; Higher education; Education; Environment; Health care; Recreation; Youth development; Human services; Community/economic development; Youth.

Type of support: Continuing support; Equipment; Program development; Seed money; Technical assistance; Employee matching gifts; Scholarships —to individuals; Matching/challenge support.
Limitations: Applications accepted. Giving limited to Menominee County, MI, and Marinette County, WI. No support for sectarian religious purposes. No grants to individuals (except for scholarships), or for routine operating expenses, endowments, annual campaigns, debt retirement, or for-profit enterprises.
Publications: Annual report; Financial statement; Grants list; Informational brochure; Newsletter.
Application information: Visit foundation Web site for online Letter of Intent form, full grant application form, and guidelines. Full grant applications are accepted only after the project is deemed eligible based on Letter of Intent. Application form required.
  Initial approach: Complete online Letter of Intent
  Copies of proposal: 1
  Deadline(s): 1 month prior to full application deadline for Letter of Intent; Jan. 26 and June 15 for senior grants and Apr. 20 for youth grants
  Board meeting date(s): Quarterly; grants committee meets in Sept.
  Final notification: May for youth grants
Officers and Trustees:* Dr. North Shetter,* Pres.; Larry Valencic,* V.P.; Mark Nygren,* 2nd V.P.; Bruce Peters,* Secy.-Treas.; Richard O'Farrell, Exec. Dir.; Arthur Baron; Michele Biehl; Dr. Stephen Caselton; Mike Dama; Jeanie Danielak; Sharon Danielson; Deb Fisher; Barb Killen; Tom Kuber; John MacIntyre; Randy Neelis; Dr. Jeffrey Orear; Jerry Schmidt; Ruth Thielen; Robin Kinzer West; Gail Wright.
Number of staff: 1 full-time professional; 3 part-time professional.
EIN: 383264725

1146
Mackinac Island Community Foundation
Twilight Inn
P.O. Box 1933
Mackinac Island, MI   49757-1933
(906) 847-3701
County: Mackinac
Contact: Robin Dorman, Exec. Dir.
FAX: (906) 847-3893; E-mail: info@micf.org;
Additional E-mail: rdorman@micf.org; URL: http://www.micf.org

Established in 1994 in MI.
Grantmaker type: Community foundation.
Financial data (yr. ended 12/31/09): Assets, $5,005,030 (M); gifts received, $363,171; expenditures, $224,715; total giving, $112,049; giving activities include $77,783 for 4+ grants (high: $57,277), and $34,266 for grants to individuals.
Purpose and activities: Recognizing the dignity and beauty of Mackinac Island, the foundation serves the general well-being of Island residents and visitors. The foundation is most interested in projects that focus on arts and humanities, social service, education, community enrichment, youth, environmental awareness and protection, health and wellness, or the horse tradition on Mackinac Island.
Fields of interest: Humanities; History/archaeology; Arts; Higher education; Education; Environment, natural resources; Environment; Health care; Housing/shelter, development; Athletics/sports, equestrianism; Recreation; Youth development; Children/youth, services; Human services;

Community/economic development; Youth; Economically disadvantaged.
Type of support: General/operating support; Continuing support; Emergency funds; Program development; Seed money; Scholarship funds.
Limitations: Applications accepted. Giving limited to the Mackinac Island area, MI. No support for organizations lacking 501(c)(3) status or for sectarian purposes. No grants to individuals (except for scholarships), or generally for deficit financing, operating expenses, or annual fundraising campaigns; no loans.
Publications: Application guidelines; Annual report (including application guidelines); Financial statement; Grants list; Informational brochure (including application guidelines); Newsletter.
Application information: Visit foundation web site for application form and guidelines. Application form required.
  Initial approach: Letter, e-mail, or telephone
  Copies of proposal: 1
  Deadline(s): Apr. 15 and Nov. 1
  Board meeting date(s): Feb., May, June, July, Aug., Sept., and Dec.
  Final notification: June and Dec.
Officers and Trustees:* Kathleen S. Lewand,* Chair.; Carole Rearick,* Vice-Chair.; R. Daniel Musser III,* Pres.; Margaret M. Doud,* Secy.; Randy Stuck,* Treas.; Robin Dorman, Exec. Dir.; Jennifer Bloswick; Brenda Bunker; Bradley T. Chambers; Jack E. Dehring; Charles F. Kleber; Wesley H. Maurer, Jr.; Mary K. McIntire; Lorna Puttkammer Straus; Michael Young.
Number of staff: 1 full-time professional.
EIN: 383179612
Selected grants: The following grants were reported in 2006.
$1,730 to Allied EMS Systems, Harbor Springs, MI. For purchase of airway mannequin to be used in training of new EMT's and paramedics.
$1,527 to Mackinac Island Medical Center, Mackinac Island, MI. For purchase of mechanical ventilator for emergency room.
$875 to Mackinac State Historic Parks, Mackinac Island, MI. For acquiring back issues of Mackinac Island Town Crier for use in the park.
$500 to Trinity Episcopal Church, Mackinac Island, MI. For program that sends author to speak with and record oral history of senor citizen in the community.
$377 to Mackinac Island Public School, Mackinac Island, MI. For purchase of handicap accessible swing for school playground.

1147
Manistee County Community Foundation
77 Spruce St.
Manistee, MI   49660-1524   (231) 723-7269
County: Manistee
Contact: Laura Heintzelman, Exec. Dir.
FAX: (231) 723-4983;
E-mail: mccf@manisteefoundation.org; URL: http://www.manisteefoundation.org

Established in 1987 in MI; in 2009 became an affiliate of Community Foundation for Muskegon County.
Grantmaker type: Community foundation.
Purpose and activities: The foundation seeks to enhance the quality of life in Manistee County for now and forever. This includes managing endowment funds, making grants and acting as a neutral convenor for the community at large.

Fields of interest: Arts; Education; Environment; Recreation; Human services; Community/economic development; Youth.
Type of support: Annual campaigns; Endowments; Seed money; Scholarship funds.
Limitations: Applications accepted. Giving limited to the Manistee County, MI, area.
Publications: Application guidelines; Annual report; Financial statement; Grants list; Informational brochure.
Application information: Grant (RFP) information is available each Feb. through the foundation's web site or by calling the foundation. Application form required.
  Initial approach: Letter or telephone
  Copies of proposal: 7
  Deadline(s): Mid-Mar.
  Board meeting date(s): Monthly
  Final notification: 6 weeks
Officers and Directors:* Beth McCarthy,* Chair.; George Wagoner,* Vice-Chair.; Tim Ervin,* Pres.; Clara D. Vargo,* Secy.; Michael Thompson,* Treas.; Laura M. Heintzelman, Exec. Dir.; Mike Acton; Ted Arens; Steve Brower; John Bueker; Dr. Charles T. Dillon; Tim Ervin; Rosalind Jaffe; By Lyon; Burt Parks; Anna Veverica.
Number of staff: 1 full-time professional; 1 part-time professional.
EIN: 382741723

1148
Marquette County Community Foundation
(formerly Marquette Community Foundation)
401 E. Fair Ave.
P.O. Box 37
Marquette, MI   49855-2951   (906) 226-7666
County: Marquette
Contact: Linda Vallier, Prog. Admin.
FAX: (906) 226-2104; E-mail: mcf@chartermi.net;
URL: http://www.mqt-cf.org

Established in 1988 in MI.
Grantmaker type: Community foundation.
Financial data (yr. ended 12/31/08): Assets, $7,196,671 (M); gifts received, $454,705; expenditures, $466,340; total giving, $286,789; giving activities include $252,068 for grants, and $34,721 for 53 grants to individuals (high: $2,500; low: $250).
Purpose and activities: The foundation supports organizations involved with the arts, education, health, human services, and other projects and programs that enhance life.
Fields of interest: Arts; Education; Health care; Health organizations, association; Recreation; Children/youth, services; Human services.
Type of support: Film/video/radio; Technical assistance; Consulting services; Capital campaigns; Building/renovation; Equipment; Program development; Seed money; Scholarship funds; Scholarships—to individuals.
Limitations: Applications accepted. Giving limited to Marquette County, MI. No support for religious programs that promote their particular religion.
Publications: Application guidelines; Annual report; Financial statement; Informational brochure; Newsletter; Program policy statement; Program policy statement (including application guidelines).
Application information: Visit foundation web site for application form and guidelines. Application form required.
  Initial approach: Telephone
  Copies of proposal: 6

Deadline(s): Apr. 1 and Oct. 1
Board meeting date(s): Six times annually
Final notification: Within one week of board meeting

Officers and Trustees:* Robert Cowell,* Pres.; Mark Canale,* V.P.; Maura Davenport,* Secy.; John Marshall,* Treas.; Dr. Carole L. Touchinski, Exec. Dir.; Marilyn Andrew; Stu Bradley; Kris Edmark; John Lenten; John Maki; Don Mourand; Mike Roy; Nancy Wiseman Seminoff; Roger Zappa.

Number of staff: 2 full-time professional.

EIN: 382826563

Selected grants: The following grants were reported in 2004.

$9,780 to Northern Michigan University, NMU Crew, Marquette, MI. For Marquette County Summer Learn-to-Row program.

$7,210 to Great Lakes Recovery Centers, Marquette, MI. For Women and Children Specialty Clinic.

$6,500 to Marquette, City of, Office of Arts and Culture, Marquette, MI. For Jayne Hiebel memorial installation.

$5,500 to American Red Cross, Marquette, MI. For volunteer database.

$5,000 to Upper Peninsula Childrens Museum, Marquette, MI. For Good Lung/Bad Lung exhibit.

$3,100 to Lake Superior Community Partnership Foundation, Marquette, MI. For Marquette Area Blues Fest youth workshops.

$2,300 to Salvation Army of Ishpeming, Ishpeming, MI. For Working Homes program.

$1,207 to Noquemanon Trail Network, Marquette, MI. For improvements.

$1,000 to Michigan Iron Industry Museum, Negaunee, MI. For capital campaign for expansion and renovation.

$750 to Ishpeming Ski Club, Ishpeming, MI. For youth ski jumping and cross country ski equipment.

1149
Marshall Community Foundation

(formerly Marshall Civic Foundation)
126 W. Michigan Ave., Ste. 202
Marshall, MI 49068-1574 (269) 781-2273
County: Calhoun
Contact: Sherry Anderson, Exec. Dir.
FAX: (269) 781-9747; E-mail: info@marshallcf.org;
URL: http://www.marshallcf.org

Established in 1970 in MI.

Grantmaker type: Community foundation.

Financial data (yr. ended 09/30/09): Assets, $8,330,112 (M); gifts received, $95,294; expenditures, $489,878; total giving, $333,986; giving activities include $333,986 for grants.

Purpose and activities: The foundation's mission is to help make the Marshall area an even better place to live, work, and raise a family. This is done by attracting permanently endowed funds from a wide range of donors serving as a conduit for special projects and distributing of grants in support of innovative programs, while always being mindful to carry out the intention of the donors.

Fields of interest: Arts; Education; Health care; Health organizations, association; Youth, services; Human services; Community/economic development; Youth; Aging.

Type of support: General/operating support; Building/renovation; Equipment; Program development; Conferences/seminars; Seed money; Curriculum development; Scholarship funds;

Technical assistance; Scholarships—to individuals; Matching/challenge support.

Limitations: Applications accepted. Giving limited to Calhoun County, MI. No support for religious or sectarian purposes. No grants to individuals (except for scholarships), or for annual fundraising drives or capital campaigns, endowments or debt reductions, or normal operating expenses (except for start-up purposes and/or special needs).

Publications: Annual report; Informational brochure.

Application information: Visit foundation web site for application forms and guidelines. Application form required.

Initial approach: Submit application form and attachments
Copies of proposal: 26
Deadline(s): Jan. 1 , Apr. 1, July 1, and Oct. 1
Board meeting date(s): Quarterly
Final notification: Within 2 months

Officers and Trustees:* Charles B. Cook,* Pres.; Mark F. Stuart,* V.P.; Kathy Tarr,* Secy.; Frank E. Boley,* Treas.; Sherry Anderson, Exec. Dir.; Morris Stulberg, Pres. Emeritus; Mary Jo Byrne; Dr. Randy Davis; Sandra J. Dobbins; Thomas F. Franke; Pastor Richard Gerten; Lynne M. Haley; Michael E. Kinter; Dr. Jay Larson; Darlene Neidlinger; James A. Pardoe; Bruce Smith; Ron Smith.

Number of staff: 1 part-time professional; 1 part-time support.

EIN: 237011281

1150
Mecosta County Community Foundation

P.O. Box 1012C
Big Rapids, MI 49307-0352 (231) 796-3065
County: Mecosta
URL: http://www.mccf.us

Established in 1991 in MI as an affiliate of Fremont Area Community Foundation.

Grantmaker type: Community foundation.

Purpose and activities: The mission of the foundation is to enhance the quality of life for all citizens in Mecosta County in the areas of art and culture, education, health, nature conservation and the environment, community development, historical resources, and social services.

Fields of interest: Historical activities; Arts; Education; Environment, natural resources; Health care; Human services; Community/economic development.

Type of support: Seed money; Scholarships—to individuals; Scholarship funds; Program development; General/operating support; Equipment; Building/renovation.

Limitations: Applications accepted. Giving limited to Mecosta County, MI. No support for organizations lacking 501(c)(3) status, or for religious organizations for solely religious purposes. No grants for general operating support.

Publications: Application guidelines; Annual report; Newsletter.

Application information: See foundation web site for application guidelines and requirements. Application form required.

Copies of proposal: 5
Deadline(s): Apr. 1 and Oct. 1 for grants; Mar. 15 for scholarships

Officers and Trustees:* John Norton,* Pres.; Gary Trimarco,* 1st V.P.; Kim Von Kronenberger,* 2nd V.P.; Glen Pepper,* Treas.; Yolanda Bellingar; Pete Chesebrough; Rita Conrad; Patsy Eisler; David Hamelund; Robert Hampson; Scott Hill-Kennedy;

Isabel Kempton; Karl Linebaugh; Michael Mohnke; Debbie Patterson; Judy Tressler; Tim Zehr.

Number of staff: None.

1151
Michigan Gateway Community Foundation

(formerly Buchanan Area Foundation)
111 Days Ave.
Buchanan, MI 49107-1609 (269) 695-3521
County: Berrien
Contact: Robert N. Habicht, C.E.O.
FAX: (269) 695-4250; E-mail: info@mgcf.org;
URL: http://www.mgcf.org

Established in 1978 in MI.

Grantmaker type: Community foundation.

Financial data (yr. ended 03/31/09): Assets, $5,013,319 (M); gifts received, $299,462; expenditures, $537,890; total giving, $274,083; giving activities include $274,083 for grants.

Purpose and activities: The foundation provides support for the arts, education, and social services. Scholarships are for local-area high school seniors for study in any field.

Fields of interest: Arts; Education; Health care; Human services.

Type of support: General/operating support; Income development; Equipment; Program development; Conferences/seminars; Seed money; Curriculum development; Program evaluation; Scholarships—to individuals; Matching/challenge support.

Limitations: Applications accepted. Giving limited to Cass County and southern Berrien County, MI.

Publications: Application guidelines; Annual report; Financial statement; Informational brochure; Newsletter.

Application information: Visit foundation web site for application information. Use of the Common Grant Application of the Council of Michigan Foundations is encouraged. Application form required.

Initial approach: Telephone
Copies of proposal: 1
Deadline(s): Feb. 1, May 1, Aug. 1, and Nov. 1 for grants; May for scholarships
Board meeting date(s): Mar., May, July, Aug., and Nov.
Final notification: Within 1 month

Officers and Trustees:* Louis A. Desenberg,* Chair.; Robert N. Habicht,* C.E.O. and Pres.; Robert Cochrane,* Treas.; Nancy Oare Butler; Karin Falkenstein; Casper Grathwohl; Pat McCollough; Don Stibbs; Judy Truesdell; Stephen K. Woods.

Number of staff: 1 full-time professional; 1 part-time support.

EIN: 382180730

1152
Midland Area Community Foundation

(formerly Midland Foundation)
76 Ashman Cir.
Midland, MI 48640 (989) 839-9661
County: Midland
Contact: Janet McGuire, C.E.O.; For grants: Ken Mault, Prog. Off.
FAX: (989) 839-9907;
E-mail: info@midlandfoundation.org; Additional tel: (800) 906-9661; Grant application E-mail: kmault@midlandfoundation.org; URL: http://www.midlandfoundation.org

Established in 1973 in MI.

Grantmaker type: Community foundation.

Financial data (yr. ended 12/31/09): Assets, $59,173,628 (M); gifts received, $2,486,909; expenditures, $2,587,083; total giving, $1,180,412; giving activities include $990,649 for 173+ grants (high: $143,584), and $189,763 for grants to individuals.

Purpose and activities: The foundation seeks to promote and enable philanthropic giving to improve the quality of life for the people in the community.

Fields of interest: Humanities; Arts; Adult/continuing education; Education; Environment, energy; Environment; Health care; Recreation; Youth, services; Human services; Economic development; Community/economic development; Infants/toddlers; Children/youth; Children; Youth; Adults; Aging; Young adults; Disabilities, people with; Physically disabled; Deaf/hearing impaired; Mentally disabled; Minorities; African Americans/Blacks; Women; Infants/toddlers, female; Girls; Adults, women; Young adults, female; Men; Infants/toddlers, male; Adults, men; Young adults, male; Military/veterans; Substance abusers; Single parents; Crime/abuse victims; Terminal illness, people with; Economically disadvantaged; Homeless.

Type of support: Building/renovation; Equipment; Seed money; Scholarship funds; Technical assistance; Consulting services; Matching/challenge support.

Limitations: Applications accepted. Giving primarily in full support services to Midland and Gladwin counties, MI, and also Clare County through affiliate. No support for sectarian religious programs or basic governmental services. No grants for operating budgets, continuing support, annual campaigns, deficit financing, endowment funds, or travel for groups such as school classes, clubs, or sports teams.

Publications: Application guidelines; Annual report; Grants list; Informational brochure; Newsletter.

Application information: Visit foundation web site for application guidelines. Application form required.

  Initial approach: Telephone Prog. Off. to discuss project

  Copies of proposal: 3

  Deadline(s): Jan. 15, Apr. 15, July 15, and Oct. 15

  Board meeting date(s): 4th Mon. of every month

  Final notification: Early in Mar., June, Sept., and Dec.

Officers and Trustees:* Jim Hop,* Chair.; Alison Goethe,* Vice-Chair.; Janet McGuire, C.E.O. and Pres.; Melissa Barnard,* Secy.; Angela Hine,* Treas.; Richard Dolinski; Carole Donaghy; Mary Draves; Bridgette Gransden; Joan Herbert; Sam Howard; Cal leuter; Craig McDonald; Just Rapanos; Mike Rush.

Number of staff: 4 full-time professional; 2 part-time professional; 2 full-time support.

EIN: 382023395

Selected grants: The following grants were reported in 2007.

$40,000 to Greater Midland Community Centers, Midland, MI. For playscape and basketball court as part of campus renovation.

$30,000 to Bullock Creek School District, Midland, MI. For training and material for Floyd Elementary School and West Midland Family Center staff in development of Diagnostic Reading Lab to serve kindergarten, first and second grade students at Floyd Elementary School.

$20,000 to Beaverton Rural Schools, Beaverton, MI. For portable, wireless computer equipment.

$17,200 to Coleman, City of, Coleman, MI. For Phase II of city's Senior Housing Project.

$12,500 to Southtown Little League, Midland, MI. For additional facilities.

$9,255 to ARC of Midland, Midland, MI. For Project Lifesaver, to assist individuals with disabilities, including age related memory loss, to purchase system that includes GPS bracelets.

$7,500 to Midland County Emergency Food Pantry Network, Midland, MI. For Backpack Buddies Program to meet needs of hungry children over the weekends during the school year.

$5,810 to Mid-Michigan Community Action Agency, Farwell, MI. For materials to improve technology ability of local women, infant, and children's clinic, including autodialer and scheduling system and child blood lead testing supplies.

$3,600 to Michigan State University Extension-Gladwin County, Gladwin, MI. For supplying nutrition information to low-income audiences in Gladwin County.

1153
Missaukee Area Community Foundation

(formerly Missaukee County Community Foundation)
P.O. Box 166
Lake City, MI   49651-0166
County: Missaukee
Contact: James Hinkamp, Pres.
E-mail: jhinkamp@i2k.com; URL: http://www.cadillacfoundation.org/missaukee.php

Established in 1999 in MI as a geographic component fund of the Cadillac Area Community Foundation.

Grantmaker type: Community foundation.

Purpose and activities: The primary purpose of the Missaukee Area Community Foundation is to develop a community-wide vehicle for permanent endowments to enhance the quality of life in the area (County of Missaukee, Michigan), and to establish and manage worthwhile funds for the benefit of our community. Support for youth activities, education, and community improvement projects.

Fields of interest: Education; Youth development; Community/economic development.

Type of support: Continuing support; Annual campaigns; Seed money; Consulting services; Matching/challenge support.

Limitations: Applications accepted. Giving limited to Missaukee County, MI. No support for sectarian programs. No grants to individuals, or generally for general operating support, fundraising campaigns, endowments, or conferences.

Publications: Application guidelines; Occasional report; Program policy statement.

Application information: See foundation Web site for application requirements, including downloadable application form. Application form required.

  Initial approach: Letter or telephone

  Copies of proposal: 8

  Deadline(s): See foundation Web site for current deadline information. Applications are only considered during specific award cycles (at least 1 per year)

  Board meeting date(s): As needed

1154
Mount Pleasant Area Community Foundation

(formerly Mount Pleasant Community Foundation)
113 W. Broadway
P.O. Box 1283
Mount Pleasant, MI   48804-1283
(989) 773-7322
County: Isabella
Contact: Amanda Schafer, Exec. Dir.
FAX: (989) 773-1517; E-mail: info@mpacf.org;
URL: http://www.mpacf.org

Established in 1990 in MI.

Grantmaker type: Community foundation.

Financial data (yr. ended 12/31/09): Assets, $8,445,418 (M); gifts received, $959,844; expenditures, $619,674; total giving, $368,259; giving activities include $322,248 for grants, and $46,011 for grants to individuals.

Purpose and activities: The foundation seeks to enhance the quality of life for all citizens of Isabella County, both current and future generations, by holding and attracting permanent, endowed funds from a wide range of donors, addressing needs through grant making, and providing leadership on key community issues.

Fields of interest: Education, research; Education; Environment; Health care; Youth development; Human services; Community development, neighborhood development.

Type of support: Capital campaigns; Building/renovation; Equipment; Land acquisition; Endowments; Emergency funds; Program development; Conferences/seminars; Publication; Seed money; Scholarship funds; Research; Technical assistance; Scholarships—to individuals; Matching/challenge support; Student loans—to individuals.

Limitations: Applications accepted. Giving limited to Isabella County, MI. No support for the promotion of religious organizations. No grants to individuals (except for scholarships), or for annual operating expenses.

Publications: Application guidelines; Annual report; Financial statement; Grants list; Informational brochure; Newsletter.

Application information: Visit foundation web site for application and guidelines. Faxed applications are not accepted. Application form required.

  Initial approach: Contact foundation staff

  Copies of proposal: 15

  Deadline(s): Jan. 26, May 25, and Sept. 28 for general grants; Mar. 11 for scholarships

  Board meeting date(s): Bimonthly

  Final notification: Within 2 weeks of board meeting

Officers and Trustees:* Nancy Ridley,* Pres.; Jan Strickler,* V.P.; Bob Long,* Secy.; Dan Boge,* Treas.; Amanda Schafer, Exec. Dir.; Jill Bourland; Bill Chilman; Shirley Martin Decker; Dan Eversole; Joanne Golden; Doug Heinze; Chuck Hubscher; Dave Keilitz; Steve Martineau; Diane Morey; Lon Morey; Darcy Orlik; Steven Pung; Laura Richards; Donald Schuster; Harold Stegman; Thomas Sullivan; Robert L. Wheeler; Terri Zitzlesberger.

Number of staff: 1 full-time professional; 1 part-time professional; 1 part-time support.

EIN: 382951873

1155
Negaunee Area Community Fund
1036 Maas St.
Negaunee, MI   49866-1504   (906) 226-7666
County: Marquette
Contact: Alan Nelson, Tr.
FAX: (906) 226-2104; E-mail: alnelson@up.net;
URL: http://
www.marquettecountycommunityfoundation.org/
nacf.html

Established in MI as an affiliate of Marquette
Community Foundation.
Grantmaker type: Community foundation.
Fields of interest: Community/economic
development.
Limitations: Giving primarily in western Marquette
County, MI.

1156
North Central Michigan Community Foundation
c/o Community Foundation for Northeast Michigan
P.O. Box 495
Alpena, MI   49707-0495   (877) 354-6881
County: Alpena
Contact: Christine Hitch
FAX: (989) 356-3319; E-mail: chitch@cfnem.org;
URL: http://www.ncmcf.org/

Established in 1998 in MI as an affiliate of the
Community Foundation for Northeast Michigan.
Grantmaker type: Community foundation.
Purpose and activities: The foundation seeks to
serve Crawford, Ogemaw, and Oscoda counties and
to preserve the charitable goals of a wide range of
donors now and for generations to come by
supporting 501(c)(3) organizations, churches for
non-religious purposes, and government agencies.
Type of support: Management development/
capacity building; Film/video/radio; Curriculum
development; Building/renovation; Equipment;
Program development; Conferences/seminars;
Publication; Seed money; Technical assistance;
Scholarships—to individuals.
Limitations: Applications accepted. Giving limited to
Crawford, Ogemaw and Oscoda counties, MI. No
support for religious purposes or political
campaigns. No grants to individuals (except for
scholarships), or for routine operating needs or
budget deficits.
Publications: Application guidelines; Annual report;
Financial statement; Grants list; Informational
brochure; Newsletter.
Application information: See foundation web site
for Common Grant Application Form and
requirements. Application form required.
  Copies of proposal: 1
  Deadline(s): June 30, for Common Grants, Dec.
    31 for YAC Grants, Dec. 31 and Mar. 30 for
    Crawford County YAC Grants
  Board meeting date(s): Every 3rd Wed. of Feb.,
    May, Aug., and Nov.
  Final notification: Within 6 weeks of grant
    deadlines
Officers and Directors: Joe Porter, Chair.; Gerald
Gosnell, Vice-Chair.; Carolyn DiPonio,
Secy.-Treas.; Hugo Burzlaff; Jeanne Cardinal; Bob
Carpenter; Jim Howard; Michael Lange; David
Marston; Philip Shaw.
Selected grants: The following grants were reported
in 2008.

$2,500 to West Branch Rose City Schools, Rose
City, MI. For theater exposure.
$1,900 to West Branch Public Library, West Branch,
MI. For Summer Reading Program.
$1,500 to Peter Pan Cooperative Pre-School Center,
Saginaw, MI. For playground renovation.
$1,000 to Crawford County Economic Development
Partnership, Grayling, MI. For Watershed Art Project.
$1,000 to Humane Society, Ogemaw County, West
Branch, MI. For start-up costs.
$500 to Crawford, County of, Family Court, Grayling,
MI. For J.U.S.T.I.C.E. (Cyber Crime Prevention).
$500 to Crisis Pregnancy Center of West Branch,
West Branch, MI. For Sexual Integrity Program.
$500 to River House Shelter and Domestic Crisis
Services, Grayling, MI. For Toys for Children's
Well-Being.

1157
Northville Community Foundation
18600 Northville Rd., Ste. 275
Northville, MI   48168   (248) 374-0200
County: Wayne
Contact: Shari Peters, Pres.
FAX: (248) 374-0403;
E-mail: nvillefoundation@aol.com; URL: http://
www.northvillecommunityfoundation.com

Established in 1997 in MI.
Grantmaker type: Community foundation.
Financial data (yr. ended 12/31/09): Assets,
$595,543 (M); gifts received, $136,835;
expenditures, $201,424; total giving, $1,950;
giving activities include $950 for grants, $1,000 for
grants to individuals, and $160,294 for
foundation-administered programs.
Purpose and activities: The foundation seeks to
benefit the Northville community through promotion
of education, arts, music, and cultural events;
support also for environmental conservation.
Fields of interest: Performing arts, music; Arts;
Education; Environment, natural resources.
Limitations: Applications accepted. Giving limited to
Northville, MI.
Application information: Application form required.
  Initial approach: Telephone
Officers and Directors: Chris Belcher, Chair.;
Shari Peters, Pres. and Exec. Dir.; Lisa Barry;
Nickie Bateson; Eric Colthurst; Andrea Daniels;
Christopher Kelly; Ted March; Steve Moore; Tom
Steele.
EIN: 383361844

1158
Norway Area Community Foundation
(formerly Norway Area Community Fund)
c/o Dickinson Area Community Foundation
427 S. Stephenson Ave.
Iron Mountain, MI   49801-0648   (906) 774-3131
County: Dickinson
FAX: (906) 774-7640; E-mail: dcacf@uplogon.com;
URL: http://
www.dickinsonareacommunityfoundation.org/
page4.asp

Established in MI; a geographic affiliate of Dickinson
Area Community Foundation.
Grantmaker type: Community foundation.
Purpose and activities: Grants are made in the
areas of advancing philanthropy, arts and the
humanities, community services, education,

conservation and the environment, health, and
human and social services.
Fields of interest: Humanities; Arts; Education;
Environment; Health care; Human services;
Community/economic development; Philanthropy/
voluntarism.
Limitations: Giving limited to Norway, MI, and its
surrounding townships. No support for sectarian
religious purposes. No grants to individuals, or for
budget deficits, routine operating expenses of
existing organizations, or endowments.
Application information: Contact foundation for
deadline and decision dates.
Officer: Grant Carlson, Mgr.
Trustees: Ray Anderson; Pastor James Britt; Duane
Manie; Allyn Thornberry; Randall Van Gasse; Robert
Wurzer.

1159
Osceola County Community Foundation
P.O. Box 37
Reed City, MI   49677-0037   (231) 342-9163
County: Osceola
E-mail: office@occf.info; URL: http://www.occf.info/

Established in MI as an affiliate of Fremont Area
Community Foundation.
Grantmaker type: Community foundation.
Purpose and activities: The mission of the
foundation is to make Osceola County a better place
in which to live and work by enhancing the quality of
life and building a strong community spirit through
support of programs in the areas of human services,
arts and culture, environment, health care, and
education.
Fields of interest: Arts; Education; Environment;
Health care; Human services; Community/economic
development.
Limitations: Applications accepted. Giving limited to
Osceola County, MI. No support for religious
organizations, except for services provided on a
secular basis, or for organizations lacking 501(c)(3)
status, except for schools, churches and
governmental bodies. No grants to individuals
(except for scholarships administered through
schools).
Application information: See foundation web site
for application guidelines, including application form
which can be completed online or downloaded.
Application form required.
  Copies of proposal: 9
  Deadline(s): Mar. 1 and Oct. 1 for grants; Mar. 15
    for scholarships
  Board meeting date(s): Apr. and Nov.
  Final notification: June and Dec.
Officers and Trustees: Joe Curtin, Pres.; Howard
Hyde, V.P.; Alan Bengry, Secy.; Theresa Rasor,
Treas.; Ron Babb; Larry Emig; Terry Gerber; Hon.
Susan Grant; Judy Hays; Dr. Amy Keller; Sally
Nelson; Lynn Salinas; Marie Wilkerson.

1160
Otsego County Community Foundation
P.O. Box 344
Gaylord, MI   49734-0344   (989) 731-0597
County: Otsego
Contact: Marilyn McFarland, Exec. Dir.
FAX: (989) 448-8377;
E-mail: contact@otsegofoundation.org; Additional
E-mail: marilyn@otsegofoundation.org; URL: http://
www.otsegofoundation.org

Established in 1995 in MI as a regional affiliate of Grand Traverse Regional Community Foundation; became an independent community foundation in 2002.

Grantmaker type: Community foundation.

Financial data (yr. ended 12/31/08): Assets, $1,976,637 (M); gifts received, $67,684; expenditures, $140,179; total giving, $78,302; giving activities include $62,802 for grants, and $15,500 for 26 grants to individuals.

Purpose and activities: The foundation's mission is to enhance the quality of life for all citizens of the Otsego County, Michigan area now and for future generations by building community endowment, awarding grants to address community needs, and convening leadership on key issues.

Fields of interest: Arts; Education; Environment; Health organizations, association; Cancer; Recreation; Children/youth, services; Community/economic development.

Limitations: Applications accepted. Giving limited to Otsego County, MI. No support for sectarian organizations. No grants for operating expenses, or loan payments.

Application information: Visit foundation Web site for application form and guidelines. Application form required.

Initial approach: Contact foundation
Copies of proposal: 4
Deadline(s): Mar. and Aug.
Final notification: May and Oct.

Officers and Directors:* Maureen Derenzy,* Chair.; Dr. David Gast,* Vice-Chair.; Kevin Reynolds,* Treas.; Marilyn McFarland, Exec. Dir.; Peter Amar; Mike Fernandez; Nick Florian; Tim Granahan; Dr. Peter Handley; Janice Lampert; Susan Premo; Matt Rooyakker; Aurora Walcheck-Arndt.

EIN: 383216235

1161
Peshtigo Area Foundation

c/o M & M Area Community Foundation
1101 11th Ave., Ste. 2
P.O. Box 846
Menominee, MI   49858-0846   (906) 864-3599
County: Menominee
URL: http://www.mmcommunityfoundation.org/Affiliate-Funds/Peshtigo-Area-Foundation

Established in 2006 in MI; a regional affiliate of M & M Area Community Foundation.

Grantmaker type: Community foundation.

Purpose and activities: The foundation was established for the purpose of assisting and promoting charitable activities in the Peshtigo, Michigan, area.

Fields of interest: Community/economic development.

Limitations: Giving limited to Peshtigo, MI.

Application information: Application form required.

Initial approach: Applications must be submitted online

Officers and Board Members:* Dick Omdahl,* Chair.; Deb Fisher,* Secy.; Dale Berman; John Berth; Teresa Brostowitz; Bill Clement; Renee Kresl; Sue Martin; Steve Motkowski; and 5 additional members.

1162
Petoskey-Harbor Springs Area Community Foundation

616 Petoskey St., Ste. 300
Petoskey, MI   49770-2779   (231) 348-5820
County: Emmet
Contact: David L. Jones, Exec. Dir.
FAX: (231) 348-5883; E-mail: info@phsacf.org; Additional E-mails: djones@phsacf.org and lwendland@phsacf.org; URL: http://www.phsacf.org

Established in 1991 in MI.

Grantmaker type: Community foundation.

Financial data (yr. ended 03/31/10): Assets, $18,549,457 (M); gifts received, $831,467; expenditures, $778,551; total giving, $427,043; giving activities include $404,693 for 250+ grants (high: $29,287), and $22,350 for 15 grants to individuals.

Purpose and activities: The foundation awards grants to nonprofit organizations, schools, and municipalities in Emmet County, MI or to those that serve a significant number of Emmet County residents.

Fields of interest: Historic preservation/historical societies; Arts; Higher education; Education; Environment; Health care; Recreation; Youth development; Human services; Economic development; Community/economic development.

Type of support: Building/renovation; Equipment; Program development; Seed money; Scholarship funds; Technical assistance; Scholarships—to individuals; Matching/challenge support.

Limitations: Applications accepted. Giving limited to Emmet County, MI. No support for sectarian religious purposes. No grants to individuals (except for scholarships), or for endowments, debt reduction, annual fundraising drives, operational phases of established programs, conferences, travel, or scholarly research; no loans.

Publications: Application guidelines; Annual report; Financial statement; Informational brochure.

Application information: Potential applicants must contact the foundation prior to submitting an application to discuss their project. Visit foundation web site for application information. Application form required.

Initial approach: Telephone
Copies of proposal: 30
Deadline(s): Mar. 1 and Oct. 1
Board meeting date(s): Monthly
Final notification: Approx. 2 months

Officers and Directors:* Charles H. Gano,* Pres.; Lisa G. Blanchard,* V.P.; David T. Buzzelli,* Secy.; Todd Winnell,* Treas.; David L. Jones, Exec. Dir.; Sandra T. Baker; J. Wilfred Cwikiel; Jane T. Damschroder; Jennifer E. Deegan; Mike Eberhart; Eden C. Erxleben; Michael J. FitzSimons; Louise T. Graham; Charles W. Johnson; Virginia B. McCoy; Philip H. Millard.

Number of staff: 3 full-time professional; 1 full-time support.

EIN: 383032185

1163
Roscommon County Community Foundation

701 Lake St.
P.O. Box 824
Roscommon, MI   48653   (989) 275-3112
County: Roscommon
Contact: Mary Fry, C.E.O.
FAX: (989) 275-8513; E-mail: rococofo@yahoo.com; URL: http://www.roscommoncountycommunityfoundation.org

Established in 1997 as an affiliate of NCMCF; recognized as an independent community foundation in 2001.

Donors: Rex Gillen†; Arlene Gillen†.

Grantmaker type: Community foundation.

Financial data (yr. ended 12/31/08): Assets, $4,634,180 (M); gifts received, $126,138; expenditures, $421,867; total giving, $266,103; giving activities include $92,278 for grants, and $173,825 for 32 grants to individuals.

Purpose and activities: The foundation seeks to improve the quality of life for all present and future residents of Roscommon County by: 1) providing stewardship and leadership; 2) attracting and holding permanent endowment funds from a wide range of donors; and 3) by making grants of the income from its permanent endowment funds. The foundation is committed to protecting the personal investments that all residents have made, demonstrating concern for youth and many issues affecting their future, recognizing the value and importance of the natural environment now and for the future, and improving and building the future for families.

Fields of interest: Arts, public education; Arts education; Education, formal/general education; Child development, education; Adult education—literacy, basic skills & GED; Education, community/cooperative; Education; Animals/wildlife, single organization support; Animals/wildlife, public education; Animals/wildlife, volunteer services; Animals/wildlife, formal/general education; Animal welfare; Animals/wildlife, special services; Animals/wildlife; AIDS; AIDS research; Crime/law enforcement, management/technical assistance; Crime/law enforcement, single organization support; Crime/law enforcement, public education; Crime/law enforcement, government agencies; Crime/law enforcement, formal/general education; Crime/law enforcement, missing persons; Crime/law enforcement, police agencies; Crime/law enforcement; Agriculture/food, single organization support; Agriculture/food, public education; Agriculture/food, government agencies; Disasters, search/rescue; Athletics/sports, training; Athletics/sports, school programs; Athletics/sports, basketball; Athletics/sports, baseball; Athletics/sports, soccer; Athletics/sports, football; Athletics/sports, golf; Boy scouts; American Red Cross; Children/youth, services; Children, day care; Children, services; Community/economic development, single organization support; Community development, women's clubs; Christian agencies & churches.

Type of support: Endowments; Scholarship funds.

Limitations: Applications accepted. Giving limited to Roscommon County, MI. No support for religious or for-profit organizations.

Publications: Application guidelines; Annual report; Annual report (including application guidelines); Financial statement; Grants list; Informational brochure; Newsletter.

Application information: Visit foundation web site for application cover sheet and guidelines. Application form required.

Initial approach: Submit application
Copies of proposal: 8
Deadline(s): Apr. 29 and Oct. 30
Board meeting date(s): Varies
Final notification: 2 months

Officers and Trustees: David Reece,* Chair.; Thomas Morleau,* Vice-Chair.; Mary Fry,* C.E.O. and Pres.; Ron Duquette,* Secy.; Katherine Hall, C.F.O.; Tom Richardson,* Treas.; Ruth Freuhauf; Clarence Harvey; Brian Hill; Matt Jernigan; Henri Junod, Jr.; Gary Long; John Sinnaeve.

Number of staff: 1 full-time professional; 2 part-time support.

EIN: 383612480

1164
Saginaw Community Foundation
100 S. Jefferson Ave., Ste. 201
Saginaw, MI   48607-1282   (989) 755-0545
County: Saginaw
Contact: Renee S. Johnston, C.E.O.
FAX: (989) 755-6524;
E-mail: info@saginawfoundation.org; URL: http://www.saginawfoundation.org

Incorporated in 1984 in MI.

Grantmaker type: Community foundation.

Financial data (yr. ended 12/31/09): Assets, $36,344,180 (M); gifts received, $2,650,495; expenditures, $2,752,188; total giving, $1,234,409; giving activities include $788,518 for 15+ grants (high: $75,000), and $445,891 for 236 grants to individuals.

Purpose and activities: Support for projects not currently being served by existing community resources and for projects providing leverage for generating other funds and community resources.

Fields of interest: Arts; Education; Environment; Health care; Recreation; Family services; Human services; Economic development; Community/economic development; General charitable giving; Youth; Aging.

Type of support: Building/renovation; Equipment; Emergency funds; Program development; Publication; Seed money; Scholarship funds; Technical assistance; Scholarships—to individuals; Matching/challenge support.

Limitations: Applications accepted. Giving limited to Saginaw County, MI. No support for churches or sectarian religious programs. No grants to individuals (except for designated scholarship funds), or for operating budgets, endowment campaigns, debt reduction, travel, or basic municipal or educational services; generally no multi-year grants.

Publications: Application guidelines; Annual report (including application guidelines); Newsletter; Occasional report.

Application information: Visit foundation Web site for application cover form and guidelines. Application form required.

Initial approach: Telephone
Copies of proposal: 3
Deadline(s): Feb. 1, May 1, Aug. 1 and Nov. 1
Board meeting date(s): Monthly
Final notification: 2 months after deadline

Officers and Directors: Joseph W. Madison,* Chair.; Mark S. Flegenheimer,* Vice-Chair.; Renee S. Johnston, C.E.O. and Pres.; Brian Jackson, V.P., Donor Rels. and Devel.; David J. Abbs,* Secy.; Heidi

A. Bolger,* Treas.; Shelby Avery; Mary Lou Benecke; Tammy L. Bernier; Andre Buckley; Paul Chaffee; Morrall M. Claramunt; Greg Cochran; Rev. Hurley J. Coleman, Jr.; Ellen E. Crane; JoAnn Crary; Desmon Daniel, Ph.D.; Craig C. Douglas, Ph.D.; James Fabiano II; Andrea L. Fisher; Richard J. Garber; Frederick C. Gardner; Jimmy E. Greene; Todd Hall; Smallwood Holoman; Timothy M. MacKay; Kala Kuru Ramasamy, M.D.; Barbara Russell; Jerry L. Seese; Kari Shaheen; James J. Shinners; Bridget Smith; Julie Case Swieczkowski; Mamie Thorns, Ph.D.; Richard T. Watson; Sean Wolohan.

Number of staff: 4 full-time professional; 2 full-time support.

EIN: 382474297

1165
Sanilac County Community Foundation
47 Austin St.
P.O. Box 307
Sandusky, MI   48471-0307   (810) 648-3634
County: Sanilac
Contact: Joan Nagelkirk, Exec. Dir.
FAX: (810) 648-4418;
E-mail: director@sanilaccountycommunityfoundation.org; Additional E-mail: joan@clearideas.biz; URL: http://www.sanilaccountycommunityfoundation.org

Established in 1994 in MI.

Grantmaker type: Community foundation.

Financial data (yr. ended 12/31/08): Assets, $2,601,293 (M); gifts received, $430,559; expenditures, $151,035; total giving, $94,737; giving activities include $43,062 for grants, and $51,675 for 75 grants to individuals.

Purpose and activities: The foundation holds a collection of endowed funds, contributed by many individuals, corporations, private foundations and government agencies to benefit the Sanilac County, MI, area.

Fields of interest: Arts; Education; Environment; Health care; Recreation; Youth development; Children/youth, services; Human services; Community/economic development; United Ways and Federated Giving Programs; Infants/toddlers; Children/youth; Children; Youth; Adults; Aging; Young adults; Disabilities, people with; Physically disabled; Blind/visually impaired; Deaf/hearing impaired; Mentally disabled; Minorities; African Americans/Blacks; Indigenous peoples; Women; Infants/toddlers, female; Girls; Adults, women; Young adults, female; Men; Infants/toddlers, male; Boys; Adults, men; Young adults, male; Substance abusers; Single parents; Crime/abuse victims; Economically disadvantaged; Homeless.

Type of support: Technical assistance; Seed money; Program development; Film/video/radio; Equipment; Emergency funds; Curriculum development; Continuing support; Building/renovation; Annual campaigns.

Limitations: Applications accepted. Giving limited to Sanilac County, MI. No support for religious or sectarian purposes. No support for loans.

Publications: Annual report; Financial statement; Grants list; Informational brochure; Informational brochure (including application guidelines); Program policy statement.

Application information: Visit foundation Web site for application information. An application form for grants of $5,000 or less is available online. Application form required.

Initial approach: Telephone

Copies of proposal: 12
Deadline(s): May 1 and Nov. 1
Board meeting date(s): 3rd Tues. of every month
Final notification: May 30 or Nov. 30

Officers and Board Members: I. Lee Cork,* Co-Chair.; Bill Sarkella,* Co-Chair.; Ed Gamache,* Vice-Chair.; Susan Dreyer,* Secy.; Joe Nartker,* Treas.; Joan Nagelkirk,* Exec. Dir.; Judy Albrecht; Bob Armstrong; Curt Backus; Robert Barnes; Louise Blasius; Henry Buxton; Dick Carncross; Steve Coffelt; Paul Cowley; Bill Coyne; Sharon Danek; Roger Dean; Katie Dunn; Judy Ferguson; David Hearsch; Linda Kelke; Duane Lange; Gary Macklem; Bill Monroe; Paul Muxlow; Dorothy Ross; Erica Sheridan; Dave Tubbs; Sandy Willis.

EIN: 383204484

1166
Schoolcraft Area Community Foundation
(formerly Schoolcraft County Community Foundation)
221 S. Maple St.
P.O. Box 452
Manistique, MI   49854-0452   (906) 341-2834
County: Schoolcraft
Contact: Paulette Demers, Treas.
FAX: (906) 341-2834;
E-mail: pdemers@uplogon.com

Established in 1995 in MI; in 2001 became a geographic affiliate of the Community Foundation of the Upper Peninsula.

Grantmaker type: Community foundation.

Purpose and activities: Primarily awards scholarships to local area youth; support also to organizations in the areas of arts and culture, education, health, human services, community development, and the environment.

Fields of interest: Arts; Education; Environment; Health care; Human services; Community/economic development.

Type of support: Equipment; Scholarships—to individuals.

Limitations: Giving limited to Manistique, MI.

Officers: John E. MacFarlene III, Chair.; Bob Panek, Pres.; Marilyn Pitts-Johnson, V.P.; Jeff Himes, Secy.; Paulette Demers, Treas.

Trustees: Marty Fuller; Rev. Pam Fulton; Rev. David Hueter; Christina Keener; Fr. Peter Menelli; Rick Wodzinski.

EIN: 383181869

1167
Shelby Community Foundation
P.O. Box 183181
Shelby Township, MI   48318-3181
(586) 909-5305
County: Macomb
Contact: Nancy Bates, Chair.
URL: http://shelbyhistory.tripod.com/id59.html

Established in 1996 in MI.

Grantmaker type: Community foundation.

Financial data (yr. ended 12/31/08): Assets, $524,748 (M); gifts received, $215,410; expenditures, $175,390; total giving, $117,877; giving activities include $117,877 for grants.

Purpose and activities: The foundation supports projects which offer innovative and practical approaches to community needs. Its major goals are to promote activities and programs that provide

residents of the township with the following opportunities: cultural enrichment, historic preservation, recreational activities, life-long education, community beautification, and support for the township library.
Fields of interest: Historic preservation/historical societies; Arts; Education, continuing education; Libraries (public); Education; Environment, beautification programs; Recreation; Community/economic development.
Limitations: Giving limited to Shelby Township, MI.
Publications: Annual report; Informational brochure; Newsletter.
Application information:
Board meeting date(s): 4th Thurs. of each month
Officers and Directors: * Nancy Bates,* Chair.; Theresa Toia,* Vice-Chair.; Thomas J. Dearlove,* Secy.; Linda Stout,* Treas.; James R. Andary; Linda Colton; Angela Freeman; Alan Meitzner; Kathleen Morehouse; Robert E. Pechur; Robert Savo; Bud Uhl; Kathleen Vallis; Rick Young.
EIN: 383341102

1168
Shiawassee Community Foundation
(formerly Shiawassee Foundation)
1350 E. Main St., Ste. 206
Owosso, MI 48867 (989) 725-1093
County: Shiawassee
FAX: (989) 729-1358;
E-mail: info@shiawasseefoundation.org;
URL: http://www.shiawasseefoundation.org

Established in 1974 in MI.
Donor: John Northway.
Grantmaker type: Community foundation.
Financial data (yr. ended 09/30/09): Assets, $4,092,502 (M); gifts received, $63,487; expenditures, $110,123; total giving, $28,824; giving activities include $9,474 for grants, and $19,350 for 38 grants to individuals.
Purpose and activities: The mission of the foundation is to enrich the quality of life in Shiawassee County by building permanently endowed funds from a wide range of donors to fund emerging community needs.
Fields of interest: Arts; Higher education; Education; Environment; Health care; Human services; Community/economic development.
Type of support: Continuing support; Endowments; Program development; Conferences/seminars; Curriculum development; Scholarship funds.
Limitations: Applications accepted. Giving limited to Shiawassee County, MI. No support for religious programs serving specific religious denominations. No grants to individuals (except for designated funds), or for routine operating expenses or expenses for established programs, fundraising drives, capital equipment, computers, video equipment, or vehicles, conference attendance, speakers, salaries, or projects that are primarily cause-related.
Publications: Annual report; Newsletter.
Application information: Upon review of letter of intent, organizations meeting the foundation's funding and priority guidelines will be invited to submit a full grant application. Application form required.
Initial approach: Telephone
Copies of proposal: 2
Deadline(s): Feb. 28 for letter of intent; Mar. 30 for full grant application

Board meeting date(s): Varies
Final notification: Annually, prior to Sept.
Officers and Trustees: * Dr. Mark E. Miller,* Chair. and Pres.; Jacqueline Flynn,* V.P.; Catherine Stevenson,* Secy.; Vearn Wenzlick,* Treas.; Carol Soule, Exec. Dir.; Richard A. Batchelor; Ann Marie Bentley; Kevin Davis; Adam Dingens; Richard Dunham; Glen Merkel; Patrick Wegman II; Barbara Williamson.
EIN: 383285624

1169
South Haven Community Foundation
228 Broadway
South Haven, MI 49090-1472 (269) 639-1631
County: Van Buren
URL: http://www.kalfound.org/page20372.cfm

Established in MI a geographic affiliate of Kalamazoo Community Foundation.
Grantmaker type: Community foundation.
Purpose and activities: The foundation makes grants to help improve the quality of life in the greater South Haven, Michigan, area.
Fields of interest: Performing arts; Elementary/secondary education; Housing/shelter; Youth development; Community/economic development.
Type of support: Equipment; Program development; Scholarship funds.
Limitations: Applications accepted. Giving limited to the greater South Haven, MI, area. No support for organizations lacking 501(c)(3) status.
Application information: Grant awards are made quarterly.
Advisory Board: Dick Averill; Bruce Barker; Tyler Dotson; Gwen DeBruyn; Dorann Fleming; Ann Habicht; Don Hixson; Jim Marcoux; Glenn Pientenpol; Bill Rockhold; Gordon D. Smith; Pamela Utke; Janice Varney; Karen Willming.
EIN: 203841038

1170
Southeast Ottawa Community Foundation
(formerly Hudsonville Community Fund)
c/o Grand Rapids Community Foundation
161 Ottawa Ave. N.W., Ste. 209-C
Grand Rapids, MI 49503-2757
County: Kent
Contact: Kate Luckert Schmid, Prog. Dir.
Tel.: (616) 454-1751, ext. 117;
E-mail: kluckert@grfoundation.org; URL: http://www.grfoundation.org/seottawa

Established in 1990 in MI; an affiliate of Grand Rapids Community Foundation.
Grantmaker type: Community foundation.
Purpose and activities: The foundation gives priority to projects that address the areas of art and culture, community development, education, environment, health, or social needs.
Fields of interest: Arts; Education; Environment; Health care; Human services; Community/economic development.
Limitations: Applications accepted. Giving limited to Georgetown Township, Hudsonville, and Jamestown Township, MI. No support for religious organizations for religious purposes, or organizations lacking 501(c)(3) status. No grants to individuals, or for annual fundraising drives, endowments or debt reduction, capital projects without site control, medical research, ongoing operating expenses of

established institutions, sabbatical leaves, scholarly research, travel, tours or trips, underwriting of conferences, films, videos or television projects, or venture capital for competitive profit-making activities.
Application information: Accepts CMF Common Grant Application Form. See foundation web site for full guidelines and requirements. Application form required.
Initial approach: Online application
Final notification: 2 months

1171
Southfield Community Foundation
25630 Evergreen Rd.
Southfield, MI 48075-1769 (248) 796-4190
County: Oakland
Contact: Raquel Robinson, Exec. Dir.
FAX: (248) 796-4195; E-mail: info@scfmi.org;
URL: http://www.scfmi.org

Established in 1989 in MI.
Grantmaker type: Community foundation.
Financial data (yr. ended 06/30/09): Assets, $1,594,523 (M); gifts received, $297,070; expenditures, $1,097,572; total giving, $895,760; giving activities include $895,760 for grants.
Purpose and activities: The foundation seeks to connect people who care with causes that matter in the local community. The foundation focuses on systematic change, enabling philanthropy and empowering collaborative efforts.
Fields of interest: Arts, cultural/ethnic awareness; Arts; Education, public education; Higher education; Education; Youth development; Civil rights, race/intergroup relations; Community/economic development; Aging.
Type of support: Emergency funds; Program development; Seed money; Curriculum development; Scholarships—to individuals.
Limitations: Applications accepted. Giving limited to the Southfield and Lathrup Village, MI, area. No support for sectarian or religious purposes or programs/projects that duplicate existing services. No grants to individuals (except for scholarships), or for endowments, debt reduction, or operational, maintenance, or ongoing program expenses, fundraising events, or advertising.
Publications: Financial statement; Grants list.
Application information: Accepts CMF Common Grant Application Form. Applicants are encouraged to call the foundation to review the scope and appropriateness of their proposals before submitting a formal application. Visit foundation web site for application guidelines. Application form not required.
Initial approach: Telephone
Copies of proposal: 1
Deadline(s): None
Board meeting date(s): Approximately 6 times annually
Final notification: Varies
Officers and Directors: * Grenae Dudley,* Chair.; Angela Patrick Wynn,* Vice-Chair.; Suzanne Dibble,* Secy.; William Steffan,* Treas.; Raquel Robinson, Exec. Dir.; Mark Adams; Tonya Allen; Chardae Caine; Caroline Chambers; Matthew E. Chope; Wanda Cook-Robinson; Tracey L. Ewing; Scott Griffin; Donald J. Gross; Linda L. Height; Shirley A. Kaigler; Stephen R. Kemp; Karen Miller; Jeffrey Mueller; Wayne Peal; Eddie G. Powers, Jr.; James Ralph, Jr.; Angela Rankin-Yohannes; Rhonda

C. Saunders; James Scharret; Cherryl R. Thames; Mike D. Waring; William Winbush.
Number of staff: 1 full-time professional; 1 part-time professional.
EIN: 382918048

1172
Sparta Community Foundation
c/o Grand Rapids Community Foundation
161 Ottawa Ave., N.W., Ste. 209-C
Grand Rapids, MI   49503-2721
County: Kent
Contact: Bill Dani
Tel.: (616) 752-2197 (for Bill Dani); URL: http://www.grfoundation.org/sparta

Established in 1996 in MI as a regional affiliate of Grand Rapids Community Foundation.
Grantmaker type: Community foundation.
Purpose and activities: The foundation gives priority to projects that address the areas of art and culture, community development, education, environment, health, or social needs.
Fields of interest: Arts; Education; Health care; Human services; Community/economic development.
Type of support: Equipment; Seed money; Building/renovation; Capital campaigns.
Limitations: Applications accepted. Giving limited to the greater Sparta, MI, area. No support for religious organizations for religious purposes, or organizations lacking 501(c)(3) status. No grants to individuals, or for annual fundraising drives, endowments or debt reduction, capital projects without site control, medical research, ongoing operating expenses of established institutions, sabbatical leaves, scholarly research, travel, tours or trips, underwriting of conferences, films, videos or television projects, or venture capital for competitive profit-making activities.
Application information: See foundation web site for information on RFP process. Application form not required.
Initial approach: Submit application online
Final notification: 2 months
Number of staff: None.

1173
Sterling Heights Community Foundation
P.O. Box 7023
Sterling Heights, MI   48311-7023
County: Macomb

Established in 1991 in MI.
Grantmaker type: Community foundation.
Financial data (yr. ended 12/31/08): Assets, $335,608 (M); gifts received, $37,683; expenditures, $154,875; total giving, $47,074; giving activities include $22,574 for grants, and $24,500 for grants to individuals.
Purpose and activities: The goals of the foundation are to: 1) initiate and coordinate functions and activities within Sterling Heights, MI to enhance the quality of life of its citizens; 2) award grants and/or support projects that are in accordance with the foundation's purpose; 3) acquire, improve and preserve historical areas, public facilities, and parks and recreational areas of Sterling Heights; 4) offer tax benefits to the foundation's contributors; and 5) develop civic leadership and initiate civic action.
Fields of interest: Arts; Education; Recreation.

Type of support: Scholarships—to individuals.
Limitations: Applications accepted. Giving primarily in Sterling Heights, MI.
Application information: Visit foundation Web site for scholarship application information.
Initial approach: Contact foundation
Deadline(s): Nov. 17 for scholarships
Officers and Board Members: Karl G. Oskoian, Pres.; Dr. Martin Brown,* V.P.; Michael Lazzara, Treas.; Ken Lampar, Exec. Dir.; Frank E. Henke, Legal Counsel; Lil Adams; John Bozymowski; Larry Calcaterra; Doug Dinning; Wallace Doebler; Mark Hurst; Michael McCurry; Steven Pomaville.
EIN: 383004613

1174
Straits Area Community Foundation
c/o Community Foundation for Northeast Michigan
P.O. Box 495
Alpena, MI   49707-0495   (877) 354-6881
County: Alpena
Contact: Christine Hitch
FAX: (989) 356-3319; E-mail: chitch@cfnem.org; URL: http://www.sacf.net/

Established in 1998 in MI as an affiliate of the Community Foundation for Northeast Michigan.
Grantmaker type: Community foundation.
Purpose and activities: The foundation seeks to serve Cheboygan County and Mackinaw City and to preserve the charitable goals of a wide range of donors now and for generations to come by supporting 501(c)(3) organizations, schools, churches for non-religious purposes, and government agencies.
Type of support: Management development/capacity building; Building/renovation; Equipment; Program development; Conferences/seminars; Film/video/radio; Publication; Seed money; Curriculum development; Technical assistance; Scholarships—to individuals.
Limitations: Applications accepted. Giving limited to Cheboygan County or Mackinaw City, MI. No support for political campaigns or programs with religious overtones. No grants to individuals (except for scholarships), or routine operating needs or budget deficits.
Publications: Application guidelines; Annual report; Financial statement; Grants list; Informational brochure; Newsletter.
Application information: See foundation Web site for Common Grant Application Form and requirements. Application form required.
Copies of proposal: 1
Deadline(s): Jan. 15 for Common Grants; Oct. 1, Jan. 1, and Apr. 1 for Youth Advisory Council
Board meeting date(s): Every 2nd Wed. of Feb., May, Aug., and Nov.
Final notification: Within 6 weeks of the grant deadlines
Officers and Trustees:* Katie Darrow,* Pres.; Dean Scheerens,* V.P.; Judy Bennett; Judy Churchill; Joann Leal; Jennifer Lee; Marilyn McFarland; Alex McVey; Joan Pepper; Kathy Scoon; Krista Siler; Lawton Smith; Debra Turnbull; Janet Weiss.
Selected grants: The following grants were reported in 2009.
$2,500 to Mackinaw City Public Schools, Mackinaw City, MI. For Project Close Up.
$1,200 to Cross of Christ Compassionate Ministries, Cheboygan, MI. For Back to School giveaway event.

$852 to Mackinaw Area Historical Society, Mackinaw City, MI. For Booklet Diary of Mary Anderson.
$396 to American Red Cross, Northern Lower Michigan Chapter, Petoskey, MI. For smoke detector distribution and battery replacement.
$300 to Wolverine Community Schools, Wolverine, MI. For Wolverine Varsity baseball equipment.

1175
Sturgis Area Community Foundation
(formerly Sturgis Foundation)
310 N. Franks Ave.
Sturgis, MI   49091-1259
County: St. Joseph
FAX: (269) 659-4539;
E-mail: sacf@sturgisfoundation.org; URL: http://www.sturgisfoundation.org

Established in 1962 in MI.
Grantmaker type: Community foundation.
Financial data (yr. ended 03/31/10): Assets, $19,402,490 (M); gifts received, $639,065; expenditures, $510,419; total giving, $332,424; giving activities include $287,182 for 8+ grants (high: $135,482), and $45,242 for 63 grants to individuals.
Purpose and activities: The foundation seeks to provide benefits to area community charitable organizations.
Fields of interest: Arts; Education; Animals/wildlife; Health care; Recreation; Human services; Community/economic development; Children/youth; Children; Youth; Disabilities, people with; Mentally disabled; Women; Substance abusers; Crime/abuse victims; Economically disadvantaged; Homeless.
Type of support: General/operating support; Capital campaigns; Building/renovation; Equipment; Endowments; Program development; Scholarship funds; Consulting services; Scholarships—to individuals; Matching/challenge support; Student loans—to individuals.
Limitations: Applications accepted. Giving limited to the Sturgis, MI, area. No support for religious organizations. No grants to individuals (except for scholarships), or for existing obligations or debts, or new business loans.
Publications: Application guidelines; Annual report; Financial statement; Grants list; Informational brochure; Informational brochure (including application guidelines).
Application information: Visit foundation Web site application form and guidelines. Application form required.
Initial approach: Contact foundation
Copies of proposal: 10
Deadline(s): May 1 and Nov. 1
Board meeting date(s): Monthly
Final notification: June 30 and Dec. 31
Officers and Trustees:* Tom Kool,* Chair.; Sheila Riley,* Secy.-Treas.; Mary Dresser, Co-Dir.; John Wiedlea, Co-Dir.; Laura Brothers; LeeAnn McConnell; Kelly Murphy; Ruth Perry; John Svendsen; Philip Ward.
Number of staff: 1 full-time professional; 1 part-time support.
EIN: 383649922

1176
Three Rivers Area Community Foundation
(formerly Three Rivers Community Foundation)
P.O. Box 453
Three Rivers, MI 49093-0453 (269) 279-7402
County: St. Joseph
Contact: Melissa J. Bliss, Admin.

Established in 1974 in MI.
Grantmaker type: Community foundation.
Financial data (yr. ended 12/31/08): Assets, $1,333,187 (M); gifts received, $117,321; expenditures, $53,803; total giving, $17,601; giving activities include $5,601 for grants, and $12,000 for 11 grants to individuals.
Purpose and activities: The Three Rivers Area Community Foundation, serving three rivers and surrounding townships, is dedicated to the growth and stewardship of donor funds, while improving the quality of life in the community through pro-active problem solving, partnerships with others of similar goals, and responsible grantmaking.
Fields of interest: Performing arts, theater; Performing arts, music; Historic preservation/historical societies; Arts; Libraries/library science; Scholarships/financial aid; Education; Hospitals (general); Health care; Health organizations; Crime/violence prevention, domestic violence; Housing/shelter, development; Recreation; Family services; Residential/custodial care, hospices; Community/economic development.
Type of support: Capital campaigns; Building/renovation; Equipment; Seed money; Scholarship funds; Scholarships—to individuals.
Limitations: Applications accepted. Giving limited to the city of Three Rivers and surrounding townships in MI. No support for religious purposes, or special interest groups that appeal only to a narrow band of citizens. No grants to individuals (except for scholarships), or for profit ventures.
Publications: Annual report; Informational brochure.
Application information: Application form required.
  Initial approach: Letter or telephone
  Copies of proposal: 8
  Deadline(s): Apr. 1 and Oct. 1
  Board meeting date(s): Feb., May, Aug., and Nov.
  Final notification: After board meeting
Officers and Trustees:* James Stuck,* Pres.; Daryl Tolbert, V.P.; Carl Howe,* Secy.; Joe Bippus,* Treas.; Carolyn Roberts, Exec. Dir.; Sally Carpenter; John Carton; Chad Corte; Jeff Gatton; Phil Hoffine; Julie Howe; Thomas Meyer; David T. Stuck.
EIN: 382051672
Selected grants: The following grants were reported in 2005.
$6,300 to Keystone Place, Centreville, MI. For furnace.
$5,000 to Three Rivers Area Mentoring, Three Rivers, MI. For mentoring program elementary students.
$3,500 to Silliman House Museum. For building restoration.
$3,000 to Domestic Assault Shelter Coalition, Three Rivers, MI. For operating support.
$2,500 to Carnegie Center Council for the Arts, Three Rivers, MI. For equipment.
$2,450 to Three Rivers, City of, Three Rivers, MI. For nature programs in park.
$2,000 to Fontana Chamber Arts, Kalamazoo, MI. For concerts.
$2,000 to Glen Oaks Community College, Centreville, MI. For program support.
$2,000 to Kalamazoo Symphony Society, Kalamazoo, MI. For concert.

$2,000 to Three Rivers, City of, Three Rivers, MI. For harmony fest.

1177
Tuscola County Community Foundation
P.O. Box 534
Caro, MI 48723-0534 (989) 673-8223
County: Tuscola
Contact: Ken Micklash, Exec. Dir.
FAX: (989) 673-8223; E-mail: tccf534@yahoo.com; URL: http://www.tuscolacountycommunityfoundation.org

Established in 1997 in MI.
Grantmaker type: Community foundation.
Financial data (yr. ended 12/31/08): Assets, $4,187,034 (M); gifts received, $1,046,628; expenditures, $298,978; total giving, $176,915; giving activities include $145,140 for grants, and $31,775 for 19 grants to individuals (high: $2,000; low: $250).
Purpose and activities: The foundation provides support in the areas of human services, recreation, education, youth, and seniors.
Fields of interest: Education; Recreation; Youth development; Human services; Children/youth; Children; Youth; Adults; Aging; Substance abusers; Economically disadvantaged; Homeless.
Type of support: Building/renovation; Equipment; Emergency funds; Program development; Seed money; Curriculum development; Scholarship funds; Matching/challenge support.
Limitations: Applications accepted. Giving limited to Tuscola County, MI. No support for sectarian religious programs. No grants for operating budgets, previously incurred debt, endowment campaigns, or fundraising activities.
Publications: Application guidelines; Annual report; Financial statement; Grants list; Informational brochure; Newsletter.
Application information: Visit foundation Web site for application form and guidelines. Application form required.
  Initial approach: Letter or telephone
  Copies of proposal: 6
  Deadline(s): Feb. 1 and Oct. 1
  Board meeting date(s): 4th Thurs., quarterly
  Final notification: 3 months
Officers and Board Members:* Rick Zimmer,* Pres.; Randy Stec,* V.P.; Dorothy Scollon,* Secy.; Sherri Diegel,* Treas.; Ken Micklash,* Exec. Dir.; Kurt Bender; Gary Crews; Pat Curtis; Sara Dost; Gary Haas; Larry Kroswek; Sue Ransford; Dorothy Scollon; Janet Thane; Ben Varney; Jill White; Dale Wingert.
Number of staff: 1 part-time professional.
EIN: 383351315
Selected grants: The following grants were reported in 2007.
$10,000 to Good Samaritan Fund, Caro, MI. For food, utilities, fuel and housing assistance to needy families.
$10,000 to Habitat for Humanity, Cass River, Caro, MI. Toward constructing home for needy family.
$6,500 to Big Brothers Big Sisters. For building energy and safety improvements.
$5,000 to American Red Cross. For purchase of car seats for low-income families.
$5,000 to Caro Community Schools, High School Photography Program, Caro, MI. For new computer and software for department.

$5,000 to Michigan State University Extension-Tuscola County, Caro, MI. For Green Thumb Master Gardeners, renovating Secret Gardens project.
$4,600 to Thumb Area Center for the Arts, Caro, MI. Toward purchase of new sound equipment.
$4,000 to Tuscola County Sheriff Department, Caro, MI. For purchase of software to verify speeds, witness statements related to crashes.
$3,150 to Almer Township Parks and Recreation, MI. For park climbing wall.
$3,000 to Caro Community Schools, High School Band, Caro, MI. For purchase of 80 music stands and 3 carts.
$1,000 to Columbia Township Library, Unionville, MI. For new copy machine.

1178
The White Pigeon Area Community Foundation
c/o Sturgis Area Community Foundation
310 N. Franks Ave.
Sturgis, MI 49091-1259
County: St. Joseph
URL: http://www.sturgisfoundation.org/affiliate_whitepigeon.php

Established in 2000 in MI; an affiliate of Sturgis Area Community Foundation.
Grantmaker type: Community foundation.
Purpose and activities: Areas of priority include the improvement of living and working conditions for the citizens of the White Pigeon area; youth and recreation; public, educational, charitable or benevolent purposes; and care of the sick or aged.
Fields of interest: Education; Health care; Recreation; Youth development; Human services; Aging, centers/services; Community/economic development.
Type of support: Program development; Seed money.
Limitations: Applications accepted. Giving limited to the White Pigeon, MI, area. No support for organizations lacking 501(c)(3) status or for religious programs that appear to serve a specific religious denomination. No grants to individuals, or for fundraising events or existing obligations or debts.
Application information: See foundation web site for full application guidelines and requirements. Application form required.
  Copies of proposal: 8
Officer: Susan Cline, Advisory Board Chair.
Directors: Mary Dresser; John Wiedlea.

1179
Wyoming Community Foundation
c/o Grand Rapids Community Foundation
161 Ottawa Ave. N.W., Ste. 209-C
Grand Rapids, MI 49503-2721
County: Kent
Contact: Kate Luckert Schmid, Prog. Dir.
Tel.: (616) 454-1751, ext. 117;
E-mail: kluckert@grfoundation.org; URL: http://www.grfoundation.org/wyoming

Established in 1992 in MI as an affiliate of the Grand Rapids Community Foundation.
Grantmaker type: Community foundation.
Purpose and activities: The foundation gives priority to projects that address the areas of art and culture,

community development, education, environment, health, or social needs.

Fields of interest: Arts; Education; Environment; Health care; Human services; Community/economic development.

Type of support: Seed money; Equipment; Building/renovation; Capital campaigns.

Limitations: Applications accepted. Giving limited to the Wyoming, MI, area. No support for religious organizations for religious purposes, or for organizations lacking 501(c)(3) status. No grants to individuals, or for annual fundraising drives, endowments or debt reduction, capital projects without site control, medical research, ongoing operating expenses of established institutions, sabbatical leaves, scholarly research, travel, tours or trips, underwriting of conferences, films, videos or television projects, or venture capital for competitive profit-making activities.

Publications: Application guidelines; Informational brochure.

Application information: See foundation Web site for RFP information. Application form required.

Initial approach: Submit application online
Final notification: 2 months
Number of staff: None.

1180
Ypsilanti Area Community Fund
c/o Ann Arbor Area Community Foundation
301 N. Main St., Ste. 300
Ann Arbor, MI   48104-2113   (734) 663-0401
County: Washtenaw
Contact: Martha Bloom, AAACF V.P.
FAX: (734) 663-3514; E-mail: info@aaacf.org;
E-mail: mbloom@aaacf.org; URL: http://aaacf.org/yacf.asp

Established in 2001 in MI as a regional affiliate fund of the Ann Arbor Area Community Foundation.
Grantmaker type: Community foundation.
Purpose and activities: The fund is a geographic affiliate fund of the Ann Arbor Area Community Foundation to serve residents of the Ypsilanti area.

The fund is a permanent endowment established to support programs, events and projects in the greater Ypsilanti area.

Fields of interest: Community/economic development.

Type of support: Student loans—to individuals; Research; Publication; Program development; Matching/challenge support; Management development/capacity building; Income development; Emergency funds; Conferences/seminars.

Limitations: Applications accepted. Giving limited to the greater Ypsilanti, MI, area.

Publications: Annual report; Grants list; Newsletter.

Application information:

Deadline(s): Oct. 1 for letter of intent
Final notification: Dec.

Advisory Committee: Richard Robb, Chair.; Dr. Daniel Cox; Larry Doe; Marcia Harrison; Tom Harrison; Derrick Jackson; Diane Keller; Patricia Horne McGee; James Nelson; Peter Rinehart; Naz Sesi; Pat Tamblyn; Larry Whitworth; Laura Wilbanks.

PUBLIC CHARITIES

1181
ACI Foundation
(also known as American Concrete Institute Foundation)
(formerly Concrete Research & Education Foundation)
38800 Country Club Dr.
Farmington Hills, MI 48331-3439
County: Oakland
E-mail: scholarships@concrete.org; URL: http://www.concrete.org/ABOUT/AB_awards.HTM

Supporting organization of American Concrete Institute.
Grantmaker type: Public charity.
Financial data (yr. ended 12/31/09): Revenue, $404,947; assets, $4,439,440 (M); gifts received, $298,312; expenditures, $423,250; total giving, $119,500; giving activities include $50,000 for grants, and $69,500 for grants to individuals.
Purpose and activities: The foundation supports educational, research, scientific, and charitable purposes; building knowledge for improvements in concrete design and construction.
Fields of interest: Higher education; Engineering school/education; Business/industry.
Type of support: Fellowships; Scholarship funds; Research; Scholarships—to individuals.
Limitations: Applications accepted. Giving on a national basis.
Application information: Only students nominated by faculty members who are also ACI members will be eligible to receive applications for the ACI Student Fellowship Program. After a student is formally nominated, the foundation will convey an official application directly to the nominated student. Application form required.
Officers: Claude Bedard,* Chair.; Debrethann R. Orsak,* Vice-Chair.; William R. Tolley,* Pres.; Florian G. Barth,* V.P.; Luis E. Garcia,* V.P.; Donna G. Halstead,* Treas.
EIN: 382986800

1182
African American Endowment Fund
c/o Ann Arbor Area Community Foundation
301 North Main St., Ste. 300
Ann Arbor, MI 48104 (734) 663-0401
County: Washtenaw
Contact: Neel Hajra, C.OO. and V.P., Community Invest.
E-mail: nhajra@aaacf.org; URL: http://www.aaacf.org/about-aaacf/our-funds/aaacf-field-interest-funds/african-american-endowment-fund

Established in 1993 in MI; Component Fund of the Ann Arbor Area Community Foundation.
Grantmaker type: Public charity.
Financial data (yr. ended 12/31/10): Total giving, $3,000 Giving activities include $3,000 for 1 grant.
Purpose and activities: The fund aims to improve the physical, economic, social and educational conditions that affect the quality of life for African Americans in the Ann Arbor area.

Fields of interest: Community/economic development; African Americans/Blacks.
Limitations: Applications accepted. Giving primarily in Ann Arbor, MN.
Application information:
Initial approach: Contact foundation prior to submitting online application
Deadline(s): Oct. 5
Officer: Neel Hajra, C.O.O. and V.P. for Community Investment.

1183
Albion-Homer United Way
203 S. Superior St.
P.O. Box 55
Albion, MI 49224-0055
County: Calhoun
Contact: John Ropp, Exec. Dir.
Tel./FAX: (517) 629-2645; URL: http://www.albionhomerunitedway.org/

Established in 1947 as the Community Chest; became a United Way affiliate in 1987.
Grantmaker type: Public charity.
Financial data (yr. ended 06/30/09): Revenue, $192,564; assets, $168,528 (M); gifts received, $191,363; expenditures, $176,732; total giving, $90,402; giving activities include $90,402 for grants.
Purpose and activities: The organization seeks to increase the organized capacity of people to care for one another by uniting together to improve lives.
Fields of interest: Education; Health care; Employment; Family services; Community/economic development.
Type of support: Annual campaigns; Emergency funds; In-kind gifts.
Limitations: Applications accepted. Giving limited to the Albion and Homer area, MI. No support for health services or human services organizations.
Publications: Application guidelines; Annual report; Financial statement; Grants list; Informational brochure; Occasional report; Program policy statement.
Application information: Application form not required.
Initial approach: Cover letter with grant application
Copies of proposal: 12
Deadline(s): Jan. 15
Board meeting date(s): 3rd Monday
Final notification: 2 weeks
Officers and Directors: Melissa Hoath,* Pres.; Martin P. Blashfield,* V.P.; Scott Stephen,* Secy.; Barbara Frederick,* Treas.; John Ropp, Exec. Dir.; Andrew Dobbins; M. Sue Klepper; Walter Nichols; Paul Phelan; Eusebio Solis, Jr.; Pauline Story.
Number of staff: 1 full-time professional.
EIN: 381841180

1184
Allegan County United Way
650 Grand St.
Allegan, MI 49010-9060 (269) 673-6545
County: Allegan
FAX: (269) 686-5912; E-mail: info@acuw.org; URL: http://www.acuw.org

Established in MI.
Grantmaker type: Public charity.
Financial data (yr. ended 06/30/10): Revenue, $895,951; assets, $1,241,351 (M); gifts received, $829,530; expenditures, $781,208; total giving, $506,212; giving activities include $506,212 for grants.
Purpose and activities: The organization seeks to increase the impact of people's caring in Allegan County and further those efforts by connecting and supporting volunteers and groups for the betterment of the community.
Fields of interest: Community/economic development.
Type of support: In-kind gifts.
Limitations: Giving primarily in Allegan County, MI.
Application information:
Board meeting date(s): 3rd Wed. of each month
Officers and Directors: * Cathy Burton-Snell,* Pres.; John Mellein,* V.P.; Barb Boot,* Secy.; Rebecca Lamper,* Treas.; Heather Boswell; Robert Carlson; Timothy Dickinson, M.D.; Larry Johnson; Brian Kilbane; Larry Nameche.
Number of staff: 2 full-time professional; 1 full-time support.
EIN: 386063214

1185
Alternatives for Children and Families, Inc.
2065 S. Center Rd.
P.O. Box 190238
Burton, MI 48519-0238 (810) 250-3800
County: Genesee
FAX: (810) 250-3836; E-mail: info@acfinc.org; URL: http://www.acfinc.org/

Established in 1988 in MI.
Grantmaker type: Public charity.
Financial data (yr. ended 12/31/09): Revenue, $4,124,722; assets, $2,430,193 (M); gifts received, $20,453; expenditures, $3,750,054; total giving, $1,332,157; giving activities include $1,332,157 for grants to individuals.
Purpose and activities: The organization works to provide a safe, nurturing, and therapeutic environment for children who require out-of-home placement; and to help their parents gain the necessary skills to parent effectively when the children are returned home.
Fields of interest: Children/youth, services; Children, foster care.
Officers and Directors: * Robert Wesley,* Chair.; Patrick Hughes,* Vice-Chair.; Ywania Richardson, C.E.O.; Larry Sutter, C.O.O.; Grover Croom,* Secy.; Tina Fielder-Gibson,* Treas.; Deena Christensen,* C.F.O.; Elonzo Duncan; Patricia Henkel-Primozic;

Manual Holcolm; Gloria Quinney; Randy Veenhuis; Don Wiggins; Tracy L. Wilmont.
EIN: 382785946

1186
American Dysautonomia Institute
2135 Oakbrook Blvd.
Commerce Township, MI   48390-3272
(248) 470-3992
County: Oakland
Contact: Gilbert M. Chinitz J.D., M.L.I.S, Grant/Fdn. Librarian
FAX: (248) 438-6108; E-mail: staff@adiwebsite.org;
Additional addresses: California office: 3544 28th St.,, San Diego, CA 92104, Florida office: 2760 Night Hawk Ct., Longwood, FL 32779, Illinois office: 1411 W. Ohio St., No. 1R, Chicago, IL 60622, South Carolina office: 1578 Dowden Ct., Charleston, SC 29407; URL: http://www.adiwebsite.org/index2.html

Established in 2004 in MI.
Donors: Michael and Elaine Serling Philanthropic Fund; Wal-Mart Stores, Inc.; Macomb County, MI, Staff Charitable Contribution Program.
Grantmaker type: Public charity.
Financial data (yr. ended 12/31/08): Revenue, $32,314; assets, $46,309 (M); gifts received, $31,294; expenditures, $8,005; total giving, $2,421; program services expenses, $7,685; giving activities include $2,421 for grants.
Purpose and activities: The institute funds non-familial dysautonomia research, a disease of the autonomic nervous system. The institute also advocates for increased research funding and disease awareness.
Fields of interest: Health care, public policy; Medicine/medical care, public education; Medical research.
Type of support: Research.
Limitations: Applications accepted. Giving on a national basis.
Publications: Informational brochure; Newsletter.
Application information: Applicant institution must be headed by a medical doctor, osteopathic physician, or an individual with an with an appropriately related earned Ph.D., and must have a track record of research regarding or treatment of non-familial dysautonomia. Application form not required.
  Initial approach: Letter
  Copies of proposal: 3
  Deadline(s): None
  Board meeting date(s): Dec.
  Final notification: 90 days
Officers and Trustees:* Jon Stern,* Pres.; Shirlee Berman,* V.P.; Steven Siman,* Secy.-Treas.; J.A. Chinitz, Emeritus.
Number of staff: 1 part-time professional.
EIN: 320129358

1187
American Federation of Muslims of Indian Origin
29008 W. 8-Mile Rd.
Farmington, MI   48336-5910   (248) 442-2364
County: Oakland
URL: http://www.afmi.org

Established in 1989.
Grantmaker type: Public charity.

Financial data (yr. ended 06/30/09): Revenue, $559,340; assets, $408,897 (M); gifts received, $577,025; expenditures, $1,134,775; total giving, $1,047,238; program services expenses, $1,072,979; giving activities include $25,741 for foundation-administered programs.
Purpose and activities: The federation works to improve the socio-economic status of underprivileged Indian Muslim minorities through education.
Fields of interest: Education; Minorities.
Officers and Trustees:* Shaukat Khan,* Pres.; Ayub Khan,* Secy.; Dr. Iqbal Ahmed,* Treas.; Dr. Aslam Abdullah; Dr. A.S. Nakadar; Ali Quraishi; Dr. Syed Samee.
EIN: 382959299

1188
American Indian College Fund
8333 Greenwood Blvd.
Denver, CO   80221-4488   (303) 426-8900
County: Adams
FAX: (303) 426-1200; E-mail: info@collegefund.org;
Toll-free tel.: (800) 776-3863; URL: http://www.collegefund.org

Founded in 1989.
Grantmaker type: Public charity.
Financial data (yr. ended 06/30/10): Revenue, $17,594,300; assets, $58,232,043 (M); gifts received, $13,230,694; expenditures, $15,575,974; total giving, $9,080,896; giving activities include $9,080,896 for grants.
Purpose and activities: The fund's mission is to raise scholarship funds for American Indian students at qualified tribal colleges and universities and to generate broad awareness of those institutions and the fund itself; the organization also raises money and resources for other needs at the schools, including capital projects, operations, endowments or program initiatives.
Fields of interest: Higher education; Native Americans/American Indians.
Type of support: Scholarship funds.
Limitations: Giving limited to AK, AZ, KS, MI, MN, MT, ND, NE, NM, SD, WA, and WI.
Officers and Trustees:* Dr. Cynthia Linquist Mala,* Chair.; Dr. Richard Littlebear, Ph.D.*, Vice-Chair.; Steve Denson; Dr. Verna Fowler; David M. Gipp; Barbara Gohr; Daniel Gutstein; Brian C. McK. Henderson; David Kennedy; Dr. Joseph McDonald; Michael Oltrogge; and 6 additional trustees.
EIN: 521573446

1189
American Ramallah Federation Educational and Charitable Fund
27484 Ann Arbor Trail
Westland, MI   48185-5515   (734) 425-1600
County: Wayne
Contact: Roy Watts
FAX: (734) 425-3985; URL: http://www.afrp.org/funds/endowmentfund/
E-mail address for essay contest: essaycontest@afrp.org

Grantmaker type: Public charity.
Financial data (yr. ended 05/31/10): Revenue, $537,792; assets, $2,296,350 (M); gifts received, $175,454; expenditures, $142,744.

Purpose and activities: The fund fosters cooperation in the Ramallah community to perpetuate and enhance closer ties to Ramallah people and to enhance appreciation of the culture and history of the Ramallah community.
Fields of interest: Arts, cultural/ethnic awareness.
Application information: Application form required.
  Deadline(s): May 31
Officers and Directors:* David Batch,* Pres.; Terry Ahwal-Morris,* Secy.; Hanna Faris,* Treas.; Salem Abdelnour; Karim Ajloni; Sonya Kassis; George N. Khoury; Michael Mufarreh; Hala Taweel.
EIN: 386096449

1190
Ann Arbor Film Festival
308 1/2 S. State St., Ste. 31
Ann Arbor, MI   48104-2432   (734) 995-5356
County: Washtenaw
Contact: Donald Harrison, Exec. Dir.
FAX: (734) 995-5396; E-mail: info@aafilmfest.org;
Application address: P.O. Box 8232, Ann Arbor, MI 48107-8232; URL: http://aafilmfest.org

Established in 1963 in MI.
Grantmaker type: Public charity.
Financial data (yr. ended 05/31/09): Revenue, $299,997; assets, $57,385 (M); gifts received, $125,868; expenditures, $304,384.
Purpose and activities: The mission works to support bold, visionary filmmakers, advance the art form of film, and engage communities with remarkable cinematic experiences; and seeks to encourage (through awards and prizes) the work of the independent and experimental filmmaker, promote the concept of film as art, and organize and present an annual film festival of 16mm independent and experimental film.
Fields of interest: Media, film/video.
Type of support: Grants to individuals.
Limitations: Applications accepted. Giving limited to Ann Arbor, MI.
Publications: Informational brochure (including application guidelines); Newsletter.
Application information: An entry form must be completed for each film entered, accompanied by a submission fee ranging from $30 to $50 for each film. Application form required.
  Initial approach: Letter or telephone for guidelines
  Deadline(s): Entry for the festival takes place from July 1 to Nov. 1
  Final notification: All filmmakers are notified of selection for the festival by Mar. 1
Officers: Jay Nelson, Pres.; Heidi Kumao, Secy.; Myrna Rugg, Treas.; Donald Harrison, Exec. Dir.
Trustees: Steve Bergman; Tom Bray; Tara McComb; Edward McDonald; Bryan Rogers; Joe Tiboni.
Number of staff: 3
EIN: 382379836

1191
Applebaum Family Support Foundation
P.O. Box 2030
6735 Telegraph Rd.
Bloomfield Hills, MI   48303-2030
County: Oakland

Established in 1989; supporting organization of Jewish Federation of Metropolitan Detroit.
Grantmaker type: Public charity.

Financial data (yr. ended 05/31/10): Expenditures, $17,914.

Fields of interest: Arts; Higher education; Medical research; Jewish federated giving programs; Jewish agencies & synagogues.

Type of support: General/operating support; Research.

Limitations: Giving limited to Detroit, MI.

Officers and Directors:* Eugene Applebaum,* Pres.; Marcia Applebaum,* V.P.; Robert R. Aronson,* Secy.; Dorothy Benyas,* Treas.; Lisa Applebaum; Pamela Applebaum; Robert R. Aronson; Penny Blumenstein; Mark Hauser; Doreen Hermelin; Lawrence S. Jackier.

EIN: 382870708

1192
Arab Community Center for Economic and Social Services

2651 Saulino Ct.
Dearborn, MI 48120-1556   (313) 842-7010
County: Wayne
Contact: Hassan Jaber, Exec. Dir.
FAX: (313) 342-5150; URL: http://www.accesscommunity.org

Established in 1974 in MI.

Grantmaker type: Public charity.

Financial data (yr. ended 09/30/10): Revenue, $20,334,716; assets, $6,748,361 (M); expenditures, $17,550,841; total giving, $546,718; giving activities include $178,090 for grants, and $368,628 for grants to individuals.

Purpose and activities: The organization is dedicated to empowering and enabling individuals, families, and communities to lead informed, productive, culturally sensitive, and fulfilling lives.

Fields of interest: Children/youth; Minorities; Immigrants/refugees; Economically disadvantaged.

Type of support: Grants to individuals; In-kind gifts.

Limitations: Applications accepted. Giving on a national basis with primary focus on MI.

Publications: Annual report; Newsletter.

Application information:

Initial approach: Contact Sandy Al for an appointment

Officers and Directors:* Hussein Berry, Pres.; Wadad Abed, V.P.; Amal M. Berry-Brown, Arabic Secy.; Edward Bagale, Eng. Secy.; Yasser Al-Soofi, Treas.; David Allen; Ramzi Chraim; Greg Clark; Amal David, Ph.D.; Rasha Demashkieh; Aoun Jaber; and 19 additional directors.

EIN: 237444497

1193
Arts Council of Greater Grand Rapids, Inc.

532 Ottawa Ave.
Grand Rapids, MI 49501-2265   (616) 459-2787
County: Kent
FAX: (616) 459-7160; Mailing address: P.O. Box 2265, Grand Rapids, MI 49503; URL: http://www.artsggr.org

Established in 1967.

Grantmaker type: Public charity.

Financial data (yr. ended 09/30/09): Revenue, $218,752; assets, $821,198 (M); gifts received, $193,941; expenditures, $284,285; total giving, $80,401; giving activities include $80,401 for grants to individuals.

Purpose and activities: The council works to make the arts central to the lives of everyone in the community.

Fields of interest: Arts education; Arts.

Limitations: Applications accepted. Giving primarily in MI.

Publications: Application guidelines.

Application information:

Deadline(s): Feb. 1 and Aug. 1 for Minigrants

Officers: Susan K. Jones, Pres.; Heidi Lyon, V.P.; Paul Hense, Secy.; Michael Puerner, Treas.; Caroline Older, Exec. Dir.

EIN: 386160845

1194
Arts Council of Greater Kalamazoo

359 S. Kalamazoo Mall, Ste. 203
Kalamazoo, MI 49007-4842   (269) 342-5059
County: Kalamazoo
FAX: (269) 342-6531;
E-mail: info@kalamazooarts.com; URL: http://www.kalamazooarts.com/services

Established in 1966 in MI.

Grantmaker type: Public charity.

Financial data (yr. ended 09/30/09): Revenue, $933,818; assets, $1,329,874 (M); gifts received, $891,093; expenditures, $2,984,518; total giving, $2,289,684; giving activities include $2,282,884 for grants, and $6,800 for grants to individuals.

Purpose and activities: The council funds, promotes, and supports the arts and culture of Kalamazoo County, Michigan, through its involvement in many activities for individual artists and member arts and cultural organizations, such as arts management, audience development, cultural tourism, and educational programs.

Fields of interest: Arts, artist's services; Arts.

Type of support: General/operating support; Continuing support; Income development; Management development/capacity building; Equipment; Program development; Conferences/seminars; Film/video/radio; Publication; Internship funds; Scholarship funds; Technical assistance; Consulting services; Program evaluation; Grants to individuals; Matching/challenge support.

Limitations: Applications accepted. Giving limited to residents of Kalamazoo County, MI, for most programs and to Barry, Berrien, Cass, Kalamazoo, St. Joseph, and Van Buren counties, MI, for State Regional minigrant (decentralized) program. No grants for capital improvements, endowment, publication, fundraising, or for existing deficits of more than two years.

Publications: Application guidelines; Annual report; Biennial report; Grants list; Informational brochure; Informational brochure (including application guidelines); Multi-year report; Newsletter; Program policy statement.

Application information: First-time applicants for Arts Council grants, and repeat applicants whose prior applications were not funded, must schedule an appointment to discuss application criteria and procedures. The council prefers applications in English, however they are open to translation if necessary and possible. Application form required.

Initial approach: Telephone or e-mail
Deadline(s): Feb. 1 and Aug. 1 for MCACA Region Mini-Grants; Mar. 1 for Arts Outreach Fund; Nov. 30 for MAGIK; Dec. 1 for Arts Fund
Board meeting date(s): 2nd Thurs. of each month
Final notification: Varies

Officers and Directors:* Norman L. Hamann, Jr.,* Pres.; Peter Seaver, V.P.; Dee Velkoff,* Secy.; Dori Kunkle,* Treas.; Anne Berquist, Exec. Dir.; Don Desmet; Robert S. Doud; Sidney Ellis; Carole Spight Greene; Dr. Jeffrey Harkins; Julie Lehman Peterson; James M. Marquardt; James McIntyre; Chris Middleton; Bernard Palchick; and 3 additional directors.

Number of staff: 6 full-time professional.

EIN: 386121183

1195
Arts Midwest

2908 Hennepin Ave., Ste. 200
Minneapolis, MN 55408-1987   (612) 341-0755
County: Hennepin
Contact: David J. Fraher, Exec. Dir.
FAX: (612) 341-0902;
E-mail: general@artsmidwest.org; Additional tel. (for Performing Arts Fund) (816) 421-1388; TDD: (612) 822-2956; URL: http://www.artsmidwest.org

Established in 1985 in MN.

Grantmaker type: Public charity.

Financial data (yr. ended 06/30/09): Revenue, $13,344,513; assets, $8,441,474 (M); gifts received, $12,427,039; expenditures, $12,519,775; total giving, $6,393,495; giving activities include $6,393,495 for 290 grants.

Purpose and activities: The organization enables individuals and families throughout America's heartland to share in and enjoy the art and culture of their region and the world.

Fields of interest: Performing arts.

Type of support: Matching/challenge support.

Limitations: Applications accepted. Giving limited to IA, IL, IN, MI, MN, ND, OH, SD, and WI.

Publications: Application guidelines.

Application information: Applications will be reviewed on a first-come, first-served basis; early application may increase the likelihood of funding. Application form required.

Initial approach: Download application form
Deadline(s): Feb. 2 for The Big Read Grants; Mar. 24 (beginning of review of application) for Performing Arts Fund
Board meeting date(s): May and Nov.
Final notification: Mid-Apr. for The Big Read Grants

Officer: David J. Fraher, Exec. Dir.

Directors: Tom Benson; Peter Capell; Loann Crane; Ken Fischer; Dennis Holub; William H. Jackson; Sylvia C. Kaufman; Leonard Pas; Rhoda A. Pierce; Barbara Robinson; Anita Walker; Pam Perri Weaver; Jan Webb; Woodie T. White.

Number of staff: 9 full-time professional; 3 full-time support.

EIN: 411000424

1196
ArtServe Michigan

Riley Broadcast Ctr.
1 Clover Ct.
Wixom, MI 48393-2247   (248) 912-0760
County: Oakland
Contact: Jennifer H. Goulet, Pres.
FAX: (248) 912-0768;
E-mail: jennifer@artservemichigan.org; Toll-free tel.: (800) 203-9633; URL: http://www.artservemichigan.org

Established in 1997 in MI through a merger of Arts Foundation of Michigan, Business Volunteers for the Arts, Concerned Citizens for the Arts in Michigan, and Michigan Alliance for Arts Education.
Grantmaker type: Public charity.
Financial data (yr. ended 09/30/09): Revenue, $703,677; assets, $867,844 (M); gifts received, $581,219; expenditures, $771,870.
Purpose and activities: The organization serves, supports, and advocates for an enriched cultural environment, and promotes the arts as a valuable state and community resource in Michigan through education, professional services, networking, support of artists and cultural organizations, volunteer assistance, and collaborations.
Fields of interest: Arts education; Arts.
Type of support: Conferences/seminars; Grants to individuals.
Limitations: Giving limited to MI.
Publications: Financial statement; Informational brochure; Newsletter.
Application information:
  Board meeting date(s): Quarterly
Officers and Directors: * Randy Paschke,* Chair.; Melonie B. Colaianne,* Vice-Chair., Devel.; Deborah Pfliegel,* Vice-Chair., Admin. and Finance; Jennifer H. Goulet, Pres.* Eugene Jenneman,* Secy.; Steven Antoniotti; Bruce Ashley; Nancy Barker; Hedy Blatt; James Bridenstine; and 39 additional directors.
Number of staff: 6 full-time professional.
EIN: 382537585

1197
Asthma & Allergy Foundation of America - Michigan Chapter
2075 Walnut Lake Rd.
West Bloomfield, MI 48323-3733
(248) 406-4254
County: Oakland
Contact: Kathleen Felice Slonager R.N., Exec. Dir.
FAX: (248) 737-8862;
E-mail: aafamich@sbcglobal.net; Toll-free tel.: (888) 444-0333; URL: http://www.aafamich.org

Established in 1984 in MI.
Grantmaker type: Public charity.
Financial data (yr. ended 12/31/09): Revenue, $74,973; assets, $25,345 (M); gifts received, $50,826; expenditures, $78,111.
Purpose and activities: The foundation seeks to improve the quality of life for individuals affected by asthma and allergic diseases and to promote awareness of these disorders.
Fields of interest: Education; Environment; Public health; Allergies; Asthma.
Type of support: Annual campaigns; Scholarships—to individuals.
Limitations: Applications accepted. Giving limited to MI.
Publications: Application guidelines; Annual report; Informational brochure; Newsletter.
Application information: Application form not required.
  Initial approach: Download application form
  Deadline(s): Mar. 10 for Camp Michi-MAC; Sept. 1 for Jean Yonke Scholarship Fund
  Board meeting date(s): Quarterly
  Final notification: Apr. 1 for Camp Michi-MAC; Sept. 15 for Jean Yonke Scholarship Fund
Officers and Directors: * Irving Miller, M.D.*, Pres.; Clyde Flory, M.D.*, V.P., Comms. and Legislative Affairs; Jacqueline Moore, M.D.*, V.P., Medical

Affairs; Susan Stridiron, R.N., B.S.N.*, Secy.; Matthew Hunter,* Treas.; Kathleen Felice Slonager, R.N., Exec. Dir.; Carol Finkelstein; Lana Hardin; Lawrence Pasik, M.D.; Allen Sosin, M.D.; and 7 additional directors.
Number of staff: 1 part-time professional.
EIN: 382534175

1198
Avondale Foundation
2940 Waukegan St.
Auburn Hills, MI 48326-3264
County: Oakland
E-mail: AvondaleFoundation@avondale.k12.mi.us;
URL: http://www.avondalefoundation.org/

Established in MI.
Grantmaker type: Public charity.
Financial data (yr. ended 06/30/09): Revenue, $64,358; assets, $98,048 (M); gifts received, $54,982; expenditures, $47,111; total giving, $46,254; giving activities include $46,254 for grants.
Purpose and activities: The foundation works to support student development, promote excellence through creative teaching, and foster community/school partnerships by securing and allocating financial and other resources to create and/or expand education related enrichment projects and programs offered through the Avondale School District.
Fields of interest: Higher education; Scholarships/financial aid; Education.
Type of support: Scholarships—to individuals.
Limitations: Applications accepted. Giving limited to the Oakland County municipalities of Auburn Hills, Rochester Hills, Troy, and Bloomfield Township, MI.
Publications: Application guidelines.
Application information: Applications are only available to students of the Avondale school district.
  Board meeting date(s): 2nd Tuesday of each month
Officers and Directors: * Julie Tingley,* Pres.; Terry Statz,* V.P., Fund Devel.; Jim Tebbe,* V.P., Projects; Barb Sucher, Secy.; Tina Abbate-Marzolf; Sue Briggs; Tom DelPup; George Heitsch; Debra LaMothe; Kim Nash; John Nofs; Chris Scott.
EIN: 383039178

1199
Baraga-Houghton-Keweenaw Community Action Agency, Inc.
926 Dodge St.
Houghton, MI 49931-1944
County: Houghton

Established in 1965.
Grantmaker type: Public charity.
Financial data (yr. ended 09/30/09): Revenue, $1,743,032; assets, $412,176 (M); gifts received, $1,687,218; expenditures, $1,734,819.
Purpose and activities: The agency administers various governmental programs for the low-income and elderly population in Baraga, Houghton, and Keweenaw counties.
Fields of interest: Human services.
Type of support: Grants to individuals.
Officers: Terry Langston, Pres.; Alfred Brewer, Treas.; Jerry Jackovac, Exec. Dir.
EIN: 381800879

1200
The Battier Family Foundation
c/o Greater Houston Community Foundation
4550 Post Oak Pl., Ste. 100
Houston, TX 77027-3143   (713) 333-2200
County: Harris
E-mail: battierfoundation@givingback.org

Donor-advised fund of the Houston Community Foundation.
Grantmaker type: Public charity.
Purpose and activities: The foundation provides college scholarships to Detroit-area students, and works to improve the quality of life for children in Detroit, Michigan and Houston, Texas.
Fields of interest: Higher education; Scholarships/financial aid; Boys & girls clubs; Children/youth.
Type of support: Scholarships—to individuals.
Limitations: Giving primarily in Detroit, MI.
Publications: Application guidelines.

1201
Edgar and Marion Beck Foundation
9861 Meisner Ln.
Casco, MI 48064-2911   (586) 727-4681
County: St. Clair
E-mail: rturgeon@beckfoundation.com; URL: http://www.beckfoundation.com/index.htm

Established in 2005 in MI.
Grantmaker type: Public charity.
Financial data (yr. ended 12/31/08): Revenue, $77,456; assets, $29,924 (M); gifts received, $25,100; expenditures, $102,498; total giving, $10,755; program services expenses, $88,359; giving activities include $10,755 for grants, and $77,604 for foundation-administered programs.
Purpose and activities: The foundation strives to raise funding in support of Wayne State University Brain Tumor Research Program and other local charitable organizations.
Fields of interest: Higher education, university; Brain research.
Type of support: Research.
Officer: Marion Beck, Chair.
Board Members: Wayne Stewart; Richard Turgeon; Sharon Turgeon; Jill Wald; David Wilkie.
EIN: 300339215

1202
The Gerald Beckwith Constitutional Liberties Fund
259 Clarendon Rd.
East Lansing, MI 48823-2616
County: Ingham

Established in 1984 in MI.
Grantmaker type: Public charity.
Financial data (yr. ended 06/30/10): Revenue, $38,641; assets, $18,908 (M); gifts received, $38,525; expenditures, $32,781; total giving, $32,750; giving activities include $32,750 for grants.
Purpose and activities: The fund offers support for the advancement of constitutional liberties and the protection of civil rights; projects which involve education, litigation, legislation, and public policy formulation or advocacy.
Fields of interest: Civil liberties, advocacy; Civil/human rights.

Limitations: Giving limited to MI, with emphasis on Clinton, Eaton, Ingham, and Jackson counties.
Officers and Directors:* Carolyn Koenig,* Pres.; Erick Williams,* V.P.; Mary Pollock,* Secy.; Joseph S. Tuchinsky,* Treas.; Cindie L. Alwood; Susan Anderson; Ed Bladen; Joy Brown; Joseph Finkbeiner; and 21 additional directors.
EIN: 382536385

1203
The Jerome Bettis "Bus Stops Here" Foundation
2615 W. 12 Mile Rd.
Berkley, MI 48072 (248) 354-3636
County: Oakland
Contact: Gloria Bettis, Dir.
E-mail: foundation@thebus36.com; URL: http://www.thebus36.com

Established in 1996 in MI.
Grantmaker type: Public charity.
Financial data (yr. ended 12/31/09): Revenue, $96,633; assets, $111,639 (M); gifts received, $12,822; expenditures, $108,844.
Purpose and activities: The foundation provides programs, activities, and services that continue to help youngsters reach their goals and improve their quality of life.
Fields of interest: Education; Recreation, centers; Athletics/sports, academies.
Type of support: Scholarship funds.
Limitations: Giving limited to Detroit, MI.
Officers and Directors:* Gladys Bettis,* Pres.; Jerome "The Bus" Bettis,* V.P.; Lasundres Davis,* Secy.; Gloria Bettis.
EIN: 383378049

1204
Birmingham Student Loan & Scholarship Fund
550 W. Merrill St.
Birmingham, MI 48009-1443
County: Oakland

Grantmaker type: Public charity.
Financial data (yr. ended 09/30/09): Assets, $868,794 (M); gifts received, $20,827; expenditures, $63,841; total giving, $59,450; giving activities include $59,450 for grants to individuals.
Purpose and activities: The fund awards college scholarships.
Fields of interest: Higher education, college.
Type of support: Scholarships—to individuals.
Officers: Steve Johnston, Pres.; Sarah Rosso McCaughey, V.P.; Eileen Cooney, Secy.; John Boukamp, Treas.
Trustees: Marlene Bodary; John Hoeffler; Janna Keyes; Renee Koehn; Ann Swartwout; Thomas F. Sweeney; Shelli Weisberg; Daniel Yuhn.
EIN: 386091548

1205
Birmingham-Bloomfield Symphony Orchestra
P.O. Box 1925
Birmingham, MI 48012-1925 (734) 525-7578
County: Oakland
Contact: Sebastian Kruger, Asst. Exec. Dir.

E-mail: bbso@bbso.org; Application address: c/o Millicent Berry, 25435 Wareham, Huntington Woods, MI 48070; URL: http://www.bbso.org/

Established in 1975 in MI.
Grantmaker type: Public charity.
Financial data (yr. ended 06/30/09): Revenue, $98,893; assets, $14,472 (M); gifts received, $49,975; expenditures, $65,702; program services expenses, $46,246.
Purpose and activities: The orchestra maintains a high quality professional orchestra in the Birmingham-Bloomfield community and surrounding areas, and provides the opportunity to experience quality performances featuring distinguished artists.
Fields of interest: Performing arts, orchestras.
Limitations: Giving primarily in MI.
Publications: Informational brochure; Informational brochure (including application guidelines).
Application information:
Board meeting date(s): 1st Wed. of every month
Officers and Directors:* Rich Tropea,* Chair.; Ward Lamphere,* V.P.; Michael A. Lochricchio, J.D.*, Treas.; Carla D. Lamphere,* Exec. Dir.; Millicent R. Berry; Wendy Cleland; Bill Close; Barbara Diles; Charles Greenwell; Marvin Hirsch; Julia Kurtya; June McGregor; Robert Pliska; Felix Resnick; John Rohrbeck; Kent Shafer; Ted Stacey.
Number of staff: 2 part-time professional.
EIN: 382088537

1206
Black United Fund of Michigan, Inc.
2187 W. Grand Blvd.
Detroit, MI 48208-1115 (313) 894-2200
County: Wayne
FAX: (313) 894-7562; E-mail: info@bufmi.org; URL: http://www.bufmi.org

Established in 1971 in MI.
Grantmaker type: Public charity.
Financial data (yr. ended 12/31/09): Revenue, $571,037; assets, $390,678 (M); gifts received, $562,198; expenditures, $538,906; total giving, $126,401; program services expenses, $449,806; giving activities include $126,401 for 6 grants (high: $10,000; low: $5,000), and $323,405 for foundation-administered programs.
Purpose and activities: The organization is committed to impact positive changes in a diverse community by providing funding.
Fields of interest: African Americans/Blacks.
Type of support: Program development.
Limitations: Giving primarily in MI.
Officers: Lawrence Patrick, Esq., Chair.; Alphonso Bell, Vice-Chair.; Kenneth W. Donaldson, Pres. and C.E.O.; Gia L. Todd, Secy.; Shaundralyn Hughes, Treas.
Directors: Tamika Bryant Cromer, Esq.; Grenae Dudley; Darryl W. Johnson; LaTonja Muhammad; Stanley Pitts, Esq.; Cynthia Reynolds; Phyllis Ross; Deierdre L. Weir.
EIN: 381964012

1207
D. A. Blodgett for Children
805 Leonard St. N.E.
Grand Rapids, MI 49503-1184 (616) 451-2021
County: Kent
FAX: (616) 451-8936;
E-mail: generalemail@dablodgett.org; URL: http://www.dablodgett.org

Established in 1887 in MI.
Grantmaker type: Public charity.
Financial data (yr. ended 12/31/09): Revenue, $9,203,748; assets, $7,989,977 (M); gifts received, $891,103; expenditures, $9,020,303; total giving, $2,406,237; giving activities include $2,406,237 for grants to individuals.
Purpose and activities: The organization works to enhance the well-being of children and their families by providing traditional and innovative programs that will assure them the best opportunity to realize their potential as human beings.
Fields of interest: Children/youth, services; Family services; Human services.
Type of support: Grants to individuals.
Limitations: Giving limited to Grand Rapids, MI.
Publications: Annual report; Informational brochure; Newsletter.
Officers and Directors:* Larry A. Pinckney,* Pres.; Anne Rothwell,* V.P.; Thomas D. Burr,* Secy.; E. Greer Candler,* Treas.; Robert G. Clark; Maria del Carmen Cruz; Tony Gates; Mary Grady; Kurt M. Graham; William R. Hineline; Dr. Thomas R. Kimball; Charles W. Lott; Christopher Macon; Tari Reinink; Alan Ryan; and 7 additional directors.
EIN: 381358163

1208
Blue Cross Blue Shield of Michigan Foundation
(formerly Michigan Health Care Education and Research Foundation/MHCERF)
600 Lafayette E., Ste. X520
Detroit, MI 48226-2998 (313) 225-8706
County: Wayne
Contact: Ira Strumwasser Ph.D., C.E.O. and Exec. Dir.
FAX: (313) 225-7730;
E-mail: foundation@bcbsm.com; Additional tel.: (313) 225-7560; URL: http://www.bcbsm.com/foundation/

Established in 1980 in MI.
Donor: Blue Cross and Blue Shield of Michigan.
Grantmaker type: Public charity.
Financial data (yr. ended 12/31/08): Revenue, $1,864,976; assets, $41,526,685 (M); gifts received, $3,800; expenditures, $3,824,993; total giving, $2,581,998; giving activities include $2,516,748 for grants, and $65,250 for grants to individuals.
Purpose and activities: The foundation supports projects that focus on enhancing the quality of health care, and improving access to and containing the cost of health care.
Fields of interest: Health care; Medical research, institute.
Type of support: Income development; Program development; Seed money; Fellowships; Research; Technical assistance; Grants to individuals; Matching/challenge support.
Limitations: Applications accepted. Giving primarily in MI.

Publications: Application guidelines; Annual report (including application guidelines); Informational brochure (including application guidelines).
Application information: See web site for current requests for proposals and application guidelines/deadlines. Application form required.
Deadline(s): Jan. 1 for Excellence in Research Awards and Excellence in Research Awards for Students; Apr. 3 for Research Award for Improving Patient Safety and Research Award for Identification and Treatment of Depression; and Apr. 30 for Student Awards Program
Board meeting date(s): May, Aug., and Nov.
Final notification: Aug. for Student Awards Program; quarterly for Matching Grants Program
Officers and Directors:* Shauna Ryder Diggs, M.D.*, Chair.; Joel I. Ferguson,* Vice-Chair.; Ira Strumwasser, Ph.D., C.E.O. and Exec. Dir.; Kevin L. Seitz,* Pres.; Marla Larkin, Secy.; Peter B. Ajluni, D.O.*, Treas.; Haifa Fakhouri, Ph.D.; Joel I. Ferguson; John M. MacKeigan, M.D.; Willard S. Stawski, M.D.
Number of staff: 3 full-time professional; 2 full-time support.
EIN: 382338506

1209
Boysville of Michigan, Inc.
(doing business as Holy Cross Children's Services)
8759 Clinton-Macon Rd.
Clinton, MI   49236-9572
County: Lenawee
Contact: Gary Tester, V.P., Advocacy
E-mail: gtester@hccsnet.org; URL: http://www.hccsnet.org

Established in 1948 in MI.
Grantmaker type: Public charity.
Financial data (yr. ended 12/31/08): Revenue, $45,940,129; assets, $25,713,782 (M); gifts received, $2,892,992; expenditures, $46,429,637; total giving, $3,812,763; program services expenses, $41,665,530; giving activities include $3,812,763 for grants to individuals, and $37,852,767 for foundation-administered programs.
Purpose and activities: The organization conducts residential- and community-based programs throughout Michigan that help to serve the needs of Michigan families and children without regard to race, creed, or economic status, with the goal of empowering children and families to function effectively in their community.
Fields of interest: Youth development, adult & child programs; Youth development; Family services; Residential/custodial care; Youth.
Type of support: Grants to individuals.
Limitations: Giving limited to MI.
Officers and Directors:* William P. Bolton,* Chair.; Francis Boylan, C.S.C.*, Pres.; Tim Lynch, Treas.; Loren P. Brown,* Exec. Dir.; Benjamin Lee Anderson; Rev. Moses B. Anderson, S.S.E.; Thomas J. Armstead; James V. Bellanca, Jr.; Bro. Robert Fillmore, C.S.C.; Carne L.P. Gray Gaines; James L. Hughes; John P. Jacobs; Msgr. Michael C. LeFevre; Dr. Lyn Lewis; Phyllis Marra; and 10 additional directors.
EIN: 381368326

1210
Branch County United Way, Inc.
P.O. Box 312
Coldwater, MI   49036-0312
County: Branch

Established in MI.
Grantmaker type: Public charity.
Financial data (yr. ended 12/31/09): Revenue, $254,485; assets, $125,219 (M); gifts received, $250,492; expenditures, $252,939; total giving, $176,285; giving activities include $176,285 for grants.
Fields of interest: Health care; Multiple sclerosis; Big Brothers/Big Sisters; Boy scouts; Girl scouts; American Red Cross; Community/economic development.
Limitations: Giving primarily in Branch County, MI.
Officers: Sonya Sayles, Pres.; Ron Rose, V.P.; Jill Smoker, Treas.
Board Members: Eric Anglin; Keith Baker; Robin Glascock; Melissa Lafferty; Mark Ludlow; David O'Rourke; Susan Morton; Sara Roper; Bill Stewart; Eric Zuzga; and 4 additional board members.
EIN: 381554662

1211
Bronson Health Foundation
301 John St., Box C
Kalamazoo, MI   49007-5295   (269) 341-8100
County: Kalamazoo
Contact: Angela Graham, Exec. Dir.
E-mail: johnsonh@bronsonhg.org; URL: https://www.bronsonhealth.com/WaysToGive/Bronson%20Health%20Foundation/page3082.html.html

Established in 1983 in MI.
Grantmaker type: Public charity.
Financial data (yr. ended 12/31/09): Revenue, $263,725; assets, $9,742,416 (M); gifts received, $355,482; expenditures, $430,921; total giving, $106,923; giving activities include $106,923 for grants.
Purpose and activities: The foundation supports Bronson Methodist Hospital and Bronson Vicksburg Hospital in their efforts to improve the health of the individual and the Bronson community.
Fields of interest: Public health; Health care.
Limitations: Applications accepted. Giving primarily in Kalamazoo, MI. No support for medical research or religious or political organizations. No grants to individuals, or for capital campaigns, fund raising events, annual fund appeals, operating expenses, or endowments.
Application information: Application form required.
Initial approach: Telephone
Copies of proposal: 1
Deadline(s): Mar., June, Sept., and Dec.
Board meeting date(s): Jan., Apr., July, and Oct.
Final notification: 8 to 12 weeks
Officers and Directors:* Jerry L. Miller,* Chair.; Michael F. Odar,* Vice-Chair.; Gene Conrad; Dennis DeHaan; William T. DeNooyer; Steven A. East; Carole Harroun-Holmes; Judy K. Jolliffe; Allan R. LaReau, M.D.; Carl E. Lee; Michele Marquardt; John G. Polzin.
Number of staff: 1 full-time professional; 1 part-time professional; 1 part-time support.
EIN: 382415081

1212
Byron Center Fine Arts Foundation
P.O. Box 13
Byron Center, MI   49315-0013   (616) 878-6818
County: Kent
Contact: Jonathan Bower, Pres.

Established in 1999 in MI.
Grantmaker type: Public charity.
Financial data (yr. ended 12/31/09): Revenue, $12,337; assets, $108,589 (M); gifts received, $2,502; expenditures, $7,702; total giving, $2,000; giving activities include $2,000 for grants.
Purpose and activities: The foundation provides funds for scholarships and grants, and promotes education, training, and performing in the performing and visual arts.
Fields of interest: Visual arts; Performing arts.
Type of support: General/operating support; Scholarships—to individuals.
Limitations: Applications accepted. Giving primarily in Kent County, MI.
Application information: Application form required.
Initial approach: Letter or telephone requesting application
Deadline(s): Early Mar. for Scholarships
Board meeting date(s): 3rd Wed. of each month
Final notification: End of Apr. for Scholarships
Officers: Jonathan Bower, Pres.; Joyce Winchester, V.P.; David Hart, Secy.; Leon De Lange, Treas.
Board Members: Ed Elderkin; Hank Haan; Tim Hitson; Tim Newhouse; Joanne Voorhees.
Number of staff: 1 part-time professional.
EIN: 383498857

1213
Capital Area United Way
1111 Michigan Ave., Ste. 300
East Lansing, MI   48823-4050   (517) 203-5000
County: Ingham
FAX: (517) 203-5001; URL: http://www.capitalareaunitedway.org

Grantmaker type: Public charity.
Financial data (yr. ended 06/30/09): Revenue, $4,637,642; assets, $4,129,490 (M); gifts received, $4,402,707; expenditures, $4,372,517; total giving, $2,687,417; giving activities include $2,687,417 for grants.
Purpose and activities: The organization works to unite people and resources to solve defined problems and improve the quality of life for individuals and families in need.
Fields of interest: Crime/violence prevention, domestic violence; Employment, services; Youth development; Human services; Family services; Family services, parent education; Human services, emergency aid; Aging, centers/services.
Limitations: Giving limited to the greater Lansing, MI area.
Publications: Annual report.
Officers and Directors:* Jerry King,* Chair.; Michael Brown, Pres.; Janet Gibbons, C.E.O., Internal Opers.; Sharon Granger, V.P., Community Impact; Teresa Kmetz, V.P., Campaign & Comms.; Jerry Ambrose; Joan Bauer; Ken Beall; Angela Brown; James Butler; and 40 additional directors.
EIN: 381363572

1214
Caravan Youth Center
1706 Willowbrook
Lansing, MI   48917-1220
County: Eaton

Grantmaker type: Public charity.
Financial data (yr. ended 08/31/09): Revenue, $10,643; assets, $244,118 (M); gifts received, $680; expenditures, $27,382.
Purpose and activities: The organization aims to improve the lives of youth.
Fields of interest: Youth, services.
Type of support: In-kind gifts.
Limitations: Giving primarily in MI.
Directors: Wayne Caruss; Lester Florida; W. Monte Ream; Robert R. Smith; William Turney; Francis E. Walker.
EIN: 386099677

1215
Career Alliance, Inc.
711 N. Saginaw St., Ste. 300
Flint, MI   48503-1769
County: Genesee

Grantmaker type: Public charity.
Financial data (yr. ended 06/30/09): Revenue, $25,041,845; assets, $8,362,687 (M); gifts received, $25,539,913; expenditures, $25,730,351; total giving, $21,760,896; giving activities include $18,559,171 for grants, and $3,201,725 for grants to individuals.
Purpose and activities: The alliance seeks to foster systemic reform in workforce development that ensures continuous economic growth for all employers and residents.
Fields of interest: Employment.
Officer: Jimmy King, Chair.; Alicia Booker, Pres. and C.E.O.
EIN: 382498451

1216
CareLink Network, Inc.
1333 Brewery Park Blvd,. Ste. 300
Detroit, MI   48207-4544   (313) 656-0000
County: Wayne
Toll-free tel.: (888) 711-5465; URL: http://www.bhpnet.org/carelink.asp

Grantmaker type: Public charity.
Financial data (yr. ended 09/30/09): Revenue, $100,059,512; assets, $5,565,006 (M); gifts received, $349,037; expenditures, $100,702,477; total giving, $96,262,052; giving activities include $96,262,052 for grants to individuals.
Purpose and activities: The network coordinates services for children and adults with mental illness throughout Wayne County, Michigan, including outpatient therapy, in-patient hospitalizations, crisis screening and services, residential services, partial hospitalization, housing supports, consultations, and referral services.
Fields of interest: Family services; Developmentally disabled, centers & services; Human services.
Limitations: Giving limited to Wayne County, MI.
Officer: Deborah Snyder, Exec. Dir.
Directors: Judith Chapman; Sarah Clark; Sheilah Clay; Cheryl Coleman; Ed Forry; James Lloyd; Michael Lott; Elijah Sherman Lyons; Debora

Matthews; Roberta Sanders; Dr. Robert Shaw; John van Camp.
EIN: 383653299

1217
Caring Athletes Team for Children's and Henry Ford Hospitals
(also known as CATCH)
223 Fisher Bldg.
3011 W. Grand Blvd.
Detroit, MI   48202-1601   (313) 876-9399
County: Wayne
Contact: Jim Hughes, Exec. Dir.
FAX: (313) 876-9241;
E-mail: jhughes@catchcharity.org; Additional E-mail: info@catchcharity.org; URL: http://www.catchcharity.org

Established in 1987 in MI.
Grantmaker type: Public charity.
Financial data (yr. ended 12/31/09): Revenue, $580,758; assets, $6,248,555 (M); gifts received, $483,611; expenditures, $596,384; total giving, $290,000; giving activities include $265,000 for grants, and $25,000 for grants to individuals.
Purpose and activities: The organization is dedicated to improving the quality of life of pediatric patients at Children's Hospital and Henry Ford Hospital and through the development of a board-designated endowment fund, the organization will provide needy pediatric patients with assistance which is not otherwise available.
Fields of interest: Hospitals (specialty); Pediatrics.
Limitations: Giving limited to MI.
Officers and Trustees:* Jim Berline,* Chair.; David B. Bergman,* Vice-Chair.; David Levy,* Vice-Chair.; Thomas F. McNulty,* Treas.; James F. Hughes, Exec. Dir.; Hon. Dennis W. Archer; Charles J. Barone, M.D.; Marvin W. Beatty; Kathy Brennan; Maureen Mara Brown; Brian T. Coughlin; Del deWindt; Michael S. Dietz; David Dombrowski; Tiffany S. Douglas; and 33 additional trustees.
EIN: 382746810

1218
Cash for Kids
1985 Lincoln Way, Ste. 23-176
White Oak, PA   15131-2418   (412) 238-0096
County: Allegheny
Contact: Lisa Pelofsky
E-mail: lisa@swincash.com; URL: http://swincash.com/cashforkids/cfkmission.html

Donor: Swintalya "Swin" Cash.
Grantmaker type: Public charity.
Purpose and activities: The organization works to provide the essential tools for kids to 'get in the game,' both educationally and on the court, by providing financial support to the arts while focusing on culture, literacy, athletics, and youth development initiatives.
Fields of interest: Arts; Education; Athletics/sports, basketball; Youth development.
Limitations: Applications accepted. Giving primarily in the Detroit, MI area and McKeesport, PA.
Application information:
  Initial approach: Submit proposal
EIN: 202862814

1219
Catholic Healthcare Partners Foundation
615 Elsinore Pl.
Cincinnati, OH   45202
County: Hamilton

Grantmaker type: Public charity.
Financial data (yr. ended 12/31/09): Revenue, $1,971,038; assets, $15,469,677 (M); gifts received, $1,577,515; expenditures, $1,465,299; total giving, $1,354,423; giving activities include $1,354,423 for grants.
Purpose and activities: The foundation supports the operations of Catholic Healthcare Partners by encouraging charitable giving and effectively managing gift resources, with the goal of bringing life-enhancing hope and help to those in need.
Fields of interest: Health care; Community/economic development.
Type of support: Program development.
Limitations: Giving in CHP communities in IN, KY, northeast PA, eastern TN, and southwest, western, west central, north central, northeast, and northwest OH (including southern MI), with emphasis on OH.
Officer and Trustees:* Sr. Marjorie Bosse; Michael Connelly; Jane D. Crowley; Sr. Doris Gottemoeller; A. David Jimenez; Susan Makos; William Shuttleworth.
EIN: 201072726

1220
Center for Arab-American Philanthropy
2651 Saulino Ct.
Dearborn, MI   48120-1556   (313) 842-7010
County: Wayne
Contact: Katherine Hanway, Program Coord.
FAX: (313) 842-5150; E-mail: caap@centeraap.org; URL: http://www.centeraap.org/

Established in 2006 in MI.
Grantmaker type: Public charity.
Purpose and activities: CAAP promotes, facilitates and celebrates Arab-American giving through education, training and donor outreach and services.
Fields of interest: Arts, single organization support; Arts, cultural/ethnic awareness; Museums (ethnic/folk arts); Youth development; Human services, single organization support; Minorities/immigrants, centers/services; Civil/human rights, immigrants; Voluntarism promotion; Philanthropy/voluntarism; Minorities.
Type of support: General/operating support; Program development; Technical assistance.
Limitations: Giving limited to the U.S., serving the Arab-American community. No support for organizations lacking 501(c)(3) status, religious organizations for religious purposes, or non U.S.-based organizations. No grants to individuals, or for fundraising events; no re-granting or loans.
Application information: See web site for Request for Proposals.

1221
Char-Em United Way
P.O. Box 1701
Petoskey, MI   49770-1701   (231) 487-1006
County: Emmet
Contact: Martha Lancaster, Exec. Dir.; Julie Voci, Admin. and Prog. Asst.

FAX: (231) 487-0795;
E-mail: info@charemunitedway.org; URL: http://www.charemunitedway.org

Established in MI.
Grantmaker type: Public charity.
Financial data (yr. ended 06/30/09): Revenue, $307,426; assets, $280,537 (M); gifts received, $304,384; expenditures $301,603; total giving, $195,765; giving activities include $195,765 for grants.
Fields of interest: Community/economic development.
Limitations: Applications accepted. Giving primarily in Charlevoix and Emmet counties, MI. No grants for religious purposes, capital expenses, or debt reduction.
Publications: Application guidelines; Financial statement; Grants list; Informational brochure; Newsletter.
Application information: Application form required.
  Initial approach: Letter, telephone, or e-mail
  Copies of proposal: 5
  Deadline(s): Feb.
  Board meeting date(s): Monthly
  Final notification: Two months
Officers: Bob Carlie, Pres.; Steve Andreae, V.P.; Jennifer Archamba, Secy.; Barb Perreault, Treas.; Martha Lancaster, Exec. Dir.
Directors: Mark Gray; Doug Hall; Jim Rudolph; Karen Sherard; Kendall Stanley; Dena Sydow; Dee Vincent.
Number of staff: 1 part-time professional; 1 part-time support.
EIN: 237049778

1222
Charity Motors, Inc.
10431 Grand River Ave.
Detroit, MI 48204-2005   (313) 933-4000
County: Wayne
Contact: Gary E. Bowersox, Exec. Dir.; Stephen Hendrix, Mgr., Business Opers.
FAX: (313) 933-3754;
E-mail: gbowersox@charitymotors.org; Toll-free tel.: (888) 908-2277; URL: http://www.charitymotors.org

Established in 1995 in MI.
Grantmaker type: Public charity.
Financial data (yr. ended 12/31/09): Revenue, $8,199,327; assets, $3,061,038 (M); gifts received, $7,337,282; expenditures, $8,034,784; total giving, $5,203,910; giving activities include $1,492,421 for grants, and $3,711,489 for grants to individuals.
Purpose and activities: The organization is dedicated to helping the underprivileged with transportation, and provides funding to other 501(c)(3) organizations from vehicle sales proceeds.
Fields of interest: Human services; Economically disadvantaged.
Limitations: Applications accepted. Giving primarily in MI and TX. No support for political organizations or organizations lacking 501(c)(3) status.
Publications: Annual report.
Application information: Application form not required.
  Initial approach: Letter or telephone
  Board meeting date(s): Jan., Apr., July, and Oct.
Officers: Norman A. Yatooma, Chair.; Bob R. Ivory, Jr., Vice-Chair.; John Hale, Sr., Secy.; Ramzi Faraj, Treas.; Gary E. Bowersox, Exec. Dir.

Number of staff: 8 full-time professional; 14 full-time support; 6 part-time support.
EIN: 383251827

1223
Cheboygan County United Way
224 N. Main St.
P.O. Box 488
Cheboygan, MI 49721-1640   (231) 627-2288
County: Cheboygan
Contact: Burnice F. Myers, Exec. Dir.
FAX: (231) 627-2062; E-mail: ccuw@hotmail.com

Grantmaker type: Public charity.
Financial data (yr. ended 09/30/09): Revenue, $51,278; assets, $151,519 (M); gifts received, $52,795; expenditures, $63,880; total giving, $27,533; giving activities include $27,533 for grants.
Purpose and activities: The Cheboygan County United Way activates community resources to assist various local charitable organizations to help children and youth succeed, strengthen families, and support vulnerable and aging populations.
Fields of interest: Youth development; Human services; Children/youth, services; Family services; Aging, centers/services; Developmentally disabled, centers & services.
Type of support: In-kind gifts; Annual campaigns; Grants to individuals.
Limitations: Applications accepted. Giving limited to Cheboygan County, MI.
Publications: Annual report; Financial statement; Informational brochure; Program policy statement.
Application information: Application form required.
  Board meeting date(s): 2nd Wed. of each month
Officers and Directors:* Jean Boucher,* Pres.; Susan Caswell,* Treas.; Burnice F. Myers, Exec. Dir.; Twyla Brooks; Lew Crusoe; Theresa Dilts; Cheryl Kennedy; Carol Northcott.
Number of staff: 1 part-time professional.
EIN: 386094846

1224
Chelsea Education Foundation, Inc.
(also known as C.E.F.)
P.O. Box 295
Chelsea, MI 48118-0295
County: Washtenaw
E-mail: OBallow@ChelseaEducationFoundation.org; URL: http://chelseaeducationfoundation.org/

Established in 1990 in MI.
Grantmaker type: Public charity.
Financial data (yr. ended 06/30/09): Revenue, $2,146; assets, $478,580 (M); gifts received, $14,509; expenditures, $75,083; total giving, $62,339; giving activities include $62,339 for grants.
Purpose and activities: The foundation provides funding for a wide spectrum of educational activities to benefit the residents of Chelsea, Michigan, including scholarships to individuals, innovative school programs, community forums, building projects, and extra-curricular classes and experiences.
Fields of interest: Education.
Type of support: Program development; Scholarships—to individuals.
Limitations: Applications accepted. Giving primarily in Chelsea, MI.

Publications: Application guidelines.
Application information: Application form required.
  Initial approach: Download application form
  Copies of proposal: 12
  Deadline(s): Apr. 10 for scholarships; Nov. 2 for grants
Officers: Owen Ballow, Pres.; Julie Herman, Secy.; Bill Wells, Treas.
Board Members: Bill Arons; Stacie Battaglia; Matt Cole; Peg Bravo; Jolene Everard; Beth Ewald; Kristin Hall; Dave Mahoney; Jon Mykala; Nancy Salatin; Angela Sujek; Juli Turner.
EIN: 382953926

1225
Chelsea United Way
P.O. Box 176
Chelsea, MI 48118-0176   (734) 475-0020
County: Washtenaw
E-mail: webmaster@chelseaunitedway.org; URL: http://chelseaunitedway.org/

Established in MI.
Grantmaker type: Public charity.
Financial data (yr. ended 12/31/09): Revenue, $92,476; assets, $53,470 (M); gifts received, $92,077; expenditures, $100,214; total giving, $90,221; giving activities include $90,221 for grants.
Purpose and activities: The organization seeks to raise and disburse funds to qualified nonprofit and volunteer organizations in the community.
Fields of interest: Boy scouts; Girl scouts; American Red Cross; Salvation Army; Aging, centers/services; Human services; Community/economic development; Catholic agencies & churches.
Limitations: Giving primarily in MI.
Officers and Directors:* Doug Worthington,* Pres.; Rick Ader,* V.P.; Allison Pollard,* Secy.; Christine Sing,* Treas.; Robert Frayer; Annette Houle; Scott Moore; and 12 additional directors.
EIN: 237128098

1226
Children's Charities at Adios
30435 Groesbeck Hwy.
Roseville, MI 48066-1546
County: Macomb
Contact: Michael Pannuto, Pres.

Established in 1991.
Grantmaker type: Public charity.
Financial data (yr. ended 12/31/08): Revenue, $219,420; assets, $52,638 (M); gifts received, $109,005; expenditures, $183,820; total giving, $104,500; giving activities include $104,500 for grants.
Purpose and activities: The organization raises funds to support children's charities.
Fields of interest: Children, services.
Limitations: Giving on a national basis.
Officers: Michael Pannuto, Pres.; Onorio Moscone, V.P.; William Bender, Secy.; William I. Minoletti, Treas.
EIN: 382924503

1227
Children's Leukemia Foundation of Michigan
5455 Corporate Dr., Ste. 306
Troy, MI 48098-7650   (248) 353-8222
County: Oakland
Contact: William D. Seklar, Pres. and C.E.O.
FAX: (248) 353-0157;
E-mail: info@leukemiamichigan.org; Toll-free tel.:
(800) 825-2536; URL: http://
www.leukemiamichigan.org
Additional tel. for assistance: Patient Services Dept.,
(800) 825-2536

Established in 1952 in MI.
Grantmaker type: Public charity.
Financial data (yr. ended 06/30/10): Revenue,
$1,025,482; assets, $287,868 (M); gifts received,
$1,214,874; expenditures, $930,162; total giving,
$65,443; giving activities include $65,443 for
grants to individuals.
Purpose and activities: The foundation seeks to
provide and promote compassionate, personalized
support to people in Michigan affected by leukemia
and other related disorders.
Fields of interest: Cancer, leukemia.
Type of support: Grants to individuals; Research.
Limitations: Giving limited to MI.
Publications: Annual report; Informational brochure;
Newsletter.
Officers and Directors:* Gary H. Gonzalez,* Chair.;
Richard Astrein,* Vice-Chair.; Glen R. Trevisian,
Pres. and C.E.O.; Denise M. Glassmeyer,* Secy.;
Michael Ansley; Jim Berline; Rob Bluthardt; Michele
Compton; Jason Curtis; Chuck Fortinberry; Karen
Hammelef, M.S.W.; Cindy Obron Kahn; Dr. Charles
Main, M.D.; Brett Rendeiro; Denice Richmond.
EIN: 381682300

1228
Collectors Foundation
141 River's Edge Dr., Ste. 200
Traverse City, MI 49684-3299   (231) 932-6835
County: Grand Traverse
Contact: Bob Knechel, Exec. Dir.
FAX: (231) 932-6857;
E-mail: bob@collectorsfoundation.org; URL: http://
www.collectorsfoundation.org

Established in 2005 in MI.
Donors: Franklin Adkins; Bruce Anderson; Jon
Bartel; Bruce Benson; Bruce Bone; Kristin Boyer;
Arthur Braida; Thomas Case; Barbara Carper; Klaus
Chavanne; Richie Clyne; H. Gene Drecktrah; Rick
Eagan; Linda Edelman; Jim Eidsvold; Automotive
Appraisal Group; James Craft, Inc.; CoachNet; FedEx
Custom Critical Passport Transport; Ford Motor
Company Fund; Great Lakes Motorworks; Hagerty
Insurance; Holy Cross Classic Cruisers; Intrigue
Collection, LLC; Jaguar Clubs of North America;
Mammel Family Foundation; Manitou Boatworks and
Engineering; Mecum Auctions; Mosaic Foundation;
Mustang Northwest Club; Panhandle Cruisers;
Specialty Vehicle Dealers Association; SPEED
Channel; Sports Car Market Magazine; Woodside
Credit.
Grantmaker type: Public charity.
Financial data (yr. ended 12/31/09): Revenue,
$355,938; assets, $190,425 (M); gifts received,
$355,820; expenditures, $247,476; total giving,
$190,648; giving activities include $190,648 for
grants.

Purpose and activities: The foundation's mission is
to serve the long-term interest of collector vehicle
and classic boat enthusiasts by funding educational
institutions, museums, libraries, and clubs that are
actively engaged in educational programming for
children, youth, young adults, and adults where
historic vehicles and classic boats are the
centerpiece for learning.
Fields of interest: Museums (sports/hobby);
Humanities; Arts; Vocational education; Youth
development; Human services; Children/youth;
Youth; Young adults; Young adults, female; Young
adults, male; Economically disadvantaged.
Type of support: Continuing support; Building/
renovation; Equipment; Program development; Seed
money; Internship funds; Scholarship funds;
Matching/challenge support.
Limitations: Applications accepted. Giving on a
worldwide basis. No support for political
organizations. No grants to individuals.
Publications: Annual report; Financial statement;
Grants list; Informational brochure; Newsletter;
Newsletter (including application guidelines);
Program policy statement.
Application information: Application form is
available on the foundation's web site. Application
form required.
> *Initial approach:* E-mail, telephone, or letter
> *Copies of proposal:* 1
> *Deadline(s):* Jan. 1, Apr. 1, July 1, and Oct. 1
> *Board meeting date(s):* Jan., Apr., July, and Oct.
> *Final notification:* Three to five business days
> after board meetings
Officers and Trustees:* John Hollansworth,* Pres.;
Bruce Knox,* Secy.; Mike Stowe,* Treas.; Bob
Knechel, Exec. Dir.; Ken Gross; McKeel Hagerty;
Jean Hoffman; Keith Martin; Raffi Minasian.
EIN: 202102643
Selected grants: The following grants were reported
in 2007.
$45,000 to Montana Automotive Technologies,
Missoula, MT. For general support, payable over
3.00 years.
$15,000 to Berks Career and Technology Center,
Leesport, PA. To combine developing restoration
technology curriculum within automotive technology
department.
$10,000 to Art Center College of Design, Pasadena,
CA. For scholarship for future classic designer.
$10,000 to Chris-Craft Antique Boat Club, Cedar
Rapids, IA. For matching challenge grant for
scanning literature.
$10,000 to College for Creative Studies, Detroit, MI.
For scholarship for 2 students in transportation
design.
$10,000 to Landing School of Boatbuilding and
Design, Kennebunkport, ME. For scholarship shared
by four students.
$10,000 to Washtenaw Community College, Ann
Arbor, MI. For scholarship to be shared among
students majoring in Rod & Custom Design/
Building.
$5,000 to Indiana State University, Terre Haute, IN.
For students attending Youth Summer Motorsports
Camp.
$3,740 to Auburn Cord Duesenberg Automobile
Museum, Auburn, IN. For summer intern from
McPherson College.
$3,038 to Yuba County Career Preparatory Charter
School, Marysville, CA. For special equipment in
auto program.

1229
John Coltrane Foundation
c/o Michelle A. Coltrane
21777 Ventura Blvd., Ste. 253
Woodland Hills, CA 91364-1843
County: Los Angeles
FAX: (818) 226-9996; E-mail: jcf@dslextreme.com;
URL: http://www.johncoltrane.com/htm/
jc_foundp.htm

Grantmaker type: Public charity.
Financial data (yr. ended 12/31/08): Revenue,
$9,735; assets, $13,200 (M); expenditures,
$13,796; total giving, $11,453; program services
expenses, $11,453; giving activities include
$11,453 for grants to individuals.
Purpose and activities: The foundation works to
encourage and advance the performance of jazz
music and other forms of artistic expression in the
jazz idiom, by providing scholarships to outstanding
young musicians and creating venues for them to
perform.
Fields of interest: Performing arts, music; Arts,
artist's services; Scholarships/financial aid.
Type of support: Scholarships—to individuals.
Limitations: Giving limited to Los Angeles and
Valencia, CA; Washington, DC; Bloomington, IN; Ann
Arbor, MI; Durham, NC; and New York, NY.
Officers and Directors:* Michelle Coltrane,* Pres.;
Michelle Coltrane-Carbonell,* V.P.; Gloria
Hartman-Ali, Ph.D.; Carl Hickson, H.Y.T.; Sylvia
Roberts, B.A.C.
EIN: 954862331

1230
Community Foundation Alliance of Calhoun County
104 S. Hillsdale St.
P.O. Box 101
Homer, MI 49245-1026   (517) 568-5222
County: Calhoun
Contact: Carol Petredean-DiSalvio, Admin.
FAX: (517) 568-5453; E-mail: cfa@cc.org;
URL: http://www.cfa-cc.org/

Established in 1998 in MI as a supporting
organization of Calhoun County; now a supporting
organization of Battle Creek Community Foundation,
Albion Community Foundation, Athens Area
Community Foundation, Homer Area Community
Foundation, and Marshall Community Foundation.
Grantmaker type: Public charity.
Financial data (yr. ended 03/31/09): Revenue,
$337,283; assets, $427,690 (M); gifts received,
$326,683; expenditures, $423,219; total giving,
$324,545; giving activities include $324,545 for
grants.
Purpose and activities: To improve the quality of life
and access to opportunity in Calhoun County, MI,
with an emphasis on youth.
Fields of interest: Elementary/secondary
education; Mental health, smoking; Athletics/
sports, school programs; Recreation; Youth
development; Community/economic development;
Foundations (community); Youth.
Type of support: Program development; Scholarship
funds.
Limitations: Applications accepted. Giving primarily
in Calhoun County, MI.
Publications: Annual report.
Application information:

Initial approach: Download proposal
Deadline(s): Feb. 1 for Positive Youth Development Fund; Apr. 20 for Calhoun County Republican Party Scholarship; Apr. 28 for Community Foundation Alliance Scholarship; July 1 for Calhoun County Swine Club Scholarship Fund; Dec. 28 for Healthy Youth, Healthy Seniors Fund
Officer and Directors: * Rachel Maksimchuk,* Pres.; Betsy Briere,* V.P. and Secy.; Lynn Haley,* Treas.; Sherry Anderson; Carolyn Ballard; Holly Blashfield; Paul Frederick; Cindy Leach; Elizabeth Schultheiss; Karen Yankie.
EIN: 043597340

1231
Community Network Services, Inc.
38855 Hills Tech Dr., Ste. 200
Farmington Hills, MI   48331-3428
(248) 994-8001
County: Oakland
FAX: (248) 994-8005; Toll-free tel. (Farmington Hills area): (800) 615-0411; toll-free tel. (Waterford area): (800) 273-0258; URL: http://www.cnsmi.org

Established in 2002 in MI.
Grantmaker type: Public charity.
Financial data (yr. ended 09/30/09): Revenue, $30,368,410; assets, $3,361,862 (M); gifts received, $11,551; expenditures, $30,259,425; total giving, $696,095; program services expenses, $28,162,138; giving activities include $696,095 for grants to individuals, and $27,466,043 for foundation-administered programs.
Purpose and activities: The organization is a mental health care provider that identifies, supports, and promotes opportunities for eligible persons in Oakland County, Michigan, with mental illness, including substance use; services include assessment, case management, psychiatric, therapy, and recovery services.
Fields of interest: Mental health, clinics; Mental health, counseling/support groups; Mentally disabled.
Limitations: Giving primarily in Oakland County, MI.
Publications: Newsletter.
Officers and Directors: * Manuel Alfonso,* Co-Chair.; Artie Davenport,* Co-Chair.; Evelyn Reinke,* Secy.; Benjamin Anderson,* Treas.; Dr. Lauren Hicks Barton; Susan F. Cuevas; Mark William Foss; James Johnson; Linda Koch; Lillie Leverett; Harold Nevils.
EIN: 431969008

1232
Copper Country United Way
604 Shelden Ave.
P.O. Box 104
Houghton, MI   49931-0104   (906) 482-3276
County: Houghton

Grantmaker type: Public charity.
Financial data (yr. ended 02/28/09): Revenue, $138,730; assets, $193,530 (M); gifts received, $136,006; expenditures, $146,569.
Purpose and activities: The Copper Country United Way allocates funds to charitable agencies in the Keweenaw Peninsula, Michigan.
Fields of interest: Human services; Community/ economic development.

Limitations: Giving limited to Keweenaw Peninsula, the northwestern end of the Upper Peninsula of MI.
Officers and Directors: * Frank J. Stipech,* Pres.; Nancy Archambeau,* V.P.; Jan Woodbeck,* Secy.; Rick West,* Treas.; Lois Gemignani; Mark Jalkannen; Chen Raasio; Brian Rimpela; Virginia Schaller; and 12 additional directors.
EIN: 386030235

1233
Corporation for Supportive Housing
50 Broadway, 17th Fl.
New York, NY   10004-3816   (212) 986-2966
County: New York
Contact: Deborah DeSantis, Pres. and C.E.O.; Connie Tempel, C.O.O.
FAX: (212) 986-6552; E-mail: info@csh.org; URL: http://www.csh.org

Established in 1991.
Grantmaker type: Public charity.
Financial data (yr. ended 12/31/09): Revenue, $19,846,868; assets, $75,019,343 (M); gifts received, $10,310,886; expenditures, $21,757,734; total giving, $2,801,346; giving activities include $2,801,346 for grants.
Purpose and activities: The organization works to help communities create permanent housing with services to prevent and end homelessness by providing high-quality advice and development expertise, making loans and grants to supportive housing sponsors, strengthening the supportive housing industry, and reforming public policy to make it easier to create and operate supportive housing.
Fields of interest: Housing/shelter, expense aid; Housing/shelter; Children/youth; Young adults; Disabilities, people with; Mentally disabled; Native Americans/American Indians; Military/veterans; Offenders/ex-offenders; Economically disadvantaged; Homeless.
Type of support: Program development; Management development/capacity building; Program-related investments/loans.
Limitations: Giving limited to CA; CT; Washington, DC; IL; IN; MI; MN; NJ; NY; OH; RI; and TX.
Publications: Annual report; Financial statement; Newsletter.
Officers and Directors: * Denise O'Leary,* Chair.; David P. Crosby,* Vice-Chair.; Deborah De Santis,* Pres. and C.E.O.; Connie Tempel, C.O.O.; Ellen Baxter,* Secy.; Kenneth J. Bacon; Pete Earley; Gary R. Eisenman; Alicia K. Glen; Marc R. Kadish; Mitchel R. Levitas; James L. Logue III; Evelyn Lundberg Stratton; Douglas M. Weill.
EIN: 133600232

1234
Crawford County United Way
P.O. Box 171
Grayling, MI   49738-0171   (989) 344-9300
County: Crawford

Established in MI.
Donors: Consumer's Power; DTE Energy; Mercy Hospital; Weyerhaeuser Company.
Grantmaker type: Public charity.
Financial data (yr. ended 12/31/09): Revenue, $42,622; assets, $30,599 (M); gifts received, $41,256; expenditures, $31,893; total giving,

$27,004; giving activities include $27,004 for 27 grants (high: $3,900; low: $35).
Purpose and activities: The organization works to provide support to local nonprofits, to improve the community.
Fields of interest: Human services; Community/ economic development.
Limitations: Giving primarily in MI.
Publications: Informational brochure; Newsletter.
Officers: Karen Hatley, Pres.; Jason Alexander, V.P.; Kirk Wakefield, Secy.; Bonnie French, Treas.
EIN: 382777940

1235
Cutaneous Lymphoma Foundation, Inc.
(formerly Mycosis Fungoides Foundation, Inc.)
P.O. Box 374
Birmingham, MI   48012-0374
County: Oakland
Tel./FAX: (248) 644-9014; URL: http:// www.clfoundation.org

Established in 1998.
Grantmaker type: Public charity.
Financial data (yr. ended 06/30/10): Revenue, $1,043,697; assets, $1,187,671 (M); gifts received, $1,039,040; expenditures, $535,978; total giving, $14,300; giving activities include $1,800 for grants.
Purpose and activities: The foundation supports patients with mycosis fungoides, Sezary syndrome, and other forms of cutaneous T-cell lymphomas by promoting awareness and education, advancing patient care, and facilitating research.
Fields of interest: Medical research.
Officers and Directors: * Claudia Day,* Pres.; Christopher Shipp,* V.P.; Rick Megargell,* Secy.; Richard Bradlow,* Treas.; Judy Jones, Exec. Dir.; Margie Legowski; Leora Lowenthal.
EIN: 383443135

1236
Costantino Del Signore Foundation
39000 Schoolcraft
Livonia, MI   48150-1036
County: Wayne

Established in 1996.
Grantmaker type: Public charity.
Financial data (yr. ended 12/31/09): Revenue, $71,494; assets, $5,678 (M); expenditures, $80,773; total giving, $21,770; giving activities include $21,770 for grants.
Purpose and activities: The foundation provides funds for the advancement of medical research.
Fields of interest: Hospitals (general); Cancer; Medical research.
Limitations: Giving primarily in MI.
Officers: Costantino Del Signore, Pres.; Angelo Colone, Secy.; Jim Carver, Treas.
EIN: 383331000

1237
Delta College Foundation
1961 Delta Rd.
University Center, MI   48710-0001
(989) 686-9224
County: Bay
URL: http://www.delta.edu/foundation.aspx

Established in 1978 in MI.
Grantmaker type: Public charity.
Financial data (yr. ended 06/30/09): Revenue, $1,223,126; assets, $1,896,155 (M); gifts received, $1,216,259; expenditures, $1,050,825; total giving, $926,132; giving activities include $897,226 for grants, and $28,906 for grants to individuals.
Purpose and activities: The foundation seeks to change lives by supporting opportunities and innovation at Delta College.
Fields of interest: Higher education, college; Scholarships/financial aid.
Type of support: Scholarship funds; Scholarships—to individuals; In-kind gifts.
Limitations: Applications accepted. Giving limited to MI.
Publications: Application guidelines.
Application information:
  Initial approach: Download application form
  Deadline(s): May 9
Officers and Directors:* James L. Wolohan,* Chair.; Robert H. Monroe,* Vice-Chair.; Mary J. Goodnow,* Secy.-Treas.; Karen M. MacArthur, Exec. Dir.; Donald Halog; Susan A. Pumford; Eileen C. Starks; James M. VanTiflin; and 12 additional directors.
EIN: 382274366

1238
Delta Dental Foundation
(formerly Delta Dental Fund)
P.O. 30416
Lansing, MI 48909-7916 (517) 349-6000
County: Ingham
Contact: Lawrence D. Crawford D.D.S., Vice-Chair.
E-mail: ddfund@ddpmi.com; URL: http://www.deltadentalmi.com/ddf/index.htm

Established in 1980 in MI; supporting organization of Delta Dental Plan of Michigan, Inc.
Grantmaker type: Public charity.
Financial data (yr. ended 12/31/09): Revenue, $844,493; assets, $25,582,158 (M); gifts received, $26,495; expenditures, $896,952; total giving, $532,733; giving activities include $356,106 for grants, and $176,627 for grants to individuals.
Purpose and activities: The fund supports education and research for the advancement of dental science and promotes the oral health of the public through education and service activities, particularly for those with special needs.
Fields of interest: Dental school/education; Dental care; Cancer; Cancer research; Economically disadvantaged.
Type of support: Conferences/seminars; Fellowships; Scholarship funds; Research.
Limitations: Applications accepted. Giving limited to IN, MI, and OH. No support for political organizations or organization that discriminate by race, religion, color, creed, gender, age, or national origin. No grants for capital campaigns, overhead/administrative expenses, endowments, advertising, fundraising activates, or projects developed for commercial and proprietary purposes; no loans.
Publications: Application guidelines; Biennial report (including application guidelines).
Application information: Application form required.
  Initial approach: Download application form
  Deadline(s): Apr. 15 and Oct. 15 for Research Grants; Sept. 30 for Thomas P. Moore II

Memorial Grant; Nov. 1 for Community Mini-Grants
Final notification: Nov. for Community Mini-Grants and Thomas P. Moore II Memorial Grant
Officers and Trustees:* Jack W. Gottschalk, D.D.S.*, Chair.; Lawrence D. Crawford, D.D.S.*, Vice-Chair.; Penelope K. Majeske, Ph.D.*, Secy.; James P. Hallan,* Treas.; Stephen A. Eklund, D.D.S.; Lonny E. Zietz; and 6 additional trustees.
EIN: 382337000

1239
Detroit & Wayne County Tuberculosis Foundation
(doing business as Respiratory Foundation of Southeast Michigan)
100 Maple Park Blvd., Ste. 152
St. Clair Shores, MI 48081-2253
(586) 498-1286
County: Macomb

Grantmaker type: Public charity.
Financial data (yr. ended 12/31/08): Revenue, $1,039,185; assets, $17,599,453 (M); expenditures, $1,161,514; total giving, $1,098,234; giving activities include $1,098,234 for grants.
Purpose and activities: The foundation exists to receive and administer funds for scientific, educational, and charitable purposes connected with the investigation, prevention, detection, treatment and cure of Tuberculosis and rehabilitation of those affected, with special reference to the support of such activities as are now carried on my Detroit Tuberculosis Sanatorium.
Fields of interest: Lung diseases.
Limitations: Giving limited to Detroit, MI.
Officers: Thomas J. Petz, Pres.; William L. Hurley, V.P.; Patrick J. Mansfield, V.P.; Michael Owsiany, Secy.; Robert D. Kemp, Jr., Treas.
Trustees: Edmund M. Brady, Jr.; Ruth Roby Glancy; Carol C. Marantette; Mrs. Ralph T. McElvenny; John R. Nicholson; Alfonso V. O'Neill; Mark K. Wilson.
EIN: 386088988

1240
Detroit Area Agency on Aging
1333 Brewery Park Blvd.
Detroit, MI 48207-2635
County: Wayne
URL: http://www.daaa1a.org

Established in 1981 in MI.
Grantmaker type: Public charity.
Financial data (yr. ended 09/30/09): Revenue, $28,206,637; assets, $6,966,412 (M); gifts received, $28,166,569; expenditures, $28,039,666; total giving, $18,729,275; program services expenses, $26,694,304; giving activities include $18,729,275 for 31 grants (high: $180,386; low: $6,809), and $7,965,029 for foundation-administered programs.
Purpose and activities: The organization works to educate, advocate, and promote healthy aging to enable people to make choices about home- and community-based services and long-term care that will improve their quality of life.
Fields of interest: Aging.
Type of support: In-kind gifts.
Limitations: Giving primarily in Detroit, MI.
Publications: Annual report; Financial statement.

Officers and Directors:* Wayne W. Bradley, Sr.,* Chair.; Elaine Williams,* 1st Vice-Chair.; Mark Wollenweber, 2nd Vice-Chair.; Paul Bridgewater, Pres. and C.E.O.; Frances Schonenberg,* Secy.; Lorenzer Frazier,* Treas.; Barbara Atkins-Smith; Kathleen Carlson; Patricia Carter; Denise Christy; Carol Coulton; Marvin Davis, Ed.D.; Juliette Okotie Eboh, Ph.D.; Loretta France; Louis Green; and 5 additional directors.
EIN: 382320421

1241
Detroit Auto Dealers Association Charity Preview
1900 W. Big Beaver Rd.
Troy, MI 48084-3508
County: Oakland

Established in 1976 in MI.
Grantmaker type: Public charity.
Financial data (yr. ended 06/30/09): Revenue, $2,601,795; assets, $819,605 (M); gifts received, $2,615,936; expenditures, $2,851,107; total giving, $2,349,039; giving activities include $2,349,039 for grants.
Purpose and activities: The organization supports charitable purposes in the Detroit area.
Fields of interest: Youth development; Human services.
Limitations: Giving primarily to Detroit, MI.
Officers: Carl Galeana, Pres.; Joe Serra, V.P.; Doug Fox, Secy.; Barron Meade, Treas.
Board Members: Rod Alberts; Bill Perkins.
EIN: 383435764

1242
Detroit Firemens Fund Association for Relief of Disabled Firemen
250 W. Larned St., Ste. 202
Detroit, MI 48226-4469 (313) 961-2988
County: Wayne
FAX: (313) 961-0215; Toll-free tel.: (877) 961-2988; URL: http://www.detroitfiremensfund.com

Established in 1866 in MI.
Grantmaker type: Public charity.
Financial data (yr. ended 11/30/09): Revenue, $963,817; assets, $3,490,445 (M); gifts received, $902,604; expenditures, $1,358,289.
Purpose and activities: The organization provides aid to the widows and orphans of fallen fire fighters.
Fields of interest: Safety/disasters, association.
Limitations: Giving primarily in Detroit, MI.
Publications: Newsletter.
Officers and Trustees:* Donald Domin,* Pres.; Christopher Dixon,* V.P.; John Fred Anderson,* Secy.; Jim Montgomery,* Treas.; John Cowan; Kim Fett; Terrill Hardaway; Richard Lancaster; Debbie Lyon; Tom Suchora.
EIN: 381681020

1243
Detroit Lions Charities
222 Republic Dr.
Allen Park, MI 48101-3650
County: Wayne
Contact: William Clay Ford, Pres.
URL: http://www.detroitlions.com/document_display.cfm?document_id=3588

Established in 1990 in MI.
Grantmaker type: Public charity.
Financial data (yr. ended 02/28/10): Revenue, $306,576; assets, $988,030 (M); gifts received, $291,632; expenditures, $347,873; total giving, $334,539; giving activities include $334,539 for grants.
Purpose and activities: The organization assists charitable and worthwhile causes in Michigan, and supports activities and programs that benefit all age groups in education, civic affairs, and health and human services.
Fields of interest: Education; Health care; Human services; Community/economic development.
Limitations: Applications accepted. Giving primarily in Detroit, MI. No support for political campaigns and activities. No grants to individuals (including loans and scholarships), or for building, raffles, banquets, advertising, equipment, or endowments.
Publications: Application guidelines.
Application information:
    Initial approach: Letter (no more than two pages)
    Deadline(s): Between Oct. 1 and Dec. 31
    Board meeting date(s): Feb.
    Final notification: Mar.
Officers: William Clay Ford, Pres.; William Clay Ford, Jr., V.P.; J. Thomas Lesnau, Treas.
Trustee: Timothy A. Pendell.
EIN: 382945709

1244
Detroit Tigers Players Home Clubhouse Scholarship Fund

16845 Kercheval Ave., Ste. 5
Grosse Pointe, MI   48230-1551
County: Wayne

Grantmaker type: Public charity.
Financial data (yr. ended 12/31/09): Revenue, $731; assets, $28,312 (M); gifts received, $200; expenditures, $2,615; total giving, $2,000; giving activities include $2,000 for grants.
Purpose and activities: The foundation provides scholarships to student athletes at high-school and college levels.
Fields of interest: Higher education; Scholarships/financial aid; Athletics/sports, school programs.
Type of support: Scholarships—to individuals.
Officers: David Bergman, Pres.; James Schmakel, V.P.; S. Gary Spicer, Secy.; Alan Trammel, Treas.
EIN: 383003854

1245
Detroit Zoological Society

8450 W. 10 Mile Rd.
Royal Oak, MI   48067-3001   (248) 541-5717
County: Oakland
URL: http://www.detroitzoo.org

Grantmaker type: Public charity.
Financial data (yr. ended 03/31/09): Revenue, $27,647,257; assets, $21,304,533 (M); gifts received, $15,364,636; expenditures, $23,748,860; total giving, $97,736.
Purpose and activities: The society primarily supports the Detroit Zoological Institute, and also makes small cash grants to other conservation organizations and programs.
Fields of interest: Animal welfare; Animals/wildlife, preservation/protection; Zoos/zoological societies; Animals/wildlife.

Limitations: Giving primarily in MI.
Officers and Directors:* Gail L. Warden,* Chair.; Michael W. Jamieson,* Vice-Chair. and Treas.; Linda Wasserman Aviv,* Vice-Chair.; Denise J. Lewis,* Vice-Chair.; Stephen R. Polk,* Vice-Chair.; Lynn Ford Alandt; Barbara S. Beresford; Madeleine H. Berman; and 24 additional directors.
EIN: 386027356

1246
Easter Seals of Michigan, Inc.

2399 E. Walton Blvd.
Auburn Hills, MI   48326   (245) 475-6400
County: Oakland
Toll-free tel.: (800) 75-SEALS; URL: http://www.essmichigan.org

Grantmaker type: Public charity.
Financial data (yr. ended 08/31/09): Revenue, $33,006,370; assets, $5,396,000 (M); gifts received, $1,097,196; expenditures, $33,114,597; total giving, $9,318,569; giving activities include $9,318,569 for grants to individuals.
Purpose and activities: The organization's mission is to create solutions that change lives of children and adults with disabilities or other special needs and their families.
Fields of interest: Family services; Family resources and services, disability; Disabilities, people with.
Limitations: Giving primarily in MI.
Officers and Directors:* Randy Velzen,* Chair.; Larry D'Angelo,* Vice-Chair.; John Coccione, Pres. and C.E.O.; Greg Fronizer, C.O.O.; Leonard Sokolowski, Secy.; John Zerbo, Treas.; Ken Gabriel; Elizabeth Kersten; and 10 additional directors.
EIN: 381402860

1247
Eastpointe Community Chest/Networking Forum

P.O. Box 442
Eastpointe, MI   48021-0442
County: Macomb

Established in MI.
Grantmaker type: Public charity.
Financial data (yr. ended 12/31/09): Revenue, $6,912; assets, $108,942 (M); gifts received, $3,508; expenditures, $9,778; total giving, $9,146; giving activities include $9,146 for grants.
Purpose and activities: The organization works to enhance the lives of local residents by meeting community needs.
Fields of interest: Education; Recreation, parks/playgrounds; Community/economic development.
Limitations: Giving primarily in Eastpointe and East Detroit, MI.
Officers: Chief Michael Lauretti, Pres.; Margaret Torp, V.P.; Robert Kern, Treas.
Directors: Rev. Susan Boch; Rev. Peter Conln; Neil Druzinski; Rev. James Friedman; Judy Helm; Rev. Kevin Lancaster; Suzanne Pixley; Teresa West; Sue Young; Diane Reece.
EIN: 383203070

1248
Eaton County United Way

350 Lansing St., Ste. B
P.O. Box 14
Charlotte, MI   48813-1694   (517) 543-5402
County: Eaton
FAX: (517) 543-5651; E-mail: ecuw@ecuw.org; URL: http://www.ecuw.org

Established in MI.
Grantmaker type: Public charity.
Financial data (yr. ended 06/30/09): Revenue, $494,948; assets, $638,075 (M); gifts received, $402,633; expenditures, $402,973; total giving, $171,460; giving activities include $171,460 for grants.
Purpose and activities: The organization's mission is to focus community resources to meet community needs.
Fields of interest: Health care; Independent living, disability; Human services; Community/economic development.
Limitations: Applications accepted. Giving primarily in Eaton County, MI. No support for political organizations.
Publications: Annual report; Financial statement; Informational brochure; Newsletter.
Application information: Application form required.
    Deadline(s): Apr. 21 for Health and Human Service Grants
    Board meeting date(s): 3rd Wed. of each month
Officers and Directors:* Larry Mengerink,* Pres.; Tracy Freeman, V.P.; Alison Walters, Secy.; Mary M. Douma, Treas.; Joni Risner, Exec. Dir.; Wayne Buletza; Sean Cotter; Bill Elis; Dave Harwood; Janine Nierenberger; Ronda Rucker; Mary Wright.
Number of staff: 1 full-time professional; 2 part-time professional.
EIN: 383483965

1249
Educational Services of America, Inc.

(also known as ESA)
1321 Murfreesboro Pike, Ste. 702
Nashville, TN   37217-2626   (615) 361-4000
County: Davidson
FAX: (615) 577-5695; Toll-free tel.: (888) 979-0004; URL: http://www.esa-education.com

Established in 1994 in TN.
Grantmaker type: Public charity.
Financial data (yr. ended 12/31/09): Revenue, $66,814,249; assets, $1,292,720,616 (M); expenditures, $57,379,552; total giving, $1,927,745; program services expenses, $45,850,633; giving activities include $1,927,745 for 774 grants to individuals, and $43,922,888 for foundation-administered programs.
Purpose and activities: The organization seeks to provide excellent educational services in a structured and encouraging environment.
Fields of interest: Education.
Type of support: Scholarships—to individuals; Student loans—to individuals.
Limitations: Giving limited to AL, AR, AZ, CA, CO, FL, GA, IL, IN, MI, MO, MS, NC, NE, NH, OH, OK, PA, TN, and TX.
Officers: Mark Claypool, Pres. and C.E.O.; Shirley W. Hanback, Exec. V.P., Human Resources; Karen LeFever, Ed.D., Exec. V.P. and Chief Devel. Off.; Cate Lewandowski, Exec. V.P. and Chief Mktg. Officer; John M. McLaughlin, Ph.D., Exec. V.P.; Bryan Skelton, Exec. V.P. and C.F.O.; Alan D. Watson,

Exec. V.P. and C.I.O.; Donald B. Whitfield, Exec. V.P. and C.A.O.
EIN: 621586836

1250
Ennis Center for Children, Inc.
129 E. 3rd St.
Flint, MI 48502 (810) 233-4031
County: Genesee
FAX: (810) 233-0008; URL: http://www.enniscenter.org

Established in 1978.
Grantmaker type: Public charity.
Financial data (yr. ended 09/30/09): Revenue, $10,544,581; assets, $3,030,396 (M); gifts received, $139,193; expenditures, $10,430,474; total giving, $2,685,300; giving activities include $2,685,300 for grants to individuals.
Purpose and activities: The center works to preserve and reunify families whenever possible, and to create new families when needed.
Fields of interest: Children, foster care.
Type of support: Grants to individuals.
Officers and Board Members: Kimberly Stout,* Chair.; Bruce Brownlee,* Vice-Chair.; Robert Ennis, Pres.; Janet Hayward-Frost, Sr. V.P.; Gale Schempf, V.P., Finance and Human Resources; Gary Wend, V.P., Programming; Denise Brooks-Williams, Secy.; Jeffrey Williams, Treas.; Eleanor Austin; Dennis Brewer; and 4 additional board members.
EIN: 382222428

1251
Face to Face Scholarship Fund, Inc.
31500 Schoolcraft Rd.
Livonia, MI 48150-1805 (248) 467-9946
County: Wayne
FAX: (734) 422-9353; E-mail: ksendi@voyager.net; URL: http://facetofacefoundation.com

Established in 2006 in MI as an operating foundation; status changed to a public charity in 2007.
Grantmaker type: Public charity.
Financial data (yr. ended 12/31/09): Revenue, $11,601; assets, $33,060 (M); gifts received, $6,374; expenditures, $2,428.
Purpose and activities: The foundation aims to provide underprivileged, under/uninsured children, adolescents and families throughout metropolitan Detroit with the critical crisis intervention psychiatric services that they desperately need.
Fields of interest: Mental health/crisis services; Family services; Children/youth.
Limitations: Applications accepted. Giving in the metropolitan Detroit, MI, area.
Application information: Information concerning access and application will be publicized in various periodicals, program literature, local mental health agencies and hospitals, as well as on various web sites. Application form required.
  Initial approach: Request application
  Deadline(s): At least 24 hours prior to event the scholarship is needed for
Officers and Directors:* Martha Adair,* Pres.; Pamela Baskel,* Secy.; Kimberly Smith,* Treas.
EIN: 205439061

1252
Fallen and Wounded Soldier Fund
4835 LAHSER
Bloomfield Hills, MI 48304-2622
County: Oakland
Contact: Tino Del Signore, Chair.
Additional Telephone: (734) 462-0770

Established in 2006 in MI.
Grantmaker type: Public charity.
Financial data (yr. ended 12/31/09): Revenue, $150,076; assets, $245,656 (M); gifts received, $18,542; expenditures, $110,610; total giving, $97,100; program services expenses, $97,100; giving activities include $20,000 for 1 grant, and $77,100 for grants to individuals.
Purpose and activities: The fund assists families injured or killed during militay service.
Fields of interest: Military/veterans' organizations.
Limitations: Giving primarily in MI.
Officer: Tino Del Signore, Chair.
EIN: 204882017

1253
Farmington/Farmington Hills Foundation for Youth and Families
(formerly Farmington Hills/Farmington Community Foundation)
36520 W. 12 Mile Rd.
Farmington Hills, MI 48331-3169
(248) 345-9090
County: Oakland
Contact: Barbara G. Yuhas, Exec. Dir.
FAX: (248) 478-7461; E-mail: info@ffhfoundation.org; URL: http://www.ffhfoundation.org

Established in 1995 in MI as the Farmington Hills Community Foundation for Children, Youth and Families; name changed in 1999 to the Farmington Hills/Farmington Community Foundation, reflecting a broader outreach to both communities; name changed again in 2006 to current name, and became affiliated with the Community Foundation for Southeast Michigan.
Grantmaker type: Public charity.
Financial data (yr. ended 12/31/09): Revenue, $116,020; assets, $284,842 (M); gifts received, $114,730; expenditures, $128,833; total giving, $59,639; giving activities include $59,639 for grants.
Purpose and activities: The foundation provides the opportunity for organized philanthropy that enriches the quality of life in the communities of Farmington Hills and Farmington by making strategic grants to organizations that serve families, youth, and children.
Fields of interest: Boys & girls clubs; Youth development; Children/youth, services; Family services.
Limitations: Applications accepted. Giving limited to Farmington and Farmington Hills, MI. No grants to individuals.
Application information: Visit foundation web site for additional application information. Application form required.
  Initial approach: Telephone or e-mail for application form
  Deadline(s): Apr. 15 and Oct. 15
Officers and Trustees:* David Steinberg, Pres.; Robin Waldman, V.P.; Jan Dolan,* Treas.; Marla Parker, Secy.; Barbara G. Yuhas, Exec. Dir.; Mark

Burns; Gerson Cooper; Jan Dolan; Kimberly Riley Fouts; William T. McCarthy; Richard Miller; James K. Mitchell; Greg Murtland; Theresa Rich; Joanne Smith; Susan Zurvalec; and 10 additional trustees.
EIN: 383254708

1254
First Nations Development Institute
351 Coffman St., Ste. 200
Longmont, CO 80501-5457 (303) 774-7836
County: Boulder
Contact: Michael E. Roberts, Pres.
FAX: (303) 774-7841; E-mail: info@firstnations.org; Additional address: 2217 Princess Anne St., Ste. 111-1, Fredericksburg, VA 22401-3350, tel.: (540) 371-5615, fax: (888) 371-3686; URL: http://www.firstnations.org

Established in 1983 in VA.
Donors: Robert E. Ackerberg; William C. Adams, USN Ret.; Gerard Adams-Lyons; Marion Ajjan; Dorinda D. Alcaraz; Michael L. Allmon; Nathan Altucher; Thereasa M. Anderson; Milton Andrews; Antonio Antomattey; Florese Applebaum; Ilda Arcari; Fred Arney; Margarita Aras; Beatrice A. Arrowsmith; Charles G. Arthur; Mrs. Charles G. Arthur; and 500 additional donors.
Grantmaker type: Public charity.
Financial data (yr. ended 06/30/10): Revenue, $2,952,678; assets, $3,792,498 (M); gifts received, $2,803,703; expenditures, $3,285,322; total giving, $1,035,989; giving activities include $1,035,989 for 54 grants (high: $56,000; low: $5,000).
Purpose and activities: The institute helps Native American tribal members to mobilize enterprises that are reform-minded, culturally suitable, and economically feasible by coordinating local grassroots projects with national program and policy development initiatives to build capacity for self-reliant reservation economies.
Fields of interest: Education; Youth development; Economic development; Rural development; Community development, business promotion; Native Americans/American Indians.
Limitations: Applications accepted. Giving limited to Native American reservations and rural Native American communities, including but not limited to those in AK, AZ, CA, CO, MI, MT, ND, NE, NH, NJ, NM, NV, OK, OR, SD, VA, WA, and WI. No support for non-Native Americans or media campaigns/projects (unless part of an overall project). No grants for scholarships, fellowships, construction, renovation, land acquisition, capital or endowment campaigns, or research which has no direct practical application.
Publications: Application guidelines; Annual report; Financial statement; Grants list; Informational brochure; Newsletter; Occasional report.
Application information: Applicants must be Native American nonprofit or tribal programs on or near a reservation to be eligible for grants. Application form required.
  Initial approach: Telephone (letter of intent form will be mailed to applicant afterwards)
  Copies of proposal: 1
  Deadline(s): June 2 for Little Eagle Staff Fund; Nov. 21 for 7871 Organization Grants Program; rolling basis for all others
  Board meeting date(s): Mar. June, Sept., and Nov.
  Final notification: 30 days or fewer
Officers and Directors:* B. Thomas Vigil,* Chair.; Marguerite Smith,* Vice-Chair.; Michael E. Roberts,* Pres.; A. David Lester,* Secy.; Donald G.

Sampson,* Treas.; W. Ron Allen; Chandra Hampson; Siobhan Oppenheimer-Nicolau; Shyla Grace Sheppar; Gelvin Stevenson.
Number of staff: 9 full-time professional; 2 part-time professional; 3 full-time support; 3 part-time support.
EIN: 541254491
Selected grants: The following grants were reported in 2009.
$56,000 to Native American Youth and Family Center, Portland, OR. For Leadership Entrepreneurial Apprenticeship Development (LEAD) program.
$56,000 to Potlatch Fund, Seattle, WA. For Leadership Entrepreneurial Apprenticeship Development (LEAD) program.
$40,000 to Oregon Native American Business and Entrepreneurial Network, Tigard, OR. For three variations on tribal entrepreneurship development system.
$40,000 to Sitting Bull College, Tribal Business Information Center, Fort Yates, ND. For financial education and entrepreneur development.
$25,000 to Turtle Mountain Band of Chippewa Indians, Belcourt, ND. To develop better control over tribal land records to enable them to utilize their land more effectively for housing, food production, and/or economic development.
$20,000 to California Indian Basketweavers Association, Woodland, CA. To continue and further develop basketry activities.
$20,000 to Native American Community Board, Lake Andes, SD. For Yankton Sioux and Heritage Preservation Program.
$20,000 to Washoe Tribe of Nevada and California, Gardnerville, NV. For Washoe Language Program.
$20,000 to Western Shoshone Defense Project, Crescent Valley, NV. To Seventh Generation Fund, to educate and empower Western Shoshone and other native youth.
$10,000 to Native American Fish and Wildlife Society, Broomfield, CO. For intensive hands-on indigenous environmental education for Native American high school students.

1255
Flint Cultural Center Corporation, Inc.
1198 Longway Blvd.
Flint, MI 48503-1851 (810) 237-7333
County: Genesee
FAX: (810) 237-7335; URL: http://www.flintculturalcenter.com

Grantmaker type: Public charity.
Financial data (yr. ended 06/30/09): Revenue, $8,359,568; assets, $35,058,508 (M); gifts received, $5,681,783; expenditures, $9,577,681; total giving, $2,119,583; giving activities include $2,081,883 for grants, and $37,700 for grants to individuals.
Purpose and activities: The center works to provide a distinguished and diverse array of cultural, scientific, historical, and artistic experiences to promote cultural appreciation.
Fields of interest: Arts.
Type of support: Scholarships—to individuals.
Limitations: Giving primarily in Flint, MI.
Publications: Informational brochure.
Officers and Directors:* Tim Keener,* Chair.; Jeanne Pepper,* Vice-Chair.; Cindy Ornstein, Pres. and C.E.O.; Claire White,* Secy.; Jim Johnson,*

Treas.; Sarah Abdallah; Abd Alghanem; Johanna Brown; David Doherty; and 10 additional directors.
EIN: 386089075

1256
Foodbank of South Central Michigan
5451 Wayne Rd.
Battle Creek, MI 49037-7327 (269) 964-3663
County: Calhoun
FAX: (269) 966-4147; E-mail: fbscm@wmis.net; Mailing address: P.O. Box 408, Battle Creek, MI 49016-0408; URL: http://www.foodbankofscm.org

Established in 1983.
Grantmaker type: Public charity.
Financial data (yr. ended 12/31/09): Revenue, $12,040,774; assets, $3,857,437 (M); gifts received, $11,028,273; expenditures, $11,816,140; total giving, $9,379,893; giving activities include $9,379,893 for grants.
Purpose and activities: The organization's mission is to feed hungry people by collecting and distributing food and grocery products, advocating for hunger-relief programs and collaborating with others who address basic human needs.
Fields of interest: Food services.
Type of support: In-kind gifts.
Limitations: Giving limited to Barry, Branch, Calhoun, Hillsdale, Jackson, Kalamazoo, Lenawee, and St. Joseph counties, MI.
Publications: Newsletter.
Officers and Board Members:* Sandi Jasper,* Chair.; Patty Parker,* Vice-Chair.; Jim Clark,* Secy.; Tim Czerney, Treas.; Dennis Berkebile; Gary Crist; Kathy DeVine; Jim Feldpausch; Dave Flook; Bonnie Garbrecht; and 9 additional board members.
EIN: 382445948

1257
Gerald R. Ford Foundation
303 Pearl St., N.W.
Grand Rapids, MI 49504-5343
County: Kent
Contact: Diane van Allsburg, Admin. Asst.
E-mail: geraldrfordfoundation@nara.gov; URL: http://www.geraldrfordfoundation.org
Additional tel.: (616) 254-0373, e-mail address: barbara.mcgregor@nara.gov (Prizes); Contact Helmi Raaska, c/o Gerald R. Ford Presidential Library, 1000 Beal Ave., Ann Arbor, MI 48109-2114, tel.: (734) 205-0555, e-mail address: helmi.raaska@nara.gov (Travel).

Established in 1981 in MI.
Grantmaker type: Public charity.
Financial data (yr. ended 12/31/09): Revenue, $1,115,781; assets, $23,665,512 (M); gifts received, $1,109,986; expenditures, $1,375,986; total giving, $42,980; giving activities include $42,980 for grants to individuals.
Purpose and activities: The foundation supports the Gerald R. Ford Library and Museum through historical exhibits, educational programs, conferences, research grants, and awards.
Fields of interest: Media/communications; Museums (history); Elementary/secondary education; Higher education; Libraries (academic/research).
Type of support: Research; Grants to individuals; Scholarships—to individuals.
Publications: Informational brochure.

Application information: Application form required.
 Copies of proposal: 7
 Deadline(s): Mar. 7 for Gerald R. Ford Journalism Prizes
 Board meeting date(s): Annually, 1st Mon. of June
Officers and Trustees:* John G. Ford,* Chair.; Hank Meijer,* Vice-Chair.; Gregory D. Willard,* Secy.; David G. Frey,* Treas.; Susan Ford Bales; Robert E. Barrett; Benton L. Becker; and 45 additional trustees.
Number of staff: 1 part-time support.
EIN: 382368003

1258
Foundation for Saline Area Schools
P.O. Box 5
Saline, MI 48176-0005 (734) 429-7378
County: Washtenaw
Contact: Dan Ouellette, Pres.
E-mail: superdeb@gmail.com; URL: http://www.foundationforsalineareaschools.org/

Established in 1987 in MI.
Grantmaker type: Public charity.
Financial data (yr. ended 12/31/09): Revenue, $29,955; assets, $319,761 (M); gifts received, $19,575; expenditures, $46,327; total giving, $45,771; giving activities include $45,771 for grants.
Purpose and activities: The foundation enhances the quality of education and educational opportunities to Saline area schools through enrichment programs and other projects which promote student learning opportunities, encourage excellence and growth of all staff, and facilitate community/school partnerships.
Fields of interest: Education.
Type of support: Seed money; Grants to individuals.
Limitations: Applications accepted. Giving limited to Saline, MI. No support for religious programs.
Publications: Application guidelines.
Application information: See web site for application information. Application form required.
 Initial approach: Proposal
 Copies of proposal: 5
 Deadline(s): 2nd Tues. of Apr. and Oct.
Officers and Trustees:* Daniel J. Ouellette,* Pres.; Nancy T. Byers,* V.P.; Abha Wiersba,* Treas.; Scott E. Fosdick; Elaine T. Heiserman; Beth Henschen; Thomas S. Kirvan; Mary Laidlaw; Bernice "Woodie" Merchant; Cathy Redies; Kenneth H. Rogers, Jr.; Nancy Schmerberg; Norma M. Smith; Terry Walters.
EIN: 382733854

1259
Foundation of Michigan Association of Physicians of Indian Origin
28230 Orchard Lake Rd., Ste. 203
Farmington Hills, MI 48334-3764
(248) 539-3604
County: Oakland
FAX: (248) 539-3638; E-mail: office@mapiusa.org; URL: http://www.mapiusa.org/fomapi

Established in 1989 in MI.
Grantmaker type: Public charity.
Financial data (yr. ended 12/31/09): Revenue, $193,321; assets, $275,872 (M); gifts received, $164,629; expenditures, $58,420; total giving, $35,000; program services expenses, $43,000;

giving activities include $12,000 for 1 grant, and $18,000 for foundation-administered programs.

Purpose and activities: The foundation is devoted to raising funds for charities that support medical clinics in India and Michigan.

Fields of interest: Health care, clinics/centers; Health care.

Limitations: Giving limited to MI and India.

Officer: Dinesh Shah, M.D., Pres.

EIN: 383032459

1260
Samuel and Jean Frankel Support Foundation

6735 Telegraph Rd.
P.O. Box 2030
Bloomfield Hills, MI 48301-3141
County: Oakland
Contact: Samuel Frankel, Pres.

Established in 1985 in MI; supporting organization of the Jewish Federation of Metropolitan Detroit.

Grantmaker type: Public charity.

Financial data (yr. ended 05/31/10): Revenue, $5,241,265; assets, $11,287,790 (M); gifts received, $4,000,000; expenditures, $2,566,431; total giving, $2,543,457; giving activities include $2,543,457 for grants.

Fields of interest: Jewish federated giving programs.

Limitations: Giving primarily in MI.

Officers and Directors:* Stanley D. Frankel, Pres. and V.P.; Robert P. Aronson, Secy.; Dorothy Benyas, Treas.; Jean Frankel; Lawrence S. Jackier; Arthur A. Weiss.

EIN: 382582299

1261
Frischkorn Memorial Fund Number III

c/o Comerica Bank
P.O. Box 7500
Detroit, MI 48275-0001
County: Wayne

Supporting organization of Defenders of Wildlife.

Grantmaker type: Public charity.

Financial data (yr. ended 09/30/09): Assets, $603,608 (M); expenditures, $27,926; total giving, $12,727; giving activities include $12,727 for grants.

Fields of interest: Environment.

Limitations: Giving limited to Washington, DC.

Trustees: Dr. George Stege III; Comerica Bank.

EIN: 386646188

1262
Gay, Lesbian, Bisexual, and Transgender Equality Fund

c/o Kalamazoo Community Foundation
151 S. Rose St., Ste. 332
Kalamazoo, MI 49007-4775 (269) 381-4416
County: Kalamazoo
Contact: Sharon Anderson Ph.D., Sr. Community Investment Officer, Kalamazoo Community Foundation
FAX: (269) 381-3146; E-mail: info@kalfound.org;
URL: http://www.kalfound.org/page10004039.cfm

Component fund of the Kalamazoo Community Foundation.

Grantmaker type: Public charity.

Financial data (yr. ended 12/31/10): Total giving, $19,795 Giving activities include $19,795 for 6 grants (high: $5,145; low: $500).

Purpose and activities: The fund seeks to foster new connections between the gay/lesbian/bisexual/transgender (GLBT) community of Kalamazoo and other communities, and serves to build and strengthen bonds among GLBT communities.

Fields of interest: Community/economic development; LGBTQ.

Limitations: Giving limited to the Kalamazoo, MI area.

Application information:

Initial approach: Contact Sharon Anderson for grantmaking guidelines

---

1263
Glen Arbor Art Association

P.O. Box 305
Glen Arbor, MI 49636-0305 (231) 334-6112
County: Leelanau
Contact: Peg McCarty, Dir.
E-mail: info@glenarborart.org; URL: http://www.glenarborart.org

Established in MI.

Grantmaker type: Public charity.

Financial data (yr. ended 12/31/09): Revenue, $133,908; assets, $296,859 (M); gifts received, $52,737; expenditures, $136,702.

Purpose and activities: The association is dedicated to furthering the arts in the Glen Lake, Michigan area by providing residencies, in which no monetary support is given.

Fields of interest: Visual arts, photography; Visual arts, sculpture; Visual arts, painting; Visual arts, ceramic arts; Performing arts, music; Philosophy/ethics.

Type of support: Use of facilities.

Limitations: Applications accepted. Giving on a national basis.

Publications: Application guidelines; Newsletter.

Application information: Application form required.

Initial approach: Letter of intent
Copies of proposal: 1
Deadline(s): Mar. 1 for Artists in Residence
Final notification: Six weeks from deadline

Officers: Linda Young, Pres.; Joan Schloop, V.P.; Kathy Drabik, Secy.; Bill Stege, Treas.

Board Members: Beth Bricker; Michael Buhler; Missi Missad; Linda Peppler; Becky Thatcher; Rob Turney; Karen van Nort; Betsy Wagner; Paul Walters; Ann Wettlaufer.

Number of staff: 1 part-time professional.

EIN: 382886660

1264
Global Philanthropy Alliance

P.O. Box 890
St. Joseph, MI 49085-0890 (202) 470-0716
County: Berrien
E-mail: info@globalphilanthropyalliance.org;
URL: http://www.globalphilanthropyalliance.org

Established in 2006 in MI.

Grantmaker type: Public charity.

Financial data (yr. ended 09/30/09): Revenue, $10,015; assets, $80,940 (M); gifts received, $9,900; expenditures, $27,614; total giving, $20,877; program services expenses, $24,939;

giving activities include $4,062 for foundation-administered programs.

Purpose and activities: The organization aims to develop partnerships between people in the United States and Africa, through mutual exchange of ideas and resources to support local organizations, empower youth, promote philanthropy, share knowledge and encourage innovation to achieve sustainable community development.

Fields of interest: Community/economic development; Philanthropy/voluntarism.

International interests: Kenya; Nigeria; South Africa.

Limitations: Applications accepted. Giving primarily in Kenya, Nigeria, and South Africa.

Publications: Application guidelines.

Application information: Application form required.

Initial approach: Download application
Deadline(s): Sept. 1

Officers and Board Members:* Anne C. Petersen,* Pres.; Robert L. Judd,* V.P. and Secy.; John C. Goff,* Treas.; Erin Brandt, Exec. Dir.; Karen Stone.

EIN: 205715805

1265
Gogebic Range United Way

P.O. Box 248
Ironwood, MI 49938-0248
County: Gogebic

Grantmaker type: Public charity.

Financial data (yr. ended 12/31/09): Revenue, $34,137; assets, $27,333 (M); gifts received, $33,915; expenditures, $33,824; total giving, $27,775; giving activities include $27,775 for grants.

Fields of interest: Community/economic development.

Limitations: Giving limited to Gogebic County, MI.

Officers: Anneito Grosso, Pres.; Carolyn Carlson, V.P.; Cindy Simmons, Secy.-Treas.

Directors: Margaret Celeski; Robert Hautala; Dale Kangas; Joseph Karius; Gina Kretschmar; Sandra Machesky; Marge Mickelson; Velda Sclafini; Jim Vanderspool.

EIN: 381940876

1266
Grand Kids Foundation

c/o John Fuller
2233 Park Ave., Ste. 5A
Detroit, MI 48201-3426
County: Wayne
Contact: John Fuller, V.P.
E-mail: fullerjoh@gmail.com; URL: http://www.grandkidsfoundation.org/

Established in 2008.

Donor: Curtis Granderson.

Grantmaker type: Public charity.

Purpose and activities: The organization works to enforce educational initiatives to youth and to help bring the sport of baseball back to the nation's inner cities.

Fields of interest: Education; Athletics/sports, baseball; Children/youth.

Officers and Directors:* Curtis Granderson, Pres.; John Fuller, V.P.; Mary Granderson, Treas.

EIN: 262086876

1267
Grand Rapids E.C. Foundation, Inc.
2944 Fuller Ave. N.E., Ste. 202
Grand Rapids, MI 49505-3784
County: Kent

Established in 1997 in MI.
Grantmaker type: Public charity.
Financial data (yr. ended 08/31/09): Revenue, $7,285; assets, $2,521 (M); gifts received, $6,450; expenditures, $8,274; total giving, $4,948; program services expenses, $5,091; giving activities include $4,948 for in-kind gifts, and $143 for foundation-administered programs.
Purpose and activities: The organization provides shoes and boots to needy children.
Fields of interest: Performing arts, music; Human services, gift distribution; Human services, emergency aid.
Officers: Aaron Pike, Pres.; James Hughes, V.P.; John Laninga, Secy.; Rusty S. Snyder, Treas.
EIN: 383110178

1268
Grand Rapids Jaycees Foundation
2774 Birchcrest Dr. S.E.
Grand Rapids, MI 49506-5477 (616) 949-8412
County: Kent
FAX: (616) 949-8742; URL: http://www.grjayceesfoundation.org

Established in 1983 in MI.
Grantmaker type: Public charity.
Financial data (yr. ended 12/31/09): Revenue, $325; assets, $1,327,737 (M); gifts received, $3,566; expenditures, $42,682; total giving, $16,988; giving activities include $16,988 for grants.
Purpose and activities: The foundation provides assistance to promote community involvement in community affairs and to promote the community's welfare; support is given primarily for cancer services, housing and shelter, youth development, and children's services.
Fields of interest: Cancer; Housing/shelter; Youth development; Children/youth, services.
Type of support: Capital campaigns.
Limitations: Applications accepted. Giving limited to western MI. No grants to individuals, or for religious or political purposes, contingency funds, or operational funds.
Publications: Newsletter.
Application information: Application form required.
  Initial approach: Application
  Deadline(s): Sept. 30 for Grants
  Board meeting date(s): Monthly
Officers and Directors:* Kris Nylaan,* Chair.; Dan McFarland,* Pres.; Michael Maloney,* Treas.; Becky Cayka; Brandi Grimmer; John Greko; Krista Rye; Jud Wierenga; Stacy Wierenga.
EIN: 382425009

1269
Grand Rapids Urban League
745 Eastern Ave., S.E.
Grand Rapids, MI 49503-5544 (616) 245-2207
County: Kent
FAX: (616) 245-6510;
E-mail: info@grurbanleague.org; URL: http://grurbanleague.org

Grantmaker type: Public charity.
Financial data (yr. ended 12/31/09): Revenue, $3,707,349; assets, $526,090 (M); gifts received, $3,698,357; expenditures, $3,748,570; total giving, $2,791,604; giving activities include $2,791,604 for grants to individuals.
Purpose and activities: The league provides food and daycare assistance for child care providers, housing assistance, and on-the-job training to residents of the Grand Rapids, Michigan, area.
Fields of interest: Employment, training; Food services; Housing/shelter, services; Children, day care; Children, services.
Limitations: Giving limited to Grand Rapids, MI.
Officers and Directors:* Dr. George Grant, Jr.,* Chair.; Dr. Walter M. Brame,* Pres. and C.E.O.; Mark Baker; Betty Smith Banks; Phil Barnes; Brian Chisholm; Walter Gutowski, Jr.; Armando Hernandez; Thomas Kohn; Patrick Lonergan; Larry Love; Dr. Lisa Lowery; Hon. William Murphy; Daniel Oglesby; Patricia Oldt, Ph.D.; Gordon Oosting; Michael Ramirez; Rev. Doug van Doren; Lamont Walker; Matilda Weddle; Fred Wooten.
EIN: 381359259

1270
Great Lakes Center for Youth Development
(also known as GLCYD)
(formerly Marquette-Alger Youth Foundation)
307 S. Front St.
Marquette, MI 49855-4613 (906) 228-8919
County: Marquette
Contact: Judy Watson Olson, Pres.
FAX: (906) 228-7712; E-mail: jwatson@glcyd.org; Toll-free tel.: (877) 33YOUTH; URL: http://www.glcyd.org/

Established in 2000 in MI as a part of the Kellogg Youth Initiative Partnerships through the W.K. Kellogg Foundation.
Grantmaker type: Public charity.
Financial data (yr. ended 06/30/10): Revenue, $465,721; assets, $8,066,628 (M); gifts received, $480,558; expenditures, $1,142,318; total giving, $210,192; giving activities include $210,192 for grants.
Purpose and activities: The organization is committed to helping rural communities build healthy youth environments by strengthening organizations that serve youth.
Fields of interest: Youth development.
Type of support: Scholarship funds.
Limitations: Applications accepted. Giving limited to the Upper Peninsula region in MI.
Application information:
  Initial approach: Telephone
Officers: Connie Koutouzos,* Chair.; Betsy Wesselhoft, Vice-Chair.; Judy Watson Olson,* Pres.; Anna Irish Burnett, Secy.; Don Mourand, Treas.
Directors: Paula Ackerman; Caleb Carlson; Pryce Hadley; Laurie Kaufman; Pete Kelto; June Schaefer, Ph.D.; and 3 additional directors.
EIN: 383522344

1271
Great Lakes Chapter of Links, Inc.
P.O. Box 4296
Southfield, MI 48037-4296
County: Oakland
URL: http://www.greatlakeslinks.org/

Established in 2008 in MI.
Grantmaker type: Public charity.
Financial data (yr. ended 04/30/10): Revenue, $50,882; assets, $32,658 (M); gifts received, $36,117; expenditures, $57,440; total giving, $2,500; program services expenses, $57,440; giving activities include $2,500 for grants to individuals, and $54,940 for foundation-administered programs.
Purpose and activities: The chapter promotes service and friendship in the Great Lakes community.
Fields of interest: Community development, service clubs.
Limitations: Giving primarily to the metropolitan Detroit, MI area.
Officers: Judi Caliman, Pres.; Veronica Murf, V.P.; Pauline Given, Treas.
EIN: 382922101

1272
Great Lakes Energy People Fund
1323 Boyne Ave.
P.O. Box 70
Boyne City, MI 49712-8940
County: Charlevoix
Contact: Terry Distel, Pres.
FAX: (231) 582-6213;
E-mail: glenergy@glenergy.com; Toll-free tel.: (888) 485-2537; URL: http://www.gtlakes.com/people-fund/program-details

Established in 1996 in MI.
Donor: Customers of Great Lakes Energy.
Grantmaker type: Public charity.
Financial data (yr. ended 12/31/09): Revenue, $130,465; assets, $231,993 (M); gifts received, $128,406; expenditures, $205,902; total giving, $205,902; giving activities include $205,902 for grants.
Purpose and activities: The fund part of Operation RoundUp, a voluntary charitable contribution program sponsored by Great Lakes Energy customers, awards grants to nonprofit organizations and charitable activities within the geographical area served by Great Lakes Energy.
Fields of interest: Community/economic development.
Limitations: Applications accepted. Giving limited to Allegan, Antrim, Barry, Charlevoix, Cheboygan, Clare, Crawford, Emmet, Grand Traverse, Kalkaska, Kent, Lake, Manistee, Mason, Mecosta, Missaukee, Montcalm, Montgomery, Muskegon, Newaygo, Oceana, Osceola, Oscoda, Otsego, Ottawa, and Wexford counties, MI. No support for religious activities or for continuing school projects. No grants to individuals, or generally for normal operating expenses of established programs, annual fundraising campaigns, endowment funds, or deficit spending; no loans.
Publications: Application guidelines; Annual report.
Application information: Applications will not be accepted by fax or email. Application form required.
  Initial approach: Submit application
  Deadline(s): Feb. 1, June 1, and Oct. 1
Officers and Directors:* Kathleen Anderson,* Pres.; Tom Walenta,* V.P.; Sharon Templar, Secy.; Mike Stowe,* Treas.; Laura Beyer; Wayne Bumstead; Beverly Cassidy; Terry Distel; Shirley Farrier; Carol Holtrop; Shelley Myers; Al Quaal; Pat Stapp; David Wagner.
EIN: 383220304

1273

Great Lakes Fishery Trust

c/o Public Sector Consultants
600 W. St. Joseph St., Ste. 10
Lansing, MI 48933-2265 (517) 371-7468
County: Ingham
Contact: Holly Madill, Opers. Mgr.
FAX: (517) 484-6549; E-mail: glft@glft.org;
URL: http://www.glft.org/

Established in 1996 in MI.
Grantmaker type: Public charity.
Financial data (yr. ended 12/31/09): Revenue,
$3,199,078; assets, $20,305,752 (M); gifts
received, $111,250; expenditures, $4,481,033;
total giving, $3,739,808; program services
expenses, $4,032,502; giving activities include
$3,739,808 for 26 grants (high: $900,000; low:
$9,939), and $292,694 for
foundation-administered programs.
Purpose and activities: The trust provides funding
to enhance, protect, and rehabilitate Great Lakes
fishery resources, and to mitigate for lost use and
enjoyment of the Lake Michigan fishery resulting
from the operation of the Ludington Pumped Storage
Plant.
Fields of interest: Environment, research;
Environment, public education; Environment, water
resources; Animals/wildlife, preservation/
protection; Animals/wildlife, fisheries.
Type of support: Continuing support; Building/
renovation; Equipment; Land acquisition; Program
development; Conferences/seminars; Publication;
Seed money; Curriculum development; Fellowships;
Internship funds; Scholarship funds; Research;
Technical assistance; Program evaluation;
Matching/challenge support.
Limitations: Applications accepted. Giving limited to
MI, with Lake Michigan and its tributaries the
primary geographic target for projects; secondary
consideration given to projects that primarily benefit
fisheries or fishing access outside the Lake
Michigan watershed. No support for lobbying. No
grants to individuals.
Publications: Application guidelines; Annual report;
Financial statement; Grants list; Informational
brochure; Occasional report.
Application information: Proposals are accepted by
e-mail. Application form required.
   Initial approach: Application form, letter, or
      telephone
   Copies of proposal: 1
   Deadline(s): Jan. for Ecosystem Health and
      Sustainable Fish Populations; Sept. for Fishing
      Access; two weeks prior to board meetings for
      Great Lakes Stewardship Initiative
   Board meeting date(s): Feb., May, Aug., and Nov.
   Final notification: Feb. for Stewardship; Nov. for
      Fishing Access
Trustees: Andy Buchsbaum; Peter Manning; Eric
McDonough; Brian Napont; Robert Reichel; Bill
Schuette; Kelley Smith; Charles Wooley.
Number of staff: 1 full-time professional; 4 part-time
professional.
EIN: 383331471

1274

Irwin and Bethea Green Support Foundation

6735 Telegraph Rd.
P.O. Box 2030
Bloomfield Hills, MI 48301-3141
(248) 642-4260
County: Oakland
Contact: Bethea Green, Pres.

Established in 1984 in MI; supporting organization
of the Jewish Federation of Metropolitan Detroit.
Grantmaker type: Public charity.
Financial data (yr. ended 05/31/10): Revenue,
$348,993; assets, $2,363,460 (M); gifts received,
$3,737; expenditures, $833,156; total giving,
$814,492; program services expenses, $814,492;
giving activities include $130,000 for 3 grants (high:
$55,000; low: $25,000).
Fields of interest: Jewish federated giving programs;
Jewish agencies & synagogues.
Limitations: Giving on a national and international
basis.
Officers and Directors:* Irwin Green,* Pres.; Robert
P. Arnson,* Secy.; Dorothy Benyas, Treas.; Mandell
Berman; Stacey A. Crane; Don Green; Margo Green.
EIN: 382490337

1275

Habitat for Humanity of Kent County, Inc.

539 New Ave. S.W.
Grand Rapids, MI 49503-4925 (616) 774-2431
County: Kent
FAX: (616) 774-4120; URL: http://habitatkent.org/

Established in 1983.
Grantmaker type: Public charity.
Financial data (yr. ended 06/30/10): Revenue,
$7,043,267; assets, $10,184,264 (M); gifts
received, $3,862,515; expenditures, $5,791,676;
total giving, $3,667,849; giving activities include
$65,025 for grants, and $3,602,824 for grants to
individuals.
Purpose and activities: The organization's mission
is to strengthen the families and neighborhoods of
Kent County through partnership, house building,
and affordable homeownership.
Fields of interest: Housing/shelter.
Type of support: Grants to individuals.
Limitations: Giving primarily in Kent County, MI.
Officers and Board Members:* Matt Wey, Pres.; Ted
Adornado,* V.P.; Laurie Termaat,* Secy.; Ben
Irwin,* Treas.; Sonali Allen; Brian Chisholm; Sanjay
Dutta; Charles Fridsma; Mark Greiner; Daniel C.
Molhoek; Andrew Rassi; Julie Ridenour; Julie
Towner; Craig VanEss; Aaron VanSoest.
EIN: 382527968

1276

Harbor Springs Educational Foundation

P.O. Box 844
Harbor Springs, MI 49740-0844
County: Emmet
Contact: Frank Shumway, Pres.

Grantmaker type: Public charity.
Financial data (yr. ended 12/31/09): Revenue,
$6,380; assets, $37,911 (M); gifts received,
$6,227; expenditures, $55,474; total giving,
$48,262; giving activities include $48,262 for
grants.

Purpose and activities: The foundation supports the
educational enhancement of students in the Harbor
Springs school district.
Fields of interest: Education.
Type of support: Curriculum development;
Scholarships—to individuals; In-kind gifts.
Limitations: Giving primarily in Harbor Springs, MI.
Application information:
   Board meeting date(s): 2nd Wed. of every month
Officers: Danielle Ottimer, Pres.; Susan Clarke,
Secy.; Kathie Breighner, Treas.
Directors: Larry Cuminings; Gordon Fearon; Jill
Hanna; Linda Heminger; Sheila Luplow; Frank
Shumway; David Walsh.
EIN: 383458936

1277

Heart of West Michigan United Way

118 Commerce Ave., S.W.
Grand Rapids, MI 49503-4106 (616) 459-6281
County: Kent
FAX: (616) 459-8460; URL: http://
www.waybetterunitedway.org/

Established in 1917 in MI; supporting organization
of American Red Cross, Arbor Circle Corporation,
Association for the Blind and Visually Impaired,
Baxter Community Center, Boy Scouts of America -
Gerald R. Ford Council, Camp Fire-West Michigan
Council, Catholic Social Services, Child and Family
Resource Council, D.A. Blodgett Services for
Children and Families, Dwelling Place of Grand
Rapids, Family Outreach Center, Girl Scouts -
Michigan Trails Council, Grand Rapids Urban
League, Life Guidance Services, Project Rehab,
Salvation Army, Senior Neighbors, United Methodist
Community House, Visiting Nurse Association of
Western Michigan, Young Men's Christian
Association, Young Women's Christian Association,
and 38 other affiliated agencies.
Grantmaker type: Public charity.
Financial data (yr. ended 06/30/09): Revenue,
$15,082,427; assets, $25,583,631 (M); gifts
received, $14,697,577; expenditures,
$16,174,787; total giving, $10,571,108; giving
activities include $10,571,108 for grants.
Purpose and activities: The organization partners
with local human service providers and volunteers to
identify community needs and implement effective
solutions in five target areas: ensuring the healthy
development and school readiness of children,
preparing youth to become accountable adults,
equipping adults with skills for independence and
changing life stages. helping senior adults find
support and maintain independence, and supporting
families to achieve well-being and success.
Fields of interest: Education, early childhood
education; Adult education—literacy, basic skills &
GED; Education, reading; Education; Health care;
Youth development; Children/youth, services;
Family services; Aging, centers/services.
Type of support: General/operating support;
Program development.
Limitations: Giving limited to Kent County, MI. No
support for political purposes or purposes other
than health or human services.
Publications: Grants list.
Officers and Directors:* Lou Moran,* Chair.; Bert
Bleke,* Interim Pres.; Tony Campbell, V.P., Focused
Impact; Richard Liberatore, V.P., Agency Impact;
Sue Stoddard, V.P., Finance and Opers.; Christine
Arnold; Dr. Jeanne Arnold; Debra Bailey; Stacie
Behler, Esq.; Carla Blinkhorn; Dana Boals; Brian

Bosak; Sean M. Egan; Dennis Eidson; Rev. Dallas Lenear; John Meilner; Nelson Miller; Daniel Oglesby; Sean Welsh.
Number of staff: 49 full-time professional; 7 part-time professional.
EIN: 381360923

1278
The Heat and Warmth Fund
(also known as THAW)
607 Shelby, Ste. 400
Detroit, MI 48226-1848   (313) 226-9467
County: Wayne
Contact: John X. Miller, C.E.O.
FAX: (313) 963-2777; E-mail: info@thawfund.org; Toll-free tel.: (800) 866-8429; URL: http://www.thawfund.org

Grantmaker type: Public charity.
Financial data (yr. ended 06/30/09): Revenue, $17,169,934; assets, $3,257,280 (M); gifts received, $16,487,677; expenditures, $17,325,896; total giving, $14,772,776; giving activities include $14,772,776 for grants to individuals.
Purpose and activities: The fund seeks to improve the quality of life in Michigan and prevent human suffering by providing low-income families with energy assistance during crisis and by advocating for long term solutions to energy issues that affect the poor.
Fields of interest: Housing/shelter; Human services; Economically disadvantaged.
Type of support: Emergency funds.
Limitations: Applications accepted. Giving limited to MI.
Application information:
 Initial approach: Telephone
Officers and Directors:* Edd Snyder,* Pres.; Jonathan X. Miller, C.E.O.; Donald Jones, Secy.; Mark Steirs,* Treas.; David Ellis; Susan Foley; Dan Forsyth; Louise Guyton; Joseph Kowalski; Paul Livernois; Wayne Lynn; Bertram Marks; Jane Frances Morgan; Terry Oprea; Ed Ptasznik, Jr.; Ramona H. Richard; James Roberts.
Number of staff: 13
EIN: 382646924

1279
Hemophilia Foundation of Michigan
1921 W. Michigan Ave.
Ypsilanti, MI 48197-4816   (734) 544-0015
County: Washtenaw
Contact: Ivan C. Harner FACHE, Exec. Dir.
FAX: (734) 544-0095; E-mail: hfm@hfmich.org; Toll-free tel.: (800) 482-3041; URL: http://www.hfmich.org

Established in 1997 in MI.
Grantmaker type: Public charity.
Financial data (yr. ended 12/31/09): Revenue, $2,222,892; assets, $2,551,261 (M); gifts received, $1,595,438; expenditures, $2,154,235; total giving, $1,097,486; giving activities include $1,097,486 for grants.
Purpose and activities: The organization is dedicated to improving the quality of life for all those affected by hemophilia and hereditary bleeding disorders and related complications, including HIV infection and AIDS, through the support of

individual, family, and community services; education; health care; advocacy; and research.
Fields of interest: Health care; Hemophilia; AIDS; Hemophilia research.
Type of support: Research; Grants to individuals.
Limitations: Applications accepted. Giving limited to MI.
Publications: Annual report.
Application information: Application form required.
 Initial approach: Download application
 Deadline(s): Mar. 24
 Final notification: Apr. 10
Officers and Directors:* Jennifer Faunce,* Pres.; Adam Wilmers,* 2nd V.P.; Lauren Shellenberger,* Secy.; Peter Deininger,* Treas.; Ivan C. Harner, FACHE, Exec. Dir.; Amy Denton, M.S.A.; Jessica Foley, M.D.; Angie Guadagnini; Mark Higgins; Allan Kucab, R.N.; Harvey Liverman; Barbara Menzies, M.D.; Jennifer Wakefield.
EIN: 381905673

1280
Henry Ford Health System
1 Ford Pl., S.F.
Detroit, MI 48202-3450   (313) 876-8714
County: Wayne
URL: http://www.henryfordhealth.org

Established in 1915 in MI.
Grantmaker type: Public charity.
Financial data (yr. ended 12/31/09): Revenue, $2,118,447,816; assets, $1,805,786,268 (M); gifts received, $41,118,975; expenditures, $2,091,627,335; total giving, $33,423,072; giving activities include $1,540,038 for grants, and $31,883,034 for grants to individuals.
Purpose and activities: The system works to improve life through excellence in the science and art of health care and healing.
Fields of interest: Hospitals (general); Health care.
Type of support: Grants to individuals.
Limitations: Giving limited to Detroit, MI.
Officers and Trustees:* Cary C. Valade,* Chair.; Edward D. Callaghan, Ph.D.*, Vice-Chair.; Walter E. Douglas,* Vice-Chair.; Anthony F. Earley, Jr.,* Vice-Chair.; Jack Martin, Vice-Chair.; Mariam C. Noland,* Vice-Chair.; Sandra E. Pierce,* Vice-Chair.; Nancy M. Schlichting,* Pres. and C.E.O.; Edith L. Eisenmann,* Secy.; James M. Connelly,* Treas. and C.F.P.; N. Charles Anderson; Lynn Ford Alandt; Penny B. Blumenstein; David M. Hempstead; Albert L. Lorenzo, Ph.D.; and 9 additional trustees.
EIN: 381357020

1281
Hermelin Family Support Foundation
(formerly Hermelin Family Foundation)
6735 Telegraph Rd.
P.O. Box 2030
Bloomfield Hills, MI 48301-3141
County: Oakland

Established in 1985 in MI; supporting organization of the Jewish Federation of Metropolitan Detroit.
Donor: David B. Hermelin.
Grantmaker type: Public charity.
Financial data (yr. ended 05/31/10): Revenue, $591,017; assets, $3,157,013 (M); gifts received, $244,120; expenditures, $546,043; total giving, $528,129; program services expenses, $528,129;

giving activities include $528,129 for 64 grants (high: $97,333; low: $250).
Fields of interest: History/archaeology; Arts; Education; Health care; Medical research; Jewish federated giving programs; Jewish agencies & synagogues.
Limitations: Giving primarily in New York, NY, and MI. No grants to individuals.
Officers and Directors:* Doreen Hermelin,* Pres.; Brian Hermelin,* V.P.; Francine G. Hermelin, Secy.; Julie C. Hermelin, Treas.; Eugene Applebaum; Penny Blumenstein; Karen B. Hermelin; Marcie Hermelin Orley; Arthur Weiss.
EIN: 382574834

1282
F. W. & Elsie Heyl Science Scholarship Fund
c/o National City Bank
200 Public Sq., 5th Fl.
Cleveland, OH 44114-2332
County: Cuyahoga
Contact: For Kalamazoo College applicants: Dr. Diane R. Kiino, Exec. Dir.; For WMU Bronson School of Nursing applicants: Dr. Marie Gates
URL: http://www.kzoo.edu/heyl/

A supporting organization of Kalamazoo College, Western Michigan University Bronson School of Nursing, and Yale University.
Donors: Frederick W. Heyl†; Mrs. Frederick W. Heyl†.
Grantmaker type: Public charity.
Financial data (yr. ended 12/31/09): Assets, $32,427,914 (M); expenditures, $1,276,530; total giving, $1,154,106; giving activities include $1,154,106 for grants.
Purpose and activities: Scholarships for tuition, fees, college housing and a book allowance are available for study in the natural sciences, mathematics, computer science or health sciences at Kalamazoo College and for nursing at Western Michigan University Bronson School of Nursing. The fund also provides fellowships (renewable for a maximum of four years) for graduate study in certain (usually chemistry-related) disciplines at Yale University. These are available to any graduate of Kalamazoo College majoring in one of the exact sciences.
Fields of interest: Nursing school/education; Health sciences school/education; Science; Chemistry; Mathematics; Computer science.
Type of support: Fellowships; Scholarships—to individuals.
Limitations: Applications accepted. Giving primarily for the benefit of residents of Kalamazoo, MI.
Application information: See fund web site for application requirements. Application form required.
Officers: Eileen Wilson-Oyelaran, Pres.; David Tomko, V.P.; Scott Campbell, Secy.-Treas.; Diane Kiino, Exec. Dir.
Directors: Randall Ackerman; Henry Holland; Marian Klein; Cindy Kole; Jon Streeter; James Walter.
Trustee: National City Bank.
EIN: 386194019

1283
Hillsdale County United Way
43 North St.
P.O. Box 203
Hillsdale, MI 49242-1621 (517) 439-5050
County: Hillsdale
FAX: (517) 439-0836;
E-mail: lbenzing@hillsdalecountyunitedway.org;
URL: http://www.hillsdalecountyunitedway.org/

Established in MI.
Grantmaker type: Public charity.
Financial data (yr. ended 03/31/10): Revenue, $142,276; assets, $117,602 (M); gifts received, $123,063; expenditures, $146,592; total giving, $52,841; giving activities include $52,841 for grants.
Purpose and activities: Hillsdale County United Way provides funding for programs and services that address critical community needs to human service agencies in Hillsdale County, MI.
Fields of interest: Health care; Human services; Community/economic development.
Limitations: Giving limited to Hillsdale County, MI.
Officers and Directors: * Eric Moore,* Pres.; Bill Van Arsdalen,* V.P.; Sandra Grimm,* Secy.; Brenda Cole,* Treas.; Laurie Benzing, Exec. Dir.; Richard Ames; Harold Campbell; Rev. Julie Carey; Julie Gaier; and 8 additional directors.
EIN: 237218311

1284
Home Builders Association of Livingston County Foundation, Inc.
(also known as HBALC Foundation)
132 E. Grand River Ave.
Brighton, MI 48116-1510 (810) 227-6210
County: Livingston
Contact: Diane Korona, Exec. Dir.
FAX: (810) 227-1840; E-mail: diane@hbalc.com;
URL: http://www.hbalc.com/charitablefound.cfm

Established in 1998 in MI.
Grantmaker type: Public charity.
Financial data (yr. ended 12/31/08): Revenue, $910; assets, $1,355 (M); expenditures, $545.
Purpose and activities: Provides training and education for students pursuing a career in the building industry, as well as assisting in community service programs focusing on special housing needs.
Fields of interest: Housing/shelter, development.
Type of support: General/operating support; Scholarships—to individuals.
Limitations: Applications accepted. Giving limited to Livingston, County, MI.
Application information: Application form required.
Initial approach: Download application
Deadline(s): Mar. 23
Officers and Directors: * Bryce Palo,* Pres.; Kyle Sober,* V.P.; John Noel,* Secy.; Darlene Lane,* Treas.; Tom Boyle, C.G.R.; Dale Brewer; Boyd Buchanan; Ivy Glynn; Dianne Nance; Marie Karas.
EIN: 383466735

1285
Hope Network Foundation
(formerly Hope Foundation, Inc.)
755 36th St., S.E.
P.O. Box 890
Grand Rapids, MI 49518-0890 (616) 248-5205
County: Kent
URL: http://www.hopenetwork.org/Give-to-Hope-Network/About-the-Foundation.aspx

Established in 1987.
Grantmaker type: Public charity.
Financial data (yr. ended 09/30/09): Revenue, $1,601,113; assets, $1,975,116 (M); gifts received, $1,180,611; expenditures, $1,447,806; total giving, $784,993; giving activities include $784,993 for grants.
Purpose and activities: The foundation works to support Hope Network in its mission of empowering people with disabilities and disadvantages, allowing them to achieve their highest level of independence.
Fields of interest: Disabilities, people with.
Limitations: Giving limited to MI.
Officers: Dan de Vos,* Pres.; Jeffrey Bennett,* V.P.; Kathy Dunlap, Secy.; Michael Lettinga,* Treas.; John Canepa; Dan Coffield; Randolph Flechsig; Mike Jandernoa; Mark Lancaster; Wilbur Lettinga; Adrienne Stevens; Thomas Svitkovich; John Vander Ploeg.
EIN: 382731395

1286
Human Development Commission
429 Montague Ave.
Caro, MI 48723-1921 (989) 673-4121
County: Tuscola
FAX: (989) 673-2031; E-mail: keithp@hdc-caro.org; Additional address (Sanilac County office): 227 N. Elk St., P.O. Box 207, Sandusky, MI 48471-1106, tel.: (989) 673-4121, fax: (989) 673-2031; additional address (Huron County office): 150 Nugent Rd., Bad Axe, MI 48413-8705, tel.: (810) 648-4497, fax: (810) 648-5422; additional address (Lapeer County office): 1559 Imlay City Rd., Lapeer, MI 48446-3175, tel.: (810) 664-7133, fax: (810) 664-2649; URL: http://www.hdc-caro.org

Established in 1965 in MI.
Grantmaker type: Public charity.
Financial data (yr. ended 09/30/09): Revenue, $11,041,195; assets, $4,961,943 (M); gifts received, $9,123,111; expenditures, $10,922,861; total giving, $3,540,692; giving activities include $3,540,692 for grants to individuals.
Purpose and activities: The organization attempts to empower individuals and communities to identify their needs and secure the resources necessary to achieve their goals of self-sufficiency and improved quality of life.
Fields of interest: Dispute resolution; Housing/shelter, services; Family services; Aging, centers/services; Transportation.
Limitations: Applications accepted. Giving limited to Huron, Lapeer, Sanilac, and Tuscola counties, MI.
Publications: Annual report.
Application information:
Initial approach: Telephone
Officers and Directors: * Della Hammond,* Chair.; Christopher Taylor,* Vice-Chair.; Ron Wruble,* Secy.; Leo W. Dorr,* Treas.; Elmer Bussema; Bill Butler; Jamie Davis; Leo W. Dorr; Kim Glaspie; Carl

Holmes; Beth Hunter; Linda Jarvis; Tom Kern; Al Long; George Loomis; and 8 additional directors.
EIN: 381792679

1287
I.N. Network
10432 Chicago Dr., Ste. 2
Zeeland, MI 49464-8371 (616) 748-9620
County: Ottawa
FAX: (616) 748-9641;
E-mail: info@innetworkusa.org; Toll-free tel.: (800) 738-2912; URL: http://www.innetworkusa.org

Established in 1974.
Grantmaker type: Public charity.
Financial data (yr. ended 12/31/09): Revenue, $2,274,453; assets, $604,067 (M); gifts received, $2,268,380; expenditures, $2,303,187; total giving, $1,299,998.
Purpose and activities: The network seeks to connect front-line and supply-line partners in effective evangelism, discipleship, and community development.
Fields of interest: Christian agencies & churches.
Limitations: Giving on an international basis.
Publications: Financial statement.
Officers and Board Members: * D. James Barton,* Chair.; Robert Dean,* Vice-Chair.; LaDoyt "Rody" Rodeheaver, Pres. and C.F.O.; Teri Van Hekken, Sr. V.P., Ministry Advancement; William VerWys,* Secy.; Curt VanSolkema,* Treas.; Mark Bleyer; Kent Dale; Carl H. De Witt; Donald Engram; and 6 additional board members.
EIN: 911080666

1288
Ilitch Charities, Inc.
(formerly Ilitch Charities for Children, Inc.)
2211 Woodward Ave.
Detroit, MI 48201-3400 (313) 983-6340
County: Wayne
Contact: Anne Marie Krappmann, V.P.
URL: http://www.ilitchcharitiesforchildren.com

Grantmaker type: Public charity.
Financial data (yr. ended 12/31/09): Revenue, $637,917; assets, $2,919,380 (M); gifts received, $497,770; expenditures, $349,178; total giving, $219,566; giving activities include $219,566 for grants to individuals.
Purpose and activities: The organization is dedicated to improving the lives of children in the areas of health, education, and recreation.
Fields of interest: Arts, association; Education; Health care; Recreation.
Type of support: Scholarships—to individuals.
Limitations: Applications accepted. Giving primarily in the metropolitan Detroit, MI, area.
Publications: Application guidelines.
Application information:
Initial approach: Letter of inquiry for grants; Download application form for Hockey Scholarship
Deadline(s): Four months prior to project start date for letter of inquiry; Mar. 1 for Hockey Scholarship
Officers and Directors: * Christopher Ilitch,* Chair.; David Agius,* Pres. and Treas.; Michael J. Healy,* V.P.; Anne Marie Krappmann,* V.P.; Robert Carr,*

Secy.; Rick Fenton; Jordan Field; and 7 additional directors.
EIN: 383548144

1289

Atanas Ilitch Osteosarcoma Foundation
2211 Woodward Ave.
Detroit, MI 48201-3460
County: Wayne

Grantmaker type: Public charity.
Financial data (yr. ended 12/31/09): Revenue, $1,851; assets, $130,730 (M); gifts received, $1,246; expenditures, $12,520; total giving, $12,500; giving activities include $12,500 for grants.
Purpose and activities: The foundation provides assistance to individuals and organizations dedicated to research and treatment of people diagnosed with osteosarcoma.
Fields of interest: Cancer, leukemia.
Type of support: Grants to individuals; Research.
Limitations: Giving primarily in MI.
Officers: Atanas Ilitch, Pres.; Robert Carr, V.P.; Christopher Ilitch, V.P.
EIN: 383514195

1290

Indo-American Health & Education Foundation, Inc.
5206 Gateway Ctr., Ste. 100
Flint, MI 48507 (810) 257-9828
County: Genesee

Grantmaker type: Public charity.
Financial data (yr. ended 12/31/09): Revenue, $3,822,823; assets, $315,939 (M); gifts received, $3,822,563; expenditures, $4,202,604; total giving, $3,920,476; giving activities include $210,989 for grants.
Purpose and activities: The organization seeks to support a nonprofit hospital in India and other humanitarian projects elsewhere.
Fields of interest: Hospitals (general).
Limitations: Giving on a national and international basis, with emphasis on India.
Officers: Jitendra Kateni, Pres.; Sairamesh Bikkina, V.P.; Suresh Anne, Secy.; Apparao Mukkamala, Treas.
EIN: 481305451

1291

International Aid, Inc.
17011 W. Hickory
Spring Lake, MI 49456-9712 (616) 846-7490
County: Ottawa
FAX: (616) 846-3842; Toll-free tel.: (800) 968-7490; URL: http://www.internationalaid.org

Established in 1980 in MI.
Grantmaker type: Public charity.
Financial data (yr. ended 06/30/10): Revenue, $73,899,297; assets, $1,216,113 (M); gifts received, $72,522,612; expenditures, $73,669,080; total giving, $71,238,902; giving activities include $67,275,324 for grants, and $3,844,117 for grants to individuals.
Purpose and activities: The organization is committed to improving global health care by making quality health services available to the world's poor.

Fields of interest: Health care; Economically disadvantaged.
Limitations: Giving primarily on an international basis.
Publications: Annual report; Financial statement.
Officers and Directors:* Roger Spoelman,* Chair.; Robert Holmes Bell,* Vice-Chair.; Rev. Myles D. Fish,* Pres. and C.E.O.; Myron Aldrink, V.P., Procurement; Sonny Enriquez, V.P., Progs.; Scott Whiting, V.P., Opers.; Robert Wiersma,* Secy.; James B. Wynsma,* Treas.; Robert A. Berkhof; Tim Coan; David L. Dull, M.D.; Peter Egbert, M.D.; James Haveman, Jr.; Cathy Masamitsu; Wally Olsson; Randall G. Veltkamp.
EIN: 382323550

1292

International Development Fund for Higher Education
615 N. Fox Hills Dr.
Bloomfield Hills, MI 48304-1313
County: Oakland
Contact: Dr. Venkateswarlu Jasti, Pres.

Donors: Dr. J. Rao Divvela; Mrs. Kalpana Enduri; Dr. Ramesh Jasti; Dr. Venkateswarlu Jasti; Dr. Subbaiah Perla; Boppana D. Prasad; Dr. Bin Raju; Dr. Sitaram Ravipati; Dr. Somayajulu Yadavalli.
Grantmaker type: Public charity.
Financial data (yr. ended 12/31/09): Revenue, $2,010; assets, $194,124 (M); expenditures, $8,241; total giving, $8,102; giving activities include $8,102 for grants.
Purpose and activities: The fund provides fellowship grants to economically disadvantaged students, and also supports schools and orphanages who help disadvantaged children.
Fields of interest: Education; Economically disadvantaged.
Type of support: Fellowships; Scholarships—to individuals.
Limitations: Applications accepted. Giving limited to Andhra Pradesh state, India. No support for religious or political organizations.
Publications: Annual report; Financial statement; Grants list.
Application information: Any student in good academic standing and from an economically-disadvantaged family from Andhra Pradesh, India, may apply. Application form not required.
   Initial approach: Letter
   Deadline(s): Rolling, during the academic year
   Board meeting date(s): September
   Final notification: One month
Officers: Dr. Venkateswarlu Jasti, Pres.; Rao N. Guthikonda, V.P.; Dwaraka Prasad Boppana, Co-Secy.; Satish Jasti, Co-Secy.; K.C. Prasad, Treas.
Directors: Kondareddy Baddigam; Rama Rao Cherukuri; Udayalakshmi Nallamouthu; Kottamasu S. Rao; Lakshmi Tummala.
EIN: 382305676

1293

Ironwood Area Scholarship Foundation
650 E. Ayer St.
Ironwood, MI 49938-2206
County: Gogebic
Contact: Tim Kolesar, Pres.

Grantmaker type: Public charity.

Financial data (yr. ended 06/30/09): Revenue, $89,251; assets, $742,844 (M); gifts received, $61,717; expenditures, $22,162; total giving, $14,250; giving activities include $14,250 for grants.
Purpose and activities: The foundation provides scholarships to high school graduates based on their performances, grades, and achievements.
Fields of interest: Education.
Type of support: Scholarships—to individuals.
Application information: Application form required.
Officers: Tim Kolesar, Pres.; Darlene Dugan, V.P.; Wendy Stolt, Secy.; Sue Murphy, Treas.
Directors: James Anderson; Dan Corullo; John Garske; Dan Hannigan; Shirley Pertile; and 5 additional directors.
EIN: 382822183

1294

Italian American Delegates, Inc.
15985 Canal Rd., Ste. 5
Clinton Township, MI 48038-5021
(586) 228-5800
County: Macomb
Contact: Vito Tocco, Pres.

Established in 1986 in MI.
Grantmaker type: Public charity.
Financial data (yr. ended 10/31/09): Revenue, $29,632; assets, $32,306 (M); gifts received, $13,595; expenditures, $40,590; total giving, $39,000; program services expenses, $39,000; giving activities include $33,900 for 11 grants, and $5,100 for 2 grants to individuals (high: $5,000; low: $100).
Purpose and activities: The organization supports cultural and educational programs and provides assistance to the disadvantaged, especially to those of Italian American heritage, children and senior citizens.
Fields of interest: Arts, cultural/ethnic awareness; Disabilities, people with; Economically disadvantaged.
International interests: Italy.
Type of support: Endowments; Grants to individuals.
Limitations: Giving limited to the Detroit metropolitan area, MI.
Officers: Salvatore Ventimiglia, Pres.; Daniel Patrona, Sr., V.P.; Ted Barrie, Secy.; Frank Coppola, Treas.
EIN: 382840038

1295

Jewish Federation of Grand Rapids
2727 Michigan N.E.
Grand Rapids, MI 49506-1240 (616) 942-5553
County: Kent
Contact: Jeff Slotnick, Exec. Dir.
FAX: (616) 942-5780; URL: http://www.jewishgrandrapids.org/

Established in 1947 in MI.
Grantmaker type: Public charity.
Financial data (yr. ended 06/30/09): Revenue, $817,933; assets, $3,124,508 (M); gifts received, $614,190; expenditures, $766,127; total giving, $285,733; program services expenses, $609,507; giving activities include $285,733 for 3 grants (high: $236,281; low: $7,500), and $323,774 for foundation-administered programs.

Purpose and activities: The federation seeks to strengthen and unify the Jewish community and function as an umbrella organization to provide for the cultural, social and financial needs of its community, world Jewry and the state of Israel; areas of focus include social services, senior assistance, immigrant assistance, singles involvement, youth and family activities, and summer camp for younger children.

Fields of interest: Youth development; Human services; Family services; Jewish agencies & synagogues; Aging; Immigrants/refugees.

Limitations: Giving in the U.S., with some emphasis on Grand Rapids, MI and in Israel.

Officers and Trustees: * Dan Hurwitz,* Chair.; Judith Joseph,* Vice-Chair.; Greg Kaufman,* Vice-Chair.; Andrew Samrick,* Vice-Chair.; Claude Titche III,* Treas.; Jeff Slotnick, Exec. Dir.; David Alfonso; Glenn Barkan; Stuart Berman; Davida Dennen; Mark Finkelstein; Machelle Hammond; Norm Kravitz; Marisa Krishef; Michael Presant; and 3 additional trustees.

Number of staff: 1 full-time professional; 5 part-time professional.

EIN: 386099686

1296
Jewish Federation of Metropolitan Detroit

6735 Telegraph Rd.
P.O. Box 2030
Bloomfield Hills, MI   48303-2030
(248) 642-4260
County: Oakland
FAX: (248) 642-4941; Toll-free tel.: (888) 902-4673;
URL: http://www.thisisfederation.org

Established in 1926 in MI.

Grantmaker type: Public charity.

Financial data (yr. ended 05/31/10): Revenue, $41,154,211; assets, $36,196,249 (M); gifts received, $39,231,592; expenditures, $44,101,798; total giving, $32,600,409; program services expenses, $39,176,063; giving activities include $32,027,409 for 48 grants (high: $10,337,426; low: $7,905), and $6,575,654 for foundation-administered programs.

Purpose and activities: The foundation, in partnership with its agencies, plays the leadership role in identifying needs within the metropolitan Detroit Jewish community and in mobilizing human and financial resources, engaging in communal planning, and allocating and advocating to meet those needs.

Fields of interest: Philanthropy/voluntarism; Jewish federated giving programs; Jewish agencies & synagogues.

International interests: Israel.

Type of support: Annual campaigns; Capital campaigns; Program development.

Limitations: Giving on a national and international basis.

Publications: Annual report; Financial statement; Newsletter.

Officers and Directors: * Nancy Grosfeld,* Pres.; Michael P. Horowitz,* Pres.-Elect; Ronald A. Klein,* V.P.; Ronald Krugel,* V.P.; Lawrence S. Lax,* V.P.; Matthew B. Lester,* V.P.; Beverly Liss,* V.P.; Gary Torgow,* V.P.; Marcie Orley,* Secy.; James B. Bellinson,* Treas.; Dr. Lynda Giles; Florine Mark; Marta Rosenthal; Jane Sherman; Paul r. Silverman.

EIN: 381359214

1297
The Jewish Fund

6735 Telegraph Rd.
Bloomfield Hills, MI   48301-3141
(248) 203-1487
County: Oakland
Contact: Margo Pernick, Exec. Dir.
FAX: (258) 645-7843; URL: http://www.thejewishfund.org

Established in 1997 in MI; supporting organization of the Jewish Federation of Metropolitan Detroit.

Grantmaker type: Public charity.

Financial data (yr. ended 05/31/10): Revenue, $3,677,532; assets, $56,160,054 (M); expenditures, $2,782,341; total giving, $2,537,917; giving activities include $2,537,917 for grants.

Fields of interest: Palliative care; Health care; Family services; Aging, centers/services; Human services; Jewish agencies & synagogues; Aging.

Type of support: Program development; Seed money; Curriculum development; Technical assistance; Program evaluation; Matching/challenge support.

Limitations: Applications accepted. Giving limited to southeastern MI, primarily metropolitan Detroit. No grants to individuals, or for annual campaigns, religious activities, sectarian education, overseas projects, capital campaigns, equipment, endowments, or debt reduction; no loans.

Publications: Application guidelines; Annual report.

Application information: Application form required.

Initial approach: Letter of intent
Copies of proposal: 1
Deadline(s): Mar. 7 and Sept. 4 for letters of intent; June 4 and Oct. 30 for full proposals
Board meeting date(s): Jan., May, Aug., Nov., and Dec.
Final notification: Aug. and Dec.

Officers and Board Members: * Robert Naftaly,* Chair.; Michael Maddin,* Vice-Chair.; Dorothy Benyas, Secy.-Treas.; Margo Pernick, Exec. Dir.; David Aronow; Selwyn Isakow; Mark Schlussel; Jerry Schostak; Gary Torgow; and 20 additional board members.

Number of staff: None.

EIN: 383323875

Selected grants: The following grants were reported in 2006.

$288,528 to Jewish Family Service, West Bloomfield, MI. For Project Chessed, a network of free and reduced price medical care for uninsured Jewish adults in metro Detroit.

$95,000 to City Year Detroit, Detroit, MI. For obesity prevention program in Detroit Public Schools in partnership with Henry For Health System.

$80,000 to Jewish Hospice and Chaplaincy Network, West Bloomfield, MI. For development of palliative care program for Detroit Jewish community.

$67,000 to Jewish Family Service, West Bloomfield, MI. For Escorted Transportation program for frail older adults.

$45,000 to Dr. Gary Burnstein Community Health Clinic, Pontiac, MI. For start-up costs for new free medical clinic.

$45,000 to JARC, Farmington Hills, MI. For CHEERS, program providing meaningful social inclusion opportunities for people with developmental disabilities.

$35,000 to Friendship Circle, West Bloomfield, MI. For adult volunteer coordinator for new Life Village.

$25,000 to Humanitarian Aid Foundation, Huntington Woods, MI. For in-home services for holocaust survivors in metro Detroit.

$25,000 to Kadima: Jewish Support Services for Adults with Mental Illness, Southfield, MI. For support program for families of children who struggle with emotional disorders.

$18,000 to Jewish Community Center of Metropolitan Detroit, West Bloomfield, MI. For summer recreational and vocational program for older teens with special needs.

1298
Jewish Women's Foundation of Metropolitan Detroit

6735 Telegraph Rd.
P.O. Box 2030
Bloomfield Hills, MI   48303-2030
(248) 203-1483
County: Oakland
Contact: Helen Katz, Dir.
FAX: (248) 642-4941; E-mail: katz@jfmd.org;
URL: http://www.jewishdetroit.org/jwf/

Established in 1999 in MI; a component fund of Jewish Federation of Metropolitan Detroit.

Grantmaker type: Public charity.

Financial data (yr. ended 05/31/09): Total giving, $240,700 Giving activities include $240,700 for grants.

Purpose and activities: The Jewish Women's Foundation of Metropolitan Detroit, a special grantmaking fund within the United Jewish Foundation of Metropolitan Detroit, seeks to expand and improve opportunities and choices in all aspects of Jewish women's and girls' lives through strategic and effective grantmaking. The foundation endeavors to empower women as funders, decision makers, and agents for change through projects and programs that promote change among, and address the unmet needs of, Jewish women and girls, such as domestic abuse, health concerns, employment, resettlement, aging, poverty, and single-parent support.

Fields of interest: Health care; Crime/violence prevention, domestic violence; Employment; Family services, single parents; Aging; Women; Immigrants/refugees; Economically disadvantaged.

Type of support: Continuing support; Program development; Conferences/seminars; Seed money; Curriculum development; Research; Technical assistance.

Limitations: Applications accepted. Giving currently limited to programs, projects or initiatives in MI. No support for political campaigns or organizations. No grants to individuals, or for scholarships or tuition reimbursement, capital campaigns, sponsorships for special events, or purchase of tickets or tables for events; no loans.

Publications: Application guidelines; Informational brochure (including application guidelines); Program policy statement.

Application information: See foundation web site for full application guidelines, deadlines, and requirements, including Letter of Intent. Application form required.

Initial approach: Letter of Intent (available on foundation web site); full grant application should be submitted only upon invitation.
Copies of proposal: 1
Deadline(s): See foundation web site for current deadline for Letter of Intent

Officers and Trustees: * Sharon Hart,* Chair.; Lisa Lis,* Assoc. Chair.; Helen Katz,* Dir.; and 115 additional trustees.
Number of staff: 1 part-time professional; 1 full-time support.

1299
John Ball Zoological Society

1300 W. Fulton St.
P.O. Box 2506
Grand Rapids, MI 49504-6100 (616) 336-4301
County: Kent
E-mail: info@johnballzoosociety.org; URL: http://www.johnballzoosociety.org

Established in 1950 in MI.
Grantmaker type: Public charity.
Financial data (yr. ended 06/30/09): Revenue, $1,839,949; assets, $2,976,329 (M); gifts received, $1,109,826; expenditures, $2,141,698; total giving, $12,923; program services expenses, $1,687,263; giving activities include $12,923 for 10 grants to individuals, and $1,674,340 for foundation-administered programs.
Purpose and activities: The society supports the operation and maintenance of the John Ball Zoo, and works to provide funds for conservation efforts around the world.
Fields of interest: Animals/wildlife, research; Animal welfare.
Type of support: Scholarships—to individuals; Research.
Limitations: Applications accepted. Giving on a national and international basis.
Publications: Application guidelines.
Application information: Application form required.
Initial approach: Submit proposal
Deadline(s): Mar. 1 for Wildlife Conservation Fund
Officers: Cathy Bissell, Co-Chair., Devel.; Gary Burbridge, Co-Chair., Community; Kyle Irwin, Co-Chair., Devel. and Secy.; Gary K. Milligan, Co-Chair., Admin.; Robert Tholl, Jr., Pres.; John Green, V.P.; Craig Terpestra, Treas.; Brenda Stringer, Exec. Dir.
Board Members: Anthony Barnes; Ryan Cook; Marilyn Crawford; Lori Crook; Mimi Cummings; Gilbert De Padula; Dr. Matthew Douglas; Candance Dugan; Randall Dykstra; Bill Hineline; Tracey Hornbeck; Dan Hurwitz; Barbara Lindquist; Dan Molhoek; Ed Pynnonen; and 7 additional board members.
EIN: 386076879

1300
Junior League of Saginaw Valley

5800 Gratiot Rd., Ste. 104
Saginaw, MI 48638-6090 (989) 790-3763
County: Saginaw
URL: http://jlsv.org/

Established in 1929 in MI.
Grantmaker type: Public charity.
Financial data (yr. ended 05/31/10): Revenue, $78,111; assets, $175,472 (M); expenditures, $54,023; total giving, $10,439; giving activities include $10,439 for grants.
Purpose and activities: The Junior League of Saginaw Valley is an organization of women committed to promoting voluntarism, developing the potential of women and improving the community through the effective action and leadership of

trained volunteers. Its purpose is exclusively educational and charitable. Focus areas include health and education of women and children, violence and prevention, and women in leadership.
Fields of interest: Children/youth, services; Women, centers/services; Community/economic development; Philanthropy/voluntarism; Women.
Limitations: Applications accepted. Giving limited to the Saginaw Valley, MI, area.
Publications: Application guidelines.
Application information: Application form required.
Initial approach: Download application
Officers and Directors: * Sara Robles,* Pres.; Elizabeth Stuber,* Pres.-Elect; Carrie Kessel,* Secy.; Lisa Beird,* Treas.; Julie Brown,* Membership Chair.; Tara Stewart,* Program Chair.; Sarah Nothelfer,* Public Rels.; Kari Shaheen,* Nominating & Placement.
Sustaining Advisors: Cyndy Lange; Andrea Muladore.
EIN: 381513320

1301
Justice Foundation of West Michigan

(formerly Grand Rapids Bar Foundation)
c/o Grand Rapids Bar Assn.
161 Ottawa Ave. N.W., Ste. 203B
Grand Rapids, MI 49503-2714 (616) 454-5550
County: Kent
Contact: Mark Petz
URL: http://www.grbar.org/displaycommon.cfm?an=1&subarticlenbr=62

Established in 1978 in MI.
Grantmaker type: Public charity.
Financial data (yr. ended 12/31/09): Revenue, $64,090; assets, $375,796 (M); gifts received, $67,734; expenditures, $60,830; total giving, $25,117; giving activities include $25,117 for grants.
Purpose and activities: Support for programs that promote or provide legal services to the disadvantaged, improve the administration of justice, and educate the public about democratic values.
Fields of interest: Courts/judicial administration.
Type of support: Seed money; Program development.
Limitations: Applications accepted. Giving limited to western MI, primarily in Kent County. No support for partisan political organizations. No grants to individuals, or for general operating costs, capital construction projects or endowment campaigns, fundraising events or sponsorships, or honorariums and/or speaker fees.
Publications: Application guidelines.
Application information: See foundation web site for full application guidelines and requirements; application form may be downloaded or submitted online. Application form required.
Initial approach: Letter
Copies of proposal: 2
Deadline(s): Mar. 1 and Sept. 1
Board meeting date(s): Mar. and Sept.
Final notification: Within 90 days
Officers: Hon. Paul J. Sullivan, Pres.; Paul T. Sorensen, V.P.; Miles J. Postema, Secy.; Terence J. Ackert, Treas.
Trustees: Jane M. Beckering; Karl W. Butterer; Charles E. Chamberlain; Scott E. Dwyer; Anthony P. Gauthier, Jr.; Dwight K. Hamilton; Wendell P.

Russell, Jr.; Kristin M. Vandenberg; Matthew L. Vicari.
EIN: 382245940

1302
The Kalamazoo Aviation History Museum

6151 Portage Rd.
Portage, MI 49002-3003 (269) 382-6555
County: Kalamazoo
Toll-free tel.: (866) 524-7966; URL: http://www.airzoo.org/

Classified as a private operating foundation in 1977.
Donors: Preston S. Parish; Suzanne D. Parish; Bowers Manufacturing Co.; Diane Patriacca; George Polla; Albert Schiffer; Anna Schiffer; Mrs. Michael Schiffer; Michael Schiffer; Preston Parish; Vlado Lenoch; Arnold Herskovic; Ronda E. Stryker; William D. Johnson; Ley Smith; Lois Smith; Dorothy U. Dalton Foundation.
Grantmaker type: Public charity.
Financial data (yr. ended 12/31/09): Revenue, $4,529,273; assets, $22,112,838 (M); gifts received, $1,897,781; expenditures, $4,973,540.
Purpose and activities: The museum works to preserve the legacy of flight for present and future generations.
Fields of interest: Museums (science/technology); Transportation.
Officers and Directors: * Preston S. Parish,* Chair.; Suzanne D. Parish,* Vice-Chair.; David Hatfield, 2nd Vice-Chair.; Robert E. Ellis, Pres. and Exec. Dir.; James Bridenstine, Secy.; Ronald N. Kilgore, Treas.
Board Members: Jon Bowers; Dr. Randall W. Eberts; Donald Parfet; Barry Smith; Mary Tyler; Jon van der Molen.
EIN: 382144402

1303
Kalamazoo Communities in Schools Foundation

(formerly Kalamazoo Public Education Foundation)
714 S. Westnedge Ave., Ste. 214
Kalamazoo, MI 49007-5094 (269) 337-0498
County: Kalamazoo
Contact: Pamela Kingery, Exec. Dir.
FAX: (269) 337-0496; E-mail: kpefcec@aol.com; URL: http://www.kcisfkidsfirst.org

Established in 1991.
Grantmaker type: Public charity.
Financial data (yr. ended 06/30/09): Revenue, $1,693,663; assets, $3,176,023 (M); gifts received, $1,459,082; expenditures, $1,586,197.
Purpose and activities: The foundation supports programs to benefit students in Kalamazoo public schools.
Fields of interest: Elementary/secondary education.
Type of support: Program development; Scholarships—to individuals.
Limitations: Giving limited to Kalamazoo, MI.
Publications: Application guidelines; Grants list.
Application information: See web site for additional application information. Application form required.
Deadline(s): Varies
Officers and Directors: * Larry Lueth,* Chair.; Jim Harrington,* Vice-Chair.; Rebekah Fennell,* Secy.-Treas.; Pamela Kingery, Exec. Dir.; Janice

Brown; Kevin Campbell; Stephen Denenfeld; James A. Harrington; and 25 additional directors.
EIN: 382873188

1304
Kalamazoo County Health Plan Corporation

c/o Family Health Center
117 W. Paterson St.
Kalamazoo, MI 49007-2557
County: Kalamazoo

Established in MI.
Grantmaker type: Public charity.
Financial data (yr. ended 09/30/09): Revenue, $5,239,413; assets, $1,861,226 (M); gifts received, $5,082,789; expenditures, $5,357,609; total giving, $1,216,241; giving activities include $1,216,241 for grants.
Purpose and activities: The organization seeks to insure the delivery of basic preventative healthcare to low income persons without insurance and/or who are ineligible for other government programs.
Fields of interest: Health care; American Red Cross; Residential/custodial care, hospices; Economically disadvantaged.
Limitations: Giving limited to Kalamazoo, MI.
Officers: Denise Crawford,* Pres.; Moses Walker, Secy.-Treas.; Lucinda Stinson, Exec. Dir.
Directors: Earl Burhans, M.D.; Bob Doud; Eric Dewey; Jeff Patton; Lowell Rinker; Sherry Thomas-Cloud; Rick Tooker.
EIN: 383620947

1305
Kalamazoo Loaves and Fishes

913 E. Alcott
Kalamazoo, MI 49001-3853 (269) 488-2617
County: Kalamazoo
FAX: (269) 343-3669; URL: http://www.kzoolf.org

Established in 1982 in MI.
Grantmaker type: Public charity.
Financial data (yr. ended 06/30/10): Revenue, $2,469,259; assets, $1,938,010 (M); gifts received, $2,448,127; expenditures, $2,170,406.
Purpose and activities: The organization works to expand the availability of emergency food resources and to promote the ability of hungry people to feed themselves.
Fields of interest: Food services; Food services, commodity distribution; Nutrition; Human services, emergency aid.
Limitations: Giving limited to south-central MI.
Publications: Annual report; Newsletter.
Officers: Harvey Meyers,* Pres.; Maija Petersons,* Secy.; Anne Lipsey, Exec. Dir.; Leatta Byrd; Patricia Carlin; Bob Ezelle; Bruce Gelbaugh; Martin Glitsa; Lynn Jessell; Cheryl Knapp; Sam Lealofi; Donna McClurken; Helen Norris; Martha Simpson.
EIN: 382420575

1306
Kalamazoo Regional Catholic Schools Foundation

1000 W. Kilgore Rd.
Kalamazoo, MI 49008-3616
County: Kalamazoo

Grantmaker type: Public charity.

Financial data (yr. ended 06/30/08): Revenue, $467,141; assets, $2,310,139 (M); gifts received, $291,522; expenditures, $119,738; total giving, $112,011; program services expenses, $112,011; giving activities include $112,011 for 2 grants (high: $107,011; low: $5,000).
Purpose and activities: The foundation provides educational funds for Catholic schools in the greater Kalamazoo area.
Fields of interest: Elementary/secondary education; Catholic agencies & churches.
Type of support: Endowments; Scholarship funds.
Limitations: Giving limited to Kalamazoo, MI.
Publications: Financial statement.
Officers: Daniel DeMent, Pres.; Julie Sullivan, V.P.; Joseph Spoerl, Treas.
EIN: 382476783

1307
Kalamazoo Rotary Club Charities

P.O. Box 50251
Kalamazoo, MI 49005-0251
County: Kalamazoo

Grantmaker type: Public charity.
Financial data (yr. ended 06/30/09): Revenue, $37,774; assets, $95,159 (M); gifts received, $36,285; expenditures, $21,851; total giving, $21,321; giving activities include $21,321 for grants.
Fields of interest: Community/economic development.
Type of support: Seed money.
Limitations: Giving primarily in Kalamazoo, MI.
Officers: Judith Moore, Pres.; Rex Bell, V.P.; Barbara Walters, Secy.; Robert Kent, Treas.
Directors: Sandra Bliesner; Drew Elliott; Lisa Godfrey; Mary Jo Hawk; Brian Kaufman; Ann Nieuwenhuis; Michael Williams.
EIN: 386089188

1308
Kalamazoo Symphony Orchestra

359 S. Kalamazoo Mall, Ste. 100
Kalamazoo, MI 49007-4843 (269) 349-7759
County: Kalamazoo
FAX: (269) 349-9229; URL: http://www.kalamazoosymphony.com

Grantmaker type: Public charity.
Financial data (yr. ended 05/31/09): Revenue, $2,774,266; assets, $13,173,572 (M); gifts received, $1,354,238; expenditures, $2,581,094; total giving, $7,880; giving activities include $7,880 for grants.
Fields of interest: Performing arts, orchestras.
Type of support: Scholarships—to individuals.
Officers and Directors: Darren Timmeney,* Pres.; Christopher Haenicke,* V.P., Finance, and Treas.; Robert Beam,* V.P., Opers.; Linda Depta,* V.P., Devel.; Jay Heckler,* V.P., Opers.; Fred Schubkegel,* V.P., Education; Janet Karpus,* Secy.; Jane Baley; Callie Baskerville-Jones; Sandra Blix; and 25 additional directors.
EIN: 386005710

1309
Greater Kalamazoo United Way

709 S. Westnedge Ave.
Kalamazoo, MI 49007-6003 (269) 343-2524
County: Kalamazoo
FAX: (269) 344-7250;
E-mail: information@KalamazooUnitedWay.org;
URL: http://www.kalamazoounitedway.org/

Established in 1945 in MI.
Grantmaker type: Public charity.
Financial data (yr. ended 03/31/10): Revenue, $352,726; assets, $11,293,594 (M); gifts received, $284,556; expenditures, $438,090; total giving, $25,280; giving activities include $25,280 for grants.
Purpose and activities: The GKUW makes an impact by investing time and resources in initiatives, collaborations and programs in seven target areas: health care, healthy families, addressing basic needs, coping with crisis, increasing self-sufficiency, youth development, and community building.
Fields of interest: Health care; Youth development; Human services; Family services; Community/economic development.
Limitations: Applications accepted. Giving limited to the greater Kalamazoo, MI, area.
Application information: See web site for application guidelines and requirements, including downloadable application form. Application form required.
Deadline(s): See web site for current deadlines for grants for permanent supportive housing, addressing grief and loss for children, early childhood systems change, and cultural understanding.
Officers and Directors: Don Parfet,* Chair.; Paul Sapude,* Vice-Chair.; Eric Dewey, Pres.; Rich MacDonald,* Secy.; David Furgason, Treas.; James Barnum; Robert Beam; John Boss; Joel Brooks; Cecily Cagle; Doug Callander; Ken Collard; Niall Condon; Dawnanne Corbit; John Dunn; and 26 additional directors.
EIN: 381359193

1310
The Kelly Relief Fund

999 W. Big Beaver Rd.
Troy, MI 48084
County: Oakland

Grantmaker type: Public charity.
Financial data (yr. ended 12/31/07): Revenue, $50; assets, $20,044 (M); gifts received, $50; expenditures, $6,269; total giving, $6,250; program services expenses, $6,250; giving activities include $6,250 for grants to individuals.
Purpose and activities: The fund provides assistance to disaster victims.
Fields of interest: Safety/disasters.
Type of support: Grants to individuals.
Officers and Directors: Terence E. Adderley,* Chair.; Carl T. Camden,* Pres. and C.E.O.; William K. Gerber,* Exec. V.P. and C.F.O.; Michael L. Durik,* Exec. V.P. and C.A.O.; Daniel T. Lis,* Sr. V.P. and Secy.; Michael F. Orsini, V.P., Tax, and Treas.; Sandra W. Galac, V.P.; Nicole Beck; Cathleen Brook.
EIN: 203414345

1311
Kent Regional Community Coordinated Child Care, Inc.
233 E. Fulton St., Ste. 107
Grand Rapids, MI   49503-3262   (616) 451-8281
County: Kent
FAX: (616) 451-8327; Toll-free tel.: (800) 448-6995

Grantmaker type: Public charity.
Financial data (yr. ended 09/30/09): Revenue, $5,495,016; assets, $1,346,556 (M); gifts received, $5,350,356; expenditures, $5,452,558; total giving, $3,797,891; giving activities include $3,797,891 for grants.
Purpose and activities: The organization works in partnership with other organizations to ensure the availability of affordable, accessible, and quality child care which is compatible with the needs of the family, and to provide information and referral for dependent care.
Fields of interest: Children/youth, services; Children, day care; Children/youth.
Limitations: Giving limited to Allegan, Barry, Ingham, Ionia, Kalamazoo, Kent, Lake, Mason, Mecosta, Montcalm, Muskegon, Newaygo, Oceana, Ottawa, and Wexford counties, MI.
Officers and Board Members:* Dan Fogel,* Chair.; Shlynn Rhodes,* Vice-Chair.; Kathi Harris, Treas.; Michael Chielens; Amy Combs; Dan Gerrity; Mary Beth Kozak; Gayle Orange; Karen Schneider; Dr. Pat Seiler; Diane Sparks.
EIN: 382066096

1312
King Trust Charitable Gift Fund
P.O. Box 580
Spring Arbor, MI   49283-0580
County: Jackson

Established in MI.
Grantmaker type: Public charity.
Financial data (yr. ended 12/31/08): Revenue, $818,147; assets, $3,819,232 (M); gifts received, $607,266; expenditures, $674,285; total giving, $550,701; giving activities include $550,701 for grants.
Limitations: Giving on a national and international basis.
Officers: Gene E. Keene, Chair.; Tim Burkhart, Pres. and C.E.O.; Dan Kurtz, C.F.O. and V.P.; Kerry Hettinger, Secy.
EIN: 386753798

1313
Kiwanis Foundation of Harbor Springs
P.O. Box 485
Harbor Springs, MI   49740-0485
County: Emmet

Grantmaker type: Public charity.
Financial data (yr. ended 09/30/09): Assets, $300,079 (M); gifts received, $4,135; expenditures, $15,708; total giving, $12,591; giving activities include $12,591 for grants.
Purpose and activities: Support for education, including scholarships to high school graduates for college.
Fields of interest: Education.
Type of support: Program development; Scholarships—to individuals.
Limitations: Giving primarily in Harbor Springs, MI.

Officers and Directors:* Bob Kickel,* Pres.; Matthew Keene,* V.P.; Hal Dorf,* Secy.; Gary Kent,* Treas.; Steve Hoffman.
EIN: 382577262

1314
Kolo Charities, Inc.
2410 Correll Dr.
Lake Orion, MI   48360-2258   (248) 891-4766
County: Oakland
Contact: Scott Kowalkowski, Pres.
E-mail: info@kolocharities.org; URL: http://www.kolocharities.org

Established in 1991 in MI.
Grantmaker type: Public charity.
Financial data (yr. ended 12/31/09): Revenue, $34,293; assets, $96,384 (M); expenditures, $31,163; total giving, $27,500; giving activities include $27,500 for grants.
Purpose and activities: The organization provides funds for charitable and educational purposes.
Fields of interest: Education.
Limitations: Giving limited to the Houghton Lakes area, MI.
Officers and Directors:* Scott Kowalkowski,* Pres.; Judy Kowalkowski,* Secy.; J. Thomas Lesnau,* Treas.; Daniel Jaroshewich; Terry Kazakos.
EIN: 382999444

1315
Lakeland Health Foundation, Niles
(formerly Pawating Health Foundation)
1234 Napier Ave.
St. Joseph, MI   49085-2112
County: Berrien
Contact: Douglas Law, Chair.
URL: http://www.lakelandhealth.org/body.cfm?id=44

Established in 1992 in MI; converted from Pawating Hospital.
Grantmaker type: Public charity.
Financial data (yr. ended 09/30/09): Revenue, $225,990; assets, $1,103,422 (M); gifts received, $247,536; expenditures, $73,629; total giving, $33,006; giving activities include $22,506 for grants, and $10,500 for grants to individuals.
Purpose and activities: The foundation seeks to promote and assist in providing health care services.
Fields of interest: Health care.
Type of support: Equipment; Scholarships—to individuals.
Limitations: Applications accepted. Giving limited to southwestern MI.
Publications: Application guidelines.
Application information: Application form required.
  Initial approach: Telephone or email foundation for application materials for Allied Health Careers Scholarship/Loan Fund
Officers and Directors:* Douglas Law,* Chair.; Robert Habicht,* Vice-Chair.; Leo Soorus,* Pres.; Thomas Grant,* Secy.-Treas.; Ishwara Bhat, M.D.; Michele Boyd; Nancy Butler; Tim Childs; John Colip; Gloria Cooper; Terry Eull; Robert Feldman; Harold Finley; Jerry French; Ted Halbritter III; and 14 additional directors.
EIN: 383130558

1316
Lansing Art Gallery, Inc.
113 S. Washington Sq.
Lansing, MI   48933-1703   (517) 374-6400
County: Ingham
Contact: Catherine Allswede-Babcock, Exec. Dir.
E-mail: lansingartgallery@yahoo.com; URL: http://www.lansingartgallery.org

Established in 1964 in MI.
Grantmaker type: Public charity.
Financial data (yr. ended 06/30/10): Revenue, $315,030; assets, $154,636 (M); gifts received, $267,787; expenditures, $120,390.
Purpose and activities: The gallery promotes public awareness, enjoyment and education of the visual arts through the support of Michigan artists.
Fields of interest: Visual arts.
Type of support: Scholarships—to individuals.
Limitations: Applications accepted. Giving limited to Lansing, MI.
Application information: See web site for additional application information.
  Initial approach: Submit portfolio for Art Scholarship Alert
Officers and Directors:* Daniel Warmels,* Pres.; Anne E. Hodgins,* Treas.; Catherine Allswede-Babcock, Exec. Dir.; Connie Christy; Gary McRay; and 15 additional directors.
EIN: 381889973

1317
Latvian Foundation, Inc.
1907 Autumn Crest Ln.
Kalamazoo, MI   49008-4810
County: Kalamazoo

Established in 1976.
Grantmaker type: Public charity.
Financial data (yr. ended 04/30/10): Revenue, $63,844; assets, $724,612 (M); gifts received, $18,952; expenditures, $40,894; total giving, $14,721; giving activities include $14,721 for grants.
Purpose and activities: The foundation seeks to preserve Latvian culture.
Fields of interest: Arts; Education.
International interests: Latvia.
Type of support: Grants to individuals.
Limitations: Giving limited to Latvia.
Officers: Valdis Berzins, Pres.; Astrida Levensteins, V.P.; Alfs Berztiss, Secy.; Tua Karklis, Treas.
EIN: 237089477

1318
Lenawee United Way
1354 N. Main St.
Adrian, MI   49221-1724   (517) 263-4696
County: Lenawee
FAX: (517) 265-3039;
E-mail: info@lenaweeunitedway.org; URL: http://www.lenaweeunitedway.org

Established in MI.
Grantmaker type: Public charity.
Financial data (yr. ended 07/31/10): Revenue, $881,748; assets, $872,260 (M); gifts received, $851,113; expenditures, $1,030,857; total giving, $675,812; giving activities include $675,812 for grants.

Fields of interest: Community/economic development, fund raising/fund distribution; Community/economic development; Philanthropy/voluntarism, fund raising/fund distribution.
Type of support: Annual campaigns.
Limitations: Applications accepted. Giving primarily in Lenawee County, MI.
Application information:
Initial approach: Telephone or e-mail
Officers and Board Members:* Jan Parson,* Pres.; Jay VanBuren,* 1st V.P.; Tom Kavanagh,* 2nd V.P.; Anne Rospo,* Treas.; Kathleen Schanz, Exec. Dir.; and 15 additional board members.
Number of staff: 4 full-time professional.
EIN: 381598949

1319
Life Giving Ministries
3510 Apache Ct.
Grandville, MI   49418-1924
County: Kent

Established in 2005 in MI.
Donors: Steve Maas; Lisa Maas.
Grantmaker type: Public charity.
Financial data (yr. ended 12/31/09): Revenue, $9; assets, $130 (M); expenditures, $2,214.
Fields of interest: Religion.
Officers: Dora Meendering, Co-Pres.; Rajeswari Sonni, Co-Pres.; Ashok Sonni, V.P.; Steve Maas, Treas.
Directors: June Blums; Dean Wheeler.
EIN: 202933800

1320
Lifestyle Lift Foundation
100 Kirts Blvd., Ste. A
Troy, MI   48084-5217
County: Oakland
URL: http://www.lifestyleliftfoundation.com/

Established in 2007 in MI; supporting organization Hemangioma Treatment Foundation, Inc.
Grantmaker type: Public charity.
Financial data (yr. ended 12/31/09): Revenue, $34,000; assets, $2,000 (M); gifts received, $34,000; expenditures, $33,000; total giving, $33,000; giving activities include $33,000 for grants.
Purpose and activities: The foundation's mission is to help children suffering from disfiguring diseases, particularly hemangioma, so that they may lead happier and healthier lives.
Fields of interest: Genetic diseases and disorders; Children.
Director: Justin Berger; Marcelo Hochman; Jane Milner.
EIN: 205597767

1321
Lighthouse Emergency Services, Inc.
46156 Woodward Ave.
Pontiac, MI   48342-5033   (248) 920-6100
County: Oakland
E-mail: tlukens@lighthouseoakland.org;
URL: http://www.lighthouseoakland.org/les.php

Established in 1972 in MI.
Grantmaker type: Public charity.

Financial data (yr. ended 06/30/09): Revenue, $2,795,276; assets, $396,488 (M); gifts received, $2,725,009; expenditures, $2,827,906; total giving, $1,740,480; program services expenses, $2,627,259; giving activities include $762,924 for grants to individuals, $977,556 for in-kind gifts, and $886,779 for foundation-administered programs.
Purpose and activities: The organization seeks to help transform the lives of low-income families and individuals by providing both immediate and long-term help and support from emergency and supplemental food to permanent housing, counseling, and education.
Fields of interest: Education; Agriculture/food; Housing/shelter; Human services; Economically disadvantaged.
Type of support: Grants to individuals.
Officers: William Johnson, Pres.; John Wright, V.P.; Lori Wigler, C.P.A., Secy.; Julie Johnson, Treas.; Tom Stowell, Exec. Dir.
Directors: Wilma D. Abney; Michael Baskin; Julie Beaty; Joy D. Calloway; John R. Clemmer; James LeBlanc; Chris Liparoto, CIMA, CRPC; Neran Shaya; Dennis Winkler; John Ziraldo.
EIN: 383327797

1322
Livingston County United Way
2980 Dorr Rd.
Brighton, MI   48116-9459   (810) 494-3000
County: Livingston
FAX: (810) 494-3004; *Additional tel.:* (810) 494-3003; *URL:* http://www.lcunitedway.org/

Established in 1977 in MI.
Grantmaker type: Public charity.
Financial data (yr. ended 06/30/10): Revenue, $1,345,105; assets, $2,577,104 (M); gifts received, $1,312,162; expenditures, $1,285,493; total giving, $868,851; giving activities include $868,851 for grants.
Purpose and activities: The mission of the Livingston County United Way is to represent and serve the overall interests of the citizens of Livingston County in matters concerning individual and community health and well being; current areas of focus include funding programs in the need areas of healthy aging, meeting basic needs, strengthening families, and youth services.
Fields of interest: Medical care, community health systems; Health care, clinics/centers; Public health; Health care; Children/youth, services; Family services; Human services, emergency aid; Aging, centers/services.
Limitations: Giving limited to Livingston County, MI.
Publications: Application guidelines; Annual report; Informational brochure; Newsletter.
Application information:
Board meeting date(s): 4th Wed. of each month
Officers and Directors:* Chuck Breiner,* Pres.; Becky Best,* V.P.; Greg Clum,* Secy.-Treas.; Nancy A. Rosso, Exec. Dir.; Gladys Bottum; Patricia Claffey; Greg Earl; Dennis Gehringer; Lauraine Hoensheid; Tom Lawrence; and 11 additional directors.
Number of staff: 4 full-time professional; 1 full-time support.
EIN: 382174453

1323
Local Initiatives Support Corporation
(also known as LISC)
501 7th Ave., 7th Fl.
New York, NY   10018-5903   (212) 455-9312
County: New York
FAX: (212) 682-5929; *E-mail:* info@lisc.org; *E-mail for Lea Palabrica, Prog. Off.:* lpalabrica@lisc.org;
URL: http://www.lisc.org

Established in 1979.
Grantmaker type: Public charity.
Financial data (yr. ended 12/31/09): Revenue, $113,673,475; assets, $443,477,699 (M); gifts received, $86,896,011; expenditures, $110,145,901; total giving, $36,637,310; giving activities include $36,637,310 for grants.
Purpose and activities: The corporation helps community development organizations transform distressed communities and neighborhoods into healthy and sustainable communities that are good places to live, do business, work, and raise families.
Fields of interest: Child development, education; Crime/violence prevention; Employment; Housing/shelter, development; Housing/shelter; Community/economic development, management/technical assistance; Community development, neighborhood development; Community development, citizen coalitions; Economic development; Urban/community development; Rural development; Community development, business promotion; Community development, small businesses; Community development, real estate; Community/economic development.
Type of support: Income development; Program development; Conferences/seminars; Seed money; Technical assistance; Program-related investments/loans.
Limitations: Applications accepted. Giving limited to AK, AL, AR, AZ. CA, CO, CT, DC, FL, HI, IL, IN, KS, KY, LA, MA, MD, ME, MI, MN, MO, MS, MT, NC, NE, NH, NJ, NM, NY, OH, PA, RI, SC, SD, TN, TX, VA, VT, WA, WI, and WV.
Publications: Annual report; Newsletter.
Application information:
Copies of proposal: 3
Deadline(s): Feb. 28 for (preliminary proposal) for MetLife Foundation Community-Police Partnership Awards Program; Oct. 25 for Financial Opportunity Center Social Innovation Fund; Dec. 15 for NFL Grassroots Program
Officers and Directors:* Robert E. Rubin,* Chair.; Michael Rubinger, Pres. and C.E.O.; Michael Tierney, C.O.O. and Exec. V.P.; Michael Levine, Exec. V.P. and Genl. Counsel; Betsy Pugh, Exec. V.P. & C.F.O; Mary Jo Allen, Sr. V.P., Human Resources; Evelyn Brown, Sr. V.P., Progs., Gulf Coast Rebuilding Initiative; Joe DiFilippi, Sr. V.P., Inf. Tech.; and C.I.O.; Joseph Hagan, Sr. V.P., LISC; Greg Maher, Sr. V.P., Lending; Stephanie O'Keefe, Sr. V.P., Ext. Affairs; Benson "Buzz" Roberts, Sr. V.P., Policy and Prog. Devel.; Sandra Rosenblith, Sr. V.P., Rural; Paul Williams, Sr. V.P., Field Strategies and Devel.; Sandra Abramson, V.P., Field Resources and Learning; Denise Altay, V.P., Finance; Reena Bhatia, V.P., Ed. Progs.; Mariano Diaz, V.P., Western Regional; Anika Goss-Foster, V.P., Sustainable Communities; Greta Harris, V.P., Progs.-Southeast Region; Elise Hoben, V.P., Progs.-Rural; Lily Lim, V.P. and Cont.; Richard Manson, V.P., Progs.; Vincent O'Donnell, V.P., Affordable Housing Preservation Initiative; Janet Ozarchuck, V.P. and Treas.; Margaret Slane, V.P., Govt. Contracts; Chuck Vliek, V.P., Progs.-Midwest Region; Larry H. Dale;

William M. Daley; John G. Finneran; Pamela P. Flaherty; Colvin W. Grannum; and 18 additional directors.
Number of staff: 310 full-time professional.
EIN: 133030229

1324
Love, Inc. of the Tri-Cities
1106 Fulton St.
Grand Haven, MI   49417-1530   (616) 846-2701
County: Ottawa
FAX: (616) 846-8009;
E-mail: eric@loveinctricities.org; URL: http://
www.loveinctricities.org

Grantmaker type: Public charity.
Financial data (yr. ended 02/28/10): Revenue, $3,477,617; assets, $1,959,168 (M); gifts received, $3,464,401; expenditures, $3,232,469.
Purpose and activities: The organization works to serve the spiritual, emotional, and physical needs of those in the greater Grand Haven area.
Fields of interest: Human services; Christian agencies & churches.
Limitations: Giving primarily to Grand Haven, MI.
Publications: Newsletter.
Officers and Directors:* Mark Green,* Pres.; Mike Leak,* V.P.; Abby Reeg,* Secy.; Kevin Youngquist,* Treas.; Eric Morgan,* Exec. Dir.; Debbie Reynolds; Bonnie Roth.
EIN: 382856482

1325
Lowell Area Community Fund
c/o Grand Rapids Community Foundation
161 Ottawa Ave. N.W., Ste. 209-C
Grand Rapids, MI   49503-2721
County: Kent
Contact: Kate Luckert Schmid, Prog. Dir.
E-mail: onlinegrants@grfoundation.org; Tel.: (616) 454-1751, ext. 117; E-mail: kluckert@grfoundation.org; URL: http://
www.grfoundation.org/lowell/

Established in 1997 in MI as a fund adminstered by Grand Rapids Community Foundation.
Grantmaker type: Public charity.
Purpose and activities: The fund's mission is to assure community cooperation and participation that supports a healthy, dynamic community. It places an emphasis on broad educational initiatives, but also supports initiatives in the areas of arts and culture, community development, environment, health, human services, and recreation.
Fields of interest: Arts; Education; Environment; Health care; Recreation; Human services; Community/economic development.
Limitations: Applications accepted. Giving limited to the Lowell, MI, area (currently defined as the City of Lowell, the Township of Lowell, and the Township of Vergennes). No support for religious organizations for religious purposes, or for organizations lacking 501(c)(3) status. No grants to individuals.
Publications: Application guidelines.
Application information: See foundation web site for online application form. Application form required.
   Initial approach: Submit online application form
   Deadline(s): 3rd Fri. in Apr., Aug., and Dec.
   Final notification: 2 months

Selected grants: The following grants were reported in 2009.
$74,000 to Lowell Area Schools, Lowell, MI. To help families prepare their preschool children to enter school healthy and ready to learn.
$72,500 to Lowell, City of, Lowell, MI. To create walking path along Gee Drive and provide funding for engineering and added retaining walls.
$20,000 to Lowell Area Schools Education Foundation, Lowell, MI. For innovative projects that support and enhance education.
$17,420 to Greater Lowell Chamber Foundation, Lowell, MI. To publish Kaleidoscope brochure and community base website.
$13,125 to Greater Lowell Chamber Foundation, Lowell, MI. For 2009 Summer Concert Series.
$12,500 to Lowell Area Arts Council, Lowell, MI. For new and on-going administrative costs.
$10,000 to Flat River Outreach Ministries, Lowell, MI. To continue fund development mentoring, completion of the organizational structure and fund development planning.

1326
Lutheran Child & Family Service of Michigan, Inc.
6019 W. Side Saginaw Rd.
P.O. Box 48
Bay City, MI   48707-0048
County: Bay
E-mail: information@lcfsmi.org; Toll-free tel.: (800) 625-7650

Established in 1899 in MI.
Grantmaker type: Public charity.
Financial data (yr. ended 12/31/09): Revenue, $20,809,871; assets, $11,954,158 (M); gifts received, $1,114,205; expenditures, $21,501,115; total giving, $2,994,530; giving activities include $2,994,530 for grants to individuals.
Purpose and activities: The organization provides hope through quality services, adoption services, foster care placements, family preservation services, individual and family counseling, substance abuse services, group homes for emotionally- and mentally-impaired young people, and pregnancy and teen parent support services.
Fields of interest: Substance abuse, services; Mental health, counseling/support groups; Children/youth, services; Children, adoption; Children, foster care; Family services; Family services, adolescent parents; Family services, counseling.
Officers and Directors:* Paul F. Nyquist,* Chair.; Roger C. Johr,* Vice-Chair.; Dr. Donald A. Meier,* Secy.; Ritch R. Cushway,* Treas.; John Davis; Dr. Thomas V. Focker; Michael Jessamy; Thomas Kissling; Rev. David P.E. Maier; William T. McCarthy; James E. Miller; Thomas F. Neusiis; G. Joseph Pasman, Jr.; Mattew A. Resch; Sen. Tony N. Stamas; Gerald A. Westgate; Alicia J. Winget.
EIN: 381359524

1327
The Macomb Charitable Foundation
(formerly The Macomb Lutheran Charitable Foundation)
18215 24 Mile Rd.
Macomb, MI   48042-2909   (586) 232-3473
County: Macomb
E-mail: macombcharitable@comcast.net;
URL: http://macombcharitablefoundation.org

Established in 2002 in MI.
Grantmaker type: Public charity.
Financial data (yr. ended 12/31/09): Revenue, $96,147; assets, $64,160 (M); gifts received, $96,147; expenditures, $60,937; total giving, $57,105; giving activities include $57,105 for grants.
Purpose and activities: The foundation works to help children living at or below the poverty level in Macomb County.
Fields of interest: Human services, emergency aid; Protestant agencies & churches; Children/youth.
Type of support: Emergency funds.
Limitations: Giving limited to Macomb County, MI.
Publications: Newsletter.
Officers and Board Members:* Shelly Penzien,* Pres.; Mitch Vogeli,* V.P.; Susan Schwark,* Treas.; Wayne Oehmke; Julie Wright.
EIN: 383618892

1328
Make-A-Wish Foundation of Michigan
2300 Genoa Business Pk. Dr., Ste. 290
Brighton, MI   48114-7369   (734) 994-8620
County: Livingston
FAX: (734) 994-8025; E-mail: wish@wishmich.org; Toll-free tel. (Brighton office): (800) 622-9474; additional address (Grand Rapids office) 2900 E. Beltline N.E., Ste. E, Grand Rapids, MI 49525-9403, tel.: (616) 363-4607, fax: (616) 363-5415, toll-free tel.: (877) 631-9474; additional address (Detroit office): Old Hutzel Bldg., 4707 St. Antoine St., Detroit, MI 48201-1427, tel.: (313) 833-9100, fax: (313) 833-9103, toll-free tel.: (888) 857-9474; URL: http://www.wishmich.org

Established in 1984 in MI.
Grantmaker type: Public charity.
Financial data (yr. ended 08/31/09): Revenue, $5,669,421; assets, $3,594,539 (M); gifts received, $5,637,909; expenditures, $6,295,371; total giving, $338,040; program services expenses, $5,263,815; giving activities include $338,040 for 221 grants to individuals, and $4,925,775 for foundation-administered programs.
Purpose and activities: The foundation grants the wishes of children between the ages of 2 and 1/2 and 18 years old with life-threatening medical conditions to enrich the human experience with hope, strength, and joy.
Fields of interest: Children.
Limitations: Applications accepted. Giving primarily in MI.
Publications: Application guidelines.
Application information:
   Initial approach: Complete online child referral form
Officers and Directors:* James Fahner, M.D.*, Chair.; Karen Davis,* Pres. and C.E.O.; Jim Berline; Valerie Castle, M.D.; Suie Elwood; Christine Farah; Janette Ferrantino; Deborah Gray; Steve Heacock; Susan Jandernoa; David R. Morlock; Walter F.

"Chip" Perschbacher; Michael Pettibone; Meg Miller Willit.
EIN: 382505812

1329
Marquette Area Public Schools Education Foundation
1201 W. Fair Ave.
Marquette, MI   49855-2668
County: Marquette

Grantmaker type: Public charity.
Financial data (yr. ended 06/30/09): Revenue, $58,128; assets, $689,334 (M); gifts received, $40,121; expenditures, $37,834; total giving, $24,609; giving activities include $24,609 for grants.
Purpose and activities: The foundation acquires and distributes financial and other resources to the Marquette Public Schools for unique programs and activities which supplement and enhance the quality of education and provide students with extended learning opportunities.
Fields of interest: Education.
Type of support: Scholarships—to individuals.
Limitations: Applications accepted. Giving limited to Marquette, MI.
Publications: Application guidelines; Grants list.
Application information: Application form required.
  Initial approach: Download application
  Copies of proposal: 10
  Deadline(s): Jan. 1, Mar. 1, May 1, and Oct. 1
  Board meeting date(s): Quarterly
  Final notification: Jan., Mar., May, and Oct.
Officers and Trustees: * Linda Winslow,* Pres.; Laura Goodney,* V.P.; Michael Anderegg; Jackie Mahennick,* Treas.; Thomas L. Baldini; and 9 additional trustees.
EIN: 382972673

1330
Marshall United Way
124 W. Michigan Ave.
P.O. Box 190
Marshall, MI   49068-0190   (616) 781-3325
County: Calhoun
E-mail: marshallunitedway@sbcglobal.net;
URL: http://www.marshallunitedway.org

Grantmaker type: Public charity.
Financial data (yr. ended 08/31/09): Revenue, $156,860; assets, $220,585 (M); gifts received, $146,766; expenditures, $139,302; total giving, $120,693; giving activities include $120,693 for grants.
Purpose and activities: Marshall United Way provides funding to various charities in Calhoun County, Michigan and the surrounding areas.
Fields of interest: Health care; Legal services; Youth development; Human services; Family services.
Limitations: Giving limited to Calhoun County, MI, and surrounding areas.
Officers and Directors: * Mindy Deno,* Pres.; Nancy Stulberg,* Pres.-Elect; Kevin Giannunzio,* V.P.; Jean Rogers,* Exec. Dir.; Sherry Anderson; Linda Bennick; Peggy Day; David DeGraw; and 10 additional directors.
EIN: 237161104

1331
Mason Area United Way
P.O. Box 13
Mason, MI   48854-0013
County: Ingham

Grantmaker type: Public charity.
Financial data (yr. ended 01/31/10): Revenue, $101; assets, $449,380 (M); expenditures, $57,429; total giving, $55,042; giving activities include $55,042 for grants.
Fields of interest: Crime/violence prevention, abuse prevention; Recreation; Youth development; Human services; Family services; Aging, centers/ services; Christian agencies & churches.
Limitations: Giving limited to the greater Mason, MI area.
Officers: Mark Emmert, Chair.; Mike Kollin, Vice-Chair.; Donna Rehbeck, Secy.; Tom Peterson, Treas.
EIN: 382844122

1332
Masonic Foundation of Michigan, Inc.
1204 Wright Ave.
Alma, MI   48801-1133   (989) 966-4440
County: Gratiot
Contact: David Neff, Pres.
E-mail: mmhcf@masonichome.com

Established in 1980 in MI.
Grantmaker type: Public charity.
Financial data (yr. ended 03/31/07): Revenue, $212,375; assets, $2,640,768 (M); gifts received, $104,248; expenditures, $252,202; total giving, $95,648; program services expenses, $157,161; giving activities include $76,175 for grants, $19,473 for 238 grants to individuals (high: $3,000; low: $300), and $61,513 for foundation-administered programs.
Purpose and activities: The foundation supports and maintains a library and museum, and provides funds for educational scholarships.
Fields of interest: Museums; Libraries/library science.
Type of support: Scholarship funds; Scholarships—to individuals.
Limitations: Giving primarily in MI.
Officers: David Neff, Pres.; W. Johnson, V.P.; Robert Stevens, Secy.; T. Hamlin, Treas.
Trustees: W. Keith Bankwitz; Robert Helmic; A. Meyer; R. Ruhland; I. Slaven; B. Valentine; R. Watts; W. Wheeler; D. Williamson.
EIN: 382284259

1333
McCarty Cancer Foundation
P.O. Box 1874
Royal Oak, MI   48068-1874   (248) 336-2500
County: Oakland
FAX: (248) 336-2330; *Toll-free tel.:* (800) 746-0355; additional address (Canada office): P.O. Box 63, Leamington, ON N8H 3W1, tel.: (519) 324-9834

Established in 1997 in MI.
Grantmaker type: Public charity.
Financial data (yr. ended 06/30/09): Revenue, $52,456; assets, $207,364 (M); gifts received, $52,335; expenditures, $494,412; total giving, $32,000; program services expenses, $32,000;

giving activities include $32,000 for 2 grants (high: $30,000; low: $2,000).
Purpose and activities: The foundation is dedicated to raising awareness of multiple myeloma and improving the quality of life of myeloma cancer patients, while working toward prevention and a cure.
Fields of interest: Cancer; Cancer research.
Type of support: Research.
Limitations: Giving on a national basis.
Publications: Newsletter.
Officer and Directors: * Roberta McCarty,* Pres.; Patrick Kelly; Darren McCarty; Patricia Vincent.
EIN: 383359447

1334
Mecosta-Osceola United Way, Inc.
315 Ives Ave.
P.O. Box 311
Big Rapids, MI   49307-2001   (231) 592-4144
County: Mecosta
FAX: (231) 592-1138;
E-mail: unitedway@tucker-usa.com

Grantmaker type: Public charity.
Financial data (yr. ended 09/30/08): Revenue, $385,814; assets, $298,192 (M); gifts received, $384,961; expenditures, $392,305; total giving, $295,827; program services expenses, $313,845; giving activities include $295,827 for grants, and $18,018 for foundation-administered programs.
Purpose and activities: The organization seeks to increase the organized capacity of people to care for one another.
Fields of interest: Community/economic development.
Officers and Directors: * Jeremy Mishler,* Pres.; Duane Shafer,* V.P.; Margaret Taylor,* Secy.; Jean Misenar,* Treas.; Jim Becker; John Calabrese; Gerald Flessland; Hon. Susan H. Grant; Susan Haut; Bob Hodge; Tom Hogenson; Steven Petersmark.
EIN: 382489813

1335
Metropolitan Foundation
(also known as Metro Health Hospital Foundation)
5900 Byron Center Ave., S.W.
Wyoming, MI   49519-9606   (616) 252-5000
County: Kent
E-mail: foundation@metrogr.org; URL: http:// www.metrohealth.net/foundation

Established in 1990 in MI.
Grantmaker type: Public charity.
Financial data (yr. ended 06/30/09): Revenue, $439,011; assets, $9,323,851 (M); gifts received, $1,355,816; expenditures, $1,626,762; total giving, $1,626,762; program services expenses, $1,626,762; giving activities include $1,626,762 for 1 grant.
Purpose and activities: The foundation supports Metro Health Hospital in its mission of providing life-saving education and services to improve the health and well-being of the communities it serves.
Fields of interest: Health care, single organization support; Hospitals (general); Health care.
Limitations: Giving limited to Wyoming, MI.
Publications: Newsletter.
Officers: Stephen Klotz, Chair.; Dan Pfeiffer, Vice-Chair.; Michael Faas, C.E.O.; Laura

Staskiewicz, V.P.; John van Singel, Secy.-Treas.; Timothy Susterich, C.F.O.
Directors: Jan Aardema; Ellen Arlinsky; Dan Behm; Robert G. Bowman, D.O.; Tommy Brann; Chris Branoff; James Clay; Lindsey Dodd; Paul Dwyer, M.D.; Jennifer Hascall; Carol Karr; John Leegwater; Christos Panopoulos; David Rodriguez; Luanne Thodey; and 14 additional directors.
EIN: 383033329

1336
MGM Mirage Voice Foundation
3260 Industrial Rd.
Las Vegas, NV 89109-1132 (702) 650-7469
County: Clark
Contact: Christina Roth, Dir., Corp. Philanthropy
FAX: (702) 650-7401; Application address for southern MS: c/o Sara Miller, P.O. Box 7777, Biloxi, MS 39540-7777; Toll-free tel.: (800) 477-5110; URL: http://www.mgmmiragevoice.com/pages/eg_foundation.asp

Established in 2002.
Donor: MGM Mirage.
Grantmaker type: Public charity.
Financial data (yr. ended 04/30/10): Revenue, $4,408,327; assets, $2,724,023 (M); gifts received, $4,408,152; expenditures, $3,636,112; total giving, $3,614,036; giving activities include $3,368,299 for grants, and $245,737 for grants to individuals.
Purpose and activities: The foundation supports charitable organizations in the communities where MGM Mirage employees live, work, and care for their families.
Fields of interest: Education; Safety/disasters; Human services; Community/economic development; Foundations (community).
Limitations: Applications accepted. Giving limited to Detroit, MI; southern MS; and southern NV. No support for individual public or private schools or governmental entities. No grants for sponsorship of fundraising events, capital campaigns, or endowments.
Application information: For Nevada or the Detroit, Michigan area, submit original application plus 10 copies; for Mississippi, submit original applications plus 8 copies. Application form required.
Initial approach: Completed application form
Deadline(s): May 5
Officers and Directors:* Merlinda Gallegos,* Pres.; Jeanette Renard,* Secy.; Keri King; Punam Mathur.
EIN: 010640027

1337
Michigan Accountancy Foundation
5480 Corporate Dr., Ste. 200
Troy, MI 48098-2642 (248) 267-3700
County: Oakland
FAX: (248) 267-3737; E-mail: macpa@michcpa.org; URL: http://www.michcpa.org/Content/home.aspx
Application address: c/o MAF Accounting Scholarship Prog., P.O. Box 5068, Troy, MI 48007-5068

Established in 1961 in MI.
Grantmaker type: Public charity.
Financial data (yr. ended 06/30/10): Revenue, $115,468; assets, $305,598 (M); gifts received, $95,859; expenditures, $118,139; total giving,

$96,983; giving activities include $96,983 for grants.
Purpose and activities: The foundation gives out awards through its scholarship program to assist current college accounting majors in funding their fifth/graduate year.
Fields of interest: Business school/education.
Type of support: Scholarships—to individuals.
Limitations: Applications accepted. Giving limited to U.S. citizens enrolled in an accredited MI college or university.
Publications: Application guidelines.
Application information: Application form required.
Initial approach: Download application form
Deadline(s): Jan. 31
Final notification: Mar. 15
Officers and Trustees:* Stephen H. Epstein,* Pres.; Peggy A. Dzierzawski,* Secy.; Gadis J. Dillon,* Treas.; Robert A. Bogan, Jr.; Richard E. Czarnecki; Richard G. David, C.P.A.; Edward J. Dupke, C.P.A., A.B.V.; Dennis M. Echelbarger, C.P.A.; William H. Harvey, C.P.A.; Raymond E. Howard, C.P.A.; and 14 additional trustees.
EIN: 386090334

1338
Michigan Community Coordinated Child Care Association
(also known as Michigan 4C Association)
839 Centennial Way
Lansing, MI 48917-9277 (517) 351-4171
County: Eaton
FAX: (517) 351-0157; E-mail: mich4c@mi4c.org; URL: http://www.mi4c.org

Established in 1972 in MI.
Grantmaker type: Public charity.
Financial data (yr. ended 09/30/09): Revenue, $8,190,338; assets, $1,595,651 (M); gifts received, $7,985,419; expenditures, $8,225,255; total giving, $7,332,518; giving activities include $5,904,366 for grants, and $1,428,152 for grants to individuals.
Purpose and activities: The association promotes and advocates for the optimal care and development of Michigan's children and families through the statewide Community Coordinated Child Care (4C) Network.
Fields of interest: Youth development, services; Children/youth, services; Children, day care.
Limitations: Applications accepted. Giving limited to MI.
Publications: Application guidelines; Annual report.
Application information: Application form required.
Deadline(s): Rolling basis
Officers and Directors:* Bob Parks,* Chair.; Jacqueline Wood,* Vice-Chair.; Kendra Curtiss,* Secy.; Joan Deschamps,* Treas.; J. Mark Sullivan, Exec. Dir.; Sue Allen; Linda Dielman; Ella Fabel-Ryder; Jeff Minore; Laurie Nickson; Wynne Noble; K.P. Pelleran; Sharon Peters; Hubert Price.
EIN: 382768272

1339
Michigan Council on Economic Education
c/o Walsh College
41500 Gardenbrook Rd.
Novi, MI 48375-1313 (248) 596-9560
County: Oakland
Contact: David A. Dieterle Ph.D., Pres.

FAX: (248) 596-9562;
E-mail: david@mceeonline.org; URL: http://www.mceeonline.org

Established in 1978 in MI.
Grantmaker type: Public charity.
Financial data (yr. ended 08/31/10): Revenue, $208,309; assets, $40,119 (M); gifts received, $196,941; expenditures, $245,148.
Purpose and activities: The council provides leadership promoting and strengthening economic education in the state of Michigan.
Fields of interest: Education; Economics.
Limitations: Giving primarily in MI.
Officers and Directors:* Robert E. Hoisington,* Chair.; Patrick McQueen,* Vice-Chair.; David A. Dieterle, Ph.D.*, Pres.; Jon Sudduth,* Secy.-Treas.; Jon Anibal; Thomas H. Bergh; William E. Bjork; Donald Booth; Robert Burgess; Dr. Lisa Donnini; Peggy A. Dzierzawski; Kurt Gallagher; Chris Georvassilis; Daniel Graf; Jeff Guilfoyle; and 15 additional directors.
EIN: 382183524

1340
Michigan Dental Association Relief Fund
230 N. Washington Ave., Ste. 208
Lansing, MI 48933-1302
County: Ingham
Contact: Andrew Eason C.A.E., Exec. Dir.; Josh Lord, Dir., Member and Student Affairs
E-mail: jlord@michigandental.org; Email for Andrew Eason: deason@michigandental.org

Established in 1966; supporting organization of Michigan Dental Association.
Grantmaker type: Public charity.
Financial data (yr. ended 12/31/08): Revenue, $11,475; assets, $300,051 (M); gifts received, $25; expenditures, $21,442; total giving, $14,343; giving activities include $14,343 for grants to individuals.
Fields of interest: Human services; Economically disadvantaged.
Type of support: Grants to individuals.
Limitations: Applications accepted. Giving limited to MI.
Application information: Applicant must be a Michigan resident. Application form required.
Initial approach: Telephone
Copies of proposal: 1
Deadline(s): None
Board meeting date(s): Varies
Final notification: Immediately for qualified applicants
Officers and Trustees:* Joanne Dawley, D.D.S.*, Pres.; William Wright, D.D.S., M.S.*, Pres.-Elect; Gary Jeffers, D.D.S., M.S.*, V.P.; Norman Palm, D.D.S., M.S.*, Secy.; Connie Verhagen, D.D.S., M.S.*, Treas.; Andrew Eason, C.A.E., Exec. Dir.; Patricia Boy; and 12 additional trustees.
Number of staff: 1 part-time professional; 1 part-time support.
EIN: 386112478

1341
Michigan Dental Foundation

c/o Lori Kleinfelt
3657 Okemos Rd., Ste. 200
Okemos, MI 48864-3927 (517) 372-9070
County: Ingham
URL: http://foundation.smilemichigan.com/

Established in 1998 in MI; supporting organization of the Michigan Dental Association.
Grantmaker type: Public charity.
Financial data (yr. ended 12/31/09): Revenue, $160,127; assets, $1,242,470 (M); gifts received, $103,490; expenditures, $126,866; total giving, $26,061; program services expenses, $76,230; giving activities include $22,061 for 4 grants (high: $7,061; low: $5,000), $4,000 for 5 grants to individuals (high: $1,000; low: $500), and $50,169 for foundation-administered programs.
Purpose and activities: The foundation works to provide the people of Michigan with access to care programs, oral health initiatives, and dental scholarships.
Fields of interest: Medical school/education; Dental care.
Type of support: Scholarships—to individuals; In-kind gifts.
Limitations: Applications accepted. Giving primarily in MI.
Publications: Application guidelines.
Application information: Application form required.
Initial approach: Submit application
Deadline(s): Feb. 15 (for dental and dental assisting students) and Nov. 15 (for dental hygiene students) for Scholarships; June 1 for Grants
Officers and Directors:* Ronald Paler, D.D.S.*, Pres.; Susan Carron, D.D.S., M.S.*, V.P.; Grace Curcuru, D.D.S.*, Secy.; Michael D. Jennings, D.D.S.*, Treas.; Drew Eason, C.A.E., Exec. Dir.; Arnold Baker, D.D.S.; Kevin Cook; Ghabi Kaspo, D.D.S.; Jill Loewen, C.D.A., M.S.; Joan McGowan, Ph.D.; Kathy Mielke, B.S., R.D.H.; Kris Nicholoff; Charles Owens, D.D.S.; Curt S. Ralstrom, D.D.S., M.S.; Donald Smith, D.D.S., M.S.; Mark Stephens; Matt Uday, D.D.S.
EIN: 383421257

1342
Michigan Education Association Scholarship Fund

1216 Kendale Blvd.
P.O. Box 2573
East Lansing, MI 48826-2573 (517) 332-6551
County: Ingham
Toll-free tel.: (800) 292-1934; *URL:* http://www.mea.org/awards/meascholarship.html

Established in MI; a supporting organization of Michigan Education Association.
Grantmaker type: Public charity.
Financial data (yr. ended 08/31/10): Revenue, $69,882; assets, $982,692 (M); gifts received, $8,878; expenditures, $52,198; total giving, $30,000; giving activities include $30,000 for grants.
Type of support: Scholarships—to individuals.
Limitations: Applications accepted. Giving limited to MI.
Publications: Application guidelines.
Application information: Application form required.

Initial approach: Download application
Deadline(s): Feb. 18
Officers and Trustees:* Mary Christian,* Chair.; Linda Carter,* Vice-Chair.; Pattie Bayless; Cathy King; E. Craig Lesley; Lillian McFadden; Leo Sell.
EIN: 383285500

1343
Michigan Friends of Education

P.O. Box 183
Gregory, MI 48137-0183 (734) 498-3003
County: Livingston
FAX: (734) 498-3005;
E-mail: mifriends@charterinternet.com; Toll-free tel.: (800) 846-8876; URL: http://www.mifriends.org/mifriends/index3.html

Established in 1984 in MI.
Grantmaker type: Public charity.
Financial data (yr. ended 09/30/09): Revenue, $6,233,025; assets, $6,264,531 (M); gifts received, $6,221,293; expenditures, $7,280,074; total giving, $7,095,922; giving activities include $7,095,922 for grants.
Purpose and activities: The organization is committed to serving the people of Michigan by promoting literacy with the distribution of free books to those in need.
Fields of interest: Education, reading.
Type of support: In-kind gifts.
Limitations: Giving limited to MI. No grants to individuals directly.
Publications: Annual report; Newsletter.
Application information:
Initial approach: Submit completed request for materials form
Board meeting date(s): Dec.
Officers and Directors:* Mike Burtch,* Pres.; Kristen McDonald Stone,* V.P.; Joe Lentine,* Secy.-Treas.; Donald H. Porter, Exec. Dir.
Number of staff: 4 full-time professional; 2 part-time professional.
EIN: 382547207

1344
Michigan Humanities Council

119 Pere Marquette Dr., Ste. 3B
Lansing, MI 48912-1270 (517) 372-7770
County: Ingham
Contact: Jan Fedewa, Exec. Dir.
FAX: (517) 372-0027;
E-mail: contact@mihumanities.org; URL: http://michiganhumanities.org

Established in 1975 in MI.
Grantmaker type: Public charity.
Financial data (yr. ended 10/31/09): Revenue, $1,235,121; assets, $1,090,519 (M); gifts received, $1,231,466; expenditures, $1,179,646; total giving, $415,691; giving activities include $415,691 for grants.
Purpose and activities: The council aims to connect people and communities by fostering and creating cultural programs. The Council accomplishes its mission by awarding grants, conducting programs, initiating collaborations, and serving as the public voice for the humanities in Michigan.
Fields of interest: Humanities; Arts; Education.
Type of support: Program development.
Limitations: Applications accepted. Giving limited to MI. No support for advocacy or action programs. No

grants to individuals, or for equipment, travel, or capital purchases.
Publications: Application guidelines; Annual report; Grants list; Newsletter.
Application information: Applicants must use grant applications available for download from council web site. Application form required.
Initial approach: Letter, telephone, or e-mail
Deadline(s): Mar. 15 and Sept. 15 for Michigan People, Michigan Places Grant Program; Sept. 10 and Mar. 10 for Touring Program grants; four weeks in advance of program/travel for Quick and Transportation Grants
Board meeting date(s): 3 times per year
Final notification: Mar. 15 and Nov. 15 for Grants Program and We the People grants; Apr. 15 and Oct. 15 for Touring Program grants
Officers and Trustees:* Timothy Chester,* Chair.; Erik Nordberg, Secy.-Treas.; Jan Fedewa, Exec. Dir.; Christine Albertini; Ed Bagale; Amy DeWys-VanHecke; Eva Evans; Suzanne M. Janis; James Karshner; Michael Margolin; Craig McDonald; Patricia Anne Shaheen; Shaun Nethercott; Karen Smith.
Number of staff: 4 full-time professional; 2 part-time professional; 1 part-time support.
EIN: 510164775

1345
Michigan Masonic Charitable Foundation

(formerly Michigan Masonic Home Charitable Foundation)
1200 Wright Ave.
Alma, MI 48801-1133 (989) 466-4339
County: Gratiot
Contact: Keith Bankwitz, Dir., Philanthropy
FAX: (989) 466-4340; Tel. for Keith Bankwitz: (800) 994-7400 ext. 3802;
e-mail:kbankwitz@michiganmasonsfoundation.org; URL: http://www.michiganmasonsfoundation.org/

Established in MI.
Grantmaker type: Public charity.
Financial data (yr. ended 03/31/10): Revenue, $3,760,261; assets, $109,028,721 (M); gifts received, $1,874,038; expenditures, $6,872,801; total giving, $5,191,780; giving activities include $5,191,780 for grants.
Purpose and activities: The organization aims to invest programs and services to make life better for Michigan Masons, their families, and their communities.
Fields of interest: Higher education.
Limitations: Applications accepted. Giving limited to Alma, MI.
Publications: Application guidelines.
Application information: Application form required.
Initial approach: Download application
Deadline(s): Mar. 31
Officers and Trustees:* Kenneth Carroll, P.M.*, Pres.; Roger L. Meyers,* V.P.; Theodore F. Boyden, P.M.; Thomas Hamlin, R.W.G.T; Robert N. Osborne, P.G.M.; Richard K. Rappleye; Richard P. Ruhland, M.W.G.M.; Lloyd A. Semple; Robert W. Stevens, P.G.M., R.W.G.S.
EIN: 383266089

1346
Michigan Minority Business Development Council, Inc.
3011 W. Grand Blvd., Ste. 230
Detroit, MI 48202-3042 (313) 873-3200
County: Wayne
FAX: (313) 873-4783; E-mail: mail@mmbdc.com;
URL: http://www.mmbdc.com

Established in MI.
Grantmaker type: Public charity.
Financial data (yr. ended 12/31/09): Revenue, $2,122,841; assets, $3,948,136 (M); gifts received, $1,850,780; expenditures, $2,315,608; total giving, $6,000; giving activities include $6,000 for grants to individuals.
Purpose and activities: The organization aims to enhance business opportunities and professional development.
Fields of interest: Economic development; Community development, small businesses; Minorities.
Limitations: Giving limited to MI.
Publications: Application guidelines; Newsletter.
Application information:
Initial approach: Contact organization for scholarship application form
Officers: Bo I. Anderson, Chair.; Robert Fisher, Vice-Chair.; Louis Green, Pres. and C.E.O.; Mary Brown, Exec. V.P. and C.F.O.; James Franklin, V.P., Member Svcs. and Govt. Rels.; Robert Scavone, V.P., Corp. Svcs.; Hector Shamley, V.P., Strategic Initiatives; Arthur Dudley, Secy.; Don P. Alessi, Treas.
Board Members: Arnold Andrews; George Barnes; Sarah Bates; Kevin L. Bell; Jackie Burnley; Sharon Cannarsa; Walter Elloitt, Jr.; Helen Ford; Joseph Garcia; Joan Gossman; Don Groth; John James; Ram Kancharla; Cathy L. Kutch; Thomas E. Lake; and 18 additional board members.
EIN: 382292187

1347
Michigan Parkinson Foundation
30400 Telegraph Rd., Ste. 150
Bingham Farms, MI 48025-5819
(248) 433-1011
County: Oakland
FAX: (248) 433-1150; E-mail: mpfdir@yahoo.com;
Toll-free tel.: (800) 852-9781; URL: http://www.parkinsonsmi.org

Grantmaker type: Public charity.
Financial data (yr. ended 12/31/09): Revenue, $374,194; assets, $319,625 (M); gifts received, $280,268; expenditures, $369,192.
Purpose and activities: The foundation's mission is to educate and provide support to people with Parkinson's and related disorders, their loved ones and care partners, and the physicians and other allied health professionals who diagnose and treat those affected by the illness; to support research into the mechanisms underlying the disease and therapeutic strategies aimed at reducing the burden of illness; and to engage and enlist the support of institutions and individuals whose activities impact the needs of people with Parkinson's and related disorders.
Fields of interest: Parkinson's disease; Parkinson's disease research.
Type of support: Fellowships; Grants to individuals.
Limitations: Giving primarily in MI.

Officers and Directors:* Leonard S. Borman,* Chair.; Paul A. Cullis, M.D.*, Vice-Chair.; Peter A. LeWitt, M.D.*, Pres.; Hon. Gail McKnight,* Secy.; Lawrence Millman,* Treas.; David Bartczak; Peter Hasbrook; Richard McKnight, J.D.; and 10 additional directors.
EIN: 382494280

1348
Michigan State Bar Foundation
306 Townsend St.
Lansing, MI 48933-2012 (517) 346-6400
County: Ingham
Contact: Linda K. Rexer, Exec. Dir. and Asst. Secy.
FAX: (517) 371-3325; E-mail: msbf@msbf.org;
Toll-free tel.: (800) 968-6723; URL: http://www.msbf.org

Established in 1947 in MI.
Grantmaker type: Public charity.
Financial data (yr. ended 09/30/09): Revenue, $2,458,708; assets, $11,347,545 (M); gifts received, $632,963; expenditures, $3,283,397; total giving, $2,666,729; giving activities include $2,666,729 for grants.
Purpose and activities: The foundation promotes improvements in the administration of justice; makes advancements in the science of jurisprudence; promotes improvements in the uniformity of judicial proceedings and decisions; elevates judicial standards; advances professional ethics; improves relations between members of the bar, the judiciary, and the public; preserves the American constitutional form of government through education, scientific research, and publicity; and furthers the delivery of legal services to the poor.
Fields of interest: Legal services.
Type of support: General/operating support.
Limitations: Applications accepted. Giving limited to MI. No grants to individuals, or for endowments or capital expenses.
Publications: Application guidelines; Annual report; Informational brochure; Newsletter; Occasional report.
Application information: Applicants should submit one hard copy and one electronic copy of application. Application form required.
Deadline(s): Varies
Board meeting date(s): 5 times per year
Final notification: Varies
Officers and Trustees:* Margaret J. Nichols,* Pres.; Hon. Alfred M. Butzbaugh,* V.P.; Stefani A. Carter,* Secy.; Lamont E. Buffington,* Treas.; Linda K. Rexer, Exec. Dir.; Kimberly Cahill; Peter H. Ellsworth; Julie I. Fershtman; Michael G. Harrison; Hon. Harold Hood; Ronald Keefe; Hon. William B. Murphy; Jon R. Muth; Richard K. Rappleye; Hon. Victoria A. Roberts; Richard A. Soble; Hon. Clifford Taylor.
Number of staff: 3 full-time professional; 2 full-time support; 1 part-time support.
EIN: 381459016

1349
Michigan State Medical Society Foundation
(formerly Health Education Foundation)
c/o Michigan State Medical Society
120 W. Saginaw St.
East Lansing, MI 48823-2605 (517) 336-5745
County: Ingham
Contact: Sheri W. Greenhoe, Secy.

FAX: (517) 337-2490; E-mail: msms@msms.org;
E-mail for Sheri W. Greenhoe: sgreenhoe@msms.org

Established in 1945 as Michigan Foundation for Medical & Health Education; status changed to a public charity in 2004; supporting organization of the Michigan State Medical Society.
Grantmaker type: Public charity.
Financial data (yr. ended 11/30/08): Revenue, $785,407; assets, $972,976 (M); gifts received, $31,534; expenditures, $696,425; total giving, $35,350; program services expenses, $681,220; giving activities include $35,350 for grants, and $645,870 for foundation-administered programs.
Purpose and activities: Support for community-based programs promoting volunteerism and public health. The foundation supports both research programs and demonstration programs with short-term or start-up costs. A current focus is on wellness and healthy lifestyles.
Fields of interest: Public health; Community/economic development; Voluntarism promotion.
Type of support: Annual campaigns; Equipment; Emergency funds; Program development; Publication; Seed money; Technical assistance; Matching/challenge support.
Limitations: Applications accepted. Giving limited to MI.
Publications: Application guidelines; Grants list; Informational brochure; Occasional report (including application guidelines).
Application information: Accepts CMF Common Grant Application Form. See foundation Web site for full application guidelines and downloadable application form. Application form required.
Copies of proposal: 18
Deadline(s): Mar. 25 and Sept. 25
Board meeting date(s): Feb., Apr., and Oct.
Officers: Dorothy J. Kahkonen, M.D., Pres.; Kevin A. Kelly, V.P.; Sheri W. Greenhoe, Secy.; Henry M. Domzalski, M.D., Treas.
Trustees: Busharat Ahmad, M.D.; Rudy Ansbacher; Curtis DeRoo; Peter A. Duhamel; Gregory J. Forzley; Suzanne H. Pederson; and 4 additional trustees.
Number of staff: 1 part-time support.
EIN: 386069432

1350
Michigan Women's Foundation
18530 Mack Ave., Ste. 562
Grosse Pointe Farms, MI 48236-3254
(313) 640-0128
County: Wayne
E-mail: info@miwf.org; Toll-free tel.: (800) 404-4372; Additional address: 118 Commerce S.W., Grand Rapids, MI 49503-4106; URL: http://www.miwf.org

Established in 1986 in MI.
Grantmaker type: Public charity.
Financial data (yr. ended 09/30/09): Revenue, $455,670; assets, $951,144 (M); gifts received, $286,975; expenditures, $542,088; total giving, $71,125; giving activities include $71,125 for grants.
Purpose and activities: The foundation focuses solely on the economic barriers that prevent Michigan women and girls from becoming self-sufficient by developing emerging women leaders and providing financial and technical assistance to non-profits.

Fields of interest: Health care; Employment, training; Women, centers/services; Leadership development.
Type of support: General/operating support; Program development; Technical assistance; Consulting services.
Limitations: Applications accepted. Giving limited to MI. No support for projects that require religious participation as a condition for receiving services. No grants to individuals, or for building funds, capital campaigns, or endowments.
Publications: Application guidelines; Annual report; Grants list; Informational brochure; Newsletter; Occasional report.
Application information: Application form required.
    Initial approach: Submit proposal; telephone inquiries encouraged
    Copies of proposal: 3
    Deadline(s): July 31 for Mini-grants
    Board meeting date(s): Apr., June, Sept., and Nov.
Officers and Trustees:* Linda Forte,* Chair.; Delores Clark Givens, Pres. and C.E.O.; Vernice Davis Anthony; Beverly Hall Burns; Deborah I. Dingell; Laura Fochtman; Kathy Fore; Anika Goss-Foster; Wallis Klein; Lynn Kotecki; Emily Malloy; Kristin McLaughlin; Terry Merritt; Jacqueline Taylor; Tina Wheeler; and 5 additional trustees.
Number of staff: 3 full-time professional; 1 full-time support.
EIN: 382689979

1351
Middle East Reformed Fellowship, Inc.
P.O. Box 1904
Holland, MI   49422-1904
County: Ottawa
E-mail: usa@merf.org

Established in 1974.
Grantmaker type: Public charity.
Financial data (yr. ended 12/31/09): Revenue, $944,387; assets, $100,947 (M); gifts received, $943,168; expenditures, $913,105; total giving, $801,000.
Purpose and activities: The organization seeks to encourage and strengthen the Church throughout the Middle East.
Fields of interest: Christian agencies & churches.
Officers: Lee DeYoung, Chair.; Dr. Norman DeJong, Vice-Chair.; Rev. William J. Bouwer, Secy.; John Kuyers, Treas.
EIN: 232416249

1352
Morenci Education Foundation
500 Page St.
Morenci, MI   49256-1230
County: Lenawee
Contact: Bill Van Valkenburg, Pres.
E-mail: vanvalkenburg@morencieducationfoundatio n.org; URL: http://morencieducationfoundation.org

Established in 2004 in MI.
Grantmaker type: Public charity.
Financial data (yr. ended 12/31/09): Revenue, $101,092; assets, $223,909 (M); gifts received, $85,989; expenditures, $30,512; total giving, $18,229; giving activities include $18,229 for grants.
Purpose and activities: The foundation provides scholarships to Morenci area school graduates and

mini-grants for teachers of the Morenci area school district.
Fields of interest: Higher education.
Type of support: Grants to individuals; Scholarships —to individuals.
Limitations: Applications accepted. Giving limited to Morenci, MI.
Publications: Application guidelines.
Application information: Application form not required.
    Initial approach: Download application
    Deadline(s): Mar. 31 for Evelyn and Ronald Wirick Foundation Scholarship; the last Friday in Mar. for the Eric K. Brandeberry Memorial Scholarship
Officers: Bill Van Valkenburg, Pres.; Rosemary Dickerson, V.P.; Barbara E. Vallieu, Secy.; Philip R. Burley, Treas.
Directors: Dr. Joshua Baumgartner, D.C.; Timothy E. Bovee; Dan R. Bruggeman; Carrie A. Dillon; and 6 additional directors.
EIN: 043721858

1353
Ms. Molly Foundation
c/o Molly Maid, Inc.
3948 Ranchero Dr.
Ann Arbor, MI   48108-2775
County: Washtenaw
URL: http://www.mollymaid.com/ MainMsMollyFoundation.aspx

Established in 1996 in MI.
Grantmaker type: Public charity.
Financial data (yr. ended 12/31/09): Revenue, $125,565; assets, $10,294 (M); gifts received, $105,197; expenditures, $125,464; total giving, $119,985; giving activities include $119,985 for grants.
Purpose and activities: The foundation is dedicated to assisting victims and families affected by domestic violence through its support of hundreds of local shelters and safe houses across America providing refuge and personal care items to victims of domestic violence.
Fields of interest: Crime/violence prevention, domestic violence; Family services, domestic violence; Residential/custodial care.
Limitations: Giving on a national basis.
Officers: David Dickinson, Co-Chair.; Stephanie Zikakis, Co-Chair.
Directors: Lynn Butler; Mary Dickinson; David McKinnon; Donna Reilly; Harry Young.
EIN: 383290026

1354
Greater Muskegon Service League Foundation
1903 Marquette Ave.
Muskegon, MI   49442-1453
County: Muskegon
Contact: Barbara Grennan, Pres.; Lisa Tyler, V.P.

Established in 1991.
Grantmaker type: Public charity.
Financial data (yr. ended 08/31/09): Revenue, $62,730; assets, $37,229 (M); expenditures, $51,067; total giving, $22,130; giving activities include $22,130 for grants.
Fields of interest: Community/economic development.

Limitations: Applications accepted. Giving primarily in Muskegon, MI.
Application information: Application form required.
    Board meeting date(s): 3rd Thurs. of each month except July and Aug.
Officers: Barbara Grennan, Pres.; Jeana Kersman, V.P.; Lisa Tyler, V.P.; Priscilla Wilcox, Secy.; Harriet Oliver, Treas.
EIN: 386072774

1355
National Comprehensive Cancer Network
275 Commerce Dr., Ste. 300
Fort Washington, PA   19034-2413
(215) 690-0300
County: Montgomery
FAX: (215) 690-0280; URL: http://www.nccn.org/ index.asp

Established in 1993 in PA.
Grantmaker type: Public charity.
Financial data (yr. ended 12/31/09): Revenue, $25,511,455; assets, $29,508,232 (M); gifts received, $22,379,720; expenditures, $28,945,703; total giving, $2,336,551; giving activities include $2,336,551 for grants.
Purpose and activities: The network is a nonprofit alliance of 21 of the world's leading cancer centers, and is dedicated to improving the quality and effectiveness of care provided to patients with cancer.
Fields of interest: Cancer; Medical research, alliance/advocacy; Cancer research.
Limitations: Giving limited to San Francisco, CA; New Haven, CT; Tampa, FL; Atlanta, GA; Evanston, IL; Boston, MA; Baltimore, MD; Ann Arbor, MI; St. Louis, MO; Durham, NC; Omaha, NE; Buffalo and New York, NY; Columbus, OH; Rockledge, PA; Memphis, TN; Houston, TX; and Salt Lake City, UT.
Publications: Annual report; Informational brochure.
Officers and Directors:* Thomas A. D'Amico, M.D.*, Chair.; Samuel M. Silver, M.D., Ph.D.*, Vice-Chair.; Marcy B. Waldinger, M.H.S.A.*, Secy.; Nicolas C. Porter,* Treas.; Al B. Benson III, M.D.; Jordan D. Berlin, M.D.; Mara G. Bloom, J.D., M.P.A.; Robert W. Carlson, M.D.; Carolyn C. Carpenter, M.H.A.; William E. Carson III, M.D.; Peter F. Coccia, M.D.; Timothy Eberlein, M.D.; Stephen B. Edge, M.D.; Paul F. Engstrom, M.D., F.A.C.P.; David S. Ettinger, M.D.; and 26 additional directors.
EIN: 232818395

1356
National Kidney Foundation of Michigan, Inc.
1169 Oak Valley Dr.
Ann Arbor, MI   48108-9674   (734) 222-9800
County: Washtenaw
Contact: Daniel M. Carney, Pres. and C.E.O.
FAX: (734) 222-9801; E-mail: mgerlach@nkfm.org; Toll-free tel.(in MI): (800) 482-1455; URL: http:// www.nkfm.org

Grantmaker type: Public charity.
Financial data (yr. ended 06/30/09): Revenue, $5,560,396; assets, $6,886,461 (M); gifts received, $5,208,075; expenditures, $5,223,157; total giving, $89,869; giving activities include $50,000 for grants, and $39,869 for grants to individuals.

Purpose and activities: The foundation seeks to prevent kidney disease and improve the quality of life for those living with it.
Fields of interest: Kidney diseases; Kidney research.
Type of support: Research; Grants to individuals.
Limitations: Giving primarily in MI.
Application information:
   Initial approach: Telephone or e-mail
Officers and Trustees: * Cynthia H. Shannon,* Chair.; Mark E. Behm,* Vice-Chair.; Daniel M. Carney,* Pres. and C.E.O.; M. David Campbell,* Secy.; Andrew Boschma,* Treas.; Michael Allie; Renee T. Farhat; Janice G. Frazier; Sen. Beverly S. Hammerstrom; Hon. Kirsten Frank Kelly; Tomasine Marx; David W. Potts; Robert Provenzano, M.D.; Scott Seling; Michael S. Sisskind.
EIN: 381559941

1357
National Multiple Sclerosis Society Michigan Chapter, Inc.
21311 Civic Center Dr.
Southfield, MI   48076-3911   (248) 350-0020
County: Oakland
FAX: (248) 350-0029; E-mail: info@mig.nmss.org; Toll-free tel.: (800) 243-5767; URL: http://www.nationalmssociety.org/chapters/MIG/index.aspx

Established in 1948 in MI.
Grantmaker type: Public charity.
Financial data (yr. ended 09/30/09): Revenue, $3,768,445; assets, $863,794 (M); gifts received, $3,745,719; expenditures, $3,382,428; total giving, $563,766; giving activities include $469,457 for grants, and $94,309 for grants to individuals.
Purpose and activities: The society is organized to end the devastating effects of multiple sclerosis by supporting the national organization and its research into the cause and cure of the disease; as well as supporting those afflicted with multiple sclerosis.
Fields of interest: Multiple sclerosis; Multiple sclerosis research.
Type of support: Grants to individuals; Research.
Limitations: Applications accepted. Giving limited to MI.
Publications: Annual report; Newsletter.
Application information: Accepts applications from hospitals and clinics. Application form required.
   Initial approach: Telephone
   Deadline(s): None
   Board meeting date(s): Quarterly
Officers and Board Members: * Peter Burton,* Chair.; Dean Munger,* 1st Vice-Chair.; Jim Gismondi,* Secy.; Steven A. Micsowicz,* Treas.; Elana Sullivan, Pres.; Eugene Applebaum; Tim Blett; Michael Brady; Marc Broadnax; and 28 additional board members.
EIN: 381410476

1358
The New Day Foundation for Families
P.O. Box 81252
Rochester, MI   48306-4801   (248) 330-0471
County: Oakland
Contact: Gine Kell Spehn, Dir.
URL: http://www.foundationforfamilies.com

Established in 2007 in MI.
Grantmaker type: Public charity.
Financial data (yr. ended 12/31/09): Revenue, $30,247; assets, $38,909 (M); gifts received, $31,517; expenditures, $30,535; total giving, $8,908; program services expenses, $8,909; giving activities include $1,347 for 1 grant, and $7,561 for 3 grants to individuals (high: $4,564; low: $287).
Purpose and activities: The foundation's mission is to offer financial relief, spiritual support, and hope for young families who have lost a parent to cancer.
Fields of interest: Cancer.
Directors: Steve Elmer; Matt Preuss; Mike Schomaker; Marty Shelata; Gina Kell Spehn; Michael Spehn.
EIN: 260609040

1359
New Detroit, Inc.
3011 W. Grand Blvd., Ste. 1200
Detroit, MI   48202-3013   (313) 664-2000
County: Wayne
FAX: (313) 664-2071;
E-mail: sstancato@newdetroit.org; URL: http://www.newdetroit.org

Established in 1967 in MI.
Grantmaker type: Public charity.
Financial data (yr. ended 12/31/09): Revenue, $1,412,467; assets, $3,311,388 (M); gifts received, $1,214,441; expenditures, $2,794,969; total giving, $320,555; giving activities include $320,555 for grants.
Purpose and activities: The organization works as the coalition of Detroit area leadership to address the issue of race relations by positively impacting issues and policies that ensure economic and social equality.
Fields of interest: Civil rights, race/intergroup relations; Community development, neighborhood development.
Type of support: Technical assistance; Management development/capacity building.
Limitations: Applications accepted. Giving limited to MI.
Publications: Application guidelines; Newsletter.
Application information: Application form required.
   Initial approach: Download application
   Deadline(s): Nov. 14
Officers and Trustees: * John Rakolta, Jr.,* Chair.; Eva Garza Dewaelsche,* Vice-Chair.; Roderick D. Gillum,* Vice-Chair.; Timothy D. Leuliette,* Vice-Chair.; Shirley R. Stancato, Pres. and C.E.O.; Leatrice W. Eagleson, V.P., Admin.; Maurice Shane, V.P., Progs.; Susan Urban, V.P., Fund Devel.; Gerald K. Smith, Ed.D., Secy.-Treas.; Ruben Acosta; and 77 additional trustees.
EIN: 386159215

1360
Newaygo County Community Services
6308 S. Warner Ave.
P.O. Box 149
Fremont, MI   49412-9279   (231) 924-0641
County: Newaygo
Contact: Beverly Cassidy, Exec. Dir.
FAX: (231) 924-5594; E-mail: info@nccsweb.org; URL: http://www.nccsweb.org

Established in 1968 in MI.
Grantmaker type: Public charity.

Financial data (yr. ended 12/31/09): Revenue, $9,108,736; assets, $9,829,157 (M); gifts received, $8,540,177; expenditures, $7,802,297; total giving, $5,139,161; giving activities include $5,139,161 for grants to individuals.
Purpose and activities: The organization seeks to serve the positive development of individuals and their communities.
Fields of interest: Human services; Economically disadvantaged.
Type of support: Grants to individuals.
Limitations: Giving primarily in Newaygo County, MI.
Publications: Annual report; Financial statement.
Officers and Directors: * Scott Rumsey,* Pres.; Pam Semlow,* V.P.; Mary Lantz,* Secy.; John Cooper,* Treas.; Beverly Cassidy, Exec. Dir.; Jelanie Bush; Bob Clark; Chris Haynor; Mike Paige; Andy Paris; Sharla Schipper; Suzanne VanWieren.
EIN: 386158533

1361
Nonprofit Finance Fund
(formerly Nonprofit Facilities Fund)
70 W. 36th St., 11th Fl.
New York, NY   10018-8007   (212) 868-6710
County: New York
FAX: (212) 868-8653; E-mail: nff@nffusa.org; URL: http://www.nonprofitfinancefund.org

Established in 1980 in NY.
Grantmaker type: Public charity.
Financial data (yr. ended 12/31/09): Revenue, $20,695,992; assets, $79,496,573 (M); gifts received, $14,566,774; expenditures, $20,164,716; total giving, $5,912,290; giving activities include $5,912,290 for grants.
Purpose and activities: The fund seeks to be a national leader in financing nonprofits through strengthening their financial health; improving their capacity to serve their communities; and helping them build and renovate facilities, fund growth needs, and expand and sustain operations over time.
Fields of interest: Humanities; Arts; Education; Environment; Animal welfare; Health care; Employment; Housing/shelter, services; Housing/shelter; Recreation; Youth development; Human services; Economic development; Community/economic development; Population studies; Religion.
Type of support: Management development/capacity building; Building/renovation; Equipment; Land acquisition; Conferences/seminars; Technical assistance; Consulting services; Program-related investments/loans; Matching/challenge support.
Limitations: Applications accepted. Giving primarily on the West Coast; the greater Washington, DC, area, including MD and VA; New England; the New York City metropolitan area; NJ; the greater Philadelphia, PA, area; and the Midwest (IL, IN, MI, and OH).
Publications: Application guidelines; Annual report; Financial statement; Informational brochure; Occasional report.
Application information: Application form required.
   Initial approach: Telephone
   Board meeting date(s): Quarterly
   Final notification: Six to eight weeks
Officers and Directors: * Elizabeth C. Sullivan,* Chair.; Clara Miller,* Pres. and C.E.O.; Elizabeth Hall Ortiz,* C.O.O.; Leon E. Wilson, Exec. V.P.; Bruce Skyer, C.F.O. and C.A.O.; Daniel Ben Horin; Jim Bildner; Andrew B. Cohn; Ami Dar; Tessie Guillermo;

Maurice Jones; Robert S. Robbin; Ruth Salman; William E. Strickland, Jr.; Janet Thompson; David Vollmayer.
Number of staff: 42 full-time professional; 4 part-time professional; 31 full-time support.
EIN: 133238657

1362
Northeast Michigan Community Service Agency, Inc.
2375 Gordon Rd.
Alpena, MI   49707-4627   (989) 356-3474
County: Alpena
FAX: (989) 354-5909; E-mail: Contact@nemcsa.org; Toll-free tel.: (866) 484-7077; URL: http://www.nemcsa.org

Grantmaker type: Public charity.
Financial data (yr. ended 09/30/09): Revenue, $38,916,739; assets, $5,428,412 (M); gifts received, $33,112,456; expenditures, $38,720,045; total giving, $10,870,764; giving activities include $4,547,238 for grants, and $6,323,526 for grants to individuals.
Purpose and activities: The agency plans, establishes, coordinates and operates programs to promote health, education and welfare to residents within northeast Michigan.
Fields of interest: Education; Health care; Assistive technology.
Type of support: Technical assistance; Grants to individuals.
Limitations: Applications accepted. Giving limited to Alcona, Alpena, Arenac, Cheboygan, Crawford, Iosco, Montmorency, Ogemaw, Oscoda, Otsego, and Presque Isle counties, MI.
Application information:
   Initial approach: E-mail or telephone
Officers and Directors:* Dale A. Huggler,* Pres.; John M. Swise, C.E.O.; John E. Briggs, C.O.O.; Rev. Bill Hipwood,* V.P.; Frank Cowger,* Treas.; Terry Beardslee; Robert Cudney; Gerald Fournier; Kenneth Glasser; Pauline Hall; Pete Hennard; Herb Makima; Daniel Marcrum; Sheila Phillips; Gary Wazniak; and 21 additional directors.
EIN: 381873461

1363
Northern Michigan Hospital Foundation
360 Connable Avenue
Petoskey, MI   49770-2272   (231) 487-3500
County: Emmet
E-mail: foundation@northernhealth.org; URL: http://www.nmh-foundation.org

Supporting organization of Boulder Park Terrace, Healthshare Real Estate, Hospice of Little Traverse Bay, Northern Michigan Hematology and Oncology, Northern Michigan Hospital, Northern Michigan Regional Health System, and Petosky Community Free Clinic.
Grantmaker type: Public charity.
Financial data (yr. ended 12/31/09): Revenue, $7,486,780; assets, $17,301,157 (M); gifts received, $7,365,099; expenditures, $2,642,784; total giving, $1,570,719; giving activities include $1,449,356 for grants, and $121,363 for grants to individuals.
Fields of interest: Hospitals (general).
Limitations: Giving limited to Petoskey, MI.

Officers and Trustees:* Elise Hayes,* Chair.; James Offield,* Vice-Chair.; Thomas Mroczkowski,* Pres.; H. Gunner Deery, M.D.*, Secy.; Stephen Eilbling,* Treas.; Moon Seagren, Exec. Dir. and Chief Devel. Officer; Michael Bacon, D.O.; Lawrence Buhl; Steven Dupuis, D.O.; Ann Irish; Frederick Koehler; Patrick Leavy; William Meengs, M.D.; William Meengs, Jr.; Thomas Moran; and 6 additional directors.
EIN: 382445611

1364
Northville Educational Foundation
501 W. Main St.
Northville, MI   48167-1576
County: Wayne
URL: http://www.northville.k12.mi.us/district/educational-foundation.asp

Established in 2000 in MI.
Grantmaker type: Public charity.
Financial data (yr. ended 06/30/09): Revenue, $17,743; assets, $81,001 (M); gifts received, $10,228; expenditures, $25,559; total giving, $3,059; giving activities include $3,059 for grants.
Purpose and activities: NEF is a community-based organization managed by a board of trustees comprised of parents and community leaders. It works in partnership with the Northville Public Schools to support special programs that enhance the classroom experience, including technology integration, innovative grants for classroom initiatives, teacher leadership programs, and student and staff scholarhsips.
Fields of interest: Education.
Type of support: Scholarship funds; Scholarships—to individuals.
Limitations: Giving limited to Northville, MI.
Officers and Directors: Eric Barritt,* Pres.; Todd Knickerbocker,* V.P.; Mark Cousino,* Secy.; Amy Storm,* Treas.; Jay Dunkerley; Mike Poterala; Mark Knoth; Jerry Rupley; Jim Sourges; Judy Wollack.
EIN: 383503644

1365
Northwest Michigan Community Coordinated Child Care Council
720 S. Elmwood Ave., Ste. 4
Traverse City, MI   49684-3005   (231) 941-7767
County: Grand Traverse
URL: http://www.nwmi4c.org

Established in 1979 in MI.
Grantmaker type: Public charity.
Financial data (yr. ended 09/30/09): Revenue, $1,416,383; assets, $298,565 (M); gifts received, $1,401,374; expenditures, $1,419,937; total giving, $782,774; giving activities include $782,774 for grants to individuals.
Purpose and activities: The council serves children, families, businesses and early childhood professionals in northwestern Michigan.
Fields of interest: Food services; Children, day care; Children.
Type of support: Grants to individuals.
Limitations: Giving primarily in northwestern MI.
Officers: Barb Keelan, Chair.; Sara Weatherholt, Secy.; Kari Kahler, Treas.; Pam Ward, Exec. Dir.
EIN: 382262853

1366
Northwest Michigan Human Services, Inc.
3963 Three Mile Rd.
Traverse City, MI   49686-9164
County: Grand Traverse
FAX: (231) 947-4935; E-mail: mgordon@nmhsa.org

Grantmaker type: Public charity.
Financial data (yr. ended 09/30/09): Revenue, $18,390,176; assets, $3,436,306 (M); gifts received, $17,426,304; expenditures, $18,186,099; total giving, $4,888,667; giving activities include $404,533 for grants, and $4,484,134 for grants to individuals.
Purpose and activities: The organization strives to plan, establish, coordinate, and operate programs to promote the health and welfare of low income residents of Michigan.
Fields of interest: Health care; Human services.
Type of support: Grants to individuals.
Limitations: Giving limited to MI.
Officers and Board Members:* Shirley Roloff, Chair.; Bonnie Carlson,* Vice-Chair.; Margaret Underwood, Secy.; John K. Stephenson, Exec. Dir.; Bruce Anderson, Sr.; Larry Bargy; Shirley Dunklow; Janet Froats-Sheperd; and 19 additional board members.
EIN: 382027389

1367
Northwest Senior Resources, Inc.
P.O. Box 5946
Traverse City, MI   49696-5946
County: Grand Traverse

Established in MI.
Grantmaker type: Public charity.
Financial data (yr. ended 09/30/09): Revenue, $7,044,469; assets, $1,690,030 (M); gifts received, $6,988,486; expenditures, $6,942,650.
Purpose and activities: The organization provides various services to senior citizens.
Fields of interest: Aging, centers/services.
Limitations: Giving primarily in northwestern MI.
Officers: Ray Kadelic, Pres.; Lester Barnes, V.P.; Victor Patrick, Secy.; David Banks, Treas.; Gregory Piaskowski, Exec. Dir.
EIN: 382056710

1368
Novi Parks Foundation
P.O. Box 1169
Novi, MI   48376-1169   (888) 288-1199
County: Oakland
Contact: Jack Lewis, Deputy Dir.
FAX: (248) 474-6659; E-mail: info@noviparks.org; URL: http://www.noviparks.org/
Application address: 45175 W. Ten Mile Rd., Novi, MI 48375-3006

Established in 2004 in MI.
Grantmaker type: Public charity.
Financial data (yr. ended 12/31/08): Revenue, $192,592; assets, $324,052 (M); gifts received, $189,469; expenditures, $59,973; total giving, $6,500; giving activities include $6,500 for grants.
Purpose and activities: The foundation awards scholarships to assist needy individuals to register for recreational programs.
Fields of interest: Recreation, parks/playgrounds.
Type of support: Scholarships—to individuals.

Limitations: Applications accepted. Giving limited to Novi, MI.
Publications: Application guidelines.
Application information: Application form required.
Initial approach: Download application
Officers and Directors:* Linda Blair,* Chair. and Pres.; Charles Staab,* Vice-Chair. and V.P.; Brian Bartlett,* Secy.; Justin Fischer,* Treas.; Mark Adams; Randy Auler; Brian Burke; Hugh Crawford; Kathy Crawford; Jay F. Dooley; Angel Heard; Lou Martin; Mark Merlanti; Tim Shroyer; David Staudt.
EIN: 200902251

1369
Oakland County Bar Foundation

1760 S. Telegraph Rd., Ste. 100
Bloomfield Hills, MI 48302-0181
(248) 334-3400
County: Oakland
FAX: (248) 334-7757;
E-mail: membership@ocba.org; URL: http://www.ocba.org/barfoundation.id.19.htm

Supporting organization of the Oakland County Bar Association.
Grantmaker type: Public charity.
Financial data (yr. ended 12/31/09): Revenue, $194,203; assets, $512,529 (M); gifts received, $188,127; expenditures, $169,494; total giving, $132,000; giving activities include $132,000 for grants.
Purpose and activities: The foundation's mission is to serve the citizens of Oakland County and the legal profession through the funding of programs that foster the honor, integrity and welfare of the legal system, improve its equality, accessibility and affordability, and educate the public about the role of lawyers in our society.
Fields of interest: Crime/law enforcement, administration/regulation; Crime/law enforcement, reform; Crime/law enforcement, equal rights; Crime/law enforcement, information services; Crime/law enforcement, public education; Crime/law enforcement.
Limitations: Applications accepted. Giving primarily in MI. No support for religious activities, or political campaigns or entities designed primarily for political lobbying. Generally, no grants to individuals, or for endowment campaigns; no loans.
Publications: Application guidelines.
Application information: Application form required.
Initial approach: Download application form
Deadline(s): Feb. 4 and June 2
Final notification: 1 month
Officers and Trustees:* Francile Anderson,* Pres.; Gerald A. Fisher,* V.P.; Thomas J. Tallerico,* Secy.; Michael J. Sullivan,* Treas.; Alan T. Ackerman; Diana Dietle; Brenda M. Orlando; Lawrence R. Ternan; and 11 additional trustees.
EIN: 382170426

1370
Oakland Livingston Human Service Agency

196 Cesar E. Chavez Ave.
Pontiac, MI 48343-0598   (248) 209-2600
County: Oakland
FAX: (248) 209-2645; E-mail: info@olhsa.org; Mailing address: P.O. Box 430598, Pontiac, MI 48343-0598; URL: http://www.olhsa.org

Established in 1964 in MI.
Grantmaker type: Public charity.
Financial data (yr. ended 12/31/09): Revenue, $30,331,481; assets, $4,642,127 (M); gifts received, $30,024,912; expenditures, $30,687,201; total giving, $8,909,589; program services expenses, $28,819,362; giving activities include $3,811,721 for 13 grants (high: $717,398; low: $127,473), $5,097,868 for grants to individuals, and $19,909,773 for foundation-administered programs.
Purpose and activities: The agency works to enable the low-income, elderly, and persons with disabilities living in Oakland and Livingston counties to become self-sufficient.
Fields of interest: Aging, centers/services; Developmentally disabled, centers & services; Human services; Community/economic development; Children/youth; Aging; Economically disadvantaged.
Type of support: Grants to individuals.
Limitations: Giving limited to Livingston and Oakland counties, MI.
Publications: Annual report; Informational brochure.
Directors: Sonia Acosta; John Almstadt; Yohannes Bolds; Ursula Bolton; Cheryl Braxton; Sean Corcoran; Kathy Crawford; Nancy L. Dingeldey; Jay Drick; Dennis Griffin; Robert Griffin; Candye Hinton; Richard Holmes; Holbert Maxey; Douglas Williams; and 15 additional directors.
EIN: 381785665

1371
Oakwood Healthcare, Inc.

23400 Michigan Ave., No. 800
Dearborn, MI 48124-1985
County: Wayne
URL: http://www.oakwood.org

Established in 1948 in MI.
Grantmaker type: Public charity.
Financial data (yr. ended 12/31/09): Revenue, $996,999,998; assets, $887,015,660 (M); gifts received, $6,724,287; expenditures, $986,702,049; total giving, $10,413,115; giving activities include $225,626 for grants, and $10,187,489 for grants to individuals.
Purpose and activities: The organization works to provide excellence in care, healing, and health to the individuals and communities it serves.
Fields of interest: Hospitals (general); Health care.
Type of support: Scholarships—to individuals.
Limitations: Giving primarily to Dearborn, MI.
Officers and Trustees:* John Lewis,* Chair.; Brian Connolly,* Pres. and C.E.O.; John Furman,* V.P., Human Resources; Kenneth Trester,* V.P., Planning and Mktg.; Seth Lloyd,* Secy.; Lizabeth Ardisana; Robert Kramer; Richard Kughn; Jerry Norcia; Martin Mulloy; Robert Mentzer, M.D.; Lester Robinson; Robert Rosowski; Edgar Scribner; Bala Setty; and 4 additional trustees.
EIN: 381405141

1372
The Ontonagon Area Scholarship Foundation

P.O. Box 92
Ontonagon, MI 49953-0092
County: Ontonagon
E-mail: marilyn@oasd.k12.mi.us; URL: http://scholarship.oasd.k12.mi.us/index.htm

Grantmaker type: Public charity.
Financial data (yr. ended 05/31/10): Revenue, $288,555; assets, $843,849 (M); gifts received, $278,116; expenditures, $16,121; total giving, $14,000; giving activities include $14,000 for grants.
Purpose and activities: The foundation awards scholarships for higher education to graduates of Ontonagon Area High School.
Fields of interest: Scholarships/financial aid.
Type of support: Scholarships—to individuals.
Limitations: Applications accepted. Giving limited to residents of Ontonagon, MI.
Publications: Application guidelines; Grants list.
Application information:
Initial approach: Download application
Officers: Meredith Strong, Pres.; James Morin, V.P.; Marilyn Anderson, Secy.; Gerald Domitrovich, Treas.
Trustees: John Cane; Louis Gregory; Dean Juntunen; James Klein; Matthew Lukshaitis; James Michie; Kristina Miliu; Kathleen Preiss; Sue Preiss; James Tucker; Janis Tucker; Clarence Wilbur; Janet Wolfe.
EIN: 383525614

1373
The Optimist Club Foundation

P.O. Box 891
Clarkston, MI 48347-0891
County: Oakland

Grantmaker type: Public charity.
Financial data (yr. ended 09/30/09): Revenue, $44,965; assets, $65,085 (M); expenditures, $41,208; total giving, $3,178; giving activities include $1,182 for grants, and $1,996 for grants to individuals.
Fields of interest: Youth development.
Type of support: Scholarships—to individuals.
Officers: Kelley Kostin, Pres.; Jean Dasuqi, V.P.; Nancy Knitter, Secy.; Jeffrey Reed, Treas.
EIN: 383373756

1374
Orchards Children's Services, Inc.

30215 Southfield Rd.
Southfield, MI 48076-1300   (248) 258-0440
County: Oakland
FAX: (248) 258-0487; URL: http://www.orchards.org

Grantmaker type: Public charity.
Financial data (yr. ended 09/30/09): Revenue, $12,384,625; assets, $3,854,978 (M); gifts received, $474,307; expenditures, $11,646,618; total giving, $2,630,941; giving activities include $2,630,941 for grants to individuals.
Purpose and activities: The organization seeks to protect and nurture children and youth by providing shelter, sustenance, life- and education skills, and opportunities, with the hopes of helping them achieve stability and long-terms self-sufficiency. Assistance is provided to foster care parents.
Fields of interest: Food services; Children/youth, services; Children, adoption; Children, foster care; Children, day care; Children, services.
Publications: Financial statement.
Officers and Directors:* Shirley J. Bryant,* Chair.; David Kramer,* Vice-Chair.; Michael E. Williams, M.A., Pres. and C.E.O.; Carmine Devivo, M.S.W., C.S.W., C.O.O.; Robert Y. Blumenfeld, Sr. V.P.,

Finance and Devel.; Trudy Fortino, M.S.W., C.S.W., V.P., Placement Svcs.; George Fox,* Secy.; Steven J. Schwarz,* Treas.; Sonya Delley; Allen Einstein; Barbara Goldberg; Teresa Gueyser; Maura Jung; Carol G. Klein; David Kramer; and 11 additional directors.
EIN: 382712084

1375
Otsego County United Way, Inc.
116 E. 5th St.
Gaylord, MI 49735-1270 (989) 732-8929
County: Otsego
FAX: (989) 731-2677;
E-mail: otsegounitedway@voyager.net; URL: http://www.otsego.org/unitedway/

Established in MI.
Grantmaker type: Public charity.
Financial data (yr. ended 12/31/09): Revenue, $301,763; assets, $323,955 (M); gifts received, $280,114; expenditures, $346,470; total giving, $94,757; giving activities include $66,000 for grants, and $28,757 for grants to individuals.
Purpose and activities: The organization seeks to provide support to organizations serving the social welfare of Otsego County, Michigan.
Fields of interest: Human services.
Type of support: Grants to individuals; In-kind gifts.
Limitations: Giving primarily in Otsego County, MI.
Officers and Directors:* Laura Hansmann,* Pres.; Skip Kasprzak,* 1st V.P.; Bruce Brown, 2nd V.P.; Jennifer Hendrickson,* Secy.; Tim Hall,* Treas.; Tammie Rich, Exec. Dir.; Sandy Allison; Roland Chavey; Liz Mench; Brian Samkowiak; and 5 additional directors.
EIN: 237156104

1376
Greater Ottawa County United Way
115 Clover St., Ste. 300
Holland, MI 49423-3266 (616) 396-7811
County: Ottawa
FAX: (616) 396-5140;
E-mail: info@ottawaunitedway.org; Mailing address: P.O. Box 1349, Holland, MI 49422-1349; additional office (Grand Haven office): 700 Fulton St., Ste. B, Grand Haven, MI 49417-1573; tel.: (616) 842-7130; URL: http://ottawaunitedway.org

Established in 2000.
Grantmaker type: Public charity.
Financial data (yr. ended 03/31/10): Revenue, $2,074,804; assets, $3,225,971 (M); gifts received, $1,934,996; expenditures, $2,057,868; total giving, $1,142,359; program services expenses, $1,627,478; giving activities include $1,142,359 for 35 grants (high: $135,427; low: $5,435), and $485,119 for foundation-administered programs.
Purpose and activities: The organization seeks to improve lives by mobilizing communities to create sustained changes in community conditions, focusing on solutions in the areas of thriving kids, strong families, and healthy communities.
Fields of interest: Public health; Youth development; Human services; Children/youth, services; Family services; Community/economic development.
Limitations: Applications accepted. Giving limited to the greater Ottawa County, MI area.

Publications: Annual report.
Application information: Application form required.
Initial approach: Download letter of intent
Deadline(s): Nov. 30
Officers and Trustees:* Jack Russell,* Chair.; Pete Esser,* Vice-Chair.; Ron Veldman,* Secy.; Mike Metzger,* Treas.; Taiyoh Afrik; Brett Burza; Les Denton; David DeYoung; Sandy Ganz; Eric Kaelin; Larry Koops; Paul Thurman; Mark Wilson.
EIN: 383522782

1377
Rosa L. Parks Scholarship Foundation, Inc.
c/o The Detroit News
615 W. Lafayette Blvd.
Detroit, MI 48226-3124
County: Wayne
E-mail: rpscholarship@dnps.com; Application address: P.O. Box 950, Detroit, MI 48231; URL: http://www.rosaparksscholarshipfoundation.org

Established in 1980 in MI.
Grantmaker type: Public charity.
Financial data (yr. ended 04/30/09): Revenue, $81,572; assets, $85,664 (M); gifts received, $80,625; expenditures, $67,182; total giving, $62,000; giving activities include $62,000 for grants.
Purpose and activities: The foundation is dedicated to awarding scholarships to Michigan high school seniors who hold close to the legacy of Rosa Parks, while demonstrating academic skills, community involvement, and economic need.
Fields of interest: Scholarships/financial aid; Education; Civil/human rights.
Type of support: Scholarships—to individuals.
Limitations: Applications accepted. Giving primarily in MI.
Application information: Scholarship application form is available on the foundation's Web site. Application form required.
Deadline(s): Apr. 1
Officers and Trustees:* Delora Hall Tyler,* Pres.; Christopher Carswell,* V.P.; Marcia Hart,* Secy.; Michael Johnson,* Treas.; Bernadine Aubert; Kristi Boweden; Louise Guyton; Kimberly Trent; and 9 additional trustees.
EIN: 382339613

1378
Pennock Foundation
1009 W. Green St.
Hastings, MI 49058-1790 (269) 948-3122
County: Barry
Contact: Matthew J. Thompson

Established in 1987; supporting organization of Pennock Hospital.
Grantmaker type: Public charity.
Financial data (yr. ended 09/30/09): Revenue, $217,602; assets, $5,120,552 (M); gifts received, $81,896; expenditures, $272,922; total giving, $186,654; giving activities include $23,095 for grants, and $163,559 for grants to individuals.
Fields of interest: Health care.
Type of support: Scholarships—to individuals.
Limitations: Applications accepted. Giving limited to Hastings, MI.

Application information: Contact organization for specific grant guidelines before submitting application. Application form required.
Initial approach: Application form
Officer and Directors:* James Wiswell,* Chair.; David Baum; Bill Wallace; John Walker.
EIN: 382713275

1379
Pewabic Society, Inc.
10125 E. Jefferson Ave.
Detroit, MI 48214-3138 (313) 822-0954
County: Wayne
Contact: Terese Ireland, Exec. Dir.
FAX: (313) 822-6266;
E-mail: pewabic1@pewabic.com; URL: http://www.pewabic.com

Grantmaker type: Public charity.
Financial data (yr. ended 09/30/09): Revenue, $2,305,595; assets, $2,609,976 (M); gifts received, $690,598; expenditures, $2,298,830.
Purpose and activities: The society is dedicated to the preservation of the arts and crafts curriculum of educational programs, support of individual artists, outreach to various communities, and leadership in the exhibition of contemporary and historic collections and archiving of scholarly research.
Fields of interest: Visual arts, sculpture; Visual arts, ceramic arts.
Type of support: Grants to individuals.
Limitations: Giving on a national basis.
Application information:
Board meeting date(s): Annually
Officers: Roger Garrett, Chair.; Carey Ford, Vice-Chair.; Deborah Ferris, Secy.; Joseph Vassalio, Treas.; Terese Ireland, Exec. Dir.
Trustees: Jeff Art; Barbara Bierbusse; Edith S. Briskin; Neil Bristol; Beth Carnaghi; Sandra Coleman; Anne Crane; Annmarie Erickson; Frank Dulin; Gloria Frank; and 9 additional trustees.
EIN: 382277840

1380
Plumbers and Pipefitters Local No. 333 Scholarship Plan
3101 Allied Dr., Ste. B
Jackson, MI 49201
County: Jackson

Grantmaker type: Public charity.
Financial data (yr. ended 06/30/09): Revenue, $45,620; assets, $46,426 (M); expenditures, $49,390; total giving, $44,552; giving activities include $44,552 for grants.
Purpose and activities: The foundation provides scholarships to members of Plumbers and Pipefitters Local No. 333 and their dependents, to be used toward any approved educational activity.
Fields of interest: Scholarships/financial aid; Employment, labor unions/organizations.
Type of support: Scholarships—to individuals.
Limitations: Giving limited to Jackson, MI.
Officers and Trustees:* Tim Haggart,* Chair.; Charles Osborne, Secy.; Tom Eifert; Larry Gunthorpe; Chad Meyers; Joseph Michilizzi; Terry Potts; Michael Sliger; George van Coppenolle.
EIN: 386191955

1381
Plymouth Christian Schools Foundation
P.O. Box 150032
Grand Rapids, MI 49515-0032
County: Kent

Established in 1995 in MI.
Grantmaker type: Public charity.
Financial data (yr. ended 12/31/09): Revenue, $163,874; assets, $1,534,215 (M); gifts received, $125,038; expenditures, $57,722; total giving, $57,387; giving activities include $57,387 for grants.
Fields of interest: Elementary/secondary education; Christian agencies & churches.
Limitations: Giving primarily in Grand Rapids, MI.
Officers and Trustees:* Gary R. Bleeker,* Pres.; Ken Lugthart,* Secy.; James D. Bleeker,* Treas.; John Bazen, Jr.; Fred Kegel; Tim Kwekel; Orie VanderBoon; Richard Westrate, Jr.
EIN: 383271783

1382
Plymouth Community United Way
960 W. Ann Arbor Trail, Ste. 2
Plymouth, MI 48170-1591 (734) 453-6879
County: Wayne
E-mail: plymouthunitedway@ameritech.net;
URL: http://www.plymouthunitedway.org/

Established in 1944 in MI.
Grantmaker type: Public charity.
Financial data (yr. ended 12/31/09): Revenue, $1,016,942; assets, $3,694,346 (M); gifts received, $898,795; expenditures, $853,556; total giving, $416,900; program services expenses, $640,659; giving activities include $416,900 for 10 grants (high: $128,000; low: $7,500), and $223,759 for foundation-administered programs.
Purpose and activities: The organization works to reach out and serve human needs which go beyond the reach of government or private service groups, through various nonprofit health and welfare organizations.
Fields of interest: Health care; Human services; Community/economic development.
Limitations: Giving primarily in Plymouth, MI.
Publications: Annual report; Informational brochure; Newsletter.
Officers and Board Members:* Arthur Butler,* Pres.; Paul Hood,* V.P.; Jerry Schoenle, Secy.; Howard Behr,* Treas.; Trayce Dillard-Parker; Gregory Foster; Maria Holmes; Alison Hug; Martha Logan; Louis Whitlock.
EIN: 237327248

1383
Plymouth Rotary Foundation, Inc.
1095 S. Main St.
P.O. Box 701308
Plymouth, MI 48170-2022 (734) 453-6280
County: Wayne

Established in 1965.
Grantmaker type: Public charity.
Financial data (yr. ended 06/30/09): Revenue, $92,917; assets, $296,155 (M); gifts received, $83,362; expenditures, $63,198; total giving, $57,524; program services expenses, $57,524; giving activities include $32,285 for grants, and $25,239 for 10 grants to individuals.

Purpose and activities: The foundation supports charitable, religious, scientific, literary, and educational purposes.
Fields of interest: Literature; Education; Science; Religion.
Officers and Directors:* Dale Knab,* Pres.; Dale Yagiela, V.P.; Ron Lowe,* Secy.; David Williams,* Treas.; Chuck Bares; Art Gulick; Julie Howell-Romein; Thomas Kennedy; Ian McCluskey; Habib Zuberi.
EIN: 386107391

1384
Portland Community Fund Association
P.O. Box 524
Portland, MI 48875-0524
County: Ionia
E-mail: info@portlandcommunityfund.org;
URL: http://www.portlandcommunityfund.org

Established in MI.
Grantmaker type: Public charity.
Financial data (yr. ended 06/30/10): Revenue, $21,883; assets, $60,576 (M); gifts received, $21,084; expenditures, $21,328; total giving, $19,466; giving activities include $19,466 for grants.
Purpose and activities: The association seeks to support charitable activities for residents of the Portland School District.
Fields of interest: Human services; Community/economic development.
Limitations: Applications accepted. Giving primarily in MI.
Publications: Application guidelines; Newsletter.
Application information: See website for application information.
Officers: Sandra Olson, Pres.; Julie Hughes, V.P.; Sandy Klein, Secy.; Keith Neller, Co-Treas.; Jim Smith, Co-Treas.
Board Members: Julie Balderson; Lisa Balderson; Sheri Gensterblum; Tom Kreiner; Rose Mary Leik; Douglas Logel; Suzanne Maystead; Rosie Neller; Marlene Thomas; Kim Thorp; Joe Wright.
EIN: 237168046

1385
Promedica Physicians Group, Inc.
5855 Monroe St.
Sylvania, OH 43560-2269
County: Lucas
URL: http://www.ppgdocs.org

Established in 1992.
Grantmaker type: Public charity.
Financial data (yr. ended 12/31/09): Revenue, $130,567,058; assets, $25,315,851 (M); gifts received, $15,424,000; expenditures, $131,643,827; total giving, $11,942,363; giving activities include $11,942,363 for grants.
Purpose and activities: The group is a network of physicians and specialists that serves northwestern Ohio and southeastern Michigan.
Fields of interest: Medical care, community health systems; Health care.
Limitations: Giving limited to northwestern OH and southeastern MI.
Officers and Trustees:* James Murray,* Chair.; Lee Hammerling,* Pres.; Dawn Buskey, V.P., Opers.; Martin Dansack, V.P., Finance and Practice Mgmt.; Jeffrey Kuhn,* Secy.; Kathleen Hanley,* Treas.;

Edward Bardi; Brian Bucher; Gary Collins, M.D.; Robert Gatchel; Robert Gray; Kenneth Joyce; Jane Miller; Emory Schmidt; Byron West.
EIN: 341899439

1386
Racing for Kids
c/o J. Patrick Wright
93 Kercheval, Ste. 4
Grosse Pointe Farms, MI 48236
(313) 882-3403
County: Wayne
FAX: (313) 882-2193; URL: http://www.racingforkids.org

Established in 1989 in MI.
Grantmaker type: Public charity.
Financial data (yr. ended 12/31/09): Revenue, $283,514; assets, $89,600 (M); gifts received, $164,582; expenditures, $270,975; total giving, $31,724; giving activities include $31,724 for grants.
Purpose and activities: The organization uses motorsports to focus public attention and funding on the health care needs of children.
Fields of interest: Health care; Recreation; Children/youth.
Limitations: Giving on a national and international basis.
Officers: William Pinsky, Pres.; Robert P. Buhl, V.P.; J. Patrick Wright, Secy.-Treas.
EIN: 383457448

1387
Walter and May Reuther Memorial Fund
c/o Comerica Bank
P.O. Box 75000, MC 3462
Detroit, MI 48275-3462 (313) 222-4085
County: Wayne

Established in 1970.
Grantmaker type: Public charity.
Financial data (yr. ended 12/31/09): Revenue, $27,615; assets, $815,144 (M); gifts received, $7,346; expenditures, $96,847; total giving, $92,566; giving activities include $75,000 for grants, and $17,566 for grants to individuals.
Purpose and activities: The fund provides scholarships and grants to individuals and institutions for the study or provider of educational services in the fields of labor, human relations, and betterment of mankind.
Fields of interest: Education; Labor studies; Social sciences.
Type of support: Scholarships—to individuals.
Application information: Scholarship applicants must be a member or dependent of a member of the UAW or another labor organization, or be a student in an accredited educational institution.
Officers and Trustees:* Ron Gettelfinger,* Pres.; Elizabeth Bunn,* Secy.-Treas.; Douglas A. Fraser; Carly Murdy; Elizabeth Reuther; Linda Reuther; Victor G. Reuther; Comerica Bank.
EIN: 237067164

1388
Rochester Area Neighborhood House, Inc.
1234 Inglewood
P.O. Box 80112
Rochester, MI 48308-0112 (248) 651-5836
County: Oakland
FAX: (248) 651-5310;
E-mail: ranhranh@sbcglobal.net; URL: http://
www.ranh.org

Established in 1972 in MI.
Grantmaker type: Public charity.
Financial data (yr. ended 12/31/08): Revenue,
$420,271; assets, $354,172 (M); gifts received,
$425,786; expenditures, $430,596; total giving,
$237,543; program services expenses, $369,584;
giving activities include $237,543 for grants to
individuals.
Purpose and activities: The organization provides
the basic needs and other support for its residents
in times of crisis and coordinates available
resources to meet those needs.
Fields of interest: Food services; Housing/shelter,
services; Human services; Transportation.
Limitations: Giving limited to the greater Rochester,
MI, area.
Officers and Directors:* Tom Mines,* Chair.; Karen
Charles, Vice-Chair.; Kathy Losinski, Secy.; Patricia
Botkin, Treas.; Susan Vidican, Exec. Dir.; Bob
Beiver; Pat Botkin; Karen Charles; Penny Crissman;
Nancy Drapalski; Rob Laing; Kay Smith; Joe
Soncrant; David Wheeler; Ravi Yalamanchi.
EIN: 381956214

1389
Roscommon County United Way
P.O. Box 324
Roscommon, MI 48653-0324
County: Roscommon

Grantmaker type: Public charity.
Financial data (yr. ended 12/31/09): Revenue,
$46,059; assets, $47,265 (M); gifts received,
$46,017; expenditures, $46,594; total giving,
$37,213; giving activities include $37,213 for
grants.
Purpose and activities: The organization collects
public contributions to be distributed to charitable
organizations throughout Roscommon County.
Fields of interest: Community/economic
development.
Officers: Cherie Johnson, Pres.; Arlene Williams,
Secy.; Gregory Bush, Treas.
Board Members: Robert Bennett; Al Cambridge;
Larry Meier; Adam Slosar; Pam Stephan; Frank
Walsh.
EIN: 382977871

1390
The Jalen Rose Foundation
c/o The Giving Back Fund
6033 W. Century Blvd., Ste. 350
Los Angeles, CA 90045-6444 (310) 649-5222
County: Los Angeles
FAX: (310) 649-5070;
E-mail: jalenrosefoundation@givingback.org;
URL: http://www.jalenrosefoundation.org/

Donor-advised fund of The Giving Back Fund.
Grantmaker type: Public charity.

Purpose and activities: The foundation works to
create life-changing opportunities for underserved
youth through the development of unique programs
and the distribution of grants to qualified nonprofit
organizations, especially those focusing on sports
and education.
Fields of interest: Education; Recreation; Children/
youth.
Type of support: Scholarships—to individuals;
Program development.
Limitations: Applications accepted. Giving primarily
in Detroit, MI.
Publications: Application guidelines.
Application information:
  Initial approach: Letter of inquiry via e-mail for
  Grants Program; application for Scholarship
  Program
  Deadline(s): Apr. 30 for Scholarship Program;
  none for Grants Program

1391
Rotary Charities of Traverse City
202 E. Grandview Pkwy., Ste. 200
Traverse City, MI 49684-2510 (231) 941-4010
County: Grand Traverse
Contact: Marsha J. Smith, Exec. Dir.
FAX: (231) 941-4066;
E-mail: msmith@rotarycharities.org; URL: http://
www.rotarycharities.org

Established in 1976; supporting organization of the
Rotary Club of Traverse City.
Donor: Rotary Club of Traverse City.
Grantmaker type: Public charity.
Financial data (yr. ended 06/30/09): Revenue,
$1,506,590; assets, $34,184,306 (M);
expenditures, $1,776,336; total giving,
$1,222,378; giving activities include $1,222,378
for grants.
Fields of interest: Arts; Education; Environment,
management/technical assistance; Housing/
shelter, search services; Recreation; Family
services.
Type of support: Management development/
capacity building; Capital campaigns; Building/
renovation; Equipment; Land acquisition; Program
development; Seed money; Technical assistance;
Matching/challenge support.
Limitations: Applications accepted. Giving limited to
Antrim, Benzie, Grand Traverse, Kalkaska, and
Leelanau counties, MI. No support for religious
activities or programs. No grants to individuals, or
for endowment funds or ongoing support; no loans
to individuals.
Publications: Application guidelines; Annual report
(including application guidelines); Financial
statement; Grants list.
Application information: Pre-application telephone
conversations are strongly encouraged. Application
form required.
  Initial approach: Online application
  Copies of proposal: 1
  Deadline(s): Mar. 2 for Program Grants; Mar. 3 for
  Capacity Grants; Sept. 2 for Capital Grants;
  none for Planning Grants
  Board meeting date(s): Monthly
  Final notification: 30 to 90 days
Officers and Trustees:* Don Fraser,* Chair.; Ed
Downing,* Vice-Chair.; George Powell,*
Secy.-Treas.; Marsha J. Smith, Exec. Dir.; Mack
Beers; Al Bonney; Homer Nye; Bob Portenga; Gregg
Smith; Elaine Wood.

Number of staff: 2 full-time professional; 1 full-time
support.
EIN: 382170564

1392
Rotary Club of Lowell Community Foundation
P.O. Box 223
Lowell, MI 49331-0223
County: Kent

Grantmaker type: Public charity.
Financial data (yr. ended 12/31/09): Revenue,
$71,416; assets, $140,290 (M); gifts received,
$69,704; expenditures, $85,436; total giving,
$73,084; giving activities include $73,084 for
grants.
Purpose and activities: The foundation awards
individual scholarships and makes charitable
contributions to organizations.
Fields of interest: Community/economic
development.
Type of support: Scholarships—to individuals.
Officers: Gregory Flick, Pres.; R. Tony Asselta, V.P.;
Roger Chapman, Secy.; Betty Morlock, Treas.
EIN: 383563288

1393
Rotary District 6360 Foundation
316 Beech St.
Charlotte, MI 48813-1006 (517) 543-7929
County: Eaton
FAX: (517) 543-3041;
E-mail: district6360@cablespeed.com; URL: http://
www.district6360.com/district_foundation/
index.htm

Established in 1992 in MI.
Grantmaker type: Public charity.
Financial data (yr. ended 06/30/09): Revenue,
$67,036; assets, $201,850 (M); gifts received,
$46,896; expenditures, $18,553; total giving,
$14,041; giving activities include $14,041 for
grants.
Purpose and activities: The foundation supports
local area literacy programs and other community
service projects, and provides aid for educational
and capital improvements in Nicaragua and Mexico.
Fields of interest: Adult education—literacy, basic
skills & GED; Education.
International interests: Mexico; Nicaragua.
Type of support: Capital campaigns; Equipment;
Program development; Seed money; Matching/
challenge support.
Limitations: Applications accepted. Giving on a
national and international basis. No grants to
District 6360 Rotarians, a Rotary employee or a
parent, grandparent, child, grandchild of a Rotarian,
or their spouses, or for individual travel expenses,
salaries, personnel costs, research consultant fees,
operating administrative expenses, or pre-project
planning costs.
Publications: Annual report (including application
guidelines); Informational brochure; Program policy
statement.
Application information: Application form required.
  Initial approach: Download application form
  Copies of proposal: 1
  Deadline(s): None

Board meeting date(s): Apr. 25, June 10, Aug. 10, Oct. 24, and Dec. 12

Final notification: Within 30 to 60 days

Officers and Board Members: Terrence J. Allen,* Pres.; Teresa Fitzwater,* Pres.-Elect; Marjorie R. Haas,* Secy.; Nancy L. Thompson Commissaris,* Treas.; Thomas A. Faulkner; James H. Hines; James W. McIntyre; James E. Miyagawa; Carl A. Schoessel; Donald G. Siegel.

Number of staff: 1 part-time support.

EIN: 383002325

1394
Saint Mary's Doran Foundation

c/o St. Mary's Health Care
200 Jefferson St. S.E.
Grand Rapids, MI 49503-4502 (616) 752-6762
County: Kent
Contact: Michelle Rabideau, Exec. Dir.
E-mail: rabideaa@trinity-health.org; URL: http://www.smmmc.org/foundation/

Grantmaker type: Public charity.

Financial data (yr. ended 06/30/09): Revenue, $2,526,055; assets, $13,332,898 (M); gifts received, $2,961,528; expenditures, $6,655,263; total giving, $5,989,273; giving activities include $5,987,273 for grants, and $2,000 for grants to individuals.

Purpose and activities: The organization receives and administers funds in order to promote and support the health care mission and philosophy of Saint Mary's Health Care.

Fields of interest: Health care.

Limitations: Giving primarily in MI.

Publications: Annual report.

Officers and Directors:* William J. Passinault, M.D.*, Chair.; David D. Baumgartner, M.D.*, Vice-Chair.; Lawrence P. Burns,* Secy.; Lisa Wurst,* Treas.; Michelle Rabideau, Exec. Dir.; Micki Benz; Harold E. Bowman, M.D.; Ellamae Braun; Robert D. Burton, M.D.; Steven A. Crane, M.D.; and 21 additional directors.

EIN: 381779602

1395
Shaevsky Family Foundation

(formerly Shaevsky Family Support Foundation)
6735 Telegraph Rd.
P.O. Box 2030
Bloomfield Hills, MI 48301-3141
County: Oakland

Established in 1998 in MI; a supporting organization of Jewish Federation of Metropolitan Detroit.

Grantmaker type: Public charity.

Financial data (yr. ended 05/31/10): Revenue, $103,154; assets, $770,292 (M); expenditures, $100,314; total giving, $82,400; giving activities include $82,400 for grants.

Purpose and activities: The foundation supports Jewish federated programs, with giving also for the arts and human services.

Fields of interest: Performing arts; Historic preservation/historical societies; Arts; Animals/wildlife; Human services; Children, services; Jewish federated giving programs; Jewish agencies & synagogues.

Type of support: General/operating support; Annual campaigns.

Limitations: Giving on a national basis.

Officers: Lois L. Shaevsky, Pres.; Robert P. Aronson, V.P.; Jonathan Lowe, Secy.; Dorothy Benyas, Treas.

Directors: Penny Blumenstein; Mark Hauser; Lawrence Jackier; Lawrence K. Shaevsky; Mark Shaevsky; Thomas L. Shaevsky.

EIN: 383423716

1396
Joel H. and Loraine Shapiro Family Foundation

6735 Telegraph Rd.
P.O. Box 2030
Bloomfield Hills, MI 48301-3141
County: Oakland
Contact: Loraine Shapiro, Pres.

Established in 1989; supporting organization of the Jewish Federation of Metropolitan Detroit.

Grantmaker type: Public charity.

Financial data (yr. ended 05/31/10): Revenue, $57,032; assets, $409,128 (M); expenditures, $72,907; total giving, $54,993; giving activities include $54,993 for grants.

Fields of interest: Jewish federated giving programs.

Limitations: Giving primarily in MI.

Officers and Directors:* Loraine Shapiro,* Pres.; Aaron L. Shapiro,* V.P.; Bonnie L. Shapiro,* V.P.; Phyllis A. Shapiro Siegal,* V.P.; Robert P. Aronson,* Secy.; Dorothy Benyas,* Treas.; Penny Blumenstein; Mark R. Hauser; Michael W. Maddin; Joel Shapiro.

EIN: 382870707

1397
Shiawassee United Way

1302 W. Main St.
P.O. Box 664
Owosso, MI 48867-2042 (989) 723-4987
County: Shiawassee
Contact: Sheila Shegos, Exec. Dir.
FAX: (989) 723-7512;
E-mail: info@shiawasseeunitedway.org;
URL: http://www.shiawasseeunitedway.org/

Established in MI.

Grantmaker type: Public charity.

Financial data (yr. ended 12/31/09): Revenue, $227,436; assets, $254,772 (M); gifts received, $206,074; expenditures, $207,340; total giving, $43,591; giving activities include $41,789 for grants, and $1,802 for grants to individuals.

Purpose and activities: The organization seeks to unite people and other resources to improve and strengthen the quality of life for all people in Shiawassee County.

Fields of interest: Community/economic development.

Limitations: Giving primarily in Owosso, MI.

Application information:

Initial approach: Download application

Board meeting date(s): 4th Tues. of every month

Officers and Directors:* David Hood,* Pres.; Ed Brush,* Secy.; Retta Parsons, Exec. Dir.; Tom Bridges; Laurie Cook; Deana Doan; Mark Erickson; Joane Ford; Michelle Schwab; Cathy Stevenson; Joy Welty; Ron Zimmerman.

Number of staff: 1 full-time professional; 2 part-time professional; 1 full-time support; 2 part-time support.

EIN: 386006199

1398
The Shop Rat Foundation, Inc.

11855 Bunkerhill Rd.
Pleasant Lake, MI 49272-9798 (517) 769-2100
County: Jackson
FAX: (517) 769-6902; E-mail: shoprat@gmail.com;
URL: http://www.shoprat.org/foundation.php

Established in 2004 in MI.

Grantmaker type: Public charity.

Financial data (yr. ended 12/31/09): Revenue, $106,081; assets, $61,164 (M); gifts received, $87,693; expenditures, $150,345.

Purpose and activities: The foundation's mission is to advance the skilled trades industries by opening the minds of our youth through building innovative and unique projects from concept to completion.

Fields of interest: Vocational education; Neighborhood centers.

Officers: Stan Dzierwa, Chair. and Treas.; Christopher Salow, Pres.; Amanda Proctor, Secy.

EIN: 383700259

1399
Shopko Foundation, Inc.

P.O. Box 19060
Green Bay, WI 54307-9060
County: Brown
E-mail: GreenBayAreaCommunityGrants@Shopko.com; URL: http://www.shopko.com/company/community-giving-shopko-foundation

Established in 2005 in WI.

Grantmaker type: Public charity.

Financial data (yr. ended 12/31/09): Revenue, $799,695; assets, $9,291,982 (M); gifts received, $792,650; expenditures, $785,884; total giving, $677,066; giving activities include $627,066 for grants, and $50,000 for grants to individuals.

Fields of interest: Education; Athletics/sports, Special Olympics; Youth development; Human services.

Limitations: Applications accepted. Giving limited to CA, IA, ID, IL, MI, MN, MT, NE, OR, SD, UT, WA, and WI.

Application information:

Initial approach: Letter on organization's letterhead

Deadline(s): Quarterly

Officers: Michael MacDonald, Pres.; Michael J. Bettiga, V.P.; Sara Stensrud, Secy.; Mary Meixelsperger, Treas.

EIN: 200917227

Selected grants: The following grants were reported in 2007.

$30,000 to March of Dimes Foundation, White Plains, NY.

$15,000 to Chamber of Commerce Foundation, Green Bay Area, Green Bay, WI.

$12,000 to Bellin Foundation, Green Bay, WI.

$10,000 to New North, Inc., De Pere, WI.

$5,000 to Boys and Girls Club of Green Bay, Green Bay, WI.

$2,500 to University of Wisconsin, Eau Claire, WI.

$2,500 to University of Wisconsin, Eau Claire, WI.

$2,500 to University of Wisconsin-Fox Valley, Menasha, WI.

$2,000 to Make-A-Wish Foundation of Idaho, Boise, ID.

$1,000 to Multiple Sclerosis Society, National, Wisconsin Chapter, Hartland, WI.

1400
Social Venture Investors
(formerly Social Venture Philanthropy)
c/o Grand Rapids Community Foundation
161 Ottawa Ave. N.W., Ste. 209C
Grand Rapids, MI 49503-2721
County: Kent
Contact: Gina Bovee, Dir., Devel.
E-mail for Gina Bovee: gbovee@grfoundation.org;
URL: http://www.grfoundation.org/svi.php

Established in 2001 in MI; component fund of Grand Rapids Community Foundation.
Grantmaker type: Public charity.
Financial data (yr. ended 06/30/08): Total giving, $98,400 Giving activities include $98,400 for 3 grants (high: $32,800; low: $32,800).
Purpose and activities: The giving circle invests in innovative programs to improve the quality of life in Grand Rapids and address the needs of children and youth, education, community/economic development, health, and human services.
Fields of interest: Education; Health care; Children/youth, services; Human services; Economic development; Community/economic development.
Type of support: Seed money; Program development.
Limitations: Applications accepted. Giving limited to Kent County, MI. No grants for capital improvements or solely for purchase of equipment.
Application information: Application form required.
Initial approach: Online application
Deadline(s): Jan.
Final notification: May

1401
Society for Research in Child Development, Inc.
(also known as SRCD)
2950 S. State St., Ste. 401
Ann Arbor, MI 48104-6773 (734) 926-0600
County: Washtenaw
FAX: (734) 926-0601; E-mail: info@srcd.org;
URL: http://www.srcd.org

Established in 1933.
Grantmaker type: Public charity.
Financial data (yr. ended 06/30/09): Revenue, $4,081,601; assets, $7,780,011 (M); gifts received, $1,269,078; expenditures, $4,263,229; total giving, $103,163; giving activities include $103,163 for grants to individuals.
Purpose and activities: The society promotes multidisciplinary research in the field of human development, fosters the exchange of information among scientists and other professionals of various disciplines, and encourages applications of research findings.
Fields of interest: Education, research; Child development, education; Child development, services.
Type of support: Fellowships.
Limitations: Applications accepted. Giving on a national and international basis.
Publications: Application guidelines.
Application information: Application form required.
Initial approach: Download application
Deadline(s): Dec. 1 for SECC Dissertation Funding Research Awards; Dec. 15 for Fellowships
Officers and Council Members:* Greg Duncan,* Pres.; Ann Masten,* Pres.-Elect; Nancy Hill,* Secy.; Lonnie Sherrod, Ph.D., Exec. Dir.; Oscar Barbarin;

Patricia Bauer; Marc Bornstein; Nancy E. Hill; Jennie K. Grammer; Melanie Killen; Richard M. Lerner; Kenneth H. Rubin; Elizabeth Susman; Thomas S. Weisner.
EIN: 356005842

1402
Society of Manufacturing Engineers Education Foundation
(also known as SME Education Foundation)
1 SME Dr.
P.O. Box 930
Dearborn, MI 48121-0930 (313) 425-3300
County: Wayne
Contact: Bart A. Aslin, Dir.
FAX: (313) 425-3411; E-mail: foundation@sme.org;
E-mail for Bart A. Aslin: baslin@sme.org;
URL: http://www.smeef.org

Established in 1979 in MI.
Donors: E. Wayne Kay; Ford Motor Company Fund; Caterpillar Foundation; Toyota Motor Corp.; Albert F. Wright; General Motors Foundation; Earl E. Walker; Emerson Charitable Trust; Allen Weber; Bush Foundation.
Grantmaker type: Public charity.
Financial data (yr. ended 12/31/08): Revenue, $2,680,073; assets, $16,448,668 (M); gifts received, $1,522,193; expenditures, $4,100,374; total giving, $2,631,363; program services expenses, $3,245,815; giving activities include $2,631,363 for grants to individuals.
Purpose and activities: As an arm of the Society of Manufacturing Engineers (SME), the foundation's mission is to prepare the next generation of manufacturing engineers and technologists through outreach programs to enrich students to study Science, Technology, Engineering, and Mathematics (STEM) as well as Computer Integrated Manufacturing (CIM) education. Providing scholarships to these students ensure that we enrich the pipeline of students pursuing manufacturing engineering and engineering technology degrees.
Fields of interest: Elementary/secondary education; Engineering school/education; Scholarships/financial aid; Engineering/technology; Youth.
Type of support: Annual campaigns; Capital campaigns; Equipment; Program development; Seed money; Curriculum development; Fellowships; Scholarship funds; Research; Scholarships—to individuals.
Limitations: Applications accepted. Giving limited to the U.S. and Canada.
Publications: Application guidelines; Annual report; Grants list; Program policy statement.
Application information: Application form required.
Initial approach: Download application and nomination forms
Deadline(s): Feb.1 for SME Education Foundation Family Scholarships; Dec. 5 for M. Eugene Merchant Manufacturing Textbook Award and Sargeant Americanism Award; Feb. 1 for all others
Board meeting date(s): Apr. and Sept.
Final notification: May
Officers and Directors:* Glen H. Pearson,* Pres.; Sandra L. Bouckley,* V.P.; Angela Nardozzi,* Sr. Secy.; Winston F. Erevelles, Ph.D.*, Secy.; Peter F. Mackie,* Treas.; Patty Antoun; Douglas E. Booth, FSME; Cece Brueckman; Charles M. Chambers, Ph.D., J.D.; Marcus B. Crotts; Gregg O. Ekberg;

Steve Megli; Connie J. Robinson; Pamela J. Ruschau; Cecil W. Schneider; William R. Segar; Khalil S. Taraman, Ph.D.; Kenneth Vedra, Ph.D.; Albert Wavering; Sherril West; Robert T. Williams.
Number of staff: 3 full-time professional; 1 part-time professional.
EIN: 382746841

1403
Sojourner Foundation
25940 Grand River Ave.
Detroit, MI 48240-1485 (313) 534-4263
County: Wayne
Contact: Helen Hicks, Pres.
E-mail: sojournerfound@sbcglobal.net; URL: http://sojournerfoundation.org

Established in 1985 in MI.
Grantmaker type: Public charity.
Financial data (yr. ended 12/31/08): Revenue, $11,150; assets, $12,171 (M); gifts received, $6,963; expenditures, $20,157; total giving, $13,625; program services expenses, $17,663; giving activities include $13,625 for grants to individuals, and $4,038 for foundation-administered programs.
Purpose and activities: The foundation provides funds to worthwhile organizations serving women and girls that encounter difficulty in raising adequate support from traditional sources. Grants are awarded to organizations which seek to eliminate the barriers preventing women and girls from exercising their full human rights.
Fields of interest: Health care, infants; Reproductive health; Crime/violence prevention, domestic violence; Crime/violence prevention, child abuse; Youth, pregnancy prevention; Civil/human rights, women; Women; Girls.
Type of support: Continuing support; Annual campaigns; Program development; Conferences/seminars; Technical assistance; In-kind gifts.
Limitations: Applications accepted. Giving limited to Wayne, Oakland, Livingston, Washtenaw, St. Clair, Monroe, and Macomb counties, MI. No support for programs and services that do not serve population groups made up of a majority of women and girls.
Publications: Application guidelines; Grants list; Informational brochure; Newsletter.
Application information: Application form required.
Initial approach: Download application form
Copies of proposal: 5
Deadline(s): Dec. 14
Board meeting date(s): 3rd Wed. of each month
Final notification: Mar. 15
Officers and Trustees:* Helen Hicks,* Pres.; Jennifer Roberts, V.P.; LaNaita Thomas, Secy.; Susan Titus, Treas.; Kate Davis; Rosalyn Hall; Dori Hawkins; Onnie Barnes Jacque; Brenda Scoggins; Deborah Williams.
Number of staff: 1 part-time professional; 1 part-time support.
EIN: 382477123

1404
Southeast Michigan Community Alliance
25363 Eureka Rd.
Taylor, MI 48180-5051
County: Wayne
FAX: (734) 229-3501; E-mail: info@semca.org;
Toll-free tel.: (800) 285-WORKS; TTY: (800) 649-3501; URL: http://www.semca.org

Grantmaker type: Public charity.
Financial data (yr. ended 09/30/09): Revenue, $56,193,321; assets, $7,250,955 (M); gifts received, $56,183,807; expenditures, $55,191,335.
Purpose and activities: The alliance provides employment training and substance abuse services to youths.
Fields of interest: Substance abuse, services; Employment, services.
Limitations: Giving limited to Monroe and Wayne counties, MI.
Officers: John B. O'Reilly, C.E.O.; Chris Smith, C.O.O.; Beth Herzog, C.F.O.
Board Members: Pam Alexander; Rochelle Allen; Alan Anderson; Ned Fawaz; Bobbie Gelman; Tamara Harmon; Gerald Hesson; Randy Hicks; Michael Hoydie; Wayne Meehean; and 30 additional board members.
EIN: 382675191

1405
Southfield Kappa Foundation
P.O. Box 446
Southfield, MI   48037-0446
County: Oakland
E-mail: info@southfieldkappafoundation.org;
URL: http://www.southfieldkapsi.org/index.php

Established in 1993 in MI.
Donor: Members of the Southfield Alumni Chapter of Kappa Alpha Psi Frate.
Grantmaker type: Public charity.
Financial data (yr. ended 12/31/07): Revenue, $37,164; assets, $81,880 (M); gifts received, $29,501; total giving, $16,250; program services expenses, $1,724; giving activities include $16,250 for 21 grants to individuals (high: $1,000; low: $1,000).
Purpose and activities: The foundation provides financial assistance to deserving minority students in the Detroit metropolitan area.
Fields of interest: Scholarships/financial aid; African Americans/Blacks.
Type of support: Scholarships—to individuals.
Limitations: Applications accepted. Giving limited to the Detroit metropolitan area, particularly in Wayne and Oakland counties, MI.
Publications: Application guidelines.
Application information: Application form available after Oct. 1. Application form required.
  Initial approach: Download application form
  Deadline(s): Mar. 17
  Final notification: May 5
Officers and Directors:* Niko Dawson,* Chair.; Darrell Buchanan,* Vice-Chair.; Ralph Jefferson, Pres.; Carlton Powell, Secy.; Douglas Sanders, Treas.; Eddie Hoskins; Brian Jefferson; Ervin Johnson; Chad Taylor; Gregory Whiting; Tony Zerinque.
EIN: 383050851

1406
Southwest Michigan Community Action Agency
185 E. Main St., Ste. 200
Benton Harbor, MI   49022-4432
(269) 925-9077
County: Berrien
FAX: (269) 925-9271; E-mail: contact@smcaa.com;
URL: http://www.smcaa.com

Established in 1986 in MI.
Grantmaker type: Public charity.
Financial data (yr. ended 09/30/09): Revenue, $4,714,080; assets, $1,436,413 (M); gifts received, $4,703,577; expenditures, $4,665,697.
Purpose and activities: The purpose of the agency is to assist people in economic need and enable them to achieve and sustain self-sufficiency while respecting their diversity.
Fields of interest: Food services; Housing/shelter, services; Human services; Financial services.
Limitations: Applications accepted. Giving limited to Berrien, Cass, and Van Buren counties, MI.
Publications: Financial statement; Informational brochure.
Directors: Richard Accoe; Katherine Edwards; Margaret Edwards; Carol Elam; Michael Franks; Lee Gill; Adrienne Glover; Donald Hanson; and 9 additional directors.
EIN: 382415106

1407
Southwestern Michigan Urban League
172 W. Van Buren
Battle Creek, MI   49017-3005
County: Calhoun

Grantmaker type: Public charity.
Financial data (yr. ended 12/31/09): Revenue, $48,025; assets, $338,975 (M); gifts received, $20,555; expenditures, $221,794.
Purpose and activities: The league promotes the advancement of minorities in the southwestern Michigan community.
Fields of interest: Urban League; Human services; Community/economic development; Minorities.
Type of support: In-kind gifts.
Limitations: Giving limited to Battle Creek, MI.
Officers: Erick Stewart, Chair.; Joyce R. Wilson, Secy.; Lynne Haley, Treas.; Carl Word, Exec. Dir.
Board Members: Charles Coleman; Brenda Hunt; Mark Schauer; Joe Stewart.
EIN: 381817220

1408
Spaulding for Children
16250 Northland Dr., Ste. 100
Southfield, MI   48075-5226   (248) 443-7080
County: Oakland
FAX: (248) 443-7099; URL: http://www.spaulding.org

Established in 1968 in MI.
Grantmaker type: Public charity.
Financial data (yr. ended 09/30/09): Revenue, $9,459,890; assets, $3,982,516 (M); gifts received, $5,847,490; expenditures, $9,242,503; total giving, $2,381,487; giving activities include $2,305,426 for grants, and $76,061 for grants to individuals.
Purpose and activities: The organization finds permanent homes for children that have been in the foster care and adoption system the longest, and trains adoptive families for the placement of special needs children.
Fields of interest: Children, adoption.
Type of support: Scholarships—to individuals; In-kind gifts.
Officers: Addie Williams, Pres. and C.E.O.; Kay E. Brown, V.P., Finance & Business; Kris Henneman,

V.P., Spaulding Institute; Natalie Lyons, V.P., NRC; Charles Stults, V.P., Child and Family Svcs.
Directors: Jamie Bozarth; Chris Doyle; Denise Figurski; Jean Niemann.
EIN: 381871660

1409
Spectrum Human Services, Inc.
28303 Joy Rd.
Westland, MI   48185-5524   (734) 458-8736
County: Wayne
FAX: (734) 458-8836;
E-mail: info@spectrumhuman.org; URL: http://www.spectrumhuman.org

Established in 1975 in MI.
Grantmaker type: Public charity.
Financial data (yr. ended 12/31/08): Revenue, $2,879,460; assets, $5,529,514 (M); gifts received, $59,717; expenditures, $3,365,570; program services expenses, $2,429,119.
Purpose and activities: The organization supports foster care and adoption services for youth and infants with various needs, independent living and youth in transition programs for disadvantaged youth, residential group homes, and emergency shelter for abused, neglected, and disadvantaged girls.
Fields of interest: Housing/shelter, temporary shelter; Housing/shelter; Human services; Children/youth, services; Children, adoption; Children, foster care; Girls.
Publications: Annual report; Newsletter.
Officers: Arnold A. Budin, Chair.; Gary Bruhn,* Vice-Chair.; Roger I. Swaninger, ACSW, Pres. and C.E.O.; Kari A. Klinski, V.P.; Pamela E. Sawhney, Secy.; Jeffrey S. Sherbow, Treas.; Lawrence G. Poupard, C.F.O.
Directors: Mark R. Bartlett; Christine A. Derderian; Ellen Downey; Edward Foxworth III; Joe Gagnon; Marv Haupt; Samir W. Mashni.
EIN: 510154248

1410
The Sphinx Organization
(formerly Concert Competitions & Musical Development, Inc.)
400 Renaissance Ctr., Ste. 2550
Detroit, MI   48243-1679   (313) 877-9100
County: Wayne
Contact: Aaron P. Dworkin, Pres.
FAX: (313) 877-0164;
E-mail: info@sphinxmusic.org; Additional address (New York office): 2214 Frederick Douglass Blvd., Ste. 190, New York, NY 10026-1123, tel.: (646) 429-1987, fax: (646) 429-1988; URL: http://www.sphinxmusic.org

Established in 1996 in MI.
Grantmaker type: Public charity.
Financial data (yr. ended 12/31/09): Revenue, $1,922,694; assets, $2,277,762 (M); gifts received, $1,544,439; expenditures, $2,820,524; total giving, $62,300; program services expenses, $2,292,790; giving activities include $62,300 for grants to individuals, and $2,230,490 for foundation-administered programs.
Purpose and activities: The foundation develops and encourages classical musical talent in the Black and Latino communities, and among all youth.

Fields of interest: Performing arts, orchestras; African Americans/Blacks; Hispanics/Latinos.
Type of support: Scholarships—to individuals.
Limitations: Applications accepted. Giving on a national basis.
Publications: Application guidelines.
Application information: Each applicant must submit with their application a preliminary audition tape or CD which includes all of the required preliminaries repertoire for their instrument category. A $35 application fee must also be enclosed. Application form required.
  Initial approach: Download application
  Deadline(s): Nov. 15
  Board meeting date(s): Quarterly
  Final notification: Dec. 15
Officers and Directors:* Diedre Bounds,* Chair.; Howard Hertz,* Vice-Chair.; Aaron P. Dworkin, Pres.; Hon. Kurtis T. Wilder, Secy.; Anthony Glover,* Treas.; Ruben Acosta; Martha Dailing; Sally Stegeman DiCarlo; Ken Fischer; Jenice Mitchell Ford; Carl Herstein; Al McDonough; Daedia Von McGhee; David Rudolph; Juan Ramirez; Anne L. Taylor, M.D.; Kathy Weaver; Beverly Willis.
EIN: 383283759

1411
St. Joseph County United Way
132 W. Main St.
P.O. Box 577
Centreville, MI 49032-0577   (269) 467-9099
County: St. Joseph
FAX: (269) 467-7119; E-mail: info@sjcuf.com;
URL: http://www.sjcuf.com

Established in 1999 in MI as a result of the merger of The Sturgis United Way and The Western St. Joseph County Community Chest.
Grantmaker type: Public charity.
Financial data (yr. ended 12/31/09): Revenue, $410,454; assets, $601,980 (M); gifts received, $382,297; expenditures, $553,744; total giving, $337,064; giving activities include $337,064 for grants.
Purpose and activities: The organization seeks to promote the social welfare of St. Joseph County, Michigan.
Fields of interest: Family services; Human services.
Limitations: Giving primarily in St. Joseph County, MI.
Officers and Directors: Kathie Stratman,* Pres.; Pattie Bender,* 1st V.P.; Bob Brothers,* 2nd V.P.; Rick Strawser, Treas.; Kelly Hostetler, Exec. Dir.; Monte Anderson; Rick Anderson; Andy Boyd; Diana DeGraaf; Kathleen Earl; Doug Flint; David Franks; Chuck Frisbie; Marcus Gleaton; Steve Hart; and 11 additional directors.
EIN: 386095409

1412
St. Joseph/Benton Harbor Rotary Foundation, Inc.
P.O. Box 335
St. Joseph, MI 49085-0335
County: Berrien

Established in 1980 in MI.
Grantmaker type: Public charity.
Financial data (yr. ended 06/30/09): Revenue, $201,955; assets, $910,282 (M); gifts received, $180,078; expenditures, $33,466; total giving,

$26,500; giving activities include $26,500 for grants.
Purpose and activities: The mission of the foundation is to improve the quality of life, primarily in the greater St. Joseph/Benton Harbor community, through human development projects that focus on promoting the health, education and self-development of people in the community, and community development projects that focus on activities that improve and enhance physical aspects of the community.
Fields of interest: Education; Health care; Human services; Community/economic development.
Limitations: Giving primarily in the greater St. Joseph and Benton Harbor, MI, area.
Officers and Trustees:* Kurt Marzke,* Chair.; Charlotte Wenham,* Vice-Chair.; Steve Banyon, Exec. Dir.; Randy Bettich; Charles Jespersen; Nanette Kaiser; Jim Marohn; Christine Vanlandingham; Chuck Wells.
EIN: 382336366

1413
St. Mary's of Michigan Foundation
(formerly St. Mary's Hospital Foundation)
800 S. Washington Ave.
Saginaw, MI 48601-2551   (987) 907-8300
County: Saginaw
E-mail: foundation@stmarysofmichigan.org;
URL: http://www.stmarysofmichigan.org/foundation/index.php

Established in 1978 in MI; supporting organization of St. Mary's Medical Center of Saginaw Inc.
Grantmaker type: Public charity.
Financial data (yr. ended 06/30/09): Revenue, $657,255; assets, $10,453,590 (M); gifts received, $1,178,016; expenditures, $660,618; total giving, $64,137; program services expenses, $64,137; giving activities include $48,137 for 1 grant, and $16,000 for 7 grants to individuals.
Fields of interest: Health care, clinics/centers.
Type of support: Scholarships—to individuals.
Limitations: Applications accepted. Giving limited to Saginaw, MI.
Publications: Application guidelines.
Application information: Application form required.
  Initial approach: Download application online
  Deadline(s): May 18
  Final notification: Fall
Officers and Directors:* Suhasini Gudipati, M.D.*, Chair.; John Kunitzer, M.D.*, Vice-Chair.; John Graham,* Pres. and C.E.O.; Andy Richards,* Secy.; Sherry Desrosiers, Exec. Dir.; Gary Campbell; Brian Eggers; Gary Glaza; Sarge Harvey; Chip Hendrick; Charles Jessup, D.O.; Molly Ninan; David Shooltz; Kizhakepat Sukumaran, M.D.
EIN: 382246366

1414
Susan G. Komen for the Cure of Mid-Michigan
P.O. Box 4368
East Lansing, MI 48826-4368   (517) 886-4901
County: Ingham
FAX: (517) 347-7595;
E-mail: info@komenmidmichigan.org; URL: http://www.komenmidmichigan.org

Established in MI.
Grantmaker type: Public charity.

Purpose and activities: The organization is dedicated to combating breast cancer on every front.
Fields of interest: Health organizations, public education; Breast cancer; Breast cancer research.
Limitations: Giving limited to Clinton, Eaton, Ingham, Jackson, Livingston, Shiawassee, and Washtenaw counties, MI.
Publications: Application guidelines.
Application information: Contact organization for more information about applying for Small Grants, including application guidelines and deadlines.
  Initial approach: Submit application
  Deadline(s): June 14 for Grants
  Final notification: Sept. 1 for Grants
Officers and Board Members:* Dione Pena,* Pres.; Karen Holcomb-Merrill,* Secy.; Sue Schanski,* Treas.; Barbara J. Fulton, Ph.D.; Kay Randolph-Black; Kristen St. Marie; Steve Widder; Barbara Wirtz.

1415
Tahquamenon Education Foundation
P.O. Box 482
Newberry, MI 49868-0482   (906) 293-3045
County: Luce
FAX: (906) 293-3410; E-mail: teflil@lighthouse.net;
URL: http://tahquamenoned.org

Established in 1987 in MI.
Grantmaker type: Public charity.
Financial data (yr. ended 06/30/10): Revenue, $42,605; assets, $461,652 (M); gifts received, $36,557; expenditures, $65,137; total giving, $31,500; giving activities include $31,500 for grants to individuals.
Purpose and activities: The foundation provides support to the Tahquamenon Area School District through scholarships, special grants, and teacher mini-grants.
Fields of interest: Elementary/secondary education.
Type of support: Equipment; Program development; Scholarships—to individuals.
Limitations: Giving limited to the Tahquamenon Area School District, including Newberry, Hulbert, Seney, Curtis, Germfask, McMillan, Lakefield, and Deer Park, MI.
Publications: Newsletter.
Officers and Trustees:* Steven Derusha, Pres.; Michael Slaght,* V.P.; Kelly Hetrick, Secy.-Treas.; Christopher Beaulieu; Chad Peltier; Scott Pillion; Donald Stephenson.
EIN: 382744932

1416
Tawas-Whittemore-Hale Area United Fund
P.O. Box 28
East Tawas, MI 48730-0028
County: Iosco

Grantmaker type: Public charity.
Financial data (yr. ended 03/31/07): Revenue, $17,051; assets, $14,612 (M); gifts received, $16,981; expenditures, $19,574; total giving, $18,296; program services expenses, $18,296; giving activities include $18,296 for grants (high: $1,550; low: $522).
Purpose and activities: The fund collects contributions from various individuals and businesses that are subsequently disbursed to local charitable organizations based on need.

Fields of interest: Education; Health care; Youth development; Human services; Family services.
Limitations: Giving in Iosco County, MI, primarily in the Tawas, Whittemore, and Hale areas.
Officers: John Lorenz, Chair.; Peter Stoll, Vice-Chair.; Julie Westcott, Secy.; Blinda Baker, Treas.
EIN: 237149665

1417
Thornapple Kellogg Education Foundation
P.O. Box 164
MIddleville, MI 49333-0164
County: Barry

Established in 2002 in MI.
Grantmaker type: Public charity.
Financial data (yr. ended 06/30/07): Revenue, $61,443; assets, $264,501 (M); gifts received, $28,517; expenditures, $14,788; total giving, $9,850; program services expenses, $9,850; giving activities include $9,850 for grants to individuals.
Purpose and activities: Support primarily through student scholarships to promote education in Barry County, Michigan.
Fields of interest: Scholarships/financial aid; Education.
Type of support: Scholarship funds.
Limitations: Giving limited to Barry County, MI.
Officers and Directors:* Donald Williamson,* Pres.; Diane Weatherhead,* V.P.; Cheryl Peters,* Secy.; Charles Wolverton,* Treas.; Bob Bender; Joanne Dipp; Barb Dykstra; Bob Evans; Marilyn Finkbeiner; Robert WIliams.
EIN: 383051928

1418
Thresholds, Inc.
1225 Lake Dr. S.E.
Grand Rapids, MI 49506-1656 (616) 774-0853
County: Kent

Grantmaker type: Public charity.
Financial data (yr. ended 09/30/09): Revenue, $11,590,793; assets, $3,865,401 (M); gifts received, $198,234; expenditures, $11,504,733; total giving, $2,983,514; giving activities include $2,983,514 for grants to individuals.
Purpose and activities: The organization works to enable children and adults who have developmental disabilities, to live as productively and independently as possible in their community. The foundation also provides direct cash assistance to indigents.
Fields of interest: Supported living; Developmentally disabled, centers & services; Mentally disabled.
Type of support: Grants to individuals.
Limitations: Giving limited to the Grand Rapids, MI, area.
Officers and Directors:* William Vert,* Chair.; Chris Brown,* Vice-Chair.; David Macdonald,* Secy.; Al Emmons,* Treas.; Thomas Ferch, Exec. Dir.; Richard Becker; Ray Black; Carole Hoffman; Nancee Phelan; Vicki Pickel.
EIN: 382063018

1419
Tony Semple Foundation for Hope
16980 Wood Rd.
Lansing, MI 48906-1044 (517) 372-8300
County: Ingham
FAX: (517) 372-8301;
E-mail: info@tonysemplefoundation.org;
URL: http://www.tonysemplefoundation.org

Grantmaker type: Public charity.
Financial data (yr. ended 12/31/09): Revenue, $168,192; assets, $538,907 (M); gifts received, $155,221; expenditures, $113,321; program services expenses, $95,549.
Purpose and activities: The foundation works to facilitate inspiring, meaningful outdoor experiences for youth who suffer life-challenging medical conditions, and to value, promote, and continue to preserve the heritage of the 'outdoor sportsman'.
Fields of interest: Athletics/sports, fishing/hunting; Children/youth; Terminal illness, people with.
Officers and Directors:* Tony Semple,* Pres.; Craig Mortz,* V.P.; Dawn Semple,* Secy.; Todd Granger,* Treas.; Jerry Granger; Mike Leonard; Mike Ruhlig.
EIN: 203209385

1420
Training & Treatment Innovations, Inc.
1450 S. Lapeer Rd.
Oxford, MI 48371-6108 (248) 969-9932
County: Oakland
Toll-free tel.: (800) 741-1682; URL: http://www.ttiinc.org/

Established in 1987.
Grantmaker type: Public charity.
Financial data (yr. ended 09/30/09): Revenue, $23,413,482; assets, $2,033,729 (M); expenditures, $23,175,610.
Purpose and activities: The organization works to provide quality mental health services to adults, adolescents, and children with psychiatric and/or developmental disabilities, as well as those individuals who have a co-occurring disorder.
Fields of interest: Developmentally disabled, centers & services; Mentally disabled.
Limitations: Giving primarily to MI.
Officers: Patrick Hull, Chair.; Connie Vaive, Vice-Chair.; Nadine M. Harvey, Secy.; Jacquline Kiss-Wilson, Exec. Dir.
Directors: Shirley Brown; Darlene Donaldson; Philip Nicholson; Geraldine Sharp; Thomas L. Werth.
EIN: 382740431

1421
Travelers Aid Society of Metropolitan Detroit
30th Fl. Cadillac Twr.
65 Cadillac Square
Detroit, MI 48226-1900 (313) 926-6740
County: Wayne
E-mail: info@travelersaiddetroit.org; URL: http://www.travelersaiddetroit.org

Grantmaker type: Public charity.
Financial data (yr. ended 06/30/09): Revenue, $3,718,915; assets, $484,238 (M); gifts received, $3,715,811; expenditures, $3,793,719; total giving, $1,917,149; giving activities include $1,917,149 for grants to individuals.

Purpose and activities: The society provides permanent housing and supportive services to socially-economically challenged individuals and/or disconnected families and travelers by returning them to point of origin, advancing the well-being of the community and empowering them to become self-sufficient contributing members of society.
Fields of interest: Housing/shelter; International migration/refugee issues; Economically disadvantaged.
Type of support: Grants to individuals.
Publications: Annual report.
Officers and Directors:* Eric Foster,* Pres.; Nathaniel Warshay,* V.P.; Alfred J. Gittleman,* Secy.; Wendy L. Smith,* Treas.; Harriet Cosby; Monica Davie; John L. Davis II; Lamar Richardson; and 7 additional directors.
EIN: 381358052

1422
Trinity Community Services & Educational Foundation
1050 Porter St.
Detroit, MI 48226-2405
County: Wayne
Contact: Fr. Russell Kohler, Pres.

Established in 1994; status changed to a public charity.
Grantmaker type: Public charity.
Financial data (yr. ended 12/31/09): Revenue, $333,450; assets, $2,271,424 (M); gifts received, $210,898; expenditures, $439,164.
Purpose and activities: The foundation provides scholarships, based on established criteria, to elementary, primary and secondary school students living in the Corktown District of Detroit; the foundation also subsidizes the operations of the Sister Frances Cabrini Health Clinic.
Fields of interest: Elementary/secondary education; Health care, clinics/centers; Catholic agencies & churches.
Type of support: Scholarship funds; Grants to individuals; Scholarships—to individuals.
Limitations: Applications accepted. Giving limited to Detroit, MI.
Officers: Brian Coyne, Chair.; Sr. Mary Ellen Howard, Vice-Chair.; Fr. Russell Kohler, Pres.; Kevin Coyne, Treas.
Directors: Vincent Brennan; Daniel Buckley; Paul Manion.
EIN: 383129349

1423
UAW-GM Center for Human Resources
200 Walker St.
Detroit, MI 48207-4229 (313) 324-5290
County: Wayne
URL: https://www.uawgmjas.org/j/

Established in 1985.
Grantmaker type: Public charity.
Financial data (yr. ended 12/31/09): Revenue, $63,003,769; assets, $136,140,784 (M); expenditures, $73,574,654; total giving, $16,732,259; giving activities include $16,732,259 for grants to individuals.
Purpose and activities: The center works to provide for the development, delivery, coordination, and administration of strategies and joint programs

designed to educate and train both active and dislocated auto workers.

Fields of interest: Scholarships/financial aid; Employment, services; Employment, training.
Type of support: Scholarships—to individuals.
Publications: Application guidelines.
Application information:
Initial approach: Submit application
Deadline(s): None
Officers: Timothy E. Lee, Co-Pres.; Calvin Rapson, Co-Pres.; Dorothy Hennessy, Secy.; Thomas P. Hill, C.F.O.; Paul Mitchell, Treas.
Board Members: Garry Bernath; Mike Grimes; Gary Mason; Joe Ponce; Diana Tremblay.
EIN: 383211550

1424
United Arts Council of Calhoun County
(doing business as Arts & Industry Council)
77 E. Michigan Ave., Ste. 190
P.O. Box 1079
Battle Creek, MI   49016-7030   (269) 441-2700
County: Calhoun
Contact: Charlie Robertson, Exec. Dir.
FAX: (269) 441-2707;
E-mail: robertson@artsandindustrycouncil.org;
URL: http://www.artsandindustrycouncil.org

Established in 1963.
Grantmaker type: Public charity.
Financial data (yr. ended 06/30/10): Revenue, $77,862; assets, $549,166 (M); gifts received, $73,720; expenditures, $93,543; total giving, $23,773; giving activities include $23,773 for grants.
Purpose and activities: The council provides marketing and technical services, professional development programs, and grants to arts and cultural organizations and artists, with the goal of improving the quality of life through the arts.
Fields of interest: Arts.
Type of support: Annual campaigns; Program development; Technical assistance; Consulting services; Grants to individuals.
Limitations: Applications accepted. Giving primarily in Calhoun County, MI.
Publications: Application guidelines; Annual report; Grants list; Informational brochure.
Application information: Application form required.
Initial approach: Download application form
Deadline(s): Jan. 9 and Apr. 3 for Creative Industries Development Grant; Feb. 1 and Aug. 1 for MCACA Minigrant; Mar. 6 and Oct. 3 for Arts Marketing & Programming Grant
Board meeting date(s): 1st Tues. of each month
Officers and Directors:* Carol Petredean-Di Salvio,* Chair.; George Guerin, Vice-Chair.; Linda Gillespie,* Secy.; Julyette Jacobs,* Treas.; Charlie Robertson, Exec. Dir.; Tonya Arnett; Bill Birch; Greg Dunn; Velma Laws-Clay; Chris McCoy; Peggy Sindt.
Number of staff: 2 full-time professional.
EIN: 386091848

1425
United Jewish Foundation
6735 Telegraph Rd.
Bloomfield Hills, MI   48301-3141
(248) 642-4260
County: Oakland
Contact: Howard Neistein

Supporting organization of the Jewish Federation of Metropolitan Detroit.
Grantmaker type: Public charity.
Financial data (yr. ended 05/31/10): Revenue, $33,363,266; assets, $331,046,094 (M); gifts received, $19,907,987; expenditures, $35,977,391; total giving, $29,401,589; giving activities include $29,401,589 for grants.
Fields of interest: Jewish federated giving programs; Jewish agencies & synagogues.
Limitations: Giving limited to the metropolitan Detroit, MI, area. No grants to individuals.
Publications: Annual report; Financial statement.
Officers and Directors:* Allan Nachman,* Pres.; Robert P. Aronson, C.E.O.; Dorothy Benyas, C.F.O.; Mark Davidoff, Exec. Dir.; Douglas Etkin; Phillip Fisher; Margot Halperin; Terran Leemis; Norman Pappas; and 81 additional directors.
EIN: 381360585

1426
United Nations Association, Kalamazoo Chapter
1125 Tanglewood Dr.
Portage, MI   49024-5047
County: Kalamazoo

Grantmaker type: Public charity.
Financial data (yr. ended 12/31/08): Revenue, $1,412; assets, $5,543 (M); gifts received, $450; expenditures, $1,425; total giving, $400; giving activities include $400 for grants.
Purpose and activities: The organization supports education by providing scholarships.
Fields of interest: Education.
Type of support: Scholarships—to individuals.
Limitations: Giving primarily in Kalamazoo, MI.
Officers: Thomas J. Vance, Pres.; Gordan Boardman, V.P.; Richard Knapp, Secy.-Treas.
EIN: 900058942

1427
United Way for Southeastern Michigan
1212 Griswold
Detroit, MI   48226-1848   (313) 226-9200
County: Wayne
URL: http://www.uwsem.org/

Established in 2005 in MI as a result of the consolidation of operations of United Way Community Services and United Way of Oakland County.
Grantmaker type: Public charity.
Financial data (yr. ended 06/30/09): Revenue, $49,443,691; assets, $64,867,513 (M); gifts received, $49,434,762; expenditures, $53,883,242; total giving, $34,784,055; giving activities include $34,368,269 for grants, and $415,786 for grants to individuals.
Purpose and activities: The mission of United Way for Southeastern Michigan is to mobilize the caring power of Detroit and southeastern Michigan to improve communities and individual lives in measurable and lasting ways.
Fields of interest: Community/economic development.
Limitations: Giving limited to Wayne, Oakland and Macomb counties, MI.
Officers and Directors:* Reginald Turner,* Chair.; Leslie Murphy,* Vice-Chair.; Michael J. Brennan, Pres. and C.E.O.; Rick David, V.P.; Jacqueline Jones,

V.P.; Deborah Macon,* Secy.; Michael S. Hanley,* Treas.; Anthony F. Earley, Jr.; and 24 additional directors.
EIN: 203099071

1428
United Way of Bay County
909 Washington Ave.
P.O. Box 602
Bay City, MI   48708-5722   (989) 893-7508
County: Bay
Contact: Jennifer L. Carroll, Exec. Dir.
FAX: (989) 893-0087;
E-mail: jennifer@unitedwaybaycounty.org;
URL: http://www.unitedwaybaycounty.org

Established in MI.
Grantmaker type: Public charity.
Financial data (yr. ended 12/31/09): Revenue, $1,231,272; assets, $2,508,622 (M); gifts received, $1,293,237; expenditures, $1,313,334; total giving, $706,580; giving activities include $706,580 for grants.
Purpose and activities: The organization's mission is to build the community's financial and human ability to effectively and efficiently meet its human care needs and to create increased awareness in the community.
Fields of interest: Boys & girls clubs; Big Brothers/ Big Sisters; Boy scouts; Girl scouts; American Red Cross; YM/YWCAs & YM/YWHAs; Children, services; Human services; Community/economic development; Women.
Limitations: Giving primarily in Bay County, MI.
Officers: Beth Cobert, Chair.; Tim Quinn, Pres.; Joseph Liefbroer, V.P.; Robert Rajewski, Secy.; William B. Kessel, Treas.; Jennifer L. Carroll, Exec. Dir.
Directors: Judy Adair; Ellen Albrecht; Mark Bauer; Bill Bowen; Mike Dewey; Amy Doornhaag; Stephen Fralick; Alice Gerard; Bob Hagen; Barbara Hayward; and 23 additional directors.
EIN: 381360524

1429
United Way of Clare County
P.O. Box 116
106 W. 7th St.
Clare, MI   48617-0116   (989) 386-6015
County: Clare
FAX: (989) 386-6548;
E-mail: info@unitedwayclare.org; URL: http:// www.unitedwayclare.org/

Established in 1993 in MI.
Grantmaker type: Public charity.
Financial data (yr. ended 06/30/10): Revenue, $232,647; assets, $235,700 (M); gifts received, $228,506; expenditures, $260,247; total giving, $159,491; giving activities include $159,491 for grants.
Purpose and activities: Through its network of member agencies, volunteers, and community leaders, the organization takes a leadership role in addressing health and human service issues that face Clare County.
Fields of interest: Health care; Human services; Community/economic development.
Limitations: Giving limited to Clare County, MI.
Officers and Directors:* Jeff Poet,* Pres.; Ray Stover,* V.P.; Dan Timmins,* Secy.-Treas.; Sandina

Hages, Exec. Dir.; John Allen, D.D.S.; Jeff Goyt; Tom Jared; Tom House; Karen Kleinhardt; Joseph Manifold; Jeanie Mishler; Dave Peterson; Don Richards; Al White.
EIN: 383013356

1430
United Way of Delta County
1100 Ludington St., Ste. 300
Escanaba, MI 49829-3500 (906) 786-3736
County: Delta
Contact: Julie Mallard, Exec. Dir.
FAX: (906) 786-7210; E-mail: united@dsnet.us;
URL: http://www.uwdelta.org/

Established in MI.
Grantmaker type: Public charity.
Financial data (yr. ended 12/31/09): Revenue, $252,801; assets, $319,320 (M); gifts received, $251,519; expenditures, $260,722; total giving, $155,401; giving activities include $155,401 for grants.
Purpose and activities: The organization seeks to improve its community's capacity to care for one another.
Fields of interest: Museums; Health care; Crime/violence prevention, abuse prevention; Athletics/sports, Special Olympics; Boy scouts; Girl scouts; Youth development; Human services; American Red Cross; Salvation Army.
Limitations: Giving limited to Delta County, MI, primarily in Escanaba and Marquette.
Publications: Financial statement; Informational brochure.
Officers and Board Members:* Jim Wayne,* Pres.; Don Howlett,* V.P.; Paddy Fitch, Secy.; Denise Boyle,* Treas.; Julie Mallard, Exec. Dir.; Mike Birholz; Rusty Bluse; Lisa Broman; Will Carne; Richard Crofton; and 10 additional board members.
EIN: 381740320

1431
United Way of Genesee County
P.O. Box 949
Flint, MI 48501-0949 (810) 232-8121
County: Genesee
Contact: Ron Butler, Exec. Dir.
FAX: (810) 232-9370;
E-mail: rbutler@unitedwaygenesee.org; URL: http://www.unitedwaygenesee.org/

Established in 1922 in MI.
Grantmaker type: Public charity.
Financial data (yr. ended 06/30/09): Revenue, $9,556,709; assets, $12,859,893 (M); gifts received, $9,379,704; expenditures, $8,363,307; total giving, $2,249,959; program services expenses, $7,344,768; giving activities include $2,249,959 for 29 grants (high: $238,000; low: $5,500), and $5,094,809 for foundation-administered programs.
Purpose and activities: The foundation seeks to unite people, develop resources and create solutions to build stronger Flint and Genesee counties by mobilizing the community to improve people's lives.
Fields of interest: Education; Health care; Youth development; Human services; Family services; Aging, centers/services; Community/economic development; Philanthropy/voluntarism; Children/youth; Aging.

Limitations: Giving primarily to Flint, Genesee, and Lapeer counties, MI.
Publications: Annual report; Informational brochure.
Officers and Trustees: Kevin Keane, Chair.; Mike Frawley,* Vice-Chair.; Ravi Yalamanchi,* Secy.; Mike Cantor, Treas.; Rudy Armstrong; Alicia Booker; Marcy Garcia; Raul Garcia; Larry Roehrig; Karen Toler; and 11 additional trustees.
EIN: 381359516

1432
United Way of Gladwin County
234 W. Cedar Ave.
P.O. Box 620
Gladwin, MI 48624 (989) 426-9225
County: Gladwin
Contact: Tami Jenkinson, Exec. Dir.
URL: http://www.unitedwaygladwinco.org

Established in MI.
Grantmaker type: Public charity.
Financial data (yr. ended 12/31/09): Revenue, $106,451; assets, $326,310 (M); gifts received, $91,553; expenditures, $131,881; total giving, $71,890; giving activities include $71,890 for grants.
Purpose and activities: The organization seeks to be an ongoing, mobilizing source of leadership and support for improving life in Gladwin County, MI, through its member agencies.
Fields of interest: Crime/violence prevention, abuse prevention; Recreation; Boy scouts; American Red Cross; Residential/custodial care, hospices; Human services; Community/economic development.
Limitations: Giving primarily in Gladwin County, MI.
Officer: Kathy Wilton, Pres.; Bob Scott, V.P.; Barb Woodruff, Secy.; Julie Shearer, Treas.; Tamara Jenkinson, Exec. Dir.
Board Members: Kelly Armbruster; Sherry Augustine; Joyce Cummins; Tom Cummins; Liz Looker; Georgann Schuster; Jerry Whittington; Christy VanTiem.
EIN: 382476861

1433
United Way of Gratiot County
110 W. Superior St.
Alma, MI 48801-1670 (989) 463-6245
County: Gratiot
Contact: Sharon Fenton, Exec. Dir.
FAX: (989) 463-6588;
E-mail: unitedway@gratiot.com; URL: http://www.gratiotunitedway.com

Grantmaker type: Public charity.
Financial data (yr. ended 12/31/09): Revenue, $652,622; assets, $1,072,216 (M); gifts received, $645,517; expenditures, $423,513; total giving, $302,988; giving activities include $237,925 for grants, and $65,063 for grants to individuals.
Purpose and activities: The organization seeks to raise and distribute funds to local health and human service organizations; financially support programs that produce measurable success and help those at risk of becoming disconnected from society; monitor effective human service programs that benefit the needs of Gratiot County; foster the opportunity for people to care for one another by giving their time, talents, and/or money; empower volunteers to become personally involved in meeting health and

human service needs; recognize the rights of donors to direct their gifts; and research and identify grants and other funding opportunities.
Fields of interest: Health care; Human services; Community/economic development.
Type of support: Grants to individuals; Research.
Limitations: Applications accepted. Giving primarily in Gratiot County, MI.
Publications: Application guidelines; Annual report; Financial statement; IRS Form 990 or 990-PF printed copy available upon request.
Application information: Applicants should provide an electronic copy of their proposals along with 2 hard copies. Application form required.
  Initial approach: Download RFP
  Deadline(s): Aug. 29
  Final notification: Nov. 4
Officers: Bill Dilts, Pres.; Sue Gay, Secy.; Rich Rice, Treas.; Sharon Fenton, Exec. Dir.
Directors: Rick Barratt; Sue Brooks; Zachary Everitt; Janet Hunter; Brent Moeggenberg; Ray Nichols; and 27 additional directors.
EIN: 386093791

1434
United Way of Greater Battle Creek
34 W. Jackson St., Ste. 4B
P.O. Box 137
Battle Creek, MI 49017-0137 (269) 962-9538
County: Calhoun
Contact: Michael J. Larson, Pres.
FAX: (269) 962-0074; E-mail: info@uwgbc.org;
URL: http://www.uwgbc.org

Established in MI.
Grantmaker type: Public charity.
Financial data (yr. ended 06/30/10): Revenue, $5,546,264; assets, $6,402,951 (M); gifts received, $4,897,118; expenditures, $5,563,667; total giving, $4,381,013; giving activities include $4,381,013 for grants.
Purpose and activities: The organization's mission is to address some of the community's most pressing problems and improve the lives of individuals in need.
Fields of interest: Human services; Community/economic development.
Limitations: Giving primarily in the greater Battle Creek, MI area.
Officers and Directors:* Ed Haring,* Chair.; Linda Miller,* Chair.-Elect; Tim Kool, Vice-Chair.; Chris Sargent, Pres. and C.P.O.; Jan Frantz,* Secy.; Todd Turcotte,* Treas.; Kevin Andrews; Suzy Avery; Julie Bosley; Ed Feld; Frank Hardgrove; Reggie LaGrand; David Lucas; Creighton Mabry; William Muth; and 10 additional directors.
EIN: 381846794

1435
United Way of Greater Niles, Inc.
210 E. Main St.
P.O. Box 375
Niles, MI 49120-2304
County: Berrien
Contact: John Stauffer, Exec. Dir.

Established in 1953 in MI.
Grantmaker type: Public charity.
Financial data (yr. ended 03/31/10): Revenue, $308,098; assets, $242,257 (M); gifts received, $265,985; expenditures, $301,366; total giving,

$133,246; program services expenses, $271,970; giving activities include $133,246 for 18 grants (high: $32,063; low: $417), and $138,724 for foundation-administered programs.

Purpose and activities: The organization invests in the programs and services that strengthen the ability of local United Ways to identify and build a coalition around a set of community priorities and measure success based on community impact.

Fields of interest: Community/economic development.

Limitations: Giving in the greater Niles, MI, area.

Publications: Grants list.

Officers and Directors: * Wyvonne Johnson,* Pres.; Nancy Studebaker,* V.P.; Dick DeVos,* Treas.; John Stauffer, Exec. Dir.; Eric Booker; Lisa Busby; Dale Rector; and 5 additional directors.

EIN: 386065024

1436
United Way of Jackson County
536 N. Jackson St.
Jackson, MI   49201-1223   (517) 784-0511
County: Jackson
FAX: (517) 784-2430; URL: http:// www.uwjackson.org

Grantmaker type: Public charity.

Financial data (yr. ended 06/30/09): Revenue, $3,755,872; assets, $10,337,757 (M); gifts received, $3,294,076; expenditures, $4,013,235; total giving, $1,579,851; giving activities include $1,579,851 for grants.

Purpose and activities: The organization works to improve people's lives by mobilizing the caring power of Jackson County's citizens.

Fields of interest: Community/economic development; Philanthropy/voluntarism.

Limitations: Giving limited to Jackson County, MI.

Officers and Directors: * Joe Lathrop,* Pres.; Dave Mengebier,* V.P.; Randy Ramirez,* Secy.; Bryanna Tapley,* Treas.; Ken Toll, Exec. Dir.; Brendon Beer; Malachi Crane; Ron Griffith; Bart Hawley; Chad Noble; Ed Piper; Ray Snell; Randy Treacher; Jason Valente; Rev. Mark VanValin; Frank Weathers; Jeanne Wickens.

EIN: 381368341

1437
United Way of Lapeer County
220 W. Nepessing St., Ste. 201
Lapeer, MI   48446-3815   (810) 667-3114
County: Lapeer
FAX: (810) 664-2016; URL: http:// unitedwaylapeer.org/

Established in 1927 in MI.

Grantmaker type: Public charity.

Financial data (yr. ended 06/30/10): Revenue, $362,322; assets, $217,582 (M); gifts received, $321,653; expenditures, $362,987; total giving, $88,592; giving activities include $88,592 for grants.

Purpose and activities: United Way of Lapeer County is a community solutions leader, uniting its community to measurably improve people's lives and build the most vital caring community in America. Current areas of priority are helping children succeed, supporting older adults, providing basic needs, and building strong families.

Fields of interest: Human services; Children/youth, services; Family services; Aging, centers/services.

Limitations: Applications accepted. Giving limited to Lapeer County, MI.

Publications: Application guidelines; Newsletter.

Application information: See web site for additional application requirements and guidelines, including downloadable forms. Application form required.
   Initial approach: Apr. 27

Officers and Board Members: * Rick van Haaften,* Pres.; Lori Curtiss,* V.P.; Marilyn Swihart, Secy.; John Biscoe, Treas.; Barton Buxton; Victor George; Mark Glasby; Lorraine Grinnell; Kay Harris; Nick Holowka; Kenneth Johnson; Byron Konschuh; Lorraine Konschuh; Kim McComb; Steve Paterson; Bonnie Schiedegger.

EIN: 383509445

1438
United Way of Manistee County
30 Jones St.
Manistee, MI   49660-1436   (231) 723-2331
County: Manistee
Contact: Corey van Fleet, Exec. Dir.
FAX: (231) 723-3727; E-mail: info@uwmanistee.org; URL: http://www.uwmanistee.org/

Established in 1942 in MI.

Grantmaker type: Public charity.

Financial data (yr. ended 03/31/09): Revenue, $171,162; assets, $254,407 (M); gifts received, $153,518; expenditures, $228,427; total giving, $135,830; giving activities include $135,830 for grants.

Purpose and activities: The organization makes allocations to various nonprofit organizations in the Manistee community to improve lives and build stronger communities.

Fields of interest: Youth development; Human services; Community/economic development.

Limitations: Giving limited to Manistee County, MI.

Application information:
   Board meeting date(s): Third Wed. of every month

Officers and Directors: * Anna Detz,* Pres.; Miles Gerberding,* V.P.; Julie Blaney,* Secy.; Jason Verheek,* Treas.; Corey van Fleet,* Exec. Dir.; Bill Brooks; Charles Fisher; Christine Hayes; Glenn Lottie; Jeff Rose; Steve Schmeling; Jeanette Somsel; Allen Taylor.

Number of staff: 2 part-time professional.

EIN: 386032839

1439
United Way of Marquette County
401 E. Fair Ave.
P.O. Box 73
Marquette, MI   49855-2951   (906) 226-8171
County: Marquette
FAX: (906) 226-7050;
E-mail: unitedway@uwmqt.org; URL: http:// www.uwmqt.org/

Established in 1943 in MI.

Grantmaker type: Public charity.

Financial data (yr. ended 06/30/10): Revenue, $432,378; assets, $634,330 (M); gifts received, $427,145; expenditures, $447,718; total giving, $320,215; giving activities include $320,215 for grants.

Purpose and activities: The mission of the United Way of Marquette County is to improve lives by focusing community resources to meet community needs. Current areas of focus include: unemployment and underemployment, domestic violence and substance abuse, positive youth development, health education, and elderly and adults with disabilities.

Fields of interest: Public health; Substance abuse, services; Crime/violence prevention, domestic violence; Employment, services; Youth development; Aging; Disabilities, people with; Economically disadvantaged.

Limitations: Giving limited to Marquette County, MI.

Officers and Board Members: * Donna Day,* Pres.; Jeff Bero,* V.P.; Diane Giddens,* Secy.; Ward Rantala,* Treas.; Joe Burdick; Bruce Miller; Ed Sloan; Robert Toutant; and 12 additional members.

EIN: 381358204

1440
United Way of Mason County
5868 West U.S. 10
Ludington, MI   49431-2450   (231) 843-8593
County: Mason
Contact: Lynne Russell, Exec. Dir.
E-mail: lynner@uwmasoncounty.org; URL: http:// www.uwmasoncounty.org/

Established in MI.

Grantmaker type: Public charity.

Financial data (yr. ended 03/31/10): Revenue, $386,430; assets, $445,656 (M); gifts received, $367,080; expenditures, $395,908; total giving, $130,177; giving activities include $130,177 for grants.

Purpose and activities: The mission of the United Way of Mason County is to improve the lives of the people of Mason County by funding programs for: basic needs and self-sufficiency, nurturing environments for children and youth, self-sufficiency for older adults, and behavioral and physical health services.

Fields of interest: Public health; Health care; Housing/shelter, development; Youth development; Human services; Children/youth, services; Aging, centers/services; Developmentally disabled, centers & services.

Limitations: Giving limited to Mason County, MI.

Officers: Debra Kinnaird, Chair.; Jeff Mount, Vice-Chair.; Sarah Kanitz, Treas.; Lynne Russell, Exec. Dir.

Directors: Herb Cross; Doug Damkoehler; Kent Gage; Kathy Maclean; Vicki Oddo; Bobbie Spence; Cele Wood.

EIN: 382943115

1441
United Way of Midland County
220 W. Main St., Ste. 100
Midland, MI   48640-5184   (989) 631-3670
County: Midland
FAX: (989) 832-5524;
E-mail: answers@unitedwaymidland.org; URL: http://www.unitedwaymidland.org/

Grantmaker type: Public charity.

Financial data (yr. ended 12/31/09): Revenue, $5,782,087; assets, $10,639,242 (M); gifts received, $5,489,851; expenditures, $5,864,027; total giving, $4,626,902; giving activities include $4,073,267 for grants, and $553,635 for grants to individuals.

Purpose and activities: To mobilize the caring resources of the Midland, Michigan community through leadership, collaboration, and charitable fundraising. Priority areas include strengthening families, nurturing children and youth, promoting health and healing, increasing self-sufficiency, and maximizing community impact.

Fields of interest: Youth development; Neighborhood centers; Children/youth, services; Family services; Aging, centers/services; Voluntarism promotion.

Type of support: Grants to individuals.

Limitations: Giving limited to Midland County, MI.

Officers and Directors: * Bridgette Gransden,* Pres.; Clark Volz,* V.P.; Darrell Zavitz,* Secy.; Doug Ward,* Treas.; Ann Fillmore, Exec. Dir.; and 18 additional directors.

EIN: 381434224

1442
United Way of Monroe County, Inc.
216 N. Monroe St.
Monroe, MI   48162-2620   (734) 242-1331
County: Monroe
FAX: (734) 337-3378;
E-mail: uwmhoydic@monroeuw.org; Additional tel.
(First Call for Help): (734) 242-4357; URL: http://
www.monroeuw.org/

Grantmaker type: Public charity.

Financial data (yr. ended 06/30/09): Revenue, $1,194,016; assets, $1,415,791 (M); gifts received, $1,321,334; expenditures, $1,264,644; total giving, $756,763; giving activities include $756,763 for grants.

Purpose and activities: The organization works to provide financial and related management support to human service organizations providing needed community services.

Fields of interest: Human services; Community/economic development.

Limitations: Giving limited to Monroe County, MI.

Officers and Directors: * Matt Hehl,* Pres.; Jim DuBay,* 1st V.P.; Don Spencer,* 2nd V.P.; Dave Abalos,* 3rd V.P.; Tom Myers,* Treas.; Michael D. Hoydic, Exec. Dir.; Jeanine Bragg; Bob Cebina; Jeff Hensley; and 14 additional directors.

EIN: 381437937

1443
United Way of Northwest Michigan
521 S. Union St.
Traverse City, MI   49685-0694   (231) 947-3200
County: Grand Traverse
Contact: Steve Wade, Exec. Dir.
FAX: (231) 947-3201;
E-mail: steve@unitedwaynwmi.org; Application mailing address: P.O. Box 694, Traverse City, MI 49685-0694; URL: http://www.unitedwaynwmi.org

Established in MI.

Grantmaker type: Public charity.

Financial data (yr. ended 12/31/09): Revenue, $929,522; assets, $1,207,432 (M); gifts received, $866,834; expenditures, $1,017,833; total giving, $590,898; giving activities include $590,898 for grants.

Purpose and activities: To improve the lives of community members by making value-added grants in the areas of youth development, human services, and health.

Fields of interest: Public health; Health care; Youth development; Human services; Homeless, human services.

Limitations: Applications accepted. Giving limited to Antrim, Kalkaska, Grand Traverse and Leelanau counties, MI.

Publications: Application guidelines; Annual report; Grants list; Informational brochure.

Application information: Requests for proposals are e-mailed to agencies during the first week of Feb., to be included on the e-mail list contact Michelle Gallagher at michelleg@unitedwaynwmi.org. Application form required.

Initial approach: RFP
Deadline(s): Feb. 23
Board meeting date(s): 2nd Wed. of each month
Final notification: Mar. 20

Officers and Directors: * Mike Hill,* Pres.; Barbara Rowlett, Secy.; Mark Eckhoff,* Treas.; Steve Wade, Exec. Dir.; Bob Gluszewski; Doug Luciani; Patty Maxbauer; Peter Marinoff; Jayne Mohr; Sue Nelson; Bruce Reavely.

Number of staff: 6 full-time professional.

EIN: 381679060

Selected grants: The following grants were reported in 2006.

$23,750 to Catholic Human Services, Traverse City, MI. For Host Homes for Homeless Youth.

$23,750 to Community Health Clinic, MI. For Dental Access Project.

$19,000 to G.W. Homeless Services of Northern Michigan, Traverse City, MI. For Goodwill Inn Homeless Shelter.

$18,050 to Traverse City Area Public Schools, Traverse City, MI. For Achieving the Vision project.

$11,875 to Womens Resource Center for the Grand Traverse Area, Traverse City, MI.

$10,450 to YMCA of Grand Traverse Bay, Traverse City, MI. For scholarship program.

$8,075 to Girl Scouts of the U.S.A., Crooked Tree Council. For scholarships.

$7,600 to Big Brothers Big Sisters of Northwestern Michigan, Traverse City, MI. For professional staff support of volunteers.

$5,700 to Northwest Michigan Transportation Alliance, Traverse City, MI.

$4,750 to Third Level Crisis Intervention Center, Traverse City, MI. For developing internet-accessible directory of local services.

1444
United Way of Sanilac County, Inc.
217 E. Sanilac, Ste. 2
Sandusky, MI   48471-1383
County: Sanilac

Grantmaker type: Public charity.

Financial data (yr. ended 12/31/09): Revenue, $202,432; assets, $129,902 (M); gifts received, $196,598; expenditures, $177,513; total giving, $106,035; giving activities include $106,035 for grants.

Purpose and activities: The organization collects donations and redistributes the proceeds to various non-profit agencies within Sanilac County for the benefit of area residents.

Fields of interest: Community/economic development.

Limitations: Giving limited to Sanilac County, MI.

Officers and Directors: * Virgil Strickler,* Pres.; Tony Parker,* V.P.; Julie Crowell,* Secy.; Jean Morgan,* Treas.; Stuart Armstead; Wayne Bank; Arthur

Birdsall; Jim Beyer; Dennis Cargill; and 16 additional directors.

EIN: 237123395

1445
United Way of Southwest Michigan
185 E. Main St., Ste. 601
P.O. Box 807
Benton Harbor, MI   49023-0807
(269) 925-7772
County: Berrien
FAX: (269) 925-1590; E-mail: info@uwsm.org;
Additional address: P.O. Box 239, Dowagiac, MI
49047-0239; URL: http://www.uwsm.org

Established in 1942 in MI.

Grantmaker type: Public charity.

Financial data (yr. ended 12/31/09): Revenue, $2,739,804; assets, $4,517,807 (M); gifts received, $2,695,983; expenditures, $2,627,888; total giving, $1,842,038; giving activities include $1,842,038 for grants.

Purpose and activities: The organization seeks to improve lives and build stronger communities.

Fields of interest: Community/economic development.

Limitations: Giving primarily in southwestern MI.

Officers and Directors: * Kate Seaman,* Chair.; Bill Schalk, Vice-Chair.; Anna Murphy, Pres. and C.E.O.; Gary Easterling,* Treas.; David Bly, Jr.; Hal Davis; Sarah Dempsey; Todd Gustafson; Christina Hardy; Randel Pompey; Michael Ruelle; Jim Schlaman; Carl Spikner; Joy Strand; Mary Jo Tomasini.

EIN: 381358411

1446
United Way of St. Clair County
1723 Military St.
Port Huron, MI   48060-5934   (810) 985-8169
County: St. Clair
Contact: Rick R. Garcia, Exec. Dir.
FAX: (810) 982-7202;
E-mail: uwsccadm@sbcglobal.net; URL: http://
uwstclair.org/

Established in 1953 in MI.

Grantmaker type: Public charity.

Financial data (yr. ended 03/31/10): Revenue, $1,718,720; assets, $3,656,755 (M); gifts received, $1,682,286; expenditures, $1,777,601; total giving, $1,261,200; giving activities include $1,045,739 for grants, and $215,461 for grants to individuals.

Purpose and activities: The organization works to mobilize the community and to raise funds and/or resources to meet identified human service needs with the highest level of accountability and community involvement.

Fields of interest: Health care; Crime/violence prevention, abuse prevention; Employment; Youth development; Human services; Human services, emergency aid; Community/economic development; Disabilities, people with; Economically disadvantaged; Homeless.

Limitations: Giving limited to St. Clair County, MI.

Officers: Roy Klecha, Pres.; Mike Caza, V.P.; Dan Degrow, Secy.; Tim Lubbers, Treas.; Rick R. Garcia, Exec. Dir.

Board Members: Mary Berckley; Mark Bessette; Tom Brunner; Robert Cook; Richard Cummings; Joseph Dams; Larry Dent; Tim Donnellon; Bob Funk;

Dr. Connie Harrison; Peter Karadjoff; Cindy Lane; Danny Negin; Jim Nunnold; Mike Ritacca; and 9 additional board members.
EIN: 381357996

1447
United Way of the Lakeshore
(formerly United Way of Muskegon County)
313 W. Webster Ave.
P.O. Box 207
Muskegon, MI 49440-1233 (231) 722-3134
County: Muskegon
FAX: (231) 722-3137; Toll-free tel.: (877) 722-3134;
URL: http://www.unitedwaylakeshore.org

Established in MI.
Grantmaker type: Public charity.
Financial data (yr. ended 12/31/09): Revenue, $2,736,965; assets, $3,160,434 (M); gifts received, $2,603,835; expenditures, $2,799,914; total giving, $2,038,221; giving activities include $2,038,221 for grants.
Purpose and activities: The organization seeks to unite the diverse elements of the community for the delivery of human services through assessing community needs, raising funds, allocating resources, and encouraging voluntarism.
Fields of interest: Crime/violence prevention, abuse prevention; Big Brothers/Big Sisters; Boy scouts; Girl scouts; American Red Cross; Urban League; YM/YWCAs & YM/YWHAs; Children, services; Human services; Community/economic development; Catholic agencies & churches.
Limitations: Giving primarily in Muskegon County, MI.
Officers and Directors:* Mary Lou Achterhoff,* Chair.; Bill Loxterman,* Vice-Chair.; Connie Verhagen,* Secy.; Earl Geiger,* Treas.; Jim Alderink; Stan Brown; Dana Bryant; Sue Cook; Deb Dean; John DeWolf; and 18 additional directors.
EIN: 381426895

1448
United Way of the Upper Eastern Peninsula
(formerly United Way of Chippewa County)
511 Ashmun, Ste. 104
P.O. Box 451
Sault Sainte Marie, MI 49783-0451
(906) 632-3700
County: Chippewa
Contact: Molly Paquin, Exec. Dir.
FAX: (906) 632-3190;
E-mail: molly@unitedwayeup.org; URL: http://unitedwayeup.org/

Established in 1956 in MI as United Way of Chippewa County; changed to current name in 2008.
Grantmaker type: Public charity.
Financial data (yr. ended 06/30/10): Revenue, $420,565; assets, $222,324 (M); gifts received, $379,193; expenditures, $382,642; total giving, $123,021; giving activities include $123,021 for grants.
Purpose and activities: The organization strives to increase the organized capacity of people to care for one another.
Fields of interest: Youth development; Human services.

Type of support: Technical assistance; Program development; Management development/capacity building; Internship funds; General/operating support; Emergency funds.
Limitations: Applications accepted. Giving limited to Chippewa, Luce, and Mackinac counties, MI. No support for political organizations.
Publications: Application guidelines; Annual report; Financial statement; Grants list; Informational brochure.
Application information: Application form required.
   Initial approach: Telephone, e-mail, or letter to request pre-application eligibility requirements
   Deadline(s): Dec. 31 for basic eligibility for new agencies
   Board meeting date(s): 3rd Thurs. of Jan., Mar., May, July, Sept., and Nov.
   Final notification: Feb. 1 for new agencies
Officers: Tom Ewing, Pres.; Carol Boger, Secy.; Don Gerrie, Treas.; Tracey Laitinen, Exec. Dir.
Directors: Phil Becker; Dan Dasho; Barry Davis; Keith Drenth; Henry Guzzo; Colleen Horn; Keith Krahnke; Kellie LaVictor; Karen Litzner; Mary Lynch; Ruth McCord; Tom McLain; Rod Nelson; Cory Parker; Dan Reattoir; Tom Swanson; and 6 additional directors.
Number of staff: 2 full-time professional; 1 full-time support.
EIN: 381678240
Selected grants: The following grants were reported in 2007.
$31,000 to Diane Peppler Resource Center, MI. For domestic violence and sexual assault services, parent nurturing classes, and educational programs.
$30,000 to Hospice of Chippewa County, Sault Sainte Marie, MI. For patient services.
$24,000 to Big Brothers Big Sisters. For youth mentors and Kids Fishing Day.
$22,000 to American Red Cross. For disaster training classes, blood units, and certifications for health and safety courses.
$20,000 to Great Lakes Recovery Centers, New Hope Houses, Marquette, MI. For outpatient services to men and women recovering from alcohol or drug addiction.
$20,000 to Salvation Army, MI. To provide food for soup kitchen, groceries, housing/utility assistance, and clothing/household items.
$18,000 to Sault Ste. Marie Housing Commission, Safe Haven, Sault Ste. Marie, MI. For operating support.
$15,000 to Bay Cliff Health Camp, Big Bay, MI. For therapy, dental services, instruction for hearing and visually impaired and swimming and horseback riding for special campers.
$15,000 to Chippewa-Luce-Macinac Community Action Resource Authority, Sault Sainte Marie, MI. For Home Delivered Meals program.
$10,000 to Catholic Charities of Shiawassee and Genesee Counties, Flint, MI. For individual/family counseling and child welfare sessions.

1449
United Way of Tuscola County
P.O. Box 51
Cass City, MI 48726-0051
County: Tuscola
E-mail: info@unitedwaytuscola.org; URL: http://www.unitedwaytuscola.org/

Established in MI.
Grantmaker type: Public charity.

Financial data (yr. ended 12/31/09): Revenue, $62,506; assets, $30,881 (M); gifts received, $62,419; expenditures, $59,446; total giving, $57,300; giving activities include $57,300 for grants.
Purpose and activities: The organization works to provide a means by which the residents, businesses, and political organizations of Tuscola County may make contributions to health and welfare needs for local, county, state, and national charities and community services.
Fields of interest: Community/economic development.
Limitations: Giving primarily in Tuscola County, MI.
Officers and Directors: Ken Spencer,* Pres.; Susan Rickwalt-Holder,* V.P.; Shelli Pohlod,* Secy.; Dawn Prieskorn,* Treas.; Al Avram; Ray Bates; Al Dadacki; Sandy Gaudreau; Janet Raleigh; Ron Wilson.
EIN: 383004648

1450
United Way of Wexford County
117 W. Cass St.
P.O. Box 177
Cadillac, MI 49601-2186 (231) 775-3753
County: Wexford
FAX: (231) 775-0169;
E-mail: info@unitedwaywexford.org; URL: http://www.unitedwaywexford.org/

Established in MI.
Grantmaker type: Public charity.
Financial data (yr. ended 03/31/10): Revenue, $327,603; assets, $363,730 (M); gifts received, $294,760; expenditures, $292,671; total giving, $180,500; giving activities include $180,500 for grants.
Purpose and activities: The United Way of Wexford County is committed to building a better community by meeting critical needs, and working to achieve community solutions. It supports over 26 direct local health and human service programs, and a variety of emerging needs through Community Response Grants.
Fields of interest: Public health; Health care; Housing/shelter; Youth development; Children/youth, services; Family services.
Limitations: Applications accepted. Giving limited to Wexford County, MI.
Application information: Application form required.
   Initial approach: E-mail the organization
Officers and Directors:* Van Eldridge,* Pres.; Scott Crosby,* 1st V.P.; Sue Peterson,* 2nd V.P.; Melody Hurley,* Secy.; Tim McNalley,* Treas.; Diane Dykstra,* Exec. Dir.; Mary Jo Binkley; Jim Blackburn; Deb Christie; Barb Darrigan; and 10 additional directors.
EIN: 237112549

1451
W. E. Upjohn Unemployment Trustee Corp.
(also known as W.E. Upjohn Institute for Employment Research)
300 S. Westnedge Ave.
Kalamazoo, MI 49007-4630 (269) 343-5541
County: Kalamazoo
Contact: Richard Wyrwa, Publications and Mktg. Mgr.
FAX: (269) 343-3308;
E-mail: webmaster@upjohninstitute.org;
URL: http://www.upjohninstitute.org

Incorporated in 1932 in MI.
Donor: W.E. Upjohn†.
Grantmaker type: Public charity.
Financial data (yr. ended 12/31/09): Revenue, $17,283,171; assets, $135,757,313 (M); gifts received, $13,089,517; expenditures, $18,418,836; total giving, $10,578,892; giving activities include $10,547,430 for grants, and $31,462 for grants to individuals.
Purpose and activities: The corporation supports research into the causes, effects, prevention, and alleviation of unemployment; and also provides funding to support the W.E. Upjohn Institute for Employment Research, an activity of the corporation.
Fields of interest: Employment; Economics.
Type of support: Research; Grants to individuals.
Limitations: Applications accepted. Giving on a national basis; grants may be awarded to individuals internationally as well. No grants for building/renovation, endowment funds, operating budgets, scholarships, or matching gifts; no loans.
Publications: Application guidelines; Program policy statement.
Application information: Submissions via fax or e-mail are not accepted. Application form not required.
  Initial approach: 3-page description of proposed research and curriculum vitae of researchers
  Copies of proposal: 8
  Deadline(s): Feb. 1 for 3-page summary applications and Feb. 27 for full 15-page Research Grant application; Apr. 1 for full Research Grant proposals and Mini Grant proposal
  Board meeting date(s): May, Oct. and Dec.
  Final notification: 90 days
Officers and Trustees:* Donald R. Parfet,* Chair.; Randall W. Eberts, Pres.; Marilyn J. Schlack,* Secy.-Treas.; Thomas W. Lambert; William C. Richardson; Frank Sardone; Paul H. Todd; Amanda Van Dusen; B. Joseph White.
Number of staff: 24 full-time professional; 6 part-time professional; 12 full-time support; 14 part-time support.
EIN: 381360419

1452
Peter Van Haften Charitable Trust
c/o Comerica Bank
151 S. Rose St.
Kalamazoo, MI 49007-4792
County: Kalamazoo

Established in MI; a supporting organization of American Cancer Society, Michigan Division and American Diabetes Association, Michigan Affilate.
Grantmaker type: Public charity.
Financial data (yr. ended 05/31/10): Assets, $341,768 (M); expenditures, $9,969; total giving, $4,822; giving activities include $4,822 for grants.
Purpose and activities: Giving limited to American Cancer Society and American Diabetes Association.
Fields of interest: Cancer; Diabetes.
Limitations: Giving limited to MI.
Trustee: Comerica Bank.
EIN: 386527243

1453
Variety Club Charity For Children, Inc.
30161 Southfield Rd., Ste 301
Southfield, MI 48076-1448 (248) 258-5511
County: Oakland
FAX: (313) 257-5575; E-mail: Variety5@msn.com;
URL: http://www.variety-detroit.com

Grantmaker type: Public charity.
Financial data (yr. ended 09/30/09): Revenue, $1,289,252; assets, $2,320,845 (M); gifts received, $1,368,744; expenditures, $1,478,172; total giving, $1,143,434; giving activities include $1,143,434 for grants.
Purpose and activities: The charity provides vital medical and therapeutic services, recreational facilities and educational opportunities to children with special needs.
Fields of interest: Education; Health care; Recreation; Children.
Limitations: Giving limited to the greater Detroit, MI, area.
Officers and Directors:* J. Douglas Clark,* Chair.; B.N. Bahadur,* V.P.; Jeffrey King,* V.P.; Felicia Palazzolo-Shaw, V.P.; Frank Vega, V.P.; Nancy Levy, Secy.; Bruce Kridler, Treas.; Jennie Cascio,* Exec. Dir.; Heather Catallo; Eric Clark; Jon Flora; Cathy Frank; Mary Khouri; Eric Kovan; Donald Kramer; and 7 additional directors.
EIN: 382140520

1454
Veteran's Haven, Inc.
4924 Wayne Rd.
Wayne, MI 48184-3200 (734) 728-0527
County: Wayne
FAX: (734) 728-1278;
E-mail: vetshaven@earthlink.net; URL: http://www.vetshaveninfo.org/haven.htm

Established in 1994 in MI.
Grantmaker type: Public charity.
Financial data (yr. ended 12/31/09): Revenue, $187,482; assets, $511,447 (M); gifts received, $136,829; expenditures, $192,071; total giving, $131,114; giving activities include $131,114 for grants to individuals.
Purpose and activities: The organization is dedicated to helping honorably-discharged veterans by providing food, clothing, housing, transportation, medical supplies, counseling referrals, and job connections to those in need.
Fields of interest: Food services; Housing/shelter, services; Human services, emergency aid; Human services; Military/veterans; Economically disadvantaged.
Type of support: Grants to individuals; In-kind gifts.
Limitations: Giving primarily in Wayne County, MI.
Officers and Trustees:* Stefan Berna,* Pres.; Ray Plesiewicz,* V.P.; Tyrone Wiley,* Secy.; Mike Brannigan,* Treas.; Dan Murry; Ron Ruark; Jim Shaiheen.
EIN: 383176960

1455
The Village Woman's Club Foundation
190 E. Long Lake Rd.
Bloomfield Hills, MI 48304-2325
County: Oakland
Contact: Linda Wilson, Pres.

URL: http://www.thevillageclub.org/Default.aspx?p=DynamicModule&pageid=287185&ssid=165075&vnf=1

Established in 1956.
Donor: Members of the Village Club.
Grantmaker type: Public charity.
Financial data (yr. ended 04/30/10): Revenue, $278,740; assets, $1,938,183 (M); gifts received, $92,750; expenditures, $116,530; total giving, $90,000; giving activities include $90,000 for grants.
Purpose and activities: The foundation promotes philanthropic projects in the form of grants which further educational, cultural and human services in Macomb, Oakland, and Wayne counties, Michigan.
Fields of interest: Children/youth, services; Family services; Human services; Children/youth; Youth; Disabilities, people with; Women; Economically disadvantaged.
Type of support: Equipment; General/operating support; Program development; Program-related investments/loans.
Limitations: Applications accepted. Giving limited to Oakland, Wayne, and Macomb counties, MI. No support for private foundations. No grants to individuals, or for medical research, scholarship funds, or emergency appeals.
Publications: Application guidelines; Annual report; Grants list.
Application information: Application form required.
  Initial approach: Letter requesting application and guidelines
  Copies of proposal: 2
  Deadline(s): Aug. 1
  Final notification: Apr.
Officers and Trustees:* Linda Wilson,* Pres.; Sandra Pott,* V.P.; Mary Callam,* Secy.; Anne Whitelaw,* Treas.; Lynn Ferron; Sharon Frost; Margaret Lowe; Sue Steinhagen.
EIN: 381690100

1456
VSA arts of Michigan
1920 25th Ave., Ste. B
Detroit, MI 48216-1435 (313) 843-2355
County: Wayne
FAX: (313) 843-2353; E-mail: info@vsami.org;
URL: http://www.vsami.org

Established in 1977 in MI.
Grantmaker type: Public charity.
Financial data (yr. ended 06/30/10): Revenue, $486,019; assets, $138,063 (M); gifts received, $485,470; expenditures, $478,375; program services expenses, $420,821; giving activities include $420,821 for foundation-administered programs.
Purpose and activities: The organization assists in the promotion and advancement of training and education in the arts for disabled individuals.
Fields of interest: Arts; Disabilities, people with.
Limitations: Giving primarily in MI.
Publications: Newsletter.
Officers: Daniel Steele, Pres.; Mary Bevans Gillett, Pres.-Elect; Marcia Love, Secy.; Edwin Smith, Treas.; Lora Frankel, Exec. Dir.
Board Members: Cindy Babcock; Kris DeYoung; Jim Edwards; Greg Fiedler; Aleatha Kimbrough; Joann P. Leal; Carolyn White; Mary Wiklanski.
EIN: 382690117

1457
Washtenaw Health Plan Corporation
555 Towner St.
Ypsilanti, MI 48198-5752
County: Washtenaw
URL: http://www.ewashtenaw.org/government/
departments/public_health/whp/

Established in 2001 in MI.
Grantmaker type: Public charity.
Financial data (yr. ended 09/30/09): Revenue,
$9,129,810; assets, $2,620,554 (M);
expenditures, $11,364,848; total giving,
$395,913; program services expenses,
$10,375,666; giving activities include $395,913
for 7 grants (high: $97,636; low: $20,944), and
$9,979,753 for foundation-administered programs.
Purpose and activities: The corporation insures the
delivery of basic preventative health care to
low-income persons without insurance, and/or who
are ineligible for other government programs.
Fields of interest: Health care; Insurance, providers.
Limitations: Giving primarily in MI.
Officers: Robert F. Gillett, Pres.; Tom Campbell, V.P.
and Treas.; Amy Kerschbaum, Secy.
Directors: Thomas Biggs; Robert E. Guenzel; Robert
Laverty; Kathleen Rhine; David Share.
EIN: 020585175

1458
Washtenaw United Way
2305 Platt Rd.
Ann Arbor, MI 48104-5115 (734) 971-8200
County: Washtenaw
FAX: (734) 971-6230; *URL:* http://www.wuway.org/

Established in 1971 in MI.
Grantmaker type: Public charity.
Financial data (yr. ended 06/30/09): Revenue,
$6,728,149; assets, $10,557,865 (M); gifts
received, $7,026,657; expenditures, $6,664,159;
total giving, $4,779,722; program services
expenses, $5,677,605; giving activities include
$4,779,722 for 37 grants (high: $298,769; low:
$9,550), and $897,883 for
foundation-administered programs.
Purpose and activities: The organization works to
generate and allocate resources to help individuals
and families build better lives and stronger
communities.
Fields of interest: Health care; Human services;
Community/economic development.
Limitations: Giving limited to Washtenaw County,
MI.
Publications: Newsletter.
Officers and Directors:* William Brinkerhoff,*
Chair.; Mark Ouimet,* Vice-Chair.; Katie
Oppenheim,* Secy.; Tim Gretkierewicz,* Treas.;
David Behen; Jim Burns; Frank Cambria; Mark
Caruso; Laurel Champion; Steve Dobson; Gloria
Edwards; Michael Ford; Rod Gauvin; Kristen Holt;
Todd Roberts; Richard Sheridan; Marilyn Smith.
EIN: 381951024

1459
Waverly Education Foundation
515 Snow Rd.
Lansing, MI 48917-4064 (517) 321-7265
County: Eaton
Contact: Janice Cunningham, Tr.

Application address: c/o Grant Comm., P.O. Box
80353, Lansing, MI 48908-0353, tel.: (517)
482-0222; *URL:* http://
waverlyeducationfoundation.org

Established in 1993 in MI.
Grantmaker type: Public charity.
Financial data (yr. ended 06/30/09): Revenue,
$7,909; assets, $240,088 (M); gifts received,
$16,088; expenditures, $19,802; total giving,
$13,553; giving activities include $13,553 for
grants.
Purpose and activities: Support for school
programs within the Waverly school district.
Fields of interest: Elementary/secondary
education.
Limitations: Applications accepted. Giving limited to
the Waverly School District, MI.
Publications: Application guidelines.
Application information: Application form required.
  Initial approach: Download application
  Deadline(s): Last Fri. in Feb. and Sept.
  Board meeting date(s): 8 times annually; board
    meets on grant funding Apr. and Nov.
Officers and Trustees:* Cam McComb,* Chair.; Miki
Patterson,* Vice-Chair.; Becky Pease,* Secy.;
Arnold Weinfeld,* Treas.; Margie Aimery; Susan
Steiner Bolhouse; Janice Cunningham; Mike Curley;
Robert Forgrave; Calvin Jones; Tom Klein; Holly
LaPratt; Steve Slater; Will Mahoney; Sue Stock.
EIN: 383190405

1460
Wayne Rotary Foundation
2732 S. Newburgh Rd.
Westland, MI 48186-9394
County: Wayne
URL: http://www.clubrunner.ca/cprg/home/
homed.asp?cid=652

Grantmaker type: Public charity.
Financial data (yr. ended 06/30/10): Revenue,
$81,207; assets, $687,122 (M); gifts received,
$22,980; expenditures, $59,359; total giving,
$57,909; giving activities include $57,909 for
grants.
Purpose and activities: The foundation gives to
scientific, educational, and charitable causes.
Fields of interest: Youth development; Community/
economic development.
Limitations: Applications accepted. Giving primarily
in the Wayne, MI area.
Publications: Application guidelines.
Application information: Application form required.
  Initial approach: Online application form
    submitted to Pres., Secy., or Treas. of the
    foundation
  Copies of proposal: 1
Officers and Trustees: Aziz Haridy,* Chair.; John
VanStipdonk, Secy.; David Carpenter, Treas.; Tom
Lynch; Robert McLellan; Patricia Rice; Lois
VanStipdonk.
EIN: 386091615

1461
Wayne-Metropolitan Community Action Agency
2121 Biddle Ave., Ste. 102
Wyandotte, MI 48192-4064 (734) 246-2280
County: Wayne
FAX: (734) 246-2288; *E-mail:* info@waynemetro.org;
URL: http://www.waynemetro.org

Grantmaker type: Public charity.
Financial data (yr. ended 09/30/09): Revenue,
$18,423,233; assets, $9,386,202 (M); gifts
received, $866,466; expenditures, $18,238,686;
total giving, $1,860,238; giving activities include
$1,860,238 for grants.
Purpose and activities: The organization provides
financial assistance and services to low-income
individuals such as adequate housing, job
placement assistance, and after school tutoring for
at-risk youth.
Fields of interest: Human services.
Type of support: Grants to individuals.
Limitations: Giving limited to residents of MI.
Officers and Directors:* Jodi Adamovich,* Chair.;
Michael Chappell,* 1st Vice-Chair.; Michelle
DaRos,* 2nd Vice-Chair.; William Hood,* Secy.; Ivan
Louis Cotman,* Treas.; and 14 additional directors.
EIN: 381976979

1462
Nathan Weidner Memorial Foundation
1392 S. Valley Center Dr.
Bay City, MI 48706-9798
County: Bay

Grantmaker type: Public charity.
Financial data (yr. ended 12/31/09): Revenue,
$76,638; assets, $872,973 (M); gifts received,
$44,579; expenditures, $47,766; total giving,
$46,692; giving activities include $46,692 for
grants.
Purpose and activities: The foundation aids and
assists in charitable and educational activities for
the mental, moral, intellectual, and physical
development of young men and women of Bay
County.
Fields of interest: Education.
Type of support: Scholarships—to individuals.
Limitations: Giving limited to Bay County, MI.
Officers: Gavin Goetz, Pres.; Pat Hubert, V.P.; Ann
Weidner, Secy.; Jack Weidner, Treas.
Board Members: Glenn Eyre; JoAnn Kuhn; Sandy
Meyer; Barbara Powers; Hon. Ken Schmidt; Matt
Weidner.
EIN: 383262641

1463
West Michigan Strategic Alliance, Inc.
951 Wealthy St., S.E.
Grand Rapids, MI 49506-1214 (616) 356-6060
County: Kent
FAX: (616) 328-5133; *E-mail:* info@wm-alliance.org;
Mailing address: P.O. Box 68046, Grand Rapids, MI
49516-8046; *URL:* http://www.wm-alliance.org

Established in 2000 in MI.
Grantmaker type: Public charity.
Financial data (yr. ended 12/31/09): Revenue,
$2,168,781; assets, $536,934 (M); gifts received,
$2,168,774; expenditures, $2,124,122; total
giving, $880,680; program services expenses,

$1,738,706; giving activities include $880,680 for 1 grant, and $858,026 for foundation-administered programs.
Purpose and activities: The alliance works to make western Michigan a better place to live, learn, work, and play by serving as a catalyst for regional collaboration.
Fields of interest: Community/economic development, alliance/advocacy; Economic development; Community/economic development.
Limitations: Giving limited to Allegan, Barry, Ionia, Kent, Montcalm, Muskegon, Newaygo, and Ottawa counties, MI.
Publications: Annual report; Occasional report; Quarterly report.
Officers: Alan Vanderberg, Chair.; James Dunlap, Vice-Chair.; Dale Nesbary, Vice-Chair.; Greg Northrup, Pres.; Bob Garretson, Secy.; Chris Hyzer, Treas.
Directors: Jim Bachmeier; James Buck; Tony Castillo; Darby Delabbio; Candace Dugan; Kurt Dykstra; Bing Goei; Bonnie Hammersley; Lesa Hardiman; Steve Heacock; Kenneth James; Cindy Larsen; Terry Lenhardt; Mat Nguyen; Lyman Parks, Jr., A.I.S., C.S.I., C.D.T.; Milt Rohwer; Elissa Sangalli-Hillary.
EIN: 383551109

1464
Whaley Children's Center, Inc.
1201 N. Grand Traverse St.
Flint, MI 48503-1312   (810) 234-3603
County: Genesee
FAX: (810) 232-3416;
E-mail: info@whaleychildren.org; URL: http://www.whaleychildren.org/

Established in 1942.
Grantmaker type: Public charity.
Financial data (yr. ended 12/31/09): Revenue, $3,126,287; assets, $6,226,967 (M); gifts received, $3,266,997; expenditures, $3,633,726; total giving, $104,130; giving activities include $104,130 for grants to individuals.
Purpose and activities: The center is a multi-service agency serving children and families.
Fields of interest: Children/youth, services; Family services; Children.
Officers: Doug Pastor, Vice-Chair.; Raquel T. Hatter, Pres. and C.E.O.; Dr. Kenneth Ganapini, D.O., Secy.; Jeffrey Kellerman, Treas.
Directors: Francine Jara; Tanya Jefferson; Bobby Johnson; Mark Krueger; Diana K. Hedderman; James Murdock; Evelyn Nartelski; Patrick Wardell.
EIN: 381358235

1465
Alfredine Jordan Wiley Scholarship, Inc.
19785 W. 12 Mile Rd., No. 107
Southfield, MI 48076
County: Oakland

Established in 2004 in MI.
Grantmaker type: Public charity.
Purpose and activities: The organization provides scholarships for metropolitan Detroit, Michigan high school students, and offers educational seminars for students, parents, and educators regarding the process of obtaining scholarships, grants, and educational opportunities.

Fields of interest: Higher education; Scholarships/financial aid; Education.
Type of support: Scholarships—to individuals.
Limitations: Applications accepted. Giving limited to the Detroit, MI, metropolitan area.
Publications: Application guidelines; Newsletter.
Application information: Application form required.
   Initial approach: Download application form
   Deadline(s): Apr. 18
   Final notification: June
Officers and Directors:* Alfredine J. Wiley,* Chair.; Doris T. Walls,* Vice-Chair.; Hattie M. Riley, Secy.; Santrannella Anderson; Judy Bednar; Jeron Campbell; Renee Fluker; Anderson Gilmer; Craig Samuel; Lilian Samuel; Donna Thornwell.
EIN: 300257414

1466
George & Emily Harris Willard Trust
3 W. Vanburen St.
Battle Creek, MI 49017-3009
County: Calhoun

Established in 1939; supporting organization of Battle Creek Public Schools.
Grantmaker type: Public charity.
Financial data (yr. ended 06/30/09): Assets, $785,622 (M); expenditures, $31,965; total giving, $31,315; giving activities include $31,315 for grants.
Purpose and activities: The trust seeks to provide care for under-privileged children residing within the city of Battle Creek attending the public schools therein.
Fields of interest: Education.
Type of support: Grants to individuals; Scholarships—to individuals.
Limitations: Giving limited to residents of Battle Creek, MI.
Trustee: School District/City of Battle Creek.
EIN: 386053144

1467
William Beaumont Hospital
16500 W. Twelve Mile Rd.
Southfield, MI 48076-2975
County: Oakland
URL: http://www.beaumonthospitals.com

Established in 1956 in MI.
Grantmaker type: Public charity.
Financial data (yr. ended 12/31/09): Revenue, $2,078,105,665; assets, $2,647,016,596 (M); gifts received, $26,192,157; expenditures, $2,050,155,889; total giving, $20,954,640; giving activities include $309,960 for grants, and $20,644,680 for grants to individuals.
Purpose and activities: The hospital works to provide individuals with the highest-quality health care services, regardless of situation.
Fields of interest: Hospitals (general); Health care.
Officers and Directors:* Thomas G. Dernomme,* Chair.; Stephen Howard,* Vice-Chair.; Kenneth J. Matzick,* Pres. and C.E.O.; Gale R. Colwell,* Secy.; William R. James,* Treas.; Robert K. Burgess; Susan E. Cooper; Robert C. Emde; Hadley Mack French; Charles J. Ghesquiere; John P. Hartwig; Geoffrey L. Hockman; Aubrey W. Lee; Barbara J. Mahone; Harold A. Poling; and 5 additional directors.
EIN: 381459362

1468
Wolverine Human Services
15100 Mack Ave.
Grosse Pointe Park, MI 48230-6202
(313) 824-4400
County: Wayne
FAX: (313) 824-4522; E-mail: leej@wolverinehs.org; URL: http://www.wolverinehs.org

Established in 1987 in MI.
Grantmaker type: Public charity.
Financial data (yr. ended 09/30/09): Revenue, $41,052,262; assets, $37,468,822 (M); gifts received, $247,411; expenditures, $40,171,017; total giving, $2,407,752; program services expenses, $35,173,221; giving activities include $2,407,752 for 1,431 grants to individuals, and $32,765,469 for foundation-administered programs.
Purpose and activities: The organization provides safety, sustenance, nurturing, and therapeutic intervention to children.
Fields of interest: Children/youth.
Limitations: Giving primarily in MI.
Officers and Trustees:* Bruce A. Kintz,* Chair.; Ron Warhurst,* 1st Vice-Chair.; Robert E. Wollack,* 2nd Vice-Chair. and C.E.O.; James Libs,* Secy.; Jerry Meter,* Treas.; Vince Brennan; James Cavicchioli; Marty Daly; Samuel McCargo; Karen Paciorek, Ph.D.; John Wangler.
EIN: 382675330

1469
Worldwide Christian Schools
629 Ionia Ave. S.W.
Grand Rapids, MI 49503-5148   (616) 531-9102
County: Kent
Contact: Scott Vander Kooy, Pres.
FAX: (616) 531-0602; E-mail: info@wwcs.org;
Toll-free tel.: (800) 886-9000; URL: http://www.wwcs.org

Established in 1987 in MI.
Grantmaker type: Public charity.
Financial data (yr. ended 06/30/09): Revenue, $3,473,214; assets, $1,788,509 (M); gifts received, $2,742,868; expenditures, $2,624,285; total giving, $1,196,837; giving activities include $25,735 for grants.
Purpose and activities: The organization provides funding to churches and other stable, accountable nonprofits to build schools in developing countries.
Fields of interest: Teacher school/education; Education; Children, services; Christian agencies & churches.
International interests: Developing countries.
Type of support: Building/renovation; Equipment; Program development; Conferences/seminars; Curriculum development; Scholarship funds; Consulting services; Program evaluation.
Limitations: Applications accepted. Giving primarily in developing countries. No support for political organizations.
Publications: Informational brochure (including application guidelines); Newsletter; Occasional report; Program policy statement.
Application information: Application form required.
   Board meeting date(s): 4th Thurs. of every other month
Officers and Directors:* Gloria Stronks, Ph.D.*, Chair.; Melvin Busscher,* Vice-Chair.; Scott Vander Kooy,* Pres.; Ken Van Den Bosch,* Treas.; Russell Bloem; Jeni Hoekstra; Robert Jonker.

Number of staff: 8 full-time professional; 1 part-time professional; 1 full-time support.
EIN: 382693388

1470
Coleman A. Young Foundation
2111 Woodward Ave., Ste. 600
Detroit, MI 48201-3473   (313) 962-2200
County: Wayne
Contact: Claudette Y. Smith Ph.D., Exec. Dir.
FAX: (313) 962-2208; E-mail: info@cayf.org;
URL: http://www.cayf.org

Established in 1982.
Donors: John Bernard, Jr.; Charter One Bank; Comerica Bank; Louis Cunningham; DaimlerChrysler Corp.; Ford Motor Co.; Gem Foundation; General Motors; Greektown Casino; Alison Harmon, Ed.D.; John James; David Baker Lewis; Kathleen McCree Lewis†; MGM Grand; Motor City Casino; National City Bank.
Grantmaker type: Public charity.

Financial data (yr. ended 12/31/09): Revenue, $316,856; assets, $1,683,534 (M); gifts received, $304,287; expenditures, $456,667.
Purpose and activities: The foundation provides scholarships to high school students for higher education.
Fields of interest: Higher education; Children/youth.
Type of support: Scholarships—to individuals.
Limitations: Applications accepted. Giving primarily in Detroit, MI.
Publications: Application guidelines; Annual report; Financial statement; Informational brochure (including application guidelines); Newsletter.
Application information: Application form required.
Initial approach: Download application form
Copies of proposal: 1
Deadline(s): Mar. 30
Board meeting date(s): Quarterly
Officers and Trustees:* Marvin Beatty,* Pres.; Garry G. Carley,* V.P.; Fred Martin,* Secy.; William Sanders,* Treas.; Claudette Y. Smith, Ph.D., Exec. Dir.; George Aubrey; George A. Goff; Elliott Hall; John A. James; Deanna L. Naugles-Jack; Juliette Okotie-Eboh, Ph.D.; Adam A. Shakoor; Charlie J. Williams; Jermaine A. Wyrick; Carlito H. Young; and 8 additional trustees.
Number of staff: 3 full-time professional; 1 part-time professional.
EIN: 382400801

1471
Young Old United Foundation
3209 Hillgate Cir.
Lansing, MI 48912-5011
County: Ingham

Donor: H. David Dekker.
Grantmaker type: Public charity.
Financial data (yr. ended 12/31/09): Revenue, $4,650; assets, $680 (M); gifts received, $4,650; expenditures, $5,010.
Officers: H. David Dekker, Pres.; Gordon Schleicher, V.P.; Debby Steele, Secy.-Treas.
Board Member: Jim Firos.
EIN: 382710827

OPERATING FOUNDATIONS

1472
A.I.R. Foundation
3181 Packard St.
Ann Arbor, MI 48108-1951 (734) 973-0420
County: Washtenaw

Established in MI.
Donors: George H. Muller; Brigitte D. Muller.
Grantmaker type: Operating foundation.
Financial data (yr. ended 12/31/09): Assets,
$149,992 (L); gifts received, $4,056; expenditures,
$7,755; total giving, $0; qualifying distributions,
$6,656.
Officers: Frank G. Muller, Pres.; Brigitte D. Muller,
V.P.
Trustees: Christine B. Ballard; Phillip G. Muller,
Ph.D.; Steven Muller.
EIN: 386120750

1473
Akbar Waqf Foundation, Inc.
(formerly Aye-You Charitable Foundation, Inc.)
4701 Towne Centre, Ste. 303
Saginaw, MI 48604-2833
County: Saginaw
Contact: Waheed Akbar, Dir.

Established in 1994 in MI.
Donors: Waheed Akbar; Raana Akbar.
Grantmaker type: Operating foundation.
Financial data (yr. ended 12/31/09): Assets,
$21,588 (M); gifts received, $9,500; expenditures,
$14,390; total giving, $13,800; qualifying
distributions, $13,800; giving activities include
$13,800 for grants.
Purpose and activities: Giving primarily to Islamic
organizations.
Fields of interest: Education; Human services;
Islam.
International interests: Pakistan.
Limitations: Giving primarily in Pakistan; giving also
in Saginaw, MI.
Application information: Application form not
required.
   Initial approach: Letter
   Deadline(s): None
Directors: Raana Akbar, M.D.; Waheed Akbar.
EIN: 363917606

1474
Jerome S. Amber Foundation, Inc.
1610 Hanley Ct.
Birmingham, MI 48009-7267 (248) 258-6714
County: Oakland

Established in 2004.
Grantmaker type: Operating foundation.
Financial data (yr. ended 12/31/09): Assets,
$32,733 (M); gifts received, $6,000; expenditures,
$1,296; total giving, $915; qualifying distributions,
$915; giving activities include $915 for 5 grants
(high: $550; low: $25).
Officer: Jerome S. Amber, Pres.

Trustees: Allen L. Amber; Jennifer Soble.
EIN: 200809177

1475
Angels in Motion Foundation
1800 W. Big Beaver Rd., Ste. 100
Troy, MI 48084-3531 (248) 822-9010
County: Oakland
Contact: Stephen Metzler

Established in 2003 in MI.
Grantmaker type: Operating foundation.
Financial data (yr. ended 12/31/09): Assets,
$1,294 (M); gifts received, $50; expenditures,
$158; total giving, $0; qualifying distributions, $0.
Fields of interest: Family services; Homeless.
Type of support: Grants to individuals.
Application information:
   Initial approach: Letter
   Deadline(s): None
Officer: Stephen A. Metzler, Pres.
EIN: 200068383

1476
Arbor Research Collaborative for Health
(formerly University Renal Research and Education
Association)
c/o Friedrich Port, M.D., Pres.
315 W. Huron St., Ste. 360
Ann Arbor, MI 48103-4262 (734) 665-4108
County: Washtenaw
FAX: (734) 665-2103; *URL:* http://
www.arborresearch.org/

Established in 1996 in MI. Classified as a private
operating foundation in 1997.
Grantmaker type: Operating foundation.
Financial data (yr. ended 12/31/09): Assets,
$13,826,212 (M); gifts received, $11,121,240;
expenditures, $10,792,716; total giving, $0;
qualifying distributions, $0.
Officers: Friedrich Port, M.D., M.S., Pres.; Robert
Wolf, Ph.D., V.P.; Sylvia Ramirez, V.P.; Judy Kubacki,
Secy.; Deborah Vandermade, Treas.
Directors: Mark Barr; Peter De Oreo; Lee
Henderson; Maureen Michael; John Newman; Phillip
Roos.
EIN: 383289521

1477
Arjuna Institute
1507 Brooklyn Ave.
Ann Arbor, MI 48104-4416
County: Washtenaw

Established around 1982 in MI.
Grantmaker type: Operating foundation.
Financial data (yr. ended 12/31/09): Assets,
$4,645 (M); gifts received, $11,787; expenditures,
$11,787; total giving, $0; qualifying distributions,
$0; giving activities include $11,787 for
foundation-administered programs.

Officer: Richard D. Mann, Pres.
Trustee: Edward N. Mann.
EIN: 382110752

1478
Ekrem Bardha Foundation, Inc.
3300 Lone Pine Rd.
West Bloomfield, MI 48323-3324
(248) 851-7310
County: Oakland
Contact: Ekrem Bardha, Pres.

Established in 1995 in MI.
Grantmaker type: Operating foundation.
Financial data (yr. ended 12/31/09): Assets,
$22,423 (M); gifts received, $35,000;
expenditures, $80,917; total giving, $80,917;
qualifying distributions, $80,917; giving activities
include $80,917 for grants.
Fields of interest: Arts, cultural/ethnic awareness;
Christian agencies & churches; Immigrants/
refugees.
Limitations: Giving in MI, with emphasis on Oakland
and Wayne counties. No grants to individuals.
Application information:
   Initial approach: Letter or telephone
   Deadline(s): None
Officers: Ekrem Bardha, Pres.; Lumteri Bardha,
Secy.
EIN: 383212623

1479
Barros Research Foundation
2430 College Rd.
Holt, MI 48842-9704
County: Ingham

Classified as a private operating foundation in 1981
in MI.
Donors: Barnett Rosenberg; Tina Rosenberg.
Grantmaker type: Operating foundation.
Financial data (yr. ended 12/31/09): Assets,
$366,542 (M); gifts received, $350,000;
expenditures, $354,927; total giving, $0; qualifying
distributions, $341,814.
Officers: Barnett Rosenberg, Pres.; Ritta
Rosenberg, Secy.-Treas.
Directors: Paul A. Rosenberg; Tina Rosenberg.
EIN: 382380724

1480
Donald and Ethel Baughey Foundation
7620 W. U.S. Hwy. 223
Adrian, MI 49221-8421
County: Lenawee

Established in 2001.
Donors: Donald Baughey†; Ethel Baughey†.
Grantmaker type: Operating foundation.
Financial data (yr. ended 12/31/09): Assets,
$233,147 (M); expenditures, $20,591; total giving,

$12,300; qualifying distributions, $12,300; giving activities include $12,300 for grants.
Fields of interest: Hospitals (general).
Limitations: Giving primarily in Adrian, MI.
Officer: Dorcas Baughey, Secy.
Directors: Daniel Wright; Donald Baughey, Jr.
EIN: 383562947

1481
Lan Benson Foundation
11933 S. Lake Chapin Rd.
Berrien Springs, MI 49103-9232
(269) 277-3340
County: Berrien
Contact: Douglas L. Benson, Pres.

Established in 2007 in MI.
Donors: William N. Snyder; Ardith R. Jarrard-Benson; Douglas L. Benson.
Grantmaker type: Operating foundation.
Financial data (yr. ended 12/31/07): Assets, $29,992 (M); gifts received, $37,412; expenditures, $7,432; total giving, $0; qualifying distributions, $0.
Officers: Douglas L. Benson, Pres. and Treas.; Ardith R. Jarrard-Benson, V.P. and Secy.
EIN: 205772331

1482
Jesse Besser Museum
491 Johnson St.
Alpena, MI 49707-1496
County: Alpena

Classified as a private operating foundation in 1972.
Donor: Besser Foundation.
Grantmaker type: Operating foundation.
Financial data (yr. ended 06/30/10): Assets, $8,623,119 (M); gifts received, $331,027; expenditures, $649,772; total giving, $0; qualifying distributions, $504,781.
Purpose and activities: Support only for a museum and planetarium.
Officers: Ronald A. Meneghel, Pres.; Kathy Himes, 1st V.P.; Dave Musch, 2nd V.P.; Sharon Powers, Secy.; Jim Arbuckle, Treas.
EIN: 386111671

1483
The Les and Anne Biederman Foundation, Inc.
P.O. Box 564
Traverse City, MI 49685-0564
County: Grand Traverse
Contact: Chris Warren, Secy.

Established in 1986 in MI.
Donors: Lester M. Biederman‡; Anna R. Biederman; Anne Biederman Trust.
Grantmaker type: Operating foundation.
Financial data (yr. ended 12/31/09): Assets, $4,503,247 (M); gifts received, $100,200; expenditures, $205,278; total giving, $187,075; qualifying distributions, $187,075; giving activities include $187,075 for 24 grants (high: $20,000; low: $1,000).
Purpose and activities: Support for education, civic improvement, fine arts, health and human services, and recreation and youth services.

Fields of interest: Arts; Higher education; Education; Recreation; Human services; Youth, services; United Ways and Federated Giving Programs; Government/public administration.
Type of support: General/operating support; Continuing support; Building/renovation; Equipment; Land acquisition; Endowments; Program development; Scholarship funds.
Limitations: Applications accepted. Giving primarily in northern MI. No support for fraternal organizations, societies, or orders, political organizations or campaigns, or for religious organizations for sectarian purposes. No grants to individuals (except selected scholarships), or for deficit financing or debt retirement, endowment funds, travel or conferences, normal operating expenses, scientific research, or writing, publication or production of articles, books or films.
Publications: Application guidelines.
Application information: Application form required.
  Initial approach: Letter
  Copies of proposal: 7
  Deadline(s): 1 month prior to board meetings
  Board meeting date(s): 2 to 3 times annually
Officers and Trustees:* Ross Biederman,* Pres.; Lawrence E. Gorton, V.P.; Chris Warren, Secy.; Vojin Baic; Paul M. Biederman; Lee Russell.
Number of staff: None.
EIN: 382449838
Selected grants: The following grants were reported in 2009.
$20,000 to Northwestern Michigan College, Traverse City, MI.
$20,000 to Tri-County Coalition for Prevention of Child Neglect.
$15,000 to Food Rescue of NW Michigan.
$12,500 to Grand Traverse Regional Land Conservancy, Traverse City, MI.
$12,500 to YMCA of Grand Traverse Bay, Traverse City, MI.
$10,000 to Crystal Lake Art Center.
$10,000 to Goodwill Industries of Northern Michigan, Traverse City, MI.
$10,000 to Michaels Place.
$10,000 to Traverse Symphony Orchestra, Traverse City, MI.
$10,000 to Watershed Center, Traverse City, MI.

1484
Buist Foundation
8650 Byron Center Ave. S.W.
Byron Center, MI 49315-9201 (616) 878-3315
County: Kent
Contact: Brent Brinks, Pres.
URL: http://www.buistelectric.com/company_info/community/buist_foundation.php

Established as a company-sponsored operating foundation in 1998.
Donor: Buist Electric, Inc.
Grantmaker type: Operating foundation.
Financial data (yr. ended 12/31/09): Assets, $75,210 (M); gifts received, $284,974; expenditures, $345,875; total giving, $338,084; qualifying distributions, $338,084; giving activities include $63,649 for 28+ grants (high: $10,000), and $274,434 for grants to individuals.
Purpose and activities: The foundation supports organizations involved with secondary education, housing, human services, and Christianity and awards grants to needy families.
Fields of interest: Education; Housing/shelter; Human services; Christian agencies & churches.

Type of support: General/operating support; Scholarship funds; Grants to individuals.
Limitations: Applications accepted. Giving primarily in Grand Rapids, MI.
Publications: Application guidelines.
Application information: Application form not required.
  Initial approach: Proposal
  Deadline(s): None
  Board meeting date(s): Monthly
Officer and Directors: Brent Brinks, Pres.; Andy Vermunen, Secy.; Kathy Burgess; Aaron Cocco; Matt DeVries; Jim Etzinga; Dave Houseman; Vic Martinski; Cindy Meengs; John Lee.
EIN: 383314509
Selected grants: The following grants were reported in 2008.
$7,000 to South Christian High School, Grand Rapids, MI.
$5,000 to Brown-Hutcherson Ministries, Grand Rapids, MI.
$2,500 to Volunteers in Service, Grand Rapids, MI.
$2,312 to Kalamazoo Gospel Mission, Kalamazoo, MI.
$1,000 to Grand Rapids Community College, Grand Rapids, MI.

1485
Central Care Management Organization
(formerly Network Community Services)
28303 Joy Rd.
Westland, MI 48185-5524
County: Wayne
Contact: Michelle Y. Scott, Exec. Dir.
Application address: 18100 Meyers Rd., Detroit, MI 48235-1493, tel.: (313) 862-2800

Established in MI.
Donor: Wayne County Department of Child and Family Services.
Grantmaker type: Operating foundation.
Financial data (yr. ended 09/30/09): Assets, $2,496,136 (M); gifts received, $485; expenditures, $24,438,163; total giving, $0; qualifying distributions, $0.
Purpose and activities: Giving for programs that assist delinquent youth in Wayne County, Michigan.
Fields of interest: Youth, services.
Limitations: Applications accepted. Giving limited to the central Detroit, Highland Park, and Hamtramck, MI, area.
Application information:
  Initial approach: Letter or telephone
  Deadline(s): Mar. 31
Officers: Roderick L. Johnson, C.E.O.; Robert E. Ennis III, Chair.; Dr. Arthur Carter, Secy.; Charles Small, Treas.; Jen L. Fisher, Exec. Dir.
Directors: Jerome E. Crawford; V. Gail Simpson; Dr. Marvin R. Youmans.
EIN: 383050521

1486
Subir and Malini Chowdhury Foundation
1881 Heron Ridge Dr.
Bloomfield Hills, MI 48302-0725
County: Oakland

Established in 2006 in MI.
Donor: Subir Chowdhury.
Grantmaker type: Operating foundation.

Financial data (yr. ended 12/31/09): Assets, $3,037,821 (M); gifts received, $1,000,000; expenditures, $134,359; total giving, $100,000; qualifying distributions, $119,295; giving activities include $100,000 for grants.
Fields of interest: Education; Human services.
Limitations: Giving primarily in MI.
Directors: Malini Chowdhury; Subir Chowdhury.
EIN: 205991853

1487
The Coleman Family Foundation
947 Bradford Hollow N.E.
Grand Rapids, MI   49525-3303   (616) 365-1560
County: Kent
Contact: Robert D. Coleman, Pres.

Established in 2004 in MI.
Donor: Universal Forest Products, Inc.
Grantmaker type: Operating foundation.
Financial data (yr. ended 12/31/09): Assets, $21,910 (M); gifts received, $10,000; expenditures, $12,825; total giving, $12,172; qualifying distributions, $12,172; giving activities include $12,172 for grants.
Fields of interest: Education; Medical research; Christian agencies & churches.
Type of support: General/operating support.
Limitations: Giving primarily in MI. No grants to individuals.
Application information:
  Initial approach: Letter
  Deadline(s): None
Officers: Robert D. Coleman, Pres.; Rachelle L. Coleman, Secy.-Treas.
EIN: 371485573

1488
Cornucopia Family Foundation
2680 Horizon Dr. S.E., Ste. C
Grand Rapids, MI   49546-7500
County: Kent

Established in 2006 in MI.
Donor: Paulus C. Heule.
Grantmaker type: Operating foundation.
Financial data (yr. ended 12/31/09): Assets, $1,208,306 (M); gifts received, $200,000; expenditures, $88,039; total giving, $79,134; qualifying distributions, $79,134; giving activities include $79,134 for grants.
Fields of interest: Education; Christian agencies & churches; Children/youth.
Limitations: Giving primarily in MI.
Directors: Paulus C. Heule; Rosemary L. Heule.
EIN: 208080952

1489
Creative Health Institute
918 Union City Rd.
Union City, MI   49094-9753
County: Branch

Grantmaker type: Operating foundation.
Financial data (yr. ended 12/31/07): Assets, $103,749 (M); gifts received, $13,422; expenditures, $288,357; total giving, $4,209; qualifying distributions, $4,209; giving activities include $4,209 for grants.

Purpose and activities: Support only for programs that promote a healthy alternative lifestyle and diet.
Fields of interest: Health care.
Trustees: Joe Basset; James Carey; Hiawatha Cromer; Mary Moore.
EIN: 382557714

1490
Richard E. & Sandra J. Dauch Family Foundation
203 Mason St.
Charlevoix, MI   49720-1337   (231) 547-4602
County: Charlevoix
Contact: Thomas G. Bickersteth, Secy.

Established in 2002 in MI.
Donors: Richard E. Dauch; Sandra J. Dauch; Helen R. Dauch Trust.
Grantmaker type: Operating foundation.
Financial data (yr. ended 04/30/10): Assets, $4,259,072 (M); gifts received, $300,000; expenditures, $867,768; total giving, $853,188; qualifying distributions, $854,158; giving activities include $853,188 for 5 grants (high: $340,688; low: $2,500).
Fields of interest: Higher education; Health care; Medical research; Boys & girls clubs; Human services; Residential/custodial care, hospices; Protestant agencies & churches.
Limitations: Applications accepted. Giving primarily in IN, MI, and OH.
Application information: Application form not required.
  Initial approach: Letter
  Copies of proposal: 1
  Deadline(s): None
  Board meeting date(s): May
  Final notification: Following annual meeting
Officers: Richard E. Dauch, Pres.; Sandra J. Dauch, V.P. and Treas.; Thomas G. Bickersteth, Secy.
EIN: 300074517
Selected grants: The following grants were reported in 2009.
$300,000 to Purdue University, Krannert School, West Lafayette, IN.
$100,000 to Ashland First United Methodist Church, Ashland, OH.
$100,000 to Hospice of North Central Ohio, Ashland, OH.
$2,500 to Smile Train, New York, NY.
$2,500 to University of Michigan, Ann Arbor, MI.

1491
DeShano Community Foundation
P.O. Box 539
Gladwin, MI   48624-0539
County: Gladwin
Contact: Florence G. DeShano, Secy.
Application address: 4339 Round Lake Rd., Gladwin, MI 48624-9211, tel.: (989) 426-0670

Established in 2001 in MI.
Donors: Florence G. DeShano; Gary L. DeShano.
Grantmaker type: Operating foundation.
Financial data (yr. ended 12/31/09): Assets, $62,041 (M); gifts received, $30,000; expenditures, $26,632; total giving, $26,414; qualifying distributions, $26,414; giving activities include $26,414 for grants.

Fields of interest: Education; Human services; Community/economic development; Christian agencies & churches.
Limitations: Giving limited to the mid-MI region. No grants to individuals.
Application information:
  Initial approach: Letter
  Deadline(s): None
Officers: Gary L. DeShano, Pres.; Florence G. DeShano, Secy.
Trustees: Scott G. DeShano; Douglas A. Jacobson; Douglas F. Larner.
EIN: 382902743

1492
Detroit Christadelphian Bible Explorers, Inc.
14676 Berwick St.
Livonia, MI   48154-3550
County: Wayne

Grantmaker type: Operating foundation.
Financial data (yr. ended 12/31/09): Assets, $199 (M); gifts received, $6,928; expenditures, $6,798; total giving, $0; qualifying distributions, $0.
Officers: William A. Robinson, Pres.; Jared Keyes, V.P.; Pam Styles, Secy.; Ruth Robinson, Treas.
Director: Jonathon Brinkerhoff.
EIN: 383497401

1493
Detroit Metro Sports Commission, Inc.
211 W. Fort St., Ste. 1000
Detroit, MI   48226-3270
County: Wayne
E-mail: info@detroitsports.org; URL: http://www.detroitsports.org

Established in 2001 in MI.
Grantmaker type: Operating foundation.
Financial data (yr. ended 12/31/09): Assets, $176,811 (M); expenditures, $654,242; total giving, $0; qualifying distributions, $0.
Officers: Larry D. Alexander, Pres.; Michael O'Callaghan, Exec. V.P.; Sajid Zuberi, V.P., Finance.
EIN: 383584276

1494
Detroit Neurosurgical Foundation
3333 E. Jefferson Ave., Ste. 1117
Detroit, MI   48207-4237   (313) 259-0391
County: Wayne
Contact: Amy Berke, Exec. Dir.

Established in MI. Classified as a private operating foundation in 1977.
Donor: Joseph J. Berke, M.D., Ph.D.
Grantmaker type: Operating foundation.
Financial data (yr. ended 11/30/09): Assets, $1,007,129 (M); expenditures, $21,226; total giving, $4,171; qualifying distributions, $4,171; giving activities include $4,171 for grants.
Fields of interest: Medical research; Community development, neighborhood development; Jewish agencies & synagogues.
Type of support: Annual campaigns; Capital campaigns; Program development; Conferences/seminars; Research; Program evaluation; Matching/challenge support.
Limitations: Giving limited to Detroit, MI.

Publications: Informational brochure.
Application information: Application form not required.
  Initial approach: Letter
  Copies of proposal: 1
  Deadline(s): None
  Board meeting date(s): As needed
Officers and Directors:* Joseph J. Berke, M.D., Ph.D.*, Pres.; Amy Berke,* Exec. Dir.; Irving F. Keene; Herman Moehlman.
EIN: 382127946

1495
Devries Nature Conservancy

P.O. Box 608
Owosso, MI 48867-0608
County: Shiawassee

Established in 2004 in MI; funded in 2006.
Grantmaker type: Operating foundation.
Financial data (yr. ended 12/31/09): Assets, $2,318,942 (M); gifts received, $12,908; expenditures, $177,046; total giving, $0; qualifying distributions, $0.
Officers: Thomas McClear, Pres.; Richard Hanchett, Secy.; Richard Batchelor, Treas.; Kenneth Algozin, Exec. Dir.
EIN: 200631470

1496
Alden B. and Vada B. Dow Creativity Foundation

c/o \
315 Post St.
Midland, MI 48640-6615   (989) 837-4478
County: Midland

Established in 1989 in MI; funded in 1991.
Donor: Vada B. Dow‡.
Grantmaker type: Operating foundation.
Financial data (yr. ended 12/31/09): Assets, $2,905,416 (M); gifts received, $534,742; expenditures, $801,699; total giving, $0; qualifying distributions, $0.
Officers and Trustees:* Michael Lloyd Dow,* Pres.; Marry Lloyd Dow Mills,* Secy.; Kendall A. Mills, Treas.; Barbara D. Carras; Steven Carras; Diane Hullet; Chris Mills.
EIN: 382852321

1497
Evergreene Foundation

19459 Thompson Ln.
Three Rivers, MI 49093-9039
County: St. Joseph

Established in MI.
Grantmaker type: Operating foundation.
Financial data (yr. ended 12/31/09): Assets, $552,849 (M); expenditures, $15,774; total giving, $15,200; qualifying distributions, $15,200; giving activities include $15,200 for grants.
Fields of interest: Education; Health care; Human services; Community/economic development; Protestant agencies & churches.
Type of support: General/operating support.
Limitations: Applications accepted. Giving limited to MI, with some emphasis on Three Rivers. No grants to individuals.
Application information:

Initial approach: Letter or proposal
Deadline(s): July 1
Director: Blaine A. Rabbers.
EIN: 382737257

1498
Fahd Foundation

15113 S. Dixie Hwy.
Monroe, MI 48161-3770
County: Monroe

Established in 2000 in MI.
Donor: Tanvir I. Quershi.
Grantmaker type: Operating foundation.
Financial data (yr. ended 12/31/09): Assets, $890 (M); gifts received, $15,000; expenditures, $14,710; total giving, $14,700; qualifying distributions, $14,700; giving activities include $14,700 for grants.
Purpose and activities: Giving for the benefit of Pakistan.
Fields of interest: Christian agencies & churches; Economically disadvantaged.
International interests: Pakistan.
Limitations: Giving primarily in Pakistan.
Officers: Tanvir I. Quershi, Pres. and Treas.; Amber T. Quershi, Secy.
Directors: Riaz Ahmad; Shala Riaz Ahmad; Muzzamil Malik.
EIN: 383229397

1499
First Federal Community Foundation

100 S. 2nd Ave.
Alpena, MI 49707-2814   (989) 354-7319
County: Alpena
Contact: Michael W. Mahler, Pres.
URL: http://www.first-federal.com/about-us/our-community-foundation.html

Established in 2005 in MI.
Donor: First Federal of Northern Michigan Bancorp, Inc.
Grantmaker type: Operating foundation.
Financial data (yr. ended 12/31/09): Assets, $271,155 (M); expenditures, $19,028; total giving, $16,195; qualifying distributions, $245,565; giving activities include $16,195 for 17 grants (high: $2,000; low: $100).
Purpose and activities: The purpose of the foundation is to enhance the relationship between First Federal of Northern Michigan and the communities in which it operates and to enable its communities to share in its long-term growth. The foundation is dedicated to community activities and the promotion of charitable causes.
Fields of interest: Museums; Secondary school/education; Higher education; Education; Hospitals (general); Community/economic development; United Ways and Federated Giving Programs; General charitable giving.
Type of support: Capital campaigns; Building/renovation; Equipment; Program development; Seed money; Scholarship funds.
Limitations: Applications accepted. Giving limited to areas of company operations in Alcona, Alpena, Cheboygan, Charlevoix, Crawford, Emmet, Iosco, Montmorency, Ogemaw, Oscoda, Otsego, and Presque Isle counties, MI. No support for religious organizations not of direct benefit to the entire

community. No grants to individuals, or for general operating support or debt reduction.
Publications: Application guidelines.
Application information: The foundation currently accepts two types of applications. The Mini-Grant Application is available for grant requests of up to $250, and the Common Grant Application is available for grant requests of $250 to $1,500. Application form required.
  Initial approach: Download application form and mail to foundation
  Deadline(s): 1st regular workday of the month
  Board meeting date(s): Mar., June, Sept., and Dec.
Officers and Directors:* Gary C. VanMassenhove,* Chair.; Michael W. Mahler,* Pres.; Amy E. Essex,* V.P. and Secy.-Treas.; Lora Greene.
EIN: 202531733

1500
E. Root Fitch Foundation

107 Pennsylvania Ave.
Dowagiac, MI 49047-1748
County: Cass

Established in MI.
Grantmaker type: Operating foundation.
Financial data (yr. ended 12/31/09): Assets, $1,257,492 (M); gifts received, $700; expenditures, $118,443; total giving, $0; qualifying distributions, $0.
Officers: Paul Bakeman, Pres.; Denise Wierman, Secy.; John Magyar, Treas.
EIN: 386009605

1501
Maxine and Stuart Frankel Foundation for Art

1334 Maplelawn Dr.
Troy, MI 48084-5341
County: Oakland

Established in 1996 in MI. Classified as a private operating foundation in 1997; funded in 1998.
Donors: Maxine Frankel; Stuart Frankel.
Grantmaker type: Operating foundation.
Financial data (yr. ended 12/31/09): Assets, $53,176,162 (M); gifts received, $3,836,803; expenditures, $167,296; total giving, $0; qualifying distributions, $0.
Officers: Maxine Frankel, Pres.; Stuart Frankel, Secy.-Treas.
EIN: 383357965

1502
Galesburg-Augusta Education Foundation

(formerly Galesburg-Augusta Community Foundation)
1076 N. 37th St.
Galesburg, MI 49053-9762
County: Kalamazoo

Established in 1991 in MI.
Donors: Galesburg-Augusta United Way; Weisblat Foundation.
Grantmaker type: Operating foundation.
Financial data (yr. ended 06/30/09): Assets, $32,188 (M); gifts received, $5,100; expenditures, $17,244; total giving, $15,501; qualifying distributions, $17,229; giving activities include

$5,551 for 1 grant, and $9,950 for 11 grants to individuals (high: $1,250; low: $250).

Purpose and activities: Scholarship awards to graduates of Galesburg-Augusta High School, Michigan.

Fields of interest: Higher education; Environment, forests.

Type of support: Scholarships—to individuals.

Limitations: Applications accepted. Giving limited to Galesburg, MI.

Publications: Informational brochure.

Application information:

Initial approach: Letter

Deadline(s): None

Officers and Trustees:* Miriam Shannon,* Pres.; Eric Palma,* Secy.; Wanda Hartman,* Treas.; Tom Conor; Al Forrester; Cheryl Fryer; Linda Godde; Julie Howes; Sharon Kraiger; Cheryl Lemmien; Kathy Piper; Jim Schultz.

Number of staff: None.

EIN: 383082334

1503

Lloyd Ganton Auto Museum Foundation, Inc.

7925 Spring Arbor Rd.
Spring Arbor, MI 49283-9759
County: Jackson

Classified as a private operating foundation in 1989 in MI.

Donors: Lloyd G. Ganton; Joyce Ganton; Kevin J. Ganton; Scott Ganton.

Grantmaker type: Operating foundation.

Financial data (yr. ended 06/30/10): Assets, $1,324,643 (M); gifts received, $15,171; expenditures, $31,126; total giving, $0; qualifying distributions, $0.

Officers and Directors:* Lloyd G. Ganton,* Pres.; Troy L. Ganton,* V.P. and Exec. Dir.

EIN: 382837086

1504

Genesis Program, Inc.

c/o Daniel R. Slate
P.O. Box 9
Fremont, MI 49412-0009
County: Newaygo
Application address: c/o Hendon & Slate PC, Attn.: Dorothy Paris, 711 W Main St., Fremont, MI 49412-1414

Established in MI.

Donor: The Cummings Fund.

Grantmaker type: Operating foundation.

Financial data (yr. ended 12/31/09): Assets, $174,321 (M); expenditures, $17,780; total giving, $0; qualifying distributions, $0.

Purpose and activities: Loans that are Interest-free to qualified applicants to assist in the start-up of new business ventures.

Fields of interest: Business/industry.

Limitations: Giving limited to Newaygo, MI, and surrounding counties.

Application information:

Initial approach: Letter

Deadline(s): None

Officer and Trustees:* Andrew M. Cummings,* Pres.; Daniel R. Slate, Secy.-Treas.; Gay Gerber

Cummings; Harrington M. Cummings; Samuel M. Cummings; Michael Flaherty.

EIN: 383305718

1505

Genevieve and Donald Gilmore Foundation

6865 W. Hickory Rd.
Hickory Corners, MI 49060-9788
County: Barry

Classified as a private operating foundation in 1981 in MI.

Donors: William U. Parfet; MPI Research; Cole Gilmore; Off Brothers; Michael J. Welsh; William C. Holland; Patricia Ann Casey; Carol B. Coggan; Donald & Ann Parfet Family Foundation; William D. Johnston.

Grantmaker type: Operating foundation.

Financial data (yr. ended 12/31/09): Assets, $13,523,400 (M); gifts received, $5,992,160; expenditures, $1,308,903; total giving, $0; qualifying distributions, $0.

Fields of interest: Museums (specialized).

Officers and Trustees:* William U. Parfet,* Pres.; Carol B. Coggan, V.P.; Martha B. Vandermolen,* V.P.; Sydney Waldorf,* Secy.; Jay Gudebski, Jr.,* Treas.; Michael J. Spezia, Exec. Dir.; Peter Coggan; Steven H. Maloney; and 8 additional trustees.

Board Members: Sherwood M. Boudeman; Jenn Gudebski; Daniel G. Maloney; Martha G. Parfet; Courtney Vandermolen; Jon G. Vandermolen.

EIN: 386154163

1506

Gleaner Life Insurance Society Scholarship Foundation

5200 W. U.S. Hwy. 223
P.O. Box 1894
Adrian, MI 49221-9461 (517) 263-2244
County: Lenawee
FAX: (517) 265-7745;
E-mail: scholarships@gleanerlife.com; Additional tel.: (800) 992-1894; URL: http://www.gleanerlife.org/PreviewNewsMore.aspx?NewsArticleID=352

Established as a company-sponsored operating foundation in 1992 in MI.

Donors: Gleaner Life Insurance Society; Laura Viers; Charles E. Banner‡; Margaret Banner.

Grantmaker type: Operating foundation.

Financial data (yr. ended 06/30/09): Assets, $725,860 (M); gifts received, $197,590; expenditures, $131,504; total giving, $129,000; qualifying distributions, $131,225; giving activities include $129,000 for 130 grants to individuals (high: $1,000; low: $500).

Purpose and activities: The foundation awards college scholarships to high school seniors or graduates who are members of Gleaner Life Insurance Society.

Fields of interest: Higher education.

Type of support: Scholarships—to individuals.

Limitations: Applications accepted. Giving primarily in IN, MI, NE, and OH.

Publications: Application guidelines; Informational brochure.

Application information: Application form required.

Initial approach: Download application form and mail to foundation

Deadline(s): Dec.1 to Mar. 1

Officers and Directors:* David E. Sutton,* Chair.; Ellsworth L. Stout, Secy-Treas.; Richard J. Bennett; Frank Dick; Dudley L. Dauterman; Terry Garner; Suann A. Hammersmith.

EIN: 383006741

1507

Gratiot Physicians Foundation

121 N. Pine River Rd.
Ithaca, MI 48847-1039
County: Gratiot

Established in 2001 in MI.

Grantmaker type: Operating foundation.

Financial data (yr. ended 12/31/08): Assets, $143,212 (M); gifts received, $812; expenditures, $5,866; total giving, $4,390; qualifying distributions, $4,390; giving activities include $2,390 for 2 grants (high: $2,000; low: $390), and $2,000 for 2 grants to individuals (high: $1,000; low: $1,000).

Purpose and activities: Support for health, including through scholarship awards to residents of Gratiot County who live within the Gratiot Hospital's service area and who have been accepted at a professional school for training in one of the various branches of health care, such as medical or nursing school, podiatry, physical therapy, X-ray or ultrasound technology.

Fields of interest: Medical school/education; Nursing school/education; Public health school/education; Health sciences school/education.

Type of support: Equipment; Scholarships—to individuals.

Limitations: Giving limited to the Gratiot County, MI, area.

Application information: Application form required.

Deadline(s): None

Officers: David K. Austin, Pres.; Gregg Stefanek, V.P.; Louis Sando, Secy.; Mike Stack, Treas.

EIN: 383571320

1508

Hall of Fame Dance Foundation, Inc.

3160 Haggerty Rd., Ste. E.
West Bloomfield, MI 48323 (248) 668-8151
County: Oakland
URL: http://www.halloffamedance.com

Established in 2007 in MI.

Donor: The Hall of Fame Dance Challenge, Inc.

Grantmaker type: Operating foundation.

Financial data (yr. ended 12/31/09): Assets, $22 (M); gifts received, $21,500; expenditures, $22,003; total giving, $22,000; qualifying distributions, $22,000; giving activities include $22,000 for 33 grants to individuals (high: $1,000; low: $500).

Application information: Application form required.

Initial approach: Letter of Recommendation

Deadline(s): May 31, 2009

Officers: Kim Fink, Pres.; Neil Fink, V.P.; Jeffrey Fleischman, Secy.; Christine McIsaacs, Treas.

Director: Samantha Shelton.

EIN: 261539440

1509
Rose Hamlin Tennis National Honor Society Scholarship Trust
7677 W. Sharpe Rd.
Fowlerville, MI 48836-8748
County: Livingston
Contact: Ann Glover, Tr.

Classified as a private operating foundation in 1988 in MI.
Grantmaker type: Operating foundation.
Financial data (yr. ended 12/31/09): Assets, $8,429 (M); expenditures, $532; total giving, $500; qualifying distributions, $500; giving activities include $500 for grants to individuals.
Purpose and activities: Scholarship awards to students in the Fowlerville School District who are members of the National Honor Society.
Fields of interest: Higher education.
Type of support: Scholarships—to individuals.
Limitations: Applications accepted. Giving limited to the Fowlerville, MI, area.
Application information: Application form available at Fowlerville High School. Application form required.
Deadline(s): Varies
Trustees: Edward Alverson; Ann Glover.
EIN: 382777453

1510
Hand in Hand Foundation, Inc.
24200 Woodward Ave.
Pleasant Ridge, MI 48069-1144
County: Oakland

Established in 2004 in DE and MI.
Donors: Rex B. Smith; Susan Smith.
Grantmaker type: Operating foundation.
Financial data (yr. ended 11/30/09): Assets, $74,900 (M); gifts received, $6,150; expenditures, $43,920; total giving, $0; qualifying distributions, $43,920.
Officers: Rex B. Smith, Pres.; Susan Smith, Secy.
EIN: 200514227

1511
Luella Hannan Memorial Foundation
(formerly Luella Hannan Memorial Home)
4750 Woodward Ave.
Detroit, MI 48201-1352
County: Wayne
URL: http://www.hannan.org/

Established in 1935 in MI; classified as a private operating foundation in 1997.
Donors: William Hannan†; Luella Hannan†.
Grantmaker type: Operating foundation.
Financial data (yr. ended 12/31/08): Assets, $13,654,930 (M); gifts received, $846; expenditures, $112,939; total giving, $0; qualifying distributions, $0.
Officers and Trustees:* Beverly J. Holman,* Treas.; Timothy Wintermute,* Exec. Dir.
EIN: 381358386

1512
HCC Foundation
2113 N. Birch Dr.
Mears, MI 49436 (616) 928-9120
County: Oceana
Application address: c/o Ned Timmer, 301 Hoover Blvd., Holland, MI 49423, tel.: (616) 928-9120

Establishes in 2002 in MI.
Donor: Ned Timmer.
Grantmaker type: Operating foundation.
Financial data (yr. ended 12/31/09): Assets, $12,553 (M); gifts received, $350,000; expenditures, $356,251; total giving, $355,531; qualifying distributions, $355,531; giving activities include $350,000 for 1 grant, and $5,531 for 3 grants to individuals (high: $4,000; low: $134).
Purpose and activities: Giving primarily to a boys and girls club; support also for education through scholarships to individuals.
Fields of interest: Education; Boys & girls clubs; Human services.
Type of support: General/operating support; Income development; Scholarships—to individuals.
Limitations: Giving limited to Holland, MI.
Application information: Application form not required.
Initial approach: Letter
Deadline(s): None
Trustee: Ned Timmer.
EIN: 061660898

1513
Hillier Scholarship Fund of Evart
142 N. Main St.
Evart, MI 49631-5104 (231) 734-5563
County: Osceola
Contact: Lynn Salinas, Tr.
Application address: P.O. Box 608, Evart, MI 49631-0608

Established in 1996 in MI.
Donor: Hillier Family Foundation.
Grantmaker type: Operating foundation.
Financial data (yr. ended 12/31/09): Assets, $148,679 (M); expenditures, $3,320; total giving, $2,625; qualifying distributions, $2,625; giving activities include $2,625 for grants to individuals.
Purpose and activities: Scholarship awards to graduates from Evart High School, Michigan, attending an accredited undergraduate institution.
Fields of interest: Higher education.
Type of support: Scholarships—to individuals.
Limitations: Applications accepted. Giving limited to residents of Evart, MI.
Application information: Application form required.
Deadline(s): Mar. 15
Trustees: Alan Bengry; Carolyn Curtin; Charles Flachs; Lynn Salinas; Marie Wilkerson.
EIN: 383299844

1514
Historic Warbird Foundation
656 Country Club Dr.
Battle Creek, MI 49015-3651
County: Calhoun

Established in 2004 in MI.
Donor: Timothy J. Brutsche.
Grantmaker type: Operating foundation.

Financial data (yr. ended 12/31/09): Assets, $313,168 (M); gifts received, $143,794; expenditures, $80,220; total giving, $0; qualifying distributions, $0.
Officers: Timothy J. Brutsche, Pres.; Katherine I. Brutsche, V.P.
Director: David M. Mills.
EIN: 201773413

1515
Kenneth & Gwendolyn Hoving Foundation
363 Trinity Ln.
Oak Brook, IL 60523-2565
County: Dupage

Established in 1995.
Donor: Kenneth Hoving.
Grantmaker type: Operating foundation.
Financial data (yr. ended 12/31/09): Assets, $1 (M); gifts received, $70,000; expenditures, $67,000; total giving, $67,000; qualifying distributions, $67,000; giving activities include $67,000 for grants.
Fields of interest: International development; Christian agencies & churches.
International interests: India.
Limitations: Giving primarily in Grand Rapids, MI. No grants to individuals.
Directors: Gwendolyn Hoving; Kenneth Hoving.
EIN: 363993239

1516
Hubbard Memorial Museum Foundation
317 Hanover St.
P.O. Box 463
Concord, MI 49237-9576
County: Jackson

Classified as a private operating foundation in 1992 in MI.
Donor: Bruce Lindsay Co.
Grantmaker type: Operating foundation.
Financial data (yr. ended 12/31/09): Assets, $1,639,734 (M); gifts received, $3,681; expenditures, $67,474; total giving, $0; qualifying distributions, $0.
Officers: Earl Schultz, Chair.; Elizabeth Schultz, Vice-Chair.; Joan Ropp, Secy.; Don Haughey, Treas.
Trustee: John Kinney.
EIN: 656084788

1517
International Centre for Healing and the Law
(also known as The Center for Law and Renewal)
9292 W. KL Ave.
Kalamazoo, MI 49009-5316 (269) 353-0592
County: Kalamazoo
FAX: (269) 372-2163; E-mail: info@lawrenewal.org; URL: http://www.healingandthelaw.org/

Established in 2002 in MI.
Grantmaker type: Operating foundation.
Financial data (yr. ended 07/31/08): Assets, $9,838 (M); expenditures, $266,057; total giving, $0; qualifying distributions, $263,824.
Purpose and activities: The center's mission is to equip law professionals with the knowledge, skills and practices they need to serve clients and communities out of a relationship-centered ethic.

Officers and Trustees:* Michael C. Gergely,* Chair.;
Bonnie Allen, Pres. and C.E.O.; David T. Link, Pres.
Emeritus; Hon. Janine P. Geske; Richard L. Halpert;
Roland Johnson; Angela E. Oh; Hon. William G.
Schma; Bob Seng.
EIN: 611426645

1518
Investment Education Institute
711 W. 13 Mile Rd.
Madison Heights, MI 48071-1806
County: Oakland

Established in 1998 in MI.
Grantmaker type: Operating foundation.
Financial data (yr. ended 09/30/09): Assets,
$11,087 (M); expenditures, $1; total giving, $0;
qualifying distributions, $0.
Directors: Richard A. Holthaus; Donald J.
Houtakker; Kenneth S. Janke, Sr.; Kenneth S.
Janke, Jr.; Robert A. O'Hara; Thomas E. O'Hara;
Lewis A. Rockwell.
EIN: 383162028

1519
Jackson Literary & Art Association
1709 Probert Rd.
Jackson, MI 49203-5357
County: Jackson
Contact: Nan Sparks, Pres.
Application address: 1659 Kibby Rd., Jackson, MI
49203-3828

Classified as a private operating foundation in
1984.
Grantmaker type: Operating foundation.
Financial data (yr. ended 12/31/09): Assets,
$226,270 (M); expenditures, $9,426; total giving,
$8,725; qualifying distributions, $8,725; giving
activities include $8,725 for grants.
Fields of interest: Literature; Arts.
Limitations: Applications accepted. Giving primarily
in the Jackson, MI, area.
Application information:
  Initial approach: Letter
  Deadline(s): None
Officers: Nan Sparks, Pres.; Dorothy Kobs, Secy.;
Joyce Grace, Treas.
Trustees: Mary Lou Blanchard; LeeAnn Kendall;
Helen Greene; Kay Marcoux; Carol Thompson;
Beverly Walters.
EIN: 386089640

1520
Jones Trauma Research Fund
1240 Brenton Ct. S.E.
East Grand Rapids, MI 49506-4036
County: Kent

Established in 2005 in MI.
Donors: Holly K. Hirai; Clifford B. Jones, M.D.;
Medtronic Biologics.
Grantmaker type: Operating foundation.
Financial data (yr. ended 12/31/09): Assets, $0
(M); gifts received, $10,309; expenditures,
$10,996; total giving, $0; qualifying distributions,
$4,421.
Trustees: Holly K. Hirai; Clifford B. Jones, M.D.
EIN: 203649632

1521
The Knowlton Foundation
1655 Yeager St.
Port Huron, MI 48060-2577
County: St. Clair

Established in 1999 in MI.
Donors: Norman F. Knowlton; Agnes Knowlton.
Grantmaker type: Operating foundation.
Financial data (yr. ended 12/31/09): Assets,
$2,130,042 (M); gifts received, $279,720;
expenditures, $96,154; total giving, $0; qualifying
distributions, $0.
Officers and Directors: * Suzanne A. Knowlton,*
Secy.; Judith A. Campbell,* Treas.; Melissa Davis;
Curtis Karl; Agnes J. Knowlton; Charles J. Knowlton;
Norman F. Knowlton.
EIN: 383506105

1522
L & L Educational Foundation
160 McLean Dr.
Romeo, MI 48065-4919 (586) 336-1608
County: Macomb
Contact: Margaret Domenick-Muscat, Pres.
FAX: (586) 336-1635;
E-mail: edfoundation@llproducts.com; URL: http://
foundationcenter.org/grantmaker/landl/

Established in 1987 in MI.
Donors: W. Eugene Lane; Robert M. Ligon; Lane
Texas Partners; Lesle E. Cole; Susan Lane Mulka.
Grantmaker type: Operating foundation.
Financial data (yr. ended 12/31/09): Assets,
$7,023,632 (M); gifts received, $2,150;
expenditures, $344,873; total giving, $321,121;
qualifying distributions, $323,421; giving activities
include $321,121 for 109 grants to individuals
(high: $6,926; low: $251).
Purpose and activities: Scholarships only to
employees of L & L Products, Inc., and their spouses
and children.
Fields of interest: Higher education.
Type of support: Employee-related scholarships.
Limitations: Giving limited to residents of MI.
Application information: Applications available in
Jan. annually. Application form required.
  Deadline(s): Apr. 1
Officers: Margaret Domenick-Muscat, Pres.; Shelly
Lewallen, V.P.; Shelley Semren, V.P.; Susan Deeb,
Secy.; Kara Wawrowski, Treas.
Trustees: Lesle E. Cole; Claude Z. Demby; Robert
M. Ligon; Susan Lane Mulka.
EIN: 382785121

1523
La Unidad Foundation
26300 Telegraph Rd., 2nd Fl.
Southfield, MI 48034-2436
County: Oakland

Established in 2005 in MI.
Grantmaker type: Operating foundation.
Financial data (yr. ended 12/31/09): Assets,
$120,199 (M); gifts received, $20,000;
expenditures, $6,467; total giving, $5,000;
qualifying distributions, $5,000; giving activities
include $5,000 for grants.
Officer: Mohamad Bazzi, Pres.
EIN: 202650247

1524
Lahser Interspecies Research Foundation
3770 Lahser Rd.
Bloomfield, MI 48302-1535 (248) 593-9419
County: Oakland
Contact: Scott B. Karlene

Established in 2003 in MI.
Donors: Kevin J. Gaffney, M.D.; Scott B. Karlene,
M.D.
Grantmaker type: Operating foundation.
Financial data (yr. ended 12/31/09): Assets,
$1,120,118 (L); gifts received, $687,500;
expenditures, $228,272; total giving, $0; qualifying
distributions, $228,063.
Purpose and activities: The foundation provides
grants to research and elucidate the nature of
presumed infectious gastrointestinal diseases in
birds, specifically proventricular dilation disease
(PDD) and the relationship of these diseases to
human gastrointestinal disease.
Limitations: Applications accepted. Giving primarily
in MI.
Application information:
  Initial approach: letter
  Deadline(s): Dec. 31
Officers: Scott B. Karlene, M.D., Pres. and Secy.;
Kevin J. Gaffney, M.D., V.P. and Treas.
EIN: 384542343

1525
Lester and Brown Foundation
406 S. Main St.
Marine City, MI 48039-1628
County: St. Clair

Established in 2007 in MI.
Donor: E. Janet Brown.
Grantmaker type: Operating foundation.
Financial data (yr. ended 12/31/09): Assets,
$537,179 (M); expenditures, $56,932; total giving,
$0; qualifying distributions, $0.
Officers: E. Janet Brown, Pres.; William M. Brown,
Secy.; Sandra L. Brown, Treas.
EIN: 270128982

1526
Let These Animals Live, Inc.
c/o Gerald J. Jenkins
13990 Fairmont Dr.
Rapid City, MI 49676-9345
County: Kalkaska

Established in MI.
Grantmaker type: Operating foundation.
Financial data (yr. ended 05/31/09): Assets,
$228,551 (M); gifts received, $20,319;
expenditures, $15,631; total giving, $0; qualifying
distributions, $0.
Officers: Gerald J. Jenkins, Pres.; Mary Ann
Bingham, Secy.-Treas.
Directors: Rosemary Dykema; Daniel Jenkins;
Elizabeth Jenkins; Charles Lindholm; Lorlie White.
EIN: 383301656

1527
Lowell Area Housing, Inc.
P.O. Box 186
Lowell, MI 49331-0186
County: Kent

Classified as a private operating foundation in 1991 in MI.
Grantmaker type: Operating foundation.
Financial data (yr. ended 12/31/09): Assets, $1 (M); gifts received, $67,909; expenditures, $379,924; total giving, $0; qualifying distributions, $0.
Officers: Ray Zandstra, Pres.; Leo Phaller, V.P.; Jody Haybarker, Secy.
Trustees: Richard Bieri; Rev. Glenn Marks; John Timpson.
EIN: 381945437

1528
Mackenzie's Animal Sanctuary, Inc.
(formerly Mackensie's Shelter, Inc.)
8665 Thompson Rd.
Lake Odessa, MI 48849-9788
County: Ionia
URL: http://www.mackenzies.info/

Established in 2000 in MI.
Donor: James D. Azzar Foundation.
Grantmaker type: Operating foundation.
Financial data (yr. ended 12/31/09): Assets, $152,504 (M); gifts received, $937,206; expenditures, $848,747; total giving, $0; qualifying distributions, $0.
Purpose and activities: Giving for the adoption of abused, abandoned and neglected dogs.
Directors: James A. Azzar; James D. Azzar; L. Susan Azzar; Erik Bauer; Jennifer Bauer.
EIN: 383533253

1529
Stephen A. Marks Foundation, Inc.
1390 Bagley St.
Alpena, MI 49707
County: Alpena

Established in 2007 in MI.
Donor: The Marks Foundation.
Grantmaker type: Operating foundation.
Financial data (yr. ended 12/31/08): Assets, $1,343,176 (M); expenditures, $124,311; total giving, $116,700; qualifying distributions, $116,700; giving activities include $116,700 for grants.
Application information:
Deadline(s): None
Officer: Stephen A. Marks, Pres.
EIN: 261289704

1530
McDonald's Historic Automobile
Foundation
3126 Davenport Ave.
Saginaw, MI 48602-3647
County: Saginaw
Contact: Thomas W. McDonald Sr., Pres.
Application address: 1520 S. Thomas Rd., Saginaw, MI 48609-9701

Established in MI.
Donors: Thomas W. McDonald, Sr.; Ruth B. McDonald; Thomas W. McDonald, Jr.
Grantmaker type: Operating foundation.
Financial data (yr. ended 12/31/09): Assets, $562,897 (M); gifts received, $9,000; expenditures, $151,703; total giving, $40,850;

qualifying distributions, $40,850; giving activities include $40,850 for grants.
Fields of interest: Historical activities; Human services; Community/economic development.
Limitations: Giving primarily in Saginaw, MI.
Application information:
Initial approach: Letter
Deadline(s): None
Officers: Thomas W. McDonald, Sr., Pres.; Ruth B. McDonald, V.P.; Thomas W. McDonald, Jr., Secy.; William McDonald, Treas.
EIN: 382489799

1531
The Mark C. and Carolyn A. McQuiggan
Foundation
29653 Club House Ln.
Farmington Hills, MI 48334-2015
County: Oakland

Established in 1998 in MI.
Donors: Mark C. McQuiggan; Carolyn A. McQuiggan.
Grantmaker type: Operating foundation.
Financial data (yr. ended 06/30/09): Assets, $305 (M); gifts received, $800; expenditures, $725; total giving, $725; qualifying distributions, $725; giving activities include $725 for grants.
Fields of interest: Education.
Limitations: Giving primarily to MI.
Directors: Carolyn A. McQuiggan; Mark C. McQuiggan.
EIN: 383435181

1532
Memorial Nature Preserve
124 W. Allegan St., Ste. 1000
Lansing, MI 48933-1716
County: Ingham

Established in 1979; classified as a private operating foundation in 1985.
Grantmaker type: Operating foundation.
Financial data (yr. ended 12/31/09): Assets, $259,039 (M); gifts received, $7,895; expenditures, $6,152; total giving, $0; qualifying distributions, $0.
Officers and Directors:* Garry McKeen,* Pres.; Joan Ryan,* V.P.; Jane Thompson,* Secy.; J. Paul Thompson, Jr.,* Treas.; Marilyn Johnson; Ron Kuykendall; Bruce Turnbull.
EIN: 382221489

1533
Michigan Railroad Historic Preservation
Foundation, Inc.
1225 10th St.
Port Huron, MI 48060-5205
County: St. Clair

Established in MI. Classified as a private operating foundation in 1983.
Donor: Alexander G. Ruthven II, M.D.
Grantmaker type: Operating foundation.
Financial data (yr. ended 06/30/10): Assets, $367,426 (M); gifts received, $20; expenditures, $40; total giving, $0; qualifying distributions, $0.
Officer: Alexander G. Ruthven II, M.D., Pres.
EIN: 382477844

1534
Michigan Wildlife & Forest Preservation
Foundation
1939 Briarcliff Blvd.
Owosso, MI 48867-9084
County: Shiawassee

Classified as a private operating foundation in 1992.
Donors: Fred J. Van Alstine; Kathleen Van Alstine.
Grantmaker type: Operating foundation.
Financial data (yr. ended 12/31/09): Assets, $361,743 (M); gifts received, $15,500; expenditures, $15,880; total giving, $0; qualifying distributions, $0.
Officers: Fred J. Van Alstine, Pres.; Kathleen Van Alstine, Secy.
Director: Heather Dale.
EIN: 383005117

1535
Mid-Michigan Society for Animal
Protection
1520 Berkley Dr.
Holt, MI 48842-1853
County: Ingham

Established in MI.
Grantmaker type: Operating foundation.
Financial data (yr. ended 03/31/07): Assets, $1,365 (M); gifts received, $14,882; expenditures, $16,685; total giving, $0; qualifying distributions, $16,685; giving activities include $16,595 for foundation-administered programs.
Officer: Charles Ogar, Pres.
Director: Nancy Bischof; Lisa Diehl; Scott Harris.
EIN: 382920947

1536
Moholy-Nagy Foundation, Inc.
1204 Gardner Ave.
Ann Arbor, MI 48104-4321 (734) 996-4469
County: Washtenaw
Contact: Hattula Moholy-Nagy, Treas.
URL: http://www.moholy-nagy.org

Established in 2003 in IL.
Donor: Hattula Maholy-Nagy.
Grantmaker type: Operating foundation.
Financial data (yr. ended 12/31/09): Assets, $824,814 (M); gifts received, $21,247; expenditures, $58,387; total giving, $15,000; qualifying distributions, $15,000; giving activities include $15,000 for grants.
Officers: Andreas L. Hug, Pres.; Daniel C. Hug, Secy.; Hattula Moholy-Nagy, Treas.
EIN: 770612896

1537
Murff Manor, Inc.
1574 Cadillac Blvd.
P.O. Box 32539
Detroit, MI 48214-3108
County: Wayne

Established in MI.
Grantmaker type: Operating foundation.
Financial data (yr. ended 12/31/08): Assets, $32,153 (M); expenditures, $288,622; total giving,

$253,866; qualifying distributions, $253,866; giving activities include $253,866 for grants.
Officers: James Talbert, Pres.; Errol Talbert, V.P.
EIN: 382838860

1538
Nakadar Foundation
3707 Durham Ct.
Bloomfield Hills, MI   48302-1224
(248) 478-1100
County: Oakland
Contact: Abdul Rahman Nakadar, Pres.

Donor: Abdul Rahman Nakadar.
Grantmaker type: Operating foundation.
Financial data (yr. ended 12/31/09): Assets, $487,760 (M); expenditures, $46,957; total giving, $35,550; qualifying distributions, $35,550; giving activities include $35,550 for grants.
Purpose and activities: Support for medical research and to organizations promoting medical education for Muslim minorities.
Fields of interest: Medical school/education; Health care; Medical research; Islam.
Limitations: Giving primarily in MI. No grants to individuals.
Application information: Application form not required.
Deadline(s): None
Officers: Abdul Rahman Nakadar, Pres.; Najma Nakadar, V.P.
EIN: 382541935
Selected grants: The following grants were reported in 2006.
$500 to Islamic Relief USA, Buena Park, CA.
$200 to Helping Hand for Relief and Development, Detroit, MI.
$150 to Human Development Foundation, Encinitas, CA.
$50 to American Civil Liberties Union, New York, NY.
$50 to Doctors Without Borders USA, New York, NY.
$35 to Carter Center, Atlanta, GA.
$25 to UNICEF.
$20 to National Federation of the Blind of Michigan, Lansing, MI.
$20 to National Foundation for Cancer Research, Bethesda, MD.

1539
Neff Family Foundation
3890 E. 79th St.
Indianapolis, IN   46240-3457   (317) 577-3733
County: Marion
Contact: Virginia M. Neff, Secy.

Established in 1997 in IN.
Donors: Neff Engineering Co., Inc.; Harry M. Neff.
Grantmaker type: Operating foundation.
Financial data (yr. ended 12/31/09): Assets, $205,048 (M); gifts received, $8,000; expenditures, $17,500; total giving, $15,000; qualifying distributions, $15,000; giving activities include $15,000 for 19 grants (high: $2,800; low: $250).
Purpose and activities: The foundation supports zoos and camps and organizations involved with education, health, human services, and disadvantaged youth.
Fields of interest: Secondary school/education; Education; Zoos/zoological societies; Hospitals (general); Health care, patient services; Health care;

Recreation, camps; Developmentally disabled, centers & services; Human services; Youth; Economically disadvantaged.
Type of support: General/operating support.
Limitations: Applications accepted. Giving primarily in areas of company operations in MI and WI, with emphasis on Indianapolis, IN.
Application information: Application form required.
Initial approach: Contact foundation for application form
Deadline(s): Sept. 30
Officers: Betty M. Neff, Pres.; Elizabeth W. Neff, V.P.; Julia D. Neff, V.P.; Virginia M. Neff, Secy.; I. Marie Neff, Treas.
EIN: 352008774

1540
Nehru-Lincoln Human Services
c/o Jitendra M. Mishra
1400 Michigan St. N.E.
Grand Rapids, MI   49503-2032   (616) 454-5878
County: Kent

Established in 1991 in MI.
Donors: Jitendra M. Mishra; Mithilesh Mishra.
Grantmaker type: Operating foundation.
Financial data (yr. ended 12/31/09): Assets, $5,000 (M); gifts received, $5,287; expenditures, $6,694; total giving, $0; qualifying distributions, $0.
Officers: Jitendra M. Mishra, Pres.; Mithilesh Mishra, V.P.
EIN: 382968976

1541
Sara L. Nieman Scholarship Fund
c/o Argus Corp.
12540 Beech Daly
Redford, MI   48239-2469
County: Wayne
Contact: Sandra K. Nieman, Pres.
Application address: 1012 Kensington, Grosse Pointe Park, MI 48230-1403, tel.: (313) 937-2900

Established in 2000 in MI.
Donor: Divine Child High School Scholarship Fund.
Grantmaker type: Operating foundation.
Financial data (yr. ended 12/31/09): Assets, $34,361 (M); expenditures, $4,000; total giving, $4,000; qualifying distributions, $4,000; giving activities include $4,000 for grants to individuals.
Fields of interest: Higher education.
Type of support: Scholarships—to individuals.
Limitations: Applications accepted. Giving primarily to residents of MI.
Application information: Application form required.
Initial approach: Letter or telephone
Deadline(s): May 1
Officers: Sandra K. Nieman, Pres. and Treas.; Fred J. Ransford, Secy.
EIN: 383570934

1542
Northern Michigan Foundation
P.O. Box 932
Elk Rapids, MI   49629-0932   (734) 741-5858
County: Antrim
Contact: Charles S. McDowell, V.P.

Established in 1996 in MI.
Donor: Stephen L. Ranzini.

Grantmaker type: Operating foundation.
Financial data (yr. ended 12/31/09): Assets, $931,070 (M); gifts received, $17,147; expenditures, $148,895; total giving, $0; qualifying distributions, $0.
Purpose and activities: The foundation makes loans to businesses in economically distressed counties in the eastern upper and northern lower peninsula of Michigan. Applicants to be considered for loan purposes must have been denied credit by traditional lending institutions such as commercial banks and credit unions.
Fields of interest: Community development, business promotion; Community development, small businesses.
Type of support: Program-related investments/ loans.
Limitations: Applications accepted. Giving limited to MI.
Application information: Application form required.
Initial approach: Letter
Deadline(s): None
Officers: Stephen L. Ranzini, Pres. and Treas.; Robert P. Kozak, V.P.; Charles S. McDowell, V.P.
Directors: Andrew Johnson; Stuart Merillat; Sharon Teeple; Mary L. Trucks; James Trumbull.
EIN: 383136089

1543
The David O'Hare Foundation, Inc.
2701 Blackberry Ln. N.E.
Grand Rapids, MI   49525-9760   (616) 363-1441
County: Kent
Contact: Maria O'Hare, Exec. Dir.

Established in 1997 in MI.
Donors: Patrick O'Hare; Maria O'Hare.
Grantmaker type: Operating foundation.
Financial data (yr. ended 12/31/09): Assets, $39,831 (M); gifts received, $1,200; expenditures, $2,040; total giving, $1,500; qualifying distributions, $1,500; giving activities include $1,500 for grants.
Purpose and activities: Support for health and other services for visually impaired children and their caregivers.
Fields of interest: Hospitals (specialty); Children/ youth, services; Blind/visually impaired.
Limitations: Giving primarily in Grand Rapids, MI.
Application information:
Initial approach: Letter or telephone
Deadline(s): None
Officers: Patrick O'Hare, Treas.; Maria O'Hare, Exec. Dir.
Director: Dr. Patrick Droste.
EIN: 383338582

1544
The O'Neill Foundation
30801 Barrington Ave., Ste. 125
Madison Heights, MI   48071-5105
(248) 524-4119
County: Oakland
Contact: John O'Neill, Pres.

Established in 2003 in MI.
Donors: John O'Neill; Madeline S. O'Neill.
Grantmaker type: Operating foundation.
Financial data (yr. ended 12/31/09): Assets, $535,859 (M); expenditures, $48,181; total giving,

$25,475; qualifying distributions, $25,475; giving activities include $25,475 for grants.
Fields of interest: Theological school/education; Hospitals (specialty); Human services; Catholic agencies & churches; Children/youth; Homeless.
Type of support: General/operating support.
Limitations: Applications accepted. Giving primarily in MI. No grants to individuals.
Application information:
Initial approach: Letter
Deadline(s): None
Officers: John O'Neill, Pres.; Madeline S. O'Neill, Secy.
EIN: 223887218

1545
Ohana Research Foundation
P.O. Box 108
Wallace, MI 49893-0108
County: Menominee

Established in IL, FL, and MI.
Donor: Alfred M. Tenny.
Grantmaker type: Operating foundation.
Financial data (yr. ended 12/31/09): Assets, $1,645,542 (M); expenditures, $178,729; total giving, $0; qualifying distributions, $0.
Officers and Directors:* Alfred M. Tenny,* Pres.; Karen S. Tenny,* V.P. and Exec. Dir.; Dorothy Tolliver.
EIN: 943240747

1546
OneSight Research Foundation
(formerly Pearle Vision Foundation, Inc.)
2465 Joe Field Rd.
Dallas, TX 75229-3402 (972) 277-6191
County: Dallas
Contact: Trina Parasiliti, Secy.
FAX: (972) 277-6422; E-mail: tparasil@onesight.org; URL: http://www.onesight.org

Established as a company-sponsored operating foundation in 1986 in CA.
Donors: Pearle Vision, Inc.; Cole National Foundation; Luxottica Retail; Lenscrafters, Inc.
Grantmaker type: Operating foundation.
Financial data (yr. ended 12/31/09): Assets, $1,189,616 (M); gifts received, $260,454; expenditures, $322,472; total giving, $256,306; qualifying distributions, $313,379; giving activities include $236,286 for 12 grants (high: $30,000; low: $6,000), and $20,000 for grants to individuals.
Purpose and activities: The foundation supports research projects designed to find better treatments and cures for vision threatening diseases and disorders with a focus on diabetic and pediatric eye diseases; and awards scholarships to optometry students through the Dr. Stanley Pearle Scholarship Fund.
Fields of interest: Medical school/education; Eye diseases; Eye research; Diabetes research.
Type of support: Research; Scholarships—to individuals.
Limitations: Applications accepted. Giving in CA, HI, IL, MI, MT, NY, OH, PR, and VA, and in Brazil, Canada, Chile, Dominican Republic, Ecuador, El Salvador, Guatemala, Honduras, India, Mexico, Nicaragua, Panama, Paraguay, South Africa, and Thailand; block grants awarded on a national basis

in U.S. No grants for endowments or general operating support.
Publications: Application guidelines.
Application information: Only 2nd, 3rd and 4th year students eligible for Optometry Scholarships. Application form required.
Initial approach: Download application form and mail to foundation
Copies of proposal: 1
Deadline(s): Postmarked by Dec. 31 and June 30 for Block grants; Apr. 15 for Dr. Stanley Pearle Scholarship Fund
Board meeting date(s): Feb. and Aug.
Final notification: Mid-Mar. and mid-Sept.; June 15 for Dr. Stanley Pearle Scholarship Fund
Officers and Directors:* Greg Hare,* Chair.; Mark Jacquot, OD*, V.P.; Trina Parasiliti, Secy.; Kevin Boyle, Treas.; Stanley C. Pearle, OD, Exec. Dir.; Tami Hannaman, OD; Denver Kramer; Seth McLaughlin; Mike Mendoza, OD; Joe Neville.
Number of staff: 1 part-time professional.
EIN: 752173714
Selected grants: The following grants were reported in 2008.
$50,000 to Juvenile Diabetes Research Foundation International, Dallas, TX. For Pro-survival Retinal Insulin Reception Signaling in Type I Diabetes research at the Pennsylvania College of Medicine.
$47,000 to University of Texas Foundation, Department of Ophthamology, San Antonio, TX. To purchase a confocal microscope to manage patients with corneal ulcers, to educate optometry students, and for research projects.
$25,000 to American Diabetes Association, Alexandria, VA. For Doctor Yuguang Shi's research on The Role of Inflammatory Lipids in Development of Diabetic Retinopathy.
$25,000 to Duke University Medical Center, Department of Ophthalmology, Durham, NC. To support the study, Defining the Role of Ran-binding Protein-2 in Phenotypes Linked to Diabetic Retinopathy.
$24,875 to University of Illinois at Chicago, Chicago, IL. For research to develop a new therapeutic approach to reduce/prevent hypoxia stress in the diabetic retina, thereby preventing the development of retinopathy.
$20,000 to Neurological Health International, Montecito, CA. For study to develop cost-effective compound to prevent glaucoma.
$20,000 to Western University of Health Sciences, Pomona, CA. To purchase equipment for the pediatric vision therapy room to use in the education of the optometric students.
$15,000 to Carnegie Institution of Washington, Embryology Department, Washington, DC. For research aimed at identifying the genes that are mutated in retinoblastoma so that better therapies can be developed.
$12,000 to Saint Jude Childrens Research Hospital, Memphis, TN. For Doctor Michael Dyer's continued research on Retinoblastoma.
$10,000 to University of Chicago Hospitals, Department of Ophthalmology, Chicago, IL. For project, Genomic and Genetic Studies of Diabetic Retinopathy.

1547
Pardee Cancer Treatment Fund of Bay County
P.O. Box 541
Bay City, MI 48707-0541 (989) 891-8815
County: Bay
Contact: Vicki Place, Mgr.

Classified as a private operating foundation in 1991.
Donor: Elsa U. Pardee Foundation.
Grantmaker type: Operating foundation.
Financial data (yr. ended 09/30/10): Assets, $1 (M); gifts received, $179,764; expenditures, $135,060; total giving, $118,503; qualifying distributions, $118,503; giving activities include $118,503 for grants to individuals.
Purpose and activities: Financial assistance provided to help pay medical bills of cancer patients who are residents of Bay County, Michigan.
Fields of interest: Cancer.
Type of support: Grants to individuals.
Limitations: Applications accepted. Giving limited to residents of Bay County, MI.
Publications: Annual report.
Application information: Application form required.
Initial approach: Letter
Deadline(s): None
Board meeting date(s): Varies
Officers: Dominic Monastiere, Pres.; Vicki Place, Mgr.
Directors: David Foster; Elizabeth Gresch; George R. Heron; Walter L. Howland; Gay McGee; Robert Sarow; Richard Steele; Andreas Teich.
Number of staff: 1 part-time professional.
EIN: 382877951

1548
Pardee Cancer Treatment Fund of Gratiot County
c/o Gratiot Community Hospital
315 E. Warwick Dr., Ste. C
Alma, MI 48801-1014 (989) 463-9319
County: Gratiot
Contact: Lala Threloff

Donor: Elsa U. Pardee Foundation.
Grantmaker type: Operating foundation.
Financial data (yr. ended 09/30/10): Assets, $1 (M); gifts received, $214,989; expenditures, $132,657; total giving, $114,932; qualifying distributions, $114,932; giving activities include $114,932 for grants.
Fields of interest: Hospitals (general); Cancer; Health organizations; Medical research.
Limitations: Giving primarily in Gratiot County, MI.
Application information:
Deadline(s): None
Officers: Kathleen Crumbaugh, Chair.; Chuck Fortino, Vice-Chair.; Janet Sherwood, Secy.; Vicki Root, Treas.; Lala Threloff, Client Coord.
Directors: Nancy Fenn; James Hall; Becky Hirschman; Roger Keck; Mick Koutz; Don Pavlik; Jamey Seals; Bernard Siler; Brad Vibber; Robin Whitmore.
EIN: 383532130

1549
Park West Charitable Foundation
29469 Northwestern Hwy.
Southfield, MI 48034-1026 (800) 521-9654
County: Oakland
Contact: Albert Scaglione, Pres.
FAX: (248) 799-7225;
E-mail: info@parkwestfoundation.com; Additional application address: 101 W. Big Beaver Rd., Ste. 1000, Troy, MI 48084-5280, tel.: (248) 457-7204; URL: http://www.parkwestfoundation.com

Established in MI.
Donor: Albert Scaglione.
Grantmaker type: Operating foundation.
Financial data (yr. ended 12/31/09): Assets, $1,353,513 (M); gifts received, $6,590; expenditures, $112,700; total giving, $94,263; qualifying distributions, $94,263; giving activities include $94,263 for grants.
Purpose and activities: Giving to provide a range of services for children and families in the form of foster care, family preservation, family life education, counseling, teen parent services, residential placement and adoption.
Fields of interest: Children/youth, services; Family services; Women, centers/services.
Limitations: Applications accepted. Giving primarily in MI.
Application information: Application form available on foundation web site. Application form required.
 Initial approach: Letter or telephone
 Deadline(s): 6 to 8 weeks prior to need
Officer: Albert Scaglione, Pres.
EIN: 205917008

1550
The Willard G. & Jessie M. Pierce Foundation
701 W. Cloverdale Rd.
Hastings, MI 49058-8360 (269) 721-4470
County: Barry
Contact: Michelle Skedgell, Secy.

Established in 1989 in MI.
Donors: Willard G. Pierce†; Jessie M. Pierce†; Flexfab Horizons International.
Grantmaker type: Operating foundation.
Financial data (yr. ended 12/31/09): Assets, $27,533,795 (M); gifts received, $69,976; expenditures, $1,315,037; total giving, $22,045; qualifying distributions, $22,045; giving activities include $22,045 for grants.
Purpose and activities: Giving to programs that improve the quality of life for residents in Barry County, Michigan; special consideration for programs of environmental education.
Fields of interest: Elementary/secondary education; Environmental education.
Type of support: General/operating support; Capital campaigns; Endowments; Program development.
Limitations: Applications accepted. Giving limited to Barry County, MI. No support for No support generally for health care institutions or programs. No grants to individuals.
Publications: Application guidelines; Informational brochure; Newsletter.
Application information: Availability of new funding is very limited. Application form required.
 Initial approach: 1-page letter of intent prior to the submittal of a complete grant application.
 Copies of proposal: 1

Deadline(s): Sept. 1
Board meeting date(s): Oct.
Final notification: Dec.
Officers and Trustees: Carl Schoessel,* Pres.; Jeff Garrison,* V.P.; Michelle Skedgell,* Secy.; James R. Toburen,* Treas.; Christopher L. Cooley; Willard L. Pierce; Hilary F. Snell.
Number of staff: 6 full-time professional; 1 part-time professional; 2 part-time support.
EIN: 382820095

1551
The Redman Foundation
P.O. Box 630
Indian River, MI 49749-0630
County: Cheboygan

Established in 1999 in MI.
Donors: Robert Redman; Cynthia Redman.
Grantmaker type: Operating foundation.
Financial data (yr. ended 12/31/09): Assets, $1,251,649 (M); gifts received, $2,000; expenditures, $1,705; total giving, $0; qualifying distributions, $0.
Officers: Robert Redman, Pres.; Cynthia Redman, V.P. and Secy.; Thomas Redman, Treas.
EIN: 383517998

1552
The Robey Charitable Trust
(formerly The Edmund W. Robey Charitable Trust)
2986 Meadow Hill Dr.
Clearwater, FL 33761-2825
County: Pinellas
Contact: Leon J. Robey, Tr.
Application address: 9 Brisbane Ct., Savannah, GA 31411-1612, tel.: (912) 598-8202

Established in 1990 in FL. Classified as a private operating foundation in 1995.
Donors: E.W. Robey; Leon J. Robey.
Grantmaker type: Operating foundation.
Financial data (yr. ended 12/31/07): Assets, $213,108 (M); gifts received, $40,000; expenditures, $59,323; total giving, $52,900; qualifying distributions, $59,323; giving activities include $52,900 for 4 grants (high: $18,400; low: $5,000).
Purpose and activities: Giving primarily to educational institutions maintaining Better Effectiveness programs.
Fields of interest: Higher education.
Type of support: Program development; Scholarship funds.
Limitations: Giving primarily in GA, MI, and NH. No grants to individuals.
Application information:
 Initial approach: Letter or telephone
 Deadline(s): None
Trustees: A.M. Robey; E.A. Robey; Edmund W. Robey; Leon J. Robey; D.M. Wroblewski.
EIN: 596961615

1553
Sand Products Foundation
63 Kercheval Ave., Ste. 200
Grosse Pointe Farms, MI 48236-3652
County: Wayne

Established in 2006 in MI.

Grantmaker type: Operating foundation.
Financial data (yr. ended 12/31/08): Assets, $92,191 (M); gifts received, $100; expenditures, $5,427; total giving, $5,159; qualifying distributions, $5,159; giving activities include $5,159 for grants.
Officers: Max B. McKee, Pres.; Gregory A. Canestraight, V.P.; Patrick J. McKee, V.P.; Kathleen Gast, Secy.; Thomas A. Burton, Treas.
EIN: 204819901

1554
The A. Scott Foundation
(formerly The Ascott Foundation)
127 Adam St.
Ann Arbor, MI 48104-2901
County: Washtenaw

Established in 2006 in MI.
Donor: Alexander Crawford.
Grantmaker type: Operating foundation.
Financial data (yr. ended 06/30/09): Assets, $15,419 (M); gifts received, $148,700; expenditures, $168,611; total giving, $16,000; qualifying distributions, $61,848; giving activities include $16,000 for 1 grant.
Officers: Henry Lin, Pres.; M. Abdul Azad, Mgr.
Directors: John Langs; David Larsen; Michael Schmidt; Larry Seiford; Adam Wellman.
EIN: 205282308

1555
Seed the World, Inc.
3318 Windshadow Dr.
Ann Arbor, MI 48105-1068 (734) 213-2148
County: Washtenaw
Contact: Renu S. Malhotra, Pres.

Established in MI.
Grantmaker type: Operating foundation.
Financial data (yr. ended 12/31/09): Assets, $318,484 (M); gifts received, $12,999; expenditures, $17,337; total giving, $10,387; qualifying distributions, $10,387; giving activities include $10,387 for grants.
Purpose and activities: Giving to benefit youth, children and women, and for the educational and cultural advancement of the underprivileged.
Limitations: Applications accepted. Giving on an international basis, primarily in India. No grants to individuals.
Application information:
 Initial approach: Proposal
 Deadline(s): None
Officers: Renu Sophat Malhotra, Pres.; S.K. Malhotra, V.P.
Trustee: Bithika S. Kheterpal, M.D.
EIN: 383333880

1556
The Seligman Medical Institute
1 Towne Sq., Ste. 1913
Southfield, MI 48076-3733
County: Oakland

Established in 2003 in NV.
Grantmaker type: Operating foundation.
Financial data (yr. ended 12/31/09): Assets, $4,526 (M); expenditures, $4,178; total giving, $0; qualifying distributions, $0.

Officers: Scott J. Seligman, Pres.; Tammy Wong, Secy.-Treas.
Trustees: Erwin A. Rubenstein, Esq.; Sandra Seligman.
EIN: 010792167

1557
The SEMP Foundation
(also known as The Southeast Michigan Physicians Foundation)
17000 Hubbard Dr., Ste. 400
Dearborn, MI 48126-4219 (313) 593-3915
County: Wayne
FAX: (313) 593-3810;
E-mail: semp@sempdocs.com

Established in 2004 in MI.
Donors: Southeast Michigan Physicians, P.C.; SEMP Enterprises, LLC.
Grantmaker type: Operating foundation.
Financial data (yr. ended 12/31/09): Assets, $7,790 (M); expenditures, $50,400; total giving, $50,000; qualifying distributions, $50,000; giving activities include $50,000 for grants.
Fields of interest: Higher education, university; Health care.
Limitations: Giving primarily in Dearborn, MI. No grants to individuals.
Application information: Application form not required.
  Initial approach: Letter
  Deadline(s): None
Officers and Directors:* Robert C. Schwyn, M.D.*, Pres.; Steven Pickard, M.D.*, V.P.; Chilakapati Kumer, M.D.*, Treas.; Sunil Bhatia, M.D.; Sanganur V. Mahadevan; Thomas S. Siegel, M.D.
EIN: 200747612
Selected grants: The following grants were reported in 2007.
$122,500 to Oakwood Healthcare, Dearborn, MI.
$10,000 to Alternatives for Girls, Detroit, MI.
$10,000 to University of Michigan, Dearborn, MI.
$1,250 to Wayne County Medical Society Foundation, Detroit, MI.

1558
Share With The World Foundation
1417 Joliet Pl.
Detroit, MI 48207-2802
County: Wayne

Established in 1997 in MI.
Grantmaker type: Operating foundation.
Financial data (yr. ended 12/31/09): Assets, $4,573 (M); gifts received, $5,176; expenditures, $985; total giving, $965; qualifying distributions, $965; giving activities include $965 for grants.
Fields of interest: Human services.
Type of support: General/operating support.
Limitations: Giving primarily in India.
Officers: Kanji Khatana, Pres.; Shanta Khatana, Secy.
Trustees: Dinesh Mehta; Kirit Pandya; Marcella Silva; Yvan Silva; Nalin Vaidya.
EIN: 383277120

1559
Drs. Enrico and Esther Sobong Fundation
1442 Middlebrook Ave. S.E.
Grand Rapids, MI 49546-9724
County: Kent

Established in 2001 in MI.
Grantmaker type: Operating foundation.
Financial data (yr. ended 12/31/09): Assets, $71,851 (M); expenditures, $36,431; total giving, $35,450; qualifying distributions, $35,450; giving activities include $35,450 for grants.
Fields of interest: Education; Christian agencies & churches.
Limitations: Giving primarily in MI.
Officers: Enrico Sobong, Pres.; Esther Sobong, V.P. and Secy.-Treas.
EIN: 383552149

1560
Society of the Brethren
P.O. Box 472
Leslie, MI 49251-0472
County: Ingham

Established in 2002 in MI.
Donor: Diane Detore.
Grantmaker type: Operating foundation.
Financial data (yr. ended 12/31/09): Assets, $10 (M); gifts received, $11,457; expenditures, $11,536; total giving, $6,641; qualifying distributions, $6,641; giving activities include $6,641 for grants.
Fields of interest: Elementary/secondary education.
Limitations: Giving primarily in Leslie, MI.
Officer: Diane Detore, Mgr.
EIN: 382840350

1561
The Sonkin Family Foundation
121 Island Cove Way
Palm Beach Gardens, FL 33418-5773
County: Palm Beach

Established in 1996 in MI.
Donor: Joel Sonkin Trust.
Grantmaker type: Operating foundation.
Financial data (yr. ended 12/31/09): Assets, $995,864 (M); expenditures, $142,163; total giving, $123,970; qualifying distributions, $123,970; giving activities include $123,970 for grants.
Fields of interest: Museums; Performing arts; Education; Human services; Jewish federated giving programs; Jewish agencies & synagogues.
Limitations: Giving primarily in FL, MI, and NY. No grants to individuals.
Application information: Application form not required.
  Initial approach: Letter
  Deadline(s): None
Officer: Sydelle Sonkin, Pres.
EIN: 383322771

1562
Southwest Michigan Crate and Basket and Veneer Machinery Museum, Inc.
c/o Salvatore P. Monte
P.O. Box 126
Riverside, MI 49084-0126
County: Berrien

Established in 2002 in MI.
Donors: Salvatore P. Monte; Constance J. Monte.
Grantmaker type: Operating foundation.
Financial data (yr. ended 12/31/09): Assets, $350,051 (M); expenditures, $27,261; total giving, $0; qualifying distributions, $0.
Officers: Salvatore P. Monte, Pres.; Bob R. Roberts, Secy.-Treas.
Directors: Jim Behlen; Bob Hatch; Constance J. Monte; Norm Smith.
EIN: 320019445

1563
Stepping Stones Foundation
3475 Belle Chase Way
Lansing, MI 48911-4252
County: Ingham

Established in 2004 in MI.
Donors: Abide Ministries; Dewitt Community Church; Block Imaging International.
Grantmaker type: Operating foundation.
Financial data (yr. ended 12/31/09): Assets, $53,446 (M); gifts received, $46,015; expenditures, $42,674; total giving, $36,596; qualifying distributions, $36,596; giving activities include $36,596 for grants.
Director: Bruce Block.
EIN: 201183305

1564
George Stines Family Foundation
2131 Itsell Rd.
Howell, MI 48843-8808
County: Livingston

Established in 2002 in MI.
Donors: Alfred Stines; Joan Stines.
Grantmaker type: Operating foundation.
Financial data (yr. ended 12/31/09): Assets, $44,395 (M); gifts received, $116,860; expenditures, $139,674; total giving, $0; qualifying distributions, $0.
Officers and Directors:* Alfred V. Stines, D.D.S.*, Pres.; Christopher Stines, D.D.S.*, V.P.; Michelle Stines, D.D.S., Secy.; Emile Charles, M.D.; Paul Henri Talson, M.D.
EIN: 300106874

1565
Lynn Stubberfield Foundation
126 E. Church St.
Adrian, MI 49221-2720
County: Lenawee
Contact: Dan E. Bruggeman, Dir.

Grantmaker type: Operating foundation.
Financial data (yr. ended 12/31/09): Assets, $581,290 (M); expenditures, $35,900; total giving, $27,066; qualifying distributions, $27,066; giving activities include $27,066 for grants.

Fields of interest: Community/economic development.
Type of support: General/operating support.
Limitations: Applications accepted. Giving primarily in Adrian, MI. No grants to individuals.
Application information: Application form not required.
   Deadline(s): None
Director: Dan E. Bruggeman.
EIN: 383571515

1566
The Tabbaa Foundation
16959 Kings Fairway Ln.
Grand Blanc, MI   48439-3504
County: Genesee

Established in 2004 in MI.
Donor: Dr. Abdul Tabbaa.
Grantmaker type: Operating foundation.
Financial data (yr. ended 12/31/09): Assets, $2,089,326 (M); gifts received, $600,000; expenditures, $119,219; total giving, $30,330; qualifying distributions, $30,330; giving activities include $30,330 for grants.
Fields of interest: Human services; Islam.
Type of support: General/operating support.
Limitations: Giving primarily in MI and CA.
Officer: Dr. Abdul Tabbaa, Pres.
EIN: 201097781

1567
The Steve and Elizabeth Tengler
Educational Fund
(also known as S.E.T. Educational Fund)
P.O. Box 36656
Grosse Pointe Farms, MI   48236-0656
County: Wayne
E-mail: contact@setfund.org; *URL:* http://www.setfund.org/

Established in 1999 in MI.
Donors: Steve Tengler; Elizabeth Tengler; Jeff Cornell; Catherine Cornell; Joe Johnston; Susan Johnston.
Grantmaker type: Operating foundation.
Financial data (yr. ended 12/31/09): Assets, $118,687 (M); gifts received, $11,879; expenditures, $5,716; total giving, $5,000; qualifying distributions, $5,000; giving activities include $5,000 for grants to individuals.
Purpose and activities: Scholarship awards to Michigan residents attending public universities in Michigan who are not related to the trustees or a previous scholarship winner.
Fields of interest: Higher education.
Type of support: Scholarships—to individuals.
Limitations: Applications accepted. Giving limited to residents of MI.
Application information: See web site for application guidelines. Application form required.
   Initial approach: Letter
   Deadline(s): June 1
Trustees: Catherine Cornell; Jeffery Cornell; Elizabeth Tengler; Steve Tengler.
EIN: 383432884

1568
Troy Internal Medicine Foundation
4600 Investment Dr., Ste. 300
Troy, MI   48098-6368
County: Oakland

Established in 2001 in MI.
Grantmaker type: Operating foundation.
Financial data (yr. ended 12/31/09): Assets, $5,970 (M); expenditures, $1,014; total giving, $0; qualifying distributions, $0.
Directors: James Henderson; Robert Martel; Mark Wilson.
EIN: 383563184

1569
Lyle and Diane Victor Foundation
6130 Wing Lake Rd.
Bloomfield Hills, MI   48301-1531
County: Oakland

Established in 2000 in MI.
Donor: Lyle D. Victor.
Grantmaker type: Operating foundation.
Financial data (yr. ended 07/31/09): Assets, $15,159 (M); expenditures, $3,535; total giving, $3,509; qualifying distributions, $3,509; giving activities include $3,509 for grants.
Fields of interest: Human services; Jewish agencies & synagogues.
Limitations: Giving primarily in MI.
Application information:
   Initial approach: Letter
   Deadline(s): None
Directors: Diane A. Victor; Lyle D. Victor; Nadine E. Victor; Natalie N. Victor.
EIN: 383497934

1570
Lorna A. Welch Charitable Foundation
P.O. Box 390
Flushing, MI   48433-0390
County: Genesee
Application address: c/o James Wood, 121 E. Main St., Flushing, MI 48433-2023

Established in 2001 in MI.
Donor: James L. Orr.
Grantmaker type: Operating foundation.
Financial data (yr. ended 12/31/09): Assets, $546,260 (M); expenditures, $518; total giving, $25,000; qualifying distributions, $25,000; giving activities include $25,000 for 5 grants to individuals (high: $5,000; low: $5,000).
Fields of interest: Higher education.
Type of support: Scholarships—to individuals.
Limitations: Giving primarily to residents of Flushing, MI.
Trustee: James L. Orr.
EIN: 383553903

1571
Welter Foundation, Inc.
66480 High Meadow Ct.
Edwardsburg, MI   49112-9621
County: Cass
Contact: Jill Richardson

Established in 1997 in IN.
Donors: Edward P. Welter; Wilhelmina J. Welter.

Grantmaker type: Operating foundation.
Financial data (yr. ended 12/31/09): Assets, $5,248,743 (M); expenditures, $372,932; total giving, $230,735; qualifying distributions, $240,735; giving activities include $230,735 for 21 grants (high: $52,500; low: $180).
Fields of interest: Higher education, university; Diabetes research; Crime/violence prevention, child abuse; Human services; Salvation Army; Foundations (community); United Ways and Federated Giving Programs; Christian agencies & churches.
Limitations: Applications accepted. Giving primarily in IN and MI.
Application information: Application form not required.
   Initial approach: Letter
   Deadline(s): None
Officers and Directors:* Edward P. Welter,* Pres.; Cynthia S. Gillard,* Secy.; Wilhelmina J. Welter,* Treas.
EIN: 352023590
Selected grants: The following grants were reported in 2006.
$100,000 to Charlevoix County Community Foundation, East Jordan, MI.
$28,650 to Parent and Child Services, Elkhart, IN.
$20,000 to Ball State University Foundation, Muncie, IN.
$10,000 to United Way of Elkhart County, Elkhart, IN.
$600 to Mental Health America of Vigo County, Terre Haute, IN.

1572
The Gerard I. and Beverly L. Winkle
Foundation
7116 W. Lake Dr.
Lake City, MI   49651-8795
County: Missaukee
Contact: Gerard I. Winkle, Tr.

Established in MI.
Donors: Gerard I. Winkle; Beverly L. Winkle.
Grantmaker type: Operating foundation.
Financial data (yr. ended 12/31/09): Assets, $526,035 (M); gifts received, $2,000; expenditures, $38,502; total giving, $31,500; qualifying distributions, $31,500; giving activities include $31,500 for grants.
Fields of interest: Education; Protestant agencies & churches.
Limitations: Giving primarily in western MI. No grants to individuals.
Application information: Application form not required.
   Initial approach: Letter
   Deadline(s): None
Trustees: Beverly L. Winkle; Gerard I. Winkle.
EIN: 383212032

1573
Orlo H. Wright Scholarship Foundation
10225 Whittaker Rd.
Ypsilanti, MI   48197-8915
County: Washtenaw
Contact: Sharon R. Wenzel, Tr.

Grantmaker type: Operating foundation.
Financial data (yr. ended 03/31/09): Assets, $41,807 (M); gifts received, $1,000; expenditures,

$1,398; total giving, $1,000; qualifying distributions, $42,807; giving activities include $1,000 for 1 grant to an individual.
Purpose and activities: Scholarship awards to graduates of Lincoln High School, Ypsilanti, Michigan.
Fields of interest: Higher education.
Type of support: Scholarships—to individuals.
Limitations: Giving limited to residents of Ypsilanti, MI.
Application information: Application form required.
  Deadline(s): Apr. 10
Trustee: Sharon R. Wenzel.
EIN: 386432958

1574
Wyandotte Public Schools Scholarship Foundation

(also known as WPS Scholarship Foundation)
(formerly Wyandotte Public Schools Foundation)
P.O. Box 412
Wyandotte, MI 48192-0012 (734) 759-6002
County: Wayne
E-mail: wpsf@wyandotte.org; URL: http://www.wyandotte.org/wpsf.html
Application address: c/o Wyandotte Regional High School, Attn.: Principal, 540 Eureka Rd., Wyandotte, MI 48192-5709, tel.: (734) 759-5000

Established in 1989 in MI.
Grantmaker type: Operating foundation.
Financial data (yr. ended 06/30/10): Assets, $509,910 (M); gifts received, $106,719; expenditures, $73,604; total giving, $69,620; qualifying distributions, $69,620; giving activities include $69,620 for grants to individuals.
Purpose and activities: Scholarship awards to graduating seniors at Wyandotte Regional High School, Michigan.
Fields of interest: Higher education.
Type of support: Scholarships—to individuals.
Limitations: Applications accepted. Giving limited to residents of Wyandotte, MI.
Application information: Application form available in high school office. Application form required.
  Deadline(s): Apr. 28
Officers and Directors:* Al Sliwinski,* Pres.; Conrad Kreger,* V.P.; Patricia Cole,* Secy.; Lisa Kaiser,* Treas.; Marcia Aller; James Candela; William Kreger; Christine Mathews; Mary McFarlane; Wallace Merritt; Joe Peterson; Michael Quint; James Sexton; Patrick Sutka; Michael Swiecki; James Wagner.
EIN: 382898957

1575
Virginia Zynda Family Foundation
3416 Corwin Rd.
Williamston, MI 48895-9711
County: Ingham

Established in 2007 in MI.
Donor: Virginia Zynda†.
Grantmaker type: Operating foundation.
Financial data (yr. ended 04/30/08): Assets, $518,062 (M); gifts received, $601,517; expenditures, $49,696; total giving, $31,750; qualifying distributions, $46,254; giving activities include $31,750 for grants.
Fields of interest: Performing arts.
Limitations: Giving primarily in MI. No grants to individuals.
Officers: Stephen R. Zynda, Pres. and Treas.; James K. Zynda, V.P.; David P. Zynda, Secy.
EIN: 260488652

GRANTMAKER NAME INDEX

Numbers following the grantmaker names refer to the entry
sequence numbers in the Descriptive Directory.

41 Washington St. Foundation, MI, 1

A.I.R. Foundation, MI, 1472
Abbott Fund, IL, 933
Abbott Laboratories Fund, IL, see 933
Abbott Memorial Foundation, Frances H., MI, 2
Abele Memorial Fund, Edward & Marie, MI, 3
Aboudane Family Foundation, MI, 4
ACI Foundation, MI, 1181
Adray Foundation, Inc., MI, 5
AEP Corporate Giving Program, OH, 934
African American Endowment Fund, MI, 1182
Akbar Waqf Foundation, Inc., MI, 1473
Akers Foundation, The, IL, 6
Albion Civic Foundation, MI, see 1078
Albion Community Foundation, MI, 1078
Albion-Homer United Way, MI, 1183
Aletheia Foundation, The, MI, 7
Alexandrowski Family Foundation, Inc., MI, 8
Alger Regional Community Foundation, Inc., The, MI, 1079
Allegan County Community Foundation, MI, 1080
Allegan County Foundation, MI, see 1080
Allegan County United Way, MI, 1184
Allen Foundation, Inc., MI, 9
Allen Scholarship Trust, William & Louise, MI, 10
Allendale Community Foundation, MI, 1081
Alliance for Gifted Children, MI, 11
Allmerica Financial Charitable Foundation, Inc., MA, see 999
Allstate Foundation, The, IL, 935
Almansour Family Foundation, MI, 12
Almont-Dickinson Foundation, MI, 13
Alpern Foundation, E. Bryce & Harriet, MD, 14
Alternatives for Children and Families, Inc., MI, 1185
Amber Foundation, Inc., Jerome S., MI, 1474
Ambrosiani Foundation, MI, 15
American Axle & Manufacturing Holdings, Inc. Corporate Giving Program, MI, 936
American Concrete Institute Foundation, MI, see 1181
American Dysautonomia Institute, MI, 1186
American Electric Power Foundation, OH, 937
American Federation of Muslims of Indian Origin, MI, 1187
American Indian College Fund, CO, 1188
American Ramallah Federation Educational and Charitable Fund, MI, 1189
Americana Foundation, MI, 16
Amerisure Mutual Insurance Company Contributions Program, MI, 938
Amway Corporation Contributions Program, MI, 939
Amy Foundation, MI, 17
Anchor Bay Community Foundation, MI, 1082
Andersen Charitable Trust, Harold A. and Marilyn Kay, MI, 18
Andersen Foundation, Frank N., MI, 19
Anderson Charitable Foundation, Andrew F. & Mary H., MI, 20
Anderson Foundation, MI, 22
Anderson Foundation, OH, 21
Anderson Scholarship Trust, Olson L. Anderson and Catherine Bastow, MI, 23
Andrews Foundation, Rhoda Burke, The, MI, 24
Angels in Motion Foundation, MI, 1475
Ann Arbor Area Community Foundation, MI, 1083
Ann Arbor Area Community Foundation, MI, see 1083
Ann Arbor Film Festival, MI, 1190
Annis Foundation, Ted, MI, 25
Applebaum Family Foundation, Eugene, The, MI, 26
Applebaum Family Support Foundation, MI, 1191

Arab Community Center for Economic and Social Services, MI, 1192
Arbor Research Collaborative for Health, MI, 1476
Arcus Foundation, MI, 27
Arden Foundation Trust, Richard and Mary, MI, 28
Arjuna Institute, MI, 1477
Armstrong Educational Corporation, Edmund, MI, 29
Armstrong Foundation, Edmund, MI, see 29
Arnold Family Foundation, The, MI, 30
Arts & Industry Council, MI, see 1424
Arts Council of Greater Grand Rapids, Inc., MI, 1193
Arts Council of Greater Kalamazoo, MI, 1194
Arts Midwest, MN, 1195
ArtServe Michigan, MI, 1196
ArvinMeritor, Inc. Trust, MI, see 1030
Ascott Foundation, The, MI, see 1554
Ash Foundation, Stanley and Blanche, MI, 31
Asthma & Allergy Foundation of America - Michigan Chapter, MI, 1197
Attanasio Charitable Trust, Raymond V., MI, 32
AtWater Foundation, MI, 33
Avondale Foundation, MI, 1198
Aye-You Charitable Foundation, Inc., MI, see 1473
Ayrshire Foundation, The, CA, 34

Baiardi Family Foundation, Inc., MI, 35
Baker Foundation, Howard, The, MI, 36
Baker U.S.-Japan Study Foundation, MI, 37
Baldwin Foundation, MI, 38
Balk Foundation, James & Shirley, MI, 39
Ball Foundation, Inc., Edmund F. and Virginia B., IN, 40
Baraga County Community Foundation, MI, 1084
Baraga-Houghton-Keweenaw Community Action Agency, Inc., MI, 1199
Bardha Foundation, Inc., Ekrem, MI, 1478
Bardsley Charities, MI, 41
Barnes Memorial Foundation, J. Spencer, The, MI, 42
Barr Foundation, Shelley & Terry, MI, 43
Barros Research Foundation, MI, 1479
Barry Community Foundation, MI, 1085
Barstow Foundation, The, MI, 44
Barth Charitable Foundation, Charles F. and Adeline L., MI, 45
Barton-Malow Company Foundation, MI, 940
Bartsch Memorial Bank Trust, Ruth, DE, see 46
Bartsch Memorial Trust, DE, 46
Basch Family Foundation, MI, 47
Bashur Foundation, Barry, MI, 48
Basilica of St. Adalbert Foundation, MI, 49
Bates Foundation, The, MI, 50
Battier Family Foundation, The, TX, 1200
Battle Creek Community Foundation, MI, 1086
Battle Creek Foundation, Greater, MI, see 1086
Batts Foundation, The, MI, 941
Bauervic Foundation, Inc., Charles M., MI, 51
Bauervic Foundation, Peggy, MI, 52
Bauervic-Carroll Foundation, MI, see 52
Bauervic-Paisley Foundation, MI, 53
Baughey Foundation, Donald and Ethel, MI, 1480
Baxter Honorary Scholarship, Grayce David, MI, 54
Bay Area Community Foundation, MI, 1087
Bay Harbor Foundation, The, MI, 1088
Beal Scholarship Foundation, Bernard H., MI, 55
Beals Family Foundation, Joseph & Mari, MI, 56
Beauchamp Charitable Trust, Joseph E., WI, 57
Beck Foundation, Edgar and Marion, MI, 1201

Beckwith Constitutional Liberties Fund, Gerald, The, MI, 1202
Bedford Community Foundation, MI, 1089
Bedford Foundation, MI, see 1089
Bees School Foundation, John & Nesbeth, MI, 58
Bell Charitable Trust, Gloria Wille Bell and Carlos R., The, VA, 59
Bell Foundation, Brian A., MI, 60
Bellinger Scholarship Fund, Don & Iva, MI, 61
Bemis Scholarship Fund, Samuel L., MI, 62
Benson Foundation, Lan, MI, 1481
Bentley Foundation, Alvin M., MI, 63
Berkery Memorial Trust, Mary Maybury, MI, 64
Berkowitz Foundation, Hy and Greta, MI, 65
Berrien Community Foundation, Inc., MI, 1090
Berry Foundation, The, MI, 66
Bertsch Charitable Foundation, John W. and Margaret G., MI, 67
Besse Foundation, John & Melissa, MI, 68
Besser Foundation, MI, 69
Besser Museum, Jesse, MI, 1482
Betmar Charitable Foundation, Inc., MI, 70
Bettis "Bus Stops Here" Foundation, Jerome, The, MI, 1203
Biederman Foundation, Inc., Les and Anne, The, MI, 1483
Bierlein Family Foundation, Duane & Dorothy, MI, 71
Bilkie Family Foundation, Shari and Bob, MI, 72
Binda Foundation, Guido A. & Elizabeth H., MI, 73
Binion Foundation, Natalie, MI, 74
Birkenstock Family Foundation, MI, 75
Birkhill Family Foundation, F. Ross & Laura Jean, MI, 76
Birmingham Student Loan & Scholarship Fund, MI, 1204
Birmingham-Bloomfield Symphony Orchestra, MI, 1205
Birtwistle Family Foundation, MI, 77
Birtwistle Foundation, Donald B., MI, see 77
Bishop Charitable Trust, A. G., WI, 78
BJB Charitable Trust, MI, 79
Black United Fund of Michigan, Inc., MI, 1206
Blakely Foundation, Dorothy, MI, 80
Blaske-Hill Foundation, MI, 81
Blodgett for Children, D. A., MI, 1207
Blodgett Foundation, The, MI, 82
Blue Cross Blue Shield of Michigan Corporate Giving Program, MI, 942
Blue Cross Blue Shield of Michigan Foundation, MI, 1208
Blue Foundation, Inc., The, MI, 83
Bodman LLP, MI, 943
Bodman, Longley & Dahling LLP, MI, see 943
Boll Foundation, John A. & Marlene L., MI, 84
Bonisteel Foundation, MI, 85
Bonner Foundation, The, MI, 86
Bonsall Foundation, Joseph Sloan Bonsall and Mary Ann, MI, 87
Borders Group, Inc. Corporate Giving Program, MI, 944
BorgWarner Inc. Corporate Giving Program, MI, 945
Borman Fund, The, MI, see 88
Borman's, Inc. Fund, The, MI, 88
Borovoy Family Foundation, MI, 89
Bossenbroek Family Foundation, Steven and Elaine, MI, 90
Bouma Foundation, Henry Bouma, Jr. and Carolyn L., MI, 91
Boutell Memorial Fund, Arnold and Gertrude, MI, see 92
Boutell Memorial Fund, MI, 92
Boysville of Michigan, Inc., MI, 1209
Branch County Community Foundation, MI, 1091
Branch County United Way, Inc., MI, 1210
Brauer Foundation, The, MI, 93
Bray Charitable Trust, Viola E., TX, 94
Brege Memorial Foundation, Jonathan D., WI, 95

Brennan Family Charitable Trust, The, MI, 96
Brenske Scholarship Fund, C. William, MI, 97
Brenske Student Loan Fund, Anthony Stephen & Elizabeth E., MI, 98
Briggs-Fisher Foundation, The, MI, 99
Brinkerhoff-Sample Family Foundation, MI, 100
Brintnall Family Foundation, Robert L., MI, 101
Bronner Family Charitable Foundation, Wallace and Irene, MI, 102
Bronson Health Foundation, MI, 1211
Brooks Foundation, Bennie Marie, MI, 103
Brown Charitable Foundation, Gregory & Helayne, MI, 104
Brown Foundation, Inc., Richard M. & Sharon R., MI, 106
Brown Foundation, Richard H., MI, 105
Browne Foundation, MI, see 107
Browne Foundation, Robert W. & Lynn H., MI, 107
Buchanan Area Foundation, MI, see 1151
Bucknell College Scholarship Trust, Laura Schaeffer, MI, 108
Buist Foundation, MI, 1484
Burch Family Foundation, MI, 109
Burnham Family Foundation, MI, 110
Burroughs Memorial Trust, MI, 111
Busch Family Foundation, MI, 112
Butzel Long Charitable Trust, MI, 946
Butzel Long Gust & Van Zile Charitable Trust, The, MI, see 946
Byrne Family Foundation, MI, 113
Byron Center Fine Arts Foundation, MI, 1212

C.E.F., MI, see 1224
Cabot Corporation Foundation, Inc., MA, 947
Cadillac Area Community Foundation, MI, 1092
Cadillac Products Inc. Foundation, MI, 948
Caesar Puff Foundation, MI, 114
Camp Foundation, Samuel Higby, MI, 115
Campbell Foundation for Neurological Research, Kenneth H., MI, 116
Campbell Soup Foundation, NJ, 949
Campbell Soup Fund, NJ, see 949
Canaan Foundation, MI, 117
Canton Community Foundation, MI, 1093
Capital Area United Way, MI, 1213
Capital Region Community Foundation, MI, 1094
Caravan Youth Center, MI, 1214
Career Alliance, Inc., MI, 1215
CareLink Network, Inc., MI, 1216
Caring Athletes Team for Children's and Henry Ford Hospitals, MI, 1217
Carls Foundation, The, MI, 118
Carmell Scholarship Trust Fund, OH, 119
Carpenter Scholarship Trust, Norman & Ardis, WI, 120
Cash for Kids, PA, 1218
Cassie, Jr. Foundation, James C., MI, 121
CATCH, MI, see 1217
Catholic Healthcare Partners Foundation, OH, 1219
Catt Foundation, C. Glen and Barbara A., MI, 122
Center for Alternative Media and Culture, NY, 123
Center for Arab-American Philanthropy, MI, 1220
Center for Law and Renewal, The, MI, see 1517
Central Care Management Organization, MI, 1485
Central Montcalm Community Foundation, MI, 1095
Chamberlain Foundation, The, MI, 124
Chang Foundation, MI, 125
Char-Em United Way, MI, 1221
Charfoos Charitable Foundation, Lawrence S., MI, 126
Charity Motors, Inc., MI, 1222
Charlevoix County Community Foundation, MI, 1096
Charlupski Foundation, Allen and Franka, MI, 127
Charter One Bank Foundation, OH, 950
Chase Manhattan Bank Corporate Social Responsibility Program, The, OH, see 1008
Chase Scholarship Fund, Lavere Leonard and Gladys Loraine, MI, 128
Cheboygan County United Way, MI, 1223
Chelsea Education Foundation, Inc., MI, 1224
Chelsea Kiwanis Club Foundation, MI, 129
Chelsea United Way, MI, 1225
Chemical Financial Corporation Contributions Program, MI, 951
Chernick Foundation, Alan W., MI, 130
Children's Charities at Adios, MI, 1226
Children's Leukemia Foundation of Michigan, MI, 1227

Chippewa County Community Foundation, MI, 1097
Chowdhury Foundation, Subir and Malini, MI, 1486
Christian Advancement, Inc., MI, see 571
Christian Missionary Scholarship Foundation, MI, 131
Christopher Foundation, The, MI, 132
CHS Foundation, MN, 952
Cipa Foundation, The, MI, 133
Circle K Corporation Contributions Program, The, AZ, 953
Citizens First Foundation, Inc., MI, 134
Citizens First Savings Charitable Foundation, Inc., MI, see 134
CKT Foundation, NJ, 135
Clannad Foundation, MI, 136
Clare County Community Foundation, MI, 1098
Clare Foundation, The, IL, 137
Clark Fund, MI, 138
Cleveland-Cliffs Foundation, The, OH, see 954
Cliffs Foundation, The, OH, 954
Clinton Rotary Scholarship Foundation, MI, 139
Clio Area Community Fund, MI, 1099
CMS Energy Foundation, MI, 955
CNF Inc. Corporate Giving Program, MI, see 958
Cochrane Foundation, Edgar G. Cochrane M.D. and Agnes L., MI, 140
Coleman Family Foundation, The, MI, 1487
Colina Foundation, MI, 141
Collectors Foundation, MI, 1228
Coller Foundation, MI, 142
Coltrane Foundation, John, CA, 1229
Comerica Charitable Foundation, MI, 956
Comerica Incorporated Corporate Giving Program, MI, 957
Community Christian Ministries, MI, 143
Community Connection, Inc., MI, 144
Community Foundation Alliance of Calhoun County, MI, 1230
Community Foundation for Delta County, Michigan, Inc., MI, 1100
Community Foundation for Livingston County, MI, 1101
Community Foundation for Mason County, MI, 1102
Community Foundation for Muskegon County, MI, 1103
Community Foundation for Northeast Michigan, MI, 1104
Community Foundation for Oceana County, MI, 1105
Community Foundation for Southeast Michigan, MI, 1106
Community Foundation for Southeastern Michigan, MI, see 1106
Community Foundation of Greater Flint, MI, 1107
Community Foundation of Greater Rochester, MI, 1108
Community Foundation of Monroe County, MI, 1109
Community Foundation of St. Clair County, MI, 1110
Community Foundation of the Holland/Zeeland Area, The, MI, 1111
Community Foundation of the Upper Peninsula, MI, 1112
Community Foundation of Troy, MI, 1113
Community Network Services, Inc., MI, 1231
Con-way Inc. Corporate Giving Program, MI, 958
ConAgra Foods Foundation, NE, 959
ConAgra Foundation, Inc., The, NE, see 959
Concert Competitions & Musical Development, Inc., MI, see 1410
Concrete Research & Education Foundation, MI, see 1181
Connable Fund, Nancy Malcomson, MI, 145
Constantine Area Community Foundation, MI, 1114
Consumers Energy Company Contributions Program, MI, 960
Consumers Energy Foundation, MI, 961
Consumers Power Company Contributions Program, MI, see 960
Consumers Power Foundation, MI, see 961
Conway Charitable Trust, Nadalynn, MI, 146
Cook Family Foundation, MI, 147
Cook Foundation, Robert & Bess, MI, 148
Coon Foundation, Joanne Cross, MI, 149
Coopersville Area Community Foundation, MI, 1115
Copley Charitable Foundation, Allan B., MI, 150
Copper Country United Way, MI, 1232
Cornucopia Family Foundation, MI, 1488
Corporation for Supportive Housing, NY, 1233
Cott Charitable Trust, Virginia A. Cott & Richard S., MI, 151
Courtney Family Foundation, William, MI, 152
Crane Foundation, Matilda & Harold, MI, 153
Crawford County United Way, MI, 1234
Creative Health Institute, MI, 1489
Cresswell Family Foundation, Inc., The, MI, 154

Cronin Foundation, MI, 155
Crystal Falls Area Community Foundation, MI, 1116
Crystal Falls/Forest Park Area Community Fund, MI, see 1116
CSX Corporation Contributions Program, FL, 962
CT Charitable Foundation, Inc., FL, see 178
Culture Need & Heritage Foundation, MI, 156
Cummings Family Foundation, Peter D. & Julie F., MI, 157
Cummings Foundation, Peter & Julie Fisher, MI, see 157
Cunningham Scholarship Foundation, Louis, The, MI, 158
Cutaneous Lymphoma Foundation, Inc., MI, 1235
Cutler Foundation, Cecelia B. and Kenneth B., The, NY, 159
Czado Catholic Education Fund, Mary, MI, 160

D.U. Memorial Foundation, MI, 161
Dagenais Foundation, Robert & Jeanine, MI, 162
Dalton Foundation, Inc., Dorothy U., MI, 163
Dana Corporation Foundation, MI, 963
Dana Foundation, The, MI, see 164
Dana Z Foundation, The, MI, 164
Dancey Memorial Foundation, Opal, MI, 165
Daoud Foundation, The, MI, 166
Darch Ministries, Inc., Carolyn, MI, 167
Dart Energy Foundation, Inc., The, MI, 964
Dart Foundation, The, MI, 168
Dauch Family Foundation, Richard E. & Sandra J., MI, 1490
Davenport Educational Family Foundation, Henry & Sidney T., MI, 169
Davenport Educational Fund, Henry & Sidney T., MI, see 169
Davenport Foundation, M. E., MI, 170
Davis Foundation, John R. & M. Margrite, The, MI, 171
Davison Community Fund, MI, 1117
Davisson & Abelina Suarez Education Trust, Elizabeth B., MI, 172
Day Foundation, Joseph C., MI, 173
Daystar Foundation, MI, 174
Dearborn Cable Communications Fund, MI, 965
DeBower Foundation Charitable Trust, MI, 175
Deffenbaugh Foundation, George S. and Helen G., MI, 176
Deinzer Charitable Trust, Lucille B., MI, 177
Del Signore Foundation, Costantino, MI, 1236
DeLange Family Foundation, Inc., FL, 178
Delano Foundation, Mignon Sherwood, The, MI, 179
Delphi Automotive Systems Corporation Contributions Program, MI, see 966
Delphi Corporation Contributions Program, MI, 966
Delta College Foundation, MI, 1237
Delta Dental Foundation, MI, 1238
Delta Dental Fund, MI, see 1238
DENSO International America, Inc. Corporate Giving Program, MI, 967
DENSO North America Foundation, MI, 968
DeRoy Testamentary Foundation, MI, 180
DeShano Community Foundation, MI, 1491
Detroit & Wayne County Tuberculosis Foundation, MI, 1239
Detroit Area Agency on Aging, MI, 1240
Detroit Armory Corporation, MI, 181
Detroit Auto Dealers Association Charity Preview, MI, 1241
Detroit Christadelphian Bible Explorers, Inc., MI, 1492
Detroit Edison Foundation, MI, see 977
Detroit Firemens Fund Association for Relief of Disabled Firemen, MI, 1242
Detroit Industrial School, MI, 182
Detroit Lions Charities, MI, 1243
Detroit Lions, Inc. Corporate Giving Program, The, MI, 969
Detroit Metro Sports Commission, Inc., MI, 1493
Detroit Neurosurgical Foundation, MI, 1494
Detroit Pistons Basketball Company Contributions Program, MI, 970
Detroit Red Wings, Inc. Corporate Giving Program, MI, 971
Detroit Tigers Players Home Clubhouse Scholarship Fund, MI, 1244
Detroit Zoological Society, MI, 1245
Detter Family Foundation, Inc., FL, 183
Deur Endowment Fund, MI, 184
DeVlieg Foundation, Charles, The, MI, see 185
DeVlieg Foundation, The, MI, 185
DeVos Foundation, Daniel and Pamella, MI, 186
DeVos Foundation, Dick & Betsy, MI, 187
DeVos Foundation, Douglas & Maria, MI, 188
DeVos Foundation, Richard and Helen, The, MI, 189
Devries Nature Conservancy, MI, 1495
Dexter Memorial Foundation, Inc., Louis M., FL, 190

Diamond Crystal Foundation, The, MI, see 209
Dickinson Area Community Foundation, MI, 1118
Dickinson County Area Community Foundation, MI, see 1118
Dickinson County War Veterans Scholarship Association, MI, 191
Diephouse Foundation, Bruce & Rika, MI, 192
DiPonio Foundation, Angelo & Margaret, The, MI, 193
DJD Foundation, FL, 194
Doan Family Foundation, The, MI, 195
Doan Foundation, Herbert & Junia, The, MI, see 195
Doan Foundation, Herbert and Junia, The, NY, 196
Domino's Pizza, Inc. Corporate Giving Program, MI, 972
Don't Just Sit There Foundation, Inc., MI, 197
Donlin Charitable Corporation, Mildred Mary, MI, 198
Dooge Family Foundation, MI, 199
Doran Foundation, The, MI, 200
Dorfman Foundation, Henry S. & Mala, MI, 201
Dow Chemical Company Foundation, The, MI, 973
Dow Corning Corporation Contributions Program, MI, 974
Dow Corning Foundation, MI, 975
Dow Creativity Foundation, Alden B. and Vada B., MI, 1496
Dow Foundation, Herbert H. and Grace A., The, MI, 202
Doyle Family Foundation, Del & Jean, MI, 203
Drazick Foundation, Herman & Sheila, MI, 204
Dresner Foundation, Inc., Milton H., MI, 205
Drew & Mike Charitable Private Foundation, MI, 206
Drew Family Foundation, MI, 207
Driggers Foundation, MI, 208
DSLT Foundation, MI, 209
DTE Energy Company Contributions Program, MI, 976
DTE Energy Foundation, MI, 977
Duchene Foundation, Doris J. & Donald L., MI, 210
Duffy Memorial Trust, Hubert and Marie, MI, 211
Duncan Family Foundation, Richard and Barbara, The, MI, 212
Dunning Foundation, Margaret, MI, 213
Dunnings Foundation, Inc., MI, 214
Dyer-Ives Foundation, MI, 215
Dykstra Foundation, MI, 216

Earhart Foundation, MI, 217
Easter Seals of Michigan, Inc., MI, 1246
Eastpointe Community Chest/Networking Forum, MI, 1247
Eaton County Community Foundation, The, MI, 1119
Eaton County United Way, MI, 1248
Eddy Family Memorial Fund, C. K., MI, 218
Edmund T. Bott Foundation, Inc., Dr. & Mrs., MI, 219
Educational Services of America, Inc., TN, 1249
Elliott Family Foundation, R. Hugh, MI, 220
Emmenecker Charitable Foundation, Patricia and Thomas, MI, 221
En Gedi Foundation, MI, 222
Engle Foundation, The, MI, 978
Ennis Center for Children, Inc., MI, 1250
Entergy Corporation Contributions Program, LA, 979
Enterprise TFL Foundation, TX, 223
Erb Family Foundation, Fred A. and Barbara M., MI, 224
Erb Family Foundation, MI, see 224
Erlich Foundation, Joseph & Linda, The, MI, 225
Erskine Foundation, Robert Chase, TX, 226
Ervin Foundation, J. F., MI, 227
ESA, TN, see 1249
Eschbach Family Foundation, Rudolf & Ruth, The, MI, 228
Evenson Foundation, Charles Robert, MI, 229
Ever Young and Green Foundation Trust, MI, 230
Evereg-Fenesse Mesrobian-Roupinian Educational Society, Inc., MI, 231
Evergreene Foundation, MI, 1497
Ewald Foundation, H. T., MI, 232
Eyster Charitable Family Foundation, MI, 233

Fabri-Kal Foundation, MI, 980
Face to Face Scholarship Fund, Inc., MI, 1251
Fahd Foundation, MI, 1498
Faigle Charitable Foundation, Ida M., MI, 234
Falk Family Foundation, The, MI, 235
Fallen and Wounded Soldier Fund, MI, 1252
Falls Foundation, O. B. Falls and Elizabeth L., The, VA, 236
Family Foundation, Callant, MI, 237
Farago Foundation Trust, Paul, The, MI, 238
Farber Family Foundation, William and Audrey, MI, 239

Farley Memorial Foundation, Marcus Martin Farley and Mable Stone, MI, 240
Farmington Hills/Farmington Community Foundation, MI, see 1253
Farmington/Farmington Hills Foundation for Youth and Families, MI, 1253
Farver Foundation, The, MI, 241
Farwell Foundation, Drusilla, MI, 242
Fayz Family Foundation, Allie & Wanda, MI, 243
Feather Foundation, MI, 244
Federal Screw Works Foundation, Inc., MI, 981
Fedewa Foundation, C. Scott, MI, 245
Fedorov Foundation, Sergei, The, MI, 246
Fehsenfeld Charitable Foundation, Frank B. and Virginia V., WA, 247
Fenton Community Fund, MI, 1120
Ferries Family Foundation, MI, 248
Fetzer Memorial Trust Fund, John E., MI, 249
Feuer Foundation, Seymour S. & Diana M., MI, 250
Fibre Converters Foundation, Inc., MI, 982
Fifth Third Bank Corporate Giving Program, OH, 983
Fifth Third Foundation, The, OH, 984
Filmer Memorial Charitable Trust, Phillip & Elizabeth, MI, 251
Fink Foundation, George R. and Elise M., MI, 252
Finkelstein Family Charitable Foundation, Morton M., MI, 253
Firestone, Jr. Foundation, Harvey, MI, 254
First Federal Community Foundation, MI, 1499
First Nations Development Institute, CO, 1254
Fish Foundation, MI, 255
Fitch Foundation, E. Root, MI, 1500
Fitzgibbon Dermidoff Foundation, MI, 256
Flemington Scholarship Trust, Nora, MI, 257
Flint Cultural Center Corporation, Inc., MI, 1255
Flushing Community Fund, MI, 1121
Foellinger Foundation, Inc., IN, 258
Foodbank of South Central Michigan, MI, 1256
Foran Charitable Trust, Jeff, MI, 259
Ford Foundation, Gerald R., MI, 1257
Ford Foundation, Geraldine C. and Emory M., MI, 261
Ford Foundation, NY, 260
Ford Foundation, William & Lisa, MI, 262
Ford Fund, Benson and Edith, MI, 263
Ford Fund, William and Martha, MI, 264
Ford II Fund, Edsel B., MI, 265
Ford Motor Company Contributions Program, MI, 985
Ford Motor Company Fund, MI, 986
Ford, Jr. Scholarship Program, William C., MI, 266
Foremost Insurance Company Grand Rapids, Michigan Corporate Giving Program, MI, 987
Foren Family Foundation, MI, 267
Foster Family Foundation, MI, 268
Foster Foundation, MI, 269
Foster Welfare Foundation, MI, see 269
Foundation for Birmingham Senior Residents, MI, 270
Foundation for Saline Area Schools, MI, 1258
Foundation of Michigan Association of Physicians of Indian Origin, MI, 1259
Four County Community Foundation, MI, 1122
Four County Foundation, MI, see 1122
Franke Foundation, Thomas F., MI, 271
Frankel Foundation for Art, Maxine and Stuart, MI, 1501
Frankel Support Foundation, Samuel and Jean, MI, 1260
Frankenmuth Area Community Foundation, Greater, MI, see 1123
Frankenmuth Community Foundation, MI, 1123
Frazier Fund, Inc., MI, 272
Fredericksen Scholarship Fund, E., MI, 273
Freeman Foundation, The, MI, 274
Fremont Area Community Foundation, MI, 1124
Fremont Area Foundation, The, MI, see 1124
Frey Charitable Trust, Twink, MI, 275
Frey Foundation, MI, 276
Frischkorn Memorial Fund Number III, MI, 1261
Fruehauf Foundation, The, TX, 277
Fruman Foundation, Albert & Dorothy, The, MI, 278
Fund for Cancer Research, MI, 279

G. II Charities, MI, 280
Galesburg-Augusta Community Foundation, MI, see 1502
Galesburg-Augusta Education Foundation, MI, 1502
Gallant Foundation, Jon A., MI, 281

Gandhi Foundation, Harendra S., The, MI, 282
Gannett Foundation, Inc., VA, 988
Ganton Auto Museum Foundation, Inc., Lloyd, MI, 1503
Garber Family Foundation, Harold & Ruth, MI, 283
Gardner Charitable Enterprises, MI, 284
Gardner Foundation, Colin, OH, 285
Garland-Schut Foundation, MI, 286
Gary Sisters Foundation, MI, 287
Gay, Lesbian, Bisexual, and Transgender Equality Fund, MI, 1262
Geiger Foundation for Cancer Research, OH, 288
General Dynamics Corporation Contributions Program, VA, 989
General Motors Foundation, Inc., MI, 990
Generations Foundation, MI, 991
Genesis Program, Inc., MI, 1504
George Fund, MI, 289
Georgia-Pacific Foundation, Inc., GA, 992
Gerber Companies Foundation, The, MI, see 290
Gerber Foundation, The, MI, 290
Gerberding/Fackler Family Foundation, Inc., The, MI, 291
Gerstacker Foundation, Rollin M., The, MI, 292
Gertz Foundation, Herman & Irene, MI, 293
Gibbs Charitable Trust, Ruby L., MI, 294
Gibson Foundation, Kirk, MI, 295
Gilbert Memorial Scholarship Fund, Muriel, OH, 296
Gilhooly & Rowan Gilhooly Sanford Educational Foundation, Karen L., MI, see 813
Gillenwater Scholarship Fund, Mary Williams, WI, 297
Gilles Scholarship Trust, Herbert & Florence, MI, 298
Gilmore Foundation, Genevieve and Donald, MI, 1505
Gilmore Foundation, Irving S., MI, 299
Gits Foundation, Norbert and Paula, NY, 300
Glassen Memorial Foundation, Hal & Jean, MI, 301
GLCYD, MI, see 1270
Gleaner Life Insurance Society Corporate Giving Program, MI, 993
Gleaner Life Insurance Society Scholarship Foundation, MI, 1506
Glen Arbor Art Association, MI, 1263
Glick Memorial & Charitable Trust, Louis, MI, 302
Global Philanthropy Alliance, MI, 1264
GM Corporate Giving Program, MI, 994
GM Foundation, MI, see 990
Goad Foundation, Louis C., The, MI, see 303
Goad Foundation, The, MI, 303
God's Gift Foundation, MI, 304
Gogebic Range United Way, MI, 1265
Goldman Foundation, Harry & Bertha A., MI, 305
Goodrich College Education Fund, David, MI, 306
Gordon Christian Foundation, MI, 307
Gordon Food Service, Inc. Corporate Giving Program, MI, 995
Gordon Foundation, Frank & Doris, The, MI, 308
Gordy Foundation, Inc., MI, 309
Gornick Fund, The, MI, 310
Goss Educational Testamentary Trust, Beatrice I., MI, 311
Graef Foundation, Rodger A., OR, 312
Grand Blanc Community Fund, MI, 1125
Grand Haven Area Community Foundation, Inc., MI, 1126
Grand Kids Foundation, MI, 1266
Grand Rapids Bar Foundation, MI, see 1301
Grand Rapids Community Foundation, MI, 1127
Grand Rapids E.C. Foundation, Inc., MI, 1267
Grand Rapids Foundation, The, MI, see 1127
Grand Rapids Home Builders Association Foundation, Greater, MI, see 384
Grand Rapids Jaycees Foundation, MI, 1268
Grand Rapids Urban League, MI, 1269
Grand Traverse Regional Community Foundation, MI, 1128
Granger Foundation, MI, 313
Granger III Foundation, Inc., MI, 314
Gratiot County Community Foundation, MI, 1129
Gratiot Physicians Foundation, MI, 1507
Great Lakes Castings Corporation Foundation, MI, 996
Great Lakes Center for Youth Development, MI, 1270
Great Lakes Chapter of Links, Inc., MI, 1271
Great Lakes Energy People Fund, MI, 1272
Great Lakes Fishery Trust, MI, 1273
Greater Ann Arbor Omega Foundation, MI, 315
Green Bay Packers, Inc. Corporate Giving Program, WI, 997
Green Support Foundation, Irwin and Bethea, MI, 1274
Green Vision Foundation, MI, 316

Greene View Foundation, MI, 317
Greenville Area Community Foundation, MI, 1130
Greenville Area Foundation, MI, see 1130
Griffith Foundation, Donald C. & Doris G., MI, 318
Grimaldi Foundation, The, MI, 319
Grosberg Foundation, Charles, FL, 320
Guilliom Family Foundation, The, KY, 321
Gumaer Scholarship Foundation, Mary L., MI, 322
Gust Foundation, Christopher L. & M. Susan, The, IL, 323
Gutierrez Family Foundation, Ben Gutierrez and Frances, MI, 324
Guy Christian Music Ministry, Inc., Rita, TX, 325
Guzikowski Family Foundation, IL, 326

H.I.S. Foundation, MI, 327
H.O.N.O.R. Foundation, MI, 328
Haas Foundation, Carroll J., MI, 329
Haas Scholarship Fund, Clarence & Marion Wiggins, MI, 330
Habitat for Humanity of Kent County, Inc., MI, 1275
Haboush Foundation, Antoon and Nita, The, OH, 331
Hagen Family Foundation, FL, 332
Haggard Foundation, The, MI, 333
Hahn Foundation, Inc., William and Sharon, MI, 334
Halcyon Foundation, MI, 335
Hall of Fame Dance Foundation, Inc., MI, 1508
Hamar Scholarship, Marcella L., MI, 336
Hamlin Tennis National Honor Society Scholarship Trust, Rose, MI, 1509
Hammel-Delangis Scholarship Trust, MI, 337
Hammond Foundation, The, MI, 998
Hampson Foundation, MI, 338
Hamstra Charitable Foundation, Bernard and Dorothy, NJ, 339
Hancock Foundation, The, MI, 340
Hand in Hand Foundation, Inc., MI, 1510
Handleman Charitable Foundation Trust A, Joseph & Sally, WI, 341
Hannan and Eugene Kraft - Amalgamated Clothing and Textile Workers of America Educational Trust Fund, Harry, MI, 342
Hannan Foundation, MI, 343
Hannan Memorial Foundation, Luella, MI, 1511
Hannan Memorial Home, Luella, MI, see 1511
Hanover Insurance Group Foundation, Inc., The, MA, 999
Hansen Charitable Foundation, Jens and Maureen, MI, 344
Harbor Beach Student Loan Fund Association, MI, 345
Harbor Springs Educational Foundation, MI, 1276
Harding Foundation, Charles Stewart, MI, 346
Harding Foundation, Jennifer Howell, MI, 347
Harding Scholarship Fund, George, The, MI, 348
Harlan Foundation, MI, 349
Harmon Foundation, Lewis G., MI, 350
Harris Foundation, Rodney C. and Karen S., MI, 351
Hartwick Foundation, Alice Kales, MI, 352
Harvest Foundation, The, MI, 353
Harvey Memorial Foundation, MI, 354
Harwell Foundation, Ernie, The, MI, 355
Hasey Foundation, Inc., FL, 356
Hastings Mutual Insurance Company Charitable Foundation, MI, 1000
Haveman Family Foundation, Inc., MI, see 357
Haveman Family Foundation, James & Catherine, MI, 357
Haworth Inc. Corporate Giving Program, MI, 1001
HBA Foundation, MI, see 384
HBALC Foundation, MI, see 1284
HCC Foundation, MI, 1512
HCR ManorCare Foundation, Inc., OH, 1002
Health Education Foundation, MI, see 1349
Heart of Gold Charity, Inc., WI, 358
Heart of West Michigan United Way, MI, 1277
Heat and Warmth Fund, The, MI, 1278
Hebert Memorial Scholarship Fund, MI, 359
Hees Family Foundation, The, MI, 360
Helppie Family Charitable Foundation, MI, 361
Hemophilia Foundation of Michigan, MI, 1279
Hennessey Family Foundation, MI, 362
Henry Ford Health System, MI, 1280
Henry Foundation, Paul B., MI, 363
Herdegen Trust, Elizabeth A., MI, 364
Here to Help Foundation, MI, 365
Hermelin Family Foundation, MI, see 1281
Hermelin Family Support Foundation, MI, 1281
Heron Foundation, F. B., The, NY, 366

Herrick Foundation, MI, 367
Hess Charitable Trust, Myrtle E. & William G., WI, 368
Hess Charitable Trust, William G. and Myrtle E., WI, 369
Hess Scholarship Fund, Frances, MI, 370
Heyl Science Scholarship Fund, F. W. & Elsie, OH, 1282
Hickman Family Foundation, Stephen L., The, MI, 371
Higgins-Hussman Foundation, Inc., Lisa, MD, 372
Hildreth Foundation, Inc., OH, 373
Hill Foundation, Robert D., MI, 374
Hillier Scholarship Fund of Evart, MI, 1513
Hillsdale County Community Foundation, MI, 1131
Hillsdale County United Way, MI, 1283
Himmel Foundation, Clarence and Jack, MI, 375
Hire Family Foundation, The, OH, 376
Hirvonen Charitable Foundation, Ray & Peg, MI, 377
His Work Private Foundation, MI, 378
Historic Warbird Foundation, MI, 1514
Hof Charitable Foundation, Helmut and Ellen, MI, 379
Hoffman Scholarship Trust, Leonard and Ethel, MI, 380
Holden Fund, James and Lynelle, MI, 381
Holland Community Foundation, Inc., MI, see 1111
Hollenbeck Foundation, Laura Ludington, The, MI, 382
Holley Foundation, The, MI, 383
Holy Cross Children's Services, MI, see 1209
Home & Building Association Foundation, MI, 384
Home Builders Association of Livingston County Foundation, Inc., MI, 1284
Homer Area Community Foundation, MI, 1132
Honholt Family Foundation, The, MI, 385
Hood Foundation, Joseph W., The, MI, 386
Hope Foundation, Inc., MI, see 1285
Hope Network Foundation, MI, 1285
Horgan Charitable Trust, Charles & Alda, MI, 387
Hovarter Scholarship Fund Trust, Leon & Audrey, MI, 388
Hoving Foundation, Kenneth & Gwendolyn, IL, 1515
Howard Foundation, John C. and Mary Jane, MI, 389
Howe Scholarship Trust, M. & H., MI, see 390
Howe Scholarship Trust, Marjorie W. Howe & Howard C., MI, 390
Hubbard Memorial Museum Foundation, MI, 1516
Hudson Foundation, Inc., Robert P. & Ella B., MI, 391
Hudson-Webber Foundation, MI, 392
Hudsonville Community Fund, MI, see 1170
Huffines Educational Fund, Carrie & Luther, MI, 393
Huizenga Family Foundation, MI, 394
Human Development Commission, MI, 1286
Humana Foundation, Inc., The, KY, 1003
Humane Society of Macomb Foundation, Inc., MI, 395
Humbert Scholarship Trust, Paul A., MI, 396
Hunter Foundation, Edward and Irma, MI, 397
Huntington Bancshares Incorporated Contributions Program, OH, 1004
Huron County Community Foundation, MI, 1133
Hurst Foundation, The, MI, 398
Huss Memorial Fund, Theodore Huss, Sr. and Elsie Endert, MI, 399

I Have a Dream Foundation - Port Huron, MI, 400
I.N. Network, MI, 1287
Ibbetson Memorial Scholarship, Julie A., MI, 401
Idema Foundation, Bill and Bea, MI, 402
Ilitch Charities for Children, Inc., MI, see 1288
Ilitch Charities, Inc., MI, 1288
Ilitch Osteosarcoma Foundation, Atanas, MI, 1289
Imerman Foundation, John & Ella, MI, 403
Imoberstag Charitable Foundation, Frances B., MI, 404
IMRA America, Inc. Contributions Program, MI, 1005
Inbounds, Inc., MI, 405
India Foundation, MI, 406
Indo-American Health & Education Foundation, Inc., MI, 1290
Ingraham Foundation, Barton J. & Gail G., The, MI, 407
International Aid, Inc., MI, 1291
International Centre for Healing and the Law, MI, 1517
International Development Fund for Higher Education, MI, 1292
Investment Education Institute, MI, 1518
Ionia County Community Foundation, MI, 1134
Iosco County Community Foundation, MI, 1135
Ironwood Area Scholarship Foundation, MI, 1293
Irwin Foundation, The, MI, 408
Isabel Foundation, The, MI, 409
Isabella Bank and Trust Foundation, MI, 1006

Ishpeming Area Community Fund, Greater, MI, 1136
Italian American Delegates, Inc., MI, 1294
Iverson Foundation, Keith A., MI, 410

Jackson Community Foundation, MI, 1137
Jackson County Community Foundation, The, MI, see 1137
Jackson Foundation, Corwill and Margie, MI, 411
Jackson Literary & Art Association, MI, 1519
Jackson National Community Fund, MI, 1007
Jacobson Foundation, Inc., Jerome, The, MD, 412
Jafari Foundation, The, MI, 413
Jaffe Charitable Trust f/b/o Colon High School, MI, see 414
Jaffe Scholarship Fund f/b/o Colon High School, Fredrica, Neva & Abraham, MI, 414
Javitch Charitable Foundation, Karen Sokolof, MI, 415
Jeffers Memorial Education Fund, Michael, MI, 416
Jeffers Memorial Fund, John Michael, MI, 417
Jennings Memorial Foundation, MI, 418
Jensen Foundation, MI, 419
Jenuwine Family Foundation, Alan & Jeanette, MI, 420
Jewish Federation of Grand Rapids, MI, 1295
Jewish Federation of Metropolitan Detroit, MI, 1296
Jewish Fund, The, MI, 1297
Jewish Women's Foundation of Metropolitan Detroit, MI, 1298
JMJ Foundation, MI, 421
Jobst Foundation, Conrad & Caroline, OH, 422
John Ball Zoological Society, MI, 1299
Johnson Corporation Scholarship Foundation, MI, see 1011
Johnson Foundation, Paul T. and Frances B., The, MI, 423
Jones Foundation, Sherrie L., MI, 424
Jones Trauma Research Fund, MI, 1520
Jospey Foundation, Marjorie and Maxwell, MI, 425
Joy Foundation, MI, 426
Joyce Foundation, The, IL, 427
JPMorgan Chase Bank, N.A. Corporate Giving Program, OH, 1008
JPMorgan Chase Philanthropy - Michigan, MI, 1009
JSJ Foundation, MI, 1010
Juhl Scholarship Fund, George W. & Sadie Marie, MI, 428
Junior League of Saginaw Valley, MI, 1300
Justice Foundation of West Michigan, MI, 1301

Kadant Johnson, Inc. Scholarship Foundation, MI, 1011
Kahan Charitable Foundation, Leo A. Kahan and Emelie O., MI, 429
Kahn Sovel Mertz Fund, MI, 430
Kaiser Foundation, Terrence S. Kaiser and Barbara A., MI, 431
Kakarala Foundation, MI, 432
Kalamazoo Aviation History Museum, The, MI, 1302
Kalamazoo Communities in Schools Foundation, MI, 1303
Kalamazoo Community Foundation, MI, 1138
Kalamazoo County Health Plan Corporation, MI, 1304
Kalamazoo Foundation, MI, see 1138
Kalamazoo Loaves and Fishes, MI, 1305
Kalamazoo Public Education Foundation, MI, see 1303
Kalamazoo Regional Catholic Schools Foundation, MI, 1306
Kalamazoo Rotary Club Charities, MI, 1307
Kalamazoo Symphony Orchestra, MI, 1308
Kalamazoo United Way, Greater, MI, 1309
Kalt Family Foundation, IL, 433
Kantzler Foundation, The, MI, 434
Kasiewicz Foundation, Stanley J., MI, 435
Katz Family Foundation, Inc., The, IN, 436
Katzman Foundation, Barney, MI, 437
Katzman Foundation, Sidney and Robert, MI, 438
Katzman Foundation, Sidney, MI, see 438
Kaufman Endowment Fund, Louis G., NE, 439
Kaufman Foundation, MI, 440
Kaufman Memorial Trust, Chaim, Fanny, Louis, Benjamin and Anne Florence, The, WI, 441
Kawasaki Good Times Foundation, NE, 1012
Kay Charitable Trust, Helen L., MI, 442
Kay Foundation, Helen L., MI, see 442
Kay Scholarship Foundation, Ryan Michael, MI, 443
Kazrus Foundation, MI, 444
Kebok Foundation, MI, 445
Keeler Foundation, The, MI, 446
Keeler Fund, Miner S. & Mary Ann, The, MI, see 446
Keeney Trust, Hattie Hannah, WI, 447
Keller Foundation, IL, 448
Kellogg Company 25-Year Employees Fund, Inc., MI, 1013

Kellogg Company Contributions Program, MI, 1014
Kellogg Foundation, Inc., Edward and June, MI, 449
Kellogg Foundation, W. K., MI, 450
Kellogg's Corporate Citizenship Fund, MI, 1015
Kelly Charitable Trust, C. L., MI, 451
Kelly Relief Fund, The, MI, 1310
Kelly Services, Inc. Foundation, The, MI, 1016
Kemler Foundation, W. J. and Lillian, The, MI, 452
Kemp Klein Foundation, MI, 1017
Kemp, Klein, Umphrey, Endelman & May Foundation, MI, see 1017
Kent Charitable Trust, MI, 453
Kent Medical Foundation, MI, 454
Kent Regional Community Coordinated Child Care, Inc., MI, 1311
Kentwood Foundation, MI, 455
Kerkstra Family Charitable Foundation, MI, 456
Keweenaw Community Foundation, MI, 1139
Key Foundation, OH, see 1018
Key Scholarship Trust, Worth M. & Madeline C., The, MI, 457
KeyBank Foundation, OH, 1018
King Trust Charitable Gift Fund, MI, 1312
Kiwanis Foundation of Harbor Springs, MI, 1313
Klobucar and Joseph D. Klobucher Foundation, John E., MI, 458
Knabusch Charitable Trust No. 2, Edward M. and Henrietta M., MI, 459
Knabusch Scholarship Foundation, Edward M. and Henrietta M., MI, 460
Knight Foundation, FL, see 462
Knight Foundation, James A. and Faith, MI, 461
Knight Foundation, John S. and James L., FL, 462
Knowlton Foundation, The, MI, 1521
Koch Bomarko Founders Scholarship Fund, Robert & Margaret, MI, 463
Koester Charitable Trust, John and Ann L., MI, 464
Kohn-Bancroft Family Foundation, The, MI, 465
Kolo Charities, Inc., MI, 1314
Konstanzer Endowment Fund of the Kiwanis Club of Mt. Clemens, Christian W., MI, see 466
Konstanzer Endowment Fund, Christian W., MI, 466
Korman Foundation, Harry B. & Anna, MI, see 686
Kosch Foundation, Donald & Mary, MI, 467
Kosch Foundation, Donald F., MI, see 467
Koster Foundation, Daniel J. & Ardith A., MI, 468
Kowalski Sausage Company Charitable Trust, WI, 1019
Krause Foundation, Cmdr. and Mrs. Robert, MI, 469
Krause Foundation, Inc., R. & W., MI, 470
Kresge Foundation, The, MI, 471
Krishnamurti Rajghat Foundation, Inc., MI, 472
Kroger Co. Contributions Program, The, OH, 1020
Kroger Co. Foundation, The, OH, 1021
Kronlund Foundation Charitable Trust, WI, 473

L & L Educational Foundation, MI, 1522
La Unidad Foundation, MI, 1523
La-Z-Boy Chair Foundation, MI, see 1022
La-Z-Boy Foundation, MI, 1022
Lafler Foundation, Marie, MI, 474
Laflin Scholarship Fund, Inc., William T., MI, 475
Lahser Interspecies Research Foundation, MI, 1524
Lahti Family Foundation, MI, 476
Lahti Foundation for the Performing Arts, Maxine Sprague, OH, 477
Laidlaw Foundation, Helen, The, MI, 478
Lake County Community Foundation, MI, 1140
Lakeland Health Foundation, Niles, MI, 1315
Lamberson Foundation, Frank and Mary, WI, 479
LaMothe Foundation, Patricia A. & William E., MI, 480
Langbo Foundation, Arnold G. & Martha M., MI, 481
Lange Foundation, Ann H. and Robert C., MI, 482
Langley Foundation, Inc., Matt, MI, 483
Lansing Art Gallery, Inc., MI, 1316
Lansing Foundation, Greater, The, MI, 484
Lapeer County Community Foundation, MI, 1141
Lapeer County Community Fund, MI, see 1141
Larson Family Foundation, The, MI, see 485
Larson Family Fund, The, MI, 485
Larson Land Foundation, MI, 486
Larzelere Foundation, Henry E. & Annabel, MI, 487
Lasko Foundation, John C., NJ, 488
Latvian Foundation, Inc., MI, 1317
LaVictoire Memorial Scholarship, Daisy Harder, MI, 489

Law Memorial Trust, Richard Barton, MI, 490
Lay Charitable Private Foundation, Joachim, MI, 491
Lee Scholarship Trust Fund, Whilma B., MI, 492
Leelanau Township Community Foundation, Inc., MI, 1142
Lefevre Scholarship Fund, E.C., MI, 493
Legion Foundation, The, MI, 494
Leighton-Oare Foundation, Inc., MI, 495
Lemmen Foundation, Bernie J., The, MI, see 496
Lemmen Foundation, Wayne E. Lemmen, Helene Lemmen & B. J., MI, 496
Lenawee Community Foundation, MI, 1143
Lenawee United Way, MI, 1318
Lesher Scholarship Trust, Dorothy Below, MI, 497
Lester and Brown Foundation, MI, 1525
Let These Animals Live, Inc., MI, 1526
Leven Foundation, Myron P., The, MI, 498
Lewis Charitable Foundation, William R. and Susan K., The, MI, 499
Lewis Foundation, Pam, MI, 500
Life Giving Ministries, MI, 1319
Life Time Fitness Foundation, MN, 1023
Lifestyle Lift Foundation, MI, 1320
Lighthouse Emergency Services, Inc., MI, 1321
Lileikis Family Foundation, MI, 501
Lilja Family Memorial Fund, August, MI, 502
Linden Foundation, J. Stewart, MI, 503
LISC, NY, see 1323
Little Foundation, William Tedrow, MI, 504
Little Scholarship Trust, Earle and Elsie, The, MI, 505
Livingston County United Way, MI, 1322
Livonia Community Foundation, Inc., MI, 1144
Local Initiatives Support Corporation, NY, 1323
Loeb Charitable Trust, Stella & Frederick, MI, 506
Loutit Foundation, The, IL, 507
Love, Inc. of the Tri-Cities, MI, 1324
Lovelight Foundation, MI, 508
Lowell Area Community Fund, MI, 1325
Lowell Area Housing, Inc., MI, 1527
Lubin, Schwartz & Goldman Foundation, MI, 509
Ludington Foundation, Thomas L., The, MI, 510
Lugers Family Foundation, MI, 511
Lukens Family Foundation, MI, 512
Luneack Family Foundation, MI, 513
Lutheran Child & Family Service of Michigan, Inc., MI, 1326
Lynch Charitable Trust, Ray J. & Leila M., MI, 514
Lyon Foundation, Inc., MI, 515
Lyons Foundation, Bob and Jan, MI, 516

M & M Area Community Foundation, MI, 1145
MAC Valves Foundation, MI, 1024
MacCrone Trust, Edward E., MI, 517
MacDonald Scholarship Trust, George R. and Doris Engblom, MI, 518
Mackensie's Shelter, Inc., MI, see 1528
Mackenzie's Animal Sanctuary, Inc., MI, 1528
Mackinac Island Community Foundation, MI, 1146
Macomb Charitable Foundation, The, MI, 1327
Macomb Lutheran Charitable Foundation, The, MI, see 1327
MacRae Scholarship Trust, Anna M., MI, 519
Mahogany Foundation, MI, 520
Make-A-Wish Foundation of Michigan, MI, 1328
Mall Family Foundation, The, MI, 521
Mally Foundation, Chester F. and Laura L., MI, 522
Malovey Educational Scholarship Fund, C., MI, 523
Manistee County Community Foundation, MI, 1147
Manor Care Foundation, Inc., OH, see 1002
Marcks Foundation, Oliver Dewey, MI, 524
Mardigian Foundation, Edward & Helen, MI, 525
Marks Foundation, Inc., Stephen A., MI, 1529
Marquette Area Public Schools Education Foundation, MI, 1329
Marquette Community Foundation, MI, see 1148
Marquette County Community Foundation, MI, 1148
Marquette-Alger Youth Foundation, MI, see 1270
Marshall Civic Foundation, MI, see 1149
Marshall Community Foundation, MI, 1149
Marshall Rotary Foundation, Inc., MI, 526
Marshall United Way, MI, 1330
Martin Foundation, W.E., The, MI, 527
Marxer College Educational Trust, Ludgardis S., MI, 528
Marzke Family Foundation, The, MI, 529
Masco Corporation Charitable Trust, MI, see 1026
Masco Corporation Contributions Program, MI, 1025

Masco Corporation Foundation, MI, 1026
Mason Area United Way, MI, 1331
Mason State Bank Centennial Fund, Inc., MI, 1027
Masonic Foundation of Michigan, Inc., MI, 1332
Matson Trust, Lorraine D., MI, 530
Matthaei Foundation, MI, 531
Mauser Harmony with Nature Foundation, Inc., MI, 532
May Foundation, Edwin J., The, MI, 533
Mayhew Foundation, Doeren, MI, 534
McBain Foundation, Robert J., MI, 535
McCabe Charitable Foundation, Donald C. and Helene Marienthal, MI, 536
McCalla Foundation, Helen, OH, 537
McCardell Family Foundation, W. B., The, PA, 538
McCarty Cancer Foundation, MI, 1333
McClendon Family Foundation, MI, 539
McClendon Scholarship Foundation, Theo & Mable, MI, 540
McClendon Scholarship Fund, Theo and Mable, MI, see 540
McCurdy Memorial Scholarship Foundation, MI, 541
McDonald's Historic Automobile Foundation, MI, 1530
McGregor Fund, MI, 542
McIntyre Foundation, B. D. and Jane E., WI, 543
McIntyre Foundation, C. S. and Marion F., WI, 544
McIntyre Foundation, W. D. & Prudence, WI, 545
McKeen Foundation, The, MI, 546
McKibben Memorial Foundation, Verna, MI, 547
McLeod Foundation, Mary I., MI, 548
McNally Family Foundation, William F., MI, 549
McNally Memorial Foundation, William F. and Marjorie A., MI, see 549
McNally Memorial Fund, Margaret, MI, 550
McNish Family Foundation, MI, 551
McQuiggan Foundation, Mark C. and Carolyn A., The, MI, 1531
McShane Family Foundation, IL, 552
MCVI Foundation, MI, see 1033
Mecosta County Community Foundation, MI, 1150
Mecosta-Osceola United Way, Inc., MI, 1334
Meeks Foundation, Madeline Sweeney, IL, 553
MEEMIC Foundation for the Future of Education, MI, 1028
Meijer, Inc. Corporate Giving Program, MI, 1029
Memorial Nature Preserve, MI, 1532
Merillat Private Foundation, Richard D. & Lynette S., NJ, 554
Meritor Charitable Trust Fund, MI, 1030
Merkley Charitable Trust, MI, 555
Metro Health Foundation, MI, 556
Metro Health Hospital Foundation, MI, see 1335
Metropolitan Foundation, MI, 1335
Meyers Foundation, Allen H. and Nydia, MI, 557
Meyers Foundation, Allen H., MI, see 557
MGM Mirage Corporate Giving Program, NV, 1031
MGM Mirage Voice Foundation, NV, 1336
Michigan 4C Association, MI, see 1338
Michigan Accountancy Foundation, MI, 1337
Michigan Agri-Business Association Educational Trust Fund, MI, 558
Michigan Agri-Dealers Educational Trust, MI, see 558
Michigan Automotive Compressor, Inc. Corporate Giving Program, MI, 1032
Michigan Cardiovascular Institute Foundation, MI, 1033
Michigan Community Coordinated Child Care Association, MI, 1338
Michigan Council on Economic Education, MI, 1339
Michigan Dental Association Relief Fund, MI, 1340
Michigan Dental Foundation, MI, 1341
Michigan Education Association Scholarship Fund, MI, 1342
Michigan Elks Association Charitable Grant Fund, MI, 559
Michigan Friends of Education, MI, 1343
Michigan Gateway Community Foundation, MI, 1151
Michigan Health Care Education and Research Foundation/ MHCERF, MI, see 1208
Michigan Humanities Council, MI, 1344
Michigan Masonic Charitable Foundation, MI, 1345
Michigan Masonic Home Charitable Foundation, MI, see 1345
Michigan Minority Business Development Council, Inc., MI, 1346
Michigan Parkinson Foundation, MI, 1347
Michigan Railroad Historic Preservation Foundation, Inc., MI, 1533
Michigan State Bar Foundation, MI, 1348
Michigan State Medical Society Foundation, MI, 1349

Michigan Wildlife & Forest Preservation Foundation, MI, 1534
Michigan Women's Foundation, MI, 1350
Michner Educational Foundation, Joseph & Lottie, MI, 560
Mick, Jr. Education Scholarship Foundation, Claud "Bud", MI, 561
Mid-Michigan Society for Animal Protection, MI, 1535
Middle East Reformed Fellowship, Inc., MI, 1351
Midland Area Community Foundation, MI, 1152
Midland Foundation, MI, see 1152
Miller Charitable Foundation, Clyde & Betty, MI, see 562
Miller Family Foundation, C. E., MI, 562
Miller Family Foundation, J. William & Lorraine M., MI, 563
Miller Foundation, Gordon and Gayle, MI, 564
Miller Foundation, The, MI, 565
Miller Trust, Louise Tuller, MI, 566
Miller, Inc. Corporate Giving Program, Herman, MI, 1034
Mills Fund, Frances Goll, MI, 567
Mims Charitable Trust, Allan C. Mims & Margaret L., MI, 568
Miner Charitable, Katharine B., WI, 569
Minton Educational Trust, Helen Lancaster, MI, 570
Missaukee Area Community Foundation, MI, 1153
Missaukee County Community Foundation, MI, see 1153
Mistele Foundation, Inc., The, MI, 571
Mitchell Foundation, MI, 572
Mitsubishi International Corporation Contributions Program, NY, 1035
Moh Foundation, Celia, The, VA, see 573
Moh Foundation, Larry & Celia, The, VA, 573
Moholy-Nagy Foundation, Inc., MI, 1536
Mojo Foundation, MI, 574
Molinello Family Foundation, MI, 575
Molloy Foundation, Inc., MI, 576
Monroe Auto Equipment Company Foundation, MI, 1036
Monroe-Brown Foundation, MI, 577
Moore Family Foundation, Frederick S. & Lezlynne P., MI, 578
Moore Foundation, Mary, MI, 579
Moore III Foundation, Joan I. & John R., MI, 580
Morath Foundation, Inc., Carl & Irene, MI, 581
Morenci Education Foundation, MI, 1352
Morey Foundation, The, MI, 582
Morgan Memorial Trust, Barbara, MI, 583
Morley Brothers Foundation, MI, see 584
Morley Foundation, MI, 584
Morrill Scholarship Fund, James K., MI, 585
Mossner Memorial Foundation, Arno & Caroline, MI, 586
Mott Foundation, Charles Stewart, MI, 587
Mott Foundation, Ruth, MI, 588
Mount Pleasant Area Community Foundation, MI, 1154
Mount Pleasant Community Foundation, MI, see 1154
Ms. Molly Foundation, MI, 1353
Mt. Zion Lutheran Church Foundation, MI, 589
Muer and Chef Larry Memorial Scholarship Fund, Chuck, MI, 590
Mukkamala Family Foundation, MI, 591
Muntwyler Foundation For Animals, Wanda, MI, 592
Munuscong River Watershed Association, MI, 593
Murff Manor, Inc., MI, 1537
Muskegon County Community Foundation, Inc., MI, see 1103
Muskegon Service League Foundation, Greater, MI, 1354
Musser Fund, Laura Jane, The, MN, 594
Musser Fund, The, MN, see 594
Mycosis Fungoides Foundation, Inc., MI, see 1235
Myers Church Scholarship, OH, 595
Myers Foundation, Frank & Irene, MI, 596

Nakadar Foundation, MI, 1538
Nash Finch Company Contributions Program, MN, 1037
National Comprehensive Cancer Network, PA, 1355
National Healthcare Scholars Foundation, MI, 597
National Kidney Foundation of Michigan, Inc., MI, 1356
National Multiple Sclerosis Society Michigan Chapter, Inc., MI, 1357
Neal Sisters Foundation, WI, 598
Neff Family Foundation, IN, 1539
Negaunee Area Community Fund, MI, 1155
Nehru-Lincoln Human Services, MI, 1540
Nelson Family Foundation, J. N., MI, 599
Nelson Scholarship Fund, Donald E. and Margaret L., MI, 600
Network Community Services, MI, see 1485

New Day Foundation for Families, The, MI, 1358
New Detroit, Inc., MI, 1359
New York Life Foundation, NY, 1038
Newaygo County Community Services, MI, 1360
Newaygo Public Schools Educational Advancement Foundation, MI, 601
Newman Family Foundation, The, MI, 602
Newsweek, Inc. Corporate Giving Program, NY, see 1039
Newsweek/Daily Beast Company LLC Contributions Program, The, NY, 1039
Nickless Family Charitable Foundation, The, MI, 603
Nickless Memorial Foundation, Allen E. & Marie A., MI, 604
Nicolay Family Foundation, Ernest L., MI, 605
Nicolay Foundation, Joanne, MI, 606
Nieman Scholarship Fund, Sara L., MI, 1541
Nill Foundation, Inc., Dr. William F. and Mabel E., MI, 607
Nissan Foundation, The, TN, 1040
Nissan North America, Inc. Corporate Giving Program, TN, 1041
Nokomis Foundation, MI, see 275
Nonprofit Facilities Fund, NY, see 1361
Nonprofit Finance Fund, NY, 1361
Nordman Charitable Trust, Amos, MI, see 608
Nordman Foundation Charitable Trust, Amos, MI, 608
North Central Michigan Community Foundation, MI, 1156
Northeast Michigan Community Foundation, MI, see 1104
Northeast Michigan Community Service Agency, Inc., MI, 1362
Northern Michigan Foundation, MI, 1542
Northern Michigan Hospital Foundation, MI, 1363
Northville Community Foundation, MI, 1157
Northville Educational Foundation, MI, 1364
Northwest Airlines, Inc. Corporate Giving Program, MN, 1042
Northwest Michigan Community Coordinated Child Care Council, MI, 1365
Northwest Michigan Human Services, Inc., MI, 1366
Northwest Senior Resources, Inc., MI, 1367
Northwind Foundation, The, MI, 609
Norway Area Community Foundation, MI, 1158
Norway Area Community Fund, MI, see 1158
Novi Parks Foundation, MI, 1368
Nowak Family Foundation, FL, 610
Nusbaum Family Foundation, MI, 611
Nuveen Benevolent Trust, IL, 612

O'Brien-VRBA Scholarship Trust, The, OH, 613
O'Hare Foundation, Inc., David, The, MI, 1543
O'Neill Foundation, The, MI, 1544
Oakland County Bar Foundation, MI, 1369
Oakland Livingston Human Service Agency, MI, 1370
Oakwood Healthcare, Inc., MI, 1371
Obloy Foundation, Leo A. Obloy and Bernice, MI, 614
Ohana Research Foundation, MI, 1545
Okun Foundation, Marvin and Rosalie, MI, 615
Olds Foundation, R. E., MI, 616
Oleson Foundation, MI, 617
Olson Foundation, Robert G. & Celia S., MI, see 618
Olson-Kulka Foundation, MI, 618
OneSight Research Foundation, TX, 1546
Ontonagon Area Scholarship Foundation, The, MI, 1372
Optimist Club Foundation, The, MI, 1373
Orchards Children's Services, Inc., MI, 1374
Osceola County Community Foundation, MI, 1159
Oshlag Stuckey Foundation, MI, 619
Otsego County Community Foundation, MI, 1160
Otsego County United Way, Inc., MI, 1375
Ott Scholarship Fund, Annette L., MI, 620
Ottawa County United Way, Greater, MI, 1376
Owen Scholarship Trust, MI, 621
OYK Foundation, The, MI, 622

Page, Sr. Family Charitable Foundation, Lawrence C., MI, 623
Paine Family Foundation, MI, 624
Palmer Foundation, Walter E. and Maria F., MI, 625
Pamida Foundation, NE, 1043
Pappas Foundation, Inc., MI, 626
Parchment Community Tennis Association, MI, 627
Pardee Cancer Treatment Fund of Bay County, MI, 1547
Pardee Cancer Treatment Fund of Gratiot County, MI, 1548
Pardee Foundation, Elsa U., MI, 628
Parfet Family Foundation, Donald and Ann, MI, 629

Parish Foundation, Suzanne D., MI, see 630
Parish Foundation, Suzanne Upjohn Delano, MI, 630
Park Family Foundation, MI, 631
Park West Charitable Foundation, MI, 1549
Parks Scholarship Foundation, Inc., Rosa L., MI, 1377
Parks-Novitsky Memorial Scholarship Fund, Liz, The, CA, 632
Parrish Family Foundation, Stan and Jean, IN, 633
Parsons Corporation Contributions Program, CA, 1044
Pati Foundation, Raji, CA, 634
Paul Foundation, Beatrice & Reymont, MI, 635
Paulsen Trust, MI, 636
Pawating Health Foundation, MI, see 1315
Peach Foundation, J. Red, MI, 637
Pearle Vision Foundation, Inc., TX, see 1546
Pellerito, Manzella, Certa & Cusmano Family Foundation, MI, 638
Peninsula Foundation, The, NM, 639
Penner Foundation, MI, 640
Pennock Foundation, MI, 1378
Pentecost Foundation, Joe D., MI, 641
Perrigo Company Charitable Foundation, MI, 1045
Perrone Charitable Foundation, Inc., MI, 642
Perry-Morrice-Shaftsburg Emergency Relief Council, MI, 643
Peshtigo Area Foundation, MI, 1161
Peters Foundation Corp., Herman & Katherine, The, IL, 644
Peterson Family Foundation, MI, 645
Petoskey-Harbor Springs Area Community Foundation, MI, 1162
Pettibone & Associates Foundation, Inc., W. H., MI, 646
Pewabic Society, Inc., MI, 1379
Physicians' Organization of Western Michigan Foundation, Inc., MI, 647
Pierce Foundation, Willard G. & Jessie M., The, MI, 1550
Pietrasiuk Family Foundation, The, MI, 648
Pistons-Palace Foundation, The, MI, 1046
Plumbers and Pipefitters Local No. 333 Scholarship Plan, MI, 1380
Plym Foundation, MI, 649
Plymouth Christian Schools Foundation, MI, 1381
Plymouth Community United Way, MI, 1382
Plymouth Rotary Foundation, Inc., MI, 1383
PNC Bank Foundation, PA, see 1047
PNC Foundation, The, PA, 1047
Pokagon Fund, Inc., The, MI, 1048
Polakovic Charitable Trust, John, MI, 650
Polan Foundation, Jennifer Gordon, MI, 651
Polk & Co. Contributions Program, R. L., MI, 1049
Pollack Educational Trust, Sara, MI, 652
Ponting Foundation, Herbert and Elsa, MI, 653
Popeye Animal Cancer Foundation, The, MI, 654
Porter Foundation, Irwin Andrew, The, MN, 656
Porter Foundation, MI, 655
Portland Community Fund Association, MI, 1384
POWM Foundation, MI, see 647
Prentis Family Foundation, Inc., Meyer and Anna, The, MI, 657
Prevo Foundation, Dan R. and Pamela M., MI, 658
Pribil Memorial Trust, Maxwell, MI, 659
Price Foundation, Inc., Robert E., The, MI, 660
Promedica Physicians Group, Inc., OH, 1385
Pryor Foundation, The, CT, 661
Pulte Corporation Contributions Program, MI, see 1050
Pulte Homes, Inc. Corporate Giving Program, MI, 1050
Puschelberg Foundation, George, MI, 662

Quicksilver Resources Inc. Corporate Giving Program, TX, 1051

R.J. Ministries, MI, 663
Racing for Kids, MI, 1386
Rainbow Foundation, MI, 664
Raiola Foundation, Dominic J., MI, 665
Ramser-Morgan Foundation, MI, 666
Randall Charitable Trust, Mamie and Harold K., The, NJ, 667
Ransom Fidelity Company, MI, see 616
Ratner Foundation, Milton M., MI, 668
Raval Education Foundation, Inc., The, MI, 669
Rawson Foundation, Inc., MI, 670
Recreational Boating Industries Educational Foundation, MI, 671
Redies Foundation, Inc., Edward F., MI, 1052
Redman Foundation, The, MI, 1551

Reid Educational Trust, C. M. & A. A., MI, 672

Reid Foundation, Joseph D. and Jerry L., The, MI, 673

Reimer Family Charitable Trust, MI, 674, 675

Reinhardt Trust, Robert C., MI, 676

Rennie Scholarship Trust, Florence M., MI, 677

Resnal Foundation, MI, 678

Respiratory Foundation of Southeast Michigan, MI, see 1239

Reuter Foundation, Loraine & Melinese, MI, 679

Reuther Memorial Fund, Walter and May, MI, 1387

Rewold & Son Foundation, Frank, MI, 1053

Rewold Foundation, Roy and Beverly, MI, 680

Reynolds Foundation, Phyllis and Max, MI, 681

Rhee Foundation, Chi Sun, MI, 682

Rhoades Memorial Foundation, Francis P. and Nell A., MI, 683

Rhoades Memorial Foundation, Francis P., MI, see 683

Richter Foundation, Inc., R. Gene and Nancy D., MI, 684

Riley Foundation, The, MI, 685

Ring Charitable Foundation, Eunice & Milton H., MI, 686

Rislov Foundation, Sigurd & Jarmila, MI, 687

Robbins Memorial Scholarship Fund, Frank E., RI, 688

Robertson Family Foundation, MI, 689

Robey Charitable Trust, Edmund W., The, FL, see 1552

Robey Charitable Trust, The, FL, 1552

Robison Foundation, Harold & Carolyn, MI, 690

Rochester Area Community Foundation, Greater, MI, see 1108

Rochester Area Neighborhood House, Inc., MI, 1388

Rock Charitable Foundation, MI, 691

Rock Foundation, MI, see 691

Rodney Fund, The, MI, 692

Roethke Scholarship Fund, Otto & Helen, MI, 693

Rolka Scholarship Foundation, MI, 694

Roon Family Foundation, Pierson J., MI, 695

Roscommon Area Historical Society, MI, 696

Roscommon County Community Foundation, MI, 1163

Roscommon County United Way, MI, 1389

Rose Family Foundation, Carl F. and Donna M., MI, 697

Rose Foundation, Jalen, The, CA, 1390

Rotary Charities of Traverse City, MI, 1391

Rotary Club of Lowell Community Foundation, MI, 1392

Rotary District 6360 Foundation, MI, 1393

Royal Foundation, May Mitchell, MI, 698

Rudlaff Family Foundation, FL, 699

Rudy Scholarship Fund, Lillian & Harold, MI, 700

Rudy Scholarship, MI, see 700

Ruf Scholarship Trust, Clara A., MI, 701

Rupp Foundation, Nelson D., MI, 702

Rusch Family Scholarship, John, The, MI, 703

Russell Foundation, Herman, MI, 704

Ryals Foundation, MI, 705

S.E.T. Educational Fund, MI, see 1567

Sackerson Charitable Foundation, Edward J., MI, 706

Sacred Family Causes Foundation, MI, 707

Sage Foundation, MI, 708

Saginaw Community Foundation, MI, 1164

Saini Memorial Foundation, Dr. Shanti Swarup & Mrs. Chawli Devi, MI, 709

Saint Mary's Doran Foundation, MI, 1394

Salahi Foundation, The, MI, 710

Salisbury Memorial Scholarship Fund, Burl E., MI, 711

Salness Memorial Scholarship Fund, Fritchof T. Salness and Marian M., MI, 712

Salpietra Family Charitable Foundation, MI, 713

Sand Products Foundation, MI, 1553

Sanilac County Community Foundation, MI, 1165

Sankrithi Foundation, MI, 714

SANYO North America Corporation Contributions Program, CA, 1054

Sault Area Community Foundation, MI, see 1097

Schaap Foundation, A. Paul and Carol C., The, MI, 715

Schalon Foundation, The, MI, 716

Schemm Scholarship Trust, Maude Ripley, MI, 717

Schmier Foundation, Leslie & Regene, MI, 718

Schmuckal Family Foundation, Art and Mary, The, MI, 719

Schoolcraft Area Community Foundation, MI, 1166

Schoolcraft County Community Foundation, MI, see 1166

Schoonbeck Family Foundation, MI, 720

Schroeder Foundation, Fred D. & Evelyn A., MI, 721

Schultheiss Memorial Scholarship Fund, Inc., Elizabeth, MI, 722

Schuyler Estate Trust, Carrie E. Smith, MI, 723

Schwartz Family Foundation, MI, 724

Scofield Trust, Emily, MI, 725

Scott Foundation, A., The, MI, 1554

Scully Foundation, John, MI, 726

Seabury Foundation, The, IL, 727

Sebastian Foundation, MI, 728

Seed the World, Inc., MI, 1555

Seidman Family Foundation, CO, 729

Seidman Foundation, Thomas Erler, The, CO, see 729

Seifert Foundation, George & Elizabeth, The, MI, 730

Seligman Medical Institute, The, MI, 1556

Seminole Foundation, MS, see 867

SEMP Foundation, The, MI, 1557

Sequin, Jr. Family Foundation, Thomas E., MI, 731

Serra Family Foundation, MI, 732

Serwinek Foundation, Paul & Marlene, MI, 733

Shaevsky Family Foundation, MI, 1395

Shaevsky Family Support Foundation, MI, see 1395

Shapiro Family Foundation, Joel H. and Loraine, MI, 1396

Share With The World Foundation, MI, 1558

Sharing of Blessings Foundation, The, MI, 734

Shelby Community Foundation, MI, 1167

Shelby Family Foundation, IL, 735

Shelden Fund, Elizabeth, Allan and Warren, MI, 736

Shepard Scholarship Fund Foundation, Inc., Leon and Josephine Wade, MI, 737

Shepherd Foundation, The, MI, 738

Shiawassee Community Foundation, MI, 1168

Shiawassee Foundation, MI, see 1168

Shiawassee United Way, MI, 1397

Shiffman Foundation, The, MI, 739

Shin Foundation for Medical Research and Betterment of Mankind, MI, 740

Shoemaker Foundation, Edwin J. & Ruth M., MI, 741

Shoer Educational Trust, William Shoer and Jennie Smidt, NH, 742

Shop Rat Foundation, Inc., The, MI, 1398

Shopko Foundation, Inc., WI, 1399

ShopKo Stores, Inc. Corporate Giving Program, WI, 1055

Shubeck Monsour Foundation, MI, 743

Siebenthaler Foundation, MI, 744

Sigmund Foundation, Bill & Vi, MI, 745

Sigmund Foundation, Bill and Vi, MI, 746

Silverwing Foundation, MI, 747

Simmons Foundation, MI, 748

Simon Foundation, Donald R. and Esther, MI, 749

Simonis Educational Fund "D", Eleanor R., MI, 750

Sinai Medical Staff Foundation, MI, 751

Sisson Charitable Trust, Harry A., MI, 752

Skandalaris Family Foundation, MI, 753

Skiles Foundation, The, MI, 754

Skillman Foundation, The, MI, 755

Slack Foundation, D. Jerome and Margery C., The, MI, 756

Sloat and Ray Okonski Foundation, Suzanne, MI, 757

SME Education Foundation, MI, see 1402

Smith Family Foundation, Arthur L. & Carra J., MI, 758

Smith Family Foundation, Inc., Jeff & Patrice, OH, 759

Smith Foundation, Jean M. R., MI, 760

Snyder Christian Environmental Preservation Foundation, MI, 761

Snyder Foundation, Inc., The, MI, 762

Sobong Fundation, Drs. Enrico and Esther, MI, 1559

Social Venture Investors, MI, 1400

Social Venture Philanthropy, MI, see 1400

Society for Research in Child Development, Inc., MI, 1401

Society of Manufacturing Engineers Education Foundation, MI, 1402

Society of the Brethren, MI, 1560

Sojourner Foundation, MI, 1403

Sonkin Family Foundation, The, FL, 1561

Sonneveldt Foundation, The, MI, 763

Souder Family Foundation, IL, 764

South Haven Community Foundation, MI, 1169

Southeast Michigan Community Alliance, MI, 1404

Southeast Michigan Physicians Foundation, The, MI, see 1557

Southeast Ottawa Community Foundation, MI, 1170

Southeastern Michigan Chapter NECA Educational and Research Foundation, MI, 765

Southeastern Michigan Tarbut Foundation, The, MI, 766

Southfield Community Foundation, MI, 1171

Southfield Kappa Foundation, MI, 1405

Southwest Michigan Community Action Agency, MI, 1406

Southwest Michigan Crate and Basket and Veneer Machinery Museum, Inc., MI, 1562

Southwest Michigan Rehab Foundation, MI, 767

Southwestern Michigan Urban League, MI, 1407

Spark Energy, L.P., Corporate Giving Program, TX, 1056

Sparta Community Foundation, MI, 1172

Spartan Motors Private Foundation, The, MI, 1057

Spaulding for Children, MI, 1408

Speckhard-Knight Charitable Foundation, MI, 768

Spector Foundation for the Arts, Alvin B., The, MI, 769

Spector Foundation for the Arts, Lois & Alvin, MI, see 769

Spectrum Human Services, Inc., MI, 1409

Speerstra Scholarship Fund Trust, Peter and Evelyn, MI, 770

Spencer Family Foundation, MI, 771

Sphinx Organization, The, MI, 1410

Spicer, Sr. Foundation, S. Gary, MI, 772

Springview Foundation, MI, 773

SRCD, MI, see 1401

St. Clair Foundation, MI, 774

St. Deny's Foundation, Inc., MI, see 817

St. Joseph County United Way, MI, 1411

St. Joseph Kiwanis Foundation, MI, 775

St. Joseph/Benton Harbor Rotary Foundation, Inc., MI, 1412

St. Mary's Hospital Foundation, MI, see 1413

St. Mary's of Michigan Foundation, MI, 1413

Stanton Foundation, The, MI, 776

Starfish Alliance, Inc., The, MI, 777

Stauffer Kentwood Foundation, MI, see 455

Steelcase Foundation, MI, 1058

Steelcase Inc. Corporate Giving Program, MI, 1059

Stepping Stones Foundation, MI, 1563

Sterban Foundation, Richard A. and Donna L., MI, 778

Sterken Family Foundation, The, MI, 779

Sterling Heights Community Foundation, MI, 1173

Stewart Management Group Charitable Foundation, MI, 780

Stines Family Foundation, George, MI, 1564

Stockbridge Foundation, MI, 781

Stockton Charitable Foundation, North J. and Florence, WI, 782

Stoddard Trust, Alice A., MI, 783

Stoker Charitable Trust, Margaret Jane, MI, 784

Stokes Scholarship Trust, Olive A., MI, 785

Straits Area Community Foundation, MI, 1174

Strobel Foundation, Wally and Jo, The, MI, 786

Strosacker Foundation, Charles J., The, MI, 787

Stryker and William D. Johnston Foundation, Ronda E., The, MI, 788

Stryker Foundation, Jon L., MI, see 27

Stubberfield Foundation, Lynn, MI, 1565

Stubnitz Foundation, Maurice & Dorothy, MI, 789

Stulberg Foundation, David & Lois, FL, 790

Sturgis Area Community Foundation, MI, 1175

Sturgis Foundation, MI, see 1175

Sud Family Foundation, Anup and Parul, MI, 791

Sullivan Foundation, Ann Ludington, The, MI, 792

Sullivan Scholarship Fund Trust, MI, see 793

Sullivan Scholarship Fund Trust, Robert and Timothy, MI, 793

Sunrise Community Foundation, MI, 794

Susan G. Komen for the Cure of Mid-Michigan, MI, 1414

Sutar-Sutaruk-Meyer Foundation, MI, 795

Swiat Foundation, Richard J. and Frances B., The, MI, 796

Sylvia Weider-Amber Family Foundation, MI, 797

Tabbaa Foundation, The, MI, 1566

Tahquamenon Education Foundation, MI, 1415

Tassell Foundation, Leslie E., The, MI, see 798

Tassell-Wisner-Bottrall Foundation, MI, 798

Taubman Centers, Inc. Corporate Giving Program, MI, 1060

Tawas-Whittemore-Hale Area United Fund, MI, 1416

Taylor Perpetual Charitable Trust, Brent, IL, 799

Taylor Scholarship Trust, P. & H., MI, 800

TCF Foundation, MN, 1061

Team Michigan, Inc., MI, 801

Tecumseh Community Fund Foundation, MI, see 1143

Temple-Krick YFU Scholarship Fund, Inc., MI, 802

Tengler Educational Fund, Steve and Elizabeth, The, MI, 1567

Tepper Family Foundation, The, NY, 803

Ternes Foundation, Ltd., Howard and Margery, The, MI, 804

THAW, MI, see 1278

Thawani Foundation, Bhagwani, MI, 805

Thiemkey Scholarship Foundation, Jean and Stewart, NC, 806
Thoman Foundation, W. B. & Candace, MI, 807
Thomas Foundation, The, MI, 808
Thomas Scholarship Fund, Russ, MI, 809
Thome Memorial Foundation, Edward N. & Della L., MA, 810
Thompson Foundation, Mary, MI, 811
Thornapple Kellogg Education Foundation, MI, 1417
Thorrez Foundation, MI, 812
Three Rivers Area Community Foundation, MI, 1176
Three Rivers Community Foundation, MI, see 1176
Three Sisters Foundation, MI, 813
Thresholds, Inc., MI, 1418
Tigers Care Program, MI, 1062
Tim Hortons Inc., Corporate Giving Program, OH, 1063
Tiscornia Foundation, The, MI, 814
Todd Company Foundation, A. M., MI, 1064
Toll Brothers, Inc. Corporate Giving Program, PA, 1065
Tony Semple Foundation for Hope, MI, 1419
Torgow Family Foundation, MI, 815
Towsley Foundation, Harry A. and Margaret D., The, MI, 816
Toyota Motor Sales, U.S.A., Inc. Corporate Giving Program, CA, 1066
Training & Treatment Innovations, Inc., MI, 1420
Travelers Aid Society of Metropolitan Detroit, MI, 1421
Tremble Foundation, Inc., MI, 817
Trinity Community Services & Educational Foundation, MI, 1422
Trinklein Educational Trust, Otto, MI, 818
Trixie Puff Foundation, MI, 819
Trone Scholarship Trust, Blanche Barr, MI, 820
Troy Community Foundation, MI, see 1113
Troy Internal Medicine Foundation, MI, 1568
Trudell Scholarship Trust, MI, 821
Trumley Family Foundation, MI, 822
Trust f/b/o Datrmouth, et al., R. Gerstell, PA, 823
Tuesdays with Mitch Charitable Foundation, NJ, 824
Tuinstra Foundation, Doris, The, MI, 825
Tuktawa Foundation, MI, 826
Tummala Charitable Foundation, MI, 827
Turfe Family Foundation, Alexander Alan, MI, 828
Turner Memorial Trust, Alice E., MI, 829
Turtle Lake Wildlife Foundation, The, MI, 830
Tuscola County Community Foundation, MI, 1177

U of M Scholarship Fund of Bay City, MI, see 831
UAW-GM Center for Human Resources, MI, 1423
United American Healthcare Foundation, MI, see 597
United Arts Council of Calhoun County, MI, 1424
United Jewish Foundation, MI, 1425
United Nations Association, Kalamazoo Chapter, MI, 1426
United Way for Southeastern Michigan, MI, 1427
United Way of Bay County, MI, 1428
United Way of Chippewa County, MI, see 1448
United Way of Clare County, MI, 1429
United Way of Delta County, MI, 1430
United Way of Genesee County, MI, 1431
United Way of Gladwin County, MI, 1432
United Way of Gratiot County, MI, 1433
United Way of Greater Battle Creek, MI, 1434
United Way of Greater Niles, Inc., MI, 1435
United Way of Jackson County, MI, 1436
United Way of Lapeer County, MI, 1437
United Way of Manistee County, MI, 1438
United Way of Marquette County, MI, 1439
United Way of Mason County, MI, 1440
United Way of Midland County, MI, 1441
United Way of Monroe County, Inc., MI, 1442
United Way of Muskegon County, MI, see 1447
United Way of Northwest Michigan, MI, 1443
United Way of Sanilac County, Inc., MI, 1444
United Way of Southwest Michigan, MI, 1445
United Way of St. Clair County, MI, 1446
United Way of the Lakeshore, MI, 1447
United Way of the Upper Eastern Peninsula, MI, 1448
United Way of Tuscola County, MI, 1449
United Way of Wexford County, MI, 1450
Universal Companies, Inc. Education Foundation, MI, see 1067
Universal Forest Products Education Foundation, MI, 1067
University of Michigan Scholarship Fund of Bay City, MI, 831
University Renal Research and Education Association, MI, see 1476

Upjohn Foundation, Harold and Grace, MI, 832
Upjohn Institute for Employment Research, W.E., MI, see 1451
Upjohn Unemployment Trustee Corp., W. E., MI, 1451
Upper Peninsula Community Foundation Alliance, MI, see 1112
Upton Foundation, Frederick S., MI, 833

V Care Jainism & Jivdaya Foundation, MI, 834
Valassis Communications, Inc. Corporate Giving Program, MI, 1068
Van Andel Foundation, David and Carol, MI, 835
Van Andel Foundation, Steve & Cindy, MI, 836
Van Andel Fund, Inc., MI, 837
Van Den Bosch Gospel Foundation, William and Anna, MI, 838
Van Haften Charitable Trust, Peter, MI, 1452
Van Hollenbeck Foundation, Homer J., MI, 839
Van Kampen Boyer Molinari Charitable Foundation, FL, 840
Van Lunen Charitable Foundation, Richard D., MD, 841
Van Wormer Family Foundation, MI, 842
Vanderwaals Foundation, James and Almeda, MI, 843
VanderWeide Family Foundation, MI, 844
VanderWeide Foundation, Robert & Cheri, MI, see 844
Variety Club Charity For Children, Inc., MI, 1453
Varnum, Riddering, Schmidt & Howlett LLP Corporate Giving Program, MI, 1069
Venturedyne, Ltd. Foundation, WI, 1070
Veteran's Haven, Inc., MI, 1454
Victor Foundation, Lyle and Diane, MI, 1569
Village Woman's Club Foundation, The, MI, 1455
Vogt Foundation, WI, 845
Vollbrecht Foundation, Frederick A., MI, 846
Vomberg Foundation, The, MI, 847
VSA arts of Michigan, MI, 1456

Walsh Charitable Trust, Richard T. and Marianne H., MI, 848
Warchol Foundation, Jane and Frank, MI, 849
Washtenaw Health Plan Corporation, MI, 1457
Washtenaw United Way, MI, 1458
Watson Foundation, John W. and Rose E., MI, 850
Watson Foundation, Raymond E. & Evona, MI, 851
Waverly Education Foundation, MI, 1459
Wayne Rotary Foundation, MI, 1460
Wayne-Metropolitan Community Action Agency, MI, 1461
Weatherwax Foundation, MI, 852
Webster Family Foundation, Inc., Frank and Sara, MI, see 853
Webster Family Foundation, MI, 853
Webster, Jr. Endowment Fund, Arthur H., MI, 854
Weed Foundation, Irene M. & Milton R., MI, 855
Wege Foundation, MI, 856
Wehr Corporation Foundation, WI, see 1070
Weidemann Foundation, Inc., Barbara J., MI, 857
Weidner Memorial Foundation, Nathan, MI, 1462
Weigel Family Foundation, FL, 858
Weikart Family Foundation, MI, 859
Weiner Family Foundation, MI, 860
Weinlander, Fitzhugh & Schairer Foundation, Inc., MI, 861
Weisberg Family Foundation, Bernard and Helen, MI, 862
Weisblat Foundation, Inc., The, MI, 863
Weiss Family Foundation, MI, 864
Weiss, Sr. Foundation, James D., MI, 865
Weissman Education and Charitable Foundation, Evelyn & Fredrick, MI, 866
Weitzenhoffer-Seminole Foundation, MS, 867
Welch Charitable Foundation, Lorna A., MI, 1570
Welch Foundation, James A., MI, 868
Wells Trust, Leon, MI, 869
Wellspring of Hope Foundation, Inc., MI, 870
Welsh Foundation, Thomas, MI, 871
Welter Foundation, Inc., MI, 1571
West Foundation, H. O., The, PA, 1071
West Foundation, Herman O., The, PA, see 1071
West Michigan Strategic Alliance, Inc., MI, 1463
Westerman Foundation, Samuel L., MI, 872
Western Michigan Society of Professional Engineers Scholarship Fund, MI, 873
Westfall Foundation, Robert B., MI, 874
Westran Corporation Foundation, MI, see 274
Weyand 1977 Charitable Trust, Louis F. and Florence H., MN, 875
Weyerhaeuser/Day Foundation, MN, 876

Whaley Children's Center, Inc., MI, 1464
Whirlpool Foundation, MI, 1072
White Foundation, Albert A., MI, 877
White Pigeon Area Community Foundation, The, MI, 1178
Whiteley Foundation, John and Elizabeth, The, MI, 878
Whitfield Fund, Inc., The, MI, 879
Whiting Foundation, The, MI, 880
Whiting Memorial Foundation, Henry and Harriet, MI, 881
Whole Foods Market, Inc. Corporate Giving Program, TX, 1073
Wickes Foundation, Harvey Randall, MI, 882
Wickson-Link Memorial Foundation, MI, 883
Wierenga Family Foundation, Inc., The, CA, 884
Wigginton Educational Foundation, MI, 885
Wilcox Family Foundation, CA, 886
Wiley Scholarship, Inc., Alfredine Jordan, MI, 1465
Willard Trust, George & Emily Harris, MI, 1466
William Beaumont Hospital, MI, 1467
Williams Charitable Foundation, Ronald A. & Patricia M., MI, 887
Williams Foundation, Jamison, The, MI, 888
Wilson Foundation, Elizabeth Ruthruff, NJ, 889
Wilson Foundation, Karen Colina, MI, 890
Wilson Fund, Matilda R., MI, 891
Wilson Scholarship Fund, MI, 892
Wilson Scholarship Fund, Rodney B., MI, see 892
Wilson Trust, Lula C., MI, 893
Wilson, Jr. Foundation, Inc., Charles Stanley, MI, 894
Winans Foundation Trust, MI, 895
Winer Charitable Trust, Irving, MI, see 896
Winer Foundation, Irving, The, MI, 896
Winkle Foundation, Gerard I. and Beverly L., The, MI, 1572
Winkler Memorial Trust, John J., MI, 897
Winn Foundation, Bill and June, MI, 898
Winn Foundation, John and Mary Jo, MI, see 899
Winn Foundation, John and Zita, MI, 899
Winship Memorial Scholarship Foundation, MI, 900
Wirick Foundation, Evelyn and Ronald, MI, 901
Wirtz Charitable Foundation, John W. and Wanda A., MI, 902
Wirtz Family Foundation, MI, 903
Wisconsin Electric System Foundation, Inc., WI, see 1074
Wisconsin Energy Corporation Foundation, Inc., WI, 1074
Wisconsin Public Service Foundation, Inc., WI, 1075
Wise Fund, MI, 904
WMY Fund, MI, 905
Wolfe Family Foundation, Howard H. & Joan M., MI, see 906
Wolfe Family Foundation, MI, 906
Wolff Family Foundation, Jean & Lewis, MI, 907
Wolters Foundation, Kate & Richard, MI, 908
Wolverine Human Services, MI, 1468
Wolverine World Wide Foundation, MI, 1076
Wong Foundation, Lawrence and Sylvia, The, MI, 909
Workers Foundation, The, MI, 910
World Heritage Foundation, MI, 911
Worldwide Christian Schools, MI, 1469
Worsham Family Foundation, The, MI, 912
WPS Foundation, Inc., WI, see 1075
WPS Scholarship Foundation, MI, see 1574
Wren Foundation, MI, see 402
Wright Scholarship Foundation, Orlo H., MI, 1573
Wright Trust, V. Ennis, MI, 913
Wyandotte Public Schools Foundation, MI, see 1574
Wyandotte Public Schools Scholarship Foundation, MI, 1574
Wynalda Foundation, Robert & Patricia, MI, 914
Wyoming Community Foundation, MI, 1179

Xcel Energy Foundation, MN, 1077

Yaffe Foundation, Frederick and Katherine, MI, 915
Yaffe Foundation, Frederick S., MI, see 915
Yankama Feed the Children Charitable Foundation, MI, 916
Yaw Foundation, William R. & Madeleine Couzens, MI, see 905
Yeager Family Foundation, Thomas and Maria, The, MI, 917
Yeager Foundation, Inc., Charles F., MI, 918
Yeo Family Foundation, MI, 919
York Foundation, Jerome B. & Eilene M., MI, 920
Young Foundation, Coleman A., MI, 1470
Young Foundation, MI, 921
Young Old United Foundation, MI, 1471
Young Woman's Home Association of Detroit, MI, see 922
Young Woman's Home Association, MI, 922

Youth Foundation of America, The, MI, 923
Ypsilanti Area Community Fund, MI, 1180

Zampetis Family Foundation, T. K., The, OH, 924
Zelt Foundation, Beverly A., MI, 925

Zemke Scholarship Fund, MI, 926
Zimmerman-Wolff Family Foundation, MI, 927
Zionist Cultural Committee, The, MI, 928
Zoller Family Foundation, MI, 929

Zondervan Foundation, MI, see 930
Zondervan Foundation, P. J. and Mary, MI, 930
Zonta Club of Muskegon Area Foundation, MI, 931
Zurschmiede, Sr. Foundation, W. Tom, MI, 932
Zynda Family Foundation, Virginia, MI, 1575

TYPES OF SUPPORT INDEX

List of terms: Terms for the major types of support used in this index are listed below with definitions.

Index: In the index itself, grantmaker entries are arranged under each term by state location, abbreviated name, and sequence number. Grantmakers in boldface type make grants on a national, regional, or international basis. The others generally limit giving to the state or city in which they are located.

Annual campaigns: any organized effort by a nonprofit to secure gifts on an annual basis; also called annual appeals.

Building/renovation: money raised for construction, renovation, remodeling, or rehabilitation of buildings; may be part of an organization's capital campaign.

Capital campaigns: a campaign, usually extending over a period of years, to raise substantial funds for enduring purposes, such as building or endowment funds.

Cause-related marketing: linking gifts to charity with marketing promotions. This may involve donating products which will then be auctioned or given away in a drawing with the proceeds benefiting a charity. The advertising campaign for the product will be combined with the promotion for the charity. In other cases it will be advertised that when a customer buys the product a certain amount of the proceeds will be donated to charity. Often gifts made to charities stemming from cause-related marketing are not called charitable donations and may be assigned as expenses to the department in charge of the program. Public affairs and marketing are the departments usually involved.

Conferences/seminars: a grant to cover the expenses of holding a conference or seminar.

Consulting services: professional staff support provided by the foundation to a nonprofit to consult on a project of mutual interest or to evaluate services (not a cash grant).

Continuing support: a grant that is renewed on a regular basis.

Curriculum development: grants to schools, colleges, universities, and educational support organizations to develop general or discipline-specific curricula.

Debt reduction: also known as deficit financing. A grant to reduce the recipient organization's indebtedness; frequently refers to mortgage payments.

Donated equipment: surplus furniture, office machines, paper, appliances, laboratory apparatus, or other items that may be given to charities, schools, or hospitals.

Donated land: land or developed property. Institutions of higher education often receive gifts of real estate; land has also been given to community groups for housing development or for parks or recreational facilities.

Donated products: companies giving away what they make or produce. Product donations can include periodic clothing donations to a shelter for the homeless or regular donations of pharmaceuticals to a health clinic resulting in a reliable supply.

Emergency funds: a one-time grant to cover immediate short-term funding needs on an emergency basis.

Employee matching gifts: a contribution to a charitable organization by a corporate employee which is matched by a similar contribution from the employer. Many corporations support employee matching gift programs in higher education to stimulate their employees to give to the college or university of their choice. In addition, many foundations support matching gift programs for their officers and directors.

Employee volunteer services: an ongoing coordinated effort through which the company promotes involvement with nonprofits on the part of employees. The involvement may be during work time or after hours. (Employees may also volunteer on their own initiative; however, that is not described as corporate volunteerism). Many companies honor their employees with awards for outstanding volunteer efforts. In making cash donations, many favor the organizations with which their employees have worked as volunteers. Employee volunteerism runs the gamut from school tutoring programs to sales on work premises of employee-made crafts or baked goods to benefit nonprofits. Management of the programs can range from fully-staffed offices of corporate volunteerism to a part-time coordinating responsibility on the part of one employee.

Employee-related scholarships: a scholarship program funded by a company-sponsored foundation usually for children of employees; programs are frequently administered by the National Merit Scholarship Corporation which is responsible for selection of scholars.

Endowments: a bequest or gift intended to be kept permanently and invested to provide income for continued support of an organization.

Equipment: a grant to purchase equipment, furnishings, or other materials.

Exchange programs: usually refers to funds for educational exchange programs for foreign students.

Fellowships: usually indicates funds awarded to educational institutions to support fellowship programs. A few foundations award fellowships directly to individuals.

Film/video/radio: grants to fund a specific film, video, or radio production.

General/operating support: a grant made to further the general purpose or work of an organization, rather than for a specific purpose or project; also called unrestricted grants.

Grants to individuals: awards made directly by the foundation to individuals rather than to nonprofit organizations; includes aid to the needy. (See also "Fellowships," "Scholarships—to individuals," and "Student loans—to individuals.")

In-kind gifts: a contribution of equipment, supplies, or other property as distinct from a monetary grant. Some organizations may also donate space or staff time as an in-kind contribution.

Income development: grants for fundraising, marketing, and to expand audience base.

Internship funds: usually indicates funds awarded to an institution or organization to support an internship program rather than a grant to an individual.

Land acquisition: a grant to purchase real estate property.

Lectureships: see "Curriculum development."

Loaned talent: an aspect of employee volunteerism. It differs from the usual definition of such in that it usually involves loaned professionals and executive staff who are helping a nonprofit in an area involving their particular skills. Loaned talents can assist a nonprofit in strategic planning, dispute resolution or negotiation services, office administration, real estate technical assistance, personnel policies, lobbying, consulting, fundraising, and legal and tax advice.

Loans: see "Program-related investments/loans" and "Student loans—to individuals.")

Loans—to individuals: assistance distributed directly to individuals in the form of loans.

Management development/capacity building: grants for salaries, staff support, staff training, strategic and long-term planning, capacity building, budgeting and accounting.

Matching/challenge support: a grant which is made to match funds provided by another donor. (See also "Employee matching gifts.")

Operating budgets: see "General/operating support."

Professorships: a grant to an educational institution to endow a professorship or chair.

Program development: grants to support specific projects or programs as opposed to general purpose grants.

Program evaluation: grants to evaluate a specific project or program; includes awards both to agencies to pay for evaluation costs and to research institutes and other program evaluators.

Program-related investments/loans: a loan is any temporary award of funds that must be repaid. A program-related investment is a loan or other investment (as distinguished from a grant) made by a foundation to another organization for a project related to the foundation's stated charitable purpose and interests.

Public relations services: may include printing and duplicating, audio-visual and graphic arts services, helping to plan special events such as festivals, piggyback advertising (advertisements that mention a company while also promoting a nonprofit), and public service advertising.

Publication: a grant to fund reports or other publications issued by a nonprofit resulting from research or projects of interest to the foundation.

Renovation projects: see "Building/renovation."

Research: usually indicates funds awarded to institutions to cover costs of investigations and clinical trials. Research grants for individuals are usually referred to as fellowships.

Scholarship funds: a grant to an educational institution or organization to support a scholarship program, mainly for students at the undergraduate level. (See also "Employee-related scholarships.")

Scholarships—to individuals: assistance awarded directly to individuals in the form of

educational grants or scholarships. (See also "Employee-related scholarships.")

Seed money: a grant or contribution used to start a new project or organization. Seed grants may cover salaries and other operating expenses of a new project. Also known as "start-up funds."

Special projects: see "Program development."

Sponsorships: endorsements of charities by corporations; or corporate contributions to all or part of a charitable event.

Student aid: see "Fellowships," "Scholarships—to individuals," and "Student loans—to individuals."

Student loans—to individuals: assistance awarded directly to individuals in the form of educational loans.

Technical assistance: operational or management assistance given to nonprofit organizations; may include fundraising assistance, budgeting and financial planning, program planning, legal advice, marketing, and other aids to management. Assistance may be offered directly by a foundation staff member or in the form of a grant to pay for the services of an outside consultant.

Use of facilities: this may include rent free office space for temporary periods, dining and meeting facilities, telecommunications services, mailing services, transportation services, or computer services.

Annual campaigns

Connecticut: Pryor 661
Georgia: **Georgia 992**
Illinois: Kalt 433, Souder 764
Kentucky: Humana 1003
Louisiana: Entergy 979
Massachusetts: **Cabot 947**
Michigan: Albion-Homer 1183, Asthma 1197, Baldwin 38, Barry 1085, Batts 941, Berkowitz 65, Borman's 88, Burroughs 111, Butzel 946, Camp 115, Cheboygan 1223, Clannad 136, Community 1108, Cook 147, Dana 963, Dart 168, Davis 171, DeRoy 180, Detroit 1494, DeVos 186, DeVos 187, DeVos 189, Ervin 227, Farver 241, Ford 986, General 990, Gerstacker 292, Gilmore 299, Gornick 310, Granger 313, **H.I.S. 327**, Harding 346, Herrick 367, Hudson 392, Hunter 397, **Isabel 409, Jewish 1296**, JSJ 1010, Lansing 484, Lapeer 1141, Leighton 495, Lenawee 1318, Manistee 1147, Masco 1026, Michigan 1349, Miller 565, Miller 566, Missaukee 1153, Monroe 577, Moore 578, Morley 584, **National 597**, Olds 616, Oleson 617, Parfet 629, Pentecost 641, Pistons 1046, Sage 708, Sanilac 1165, Schmuckal 719, **Shaevsky 1395**, Shelden 736, **Society 1402**, Sojourner 1403, St. Clair 774, Todd 1064, Towsley 816, United 1424, Upton 833, Van 836, Vanderweide 844, Warchol 849, Weatherwax 852, Wege 856, Wickes 882, Wilson 893

Minnesota: CHS 952, TCF 1061, Weyerhaeuser 876
Nebraska: Kaufman 439
Ohio: Anderson 21, Charter 950, Cliffs 954, Fifth 984, Hildreth 373, KeyBank 1018
Pennsylvania: West 1071
Texas: Bray 94
Washington: Fehsenfeld 247
Wisconsin: Beauchamp 57, Bishop 78, Hess 368, Wisconsin 1075

Building/renovation

California: Ayrshire 34, Wilcox 886
Florida: **Knight 462**
Georgia: **Georgia 992**
Illinois: Kalt 433, Keller 448, Souder 764
Kentucky: Humana 1003
Massachusetts: **Cabot 947**, Hanover 999
Michigan: Albion 1078, Allegan 1080, Americana 16, Andersen 19, Annis 25, **Arcus 27**, Baldwin 38, Barry 1085, Barth 45, Battle Creek 1086, Batts 941, Bauervic 51, Bauervic 53, Bay 1087, Besser 69, Biederman 1483, Bilkie 72, Blodgett 82, Bonisteel 85, Burroughs 111, Cadillac 1092, Capital 1094, CMS 955, **Collectors 1228**, Community 1102, Community 1103, Community 1104, Community 1108, Community 1109, Community 1110, Community 1111, Consumers 961, Cook 147,

Cronin 155, Dagenais 162, Dalton 163, Dana 963, Dart 168, Davenport 170, Davis 171, Deffenbaugh 176, **DENSO 968**, DeRoy 180, Detroit 970, DeVos 186, DeVos 189, Dow 975, Dow 202, Fabri 980, Farver 241, First 1499, Ford 986, Foundation 270, Frankenmuth 1123, Fremont 1124, Gerstacker 292, Gilmore 299, Glassen 301, Grand 1125, Grand Rapids 1127, Grand 1128, Gratiot 1129, Great 1273, Greenville 1130, **H.I.S. 327**, Hancock 340, Harding 347, Hastings 1000, Herrick 367, His 378, Holden 381, Home 384, Hudson 391, Hudson 392, Hunter 397, Hurst 398, Idema 402, Ionia 1134, Iosco 1135, Irwin 408, **Isabel 409**, Jackson 1137, JSJ 1010, **Kakarala 432**, Kantzler 434, **Kellogg's 1015**, Knight 461, **Kresge 471**, La-Z-Boy 1022, Lake 1140, Lansing 484, Leelanau 1142, Leighton 495, Lenawee 1143, Linden 503, Lyons 516, Marquette 1148, Marshall 1149, Marshall 526, Masco 1026, McGregor 542, Mecosta 1150, Midland 1152, Miller 562, Miller 565, Monroe 577, Moore 578, Morley 584, Mount Pleasant 1154, Mount Zion 589, North 1156, Oleson 617, Parfet 629, Pentecost 641, Perrigo 1045, Petoskey 1162, Pistons 1046, Plym 649, Pokagon 1048, Ratner 668, Rawson 670, Redies 1052, Reynolds 681, Robison 690, Rotary 1391, Sage 708, Saginaw 1164, Sanilac 1165, Schalon 716, Shelden 736, Shiffman 739, Sparta 1172, **Steelcase 1058**, Straits 1174, Strosacker 787, Stubnitz 789, Sturgis 1175, Three 1176, Tiscornia 814, Todd 1064,

Towsley 816, Tuscola 1177, Upton 833, Van Den Bosch 838, Vanderwaals 843, Vanderweide 844, Warchol 849, Weatherwax 852, Wege 856, Whiting 881, Wickes 882, Wickson 883, Wilson 891, Wilson 893, **Worldwide 1469**, Wynalda 914, Wyoming 1179

New Jersey: Campbell 949

New York: Nonprofit 1361

Ohio: American 937, Anderson 21, Cliffs 954, Fifth 984

Pennsylvania: PNC 1047, West 1071

Texas: Bray 94

Wisconsin: Bishop 78, Hess 368, Kaufman 441, Wisconsin 1075

Capital campaigns

California: Ayrshire 34

Connecticut: Pryor 661

Florida: **Knight 462**

Georgia: **Georgia 992**

Illinois: Gust 323, Kalt 433, Keller 448

Kentucky: Humana 1003

Massachusetts: **Cabot 947**

Michigan: Andersen 19, **Arcus 27**, Baldwin 38, Barry 1085, Barstow 44, Barth 45, Batts 941, Bay 1087, Besser 69, Bonisteel 85, Borman's 88, Burroughs 111, Camp 115, Capital 1094, Carls 118, CMS 955, Comerica 956, Community 1102, Community 1109, Community 1111, Community 1112, Consumers 961, Cook 147, Dalton 163, Dana 963, Dart 168, Davenport 170, Davis 171, **DENSO 968**, Detroit 1494, DeVos 186, DeVos 187, DeVos 188, DeVos 189, Dow 975, DTE 977, Fabri 980, Farver 241, First 1499, Ford 986, Fremont 1124, Frey 276, Gerstacker 292, Gilmore 299, Grand Haven 1126, Grand Rapids 1127, Grand Rapids 1268, Granger 313, Greenville 1130, **H.I.S. 327**, Herrick 367, Hickman 371, Hirvonen 377, Hudson 391, Hudson 392, Idema 402, Ionia 1134, **Isabel 409**, Jackson 1137, **Jewish 1296**, JSJ 1010, Kantzler 434, Kellogg 449, Knight 461, **Kresge 471**, Lansing 484, Leelanau 1142, Lenawee 1143, Lyons 516, Marquette 1148, Masco 1026, McGregor 542, Miller 562, Miller 565, Miller 566, Monroe 577, Moore 578, Morley 584, Mount Pleasant 1154, Nelson 599, Olds 616, Oleson 617, Parfet 629, Pierce 1550, Pulte 1050, Redies 1052, Reynolds 681, Robison 690, Rotary 1391, **Rotary 1393**, Sage 708, Schmuckal 719, Shelden 736, Shepherd 738, Silverwing 747, Smith 758, **Society 1402**, Sparta 1172, **Steelcase 1058**, Sturgis 1175, Three 1176, Tiscornia 814, Todd 1064, Towsley 816, Upton 833, Van 836, Vanderweide 844, Weatherwax 852, Wege 856, Wickson 883, Wilson 893, Wolters 908, World 911, Wyoming 1179

Minnesota: TCF 1061

New York: Mitsubishi 1035

Ohio: American 937, Anderson 21, Charter 950, Cliffs 954, Fifth 984, KeyBank 1018, Kroger 1021

Pennsylvania: PNC 1047, West 1071

Virginia: **Gannett 988**

Wisconsin: Wisconsin 1074, Wisconsin 1075

Conferences/seminars

California: Ayrshire 34

Florida: Hagen 332

Georgia: **Georgia 992**

Illinois: Allstate 935, **Joyce 427**

Michigan: Americana 16, Ann Arbor 1083, **Arcus 27**, Arts 1194, ArtServe 1196, Barry 1085, Battle Creek 1086, Branch 1091, Cadillac 1092, Colina 141, Community 1104, Dearborn 965, Delta 1238, Detroit 1494, **Earhart 217**, Fremont 1124, Gilmore 299, Gratiot 1129, Great 1273, Hillsdale 1131, India 406, Iosco 1135, Jewish 1298, Lansing 484, Lenawee 1143, Marshall 1149, Michigan 1151, **Mott 587**, Mount Pleasant 1154, North 1156, Olds 616, Pokagon 1048, Shiawassee 1168, Shiffman

739, Sojourner 1403, Straits 1174, Thompson 811, Weatherwax 852, **Worldwide 1469**, Ypsilanti 1180, Zondervan 930

Minnesota: CHS 952

New York: Local 1323, Mitsubishi 1035, Nonprofit 1361

Ohio: Anderson 21

Virginia: **Gannett 988**

Consulting services

Connecticut: Pryor 661

Indiana: Foellinger 258

Michigan: **Arcus 27**, Arts 1194, Barry 1085, Blodgett 82, Charlevoix 1096, Community 1103, Dyer 215, Fremont 1124, Gilmore 299, Hudson 392, Iosco 1135, Jackson 1137, Lansing 484, Marquette 1148, Michigan 1350, Midland 1152, Miller 565, Missaukee 1153, Sturgis 1175, United 1424, Weatherwax 852, **Worldwide 1469**

New York: Nonprofit 1361

Continuing support

California: Toyota 1066

Georgia: **Georgia 992**

Illinois: **Abbott 933, Joyce 427**, Keller 448, Nuveen 612

Indiana: Foellinger 258

Kentucky: Humana 1003

Michigan: Allegan 1080, Arts 1194, Batts 941, Besser 69, Biederman 1483, Burroughs 111, Clannad 136, **Collectors 1228**, Consumers 961, Crane 153, Dalton 163, Dana 963, Dart 168, Davis 171, DeRoy 180, DeVos 186, DeVos 187, DeVos 189, Doan 195, Dow 975, DTE 977, Ervin 227, Farver 241, Ford 986, Fremont 1124, General 990, Gerstacker 292, Gilmore 299, Great 1273, **H.I.S. 327**, Harding 346, Henry 363, Herrick 367, Holden 381, Hudson 392, **Isabel 409**, Jewish 1298, JSJ 1010, Lake 1140, Leighton 495, M & M 1145, Mackinac 1146, McGregor 542, Merkley 555, Miller 566, Missaukee 1153, Molloy 576, Moore 578, Morley 584, **Mott 587**, Mott 588, Oleson 617, Parfet 629, Pokagon 1048, Ratner 668, Robison 690, Sage 708, Sanilac 1165, Shelden 736, Shiawassee 1168, Shiffman 739, Skillman 755, Sojourner 1403, Strosacker 787, Thompson 811, Tiscornia 814, Todd 1064, Towsley 816, Vanderweide 844, Vollbrecht 846, Warchol 849, Westerman 872, Whirlpool 1072, Wickson 883, Wilson 893, Wynalda 914, Young 922

Minnesota: TCF 1061

New York: **Ford 260, Heron 366**, Mitsubishi 1035, **New York 1038**

Ohio: American 937, Fifth 984, **JPMorgan 1008**, KeyBank 1018

Pennsylvania: PNC 1047, West 1071

Texas: Bray 94

Wisconsin: Beauchamp 57, Bishop 78, McIntyre 543, Wisconsin 1075

Curriculum development

Florida: Hagen 332, **Knight 462**

Illinois: Allstate 935, Keller 448

Kentucky: Humana 1003

Michigan: Albion 1078, Allegan 1080, **Arcus 27**, AtWater 33, Barry 1085, Battle Creek 1086, Bay 1087, Binda 73, Blodgett 82, Cadillac 1092, Camp 115, Central 1095, Community 1109, Community 1111, Consumers 961, Dart 168, Davenport 170, Dow 975, DTE 977, Dyer 215, **Earhart 217**, Ford 986, Fremont 1124, Grand 1128, Gratiot 1129, Great 1273, Greenville 1130, Harbor 1276, Herrick 367, Iosco 1135, Jewish 1297, Jewish 1298, Kemp 1017, Marshall 1149, Michigan 1151, Miller 566, North 1156, Oleson 617, Sanilac 1165, Shiawassee 1168, **Society 1402**, Southfield 1171, Straits 1174, Tuscola 1177, Warchol 849,

Weatherwax 852, Wege 856, **Worldwide 1469**, Young 922, Zondervan 930

Minnesota: CHS 952

New York: **New York 1038**

Ohio: HCR 1002, KeyBank 1018

Pennsylvania: PNC 1047

Debt reduction

Michigan: Camp 115, Dalton 163, Gilmore 299, Hirvonen 377, Knight 461, Wynalda 914

Wisconsin: Bishop 78

Donated equipment

Louisiana: Entergy 979

Michigan: **Dow 974**, Tigers 1062

New York: Mitsubishi 1035

Ohio: **JPMorgan 1008**

Donated products

Michigan: Consumers 960, Domino's 972, **Dow 973, Dow 974**, GM 994, Gordon 995, **Haworth 1001, Kellogg 1014**, Masco 1025, Meijer 1029, Michigan 1033, **Steelcase 1059**

Minnesota: Life 1023

Nebraska: ConAgra 959

Ohio: Charter 950, Kroger 1020, Tim 1063

Texas: **Whole 1073**

Emergency funds

Connecticut: Pryor 661

Florida: **Knight 462**

Louisiana: Entergy 979

Michigan: Albion-Homer 1183, Allegan 1080, Ann Arbor 1083, Battle Creek 1086, Bay 1087, Cadillac 1092, Charlevoix 1096, Clannad 136, Community 1100, Community 1103, Community 1108, Community 1110, Dalton 163, Dana 963, Ervin 227, Farver 241, Ford 986, Frankenmuth 1123, Fremont 1124, General 990, Gerstacker 292, Gilmore 299, Gratiot 1129, Greenville 1130, Heat 1278, Herrick 367, Hunter 397, Kalamazoo 1138, **Kellogg 1013**, Lansing 484, Mackinac 1146, Macomb 1327, Michigan 1349, Miller 565, Moore 578, Morley 584, Mount Pleasant 1154, Olds 616, Parfet 629, Pellerito 638, Perry 643, Saginaw 1164, Sanilac 1165, Southfield 1171, Stubnitz 789, Tiscornia 814, Tuscola 1177, United 1448, Warchol 849, Weatherwax 852, Whiting 881, Wilson 893, Wynalda 914, Young 922, Ypsilanti 1180

Ohio: Anderson 21

Pennsylvania: West 1071

Texas: Bray 94

Wisconsin: Bishop 78

Employee matching gifts

Florida: **Knight 462**

Illinois: **Abbott 933**, Allstate 935, **Joyce 427**

Louisiana: Entergy 979

Massachusetts: **Cabot 947**

Michigan: Amerisure 938, **Arcus 27, BorgWarner 945**, Consumers 961, Dana 963, **Dow 973, Dow 974**, Dow 975, DTE 977, Ford 986, Fremont 1124, Frey 276, General 990, Gilmore 299, Grand Rapids 1127, Hudson 392, Jackson 1007, Kalamazoo 1138, **Kellogg 1014, Kellogg 450, Kellogg's 1015, Kresge 471**, M & M 1145, Masco 1025, Masco 1026, McGregor 542, Meritor 1030, Miller 565, Morley 584, **Mott 587**, Skillman 755, **Steelcase 1058**, Towsley 816, Whirlpool 1072, Wolverine 1076

Minnesota: TCF 1061, Xcel 1077

Nebraska: ConAgra 959

New Jersey: Campbell 949
New York: **Ford 260, Heron 366,** Mitsubishi 1035, **New York 1038,** Newsweek/Daily 1039
Ohio: AEP 934, Charter 950, Cliffs 954, HCR 1002, **JPMorgan 1008,** KeyBank 1018
Pennsylvania: PNC 1047, West 1071
Tennessee: Nissan 1041
Virginia: **Gannett 988**
Wisconsin: Wisconsin 1074, Wisconsin 1075

Employee volunteer services

Arizona: Circle 953
California: SANYO 1054
Florida: CSX 962
Georgia: **Georgia 992**
Illinois: Allstate 935
Kentucky: Humana 1003
Louisiana: Entergy 979
Massachusetts: **Cabot 947,** Hanover 999
Michigan: American 936, Amerisure 938, **Amway 939,** Blue 942, **BorgWarner 945,** Chemical 951, Comerica 957, Con 958, Consumers 961, **Delphi 966,** DENSO 967, DTE 976, DTE 977, **Ford 985,** Ford 986, Foremost 987, General 990, Gleaner 993, GM 994, **Haworth 1001,** Jackson 1007, **Kellogg 1014, Kellogg's 1015,** Meritor 1030, **Miller 1034,** Pulte 1050, **Steelcase 1059,** Taubman 1060, Valassis 1068, Varnum 1069, Whirlpool 1072
Minnesota: TCF 1061, Xcel 1077
Nevada: MGM 1031
New Jersey: Campbell 949
New York: Mitsubishi 1035, **New York 1038,** Newsweek/Daily 1039
Ohio: Charter 950, Fifth 983, HCR 1002, **JPMorgan 1008,** KeyBank 1018, Kroger 1020, Kroger 1021
Pennsylvania: Toll 1065
Tennessee: Nissan 1041
Texas: Quicksilver 1051, **Whole 1073**
Virginia: **General 989**
Wisconsin: ShopKo 1055, Wisconsin 1075

Employee-related scholarships

Georgia: **Georgia 992**
Illinois: Allstate 935, Taylor 799
Kentucky: Humana 1003
Louisiana: Entergy 979
Massachusetts: Hanover 999
Michigan: Community 1111, Con 958, Dart 964, Fabri 980, Ford 986, Grand Rapids 1127, **Haworth 1001,** Kohn 465, L & L 1522, Lenawee 1143, Michigan 1032, **Steelcase 1058,** Universal 1067, Whirlpool 1072
Minnesota: TCF 1061
Nebraska: ConAgra 959
New Jersey: Campbell 949
New York: Mitsubishi 1035, **New York 1038**
Ohio: Fifth 984
Pennsylvania: West 1071
Wisconsin: Wisconsin 1075

Endowments

California: Ayrshire 34
Florida: **Knight 462**
Michigan: Adray 5, Annis 25, **Arcus 27,** Barry 1085, Batts 941, Biederman 1483, Branch 1091, Burroughs 111, Central 1095, Charlevoix 1096, Chippewa 1097, Community 1108, Doan 195, Dow 202, Fremont 1124, Gerstacker 292, Grand 1128, Greenville 1130, Henry 363, Herrick 367, Hickman 371, Holley 383, Italian 1294, JSJ 1010, Kalamazoo 1306, Lapeer 1141, Law 490, Leelanau 1142, Leighton 495, Lenawee 1143, Manistee 1147, Miller 566, Mount Pleasant 1154, Paine

624, Palmer 625, Parfet 629, Pentecost 641, Pierce 1550, Ratner 668, Roscommon 1163, Sage 708, Shelden 736, Shiawassee 1168, Strosacker 787, Sturgis 1175, Towsley 816, Wege 856, Westerman 872, Whiting 881, Wilson 891, Wolters 908
Minnesota: Weyerhaeuser 876
New York: **Ford 260**
Ohio: American 937
Pennsylvania: McCardell 538
Texas: Fruehauf 277
Wisconsin: Hess 368, Wisconsin 1074

Equipment

California: Ayrshire 34
Georgia: **Georgia 992**
Illinois: Seabury 727
Massachusetts: **Cabot 947**
Michigan: Adray 5, Albion 1078, Allegan 1080, Andersen 19, Annis 25, Arts 1194, Baldwin 38, Barry 1085, Battle Creek 1086, Bauervic 51, Bauervic 53, Bay 1087, Biederman 1483, Blodgett 82, Bonisteel 85, Boutell 92, Branch 1091, Cadillac 1092, Canton 1093, Capital 1094, Clannad 136, CMS 955, **Collectors 1228,** Comerica 957, Community 1102, Community 1104, Community 1108, Community 1109, Community 1110, Community 1111, Consumers 960, Consumers 961, Cronin 155, Dagenais 162, Dalton 163, Dana 963, Dart 168, Dearborn 965, Delano 179, **DENSO 968,** Doan 195, **Dow 973,** Dow 975, Dow 202, Eddy 218, Fabri 980, Farley 240, Farver 241, First 1499, Ford 986, Fremont 1124, General 990, Gerstacker 292, Gilmore 299, Grand 1125, Grand Haven 1126, Grand 1128, Gratiot 1507, Great 1273, Greenville 1130, **H.I.S. 327,** Hastings 1000, Herrick 367, Holden 381, Hunter 397, Hurst 398, Ionia 1134, Iosco 1135, Irwin 408, **Isabel 409,** Jackson 1137, Jennings 418, Kalamazoo 1138, Kantzler 434, Kellogg 449, **Kresge 471,** Lakeland 1315, Lansing 484, Leelanau 1142, Lenawee 1143, M & M 1145, Marquette 1148, Marshall 1149, Marshall 526, Mason 1027, McGregor 542, McNally 550, Mecosta 1150, Metro 556, Michigan 1151, Michigan 1349, Midland 1152, Miller 565, Moore 578, Morley 584, Mount Pleasant 1154, North 1156, Olds 616, Oleson 617, Parfet 629, Pellerito 638, Petoskey 1162, Pokagon 1048, Ponting 653, Ratner 668, Redies 1052, Reynolds 681, Robison 690, Rotary 1391, **Rotary 1393,** Royal 698, Sage 708, Saginaw 1164, Sanilac 1165, Schoolcraft 1166, Shelden 736, Simmons 748, **Society 1402,** South 1169, Southwest 767, Sparta 1172, St. Clair 774, **Steelcase 1058,** Straits 1174, Strosacker 787, Stubnitz 789, Sturgis 1175, Tahquamenon 1415, Thompson 811, Three 1176, Tigers 1062, Tiscornia 814, Tuscola 1177, Upton 833, Van Den Bosch 838, Village 1455, Vollbrecht 846, Weatherwax 852, Weed 855, Wege 856, Whiting 881, Wickes 882, Wilson 883, Wilson 891, Wilson 893, **Worldwide 1469,** Wyoming 1179, Young 922, Zondervan 930
Minnesota: Life 1023
New Jersey: Campbell 949
New York: Nonprofit 1361
Ohio: Fifth 984, **JPMorgan 1008**
Texas: Bray 94
Virginia: **Gannett 988**
Wisconsin: Beauchamp 57, Bishop 78, Wisconsin 1074, Wisconsin 1075

Exchange programs

Michigan: Community 1103, Community 1109, Warchol 849

Fellowships

Florida: **Knight 462**

Illinois: **Abbott 933**
Michigan: ACI 1181, Baldwin 38, Blue 1208, Delta 1238, **Earhart 217,** Great 1273, **H.I.S. 327, International 1292,** Irwin 408, Marzke 529, Michigan 1347, **Society 1401, Society 1402,** Stoddard 783
New York: Mitsubishi 1035
Ohio: Heyl 1282

Film/video/radio

California: Ayrshire 34
Illinois: Allstate 935
Michigan: Arts 1194, Battle Creek 1086, Iosco 1135, Marquette 1148, North 1156, Sanilac 1165, Straits 1174

General/operating support

Arizona: Circle 953
California: **Parsons 1044,** Pati 634, Toyota 1066, Wilcox 886
Colorado: Seidman 729
Florida: CSX 962, Detter 183, Dexter 190, Hasey 356, **Knight 462,** Nowak 610
Georgia: **Georgia 992**
Illinois: **Abbott 933,** Akers 6, Allstate 935, Gust 323, Guzikowski 326, **Joyce 427,** Kalt 433, Keller 448, Meeks 553, Nuveen 612, Seabury 727, Souder 764
Indiana: Foellinger 258, Katz 436, Neff 1539
Kentucky: Humana 1003
Massachusetts: **Cabot 947,** Hanover 999, **Thome 810**
Michigan: Adray 5, Americana 16, Amerisure 938, **Amway 939,** Amy 17, Anchor 1082, Anderson 20, Annis 25, Applebaum 1191, **Arcus 27,** Arts 1194, Baker 36, Balk 39, Barry 1085, Barstow 44, Barth 45, Barton 940, Batts 941, Bauervic 53, Bay 1087, Beals 56, Bemis 62, Bertsch 67, Besse 68, Besser 69, Biederman 1483, Birkhill 76, Birtwistle 77, Blue 942, Boll 84, Bonisteel 85, Bonner 86, Bonsall 87, Borders 944, **BorgWarner 945,** Borovoy 89, Branch 1091, Brauer 93, Brinkerhoff-Sample 100, Brintnall 101, Bronner 102, Buist 1484, Busch 112, Butzel 946, Byron 1212, Cadillac 948, Camp 115, Canaan 117, Canton 1093, Capital 1094, **Center 1220,** Chamberlain 124, Charlupski 127, Chemical 951, Citizens 134, Clannad 136, CMS 955, Cochrane 140, Coleman 1487, Comerica 956, Comerica 957, Community 1100, Community 1107, Community 1108, Con 958, Consumers 960, Consumers 961, Conway 146, Cook 147, Coon 149, Copley 150, Crane 153, Cummings 157, Dalton 163, Dana 963, Dart 964, Dart 168, Davisson 172, Dearborn 965, Deffenbaugh 176, Delano 179, **Delphi 966,** DENSO 967, DeRoy 180, Detroit 181, DeVlieg 185, DeVos 186, DeVos 187, DeVos 188, DeVos 189, Doan 195, Dooge 199, Dorfman 201, **Dow 974,** Dow 202, DTE 977, En 222, Engle 978, **Erb 224,** Ervin 227, Evergreene 1497, Ewald 232, Faigle 234, Farver 241, Federal 981, Fetzer 249, Fibre 982, Fink 252, Firestone 254, Fish 255, Ford 261, **Ford 985,** Foremost 987, Four 1122, Freeman 274, Fremont 1124, Gary 287, General 990, Generations 991, George 289, Gerstacker 292, Gibbs 294, Gilmore 299, GM 994, **Gordon 307,** Gratiot 1129, Great 996, Greene 317, Greenville 1130, Haggard 333, Hammond 998, Hampson 338, Harding 346, Harding 347, Hastings 1000, **Haworth 1001,** HCC 1512, Heart 1277, Hees 360, Hennessey 362, Herrick 367, His 378, Holden 381, Home 1284, Horgan 387, Howard 389, Hudson 391, Hudson 392, Hurst 398, Idema 402, **IMRA 1005, Isabel 409,** Isabella 1006, Jackson 1137, Jackson 1007, Jennings 418, Johnson 423, Jones 424, Joy 426, JSJ 1010, Kahn 430, **Kakarala 432,** Kalamazoo 1138, Katzman 437, **Kellogg 1014,** Kellogg 449, **Kellogg's 1015,** Kelly 451, Kelly 1016, Kemler 452, Kemp 1017, Kentwood 455, Kerkstra 456, Knight 461, Kosch 467, Krause 470, La-Z-Boy 1022, Lake 1140, Larson 486, Law 490, Lay 491,

Legion 494, Leighton 495, Lenawee 1143, Lewis 500, Linden 503, Little 504, Lugers 511, Lukens 512, Lyons 516, MAC 1024, Mackinac 1146, Marcks 524, Marshall 1149, Marshall 526, Marzke 529, Masco 1025, Masco 1026, McGregor 542, McLeod 548, McNally 550, Mecosta 1150, Meijer 1029, Metro 556, Michigan 1032, Michigan 1033, Michigan 1151, Michigan 1348, Michigan 1350, Miller 562, Miller 565, Miller 566, Mills 567, Molloy 576, Monroe 1036, Moore 578, Moore 579, Morgan 583, Morley 584, **Mott 587**, Mott 588, **Mukkamala 591**, Muntwyler 592, **National 597**, Nickless 604, Nicolay 605, Nicolay 606, O'Neill 1544, Obloy 614, Okun 615, Oleson 617, Paine 624, Parfet 629, Parish 630, Pellerito 638, Perrigo 1045, Pierce 1550, Pietrasiuk 648, Pistons 1046, Pokagon 1048, Polk 1049, Ponting 653, Porter 655, Ratner 668, Reid 673, Reimer 674, Rislov 687, Robison 690, Royal 698, Russell 704, Sage 708, Schmier 718, Schroeder 721, Scully 726, Serra 732, **Shaevsky 1395**, **Share 1558**, Shelden 736, Shepherd 738, Shiffman 739, Shubeck 743, Sigmund 745, Silverwing 747, Simmons 748, Skillman 755, **Snyder 762**, Spartan 1057, Speckhard 768, Spector 769, Spicer 772, **Steelcase 1058**, **Steelcase 1059**, Stubberfield 1565, Sturgis 1175, Swiat 796, Tabbaa 1566, Tassell-Wisner-Bottrall 798, Taubman 1060, Thoman 807, Thompson 811, Tigers 1062, Torgow 815, Towsley 816, Tremble 817, Tuinstra 825, Tuktawa 826, United 1448, Upton 833, Valassis 1068, Van Andel 835, Van 836, Vanderwaals 843, Vanderweide 844, Varnum 1069, Village 1455, Vollbrecht 846, Walsh 848, Warchol 849, Watson 850, Weatherwax 852, Webster 854, Wege 856, Weisblat 863, Weiss 865, Welch 868, Westerman 872, Whirlpool 1072, Whiteley 878, Whiting 880, Whiting 881, Wickson 883, Williams 888, Wilson 891, Wilson 893, Winn 898, Winn 899, Wirtz 902, WMY 905, Wolters 908, Wolverine 1076, World 911, Wynalda 914, **Yankama 916**, Yeager 918, York 920, Young 921, Youth 923, Zimmerman 927, Zionist 928

Minnesota: CHS 952, Nash 1037, Northwest 1042, TCF 1061, Weyand 875, Weyerhaeuser 876, Xcel 1077

Mississippi: Weitzenhoffer 867

Nebraska: Kaufman 439, Kawasaki 1012, Pamida 1043

Nevada: MGM 1031

New Hampshire: Shoer 742

New Jersey: Campbell 949

New York: Doan 196, **Ford 260, Heron 366,** Mitsubishi 1035, **New York 1038,** Newsweek/Daily 1039

Ohio: AEP 934, American 937, Anderson 21, Cliffs 954, Gardner 285, Geiger 288, HCR 1002, Hildreth 373, **JPMorgan 1008,** KeyBank 1018, Kroger 1020, Lahti 477

Oregon: Graef 312

Pennsylvania: McCardell 538, PNC 1047, Toll 1065, Trust 823, West 1071

Tennessee: Nissan 1040, Nissan 1041

Texas: Fruehauf 277, Quicksilver 1051, Spark 1056, **Whole 1073**

Virginia: Falls 236, **General 989**

Wisconsin: Beauchamp 57, Bishop 78, Green Bay 997, Hess 368, Kaufman 441, Keeney 447, McIntyre 545, ShopKo 1055, Stockton 782, Venturedyne 1070, Wisconsin 1074, Wisconsin 1075

Grants to individuals

Michigan: Amy 17, Angels 1475, Ann Arbor 1190, Arab 1192, Arts 1194, ArtServe 1196, Baraga-Houghton 1199, Blodgett 1207, Blue 1208, Boysville 1209, Buist 1484, Cheboygan 1223, Children's 1227, Drew 206, **Earhart 217,** Ennis 1250, Evereg 231, Ford 1257, Ford 986, Foundation 1258, Four 1122, Habitat 1275, Hemophilia 1279, Henry 1280, **Herdegen 364,** Here 365, I Have 400, Ilitch 1289, Italian 1294, **Kellogg 1013,** Kelly 1310, Konstanzer 466, **Latvian 1317,** Lighthouse 1321,

MEEMIC 1028, Michigan 1340, Michigan 1347, Morenci 1352, National 1356, National 1357, Nelson 599, Newaygo 1360, Newaygo 601, Northeast 1362, Northwest 1365, Northwest 1366, Oakland 1370, Otsego 1375, Pardee 1547, **Pewabic 1379,** Pollack 652, Thresholds 1418, Travelers 1421, Trinity 1422, United 1424, United 1433, United 1441, **Upjohn 1451,** Veteran's 1454, Wayne-Metropolitan 1461, Willard 1466, Winkler 897, **Yankama 916**

New York: Center 123, **Ford 260**

In-kind gifts

Arizona: Circle 953

California: SANYO 1054, Toyota 1066

Florida: CSX 962

Georgia: **Georgia 992**

Louisiana: Entergy 979

Massachusetts: **Cabot 947**

Michigan: Albion-Homer 1183, Allegan 1184, **Amway 939,** Arab 1192, Borders 944, Branch 1091, Caravan 1214, Cheboygan 1223, Community 1100, Community 1109, Community 1111, Consumers 960, Delta 1237, Detroit 1240, Detroit 969, Detroit 970, Detroit 971, **Dow 973,** DTE 976, Foodbank 1256, **Ford 985,** Foremost 987, GM 994, Harbor 1276, Hillsdale 1131, India 406, Jackson 1007, Lapeer 1141, Masco 1025, Meijer 1029, Michigan 1032, Michigan 1341, Michigan 1343, Otsego 1375, Perry 643, Pistons 1046, Polk 1049, Shiffman 739, Sojourner 1403, Southwestern 1407, Spaulding 1408, **Steelcase 1059,** Tigers 1062, Veteran's 1454, Warchol 849

Minnesota: Life 1023, Northwest 1042

Nebraska: ConAgra 959

New York: Mitsubishi 1035, Newsweek/Daily 1039

Ohio: **JPMorgan 1008,** Tim 1063

Tennessee: Nissan 1041

Wisconsin: Green Bay 997, ShopKo 1055, Wisconsin 1074

Income development

Michigan: Ann Arbor 1083, Arts 1194, Barnes 42, Blue 1208, Cadillac 1092, Detroit 970, **H.I.S. 327,** HCC 1512, Lyons 516, Michigan 1151, Ypsilanti 1180

New York: Local 1323

Internship funds

Michigan: Americana 16, Arts 1194, Bay 1087, **Collectors 1228,** Cook 147, Ford 986, Gratiot 1129, Great 1273, Henry 363, Shin 740, United 1448

Land acquisition

California: Ayrshire 34

Michigan: Battle Creek 1086, Biederman 1483, Clannad 136, Dalton 163, Dana 963, Frey 276, Gerstacker 292, Gilmore 299, Grand Haven 1126, Grand Rapids 1127, Great 1273, **H.I.S. 327,** Herrick 367, Hunter 397, Jackson 1137, Kantzler 434, **Kresge 471,** Moore 578, Mount Pleasant 1154, Oleson 617, Rotary 1391, Speckhard 768, **Steelcase 1058,** Stubnitz 789, Wynalda 914

New York: Nonprofit 1361

Wisconsin: Bishop 78

Loaned talent

Michigan: Detroit 969, Detroit 971, Tigers 1062

Minnesota: TCF 1061

Wisconsin: Green Bay 997

Loans—to individuals

Michigan: Cadillac 1092, Foundation 270

Management development/capacity building

Florida: **Knight 462**

Illinois: Allstate 935

Michigan: Albion 1078, Ann Arbor 1083, **Arcus 27,** Arts 1194, Capital 1094, Community 1103, Community 1107, Community 1110, **Erb 224,** Fremont 1124, Greenville 1130, Iosco 1135, Knight 461, Lenawee 1143, Metro 556, Miller 565, **Mott 587,** Mott 588, New 1359, North 1156, Pokagon 1048, Rotary 1391, **Steelcase 1058,** Straits 1174, United 1448, Upton 833, Wickson 883, Ypsilanti 1180

Nebraska: ConAgra 959

New York: Corporation 1233, **Ford 260,** Nonprofit 1361

Matching/challenge support

California: Ayrshire 34

Florida: Hagen 332

Illinois: Keller 448, Seabury 727

Indiana: Foellinger 258

Kentucky: Humana 1003

Massachusetts: **Cabot 947**

Michigan: Albion 1078, Allegan 1080, Allendale 1081, Americana 16, Ann Arbor 1083, **Arcus 27,** Arts 1194, Barry 1085, Barth 45, Battle Creek 1086, Batts 941, Bay 1087, Besser 69, Blodgett 82, Blue 1208, Branch 1091, Cadillac 1092, Capital 1094, Colina 141, **Collectors 1228,** Community 1100, Community 1103, Community 1107, Community 1108, Community 1109, Community 1110, Coopersville 1115, Dalton 163, Dart 168, Detroit 1494, DeVos 186, DeVos 189, Dow 202, **Erb 224,** Fremont 1124, General 990, Gerstacker 292, Gilmore 299, Grand Haven 1126, Grand Rapids 1127, Grand 1128, Great 1273, Greenville 1130, **H.I.S. 327,** Hancock 340, Hastings 1000, Herrick 367, Hillsdale 1131, Holden 381, Hudson 392, Hunter 397, India 406, Jackson 1137, Jewish 1297, Kalamazoo 1138, Kantzler 434, **Kellogg 450,** Keweenaw 1139, Kresge 471, Lansing 484, Lapeer 1141, Leighton 495, M & M 1145, Marshall 1149, Metro 556, Michigan 1151, Michigan 1349, Midland 1152, Miller 565, Missaukee 1153, Monroe 577, Moore 578, Morley 584, **Mott 587,** Mott 588, Mount Pleasant 1154, Olds 616, Oleson 617, Pellerito 638, Petoskey 1162, Plym 649, Porter 655, Ratner 668, Rotary 1391, **Rotary 1393,** Sage 708, Saginaw 1164, **Steelcase 1058,** Sturgis 1175, Towsley 816, Tuscola 1177, Vanderweide 844, Warchol 849, Weatherwax 852, Wege 856, Whirlpool 1072, Wickson 883, Wilson 891, Wilson 893, Ypsilanti 1180

Minnesota: Arts 1195, **Porter 656**

Nebraska: Pamida 1043

New Jersey: Campbell 949, Wilson 889

New York: **Heron 366,** Nonprofit 1361

Ohio: Anderson 21, HCR 1002, KeyBank 1018

Pennsylvania: PNC 1047, West 1071

Texas: Bray 94

Pro bono services - strategic management

Michigan: Varnum 1069

Professorships

California: Ayrshire 34

Kentucky: Humana 1003

Michigan: Baldwin 38, DeVlieg 185, Herrick 367, Towsley 816, World 911, Zondervan 930

Ohio: KeyBank 1018

Program development

Arizona: Circle 953

California: Ayrshire 34, Rose 1390, SANYO 1054, Toyota 1066, Wilcox 886

Florida: Hagen 332, **Knight 462**, Robey 1552

Georgia: **Georgia 992**

Illinois: Allstate 935, Gust 323, **Joyce 427**, Kalt 433, Keller 448, Seabury 727

Indiana: Foellinger 258

Kentucky: Humana 1003

Louisiana: Entergy 979

Massachusetts: **Cabot 947**, Hanover 999

Michigan: Albion 1078, Allegan 1080, Americana 16, Ann Arbor 1083, **Arcus 27**, Arts 1194, Barnes 42, Barry 1085, Barstow 44, Barth 45, Battle Creek 1086, Batts 941, Bauervic 51, Bauervic 53, Bay 1087, Berrien 1090, Biederman 1483, Binda 73, Black 1206, Blodgett 82, Blue 1208, Boutell 92, Burroughs 111, Cadillac 1092, Canton 1093, Capital 1094, **Center 1220**, Charlevoix 1096, Chelsea 1224, Chelsea 129, Chippewa 1097, Cipa 133, Citizens 134, Cochrane 140, Colina 141, **Collectors 1228**, Comerica 956, Community 1230, Community 1102, Community 1103, Community 1104, Community 1106, Community 1107, Community 1109, Community 1110, Community 1111, Constantine 1114, Consumers 960, Cook 147, Coopersville 1115, Cronin 155, Dagenais 162, Dalton 163, Dart 168, Davenport 170, Delano 179, **DENSO 968**, DeRoy 180, Detroit 1494, DeVos 186, DeVos 188, DeVos 189, **Dow 973**, Dow 975, Dow 202, DTE 977, Dyer 215, **Erb 224**, Ervin 227, Farley 240, First 1499, Ford 986, Four 1122, Frankenmuth 1123, Fremont 1124, Frey 276, General 990, Gilmore 299, Glassen 301, Grand 1125, Grand Haven 1126, Grand Rapids 1127, Grand 1128, Gratiot 1129, Great 1273, Greenville 1130, Hammond 998, Hancock 340, Hastings 1000, Heart 1277, Herrick 367, Hirvonen 377, Holley 383, Home 384, Homer 1132, Hudson 391, Hudson 392, Hurst 398, Idema 402, Iosco 1135, **Isabel 409**, Jackson 1137, Jackson 1007, **Jewish 1296**, Jewish 1297, Jewish 1298, JPMorgan 1009, JSJ 1010, Justice 1301, Kalamazoo 1303, Kalamazoo 1138, Kantzler 434, Kellogg 449, **Kellogg 450, Kellogg's 1015**, Kelly 1016, Kemp 1017, Keweenaw 1139, Kiwanis 1313, Knight 461, Konstanzer 466, Lake 1140, Lansing 484, Lenawee 1143, Leven 498, Lyons 516, M & M 1145, Mackinac 1146, Marcks 524, Marquette 1148, Marshall 1149, Marshall 526, McGregor 542, Mecosta 1150, Meritor 1030, Merkley 555, Metro 556, Michigan 1151, Michigan 1344, Michigan 1349, Michigan 1350, Miller 565, Miller 566, Mitchell 572, Monroe 577, Moore 579, Morley 584, **Mott 587**, Mott 588, Mount Pleasant 1154, Mount Zion 589, North 1156, Olds 616, Palmer 625, Parfet 629, Pentecost 641, Perrigo 1045, Petoskey 1162, Pierce 1550, Pistons 1046, Plym 649, Pokagon 1048, Ponting 653, Pulte 1050, Ratner 668, Reynolds 681, Rotary 1391, **Rotary 1393**, Sage 708, Saginaw 1164, Sanilac 1165, Schmuckal 719, Shiawassee 1168, Skillman 755, Smith 758, Social 1400, **Society 1402**, Sojourner 1403, South 1169, Southfield 1171, Speckhard 768, St. Clair 774, **Steelcase 1058**, Straits 1174, Strosacker 787, Stubnitz 789, Sturgis 1175, Tahquamenon 1415, Thoman 807, Thompson 811, Towsley 816, Tremble 817, Tuscola 1177, United 1424, United 1448, Upjohn 832, Upton 833, Van 836, Van Den Bosch 838, Vanderweide 844, Village 1455, Weed 855, Wege 856, Weiner 860, Weissman 866, Westerman 872, Whirlpool 1072, White 1178, Whiting 880, Wickson 883, Wilson 891, Wolters 908, World 911, **Worldwide 1469**, Young 921, Young 922, Ypsilanti 1180, Zondervan 930

Minnesota: CHS 952, Life 1023, Musser 594, TCF 1061, Xcel 1077

Nebraska: ConAgra 959, Kaufman 439, Pamida 1043

New Jersey: Campbell 949, Wilson 889

New York: Corporation 1233, **Ford 260, Heron 366**, Local 1323, Mitsubishi 1035, **New York 1038**

Ohio: American 937, Anderson 21, Catholic 1219, Charter 950, Fifth 983, HCR 1002, **JPMorgan 1008**, KeyBank 1018, Kroger 1021

Pennsylvania: PNC 1047

Tennessee: Nissan 1040

Texas: Fruehauf 277

Virginia: **Gannett 988**

Wisconsin: Beauchamp 57, Hess 368, Kaufman 441, Kowalski 1019, Wisconsin 1075

Program evaluation

Florida: Knight 462

Illinois: Joyce 427

Indiana: Foellinger 258

Michigan: **Arcus 27**, Arts 1194, Barry 1085, Battle Creek 1086, Blodgett 82, Cadillac 1092, Community 1107, Community 1111, Detroit 1494, Four 1122, Fremont 1124, Gilmore 299, Great 1273, Greenville 1130, Hudson 392, Iosco 1135, Jackson 1137, Jewish 1297, **Kellogg 450**, Michigan 1151, **Mott 587**, Mott 588, Weatherwax 852, **Worldwide 1469**

Minnesota: CHS 952

New York: **Ford 260, Heron 366**

Program-related investments/loans

Florida: Knight 462

Michigan: Battle Creek 1086, Community 1103, Community 1110, DeVos 187, Fremont 1124, Grand Rapids 1127, Jackson 1137, Kalamazoo 1138, Miller 565, Moore 578, **Mott 587**, Northern 1542, Shiffman 739, Skillman 755, Village 1455, Wilson 893

New York: Corporation 1233, **Ford 260, Heron 366**, Local 1323, Nonprofit 1361

Pennsylvania: PNC 1047

Publication

Illinois: Allstate 935

Michigan: Albion 1078, Americana 16, Ann Arbor 1083, **Arcus 27**, Arts 1194, Battle Creek 1086, Cadillac 1092, Canton 1093, Community 1110, Dart 168, Dyer 215, **Earhart 217**, Ford 986, Gilmore 299, Great 1273, Greenville 1130, Hillsdale 1131, Holden 381, Iosco 1135, Lansing 484, Michigan 1349, Mount Pleasant 1154, Mount Zion 589, North 1156, Saginaw 1164, Straits 1174, Ypsilanti 1180

Ohio: Anderson 21

Research

Illinois: **Abbott 933, Joyce 427**

Indiana: Foellinger 258

Michigan: **ACI 1181, American 1186**, Ann Arbor 1083, Applebaum 1191, Ash 31, Barry 1085, Battle Creek 1086, Bay 1087, Beck 1201, Blue 1208, Cadillac 1092, Campbell 116, Children's 1227, Cipa 133, Cochrane 140, Community 1103, Community 1109, Dalton 163, Dart 168, Davis 171, Delta 1238, Detroit 1494, Dow 202, **Earhart 217**, Fetzer 249, Ford 1257, Frey 276, Fund 279, General 990, **Gerber 290**, Gerstacker 292, Great 1273, Hemophilia 1279, Herrick 367, Holden 381, Ilitch 1289, Iosco 1135, Jewish 1298, **John 1299, Kellogg's 1015**, Lansing 484, Linden 503, **McCarty 1333**, Morley 584, Mount Pleasant 1154, National 1356, National 1357, Nill 607, **Pardee 628**, Pellerito 638, Ratner 668, Robison 690, Royal 698, Sage 708, Shelden 736, **Society 1402**, Stoddard 783, Strosacker 787, Towsley 816, United 1433, Upjohn 832, **Upjohn 1451**, Upton 833, Weikart 859, Westerman 872, Whirlpool 1072, Wilson 891, Ypsilanti 1180, Zondervan 930

Minnesota: CHS 952

Nebraska: ConAgra 959

Ohio: Anderson 21, HCR 1002

Pennsylvania: West 1071

Texas: OneSight 1546

Wisconsin: Bishop 78, Kaufman 441, Wisconsin 1075

Scholarship funds

California: Ayrshire 34

Colorado: **American 1188**

Florida: Detter 183, Hagen 332, Robey 1552

Georgia: **Georgia 992**

Illinois: **Abbott 933**, Kalt 433, Keller 448, Seabury 727

Kentucky: Humana 1003

Louisiana: Entergy 979

Massachusetts: **Cabot 947**, Hanover 999

Michigan: **ACI 1181**, Albion 1078, Alexandrowski 8, Anchor 1082, Andersen 19, Ann Arbor 1083, Annis 25, Arden 28, Ark 31, Baker 36, Barry 1085, Barstow 44, Barton 940, Battle Creek 1086, Batts 941, Baxter 54, Bay 1087, Bentley 63, Berkery 64, Bettis 1203, Biederman 1483, Binda 73, Bonner 86, Borovoy 89, Branch 1091, Bronner 102, Buist 1484, Butzel 946, Canton 1093, Chamberlain 124, **Chang 125**, Charlevoix 1096, Chelsea 129, Chippewa 1097, Christian 131, Citizens 134, Clare 1098, **Collectors 1228**, Comerica 956, Community 1230, Community 1100, Community 1103, Community 1104, Community 1106, Community 1107, Community 1108, Community 1109, Community 1110, Community 1111, Community 1112, Consumers 961, Cook 147, Copley 150, Crane 153, Dancey 165, Dart 964, Dart 168, DeBower 175, Deffenbaugh 176, Delta 1237, Delta 1238, DeRoy 180, Detroit 970, DeVlieg 185, Doran 200, Dow 975, Dunnings 214, Fedorov 246, First 1499, Ford 986, **Ford 266**, Four 1122, Frankenmuth 1123, Fremont 1124, General 990, Gilmore 299, Glassen 301, Grand 1125, Grand Haven 1126, Grand Rapids 1127, Grand 1128, Gratiot 1129, Great 1270, Great 1273, Greenville 1130, Grimaldi 319, **H.I.S. 327**, Harding 346, Harding 347, Henry 363, Herrick 367, Hickman 371, Hillsdale 1131, Holden 381, Hudson 391, Idema 402, Irwin 408, Jaffe 414, JSJ 1010, Kalamazoo 1138, Kantzler 434, Kellogg 449, **Kellogg's 1015**, Kelly 1016, Keweenaw 1139, Lake 1140, Lansing 484, Lapeer 1141, Lenawee 1143, Leven 498, Mackinac 1146, Mall 521, Manistee 1147, Marquette 1148, Marshall 1149, Marxer 528, Marzke 529, Masonic 1332, McNish 551, Mecosta 1150, Metro 556, Michigan 1032, Michigan 1033, Midland 1152, Miller 562, Miller 565, Miller 566, Mills 567, Mims 568, Minton 570, Morey 582, Mott 588, Mount Pleasant 1154, Muntwyler 592, Nelson 599, Nordman 608, Northville 1364, Paine 624, Parfet 629, Perrigo 1045, Petoskey 1162, Pettibone 646, Pistons 1046, Pokagon 1048, Ponting 653, Ratner 668, Rawson 670, Redies 1052, Rennie 677, Reuter 679, Robison 690, Roscommon 1163, Royal 698, Russell 704, Sage 708, Saginaw 1164, Saini 709, Schmuckal 719, Schuyler 723, Serwinek 733, Shiawassee 1168, Simmons 748, Slack 756, **Snyder 762, Society 1402**, Sonneveldt 763, South 1169, Southeastern 765, St. Clair 774, **Steelcase 1058**, Stoddard 783, Stubnitz 789, Sturgis 1175, Sullivan 793, Thornapple 1417, Three 1176, Tigers 1062, Tiscornia 814, Tremble 817, Trinity 1422, Tuscola 1177, Upjohn 832, Van 836, Van Den Bosch 838, Warchol 849, Weed 855, Wege 856, Welsh 871, Westerman 872, Westfall 874, Whirlpool 1072, Wilson 891, Wolverine 1076, **Worldwide 1469**, Zoller 929, Zondervan 930

Minnesota: CHS 952, TCF 1061

Nebraska: Kaufman 439

New Jersey: Wilson 889

New York: Mitsubishi 1035, Newsweek/Daily 1039

Ohio: American 937, Anderson 21, Cliffs 954, Gilbert 296, Haboush 331, Hildreth 373, O'Brien 613
Rhode Island: Robbins 688
Virginia: Bell 59, **Gannett 988, General 989,** Moh 573
Wisconsin: Hess 368, McIntyre 543, Venturedyne 1070, Wisconsin 1074, Wisconsin 1075

Scholarships—to individuals

California: Coltrane 1229, Parks 632, Rose 1390, Wilcox 886
Georgia: **Georgia 992**
Illinois: Meeks 553, Peters 644, Taylor 799
Massachusetts: Hanover 999
Michigan: Abbott 2, **ACI 1181,** Allen 10, Anderson 20, Anderson 23, Ash 31, Asthma 1197, Avondale 1198, Baker 37, Barr 43, Basilica 49, Battle Creek 1086, Beal 55, Bees 58, Bellinger 61, Bemis 62, Birkenstock 75, Birmingham 1204, Birtwistle 77, Blaske 81, Brenske 97, Bucknell 108, Busch 112, Byrne 113, Byron 1212, Cadillac 1092, Canton 1093, Central 1095, Charfoos 126, Charlevoix 1096, Chase 128, Chelsea 1224, Clare 1098, Clinton 139, Coller 142, Community 1104, Community 1106, Community 1108, Community 1109, Community 1110, Community 1112, Cunningham 158, Czado 160, D.U. 161, Dana 963, Davisson 172, Delta 1237, Detroit 1244, Dickinson 191, **Earhart 217,** Edmund 219, Evereg 231, Ewald 232, Fedewa 245, Flemington 257, Flint 1255, Foran 259, Ford 1257, Foster 268, Foster 269, Frankenmuth 1123, Fredericksen 273, Fremont 1124, Galesburg 1502, **Gerber 290,** Gibbs 294, Gilles 298, Gleaner 1506, Goldman 305, Goodrich 306, Goss 311, Grand Haven 1126, Grand Rapids 1127, Grand 1128, Gratiot 1507, Great 996, Grimaldi 319, Gumaer 322, Haas 330, Hamar 336, Hamlin 1509, Hammel 337, Hannan 342, Harbor 1276, Harding 348, HCC 1512, Hess 370, Hillier 1513, Hillsdale 1131, Home 384, Home 1284, Homer 1132, Horgan 387, Hovarter 388, Howe 390, Humane 395, Humbert 396, Huss 399, I Have 400, Ilitch 1288, **International 1292,** Iosco 1135, Ironwood 1293, Jackson 1137, Jackson 411, Jaffe 414, **John 1299,** Johnson 423, Juhl 428, Kadant 1011, Kalamazoo 1303, Kalamazoo 1138, Kalamazoo 1308, Kay 443, Kent 454, Key 457, Kiwanis 1313, Knabusch 460, Koch 463, Krause 469, Laflin 475, Laidlaw 478, Lakeland 1315, Langley 483, Lansing 1316, LaVictoire 489, Lee 492, Leelanau 1142, Legion 494, Lesher 497, Little 505, M & M 1145, MacDonald 518, MacRae 519, Malovey 523, Marquette 1329, Marquette 1148, Marshall 1149, Masonic 1332, Matson 530, Mayhew 534, McCabe 536, McCurdy 541, Mecosta 1150, Meyers 557, **Michigan 1337,** Michigan 558, Michigan 1341, Michigan 1342, Michigan 559, Michigan 1151, Michner 560, Mick 561, Miller 563, Morenci 1352, Morrill 585, Mount Pleasant 1154, **National 597,** Nelson 600, Newaygo 601, Nieman 1541, Nill 607, Nordman 608, North 1156, Northville 1364, Novi 1368, Oakwood 1371, Ontonagon 1372, Optimist 1373, Owen 621, Parks 1377, Paulsen 636, Pennock 1378, Petoskey 1162, Pistons 1046, Plumbers 1380, Pokagon 1048, Polakovic 650, Polan 651, Pulte 1050, Raval 669, Recreational 671, Reuther 1387, Richter 684, Rislov 687, Roethke 693, Rolka 694, Rotary 1392, Rudy 700, Ruf 701, Rusch 703, Saginaw 1164, Sallness 712, Schemm 717, Schoolcraft 1166, Scofield 725, Shepard 737, Sigmund 745, Sigmund 746, Skandalaris 753, Smith 760, **Society 1402,** Southfield 1171, Southfield 1405, Spaulding 1408,

Speerstra 770, **Sphinx 1410,** St. Joseph 775, St. Mary's 1413, Sterling 1173, Stewart 780, Stokes 785, Straits 1174, Sturgis 1175, Tahquamenon 1415, Tassell-Wisner-Bottrall 798, Taylor 800, Temple 802, Tengler 1567, Thomas 809, Three 1176, Tiscornia 814, Trinity 1422, Trinklein 818, Trone 820, Trudell 821, UAW-GM 1423, United 1426, University 831, Van Hollenbeck 839, Vomberg 847, Watson 850, Watson 851, Weidner 1462, Weissman 866, Welch 1570, Wells 869, Western 873, Westfall 874, Whiteley 878, Whitfield 879, Wigginton 885, Wiley 1465, Willard 1466, Wilson 892, Winship 900, Wirick 901, Wright 1573, Wright 913, Wyandotte 1574, Young 1470, Zemke 926
Minnesota: CHS 952
New Jersey: Lasko 488, Wilson 889
New Mexico: Peninsula 639
North Carolina: Thiemkey 806
Ohio: Carmell 119, Heyl 1282, Myers 595, O'Brien 613
Pennsylvania: West 1071
Tennessee: Educational 1249
Texas: Battier 1200, **OneSight 1546**
Virginia: Bell 59
Wisconsin: Brege 95, Carpenter 120, Gillenwater 297, Heart 358, Wisconsin 1075

Seed money

California: Ayrshire 34
Florida: Hagen 332, **Knight 462**
Illinois: Keller 448, Seabury 727
Massachusetts: **Cabot 947**
Michigan: Albion 1078, Allendale 1081, Ann Arbor 1083, Barry 1085, Battle Creek 1086, Bay 1087, Berrien 1090, Binda 73, Blue 1208, Cadillac 1092, Canton 1093, Capital 1094, Carls 118, Charlevoix 1096, Colina 141, **Collectors 1228,** Community 1100, Community 1103, Community 1104, Community 1106, Community 1107, Community 1108, Community 1109, Community 1110, Community 1111, Constantine 1114, Coopersville 1115, Dalton 163, Davenport 170, DeVos 186, DeVos 189, Dickinson 1118, **Dow 973,** Dow 975, Dow 202, Dyer 215, **Erb 224,** First 1499, Foundation 1258, Fremont 1124, Frey 276, Gerstacker 292, Gilmore 299, Grand Haven 1126, Grand Rapids 1127, Grand 1128, Gratiot 1129, Great 1273, Greenville 1130, **H.I.S. 327,** Hancock 340, Hillsdale 1131, Holley 383, Hudson 392, Hurst 398, Idema 402, India 406, Iosco 1135, Jackson 1137, Jewish 1297, Jewish 1298, Justice 1301, Kalamazoo 1138, Kalamazoo 1307, Kantzler 434, **Kellogg 450,** Lansing 484, Leelanau 1142, M & M 1145, Mackinac 1146, Manistee 1147, Marquette 1148, Marshall 1149, McGregor 542, Mecosta 1150, Michigan 1151, Michigan 1349, Midland 1152, Miller 565, Missaukee 1153, Morley 584, **Mott 587,** Mount Pleasant 1154, Mount Zion 589, North 1156, Olds 616, Parfet 629, Pellerito 638, Petoskey 1162, Pokagon 1048, Rotary 1391, **Rotary 1393,** Saginaw 1164, Sanilac 1165, Shiffman 739, Silverwing 747, Social 1400, **Society 1402,** Southfield 1171, Sparta 1172, **Steelcase 1058,** Straits 1174, Strosacker 787, Stubnitz 789, Three 1176, Tiscornia 814, Towsley 816, Tuscola 1177, Upjohn 832, Upton 833, White 1178, Wickes 882, Wilson 893, Wyoming 1179
Minnesota: CHS 952, Musser 594
New York: Local 1323, Mitsubishi 1035
Ohio: Anderson 21, HCR 1002, Kroger 1021

Texas: Bray 94
Wisconsin: Bishop 78, Kaufman 441

Sponsorships

Arizona: Circle 953
Georgia: **Georgia 992**
Michigan: American 936, Amerisure 938, Butzel 946, Comerica 957, DTE 976, DTE 977, Fedorov 246, **Ford 985,** Ford 986, Foremost 987, Gordon 995, Isabella 1006, Jackson 1007, JPMorgan 1009, **Kellogg 1014,** Kelly 1016, Pistons 1046, Pokagon 1048, Polk 1049
Minnesota: CHS 952, Northwest 1042
Nebraska: Pamida 1043
New York: Mitsubishi 1035, Newsweek/Daily 1039
Ohio: AEP 934, Charter 950, Fifth 983, **JPMorgan 1008,** Tim 1063
Pennsylvania: Toll 1065
Texas: Quicksilver 1051, **Whole 1073**
Virginia: **General 989**
Wisconsin: Wisconsin 1074

Student loans—to individuals

Michigan: Abele 3, Brenske 98, Cadillac 1092, Davenport 169, Eddy 218, Glick 302, Harbor 345, Huffines 393, Jeffers 416, Kelly 451, Kent 454, Mount Pleasant 1154, Reid 672, Salisbury 711, Sallness 712, Simonis 750, Sturgis 1175, Ypsilanti 1180
Tennessee: Educational 1249

Technical assistance

Florida: Hagen 332, **Knight 462**
Illinois: Seabury 727
Indiana: Foellinger 258
Massachusetts: **Cabot 947**
Michigan: Albion 1078, Americana 16, **Arcus 27,** Arts 1194, Barry 1085, Battle Creek 1086, Bay 1087, Blue 1208, Branch 1091, Cadillac 1092, Capital 1094, **Center 1220,** Charlevoix 1096, Community 1104, Community 1106, Community 1107, Community 1109, Community 1110, Community 1111, Community 1112, Dearborn 965, Dyer 215, Fremont 1124, Frey 276, Gilmore 299, Grand Rapids 1127, Grand 1128, Great 1273, India 406, Iosco 1135, Jackson 1137, Jewish 1297, Jewish 1298, JPMorgan 1009, Kalamazoo 1138, **Kellogg's 1015,** M & M 1145, Marquette 1148, Marshall 1149, Michigan 1349, Michigan 1350, Midland 1152, **Mott 587,** Mott 588, Mount Pleasant 1154, New 1359, North 1156, Northeast 1362, Oleson 617, Petoskey 1162, Rotary 1391, Saginaw 1164, Sanilac 1165, Shiffman 739, Sojourner 1403, Straits 1174, United 1424, United 1448, Weatherwax 852
New York: **Heron 366,** Local 1323, Nonprofit 1361
Ohio: **JPMorgan 1008**

Use of facilities

Louisiana: Entergy 979
Michigan: **Glen Arbor 1263**
Minnesota: CHS 952
Ohio: Charter 950
Texas: Quicksilver 1051

SUBJECT INDEX

List of terms: Terms used in this index conform to the Foundation Center's Grants Classification System's comprehensive subject area coding scheme. The alphabetical list below represents the complete list of subject terms found in this edition. "See also" references to related subject areas are also provided as an additional aid in accessing the giving interests of grantmakers in this volume.

Index: In the index itself, grantmaker entries are arranged under each term by state location, abbreviated name, and sequence number. Grantmakers in boldface type make grants on a national, regional, or international basis. The others generally limit giving to the state or city in which they are located.

Adult education—literacy, basic skills & GED
Adult/continuing education
Adults
Adults, men
Adults, women
Africa
African Americans/Blacks
Aging
Aging, centers/services
Agriculture
Agriculture/food
Agriculture/food, government agencies
Agriculture/food, public education
Agriculture/food, public policy
Agriculture/food, single organization support
AIDS
see also People with AIDS (PWAs)
AIDS research
AIDS, people with
Alcoholism
Allergies
Alzheimer's disease
Alzheimer's disease research
American Red Cross
Animal welfare
Animals/wildlife
Animals/wildlife, alliance/advocacy
Animals/wildlife, endangered species
Animals/wildlife, fisheries
Animals/wildlife, formal/general education
Animals/wildlife, preservation/protection
Animals/wildlife, public education
Animals/wildlife, research
Animals/wildlife, sanctuaries
Animals/wildlife, single organization support
Animals/wildlife, special services
Animals/wildlife, volunteer services
Aquariums
Art & music therapy
Arthritis
Arts
see also dance; film/video; museums; music;
    performing arts; theater; visual arts
Arts councils
Arts education
Arts, artist's services
Arts, association

Arts, cultural/ethnic awareness
Arts, equal rights
Arts, folk arts
Arts, public education
Arts, single organization support
Asia
Asians/Pacific Islanders
Assistive technology
Asthma
Athletics/sports, academies
Athletics/sports, amateur leagues
Athletics/sports, baseball
Athletics/sports, basketball
Athletics/sports, equestrianism
Athletics/sports, fishing/hunting
Athletics/sports, football
Athletics/sports, golf
Athletics/sports, school programs
Athletics/sports, soccer
Athletics/sports, Special Olympics
Athletics/sports, training
Athletics/sports, water sports
Athletics/sports, winter sports
Australia
Autism
Autism research
Belgium
Big Brothers/Big Sisters
Biology/life sciences
Blind/visually impaired
Botanical gardens
Botanical/horticulture/landscape services
Boy scouts
Boys
Boys & girls clubs
Brain research
Brazil
Breast cancer
Breast cancer research
Buddhism
Business school/education
Business/industry
Cameroon
Canada
Cancer
Cancer research
Cancer, leukemia

Catholic agencies & churches
Catholic federated giving programs
Cemeteries/burial services, burial association
Cerebral palsy
Charter schools
Chemistry
Child development, education
Child development, services
Children
Children's rights
Children, adoption
Children, day care
Children, foster care
Children, services
Children/youth
Children/youth, services
China
Christian agencies & churches
Civil liberties, advocacy
Civil liberties, first amendment
Civil liberties, reproductive rights
Civil liberties, right to life
Civil rights, race/intergroup relations
see also civil rights
Civil/human rights
Civil/human rights, aging
Civil/human rights, disabled
Civil/human rights, equal rights
Civil/human rights, immigrants
Civil/human rights, LGBTQ
Civil/human rights, minorities
Civil/human rights, women
Community development, business promotion
Community development, citizen coalitions
Community development, civic centers
Community development, neighborhood
    associations
Community development, neighborhood
    development
Community development, public/private
    ventures
Community development, real estate
Community development, service clubs
Community development, small businesses
Community development, women's clubs
Community/economic development

Community/economic development, alliance/advocacy
Community/economic development, fund raising/fund distribution
Community/economic development, management/technical assistance
Community/economic development, public education
Community/economic development, single organization support
Computer science
Courts/judicial administration
Crime/abuse victims
Crime/law enforcement
Crime/law enforcement, administration/regulation
Crime/law enforcement, equal rights
Crime/law enforcement, formal/general education
Crime/law enforcement, government agencies
Crime/law enforcement, information services
Crime/law enforcement, management/technical assistance
Crime/law enforcement, missing persons
Crime/law enforcement, police agencies
Crime/law enforcement, public education
Crime/law enforcement, reform
Crime/law enforcement, single organization support
Crime/violence prevention
see also domestic violence; gun control
Crime/violence prevention, abuse prevention
see also child abuse; domestic violence
Crime/violence prevention, child abuse
Crime/violence prevention, domestic violence
Crime/violence prevention, gun control
Crime/violence prevention, youth
Cystic fibrosis research
Deaf/hearing impaired
Dental care
Dental school/education
Developing countries
Developmentally disabled, centers & services
Diabetes
Diabetes research
Disabilities, people with
Disasters, fire prevention/control
Disasters, Hurricane Katrina
Disasters, preparedness/services
Disasters, search/rescue
Dispute resolution
Eastern & Central Europe
Economic development
Economically disadvantaged
Economics
Education
Education, association
Education, community/cooperative
Education, continuing education
Education, drop-out prevention
Education, early childhood education
Education, formal/general education
Education, fund raising/fund distribution
Education, public education
Education, reading
Education, reform
Education, research
Education, services
Education, special
Elementary school/education
Elementary/secondary education
Elementary/secondary school reform
Employment
Employment, labor unions/organizations

Employment, public policy
Employment, retraining
Employment, services
Employment, training
Employment, vocational rehabilitation
End of life care
Engineering
Engineering school/education
Engineering/technology
Environment
see also energy; natural resources
Environment, air pollution
Environment, alliance/advocacy
Environment, beautification programs
Environment, climate change/global warming
Environment, energy
Environment, forests
Environment, government agencies
Environment, land resources
Environment, management/technical assistance
Environment, natural resources
Environment, pollution control
Environment, public education
Environment, public policy
Environment, recycling
Environment, reform
Environment, research
Environment, volunteer services
Environment, water pollution
Environment, water resources
Environmental education
Europe
Eye diseases
Eye research
Family resources and services, disability
Family services
Family services, adolescent parents
Family services, counseling
Family services, domestic violence
Family services, parent education
Family services, single parents
Financial services
Food banks
Food distribution, groceries on wheels
Food distribution, meals on wheels
Food services
Food services, commodity distribution
Food services, congregate meals
Foundations (community)
Foundations (private grantmaking)
Foundations (private independent)
France
Genetic diseases and disorders
Geriatrics
Geriatrics research
Germany
Girl scouts
Girls
Goodwill Industries
Government/public administration
Graduate/professional education
Haiti
Health care
Health care, blood supply
Health care, clinics/centers
Health care, cost containment
Health care, fund raising/fund distribution
Health care, infants
Health care, patient services
Health care, public policy
Health care, reform
Health care, single organization support
Health organizations
Health organizations, association

Health organizations, public education
Health organizations, research
Health sciences school/education
Heart & circulatory diseases
Heart & circulatory research
Hemophilia
Hemophilia research
Higher education
Higher education, college
see also higher education
Higher education, college (community/junior)
see also higher education
Higher education, university
see also higher education
Hinduism
Hispanics/Latinos
Historic preservation/historical societies
Historical activities
History/archaeology
Holistic medicine
Homeless
Homeless, human services
see also economically disadvantaged; food services; housing/shelter, homeless
Hospitals (general)
Hospitals (specialty)
Housing/shelter
Housing/shelter, development
Housing/shelter, expense aid
Housing/shelter, home owners
Housing/shelter, homeless
Housing/shelter, rehabilitation
Housing/shelter, repairs
Housing/shelter, search services
Housing/shelter, services
Housing/shelter, temporary shelter
Human services
Human services, emergency aid
Human services, financial counseling
Human services, gift distribution
Human services, mind/body enrichment
Human services, single organization support
Human services, travelers' aid
Humanities
see also history/archaeology; language/linguistics; literature; museums
Hungary
Immigrants/refugees
Independent living, disability
India
Indigenous peoples
Infants/toddlers
Infants/toddlers, female
Infants/toddlers, male
Insurance, providers
International affairs
see also arms control; international peace/security
International development
International economic development
International exchange, students
International human rights
International migration/refugee issues
International relief
International studies
Ireland
Islam
Israel
Italy
Japan
Jewish agencies & synagogues
Jewish federated giving programs
Journalism school/education
Kenya
Kidney diseases
Kidney research

Labor studies
Latin America
Latvia
Law school/education
Law/international law
Leadership development
see also youth development, services
Legal services
LGBTQ
see also civil rights, gays/lesbians
Libraries (academic/research)
Libraries (public)
Libraries/library science
Literature
Lung diseases
Marine science
Mathematics
Media, film/video
Media, print publishing
Media, radio
Media, television
Media/communications
Medical care, community health systems
Medical care, in-patient care
Medical care, rehabilitation
Medical research
Medical research, alliance/advocacy
Medical research, institute
Medical school/education
see also dental school/education; nursing school/
  education
Medical specialties
Medical specialties research
Medicine/medical care, public education
Men
Mental health, clinics
Mental health, counseling/support groups
Mental health, disorders
Mental health, grief/bereavement counseling
Mental health, residential care
Mental health, smoking
Mental health, treatment
Mental health/crisis services
Mentally disabled
Mexico
Middle East
Military/veterans
Military/veterans' organizations
Minorities
see also African Americans/Blacks; Asians/Pacific
  Islanders; civil rights, minorities; Hispanics/
  Latinos; Native Americans/American Indians
Minorities/immigrants, centers/services
Monaco
Multiple sclerosis
Multiple sclerosis research
Muscular dystrophy
Museums
Museums (art)
Museums (children's)
Museums (ethnic/folk arts)
Museums (history)
Museums (marine/maritime)
Museums (natural history)
Museums (science/technology)
Museums (specialized)
Museums (sports/hobby)
Native Americans/American Indians
Neighborhood centers
Neuroscience
Neuroscience research
Nicaragua
Nigeria
Nonprofit management
Nursing care

Nursing home/convalescent facility
Nursing school/education
Nutrition
Offenders/ex-offenders
Optometry/vision screening
Orthodox agencies & churches
Pakistan
Palliative care
Parkinson's disease
Parkinson's disease research
Pediatrics
Pediatrics research
Performing arts
Performing arts centers
Performing arts, ballet
Performing arts, dance
Performing arts, education
Performing arts, music
Performing arts, music (choral)
Performing arts, music composition
Performing arts, music ensembles/groups
Performing arts, opera
Performing arts, orchestras
Performing arts, theater
Performing arts, theater (musical)
Pharmacy/prescriptions
Philanthropy/voluntarism
Philanthropy/voluntarism, fund raising/fund
  distribution
Philosophy/ethics
Physical therapy
Physical/earth sciences
Physically disabled
Poland
Political science
Population studies
Portugal
Pregnancy centers
Protestant agencies & churches
Psychology/behavioral science
Public affairs
Public affairs, alliance/advocacy
Public affairs, citizen participation
Public affairs, finance
Public affairs, political organizations
Public health
Public health school/education
Public health, obesity
Public health, physical fitness
Public policy, research
Recreation
Recreation, camps
Recreation, centers
Recreation, community
Recreation, fairs/festivals
Recreation, parks/playgrounds
Religion
see also Jewish agencies & temples; Protestant
  agencies & churches; Roman Catholic agencies &
  churches
Religion, interfaith issues
Religious federated giving programs
Reproductive health
Reproductive health, family planning
Reproductive health, OBGYN/Birthing centers
Reproductive health, sexuality education
Residential/custodial care
Residential/custodial care, hospices
Residential/custodial care, senior continuing
  care
Residential/custodial care, special day care
Rural development
Russia
Safety, automotive safety

Safety/disasters
Safety/disasters, association
Safety/disasters, public education
Salvation Army
Scholarships/financial aid
Science
see also biological sciences; chemistry; computer
  science; engineering/technology; marine science;
  physical/earth sciences
Science, formal/general education
Secondary school/education
see also elementary/secondary education
Single parents
Social entrepreneurship
Social sciences
see also anthropology/sociology; economics; political
  science; psychology/behavioral science
Social sciences, public policy
South Africa
South Korea
Space/aviation
Spain
Speech/hearing centers
Spine disorders research
Spirituality
Student services/organizations
Substance abuse, prevention
Substance abuse, services
Substance abusers
Supported living
Teacher school/education
Terminal illness, people with
Theological school/education
Theology
Transportation
Tropical diseases
Ukraine
United Kingdom
United Ways and Federated Giving Programs
Urban League
Urban/community development
Utilities
Veterinary medicine
Veterinary medicine, hospital
Visual arts
Visual arts, architecture
Visual arts, art conservation
Visual arts, ceramic arts
Visual arts, painting
Visual arts, photography
Visual arts, sculpture
Vocational education
Vocational education, post-secondary
Voluntarism promotion
Wales
Women
see also civil rights, women; reproductive rights
Women, centers/services
YM/YWCAs & YM/YWHAs
Young adults
Young adults, female
Young adults, male
Youth
Youth development
Youth development, adult & child programs
Youth development, agriculture
Youth development, business
Youth development, centers/clubs
Youth development, citizenship
Youth development, religion
Youth development, research
Youth development, scouting agencies (general)
Youth development, services
Youth, pregnancy prevention
Youth, services

Adult education—literacy, basic skills & GED

Michigan: Battle Creek 1086, Binda 73, Community 1109, Greenville 1130, Heart 1277, Jackson 1137, Knight 461, Roscommon 1163, **Rotary 1393**, Thoman 807

Adult/continuing education

Michigan: Comerica 956, Midland 1152, Miller 565

Adults

Michigan: Berrien 1090, Fremont 1124, Grand Rapids 1127, Livonia 1144, Metro 556, Midland 1152, Sanilac 1165, Tuscola 1177
Minnesota: CHS 952

Adults, men

Michigan: Metro 556, Midland 1152, Sanilac 1165

Adults, women

Michigan: Comerica 957, Metro 556, Midland 1152, Sanilac 1165, Van 836

Africa

Michigan: **Amway 939, Snyder 762**
New York: **Ford 260**

African Americans/Blacks

Michigan: African 1182, Baker 36, Black 1206, Ford 986, Grand Rapids 1127, **Kellogg 450**, Kelly 1016, Metro 556, Midland 1152, **National 597**, Sanilac 1165, Southfield 1405, **Sphinx 1410**
New York: **Ford 260**
Ohio: KeyBank 1018

Aging

California: Ayrshire 34
Kentucky: Humana 1003
Massachusetts: **Thome 810**
Michigan: Ann Arbor 1083, Berrien 1090, Blue 942, Cadillac 1092, Clannad 136, Community 1109, Community 1110, Community 1111, Community 1113, Detroit 1240, Dickinson 1118, Ervin 227, Foundation 270, Fremont 1124, Gerstacker 292, Grand Rapids 1127, Hillsdale 1131, Ionia 1134, Jackson 1007, **Jewish 1295**, Jewish 1297, Jewish 1298, Livonia 1144, Marshall 1149, Merkley 555, Metro 556, Midland 1152, Oakland 1370, Saginaw 1164, Sanilac 1165, Southfield 1171, **Steelcase 1058**, Thompson 811, Tuscola 1177, United 1431, United 1439, Van 836
Nebraska: Pamida 1043
Ohio: HCR 1002

Aging, centers/services

Massachusetts: Hanover 999
Michigan: Ann Arbor 1083, Blakely 80, Blodgett 82, Cadillac 1092, Capital 1213, Central 1095, Cheboygan 1223, Chelsea 1225, Community 1109, Community 1113, Constantine 1114, DTE 976, Ervin 227, Fabri 980, Fremont 1124, Gerstacker 292, Grand Rapids 1127, Hammond 998, Heart 1277, Hillsdale 1131, Human 1286, Jackson 1007, Jewish 1297, Lay 491, Livingston 1322, Mason 1331, Metro 556, Northwest 1367, Oakland 1370, Redies 1052, Thompson 811, United 1431,

United 1437, United 1440, United 1441, Upjohn 832, White 1178
Nebraska: Pamida 1043
Ohio: HCR 1002, McCalla 537
Wisconsin: Handleman 341, Wisconsin 1075

Agriculture

Michigan: Americana 16, Drew 207, **Ford 985**, Haas 329, **Kellogg 450**
Minnesota: CHS 952
New York: **Ford 260**
Ohio: Anderson 21

Agriculture/food

Arizona: Circle 953
Michigan: **Kellogg 450**, Lighthouse 1321
Nebraska: ConAgra 959

Agriculture/food, government agencies

Michigan: Roscommon 1163

Agriculture/food, public education

Michigan: Roscommon 1163
Nebraska: ConAgra 959

Agriculture/food, public policy

Nebraska: ConAgra 959

Agriculture/food, single organization support

Michigan: Roscommon 1163

AIDS

Illinois: **Abbott 933**
Michigan: Grand Rapids 1127, Hemophilia 1279, Metro 556, Roscommon 1163
New York: **Ford 260**

AIDS research

Michigan: Rhoades 683, Roscommon 1163

AIDS, people with

Michigan: Metro 556
New York: **Ford 260**

Alcoholism

Michigan: Grand Rapids 1127
Texas: Erskine 226
Wisconsin: Hess 368

Allergies

Michigan: Asthma 1197

Alzheimer's disease

Michigan: DiPonio 193, Sinai 751
Ohio: HCR 1002
Wisconsin: Stockton 782

Alzheimer's disease research

Michigan: Dart 168, **Erb 224**

American Red Cross

Michigan: Borovoy 89, Branch 1210, Chelsea 1225, **Cresswell 154**, Dana 963, **Delphi 966**, DTE 977, Federal 981, General 990, Howard 389, Isabella 1006, Kalamazoo 1304, **Kellogg's 1015**, Lubin 509, May 533, Perrigo 1045, Roscommon 1163, Smith 758, United 1428, United 1430, United 1432, United 1447, Whirlpool 1072
Minnesota: CHS 952
Ohio: Gardner 285, Kroger 1020
Texas: Bray 94
Wisconsin: Handleman 341

Animal welfare

Michigan: Baker 36, Bashur 48, Battle Creek 1086, Birkhill 76, Blakely 80, Bonsall 87, Burroughs 111, Caesar 114, Camp 115, DeRoy 180, Detroit 1245, Foren 267, General 990, Hillsdale 1131, Humane 395, **John 1299**, Kasiewicz 435, Kellogg 449, Kemp 1017, Lugers 511, Marcks 524, Mitchell 572, Muntwyler 592, Roscommon 1163, Trixie 819, Valassis 1068, Weiss 865, Worsham 912
New York: Nonprofit 1361

Animals/wildlife

Michigan: Besse 68, Conway 146, Detroit 1245, DeVlieg 185, DTE 976, Griffith 318, Lewis 500, Mauser 532, Olds 616, Roscommon 1163, **Shaevsky 1395**, Strobel 786, Sturgis 1175, Tremble 817, Tuktawa 826
Wisconsin: Wisconsin 1075

Animals/wildlife, alliance/advocacy

Minnesota: Xcel 1077

Animals/wildlife, endangered species

Michigan: **Arcus 27**, Wong 909

Animals/wildlife, fisheries

Michigan: Frey 276, Great 1273

Animals/wildlife, formal/general education

Michigan: Roscommon 1163

Animals/wildlife, preservation/protection

Michigan: Conway 146, Detroit 1245, Feather 244, Frey 276, Great 1273, Haas 329, Weiss 865
Minnesota: Xcel 1077

Animals/wildlife, public education

Michigan: Glassen 301, Roscommon 1163
Minnesota: Xcel 1077

Animals/wildlife, research

Michigan: **John 1299**

Animals/wildlife, sanctuaries
Michigan: **Arcus 27**

Animals/wildlife, single organization support
Michigan: Roscommon 1163

Animals/wildlife, special services
Michigan: **Arcus 27**, Jospey 425, Kemp 1017, McLeod 548, Puschelberg 662, Rewold 1053, Roscommon 1163
Virginia: Falls 236

Animals/wildlife, volunteer services
Michigan: Roscommon 1163

Aquariums
Illinois: Souder 764

Art & music therapy
Michigan: Vollbrecht 846

Arthritis
Michigan: Borovoy 89

Arts
California: Ayrshire 34, **Parsons 1044**, Toyota 1066
Colorado: Seidman 729
Connecticut: Pryor 661
Florida: CSX 962, Hagen 332, **Knight 462**, Stulberg 790, Van 840
Georgia: **Georgia 992**
Illinois: **Abbott 933**, **Joyce 427**, Loutit 507, Nuveen 612, Seabury 727, Shelby 735
Indiana: Ball 40
Louisiana: Entergy 979
Maryland: Alpern 14
Massachusetts: Hanover 999
Michigan: Albion 1078, Alger 1079, Allegan 1080, Allendale 1081, Amerisure 938, **Amway 939**, Anchor 1082, Ann Arbor 1083, Applebaum 26, Applebaum 1191, Arts 1193, Arts 1194, ArtServe 1196, AtWater 33, Baldwin 38, Balk 39, Baraga 1084, Barry 1085, Barth 45, Battle Creek 1086, Batts 941, Bay 1087, Bay Harbor 1088, Bedford 1089, Berrien 1090, Besser 69, Biederman 1483, Binda 73, Blodgett 82, Boll 84, Bonisteel 85, Borman's 88, Branch 1091, Cadillac 1092, Camp 115, Canaan 117, Charlevoix 1096, Charlupski 127, Clare 1098, Clio 1099, CMS 955, **Collectors 1228**, Community 1101, Community 1103, Community 1104, Community 1106, Community 1107, Community 1108, Community 1109, Community 1110, Community 1111, Community 1113, Connable 145, Consumers 961, Courtney 152, Crystal 1116, Cummings 157, Dalton 163, Dana 963, Davison 1117, Delano 179, DENSO 967, DeVlieg 185, DeVos 186, DeVos 187, DeVos 189, Dickinson 1118, Dow 202, DTE 977, Dyer 215, Eaton 1119, Eddy 218, **Erb 224**, Ervin 227, Fabri 980, Farver 241, Farwell 242, Firestone 254, Flint 1255, Ford 263, Ford 264, Ford 265, Ford 986, Fremont 1124, Frey 276, Gerberding 291, Gilmore 299, Glick 302, Goad 303, Grand 1125, Grand Rapids 1127, Grand 1128, Gratiot 1129, Greenville 1130, Griffith 318, Hammond 998, Hancock 340, Harding 346, Harlan 349, Hartwick 352, **Haworth 1001**, Hermelin 1281, Hickman 371, Hillsdale 1131, Himmel 375, Holden 381, Holley 383, Hudson 392, Huron 1133, Hurst 398, Ionia 1134, **Isabel 409**, Isabella 1006, Ishpeming 1136, Jackson 1137, Jackson 1519, JPMorgan 1009, JSJ 1010, Kantzler 434, Katzman 438, Kaufman 440, Keeler 446, **Kellogg's 1015**, Keweenaw 1139, Knight 461, Kosch 467, **Kresge 471**, Lahti 476, Lake 1140, Lansing 484, Lapeer 1141, **Latvian 1317**, Leelanau 1142, Leighton 495, Lenawee 1143, Leven 498, Lewis 500, Livonia 1144, Loeb 506, Lowell 1325, M & M 1145, Mackinac 1146, Manistee 1147, Marcks 524, Mardigian 525, Marquette 1148, Marshall 1149, Marshall 526, Masco 1026, McGregor 542, McKeen 546, McKibben 547, Mecosta 1150, Meritor 1030, Michigan 1151, Michigan 1344, Midland 1152, Mims 568, Monroe 577, Morley 584, Mott 588, Nelson 599, Nickless 604, Northville 1157, Norway 1158, Osceola 1159, Otsego 1160, Parfet 629, Perrigo 1045, Petoskey 1162, Pokagon 1048, Porter 655, Prentis 657, Pribil 659, Reynolds 681, Rotary 1391, Sage 708, Saginaw 1164, Sanilac 1165, Schalon 716, Schoolcraft 1166, Schwartz 724, Sebastian 728, Seifert 730, **Shaevsky 1395**, Shelby 1167, Shelden 736, Shiawassee 1168, Shiffman 739, Shubeck 743, Sisson 752, Skiles 754, Skillman 755, Sloat 757, Southeast 1170, Southfield 1171, Sparta 1172, Spector 769, **Steelcase 1058**, **Steelcase 1059**, Sterling 1173, Strobel 786, Stryker 788, Sturgis 1175, Sylvia 797, Three 1176, Tiscornia 814, Todd 1064, Towsley 816, Tremble 817, United 1424, Upjohn 832, Varnum 1069, VSA 1456, Weatherwax 852, Weiner 860, Weisblat 863, Weissman 866, Westerman 872, Whirlpool 1072, Whiting 880, Wickes 882, Wickson 883, Williams 888, Wilson 890, Wilson 891, Wilson 893, Winer 896, Winn 898, WMY 905, Wolters 908, Wolverine 1076, World 911, Wyoming 1179, Zurschmiede 932
Minnesota: Musser 594, **Porter 656**, TCF 1061, Weyand 875, Xcel 1077
New York: Center 123, Doan 196, **Ford 260**, Mitsubishi 1035, Nonprofit 1361, Tepper 803
Ohio: American 937, Anderson 21, Cliffs 954, Fifth 984, Gardner 285, Hildreth 373, **JPMorgan 1008**, KeyBank 1018
Pennsylvania: Cash 1218, PNC 1047, West 1071
Texas: Fruehauf 277, Quicksilver 1051
Virginia: Falls 236, **Gannett 988**
Washington: Fehsenfeld 247
Wisconsin: Bishop 78, Handleman 341, Hess 369, McIntyre 543, McIntyre 544, Miner 569, Wisconsin 1074, Wisconsin 1075

Arts councils
Michigan: Hammond 998

Arts education
Michigan: Arts 1193, ArtServe 1196, Community 1103, **Erb 224**, Frey 276, JPMorgan 1009, MEEMIC 1028, Morgan 583, Pollack 652, Reuter 679, Roscommon 1163, Weatherwax 852
Minnesota: Xcel 1077
Pennsylvania: PNC 1047

Arts, artist's services
California: Coltrane 1229
Michigan: Arts 1194, **Kresge 471**

Arts, association
Michigan: Hahn 334, Hartwick 352, Ilitch 1288

Arts, cultural/ethnic awareness
Louisiana: Entergy 979
Michigan: American 1189, Bardha 1478, **Center 1220**, DTE 977, Frey 276, Gornick 310, Italian 1294, JPMorgan 1009, Mott 588, Southeastern 766, Southfield 1171, Whirlpool 1072
Minnesota: Northwest 1042
Nebraska: Kawasaki 1012
Tennessee: Nissan 1040
Virginia: **Gannett 988**

Arts, equal rights
Minnesota: Xcel 1077

Arts, folk arts
Michigan: Frey 276

Arts, public education
Michigan: Roscommon 1163

Arts, single organization support
Michigan: **Center 1220**

Asia
Michigan: **Amway 939**
New York: **Ford 260**

Asians/Pacific Islanders
Michigan: Grand Rapids 1127, **Kellogg 450**, **National 597**
Nebraska: Kawasaki 1012
New York: **Ford 260**
Ohio: KeyBank 1018

Assistive technology
Michigan: Northeast 1362

Asthma
Michigan: Asthma 1197

Athletics/sports, academies
Michigan: Bettis 1203

Athletics/sports, amateur leagues
Michigan: Adray 5, Dart 964, Pistons 1046
Minnesota: Life 1023

Athletics/sports, baseball
Michigan: Grand 1266, Roscommon 1163, Tigers 1062

Athletics/sports, basketball
Michigan: Roscommon 1163
Pennsylvania: Cash 1218

Athletics/sports, equestrianism
Florida: Van 840
Michigan: Leighton 495, Mackinac 1146
Pennsylvania: McCardell 538

Athletics/sports, fishing/hunting
Michigan: Tony 1419

Athletics/sports, football
Michigan: Roscommon 1163

Athletics/sports, golf
Michigan: Roscommon 1163

Athletics/sports, school programs
Michigan: Chelsea 129, Community 1230, Detroit 1244, Roscommon 1163
Minnesota: Life 1023
Wisconsin: Kowalski 1019

Athletics/sports, soccer
Michigan: Cronin 155, Foran 259, Roscommon 1163, Whitfield 879

Athletics/sports, Special Olympics
Michigan: Amerisure 938, Basch 47, United 1430
Minnesota: Life 1023
Wisconsin: Shopko 1399

Athletics/sports, training
Michigan: McNish 551, Reynolds 681, Roscommon 1163, Winn 899

Athletics/sports, water sports
Michigan: **Kellogg's 1015**

Athletics/sports, winter sports
Colorado: Seidman 729
Michigan: Adray 5, Katzman 438, Keweenaw 1139, Smith 760

Australia
Michigan: **Amway 939**

Autism
Michigan: Mall 521

Autism research
Michigan: Detroit 970

Belgium
Michigan: **Dow 974**

Big Brothers/Big Sisters
Michigan: Branch 1210, Little 504, United 1428, United 1447

Biology/life sciences
Massachusetts: **Cabot 947**
Michigan: Camp 115, Hillsdale 1131
New York: Doan 196

Blind/visually impaired
Delaware: Bartsch 46
Michigan: Grand Rapids 1127, Idema 402, Javitch 415, Jospey 425, **Kakarala 432**, McNally 550, Metro 556, Molinello 575, O'Hare 1543, Ratner 668, Sanilac 1165
Virginia: Falls 236

Botanical gardens
Michigan: Balk 39, Frey 276, Hansen 344

Botanical/horticulture/landscape services
Illinois: Keller 448

Boy scouts
Michigan: Barton 940, Besse 68, Branch 1210, Burnham 110, Chelsea 1225, Generations 991, Haas 329, Harlan 349, Kellogg 449, MAC 1024, MacCrone 517, Perrigo 1045, Roscommon 1163, United 1428, United 1430, United 1432, United 1447
Minnesota: Xcel 1077
Mississippi: Weitzenhoffer 867

Boys
Michigan: Grand Rapids 1127, Holden 381, Metro 556, Sanilac 1165

Boys & girls clubs
Michigan: Amerisure 938, **Amway 939**, Barstow 44, Consumers 961, Dart 168, Dauch 1490, Detroit 970, Eddy 218, Farmington 1253, Ford 264, HCC 1512, Hickman 371, Meritor 1030, Thomas 808, United 1428, Whirlpool 1072
Minnesota: Life 1023
New Jersey: Randall 667
Texas: Battier 1200

Brain research
Michigan: Beck 1201, Nill 607

Brazil
Michigan: **BorgWarner 945, Dow 974, Kellogg 450**

Breast cancer
Michigan: Susan 1414
Ohio: Kroger 1021

Breast cancer research
Michigan: Amerisure 938, Detroit 970, **Ford 985**, Foremost 987, Susan 1414
Ohio: Kroger 1020

Buddhism
Michigan: Ford 262

Business school/education
Michigan: Camp 115, Comerica 956, Consumers 961, **DENSO 968**, DTE 977, General 990, Grand Haven 1126, Harding 348, **Michigan 1337**, Morley 584, Ponting 653, Richter 684, Schuyler 723, Whirlpool 1072, Wickson 883
Minnesota: Xcel 1077
Wisconsin: Handleman 341

Business/industry
Michigan: **ACI 1181**, Comerica 956, Comerica 957, DTE 977, General 990, Genesis 1504, **H.I.S. 327**, Kelly 1016, Meritor 1030
Minnesota: Xcel 1077

Cameroon
Michigan: **Wellspring 870**

Canada
Michigan: **DENSO 968, Kellogg 1013, Steelcase 1058**

Cancer
Florida: Stulberg 790, Van 840
Illinois: **Abbott 933**

Michigan:* Borovoy 89, Bronner 102, Cochrane 140, Del Signore 1236, Delta 1238, DeRoy 180, Faigle 234, Federal 981, Grand Rapids 1268, Hennessey 362, Herrick 367, Horgan 387, Idema 402, Kay 442, Little 504, **McCarty 1333, New 1358, Otsego 1160, Pardee 1547, Pardee 1548, **Pardee 628**, Perrigo 1045, Pistons 1046, Price 660, Ramser 666, Reimer 674, Royal 698, Schwartz 724, Van Haften 1452, Whiting 880, Wolverine 1076
Pennsylvania: National 1355
Wisconsin: Kowalski 1019, Venturedyne 1070

Cancer research
Michigan: Ambrosiani 15, Chemical 951, Deffenbaugh 176, Delta 1238, Foren 267, Fund 279, General 990, Hickman 371, **McCarty 1333**, Nill 607, **Pardee 628**, Puschelberg 662
Ohio: Geiger 288
Pennsylvania: National 1355

Cancer, leukemia
Michigan: Children's 1227, Ilitch 1289, Kebok 445

Catholic agencies & churches
Florida: Hasey 356, Nowak 610
Illinois: Clare 137, Guzikowski 326, McShane 552
Michigan: Abele 3, Ambrosiani 15, Attanasio 32, Basilica 49, Berkery 64, Briggs-Fisher 99, Burnham 110, Busch 112, Cadillac 948, Chelsea 1225, Cipa 133, Delano 179, Duchene 210, Duffy 211, Fruman 278, Grimaldi 319, Haas 329, Hancock 340, Kalamazoo 1306, LaMothe 480, Langbo 481, Lynch 514, Marzke 529, McNish 551, Molloy 576, Moore 580, Morath 581, Myers 596, O'Neill 1544, Obloy 614, Pellerito 638, Reid 673, Riley 685, Sage 708, Sequin 731, Stanton 776, Sterken 779, Trinity 1422, United 1447, Walsh 848, Watson 850, Webster 853, Williams 887
Ohio: O'Brien 613
Wisconsin: Hess 368, McIntyre 545, Stockton 782

Catholic federated giving programs
Illinois: Guzikowski 326
Michigan: Hancock 340
Wisconsin: Hess 368

Cemeteries/burial services, burial association
Michigan: Trumley 822

Cerebral palsy
Arizona: Circle 953
Michigan: Hill 374

Charter schools
Michigan: Ford 986

Chemistry
Massachusetts: **Cabot 947**
Michigan: **Dow 973**, Meyers 557
Ohio: Heyl 1282

Child development, education
Michigan: Battle Creek 1086, Ervin 227, Frey 276, Hillsdale 1131, Nusbaum 611, Roscommon 1163, Skillman 755, **Society 1401**, Vollbrecht 846, Wilson 893, Young 922
Minnesota: Northwest 1042
Nevada: MGM 1031
New York: Local 1323, **New York 1038**
Pennsylvania: PNC 1047
Wisconsin: Hess 368

Child development, services

Michigan: Battle Creek 1086, Ervin 227, Frey 276, Hillsdale 1131, **Mott 587**, Skillman 755, **Society 1401**, Wilson 893
Wisconsin: Hess 368

Children

Illinois: **Abbott 933**
Michigan: **Amway 939**, **BorgWarner 945**, Community 1103, Eschbach 228, **Gerber 290**, Grand Rapids 1127, Holden 381, Jackson 1007, **Kellogg 450**, Lifestyle 1320, Livonia 1144, Make-A-Wish 1328, Metro 556, Midland 1152, Northwest 1365, Pentecost 641, Sanilac 1165, Schmuckal 719, Skillman 755, Sturgis 1175, Tuscola 1177, Variety 1453, **Wellspring 870**, Whaley 1464, Wickson 883
Nebraska: ConAgra 959
New York: **New York 1038**
Ohio: McCalla 537, Tim 1063
Texas: Spark 1056

Children's rights

Texas: Spark 1056

Children, adoption

Michigan: Lutheran 1326, Orchards 1374, Spaulding 1408, Speckhard 768, Spectrum 1409

Children, day care

Michigan: Berrien 1090, Frey 276, Grand 1269, Kent 1311, Michigan 1338, Northwest 1365, Orchards 1374, Roscommon 1163

Children, foster care

Michigan: Alternatives 1185, Ennis 1250, Lutheran 1326, Orchards 1374, Speckhard 768, Spectrum 1409

Children, services

Florida: CSX 962, **Knight 462**
Kentucky: Guilliom 321, Humana 1003
Louisiana: Entergy 979
Michigan: **Amway 939**, **BorgWarner 945**, **Children's 1226**, Con 958, Dickinson 1118, Fedorov 246, Fink 252, Ford 262, Frey 276, Grand 1269, Helppie 361, Jackson 1007, MAC 1024, Mojo 574, **Mott 587**, Orchards 1374, Roscommon 1163, **Shaevsky 1395**, United 1428, United 1447, Valassis 1068, Williams 887, **Worldwide 1469**, Worsham 912, Young 921
Texas: Quicksilver 1051, Spark 1056
Wisconsin: ShopKo 1055

Children/youth

California: Ayrshire 34, Rose 1390
Florida: Rudlaff 699, Van 840
Indiana: Foellinger 258
Michigan: Alliance 11, Arab 1192, Barnes 42, Berrien 1090, Berry 66, Central 1095, **Collectors 1228**, Community 1107, Cornucopia 1488, Dart 168, Dickinson 1118, Doyle 203, Face 1251, Fremont 1124, Grand 1266, Grand Rapids 1127, Holden 381, Javitch 415, **Kellogg 1014**, **Kellogg 450**, Kent 1311, Livonia 1144, MacCrone 517, Macomb 1327, Metro 556, Midland 1152, **Mott 587**, O'Neill 1544, Oakland 1370, Pentecost 641, **Racing 1386**, Sanilac 1165, Skillman 755, Sturgis 1175, Taylor 800, Tony 1419, Tuscola 1177, United 1431, Van 836, Village 1455, Weed 855, Wickson 883, Wilson 890, Wolverine 1468, **Yankama 916**, Young 1470
Minnesota: CHS 952
Nebraska: Kaufman 439

New York: Corporation 1233, **New York 1038**
Texas: Battier 1200

Children/youth, services

California: Ayrshire 34
Florida: Van 840
Illinois: Keller 448, Seabury 727
Indiana: Ball 40, Foellinger 258
Maryland: Higgins-Hussman 372
Michigan: Albion 1078, Allegan 1080, Alternatives 1185, Amerisure 938, Ann Arbor 1083, Baker 36, Baldwin 38, Baraga 1084, Barry 1085, Barstow 44, Battle Creek 1086, Batts 941, Besser 69, Blodgett 1207, Blodgett 82, Boutell 92, Burroughs 111, Butzel 946, Cadillac 948, Camp 115, Capital 1094, Carls 118, Central 1095, Charlevoix 1096, Cheboygan 1223, Citizens 134, Clannad 136, Clark 138, CMS 955, Cochrane 140, Colina 141, Community 1104, Community 1107, Community 1109, Community 1111, Cook 147, Dana 963, Dart 964, Dart 168, Davis 171, Day 173, Detroit 182, Detroit 970, DeVos 186, DeVos 187, Eddy 218, Ervin 227, Ever 230, Farmington 1253, Farwell 242, Federal 981, Filmer 251, Ford 263, Ford 265, Foren 267, Four 1122, Fremont 1124, Frey 276, Gary 287, Gerberding 291, Gerstacker 292, Glick 302, Gornick 310, Grand Rapids 1127, Grand Rapids 1268, Greene 317, Greenville 1130, Hahn 334, Hammond 998, Heart 1277, Herrick 367, Hickman 371, Hillsdale 1131, Himmel 375, Holden 381, Holley 383, Huron 1133, Idema 402, Jackson 1137, Jeffers 417, JSJ 1010, Junior 1300, Kay 442, **Kellogg's 1015**, Kemp 1017, Kent 1311, Klobucar 458, Lahti 476, Lewis 500, Livingston 1322, Loeb 506, Lovelight 508, Lugers 511, Lutheran 1326, Lynch 514, Mackinac 1146, Mardigian 525, Marquette 1148, McKeen 546, Metro 556, Michigan 1338, Miller 565, Miller 566, Mitchell 572, Moore 579, Morley 584, Mott 588, O'Hare 1543, Orchards 1374, Otsego 1160, Ottawa 1376, Park 1549, Pellerito 638, Pistons 1046, Rawson 670, Reynolds 681, Roscommon 1163, Sanilac 1165, Skillman 755, Social 1400, Spectrum 1409, Springview 773, Stoker 784, Thomas 808, United 1437, United 1440, United 1441, United 1450, Van 836, Vanderwaals 843, Village 1455, Vollbrecht 846, Watson 850, Webster 854, Wege 856, Weikart 859, Weisblat 863, Welch 868, Westerman 872, Whaley 1464, Whiting 880, Whiting 881, Wickes 882, Wickson 883, Wilson 893, WMY 905, Wolff 907, Wolverine 1076, World 911, Yeager 918, Young 922
Minnesota: Life 1023
Mississippi: Weitzenhoffer 867
Nebraska: Kaufman 439
New Jersey: Campbell 949
Ohio: Anderson 21, Cliffs 954
Oregon: Graef 312
Texas: Bray 94
Washington: Fehsenfeld 247
Wisconsin: Bishop 78, Keeney 447, Kowalski 1019, Venturedyne 1070

China

Michigan: **BorgWarner 945**, **Dow 974**, **H.I.S. 327**

Christian agencies & churches

California: Wierenga 884
Colorado: Seidman 729
Florida: DeLange 178, Dexter 190, DJD 194, Hasey 356, Weigel 858
Illinois: Hoving 1515, Loutit 507, Peters 644, Shelby 735
Indiana: Parrish 633
Maryland: Van Lunen 841
Michigan: 41 1, Amy 17, Anderson 22, Ash 31, AtWater 33, Baldwin 38, Balk 39, Bardha 1478, Bardsley 41, Bauervic 51, Beals 56, BJB 79, Boll 84, Bossenbroek 90, Bouma 91, Boutell 92, Brennan

96, Bronner 102, Buist 1484, Caesar 114, Canaan 117, Christian 131, Cochrane 140, Coleman 1487, Community 143, Coon 149, Copley 150, Cornucopia 1488, Courtney 152, Crane 153, Daystar 174, Deffenbaugh 176, DeShano 1491, Detroit 181, DeVos 186, DeVos 187, DeVos 188, Diephouse 192, Donlin 198, Doyle 203, Duffy 211, En 222, **Fahd 1498**, Falk 235, Farago 238, Farwell 242, Fibre 982, Filmer 251, Firestone 254, Fish 255, Foren 267, G. 280, Garland 286, Gertz 293, God's 304, Granger 313, Granger 314, Greene 317, Griffith 318, Grimaldi 319, **H.I.S. 327**, His 378, Honholt 385, Horgan 387, Howard 389, **I.N. 1287**, Idema 402, **Isabel 409**, Joy 426, Kazrus 444, Keeler 446, Kellogg 449, Kerkstra 456, Klobucar 458, Kosch 467, Koster 468, Legion 494, Lemmen 496, Love, 1324, Ludington 510, Mall 521, Mardigian 525, Marshall 526, Mason 1331, May 533, Merkley 555, Middle 1351, Miller 562, Mojo 574, Molinello 575, Moore 579, Nickless 604, Oleson 617, Olson 618, Penner 640, Plymouth 1381, Rainbow 664, Resnal 678, Robertson 689, Rock 691, Roon 695, Roscommon 1163, Sackerson 706, Sacred 707, Schalon 716, Serra 732, Sharing 734, Shepherd 738, Shin 740, Shoemaker 741, Siebenthaler 744, Silverwing 747, Slack 756, Sloat 757, **Snyder 762**, Sobong 1559, Spencer 771, Springview 773, Sullivan 792, Sunrise 794, Todd 1064, Tremble 817, Trixie 819, Tuinstra 825, Upjohn 832, Van Andel 835, Van Den Bosch 838, Van Wormer 842, Vanderweide 844, Warchol 849, Weed 855, Welsh 871, Welter 1571, Whiting 881, WMY 905, **Worldwide 1469**, Wynalda 914, **Yankama 916**, Zimmerman 927, Zondervan 930
Minnesota: Weyand 875
New Jersey: Hamstra 339, Merillat 554, Randall 667
New York: Gits 300
Ohio: Gardner 285
Oregon: Graef 312
Texas: Fruehauf 277, Guy 325
Wisconsin: McIntyre 543, McIntyre 544, Venturedyne 1070, Vogt 845

Civil liberties, advocacy

Indiana: Katz 436
Michigan: Beckwith 1202

Civil liberties, first amendment

Virginia: **Gannett 988**

Civil liberties, reproductive rights

Michigan: Grand Rapids 1127

Civil liberties, right to life

Michigan: Bauervic 51, **H.I.S. 327**, Shoemaker 741

Civil rights, race/intergroup relations

Florida: **Knight 462**
Illinois: Allstate 935
Michigan: Community 1106, Grand Rapids 1127, **Mott 587**, New 1359, Shiffman 739, Southfield 1171
Minnesota: Musser 594
New York: **Ford 260**
Ohio: **JPMorgan 1008**

Civil/human rights

Michigan: **Arcus 27**, Beckwith 1202, Miller 566, Parks 1377
New York: **Ford 260**, Mitsubishi 1035

Civil/human rights, aging

Michigan: Grand Rapids 1127

Civil/human rights, disabled
Michigan: Grand Rapids 1127

Civil/human rights, equal rights
Illinois: Allstate 935
Michigan: Comerica 956, DTE 976, DTE 977, Ford 986, **Kellogg 1014**
Ohio: KeyBank 1018
Virginia: **Gannett 988**

Civil/human rights, immigrants
Michigan: **Center 1220**, Grand Rapids 1127

Civil/human rights, LGBTQ
Michigan: **Arcus 27**, Grand Rapids 1127

Civil/human rights, minorities
Michigan: Grand Rapids 1127

Civil/human rights, women
Michigan: Grand Rapids 1127, Sojourner 1403

Community development, business promotion
Colorado: First 1254
Michigan: Community 1113, Home 384, Northern 1542
New York: Local 1323

Community development, citizen coalitions
New York: Local 1323

Community development, civic centers
Michigan: Consumers 961, Frey 276

Community development, neighborhood associations
Michigan: Dyer 215

Community development, neighborhood development
Florida: **Knight 462**
Illinois: Allstate 935
Louisiana: Entergy 979
Michigan: Allegan 1080, Barry 1085, Community 1101, Consumers 961, Davison 1117, Detroit 1494, DTE 977, Dyer 215, Fabri 980, Frey 276, Grand Rapids 1127, **Kellogg 450**, McClendon 539, Miller 565, Mount Pleasant 1154, New 1359, Upjohn 832
New York: **Heron 366**, Local 1323
Virginia: **Gannett 988**

Community development, public/private ventures
Michigan: Frey 276, Kentwood 455

Community development, real estate
New York: Local 1323

Community development, service clubs
Michigan: Davison 1117, Great 1271

Community development, small businesses
Georgia: **Georgia 992**

Michigan: Comerica 956, Comerica 957, Davison 1117, JPMorgan 1009, Michigan 1346, Northern 1542
New York: Local 1323

Community development, women's clubs
Michigan: Roscommon 1163

Community/economic development
California: Ayrshire 34, Toyota 1066
Georgia: **Georgia 992**
Illinois: **Abbott 933**, Loutit 507, Seabury 727
Massachusetts: **Cabot 947**, Hanover 999
Michigan: African 1182, Albion 1078, Albion-Homer 1183, Allegan 1184, Anchor 1082, Ann Arbor 1083, Annis 25, Baraga 1084, Barry 1085, Barton 940, Battle Creek 1086, Bay 1087, Bedford 1089, Berrien 1090, Borman's 88, Branch 1091, Branch 1210, Cadillac 1092, Camp 115, Canton 1093, Capital 1094, Central 1095, Char-Em 1221, Charlevoix 1096, Chelsea 1225, Chemical 951, Citizens 134, Clare 1098, Clio 1099, CMS 955, Comerica 956, Comerica 957, Community 1230, Community 1102, Community 1103, Community 1105, Community 1106, Community 1108, Community 1109, Community 1110, Community 1111, Constantine 1114, Consumers 961, Copper 1232, Crane 153, Crawford 1234, Cronin 155, Crystal 1116, Dagenais 162, Dalton 163, Dana 963, Davison 1117, Day 173, Delano 179, DeShano 1491, Detroit 1243, DeVos 188, Dickinson 1118, **Dow 973**, **Dow 974**, Dow 975, Dow 202, DSLT 209, DTE 977, Eastpointe 1247, Eaton 1119, Eaton 1248, Eddy 218, Evergreene 1497, Farver 241, Fenton 1120, First 1499, Flushing 1121, Ford 986, Four 1122, Frankenmuth 1123, Fremont 1124, Garland 286, Gay, 1262, General 990, Gertz 293, Gilmore 299, **Global 1264**, Gogebic 1265, Grand 1125, Grand Haven 1126, Grand Rapids 1127, Grand 1128, Gratiot 1129, Great 1272, Greenville 1130, Harlan 349, Hartwick 352, Hastings 1000, Helppie 361, Hillsdale 1131, Hillsdale 1283, Homer 1132, Hudson 391, Hunter 397, Huron 1133, Hurst 398, Ionia 1134, Iosco 1135, Ishpeming 1136, Jackson 1137, Jackson 1007, Jeffers 417, Johnson 423, JPMorgan 1009, Junior 1300, Kalamazoo 1138, Kalamazoo 1307, Kalamazoo 1309, Kantzler 434, **Kellogg 1013**, Kellogg 449, **Kellogg 450**, Kelly 1016, Kemler 452, Keweenaw 1139, Lake 1140, Law 490, Lenawee 1143, Lenawee 1318, Lowell 1325, Lugers 511, M & M 1145, Mackinac 1146, Manistee 1147, Marshall 1149, Marshall 526, Masco 1026, Mason 1027, McDonald's 1530, Mecosta 1150, Mecosta-Osceola 1334, Meritor 1030, Michigan 1349, Midland 1152, Missaukee 1153, Monroe 1036, Moore 579, Morley 584, **Mott 587**, Mott 588, Muskegon 1354, Negaunee 1155, Norway 1158, Oakland 1370, Osceola 1159, Otsego 1160, Ottawa 1376, Parfet 629, Peshtigo 1161, Petoskey 1162, Plym 649, Plymouth 1382, Pokagon 1048, Portland 1384, Riley 685, Roscommon 1389, Rotary 1392, Sackerson 706, Saginaw 1164, Sanilac 1165, Schmuckal 719, Schoolcraft 1166, Schwartz 724, Seifert 730, Shelby 1167, Shiawassee 1168, Shiawassee 1397, Shiffman 739, Sisson 752, Social 1400, South 1169, Southeast 1170, Southfield 1171, Southwestern 1407, Sparta 1172, St. Clair 774, St. Joseph 1412, **Steelcase 1058**, **Steelcase 1059**, Strosacker 787, Stryker 788, Stubberfield 1565, Stubnitz 789, Sturgis 1175, Thorrez 812, Three 1176, Todd 1064, Turner 829, United 1427, United 1428, United 1429, United 1431, United 1432, United 1433, United 1434, United 1435, United 1436, United 1438, United 1442, United 1444, United 1445, United 1446, United 1447, United 1449, Van 836, Vanderweide 844, Varnum 1069, Washtenaw 1458, Wayne 1460, Wege 856, Weinlander 861, West 1463, Whirlpool 1072, White 877, White 1178, Whiting 880, Whiting 881, Wilson 893, Wyoming 1179, Yeo 919, Ypsilanti 1180

Minnesota: TCF 1061, Xcel 1077
Nebraska: Kaufman 439
Nevada: MGM 1031, MGM 1336
New Jersey: Campbell 949, CKT 135
New York: **Ford 260**, Local 1323, Nonprofit 1361
Ohio: Anderson 21, Catholic 1219, Charter 950, Fifth 983, Fifth 984, **JPMorgan 1008**
Pennsylvania: PNC 1047, West 1071
Virginia: **Gannett 988**
Wisconsin: Wisconsin 1075

Community/economic development, alliance/ advocacy
Michigan: West 1463

Community/economic development, fund raising/fund distribution
Michigan: Lenawee 1318

Community/economic development, management/technical assistance
New York: Local 1323

Community/economic development, public education
Michigan: Morgan 583

Community/economic development, single organization support
Michigan: Roscommon 1163

Computer science
Massachusetts: **Cabot 947**
Ohio: Heyl 1282

Courts/judicial administration
Michigan: Justice 1301

Crime/abuse victims
Michigan: Clannad 136, Grand Rapids 1127, Midland 1152, Sanilac 1165, Sturgis 1175

Crime/law enforcement
Michigan: Grand Haven 1126, Hillsdale 1131, Oakland 1369, Roscommon 1163

Crime/law enforcement, administration/ regulation
Michigan: Oakland 1369

Crime/law enforcement, equal rights
Michigan: Oakland 1369

Crime/law enforcement, formal/general education
Michigan: Roscommon 1163

Crime/law enforcement, government agencies
Michigan: Roscommon 1163

Crime/law enforcement, information services
Michigan: Oakland 1369

Crime/law enforcement, management/ technical assistance
Michigan: Roscommon 1163

Crime/law enforcement, missing persons
Michigan: Roscommon 1163

Crime/law enforcement, police agencies
Michigan: Roscommon 1163, Yeager 917

Crime/law enforcement, public education
Michigan: Oakland 1369, Roscommon 1163

Crime/law enforcement, reform
Michigan: Oakland 1369

Crime/law enforcement, single organization support
Michigan: Roscommon 1163

Crime/violence prevention
Illinois: **Joyce 427**
Michigan: Community 1113, Hudson 392
New York: Local 1323

Crime/violence prevention, abuse prevention
Michigan: Mason 1331, United 1430, United 1432, United 1446, United 1447
New York: **Ford 260**

Crime/violence prevention, child abuse
Michigan: Hahn 334, Redies 1052, Sojourner 1403, Vollbrecht 846, Welter 1571

Crime/violence prevention, domestic violence
Michigan: Ann Arbor 1083, Capital 1213, Jewish 1298, **Ms. 1353**, Sojourner 1403, Three 1176, United 1439

Crime/violence prevention, gun control
Illinois: **Joyce 427**

Crime/violence prevention, youth
Illinois: Allstate 935
Michigan: Ervin 227, Hillsdale 1131, Skillman 755

Cystic fibrosis research
Michigan: Raiola 665

Deaf/hearing impaired
Michigan: Fremont 1124, Grand Rapids 1127, Konstanzer 466, Metro 556, Midland 1152, Sanilac 1165

Dental care
Michigan: Community 1113, Delta 1238, Kellogg 449, Michigan 1341

Dental school/education
Michigan: Delta 1238, Kadant 1011, Kellogg 449, Lesher 497

Developing countries
Michigan: **Worldwide 1469**

Developmentally disabled, centers & services
Indiana: Neff 1539
Michigan: **Amway 939**, CareLink 1216, Cheboygan 1223, Consumers 961, Oakland 1370, Perrigo 1045, Thresholds 1418, Training 1420, United 1440
Wisconsin: Wisconsin 1075

Diabetes
Illinois: **Abbott 933**
Michigan: Barnes 42, Borovoy 89, Ford 265, Van Haften 1452, Wolverine 1076

Diabetes research
Michigan: **Ford 985**, Foremost 987, General 990, Thomas 808, Welter 1571
Texas: **OneSight 1546**

Disabilities, people with
California: Ayrshire 34
Florida: Rudlaff 699
Michigan: Barnes 42, Community 1108, Community 1109, DiPonio 193, Easter 1246, Farago 238, Fibre 982, Fremont 1124, Grand Rapids 1127, Hope 1285, Italian 1294, Lansing 484, Metro 556, Midland 1152, Pietrasiuk 648, Sanilac 1165, Southwest 767, **Steelcase 1058**, Sturgis 1175, United 1439, United 1446, Village 1455, Vollbrecht 846, VSA 1456, Wilson 893, Wolters 908, Young 922
New York: Corporation 1233
Ohio: McCalla 537
Pennsylvania: McCardell 538
Wisconsin: Keeney 447

Disasters, fire prevention/control
Georgia: **Georgia 992**
Massachusetts: **Cabot 947**
Michigan: Jennings 418

Disasters, Hurricane Katrina
Michigan: **Kellogg 1014**, Lubin 509

Disasters, preparedness/services
Georgia: **Georgia 992**
Illinois: Allstate 935
Louisiana: Entergy 979
Michigan: **Amway 939**, **BorgWarner 945**, **Delphi 966**, **Ford 985**, General 990, GM 994, Here 365
Minnesota: CHS 952, Northwest 1042
Ohio: Kroger 1020
Wisconsin: Wisconsin 1074

Disasters, search/rescue
Michigan: Roscommon 1163

Dispute resolution
Michigan: Human 1286

Eastern & Central Europe
Michigan: **Mott 587**

Economic development
Colorado: First 1254
Florida: **Knight 462**

Illinois: Allstate 935
Louisiana: Entergy 979
Michigan: Albion 1078, Ann Arbor 1083, Annis 25, Cadillac 1092, Charlevoix 1096, CMS 955, Community 1101, Community 1103, Community 1106, Community 1108, Community 1110, Community 1112, Community 1113, Crystal 1116, Dickinson 1118, Federal 981, Jackson 1137, JPMorgan 1009, Kalamazoo 1138, Leven 498, Michigan 1346, Midland 1152, Miller 565, **Mott 587**, Petoskey 1162, Saginaw 1164, Social 1400, **Steelcase 1058**, West 1463
Minnesota: Xcel 1077
New Jersey: Campbell 949
New York: **Ford 260**, **Heron 366**, Local 1323, Nonprofit 1361
Ohio: **JPMorgan 1008**
Pennsylvania: PNC 1047
Virginia: **Gannett 988**

Economically disadvantaged
Delaware: Bartsch 46
Illinois: **Abbott 933**
Indiana: Foellinger 258, Neff 1539
Louisiana: Entergy 979
Michigan: Andrews 24, Arab 1192, Berkery 64, Butzel 946, Central 1095, Charity 1222, Clannad 136, **Collectors 1228**, Comerica 956, Community 143, Community 1106, Community 1107, Community 1109, Dart 168, Delta 1238, Detroit 970, Donlin 198, **Fahd 1498**, Fremont 1124, Gerberding 291, Grand Rapids 1127, Hastings 1000, Heat 1278, Helppie 361, Here 365, Hillsdale 1131, Home 384, I Have 400, **International 1291**, **International 1292**, Italian 1294, Jewish 1298, JPMorgan 1009, Kalamazoo 1304, **Kellogg 450**, Konstanzer 466, Lansing 484, Lighthouse 1321, Lovelight 508, Mackinac 1146, Masco 1025, Masco 1026, Metro 556, Michigan 1340, Midland 1152, Molinello 575, **Mott 587**, Newaygo 1360, Oakland 1370, Perry 643, Pistons 1046, Recreational 671, Sanilac 1165, Schroeder 721, Shiffman 739, Skillman 755, **Steelcase 1058**, Strobel 786, Sturgis 1175, Thoman 807, Travelers 1421, Tuscola 1177, United 1439, United 1446, Van 836, Varnum 1069, Veteran's 1454, Village 1455, Vollbrecht 846, Weed 855, **Wellspring 870**, Wickson 883, Wilson 893, **Yankama 916**, Young 922
Minnesota: Life 1023, TCF 1061, Xcel 1077
Nebraska: Pamida 1043
Nevada: MGM 1031
New York: Corporation 1233, **Ford 260**
Ohio: Charter 950, **JPMorgan 1008**, KeyBank 1018
Pennsylvania: PNC 1047
Virginia: **Gannett 988**

Economics
Michigan: Amerisure 938, Cadillac 1092, Comerica 957, Consumers 961, **Earhart 217**, Harding 348, Hillsdale 1131, Michigan 1339, **Upjohn 1451**
New York: **Ford 260**

Education
Arizona: Circle 953
California: Ayrshire 34, Rose 1390, SANYO 1054, Toyota 1066
Colorado: First 1254
Florida: CSX 962, Detter 183, Hagen 332, Hasey 356, **Knight 462**, Sonkin 1561, Van 840, Weigel 858
Georgia: **Georgia 992**
Illinois: **Abbott 933**, Allstate 935, **Joyce 427**, Keller 448, Meeks 553, Seabury 727, Shelby 735, Souder 764
Indiana: Ball 40, Katz 436, Neff 1539
Kentucky: Humana 1003
Louisiana: Entergy 979
Massachusetts: **Cabot 947**, Hanover 999
Michigan: 41 1, Abele 3, **Akbar 1473**, Albion 1078, Albion-Homer 1183, Alger 1079, Allegan 1080,

American 936, American 1187, Amerisure 938, Anchor 1082, Andersen 19, Ann Arbor 1083, Applebaum 26, Asthma 1197, Attanasio 32, Avondale 1198, Baiardi 35, Balk 39, Baraga 1084, Barry 1085, Bashur 48, Bates 50, Battle Creek 1086, Bay 1087, Bay Harbor 1088, Bedford 1089, Berrien 1090, Besser 69, Betmar 70, Bettis 1203, Biederman 1483, Binda 73, Birtwistle 77, Borders 944, **BorgWarner 945**, Borman's 88, Branch 1091, Brooks 103, Brown 106, Buist 1484, Butzel 946, Cadillac 1092, Cadillac 948, Camp 115, Canton 1093, Capital 1094, Carls 118, Central 1095, Chamberlain 124, Charlevoix 1096, Charlupski 127, Chelsea 1224, Chowdhury 1486, Cipa 133, Citizens 134, Clare 1098, Clio 1099, Coleman 1487, Comerica 956, Comerica 957, Community 1101, Community 1103, Community 1104, Community 1106, Community 1107, Community 1108, Community 1109, Community 1110, Community 1111, Community 1113, Con 958, Constantine 1114, Consumers 961, Cook 147, Cornucopia 1488, Courtney 152, **Cresswell 154**, Cronin 155, Crystal 1116, Dana 963, Daoud 166, Dart 964, Dart 168, Day 173, Daystar 174, Delano 179, **Delphi 966**, DeShano 1491, Detroit 181, Detroit 1243, Detroit 970, DeVos 186, DeVos 187, Dickinson 1118, Dow 202, Drew 207, DSLT 209, DTE 976, DTE 977, Dunnings 214, Dyer 215, Eastpointe 1247, Eaton 1119, Eddy 218, Evergreene 1497, Fabri 980, Farago 238, Farley 240, Farver 241, Farwell 242, Feuer 250, Fibre 982, Filmer 251, Fink 252, Firestone 254, First 1499, Flushing 1121, Ford 262, Ford 263, Ford 264, Ford 265, **Ford 985**, Ford 986, Foremost 987, Foren 267, Foster 269, Foundation 1258, Four 1122, Freeman 274, Fremont 1124, Garland 286, Gary 287, General 990, Gibson 295, Gilmore 299, GM 994, Goad 303, Grand 1125, Grand 1266, Grand Rapids 1127, Grand 1128, Gratiot 1129, Greenville 1130, Griffith 318, **H.I.S. 327**, Haggard 333, Halcyon 335, Hammond 998, Hampson 338, Hancock 340, Hannan 342, Hansen 344, Harbor 1276, Harlan 349, Harris 351, Hartwick 352, **Haworth 1001**, HCC 1512, Heart 1277, Hermelin 1281, Hickman 371, Hillsdale 1131, Himmel 375, Holley 383, Horgan 387, Howard 389, Hudson 391, Hunter 397, Huron 1133, I Have 400, Idema 402, Ilitch 1288, India 406, **International 1292**, Ionia 1134, Ironwood 1293, Irwin 408, Ishpeming 1136, Jackson 1137, Johnson 423, JSJ 1010, Kalamazoo 1138, Kantzler 434, **Kellogg's 1015**, Kelly 1016, Kemp 1017, Keweenaw 1139, Kiwanis 1313, Knabusch 460, Kohn 465, Kolo 1314, Koster 468, Krause 470, **Krishnamurti 472**, La-Z-Boy 1022, Lake 1140, LaMothe 480, Lansing 484, Lapeer 1141, **Latvian 1317**, Leelanau 1142, Legion 494, Lenawee 1143, Lewis 500, Lighthouse 1321, Livonia 1144, Loeb 506, Lowell 1325, Ludington 510, Lugers 511, Lyon 515, M & M 1145, MAC 1024, Mackinac 1146, Manistee 1147, Marcks 524, Marquette 1329, Marquette 1148, Marshall 1149, Marzke 529, Mason 1027, Matthaei 531, McBain 535, McGregor 542, McQuiggan 1531, Mecosta 1150, MEEMIC 1028, Meritor 1030, Merkley 555, Michigan 1032, Michigan 1339, Michigan 1151, Michigan 1344, Midland 1152, Miller 566, Missaukee 1153, Molloy 576, Monroe 1036, Monroe 577, Morey 582, Morley 584, **Mott 587**, Mott 588, Mount Pleasant 1154, Nelson 599, Nickless 601, Nicolay 606, Northeast 1362, Northville 1157, Northville 1364, Norway 1158, Olds 616, Olson 618, Osceola 1159, Otsego 1160, Paine 624, Parfet 629, Parks 1377, Pellerito 638, Perrigo 1045, Petoskey 1162, Pettibone 646, Pistons 1046, Plym 649, Plymouth 1383, Pokagon 1048, Ponting 653, Porter 655, Prentis 657, Prevo 658, Pribil 659, Pulte 1050, Rainbow 664, Redies 1052, Reid 673, Reuther 1387, Robison 690, Rock 691, **Rodney 692**, Roscommon 1163, Rotary 1391, **Rotary 1393**, Sage 708, Saginaw 1164, Sallness 712, Sanilac 1165, Schalon 716, Schoolcraft 1166, Schwartz 724, Sebastian 728, Seifert 730, Shelby 1167,

Shelden 736, Shiawassee 1168, Shiffman 739, Shubeck 743, Sigmund 745, Simon 749, Sinai 751, Sisson 752, Skiles 754, Skillman 755, Sloat 757, **Snyder 762**, Sobong 1559, Social 1400, Southeast 1170, Southfield 1171, Sparta 1172, Spencer 771, St. Joseph 1412, **Steelcase 1058**, **Steelcase 1059**, Sterban 778, Sterling 1173, Stockbridge 781, Stryker 788, Sturgis 1175, Sunrise 794, Sylvia 797, Tawas 1416, Thoman 807, Thornapple 1417, Three 1176, Three 813, Tigers 1062, Todd 1064, Towsley 816, Tremble 817, Turner 829, Tuscola 1177, United 1426, United 1431, Valassis 1068, Vanderweide 844, Variety 1453, Varnum 1069, Watson 850, Weidner 1462, Weikart 859, Weisblat 863, Weissman 866, Welch 868, Westerman 872, Whirlpool 1072, White 1178, Whiting 880, Wickes 882, Wiley 1465, Willard 1466, Williams 888, Wilson 890, Winer 896, Winkle 1572, Winship 900, Wirtz 902, Wolff 907, Wolverine 1076, **Worldwide 1469**, Wright 913, Wyoming 1179, Young 921, Zimmerman 927, Zurschmiede 932
Minnesota: CHS 952, Life 1023, Nash 1037, **Porter 656**, TCF 1061, Weyand 875, Xcel 1077
Mississippi: Weitzenhoffer 867
Nebraska: Kaufman 439, Pamida 1043
Nevada: MGM 1336
New Jersey: Campbell 949, Randall 667
New York: Doan 196, **Ford 260**, Gits 300, Mitsubishi 1035, **New York 1038**, Newsweek/Daily 1039, Nonprofit 1361
Ohio: American 937, Anderson 21, Cliffs 954, Fifth 984, Gardner 285, **JPMorgan 1008**, Kroger 1021
Pennsylvania: Cash 1218, West 1071
Tennessee: Educational 1249, Nissan 1040, Nissan 1041
Texas: Quicksilver 1051
Virginia: **Gannett 988**
Washington: Fehsenfeld 247
Wisconsin: Handleman 341, Hess 368, Kaufman 441, McIntyre 543, McIntyre 544, Shopko 1399, Wisconsin 1074, Wisconsin 1075

Education, association

Michigan: Amerisure 938, Hillsdale 1131
Ohio: Anderson 21

Education, community/cooperative

Michigan: Roscommon 1163
Minnesota: CHS 952

Education, continuing education

Michigan: Shelby 1167

Education, drop-out prevention

Michigan: Ford 986

Education, early childhood education

Illinois: Kalt 433
Massachusetts: **Cabot 947**
Michigan: Cadillac 1092, Colina 141, Consumers 961, Frey 276, Heart 1277, Hillsdale 1131, **Kellogg 450**, Leelanau 1142, Prentis 657, Skillman 755, **Steelcase 1058**, Towsley 816, Weiner 860, Wickson 883
Ohio: American 937
Pennsylvania: PNC 1047

Education, formal/general education

Michigan: Roscommon 1163

Education, fund raising/fund distribution

Michigan: Cadillac 948

Pennsylvania: West 1071

Education, public education

Michigan: Southfield 1171
Nevada: MGM 1031

Education, reading

Florida: Hagen 332
Georgia: **Georgia 992**
Illinois: McShane 552
Louisiana: Entergy 979
Michigan: Battle Creek 1086, Binda 73, Borders 944, Community 1109, Foremost 987, Grand Rapids 1127, Heart 1277, Jackson 1137, Kemp 1017, MEEMIC 1028, Michigan 1343, Pistons 1046, Pokagon 1048, Skillman 755, Thoman 807
New York: **New York 1038**

Education, reform

Michigan: Amerisure 938, Frey 276
Ohio: **JPMorgan 1008**

Education, research

Michigan: Mount Pleasant 1154, **Rodney 692**, **Society 1401**
New York: **Ford 260**

Education, services

Michigan: Basch 47, DTE 977

Education, special

Delaware: Bartsch 46
Michigan: Thoman 807, Vollbrecht 846

Elementary school/education

Michigan: Binda 73, Cadillac 1092, Community 1108, Community 1109, Hancock 340, Hillsdale 1131, **Kellogg 450**, Morley 584, Ponting 653, Prentis 657, St. Clair 774, York 920

Elementary/secondary education

California: Toyota 1066
Delaware: Bartsch 46
Florida: DeLange 178
Georgia: **Georgia 992**
Illinois: **Abbott 933**, Clare 137, Gust 323
Massachusetts: **Cabot 947**
Michigan: Applebaum 26, AtWater 33, Batts 941, Bauervic 51, Bertsch 67, Bouma 91, Brauer 93, Burnham 110, Chelsea 129, Comerica 956, Community 1230, Copley 150, DeVos 186, **Dow 973**, Dow 975, DTE 977, Duchene 210, Engle 978, Ford 1257, Ford 986, Glassen 301, Hancock 340, Helppie 361, Hill 374, Huizenga 394, Jennings 418, Kalamazoo 1303, Kalamazoo 1306, Kay 442, **Kellogg 1014**, Kellogg 449, **Kellogg's 1015**, Kelly 1016, Koester 464, Lemmen 496, Marshall 526, Mason 1027, McNish 551, Miller 562, Mills 567, Morgan 583, Myers 596, Oleson 617, Pierce 1550, Plymouth 1381, Price 660, Reynolds 681, Roon 695, Russell 704, Sackerson 706, **Society 1402**, Society 1560, South 1169, Tahquamenon 1415, Trinity 1422, Waverly 1459, Weed 855, Wege 856, Whirlpool 1072
Minnesota: Nash 1037, Weyerhaeuser 876, Xcel 1077
Nevada: MGM 1031
New Jersey: Lasko 488
New York: **New York 1038**
Ohio: AEP 934, American 937, Hildreth 373, **JPMorgan 1008**, Kroger 1020, Kroger 1021
Pennsylvania: PNC 1047
Wisconsin: Hess 368

Elementary/secondary school reform
Michigan: Workers 910

Employment
Georgia: **Georgia 992**
Illinois: Allstate 935, **Joyce 427**
Michigan: Albion-Homer 1183, Borman's 88, Career 1215, Comerica 956, DTE 977, Dyer 215, Grand Rapids 1127, Hillsdale 1131, Hunter 397, Jewish 1298, United 1446, **Upjohn 1451**
Minnesota: Xcel 1077
New York: **Ford 260**, Local 1323, Nonprofit 1361
Ohio: **JPMorgan 1008**, KeyBank 1018
Wisconsin: Wisconsin 1075

Employment, labor unions/organizations
Michigan: Plumbers 1380

Employment, public policy
Michigan: **Rodney 692**

Employment, retraining
Minnesota: Xcel 1077

Employment, services
Illinois: Allstate 935
Michigan: Capital 1213, Community 1101, **Mott 587**, Southeast 1404, UAW-GM 1423, United 1439, Workers 910

Employment, training
Georgia: **Georgia 992**
Illinois: **Abbott 933**, Allstate 935, Seabury 727
Michigan: Comerica 956, Dart 964, Davenport 170, Grand 1269, JPMorgan 1009, Michigan 1350, UAW-GM 1423
Minnesota: Xcel 1077
Ohio: **JPMorgan 1008**, KeyBank 1018

Employment, vocational rehabilitation
Michigan: Mills 567

End of life care
Michigan: Wirtz 902

Engineering
Michigan: DENSO 967, Western 873

Engineering school/education
Michigan: **ACI 1181**, **DENSO 968**, DeVlieg 185, DTE 977, Ford 986, General 990, Kadant 1011, Meritor 1030, Meyers 557, **Society 1402**, Western 873

Engineering/technology
Massachusetts: **Cabot 947**
Michigan: **BorgWarner 945**, Consumers 961, Dart 168, **Delphi 966**, **DENSO 968**, Dow 975, Dow 202, DTE 977, Meritor 1030, **Society 1402**
Pennsylvania: West 1071

Environment
California: Ayrshire 34, SANYO 1054, Toyota 1066
Florida: Hagen 332
Georgia: **Georgia 992**
Illinois: **Joyce 427**, Seabury 727
Louisiana: Entergy 979

Massachusetts:* **Cabot 947
Michigan: Albion 1078, Alger 1079, Americana 16, Anchor 1082, Asthma 1197, Baraga 1084, Barstow 44, Bay 1087, Bay Harbor 1088, Bedford 1089, Binda 73, **BorgWarner 945**, Branch 1091, Cadillac 1092, Canton 1093, Capital 1094, Charlevoix 1096, Chippewa 1097, Clare 1098, CMS 955, Community 1100, Community 1101, Community 1103, Community 1104, Community 1106, Community 1107, Community 1108, Community 1109, Community 1111, Community 1112, Community 1113, Consumers 961, Cronin 155, Crystal 1116, Dalton 163, DENSO 967, Dickinson 1118, Doan 195, **Dow 973**, Drew 207, DTE 976, DTE 977, Dyer 215, **Erb 224**, Four 1122, Fremont 1124, Frey 276, Frischkorn 1261, General 990, Grand Haven 1126, Grand Rapids 1127, Grand 1128, Gratiot 1129, Green 316, Greenville 1130, Hammond 998, **Haworth 1001**, Hickman 371, Hillsdale 1131, Ionia 1134, Ishpeming 1136, Jackson 1137, Kalamazoo 1138, Keeler 446, Keweenaw 1139, **Kresge 471**, Lake 1140, Lapeer 1141, Lewis 500, Lowell 1325, Lugers 511, Lyon 515, M & M 1145, Mackinac 1146, Manistee 1147, Masco 1025, Michigan 1032, Midland 1152, Mount Pleasant 1154, Norway 1158, Olds 616, Oleson 617, Osceola 1159, Otsego 1160, Petoskey 1162, Pokagon 1048, Pulte 1050, Saginaw 1164, Sanilac 1165, Schoolcraft 1166, Shiawassee 1168, Southeast 1170, Speckhard 768, Spicer 772, **Steelcase 1058**, **Steelcase 1059**, Todd 1064, Tremble 817, Upjohn 832, Weisblat 863, Wolverine 1076, Wyoming 1179
Minnesota: Musser 594, **Porter 656**, Xcel 1077
Mississippi: Weitzenhoffer 867
New York: **Ford 260**, Mitsubishi 1035, Nonprofit 1361
Ohio: American 937, Anderson 21
Tennessee: Nissan 1041
Wisconsin: Lamberson 479, Wisconsin 1074, Wisconsin 1075

Environment, air pollution
Georgia: **Georgia 992**
Michigan: Community 1103, DENSO 967

Environment, alliance/advocacy
Michigan: **Kresge 471**
Minnesota: Xcel 1077

Environment, beautification programs
Michigan: Davison 1117, Frey 276, Lilja 502, Shelby 1167
Minnesota: Xcel 1077

Environment, climate change/global warming
Michigan: McKeen 546

Environment, energy
California: SANYO 1054
Michigan: Bay 1087, **BorgWarner 945**, Consumers 961, DTE 977, Feather 244, General 990, **Kresge 471**, Midland 1152
Minnesota: Xcel 1077
Wisconsin: Wisconsin 1075

Environment, forests
Michigan: DTE 977, Galesburg 1502

Environment, government agencies
Michigan: **Kresge 471**

Environment, land resources
Georgia: **Georgia 992**
Michigan: Community 1101, Community 1103, Consumers 961, DENSO 967, Driggers 208, Fabri 980, Ford 262, Frey 276, Generations 991, Larson 486, Pokagon 1048, Wolverine 1076
Minnesota: Xcel 1077

Environment, management/technical assistance
Michigan: Rotary 1391

Environment, natural resources
Colorado: Seidman 729
Georgia: **Georgia 992**
Illinois: Shelby 735
Michigan: Ann Arbor 1083, Barry 1085, Borovoy 89, Cadillac 1092, Carls 118, Clannad 136, Community 1107, Community 1108, Community 1109, Consumers 961, Cook 147, Davison 185, Dow 202, Driggers 208, DTE 977, Evenson 229, Ever 230, Frey 276, Gary 287, General 990, George 289, Griffith 318, Hillsdale 1131, Kantzler 434, Knight 461, **Kresge 471**, LaMothe 480, Larson 486, Leelanau 1142, Mackinac 1146, Mahogany 520, Marcks 524, Mecosta 1150, **Mott 587**, Northville 1157, Serra 732, Shelden 736, Skiles 754, Wege 856, Wolverine 1076, Wong 909
Minnesota: Weyerhaeuser 876
New York: **Ford 260**
Ohio: Hildreth 373
Virginia: **Gannett 988**
Washington: Fehsenfeld 247
Wisconsin: Wisconsin 1074, Wisconsin 1075

Environment, pollution control
Michigan: **Erb 224**, **Mott 587**

Environment, public education
Michigan: Community 1113, Great 1273
Minnesota: Xcel 1077

Environment, public policy
Michigan: **Kresge 471**

Environment, recycling
Georgia: **Georgia 992**
Michigan: Pokagon 1048

Environment, reform
Michigan: **Kresge 471**

Environment, research
Michigan: Great 1273

Environment, volunteer services
Michigan: Driggers 208

Environment, water pollution
Michigan: Community 1103, DENSO 967, Frey 276

Environment, water resources
Michigan: Consumers 961, Driggers 208, **Erb 224**, Frey 276, Great 1273
Minnesota: **Porter 656**, Xcel 1077

Environmental education

Georgia: **Georgia 992**
Illinois: Peters 644
Michigan: Consumers 961, Davison 1117, DTE 977, **Erb 224**, Feather 244, Glassen 301, Michigan 1032, Mills 567, Pierce 1550, Winn 899
Minnesota: Xcel 1077
Wisconsin: Wisconsin 1074

Europe

Michigan: **Amway 939**

Eye diseases

Michigan: Faigle 234, Royal 698
Texas: **OneSight 1546**
Wisconsin: Stockton 782

Eye research

Maryland: Jacobson 412
Michigan: Royal 698
Texas: **OneSight 1546**

Family resources and services, disability

Michigan: Easter 1246

Family services

Florida: CSX 962, **Knight 462**
Illinois: **Abbott 933**, Seabury 727
Indiana: Foellinger 258
Kentucky: Humana 1003
Louisiana: Entergy 979
Michigan: Albion-Homer 1183, Angels 1475, Ann Arbor 1083, Bauervic 52, Berrien 1090, Blakely 80, Blodgett 1207, Boysville 1209, Capital 1213, CareLink 1216, Cheboygan 1223, CMS 955, Community 1100, Community 1108, Community 1110, Community 1113, Consumers 961, Crane 153, DeVos 187, DeVos 188, Easter 1246, Eaton 1119, Face 1251, Farmington 1253, Filmer 251, Fremont 1124, Frey 276, George 289, Grand Rapids 1127, Hahn 334, Harvey 354, Hastings 1000, Heart 1277, Hillsdale 1131, Human 1286, **Jewish 1295**, Jewish 1297, Kalamazoo 1138, Kalamazoo 1309, Kerkstra 456, Knight 461, Livingston 1322, Lutheran 1326, Marshall 1330, Mason 1331, Mojo 574, Ottawa 1376, Park 1549, Rotary 1391, Saginaw 1164, Skillman 755, Springview 773, St. Joseph 1411, Tawas 1416, Three 1176, United 1431, United 1437, United 1441, United 1450, Upjohn 832, Vanderweide 844, Village 1455, Vollbrecht 846, Webster 854, Weiner 860, Whaley 1464, Wilson 893, Wolverine 1076, Young 921
Minnesota: Life 1023
Nebraska: Kaufman 439, Pamida 1043
New Jersey: Merillat 554
Texas: Spark 1056

Family services, adolescent parents

Michigan: Lutheran 1326

Family services, counseling

Michigan: Bauervic 51, Lutheran 1326

Family services, domestic violence

Illinois: Allstate 935
Michigan: Barstow 44, Consumers 961, Gerberding 291, **Ms. 1353**

Family services, parent education

Michigan: Capital 1213, Colina 141, Frey 276, **Mott 587**

Family services, single parents

Michigan: Jewish 1298

Financial services

Michigan: Southwest 1406
Minnesota: TCF 1061
New York: **Heron 366**

Food banks

Colorado: Seidman 729
Michigan: Barstow 44, Caesar 114, Consumers 961, Delano 179, DTE 976, Ford 986, Hastings 1000, **Kellogg 1013, Kellogg 1014, Kellogg's 1015,** Kemp 1017, Meijer 1029, Morath 581, Sullivan 792, Valassis 1068
Nebraska: ConAgra 959, Pamida 1043
Ohio: American 937
Texas: **Whole 1073**

Food distribution, groceries on wheels

Michigan: DeRoy 180

Food distribution, meals on wheels

Michigan: DTE 976, DTE 977, Valassis 1068

Food services

Illinois: Meeks 553
Massachusetts: Hanover 999
Michigan: Andersen 19, Briggs-Fisher 99, Butzel 946, Clannad 136, Community 1109, Consumers 961, Detroit 970, Federal 981, Foodbank 1256, Ford 986, Grand 1269, Hillsdale 1131, Kalamazoo 1305, **Kellogg's 1015**, Meritor 1030, Northwest 1365, Orchards 1374, Robison 690, Rochester 1388, Skillman 755, Southwest 1406, Tummala 827, Veteran's 1454, Workers 910, **Yankama 916**
Nebraska: ConAgra 959
New Jersey: Campbell 949, Hamstra 339
Ohio: American 937, Kroger 1020, Kroger 1021
Texas: **Whole 1073**
Wisconsin: Stockton 782

Food services, commodity distribution

Michigan: Kalamazoo 1305

Food services, congregate meals

Nebraska: ConAgra 959

Foundations (community)

Florida: DeLange 178
Michigan: Anderson 20, Barton 940, Birkhill 76, Birtwistle 77, Canaan 117, Cipa 133, Citizens 134, Community 1230, Consumers 961, Crane 153, Ford 264, Frey 276, Harvest 353, Haveman 357, Hollenbeck 382, Isabella 1006, Jeffers 417, Kantzler 434, Kent 453, Lyon 515, Mitchell 572, Monroe 577, Mott 588, Nickless 604, Palmer 625, Peterson 645, Pettibone 646, Ramser 666, Schmuckal 719, St. Clair 774, Stryker 788, Vanderwaals 843, Webster 854, Welter 1571, Whiting 881, Winn 899
Nevada: MGM 1336

Foundations (private grantmaking)

Michigan: Farver 241

Foundations (private independent)

Michigan: Nicolay 606
New Jersey: CKT 135

France

Michigan: **BorgWarner 945, Dow 974**

Genetic diseases and disorders

Indiana: Katz 436
Michigan: Amerisure 938, Foremost 987, Lifestyle 1320

Geriatrics

Massachusetts: **Thome 810**
Michigan: Thompson 811
Ohio: HCR 1002

Geriatrics research

Ohio: HCR 1002

Germany

Michigan: **BorgWarner 945, Dow 974**

Girl scouts

Michigan: Branch 1210, Chelsea 1225, Fabri 980, Generations 991, Idema 402, Perrigo 1045, United 1428, United 1430, United 1447

Girls

Michigan: Fremont 1124, Grand Rapids 1127, Holden 381, Knight 461, Metro 556, Midland 1152, Sanilac 1165, Schuyler 723, Sojourner 1403, Spectrum 1409

Goodwill Industries

Michigan: DiPonio 193, Fabri 980, Kay 442, Leighton 495

Government/public administration

Michigan: Biederman 1483, Camp 115, Charlevoix 1096, Community 1100, Community 1101, Community 1104, Community 1106, Dana 963, Fremont 1124, Gerstacker 292, Greenville 1130, Hunter 397, Jennings 418, La-Z-Boy 1022, Palmer 625, St. Clair 774
New York: **Ford 260**
Ohio: Anderson 21

Graduate/professional education

Michigan: **Earhart 217**, Humane 395

Haiti

Michigan: **Kellogg 450**, May 533

Health care

California: Ayrshire 34
Florida: CSX 962, Stulberg 790
Illinois: **Abbott 933**, Keller 448, Seabury 727
Indiana: Neff 1539
Kentucky: Humana 1003
Massachusetts: **Cabot 947**, Hanover 999

Michigan: Albion-Homer 1183, Alger 1079, Allegan 1080, Allendale 1081, Amerisure 938, **Amway 939**, Anchor 1082, Ann Arbor 1083, Annis 25, Applebaum 26, Baraga 1084, Barry 1085, Barton 940, Battle Creek 1086, Bauervic 52, Bay 1087, Bay Harbor 1088, Bedford 1089, Berrien 1090, Blue 942, Blue 1208, Boll 84, **BorgWarner 945**, Branch 1091, Branch 1210, Bronson 1211, Burnham 110, Cadillac 1092, Canton 1093, Capital 1094, Carls 118, Central 1095, Charlevoix 1096, Chippewa 1097, Clare 1098, Clio 1099, Comerica 956, Community 1100, Community 1101, Community 1104, Community 1106, Community 1107, Community 1108, Community 1109, Community 1111, Community 1112, Community 1113, Con 958, Constantine 1114, Creative 1489, **Cresswell 154**, Crystal 1116, Dana 963, Dauch 1490, Day 173, Delano 179, Detroit 1243, DeVos 186, DeVos 188, DeVos 189, Dickinson 1118, Eaton 1248, Ervin 227, Evergreene 1497, Farley 240, Federal 981, Fibre 982, Fink 252, Firestone 254, Ford 262, Ford 264, Ford 265, **Foundation 1259**, Four 1122, Freeman 274, Fremont 1124, General 990, Gerberding 291, Gerstacker 292, Gilmore 299, Goad 303, Grand Haven 1126, Gratiot 1129, Greenville 1130, Hastings 1000, Heart 1277, Hemophilia 1279, Henry 1280, Hermelin 1281, Herrick 367, Hickman 371, Hillsdale 1131, Hillsdale 1283, Himmel 375, Hirvonen 377, Hollenbeck 382, Honholt 385, Hudson 391, Huron 1133, Ilitch 1288, **International 1291**, Ionia 1134, Jackson 1137, Jewish 1297, Jewish 1298, JSJ 1010, Kalamazoo 1138, Kalamazoo 1304, Kalamazoo 1309, Kay 442, **Kellogg 450**, **Kellogg's 1015**, Kelly 1016, Kemp 1017, Keweenaw 1139, Knabusch 459, **Kresge 471**, La-Z-Boy 1022, Lakeland 1315, Lansing 484, Lapeer 1141, Larson 485, Law 490, Leelanau 1142, Lileikis 501, Livingston 1322, Lowell 1325, Lyons 516, M & M 1145, Mackinac 1146, Marquette 1148, Marshall 1149, Marshall 1330, Marzke 529, Mecosta 1150, Meritor 1030, Metro 556, Metropolitan 1335, Michigan 1033, Michigan 1151, Michigan 1350, Midland 1152, Miller 562, Mills 567, Molinello 575, Moore 579, Morley 584, Mott 588, Mount Pleasant 1154, Nakadar 1538, Northeast 1362, Northwest 1366, Norway 1158, Oakwood 1371, Obloy 614, Olds 616, Oleson 617, Olson 618, Osceola 1159, Paine 624, Parfet 629, Pennock 1378, Perrigo 1045, Petoskey 1162, Physicians' 647, Pietrasiuk 648, Plymouth 1382, Pokagon 1048, Prentis 657, Pulte 1050, **Racing 1386**, Rewold 1053, Russell 704, Saginaw 1164, Saint 1394, Sanilac 1165, Schoolcraft 1166, Schwartz 724, SEMP 1557, Serra 732, Shelden 736, Shiawassee 1168, Siebenthaler 744, Sinai 751, Skillman 755, **Snyder 762**, Social 1400, Southeast 1170, Sparta 1172, St. Joseph 1412, **Steelcase 1058**, Sterken 779, Strobel 786, Sturgis 1175, Sylvia 797, Tassell-Wisner-Bottrall 798, Tawas 1416, Three 1176, Tiscornia 814, Todd 1064, Turner 829, United 1429, United 1430, United 1431, United 1433, United 1440, United 1443, United 1446, United 1450, Valassis 1068, Variety 1453, Washtenaw 1457, Washtenaw 1458, Weisblat 863, Westerman 872, White 1178, Whiting 881, Wickson 883, William 1467, WMY 905, World 911, Wyoming 1179, Zurschmiede 932
Minnesota: Life 1023, **Porter 656**, Weyand 875
Nebraska: Pamida 1043
New Jersey: Campbell 949
New York: Gits 300, Mitsubishi 1035, Nonprofit 1361
Ohio: American 937, Catholic 1219, Cliffs 954, Fifth 984, Gardner 285, Hire 376, KeyBank 1018, Kroger 1020, Kroger 1021, Promedica 1385
Pennsylvania: West 1071
Texas: Fruehauf 277, Quicksilver 1051
Virginia: Falls 236, **Gannett 988**
Washington: Fehsenfeld 247
Wisconsin: Hess 369, Kaufman 441, Wisconsin 1075

Health care, blood supply

Michigan: Idema 402

Health care, clinics/centers

Michigan: Fabri 980, **Foundation 1259**, Jensen 419, Leighton 495, Livingston 1322, Marshall 526, St. Mary's 1413, Trinity 1422, Trumley 822

Health care, cost containment

Michigan: Mills 567

Health care, fund raising/fund distribution

Michigan: Leighton 495

Health care, infants

Illinois: **Abbott 933**
Michigan: **Gerber 290**, Sojourner 1403

Health care, patient services

Indiana: Neff 1539
Michigan: Amerisure 938, **BorgWarner 945**

Health care, public policy

Michigan: **American 1186**

Health care, reform

Michigan: **Kellogg 450**

Health care, single organization support

Michigan: DeRoy 180, Metropolitan 1335

Health organizations

Colorado: Seidman 729
Florida: Detter 183, Van 840
Illinois: Akers 6, McShane 552
Indiana: Ball 40
Maryland: Higgins-Hussman 372
Michigan: Annis 25, Baiardi 35, Batts 941, Community 1100, Delano 179, Farver 241, Farwell 242, **Gerber 290**, Helppie 361, Howard 389, MAC 1024, Pardee 1548, Schmier 718, Spicer 772, Thomas 808, Three 1176, Tiscornia 814, Weidemann 857, Wolters 908, Wong 909
Wisconsin: Hess 369, McIntyre 543

Health organizations, association

Michigan: Ann Arbor 1083, Ash 31, Battle Creek 1086, Betmar 70, Bronner 102, Cadillac 1092, Canaan 117, Community 1103, Community 1104, Community 1106, Community 1109, Dart 168, DeVos 186, DSLT 209, Fibre 982, Four 1122, Fremont 1124, Gerstacker 292, Gornick 310, Grand Rapids 1127, Hampson 338, Hillsdale 1131, Himmel 375, Keeler 446, **Kellogg 450**, LaMothe 480, Lansing 484, Lenawee 1143, Mardigian 525, Marquette 1148, Marshall 1149, McGregor 542, McKibben 547, Metro 556, Morley 584, Nickless 603, Otsego 1160, Ratner 668, Rock 691, Sage 708, Schwartz 724, Westerman 872, Whiting 881, Wickson 883, Wolff 907, World 911

Health organizations, public education

Michigan: Susan 1414
Nebraska: ConAgra 959

Health organizations, research

Nebraska: ConAgra 959

Health sciences school/education

Michigan: Gratiot 1507, Kent 454, Laidlaw 478
Ohio: Heyl 1282
Wisconsin: Handleman 341

Heart & circulatory diseases

Illinois: **Abbott 933**
Michigan: Amerisure 938, GM 994, Kelly 1016, Michigan 1033, Royal 698
Wisconsin: Heart 358

Heart & circulatory research

Michigan: General 990, Michigan 1033, Ratner 668

Hemophilia

Michigan: Hemophilia 1279

Hemophilia research

Michigan: Hemophilia 1279

Higher education

California: **Parsons 1044**, Pati 634, Wilcox 886
Colorado: **American 1188**, Seidman 729
Connecticut: Pryor 661
Florida: Dexter 190, Grosberg 320, Nowak 610, Robey 1552, Stulberg 790
Georgia: **Georgia 992**
Illinois: **Abbott 933**, Akers 6, Gust 323, Guzikowski 326, Kalt 433, Loutit 507, Nuveen 612, Peters 644, Seabury 727, Taylor 799
Maryland: Alpern 14, Jacobson 412, Van Lunen 841
Massachusetts: **Cabot 947**, Hanover 999
Michigan: Abbott 2, **ACI 1181**, Alexandrowski 8, **Allen 9**, Allen 10, Andersen 19, Anderson 20, Anderson 23, Ann Arbor 1083, Annis 25, Applebaum 26, Applebaum 1191, Ash 31, Avondale 1198, Baker 37, Baldwin 38, Balk 39, Bardsley 41, Barth 45, Barton 940, Batts 941, Bauervic 51, Bauervic 53, Beal 55, Bees 58, Bemis 62, Bentley 63, Berkery 64, Berry 66, Biederman 1483, Binda 73, Birkenstock 75, Blaske 81, Blodgett 82, Boll 84, Bonisteel 85, Bonner 86, Bouma 91, Brauer 93, Briggs-Fisher 99, Brintnall 101, Bronner 102, Browne 107, Bucknell 108, Burch 109, Busch 112, Byrne 113, Cadillac 948, Caesar 114, Camp 115, **Chang 125**, Charlevoix 1096, Chase 128, Clinton 139, CMS 955, Coller 142, Community 1109, Community 1113, Consumers 961, Cook 147, **Cresswell 154**, Cunningham 158, Czado 160, Dana 963, Dart 964, Dart 168, Dauch 1490, Davenport 169, Davenport 170, Davis 171, Davisson 172, DeBower 175, DENSO 967, Detroit 1244, DeVlieg 185, DeVos 186, Dickinson 191, Doan 195, Doran 200, Dow 975, Dow 202, DTE 977, Duchene 210, Edmund 219, Everge 231, Ewald 232, Fabri 980, Farber 239, Farver 241, Farwell 242, Federal 981, Fedewa 245, Fetzer 249, First 1499, Fitzgibbon 256, Flemington 257, Ford 1257, Ford 262, Ford 264, Ford 265, Ford 986, **Ford 266**, Foren 267, Foster 268, Fredericksen 273, Fruman 278, Galesburg 1502, Gary 287, General 990, George 289, Gerstacker 292, Gertz 293, Gilles 298, Glassen 301, Gleaner 1506, Goodrich 306, Gordon 308, Gornick 310, Goss 311, Grand Rapids 1127, Great 996, Gumaer 322, Haas 330, Hamar 336, Hamlin 1509, Hammond 998, Hampson 338, Harbor 345, Harlan 349, Henry 363, Herrick 367, Hess 370, Hillier 1513, Hillsdale 1131, Hirvonen 377, Holden 381, Hovarter 388, Howe 390, Huffines 393, Humbert 396, Hurst 398, Huss 399, Idema 402, **Isabel 409**, Isabella 1006, Jackson 411, Jackson 1007, Jeffers 416, Jones 424, JSJ

1010, Juhl 428, Kahan 429, Katzman 437, Katzman 438, Keeler 446, **Kellogg's 1015**, Kelly 451, Kelly 1016, Kemler 452, Kemp 1017, Key 457, Koch 463, Kohn 465, Krause 469, **Kresge 471**, L & L 1522, Laflin 475, Langbo 481, Langley 483, LaVictoire 489, Law 490, Leighton 495, Leven 498, Linden 503, Little 505, Lyons 516, M & M 1145, MAC 1024, MacCrone 517, MacDonald 518, Mackinac 1146, Mall 521, Malovey 523, Mardigian 525, Matson 530, Mauser 532, McCurdy 541, McGregor 542, McKeen 546, McLeod 548, McNally 549, Meritor 1030, Michigan 558, Michigan 559, Michigan 1345, Michner 560, Mick 561, Miller 563, Miller 564, Mills 567, Mims 568, Minton 570, Monroe 1036, Monroe 577, Morath 581, Morenci 1352, Morey 582, Morley 584, Morrill 585, Mossner 586, Mott 588, Muntwyler 592, Nelson 600, Newaygo 601, Nicolay 605, Nieman 1541, Nordman 608, Obloy 614, Oleson 617, Paine 624, Paulsen 636, Penner 640, Pentecost 641, Perrigo 1045, Petoskey 1162, Pietrasiuk 648, Plym 649, Polan 651, Ponting 653, Porter 655, Prentis 657, Price 660, Rainbow 664, Ramser 666, Ratner 668, Raval 669, Rawson 670, Recreational 671, Redies 1052, Reid 672, Rewold 1053, Riley 685, **Rodney 692**, Roethke 693, Rolka 694, Rudy 700, Ruf 701, Rusch 703, Sage 708, Saini 709, Salisbury 711, Schaap 715, Schemm 717, Schwartz 724, Scofield 725, Serra 732, Serwinek 733, Shepard 737, Shiawassee 1168, Shiffman 739, Simmons 748, Simonis 750, Skandalaris 753, Slack 756, Sloat 757, Smith 760, Sonneveldt 763, Southeastern 765, Southfield 1171, Speerstra 770, Spicer 772, St. Joseph 775, Stewart 780, Stoker 784, Stokes 785, Strosacker 787, Stryker 789, Stubnitz 789, Sullivan 792, Tassell-Wisner-Bottrall 798, Taylor 800, Tengler 1567, Thoman 807, Thomas 808, Thomas 809, Tiscornia 814, Towsley 816, Tremble 817, Trinklein 818, Trone 820, Trudell 821, Tuktawa 826, Tummala 827, Universal 1067, University 831, Upjohn 832, Van Andel 835, Van Hollenbeck 839, Vomberg 847, Walsh 848, Warchol 849, Watson 851, Wege 856, Welch 1570, Wells 869, Westerman 872, Westfall 874, Whirlpool 1072, Whiteley 878, Whitfield 879, Wickson 883, Wigginton 885, Wiley 1465, Wilson 891, Wilson 892, Wilson 893, Winn 898, Wirick 901, Wirtz 903, WMY 905, Wolfe 906, Wolters 908, Wolverine 1076, World 911, Wright 1573, Wyandotte 1574, Yaffe 915, Young 1470, Zemke 926, Zoller 929
Minnesota: CHS 952
Mississippi: Weitzenhoffer 867
Nebraska: Kawasaki 1012
New Jersey: Campbell 949, Hamstra 339, Lasko 488, Merillat 554
New Mexico: Peninsula 639
New York: Cutler 159, **Ford 260**, Tepper 803
North Carolina: Thiemkey 806
Ohio: American 937, Anderson 21, Carmell 119, Cliffs 954, Gardner 285, Hildreth 373, Jobst 422, Myers 595, O'Brien 613
Pennsylvania: West 1071
Rhode Island: Robbins 688
Texas: Battier 1200, Fruehauf 277
Virginia: Bell 59, Falls 236, Moh 573
Wisconsin: Beauchamp 57, Bishop 78, Brege 95, Carpenter 120, Gillenwater 297, Handleman 341, Lamberson 479, McIntyre 543, Neal 598, Venturedyne 1070, Vogt 845, Wisconsin 1075

Higher education, college

Michigan: 41 1, Ambrosiani 15, Baxter 54, Birmingham 1204, Delta 1237, Eyster 233, Ferries 248, Hansen 344, Miller 562, Porter 655, Scully 726, Smith 758
Wisconsin: McIntyre 544

Higher education, college (community/junior)

Michigan: Besse 68

Higher education, university

Michigan: Ash 31, Baker 36, Barstow 44, Beck 1201, Brown 104, Brown 105, D.U. 161, Fund 279, Gordy 309, Haas 329, Imoberstag 404, Marxer 528, Pentecost 641, Royal 698, SEMP 1557, Trixie 819, Welter 1571
Pennsylvania: Trust 823

Hinduism

Michigan: India 406, **Kakarala 432**, **Mukkamala 591**, **Thawani 805**

Hispanics/Latinos

Michigan: Ford 986, Grand Rapids 1127, **Kellogg 450**, **National 597**, Sphinx 1410
New York: **Ford 260**
Ohio: KeyBank 1018

Historic preservation/historical societies

Georgia: **Georgia 992**
Illinois: Souder 764
Michigan: Americana 16, Andersen 19, Carls 118, Community 1109, Community 1111, Community 1112, Davison 1117, Doan 195, Dunning 213, Feather 244, Flushing 1121, Frey 276, Gertz 293, Grand 1125, Hirvonen 377, Horgan 387, Jackson 1137, Kelly 1016, Leighton 495, Livonia 1144, Lyons 516, Oleson 617, Paine 624, Petoskey 1162, Prentis 657, **Shaevsky 1395**, Shelby 1167, Three 1176, Tuktawa 826, Warchol 849, Whiting 880
Texas: Quicksilver 1051

Historical activities

Michigan: Kantzler 434, Masco 1026, McDonald's 1530, Mecosta 1150, Nicolay 606, Spicer 772

History/archaeology

Michigan: Community 1109, **Earhart 217**, Hermelin 1281, Mackinac 1146
New York: Center 123

Holistic medicine

Michigan: Bauervic 51

Homeless

Michigan: Angels 1475, Ann Arbor 1083, Cadillac 1092, Clannad 136, Ervin 227, Grand Rapids 1127, Home 384, McGregor 542, Metro 556, Midland 1152, O'Neill 1544, Sanilac 1165, Skillman 755, Sturgis 1175, Tuscola 1177, United 1446, Van 836
New York: Corporation 1233
Texas: Spark 1056

Homeless, human services

Massachusetts: Hanover 999
Michigan: Ann Arbor 1083, Cadillac 1092, Community 1109, Consumers 961, DTE 976, Ervin 227, Hammond 998, Metro 556, Peach 637, Perrigo 1045, Rhoades 683, Skillman 755, **Steelcase 1058**, United 1443
Texas: Spark 1056

Hospitals (general)

Colorado: Seidman 729
Illinois: Souder 764
Indiana: Neff 1539
Maryland: Alpern 14
Massachusetts: **Cabot 947**

Michigan: Allen 9, Ambrosiani 15, Anderson 22, Annis 25, Baiardi 35, Baldwin 38, Barth 45, Barton 940, Battle Creek 1086, Bauervic 53, Baughey 1480, Bilkie 72, Carls 118, Catt 122, Charlupski 127, Citizens 134, Cronin 155, Dalton 163, Dart 168, Davis 171, Deffenbaugh 176, Del Signore 1236, Dykstra 216, Ervin 227, First 1499, Ford 263, Ford 264, Ford 265, Gerstacker 292, Gertz 293, Gornick 310, Henry 1280, Herrick 367, Hickman 371, Hillsdale 1131, **Indo-American 1290**, Isabella 1006, Kay 442, Keeler 446, Kosch 467, Leelanau 1142, Lubin 509, Lyons 516, McNally 549, Metropolitan 1335, Miller 564, Morey 582, Morley 584, **Mukkamala 591**, Northern 1363, Oakwood 1371, Pardee 1548, Perrigo 1045, Pistons 1046, Prentis 657, Ramser 666, Ratner 668, Redies 1052, Robison 690, Royal 698, Russell 704, Shelden 736, Shepherd 738, Sinai 751, **Snyder 762**, St. Clair 774, Three 1176, Todd 1064, Tremble 817, Tuktawa 826, Van 836, Wege 856, Westerman 872, Wickes 882, William 1467, Wilson 891
New York: Tepper 803
Ohio: American 937, Cliffs 954, Gardner 285, McCalla 537
Pennsylvania: West 1071
Texas: Fruehauf 277, Quicksilver 1051
Wisconsin: Hess 368, Keeney 447, McIntyre 544, McIntyre 545, Wisconsin 1075

Hospitals (specialty)

Florida: Nowak 610, Van 840
Maryland: Jacobson 412
Michigan: Berkowitz 65, Caring 1217, Courtney 152, Detroit 181, DeVos 186, Helppie 361, Holden 381, Hood 386, Jensen 419, MacCrone 517, O'Hare 1543, O'Neill 1544, World 911, Yeager 918

Housing/shelter

Georgia: **Georgia 992**
Louisiana: Entergy 979
Massachusetts: Hanover 999
Michigan: Bauervic 53, Bay 1087, Berrien 1090, Buist 1484, Canaan 117, Chemical 951, Comerica 956, Community 1111, Delano 179, Dyer 215, Frazier 272, Grand Rapids 1268, Habitat 1275, Heat 1278, Hees 360, Lighthouse 1321, Masco 1025, Masco 1026, Pulte 1050, South 1169, Spectrum 1409, Sunrise 794, Travelers 1421, United 1450
Minnesota: TCF 1061
New York: Corporation 1233, Local 1323, Nonprofit 1361
Ohio: American 937, Charter 950, Fifth 983, **JPMorgan 1008**
Wisconsin: Miner 569

Housing/shelter, development

Georgia: **Georgia 992**
Michigan: Community 1109, Dalton 163, Dart 964, Eddy 218, Grand Rapids 1127, Home 384, Home 1284, JPMorgan 1009, Kalamazoo 1138, Knight 461, Mackinac 1146, Masco 1026, Schalon 716, Schoonbeck 720, Stubnitz 789, Three 1176, United 1440, Whirlpool 1072, Whiting 880, Wolverine 1076
New Jersey: CKT 135
New York: **Ford 260**, Local 1323
Wisconsin: Handleman 341, McIntyre 544

Housing/shelter, expense aid

New York: Corporation 1233

Housing/shelter, home owners

New York: **Heron 366**

Housing/shelter, homeless
Michigan: Branch 1091, Home 384, Kantzler 434

Housing/shelter, rehabilitation
Michigan: Home 384
Minnesota: TCF 1061

Housing/shelter, repairs
Michigan: Home 384

Housing/shelter, search services
Michigan: Rotary 1391

Housing/shelter, services
Michigan: Grand 1269, Human 1286, Rochester 1388, Shepherd 738, Southwest 1406, Veteran's 1454
New York: Nonprofit 1361

Housing/shelter, temporary shelter
Michigan: Home 384, Spectrum 1409, Workers 910

Human services
California: **Parsons 1044**, Pati 634, Wilcox 886
Colorado: Seidman 729
Connecticut: Pryor 661
Delaware: Bartsch 46
Florida: CSX 962, Detter 183, Dexter 190, Hagen 332, Nowak 610, Rudlaff 699, Sonkin 1561, Van 840
Illinois: **Abbott 933**, Akers 6, Clare 137, Gust 323, Keller 448, Loutit 507, McShane 552, Nuveen 612, Seabury 727, Shelby 735, Souder 764
Indiana: Katz 436, Neff 1539
Kentucky: Humana 1003
Louisiana: Entergy 979
Maryland: Alpern 14, Higgins-Hussman 372
Massachusetts: **Cabot 947**, Hanover 999, **Thome 810**
Michigan: **Akbar 1473**, Alger 1079, Allegan 1080, Allendale 1081, Anchor 1082, Andersen 19, Anderson 22, Ann Arbor 1083, Annis 25, Baiardi 35, Baker 36, Baldwin 38, Balk 39, Baraga 1084, Baraga-Houghton 1199, Barry 1085, Barstow 44, Barth 45, Bates 50, Battle Creek 1086, Batts 941, Bauervic 51, Bauervic 53, Bay 1087, Bay Harbor 1088, Bentley 63, Berrien 1090, Besser 69, Betmar 70, Biederman 1483, Bierlein 71, Binda 73, Birtwistle 77, Blodgett 1207, Blodgett 82, Boll 84, Borman's 88, Bouma 91, Boutell 92, Branch 1091, Brauer 93, Brennan 96, Brintnall 101, Bronner 102, Brown 104, Brown 106, Buist 1484, Burroughs 111, Butzel 946, Cadillac 1092, Cadillac 948, Canaan 117, Canton 1093, Capital 1213, Capital 1094, CareLink 1216, Charity 1222, Charlevoix 1096, Charlupski 127, Cheboygan 1223, Chelsea 1225, Chowdhury 1486, Citizens 134, Clannad 136, Clare 1098, Clark 138, CMS 955, Cochrane 140, **Collectors 1228**, Community 143, Community 1100, Community 1101, Community 1103, Community 1104, Community 1106, Community 1107, Community 1108, Community 1109, Community 1110, Community 1111, Community 1112, Community 1113, Constantine 1114, Consumers 960, Consumers 961, Cook 147, Copley 150, Copper 1232, Courtney 152, Crane 153, Crawford 1234, **Cresswell 154**, Cronin 155, Crystal 1116, Dagenais 162, Dalton 163, Dana 963, Dart 964, Dart 168, Dauch 1490, Davis 171, Deffenbaugh 176, Delano 179, DENSO 967, DeShano 1491, Detroit 181, Detroit 1241, Detroit 1243, DeVos 186, DeVos 188, Dickinson 1118, DiPonio 193, Donlin 198, Doran 200, Dow 202, Drew 206, DSLT 209, DTE 976, DTE 977, Duffy 211, Dyer 215, Eaton 1248, Eddy 218, Evergreene 1497, Ewald 232, Fabri 980, Faigle 234, Farago 238, Farber 239, Farver 241, Farwell 242, Feuer 250, Filmer 251, Fink 252, Firestone 254, Fish 255, Ford 262, Ford 264, Ford 265, Frazier 272, Freeman 274, Fremont 1124, Gallant 281, Gary 287, General 990, Gerstacker 292, Gertz 293, Gilmore 299, Gleaner 993, Glick 302, Gornick 310, Grand Rapids 1127, Granger 313, Granger 314, Gratiot 1129, Green 316, Griffith 318, Haas 329, Hahn 334, Halcyon 335, Hammond 998, Hampson 338, Hancock 340, Harding 346, Hartwick 352, Harvey 354, Hastings 1000, HCC 1512, Heat 1278, Hees 360, Helppie 361, Henry 363, Herrick 367, Hickman 371, Hillsdale 1131, Hillsdale 1283, Himmel 375, Hirvonen 377, Hollenbeck 382, Holley 383, Horgan 387, Howard 389, Hudson 391, Hunter 397, Huron 1133, Hurst 398, Idema 402, Ionia 1134, Isabella 1006, Ishpeming 1136, Jackson 1137, Jeffers 417, Jennings 418, **Jewish 1295**, Jewish 1297, Johnson 423, JSJ 1010, Kahan 429, Kalamazoo 1309, Kantzler 434, Kay 442, Kazrus 444, Keeler 446, Kellogg 449, **Kellogg's 1015**, Kemler 452, Kemp 1017, Keweenaw 1139, Knabusch 459, Knight 461, Konstanzer 466, **Kresge 471**, La-Z-Boy 1022, Lahti 476, Lake 1140, LaMothe 480, Langbo 481, Lange 482, Lapeer 1141, Larson 485, Lenawee 1143, Lewis 500, Lighthouse 1321, Lileikis 501, Linden 503, Livonia 1144, Loeb 506, Love, 1324, Lowell 1325, Lubin 509, Ludington 510, Lugers 511, Lukens 512, Lynch 514, Lyon 515, Lyons 516, M & M 1145, Mackinac 1146, Mally 522, Manistee 1147, Marcks 524, Mardigian 525, Marquette 1148, Marshall 1149, Marshall 526, Marshall 1330, Marzke 529, Masco 1025, Masco 1026, Mason 1331, McBain 535, McClendon 539, McDonald's 1530, McGregor 542, McKibben 547, McNally 549, Mecosta 1150, Meritor 1030, Merkley 555, Michigan 1340, Michigan 1151, Midland 1152, Miller 565, Miller 566, Mills 567, Mojo 574, Molinello 575, Molloy 576, Monroe 1036, Monroe 577, Moore 578, Moore 579, Morath 581, Morey 582, Morley 584, Mossner 586, **Mott 587**, Mott 588, Mount Pleasant 1154, Newaygo 1360, Nicolay 605, Northwest 1366, Norway 1158, O'Neill 1544, Oakland 1370, Oleson 617, Olson 618, Osceola 1159, Otsego 1375, Ottawa 1376, Paine 624, Parfet 629, Pellerito 638, Perrigo 1045, Perry 643, Petoskey 1162, Physicians' 647, Pietrasiuk 648, Pistons 1046, Plym 649, Plymouth 1382, Pokagon 1048, Porter 655, Portland 1384, Prentis 657, Prevo 658, Pulte 1050, Ramser 666, Redies 1052, Rewold 1053, Reynolds 681, Riley 685, Robertson 689, Robison 690, Rochester 1388, Rock 691, **Rodney 692**, Sackerson 706, Sacred 707, Sage 708, Saginaw 1164, Sanilac 1165, **Sankrithi 714**, Schalon 716, Schmier 718, Schmuckal 719, Schoolcraft 1166, Schoonbeck 720, Schroeder 721, Schwartz 724, Sebastian 728, **Shaevsky 1395**, **Share 1558**, Sharing 734, Shelden 736, Shepherd 738, Shiawassee 1168, Shubeck 743, Siebenthaler 744, Sigmund 745, Silverwing 747, Simon 749, Skillman 755, Sloat 757, **Snyder 762**, Social 1400, Southeast 1170, Southwest 1406, Southwestern 1407, Sparta 1172, Speckhard 768, Spectrum 1409, Springview 773, St. Clair 774, St. Joseph 1411, St. Joseph 1412, **Steelcase 1058**, Sterken 779, Stoker 784, Strobel 786, Strosacker 787, Stryker 788, Stubnitz 789, Sturgis 1175, Sullivan 792, Sunrise 794, Sylvia 797, Tabbaa 1566, Tawas 1416, Thoman 807, Thomas 808, Three 813, Tiscornia 814, Todd 1064, Towsley 816, Tremble 817, Tuktawa 826, Turner 829, Tuscola 1177, United 1428, United 1429, United 1430, United 1431, United 1432, United 1433, United 1434, United 1437, United 1438, United 1440, United 1442, United 1443, United 1446, United 1447, United 1448, **V Care 834**, Valassis 1068, Van 836, Vanderwaals 843, Vanderweide 844, Varnum 1069, Veteran's 1454, Victor 1569, Village 1455, Vollbrecht 846, Warchol 849, Washtenaw 1458, Watson 850, Wayne-Metropolitan 1461, Weed 855, Wege 856, Weiner 860, Weinlander 861, Welter 1571, Westerman 872, Whirlpool 1072, White 1178, Whiting 881, Wickes 882, Wickson 883, Wilson 891, Wilson 893, Winn 898, WMY 905, Wolff 907, Wolters 908, World 911, Wyoming 1179, Yaffe 915, Yeager 918, Yeo 919, Young 921, Zimmerman 927, Zurschmiede 932
Minnesota: Life 1023, **Porter 656**, TCF 1061, Weyand 875
Nebraska: Kaufman 439
Nevada: MGM 1336
New Jersey: Campbell 949, CKT 135, Hamstra 339, Merillat 554, Randall 667, Tuesdays 824
New York: Doan 196, **Ford 260**, Mitsubishi 1035, Nonprofit 1361
Ohio: American 937, Anderson 21, Charter 950, Cliffs 954, Fifth 984, Gardner 285, Hildreth 373, **JPMorgan 1008**, KeyBank 1018, Kroger 1020
Oregon: Graef 312
Pennsylvania: PNC 1047, West 1071
Texas: Fruehauf 277
Virginia: **Gannett 988**
Washington: Fehsenfeld 247
Wisconsin: Beauchamp 57, Bishop 78, Handleman 341, Hess 368, Kaufman 441, Kronlund 473, McIntyre 544, McIntyre 545, Neal 598, Shopko 1399, Vogt 845, Wisconsin 1074, Wisconsin 1075

Human services, emergency aid
Michigan: Capital 1213, Clannad 136, Gleaner 993, Grand Rapids 1267, Kalamazoo 1305, Livingston 1322, Macomb 1327, United 1446, Veteran's 1454

Human services, financial counseling
Illinois: Allstate 935
Michigan: Comerica 956
Minnesota: TCF 1061
Ohio: Charter 950, Fifth 983, KeyBank 1018

Human services, gift distribution
Michigan: Grand Rapids 1267

Human services, mind/body enrichment
Michigan: Cochrane 140, Fetzer 249, **Thawani 805**

Human services, single organization support
Michigan: **Center 1220**

Human services, travelers' aid
Minnesota: Northwest 1042

Humanities
Michigan: Branch 1091, Capital 1094, Clannad 136, **Collectors 1228**, Community 1104, Community 1107, Davison 1117, Dyer 215, Ervin 227, Grand Rapids 1127, Jackson 1137, JSJ 1010, **Kresge 471**, Mackinac 1146, Michigan 1344, Midland 1152, Norway 1158, Young 921
New York: Nonprofit 1361

Hungary
Michigan: **BorgWarner 945**

Immigrants/refugees
Michigan: Arab 1192, Bardha 1478, Grand Rapids 1127, **Jewish 1295**, Jewish 1298, **Kellogg 450**, Metro 556
New York: **Ford 260**

Independent living, disability
Michigan: Eaton 1248, Puschelberg 662, Rewold 1053

Virginia: Falls 236

India
Illinois: Hoving 1515
Michigan: **BorgWarner 945, Kakarala 432, Mukkamala 591, Sankrithi 714**

Indigenous peoples
Michigan: **Kellogg 450,** Sanilac 1165
New York: **Ford 260**
Ohio: KeyBank 1018

Infants/toddlers
Michigan: Community 1103, **Gerber 290,** Grand Rapids 1127, **Kellogg 450,** Metro 556, Midland 1152, Sanilac 1165

Infants/toddlers, female
Michigan: Midland 1152, Sanilac 1165

Infants/toddlers, male
Michigan: Midland 1152, Sanilac 1165

Insurance, providers
Michigan: Washtenaw 1457

International affairs
New York: **Ford 260,** Mitsubishi 1035

International development
Illinois: Hoving 1515
Michigan: His 378

International economic development
Minnesota: **Porter 656**
New York: **Ford 260**

International exchange, students
Michigan: Temple 802

International human rights
Michigan: Shiffman 739
New York: **Ford 260**

International migration/refugee issues
Michigan: Travelers 1421

International relief
Michigan: May 533, **Wellspring 870**
Texas: Spark 1056

International studies
Michigan: **Earhart 217**

Ireland
Michigan: **BorgWarner 945**

Islam
Michigan: **Akbar 1473,** Almansour 12, Fayz 243, Hannan 343, Jafari 413, Nakadar 1538, Northwind 609, Stockbridge 781, Tabbaa 1566

Israel
Michigan: Borman's 88, **Jewish 1296**
Wisconsin: Handleman 341

Italy
Michigan: **BorgWarner 945,** Italian 1294

Japan
Michigan: **BorgWarner 945, Dow 974**

Jewish agencies & synagogues
Florida: Grosberg 320, Sonkin 1561, Stulberg 790
Illinois: Akers 6, Kalt 433
Indiana: Katz 436
Maryland: Alpern 14
Michigan: Applebaum 26, Applebaum 1191, Betmar 70, Borovoy 89, Brown 106, Charlupski 127, Detroit 1494, Dorfman 201, Dresner 205, Erlich 225, Farber 239, Feuer 250, Ford 263, Fruman 278, Garber 283, Glick 302, Gordy 309, **Green 1274,** Hermelin 1281, Himmel 375, Imerman 403, Javitch 415, **Jewish 1295, Jewish 1296,** Jewish 1297, Kahn 430, Katzman 437, Katzman 438, Kaufman 440, Kemler 452, Linden 503, Lubin 509, McCabe 536, Nusbaum 611, Okun 615, Pappas 626, Prentis 657, Ring 686, Schmier 718, Schwartz 724, **Shaevsky 1395,** Southeastern 766, Sylvia 797, Torgow 815, Tummala 827, United 1425, Victor 1569, Weisberg 862, Wolff 907, Yaffe 915, Zionist 928
New Hampshire: Shoer 742
New York: Doan 196, Tepper 803
Wisconsin: Handleman 341

Jewish federated giving programs
Florida: Grosberg 320, Sonkin 1561, Stulberg 790
Illinois: Akers 6
Indiana: Katz 436
Maryland: Alpern 14, Jacobson 412
Michigan: Applebaum 26, Applebaum 1191, Betmar 70, Borman's 88, Brown 106, Charlupski 127, Farber 239, Finkelstein 253, Frankel 1260, Fruman 278, Glick 302, **Green 1274,** Hermelin 1281, **Jewish 1296,** Jospey 425, Kahn 430, Katzman 438, Kaufman 440, Leven 498, Lubin 509, Nusbaum 611, Prentis 657, Ring 686, **Shaevsky 1395,** Shapiro 1396, Torgow 815, United 1425, Weisberg 862
Wisconsin: Kaufman 441

Journalism school/education
Michigan: Arden 28, Winkler 897
Virginia: **Gannett 988**

Kenya
Michigan: **Global 1264**

Kidney diseases
Michigan: National 1356, Russell 704

Kidney research
Michigan: National 1356

Labor studies
Michigan: Reuther 1387

Latin America
Michigan: **Amway 939, Kellogg 450, Mott 587**
New York: **Ford 260**

Latvia
Michigan: **Latvian 1317**

Law school/education
Michigan: Kemp 1017, Leighton 495, Ponting 653

Law/international law
Michigan: Dana 963
New York: **Ford 260**

Leadership development
Michigan: Community 1106, Community 1107, Consumers 961, DTE 977, Grand Rapids 1127, Hillsdale 1131, **Kellogg 450,** Michigan 1350, **Mott 587**
Minnesota: CHS 952
New York: **Ford 260**

Legal services
Michigan: Bodman 943, Butzel 946, Kemp 1017, Marshall 1330, Michigan 1348
New York: **Ford 260**
Wisconsin: Handleman 341

LGBTQ
Indiana: Katz 436
Michigan: **Arcus 27,** Gay, 1262, Grand Rapids 1127, Metro 556
New York: **Ford 260**
Ohio: KeyBank 1018

Libraries (academic/research)
Michigan: Ford 1257

Libraries (public)
Illinois: Loutit 507
Michigan: Barstow 44, Caesar 114, Community 1113, Consumers 961, Engle 978, Frey 276, Gary 287, Hartwick 352, JSJ 1010, Kantzler 434, Keeler 446, MacCrone 517, Marshall 526, McCabe 536, Mott 588, Pokagon 1048, Reid 673, Shelby 1167, Skiles 754, St. Clair 774

Libraries/library science
Michigan: Camp 115, Community 1104, Dow 202, Fremont 1124, Hillsdale 1131, Masonic 1332, Three 1176, Wickes 882, Wickson 883
Ohio: Lahti 477
Wisconsin: Neal 598

Literature
Michigan: Borders 944, Jackson 1519, Monroe 1036, Plymouth 1383, Wilson 890

Lung diseases
Michigan: Detroit 1239

Marine science
Michigan: Feather 244

Mathematics
Massachusetts: **Cabot 947**
Michigan: Consumers 961, **Dow 974,** Dow 975, DTE 977, Grand Haven 1126
Minnesota: Xcel 1077
Ohio: Heyl 1282

Media, film/video
Michigan: Ann Arbor 1190, Mahogany 520
New York: Center 123, **Ford 260**
Ohio: **JPMorgan 1008**

Media, print publishing
Florida: **Knight 462**
Michigan: Arden 28
New York: Newsweek/Daily 1039
Virginia: **Gannett 988**

Media, radio
Michigan: Kebok 445, Schaap 715

Media, television
Michigan: Daoud 166, Deffenbaugh 176, Harding 346, Kantzler 434, Riley 685

Media/communications
Michigan: Caesar 114, Dearborn 965, Ford 1257, Lyon 515
New York: Center 123, **Ford 260**
Virginia: **Gannett 988**

Medical care, community health systems
Michigan: DeRoy 180, George 289, Livingston 1322, Nickless 603, Schmuckal 719
Ohio: Promedica 1385

Medical care, in-patient care
Michigan: McGregor 542

Medical care, rehabilitation
Michigan: Cronin 155, Fremont 1124
Ohio: Hildreth 373

Medical research
Florida: Hasey 356
Massachusetts: Hanover 999
Michigan: **American 1186**, Applebaum 1191, Bashur 48, Berkowitz 65, Brown 106, Coleman 1487, Cutaneous 1235, Dauch 1490, Del Signore 1236, Detroit 1494, General 990, George 289, Hermelin 1281, Law 490, Nakadar 1538, Pardee 1548, Pietrasiuk 648, Rhoades 683, Shin 740, Yeager 918
Wisconsin: McIntyre 543

Medical research, alliance/advocacy
Pennsylvania: National 1355

Medical research, institute
Michigan: Blue 1208, Davis 171, **Gerber 290**, Holden 381, Katzman 437, Molinello 575, **Pardee 628**, Ratner 668, Sinai 751, Thomas 808, Towsley 816, Whiting 880, World 911
Ohio: Jobst 422

Medical school/education
Michigan: Briggs-Fisher 99, Camp 115, Gratiot 1507, Hammel 337, Irwin 408, Jaffe 414, Kadant 1011, Kent 454, Laidlaw 478, Meyers 557, Michigan 1341, **Mukkamala 591**, Nakadar 1538, **National 597**, Nill 607, Puschelberg 662, Royal 698, **Snyder 762**, Stoddard 783, Thomas 808, Towsley 816, Weed 855, Wolverine 1076
Texas: **OneSight 1546**
Wisconsin: Heart 358

Medical specialties
Michigan: Vanderweide 844

Medical specialties research
Michigan: Stoddard 783

Medicine/medical care, public education
Michigan: **American 1186**

Men
Michigan: Grand Rapids 1127, Metro 556, Midland 1152, Sanilac 1165

Mental health, clinics
Michigan: Community 1231

Mental health, counseling/support groups
Michigan: Alliance 11, Community 1231, DeRoy 180, Lutheran 1326

Mental health, disorders
Michigan: Swiat 796

Mental health, grief/bereavement counseling
New York: **New York 1038**

Mental health, residential care
Michigan: MacCrone 517

Mental health, smoking
Michigan: Cadillac 1092, Community 1230, Community 1113

Mental health, treatment
Michigan: Bertsch 67, Fink 252, Miller 566

Mental health/crisis services
Illinois: **Abbott 933**
Michigan: Dalton 163, Face 1251, Gerstacker 292
Wisconsin: Wisconsin 1075

Mentally disabled
California: Ayrshire 34
Maryland: Higgins-Hussman 372
Michigan: Community 1231, Fremont 1124, Grand Rapids 1127, Livonia 1144, Metro 556, Midland 1152, Sanilac 1165, Sturgis 1175, Swiat 796, Thresholds 1418, Training 1420
New York: Corporation 1233
Texas: Spark 1056

Mexico
Michigan: **BorgWarner 945, DENSO 968, H.I.S. 327, Kellogg 1013, Kellogg 450**, Morath 581, **Rotary 1393**
New York: **New York 1038**

Middle East
New York: **Ford 260**

Military/veterans
Michigan: Detroit 970, Dickinson 191, Drew 206, **Ford 985**, Midland 1152, Strobel 786, Valassis 1068, Veteran's 1454
New York: Corporation 1233
Texas: Spark 1056

Military/veterans' organizations
Michigan: Engle 978, Fallen 1252

Minorities
Georgia: **Georgia 992**
Illinois: **Abbott 933**
Michigan: American 1187, Arab 1192, Battle Creek 1086, **Center 1220**, Comerica 957, Community 1109, DTE 977, Ford 986, Grand Rapids 1127, I Have 400, **Kellogg 450**, Metro 556, Michigan 1346, Midland 1152, **Mott 587, National 597**, Sanilac 1165, Shiffman 739, Southwestern 1407, **Steelcase 1059**, Wickson 883
New York: **Ford 260**
Ohio: **JPMorgan 1008**, KeyBank 1018, Kroger 1020, Kroger 1021
Virginia: **Gannett 988**
Wisconsin: Wisconsin 1075

Minorities/immigrants, centers/services
Michigan: Battle Creek 1086, **Center 1220**, Community 1109, Grand Rapids 1127, **Kellogg 450**, Leven 498
New York: **Ford 260**

Monaco
Michigan: **BorgWarner 945**

Multiple sclerosis
Michigan: Borovoy 89, Branch 1210, National 1357

Multiple sclerosis research
Michigan: National 1357

Muscular dystrophy
Michigan: Little 504, Sinai 751, Wolverine 1076

Museums
Florida: Sonkin 1561
Indiana: Katz 436
Michigan: Besser 69, Blakely 80, Brennan 96, Community 1108, Community 1113, DeRoy 180, Engle 978, Evenson 229, First 1499, Ford 262, Ford 264, Ford 986, Frey 276, Grand Rapids 1127, Hancock 340, Hansen 344, Hirvonen 377, Kaufman 440, Kosch 467, Lyons 516, Masonic 1332, Morley 584, Russell 704, Sisson 752, United 1430, Van Andel 835, Vanderwaals 843, Wege 856, Williams 888, Wolverine 1076
New York: **Ford 260**, Newsweek/Daily 1039
Ohio: Cliffs 954
Wisconsin: Kaufman 441, Lamberson 479, Wisconsin 1075

Museums (art)
Illinois: Keller 448
Michigan: Crane 153, DeVos 186, Frey 276, Horgan 387, Keeler 446, MacCrone 517, McNally 549, Porter 655, Wolff 907, Wolters 908
Minnesota: **Porter 656**
Nebraska: Kawasaki 1012
Texas: Bray 94

Museums (children's)
Illinois: Souder 764
Michigan: Boutell 92, Foremost 987, Frazier 272, Frey 276

Museums (ethnic/folk arts)
Michigan: **Center 1220**, Frey 276

Museums (history)
Michigan: Americana 16, Ford 1257, Frey 276, Parish 630

Museums (marine/maritime)
Michigan: Frey 276

Museums (natural history)
Michigan: Frey 276

Museums (science/technology)
Michigan: Frey 276, Kalamazoo 1302

Museums (specialized)
Michigan: Frey 276, Gilmore 1505, Gordy 309, Michigan 1033, Van Andel 837
Nebraska: Kawasaki 1012

Museums (sports/hobby)
Michigan: **Collectors 1228**

Native Americans/American Indians
Colorado: **American 1188**, First 1254
Michigan: Grand Rapids 1127, **Kellogg 450, National 597**, Pokagon 1048
New York: Corporation 1233
Ohio: KeyBank 1018

Neighborhood centers
Michigan: Barstow 44, Shop 1398, United 1441, Vollbrecht 846

Neuroscience
Michigan: Amerisure 938, Campbell 116

Neuroscience research
Michigan: Campbell 116

Nicaragua
Michigan: **Rotary 1393**

Nigeria
Michigan: **Global 1264**

Nonprofit management
Michigan: Knight 461
Ohio: **JPMorgan 1008**

Nursing care
Massachusetts: **Thome 810**

Nursing home/convalescent facility
Michigan: **Isabel 409**, Thompson 811

Nursing school/education
Michigan: Bellinger 61, Gratiot 1507, Jaffe 414, Kadant 1011, Kelly 1016, Kent 454, Laidlaw 478, Lee 492, MacRae 519, Metro 556, **National 597**
Ohio: Heyl 1282
Wisconsin: Heart 358

Nutrition
Illinois: **Abbott 933**
Michigan: **Allen 9, Amway 939**, Blue 942, DTE 976, **Gerber 290**, Grand Rapids 1127, Kalamazoo 1305, **Kellogg 1014, Kellogg's 1015**, Michigan 1033
Nebraska: ConAgra 959
New Jersey: Campbell 949

Offenders/ex-offenders
New York: Corporation 1233

Optometry/vision screening
Michigan: **Kakarala 432**
Wisconsin: ShopKo 1055

Orthodox agencies & churches
Ohio: Zampetis 924

Pakistan
Michigan: **Akbar 1473, Fahd 1498**

Palliative care
Michigan: Jewish 1297
Ohio: HCR 1002

Parkinson's disease
Michigan: Michigan 1347

Parkinson's disease research
Michigan: Michigan 1347

Pediatrics
Michigan: Caring 1217, Eschbach 228, **Gerber 290**

Pediatrics research
Michigan: **Gerber 290**, Yeager 918

Performing arts
Florida: Dexter 190, Sonkin 1561
Illinois: Keller 448
Louisiana: Entergy 979
Massachusetts: Hanover 999
Michigan: Andersen 19, Ann Arbor 1083, Bauervic 51, Bay 1087, Blakely 80, Borders 944, Byron 1212, Canton 1093, Community 1100, Community 1108, Community 1109, Community 1113, Consumers 961, Cummings 157, Dalton 163, Davison 1117, Deffenbaugh 176, DeRoy 180, DTE 977, Evenson 229, Ford 261, Ford 986, Fremont 1124, Frey 276, Gilmore 299, Grand Rapids 1127, Hancock 340, Hartwick 352, Henry 363, Hillsdale 1131, Idema 402, Jospey 425, JPMorgan 1009, Katzman 437, Keeler 446, Leighton 495, Leven 498, Loeb 506, Masco 1026, Morley 584, Pokagon 1048, Prentis 657, **Shaevsky 1395**, Skillman 755, South 1169, Van Andel 835, Weatherwax 852, Wege 856, Williams 888, Wilson 893, Zynda 1575
Minnesota: Arts 1195
New Jersey: Campbell 949
New York: **Ford 260**
Ohio: **JPMorgan 1008**, Lahti 477

Performing arts centers
Michigan: Besse 68, Frey 276

Performing arts, ballet
Michigan: DeVos 186, Frey 276
Ohio: Hire 376

Performing arts, dance
Michigan: Dorfman 201, Frey 276, Schuyler 723, Weissman 866
New York: **Ford 260**
Ohio: **JPMorgan 1008**

Performing arts, education
Illinois: Kalt 433, McShane 552
Michigan: Armstrong 29, Frey 276, Rislov 687, Thoman 807

Performing arts, music
California: Coltrane 1229, SANYO 1054
Michigan: Community 1108, Community 1109, Dalton 163, Ford 261, Ford 986, Frey 276, **Glen Arbor 1263**, Gordy 309, Grand Rapids 1267, Green 316, Harding 346, Livonia 1144, Northville 1157, Palmer 625, Pollack 652, Reuter 679, Schuyler 723, Three 1176, Welch 868, Westerman 872, Wilson 890
Nebraska: Kawasaki 1012
New Jersey: Wilson 889
New York: **Ford 260**
Ohio: Gilbert 296, **JPMorgan 1008**, Lahti 477
Texas: Guy 325

Performing arts, music (choral)
Michigan: Frey 276

Performing arts, music composition
Michigan: Rislov 687

Performing arts, music ensembles/groups
Michigan: Frey 276

Performing arts, opera
Michigan: Federal 981, Frey 276, Meritor 1030, Schalon 716, Williams 888

Performing arts, orchestras
Michigan: Birmingham 1205, DeVos 186, Ford 261, Ford 986, Frey 276, Harding 346, Hartwick 352, Horgan 387, JSJ 1010, Kalamazoo 1308, MacCrone 517, Meritor 1030, Porter 655, Price 660, Schalon 716, Schwartz 724, **Sphinx 1410**, Stubnitz 789, Williams 888, Wolters 908, Wolverine 1076
Ohio: Cliffs 954, Jobst 422
Wisconsin: Vogt 845

Performing arts, theater
Illinois: Seabury 727
Michigan: Ann Arbor 1083, Community 1103, Community 1109, Dalton 163, Fabri 980, Frey 276, Grand Rapids 1127, Hillsdale 1131, Kantzler 434, Livonia 1144, Meritor 1030, Porter 655, Three 1176, Welch 868, Wilson 893
New York: **Ford 260**
Ohio: Cliffs 954, **JPMorgan 1008**, Lahti 477

Wisconsin: Beauchamp 57, Kaufman 441, Wisconsin 1075

Performing arts, theater (musical)
Michigan: Frey 276

Pharmacy/prescriptions
Michigan: **National 597**

Philanthropy/voluntarism
Michigan: Bodman 943, **Center 1220**, Community 1102, Frey 276, **Global 1264**, Granger 314, **Jewish 1296**, Junior 1300, Norway 1158, United 1431, United 1436
New York: **Ford 260**

Philanthropy/voluntarism, fund raising/fund distribution
Michigan: Lenawee 1318

Philosophy/ethics
Michigan: **Earhart 217**, **Glen Arbor 1263**

Physical therapy
Michigan: Southwest 767
Pennsylvania: McCardell 538

Physical/earth sciences
Michigan: Meyers 557

Physically disabled
Michigan: Bertsch 67, **Ford 985**, Fremont 1124, Livonia 1144, Midland 1152, Sanilac 1165, Tiscornia 814
Ohio: KeyBank 1018

Poland
Michigan: **BorgWarner 945**

Political science
Michigan: Consumers 961, **Earhart 217**

Population studies
New York: Nonprofit 1361

Portugal
Michigan: **BorgWarner 945**

Pregnancy centers
Michigan: Riley 685

Protestant agencies & churches
Illinois: Souder 764
Michigan: Berry 66, Bertsch 67, Bonner 86, Brauer 93, Brinkerhoff-Sample 100, Brown 105, Chamberlain 124, Christopher 132, Dauch 1490, Evergreene 1497, Ferries 248, Ford 265, Gerberding 291, Gibbs 294, Goad 303, **Gordon 307**, Gordon 308, Haggard 333, Hansen 344, Harding 347, Helppie 361, Hirvonen 377, Hollenbeck 382, Howard 389, Hurst 398, Jennings 418, Kay 442, Kelly 451, Koester 464, Krause 470, Lyons 516, Macomb 1327, McCabe 536, McKeen 546, McLeod 548, McNally 549, Mills 567, Moore 578, Mossner 586, Mott 588, Mount Zion 589, Pentecost 641, Peterson 645, Rawson 670, Rose 697, Ryals 705, Smith 758, Spicer 772, Springview 773, Sterban 778, Sterken 779, Turner 829, Vanderweide 844,

Whiteley 878, Whitfield 879, Winkle 1572, Wolfe 906, York 920, Zelt 925
New Jersey: Hamstra 339
Ohio: Jobst 422
Wisconsin: Beauchamp 57, Kronlund 473, Miner 569

Psychology/behavioral science
Michigan: Fetzer 249

Public affairs
California: Pati 634, Toyota 1066
Illinois: **Abbott 933**
Michigan: Battle Creek 1086, Capital 1094, Community 1106, Community 1109, Dart 168, JSJ 1010, **Kresge 471**, Masco 1026, Mauser 532, Meritor 1030, Plym 649, Riley 685, **Rodney 692**
New York: Mitsubishi 1035
Ohio: Cliffs 954, **JPMorgan 1008**

Public affairs, alliance/advocacy
New York: Mitsubishi 1035

Public affairs, citizen participation
Florida: **Knight 462**
New York: **Ford 260**

Public affairs, finance
Illinois: **Joyce 427**
Michigan: Comerica 957

Public affairs, political organizations
Illinois: **Joyce 427**

Public health
Michigan: Asthma 1197, Blue 942, Bronson 1211, Community 1113, DeRoy 180, DTE 976, General 990, **Kellogg 1014**, Livingston 1322, Michigan 1349, Ottawa 1376, United 1439, United 1440, United 1443, United 1450
Minnesota: Northwest 1042

Public health school/education
Michigan: Gratiot 1507, Laidlaw 478

Public health, obesity
Michigan: **Kellogg's 1015**

Public health, physical fitness
Michigan: Blue 942, **Kellogg 1014**, **Kellogg's 1015**, Michigan 1033
Nebraska: ConAgra 959

Public policy, research
Michigan: DeVos 186, DeVos 187, DeVos 189, Morey 582, Van 836
Ohio: **JPMorgan 1008**

Recreation
California: Rose 1390
Michigan: Alger 1079, Allegan 1080, Allendale 1081, Anchor 1082, Bay 1087, Biederman 1483, Cadillac 1092, Camp 115, Carls 118, Charlevoix 1096, Chippewa 1097, Clare 1098, Clio 1099, Community 1230, Community 1100, Community 1108, Community 1110, Community 1111, Community 1113, Constantine 1114, Dickinson 1118, Four 1122, Fremont 1124, Grand Rapids 1127,

Greenville 1130, Hillsdale 1131, Huron 1133, Ilitch 1288, Jackson 1137, Lapeer 1141, Leelanau 1142, Lowell 1325, M & M 1145, Mackinac 1146, Manistee 1147, Marquette 1148, Mason 1331, Midland 1152, Otsego 1160, Petoskey 1162, Pistons 1046, Pokagon 1048, **Racing 1386**, Reynolds 681, Rotary 1391, Saginaw 1164, Sanilac 1165, Shelby 1167, Skillman 755, Sterling 1173, Sturgis 1175, Three 1176, Tigers 1062, Tuscola 1177, United 1432, Variety 1453, White 1178, Wickes 882
Nebraska: Kaufman 439
New Jersey: Campbell 949
New York: Nonprofit 1361
Wisconsin: Hess 368

Recreation, camps
Indiana: Neff 1539
Michigan: Bertsch 67, En 222, Hammond 998, **Herdegen 364**, Hudson 391, **Isabel 409**, Thoman 807, Welch 868, Youth 923
New Jersey: Campbell 949

Recreation, centers
Michigan: Bettis 1203, Park 631

Recreation, community
Michigan: Schalon 716

Recreation, fairs/festivals
Michigan: Generations 991, Pokagon 1048

Recreation, parks/playgrounds
Michigan: Consumers 961, Cronin 155, Dalton 163, Eastpointe 1247, Grand 1125, Kosch 467, Lilja 502, Merkley 555, Novi 1368, Pokagon 1048, Redies 1052, White 877, Whiting 881

Religion
Florida: Hagen 332
Michigan: DeVos 189, Hancock 340, Life 1319, Pietrasiuk 648, Plymouth 1383, Simon 749, **Snyder 762**, **V Care 834**, Westerman 872, Wirtz 902, Wynalda 914
New York: Nonprofit 1361
Ohio: Anderson 21
Wisconsin: Hess 368

Religion, interfaith issues
Michigan: India 406
New York: **Ford 260**

Religious federated giving programs
Michigan: Bronner 102, Morath 581, **Snyder 762**, Wolters 908

Reproductive health
Michigan: Sojourner 1403
New York: **Ford 260**

Reproductive health, family planning
Michigan: Delano 179, Fabri 980, Hill 374, Wilson 893, Wolff 907
Texas: Bray 94
Wisconsin: Kaufman 441

Reproductive health, OBGYN/Birthing centers
Illinois: **Abbott 933**

Michigan: Cadillac 1092

Reproductive health, sexuality education
New York: **Ford 260**

Residential/custodial care
Michigan: Boysville 1209, Cadillac 948, Delano 179, JSJ 1010, **Ms. 1353**, Nicolay 606, Redies 1052
Wisconsin: Kowalski 1019

Residential/custodial care, hospices
Maryland: Higgins-Hussman 372
Massachusetts: **Cabot 947**
Michigan: Bauervic 53, Cadillac 1092, Caesar 114, Camp 115, Canaan 117, Community 1100, Dauch 1490, DeRoy 180, DiPonio 193, Dooge 199, George 289, **H.I.S. 327**, Hillsdale 1131, Isabella 1006, Kalamazoo 1304, Kemp 1017, Little 504, Lugers 511, Nusbaum 611, Pokagon 1048, Schmuckal 719, Three 1176, United 1432, Wilson 893
Ohio: HCR 1002, Hire 376
Wisconsin: Handleman 341, Venturedyne 1070

Residential/custodial care, senior continuing care
Michigan: Lay 491, Prentis 657
Ohio: HCR 1002

Residential/custodial care, special day care
Wisconsin: Neal 598

Rural development
Colorado: First 1254
Michigan: **Kellogg 450**, **Mott 587**, **Mukkamala 591**
Minnesota: CHS 952, Musser 594
New York: **Ford 260**, Local 1323

Russia
Michigan: **Mott 587**

Safety, automotive safety
Illinois: Allstate 935
Michigan: Con 958, **Ford 985**, Ford 986, General 990, GM 994

Safety/disasters
Georgia: **Georgia 992**
Illinois: Allstate 935
Massachusetts: **Cabot 947**
Michigan: Ann Arbor 1083, Kelly 1310, Weisblat 863
Nevada: MGM 1336
Ohio: American 937

Safety/disasters, association
Michigan: Detroit 1242

Safety/disasters, public education
Michigan: DTE 976

Salvation Army
Michigan: Ambrosiani 15, Amerisure 938, Chelsea 1225, Consumers 960, Consumers 961, Crane 153, Kay 442, Nicolay 605, Ramser 666, Sigmund 746, Smith 758, United 1430, Vanderwaals 843, Welter 1571, Whiteley 878

Ohio: Hire 376, Kroger 1020
Wisconsin: ShopKo 1055

Scholarships/financial aid
California: Coltrane 1229
Michigan: Avondale 1198, Boll 84, Borovoy 89, Community 1103, Delta 1237, Detroit 1244, Doran 200, Fedorov 246, Ford 986, Gibbs 294, Ontonagon 1372, Parks 1377, Plumbers 1380, Polakovic 650, Ratner 668, Redies 1052, Rennie 677, **Society 1402**, Southfield 1405, Sullivan 793, Thornapple 1417, Three 1176, UAW-GM 1423, Wiley 1465
Minnesota: Xcel 1077
Texas: Battier 1200
Virginia: Moh 573

Science
Illinois: **Abbott 933**, Shelby 735
Massachusetts: **Cabot 947**
Michigan: Bay 1087, **BorgWarner 945**, Consumers 961, **Delphi 966**, DENSO 967, **Dow 974**, Dow 202, DTE 977, **Haworth 1001**, **Kresge 471**, MEEMIC 1028, Plymouth 1383, Rhee 682, Warchol 849, Welch 868
Ohio: Heyl 1282
Pennsylvania: West 1071

Science, formal/general education
Illinois: **Abbott 933**
Michigan: Dow 975, General 990, Meritor 1030
Minnesota: Xcel 1077

Secondary school/education
Illinois: Seabury 727
Indiana: Neff 1539
Michigan: Binda 73, Cipa 133, Dagenais 162, First 1499, Grimaldi 319, Herrick 367, Hurst 398, Idema 402, Keeler 446, **Kellogg 450**, Meritor 1030, Morley 584, Palmer 625, Pietrasiuk 648, Ponting 653, Robertson 689, St. Clair 774, Tremble 817, Van Andel 835, Welch 868, Westfall 874, Wilson 893
Minnesota: Life 1023
Nebraska: Kaufman 439
New York: **Ford 260**
Ohio: Anderson 21

Single parents
Michigan: Grand Rapids 1127, **Kellogg 450**, Midland 1152, Sanilac 1165

Social entrepreneurship
Georgia: **Georgia 992**

Social sciences
Michigan: Cochrane 140, DeVos 189, Dickinson 1118, Reuther 1387, **Rodney 692**
New York: **Ford 260**

Social sciences, public policy
Michigan: **H.I.S. 327**

South Africa
Michigan: **Global 1264**, **Kellogg 1013**, **Mott 587**

South Korea
Michigan: **BorgWarner 945**, **Dow 974**

Space/aviation
Michigan: Meyers 557, Parish 630

Spain
Michigan: **BorgWarner 945**

Speech/hearing centers
Michigan: Carls 118

Spine disorders research
Ohio: Smith 759

Spirituality
Michigan: **Mukkamala 591**

Student services/organizations
Michigan: Canton 1093

Substance abuse, prevention
Michigan: Berrien 1090, Perrigo 1045

Substance abuse, services
Maryland: Higgins-Hussman 372
Michigan: Cadillac 1092, Community 1109, Community 1113, DeRoy 180, Ervin 227, Ford 264, Fremont 1124, Jackson 1137, Lutheran 1326, Skillman 755, Southeast 1404, Sullivan 792, United 1439, Wilson 893
Texas: Erskine 226

Substance abusers
Michigan: Midland 1152, Pentecost 641, Sanilac 1165, Sturgis 1175, Tuscola 1177

Supported living
Michigan: Thresholds 1418

Teacher school/education
Michigan: Kadant 1011, **Worldwide 1469**
Pennsylvania: PNC 1047

Terminal illness, people with
Michigan: Midland 1152, Tony 1419

Theological school/education
Michigan: Christian 131, Czado 160, Dancey 165, Fish 255, Granger 314, Grimaldi 319, Honholt 385, Kerkstra 456, Koester 464, Lee 492, McNally 549, O'Neill 1544, Schaap 715, Schmuckal 719, Scully 726, Shepherd 738, Sonneveldt 763, Springview 773, Zondervan 930
New Jersey: Hamstra 339
Texas: Fruehauf 277

Theology
Michigan: Borovoy 89

Transportation
Michigan: Human 1286, Kalamazoo 1302, Rochester 1388
Minnesota: Weyerhaeuser 876

Tropical diseases
Michigan: Detroit 970

Ukraine
Michigan: **Mott 587**

United Kingdom
Michigan: **BorgWarner 945**, Kellogg 1013
Virginia: **Gannett 988**

United Ways and Federated Giving Programs
Connecticut: Pryor 661
Georgia: **Georgia 992**
Illinois: **Abbott 933**, Loutit 507
Louisiana: Entergy 979
Massachusetts: **Cabot 947**
Michigan: Baiardi 35, Balk 39, Barstow 44, Barth 45, Barton 940, Biederman 1483, Boutell 92, Brintnall 101, Burroughs 111, Cadillac 1092, Chemical 951, Citizens 134, CMS 955, Consumers 960, Consumers 961, Cook 147, Cummings 157, Dana 963, **Delphi 966**, Doan 195, **Dow 973**, DSLT 209, Eddy 218, Engle 978, Fabri 980, Fedorov 246, First 1499, Fish 255, Ford 262, Ford 263, Ford 264, Ford 265, **Ford 985**, Ford 986, Foremost 987, Frankenmuth 1123, Frazier 272, General 990, Glick 302, Griffith 318, Hahn 334, Hammond 998, Hansen 344, Hartwick 352, Hill 374, Horgan 387, Howard 389, Isabella 1006, Jospey 425, JSJ 1010, Katzman 437, Keeler 446, **Kellogg 1013**, **Kellogg 1014**, **Kellogg's 1015**, Kelly 1016, Kent 453, Klobucar 458, La-Z-Boy 1022, Langbo 481, Loeb 506, Lukens 512, Meritor 1030, Michigan 1032, Monroe 1036, Moore 578, Moore 579, Mott 588, Oleson 617, Paine 624, Perrigo 1045, Plym 649, Ramser 666, Reid 673, **Rodney 692**, Sanilac 1165, Schwartz 724, Shelden 736, Sigmund 746, Strosacker 787, Todd 1064, Vanderweide 844, Welter 1571, Whirlpool 1072, Whiting 880, Whiting 881, Wilson 894, Wolters 908, Wolverine 1076
Minnesota: Xcel 1077
Mississippi: Weitzenhoffer 867
Nebraska: Kawasaki 1012
New Jersey: Campbell 949, CKT 135
Ohio: Anderson 21, Cliffs 954, Kroger 1021
Pennsylvania: West 1071
Wisconsin: Bishop 78, Miner 569, ShopKo 1055, Vogt 845, Wisconsin 1074

Urban League
Michigan: Southwestern 1407, United 1447

Urban/community development
Michigan: Community 1103, DTE 977, Frey 276, Hudson 392, Matthaei 531, Monroe 577, **Mott 587**, Shiffman 739, Wolverine 1076
New York: **Ford 260**, Local 1323

Utilities
Michigan: Consumers 960

Veterinary medicine
Michigan: Eyster 233, Glassen 301, Humane 395, Irwin 408, Muntwyler 592, Weiss 865

Veterinary medicine, hospital
Michigan: Kasiewicz 435

Visual arts
Massachusetts: Hanover 999

Michigan: Ann Arbor 1083, Bay 1087, Borders 944, Byron 1212, Fremont 1124, Frey 276, Hancock 340, Hillsdale 1131, JPMorgan 1009, Lansing 1316, Livonia 1144, Skillman 755
Ohio: **JPMorgan 1008**

Visual arts, architecture
Michigan: Binda 73, Clannad 136

Visual arts, art conservation
Michigan: Community 1111

Visual arts, ceramic arts
Michigan: **Glen Arbor 1263**, Hartwick 352, **Pewabic 1379**

Visual arts, painting
Michigan: **Glen Arbor 1263**

Visual arts, photography
Michigan: **Glen Arbor 1263**

Visual arts, sculpture
Michigan: Canton 1093, **Glen Arbor 1263**, **Pewabic 1379**

Vocational education
Michigan: **Collectors 1228**, Fredericksen 273, GM 994, Muer 590, Shop 1398

Vocational education, post-secondary
Michigan: Grand Haven 1126

Voluntarism promotion
Michigan: **Center 1220**, Community 1100, Community 1109, Fetzer 249, Grand Rapids 1127, Hillsdale 1131, Homer 1132, **Kellogg 450**, Kemp 1017, Michigan 1349, **Mott 587**, United 1441

Wales
Michigan: **Dow 974**

Women
California: Ayrshire 34
Florida: Stulberg 790
Georgia: **Georgia 992**
Maryland: Alpern 14, Higgins-Hussman 372
Michigan: Bemis 62, Berkery 64, DTE 977, Flemington 257, Fremont 1124, Grand Rapids 1127, Jewish 1298, Junior 1300, Knight 461, Metro 556, Midland 1152, Prevo 658, Sanilac 1165, Sojourner 1403, Sturgis 1175, United 1428, Village 1455, Wilson 890, Wilson 893, Young 922
New York: **Ford 260**
Ohio: Kroger 1020, Kroger 1021
Virginia: **Gannett 988**
Wisconsin: Handleman 341, Wisconsin 1075

Women, centers/services
Michigan: Canaan 117, Grand Rapids 1127, Hahn 334, Junior 1300, Knight 461, Lovelight 508, Michigan 1350, Park 1549, Wilson 893
New York: **Ford 260**
Texas: Bray 94

YM/YWCAs & YM/YWHAs
Michigan: Annis 25, Barstow 44, Barton 940, Butzel 946, Fabri 980, Frazier 272, Granger 313, Granger 314, Hickman 371, Hunter 397, Idema 402, **Kellogg's 1015**, Lahti 476, Mills 567, Mims 568, Moore 579, Plym 649, Schmuckal 719, Stryker 788, United 1428, United 1447, Welch 868, Whirlpool 1072, Whiting 881, Wirtz 902, Wolverine 1076, Youth 923
Minnesota: **Porter 656**
Texas: Bray 94

Young adults
California: Ayrshire 34
Michigan: **Collectors 1228**, Grand Rapids 1127, Metro 556, Midland 1152, **Mott 587**, Sanilac 1165
Minnesota: CHS 952
New York: Corporation 1233

Young adults, female
Michigan: **Collectors 1228**, Knight 461, Metro 556, Midland 1152, Sanilac 1165

Young adults, male
Michigan: **Collectors 1228**, Metro 556, Midland 1152, Sanilac 1165

Youth
Arizona: Circle 953
California: Ayrshire 34
Georgia: **Georgia 992**
Indiana: Foellinger 258, Neff 1539
Massachusetts: Hanover 999
Michigan: Battle Creek 1086, Bay 1087, Berrien 1090, Blue 942, Boysville 1209, **Collectors 1228**, Community 1230, Community 1108, Community 1110, Community 1112, Community 1113, DeVos 188, Fremont 1124, Grand Rapids 1127, Grand 1128, Granger 313, Hastings 1000, Homer 1132, **Kellogg 450**, Lenawee 1143, M & M 1145, Mackinac 1146, Manistee 1147, Marshall 1149, Masco 1026, Metro 556, Midland 1152, Saginaw 1164, Sanilac 1165, Skillman 755, **Society 1402**, **Steelcase 1058**, Sturgis 1175, Tuscola 1177, Village 1455, Wickson 883
Minnesota: CHS 952
Nebraska: Pamida 1043
New York: **Ford 260**

Youth development
California: SANYO 1054
Colorado: First 1254
Georgia: **Georgia 992**
Massachusetts: Hanover 999
Michigan: Alger 1079, Allendale 1081, American 936, Bauervic 53, Bedford 1089, Berkowitz 65, Berrien 1090, Boysville 1209, Bronner 102, Cadillac 1092, Capital 1213, **Center 1220**, Chamberlain 124, Cheboygan 1223, Chelsea 129, Chemical 951, Chippewa 1097, Clare 1098, Clark 138, **Collectors 1228**, Community 1230, Community 1103, Constantine 1114, Dagenais 162, Delano 179, DeRoy 180, Detroit 1241, Detroit 970, DTE 977, Eaton 1119, Farmington 1253, **Ford 985**, Frazier 272, Gilmore 299, Gleaner 993, Grand Rapids 1268, Granger 313, Gratiot 1129, Great 1270, Heart 1277, Ionia 1134, Ishpeming 1136, **Jewish 1295**, Kalamazoo 1138, Kalamazoo 1309, Lahti 476, Law 490, Lay 491, Loeb 506, M & M 1145, Mackinac 1146, Marshall 526, Marshall 1330, Mason 1331, Matthaei 531, McNish 551, Mills 567, Missaukee 1153, Mott 588, Mount Pleasant 1154, Olds 616, Optimist 1373, Ottawa 1376, Palmer 625, Petoskey 1162, Pistons 1046, Price 660, Sackerson 706, Sanilac 1165, Shepherd 738, Sigmund 745, Sloat 757, South 1169, Southfield

1171, St. Clair 774, Tawas 1416, Tigers 1062, Tuktawa 826, Turner 829, Tuscola 1177, United 1430, United 1431, United 1438, United 1439, United 1440, United 1441, United 1443, United 1446, United 1448, United 1450, Van 836, Vanderwaals 843, Vollbrecht 846, Wayne 1460, White 1178, Whiting 881, Wong 909
Minnesota: CHS 952, TCF 1061, Weyand 875
Nebraska: Kaufman 439
Nevada: MGM 1031
New York: Doan 196, **New York 1038**, Nonprofit 1361
Pennsylvania: Cash 1218
Tennessee: Nissan 1041
Virginia: **Gannett 988**
Wisconsin: Hess 369, Shopko 1399

Youth development, adult & child programs
Michigan: Boysville 1209
New York: **New York 1038**
Wisconsin: Wisconsin 1075

Youth development, agriculture
Minnesota: CHS 952
Nebraska: ConAgra 959

Youth development, business
Georgia: **Georgia 992**

Michigan: Amerisure 938, Chemical 951, Davenport 170, Foremost 987, Harlan 349, Meritor 1030, Whirlpool 1072, Wolverine 1076

Youth development, centers/clubs
Michigan: Cronin 155, Huron 1133, Oleson 617, Reynolds 681

Youth development, citizenship
New York: **New York 1038**

Youth development, religion
Michigan: En 222, **H.I.S. 327**

Youth development, research
New York: **Ford 260**

Youth development, scouting agencies (general)
Delaware: Bartsch 46
Michigan: Youth 923

Youth development, services
Michigan: Colina 141, Community 1106, Community 1107, Dyer 215, Ford 263, Grand Rapids 1127, Hillsdale 1131, **Kellogg 1014**, **Kellogg 450**, Michigan 1338

Youth, pregnancy prevention
Michigan: Berrien 1090, Sojourner 1403

Youth, services
Michigan: Anchor 1082, AtWater 33, Biederman 1483, Bouma 91, Cadillac 1092, Caravan 1214, Central 1485, Community 1106, Community 1108, Dalton 163, DeVlieg 185, Hurst 398, Kellogg 449, **Kellogg 450**, Marshall 1149, McGregor 542, Merkley 555, Midland 1152, Pettibone 646, Redies 1052, Tiscornia 814, Vanderweide 844, Wilson 891
Ohio: Gardner 285
Wisconsin: Hess 369

Zoos/zoological societies
Illinois: Keller 448, Souder 764
Indiana: Neff 1539
Michigan: Consumers 961, DeRoy 180, Detroit 1245, Eddy 218, Ford 264, Ford 265, Frey 276, Harlan 349, Hartwick 352, Horgan 387, **Kellogg 1013**, Mardigian 525, Warchol 849
Wisconsin: Lamberson 479

GEOGRAPHIC INDEX

Grantmakers in boldface type make grants on a national, regional, or international basis; the others generally limit giving to the city or state in which they are located.

ARIZONA

Phoenix: Circle 953

CALIFORNIA

La Jolla: Wilcox 886
Los Angeles: Rose 1390
Pasadena: Ayrshire 34, **Parsons 1044**
Rancho Santa Fe: Wierenga 884
Rolling Hills: Pati 634
San Diego: SANYO 1054
Torrance: Toyota 1066
Woodland Hills: Coltrane 1229
Woodside: Parks 632

COLORADO

Denver: **American 1188**
Kiowa: Seidman 729
Longmont: First 1254

CONNECTICUT

West Hartford: Pryor 661

DELAWARE

Newark: Bartsch 46

FLORIDA

Boca Raton: Grosberg 320
Clearwater: Robey 1552
Fort Lauderdale: Hagen 332
Ft. Myers: Rudlaff 699
Jacksonville: CSX 962
Lauderdale By The Sea: Hasey 356
Longboat Key: Stulberg 790
Miami: DeLange 178, **Knight 462**
Naples: Dexter 190, Nowak 610
Palm Beach Gardens: Sonkin 1561
Sarasota: DJD 194
Tampa: Detter 183
Venice: Weigel 858
Wellington: Van 840

GEORGIA

Atlanta: **Georgia 992**

ILLINOIS

Abbott Park: **Abbott 933**
Chicago: Akers 6, Clare 137, Gust 323, Guzikowski 326, **Joyce 427**, Keller 448, Loutit 507, Nuveen 612, Seabury 727, Souder 764
Glencoe: Kalt 433
Lisle: Meeks 553

Northbrook: Allstate 935
Oak Brook: Hoving 1515, McShane 552
Palatine: Peters 644
Quincy: Taylor 799
Winnetka: Shelby 735

INDIANA

Fort Wayne: Foellinger 258, Parrish 633
Indianapolis: Katz 436, Neff 1539
Muncie: Ball 40

KENTUCKY

Louisville: Humana 1003
Waddy: Guilliom 321

LOUISIANA

New Orleans: Entergy 979

MARYLAND

Bethesda: Jacobson 412
Columbia: Van Lunen 841
Ellicott City: Higgins-Hussman 372
Potomac: Alpern 14

MASSACHUSETTS

Boston: **Cabot 947**, **Thome 810**
Worcester: Hanover 999

MICHIGAN

Ada: **Amway 939**, Honholt 385, Van 836
Adrian: Baughey 1480, Gleaner 993, Gleaner 1506, Hickman 371, Lenawee 1318, Price 660, Stubberfield 1565, Stubnitz 789, Westfall 874
Albion: Albion 1078, Albion-Homer 1183
Allegan: Allegan 1080, Allegan 1184, Perrigo 1045
Allen Park: Detroit 1243, Detroit 969
Allendale: Allendale 1081, Roon 695
Allenton: Jenuwine 420
Alma: Luneack 513, Masonic 1332, Michigan 1345, Pardee 1548, Smith 758, United 1433
Almont: Four 1122
Alpena: Besser 69, Besser 1482, Community 1104, First 1499, Iosco 1135, Marks 1529, North 1156, Northeast 1362, Park 631, Straits 1174
Ann Arbor: A.I.R. 1472, African 1182, Alliance 11, Ann Arbor 1083, Ann Arbor 1190, Annis 25, Arbor 1476, Arjuna 1477, Berry 66, Blaske 81, Bonisteel 85, Borders 944, Brinkerhoff-Sample 100, **Chang 125**, Con 958, **Cresswell 154**, D.U. 161, Domino's 972, **Earhart 217**, Ervin 227, Greater 315, Halcyon 335, **IMRA 1005**, Inbounds 405, Jensen 419, Knight 461, Lovelight 508, Moholy-Nagy 1536, Molloy 576, **Ms. 1353**, National 1356, Pietrasiuk 648, Pollack 652, Rislov 687, Scott 1554, **Seed 1555**, Simmons 748, **Society 1401**, Speckhard 768, Temple 802, Washtenaw 1458, Winkler 897, Wise 904, Wolfe 906, Ypsilanti 1180
Arcadia: Gerberding 291
Au Gres: Gutierrez 324
Auburn Hills: Avondale 1198, **BorgWarner 945**, Detroit 970, Easter 1246, Elliott 220, MEEMIC 1028, Pettibone 646, Pistons 1046, Skandalaris 753
Bad Axe: Huron 1133, Smith 760
Baldwin: Lake 1140
Battle Creek: Battle Creek 1086, Binda 73, Burnham 110, Farley 240, Foodbank 1256, Historic 1514, Howard 389, **Kellogg 1013**, **Kellogg 1014**, **Kellogg 450**, **Kellogg's 1015**, Lafler 474, LaMothe 480, McCurdy 541, Michigan 559, Miller 565, Scofield 725, Southwest 767, Southwestern 1407, Trone 820, United 1424, United 1434, Willard 1466, Winship 900, **Yankama 916**
Bay City: Bay 1087, Blue 83, Kantzler 434, Law 490, Lutheran 1326, Pardee 1547, Sequin 731, United 1428, University 831, Van Wormer 842, Weidner 1462, Weinlander 861
Bay Harbor: Bay Harbor 1088
Belleville: Hees 360
Belmont: Aletheia 7, Brown 105
Benton Harbor: Southwest 1406, United 1445, Whirlpool 1072
Benzonia: Johnson 423
Berkley: Bettis 1203, Molinello 575
Berrien Springs: Benson 1481
Beverly Hills: Langbo 481, Pellerito 638
Big Rapids: Mecosta 1150, Mecosta-Osceola 1334
Bingham Farms: Birkenstock 75, Cook 148, Grimaldi 319, Katzman 438, Michigan 1347, Polakovic 650, Schmier 718, Vollbrecht 846
Birmingham: Amber 1474, Andrews 24, Armstrong 29, AtWater 33, Birmingham 1204, Birmingham 1205, Cutaneous 1235, **Erb 224**, Fedorov 246, Ferries 248, Fitzgibbon 256, Foundation 270, Goad 303, Harmon 350, Lyon 515, Matthaei 531, May 533, Popeye 654, Team 801, Weisberg 862, Williams 888, Workers 910
Blissfield: Farver 241
Bloomfield: Lahser 1524, Peterson 645
Bloomfield Hills: Adray 5, Applebaum 26, Applebaum 1191, Bates 50, Brown 106, Chowdhury 1486, Clannad 136, Davis 171, Day 173, Deffenbaugh 176, Don't 197, Dorfman 201, Drazick 204, Duffy 211, Dykstra 216, Fallen 1252, Foren 267, Frankel 1260, Garber 283, Gornick 310, **Green 1274**, Hampson 338, Helppie 361, Hermelin 1281, Holley 383, **International 1292**, **Jewish 1296**, Jewish 1297, Jewish 1298, Kasiewicz 435, Katzman 437, Larson 485, Legion 494, Lubin 509, Nakadar 1538, Oakland 1369, Pulte 1050, Rose 697, **Sankrithi 714**, **Shaevsky 1395**, Shapiro 1396, **Snyder 762**, Spector 769, Taubman 1060, Thomas 809, United 1425, Victor 1569, Village 1455, Walsh 848, Westerman 872, Wilson 893, Yaffe 915, Young 921, Zionist 928
Boyne City: Great 1272
Bridgeport: Andersen 19, McNally 549

Brighton: Community 1101, Home 1284, Livingston 1322, Make-A-Wish 1328, Sage 708, Starfish 777
Buchanan: Community 144, Michigan 1151
Burtchville: Gardner 284
Burton: Alternatives 1185
Byron Center: Bouma 91, Buist 1484, Byron 1212, Koster 468
Cadillac: Cadillac 1092, United 1450
Caledonia: Daystar 174, Fish 255, Foremost 987, Resnal 678
Canton: Basch 47, Canton 1093, Richter 684, Turfe 828
Caro: Human 1286, Rolka 694, Tuscola 1177
Casco: Beck 1201
Cass City: Rawson 670, United 1449
Centreville: St. Joseph 1411
Charlevoix: Dauch 1490, Winn 898, Winn 899
Charlotte: Eaton 1248, **Rotary 1393**, Spartan 1057
Cheboygan: Cheboygan 1223, Harding 348
Chelsea: Chelsea 1224, Chelsea 129, Chelsea 1225
Clare: United 1429
Clarkston: Driggers 208, Optimist 1373
Clinton: Boysville 1209, Clinton 139, Weikart 859
Clinton Township: Daoud 166, Italian 1294, Warchol 849
Clinton Twp: Weidemann 857
Coldwater: Branch 1091, Branch 1210, Fedewa 245, Juhl 428, Malovey 523, Salisbury 711, Taylor 800
Commerce Township: **American 1186**, Shin 740
Concord: Hubbard 1516, Thorrez 812
Constantine: Constantine 1114, Fibre 982
Coopersville: Coopersville 1115, Lemmen 496
Crystal Falls: Crystal 1116
Dearborn: Arab 1192, **Center 1220**, Doran 200, Fayz 243, **Ford 985**, Ford 986, Ibbetson 401, Kosch 467, Oakwood 1371, SEMP 1557, **Society 1402**
Dearborn Heights: Dearborn 965, Imoberstag 404
Detroit: American 936, Arden 28, Attanasio 32, Berkery 64, Birkhill 76, Black 1206, Blue 942, Blue 1208, Bodman 943, Butzel 946, Caesar 114, CareLink 1216, Caring 1217, Carls 118, Charfoos 126, Charity 1222, Chase 128, Comerica 956, Comerica 957, Community 1106, Courtney 152, Davenport 169, Detroit 1240, Detroit 1242, Detroit 1493, Detroit 1494, Detroit 971, DeVlieg 185, Drew 206, DTE 976, DTE 977, Duchene 210, Callant 237, Filmer 251, Firestone 254, Ford 262, Ford 263, Ford 264, Ford 265, **Ford 266**, Frischkorn 1261, General 990, GM 994, Gordy 309, Grand 1266, Hannan 1511, Harlan 349, Hartwick 352, Heat 1278, Hennessey 362, Henry 1280, **Herdegen 364**, Herrick 367, Hudson 392, Huffines 393, Ilitch 1288, Ilitch 1289, Jackson 411, Javitch 415, JPMorgan 1009, Kay 442, Kelly 451, Key 457, Lahti 476, Larson 486, Lay 491, MacCrone 517, Marcks 524, Mardigian 525, Marxer 528, Matson 530, McGregor 542, McKeen 546, McKibben 547, Metro 556, Michigan 1346, Miller 566, Mims 568, Minton 570, Monroe 1036, Moore 580, Murff 1537, **National 597**, New 1359, Nicolay 620, Oshlag 619, Parks 1377, **Pewabic 1379**, Ponting 653, Ramser 666, Reuter 679, Reuther 1387, Riley 685, Robison 690, Royal 698, Russell 704, Schaap 715, Schwartz 724, Scully 726, **Share 1558**, Shiffman 739, Sisson 752, Skiles 754, Skillman 755, Sojourner 1403, **Sphinx 1410**, Stokes 785, Thompson 811, Tigers 1062, Torgow 815, Travelers 1421, Trinity 1422, Trixie 819, UAW-GM 1423, United 1427, VSA 1456, Watson 851, Weiss 864, Wilson 891, Wilson 894, Winer 896, Wolff 907, Young 1470, Zimmerman 927
Dewitt: Ambrosiani 15
Dexter: Lyons 516
Dollar Bay: Hamar 336
Douglas: Lugers 511
Dowagiac: Fitch 1500
East Grand Rapids: Jones 1520
East Jordan: Charlevoix 1096

East Lansing: Beckwith 1202, Capital 1213, India 406, Larzelere 487, Michigan 558, Michigan 1342, Michigan 1349, Olds 616, Pentecost 641, Susan 1414, White 877
East Tawas: Laidlaw 478, Tawas 1416
Eastpointe: Eastpointe 1247
Edwardsburg: Welter 1571
Elk Rapids: Northern 1542
Escanaba: Community 1100, Community 1112, Dagenais 162, Sackerson 706, United 1430
Essexville: Anderson 20
Evart: Hillier 1513
Farmington: American 1187
Farmington Hills: **ACI 1181**, Amerisure 938, Community 1231, Evereg 231, Farmington 1253, **Foundation 1259**, Fund 279, Goldman 305, Kemler 452, Linden 503, McQuiggan 1531, Pappas 626, Sloat 757, **V Care 834**
Flint: Abele 3, Bees 58, Bell 60, Bellinger 61, Boutell 92, Brenske 97, Brenske 98, Brooks 103, Bucknell 108, Burroughs 111, Career 1215, Clio 1099, Community 1107, Conway 146, Davison 1117, Eddy 218, Ennis 1250, Fenton 1120, Flint 1255, Flushing 1121, Gibbs 294, Gilles 298, Grand 1125, Haas 330, Harding 346, Hoover 387, Huss 399, **Indo-American 1290**, **Isabel 409**, Jafari 413, Jaffe 414, Jeffers 416, Jeffers 417, Jennings 418, Lefevre 493, Loeb 506, McNally 550, Merkley 555, Mills 567, Morgan 582, **Mott 587**, Mott 588, Pribil 659, Reid 672, Roethke 693, Ryals 705, Schemm 717, Stoker 784, Sud 791, Trinklein 818, Tummala 827, United 1431, Watson 850, Webster 854, Welch 868, Whaley 1464, Whitfield 879, Whiting 880, Wilson 892, Wright 913
Flushing: Aboudane 4, Almansour 12, Welch 1570
Fort Gratiot: Anderson 22, I Have 400
Fowlerville: Hamlin 1509
Frankenmuth: Baxter 54, Bierlein 71, Bronner 102, Frankenmuth 1123, Klobucar 458, Koester 464, Mossner 586, Palmer 625
Franklin: Borman's 88, Farber 239, Fruman 278, Nusbaum 611, Polan 651, Ratner 668, Ring 686, **Wellspring 870**
Fremont: Freeman 274, Fremont 1124, Genesis 1504, **Gerber 290**, Newaygo 1360
Galesburg: Galesburg 1502
Garden City: Stewart 780
Gaylord: Otsego 1160, Otsego 1375
Gladstone: Besse 68
Gladwin: DeShano 1491, United 1432
Glen Arbor: Ever 230, **Glen Arbor 1263**
Grand Blanc: Hannan 343, **Mukkamala 591**, Nelson 599, Tabbaa 1566, **Thawani 805**
Grand Haven: 41 1, Grand Haven 1126, Haveman 357, JSJ 1010, Love, 1324, Sharing 734, Wigginton 885
Grand Rapids: Abbott 2, Allen 10, Almont-Dickinson 13, Arts 1193, Baldwin 38, Batik 39, Barnes 42, Basilica 49, Batts 941, Bemis 62, Berkowitz 65, BJB 79, Blodgett 1207, Blodgett 82, Browne 107, Campbell 116, Coleman 1487, Cornucopia 1488, Crane 153, Davenport 170, DeVos 186, DeVos 187, DeVos 188, DeVos 189, Diephouse 192, Dooge 199, Doyle 203, Dyer 215, En 222, Evenson 229, Falk 235, Ford 1257, Foster 269, Fredericksen 273, Frey 275, Frey 276, G. 280, God's 304, Goodrich 306, **Gordon 307**, Gordon 995, Gordon 308, Goss 311, Grand Rapids 1127, Grand Rapids 1267, Grand Rapids 1268, Grand 1269, Griffith 318, Gumaer 322, Habitat 1275, Hansen 344, Harvest 353, Heart 1277, Henry 363, Hess 370, Hill 374, Hof 379, Hoffman 380, Home 384, Hope 1285, Howe 390, Humbert 396, Idema 402, Ionia 1134, **Jewish 1295**, JMJ 421, **John 1299**, Justice 1301, Keeler 446, Kent 453, Kent 454, Kent 1311, Kentwood 455, Koch 463, Lewis 499, Lowell 1325, Lukens 512, MacRae 519, McBain 535, McCabe 536, Meijer 1029, Mojo 574, Moore 579, Morrill 585, Muntwyler 592, Nehru 1540, O'Hare 1543, Owen 621, Physicians' 647, Plymouth 1381, Porter 655, Rennie 677, Rudy 700,

Saint 1394, Schoonbeck 720, Sebastian 728, Shepard 737, Silverwing 747, Simonis 750, Sobong 1559, Social 1400, Southeast 1170, Sparta 1172, Speerstra 770, Spencer 771, St. Clair 774, **Steelcase 1058**, **Steelcase 1059**, Tassell-Wisner-Bottrall 798, Thresholds 1418, Todd 1064, Tremble 817, Universal 1067, Van Andel 835, Van Andel 837, Van Den Bosch 838, Vanderwaals 843, Vanderweide 844, Varnum 1069, Wege 856, West 1463, Western 873, Whiting 881, Wolters 908, **Worldwide 1469**, Wyoming 1179
Grandville: Andersen 18, Community 143, Life 1319, Zondervan 930
Grayling: Crawford 1234
Greenville: Ash 31, Greenville 1130, Mall 521
Gregory: Michigan 1343
Grosse Pointe: Beals 56, Bonsall 87, Detroit 1244, Ewald 232, Fink 252, Harwell 355, Jones 424, Lewis 500, McLeod 548, Sacred 707, Spicer 772, Sterban 778, Young 922
Grosse Pointe Farms: Briggs-Fisher 99, Lynch 514, Michigan 1350, Muer 590, **Racing 1386**, Sand 1553, Shelden 736, Tengler 1567
Grosse Pointe Park: Davisson 172, Gibson 295, Nicolay 606, Weed 855, Wolverine 1468
Grosse Pointe Shores: Morath 581, Zurschmiede 932
Hancock: Keweenaw 1139
Harbor Beach: Harbor 345, Krause 469
Harbor Springs: Baiardi 35, Harbor 1276, Kiwanis 1313
Hartland: Hood 386
Hastings: Barry 1085, Hastings 1000, Pennock 1378, Pierce 1550, Zemke 926
Hickory Corners: Gilmore 1505
Hillsdale: Hillsdale 1131, Hillsdale 1283
Holland: Community 1111, **Haworth 1001**, Middle 1351, Ottawa 1376, Rainbow 664, Shepherd 738, Springview 773
Holt: Barros 1479, Mid-Michigan 1535
Homer: Community 1230, Homer 1132
Houghton: Baraga-Houghton 1199, Copper 1232
Howell: Bonner 86, Kellogg 449, Stines 1564
Hudson: Engle 978
Hudsonville: Bossenbroek 90, Joy 426
Huntington Woods: Prentis 657, Zoller 929
Indian River: Bauervic 53, Redman 1551
Interlochen: Penner 640
Iron Mountain: Dickinson 1118, Dickinson 191, Flemington 257, Nelson 600, Norway 1158, Trudell 821
Iron River: Brennan 96
Ironwood: Gogebic 1265, Ironwood 1293
Ishpeming: Ishpeming 1136
Ithaca: Gratiot 1129, Gratiot 1507
Jackson: Blakely 80, Camp 115, CMS 955, Consumers 960, Consumers 961, Copley 150, Gallant 281, Glick 302, Hancock 340, Hurst 398, Jackson 1137, Jackson 1519, Michner 560, Myers 596, Plumbers 1380, Raval 669, Sigmund 745, Sigmund 746, Stanton 776, United 1436, Weatherwax 852
Jenison: Kerkstra 456
Kalamazoo: **Arcus 27**, Arts 1194, Bronson 1211, Connable 145, Dalton 163, Delano 179, Fabri 980, Gary 287, Gay, 1262, Gilmore 299, Hammond 998, International 1517, Kalamazoo 1303, Kalamazoo 1138, Kalamazoo 1304, Kalamazoo 1305, Kalamazoo 1306, Kalamazoo 1307, Kalamazoo 1308, Kalamazoo 1309, **Krishnamurti 472**, **Latvian 1317**, Little 504, Okun 615, Parchment 627, Parfet 629, Parish 630, Shubeck 743, Stryker 788, Upjohn 832, **Upjohn 1451**, Van Haften 1452, Weisblat 863, Wong 909
Kewadin: Siebenthaler 744
L'Anse: Baraga 1084
Lake City: Missaukee 1153, Winkle 1572
Lake Odessa: Mackenzie's 1528
Lake Orion: Kolo 1314
Lambertville: Bedford 1089

Lansing: Amy 17, Capital 1094, Caravan 1214, Coon 149, Czado 160, Delta 1238, Dunnings 214, Eaton 1119, Granger 313, Granger 314, Great 1273, Jackson 1007, Lansing 1316, Lansing 484, Lesher 497, Memorial 1532, Michigan 1338, Michigan 1340, Michigan 1344, Michigan 1348, Reid 673, Stepping 1563, Thoman 807, Tony 1419, Waverly 1459, Whiteley 878, Young 1471

Lapeer: Lapeer 1141, United 1437, Webster 853

Leland: Feather 244

Leslie: Society 1560

Levering: Zelt 925

Livonia: Del Signore 1236, Detroit 1492, DiPonio 193, Face 1251, H.O.N.O.R. 328, Livonia 1144, Mauser 532, Recreational 671, Valassis 1068

Lowell: Lowell 1527, Rotary 1392

Ludington: Birtwistle 77, Community 1102, Great 996, United 1440

Mackinac Island: Mackinac 1146

Macomb: Konstanzer 466, Macomb 1327

Madison Heights: Investment 1518, O'Neill 1544

Mancelona: Snyder 761

Manistee: Manistee 1147, United 1438

Manistique: Schoolcraft 1166

Marcellus: Hovarter 388, Lee 492

Marine City: Lester 1525

Marlette: Miller 564

Marquette: Frazier 272, Great 1270, Hammel 337, Hirvonen 377, Lilja 502, MacDonald 518, Marquette 1329, Marquette 1148, Reynolds 681, Rupp 702, United 1439

Marshall: Cronin 155, Franke 271, Marshall 1149, Marshall 526, Marshall 1330

Mason: Dart 964, Dart 168, Mason 1331, Mason 1027

Mears: HCC 1512

Mendon: Haas 329

Menominee: M & M 1145, Peshtigo 1161

Middleville: Thornapple 1417

Midland: **Allen 9**, Baker 37, Barstow 44, Chemical 951, Clare 1098, Doan 195, **Dow 973**, **Dow 974**, Dow 975, Dow 1496, Dow 202, Gerstacker 292, Hollenbeck 382, Ludington 510, Midland 1152, Miller 563, **Pardee 628**, Reinhardt 676, Strosacker 787, Sullivan 792, Towsley 816, United 1441

Milford: Iverson 410, Serwinek 733

Millington: Kaiser 431

Monroe: Community 1109, Deinzer 177, **Fahd 1498**, Gertz 293, Knabusch 459, Knabusch 460, La-Z-Boy 1022, Little 505, Rhee 682, Stoddard 783, United 1442, Wells 869

Morenci: Morenci 1352, Wirick 901

Mount Clemens: Irwin 408

Mount Pleasant: Isabella 1006, Martin 527, Mount Pleasant 1154

Munising: Alger 1079

Muskegon: Community 1103, DeBower 175, Kaufman 440, Muskegon 1354, Nordman 608, United 1447, Zonta 931

Negaunee: Negaunee 1155

New Baltimore: Anchor 1082

New Buffalo: Pokagon 1048

Newaygo: Deur 184, Newaygo 601

Newberry: Tahquamenon 1415

Niles: Huizenga 394, Hunter 397, Leighton 495, Peach 637, Plym 649, United 1435

Northport: Leelanau 1142

Northville: Bilkie 72, Harris 351, Kebok 445, Northville 1157, Northville 1364, Perrone 642, Raiola 665

Novi: Americana 16, Michigan 1339, Novi 1368

Oak Park: Winans 895

Oakland: York 920

Oakland Township: Salpietra 713

Okemos: Glassen 301, Michigan 1341, Nickless 603, Schultheiss 722, Trumley 822

Olivet: Vomberg 847

Ontonagon: Ontonagon 1372

Orchard Lake: Farago 238, Kahn 430, Stockbridge 781, Tuktawa 826

Owosso: Bentley 63, Cook 147, Devries 1495, Michigan 1534, Mitchell 572, Shiawassee 1168, Shiawassee 1397

Oxford: Clark 138, Training 1420

Parma: Michigan 1032

Perry: Perry 643

Petoskey: Catt 122, Char-Em 1221, Northern 1363, Petoskey 1162, Reimer 674, Reimer 675, Youth 923

Pickford: Munuscong 593

Pigeon: LaVictoire 489

Pleasant Lake: Shop 1398

Pleasant Ridge: Hand 1510

Plymouth: Dunning 213, Plymouth 1382, Plymouth 1383

Pontiac: Hahn 334, Lighthouse 1321, Mally 522, Oakland 1370

Port Huron: Citizens 134, Community 1110, Knowlton 1521, Michigan 1533, United 1446, Wirtz 902, Wirtz 903

Portage: Greene 317, Kalamazoo 1302, Monroe 577, Swiat 796, United 1426

Portland: Portland 1384

Rapid City: Let 1526

Ray Township: Page 623

Reading: Alexandrowski 8

Redford: Binion 74, Nieman 1541

Reed City: Osceola 1159

Remus: Laflin 475

Riverside: Southwest 1562

Riverview: Ott 620

Rochester: Community 1108, Duncan 212, New 1358, Rewold 1053, Rewold 680, Rochester 1388, Seifert 730

Rochester Hills: Cassie 121, Cipa 133, Obloy 614

Rockford: Byrne 113, Krause 470, Wolverine 1076, Wynalda 914

Romeo: L & L 1522

Romulus: Hannan 342

Roscommon: Roscommon 696, Roscommon 1163, Roscommon 1389, Schroeder 721

Roseville: **Children's 1226**, Ford 261

Royal Oak: Detroit 1245, Here 365, Imerman 403, Langley 483, **McCarty 1333**, McNish 551

Saginaw: **Akbar 1473**, Anderson 23, Bardsley 41, Barth 45, Beal 55, Brown 104, Burch 109, Emmenecker 221, Harvey 354, Hebert 359, Junior 1300, Kahan 429, McDonald's 1530, Michigan 1033, Morley 584, Nickless 604, Robertson 689, Saginaw 1164, Sallness 712, St. Mary's 1413, Turner 829, Wickes 882, Wickson 883, Yeo 919

Saline: Arnold 30, Busch 112, Foundation 1258, Redies 1052, Sterken 779, Strobel 786

Sandusky: Coller 142, Sanilac 1165, United 1444

Saugatuck: Green 316

Sault Sainte Marie: Chippewa 1097, Hudson 391, United 1448

Shelby: Community 1105

Shelby Township: Shelby 1167, Van Hollenbeck 839

South Haven: Bauervic 52, McClendon 539, South 1169

Southfield: Barr 43, Barton 940, Cummings 157, Cunningham 158, Dana 164, Dancey 165, DENSO 967, **DENSO 968**, DeRoy 180, Detroit 182, Dresner 205, Faigle 234, Great 1271, Himmel 375, Jospey 425, Kazrus 444, La 1523, Leven 498, McClendon 540, National 1357, Northwind 609, Olson 618, Orchards 1374, Park 1549, Polk 1049, **Rodney 692**, Salahi 710, Seligman 1556, Sinai 751, Southeastern 765, Southfield 1171, Southfield 1405, Spaulding 1408, Ternes 804, Variety 1453, Weissman 866, Wiley 1465, William 1467

Southgate: Colina 141, Wilson 890

Sparta: Garland 286

Spring Arbor: Ganton 1503, **King 1312**

Spring Lake: Bertsch 67, Brauer 93, Finkelstein 253, **International 1291**, Sonneveldt 763

St. Charles: Ruf 701

St. Clair: DSLT 209, Foster 268, Moore 578

St. Clair Shores: Boll 84, Detroit 1239, Federal 981, Puschelberg 662, Schuyler 723, Welsh 871

St. Joseph: Berrien 1090, Brintnall 101, Culture 156, **Global 1264**, Lakeland 1315, Marzke 529, Schalon 716, St. Joseph 775, St. Joseph 1412, Tiscornia 814, Upton 833, Yeager 917

Stanton: Central 1095

Sterling Heights: Detroit 181, Mount Zion 589, Nill 607, Sterling 1173

Stevensville: Kohn 465

Sturgis: Rusch 703, Sturgis 1175, Weiss 865, White 1178

Suttons Bay: Drew 207, Ingraham 407

Sylvan Lake: Christian 131, Cochrane 140

Taylor: Masco 1025, Masco 1026, Southeast 1404

Tecumseh: Lenawee 1143, Meyers 557

Three Rivers: Evergreene 1497, Kadant 1011, Three 1176

Traverse City: Biederman 1483, Canaan 117, **Collectors 1228**, Cott 151, Generations 991, Grand 1128, **H.I.S. 327**, Haggard 333, Lange 482, Mahogany 520, Miller 562, Northwest 1365, Northwest 1366, Northwest 1367, Oleson 617, Paine 624, Prevo 658, Rock 691, Rotary 1391, Schmuckal 719, Slack 756, Sunrise 794, Three 813, United 1443

Trenton: R.J. 663, World 911

Troy: Angels 1475, Bashur 48, Bauervic 51, Cadillac 948, Chamberlain 124, Children's 1227, Christopher 132, Community 1113, Darch 167, **Delphi 966**, Detroit 1241, Farwell 242, Feuer 250, Foran 259, Frankel 1501, Harding 347, Holden 381, **Kakarala 432**, Kelly 1310, Kelly 1016, Kemp 1017, **Kresge 471**, Lifestyle 1320, Mayhew 534, Meritor 1030, **Michigan 1337**, Mistele 571, Newman 602, Rhoades 683, Saini 709, Shoemaker 741, Southeastern 766, Sutar-Sutaruk-Meyer 795, Sylvia 797, Thomas 808, Troy 1568, Turtle 830, WMY 905, Yeager 918

Union City: Creative 1489

University Center: Delta 1237

Utica: Humane 395

Van Buren Township: Dana 963

Vicksburg: Fetzer 249

Wallace: Ohana 1545

Walled Lake: Baker 36, Weiner 860

Warren: Eschbach 228

Waterford: Donlin 198, Serra 732

Wayne: Veteran's 1454

West Bloomfield: Asthma 1197, Bardha 1478, Betmar 70, Borovoy 89, Charlupski 127, Chernick 130, Gandhi 282, Hall 1508, Kay 443, OYK 622, Paul 635, Simon 749, Worsham 912

Westland: American 1189, Central 1485, Spectrum 1409, Wayne 1460

White Lake: Erlich 225

Williamston: Eyster 233, Zynda 1575

Winn: Morey 582

Wixom: ArtServe 1196, George 289, MAC 1024

Wyandotte: Edmund 219, Wayne-Metropolitan 1461, Wyandotte 1574

Wyoming: His 378, Lileikis 501, Metropolitan 1335, Paulsen 636, Sullivan 793, Tuinstra 825, Williams 887

Ypsilanti: Hemophilia 1279, Mick 561, Washtenaw 1457, Wright 1573

Zeeland: **I.N. 1287**, **Miller 1034**

MINNESOTA

Chanhassen: Life 1023

Eagan: Northwest 1042

Inver Grove Heights: CHS 952

Minneapolis: Arts 1195, Musser 594, Nash 1037, **Porter 656**, Xcel 1077

St. Paul: Weyand 875, Weyerhaeuser 876

Wayzata: TCF 1061

MISSISSIPPI
Columbus: Weitzenhoffer 867

NEBRASKA
Lincoln: Kawasaki 1012
Omaha: ConAgra 959, Kaufman 439, Pamida 1043

NEVADA
Las Vegas: MGM 1031, MGM 1336

NEW HAMPSHIRE
Portsmouth: Shoer 742

NEW JERSEY
Camden: Campbell 949
Marlton: Tuesdays 824
Pennington: CKT 135, Lasko 488, Merillat 554, Wilson 889
Wayne: Randall 667
Westfield: Hamstra 339

NEW MEXICO
Santa Fe: Peninsula 639

NEW YORK
Bronxville: Cutler 159
Great Neck: Tepper 803
New York: Center 123, Corporation 1233, Doan 196, **Ford 260**, Gits 300, **Heron 366**, Local 1323, Mitsubishi 1035, **New York 1038**, Newsweek/Daily 1039, Nonprofit 1361

NORTH CAROLINA
Black Mountain: Thiemkey 806

OHIO
Brooklyn: Gilbert 296, McCalla 537
Cincinnati: Catholic 1219, Fifth 983, Fifth 984, Kroger 1020, Kroger 1021, Myers 595
Cleveland: Carmell 119, Charter 950, Cliffs 954, Haboush 331, Heyl 1282, KeyBank 1018, Lahti 477, O'Brien 613
Columbus: AEP 934, American 937, Hildreth 373, Huntington 1004, **JPMorgan 1008**
Dayton: Gardner 285
Dublin: Tim 1063
Hinckley: Zampetis 924
Lexington: Hire 376
Maumee: Anderson 21
Sylvania: Promedica 1385
Toledo: Geiger 288, HCR 1002, Jobst 422
Wooster: Smith 759

OREGON
Portland: Graef 312

PENNSYLVANIA
Fort Washington: National 1355
Horsham: Toll 1065
Jenkintown: McCardell 538
Lionville: West 1071
Pittsburgh: PNC 1047, Trust 823
White Oak: Cash 1218

RHODE ISLAND
Providence: Robbins 688

TENNESSEE
Franklin: Nissan 1040, Nissan 1041
Nashville: Educational 1249

TEXAS
Austin: **Whole 1073**
Dallas: Erskine 226, **OneSight 1546**
Fort Worth: Enterprise 223, Quicksilver 1051
Houston: Battier 1200, Bray 94, Fruehauf 277, Guy 325, Spark 1056

VIRGINIA
Charlottesville: Moh 573
Falls Church: **General 989**
McLean: **Gannett 988**
Richmond: Bell 59, Falls 236

WASHINGTON
Seattle: Fehsenfeld 247

WISCONSIN
Green Bay: Green Bay 997, Shopko 1399, ShopKo 1055, Wisconsin 1075
Milwaukee: Beauchamp 57, Bishop 78, Brege 95, Carpenter 120, Gillenwater 297, Handleman 341, Hess 368, Hess 369, Kaufman 441, Keeney 447, Kowalski 1019, Kronlund 473, Lamberson 479, McIntyre 543, McIntyre 544, McIntyre 545, Miner 569, Neal 598, Stockton 782, Vogt 845, Wisconsin 1074
Pewaukee: Venturedyne 1070
Twin Lakes: Heart 358

INDEX TO DONORS, OFFICERS, TRUSTEES

1,155 SHS, PepsiCo, 527

205 SHS, PepsiCo, 527

700 SHS, Takeda Pharmaceuticals Co., 527

A.T.&G. Co., Inc., 86
Aardema, Jan, 1335
Abalos, Dave, 1442
Abbate-Marzolf, Tina, 1198
Abbott Laboratories, 933
Abbott, John, 1094
Abbs, David J., 1164
Abdallah, Sarah, 1255
Abdelnour, Salem, 1189
Abdullah, Aslam, Dr., 1187
Abed, Wadad, 1192
Abel, Norbert C., 1089
Aberth, Joel R., 547
Abide Ministries, 1563
Ableidinger, Esther, 1104
Abney, Wilma D., 1321
Aboudane, Zakwan, 4
Abramson, Sandra, 1323
Accoe, Richard, 1406
Achterhof, James, 841
Achterhoff, Mary Lou, 1447
Achterhoff, Tim, 1103
Ackerberg, Robert E., 1254
Ackerman, Alan T., 1369
Ackerman, Paula, 1270
Ackerman, Randall, 1282
Ackert, Terence J., 1301
Acosta, Ruben, 1359, 1410
Acosta, Sonia, 1370
Acton, Mike, 1147
Acuff, A. Marshall, Jr., 587
Adair, Judy, 1428
Adair, Martha, 1251
Adamovich, Jodi, 1461
Adams, Don, 396
Adams, Frederick M., Jr., 1106
Adams, Glenn, 1136
Adams, Lil, 1173
Adams, Mark, 1171, 1368
Adams, William C., 1254
Adams-Lyons, Gerard, 1254
Adderley, Terence E., 1106, 1310
Adema, William, 1115
Ader, Rick, 1225
Adkins, Franklin, 1228
Adornado, Ted, 1275
Adray, Deborah, 5
Adray, Louise, 5
Afrik, Taiyoh, 1111, 1376
Agard, Marty, 992
Agius, David, 1288
Ahmad, Busharat, 1349
Ahmad, Riaz, 1498
Ahmad, Shala Riaz, 1498
Ahmed, Iqbal, Dr., 1187
Ahwal-Morris, Terry, 1189
Aikens, Kim, 1088
Aimery, Margie, 1459
Ajegba, Paul, 315
Ajjan, Marion, 1254
Ajloni, Karim, 1189
Ajluni, Peter B., 1208
Akbar, Raana, 1473
Akbar, Waheed, 1473
Akers, James, 6

Akers, Phyllis M., 6
Akins, Nicholas K., 937
Al-Soofi, Yasser, 1192
Alandt, Lynn Ford, 263, 1245, 1280
Alarie-Tyckoski, Stacey, 1125
Albaisa, Alfonso, 1040
Alberding, Ellen S., 427
Albertini, Christine, 1344
Alberts, Rod, 1241
Albom, Mitchel, 824
Albom, Mitchell, 824
Albrecht, Ellen, 1428
Albrecht, Judy, 1165
Albright, Amy, 732
Albrough, Kathy, 1097
Alcaraz, Dorinda D., 1254
Alderink, Jim, 1447
Aldrink, Myron, 1291
Alessi, Don P., 1346
Alexander, Gaylord D., 751
Alexander, Jason, 1234
Alexander, Larry D., 1493
Alexander, Pam, 1404
Alexander, Sue, 1135
Alexandrowski, Joseph A., 8
Alexandrowski, Muriel F., 8
Alfonso, David, 1295
Alfonso, Manuel, 1231
Alghanem, Abd, 1255
Algozin, Kenneth, 1495
Algra, Diana Rodriguez, 1094
Alhadidi, Mahmoud, 781
Alkhatib, Hala, 164
Allen, Bonnie, 1517
Allen, Bryan D., 999
Allen, Carol Ann Wilson, 894
Allen, Carol Jean Wilson, 894
Allen, Chris, 894
Allen, David, 1192
Allen, Eric, 1117
Allen, Georgia Louise, 10
Allen, Jason, Sen., 1088
Allen, John, 1429
Allen, Mary Jo, 1323
Allen, Monica Y., 597
Allen, Nelson R., 636
Allen, Richard, 767
Allen, Rochelle, 1404
Allen, Sonali, 1275
Allen, Sue, 1338
Allen, Terrence J., 1393
Allen, Tonya, 755, 1171
Allen, W. James, 628
Allen, W. Ron, 1254
Allen, William James, 9
Aller, Marcia, 1574
Allesee, Margaret Acheson, 1106
Alley, Mark E., 1094
Allie, Michael, 1356
Allison, Jane, 1140
Allison, Sandy, 1375
Allmon, Michael L., 1254
Allstate Corp., The, 935
Allstate Insurance Co., 935
Allswede-Babcock, Catherine, 1316
Allushuski, Barbara E., 1106
Almansour, Muhammad, 12
Almirall, Katherine, 354
Almstadt, John, 1370
Alpern, Abbey, 14
Alpern, Dwight, 14
Alpern, E. Bryce, 14
Alpern, Harriet, 14
Alro Steel Corp., 302
Altamore, Ellen, 179

Altay, Denise, 1323
Alterman, Irwin M., 1017
Alticor Inc., 189
Altucher, Nathan, 1254
Alvarez, Cesar L., 462
Alvarez, Jose B., 427
Alverson, Edward, 1509
Alvery, Mary, 802
Alwood, Cindie L., 1202
Alzohalli, Opada, 164
Alzohalli, Siba, 164
Amante, Char, 1111
Amar, Peter, 1160
Amber, Allen L., 1474
Amber, Betty, 797
Amber, Jerome S., 1474
Amber, Rhonda J., 797
Amber, Sylvia W., 797
Ambrose, Jerry, 1213
Ambrosiani, F. Peter, 15
Ambrosiani, Irene P., 15
American Electric Power Service Corp., 937
Ames, Richard, 1283
Anantbhai, Koradia Chetan, 834
Andary, James R., 1167
Anderegg, Michael, 1329
Andersen, Frank N., 19
Anderson, Alan, 1404
Anderson, Ashley, 20
Anderson, Benjamin, 1231
Anderson, Benjamin Lee, 1209
Anderson, Bo I., 1346
Anderson, Bruce, 952, 1228
Anderson, Bruce, Sr., 1366
Anderson, Carl, 1102
Anderson, Charlene, 1116
Anderson, Charles W., 21
Anderson, Doris B., 616
Anderson, Francile, 1369
Anderson, Gary R., 694
Anderson, Geraldine L., 353
Anderson, Gerard M., 542
Anderson, James, 1293
Anderson, Jeffrey W., 21
Anderson, John Fred, 1242
Anderson, John T., 427
Anderson, Kathleen, 1272
Anderson, Linda, 22
Anderson, Marilyn, 1372
Anderson, Mary, 1140
Anderson, Mary H., 20
Anderson, Matthew C., 21
Anderson, Monica, 155
Anderson, Monte, 1411
Anderson, Moses B., Rev., 1209
Anderson, N. Charles, 1280
Anderson, Ray, 1158
Anderson, Richard M., 21
Anderson, Richard P., 21
Anderson, Richard T., 22
Anderson, Rick, 1411
Anderson, Santrannella, 1465
Anderson, Sherry, 1149, 1230, 1330
Anderson, Susan, 1202
Anderson, Thereasa M., 1254
Anderson, Tim, 1108
Andreae, Steve, 1221
Andresen, Harold, 18
Andresen, Marilyn, 18
Andrew, Marilyn, 1136, 1148
Andrews, Arnold, 1346
Andrews, Charles J., 826
Andrews, Christopher C., 826
Andrews, Colleen M., 24

Andrews, Delphine J., 826
Andrews, Edward F., Jr., 24, 910
Andrews, Kevin, 1434
Andrews, Milton, 1254
Andrews, Scott I., 538
Andrews, Tina M., 538
Andrews, Tracey, 826
Andruccidi, Barbara, 1108
Angle, Steve, 1080
Anglin, Eric, 1210
Anglin, Melvin, 315
Angner, Dennis P., 1006
Angood, Arthur W., 565
Anibal, Jon, 1339
Anne, Suresh, 1290
Annis, Ann, 25
Annis, Ted C., 25
Ansbacher, Rudy, 1349
Ansley, Michael, 1227
Antenucci, Basil, 1142
Anthony, Donald, 952
Anthony, Vernice Davis, 1350
Antomattey, Antonio, 1254
Antoniotti, Steven, 1196
Antoun, Patty, 1402
Appel, Phillip M., 213
Appel, Robert, 213, 790
Appenteng, Kofi, 260
Applebaum Charitable Lead Trust, Eugene, 26
Applebaum, Eugene, 26, 1191, 1281, 1357
Applebaum, Florese, 1254
Applebaum, Lisa, 1191
Applebaum, Lisa S., 26
Applebaum, Marcia, 26, 1191
Applebaum, Pamela, 26, 1191
Applebaum, Pamela A., 26
Appold, Lori, 20
Aras, Margarita, 1254
Arbuckle, Jim, 1482
Arbury, Julie Carol, 202
Arcari, Ilda, 1254
Archamba, Jennifer, 1221
Archambeau, Nancy, 1232
Archer, Dennis W., Hon., 1217
Arden, Mary, 28
Arden, Richard, 28
Ardisana, Lizabeth, 755, 1371
Arellano, Stephen, 1107
Arends, Jim, 184
Arens, Ted, 1147
Arfstrom, Robert, 391
Arlinsky, Ellen, 1335
Armbruster, Kelly, 1432
Armstead, Stuart, 1444
Armstead, Thomas J., 1209
Armstrong, Bob, 1165
Armstrong, Rudy, 1431
Arnett, Tonya, 1424
Arney, Fred, 1254
Arnold Trust, Barbara J., 30
Arnold, Barbara J., 30
Arnold, Bobbie N., 787
Arnold, Charles B., 30
Arnold, Christine, 1277
Arnold, David J., 787
Arnold, Jeanne, Dr., 1277
Arnson, Robert P., 1274
Aronow, David, 1297
Arons, Bill, 1224
Aronson, Robert P., 1260, 1395, 1396, 1425
Aronson, Robert R., 1191
Arrendale, Deborah, 1002

Arrington, Sharon, 451
Arrowsmith, Beatrice A., 1254
Arslanian, Paul, 645
Art, Jeff, 1379
Arthur, Charles G., 1254
Arthur, Charles G., Mrs., 1254
ArvinMeritor, Inc., 1030
Asand, Matsuhiro, 1012
Ash, Blanche E., 31
Ash, Janet E., 93
Ash, Jennifer K., 31
Ash, Stanley P., 31
Ashbrook, Lois, 1090
Ashley, Art, 765
Ashley, Bruce, 1196
Askew, Lauretha, 144
Asselta, R. Tony, 1392
Astrein, Richard, 1227
Aten, Bill, 1096
Aten, Marcia, 1104
Atkins-Smith, Barbara, 1240
Atkins-Wagner, Sue, 1097
Attanasio, Raymond V., 32
Atwater Entertainment, 597
Aubert, Bernadine, 1377
Aubrey, George, 1470
Aucker-Tykocki, Andria, 1125
Augustine, Sherry, 1432
Auler, Randy, 1368
Austin, David K., 1507
Austin, Douglas, 877
Austin, Douglas R., 1110
Austin, Eleanor, 1250
Auto Specialties Manufacturing Co., 814
Automotive Appraisal Group, 1228
Averill, Dick, 1169
Avery, Anita, 454
Avery, Shelby, 1164
Avery, Suzy, 1434
Aviv, Linda Wasserman, 1245
Avram, Al, 1449
Ayaub, John J., 708
Ayers, Chad, 1081
Aymond, Charles H., 80
Ayres, Susan, 1130
Azad, M. Abdul, 1554
Azzar Foundation, James D., 1528
Azzar, James A., 1528
Azzar, James D., 1528
Azzar, L. Susan, 1528

B&B Beer Distributing Co., 793
Baar, Sarah, 384
Babb, Ron, 1159
Babcock, Cindy, 1456
Babington, Catherine V., 933
Bach, Jens, 411
Bach, Margie N., 411
Bachman, Christopher, 1133
Bachman, Lois V., 875
Bachmeier, Jim, 1463
Bacigalupi, Tracy, 1088
Backus, Curt, 1165
Bacon, Kenneth J., 1233
Bacon, Michael, 1363
Bacon, Robert, 200
Baczewski, Kimberlee K., 787
Badalament, John, 198
Badalament, Kathleen Donlin, 198
Baddigam, Kondareddy, 1292
Badgero, James, 601
Bagale, Ed, 1344
Bagale, Edward, 1192
Bahadur, B.N., 1453
Baiardi, Angelo, 35
Baiardi, Chris A., 35
Baiardi, Cindy J., 35
Baiardi, Kristen L., 35
Baiardi, Suzanne M., 35
Baic, Vojin, 1483
Bailey, Debra, 1277
Bakeman, Paul, 1500
Baker Trust, Howard, 36

Baker, Arnold, 1341
Baker, Beverly, 928
Baker, Blinda, 1416
Baker, Frederick M., 807
Baker, George R., 37
Baker, Jana, 194
Baker, Jane, 577
Baker, Keith, 1210
Baker, Mark, 1269
Baker, Michelle L., 36
Baker, Paula, 1080
Baker, Sandra T., 1162
Baker, Tracy A., 290
Baker, Vernon G., II, 1030
Bakken, Douglas A., 40
Balas, David, 1080
Balderson, Julie, 1384
Balderson, Lisa, 1384
Baldini, Thomas L., 1329
Baldwin, Dana, II, 38
Baldwin, Susan, 1086
Bales, Robert, Jr., 923
Bales, Susan Ford, 1257
Baley, Jane, 1308
Balk, James H., 39, 344
Balk, James H., II, 39, 344
Balk, Martin, 39, 344
Balk, Shirley, 39, 344
Balk, Steven, 39, 344
Ball, Anne F., 254
Ball, Edmund F., 40
Ball, Frank E., 40
Ball, George, 1015
Ball, Melinda, 1121
Ball, Robert B., 40
Ball, Virginia B., 40
Ballard, Carolyn, 1230
Ballard, Christine B., 1472
Ballard, Christopher, 461
Ballien, Heather, 701
Ballios, Alex, 1113
Ballow, Owen, 1224
Bancroft, Robert W., 465
Bancroft, William R., Jr., 465
Banholzer, Bill, 973
Bank of America, N.A., 226, 326, 507, 688, 810
Bank One, N.A., 1046
Bank, Wayne, 1444
Banks, Betty Smith, 1269
Banks, David, 1367
Bankwitz, W. Keith, 1332
Bannan, Denise, 63
Banner, Charles E., 1506
Banner, Margaret, 1506
Banyon, Steve, 1412
Barbarin, Oscar, 1401
Barber, Gerald, 19
Barberi, Alison, 1130
Barbo, Sally, 595
Barbour, Betty, 213
Barck, Rick, 1097
Barco, Lawrence, 1098
Bardha, Ekrem, 1478
Bardha, Lumteri, 1478
Bardi, Edward, 1385
Bardolph, Mary, 190
Bardsley, Ailene, 41
Bardsley, P.E., 41
Bardsley, William, 41
Bares, Chuck, 1383
Bargy, Larry, 1366
Bark, Dennis L., 217
Barkan, Glenn, 1295
Barker, Bruce, 1169
Barker, Nancy, 1196
Barnard, Melissa, 1152
Barnes, Anthony, 1299
Barnes, George, 1346
Barnes, Judy, 384
Barnes, Lester, 1367
Barnes, Phil, 1269
Barnes, Robert, 1165
Barnes, William, 870

Barnett, Brian, 1108
Barnett, John, 636
Barney, Bruce, 900
Barnum, James, 1309
Baron, Arthur, 1145
Baron, Rick, 1086
Barone, Charles J., 1217
Baroni, Tim, 1139
Barr, Mark, 1476
Barr, Shelley E., 43
Barr, Terry A., 43
Barratt, Rick, 1433
Barrett, Clint, 1131
Barrett, John, 1131
Barrett, Robert E., 1257
Barrie, Ted, 1294
Barritt, Eric, 1364
Barry, Lisa, 1157
Barry, Michael, 57
Barstow, David O., 44
Barstow, Florence K., 44
Barstow, John C., 44
Barstow, Richard G., 44
Barstow, Robert G., 44
Bartczak, David, 1347
Bartel, Jon, 1228
Barth, Adeline L., 45
Barth, Florian G., 1181
Barth, Jane, 45
Bartlett, Brian, 1368
Bartlett, Christine, 642
Bartlett, Mark R., 1409
Barton, D. James, 1287
Barton, Lauren Hicks, Dr., 1231
Barton, Roxanne, 1132
Barton-Malow Enterprises, Inc., 940
Bartos, John N., 787
Bartsch, Ruth, 46
Barz, Richard J., 1006
Basch, Dawn, 47
Basch, Jeffrey, 47
Bashur, John, 48
Bashur, Margaret Barry, 48
Baskel, Pamela, 1251
Baskerville-Jones, Callie, 1308
Baskin, Michael, 1321
Bass, John, 613
Bass, Robert, 952
Basset, Joe, 1489
Batch, David, 1189
Batcheler, Colleen, 959
Batchelor, Richard, 1495
Batchelor, Richard A., 63, 1168
Bateman, Sharon A., 481
Bates, Gwendolyn H., 50
Bates, Martha J., 50
Bates, Nancy, 1167
Bates, Paula, 497
Bates, Ray, 1449
Bates, Sarah, 1346
Bateson, Nickie, 1157
Bath, Margaret, 1013
Battaglia, Stacie, 1224
Batts Group, Ltd., The, 941
Batts, James L., 941
Batts, John H., 941
Batts, John T., 941
Batts, Michael A., 941
Batts, Robert H., 941
Bauder, Lillian, 755
Bauer, Erik, 1528
Bauer, Janet, 1122
Bauer, Jennifer, 1528
Bauer, Joan, 1213
Bauer, Mark, 1428
Bauer, Patricia, 1401
Bauernfeind, George G., 1003
Bauervic, Charles M., 51
Baughey, Donald, 1480
Baughey, Donald, Jr., 1480
Baughey, Dorcas, 1480
Baughey, Ethel, 1480
Baum, Alexio R., 292
Baum, Dale, 9

Baum, David, 1378
Bauman, Marvin J., 1022
Baumgartner, David D., 1394
Baumgartner, Joshua, D.C., Dr., 1352
Baxter, Ellen, 1233
Bay Fire Protection, Inc., 842
Bayer, Howard, 70
Bayer, Mary Ann, 1082
Bayless, Pattie, 1342
Bazaj, Alka, 472
Bazaj, Suresh, 472
Bazen, John, Jr., 1381
Bazzi, Mohamad, 1523
Beall, Ken, 1213
Beals, Joseph, 683
Beals, Joseph M., 56
Beam, Robert, 1308, 1309
Bean, Judith, 556
Beardslee, Terry, 1362
Beatty, Marvin, 1470
Beatty, Marvin W., 1217
Beaty, Julie, 1321
Beaubien, Anne K., 66
Beauchine, Margi, 1079
Beaulieu, Christopher, 1415
Beaumier, John, 1100
Beaver, Thomas, 249
Beaverson, Russell, 901
Beck, Carol Morley, 584
Beck, Marion, 1201
Beck, Nicole, 1310
Becker, Benton L., 1257
Becker, Charles, 1100
Becker, Jim, 1334
Becker, Phil, 1448
Becker, Richard, 1418
Becker, Scott, 1040
Beckering, Jane M., 1301
Beckman, Hugh, 751
Beckwith, Ron, 616
Bedard, Claude, 1181
Bednar, Judy, 1465
Beer, Brendon, 1436
Beers, Mack, 1391
Beers, Timothy, 1125
Begick, Vaughn, 831
Behen, David, 1458
Behlen, Jim, 1562
Behler, Stacie, 1277
Behm, Dan, 1335
Behm, Mark E., 1356
Behr, Howard, 1382
Beil, Leo J., 590
Beil, Michael, 557
Beird, Lisa, 1300
Beiver, Bob, 1388
Belanger, Beth A., 1110
Belanger, Lauren, 1100
Belay, Valerie Herod, 556
Belcher, Chris, 1157
Belevender, Jenna, 1097
Belew, Patricia F., 271
Bell, Alphonso, 1206
Bell, Carlos R., 59
Bell, Jane A., 947
Bell, Kevin L., 1346
Bell, Rex, 1307
Bell, Robert Holmes, 1291
Bell, Sue E., 562
Bellairs, Robert J., Jr., 78
Bellanca, James V., Jr., 1209
Belle Tire, 1046
Bellingar, Yolanda, 1150
Bellinger, Iva, 61
Bellinger, Vickie, 1113
Bellinson, James B., 1296
Belote, Linda, 1139
Bemiller, F. Loyal, 661
Ben Horin, Daniel, 1361
Bender, Bob, 1417
Bender, Kurt, 1177
Bender, Pattie, 1411
Bender, William, 1226
Benecke, Mary Lou, 975, 1164

Bengry, Alan, 1159, 1513
Bennett, Faith H., 339
Bennett, Jeffrey, 1285
Bennett, John K., 339
Bennett, Judy, 1174
Bennett, Richard J., 1506
Bennett, Robert, 1389
Bennett, Robert, Hon., 1144
Bennett, Stephen, 27
Bennett, Thompson, 163
Bennick, Linda, 1330
Bennyhoff, George R., 1071
Benson, Al B., III, 1355
Benson, Barbara F., 719
Benson, Bruce, 1228
Benson, Douglas L., 1481
Benson, Ericka L., 637
Benson, Tom, 1195
Bentley, Alvin M., 63
Bentley, Alvin M., IV, 63
Bentley, Ann Marie, 63, 1168
Bentley, Arvella D., 63
Bentley, Susan, 63
Benyas, Dorothy, 1191, 1260, 1274,
  1297, 1395, 1396, 1425
Benz, Micki, 1394
Benz, William, 789
Benzing, Laurie, 1283
Berca, Jane J. Hampson, 338
Berckley, Mary, 1446
Beresford, Barbara S., 1245
Berger, Justin, 1320
Bergh, Thomas H., 1339
Bergman, David, 1244
Bergman, David B., 1217
Bergman, Steve, 1190
Berke, Amy, 1494
Berke, Joseph J., 1494
Berkebile, Dennis, 1256
Berkery Trust, 64
Berkhof, Robert A., 1291
Berkowitz Foundation, Alfred, 651
Berkowitz, Greta, 65
Berkowitz, Hyman, 65
Berlin, Jordan D., 1355
Berlin, Thomas, 179
Berline, Jim, 1217, 1227, 1328
Berman, Dale, 1161
Berman, Madeleine H., 1245
Berman, Mandell, 1274
Berman, Shirlee, 1186
Berman, Stuart, 1295
Berna, Stefan, 1454
Bernard, John, Jr., 1470
Bernath, Garry, 1423
Berndt, Richard O., 484
Bernier, Tammy L., 1164
Bero, Jeff, 1439
Berquist, Anne, 1194
Berriz, Albert M., 1106
Berry, Hussein, 1192
Berry, Michael J., 534
Berry, Millicent R., 1205
Berry, Philip C., 66
Berry, Philip K., 66
Berry-Brown, Amal M., 1192
Berth, John, 1161
Bertsch, J.R., 67
Bertsch, John W., 67
Berzins, Valdis, 1317
Berztiss, Alfs, 1317
Beschloss, Afsaneh M., 260
Bess, Barry R., 618
Besse, John D., 68
Besse, Melissa, 68
Bessemer Trust Co., N.A., 300
Besser Co., 69
Besser Foundation, 1482
Besser, J.H., 69
Bessette, Mark, 1446
Best, Becky, 1322
Beswick, Jeffrey, 1126
Bettich, Randy, 1412
Bettiga, Michael J., 1399

Bettis, Gladys, 1203
Bettis, Gloria, 1203
Bettis, Jerome "The Bus", 1203
Betts, Thomas A., Jr., 568
Beusse, Blake, 655
Beusse, Heather, 655
Beusse, Margaret, 655
Beyer, Jim, 1444
Beyer, Laura, 1272
Beyerlein, David, 586, 883
Beyerlein, David A., 604
Bhat, Ishwara, 1315
Bhatia, Reena, 1323
Bhatia, Sunil, 1557
Bianchi, Michelle, 1131
Bickersteth, Thomas G., 1490
Bicum, Truman, 1128
Biddinger, Mary E., 404
Biederman Trust, Anne, 1483
Biederman, Anna R., 1483
Biederman, Lester M., 1483
Biederman, Paul M., 1483
Biederman, Ross, 1483
Biehl, Michele, 1145
Bierbusse, Barbara, 1379
Bieri, Richard, 1527
Bierlein, Barbara, 71
Bierlein, Dorothy P., 71
Bierlein, Duane, 71
Bierlein, Randall D., 71
Bietler, Charles E., 193
Bigford, Paul, 1140
Biggs, Thomas, 1457
Bikkina, Sairamesh, 1290
Bildner, James L., 471
Bildner, Jim, 1361
Bilkie, Ashley, 72
Bilkie, Megan, 72
Bilkie, Robert, 72
Bilkie, Shari, 72
Bilodeau, Ken, 1108
Bilstrom, Jon W., 956
Binda, Guido A., 73
Binda, Robert, 73
Bing, Dave, 542
Bingham, Mary Ann, 1526
Binion, Natalie, 74
Binkley, David, 1072
Binkley, Mary Jo, 1450
Bippus, Joe, 1176
Birch, Bill, 1424
Birchler, D. Keith, 831
Birdsall, Arthur, 1444
Birholz, Mike, 1430
Birkenstock Trust, Horace C., 75
Birkhill, Frederick, Jr., 76
Birkhill, Laura Jean, 76
Birkhill, William, 76
Birtwistle, Donald B., 77
Birtwistle, Joclyn, 77
Bischof, Nancy, 1535
Biscoe, John, 1437
Bisher, Sharon E., 1131
Bishop, Arthur Giles, 78
Bishop, John, 1092
Bishop-Yanke, Kimber, 870
Bissell, Cathy, 1299
Bittner, Sally, 1100
Bivens, Mike L., 1013
Bjork, William E., 1339
Black, Lynne, 1127
Black, Ray, 1418
Blackburn, Jim, 1450
Blackman, Lou Uzzle, 568
Bladen, Ed, 1202
Blair, Ian D., 1064
Blair, Linda, 1368
Blakely, Dorothy M., 80
Blanchard, Lisa G., 1162
Blanchard, Mary Lou, 1519
Bland, Elizabeth, 1093
Blaney, Julie, 1438
Blashfield, Holly, 1132, 1230
Blashfield, Martin P., 1183

Blasius, Louise, 1165
Blaske, E. Robert, 81
Blaske, Thomas H., 81
Blatch, Libby, 1135
Blatt, Hedy, 1196
Blazczynski, Keane, 1130
Blazo, Michael, 1141
Bleeker, Gary R., 1381
Bleeker, James D., 1381
Bleke, Bert, 1277
Blesch, Thomas C., 847
Blett, Tim, 1357
Bleyer, Mark, 1287
Bliesner, Sandra, 1307
Blight, Ken, 1078
Blinkhorn, Carla, 1277
Blinkilde, Peter, Dr., 1130
Bliss, Rosalyn, 215
Blix, Sandra, 1308
Block Imaging International, 1563
Block, Bruce, 1563
Blockett, Charles, Jr., 1094
Blodgett, Edith I., 82
Bloem, James H., 1003
Bloem, Russell, 1469
Blohm, Donald E., 1022
Bloodworth, Carolyn A., 955, 961
Bloom, Bruce, 1091
Bloom, Charles M., 107
Bloom, Mara G., 1355
Bloom, Martha L., 1083
Bloom, Susan, 322
Bloswick, Jennifer, 1146
Blue Cross and Blue Shield of Michigan,
  1208
Bluhm, Bill, 1105
Bluhm, Gilbert B., 683
Blum, Eva T., 1047
Blumenfeld, Robert Y., 1374
Blumenstein, Penny, 1191, 1281, 1395,
  1396
Blumenstein, Penny B., 1106, 1280
Blums, June, 1319
Bluse, Rusty, 1430
Bluthardt, Rob, 1227
Bly, David, Jr., 1445
BNY Mellon, N.A., 823
Boals, Dana, 1277
Boardman, Gordan, 1426
Bobier, Bill, 1105
Bobilya, David A., 258
Bocanegra, Juanita, 1111
Boch, Susan, Rev., 1247
Bocher, Durwood, 926
Bocher, Jeanne, 926
Bodary, Marlene, 1204
Bode, Bill, 1095
Bodman, Ralph I., 746
Bodman, Ralph L., 745
Boerger, John, 1121
Boes, James, 1100
Bogan, Robert A., Jr., 1337
Boge, Dan, 1154
Boger, Carol, 1448
Boileau, Randy, 1069
Bok, Melissa, 884
Bokram, Heather, 1110
Bolds, Yohannes, 1370
Boley, Frank E., 1149
Bolger, Heidi A., 1164
Bolhouse, Susan Steiner, 1119, 1459
Bolker, Cynthia, 1038
Boll, John A., 84
Boll, Marlene L., 84
Bollinger, Lee C., 471
Bollman, Robert, 390
Bolser, Benjamin, 1104
Bolton, Kathryn R., 51
Bolton, Ursula, 1370
Bolton, William P., 1209
Bone, Bruce, 1228
Bonisteel, Lillian, 85
Bonisteel, Roscoe O., Sr., 85
Bonn, Nicholas, 1144

Bonner, Asa W., Sr., 86
Bonner, Christine, 86
Bonney, Al, 1391
Bonsall, Joseph Sloan, 87
Bonsall, Mary Ann, 87
Book, E. L., Mrs., 811
Booker, Alicia, 1215, 1431
Booker, Eric, 1435
Boone, Emily, 1215
Boone, Robert S., 727
Boone, Terra Lynn, 582
Boos, Phil, 395
Boot, Barb, 1184
Booth, Donald, 1339
Booth, Douglas E., 1402
Boppana, Dwaraka Prasad, 1292
Borden, Bernard, 1099
Bordine, Corey, 1108
Borg, Lynn, 1110
Borin, James L., 787
Borman's, Inc., 88
Borman, Gilbert, 88
Borman, Leonard S., 1347
Borman, Marlene, 88
Borman, Paul, 88
Born, Christopher, 332
Born, Patricia, 332
Bornstein, Marc, 1401
Borough, Kathy, 701
Borovoy, Joyce, 89
Borovoy, Marc A., 89
Borovoy, Mathew, 89
Bosak, Brian, 1277
Bosch, Robert, 1081
Boschma, Andrew, 1356
Boschma, Sue, 1
Bosgraaf, Brian, 384
Bosley, Julie, 1434
Bosman, Calvin, Hon., 1126
Boss, John, 1309
Boss, LaVerne H., 73
Boss, Vern, 269
Bosse, Marjorie, Sr., 1219
Bossenberry, Earl C., 575
Bossenbroek, Elaine K., 90
Bossenbroek, Geoffrey, 90
Bossenbroek, Steven L., 90
Bossenbroek, Steven L., II, 90
Boswell, Heather, 1184
Bothwell, Henry, 439
Botkin, Pat, 1388
Botkin, Patricia, 1108, 1388
Bott, Edmund T., Dr., 219
Bott, Edmund T., Mrs., 219
Bottoms, Robert G., 427
Bottrall, David C., 455, 798
Bottum, Gladys, 1322
Boucher, Jean, 1223
Bouckley, Sandra L., 1402
Boudeman, Sherwood M., 1505
Boufford, Thomas, 184
Boukamp, John, 1204
Bouma, Carolyn L., 91
Bouma, Douglas J., 174
Bouma, Henry, Jr., 91
Bouma, Sherri L., 174
Bounds, Diedre, 1410
Bourland, Jill, 1154
Bourque, Paul, 1089
Boutell, Arnold, 92
Boutell, Gertrude, 92
Bouwer, William J., Rev., 1351
Bouwman, Laurie, 9
Bouwman, Laurie G., 628
Bovee, Timothy E., 1352
Boven, Thomas M., 507
Bow, Dennis, 1121
Boweden, Kristi, 1377
Bowen, Beth, 345
Bowen, Bill, 1087, 1428
Bowen, Susan, 640
Bower, Jonathan, 1212
Bowerman, Mary, 1079, 1112
Bowers Manufacturing Co., 1302

Bowers, Jon, 1302
Bowers, Sharon, 1095
Bowersox, Gary E., 1222
Bowman, Harold E., 1394
Bowman, Paul, 1141
Bowman, Robert G., 1335
Boy, Patricia, 1340
Boyd, Andy, 1411
Boyd, Michele, 1315
Boyden, Theodore F., 1345
Boyer, Frederic Jacques, 840
Boyer, Kimberly Van Kampen, 840
Boyer, Kristin, 1228
Boyer, Margaret G., 34
Boyer, Peter S., 34
Boyer, Thomas L., 1017
Boylan, Francis, 1209
Boylan, Rebecca, 1083
Boyle, Christopher, 1133
Boyle, Denise, 1430
Boyle, Kevin, 1546
Boyle, Tom, 1284
Bozarth, Jamie, 1408
Bozymowski, John, 1173
Braaten, David A., 897
Braco, Holly, 1040
Bradley, H. Elizabeth, 661
Bradley, Stu, 1148
Bradley, Wayne W., Sr., 1240
Bradlow, Richard, 1235
Bradshaw, Conrad A., 843
Bradshaw, Margaret S., 843
Brady, Edmund M., Jr., 1239
Brady, Michael, 1357
Brady, Thomas C., Rev., 613
Bragg, Jeanine, 1442
Braida, Arthur, 1228
Braman, Bill, 1130
Bramante, Christina, 947
Brame, Walter M., Dr., 1269
Bramer, Lara, 572
Brand, Chase, 584
Brand, Michael Morley, 584
Brandt, Chad, 1104, 1135
Brandt, E.N., 292
Brandt, Erin, 1264
Brandt, Jery, 1098
Brann, Tommy, 1335
Brannigan, Mike, 1454
Branoff, Chris, 1335
Brauer, Carl A., Jr., 93
Brauer, Jan E., 563
Brauer, Richard D., 93
Braun, Ellamae, 1394
Braun, Hugo E., Jr., 582, 882
Braunlich, Paul, 1109
Bravo, Peg, 1224
Braxton, Cheryl, 1370
Bray, Theresa, 1080
Bray, Thomas J., 217
Bray, Tom, 1190
Bray, Viola E., 94
Brege, Donald R., 95
Breighner, Kathie, 1276
Breiner, Chuck, 1322
Bremer, Colleen, 1098
Brennan, James R., 96
Brennan, Kathy, 1217
Brennan, Margaret M., 96
Brennan, Michael J., 1427
Brennan, Vince, 1468
Brennan, Vincent, 1422
Brewer, Alfred, 1199
Brewer, Dale, 1284
Brewer, Dennis, 1250
Brey, Ingrid K., 423
Brice, Susan Mary, 154
Bricker, Beth, 1263
Bridenstine, James, 1196, 1302
Bridges, Tom, 1397
Bridgewater, Paul, 1240
Briere, Betsy, 1230
Briggs, John C., 868
Briggs, John E., 1362

Briggs, Robert W., 462
Briggs, Sue, 1198
Brink, Melinda, 1126
Brinkerhoff, Jonathon, 1492
Brinkerhoff, William, 1458
Brinkerhoff, William F., 100
Brinks, Ben, Jr., 384
Brinks, Brent, 1484
Brintnall, Helene W., 101
Brintnall, James W., 101
Brintnall, Robert L., 101
Briskin, Edith S., 1379
Bristol, Barbara F., 277
Bristol, Neil, 1379
Britt, James, Pastor, 1158
Britt, Wayman P., 1127
Brlas, Laurie, 954
Broadnax, Marc, 1357
Brock, Clark, 1133
Brock, Jim, 143
Brodersen, Regina, 148
Brodhead, William M., 755
Brodie, Robyn J., 763
Brody, Jay Howard, 808
Broeckel, Julie, 997
Broering, Noreen, 1128
Broman, Lisa, 1430
Broman, Susan K., 1058
Brondyke, Dolores, 931
Bronner Family Trust, Wallace and Irene, 102
Bronner, Carla, 102
Bronner, Irene R., 102
Bronner, Maria, 102
Bronner, Randy, 102
Bronner, Wayne, 102
Bronson, George A., 181
Brook, Cathleen, 1310
Brooks, Bill, 1438
Brooks, Blake, 1128
Brooks, Frank, 251
Brooks, Joel, 1309
Brooks, Joseph, Jr., 1140
Brooks, Kathy, 17
Brooks, Keefe, 946
Brooks, Lance, 103
Brooks, Lance C., 103
Brooks, Sue, 1433
Brooks, Twyla, 1223
Brooks-Williams, Denise, 1250
Brosch, Sharon, 968
Brostowitz, Teresa, 1161
Brothers, Bob, 1411
Brothers, Laura, 1175
Broucek, Gwenda, 308
Brower, Steve, 1147
Brown Charitable Lead Trust, Robert J., 577
Brown, Albertine M., 577
Brown, Alice M., 600
Brown, Angela, 1213
Brown, Bruce, 1375
Brown, Carolyn, 1086
Brown, Charles C., 105
Brown, Chris, 1418
Brown, Denise L., 657
Brown, E. Janet, 1525
Brown, Evelyn, 1323
Brown, Frederick O., 577
Brown, Geraldine C., 105
Brown, Gordon, 466
Brown, Gregory S., 104
Brown, Helayne, 104
Brown, J. Christopher, 977
Brown, James H., 637
Brown, Janice, 1303
Brown, Johanna, 1255
Brown, Joy, 1202
Brown, Judy L., 1045
Brown, Julie, 1300
Brown, Kay E., 1408
Brown, Kim R., 1141
Brown, Lee J., 1092
Brown, Loren P., 1209

Brown, Martin, Dr., 1173
Brown, Mary, 1346
Brown, Maureen Mara, 1217
Brown, Michael, 1213
Brown, Montgomery B., 217
Brown, Nancy, 105
Brown, Norman, 16, 73
Brown, Paul, 63
Brown, Paul W., 923
Brown, Richard H., 105
Brown, Richard M., 106
Brown, Robert, 315
Brown, Robert J., 577
Brown, Robert M., 577
Brown, Robert M., Jr., 577
Brown, Robin Oare, 637
Brown, Sandra L., 1525
Brown, Sharon R., 106
Brown, Shirley, 1420
Brown, Stan, 1447
Brown, Terri, 182
Brown, William M., 1525
Browne Trust, Franklin C., 923
Browne, James R., 107
Browne, Lynn H., 107
Browne, Robert W., 107
Brownlee, Bruce, 1250
Brubaker, Kim, 900
Brueckman, Cece, 1402
Bruggeman, Dan E., 1565
Bruggeman, Dan R., 1352
Bruhn, Gary, 1409
Brumley, Lyle, 592
Brummund, Carolyn, 1104
Bruner, Donna, 737
Brunner, James E., 955, 961
Brunner, Tom, 1446
Brunt, Dale, 1109
Brush, Ed, 1397
Bruski, Larry, 1104
Brutsche, Katherine I., 1514
Brutsche, Timothy J., 1514
Bryan, Jay, 1105
Bryant, Dana, 1447
Bryant, Juanita, 103
Bryant, Shirley J., 1374
Brzozowski, John, 1122
Bubb, Hillary, 1090
Buchanan, Boyd, 1284
Buchanan, Darrell, 1405
Bucher, Brian, 1385
Buchsbaum, Andy, 1273
Buck, James, 1463
Buckler, Robert J., 977
Buckley, Andre, 1164
Buckley, Daniel, 1422
Buckley, Jerry S., 949
Buckridge, Steeve O., 215
Buddendeck, Alan, 1040
Budin, Arnold A., 1409
Bueche, Virginia, 1121
Bueker, John, 1147
Buffington, Lamont E., 1348
Bugge, Mark, 837
Bugge, Mark J., 835
Buhl, Lawrence, 1363
Buhl, Robert P., 1386
Buhl, Thomas C., 1106
Buhler, Michael, 1263
Buisch, Dorenda R., 899
Buist Electric, Inc., 1484
Buletza, Wayne, 1248
Bullen, Lawrence, 852
Bullock, Robert, 309
Bumstead, Wayne, 1272
Bunbury, Barbara K., 470
Bunbury, John D., 470
Bunce, Jack D., 340
Bunch, Charles E., 484
Bunker, Brenda, 1146
Bunn, Elizabeth, 1387
Bunten, Paul, 1052
Burbridge, Gary, 1299
Burch, Michael, 109

Burch, Wilbur, 109
Burde, Ralph, 601
Burdick, Douglas, 80
Burdick, Joe, 1439
Burdiss, Paul, 956
Buresh, Shelley, 1135
Burgess, Kathy, 1484
Burgess, Robert, 1339
Burgess, Robert K., 1467
Burgess, Shirley, 395
Burgwyn, Margot Y., 905
Burhans, Earl, 1304
Burke, Brian, 1368
Burket, Jack, 29
Burkhart, Tim, 1312
Burks, Kay, 1087
Burks, Lawrence, 787, 1128
Burley, Philip R., 1352
Burmeister, Richard F., 878
Burnett, Anna Irish, 1270
Burnett, Harriet F., 236
Burnett, Laird, 236
Burnett, Rebecca, 179
Burnham, Charles C., 110
Burnham, M. Anne, 110
Burnley, Jackie, 1346
Burns, Beverly Hall, 1350
Burns, Jim, 1458
Burns, Lawrence P., 1394
Burns, Mark, 1253
Burns, Richard, 27
Burns, Stephanie A., 787
Burns, Sue Ann, 1000
Burr, Thomas D., 1207
Burrough, Rick, 1141
Burroughs, Jonathan E., II, 111
Burroughs, Jonathan, III, 111
Burroughs, Joseph S., 111
Burtch, Mike, 1343
Burton, Ann, 1104
Burton, Peter, 1357
Burton, Robert D., 1394
Burton, Thomas A., 1553
Burton, Yvette C., Dr., 27
Burton-Snell, Cathy, 1184
Burtrum, Marilyn, 900
Burza, Brett, 1376
Burzlaff, Hugo, 1156
Busby, Lisa, 1435
Busch, Stephan L., 112
Busch, Timothy R., 112
Bush Foundation, 1402
Bush, Gregory, 1389
Bush, Jelanie, 601, 1360
Bush, Lori, 1111
Bush, William L., 290
Buskey, Dawn, 1385
Buskirk, Wayne, 1102
Busman, Denise, 1115
Buss, Eric, 1023
Busscher, Melvin, 1469
Bussema, Elmer, 1286
Butch, Alice, 1100
Butcher, Barbara J., 474
Butler, Arthur, 1382
Butler, Bill, 1286
Butler, James, 1213
Butler, John M., 955, 961
Butler, Kevin J., 495
Butler, Lynn, 1353
Butler, Nancy, 1315
Butler, Nancy O., 495
Butler, Nancy Oare, 637, 1151
Butterer, Karl W., 1301
Butterfield, Gaye, 1141
Butzbaugh, Alfred M., Hon., 1348
Butzel Long, 946
Buxton, Barton, 1437
Buxton, Henry, 1165
Buzzelli, David T., 1162
Byers, Nancy T., 1258
Byington, Bob, 1085
Byker, Gaylen, 131
Byl, Mary C., 85

Byle, Tom, 873
Byrd, Leatta, 1305
Byrne, Dana W., 954
Byrne, Mary Jo, 1149
Byrne, Norman, 113
Byrne, Rosemary, 113
Byrns, Priscilla Upton, 833
Byrum, James E., 558

Cablevision of Michigan, Inc., 965
Cabot Corp., 947
Cadillac Products Inc., 948
Cagle, Cecily, 1309
Cahill, Kimberly, 1348
Caine, Chardae, 1171
Calabrese, John, 1334
Calcaterra, Larry, 1173
Calcei, Elizabeth L., 730
Calfee, William R., 954
Caliman, Judi, 1271
Callaghan, Edward D., 1280
Callam, Mary, 1455
Callander, Doug, 1309
Callant, Laurence G., 237
Callant, Mary A., 237
Calloway, Joy D., 1321
Calvert, Ann O., 654
Calvert, Kenneth A., 654
Cambria, Frank, 1458
Cambridge, Al, 1389
Camden, Andrew L., 1106
Camden, Carl T., 1016, 1310
Cameron, Lynn, Mrs., 811
Camp, Donna Ruth, 115
Campana, Mary Lou, 819
Campana, Virginia A., 114
Campanale, Frank, 238
Campau, Anne E., 1137
Campbell Soup Co., 949
Campbell, Brian, 1083
Campbell, C. David, 542
Campbell, Gary, 1413
Campbell, Harold, 1283
Campbell, J. Michael, 830
Campbell, Jeron, 1465
Campbell, John M., 649
Campbell, Judith A., 1521
Campbell, Kevin, 1303
Campbell, M. David, 1356
Campbell, Margaret, 404
Campbell, Mark, 965
Campbell, Marshall J., 134, 1110
Campbell, Martha Larzelere, 487
Campbell, Mary Alice, 63
Campbell, Scott, 737, 1282
Campbell, Tom, 1457
Campbell, Tony, 1277
Canaan Foundation, 691, 991
Canale, Mark, 1148
Candela, James, 1574
Candler, E. Greer, 1207
Cane, John, 1372
Canepa, John, 1285
Canestraight, Gregory A., 1553
Cannarsa, Sharon, 1346
Cannon, Sally, 1088
Cantor, Mike, 1431
Cantrell, Hugh, 968
Capell, Peter, 1195
Capital Ventures of NV, 131
Caplan, Marianne, 686
Carattini, Dwight M., 1086
Cardimen, Frank, 1108
Cardinal, Jeanne, 1156
Carey, James, 1489
Carey, Julie, Rev., 1283
Carey, Tammy, 1105
Cargill, Dennis, 1444
Cari, William J., 408
Carley, Garry G., 1470
Carlie, Bob, 1221
Carlin, Patricia, 1305
Carls, William, 118

Carlson, Betty, 1120
Carlson, Bonnie, 1366
Carlson, Caleb, 1270
Carlson, Carolyn, 1265
Carlson, Dennis, 952
Carlson, Grant, 1118, 1158
Carlson, Jay, 1091
Carlson, Kathleen, 1240
Carlson, Robert, 1184
Carlson, Robert W., 1355
Carlton, Ren J., 1113
Carnaghi, Beth, 1379
Carncross, Dick, 1165
Carne, Will, 1430
Carne, Willard, Sr., 1100
Carnes, Richard, 1105
Carney, Daniel M., 1356
Carolus, Robert, 151
Carpene, Gregg, 261
Carpenter, Ardis, 120
Carpenter, Bob, 1156
Carpenter, Carolyn C., 1355
Carpenter, David, 1460
Carpenter, Lynn, 252
Carpenter, Rob, 1048
Carpenter, Sally, 1176
Carpenter, Vivian L., 33
Carper, Barbara, 1228
Carr, Robert, 1288, 1289
Carrabba, Joseph A., 954
Carras, Barbara D., 1496
Carras, Steven, 1496
Carrier, Mary Jo, 203
Carroll, George, 644
Carroll, Jennifer L., 1428
Carroll, Joe, 573
Carroll, Kenneth, 1345
Carron, Susan, 1341
Carson, Charles J., 350
Carson, James C., 350
Carson, William E., III, 1355
Carswell, Christopher, 1377
Carter, Arthur, Dr., 1485
Carter, Curt, 1141
Carter, George, 690
Carter, Linda, 1342
Carter, Patricia, 1240
Carter, Stefani A., 1348
Carter-Robinson, Kira, 1094
Carton, John, 1176
Caruso, Mark, 1458
Caruss, Wayne, 1214
Carver, Jim, 1236
Carvey, Gerald, 1108
Cascio, Jennie, 1453
Case, Mary Lou, 882
Case, Thomas, 1228
Case, Ursula, 1086
Caselton, Stephen, Dr., 1145
Casey, Patricia Ann, 1505
Cash, Swintalya "Swin", 1218
Caskey-Kostecki, Amanda, 700
Cassidy, Beverly, 1272, 1360
Cassidy, John, 915
Cassie, James C., Jr., 121
Castelli, Ralph A., Jr., 1017
Castignetti, Albert, 1040
Castillo, Tony, 1463
Castle, Valerie, 1328
Caswell, Susan, 1223
Catallo, Heather, 1453
Caterpillar Foundation, 1402
Catt, Barbara A., 122
Catt, C. Glenn, 122
Cattran, Cynthia L., 1083
Cavanaugh, Camilla A., 560
Cavicchioli, James, 1468
Cayka, Becky, 1268
Caza, Mike, 1446
Cebina, Bob, 1442
Cecil, Jennifer, 208
Cedar, William, 774
Celeski, Margaret, 1265
Cenex Harvest States Cooperatives, 952

CENEX, Inc., 952
Century Bank and Trust, 523, 800
Chadwick, Colette, 138
Chadwick, Donald J., 138
Chaffee, Paul, 1164
Chahbazi, John, 1121
Chamberlain, Calvin M., 124
Chamberlain, Charles E., 1301
Chamberlain, Janet R., 124
Chambers, Bradley T., 1146
Chambers, Caroline, 1171
Chambers, Caroline E., 956
Chambers, Charles M., 1402
Champagne, Joe, 1108
Champagne, Laura, 556
Champassak, Thun, 1111
Champion, Laurel, 1458
Chandler, Cheryl, 556
Chang, Cheng-Yang, 125
Chang, Shirley, 125
Chapaton, Jean, 607
Chapaton, Oscar, 607
Chapla, Robert, 1103
Chapman, Judith, 1216
Chapman, Kelly Boles, 1086
Chapman, Roger, 1392
Chappell, Michael, 1461
Chaprnka, Karen A., 1137
Charfoos, Lawrence S., 126
Charles, Emile, 1564
Charles, Karen, 1388
Charlupski, Allen, 127
Charlupski, Franka, 127
Charlupski, Helen, 127
Charlupski, Lawrence, 127
Charter One Bank, 1470
Chartier, Denny, 191
Chartier, Ruth L., 486
Chase, John M., Jr., 524
Chase, Lavere Leonard, 128
Chavanne, Klaus, 1228
Chavey, Roland, 1375
Chebbani, Ahmad, 1106
Chellgren, Paul W., 484
Cheney, Arta, 656
Chernick, Alan W., 130
Cherry, Elesha, 309
Cherukuri, Rama Rao, 1292
Chesebrough, Pete, 1150
Chessin, Vicki, 1129
Chester, Timothy, 1344
Chevrolet, Joseph, Inc., 386
Chielens, Michael, 1311
Childs, Tim, 1315
Chilman, Bill, 1154
Chinitz, J.A., 1186
Chisholm, Brian, 1269, 1275
Choksi, Kalpanaben Ashokbhai, 834
Chope, Matthew E., 1171
Chowdhury, Malini, 1486
Chowdhury, Subir, 1486
Chraim, Ramzi, 1192
Christ, Chris T., 73
Christensen, Deena, 1185
Christensen, William, 770
Christian, John, 558
Christian, Mary, 1342
Christie, Deb, 1450
Christopher, Carroll J., 132
Christopher, Gail C., 450
Christopher, Kimberly A., 132
Christy, Connie, 1316
Christy, Denise, 1240
Chrysler Motor Co., 597
CHS Inc., 952
Church, Chuck, 1113
Churchill, Judy, 1174
Cipa, Bernard D., 133
Cipa, Bernard J., 133
Cipa, Drew M., 133
Cipa, Eleanor R., 133
Cipa, Lisa, 133
Cipa, Scott, 133
Cischke, Susan M., 986

Citibank, N.A., 365
Citizens Bank, 58, 61, 92, 97, 98, 108, 218, 330, 387, 399, 414, 416, 418, 506, 555, 567, 583, 672, 693, 712, 717, 818, 850, 854, 892
Citizens Bank Wealth Management, N.A., 3, 111, 221, 294, 417, 493, 550, 659, 784
Citizens Bank, N.A., 298, 913
Citizens First Savings Bank, 134
City of Scottville, 1102
Civgin, Don, 935
Clabaugh, Gavin T., 587
Clabuesch, Paul, 489
Claffey, Patricia, 1322
Clappe, Joel, 1099
Claramunt, Morrall M., 1164
Clark, Armand M., 472
Clark, Bob, 1360
Clark, Celeste A., 1013, 1015
Clark, Eric, 1453
Clark, Greg, 1192
Clark, J. Douglas, 1453
Clark, James F., 181
Clark, Jim, 1256
Clark, Peter B., 217
Clark, Randall, 647
Clark, Robert G., 1207
Clark, Sarah, 1216
Clark, Walter W., 138
Clarke, Susan, 1276
Clarke, Tom, 1118
Classen, Peter K., 1047
Clay, James, 1335
Clay, Phillip L., 471
Clay, Robert N., 484
Clay, Sheilah, 1216
Claypool, Mark, 1249
Cleland, Wendy, 1205
Clement, Bill, 1161
Clemmer, John R., 1321
Cleveland-Cliffs Inc., 954
Clevenger, Phyllis, 1139
Cliffs Natural Resources, 954
Cline, Bud, 1128
Cline, Susan, 1178
Close, Bill, 1205
Clouse, Robert, 1124
Clover, Ken, 802
Cloverdale Equipment Co., 940
Clow, Diane, 1131
Clow, Sue, 1097
Clum, Greg, 1322
Clyne, Richie, 1228
CMS Energy Corp., 955
CoachNet, 1228
Coan, Tim, 1291
Cobb, Kevin W., 990
Cobb, Susan, 215
Cobb, William, 1088
Cobert, Beth, 1428
Coburn, James A., 671
Coccia, Peter F., 1355
Cocciolone, John, 1246
Cocco, Aaron, 1484
Cochran, Greg, 1164
Cochran, Raymond, 556
Cochrane Trust, Agnes L., 140
Cochrane, Robert, 1151
Coffelt, Steve, 1165
Coffield, Dan, 1285
Coffield, Daniel, 1107
Coggan, Carol B., 1505
Coggan, Peter, 1505
Cogswell, Susan, 1128
Cohen, Cathy J., 27
Cohn, Andrew B., 1361
Colaianne, Melonie B., 1026, 1196
Colborn, John L., 260
Colburn, David, 509
Colburn, Robert, 509
Cole National Foundation, 1546
Cole, Brenda, 1283
Cole, Charles R., 1074

Cole, Daniel, 700
Cole, David, 13, 968
Cole, Kenneth W., 990
Cole, Lesle E., 1522
Cole, Matt, 1224
Cole, Michael R., 1067
Cole, Patricia, 1574
Cole, Ralph A., 787
Cole, Robert, 1120
Coleman, Amy B., 471
Coleman, Charles, 1407
Coleman, Cheryl, 1216
Coleman, Hurley J., Jr., Rev., 1164
Coleman, Mary Sue, 462
Coleman, Rachelle L., 1487
Coleman, Robert D., 1487
Coleman, Sandra, 1379
Coles, Gloria, 588
Colett, Patricia, 922
Colina, John, 141
Colina, Nancy, 141
Colina-Lee, Lori, 141
Colip, John, 1315
Collard, Ken, 1309
Colley, John, 765
Collier, Tina, 1105
Collins, Gary, 1385
Collins, Jerry, 1108
Collins, John F., 1033
Collins, Laura, 1089
Collison, Kevin, 1129
Colone, Angelo, 1236
Colthurst, Eric, 1157
Colton, Linda, 1167
Coltrane, Michelle, 1229
Coltrane-Carbonell, Michelle, 1229
Colwell, Gale R., 1467
Comai, Barbara L., 565
Comai, William, 767
Combs, Alice G., 597
Combs, Amy, 1311
Combs, Julius V., 597
Comerford, Janet, 199
Comerica Bank, 28, 32, 64, 114, 128,
    152, 169, 206, 251, 364, 393,
    415, 442, 451, 476, 486, 491,
    517, 528, 530, 541, 546, 547,
    568, 570, 580, 597, 605, 679,
    685, 698, 715, 726, 752, 785,
    817, 819, 851, 852, 900, 956,
    1026, 1036, 1103, 1261, 1387,
    1452, 1470
Comerica Bank & Trust, N.A., 237, 457,
    619
Comerica Inc., 956
Commissaris, Nancy L. Thompson, 1393
Community Foundation of Northeast
    Michigan, 631
Compton, Michele, 1227
Comstock, Mishelle, 1105
Comstock, Richard, 1094
Comstock, Todd, 1105
ConAgra Foods, Inc., 959
ConAgra, Inc., 959
Condit, Martha, 870
Condon, Niall, 1309
Conklin, Hugh, 1096
Conklin, Mike, 627
Conln, Peter, Rev., 1247
Connable Trust, Nancy, 145
Connelly, James M., 1280
Connelly, Michael, 1219
Conner, William, 1088
Connolly, Brian, 1371
Conor, Tom, 1502
Conquest, Daniel, 1125
Conrad, Ann, 251
Conrad, Gene, 1211
Conrad, Rita, 1150
Consumer's Power, 1234
Consumers Energy Co., 961
Consumers Power Co., 961
Conway, Greg, 38
Cook Charitable Trust, Donald O., 147

Cook, Bret, 1098
Cook, Bruce L., 147
Cook, Byron, 1130
Cook, Carlton, Dr., 1143
Cook, Charles B., 1149
Cook, Christopher W., 532
Cook, Constance E., 63
Cook, Donald O., 147
Cook, Florence-Etta, 147
Cook, Heather M., 532
Cook, Jacqueline P., 147
Cook, Kevin, 1341
Cook, Laurie, 1397
Cook, Laurie Caszatt, 147
Cook, Les, 1139
Cook, Margaret, 926
Cook, Paul C., 147
Cook, Robert, 1446
Cook, Rose M., 532
Cook, Ryan, 1299
Cook, Sue, 1447
Cook, Thomas B., 147
Cook, William T., 532
Cook-Robinson, Wanda, 1171
Cooley, Christopher L., 1550
Cooley, Ronald W., 134
Coombs, Nancy, 1104
Coon, Jeff A., 149
Coon, Joanne L., 149
Coon, Max A., 149
Cooney, Eileen, 1204
Cooper, Becky, 621
Cooper, Cara, 621
Cooper, Colleen, 1142
Cooper, Eva Aguirre, 1127
Cooper, Gerson, 1253
Cooper, Gloria, 1315
Cooper, Jeff, 621
Cooper, John, 1360
Cooper, Susan E., 224, 1467
Cooper, William A., 1061
Cooper-Boyer, Karen, 968
Copeland, Margot James, 1018
Copley, Allan B., 150
Coppola, Frank, 1294
Corbin, Tonya, 597
Corbit, Dawnanne, 1309
Corbitt, Tonya M., 597
Corcoran, Sean, 1370
Cork, I. Lee, 1165
Cornell, Catherine, 1567
Cornell, Jeff, 1567
Cornell, Jeffery, 1567
Cornille, Christopher, 947
Corte, Chad, 1176
Corullo, Dan, 1293
Cosby, Harriet, 1421
Costin, Eleanor Lynn, 154
Cotman, Ivan Louis, 1461
Cott, Virginia A., 151
Cotter, Sean, 1248
Couf, Herbert, 29
Coughlin, Brian T., 1217
Coulton, Carol, 1240
Courtney, Christopher, 152
Courtney, Frank, 152
Courtney, William F., 152
Cousino, Mark, 1364
Coval, Jeffrey, 1113
Covrett, C. Craig, 304
Cowan, John, 1242
Cowart, Greta I., 291
Cowdin, Christi L., 1076
Cowell, Robert, 1148
Cowger, Frank, 1362
Cowley, Paul, 1165
Cowsette, Alena, 405
Cox, Daniel, Dr., 1180
Cox, Edward L., Jr., 181
Cox, Sam, 1125
Cox, Samuel J., 1107
Coyne, Bill, 1165
Coyne, Brian, 1422
Coyne, Kevin, 1422

Craft, Deborah Ann, 1137
Craft, James, Inc., 1228
Craig, Jeffrey A., 1030
Crandall, Nancy L., 1103
Crane, Anne, 1379
Crane, Ellen, 882
Crane, Ellen E., 1164
Crane, Harold D., Jr., 153
Crane, Loann, 1195
Crane, Malachi, 1436
Crane, Marilyn J., 153
Crane, Marjorie Knight, 462
Crane, Matilda, 454
Crane, Matilda M., 153
Crane, Stacey A., 1274
Crane, Steven, 647
Crane, Steven A., 1394
Crary, JoAnn, 1164
Crawford, Alexander, 1554
Crawford, Denise, 1304
Crawford, Hugh, 1368
Crawford, Jerome E., 1485
Crawford, Kathy, 1368, 1370
Crawford, Lawrence D., 1238
Crawford, Marilyn, 1299
Crawford, Mark, 534
Creal, Paul, 1091
Creason, Kennard, 507
Cresswell, Margaret B., 154
Cresswell, Ronald M., 154
Cresswell, Sheena Livingstone, 154
Creswell, Thomas, 1126
Crews, Gary, 1177
Crews, Gary J., 694
Crissman, Penny, 1108, 1388
Crist, Gary, 1256
Crist, Robert, 1129
Crofton, Richard, 1430
Cromer, Hiawatha, 1489
Cromer, Tamika Bryant, 1206
Cronin, Charles F., 999
Cronin, Elizabeth, 155
Cronin, Mary Virginia, 155
Crook, Lori, 1299
Croom, Grover, 1185
Crosby, Dana A., 691
Crosby, David P., 1233
Crosby, Jonathan, 991
Crosby, Jonathan E., 691
Crosby, Scott, 1450
Cross, Herb, 1440
Crotts, Marcus B., 1402
Crotty, Cindy P., 1018
Crowell, Julie, 1444
Crowley, Jane D., 1219
Crowther, Morgan, 531
Cruickshank, Christopher, 873
Crumbaugh, David, 1129
Crumbaugh, Kathleen, 1548
Crusoe, Lew, 1223
Crutchfield, James N., 462
Cruz, Maria del Carmen, 1207
Cryderman, Valerie, 1135
Cudney, Robert, 1362
Cuevas, Susan F., 1231
Cullen, Matthew P., 392, 1106
Cullis, Paul A., 1347
Cumings, Larry, 1276
Cumming, Michael G., 839
Cumming, R. Malcolm, 215
Cummings Fund, The, 1504
Cummings, Andrew M., 1504
Cummings, Anthony F., 157
Cummings, Caroline, 508
Cummings, Caroline B., 157
Cummings, Dina, 508
Cummings, Gay Gerber, 1504
Cummings, Harrington M., 1504
Cummings, Julie F., 508
Cummings, Julie Fisher, 157
Cummings, Keith L., 157
Cummings, Mimi, 1299
Cummings, Peter D., 157, 508
Cummings, Richard, 1446

Cummings, Samuel M., 1504
Cummins, F. James, 1107
Cummins, Joyce, 1432
Cummins, Linda M., 1030
Cummins, Tom, 1432
Cunningham, Deborah Sue, 171
Cunningham, Debra, 171
Cunningham, Janice, 1459
Cunningham, Louis, 1470
Cunningham, Louis E., 158
Cunningham, Raymond C., Jr., 171
Curcuru, Grace, 1341
Curley, Mike, 1459
Curoe, Megan, 551
Curphey, John M., 422
Curtin, Carolyn, 1513
Curtin, Joe, 1159
Curtis, Carol, 257
Curtis, Deborah T., 802
Curtis, Eileen A., 1087
Curtis, Gaylen, 140
Curtis, Jason, 1227
Curtis, Pat, 1177
Curtiss, Kendra, 1338
Curtiss, Lori, 1437
Cushway, Ritch R., 1326
Cutler, Cecelia B., 159
Cutler, Kenneth B., 159
Cwikiel, J. Wilfred, 1162
Cyrulewski, Jim, 1113
Czarnecki, Richard E., 1337
Czerney, Tim, 1256
Czuprenski, Shelagh K., 232

D&J Properties, 203
D'Amico, Thomas A., 1355
D'Angelo, Larry, 1246
D'Arcy, Stephen R., 392
Daane, David A., 194
Daane, L. Jean, 194
Daavettila, Joseph, 1139
Dab, John M., 1040
Dadacki, Al, 1449
Daetz, Alta, 1103
Dagenais, Jeanine K., 162
Dagenais, Matthew A., 162
Dagenais, Paul R., 162
Dagenais, Robert A., 162
Dagenais, Timothy R., 162
Daher, Nancy, 965
Dahling, William D., Mrs., 811
Dailing, Martha, 1410
DaimlerChrysler Corp., 1470
Dalati, Sarih, 609
Dale, Heather, 1534
Dale, Kent, 1287
Dale, Larry H., 1323
Daley, William M., 1323
Dall'Olmo, Gail, 1128
Dallakian, Stephanie, 231
Dalton Foundation, Dorothy U., 1302
Dalton, Cara, 817
Dalton, Dillon, 817
Dalton, Dorothy U., 163
Dalton, Dustin, 817
Dalton, Lynn, 817
Dalton, Thomas, 817
Daly, Charles U., 427
Daly, Marty, 1468
Dama, Mike, 1145
Damkoehler, Doug, 1440
Dams, Joseph, 1446
Damschroder, Jane T., 1162
Dana Corporation, 963
Dancey, Russell V., 165
Danek, Sharon, 1165
Danicek, Lisa, 885
Daniel, Desmon, 1164
Danielak, Jeanie, 1145
Daniels, Andrea, 1157
Daniels, Nicole J., 1070
Daniels, Penny, 1129
Danielson, Sharon, 1145

Danko, Jennifer D., 859
Dansack, Martin, 1385
Daoud, Helen C., 166
Daoud, Tarik S., 166
Dar, Ami, 1361
Darch, Carolyn, 167
Darch, Dennis, 167
Darland, Tye, 992
Darling, Andrea, 190
Darling, Martha, 1083
DaRos, Michelle, 1461
Darrigan, Barb, 1450
Darrigan, Barbara, 1092
Darrow, Katie, 1174
Darrow, Kurt L., 1022
Dart Foundation, William & Claire, 168
Dart, Claire T., 168
Dart, Justin N., 964
Dart, Kenneth B., 168
Dart, William A., 168
Dasho, Dan, 1448
Dasuqi, Jean, 1373
Dauch Trust, Helen R., 1490
Dauch, Richard E., 1490
Dauch, Sandra J., 1490
Dauterman, Dudley L., 1506
Davenport, Artie, 1231
Davenport, Henry N., 169
Davenport, Maura, 1148
Davenport, Sidney T., 169
David, Amal, 1192
David, Richard G., 1337
David, Rick, 1427
Davidoff, Mark, 1425
Davidson, Ethan, 1046
Davidson, Sheila K., 1038
Davidson-Karimipour, Marla, 1046
Davie, Monica, 1421
Davies, Frederick, 115
Davies, Helen R., 373
Davies, Rick, 1137
Davis, Ann S., 1083
Davis, Barry, 1448
Davis, Daniel, 49
Davis, Gilbert, 269
Davis, Hal, 1445
Davis, Jamie, 1286
Davis, John, 1326
Davis, John L., II, 1421
Davis, John R., 171
Davis, Karen, 1328
Davis, Kate, 1403
Davis, Kevin, 1168
Davis, Kristina, 308
Davis, Lasundres, 1203
Davis, Lyle, II, 54
Davis, M. Margrite, 171
Davis, Marvin, 1240
Davis, Maurice W., 54
Davis, Melissa, 1521
Davis, Randall, Dr., 155
Davis, Randy, Dr., 1149
Davis, Sam L., 1094
Davis, Sandra, 1091
Davis, Ted C., 290
Dawdy, Steve, 1095
Dawley, Gary C., 69
Dawley, Joanne, 1340
Dawson, Dennis, 968
Dawson, Niko, 1405
Day, Claudia, 1235
Day, Diana Gornick, 310
Day, Donna, 1439
Day, Frederick K.W., 876
Day, Joseph C., 173
Day, Lincoln W., 876
Day, Lynn Weyerhaeuser, 876
Day, Peggy, 1330
Day, Stanley R., 876
Day, Stanley R., Jr., 876
Day, Vivian W., 876
De Lange, Leon, 1212
De Oreo, Peter, 1476
De Padula, Gilbert, 1299

De Santis, Deborah, 1233
de Steiger, David, 1108
de Vos, Dan, 1285
De Witt, Carl H., 1287
Deal-Koestner, Janet J., 832
Dean, Deb, 1447
Dean, Robert, 1287
Dean, Roger, 1165
Dean-Jones, Lesley, 897
Dearlove, Thomas J., 1167
Debelak, Richard J., 1118
Deboer, James N., 107
DeBruyn, Barbara L., 1103
DeBruyn, Gwen, 1169
Debs, Michael E., 1016
Decker, John, Jr., 1089
Decker, Nicole L., 689
Decker, Shirley Martin, 1154
Deeb, Susan, 1522
Deegan, Jennifer E., 1162
Deep, Said, 965
Deery, H. Gunner, 1363
DeGennaro, Joseph C., 534
DeGood, Nancy, 1067
DeGraaf, Diana, 1411
DeGraw, David, 1330
DeGraw, Ronald J., 155
Degrow, Dan, 1446
DeHaan, Dennis, 1211
Dehring, Jack E., 1146
Deininger, Peter, 1279
DeJong, Michael J., 454
DeJong, Norman, Dr., 1351
DeJong, Pam, 1081
Dekker, H. David, 1471
DeKoning, Mary Beth, 308
Del Signore, Costantino, 1236
Del Signore, Tino, 1252
Del Sol, Carlos M., 949
Delabbio, Darby, 1463
DeLange, Daniel, 178
Delano, Earl, 1080
Delano, Mignon Sherwood, 179
Delapa, Joseph A., 156
Delapa, Judith A., 156
Delehanty, Mary, 287
Delgado, Jane L., 471
Delley, Sonya, 1374
DelPup, Tom, 1198
Demashkieh, Rasha, 1192
Demashkieh, Walid, 134
Demby, Claude Z., 1522
DeMent, Daniel, 1306
Demers, Paulette, 1166
Demmer, Jack, 1093
DeMoor, Barbara, 170
Dempsey, Sarah, 1445
Den Herder, Susan, 1111
Denenfeld, Stephen, 1303
Denise Trust, Ardis, 484
Dennen, Davida, 1295
Denney, Timothy, 1141
Dennis, Kimberly O., 217
Deno, Mindy, 1330
Denomme, Thomas, 911
DeNooyer, William T., 1211
Denski, Paul, Jr., 1093
DENSO International America, Inc., 968
Denson, Lawrence, 894
Denson, Steve, 1188
Dent, Larry, 1446
Denton, Amy, 1279
Denton, Les, 1376
DePree, Barbara, 738
DePree, Esther, 738
DePree, Kris, 738
DePree, Max O., 738
Depta, Linda, 1308
Derderian, Christine A., 1409
Derenzy, Maureen, 1160
Derfiny, Daniel, 670
Derisley, Arthur B., 118
Derisley, Brian A., 118
Dernomme, Thomas G., 1467

DeRoo, Curtis, 1349
DeRoo, Curtis J., 185
DeRoy, Helen L., 180
Derusha, Steven, 1415
Deschamps, Joan, 1338
Desenberg, Louis A., 1151
DeShano, Florence G., 1491
DeShano, Gary L., 1491
DeShano, Scott G., 1491
Deshetsky, Ralph, 1141
Desmett, Don, 1194
Desrochers, Timothy, 702
Desrosiers, Sherry, 1413
Detore, Diane, 1560
Detroit Edison Co., The, 977
Detroit Pistons Basketball Co., 1046
Detter, Gerald, 183
Detter, Iris F., 183
Detter, Jason, 183
Dettloff, Jocelyn, 215
Detz, Anna, 1438
Deuel, Larry, 1095
Devendorf, David C., 134
Devine, James P., Jr., 644
DeVine, Kathy, 1256
Devivo, Carmine, 1374
DeVlieg Machine Co., 185
DeVlieg, Charles B., 185
DeVlieg, Charles R., 185
DeVlieg, Julia C., 185
DeVlieg, Kathryn S., 185
DeVos Foundation, Richard and Helen,
The, 186
DeVos, Betsy, 187
DeVos, Daniel, 186
DeVos, Daniel G., 186
DeVos, Dick, 187, 1435
DeVos, Douglas, 188
DeVos, Elisabeth, 187
DeVos, Helen J., 189
DeVos, Maria, 188
DeVos, Pamella, 186
DeVos, Richard M., 189
DeVos, Richard M., Jr., 187
deVries, Ben, 383
deVries, Daane, 383
DeVries, Matt, 1484
DeVries, Mike, 143
DeVries, Robert A., 1086
Dewaelsche, Eva Garza, 1359
Dewey, Eric, 1304, 1309
Dewey, Mike, 1087, 1428
deWindt, Del, 1217
Dewitt Community Church, 1563
DeWolf, John, 1447
Dewyer, Rod, 129
DeWys-VanHecke, Amy, 1344
DeYoung, David, 1376
DeYoung, Janet, 1111
DeYoung, Kris, 1456
DeYoung, Lee, 1351
Diaz, Mariano, 1323
Dibble, Suzanne, 1171
DiBianco, Marti, 236
DiCarlo, Sally Stegeman, 1410
Dice, James R., 116
Dick, Frank, 1143, 1506
Dickerson, Rosemary, 1352
Dickinson, David, 1353
Dickinson, Mary, 1353
Dickinson, Timothy, 1184
Diegel, Sherri, 1177
Diehl, Lisa, 1535
Dielman, Linda, 1338
Diephouse, Bruce, 192
Diephouse, Rika, 192
Dietel, William M., 366
Dieterle, David A., 1339
Dietle, Diana, 1369
Dietrich, G. Philip, 539
Dietsch, Janet L., 512
Dietz, Eric, 1113
Dietz, Michael S., 1217
DiFilippi, Joe, 1323

DiFranco, Jack, 1108
Diggs, Shauna Ryder, 1208
Diles, Barbara, 1205
Dillard-Parker, Trayce, 1382
Dilley, Cele, 1113
Dillman, Dave, 541
Dillman, Joan, 541
Dillon, Carrie A., 1352
Dillon, Charles T., Dr., 1147
Dillon, David B., 1021
Dillon, Gadis J., 1337
Dillon, Kenneth A., 745, 746
Dillon, Pat, 1131
Dilts, Bill, 1433
Dilts, Theresa, 1223
Dimond, Paul R., 1106
Dingeldey, Nancy L., 1370
Dingell, Deborah I., 990, 1106, 1350
Dingens, Adam, 1168
Dinges, Victoria A., 935
Dinning, Doug, 1173
DiPonio, Carolyn, 1156
DiPonio, Margaret E., 193
Dipp, Joanne, 1417
DiSilvestro, Anthony P., 949
Diskin, Cynthia R., 89
Disselkoen, Terri J., 153
Dissinger, Ron, 1013
Distel, Terry, 1272
Divine Child High School Scholarship
Fund, 1541
Divins, Edwina, 1137
Divvela, J. Rao, Dr., 1292
Dixon, Christopher, 1242
Dixon, Ruth M., 44
Dixon, William R., 44
Doan Family Foundation, The, 196
Doan, Alexandra A.A., 196
Doan, Anna Junia, 195, 196
Doan, Deana, 1397
Doan, Herbert D., 195
Doan, Jeffrey, 195
Doan, Michael, 195
Doan, Ruth Alden, 202
Dobbins, Andrew, 1183
Dobbins, Ronald R., 597
Dobbins, Sandra J., 1149
Dobias, Mark, 1080
Dobson, Steve, 1458
Docherty, Susan E., 990
Dodd, Jeanne D., 975
Dodd, Lindsey, 1335
Dodge, Scott, 886
Doe, Larry, 1180
Doebler, Wallace, 1173
Doelle, Kurt, 965
Doerfler, Ann H., 906
Doherty, David, 1255
Doherty, Jim, 1098
Dolan, Jan, 1253
Dolinski, Richard, 1152
Doll, Robert, 556
Dombrowski, David, 1217
Domenick-Muscat, Margaret, 1522
Domin, Donald, 1242
Domitrovich, Gerald, 1372
Domzalski, Bruno F., 855
Domzalski, Henry M., 1349
Donaghy, Carole, 1152
Donaldson, Darlene, 1420
Donaldson, Kenneth W., 1206
Donlin, Peter J., 198
Donnellon, Tim, 1446
Donnelly, John, Jr., 1111
Donnini, Lisa, Dr., 1339
Donovan, David J., 1094
Donovan, Timothy R., 1036
Dooge, Carol A., 199
Dooge, Lawrence E., Jr., 199
Dooge, Lawrence, Jr., 199
Dooley, Jay F., 1368
Doorn, Larry, 1140
Doornhaag, Amy, 1428
Doppstadt, Eric, 260

Doran, Maureen K., 200
Doran, Wayne S., 200
Dorf, Hal, 1313
Dorfman, Carolyn, 201
Dorfman, Gayle, 201
Dorfman, Henry, 201
Dorfman, Joel, 201
Dorfman, Mala, 201
Dorman, Robin, 1146
Dorr, Leo W., 1286
Dossman, Curley M., Jr., 992
Dost, Sara, 1177
Dotson, Greg D., 565
Dotson, Norma Y., Hon., 597
Dotson, Sonja, 541
Dotson, Sonja F., 1086
Dotson, Tyler, 1169
Dotterweich, Maria Miceli, 852
Doud, Bob, 1304
Doud, Margaret M., 1146
Doud, Robert S., 1194
Douglas, Craig C., 1164
Douglas, Matthew, Dr., 1299
Douglas, Tiffany S., 1217
Douglas, Walter E., 1280
Douma, Mary M., 1248
Dow Chemical Co., The, 973
Dow Corning Corp., 975
Dow, Grace A., 202
Dow, Michael Lloyd, 202, 1496
Dow, Peter A., 352
Dow, Vada B., 1496
Dowler, David, 870
Dowler, Marie, 870
Downer, Margaret, 49
Downey, Ellen, 1409
Downing, Ed, 1391
Downing, Merlyn H., 1143
Doyle & Ogden, Inc., 203
Doyle, Chris, 1408
Doyle, Eileen M., 203
Doyle, James R., 613
Doyle, Jean B., 203
Doyle, John B., 203
Doyle, Maureen J., 203
Doyle, Michael K., 203
Doyle, Paul, 1127
Doyle, Sarah Ann, 203
Doyle, Thomas B., 203
Doyle, Timothy P., 203
Doyle, William G., 203
Drabik, Kathy, 1263
Drain, Scott, 461
Drake, Amy, 244
Drake, John, 1140
Drapalski, Nancy, 1388
Draves, Mary, 1152
Drazick, Herman, 204
Drazick, Sheila, 204
Drean, Tom, 594
Drecktrah, H. Gene, 1228
Drenth, Keith, 1448
Drenth, Kenneth, Dr., 1112
Dresner, Milton H., 205
Dresser, Mary, 1114, 1175, 1178
Drew, Gary, 207, 1128
Drew, Sandra, 207
Drewes, Susan K., 471
Drewry, Paul, Dr., 1102
Dreyer, Susan, 1165
Drick, Jay, 1370
Driggers, John S., 208
Driggers, Joy M., 208
Driggers, Nathan B., 208
Droste, Patrick, Dr., 1543
Drumm, Shannon Day, 173
Drushel, Bill, 558
Druzinski, Neil, 1247
Dryburgh, Harriet, 443
DTE Energy, 1234
DTE Energy Ventures, Inc., 977
DuBay, Jim, 1442
Dubiel, Mandy, 1078
Dubow, Craig A., 988

Dubravec, Vincent A., 647
Dubs, Cindie, 694
Duchene, Donald L., Sr., 210
Duchene, Doris, 210
Dudas, David, 165, 444
Dudas, Susan, 165, 444
Dudek, Gregory, 466
Dudiak, Rosann, 1048
Dudley, Arthur, 1346
Dudley, Grenae, 1171, 1206
Dudley, Kenneth, 647
Duerksen, Rick, 761
Duffy, Marie, 211
Dufner, Richard F., 400
Dugan, Candace, 1463
Dugan, Candance, 1299
Dugan, Darlene, 1293
Duhamel, Peter A., 1349
Duke, Lisa, 594
Dulin, Frank, 1379
Dull, David L., 1291
Dunbar, Mary L., 1048
Dunbar, Wendell, 816
Duncan, Barbara, 212
Duncan, Elonzo, 1185
Duncan, Greg, 1401
Duncan, Richard, 212
Dunham, Charles D., 874
Dunham, Richard, 1168
Dunkerley, Jay, 1364
Dunklow, Shirley, 1366
Dunlap, James, 1463
Dunlap, Kathy, 1285
Dunlap, Peter, 1119
Dunn, David H., 787
Dunn, Greg, 1424
Dunn, John, 1309
Dunn, Katie, 1165
Dunn, Michael, 949
Dunning, Margaret, 213, 790
Dunning, Richard, 1124
Dunnings, Stuart J., Jr., 214
Dunnings, Susan, 214
Dupke, Edward J., 1337
Dupuis, Steven, 1363
Duquette, Ron, 1163
Durack, Daniel G., 1093
Durand, Carolyn Thrune, 787
Durant, Susan, 922
Durik, Michael L., 1016, 1310
Duszynski, Tom, 1113
Dutcher, Christi, 847
Dutta, Sanjay, 1275
Dworak, Cathy A., 997
Dworkin, Aaron P., 1410
Dwyer, Paul, 1335
Dwyer, Scott, 42
Dwyer, Scott E., 1301
Dygert, G. Paul, 487
Dygert, Mary Larzelere, 487
Dykema, Rosemary, 1526
Dykema, Sara E., 773
Dykema, Timothy J., 773
Dykes, Marie Draper, 597
Dykstra, Barb, 1417
Dykstra, Diane, 1450
Dykstra, Kurt, 1463
Dykstra, Randall, 1299
Dzierwa, Stan, 1398
Dzierzawski, Peggy A., 1337, 1339
Dziubinski, Gene, 1116, 1118
Dziurman, Kathy, 1108

Eagan, Rick, 1228
Eagleson, Leatrice W., 1359
Earhart, Harry Boyd, 217
Earl, Anthony S., 427
Earl, Greg, 1322
Earl, Kathleen, 1411
Earley, Anthony F., 392
Earley, Anthony F., Jr., 1106, 1280, 1427
Earley, Pete, 1233

Eason, Andrew, 1340
Eason, Drew, 1341
East, Steven A., 1211
Easter, Eve, 497
Easterling, Gary, 1445
Easton, Ray A., 314
Eaton, Donald S., 703
Eberhard, Lynn, 240
Eberhart, Mike, 1162
Eberlein, Timothy, 1355
Ebert, Julie, 1107
Ebert, Michael J., 290
Eberts, Randall W., 832, 1451
Eberts, Randall W., Dr., 1302
Eboh, Juliette Okotie, 1240
Echelbarger, Dennis M., 1337
Ecke, Keith H., 1074
Eckert, Carl, 352
Eckert, Kathryn, 16
Eckhoff, Mark, 1443
Eddy, Arthur D., 218
Edelman, Linda, 1228
Edge, Stephen B., 1355
Edmark, Kris, 1148
Edmark, Shannon, 1136
Edmundson, Diane, 323
Edvenson, Roger, 647
Edwards, Esther G., 309
Edwards, Gloria, 1458
Edwards, Jim, 1456
Edwards, Katherine, 1406
Edwards, Margaret, 1406
Egan, Sean M., 1277
Egbert, Peter, 1291
Eggers, Brian, 1413
Egly, Robert P., Jr., 664
Egner, David O., 392
Ehrman, Daniel S., 988
Eidson, Dennis, 1277
Eidsvold, Jim, 1228
Eifert, Tom, 1380
Eilbling, Stephen, 1363
Einstein, Allen, 1374
Eischens, Curt, 952
Eisele, Lisa, 358
Eisenman, Gary R., 1233
Eisenmann, Edith L., 1280
Eisenreich, Bobbi Jo, 997
Eisler, Patsy, 1150
Ekberg, Gregg O., 1402
Eklund, Stephen A., 1238
Eklund, Wes, 1103
Elam, Carol, 1406
Elder, Irma B., 1106
Elderkin, Ed, 1212
Eldridge, Loyal A., III, 145
Eldridge, Van, 1450
Electrical Industry Educational Fund, 765
Eley, Hillary, 1091
Elis, Bill, 1248
Elkins, Connie, 1117
Elkins, Scott, 656
Elkins, Timothy, 1117
Ellafrits, Richard, 1130
Elliott, Beth, 1087
Elliott, Chad K., 220
Elliott, Cheryl W., 1083
Elliott, Drew, 1307
Elliott, Janice C., 299
Elliott, Nancy N., 220
Elliott, R. Hugh, 220
Ellis, David, 1278
Ellis, James, 841
Ellis, Paula, 462
Ellis, Phil, 1128
Ellis, Robert E., 1302
Ellis, Sidney, 1194
Elloitt, Walter, Jr., 1346
Ellsworth, Peter H., 1348
Ellyn, Lynne, 977
Elmer, Steve, 1358
Elsesser, Edward R., 219
Elsesser, Joseph, 219
Elsworth, James M., 504

Elwood, Nancy A., 1094
Elwood, Suie, 1328
Embry, Cynthia V., 859
Emde, Robert C., 1467
Emerson Charitable Trust, 1402
Emig Trust A, John, 774
Emig Trust B, John, 774
Emig, Gerald M., 774
Emig, Larry, 1159
Emley, Margaret, 1088
Emmert, Mark, 1331
Emmons, Al, 1418
Emory, Howard O., 683
Empire Iron Mining Partnership, 954
Enderby, Lucinda, 1139
Enders, Elizabeth G., 303
Enduri, Kalpana, Mrs., 1292
Engebretson, Jack R., Hon., 1144
Engel, Kristine, 640
Engelhart, John, 1099
Engle, Edward J., Jr., 978
Engle, Edward, II, 978
Engle, Jennifer, 978
English, Brian, 673
English, Carl L., 937
Engram, Donald, 1287
Engstrom, Paul F., 1355
Enholm, David, 1043
Ennis, Dolores, 588
Ennis, Robert, 1250
Ennis, Robert E., III, 1485
Eno, Paul, 601
Enright Irrevocable Trust, Kenneth, 137
Enright, Kenneth, 137
Enright, Tim, 137
Enriquez, Sonny, 1291
Epner, Patrice, 190
Eppinger, Frederick H., 999
Epstein, Jan, 935
Epstein, Stephen H., 1337
Erb, Barbara M., 224
Erb, Debbie D., 224
Erb, Fred A., 224
Erb, John M., 224, 1106
Erb, Wendy Elaine, 224
Erdman, Vickie, 345
Erevelles, Winston F., 1402
Erichsen, Janice, 289
Erickson, Annmarie, 1379
Erickson, Mark, 1397
Erickson, Peggy, 1100
Erlich, Joseph E., 225
Erlich, Linda, 225
Erskine Trust, R.C., 226
Erskine, Christine, 501
Ervin, J.F., 227
Ervin, Tim, 1147
Erxleben, Eden C., 1162
Esch, Rosemary, 760
Eschbach, Dietmar, 228
Eschbach, Lisa, 228
Eschbach, Monica, 228
Eschbach, Reinhard, 228
Eschbach, Roland, 228
Eschbach, Ruth, 228
Eshleman, Jon W., 507
Esser, Pete, 1376
Essex, Amy E., 1499
Estes, Deonna F., 1086
Etheridge, Lynn, 1080
Etienne, Christine, 1088
Etkin, Douglas, 1425
Ettinger, David S., 1355
Etzinga, Jim, 1484
Eull, Terry, 1315
Evans, Bob, 1417
Evans, Eva, 1344
Evans, James, 1125
Evans, Joseph, 1139
Evans, Michael J., 900
Eveland, Thomas S., Hon., 1119
Evenson, Robert, Jr., 229
Everard, Jolene, 1224
Everest, Sharon S., 763

Everitt, Zachary, 1433
Eversole, Dan, 1154
Eves, David, 1077
Ewald, Beth, 1224
Ewald, Cliff, 232
Ewald, Henry T., 232
Ewald, Holly S., 232
Ewald, Judy, 232
Ewald-Kratzet, Carolyn, 232
Ewend, Peter, 882
Ewing, Stephen E., 755, 977
Ewing, Tom, 1448
Ewing, Tracey L., 1171
Eyre, Glenn, 1462
Eyster, George E., 233
Eyster, Janet Tolson, 233
Ezelle, Bob, 1305

Faas, Michael, 1335
Fabel-Ryder, Ella, 1338
Fabiano, James, II, 1164
Fabri-Kal Corp., 980
Facione, Roger, 1082
Fackler, Steven W., 291
Fadim, Melissa Sage, 708
Fahner, James, 1328
Faigle, Ida M., 234
Fairbanks, Marri, 173
Fakhouri, Haifa, 1208
Falcone, Colleen M., 777
Falcone, Joseph, 777
Falconer, Daniel P., 520
Falconer, Erik J., 520
Falconer, Meridith I., 520
Falk, Daniel C., 235
Falk, Matthew, 235
Falk, Michael, 235
Falk, Susan G., 235
Falkenstein, Karin, 1151
Fallat, Dale W., 21
Fallon, Brian, 1040
Falls, Donald L., 236
Fantazian, Ilene, 231
Fantazian, Vahram, 231
Farah, Christine, 1328
Farah, Troy, 1107
Faraj, Ramzi, 1222
Farber, Audrey, 239
Farber, William, 239
Farhat, Renee T., 1356
Farias, Pablo J., 260
Faris, Hanna, 1189
Farley, James D., 1106
Farmers Union Central Exchange, Inc., 952
Farrell, Chris, 497
Farrier, Shirley, 1272
Farver, Constance, 241
Farver, Herbert, 241
Farver, Michael, 241
Farver, Orville W., 241
Farver, Patrick, 241
Fatal, Peter, 1033
Faulkner, Thomas A., 1393
Faunce, Jennifer, 1279
Fausone, James, 1093
Fawaz, Ned, 1404
Fawcett, Jack, 270
Fayz, Allie, 243
Fayz, Wanda, 243
Fearon, Gordon, 1276
Federal Screw Works, 981
Fedewa, C. Scott, 245
Fedewa, Jan, 1344
Fedewa, Jonathan, 245
Fedewa, Philip, 245
FedEx Custom Critical Passport Transport, 1228
Fedorov, Natalya, 246
Fedorov, Sergei, 246
Fedorov, Victor, 246
Feeney, James L., 789
Feenstra, Roger, 1081

Fegley, Susan, 236
Fehsenfeld, Cecile C., 1127
Fehsenfeld, Frank, 247
Fehsenfeld, John A., 247
Fehsenfeld, Thomas V., 247
Fehsenfeld, Virginia V., 247
Fehsenfeld, William, 247
Feld, Ed, 1434
Feldman, Robert, 1315
Feldpausch, Jim, 1256
Fell, Doris M., 556
Fell, Lloyd C., 348
Feller, Nancy P., 260
Fellows, Elizabeth, 686
Felts, Thomas J., Hon., 258
Fenn, Nancy, 1548
Fennell, Rebekah, 1303
Fenton, Rick, 1288
Fenton, Sharon, 1433
Ferch, Thomas, 1418
Fergemann, Ann, 1138
Ferguson, Joel I., 1208
Ferguson, Judy, 1165
Ferguson, Robert, 990
Fernandez, Mike, 1160
Ferns, Pauline, 1135
Ferrando, Richard, 37
Ferrantino, Janette, 1328
Ferriby, Robin D., 1106
Ferries, Alexander, 248
Ferries, Donna, 248
Ferries, Jason, 248
Ferries, John C., 248
Ferries, Karen, 248
Ferris, Deborah, 1379
Ferris, Mary E., 901
Ferris, Ralph R., 901
Ferris, Vince, 1119
Ferris, Vincent J., 1094
Ferron, Lynn, 1455
Fershtman, Julie I., 1348
Fesenmyer, Bob, 963
Fessenden, Scott, 1040
Fest, Marc, 462
Festa, John, 775
Fetcher Co., M.S., 86
Fett, Kim, 1242
Fetzer Revocable Trust, John E., 249
Fetzer, Bruce, 249
Feuer, Diana M., 250
Feuer, Seymour S., 250
Fibre Converters, Inc., 982
Fiedler, Greg, 1456
Field, Jordan, 1288
Fielder-Gibson, Tina, 1185
Fields, Randolph, 242
Fifelski, Nancy, 1080
Fifth Third Bank, 2, 10, 62, 116, 273, 306, 311, 322, 370, 380, 390, 396, 402, 453, 463, 579, 585, 592, 595, 621, 677, 700, 750, 770, 984, 1064, 1103
Figurski, Denise, 1408
Fillion, Steve, 598
Fillmore, Ann, 1441
Fillmore, Robert, Bro., 1209
Filmer Estate Trust, Elizabeth, 251
Finch, Nancy, 257
Fink, Elise M., 252
Fink, George R., 252
Fink, John M., 252
Fink, Kim, 1508
Fink, Neil, 1508
Finkbeiner, Joseph, 1202
Finkbeiner, Marilyn, 1417
Finkelstein, Carol, 1197
Finkelstein, Mark, 1295
Finkelstein, Morton M., 253
Finley, Harold, 1315
Finneran, John G., 1323
Finnerty, Tom, 1108
Finney, Michael, 1083
Firos, Jim, 1471

First Allmerica Financial Life Insurance Co., 999
First Federal of Northern Michigan Bancorp, Inc., 1499
First National Bank & Trust Co., 821
First National Bank of Howell, 75
Fischer, Chari, 1112
Fischer, David T., 1106
Fischer, Justin, 1368
Fischer, Ken, 1195, 1410
Fischer, Tim, 996
Fish, Myles D., Rev., 1291
Fisher Trust, Mary Elizabeth, 99
Fisher, Andrea L., 1164
Fisher, Charles, 1438
Fisher, Charles T., III, 99
Fisher, Chris, 244
Fisher, Deb, 1145, 1161
Fisher, Gerald A., 1369
Fisher, Jeffrey E., 244
Fisher, Jen L., 1485
Fisher, Marjorie S., 157
Fisher, Mark, 509
Fisher, Michael J., Jr., 40
Fisher, Nancy Boynton, 244
Fisher, Phillip, 1425
Fisher, Phillip W., 1106
Fisher, Robert, 1140, 1346
Fisher, Sarah W., 99
Fisher, Walter B., 99
Fisk, Shannon, 727
Fisk, Stephen G., 727
Fitch, Paddy, 1430
Fitzgibbon, Jane, 256
Fitzpatrick, Sue, 1104
Fitzsimons, Candace, 1088
FitzSimons, Michael J., 1162
Fitzwater, Teresa, 1393
Flachs, Charles, 1513
Flaherty, Michael, 1504
Flaherty, Pamela P., 1323
Flannery, Debra J., 1118
Flechsig, Randolph, 1285
Fleet, Corey van, 1438
Flegenheimer, Mark S., 1164
Fleischer, Henry, 118
Fleischman, Jeffrey, 1508
Fleming, Dorann, 1169
Flessland, Gerald, 1334
Fletcher, Don C., 1110
Flexfab Horizons International, 1550
Flick, Gregory, 1392
Fliehman, Dennis W., 1094
Flint, Doug, 1411
Flood-Dziubinski, Susan, 1116
Flook, Dave, 1256
Flora, Jon, 1453
Flores-New, Fernando, 290
Florian, Nick, 1160
Florida, Lester, 1214
Flory, Clyde, 1197
Fluharty, Marlene J., 16
Fluker, Renee, 1465
Flynn, Jacqueline, 1168
Fochtman, Laura, 1350
Focker, Thomas V., Dr., 1326
Foellinger, Esther A., 258
Foellinger, Helene R., 258
Fogel, Dan, 1311
Fojtasek, Travis, 1137
Foley, Jessica, 1279
Foley, Susan, 1278
Folk, Richard, 1132
Fong, Diane M., 1033
Forbes, Patricia, 1090
Ford Motor Co., 597, 986, 1470
Ford Motor Company Fund, 1228, 1402
Ford Motor Credit Co., 986
Ford, Adelaide, 826
Ford, Alfred B., 986
Ford, Ann M., 863
Ford, Benson, 263
Ford, Benson, Jr., 263
Ford, Carey, 1379

Ford, Cynthia N., 542
Ford, Edsel, 260
Ford, Edsel B., II, 265, 755
Ford, Eleanor C., 262
Ford, Geraldine C., 261
Ford, Helen, 1346
Ford, Henry, 260
Ford, Jenice Mitchell, 1410
Ford, Joane, 1397
Ford, John G., 1257
Ford, Jr., William C., 266
Ford, Lisa V., 262
Ford, Martha F., 254, 264
Ford, Martha Firestone, 264
Ford, Michael, 1458
Ford, Richard, 617
Ford, William C., Jr., 266
Ford, William Clay, 264, 1243
Ford, William Clay, Jr., 262, 1243
Fore, Kathy, 1350
Foren Irrevocable Trust, Frazier C., 267
Foren, Belinda, 267
Foren, Donald, 267
Forgrave, Robert, 1459
Forman, Jeffrey D., 279
Forquer, Ward, 558
Forrester, Al, 1502
Forry, Ed, 1216
Forster, Kathy, 922
Forsyth, Dan, 1278
Forte, Linda, 1350
Forte, Linda D., 956
Fortinberry, Chuck, 1227
Fortino, Charles, 513, 1129
Fortino, Chuck, 1548
Fortino, Trudy, 1374
Forzley, Gregory J., 1349
Fosdick, Scott E., 1258
Foss, John H., 1022
Foss, Mark William, 1231
Foster, Chesley, 1129
Foster, Clara J., 269
Foster, David, 1547
Foster, Eric, 1421
Foster, Gregory, 1382
Foster, Henry W., 597
Foster, Jennifer, 268
Foster, John, 268
Foster, John M., 410
Foster, Michele, 268
Foster, Richard, 268
Foster, Tom, 268
Foster, Virginia, 268
Foster-Cummins, Marjorie, 268
Founders Bank and Trust, 38
Fountain, W. Frank, 392, 1106
Four Winds Casino Resort, 1048
Fournier, Gerald, 1362
Fouts, Kimberly A., 685
Fouts, Kimberly Riley, 1253
Fowler, Matt, 833
Fowler, Verna, Dr., 1188
Fox, David, 589
Fox, Doug, 1241
Fox, George, 1374
Foxworth, Edward, III, 1409
Foy, Douglas J., 40
Fradkin, Andy, 965
Fragnoli, Stephen, 646
Fraher, David J., 1195
Fraley, Bernam G., 139
Fralick, Stephen, 1428
France, Donald R., 388, 492
France, Loretta, 1240
Francoeur, Eli, 1143
Frank Rewold and Son, Inc., 1053
Frank, Alice, 293
Frank, Barbara K., 383
Frank, Cathy, 1453
Frank, Gloria, 1379
Franke, Marsha L., 271
Franke, Thomas F., 271, 1149
Frankel, Jean, 1260
Frankel, Lora, 1456

Frankel, Maxine, 1501
Frankel, Stanley D., 1260
Frankel, Stuart, 1501
Franklin, James, 1346
Franks, David, 1411
Franks, Michael, 1406
Frantz, Jan, 1434
Fraser, Don, 1391
Fraser, Douglas A., 1387
Frauenthal, Harold, 1103
Frawley, Mike, 1431
Frayer, Robert, 1225
Frazier, Anne M., 272
Frazier, Janice G., 1356
Frazier, Julia Q., 272
Frazier, Lincoln B., Jr., 272
Frazier, Lorenzer, 1240
Frazier, Peter W., 272
Frederick, Barbara, 1183
Frederick, LaMar, 1089
Frederick, Paul, 1230
Fredericks, James, 774
Frederickson, Mark A., 647
Freeman, Angela, 1167
Freeman, Emery, 269
Freeman, Lois Spector, 769
Freeman, Tracy, 1248
Freiwald, Gregory M., 973
French, Bonnie, 1234
French, Hadley Mack, 1467
French, Jerry, 1315
French, Jerry E., 397
Frenkel, Cindy P., 657
Frenkel, Dale P., 657
Frenkel, Marvin A., 657
Frenkel, Ronald E.P., 657
Frescoln, Tina, 1088
Freshwater, Paul, 1139
Freude, Michael, 1114
Freuhauf, Ruth, 1163
Freund, Judith, 283
Frey, David G., 276, 1257
Frey, Edward J., Jr., 276
Frey, Edward J., Sr., 276
Frey, Frances T., 276
Frey, John M., 276
Frey, Mary Caroline, 275
Frey, Mary Caroline "Twink", 276
Frick, Heather, 1088
Fridsma, Charles, 1275
Fried, William C., 1144
Friedman, James, Rev., 1247
Frieling, Gerald H., Jr., 397
Frigo, Gary, 1040
Frisbie, Chuck, 1411
Frissora, Mark P., 1036
Fritel, Steve, 952
Fritz, Edward T., 223
Froats-Sheperd, Janet, 1366
Froelich, Dianne, 557
Froh, Richard D., 758
Froh, Tracy N., 758
Froning, Susan Katz, 450
Fronizer, Greg, 1246
Fross, Roger R., 427
Frost, Sharon, 1455
Fruehauf, Angela, 277
Fruehauf, Harvey C., Jr., 277
Fruehauf, Martha S., 277
Fruehauf, Susanne M., 277
Fruman, Dorothy, 278
Fruman, Lee, 278
Fry, Mary, 1163
Fryer, Cheryl, 1502
Fulcher, Dan, 1117
Fuller, John, 1266
Fuller, Marty, 1166
Fulton, Barbara J., 1414
Fulton, Pam, Rev., 1166
Fung Foundation, The, 915
Funk, Bob, 1446
Furgason, David, 1309
Furman, John, 1371

Gabier, Russell L., 299
Gabrian, Dennis, 36
Gabriel, Ken, 1246
Gabriel, Nicholas M., 260
Gabrys, Richard M., 1022
Gaff, Tom P., 990
Gaffner, Kathy, 475
Gaffney, Kevin J., 1524
Gage, Kent, 1440
Gagnon, Joe, 1409
Gaier, Julie, 1283
Gaines, Carne L.P. Gray, 1209
Galac, Sandra W., 1310
Galeana, Carl, 1241
Galesburg-Augusta United Way, 1502
Galia, Gary C., 980
Galiette, Cynthia F., 241
Gallagher, Donald J., 954
Gallagher, John J., 565
Gallagher, Kurt, 1339
Gallant, Thomas, 281
Gallegos, Merlinda, 1336
Gamache, Ed, 1165
Gambka, Paul J., 36
Gamble, James N., 34
Ganakas, Gail, 868
Ganapini, Kenneth, Dr., 1464
Gannett Co., Inc., 988
Gano, Charles H., 1162
Gansen, Cindy, 1121
Ganton, Joyce, 1503
Ganton, Kevin J., 1503
Ganton, Lloyd G., 1503
Ganton, Scott, 1503
Ganton, Troy L., 1503
Ganz, Sandy, 1376
Garapati, Bhavani P., 432
Garay, James, 1086
Garbarini, Sue, 497
Garber, Arnold P., 498
Garber, Richard J., 1164
Garber, Ruth, 283
Garber, Stanley, 283
Garbrecht, Bonnie, 1256
Garcia, Bo, 1094
Garcia, Cathy G., 1036
Garcia, Dick, 1128
Garcia, Joseph, 1346
Garcia, Juliet V., 260
Garcia, Luis E., 1181
Garcia, Marcy, 1431
Garcia, Raul, 1431
Garcia, Rick R., 1446
Gardey, Kim M., 359
Gardner, Colin, IV, 285
Gardner, Donald, 284
Gardner, Frederick C., 1164
Gardner, Marilyn C., 285
Gardner, Patricia, 69
Gardner, Stephen V., 285
Garemk, Debra L., 89
Garfield, Joan, 1120
Gargaro, Eugene A., Jr., 1026
Garin, Susan H., 635
Garner, Terry, 1506
Garretson, Bob, 1463
Garrett, Roger, 1379
Garrison, Jeff, 1550
Garrow, Gerald, 593
Garske, John, 1293
Gascho, Dwight, 489
Gase, Brian, 161
Gase, Gerald R., 211
Gast, David, Dr., 1160
Gast, Kathleen, 1553
Gatchel, Robert, 1385
Gates, John "Bruce", 1113
Gates, Tony, 1207
Gatton, Jeff, 1176
Gaudreau, Sandy, 1449
Gaunt, Michael, 336
Gauthier, Anthony P., Jr., 1301
Gauvin, Rod, 1458
Gay, Sue, 1433

Gaynor, Sylvin J., 181
Geddes, John, 1072
Gehringer, Dennis, 1322
Geier, Sheila P., 653
Geiger, Earl, 1447
Geiger, Mary Ellen, 288
Gelbaugh, Bruce, 1305
Gelman, Bobbie, 1404
Gem Foundation, 1470
Gemignani, Lois, 1232
Genco, Christopher, 1033
Gendernalik, Patricia L., 1082
General Motors, 1470
General Motors Corp., 597, 910, 990
General Motors Foundation, 1402
Generations Management LLC, 991
Gensel, Janice, 1107, 1121
Gensterblum, Sheri, 1384
George, Henry E., 289
George, Jeanne, 1132
George, Victor, 1437
Georgia-Pacific Corp., 992
Georvassilis, Chris, 1339
Gerace, Frank, 292
Gerard, Alice, 1428
Gerber, Terry, 1159
Gerber, William K., 1310
Gerberding, Brian K., 291
Gerberding, Joan W., 291
Gerberding, Joan W. Fackler, 291
Gerberding, Kent E., 291
Gerberding, Miles, 1438
Gerberding, Miles C., 291
Gerend, Michael, 1023
Gergely, Michael, 249
Gergely, Michael C., 1517
Gerrie, Don, 1448
Gerrity, Dan, 1311
Gersch, Nicole V., 956
Gershenson, Bruce, 279
Gerson, Byron, 1046
Gerson, Dorothy, 1046
Gerson, Ralph J., 1046
Gerstacker, Carl A., 292
Gerstacker, Eda U., 292
Gerstacker, Lisa J., 292, 628
Gerstell Trust, Richard, 823
Gerten, Richard, Pastor, 1149
Gertz, H. F., 1022
Gertz, Herman F., 293
Gertz, Irene, 293
Gertz, Marjorie, 293
Gervasio, Julia, 1097
Gerych, Jon, 1120
Geske, Janine P., Hon., 1517
Gettelfinger, Ron, 1387
Ghesquiere, Charles J., 1467
Ghosn, Rita, 1040
Giannunzio, Kevin, 1330
Gibb, Russ, 965
Gibbons, Janet, 1213
Gibbs Trust, Ruby, 294
Gibbs, Dave, 1102
Gibson, JoAnn, 295
Gibson, Kirk, 295
Giddens, Diane, 1439
Giguere, Vicky, 1100
Giles, Lynda, Dr., 1296
Gill, Lee, 1406
Gillard, Cynthia S., 1571
Gillard, Richard C., 608
Gillen, Arlene, 1163
Gillen, Rex, 1163
Gillenwater, Mary N., 297
Gilles, Herbert A., 298
Gillespie, Deborah, 427
Gillespie, Linda, 1424
Gillespie, Pat, 1094
Gillett, Mary Bevans, 1456
Gillett, Robert F., 1457
Gillum, Roderick D., 450, 1359
Gilmer, Anderson, 1465
Gilmore, Cole, 1505
Gilmore, Irving S., 299

Gilmour, Allan D., 1106
Gilmour, John, 19
Gipp, David M., 1188
Giroux, Anne, 1136
Gismondi, Jim, 1357
Gits, Norbert, 300
Gits, Paula, 300
Gittleman, Alfred J., 1421
Given, Pauline, 1271
Givens, Delores Clark, 1350
Glancy, Alfred R., III, 1106
Glancy, Ruth R., 542
Glancy, Ruth Roby, 1239
Glasby, Mark, 1437
Glascock, Robin, 1210
Glaspie, Kim, 1286
Glass, Jane, 437
Glass, Marcus E., 1086
Glass, Michael, 1108
Glassen, Harold, 301
Glasser, Kenneth, 1362
Glassmeyer, Denise M., 1227
Glaza, Gary, 1413
Gleaner Life Insurance Society, 1506
Gleason, James, 11
Gleaton, Marcus, 1411
Glen, Alicia K., 1233
Glenn, Glenda, 1067
Glick Iron and Metal Co., 302
Glick, Barry J., 302
Glick, Carlton L., 302
Glick, Edith, 302
Glitsa, Martin, 1305
Globe Technologies, Inc., 842
Glover, Adrienne, 1406
Glover, Ann, 1509
Glover, Anthony, 1410
Glover, Gleason, 656
Gluhanich, Michael D., 1103
Gluszewski, Bob, 1443
Glynn, Ivy, 1284
Glynn, Kathleen, 123
Goad, Clarissa A., 303
Goad, Douglass C., 303
Goad, Theodore C., 303
Goad, Thomas C., 303
God's Gift Foundation of Ohio, 304
Godard, Betty D., 165
Godard, Kathy, 165
Godard, Timothy F., 165
Godde, Linda, 1502
Godfrey, Lisa, 1307
Godke, Daryl, 775
Goebel, Barbara, 1121
Goedtel, Marie B., 1017
Goei, Bing, 1463
Goerge, JoMarie, 141
Goerge, Michael, 141
Goethe, Alison, 1152
Goetz, Gavin, 1462
Goff, George A., 1470
Goff, John C., 1264
Gofrank, Shirley, 1108
Gohr, Barbara, 1188
Goldberg, Barbara, 1374
Goldberg, Jay, 656
Golden, Joanne, 1154
Goldman, Irving, 305
Goldman, Sheldon, 509
Goldsen, Sue, 1143
Goldstein, Kari Wolff, 907
Golick, Edward A., 1108
Gonte-Silver, Ann, 928
Gonzalez, Gary H., 1227
Goodman, Debi, 1088
Goodney, Laura, 1329
Goodnow, Charles, 1103
Goodnow, Daniel, 707
Goodnow, Mary J., 1237
Goodnow, Susan, 707
Gordon Food Service Inc., 280
Gordon Food Service, Inc., 307
Gordon, Daniel A., 222
Gordon, Doris M., 308

Gordon, James D., 280
Gordon, John M., Jr., 280, 307
Gordon, Joseph P., 308
Gordon, Marguerite B., 222
Gordon, Paul B., 307
Gordon, Philip M., 307
Gordon, Ted, 1091
Gordy, Berry, 309
Gorman, Christopher, 1018
Gornick, Alan L., 310
Gornick, Keith H., 310
Gorton, Lawrence E., 1483
Goslin, Karolyn, 1087
Gosnell, Gerald, 1156
Gosnell, Jerry, 1104
Goss, Beatrice I., 311
Goss, Carol A., 755
Goss-Foster, Anika, 1323, 1350
Gossman, Joan, 1346
Gottemoeller, Doris, Sr., 1219
Gottschalk, Jack W., 1238
Goulet, Jennifer H., 1196
Goyt, Jeff, 1429
Grabowski, Edward, 326
Grabowski, Marjorie, 326
Grace, Joyce, 1519
Grady, Jerry, 1093
Grady, Kenneth A., 1076
Grady, Mary, 1207
Graef, Rodger, 312
Graf, Daniel, 1339
Graham, Annie West, 136
Graham, Jeanne H., 136
Graham, John, 1413
Graham, Judy N., 603
Graham, Kurt M., 1207
Graham, Libby, 148
Graham, Louise T., 1162
Graham, Ralph A., 136
Graham, W. Thomas, 1089
Graham, William, 136
Graham-Henry, Diane, 411
Grammer, Jennie K., 1401
Granahan, Tim, 1160
Granderson, Curtis, 1266
Granderson, Mary, 1266
Granger Associates, Inc., 313, 314
Granger Construction Co., 313
Granger Electric, 314
Granger Energy, 314
Granger Energy of Decatur, LLC, 314
Granger Energy of Honeybrook, LLC, 314
Granger Holdings, LLC, 314
Granger Meadows, LLC, 314
Granger, Alton L., 313
Granger, Donna, 313
Granger, Gary, 378
Granger, Janice, 313
Granger, Jerry, 1419
Granger, Jerry P., 313
Granger, Keith L., 314
Granger, Lynne, 313
Granger, Ronald K., 313
Granger, Sharon, 1213
Granger, Todd, 1419
Granger, Todd J., 314
Grannum, Colvin W., 1323
Gransden, Bridgette, 1152, 1441
Grant, George, Jr., Dr., 1269
Grant, Jill, 1132
Grant, Susan H., Hon., 1334
Grant, Susan, Hon., 1159
Grant, Thomas, 1315
Grant, Vedra, 1140
Grashuis, Edith, 926
Grathwohl, Casper, 1151
Graves, Liana, 1079
Gray, Deborah, 1328
Gray, Donna, 900
Gray, Herman B., 755
Gray, Kathleen A., 329
Gray, Mark, 1221
Gray, Robert, 1385

Great Atlantic & Pacific Tea Co., Inc., The, 88
Great Lakes Castings Corp., 996
Great Lakes Management, 172
Great Lakes Motorworks, 1228
Greektown Casino, 597, 1470
Green, Don, 1274
Green, Irwin, 1274
Green, John, 1299
Green, Louis, 1240, 1346
Green, Margo, 1274
Green, Mark, 1324
Green, Robert, 670
Greene, Amanda L., 304
Greene, Bonnie Jane, 304
Greene, Carl F., 767
Greene, Carole Spight, 1194
Greene, Helen, 1519
Greene, Jeffrey W., 304
Greene, Jimmy E., 1164
Greene, Kenneth W., 304
Greene, Lora, 1499
Greeney, Wendy, 82
Greenhoe, Sheri W., 1349
Greenville Tool and Die Co., 31
Greenwell, Charles, 1205
Greffin, Judith P., 935
Gregels, Priscilla Hill, 374
Gregg, Ingrid A., 217
Gregory, Louis, 1372
Greiner, Mark, 1275
Greko, John, 1268
Grenke, John, 48
Grenke, John E., 267
Grennan, Barbara, 1354
Gresch, Elizabeth, 1547
Gretkierewicz, Tim, 1458
Grice, Eugene, 868
Grider, Stephen, Dr., 1109
Griffin, Dennis, 1370
Griffin, Robert, 1370
Griffin, Scott, 1171
Griffith, Doris G., 318
Griffith, Douglas T., 318
Griffith, H. Ronald, 1137
Griffith, Kim A., 318
Griffith, Ron, 1436
Grimaldi, Ruth E., 319
Grimaldi, Thomas J., 319
Grimes, Donald T., 1076
Grimes, Mike, 1423
Grimm, Sandra, 1283
Grimmer, Brandi, 1268
Grinnell, Lorraine, 1437
Grodus, Edward, 601
Groeb, Ernie, 1143
Groeneveld, Frank, 1116
Grogan, Paul S., 462
Grosberg, Merwin K., 320
Grosfeld, Nancy, 1296
Gross, Betty, 789
Gross, Charles E., 789
Gross, Charles H., 1143
Gross, Donald J., 1171
Gross, Ken, 1228
Grosso, Anneito, 1265
Groth, Don, 1348
Group W Cable, Inc., 965
Grow, Minnette, 148
Gruener, Patricia, 868
Grumaer, Mary L., 322
Grzywacz, Daniel N., 384
Guadagnini, Angie, 1279
Guardian Industries Corp., 1046
Gudas, Viki, 1048
Gudebski, Jay, Jr., 1505
Gudebski, Jenn, 1505
Gudipati, Rao V.C., 1033
Gudipati, Suhasini, 1413
Guenther, Harry, 722
Guenzel, Robert E., 1457
Guerin, George, 1424
Gueyser, Teresa, 1374
Guilfoyle, Jeff, 1339

Guillermo, Tessie, 1361
Guilliom, Anthony, 321
Guilliom, Gregory, 321
Guilliom, Heather, 321
Gulick, Art, 1383
Gulley, Joan L., 1047
Gunnell, Peggy, 1124
Gunnink, Duane, 384
Gunthorpe, Larry, 1380
Gupta, Kamal, 1125
Gurecki, Ginger, 1095
Gurwitch, Janet, 1022
Gust, Christopher L., 323
Gust, M. Susan, 323
Gustafson, Todd, 1445
Guthikonda, Rao N., 1292
Guthrie, Carlton L., 427
Gutierrez, Ben, 324
Gutierrez, Frances, 324
Gutowski, Walter, Jr., 1269
Gutstein, Daniel, 1188
Guttowsky, Lois K., 584
Guy, Andy, 215
Guyaux, Joseph C., 1047
Guyton, Louise, 1278, 1377
Guzikowski, Frank, 326
Guzikowski, Jane, 326
Guzzo, Henry, 1448
Gwinn, Daniel, 690

H.I.S. Foundation, 117
Haan, Hank, 1212
Haas, Carroll J., 329
Haas, Carroll J., II, 329
Haas, Gary, 1177
Haas, James H., 329
Haas, Marjorie R., 1393
Haas, Robert G., 329
Haas, Theresa, 329
Habicht, Ann, 1169
Habicht, Robert, 1315
Habicht, Robert N., 1151
Haboush Charitable Trust, Antoon & Nita, 331
Hack, Jay, 1083
Hackett, Dennis, 1021
Hackett, James P., 1058
Hadid, Fayiz, 622
Hadley, Pryce, 1270
Haefling, Karen R., 1018
Haenicke, Christopher, 1308
Haering, Janet, 491
Hagan, Joseph, 1323
Hagen, Andrew, Rev. Dr., 332
Hagen, Bob, 1428
Hagen, David F., 332
Hagen, Jeanette, 1133
Hagen, Laura C., 332
Hagen, Susan Dingle, Dr., 332
Hagen, Virginia, 332
Hagerty Insurance, 1228
Hagerty, McKeel, 1228
Hages, Sandina, 1429
Haggard, Dee Bowman, 333
Haggard, Ward M., Jr., 333
Haggart, Tim, 1380
Haggerty, Gwen, 1088
Hahn, Sharon, 334
Hahn, William, 334
Haines, Barbara, 919
Hajra, Neel, 1083, 1182
Halbritter, Ted, III, 1315
Hale, Craig M., 780
Hale, John, Sr., 1222
Hales, Andrea, 434
Haley, Dennis, 868
Haley, Lynn, 1230
Haley, Lynne, 1407
Haley, Lynne M., 1149
Hall of Fame Dance Challenge, Inc., The, 1508
Hall, Bill, 1113
Hall, Chrissie, 411

Hall, David J., 411
Hall, Doug, 1221
Hall, Elliott, 1470
Hall, James, 1548
Hall, Karla D., 977
Hall, Katherine, 1163
Hall, Kristin, 1224
Hall, Neil, 1047
Hall, Pauline, 1362
Hall, Rosalyn, 1403
Hall, Thomas, 411
Hall, Tim, 1375
Hall, Todd, 1164
Hallan, James P., 1238
Halligan, Susan M., 1017
Halog, Donald, 1237
Halperin, David M., 897
Halperin, Margot, 1425
Halpert, Richard L., 1517
Halstead, Donna G., 1181
Halvorsen, James, 391
Ham, Bill, 1130
Hamann, Norman L., Jr., 1194
Hamar, Douglas J., 336
Hamar, John C., 336
Hamar, Julie A., 336
Hamelund, David, 1150
Hamilton, Anne, 850
Hamilton, Dwight K., 1301
Hamilton, Peggy, 1108
Hamlin, Mark D., 410
Hamlin, T., 1332
Hamlin, Thomas, 1345
Hamm, David D., 647
Hammelef, Karen, 1227
Hammerling, Lee, 1385
Hammersley, Bonnie, 1463
Hammersmith, Suann A., 1506
Hammersmith, Suann D., 1143
Hammerstrom, Beverly, 1109
Hammerstrom, Beverly S., Sen., 1356
Hammond Machinery, Inc., 998
Hammond, Christine A., 998
Hammond, Della, 1141, 1286
Hammond, Jeremy, 998
Hammond, Kay G., 318
Hammond, Machelle, 1295
Hammond, Robert E., 998
Hamp, Sheila Ford, 986
Hamp, Steven K., 471, 1106
Hampson, Chandra, 1254
Hampson, Robert, 1150
Hampson, Robert J., 338
Hampson, Sadie G., 338
Hamstra, Bernard, 339
Hamstra, Frances K., 339
Hanback, Shirley W., 1249
Hanchett, Richard, 1495
Hancock, Arline M., 340
Handleman, Charlene, 813
Handleman, David, 813
Handley, Peter, Dr., 1160
Hanflik, Nancy, 1107
Hanisho, Louis, 883
Hanisko, Michael L., 861
Hanley, David, 1113
Hanley, Kathleen, 1385
Hanley, Michael S., 1427
Hanley, Sally J., 796
Hanna, Jill, 1276
Hannaman, Tami, 1546
Hannan, Ahmad, 343
Hannan, Luella, 1511
Hannan, William, 1511
Hannigan, Dan, 1293
Hanover Insurance Co., The, 999
Hanse, Brian W., 667
Hanse, William C., 667
Hansen Marital Trust, Jens, 344
Hansen Qualified Domestic Trust, M., 344
Hansen Residuary Trust, Jens, 344
Hansen Trust, Margaret M., 344
Hansen, Chip, 1096

Hansmann, Laura, 1375
Hanson, Donald, 1406
Hanson, Lee C., 1110
Hanson, William C., 494
Hard, Rachel, 1091
Hardaway, Terrill, 1242
Harden, Wanda D., 1107
Hardgrove, Frank, 1434
Hardiman, Lesa, 1463
Hardin, Lana, 1197
Hardy, Christina, 1445
Hare, Greg, 1546
Haridy, Aziz, 1460
Haring, Ed, 1434
Harkins, Jeffrey, Dr., 1194
Harlan, John M., 349
Harlow, Scott, 764
Harmelink, Kevin, 1127
Harmes, James, 1125
Harmon, Alison, 1470
Harmon, Debra A., 961
Harmon, Lewis G., 350
Harmon, Tamara, 1404
Harner, Ivan C., 1279
Harper, Kate, 16
Harper, Sheila M., 160
Harrington, Andrew, 1141
Harrington, Barbara, 1109
Harrington, James A., 1303
Harrington, Jim, 1303
Harris, Alan, 755
Harris, Greta, 1323
Harris, Karen S., 351
Harris, Kathi, 1311
Harris, Kay, 1437
Harris, Maya L., 260
Harris, Paul, 1018
Harris, Rodney C., 351
Harris, Sam, 1090
Harris, Scott, 1535
Harrison, Connie, Dr., 1446
Harrison, Dennis, 1100
Harrison, Donald, 1190
Harrison, Marcia, 1180
Harrison, Michael G., 1348
Harrison, Tom, 1180
Harroun-Holmes, Carole, 1211
Hart, Cathy J., 1077
Hart, David, 1212
Hart, Marcia, 1377
Hart, Michael A., 988
Hart, Sharon, 1298
Hart, Steve, 1411
Hartley, Susan J., 698
Hartman, Wanda, 1502
Hartman-Ali, Gloria, 1229
Hartmann, E. Jan, 279
Hartwick Unitrust, Alice Kales, 352
Hartwig, John P., 1467
Harvey, Albert S., 354
Harvey, Clarence, 1163
Harvey, Nadine M., 1420
Harvey, Sarge, 1413
Harvey, Thomas C., Jr., 354
Harvey, William H., 1337
Harvey, William L., 354
Harwell, Ernie, 355
Harwood, Dave, 1248
Hasbrook, Peter, 1347
Hascall, Jennifer, 1335
Haserot, F.H., 1142
Hasey, Martin J., 356
Hasey, Regina M., 356
Haskin, Nancy, 1123
Haslett, William D., 397
Hasnedl, Jerry, 952
Hass, Cyndy, 644
Hastings Mutual Insurance Co., 1000
Hatch, Bob, 1562
Hatfield, Dave, 1085
Hatfield, David, 1302
Hatfield, John, 671

Hathaway, Linda, 1120
Hatley, Karen, 1234
Hatter, Raquel T., 1464
Hattori, Kazushi, 1012
Haugen, Jon M., 423
Haughey, Don, 1516
Haupt, Marv, 1409
Hauser, Dan, 1046
Hauser, Mark, 1191, 1395
Hauser, Mark R., 1396
Hauser-Hurley, Gail, 1089
Hauswirth, Mike, 1139
Haut, Susan, 1334
Hautala, Robert, 1265
Haveman, Catherine, 357
Haveman, James, 357
Haveman, James, Jr., 1291
Hawk, George W., Jr., 954
Hawk, Mary Jo, 1307
Hawkins, Dori, 1403
Hawkins, Marion, 216
Hawley, Bart, 1436
Haworth Foundation, Richard and
    Ethelyn, 773
Haworth, Anna, 773
Haworth, Anna C., 773
Haworth, Ethelyn L., 773
Haworth, Jennifer L., 773
Haworth, Matthew R., 773
Haworth, Richard G., 773
Haybarker, Jody, 1527
Hayes, Christine, 1438
Hayes, Elise, 1363
Hayes-Giles, Joyce V., 977
Haynor, Chris, 1360
Hays, Judy, 1159
Hayward, Barbara, 1428
Hayward-Frost, Janet, 1250
Haywood, Jennifer, 1085
Hazleton, Richard, 787
HCR Manor Care, Inc., 1002
Heacock, Steve, 1328, 1463
Healer, Erin Day, 173
Healy, Michael J., 1288
Heard, Angel, 1368
Hearsch, David, 1165
Heath, Karen, 1085
Heaton, Mary Alice J., 880
Heckler, Jay, 1308
Hedderman, Diana K., 1464
Heemstra, Linda R., 434
Heenan, Earl I., III, 217
Hees, Daniel A., 360
Hees, David G., 360
Hees, Michael D., 360
Hees, Ronald D., 360
Hegarty, Neal R., 587
Hehl, David. K., 1022
Hehl, Matt, 1442
Height, Linda L., 1171
Heinen, Susan, 922
Heintzelman, Laura M., 1147
Heinze, Doug, 1154
Heiserman, Elaine T., 1258
Heisler, Christina M., 847
Heitsch, George, 1198
Heldman, Paul W., 1021
Helfrich, Thomas E., 1018
Helgerud, Frode, 1056
Helm, Judy, 1247
Helmic, Robert, 1332
Helppie Trust, Richard D., 361
Helppie, Leslie S., 361
Helppie, Richard, 361
Helppie, Richard D., Jr., 361
Helsley, John, 775
Heminger, Linda, 1276
Hemlock Semiconductor Corp., 975
Hempstead, David M., 262, 263, 264,
    265, 266, 736, 891, 1106, 1280
Henderson, Brian C. McK., 1188
Henderson, James, 1568
Henderson, Lee, 1476
Henderson, Scott M., 1021

Hendrick, Chip, 1413
Hendrick, William A., 882
Hendrick, Wliam A., 882
Hendrickson, Jennifer, 1375
Hendrickson, John T., 1045
Henke, Carol, 996
Henke, Frank E., 1173
Henkel-Primozic, Patricia, 1185
Hennard, Pete, 1362
Henneman, Kris, 1408
Hennessey, Frank Michael, 362
Hennessey, Michael I., 362
Hennessy, Dorothy, 1423
Hennon, Marilyn, 1078
Henry, Jordan, 363
Henry, Kara, 363
Henry, Megan, 363
Henschen, Beth, 1258
Hense, Paul, 1193
Hensick, Helen L., 155
Hensley, Jeff, 1442
Hephner, Tracy S., 729
Herbert, Bruce, 1096
Herbert, Joan, 1152
Herlich, Harild N., 439
Herman, Julie, 1224
Hermann, William M., 1106
Hermelin, Brian, 1281
Hermelin, David B., 1281
Hermelin, Doreen, 1191, 1281
Hermelin, Francine G., 1281
Hermelin, Julie C., 1281
Hermelin, Karen B., 1281
Hernandez, Armando, 1269
Heron, George R., 1547
Herrick, Hazel M., 367
Herrick, Kent B., 367
Herrick, Ray W., 367
Herrick, Todd W., 367
Herriman, Dan, 886
Herriman, Daniel, 886
Hershey, David E., 270
Herskovic, Arnold, 1302
Herstein, Carl, 1410
Herter, Ulrich, 870
Hertz, Howard, 1410
Herzog, Beth, 1404
Hess, Frances P., 370
Hess, Myrtle, 369
Hess, Myrtle E., 368
Hess, William, 369
Hesson, Gerald, 1404
Hetico, Rachel S., 377
Hetrick, Kelly, 1415
Hettinger, Kerry, 1312
Hetzler, Robert, 1087
Heule, Paulus C., 1488
Heule, Rosemary L., 1488
Heuschele, Richard, 882
Heydenberk, Richard, 1092
Heyl, Frederick W., 1282
Heyl, Frederick W., Mrs., 1282
Heyse, Pete, 1102
Hibbard, John D., Jr., 215
Hibben, Seabury J., 727
Hibbing Taconite Co., 954
Hickman, David S., 1143
Hickman, Sally D., 371
Hickman, Stephen L., 371
Hickman, Tracy L., 371
Hickman-Boyse, Stephanie L., 371
Hicks, Gerald, 142
Hicks, Helen, 1403
Hicks, Randy, 1404
Hicks, Romayne E., 878
Hickson, Carl, 1229
Hiemenga, Judith, 454
Higgins, Lisa Marie, 372
Higgins, Mark, 1279
Hilboldt, James S., 145
Hildebrand, Georgene, 1104
Hildebrandt, Leslie, 9
Hildner, Tom, 1123
Hildreth, Bonnie, 1085

Hildreth, James A., 80, 340
Hildreth, Louis, II, 373
Hill, Brian, 1163
Hill, Donald E., Jr., 637
Hill, Jamie, 874
Hill, Lori, 541
Hill, Lori A., 900
Hill, Mike, 1443
Hill, Nancy, 1401
Hill, Nancy E., 1401
Hill, Penny, 1128
Hill, Scott, 1143
Hill, Steve L., 1110
Hill, Thomas P., 1423
Hill-Kennedy, Scott, 1150
Hillegonds, Nancy, 1093
Hillegonds, Paul C., 471, 977
Hiller, Tim, 358
Hillier Family Foundation, 1513
Hilliker, Thomas R., 1127
Hillman, Edith, 486
Hilt, George, 1103
Hilt, Jack, 1103
Hilt, John, 1103
Hiltz, John, 1144
Himes, Jeff, 1166
Himes, Kathy, 1482
Himmel, Clarence, 375
Hinckfoot, Walter G., Jr., 181
Hine, Angela, 1152
Hineline, Bill, 1299
Hineline, William R., 1207
Hines, James H., 1393
Hines, Kimberly, 923
Hinken, Doug, 1130
Hinkle, Mike, 1096
Hinkley, Bernie, 184
Hinsdale-Knisel, Ann, 557
Hinterman, Richard, 289
Hinton, Candye, 1370
Hipwood, Bill, Rev., 1362
Hirai, Holly K., 1520
Hirano Inouye, Irene, 260
Hirano, Irene Y., 471
Hire, John S., 376
Hire, Phyllis F., 376
Hirrel, Richard J., 34
Hirrel, Tracy G., 34
Hirsch, Marvin, 1205
Hirschman, Becky, 1548
Hirvonen, Linda, 377
Hirvonen, Mark, 377
Hirvonen, Matt, 377
Hirvonen, Peg, 377
Hirvonen, Ray, 377
His Foundation, 691
HIS Foundation, 991
Hitchcock, William, 79
Hitson, Tim, 1212
Hixson, Don, 1169
Hoagland, John, 1128
Hoard, Doug, 513
Hoath, Melissa, 1183
Hobbs, Anita, 228
Hoben, Elise, 1323
Hochman, Marcelo, 1320
Hockman, Geoffrey L., 1467
Hoddy, George W., 63
Hodge, Bob, 1334
Hodgins, Anne E., 1316
Hodshire, Jeremiah, 1131
Hoeffler, John, 1204
Hoekenga, JoAnne, 931
Hoekstra, Jeni, 1469
Hoensheid, Gary, 1128
Hoensheid, Lauraine, 1322
Hof, Ellen, 379
Hof, Helmut, 379
Hofbauer, Gregory J., 348
Hoff, Rackeline, 270
Hoffer, Marilyn, 511
Hoffine, Phil, 1176
Hoffius, Dirk, 1069
Hoffman, Carole, 1418

Hoffman, Jack, 184
Hoffman, James, 1018
Hoffman, Jean, 1228
Hoffman, Julius J., 560
Hoffman, Michael S., 1127
Hoffman, Steve, 1313
Hofman, Thomas D., 314
Hogenson, Tom, 1334
Hoisington, Robert E., 1339
Holaday, Alan, 1072
Holbrook, Deborah, 291
Holcolm, Manual, 1185
Holcomb-Merrill, Karen, 1414
Holden, James S., 381
Holden, Lynelle A., 381
Holkeboer, Jim, 143
Holland, Henry, 1282
Holland, V. Vaughn, 451
Holland, William C., 1505
Hollansworth, John, 1228
Holleman, Brett, 131
Hollenbeck, Laura L., 382
Hollenbeck, Martyn T., 382
Holley, George M., 383
Holley, George M., III, Rev., 383
Holley, John C., Jr., 383
Holley, Margaret E., 383
Holley, Stephen, 383
Holloway, Deborah Seabury, 727
Hollowell, Melvin, 683
Holly, Julie A. Rodecker, 180
Holman, Beverly J., 1511
Holman, Edwin, 1022
Holmes, Carl, 598, 1286
Holmes, Maria, 1382
Holmes, Richard, 1370
Holoman, Smallwood, 1164
Holowka, Nick, 1437
Holowka, Nick O., 1141
Holt, Kristen, 1458
Holthaus, Richard A., 1518
Holton, Earl D., 1058
Holtrop, Carol, 1272
Holtsford, Jeanine, 644
Holub, Dennis, 1195
Holvick, Gary C., 350
Holy Cross Classic Cruisers, 1228
Honasoge, Mahalakshmi, 714
Honasoge, Nataraj, 714
Honholt, Douglas P., 385
Honholt, Karen L., 385
Honn, Ken, 279
Hood, David, 1397
Hood, Harold, Hon., 1348
Hood, Joseph W., 386
Hood, Kevin, 386
Hood, Lynn, 1002
Hood, Nancy, 386
Hood, Paul, 1382
Hood, William, 1461
Hoogeboom, Marge, 131
Hoogeboom, Marjorie G., 664
Hoogeboom, Sarah, 838
Hoogeboom, Thomas J., 664
Hoogewind, Cheryl L., 664
Hoover, Chuck, 1108
Hop, Jim, 1152
Hopping, Andy, 1094
Horn, Colleen, 1448
Horn, Craig W., 882
Hornbeck, Tracey, 1299
Horowitz, Michael P., 1296
Horton, Kathi, 1107
Horvitz, David W., 471
Hosking, John, 73
Hoskins, Eddie, 1405
Hostetler, Kelly, 1411
Houghton, Ralph H., Jr., 193
Houle, Annette, 1225
Houle, Julia, 885
House, Tom, 1429
Houseman, Cathy, 175, 608
Houseman, Dave, 1484
Houston-Philpot, Kimberly R., 975

Houtakker, Donald J., 1518
Hoving, Gwendolyn, 1515
Hoving, Kenneth, 1515
Hovinga Charitable Foundation, James P.
    and Debra K., The, 1
Hovinga, Debra K., 1
Hovinga, James P., 1
Howard, Andrew T., 389
Howard, Ann E., 389
Howard, Jim, 1156
Howard, Mary Ellen, Sr., 1422
Howard, Mary Jane, 389
Howard, Michael J., 389
Howard, Pat, 900
Howard, Raymond E., 1337
Howard, Sam, 1152
Howard, Shirley, 475
Howard, Stephen, 1467
Howard, Winship C., 389
Howe, Carl, 1176
Howe, J. Patrick, 911
Howe, John J., 36
Howe, Julie, 1176
Howell, Don N., 347
Howell, Jim, 1096
Howell-Romein, Julie, 1383
Howes, Julie, 1502
Howes, Randall, 1140
Howland, Walter L., 1547
Howlett, Don, 1430
Hoydic, Michael D., 1442
Hoydie, Michael, 1404
Hubbard, Amy L., 656
Hubbell Steel, 278
Hubert, Pat, 1462
Hubscher, Chuck, 1154
Huck, Nancy E., 478
Huck, Thomas B., 478
Huckle, Chris, 1092
Hudolin, Kimberly K., 990
Hudsek, Phillis, 614
Hudson Co., J.L., The, 392
Hudson, Gilbert, 392
Hudson, J. Clifford, 260
Hudson, Joseph L., IV, 392
Hudson, Joseph L., Jr., 392
Huebner, Carl, 1135
Huebner, Cynthia, 182
Hueter, David, Rev., 1166
Huffines, Robert L., Jr., 393
Hug, Alison, 1382
Hug, Andreas L., 1536
Hug, Daniel C., 1536
Huggler, Dale A., 1362
Huggler, Tom, 301
Hughes, Carla, 1002
Hughes, Carolyn R., 258
Hughes, Holly J., 1103
Hughes, James, 1267
Hughes, James F., 1217
Hughes, James L., 1209
Hughes, Julie, 1384
Hughes, Patrick, 1185
Hughes, Robert, 589
Hughes, Shaundralyn, 1206
Hughey, Richard M., Jr., 299
Hughey, Richard M., Sr., 299
Huiskens, David, 831
Huizenga, Charles B., 394
Huizenga, Douglas L., 394
Hull, Patrick, 1420
Hullet, Diane, 1496
Hullet, Diane Dow, 202
Humana Inc., 1003
Humbarger, Robert, 767
Humbert, Ines M., 396
Humphreys, B.J., 604, 829, 883
Humphreys, John, 604, 829, 883
Hunt, Brenda, 1407
Hunt, Brenda L., 1086
Hunter, Andrew, 1122
Hunter, Beth, 1286
Hunter, Brian, 1108
Hunter, Edward, 397

Hunter, Irma, 397
Hunter, Janet, 1129, 1433
Hunter, Matthew, 1197
Hunter, Scott, 1092
Hunter, Thomas, 179
Hunter, Thomas A., 1110
Hunting, John R., 215
Hunting, Mary Anne, 1058
Huntington National Bank, The, 1103
Hupert, Ann, 613
Hurley, Melody, 1450
Hurley, William L., 1239
Hurst, Anthony P., 398
Hurst, Elizabeth S., 398
Hurst, Mark, 1173
Hurst, Peter F., 398
Hurwitz, Dan, 1295, 1299
Hurwitz, Shirley B., 65
Husband, Timothy, 557
Huschke, Kathryn L., 617
Hussman, John P., 372
Huston, Barbara T., 488
Hutchins, Jane, 41
Hutchinson, Dolores Rock, 598
Hutchinson, Les, 1131
Hutchinson, Raymond J., 290
Hyde, Howard, 1159
Hyland, Diane Wynsma, 153, 507
Hyzer, Chris, 1463

Iaquinto, Anthony, 1113
Ibarguen, Alberto, 462
ICAT Investments, LLC, 822
Idema, Beatrice A., 402
Idema, William W., 402
Idziak, Eileen L., 150
Ieuter, Cal, 1152
Ilitch, Atanas, 1289
Ilitch, Christopher, 1288, 1289
Ilitch, Denise, 755
Imoberstag, Frances B., 404
Indenbaum, Michael A., 367
Inglish, David, 816
Inglish, Douglas, 816
Ingraham, Barton, 407
Ingraham, Gail, 407
Inman, Bill, 1112
Inosencio, Bruce A., 1137
Intrigue Collection, LLC, 1228
Ireland, Terese, 1379
Irish, Ann, 1363
Irish, Ann K., 217
Irvin, Kathleen B., 66
Irwin, Ben, 1275
Irwin, Claire, 408
Irwin, James, 408
Irwin, Kyle, 1299
Isabella Bank and Trust, 1006
Isakow, Selwyn, 1297
Ittigson, Mary, 1107
Ivens, Barbara J., 290
Iverson, Amy M., 410
Iverson, Clifford T., 410
Iverson, Keith A., 410
Ives, G. Allen, III, 568
Ivory, Bob R., Jr., 1222

Jaber, Aoun, 1192
Jackier, Lawrence, 1395
Jackier, Lawrence S., 1191, 1260
Jackoboice, Barbara, 269
Jackovac, Jerry, 1199
Jackson, Brian, 1164
Jackson, Claudia, 270
Jackson, Corwill, 411
Jackson, Derrick, 1180
Jackson, Doug, 526
Jackson, Margie, 411
Jackson, Sandra, 1091
Jackson, William H., 1195
Jacobs, Allan, 70
Jacobs, Goldie, 70

Jacobs, John P., 1209
Jacobs, Julyette, 1424
Jacobs, Steve, 184
Jacobs, Wesley, 1128
Jacobson, Douglas A., 1491
Jacobson, Janice, 190
Jacobson, Jerome, 412
Jacobson, Joshua, 412
Jacobson, Lana, 1126
Jacobson, Nelson C., 1010
Jacque, Onnie Barnes, 1403
Jacquot, Mark, 1546
Jafari, Jehad, 413
Jafari, Tharaa Chanda, 413
Jaffe, Ira J., 224, 542
Jaffe, Rosalind, 1147
Jaffe, Ruth M., 434
Jaffke, Thomas A., 625
Jaguar Clubs of North America, 1228
Jain, Krishna M., 472
Jakaus, Janice, 663
Jalkannen, Mark, 1232
James, Barbara L., 1138
James, John, 1346, 1470
James, John A., 1470
James, John J., 290
James, Kay Coles, 484
James, Kenneth, 1463
James, William R., 1467
Jamieson, Michael W., 1245
Jampel, Joan, 403
Jampel, Robert, Dr., 403
Jandernoa, Mike, 1285
Jandernoa, Susan, 1328
Janis, Suzanne M., 1344
Janke, Kenneth S., Jr., 1518
Janke, Kenneth S., Sr., 1518
Janners, Martha, 1139
Janson, Robert, 16
Januzelli, Eric, 1130
Jara, Francine, 1464
Jared, Tom, 1429
Jaroshewich, Daniel, 1314
Jarrard-Benson, Ardith R., 1481
Jarvis, Linda, 1286
Jasper, Sandi, 1256
Jasper, Thomas F., 1061
Jasti, Ramesh, Dr., 1292
Jasti, Satish, 1292
Jasti, Venkateswarlu, Dr., 1292
Jay, Ann F., 9
Jeannero, Jane M., 290
Jeffers Memorial Fund, Michael, 416
Jeffers, Gary, 1340
Jefferson, Brian, 1405
Jefferson, Ralph, 1405
Jefferson, Tanya, 1464
Jeffery, Donald B., Jr., 348
Jenkins, Daniel, 1526
Jenkins, Elizabeth, 1526
Jenkins, Gerald J., 1526
Jenkins, Michael, 1098
Jenkinson, Tamara, 1432
Jenneman, Eugene, 1196
Jennings Trust, Edith, 418
Jennings Trust, Wyman, 418
Jennings, Michael D., 1341
Jensen, A. Paul, 419
Jensen, Gustav, 589
Jensen, James, 419
Jensen, Keith C., 419
Jensen, Keith D., 419
Jensen, Thomas, 419
Jenuwine, Alan, 420
Jernigan, Matt, 1163
Jerue, Richard A., 185
Jespersen, Charles, 1412
Jessamy, Michael, 1326
Jessell, Lynn, 1305
Jesser, Carl, 1081
Jessup, Charles, 1413
Jeter, Mark L., 1061
Jewell, William R., 454

Jewish Welfare Federation Metro Detroit, 928
Jimenez, A. David, 1219
Jobete Music Co., Inc., 309
Johns, Karley D., 269
Johnson Corp., The, 1011
Johnson, Andrew, 1542
Johnson, Arnold L., 19
Johnson, Bari, 507
Johnson, Bari S., 1010
Johnson, Betty B., 85
Johnson, Bill, 1124
Johnson, Bobby, 1464
Johnson, Chacona W., 224
Johnson, Charles W., 1162
Johnson, Cherie, 1389
Johnson, Darryl W., 1206
Johnson, Dave, 1142
Johnson, David V., 1088
Johnson, Donald, 446
Johnson, Donald E., Jr., 880
Johnson, Dorothy A., 450
Johnson, Erick P., 1010
Johnson, Ervin, 1405
Johnson, Frances, 423
Johnson, George G., 1106
Johnson, Gerald A., 348
Johnson, Gregory, 647
Johnson, James, 94, 1231
Johnson, Jill, 466
Johnson, Jim, 1255
Johnson, Joan Jackson, 1094
Johnson, Julie, 1321
Johnson, Kadant, 1011
Johnson, Kadant, Inc., 1011
Johnson, Kenneth, 1437
Johnson, Larry, 1184
Johnson, Marilyn, 1532
Johnson, Melinda E., 1010
Johnson, Michael, 1377
Johnson, Nancy L., 1070
Johnson, Paul, 423
Johnson, Paul C., 1103
Johnson, Paula A., 1071
Johnson, Roderick L., 1485
Johnson, Roland, 1517
Johnson, Si, 1138
Johnson, W., 1332
Johnson, William, 1321
Johnson, William D., 1302
Johnson, Wyvonne, 1435
Johnston, Anne E., 788
Johnston, David S., 741
Johnston, James W., 1022
Johnston, Joe, 1567
Johnston, Mary Kaye, 741
Johnston, Megan M., 788
Johnston, Michael B., 788
Johnston, Renee S., 1164
Johnston, Steve, 1204
Johnston, Susan, 1567
Johnston, William, 788
Johnston, William D., 788, 1505
Johnston, William R., Jr., 568
Johr, Roger C., 1326
Jolliffe, Judy K., 1211
Jonaitis, Simone, 215
Jones, Allen, 142
Jones, Calvin, 1459
Jones, Clifford B., 1520
Jones, David A., 1003
Jones, David A., Jr., 1003
Jones, David L., 1162
Jones, Donald, 1278
Jones, Elyse F., 252
Jones, Hendrick, 1124
Jones, Jacqueline, 1427
Jones, Judy, 1235
Jones, Margaret, 257
Jones, Maurice, 1361
Jones, Sandy, 1125
Jones, Sherrie L., 424
Jones, Steven, 522
Jones, Susan K., 1193

Jones, Thomas, 116
Jones, William, 13
Jonker, Robert, 1469
Joos, David W., 955, 961
Jordan, Ann Kaufman, 439
Jordan, Gloria Perez, 656
Jordan, Maria, 588
Jordan, Michael C., 725
Jordan, Robert, 1124
Jorgensen, Kim M., 1122
Joseph, James A., Amb., 366
Joseph, Judith, 1295
Joseph, Paul T., 722
Joslin, David C., 290
Jospey, Marjorie R., 425
Jospey, Maxwell, 425
Joyce, Kenneth, 1385
Joyce, Robert, 1128
JPMorgan Chase & Co., 1009
JPMorgan Chase Bank, N.A., 46, 57, 78,
    95, 120, 254, 297, 341, 368, 369,
    441, 447, 473, 479, 543, 544,
    545, 566, 569, 598, 612, 782,
    833, 893, 968, 1019
JSJ Corp., 1010
Judd, Albert Randolph, 515
Judd, John Terrill, 515
Judd, Robert L., 1264
Judd, Virginia K., 1003
Julien, Michael R., 798
Jung, Maura, 1374
Junod, Henri, Jr., 1163
Juntunen, Dean, 1372
Justice, Barbara, 556
Justice, Tracy, 1120
Justin, Robert, 1108

Kabat, Orv, 1097
Kabobel, Janet, 429
Kaczor, Beth, 1002
Kadelic, Ray, 1367
Kadish, Marc R., 1233
Kaelin, Eric, 1376
Kahan, Emelie O., 429
Kahan, Leo A., 429
Kahkonen, Dorothy J., 1349
Kahler, Kari, 1365
Kahn, Cindy Obron, 1227
Kahn, Kopel I., 430
Kaigler, Shirley A., 1171
Kain, Robert L., 975
Kaiser, Barbara A., 431
Kaiser, Erik M., 431
Kaiser, James, 423
Kaiser, Lisa, 1574
Kaiser, Nanette, 1412
Kaiser, Terrence S., 431
Kaiser-Winslow, Stephanie A., 431
Kakabadse, Yolanda, 260
Kakarala, Chandrasekhara Rao, Dr., 432
Kakarala, Raghuram, 432
Kakarala, Ramani, 432
Kakarala, Ramesh, 432
Kakarala, Sriman N., 432
Kakarala, Vijaya, 432
Kalchik-Tenbrock, Joan, 1142
Kalleward, Howard, 163
Kalleward, Howard D., 299
Kalt, David S., 433
Kalt, Mark, 433
Kalt, Susan, 433
Kaminski, Mark A., 522
Kaminski, Nancy, 589
Kammeraad, Aldonna H., 153
Kammeraad, David, 153
Kamphuis, Daniel J., 79
Kamphuis, Rhonda, 79
Kanagawa, Chihiro, 37
Kancharla, Ram, 1346
Kang, Matt, 1002
Kangas, Arlene, 589
Kangas, Dale, 1265
Kangas, Paul, 706

Kanitz, Sarah, 1440
Kantzler, Leopold J., 434
Kaplan, Robert S., 260
Kapnick, Jim, 1143
Karadjoff, Peter, 1446
Karas, Agnes, 636
Karas, Carol, 1128
Karas, Marie, 1284
Karbel, Robert A., 375
Karinen, Margaret, 696
Karius, Joseph, 1265
Karklis, Tua, 1317
Karl, Curtis, 1521
Karlene, Scott B., 1524
Karpinski, Donald G., 49
Karpus, Janet, 1308
Karpus, Janet M., 832
Karr, Carol, 1335
Karr, Carol J., 1127
Karshner, James, 1344
Kasdorf, Gail B., 577
Kashian, David, 1118
Kasiewicz, Andrea M., 435
Kasiewicz, Sandra M., 435
Kasiewicz, Stanley J., 435
Kasper, E. Doran, 1120
Kaspo, Ghabi, 1341
Kasprzak, Skip, 1375
Kassis, Sonya, 1189
Kastner, Howard, 256
Kaszubski, Marc, 1113
Kaszubski, Michael A., 1113
Kaszubski, Thomas, 1113
Kateni, Jitendra, 1290
Katona, Michael F., 965
Katz Family Charitable Trust, Ann, 436
Katz, Ann, 436
Katz, Donald, 436
Katz, Helen, 1298
Katz, Irwin, 436
Katz, Nancy, 436
Katz, Richard, 882
Katzman, Barney, 437
Katzman, Betty, 438
Katzman, Jeanette, 437
Katzman, Richard, 437
Katzman, Robert, 438
Kauffman, John, Jr., 1109
Kaufman Trust, L.G., 439
Kaufman, Anne F., 441
Kaufman, Audrey, 439
Kaufman, Brian, 1307
Kaufman, Greg, 1295
Kaufman, Laurie, 1270
Kaufman, Peter, 439
Kaufman, Richard F., 440
Kaufman, Sylvia C., 440, 1195
Kautz, Chris, 1117
Kavanagh, Tom, 1318
Kawasaki Heavy Industries (USA), Inc.,
    1012
Kawasaki Motors Corp., U.S.A., 1012
Kawasaki Motors Manufacturing Corp.,
    U.S.A., 1012
Kawasaki Rail Car, Inc., 1012
Kawasaki Robotics (USA) Inc., 1012
Kay Family, 443
Kay, Christine, 443
Kay, Colleen W., 973
Kay, E. Wayne, 1402
Kay, Neil, 443
Kayser, David, 952
Kazakos, Terry, 1314
Kean, Beatrice Joyce, 427
Keane, Fay, 1096
Keane, Kevin, 1431
Kearney, Daniel P., 427
Keck, Merel, 1109
Keck, Roger, 1129, 1548
Keefe, Ronald, 1348
Keelan, Barb, 1365
Keeler Fund, The, 446
Keeler, Isaac S., 446
Keeler, Mary Ann, 446

Keeler, Miner S., II, 446
Keenan, James F., 397, 649
Keene, Gene E., 1312
Keene, Irving F., 1494
Keene, Matthew, 1313
Keener, Christina, 1166
Keener, Tim, 1255
Keeney, Hattie Hannah, 447
Keevan, Sally, 199
Kegel, Fred, 1381
Kehoe, Geoffrey, 656
Kehoe, Jack, 129
Keilitz, Dave, 1154
Keilty, Nancy B., 40
Keiser, Nanette, 1090
Keiswetter, Paul, 1088
Kelke, Linda, 1165
Keller, Amy, Dr., 1159
Keller, Bernadine J., 448
Keller, Christina L., 448
Keller, Diane, 1180
Keller, Fred P., 450
Keller, Frederick P., 448
Keller, John, 647
Keller, Linn Maxwell, 448
Keller, Sue, 1104
Kellerman, Jeffrey, 1464
Kellogg Co., 1015
Kellogg Foundation Trust, W.K., 450
Kellogg Trust, Carrie Staines, 450
Kellogg, June, 449
Kellogg, Ryan, 449
Kellogg, Thea, 1142
Kellogg, Thomas A., 449
Kellogg, W.K., 450, 1013
Kelly Services, Inc., 1016
Kelly, C.L., Sr., 451
Kelly, Carl, 215
Kelly, Charles G., 1110
Kelly, Christopher, 1157
Kelly, Kevin A., 1349
Kelly, Kirsten Frank, Hon., 1356
Kelly, Mike, 1087
Kelly, Patrick, 1333
Kelly, Richard C., 1077
Kelly, Sean P., 408
Kelly, William G., Hon., 455
Kelson, Richard B., 484
Kelto, Pete, 1079, 1270
Kemler, Lillian, 452
Kemner, Ray, 129
Kemp, Klein, Umphrey, Endelman & May,
    1017
Kemp, Robert D., Jr., 1239
Kemp, Stephen R., 1171
Kempa, Sandra, 295
Kempe, Enid, 592
Kempton, Isabel, 1150
Kempton, John, 1096
Kendall, Charles B., 9
Kendall, James A., 628
Kendall, LeeAnn, 1519
Kennedy, Cheryl, 1223
Kennedy, David, 1188
Kennedy, David B., 217
Kennedy, Dick, 1128
Kennedy, Thomas, 1383
Kennerly, Michael, 698
Kennerly, Ross, 698
Kent County Medical Society, 454
Kent, Gary, 1313
Kent, Robert, 1307
Kenworthy, Harriet, 588
Kepler, Dave E., 973
Kerans, Ellen, 1140
Kerkstra, Lawrence, 456
Kerkstra, Virginia, 456
Kern, Robert, 1247
Kern, Tom, 1286
Kernan, Joseph E., 495
Kerr, Eileen, 1099
Kerr, Janet, 1022
Kerr, Jennie, 1104
Kerschbaum, Amy, 1457

Kersman, Jeana, 1354
Kersten, Elizabeth, 1246
Kessel, Carrie, 1300
Kessel, William B., 1428
Kessler, John E., 44
Kessler, Phillip, 946
Kettler, James, 868
Key, Medline C., 457
KeyBank N.A., 285, 296, 422, 537, 1018
KeyCorp, 1018
Keyes, Janna, 1204
Keyes, Jared, 1492
Keyser, David N., 843
Keyser, Mary E., 389
Khan, Ayub, 1187
Khan, Shaukat, 1187
Khatana, Kanji, 1558
Khatana, Shanta, 1558
Kheterpal, Bithika S., 1555
Khouri, Mary, 1453
Khouri, Naif A., 977
Khoury, George N., 1189
Kickel, Bob, 1313
Kidder, Rushworth M., 587
Kienholz, Corey, 661
Kiino, Diane, 1282
Kilbane, Brian, 1184
Kile, James, 952
Kilgore, Ronald N., 163, 630, 1302
Killen, Barb, 1145
Killen, Melanie, 1401
Killips, Rob, 996
Kim, Bouh H., 445
Kimball, Thomas R., Dr., 1207
Kimbel, Linda L., 1092
Kimbrough, Aleatha, 1456
Kimpel, Henry D. "Bud", 1144
King, Cathy, 1342
King, Jeffrey, 1453
King, Jerry, 1213
King, Jimmy, 1215
King, John L., 653
King, Keri, 1336
King, Leroy, 640
King, Roberta F., 1127
King, Sarah, 786
Kingery, Pamela, 1303
Kingma, Todd W., 1045
Kinnaird, Debra, 1440
Kinnary, Michael T., 1000
Kinnear, Constance M., 576
Kinney, John, 1516
Kinter, Michael E., 1149
Kintz, Bruce A., 1468
Kircher, Christopher P., 959
Kirila, Virginia L., 277
Kirk, Madeleine Yaw, 905
Kirkbride, Cindy, 1132
Kirkpatrick, Frederick S., 587
Kirksey, Jack, Hon., 1144
Kirvan, Thomas S., 1258
Kiss-Wilson, Jacquline, 1420
Kissling, Thomas, 1326
Kittredge, Robert P., 980
Kladder, Tom, 930
Klappa, Gale E., 1074
Klebba, Kenneth J., 846
Kleber, Charles F., 1146
Klecha, Roy, 1446
Klecha, Roy W., Jr., 1110
Klein, Carol A., 1374
Klein, James, 1372
Klein, Marian, 1282
Klein, Ronald A., 1296
Klein, Sandy, 1384
Klein, Tom, 1459
Klein, Wallis, 1350
Kleinhardt, Karen, 1429
Klepper, M. Sue, 1183
Klimek, David, 11
Klinski, Kari A., 1409
Klobucar, John E., 458
Klobucher, Joseph D., 458

Klooster, Henry, 1103
Klotz, Stephen, 1335
Kmetz, Teresa, 1213
Knab, Dale, 1383
Knabusch Charitable Trust No. 2, Edward M. & Henrietta M., 460
Knabusch Marital Trust, Edward M., 459
Knabusch, Bob, 1109
Knabusch, Charles T., Jr., 459
Knabusch, Chris, 1109
Knabusch, E. M., 1022
Knabush-Taylor, June E., 1022
Knapp, Cheryl, 1305
Knapp, James, 1057
Knapp, Paul, 1088
Knapp, Richard, 1426
Knechel, Bob, 1228
Knecht, Jean B., 85
Knecht, Randy, 952
Knecht, Timothy H., 1107, 1120
Knickerbocker, Todd, 1364
Knight Trust, James L., 461
Knight, Colleen, 1091
Knight, Gerald, 768
Knight, James L., 462
Knight, John S., 462
Knight, Maureen, 768
Knight-Drain, Carol, 461
Knitter, Nancy, 1373
Knoll, Alan, 1123
Knoop, Frances A., 404
Knoth, Mark, 1364
Knowlton, Agnes, 1521
Knowlton, Agnes J., 1521
Knowlton, Charles J., 1521
Knowlton, Norman F., 1521
Knowlton, Suzanne A., 1521
Knowlton, Timothy S., 1013, 1015
Knox, Bruce, 1228
Knox, John, 129
Kobayashi, Kazuhiro, 1012
Kobs, Dorothy, 1519
Koch, Kim, 557
Koch, Linda, 1231
Koch, Margaret, 463
Koch, Robert, 463
Kochen, Manfred, 904
Kochen, Paula, 904
Kociba, Marvin, 1133
Koehler, Frederick, 1363
Koehler, Michael, 627
Koehn, Renee, 1204
Koenig, Carolyn, 1202
Koerner, Jodi, 183
Koester, Ann Leone, 464
Koester, John C., 464
Kohler, Russell, Fr., 1422
Kohn, Elizabeth J., 465
Kohn, Robert A., 465
Kohn, Thomas, 1269
Kolanowski, Mark A., 1000
Kole, Cindy, 1282
Kolesar, Tim, 1293
Kolinski, Carol, 1100
Kollin, Mike, 1331
Kolman, Duane, 237
Kolt, Robert, 1094
Kolwalski, Lawrence, 161
Konkle, Bernie, Jr., 1078
Konschuh, Byron, 1437
Konschuh, Lorraine, 1437
Kooi, Andrew, 1078
Kool, Tim, 1434
Kool, Tom, 1175
Koops, Larry, 1376
Korman, Harry B., 686
Korson, Vicki, 1095
Korstange, Jason E., 1061
Kosch, Donald F., 467
Kosch, Mary T., 467
Kosch-Meier, Susan L., 467
Kosiba, Patricia, 1116
Kosier, Susan, 1027
Kossick, Glenn F., 556

Koster, Ardith A., 468
Koster, Cheryl, 468
Koster, Daniel J., 468
Koster, Greg, 468
Koster, Kurt, 468
Koster, Linda, 468
Koster, Rick, 468
Koster, Susan, 468
Kostin, Kelley, 1373
Kotecki, Lynn, 1350
Koutouzos, Connie, 1270
Koutz, Mick, 1548
Kovach, David, 15
Kovach, Sherrill Ambrosiani, 15
Kovan, Eric, 1453
Kowalkowski, Judy, 1314
Kowalkowski, Scott, 1314
Kowalski Sausage Co., 1019
Kowalski, Agnes, 1019
Kowalski, Donald, 1019
Kowalski, Joseph, 1278
Kowalski, Kenneth, 1019
Kowalski, Stephen, 1019
Kowles, Carolyn Ford, 826
Kozak, Mary Beth, 1311
Kozak, Robert P., 1542
Krafft, Dennis, 1123
Kraft, Lawrence H. "Larry", 342
Krahnke, Keith, 1448
Kraiger, Sharon, 1502
Kraker, Candy, 1081
Kramer, David, 1374
Kramer, Denver, 1546
Kramer, Donald, 1453
Kramer, Gerald J., 1110
Kramer, Mary L., 755
Kramer, Robert, 1371
Kranz, Mary Jo, 1091
Krappmann, Anne Marie, 1288
Kratz, Bill, 1102
Kraus, John P., 21
Kraus, Karl E., 1133
Kravitz, Norm, 1295
Kravutske, Mary C., 43
Kreger, Conrad, 1574
Kreger, William, 1574
Kreh, Tom, 1133
Kreiner, Tom, 1384
Krell, Joanne K., 450
Kresge, Bruce, 1108
Kresge, Sebastian S., 471
Kresl, Renee, 1161
Kresnak, Diane M., 1106
Kretschmar, Gina, 1265
Krick, Barbara T., 802
Krick, James H., 802
Krick, Rebecca, 802
Kridler, Bruce, 1453
Krieger, Teresa R., 118
Krishef, Marisa, 1295
Kroger Co., The, 1021
Krohn, Nancy, Dr., 1133
Kronlund, Louise B., 473
Kroswek, Larry, 1177
Krueger, Blake W., 1076
Krueger, Greg, 952
Krueger, Gregory, 671
Krueger, Mark, 1464
Krugel, Ronald, 1296
Krugman, Lynn, 383
Kruis, David S., 145
Kubacki, Judy, 1476
Kuber, Tom, 1145
Kucab, Allan, 1279
Kuehn, Charlie, 383
Kuehn, Gregg, Jr., 383
Kuester, Frederick D., 1074
Kughn, Richard, 1371
Kuhl, Peter A., 647
Kuhn, Bernard, 774
Kuhn, Elizabeth, 176
Kuhn, Jeffrey, 1385
Kuhn, JoAnn, 1462
Kuhn, Joellyn D., 176

Kuhn, John, 176
Kulju, Vicki, 1136
Kulka, Justine Olson, 618
Kulka, Robert, 618
Kulkarni, Bhushan, 1083
Kumao, Heidi, 1190
Kumbier, Norma, 690
Kumer, Chilakapati, 1557
Kump, Marsha A., 880
Kunde, Paul, 885
Kunitzer, John, 604, 1413
Kunkle, Dori, 1194
Kurt, James C., 348
Kurtya, Julia, 1205
Kurtz, Dan, 1312
Kurzweil, Chris M., 400
Kurzweil, Joanne, 400
Kutch, Cathy L., 1346
Kuwata, Toshio, 1012
Kuyers, John, 1351
Kuykendall, Ron, 1532
Kwekel, Tim, 1381

La-Z-Boy Chair Co., 1022
La-Z-Boy Foundation, 460
La-Z-Boy Inc., 1022
LaBine, Jay, 454
Lacher, Joseph P., Jr., 935
LaCroix, Sara Morley, 584
LaFernier, Susan, 1084
Lafferty, Melissa, 1210
LaForest, Robert, 1072
LaGrand, Reggie, 1434
Lahti, Martha, 476
Laidlaw, Barbara G., 478
Laidlaw, James C., 478
Laidlaw, Mary, 1258
Laidlaw, W. William, 478
Laidler, Lisa, 38
Laing, Rob, 1388
Laitinen, Tracey, 1448
Lake, Thomas E., 1346
Lake, William W., 1112
Lake, William W., Jr., 1100
Laker, Irving, 279
Lamberson, Frank A., 479
Lamberson, Mary T., 479
Lambert Brake Corp., 814
Lambert, Cassie, 103
Lambert, Jeffery K., 186
Lambert, Jeffrey K., 187, 188, 189
Lambert, Thomas W., 1451
LaMendola, Sal, 1108
Lammers, James D., 168
LaMothe, Alexis, 480
LaMothe, Debra, 1198
LaMothe, Patricia A., 480
LaMothe, William E., 480
Lampar, Ken, 1173
Lamper, Rebecca, 1184
Lampert, Janice, 1160
Lamphere, Carla D., 1205
Lamphere, Ward, 1205
Lancaster, Kevin, Rev., 1247
Lancaster, Mark, 1285
Lancaster, Martha, 1221
Lancaster, Richard, 1242
Lande, Nelson P., 657
Landgraf, William R., 394
Lane Texas Partners, 1522
Lane, Cindy, 1446
Lane, Darlene, 1284
Lane, John, 870
Lane, Thomas H., 975
Lane, W. Eugene, 1522
Laneve, Mark R., 990
Lang, Richard L., 1142
Langbo, Arnold G., 481
Langbo, Keith, 481
Langbo, Martha M., 481
Langbo, Maureen, 481
Lange, Ann H., 482
Lange, Cyndy, 1300

Lange, Duane, 1165
Lange, Michael, 1156
Lange, Robert, 482
Langholz, David E., 647
Langhorne, Susan, 45
Langley, Charles Clay, 483
Langley, Charles O., 483
Langlois, Paul, 694
Langolf, Deborah, 564
Langs, John, 1554
Langston, Terry, 1199
Laninga, John, 1267
Lanphear, Gail E., 9, 292, 628
Lanser, Janet L., 678
Lanser, Peter L., 678
Lantis, Jeff, 1131
Lantz, Mary, 1360
LaPlant, Gary, 1100, 1112
LaPointe, Carol, 1084
LaPonsie, Margaret, 1097, 1112
Lappan, Steve, 1104
LaPratt, Holly, 1459
LaReau, Allan R., 1211
Larisch, Linda C. Goad, 303
Larkin, Marla, 1208
Larner, Douglas F., 1491
Larsen, Cindy, 1463
Larsen, Daryl, 224
Larsen, David, 1554
Larsen, David P., 891
Larson, Claudia K., 335
Larson, Eric B., 485, 1106
Larson, Jay, Dr., 1149
Larson, Jonathan B., 335
Larson, Kathryn W., 485
Larson, Robert C., 485
Larson, Scott T., 335
Larson, Thomas R., 335
Larvick, Jeanne, 160
Larzelere, Annabel S., 487
Larzelere, John H., 487
Lashley, Elinor, 285
Lasko, John C., 488
Lathrop, Joe, 1436
Latture, Fay, 1099
Lauderbach, William, 9
Laughlin, David, 136
Lauretti, Michael, Chief, 1247
LaVergne, Lance, 1038
Laverty, Robert, 1457
Lavery, Frederick A., Jr., 801
Lavictoire Trust, Daisy Harder, 489
LaVictor, Kellie, 1448
Law, Bruce, 490
Law, D. Brian, 434
Law, Douglas, 1315
Law, Jacquelyn D., 490
Lawler, John J., 947
Lawrence, Belinda Turner, 462
Lawrence, Charles, 647
Lawrence, David L., 397
Lawrence, Donald B., Jr., 878
Lawrence, Tom, 1322
Laws-Clay, Velma, 1424
Lawter, Kathryn L., 1141
Lax, Lawrence S., 1296
Layne, Brenda, 1090
Lazzara, Michael, 1173
Lazzara, Michael J., 166
Leach, Cindy, 1230
Leach, Dustin, 1109
Leach, Gwen, 443
Leach, Lloyd, 213
Leaders, Rance L., 565
Leak, Mike, 1324
Leal, Joann, 1174
Leal, Joann P., 1456
Lealofi, Sam, 1305
Learmond, Alexis A., 964
Leavy, Patrick, 1363
LeBlanc, James, 1321
Lecznar, John F., 259
Lecznar, Mary R., 259
Ledy, Sharon, 643

Ledyard, Phyllis, 1110
Lee, Anna Mae, 1002
Lee, Aubrey W., 1467
Lee, Carl E., 1211
Lee, Jennifer, 1104, 1174
Lee, John, 1484
Lee, Judy, 1099
Lee, Leesa, 1099
Lee, Simon, 141
Lee, Timothy E., 990, 1423
Lee, Whilma B., 492
Leeburg, Louis, 249
Leece, Phillip, 964
Leegwater, John, 1335
Leemis, Terran, 1425
LeFever, Karen, 1249
LeFevre, Michael C., Msgr., 1209
Legg, Louis E., 807
Legowski, Margie, 1235
Lehman, Jan, 384
Lehman, Robert, 249
Lehmann, Mary, 1030
Lehnert, Amanda, 72
Leighton, Judd C., 495
Leighton, Mary Morris, 495
Leik, Rose Mary, 1384
Leitch, David G., 986
Lemen, Margaret K., 639
LeMieux, Linda J., 880
LeMieux, Norman, 1115
LeMire, William A., III, 1100
LeMire, William, III, 1112
Lemmen, Helene, 496
Lemmen, Karen, 1115
Lemmen, Ray, 877
Lemmen, Wayne E., 496
Lemmien, Cheryl, 1502
Lenahan, Joan O., 1003
Lenear, Dallas, Rev., 1277
Lenhardt, Terry, 1463
Lenoch, Vlado, 1302
Lenscrafters, Inc., 1546
Lenten, John, 1148
Lentine, Joe, 1343
Leonard, John C., 51
Leonard, Mike, 1419
Leonard, Patricia A., 51
Leonard, Scot A., 644
Leonard, Theodore, 51
Leonard, Timothy J., 51
Lepard, Matthew, 1111
Leppanen, Karen L., 1106
Lerner, Richard M., 1401
Lesley, E. Craig, 1342
Leslie Metal Arts Co., Inc., The, 798
Lesnau, J. Thomas, 1243, 1314
Lesperance, Kenneth, 1113
Lester, A. David, 1254
Lester, Matthew B., 1296
Lethorn, Larry J., 601
Lettinga, Michael, 1285
Lettinga, Wilbur, 1285
Leuliette, Timothy D., 1359
Leutz, Gordette, 1084
Leven, Myron P., 498
Levensteins, Astrida, 1317
Leverett, Allen L., 1074
Leverett, Lillie, 1231
Levey, Richard H., 739
Levine, Joel, 6
Levine, Michael, 1323
Levitas, Mitchel R., 1233
Levy, David, 1217
Levy, H. George, 1022
Levy, Nancy, 1453
Lewallen, Shelly, 1522
Lewand, Kathleen S., 1146
Lewandowski, Cate, 1249
Lewis, Clara M., Rev., 325
Lewis, David Baker, 755, 1106, 1470
Lewis, Denise J., 542, 1245
Lewis, Jean E., 129
Lewis, John, 500, 1371
Lewis, John D., 1106

Lewis, Karen, 1108
Lewis, Karen J., 949
Lewis, Kathleen McCree, 1470
Lewis, Lassie, 251
Lewis, Lyn, Dr., 1209
Lewis, Pam, 500
Lewis, Susan K., 499
Lewis, William R., 499
LeWitt, Peter A., 1347
Leyder, Dennis, 1120
Liberatore, Richard, 1277
Liberty, Stanley, 1107
Libs, James, 1468
Liedtke, Leslie Erb, 224
Liefbroer, Joseph, 1428
Lieffers, Lori, 1115
Liggett, Robert G., Jr., 671
Light, Timothy, 832
Ligon, Robert M., 1522
Lileikis, Frank, 501
Lileikis, Katherine, 501
Lileikis, Thomas, 501
Lim, Henry W., 1106
Lim, Lily, 1323
Lin, Henry, 1554
Lincoln, Barbara, 19
Linden, Allan J., 503
Linden, Hanna, 503
Linden, J. Stewart, 503
Linden, Sanford J., 503
Linder, Maureen, 949
Lindholm, Charles, 1526
Lindholm, John T., 880
Lindquist, Barbara, 1299
Lindsay Co., Bruce, 1516
Lindsay, Bruce C., 484
Lindsay, Sue, 1102
Linebaugh, Karl, 1150
Link, David T., 1517
Liparoto, Chris, 1321
Lipford, Rocque E., 545, 741
Lipford, Rocque L., 543, 544
Lipsey, Anne, 1305
Lis, Daniel T., 381, 1016, 1310
Lis, Lisa, 1298
Lishman, Ruth, 698
Liss, Beverly, 1296
Little, Elsie, 505
Little, Fran, 287
Little, Frances A., 504
Little, Kristi, 1097
Little, Nancy L., 1094
Little, Patricia A., 1016
Little, Virginia S., 504
Little, William T., 287
Little, William Tedrow, 504
Littlebear, Richard, Dr., 1188
Litzner, Karen, 1448
Liu, Hanmin, 450
Liveris, Andrew N., 202
Liveris, Paula A., 292
Liverman, Harvey, 1279
Livernois, Paul, 1278
Livingston, Pete, 1069
Llewellyn, Rebecca, 274
Lloyd, James, 1216
Lloyd, Seth, 1371
Lloyd, Shirley, 561
Lloyd, Thomas T., 1078
Lochricchio, Michael A., 1205
Locker, Katy, 392
Lockwood, Dan, 1110
Lockwood, Ned, 1099
Lockwood, Patricia, 1120
Locniskar, Dana M., 1106
Loeb, Frederick, 506
Loeding, Dahna, 1141
Loerup, Richard, 595
Loesel, Robert A., 71
Loewen, Jill, 1341
Logan, Jim, 1057
Logan, Martha, 1382
Logan, Nancy, 973
Logel, Douglas, 1384

Logue, James L., III, 1233
Loiacono, Joseph, 372
Loiacono, Stacy, 372
London-Wilson, Roberta, 1047
Lonergan, Patrick, 1269
Long, Al, 1286
Long, Bob, 1154
Long, Gary, 1163
Long, George P., III, 1047
Looker, Liz, 1432
Loomis, George, 1286
Loomis, Robert F., 701
Lopez, Eleanor, 1111
LoPrete, James H., 50, 136, 171, 872
LoPrete, Kent G., 872
LoPrete, Ruth, 872
Lord Trust Fund, Mary Louise and
    Marjori, 1002
Lorencen, Richard, 1119
Lorenz, John, 1416
Lorenzo, Albert L., 1280
Losinski, Kathy, 1388
Lossing, David, 1120
Lossing, David E., 1107
Lothian, Charlotte, 1130
Lott, Charles W., 1207
Lott, Michael, 1216
Lottie, Glenn, 1438
Loubert, Anna Marie, 701
Loudon, Michael R., Dr., 1086
Loutit Memorial Trust, William, 507
Loutit, William R., 507
Love, Larry, 1269
Love, Marcia, 1456
Lovellette, Anson, 1090
Lovett, Tiffany W., 346, 409, 587
Lowe, Jonathan, 1395
Lowe, Margaret, 1455
Lowe, Olivia, 1119
Lowe, Ron, 1383
Lowenstein, Glenn, 349
Lowenthal, Leora, 1235
Lowery, Lisa, Dr., 1269
Lowney, Ann, 732
Lowrie, James, 1139
Loxterman, Bill, 1447
Lubbers, Tim, 1446
Lubig, Kimberly, 1144
Lubin, Joel, 509
Lucas, David, 1434
Lucas, David P., 900
Lucassian, Laura Negosian, 231
Lucente, Tony, 1040
Luciani, Doug, 1443
Luckey, Thomas, 1079
Luckey, Tom, 1112
Ludington, John S., 382, 510, 787, 792
Ludington, Katrina K., 510
Ludington, Thomas L., 292, 510
Ludlow, Mark, 1210
Lueder, Michael S., Dr., 1092
Lueth, Larry, 1303
Lugers, Janet, 511
Lugthart, Ken, 1381
Luke, Bill, 627
Lukens, Jack G., 512
Lukens, Katherine, 512
Lukshaitis, Matthew, 1372
Lumpart, Molly, 1109
Lund, Lisa, 1095
Luneack, Ken, 513
Luneack, Paul, 513
Lunger, Terrance, 900
Luoma, Tim, 1084
Luplow, Sheila, 1276
Lusardi, Marion Ashen, 1082
Luttman, Cheryl, 386
Lutz, Calvin C., 641
Lutz, Cheryl, 685
Lutz, Debra, 1087
Lutz, Milton "Mick", 1137
Luxottica Retail, 1546
Luzzi, Richard D., 1071
Lykins, Elizabeth Welch, 1058

Lynch, Leila M., 514
Lynch, Mary, 1448
Lynch, Ray J., 514
Lynch, Tim, 1209
Lynch, Tim J., 514
Lynch, Tom, 1460
Lynch, Wendy J., 888
Lyneis, Mary M., 171
Lyneus, Mary M., 872
Lynn, Wayne, 1278
Lyon, By, 1147
Lyon, Debbie, 1242
Lyon, G. Albert, Sr., 515
Lyon, Heidi, 1193
Lyon, Linda, 1088
Lyons, Elijah Sherman, 1216
Lyons, Jan, 516
Lyons, Natalie, 1408
Lyons, Richard, 890
Lyons, Robert C., 516
Lyons, Trudee (Gertrude), 890
Lysinger, Todd, 1112
Lytle, Carol, 182

Maas, Lisa, 1319
Maas, Steve, 1319
Mabry, Creighton, 1434
MacAllister, Lorissa K., 448
MacAllister, Wes, 448
MacArthur, Karen M., 1237
Macchia, John, 745, 746
MacCrone, Edward E., 517
Macdonald, David, 1418
MacDonald, Michael, 1399
MacDonald, Rich, 1309
MacFarlene, John E., III, 1166
Machesky, Sandra, 1265
MacIntyre, John, 1145
MacKay, Timothy M., 1164
MacKeigan, John M., 1208
Mackie, Peter F., 1402
Macklem, Gary, 1165
Maclean, Kathy, 1440
MacLeod, Patricia, 81
Macomb County, MI, Staff Charitable
    Contribution Program, 1186
Macon, Christopher, 1207
Macon, Deborah, 1427
Macrie, San L., 935
Macumber, Peggy, 564
Madaj, Kim, 968
Madden, Sheryl, 471
Maddin, Michael, 1297
Maddin, Michael W., 1396
Madhaven, Ashok, 949
Madigan, Kris, 1079
Madison, Joseph W., 1164
Magnuson, Michaelina, 1048
Magrum, Ted, Dr., 1089
Magyar, John, 1500
Mahadevan, Sanganur V., 1557
Mahan, John, 1080
Mahennick, Jackie, 1329
Maher, Greg, 1323
Mahler, Michael W., 1499
Maholy-Nagy, Hattula, 1536
Mahone, Barbara J., 1467
Mahoney, Dave, 1224
Mahoney, Will, 1459
Maibach, Douglas, 940
Maier, David P.E., Rev., 1326
Maiers, Randy D., 1110
Maile, Larry, 184
Main, Charles, Dr., 1227
Maine, Donald, 170
Maiorana, William J., 181
Maitland, Peggy L., 52
Maitland, Stuart, 52
Majeske, Penelope K., 1238
Maki, John, 1148
Makima, Herb, 1362
Makos, Susan, 1219
Maks, Susan C., 481

Maksimchuk, Rachel, 1132, 1230
Makupson, Amyre, 755
Mala, Cynthia Linquist, Dr., 1188
Malhotra, Renu Sophat, 1555
Malhotra, S.K., 1555
Malik, Muzzamil, 1498
Mall, Catherine S., 521
Mall, Thomas, 1095
Mall, Thomas H., 521
Mallard, Julie, 1430
Malloy, Emily, 1350
Mally, C. Lane, 522
Maloney, Daniel G., 1505
Maloney, Michael, 1268
Maloney, Sean, 1028
Maloney, Steven H., 1505
Malovey, Clement, 523
Mammel Family Foundation, 1228
Mamon, Catherine, 1038
Manderfield, Marianne, 63
Maness, Michael, 462
Manie, Duane, 1158
Manifold, Joseph, 1429
Manilla, Robert J., 471
Manion, Paul, 1422
Manitou Boatworks and Engineering,
    1228
Mann, Charlie, 1141
Mann, Edward N., 1477
Mann, George P., 928
Mann, Richard D., 1477
Manning, Chuck, 1104
Manning, Pam, 497
Manning, Peter, 1273
Manoogian, Richard A., 1026
Manor Care, Inc., 1002
Mansfield, Bud, 1097
Mansfield, Patrick J., 1239
Manson, Richard, 1323
Marable, Poppy, 894
Marantette, Carol C., 1239
Marcel Callant Estate Trust, 237
March, Harold, 1131
March, Ted, 1157
Marchlewicz, Marge, 831
Marcin, Robert, 963
Marciniak, Rob, 1080
Marcks, Eula D., 524
Marcks, Oliver Dewey, 524
Marcoux, Jim, 1169
Marcoux, Kay, 1519
Marcrum, Daniel, 1362
Mardigian, Arman, 525
Mardigian, Edward S., 525
Mardigian, Helen, 525
Mardigian, Robert D., 525
Margolin, Michael, 1344
Marinoff, Peter, 1443
Mark, Florine, 1106, 1296
Markiewicz, John, 161
Markoff, David, 149
Markoff, Patricia A., 149
Marks Foundation, The, 1529
Marks, Bertram, 1278
Marks, Glenn, Rev., 1527
Marks, Stephen A., 1529
Marmer, Lynn, 1021
Marohn, Jane, 1090
Marohn, Jim, 1412
Marquardt, James M., 1194
Marquardt, Michele, 1211
Marquis, John R., 1111
Marr, Brian, 1080
Marra, Phyllis, 1209
Marriott, Susan, 1088
Marsden, Harry, 677
Marsden, K. Gerald, Dr., 1112
Marsh, Les, 1089
Marshall, John, 1148
Marshall, John F., 681
Marshall, Thurgood, Jr., 260
Marston, David, 1156
Martel, Robert, 1568
Martin Trust, Alice L., 527

Martin, Eleanor, 527
Martin, Fred, 1470
Martin, Jack, 1106, 1280
Martin, Jeffrey, 1087
Martin, John, 527
Martin, John H., 153
Martin, Keith, 1228
Martin, Laura Keidan, 860
Martin, Lou, 1368
Martin, Mary Lynn, 606
Martin, Michael, 527
Martin, Sue, 1161
Martin, Thomas J., 1144
Martin, Wade, 486
Martin, Webb F., 587
Martin, William L., 527
Martineau, Steve, 1154
Martinez, Juan J., 462
Martinski, Vic, 1484
Martore, Gracia C., 988
Marx, Tomasine, 1356
Marxer Ludgardis S. Trust, 528
Marxer, John E., 528
Marzke, Christopher J., 529
Marzke, Craig S., 529
Marzke, Kevin W., 529
Marzke, Kurt, 1412
Marzke, Kurt R., 529
Marzke, L. Richard, 529
Marzke, Nancy Ann, 529
Marzke-Fletcher, Lynn Ann, 529
Marzke-Schmidt, Lynn Ann, 529
Masamitsu, Cathy, 1291
Masco Corp., 1026
Mashni, Samir W., 1409
Mason County Central Senior Center,
    1102
Mason State Bank, 1027
Mason, Dick, 37
Mason, Gary, 1423
Mason, Kathleen B., 217
Mason, Lilian, 1125
Mason, Marilyn, 889
Massaro, Anthony A., 484
Massingill, Shirley, 1109
Masten, Ann, 1401
Mastracci, Laura, 690
Mathas, Theodore A., 1038
Matheson, Bonnie B., 202
Mathews, Christine, 1574
Mathur, Punam, 1336
Mathur, Ritu, 1111
Mattens, Roger, 767
Matthaei, Amy F., 531
Matthaei, Frederick C., Jr., 531
Matthaei, Julie A., 531
Matthaei, Konrad H., 531
Matthaei, Mary K., 531
Matthews, Debora, 1216
Mattson, Stephen, 439
Matzick, Kenneth J., 1467
Mauer, Kent, 745, 746
Maurer, Wesley H., Jr., 1146
Maxbauer, Patty, 1443
Maxey, Holbert, 1370
Maxwell, David E., 1143
Maxwell, Dorothy E., 1094
May, Alan A., 126
May, Brian S., 533
May, Daniel, 533
May, Dianne S., 533
Mayer, Bob, 1091
Mayes, Jane, 1133
Mayes, Michele Coleman, 935
Mayman, Todd A., 988
Maynard, Olivia P., 587
Maystead, Suzanne, 1384
McBain, Gwendolyn, 535
McBain, Robert J., 535
McBee, Mary Ann, 1089
McBride, Kathryn M., 990
McCalla, Helen, 537
McCallister, Michael B., 1003
McCalpin, William F., 366

McCardell, Ann-Marie, 538
McCardell, Bradley W., 538
McCardell, Kenneth W., 538
McCardell, Sheran M., 538
McCardell, Steven R., 538
McCardell, Tracy L., 538
McCardell, Willard B., Jr., 538
McCargo, Samuel, 1468
McCarren, Carolyn, 452
McCartan, Michael, 1110
McCarthy, Beth, 1147
McCarthy, Denis, 1122
McCarthy, Terri, 856
McCarthy, William T., 1253, 1326
McCartney, James, 418
McCartney, James E., 603
McCarty, Darren, 1333
McCarty, Roberta, 1333
McCaughey, Sarah Rosso, 1204
McClafferty, Charles C., 745, 746
McClear, Thomas, 1495
McClelland, Dale E., 146
McClendon, Joanne, 539
McClendon, Margaret, 539
McClendon, Mark, 539
McClendon, Robert "Bob", 539
McClimans, William, 454
McClure, Charles G. "Chip", 1030
McClurken, Donna, 1305
McCluskey, Ian, 1383
McCollough, Pat, 1151
McCollough, W. Alan, 1022
McComb, Cam, 1459
McComb, Kim, 1437
McComb, Tara, 1190
McConnell, LeeAnn, 1175
McCord, Ruth, 1448
McCormick, Joseph, 845
McCormick, Molly Bray, 94
McCorry, David F., 647
McCoy, Chris, 1424
McCoy, Christopher, 69
McCoy, Paul L., 319
McCoy, Virginia B., 1162
McCoy-Jacobs, Gloria, 103
McCracken, Paul W., 217
McCulley, Patricia A., 474
McCurdy, David, 1092
McCurley, Desiree, 1097
McCurry, Michael, 1173
McDonald, Charles R., 668
McDonald, Craig, 1152, 1344
McDonald, Edward, 1190
McDonald, Fred, 1083
McDonald, Joseph, Dr., 1188
McDonald, Lowell, 1133
McDonald, Ruth B., 1530
McDonald, Thomas W., Jr., 1530
McDonald, Thomas W., Sr., 1530
McDonald, William, 1530
McDonald, William I., 272, 681
McDonough, Al, 1410
McDonough, Eric, 1273
McDowell, Boyd, III, 727
McDowell, Charles S., 1542
McDowell, David, 63
McDowell, Deborah, 1108
McEachin, Charlene, 1082
McElvenny, Ralph T., Mrs., 1239
McFadden, Lillian, 1342
McFarland, Dan, 1268
McFarland, John, 1088
McFarland, Marilyn, 1160, 1174
McFarlane, Mary, 1574
McGee, Gay, 1547
McGee, Patricia Horne, 1180
McGhee, Daedia Von, 1410
McGinty, Ann Skiles, 754
McGlynn, Joseph, 251
McGlynn, Joseph M., 5
McGowan, Joan, 1341
McGowan, Linda M., 999
McGraw, Joshua D., 574

McGraw, Michael A., 574
McGraw, Michael R., 574
McGregor, June, 1205
McGregor, Katherine W., 542
McGregor, Tracy W., 542
McGrew, Dana, 1105
McGuigan, Chris Ann, 1103
McGuire, Janet, 1152
McGuire, Janet M., 1098
McGuire, Mildred M., 360
McHale, James E., 450
McIntire, Mary K., 1146
McIntyre, C.S., 1036
McIntyre, C.S., III, 543
McIntyre, David L., 544
McIntyre, James, 1194
McIntyre, James T., 544
McIntyre, James W., 1393
McIntyre, William D., Jr., 545
McKanders, Kenneth A., 158
McKay, Jim, 275
McKay, Lawrence I., III, 423
McKay, Patrick, 1108
McKee, Mary Jo, 329
McKee, Max B., 1553
McKee, Patrick J., 1553
McKeen, Alexander, 546
McKeen, Evelyn, 546
McKeen, Garry, 1532
McKenzie, Barbara, 1129
McKeough, Mike, 1126
McKeown, Connie, 1095
McKeown, Deb, 1085
McKibben, Verna, 547
McKibbon, Ed, 1108
McKindles, Norm, III, 1084
McKinnon, David, 1353
McKnight, Gail, Hon., 1347
McKnight, Richard, 1347
McKnight, Sid, 1102
McKree, Ed, 616
McLain, Tom, 1448
McLaughlin, John M., 1249
McLaughlin, Kristin, 1350
McLaughlin, Seth, 1546
McLean, Neil A., 301
McLellan, Robert, 1460
McLeod, Mary I., 548
McIsaacs, Christine, 1508
McMacken, David, 1129
McMahon, Mary, 732
McManus, Sydney, 480
McMichael, Matthew, 1099
McMorran, Hugh, 209
McNalley, Tim, 1450
McNally, Brian, 549
McNally, Dwight, 549
McNally, Jeff, 54
McNally, William F., 19, 549
McNinch, Charles, Dr., 1130
McNish, C.A., 551
McNish, Carol A., 551
McNish, Christine, 551
McNish, Elizabeth, 551
McNish, W.J., 551
McNulty, Thomas F., 1217
McPherson, Mary Ann Smith, 230
McPherson, R. Duncan, 230
McQueen, Patrick, 1339
McQuiggan, Carolyn A., 1531
McQuiggan, Mark C., 1531
McRay, Gary, 1316
McShane, Erin, 552
McShane, Kathleen, 552
McShane, Stephen J., 552
McVey, Alex, 1174
McWain, Teresa L., 937
McWilliams, Jim, 817
Meade, Barron, 1241
Meader, Edwin, 832
Meader, Mary, 832
Meador, David E., 392
Meadowbrook Investment Advisors, 668
Meakin, Brian, 1144

Meares, Tracey L., 427
Mecum Auctions, 1228
Medtronic Biologics, 1520
Meehean, Wayne, 1404
Meeks, Andrew, 553
Meeks, Debra, 553
Meeks, Jenny Lynn, 553
Meeks, Robert, 553
MEEMIC Insurance Co., 1028
Meendering, Dora, 1319
Meengs, Cindy, 1484
Meengs, William, 1363
Meengs, William, Jr., 1363
Megargell, Rick, 1235
Megli, Steve, 1402
Mehta, Dinesh, 1558
Meier, Donald A., Dr., 1326
Meier, Larry, 1389
Meijer, Hank, 1257
Meilner, John, 1277
Meinz, Thomas P., 1075
Meitzner, Alan, 1167
Meixelsperger, Mary, 1399
Mellein, John, 1184
Mellen, Anita, 279
Mello, Denise, 1082
Melnick, Joe, 946
Melstrom, Laurie, 1092
Melvin, James C., 145
Mench, Liz, 1375
Mendenhall, M. Karen, 396
Mendoza, Mike, 1546
Meneghel, Ronald A., 1482
Menelli, Peter, Fr., 1166
Mengebier, Dave, 1436
Mengebier, David G., 955, 961
Mengerink, Larry, 1248
Mennie, Douglas, 13
Mensching, Teresa, 1128
Mentzer, Robert, 1371
Meny, Edward E., 775
Menzies, Barbara, 1279
Mercantile Bank, 799
Merchant, Bernice "Woodie", 1258
Mercy Hospital, 1234
Merillat, Lynette S., 554
Merillat, Richard D., 554
Merillat, Stuart, 1542
Meritor Automotive, Inc., 1030
Merkel, Glen, 1168
Merkle, Mark, 373
Merkley, Martha K., 555
Merlanti, Mark, 1368
Merriam, Guy, 37
Merrill Lynch Trust Co., 94
Merrill, Danielle, 1124
Merritt, Gregory, 1113
Merritt, Terry, 1350
Merritt, Wallace, 1574
Merszei, Geoffery E., 973
Mertz, Alyssa, 430
Mesereau, Robert J., 1010
Mestdagh, Kristine B., 84
Meston, Susan, 1103
Meter, Jerry, 1468
Mettler, Constance, 245
Metz, Douglas, 422
Metzger, Mike, 1376
Metzler, Stephen A., 1475
Meyer, A., 1332
Meyer, Adolph H., 16
Meyer, Ida M., 16
Meyer, Jonathon, 795
Meyer, Kathleen, 795
Meyer, Sandy, 1462
Meyer, Sheryl, 1124
Meyer, Thomas, 795, 1176
Meyers, Chad, 1380
Meyers, Hannes, Jr., 1111
Meyers, Harvey, 1305
Meyers, Nydia, 557
Meyers, Roger L., 1345
Meyers, Scott, 1105
Meyers, Susan, 411

Meyersieck, Sue, 1133
MGM Grand, 1470
MGM Grand Casino, 597
MGM Mirage, 1336
Micallef, Joseph S., 594
Michael, Maureen, 1476
Michaels, Robert S., 751
Michaels, Ronald F., 36
Michie, James, 1372
Michigan Boating Industries Assn., 671
Michigan Cardiovascular Institute PC, 1033
Michigan Educational Employees Mutual Insurance Co., 1028
Michigan Elks Assn., 559
Michilizzi, Joseph, 1380
Michlash, Kenneth, 142
Michner, Walter J., 560
Michod, Charles L., Jr., 612
Mick, Debra J., 561
Mickelson, Marge, 1265
Mickens, Helen Pratt, 807, 1094
Micklash, Ken, 1177
Micklow, Patricia L., 681
Micsowicz, Steven A., 1357
Mida, Richard E., 846
Middleton, Chris, 1194
Mieitinen, Richard M., 760
Miel, Mary, 1095
Mielke, Kathy, 1341
Mielock, Douglas A., 1094
Milanese, Wendy A., 949
Milbeck, Steve, 666
Milbrodt, Bob, 129
Miles, Patrick, Jr., 454
Miliu, Kristina, 1372
Millan, Eugenie, 285
Millard, Philip H., 1162
Miller, Allen B., 565
Miller, Betty E., 562
Miller, Bill, 1118
Miller, Bonnie K., 1127
Miller, Bruce, 1439
Miller, C.E., 562
Miller, Catherine M., 648
Miller, Clara, 366, 1361
Miller, Clyde E., 562
Miller, Daniel R., 562
Miller, David, 564
Miller, David A., 562
Miller, Deb Clark, 1111
Miller, Donald J., 381
Miller, Edward J., 1106
Miller, Eugene A., 542, 1106
Miller, Glen, 301
Miller, Irving, 1197
Miller, J. William, 563
Miller, James E., 1326
Miller, Jane, 1385
Miller, Jerry L., 1211
Miller, Joan R., 681
Miller, Joe, 1132
Miller, Jonathan X., 1278
Miller, Karen, 1171
Miller, Katharine P., 630
Miller, Katherine S., 720
Miller, Kelly E., 562
Miller, Larry, 1128
Miller, Linda, 1434
Miller, Lloyd, 557
Miller, Lorraine M., 563
Miller, Louise B., 565
Miller, Louise Tuller, 566
Miller, Mark E., Dr., 1168
Miller, Nancy, 1111
Miller, Nelson, 1277
Miller, Patrick D., 648
Miller, Phillip D., 316
Miller, R.N. "Bo", 973
Miller, Richard, 1253
Miller, Rita L., 446
Miller, Robert B., 565
Miller, Robert, III, 1082
Miller, Sharon, 1033

Miller, Shelly, 1086
Miller, Tim, 1129
Miller, W. Gordon, 564
Milligan, Cynthia H., 450
Milligan, Gary K., 1299
Millman, Lawrence, 1347
Mills, Chris, 1496
Mills, David M., 1514
Mills, Frances Goll, 567
Mills, Kendall A., 1496
Mills, Marry Lloyd Dow, 1496
Milner, Jane, 1320
Milster, Richard, 1087
Minasian, Raffi, 1228
Mines, Tom, 1108, 1388
Mingerink, Ciri, 90
Mingerink, Marv, 143
Minkin, Philip, 279
Minoletti, William I., 1226
Minore, Jeff, 1338
Minter, Benda, 1086
Minton, Helen Lancaster, 570
Miramonti, Dina, 1122
Misenar, Jean, 1334
Mishler, Jeanie, 1429
Mishler, Jeremy, 1334
Mishra, Jitendra M., 1540
Mishra, Mithilesh, 1540
Missad, Missi, 1263
Mistele, Elisabeth M., 571
Mistele, Harold E., 571
Mistele, Henry E., 571, 660
Mitchell, Ann Marie, 1142
Mitchell, Christine L., 572
Mitchell, James K., 1253
Mitchell, Paul, 1423
Mitchell, William F., 572
Mitra, Sid, 730
Mittra, Sid, 1108
Mitzel, Dennis M., 653
Mitzelfeld, Pamela, 1108
Mixer, John L., Dr., 1103
Miyagawa, James E., 1393
Mleko, JoAnn, 1084
Moceri, Gregory, 170
Moceri, Gregory C., 170
Moceri, Margaret, 170
Moceri, Margaret E., 170
Moceri, Suzanne McNish, 551
Modetz, John, 1108
Modrall, Jim, 1128
Moeggenberg, Brent, 1433
Moehlman, Herman, 1494
Mogdis, Franz, 1095
Moh, Celia, 573
Moh, Michael, 573
Mohnke, Michael, 1150
Moholy-Nagy, Hattula, 1536
Mohr, Jayne, 1443
Moilanen, Jennifer Andrews, 826
Molhoek, Dan, 1299
Molhoek, Daniel C., 1275
Molinari, Michael William, 840
Molinello Revocable Trust, John, 575
Molinello Revocable Trust, Richard, 575
Molloy, Brian J., 576
Molloy, Catherine B., 576
Molloy, Mary Alice, 576
Molloy, Stephen P., 576
Molloy, Thomas C., 576
Molnar, Bill, 870
Molnar, Marie, 870
Monaghan, John R., Hon., 1110
Monahan, Michael T., 1106
Monastiere, Dominic, 434, 1547
Monroe Auto Equipment Co., 1036
Monroe Bank & Trust, 293, 505, 783, 869
Monroe Bank and Trust, 177
Monroe, Bill, 1165
Monroe, Robert H., 1237
Monsour, Nancy A., 743
Monte, Constance J., 1562
Monte, Salvatore P., 1562

Montgomery, Jim, 1242
Montgomery-Tabron, La June, 450
Moody, Nancy J., 83
Moon, Lawrence E., 588, 1107
Mooney, Joe, 1108
Moore, Alice W., 774
Moore, David, 1088
Moore, Dorian, 315
Moore, Edward J., 760
Moore, Eric, 1283
Moore, Franklin H., 578, 1110
Moore, Franklin H., Jr., 209, 579, 774, 881
Moore, Frederick S., 209, 578, 579, 881
Moore, Frederick S., Jr., 1110
Moore, Jacqueline, 1197
Moore, John, 1133
Moore, John H., 217
Moore, Judith, 1307
Moore, Judith H., 299
Moore, Kenneth, 1140
Moore, Lezlynne P., 578
Moore, Mary, 1489
Moore, Michael, 123
Moore, Robert H., 340
Moore, Scott, 1225
Moore, Sidney L., 315
Moore, Steve, 1157
Moore, Terence F., 202
Moore, Wenda Weekes, 450
Moore, Winn Lyon, 515
Moorehead, Marion, 443
Moote, Kim, 1079
Moran, Lou, 1277
Moran, Thomas, 1363
Morath, Carl, 581
Morath, Frederick, 581
Morath, Irene, 581
Morath, Lawrence, 581
Morath, Paul, 581
Moraw, Elizabeth A., 335
Morby, Carolyn R., 290
Morehouse, Kathleen, 1167
Morelli, Rita, 575
Morey, Diane, 1154
Morey, Krista, 582
Morey, Lon, 582, 1154
Morey, Norval, 582
Morford, Bill, 1104
Morgan Bradley LLC, 1046
Morgan Trust, Barbara, 583
Morgan, Eric, 1324
Morgan, Hugh, 1083
Morgan, Jane Frances, 1278
Morgan, Jean, 1444
Morgan, Kim, 1091
Morgan, M. Louise, 666
Morgan, Sandra, 541
Morgan, William, 1099
Morin, James, 1372
Morleau, Thomas, 1163
Morley, Bobbe Dale, 721
Morley, Burrows, III, 584
Morley, Burrows, Jr., 584
Morley, Christopher, 584
Morley, David H., 584
Morley, George B., Jr., 584
Morley, Katharyn, 584
Morley, Peter, 584
Morley, Peter, Jr., 584
Morley, Ralph Chase, Sr., 584
Morley, Ralph Chase, Sr., Mrs., 584
Morlock, Betty, 1392
Morlock, David R., 1328
Morning, John, 587
Morris, Donna T., 787
Morris, Michael G., 937
Morris-Belford, Linda, 1125
Morrison, Scot, 1088
Morrison, Virginia, 563
Morton, Susan, 1210
Mortz, Craig, 1419
Mosaic Foundation, 1228
Moscone, Onorio, 1226

Moser, Bobby, 450
Moser, Monica M., 1137
Moss, Ronald H., 130
Mossner, Caroline, 586
Mossner, William A., 586
Motkowski, Steve, 1161
Motor City Casino, 1470
Mott, C.S. Harding, 346
Mott, C.S. Harding, II, 346
Mott, Charles Stewart, 587
Mott, Maryanne, 587
Mott, Maryanne T., 588
Mott, Ruth R., 588
Mott, Willard, 202
Mouch, Virginia, 1128
Mount, Jeff, 1440
Mourand, Don, 1148, 1270
MPI Research, 1505
Mroczkowski, Thomas, 1363
Mueller, Arvin F., 830
Mueller, Jeffrey, 1171
Mueller, Linda, 1096
Mueller, Sue, 885
Mueller, Victoria R., 906
Mufarreh, Michael, 1189
Muha, Joseph, 1128
Muhammad, LaTonja, 1206
Muir, Cameron K., 872
Muir, Cathy, 448
Muir, David F., 448
Muir, Elizabeth M., 448
Muir, Gordon J., 872
Muir, Kathleen K., 448
Muir, Martha M., 872
Muir, William M., 448
Muir, William W., Jr., 448
Mukherjee, Dipankar, 656
Mukkamala, Aparna, 591
Mukkamala, Apparao, 591, 1290
Mukkamala, Bobby, Dr., 1107
Mukkamala, Srinivas, 591
Mukkamala, Sumathi, 591
Muladore, Andrea, 1300
Mulcahey, Michael, 952
Mulcahy, Michael D., 538
Mulder, Henry J., 647
Mulder, P. Haans, 1111
Mulders, William, 1087
Mulka, Susan Lane, 1522
Muller, Brigitte D., 1472
Muller, Frank G., 1472
Muller, George H., 1472
Muller, Katherine R., 681
Muller, Marci, 384
Muller, Phillip G., 1472
Muller, Steven, 1472
Mullings, Candice A., 894
Mullins, Susan M., 223
Mulloy, Martin, 1371
Mulloy, Martin J., 986
Mulvoy, James E., 494
Mulvoy, Maree R., 494
Munger, Dean, 1357
Munro, John, 765
Munroe, Kirk, 190
Munson, Eddie R., 755
Muntwyler, Wanda, 592
Muraski, Edwardine A., 421
Muraski, Kenneth J., 421
Murdock, James, 1464
Murdy, Carly, 1387
Murf, Veronica, 1271
Murguia, Ramon, 450
Murphy, Alice D., Rev., 165
Murphy, Anna, 1445
Murphy, Bruce D., 1018
Murphy, Kelly, 1175
Murphy, Leslie, 1427
Murphy, Sue, 1293
Murphy, William B., Hon., 1348
Murphy, William, Hon., 1269
Murray, Helen, 258
Murray, James, 1385
Murray, Margaret, 1048

Murray, Michael D., 871
Murray, Pat, 696
Murry, Dan, 1454
Murthy, N.R. Narayana, 260
Murtland, Greg, 1253
Musch, Dave, 1482
Musgrove, Clare, 775
Musilli, Lynne Hoover, 1082
Musser, Laura J., 594
Musser, R. Daniel, III, 1146
Mustang Northwest Club, 1228
Musto, Catherine, 1088
Muth, Jon R., 1348
Muth, William, 1434
Muxlow, Paul, 1165
Muzzin, Alberta, 1102
Myers, Burnice F., 1223
Myers, Irene, 596
Myers, Keith T., 595
Myers, Margaret, 596
Myers, Martha, 596
Myers, Nathan, 596
Myers, Shelley, 1272
Myers, Tom, 1442
Mykala, Jon, 1224

Nachman, Allan, 1425
Nader, Erica, 197
Nader, Frederick, 197
Nader, Rita, 197
Nadosy, Peter A., 260
Naftaly, Robert, 1297
Nagelkirk, Joan, 1165
Nagy Family Foundation, 11
Nagy, Kathy S., 11
Nahey, Brian L., 1070
Nakadar, A.S., Dr., 1187
Nakadar, Abdul Rahman, 1538
Nakadar, Najma, 1538
Nallamouthu, Udayalakshmi, 1292
Nameche, Larry, 1184
Nance, Dianne, 1284
Napont, Brian, 1273
Nardozzi, Angela, 1402
Nartelski, Evelyn, 1464
Nartker, Joe, 1165
Nash, Kim, 1198
Nasr, Bassam G., Dr., 1110
Nass, Joel M., 766
Naswell, Patrick, 1107
Nath, Radha, 1093
National Basketball Association, 1046
National City Bank, 55, 119, 331, 477, 519, 536, 613, 737, 1103, 1282, 1470
National City Bank of the Midwest, 1123
Naugles-Jack, Deanna L., 1470
Naz, Mary D., 348
Neal, Eleanor, 598
Nedd, Khan J., 647
Neef, Allan, 662, 723
Neelis, Randy, 1145
Neely, Mary M., 9, 628
Neff Engineering Co., Inc., 1539
Neff, Betty M., 1539
Neff, David, 1332
Neff, Elizabeth W., 1539
Neff, Harry M., 1539
Neff, I. Marie, 1539
Neff, Julia D., 1539
Neff, Michelle, 1098
Neff, Robert, 1024
Neff, Virginia M., 1539
Negin, Danny, 1446
Negosian, Mary, 231
Neidlinger, Darlene, 1149
Neill, Rolfe, 462
Neiman, Sandra K., 1541
Neller, Keith, 1384
Neller, Rosie, 1384
Nelms, Charlie, 587
Nelson, Allen J., 600
Nelson, Bonnie S., 599

Nelson, David N., 599
Nelson, Donald J., 600
Nelson, Gerald, 74
Nelson, Gordon E., 325
Nelson, Irving T., 600
Nelson, James, 1180
Nelson, Jay, 1190
Nelson, Jay N., 599
Nelson, Jerry, 557
Nelson, Kenneth, 647
Nelson, Marilyn S., 599
Nelson, Mary Goodwillie, 856, 1058
Nelson, Merlin A., 600
Nelson, Robin N., 599
Nelson, Rod, 1448
Nelson, Sally, 1159
Nelson, Shirley A., 600
Nelson, Sue, 1443
Nelson, Thor, 1111
Nelson, William J., 952
Nesbary, Dale, 1463
Nethercott, Shaun, 1344
Neuhard, Thomas, 1141
Neuhauser, Charlotte, 683
Neusiis, Thomas F., 1326
Neve, Keith, 1097
Neville, Joe, 1546
Nevils, Harold, 1231
Nevin-Folino, Nancy, 290
New York Life Insurance Co., 1038
Newberry, Joan, 229
Newberry, William, 229
Newby, Barbara Hill, 374
Newhouse Foundation, Samuel I., Inc., 384
Newhouse, Tim, 1212
Newman, Ann, 1046
Newman, Donald L., 602
Newman, Jan Barney, 63
Newman, John, 1476
Newman, Max K., 602
Newman, Ruth A., 181
Newman, Steven E., 602
Neydon, Peter, 1111
Nguyen, Mat, 1463
Nicholoff, Kris, 1341
Nichols, Hank, 1122
Nichols, Karen, 212
Nichols, Margaret J., 1348
Nichols, Ray, 1433
Nichols, Walter, 1183
Nicholson, Ann, 922
Nicholson, James B., 542, 1106
Nicholson, John R., 1239
Nicholson, Philip, 1420
Nickless, Allen E., 604
Nickless, Arthur H., 603
Nickless, Charles, 604, 883
Nickless, Darcy, 604
Nickless, Marie A., 604
Nickson, Laurie, 1338
Nicola, Nick, 384
Nicolay, Ernest L., III, 605
Nicolay, Ernest L., Jr., 605
Nicolay, JoAnn, 605
Nicolay, Joanne, 606
Nielson Enterprises Corp., 327
Nielson, Barbara A., 117
Nielson, Cori, 991
Nielson, Cori E., 691
Nielson, Dale M., 117, 327
Nielson, Keith, 991
Nielson, Keith M., 117
Nielson, Melvin K., 327, 991
Nielson, Ruth E., 327
Niemann, Jean, 1408
Nierenberger, Janine, 1248
Nierenberger, Janine L., 1057
Niester, Donna M., 1110
Nietzke, Allan, 1133
Nieuwenhuis, Ann, 1307
Nill Trust, Mabel E., 607
Nill, Mabel E., 420
Nill, William F., Dr., 420

Ninan, Molly, 1413
Ninomiya, Chris, 191
Nissan Motor Corp. U.S.A., 1040
Nissan North America, Inc., 1040
Nixon, Barbara P., 259
Nixon, William R. "Bill", Jr., 259
Nobach, Michael, 1094
Noble, Chad, 1436
Noble, Wynne, 1338
Noch, Larry H., 582
Noel, D. Jeffrey, 1072
Noel, John, 1284
Nofs, John, 1198
Nolan, Daniel P., 83
Nolan, Matt, 83
Nolan, Matthew J., 83
Noland, Mariam C., 462, 1106, 1280
Nolf, Patricia A., 600
Norcia, Jerry, 755, 1371
Nordberg, Erik, 1344
Noricks, Joan, 1093
Norman, Paul, 1015
Norris, Helen, 1305
Norris, Kimberly M., 1085
North, Jim, 1112
North, Walter, 1097
Northcott, Carol, 1223
Northern Michigan Bank & Trust Co.,
    337, 502, 518
Northern Trust Co., The, 727
Northrup, Greg, 1463
Northshore Mining Co., 954
Northway, John, 1168
Norton, Dale, 1091
Norton, John, 1150
Nothelfer, Sarah, 1300
Novak, Barbara Griffin, 1030
Novitsky, John, 632
Novitsky, John F., 632
Nowak, John M., 610
Nowak, Judy K., 782
Nowak, Maureen K., 610
Nunnold, Jim, 1446
Nusbaum, Barbara, 611
Nusbaum, Irving, 611
Nuveen, John, 612
Nuveen, John S., 612
Nyberg, Bruce E., 1106
Nye, Homer, 1391
Nye, Homer E., Dr., 118
Nygren, Mark, 1145
Nylaan, Kris, 1268
Nyquist, Paul F., 1326

O'Brien, Elizabeth, 1002
O'Brien, John, 352
O'Brien, Martha A., 318
O'Brien, Pat, 1096
O'Bryan, Sean, 1122
O'Callaghan, Michael, 1493
O'Callaghan, Patrick, 1121
O'Connell, Christine, 175
O'Connell, Kathleen M., 150
O'Connor, David P., 1110
O'Connor, Kerry, 1097
O'Connor, Thomas J., 1017
O'Donald, John, 1130
O'Donnell, Vincent, 1323
O'Farrell, Richard, 1145
O'Grady, John B., 59
O'Hara, Robert A., 1518
O'Hara, Thomas E., 1518
O'Hare, Maria, 1543
O'Hare, Patrick, 1543
O'Keefe, Brian D., 246
O'Keefe, Stephanie, 1323
O'Leary, Denise, 1233
O'Leary, Joseph, 1084
O'Leary, Joseph P., 1075
O'Neill, Alfonso V., 1239
O'Neill, David, 1128
O'Neill, John, 1544
O'Neill, Madeline S., 1544

O'Neill, Romany, 185
O'Reilly, John B., 1404
O'Rourke, David, 1210
Oakes, Michael, 1102
Oare, Carol F., 495
Oare, Ernest A., 495
Oberman, William, 391
Obloy, Bernice, 614
Obloy, Leo A., 614
Obloy, Michael H., 614
Ochoa, Greg, 590
Odar, Michael F., 1211
Oddo, Vicki, 1440
Oehmke, Wayne, 1327
Oetting, Martin C., 690
Oetting, Roger H., 353
Off Brothers, 1505
Offield, James, 1363
Ogar, Charles, 1535
Oglenski, Debbie, 1133
Oglesby, Daniel, 1269, 1277
Oh, Angela E., 1517
Ohm, Paul R., 565
Ohmer, Dan, 1078
Ojakli, Ziad S., 986
Okonski, Raymond N., 757
Okotie-Eboh, Juliette, 1470
Okun, Marvin, 615
Okun, Rosalie, 615
Older, Caroline, 1193
Oldford, Will G., Jr., 1110
Olds, Ransom E., 616
Oldt, Patricia, 1269
Olekszyk, Danielle, 755
Oleson, Don, 617
Oleson, Donald W., 617
Oleson, Frances M., 617
Oleson, Gerald, 617
Oleson, Gerald E., 617
Oleson, Gerald W., 617
Olinger, Allen, 261
Olinger, Deborah, 261
Olivares, Jay, 1118
Olivarez, Juan, 1138
Oliver, Elizabeth J., 1018
Oliver, Harriet, 1354
Olsen, Gary, 706
Olsen, Stephen G., 1103
Olson, Beverly Knight, 462
Olson, Clarine, 1128
Olson, Judy Watson, 1270
Olson, Michael, 701
Olson, Sandra, 1384
Olson, Stephanie Mallak, 1135
Olsson, Stephan, 1139
Olsson, Wally, 1291
Olsson, Walter, 131
Olthoff, Kay, 1103
Oltrogge, Michael, 1188
Omdahl, Dick, 1161
OmniCare Health Plan, 597
Oosting, Gordon, 1269
Oppenheim, Katie, 1458
Oppenheimer-Nicolau, Siobhan, 1254
Oprea, Terry, 1278
Orange, Gayle, 1311
Orchard, Dale O., 559
Orear, Jeffrey, Dr., 1145
Oreffice, Paul F., 292
Oriel, Pat, 9
Orlando, Brenda M., 1369
Orley, Marcie, 1296
Orley, Marcie Hermelin, 1281
Orlik, Darcy, 1154
Ormand, Kirk, 897
Ornstein, Cindy, 1255
Orosz, Florence Upjohn, 832
Orosz, Joel, 73
Orr, James L., 1570
Orsak, Debrethann R., 1181
Orsini, Michael F., 1016, 1310
Ortiz, Elizabeth Hall, 1361
Osborne, Charles, 1380
Osborne, Robert N., 1345

Oskoian, Karl G., 1173
Ostahowski, Mark, 9
Osterink, Bruce J., 1000
Osterling, Howard, 139
Ostrander, Jane, 1036
Ostwald, David, 1118
Ostwald, Johana, 191
Ostyn, Leslie, 184
Ott, Alan W., 292, 628
Ott, Richard E., 620
Ott, Richard E., Jr., 620
Otterlei, John, 366
Ottimer, Danielle, 1276
Ouellette, Daniel J., 1258
Ouimet, Mark, 1458
Overly, Alice, 1048
Owen, Richard, 952
Owens, Anna E., 147
Owens, Charles, 1341
Owsiany, Michael, 1239
Ozarchuck, Janet, 1323

Paciorek, Karen, 1468
Page, David K., 1106
Page, Lawrence C., Sr., 623
Pahnke, Brian, 1100
Pahssen, Wayne A., 244
Paige, Mike, 1360
Paine, G. William, 624
Paine, Martha L., 624
Paine, Tom, 1102
Paine-McGovern, Carol, 624
Paisley, Beverly, 53
Paisley, Bonnie, 53
Paisley, Charles, 53
Paisley, Martha, 53
Paisley, Peter, 53
Paisley, Peter, Jr., 53
Palace of Auburn Hills, The, 1046
Palace Sports & Entertainment, Inc.,
    1046
Palazzolo-Shaw, Felicia, 1453
Palchick, Bernard, 1194
Paler, Ronald, 1341
Palm, Norman, 1340
Palma, Eric, 1502
Palmer, David, 561
Palmer, Maria F., 625
Palmer, Shirley, 287
Palmer, Walter E., 625
Palmer, Walter E., Sr., 625
Palo, Bryce, 1284
Pamida, Inc., 1043
Pandya, Kirit, 1558
Panek, Bob, 1166
Panhandle Cruisers, 1228
Pannuto, Michael, 1226
Panopoulos, Christos, 1335
Paoli, Francis E., 1112
Papa, Joseph C., 1045
Pappas, Charles N., 626
Pappas, Norman, 1425
Pappas, Norman A., 626
Pappas, Susan L., 626
Paragon Die & Engineering Co., 448
Parasiliti, Trina, 1546
Pardee Foundation, Elsa U., 1547, 1548
Pardee, Elsa U., 628
Pardoe, James A., 1149
Parfet Family Foundation, Donald & Ann,
    1505
Parfet, Ann V., 629
Parfet, Don, 1309
Parfet, Donald, 1302
Parfet, Donald R., 629, 1451
Parfet, Martha G., 1505
Parfet, William U., 1088, 1505
Paris, Andy, 1360
Paris, Roger L., 391
Parish, Preston, 1302
Parish, Preston L., 630
Parish, Preston S., 1302
Parish, Suzanne D., 163, 1302
Parish, Suzanne U.D., 630

Park, Christine, 1038
Park, James C., 69, 631
Park, Kimberly A., 631
Park, Philip Scott, 631
Parke, Jennifer Hudson, 392
Parker, Barbara, 965
Parker, Cory, 1448
Parker, Lynne, 732
Parker, Marla, 1253
Parker, Mary Webber, 392
Parker, Patric, 1120
Parker, Patty, 1256
Parker, Timothy, 1126
Parker, Tony, 1444
Parker-Moore, Jennifer, 1122
Parks, Bob, 1338
Parks, Burt, 1147
Parks, Floyd L., 299, 832
Parks, Hugh, 766
Parks, Liz, 632
Parks, Lyman, Jr., A.I.S., 1463
Parmenter, Nancy, 1122
Parr, Gale, 1095
Parrish, Debra, 1084
Parrish, Jean, 633
Parrish, Stan, 633
Parson, Jan, 1318
Parsons, Retta, 1397
Partain, Kristi, 890
Partain, Robert, 890
Pas, Leonard, 1195
Paschke, Randy, 1196
Pasik, Lawrence, 1197
Pasky, Cynthia J., 1106
Pasman, G. Joseph, Jr., 1326
Passaro, T.J., 917
Passaro, Tim, 1090
Passinault, William J., 1394
Pastor, Doug, 1464
Patel, Mayur, 462
Patenaude, Linda, 1086
Paterson, John, 142
Paterson, Steve, 1437
Patino, Douglas X., 587
Patriacca, Diane, 1302
Patrias, Rebecca, 11
Patrick, Jed, 702
Patrick, Katherine, 1137
Patrick, Lawrence, 1206
Patrick, Victor, 1367
Patrona, Daniel, Sr., 1294
Patterson, Brad, 1094
Patterson, Debbie, 1150
Patterson, Jane R., 427
Patterson, Linda B., 215
Patterson, Melissa, 588
Patterson, Miki, 1459
Patterson, Samuel R., 1047
Patterson, William R., 349
Patton, Douglas, 968
Patton, Jeff, 1304
Paul, Beatrice, 635
Pauling, Delayne H., Rev., 118
Pavlicek, Michele, 882
Pavlick, John, 595
Pavlik, Don, 1548
Payne, Brenda, 240
Payne, Harold, 1116
Payne, Larry L., 240
Payne, Thomas W., 75, 368, 473, 666
Payovich, Julie Kay, 917
Peal, Wayne, 1171
Pearle Vision, Inc., 1546
Pearle, Stanley C., 1546
Pearson, Debra A., 227
Pearson, Glen H., 1402
Pearson, Heidi, 227
Pearson, James T., 227
Pearson, John E., 227
Pearson, Susan R., 227
Pease, Becky, 1459
Pechur, Robert E., 1167
Peck, Paul, 561
Pederson, Suzanne H., 1349

Pelfresne, Sarah, 77
Pelleran, K.P., 1338
Pellerito, Coleen O., 638
Pellerito, Frank A., 638
Peltier, Chad, 1415
Peltz, Charles, 242
Pena, Dione, 1414
Pence, Robin, 988
Pendell, Timothy A., 1243
Penner, Jonathon, 640
Penner, Marsha, 1083
Penner, Ruth, 640
Pennington, Alan, 873
Penny, Dale A., 423
Pentecost, Joe D., 641
Penzien, Shelly, 1327
Pepper, Glen, 1150
Pepper, Jane G., 484
Pepper, Jeanne, 1255
Pepper, Joan, 1174
Pepper, Michael A., 1103
Peppler, Linda, 1263
Perino, Robert, 1085
Perkins, Bill, 1241
Perkins, Janice L., 1015
Perkins, R. Clay, 1117
Perla, Subbaiah, Dr., 1292
Pernick, Margo, 1297
Perreault, Barb, 1221
Perrigo Co., L., 1045
Perrone, Dianne C., 642
Perrone, John, 642
Perry, Jason, 1002
Perry, Mark, 1040
Perry, Marnette, 1021
Perry, Marvin, 315
Perry, Ruth, 1175
Perschbacher, Walter F. "Chip", 1328
Pertile, Shirley, 1293
Peruyeso, Jane, 52
Peruyeso, Jose, 52
Pestronk, Robert, 588
Peterman, Donna C., 1047
Peters Trust, Katherine, 644
Peters, Bonnie, 139
Peters, Bruce, 1145
Peters, Cheryl, 1417
Peters, Jane, 1135
Peters, Katherine, 644
Peters, Phillip H., 587
Peters, Richard W., 1103
Peters, Shari, 1157
Peters, Sharon, 1338
Peters, Steven, 737
Petersen, Anne C., 1264
Petersen, Thomas, 454
Petersmark, Steven, 1334
Peterson, Brent, 1139
Peterson, Bruce D., 977
Peterson, Dan A., 191
Peterson, Dave, 1429
Peterson, David R., 1092
Peterson, Joe, 1574
Peterson, Julie Lehman, 1194
Peterson, Mark R., 645
Peterson, Robert, 645
Peterson, Sue, 1450
Peterson, Tom, 1331
Petersons, Maija, 1305
Petredean-Di Salvio, Carol, 1132, 1424
Petrie, Jennifer Margaret, 154
Petroff, George J., 878
Petry, Kristi, 232
Petschar, Patti, 1118
Petska, Lois, 358
Petska, Richard, 358
Petska, Stephanie, 358
Pettibone, Michael, 646, 1328
Pettibone, William, Jr., 646
Petty, Brian, 1120
Petz, Thomas J., 1239
Pew, Robert C., 908
Pew, Robert C., III, 1058
Pfahler, Carol, 1115

Pfeiffer, Dan, 1335
Pfliegel, Deborah, 1196
Phaller, Leo, 1527
Phelan, Daniel J., Dr., 1137
Phelan, Nancee, 1418
Phelan, Paul, 1183
Phelps, Steve, 401
Phillips, Jeff, 1120
Phillips, Judy, 1088
Phillips, Nancy A., 865
Phillips, Rodney, 1088
Phillips, Sheila, 1362
Phipps, Robert J., 641
Physicians' Organization of Western
    Michigan, 647
Piaskowski, Gregory, 1367
Pickard, Steven, 1557
Pickard, Vivian, 990
Pickard, William F., 1106
Pickel, Vicki, 1418
Pickett, Jason A., 540
Pickett, Kiatra M., 540
Pickett, Sherry, 540
Pickett-Erway, Carrie, 1138
Pieczynski, Judith, 1120
Pientenpol, Glenn, 1169
Pierce, Barbara, 770
Pierce, Elsie, 170
Pierce, Jessie M., 1550
Pierce, Rhoda A., 1195
Pierce, Richard B., 258
Pierce, Sandra E., 1280
Pierce, Watson, 170
Pierce, Willard G., 1550
Pierce, Willard L., 1550
Piersma, Carl, 1081
Pierson, Lois, 1082
Piesko, Susan, 883
Pietras, Scott, 749
Pike, Aaron, 1267
Pillion, Scott, 1415
Pilnick, Gary H., 1015
Pinckney, Larry A., 1207
Pinderski, Louis A., 775
Pino, Catherine, 27
Pinsky, William, 1386
Piper, Ed, 1436
Piper, Kathy, 1502
Piper, William H., 587
Pitt, Tom, 1078
Pitts, Stanley, 1206
Pitts-Johnson, Marilyn, 1166
Pixley, Don, 1108
Pixley, Suzanne, 1247
Pixley, Vern, 1108
Place, Vicki, 1547
Plante, Max J., 1082
Plaskey, Wade C., 981
Platt, Harry, 325
Plesiewicz, Ray, 1454
Pliska, Robert, 1205
Plumb, Stephen D., 878
Plummer, Katy, 1108
Plym, Francis J., Mrs., 649
Plym, J. Eric, 649
Plym, John E., Jr., 649
Plym, Nancy S., 649
PNC Bank, 1138
PNC Bank, N.A., 23, 179, 484, 1047
PNC Financial Services Group, Inc., The,
    1047
Poddar, Devesh Darshan, 406
Poddar, Mayurika, 406
Poddar, Shrikumar, 406
Poet, Jeff, 1429
Poferl, Judy, 1077
Pohl, Judy C., 794
Pohl, Ronald R., 794
Pohlod, Shelli, 1449
Poisson, Thomas, 702
Polan, Jesse N., 651
Poling, Harold A., 1467
Polk, Stephen R., 1245
Polla, George, 1302

Pollack, Henry N., 652
Pollack, Lana B., 652
Pollard, Allison, 1225
Pollock, Mary, 1202
Polyak, Philip G., 955
Polzin, John G., 1211
Pomaville, Steven, 1173
Pompey, Randel, 1445
Ponce, Joe, 1423
Pontiac, Joseph, Inc., 386
Ponting Trust, William Fitzherbert, The,
    653
Poole, Charles W., Rev., 1103
Poole, Steven W., 290
Popa, Nancy A., 961
Pope, David, 1131
Pope, James, 185
Pope, Janet DeVlieg, 185
Pope, Kathy, 1124
Popielarz, Don, 850
Port, Friedrich, 1476
Portenga, Bob, 1391
Porter Machinery Co., Burke E., 655
Porter Trust, Burke, 655
Porter, Donald H., 1343
Porter, Jack, 662
Porter, Joe, 1156
Porter, John W., 587
Porter, Margaret, 901
Porter, Michael C., 977
Porter, Nicolas C., 1355
Poslajko, Julie, 219
Post, Beth, 511
Post, Dave, 1104
Post, Deborah, 135
Post, Gary, 1103
Post, Martha, 687
Postema, Miles J., 1301
Poteat, Jennifer, 1083
Poteat-Flores, Jennifer R., 816
Poterala, Mike, 1364
Pott, Sandra, 1455
Potter, Sharon L., 408
Potts, Al, 1128
Potts, David W., 1356
Potts, Terry, 1380
Poulton, Shirley, 1126
Poupard, Lawrence G., 1409
Powazek, Barbara Haveman, 357
Powell, Carlton, 1405
Powell, Dick, 595
Powell, Earl W., 462
Powell, George, 1391
Powell, Mavis C., 600
Power, Jeff, 402
Powers, Barbara, 1462
Powers, Eddie G., Jr., 1171
Powers, Robert M., 937
Powers, Sharon, 1482
Powers, Sheri, 889
Powers, Theresa, 889
Prairie, Pam, 1128
Prasad, Boppana D., 1292
Prasad, K.C., 1292
Pratt, Carolyn M., 745, 746
Prawozik, Bernard, 49
Pray, Joe E., 1119
Prechter Charitable Lead Trust, Heinz C.,
    911
Prechter, Heinz C., 911
Prechter, Paul, 911
Prechter, Stephanie, 911
Prechter, Waltraud, 911
Prechter, Waltraud E., 911
Predhomme, Michael J., 524
Preede, Linda, 1108
Preiss, Kathleen, 1372
Preiss, Sue, 1372
Premo, Susan, 1160
Presant, Michael, 1295
Prestage, Richard, 513
Preston, L.A., 563
Preuss, Matt, 1358
Prevo's Family Markets, Inc., 658

Prevo, Aaron P., 658
Prevo, Dan R., 658
Prevo, Pamela M., 658
Prevost, Patrick, 947
Price, Anne Sage, 708
Price, Glenda D., Dr., 1106
Price, Hubert, 1338
Price, Jody, 856
Price, Robert, 31
Price, Robert E., 660
Pricewaterhouse Coopers LLP, 1046
Prieskorn, Dawn, 1449
Priester, Brian, 1094
Prince Foundation, 187
Pringle, Sherry, 944
Printek, Inc., 917
Proctor, Amanda, 1398
Productions, D&M, 206
Prophet, James T., 1136
Prost, Lucinda, 182
Provenzano, Robert, 1356
Pryor, Daniel A., 661
Pryor, Esther A., 661
Pryor, Frederic L., 661
Pryor, Mary S., 661
Pryor, Millard H., 661
Pryor, Millard H., Jr., 661
Ptasznik, Ed, Jr., 1278
Puerner, Michael, 1193
Puerner, Michael W., 1000
Puff, Erich, 395
Pugh, Betsy, 1323
Pulles, Gregory J., 1061
Pumford, Susan A., 1237
Pung, Steven, 1154
Pung, Steven D., 1006
Purman, Timothy, 1121
Puro, Kristin M., 753
Putman, Dan, 1144
Pylman, Norman, 930
Pynnonen, Ed, 1299

Quaal, Al, 1272
Quain, Barbara, 1122
Qubein, Nido R., 1022
Queller, Robert L., 217
Quershi, Amber T., 1498
Quershi, Tanvir I., 1498
Query, Ann, 1111
Quicken Loans, 1046
Quimby, David D., 861
Quinn, Cindi, 1144
Quinn, Kevin M., 559
Quinn, Tim, 1428
Quinney, Gloria, 1185
Quint, Michael, 1574
Quraishi, Ali, 1187

R&B Machine Tool Co., 1052
Raasio, Chen, 1232
Rabbers, Blaine A., 1497
Rabideau, Michelle, 1394
Racette, Karen, 1138
Racine, William, 397
Raese, Robert, 640
Ragin, Luther M., Jr., 366
Rahaley, Dennis, 683
Raines, Jodee Fishman, 224
Rainey, Bartley J., 277
Raiola, Anthony J., 665
Raiola, Dominic J., 665
Raiola, Wendy S., 665
Raiola, Yvonne, 665
Rajewski, Robert, 1428
Raju, Bin, Dr., 1292
Raker, Tim, 1131
Rakolta, John, Jr., 1106, 1359
Raleigh, Janet, 1449
Ralph, James, Jr., 1171
Ralstrom, Curt S., 1341
Ramasamy, Kala Kuru, 1164
Ramer, James T., 1088

Ramirez, Juan, 1410
Ramirez, Michael, 1269
Ramirez, Randy, 1436
Ramirez, Sylvia, 1476
Ramsey, Cherry, 561
Randall, David, 1140
Randall, Harold K., 667
Randall, Judy J., 901
Randolph-Black, Kay, 1414
Ranger, Thomas F., 16
Rankin-Yohannes, Angela, 1171
Ransford, Fred J., 1541
Ransford, Sue, 1177
Rantala, Ward, 1439
Ranzini, Stephen L., 1542
Rao, Kottamasu S., 1292
Rapanos, Just, 1152
Rapp, Marcia, 1127
Rappe, Kristine A., 1074
Rappleye, Richard K., 471, 1345, 1348
Rapson, Calvin, 1423
Rapson, Rip, 471
Rasor, Theresa, 1159
Rassel, Richard E., 514, 946
Rassi, Andrew, 1275
Ratner, Milton M., 668
Rautenberg, Steven, 1038
Raval, Sudha, 669
Raval, Tejas H., 669
Ravipati, Sitaram, Dr., 1292
Rawal, Harish, 669
Ray, Chester, 1080
Raye, Glenda Byers, 1108
RDV Foundation, 747
Ream, W. Monte, 1214
Rearick, Carole, 1146
Reattoir, Dan, 1448
Reavely, Bruce, 1443
Rector, Dale, 1435
Rector, Ed, 1013
Redding, Brenda, 478
Reddy, Damoder, 634
Reddy, Sushma, Dr., 1110
Redies, Cathy, 1258
Redies, Elizabeth J., 1052
Redies, Karen, 1052
Redies, R. Edward, 1052
Redies, Robert D., 1052
Redies, Thomas D., 1052
Redies, William D., 1052
Redman, Cynthia, 1551
Redman, Robert, 1551
Redman, Thomas, 1551
Reece, David, 1163
Reece, Diane, 1247
Reed, Budde, 1102
Reed, Jeffrey, 1373
Reed, Kori E., 959
Reed, Lawrence, 692
Reed, Stephan, 682
Reeder, Breinne, 1143
Reeg, Abby, 1324
Reese, Wayne, 1091
Reese-Pumford, Mary, 601
Reeves, Karen, 541
Regan, Timothy D., 134
Rehbeck, Donna, 1331
Reichel, Robert, 1273
Reid, Alex, 672
Reid, Alice Serra, 732
Reid, Colleen, 673
Reid, Cristin, 673
Reid, Jerry, 673
Reid, Joseph D., 673
Reid, Joseph D., III, 673
Reilly, Donna, 1353
Reilly, Karen Dermidoff, 256
Reimer, Borge R., 674, 675
Reimer, Hennie, 674, 675
Reinhardt, Carsten J., 1030
Reinink, Tari, 1207
Reinke, Evelyn, 1231
Reitmeyer, Michele, 219
Remis, Justin A., 742

Remsen, Katherine W., 723
Renard, Jeanette, 1336
Rendeiro, Brett, 1227
Rennie, George, 219
Renstrom, Stig, 820
Renterghem, Lemont, 1130
Rentrop, Gary, 16
Republic Die & Tool Co., 488
Resch, Mattew A., 1326
Resnick, Felix, 1205
Resnik, Molly, 1083
Reuss, Mark L., 990
Reuter Estate Trust, Loraine, 679
Reuther, Elizabeth, 1387
Reuther, Linda, 1387
Reuther, Victor G., 1387
Rewold, Beverly J., 680
Rewold, Frank H., 1053
Rewold, Roy E., 680
Rexer, Linda K., 1348
Reynolds, Alice M., 681
Reynolds, Cynthia, 1206
Reynolds, Debbie, 1324
Reynolds, Frances, 681
Reynolds, Kevin, 1160
Reynolds, Phyllis M., 681
Reynolds, Richard M., 787
Reynolds, Thomas, 612
Reynolds, Tim, 1072
Reznick, Stephen, Dr., 1092
Rhee, Chi Sun, 682
Rhee, Robert, 682
Rhee, Sung Hi, 682
Rhine, Kathleen, 1457
Rhoades, Nell, 683
Rhoders, Paul F., 839
Rhodes, Shlynn, 1311
Rice, Donna, 405
Rice, Michael N., 623
Rice, Patricia, 1460
Rice, Rich, 1129, 1433
Rice, Sheryl, 77
Rich, Tammie, 1375
Rich, Theresa, 1253
Richard, Margaret A., 310
Richard, Ramona H., 1278
Richards, Andy, 1413
Richards, Barbara, 1082
Richards, Cecile, 260
Richards, Don, 1429
Richards, Gary, 1122
Richards, Jennifer, 1085
Richards, Laura, 1154
Richards, Mark S., 46
Richards, Vincent William, Jr., 46
Richardson, Evelyn K., 719
Richardson, Lamar, 1421
Richardson, Suzy A., 316
Richardson, Tom, 1163
Richardson, William C., 1451
Richardson, Yvwania, 1185
Richmond, Denice, 1227
Richey, Elise, 138
Richter, Kathleen, 203
Richter, Nancy D., 684
Ricker, Sally Richards, 94
Ricker, William L., 94
Rickwalt-Holder, Susan, 1449
Ridenour, Julie, 1275
Rider, Jeffrey, Rev., 165
Ridgeway, Rob, 1132
Ridley, Nancy, 1154
Riecker, Margaret Ann, 202, 816
Riecker, Steven Towsley, 816
Riegel, Steve, 952
Rifai, Samir, 343
Rigg, Remus, 1091
Riker, Bernard, 179
Riley, Anne Marie, 963
Riley, Daniel G., 685
Riley, Dolores, 685
Riley, George, 685
Riley, George K., 685
Riley, Hattie M., 1465

Riley, Sheila, 1175
Riley, William D., 685
Rima Manufacturing Co., The, 978
Rimpela, Brian, 1232
Rinehart, Peter, 1180
Ring, Eunice, 686
Ring, Milton, 686
Rinker, Lowell, 1304
Risner, Joni, 1248
Ritacca, Mike, 1446
Ritchie, Marilyn, 345
Ritter, Tom, 129
Rittmueller, Franklin, 625
Rivette, Clarence M., 1033
Roach, Jeff, 358
Robb, Richard, 1180
Robbin, Robert S., 1361
Robbins, Bob, 1128
Robbins, Edith M., 688
Robert Cook Trust, 148
Roberts, Benson "Buzz", 1323
Roberts, Bob R., 1562
Roberts, Carla, 1124
Roberts, Carolyn, 1176
Roberts, James, 1278
Roberts, Jennifer, 1403
Roberts, Jessie Castle, 922
Roberts, Michael E., 1254
Roberts, Sylvia, 1229
Roberts, Todd, 1458
Roberts, Victoria A., Hon., 1348
Robertson Institute, Ltd., 689
Robertson, Brooke J., 689
Robertson, Charlie, 1424
Robertson, David, 643
Robertson, Gloria J., 565
Robertson, Heidi L., 689
Robertson, Joel C., 689
Robertson, Marjorie, 867
Robertson, Vickie L., 689
Robey, A.M., 1552
Robey, E.A., 1552
Robey, E.W., 1552
Robey, Edmund W., 1552
Robey, Leon J., 1552
Robinson, Barbara, 1195
Robinson, Connie J., 1402
Robinson, Gloria, 556
Robinson, Jack A., 1106
Robinson, Jon, 1137
Robinson, Joseph R., 588
Robinson, Lester, 1371
Robinson, Lynne, 1124
Robinson, Michael, 1023
Robinson, Raquel, 1171
Robinson, Ruth, 1492
Robinson, William A., 1492
Robison, Harold, 690
Robles, Sara, 1300
Roby, Douglas F., Jr., Mrs., 811
Rock Charitable Foundation, 991
Rock, Cinda, 1140
Rockhold, Bill, 1169
Rockwell, Lewis A., 1518
Rodecker, Arthur, 180
Rodeheaver, LaDoyt "Rody", 1287
Rodenberg, Barbara M., 1093
Rodgers, Pamela, 1106
Rodkin, Barbara, 959
Rodkin, Gary M., 959
Rodney, James M., 692
Rodney, Leigh, 692
Rodriguez, Amy, 1087
Rodriguez, David, 1335
Rodriguez, Ray, 462
Roehrig, Larry, 1431
Roethke, Otto, 693
Rogers Department Store, 65
Rogers, Bryan, 1190
Rogers, Gary, 847
Rogers, Jean, 1330
Rogers, Jeff, 1096
Rogers, John W., Jr., 462
Rogers, Kenneth H., Jr., 1258

Rogers, Margot M., 427
Rohr, James E., 484, 1047
Rohrbeck, John, 1205
Rohwer, Milt, 1463
Rohwer, Milton W., 276
Rolf, Ramon F., Jr., 37
Rolka, James, 694
Rolka, James L., 694
Rolland, James M., 139
Roloff, Shirley, 1366
Roman, Anne, 944
Roman, Kenneth, 1038
Roman, Norman T., Rabbi, 766
Romence, Jack L., 454
Ronan, Arthur, 830
Rondeau, Terri, 1104
Rondo, Denise, 1113
Roof, Valerie, 434
Roon, Idamarie, 695
Roon, Pierson J., 695
Roos, Phillip, 1476
Roosevelt, Benjamin, 1086
Root, Richard, Mayor, 455
Root, Vicki, 1548
Rooyakker, Matt, 1160
Roper, Sara, 1210
Ropp, Joan, 1516
Ropp, John, 1183
Rose, Barbara, 1139
Rose, Carl F., 697
Rose, Donna M., 697
Rose, Jeff, 1438
Rose, Ron, 1091, 1210
Rosen, Elaine D., 471
Rosenberg, Barnett, 1479
Rosenberg, Paul A., 1479
Rosenberg, Ritta, 1479
Rosenberg, Tina, 1479
Rosenblith, Sandra, 1323
Rosenstein, Susan A., 790
Rosenthal, Marta, 1296
Roskam, Robert, 1088
Rosloniec, James, 747
Roslund, Becky, 1129
Rosowski, Robert, 1371
Rospo, Anne, 1318
Ross, Charles, 804
Ross, Dorothy, 1165
Ross, Pearl, 1116
Ross, Phyllis, 1206
Rossen, Mary Jo, 668
Rossman, Dan, 1129
Rosso, Nancy A., 1322
Rotary Club of Traverse City, 1391
Roth, Bonnie, 1324
Roth, Michael, 611
Roth, Robert T., 1127
Rotha, Diane, 589
Rotha, Norman, 589
Rothmal, Paul, 1043
Rothstein & Karbel, P.C., 751
Rothstein, Ronald A., 375
Rothwell, Anne, 1207
Rothwell, Sharon, 1026
Rottschafer, Tim, 384
Routson, Rosalyn, 497
Rowlett, Barbara, 1443
Roy, Mike, 1148
Royal Trust, May Mitchell, 698
Royce, Janet, 603
Rozum, Lisa, 1093
Ruark, Ron, 1454
Rubenstein, Erwin A., 1556
Rubin, Kenneth H., 1401
Rubin, Linda, 1140
Rubin, Robert E., 1323
Rubinger, Michael, 1323
Ruble, Cindy S., 73
Rucker, Ronda, 1248
Ruddell, John, 475
Rudlaff, F. Richard, III, 699
Rudolph, David, 1410
Rudolph, Jim, 1221
Ruelle, Michael, 1445

Ruger, William L., 850
Rugg, Carol D., 587
Rugg, Myrna, 1190
Ruhland, R., 1332
Ruhland, Richard P., 1345
Ruhlig, Mike, 1419
Rumelhart, Judith D., 816
Rummer, Sheila, 1129
Rump, Rick, 1002
Rumsey, Scott, 1360
Rumsey, Todd, 258
Runschke, Anne, 885
Rupley, Jerry, 1364
Rupp, Nelson D., 702
Ruschau, Pamela J., 1402
Rush, Mike, 1152
Russ, Randy J., 314
Russeau, Kathleen, 1109
Russell, Barbara, 1164
Russell, Evelyne, 589
Russell, Herman, 704
Russell, Jack, 1376
Russell, James A., 17
Russell, John, 663
Russell, Lee, 1483
Russell, Lynne, 1440
Russell, Michael H., 410
Russell, Phyllis M., 17
Russell, Ronda, 663
Russell, Sandra, 1027
Russell, Walter J., 17
Russell, Wendell P., Jr., 1301
Russo, Renie, 497
Rutherford, Ira A., 1107
Ruthven, Alexander G., II, 1533
Ryals, Kassondra, 705
Ryals, Marqueretta, 705
Ryals, Patrick L., Sr., 705
Ryan, Alan, 1207
Ryan, Joan, 1532
Ryan, Paul, 402
Ryason, Louis H., 541
Rye, Krista, 1268

Saad, Joseph G., 181
Saccomanno, Salvatore, 700
Sackerson, Edward J., 706
Sackerson, Helen A., 706
Sadoff, Joan, 341
Sadoff, Joan Ara, 341
Sage, Charles F., 708
Sage, Effa L., 708
Sagese, Margaret A., 1017
Saini, Inder Jit, 709
Saini, Inder, Mrs., 709
Saini, Krishan, 709
Saini, Rashmi, 709
Saini, Robert, 709
Sajdak, Robert, 486, 666, 760
Sajdak, Robert A., 118
Salahi, Farouk, 710
Salatin, Nancy, 1224
Salinas, Lynn, 1159, 1513
Salman, Ruth, 1361
Salow, Christopher, 1398
Salpietra, Andrea, 713
Salpietra, John M., 713
Salpietra, John M., Jr., 713
Salpietra, Mary, 713
Samee, Syed, Dr., 1187
Samelson, Linda, 640
Samkowiak, Brian, 1375
Sampanes, Theodore, 671
Sample, Kathleen, 100
Sampson, Donald G., 1254
Samrick, Andrew, 1295
Samuel, Craig, 1465
Samuel, Lilian, 1465
Sanders, Douglas, 1405
Sanders, Janet, 1102
Sanders, Roberta, 1216
Sanders, William, 1470
Sanderson, Don, 1131

Sando, Louis, 1507
Sands, Patricia, 701
Sanford, Kurt, 813
Sanford, Louis H., 373, 1128
Sanford, Todd, 813
Sangalli-Hillary, Elissa, 1463
Santacreu, Marjory, 283
Santini, Carol, 1098
Sapude, Paul, 1309
Sardone, Frank, 1138, 1451
Sargent, Chris, 1434
Sarkella, Bill, 1165
Sarmiento, Gil M., 427
Sarns, David, 1083
Sarow, Robert, 1547
Sarow, Robert D., 434
Satterlee, Ellen, 856
Sauer, Fran, 621
Sauer, Jonathan B., 775
Saunders, Rhonda C., 1171
Sauter, Lawrence J., 348
Savage, James, 452
Savage, Margaret, 452
Savas, Sue Ann, 687
Savas, Zachary, 687
Savio, John, 1108
Savo, Robert, 1167
Sawhney, Pamela E., 1409
Sayles, Sonya, 1210
Scaglione, Albert, 1549
Scarpone, James F., 394
Scavone, Robert, 1346
Schaap, A. Paul, 715
Schaap, Carol C., 715
Schad, Rex, 1085
Schad, Vernis, 269
Schaefer, June, 1270
Schaeffer, Taylor M., 223
Schafer, Amanda, 1154
Schalk, Bill, 1445
Schaller, Virginia, 1232
Schalon, Edward I., 716
Schalon, Marcella J., 716
Schalon, Scott, 716
Schalon, Susan K., 716
Schanski, Sue, 1414
Schanz, Kathleen, 1318
Schapman, Laura, 1122
Scharret, James, 1171
Schastok, Sara L., 863
Schaub, Nancy, 257
Schauer, Kathryn Haveman, 357
Schauer, Mark, 1407
Schecter, Susan, 931
Scheer, Daniel, 1122
Scheerens, Dean, 1174
Scheloski, Shannon, 1017
Schempf, Gale, 1250
Schiedegger, Bonnie, 1437
Schierbeek, Robert H., 186, 187, 188, 189, 844
Schiffer, Albert, 1302
Schiffer, Anna, 1302
Schiffer, Michael, 1302
Schiffer, Michael, Mrs., 1302
Schipper, Sharla, 1360
Schlachtenhaufen, Harold, 589
Schlachtenhaufen, Kari, 589
Schlack, Marilyn J., 1451
Schlaman, Jim, 1445
Schlattman, Daniel, 1027
Schleicher, Gordon, 1471
Schlichting, Nancy M., 471, 1280
Schloop, Joan, 1263
Schloss, Neil M., 986
Schlott, Stephen, 868
Schlussel, Mark, 1297
Schma, William G., Hon., 1517
Schmakel, James, 1244
Schmeling, Steve, 1438
Schmerberg, Nancy, 1258
Schmidt, Buzz, 366
Schmidt, Carol D., 93
Schmidt, Don, 1116

Schmidt, Emory, 1385
Schmidt, Harold C., 93
Schmidt, Jerry, 1145
Schmidt, Ken, Hon., 1462
Schmidt, Michael, 1554
Schmidt, Miles, 49
Schmiege, Phil, 558
Schmier, Regene, 718
Schmuckal Land Co., 719
Schmuckal, Arthur M., 719
Schmuckal, Donald A., 719
Schmuckal, Paul M., 719
Schneider, Cecil W., 1402
Schneider, John P., 455
Schneider, Judy, 115
Schneider, Karen, 1311
Schockley, Stuart, 42
Schoenle, Jerry, 1382
Schoessel, Carl, 1550
Schoessel, Carl A., 1393
Scholl, Dennis, 462
Schollaart, Ronald J., 1067
Scholma, Lee, 1081
Scholten, Herm, 143
Schomaker, Mike, 1358
Schonenberg, Frances, 1240
School District/City of Battle Creek, 1466
Schooley, Susan, 542
Schoonbeck, Caroline P., 720
Schoonbeck, Fredrick, 720
Schostak, Jerry, 1297
Schouten, Mary Beth, 930
Schrader, Win, 886
Schreibman, Jay, 509
Schrock, Charles A., 1075
Schroeder, Denise, 1094
Schroeder, Fred D., 721
Schubkegel, Fred, 1308
Schuette, Bill, 1273
Schuette, William D., 292, 628
Schuleit, Fran, 1130
Schuler, Larry, 1090
Schultheiss, Elizabeth, 1230
Schultheiss, Elizabeth N., 1078
Schultz, Earl, 1516
Schultz, Elizabeth, 1516
Schultz, Isabelle, 1109
Schultz, Jim, 1502
Schultz, John, 1108
Schultz, Roxanne, 1006
Schumacher, George T., 287
Schupra, Gregory A., 1093
Schurr, Dan, 952
Schuster, Donald, 1154
Schuster, Georgann, 1432
Schut, D. Maxine, 286
Schut, Dorothy, 286
Schut, Warren H., 286
Schutt, Paul, 1083
Schuur, Hendrik, 1137
Schwab, Cindy, 933
Schwab, Michelle, 1397
Schwark, Susan, 1327
Schwartz, Adam, 365
Schwartz, Alan E., 724, 1106
Schwartz, Ilene, 365
Schwartz, Leonard, 365
Schwartz, Marc A., 724
Schwartz, Marianne S., 724
Schwartz, Robert, 365, 509
Schwartz, Robin, 365
Schwartz, Sheila D., 1143
Schwarz, Steven J., 1374
Schwedler, John, 760
Schwendener, Benjamin O., Jr., 807
Schwind, Carl, 1098
Schwyn, Robert C., 1557
Sclafini, Velda, 1265
Scofield, Emily, 725
Scoggins, Brenda, 1403
Scolatti, Norma T., 600
Scollon, Dorothy, 1177
Scoon, Kathy, 1174

Scott, Arthur V., 1103
Scott, Asaline, 1103
Scott, Bob, 1432
Scott, Chris, 1198
Scott, William H., Jr., 1040
Scribner, Edgar, 1371
Scully, John, 726
Seabury, Charles Ward, 727
Seabury, Louise Lovett, 727
Seagren, Moon, 1363
Seals, James, Dr., 1129
Seals, Jamey, 1548
Seaman, Kate, 1445
Seaver, Peter, 1194
Seavoy, Kenneth, 439
Sebastian, Audrey M., 728
Sebastian, David S., 728
Sebastian, James R., 728
Sebastian, John, 728
Sebesta, Carol, 933
Seese, Jerry L., 1164
Segar, William R., 1402
Seger, Robert C., 910
Seidman, B. Thomas, 729
Seidman, Esther L., 729
Seidman, Frank E., 729
Seidman, Nancy C., 729
Seidman, Sarah M., 729
Seifert, Elizabeth J., 730
Seifert, George, 1108
Seifert, George H., 730
Seifert, George K., 730
Seiford, Larry, 1554
Seiler, Pat, Dr., 1311
Seitz, Kevin L., 1208
Sekerke, Linda S., 115
Selden, Daniel L., 897
Seligman, Sandra, 1556
Seligman, Scott J., 1556
Seling, Scott, 1356
Sell, Leo, 1342
Selley, Rick, 1120
Seltzer, Marian Keidan, 180, 860
Seman, Jean, 850
Semany, Joseph, 1113
Semlow, Pam, 1360
SEMP Enterprises, LLC, 1557
Semple, Dawn, 1419
Semple, Lloyd A., 1345
Semple, Tony, 1419
Semren, Shelley, 1522
Seng, Bob, 1517
Senger, Brian, 1023
Sequin Lumber Corp., 731
Sequin, Denise A., 731
Sequin, Thomas E., Jr., 731
Serling Philanthropic Fund, Michael and Elaine, 1186
Serra, Albert, 732
Serra, Jesakkah, 879
Serra, Joe, 1241
Serra, Lois, 732
Serra, Rebekkah, 879
Serwinek, Marlene, 733
Serwinek, Paul, 733
Sesi, Naz, 1180
Setchfield, James, 170
Settle, Ernest, 1103
Settles, Shanay A., 1086
Setty, Bala, 1371
Sewell, Beverly D., 51
Sexton, James, 1574
Seyburn, Bruce H., 611
Seydel, Catherine, 356
Seydlitz, Orval, 422
Seyferth, Thomas, 353
Seymour, Marcy Carolyn, 690
Shaevsky, Lawrence K., 1395
Shaevsky, Lois L., 1395
Shaevsky, Mark, 1395
Shaevsky, Thomas L., 1395
Shafer, Duane, 1334
Shafer, Kent, 1205
Shaffer Administration Trust, Ula G., 787

Shah, Dinesh, 1259
Shaheen, Kari, 1164, 1300
Shaheen, Patricia Anne, 1344
Shaiheen, Jim, 1454
Shakoor, Adam A., 1470
Shaltz, T. Ardele, 1107
Shamley, Hector, 1346
Shane, Maurice, 1359
Shannon, Cynthia H., 1356
Shannon, Miriam, 1502
Shapiro, Aaron L., 1396
Shapiro, Bonnie L., 1396
Shapiro, Jennifer, 424
Shapiro, Joel, 1396
Shapiro, Loraine, 1396
Share, Daniel, 279
Share, David, 1457
Share, Harvey, 613
Sharp, Geraldine, 1420
Sharp, Marilyn, 767
Sharp, Roger, 1120
Sharp, Terry, 1124
Shaw, Kathy, 900
Shaw, Philip, 1156
Shaw, Robert, Dr., 1216
Shaw, Shirley, 643
Shaw, T.R., Jr., 1086
Shaw, Tim, 765
Shaya, Neran, 1321
Shearer, Julie, 1432
Shedd, John, 1078
Shelata, Marty, 1358
Shelby, Carole, 735
Shelby, Christian, 735
Shelby, David, 735
Shelby, David T., 735
Shelby, Justin, 735
Shelby, Kaylynn, 735
Shelby, Paige, 735
Shelby, Sarah, 735
Shelden, Allan, III, 736
Shelden, Elizabeth Warren, 736
Shelden, W. Warren, 736
Shelden, William W., Jr., 542, 736, 1106
Sheldon, Brenda, 396
Sheldon, Sally S., 736
Shell, Frederick E., 977
Shellenberger, Lauren, 1279
Shelton, Lisa, 920
Shelton, Mike, 885
Shelton, Russ, 1108
Shelton, Samantha, 1508
Shepard, Donald J., 484
Sheppar, Shyla Grace, 1254
Sherard, Karen, 1221
Sherbow, Jeffrey S., 1409
Sheridan, Erica, 1165
Sheridan, Richard, 1458
Sherin, Margaret Winer, 896
Sherin, Peter M., 896
Sherman, Jane, 1296
Sherman, Marty, 13
Sherriff, Horst, 671
Sherrod, Lonnie, 1401
Sherry, Peter J., Jr., 986
Sherwood, Janet, 1548
Sherwood, Lynne, 1010
Sherwood, Mark F., 1010
Shetter, North, Dr., 1145
Shiffman, Abraham, 739
Shiffman, Douglas, 70
Shin, Chae S., 740
Shin-Etsu, Inc., 37
Shinners, James J., 1164
Shiozaki, Richard, 968
Shipp, Christopher, 1235
Shirk, Christopher C., 975
Shoemaker, Dale, 741
Shoemaker, Dale A., 741
Shoemaker, Edwin J., 741, 1022
Shoemaker, Erich C., 741
Shoemaker, Patricia, 1091
Shoemaker, Robert L., 741
Shoer, Jennie, 742

Shoer, Martin J., 742
Sholl, James K., 1086
Shooltz, David, 1413
Shorters, Trabian, 462
Shreve, Keith, 605
Shroyer, Tim, 1368
Shubeck, Emily, 743
Shubeck, Michael B., 743
Shumway, Frank, 1276
Shuttleworth, William, 1219
Sias, Thelma A., 1074
Sibal, Judy, 497
Sibert, Marty, 1108
Sickles, Mary Ellen, 497
Sicora, Jennifer, 1108
Siebenthaler, Elizabeth C., 744
Siebenthaler, William A., 744
Siegal, Phyllis A. Shapiro, 1396
Siegel, Alan, 647
Siegel, Donald G., 1393
Siegel, Thomas S., 1557
Sieger, Diana R., 1127
Siena, Pamela, 923
Sigmund Trust, Violet S., 745
Sigmund Trust, W.A., 745
Sigmund, William A., 745
Siler, Bernard, 1548
Siler, Krista, 1174
Silk, Dorothy, 807
Silky, Charles E., Jr., 175, 608
Silsby, Larry, 1027
Silva, Marcella, 1558
Silva, Yvan, 1558
Silver, Samuel M., 1355
Silverman, Paul r., 1296
Silverman, Sidney, 928
Siman, Steven, 1186
Simmers, Michael, 870
Simmers, Sue, 870
Simmers, Susan, 870
Simmons, Cindy, 1265
Simmons, Clifford, 748
Simmons, David T., 748
Simmons, Suezahn Lyons, 516
Simmons, Ted, 406
Simon, Charles, Hon., 1095
Simon, Cindy, 963
Simon, Donald R., 749
Simon, Esther, 749
Simonds, William W., 1086
Simons, Donald L., 405
Simpson, Jon, 1085
Simpson, Martha, 1305
Simpson, Sharon, 597
Simpson, V. Gail, 1485
Sims, Gretchen Crosby, 427
Sims, Joanne, 1090
Sindt, Peggy, 1078, 1424
Sing, Christine, 1225
Sinnaeve, John, 1163
Sisco, Robby D., 947
Sisskind, Michael S., 1356
Sisson, Garry, 775
Sisson, Harry A., 752
Sitler, Scott, 595
Sitts, Heidi, 1129
Skandalaris, Julie A., 753
Skandalaris, Robert J., 753
Skedgell, Michelle, 1550
Skelton, Bryan, 1249
Skiles, Elwin L., Jr., 754
Skillman, Rose P., 755
Skulsky, Craig, 797
Skulsky, Craig S., 602
Skyer, Bruce, 1361
Slack, D. Jerome, 756
Slack, Margery C., 756
Slaggert, Jeff, 77
Slagh, Pamela K., 18
Slaght, Michael, 1415
Slane, Margaret, 1323
Slate, Daniel R., 1504
Slater, Steve, 1459
Slater, Susan R., 1117

Slaven, I., 1332
Sliger, Michael, 1380
Sliwinski, Al, 1574
Sloan, Ed, 1439
Sloat, Suzanne M., 757
Slonager, Kathleen Felice, 1197
Sloper, Kurt, 1117
Slosar, Adam, 1389
Slotnick, Jeff, 1295
Small, Charles, 1485
Smidt, Stephen, 742
Smies, David J., 255
Smies, Deborah, 255
Smith, Alilah, 643
Smith, Anne, 1098
Smith, Arthur L., 758
Smith, Barry, 1302
Smith, Benedict J., 270
Smith, Brian J., 933
Smith, Bridget, 1164
Smith, Bruce, 155, 1149
Smith, Carra J., 758
Smith, Chris, 1404
Smith, Claudette Y., 1470
Smith, Corey, 1130
Smith, Donald, 1341
Smith, E.A., 759
Smith, Edwin, 1456
Smith, Gerald K., 1359
Smith, Gordon D., 1169
Smith, Gregg, 1391
Smith, H. Warren, 247
Smith, Jan, 767
Smith, Jean M.R., 760
Smith, Jeffrey, 759
Smith, Jim, 1384
Smith, Joanne, 1253
Smith, John F., 990
Smith, Judith, 1111
Smith, Karen, 1344
Smith, Karen L., 758
Smith, Karla M., 291
Smith, Kay, 1388
Smith, Kelley, 1273
Smith, Kimberly, 1251
Smith, Lawton, 1174
Smith, Ley, 1302
Smith, Lois, 1302
Smith, Madeline, 589
Smith, Margaret "Meg", 1089
Smith, Marguerite, 1254
Smith, Marilyn, 1254
Smith, Marsha J., 1391
Smith, Matt N., Jr., 706
Smith, Matt, Jr., 1100, 1112
Smith, Michael, 52
Smith, Michael J., 587
Smith, Nancy Fehsenfeld, 247
Smith, Norm, 1562
Smith, Norma M., 1258
Smith, Patrice, 759
Smith, Rex B., 1510
Smith, Robert, 489
Smith, Robert R., 1214
Smith, Ron, 1149
Smith, Stanley, 589
Smith, Susan, 1510
Smith, Terri, 1136
Smith, Wendy L., 1421
Smoker, Jill, 1210
Smyth, Maureen H., 587
Smythe, John, 878
Sneden Foundation, Robert W. and
    Margaret D., 170
Sneden, Kathleen, 170
Sneden, Marcia A., 170
Snell, Hilary, 363
Snell, Hilary F., 798, 1550
Snell, Hillary F., 845
Snell, Ray, 1436
Snide, Donald A., 418
Snide, Donald W., 418
Snider, Van W., Jr., 671
Snoap, Dana L., 793

Snyder, Arthur H., 762
Snyder, Clarence A., 762
Snyder, Clarence A., Mrs., 762
Snyder, Deborah, 1216
Snyder, Edd, 1278
Snyder, Edd G., 990
Snyder, Harold, 762
Snyder, Harold Z., 761
Snyder, James, 762
Snyder, James A., 761
Snyder, John, Mrs., 811
Snyder, Mary Beth, 1108
Snyder, Rusty S., 1267
Snyder, Sallie F., 404
Snyder, Steve, 761
Snyder, Valerie, 1096
Snyder, William N., 1481
Sobeck, Tom, 1104
Sober, Kyle, 1284
Soble, Jennifer, 1474
Soble, Richard A., 1348
Sobol, Scott, 1125
Sobong, Enrico, 1559
Sobong, Esther, 1559
Socia, Mary R., 1082
Socia, Oscar F., 1082
Society Capital Corp., 1018
Society Corp., 1018
Soderberg, Cal, 1118
Soimar, Michael S., 1103
Sokolof, Phil, 415
Sokolowski, Leonard, 1246
Solis, Eusebio, Jr., 1183
Solmes, Dave, 1085
Somerlott, Bambi, 1131
Sommer, Anthony G., 847
Somsel, Jeanette, 1438
Soncrant, Joe, 1388
Sonkin Trust, Joel, 1561
Sonkin, Sydelle, 1561
Sonneveldt, Carol A., 763
Sonneveldt, Lance C., 763
Sonni, Ashok, 1319
Sonni, Rajeswari, 1319
Soorus, Leo, 1315
Sorensen, Ken, 1024
Sorensen, Paul T., 1301
Sorgente Investments LLC, 573
Sorgente No. 3 Trust, 573
Sosin, Allen, 1197
Sosnowski, Julie, 179
Sotsky, Jonathan, 462
Souder Charitable Lead Trust, Susanna,
    764
Souder, Jr. Charitable Lead Trust,
    William F., 764
Souder, Susanna J., 764
Souder, William F., Jr., 764
Soule, Carol, 1168
Sourges, Jim, 1364
Southeast Michigan Physicians, P.C.,
    1557
Southern Michigan Bank & Trust, 428,
    711
Southwest Regional Rehabilitation
    Center, 767
Sovel, Susan, 430
Sparks, Diane, 1311
Sparks, Harvey, Dr., 807
Sparks, Nan, 1519
Sparrow, Susan, 1091
Spartan Motors, Inc., 1057
Spartz, Jane, 52
Spear, Al, 559
Specialty Vehicle Dealers Association,
    1228
Spector, Neal J., 769
SPEED Channel, 1228
Speer, Bill, 1104
Spehn, Gina Kell, 1358
Spehn, Michael, 1358
Speirn, Sterling K., 450
Spence, Bobbie, 1440
Spencer, Carol, 771

Spencer, Don, 1096, 1442
Spencer, Hildreth, 789
Spencer, Ken, 1449
Spencer, Kenneth, 771
Spezia, Michael J., 1505
Spicer, Gary, 210
Spicer, Joyce, 1078
Spicer, S. Gary, 87, 355, 548, 772, 778, 1244
Spicer, S. Gary, Sr., 500, 606
Spikner, Carl, 1445
Spoelhof, Scott Alan, 1111
Spoelman, Paul, 1115
Spoelman, Roger, 1103, 1291
Spoerl, Joseph, 1306
Sports Car Market Magazine, 1228
Sprague, Frederick O., 1092
Springgate, Susan, 1138
Sproles, Joe, 1088
St. Marie, Kristen, 1414
Staab, Charles, 1368
Stabile, Joseph D., 1082
Stacey, Ted, 1205
Stack, Mike, 1507
Staiger, Charles, 881
Staiger, Charles W., 579
Stallone, Kristine, 27
Stamas, Tony N., Sen., 1326
Stamps, E. Roe, IV, 462
Stancati, Joe, 963
Stancato, Shirley R., 1359
Standard Federal Bank N.A., 597
Stankey, Charles, 761
Stanley, Iola, 443
Stanley, Kendall, 1221
Stanley, Mandel, 443
Stanton, David J., 776
Stanton, Laura M., 776
Stapp, Pat, 1272
Stark, Amy, 1098
Stark, Harry S., 566
Starks, Eileen C., 1237
Starr, Joel D., 1016
Starr, Kathleen, 366
Stasker, R. Louis, Rev., 49
Staskiewicz, Laura, 1335
Statz, Terry, 1198
Staudt, David, 1368
Stauffer, John, 1435
Stavropoulos, William S., 292
Stawski, Willard S., 454, 1208
Stebbins, Mary J., 135
Stebbins, Ralph S., 135
Stec, Randy, 1177
Steelcase Inc., 1058
Steele, Betty, 216
Steele, Daniel, 1456
Steele, Debby, 1471
Steele, John O., 216
Steele, Richard, 1547
Steele, Tom, 1157
Stefanek, Gregg, 1507
Steffan, William, 967, 1171
Steffel, Sheila, 1126
Steffes, Lorene K., 484
Stege, Bill, 1263
Stege, George, III, Dr., 1261
Stegman, Harold, 1154
Steiber, Lucy, 129
Steiger, Paul, 462
Steinberg, David, 1253
Steiner, Jennifer, 1002
Steinhagen, Sue, 1455
Steinhauer, Bruce W., 542
Steirs, Mark, 1278
Stemen, Milton, 1052
Stemper, Steve, 996
Stensrud, Sara, 1399
Stenzel, Duane, 952
Stephan, Pam, 1389
Stephen, Scott, 1183
Stephens, David B., 891
Stephens, Deborah, 616
Stephens, Mark, 1341

Stephens, Sherri E., 1107
Stephenson, Ardith A., 468
Stephenson, Donald, 1415
Stephenson, John K., 1366
Sterban, Donna L., 778
Sterban, Richard A., 778
Sterken, Gwynn, 779
Sterken, Gwynn E., 779
Sterken, James, 779
Sterken, James J., 779
Stern, Jon, 1186
Stetler, Gary, 185
Stetler, Gerald, 185
Stetler, John, 900
Stevens, Adrienne, 1285
Stevens, Mariene, 358
Stevens, Robert, 1332
Stevens, Robert W., 1345
Stevens, Theresa J., 812
Stevenson, Catherine, 1168
Stevenson, Cathy, 1397
Stevenson, Gelvin, 1254
Stevenson, Patricia, 1081
Stevenson, Robert, 270
Steward, Hyun A. Rhee, 682
Steward, Jim, 1136
Steward, Larry E., 977
Stewart, Bill, 1210
Stewart, C. Allan, 301
Stewart, Erick, 900, 1407
Stewart, Gordon L., 780
Stewart, Joe, 1407
Stewart, Joseph M., 450
Stewart, Linda A., 780
Stewart, Marise M.M., 587
Stewart, Michael R., 1045
Stewart, Samuel S., III, 111
Stewart, Tara, 1300
Stewart, Wayne, 458, 607, 857, 918, 1201
Stibbs, Don, 1151
Stieg, Edward C., 118
Stieg, Elizabeth A., 118
Stieg, Harold E., 118
Stines, Alfred, 1564
Stines, Alfred V., 1564
Stines, Christopher, 1564
Stines, Joan, 1564
Stines, Michelle, 1564
Stinson, Lucinda, 1304
Stipech, Frank J., 1232
Stock, Sue, 1459
Stockbridge Enterprise Inc., 781
Stockton, Florence, 782
Stoddard, Alice A., 783
Stoddard, Sue, 1277
Stokes, Karen Henry, 363
Stoll, Peter, 1416
Stolt, Wendy, 1293
Stone, David, 623
Stone, Ethol, 1080
Stone, Karen, 1264
Stone, Kristen McDonald, 1343
Stoneman, Martin, 438, 718
Stoner, Michael, 1087
Stoor, Roger, 1116
Storm, Amy, 1364
Stormer, Dale, 901
Story, Pauline, 1183
Stoskopf, Rita F., 641
Stout, Ellsworth L., 1506
Stout, Howard, 60
Stout, Kimberly, 1250
Stout, Linda, 1167
Stover, Betsy, 833
Stover, Ray, 1429
Stowe, Mike, 1228, 1272
Stowell, Tom, 1321
Straitor, George A., 265
Strand, Joy, 1445
Strasburg, Robert, 594
Stratman, Kathie, 1411
Stratton, Evelyn Lundberg, 1233
Straus, Lorna Puttkammer, 1146

Strawser, Rick, 1411
Streeter, Jon, 1282
Strickland, William E., Jr., 1361
Strickler, Jan, 1154
Strickler, Virgil, 1444
Strickler, William J., 1006
Stridiron, Susan, 1197
Strigl, Dennis P., 484
Stringer, Brenda, 1299
Stringer, Dick, 45
Strobel, Josephine, 786
Stroh, Vivian Day, 1106
Strong, Meredith, 1372
Stronks, Gloria, 1469
Strosacker, Charles J., 787
Strumwasser, Ira, 1208
Strunk, Gail J., 730
Stryker, Jon L., 27
Stryker, Ronda E., 788, 1138, 1302
Stuart, Douglas, 1139
Stuart, Mark F., 1149
Stuber, Elizabeth, 1300
Stuck, David T., 317, 982, 1176
Stuck, James, 1176
Stuck, James D., 982
Stuck, Lois A., 317
Stuck, Randy, 1146
Stuckey Charitable Remainder Unitrust, Oshlag, 619
Studebaker, Nancy, 1435
Stuit, Thomas, 131
Stulberg, David A., 790
Stulberg, Lois, 213, 790
Stulberg, Morris, 1149
Stulberg, Nancy, 1330
Stulberg, Robert M., 213, 790
Stults, Charles, 1408
Styles, Pam, 1492
Suchecki, Bonnie, 1126
Sucher, Barb, 1198
Suchodolski, James R., 558
Suchora, Tom, 1242
Sud, Anup, 791
Sud, Parul, 791
Sudduth, Jon, 1339
Sugiyama, Andrea K., 269
Sujek, Angela, 1224
Sukumaran, Kizhakepat, 1413
Sullivan, Ann L., 792
Sullivan, Elana, 1357
Sullivan, Elizabeth C., 1106, 1361
Sullivan, J. Mark, 1338
Sullivan, Julie, 1306
Sullivan, Mary P., 170
Sullivan, Mary Sneden, 170
Sullivan, Michael J., 1369
Sullivan, Patrick M., 792
Sullivan, Paul J., Hon., 1301
Sullivan, Robert, 793
Sullivan, Thomas, 1154
Susman, Elizabeth, 1401
Susterich, Timothy, 1335
Sutar, William, 795
Sutar-meyer, Olga, 795
Sutka, Patrick, 1574
Sutter, Larry, 1185
Sutton, David E., 1506
Svendsen, John, 1175
Svitkovich, Thomas, 1285
Swain, Ronald, 696
Swaninger, Roger I., 1409
Swanson, John W., II, 1103
Swanson, Tom, 1448
Swantek, Shauna, 1085
Swartwout, Ann, 1204
Sweeney, Thomas F., 1204
Swerc, David C., 981
Swiat, James R., 796
Swiat, Richard G., 796
Swiat, Richard J., 796
Swiat, Shelly, 796
Swiecicki, Steve, 1095
Swiecki, Michael, 1574
Swieczkowski, Julie Case, 1164

Swierenga, Donald J., 153
Swihart, Marilyn, 1437
Swindell, Charles R., 451
Swise, John M., 1362
Swiss, Rachel, 1096
Sydnor, Bernice L., 1103
Sydow, Dena, 1221
Synder, Thomas, 762
Synor, Susan M., 361
Sytsma, Fredric, 229
Szalkiewicz, Diane, 1017
Szeman, Judy, 129
Sztykiel, John E., 1057
Szulwach, Joseph, Rev., 32
Szura, Patricia M., 203

Tabbaa, Abdul, Dr., 1566
Taber, Nancy, 73
Tabor, Ann Irish, 1126
Tabor, Lillie M., 556
Taj, Syed, 1093
Talbert, Errol, 1537
Talbert, James, 1537
Talburtt, Margaret A., 461
Talburtt, Peg, 508
Tallerico, Thomas J., 1369
Tallman, Lori, 1107
Tallman, Lori A., 1117
Talson, Paul Henri, 1564
Tamblyn, Pat, 1180
Tanis, Ruth, 1081
Tankersley, Joan N., 603
Tannel, Diane M., 734
Tannel, Jerald A., 734
Tapley, Bryanna, 1436
Taraman, Khalil S., 1402
Tarnecki, Duane L., 355
Tarpoff, Diane Anderson, 616
Tarr, Gregory, 1122
Tarr, Kathy, 1149
Tassell, Leslie E., 798
Taubman, Robert S., 755
Tavenner, Terri, 593
Taweel, Hala, 1189
Taylor Irrevocable Trust, Helen, 800
Taylor Unitrust, Percy, 800
Taylor, Allen, 1438
Taylor, Anne L., 1410
Taylor, Chad, 1405
Taylor, Cheryl K., 258
Taylor, Christopher, 1286
Taylor, Clifford, Hon., 1348
Taylor, Gregory B., 450
Taylor, Jacqueline, 1350
Taylor, Jane, 594
Taylor, Janis, 1079
Taylor, Margaret, 1334
Taylor, Maurice, 799
Taylor, Michelle, 799
Taylor, Robert N., 258
TCF Financial Corp., 1061
TCF National Bank, 1061
TCF National Bank Minnesota, 1061
Tebbe, Jim, 1198
Tech, Polly, 182
Teeple, Donald, 142
Teeple, Sandra, 885
Teeple, Sharon, 1542
Teich, Andreas, 1547
Tellado, Marta L., 260
Temby, Lynn Marie, 206
Tempel, Connie, 1233
Templar, Sharon, 1272
Templin, Dan, 1119
Tengler, Elizabeth, 1567
Tengler, Steve, 1567
Tenneco Automotive Inc., 1036
Tenneco Inc., 1036
Tenny, Alfred M., 1545
Tenny, Karen S., 1545
Tepper, Edward M., 803
Tepper, Elise C., 803
Tepper, Jacqueline G., 803

Tepper, Marvin B., 803
Teranishi, Takeshi, 1012
TerAvest, Robert, 1115
Termaat, Laurie, 1275
Ternan, Lawrence, 1108
Ternan, Lawrence R., 1369
Ternes, Howard, 804
Ternes, Margery, 804
Terpestra, Craig, 1299
Terreburg, Sue, 203
Terrell, Jeffrey D., 744
Terry, Robin, 309
Tersteeg, Edward, 541
Texley, Juliana, 1082
Thacker, Brad, 1040
Thames, Cherryl R., 1171
Thane, Janet, 1177
Thatcher, Becky, 1263
Thawani, Hermant, 805
Thekan, Karen, 1118
Thelan, Randy, 1111
Theunick-Perley, Connie, 1140
Thewes Charitable Annuity Lead Trust, The, 494
Thewes Trust, The, 494
Thieke, Stephen G., 484
Thielen, Ruth, 1145
Thiemkey, Richard, 806
Thiemkey, Roberta, 806
Thiemkey, William, 806
Thodey, Luanne, 1335
Thodey, Luanne B., 65
Tholl, Robert, Jr., 1299
Thoma, Henry, 1121
Thoman, Candace, 807
Thoman, W.B., 807
Thomas Revocable Trust, Harriet Kay, 808
Thomas, Bill J., 429
Thomas, Dorothy, 474
Thomas, Dorothy S., 809
Thomas, Gary R., 328
Thomas, James E., 809
Thomas, John R., 809
Thomas, John, Jr., 809
Thomas, Jonathan, 16
Thomas, LaNaita, 1403
Thomas, Laura L., 328
Thomas, Lisa, 788
Thomas, Lorna L., 597
Thomas, Marlene, 1384
Thomas-Cloud, Sherry, 1304
Thome, Robert P., 810
Thompson, Bob, 475
Thompson, Carol, 1519
Thompson, David, 647
Thompson, J. Paul, Jr., 1532
Thompson, Jane, 1532
Thompson, Janet, 1361
Thompson, Jessica E., 744
Thompson, Levi, Dr., 1083
Thompson, Margaret E., 202, 816
Thompson, Mary, 811
Thompson, Michael, 1147
Thompson, Ronald G., 975
Thomson, Lucy, 584
Thomson, Richard B., Jr., 584
Thorn, Therese M., 668
Thornberry, Allyn, 1158
Thorns, Mamie, 1164
Thornwell, Donna, 1465
Thorp, Kim, 1384
Thorrez Industries, C., Inc., 812
Thorrez, Camiel E., 812
Thorrez, Jeoffrey A., 812
Thorrez, Phyllis J., 812
Thorrez-Wheeler, Mary C., 812
Threadgill, William J., 867
Threloff, Lala, 1548
Throm, Sharon, 1089
Throop, Barbara, 1115
Thrune, Charles J., 787
Thrune-Durand, Carolyn, 787
Thrune-Lundquist, Charlie C., 787

Thunstrom, Jason, 1023
Thurman, John, 554
Thurman, Paul, 1376
Thurston, Martha, 598
Thwaites, Kris, 1095
Tibbotts, Terry, 1120
Tiboni, Joe, 1190
Ticketmaster Group, Inc., 1046
Ticknor, William S., 900
Tierney, Brian X., 937
Tierney, Michael, 1323
Tilden Mining Co., 954
Timmeney, Darren, 1308
Timmer, Ned, 1512
Timmins, Dan, 1429
Timmins, Daniel J., 1098
Timpson, John, 1527
Tingley, Julie, 1198
Tintera, Evelyn, 650
Tintera, James B., 650
Tippett, Susan, 1107
Tipping, Matt, 873
Tiscornia, Christopher, 814
Tiscornia, Edward C., 814
Tiscornia, James W., 814
Tiscornia, James Winston, 814
Tiscornia, Jeanne, 814
Tiscornia, Joanne, 814
Tiscornia, Waldo V., 814
Tisserand, Katherine Ann, 154
Titche, Claude, III, 1295
Titley, Larry J., 1069
Titus, Susan, 1403
Tobin, John, 617
Toburen, James, 1000
Toburen, James R., 1550
Toburen, Jim, 1085
Todd Co., A.M., 1064
Todd, A. John, 577
Todd, A.J., III, 1064
Todd, Gia L., 1206
Todd, Jane B., 577
Todd, Paul H., 1451
Toelle, Michael, 952
Toeman, Gerry, 696
Toia, Theresa, 1167
Tolbert, Daryl, 1176
Toler, Karen, 1431
Toll, Ken, 1436
Tolley, William R., 1181
Tolliver, Dorothy, 1545
Tomasini, Mary Jo, 1445
Tomasky, Susan, 937
Tomko, David, 1282
Tomlinson, Mitchell, 1094
Tompkins, Gary, 1132
Tooker, Rick, 1304
Torgow, Eliezer, 815
Torgow, Gary, 815, 1106, 1296, 1297
Torgow, Malka, 815
Torgow, Yonah, 815
Torp, Margaret, 1247
Torres, Abel, 1087
Totte, Thomas L., 1016
Tottingham, Sarah, 449
Touchinski, Carole L., Dr., 1148
Touma, Douglas S., 1110
Toutant, Robert, 1439
Toutant, Robert J., 272, 681
Tower, Phil, 1130
Towner, Julie, 1275
Townley, Marilyn S., 469
Townsend, Robert, 968
Towsley, Margaret D., 816
Toyne, Arlene, 1089
Toyota Motor Corp., 1402
Trahan, Anne, 1087
Trammel, Alan, 1244
Trammell, Kenneth, 1036
Trautner, Carol R., 600
Travis, Tina M., 1129
Treacher, Randy, 1436
Treadwell, Cheri, 144
Tremblay, Diana, 1423

Tremblay, Diane D., 990
Tremble, Helen R., 817
Trent, Kimberly, 1377
Tressler, Judy, 1150
Trester, Kenneth, 1371
Trevisian, Glen R., 1227
Tribble, Anita, 109
Tribble, Michael, 829
Trimarco, Gary, 1150
Tripp, Ann K., 999
Tripp, Daniel T., 765
Tropea, Rich, 1205
Trotter, Jessica, 267
Trucks, Mary L., 1542
Trudell, William, 1118
Truesdell, Judy, 1151
Trumbull, James, 1542
Trumley, Beverly R., 822
Trumley, Richard L., 822, 847
Trumley, Stephen R., 822
Tsoumas, Richard, 73
Tsoumas, Richard M., 450
TT Trust, The, 494
Tubbs, Dave, 1165
Tubergen, Jerry L., 186, 187, 188, 189, 844
Tuchinsky, Joseph S., 1202
Tucker, James, 1372
Tucker, Janis, 1372
Tuckey, Robert L., 670
Tuefel, Robert, Dr., 1089
Tuinstra, Jacob, 825
Tummala, Lakshmi, 1292
Tummala, Madhusudana Rao, 827
Tummala, Pradyumna E., 827
Tummala, Sabita, 827
Tummala-Narra, Pratyusha, 827
Tupper, Ronald, 516
Turcotte, Todd, 1434
Turfe, Alexander Alan, 828
Turfe, Lenda, 828
Turgeon, Richard, 1201
Turgeon, Sharon, 1201
Turnbull, Bruce, 1532
Turnbull, Debra, 1174
Turner & Turner, P.C., 1017
Turner, Alice E., 829
Turner, Carmen, 1094
Turner, Juli, 1224
Turner, Kathi, 103
Turner, Peter M., 1103
Turner, Reginald, 1427
Turner, Reginald M., 1106
Turner, Reginald M., Jr., 392
Turney, Rob, 1263
Turney, William, 1214
Turrentine, Paula M., 346
Twing, Dale, 1124
Tyler, Delora Hall, 1377
Tyler, Lisa, 1354
Tyler, Mary, 1302
Tyson, Geroge, 1077

U.S. Bank, N.A., 312, 594, 875
Ubinas, Luis A., 260
Uday, Matt, 1341
Uhl, Brad, 384
Uhl, Bud, 1167
Uhlig, Janice K., 990
Uihlein, Margery H., 383
Uncapher, Chester L., 808
Underwood, Margaret, 1366
Underwood, Ray L., 671
United American Healthcare Corp., 597
Universal Forest Products, Inc., 385, 1067, 1487
Upjohn, Grace G., 832
Upjohn, W.E., 1451
Upton, Ben, 833
Upton, Brad, 1108
Upton, Fred, 833
Upton, Frederick S., 833
Upton, Stephen E., 833

Urban, Susan, 1359
Usey, Michael, 640
Usher, Thomas J., 484
Utke, Pamela, 1169

Vaidya, Nalin, 1558
Vaive, Connie, 1420
Valade, Cary C., 1280
Valencic, Larry, 1145
Valente, Jason, 1436
Valenti, Dennis, 1052
Valentine, B., 1332
Valentine, Marion, 524
Valkenburg, Bill Van, 1352
Vallieu, Barbara E., 1352
Vallis, Kathleen, 1167
Van Alstine, Fred J., 1534
Van Alstine, Kathleen, 1534
Van Andel Foundation, Jan & Betty, 837
Van Andel Foundation, Jay and Betty, 747, 835, 836
Van Andel Trust, Jay, 747, 835
Van Andel, Cynthia, 836
Van Andel, David, 835, 837
Van Andel, Kristen, 838
Van Andel, Nan, 747
Van Andel, Steve, 837
Van Arsdalen, Bill, 1283
van Camp, John, 1216
van Coppenolle, George, 1380
Van Dellen, Robert J., Dr., 1092
Van Den Bosch, Anna, 838
Van Den Bosch, Ken, 1469
Van Den Bosch, Mark, 838
Van Den Bosch, William, Jr., 838
Van Den Bosch, William, Sr., 838
Van Der Brug, Gordon, 841
van der Molen, Jon, 1302
Van Dommelen, Patricia, 148
van Doren, Doug, Rev., 1269
Van Doren, James E., 708
Van Dusen, Amanda, 392, 1451
Van Dusen, Barbara C., 1106
Van Dyke, Clifford C., 434
Van Gasse, Randall, 1158
Van Gilder, Paul, 1120
Van Haaften, Ken, 384
van Haaften, Rick, 1437
Van Haren, W. Michael, 856
Van Hekken, Teri, 1287
Van Hollenbeck, Homer J., 839
Van Kampen, Judith, 734
Van Lunen, Richard D., 841
Van Manen, Jan, 143
van Nort, Karen, 1263
Van Putten, James, 116
Van Reken, Calvin P., 131
Van Reken, Randall, 131
Van Reken, Randall S., 131
Van Reken, Stanley, 131
Van Reken, Stanley R., 131
van Singel, John, 1335
Van Tassel, Ann, 1103
Van Wormer, Jason S., 842
Van Wormer, Melissa, 842
Van Wormer, Norman C., 842
Vana, Kent, 1069
VanBuren, Jay, 1318
Vance, Doug, 1099
Vance, Douglas B., 1107
Vance, Thomas J., 1426
Vancleff, Emily, 870
Vandenberg, Kristin M., 1301
Vandeputte, Gary, 718
Vander Hart, Ginny, 186, 187, 188, 189
Vander Kooy, Donald J., 1138
Vander Kooy, Scott, 1469
Vander Molen, Kenneth, 825
Vander Ploeg, John, 1285
Vander Weide, Jan, 143
Vanderberg, Alan, 1463
VanderBoon, Orie, 1381
Vanderkooi, Joel, 1013

Vanderlaan, Karen J., 664
Vandermade, Deborah, 1476
Vandermolen, Courtney, 1505
Vandermolen, Jon G., 1505
Vandermolen, Martha B., 1505
Vanderploeg, David, 917
Vanderroest, James, 909
VanderRoest, Stan M., 290
Vanderspool, Jim, 1265
VanderVeen, Jim, 1081
VanderVeen, Robert A., 844
Vanderweide, Suzanne C., 844
Vanderweide, Suzanne DeVos, 844
VanDerwel, Jody, 738
VanDongen, Robert, 269
Vandrie, Douglas, 647
VanDuyne, AnnMarie, 1107
VanDyke, Karin, 1139
VanEss, Craig, 1275
VanGilder, Russell H., 122
Vankoevering, Marilyn, 184
Vanlandingham, Christine, 1412
VanMassenhove, Gary C., 1499
VanNoy, Lonnie G., 181
VanSoest, Aaron, 1275
VanSolkema, Curt, 1287
VanStipdonk, John, 1460
VanStipdonk, Lois, 1460
VanTiem, Christy, 1432
VanTiflin, James M., 1237
VanValin, Mark, Rev., 1436
VanVliet, Mary Jane, 670
VanWieren, Suzanne, 1360
Varda, Darryl J., 647
Vardigan, Mary, 230
Vargo, Clara D., 1147
Vargo, Sharon, 1090
Varin, Lynda, 931
Varney, Ben, 1177
Varney, Janice, 1169
Vassalio, Joseph, 1379
Vaughn, Gregory C., 1090
Vazquez, George, 1040
Vebrigge, Martha, 1079
Vedra, Kenneth, 1402
Veenhuis, Randy, 1185
Veenstra, Janice, 838
Veenstra, Joel, 838
Veenstra, Michael, 838
Veenstra, Timothy W., 838
Vega, Frank, 1453
Velasquez, Christian A., 975
Velasquez, Jenee, 202
Veldman, Ron, 1115, 1376
Velie, Carroll, 275
Velkoff, Dee, 1194
Vella, James G., 266, 986
Veltkamp, Randall G., 1291
Velzen, Randy, 1246
Vennema, Ame, 639
Vennema, Catherine S., 639
Vennema, John, 639
Vennema, Peter A., 639
Ventimiglia, Salvatore, 1294
Venturedyne, Ltd., 1070
Verhage, Patricia, 419
Verhagen, Connie, 1340, 1447
Verheek, Jason, 1438
Verlinde, Al, 1122
Vermunen, Andy, 1484
Verney, Steven C., 935
Vernier, Ingrid O., 381
Verplank, L.J., 1126
Versluis, Chad, 402
Versluis, Joyce, 402
Versluis, Peter, 402
Vert, William, 1418
VerWys, William, 1287
Veverica, Anna, 1147
Vibber, Brad, 1548
Vicari, Matthew L., 1301
Victor, Diane A., 1569
Victor, Lyle D., 1569
Victor, Nadine E., 1569

Victor, Natalie N., 1569
Vidican, Susan, 1388
Viers, Laura, 1506
Vigil, B. Thomas, 1254
Vill, Carrie, 833
Vincent, Dee, 1221
Vincent, Patricia, 1333
Virginia Hill Trust, 1002
Virgne, Joanna Ford, 826
Virkler, Kim, 1120
Vliek, Chuck, 1323
Vogel, Bob, 1143
Vogel-Vanderson, Susan, 402
Vogeli, Mitch, 1327
Vogt, Frederick J., Jr., 845
Vogt, James B., 845
Vollbrecht, Frederick A., 846
Vollmayer, David, 1361
Volock, Jane R., 729
Volz, Clark, 1441
von Holt, Eugene Scott, 1142
Von Kronenberger, Kim, 1150
Vondra, Shawn, 1131
Voorhees, Joanne, 1212
Vora, Ami Anand, 834
Vora, Kirti M., 834
Vora, Mahesh H., 834
Vora, Sejal Parag, 834
Vosgerchian, Aram, 498
Voss, Kimberly Combs, 597

Waalkes, Tom, 143
Wachovia Bank, N.A., 533
Wade, Lori, 1057
Wade, Steve, 1443
Wadhams, Timothy, 11
Wadhams, Timothy J., 1026
Wagner, Betsy, 1263
Wagner, David, 1272
Wagner, Doug, 1116
Wagner, James, 1574
Wagner, Mark, 1015
Wagner, Vickie, 1048
Wagoner, George, 1147
Waichunas, Ken, 1128
Wakefield, Jennifer, 1279
Wakefield, Kirk, 1234
Wal-Mart Stores, Inc., 1186
Walainis, Randy, 556
Walcheck-Arndt, Aurora, 1160
Wald, Jill, 1201
Waldinger, Marcy B., 1355
Waldman, Robin, 1253
Waldorf, C. MacKenzie, 629
Waldorf, Clayton, 1088
Waldorf, Sydney, 1505
Waldorf, Sydney E., 629
Walenta, Tom, 1272
Walker, Anita, 1195
Walker, Darren, 27, 260
Walker, Drew, 594
Walker, Earl E., 1402
Walker, Francis E., 1214
Walker, Joan H., 935
Walker, John, 1378
Walker, Lamont, 1269
Walker, Linda, 931
Walker, Meg, 594
Walker, Moses, 1304
Walker, Robert S., 1142
Walker, Ruth Steele, 1142
Walker, Tim, 594
Wallace, Bill, 1378
Wallace, David, 375
Wallace, Harvey B., II, 277
Wallace, William H., 1000
Walldorf, Irene, 213
Walls, Doris T., 1465
Walls, George H., Jr., 484
Walls, Harold, 1098
Walsh, David, 1276
Walsh, Frank, 1389
Walsh, Marianne H., 848

Walsh, Richard T., 848
Walter, Donald F., 397, 649
Walter, James, 1282
Walters, Alison, 1248
Walters, Barbara, 1307
Walters, Beverly, 1519
Walters, Paul, 1263
Walters, Terry, 1258
Waltman, John, 889
Walton, Ric, 1137
Walz-Lefere, Carlene, 1137
Wanczyk, Stefan, 839
Wangler, John, 1468
Wannemacher, Paul, 1109
Wanninger, Chuck, 1110
Warchol, Frank L., 849
Warchol, Jane, 849
Warchol, Virginia J., 849
Ward, Doug, 1441
Ward, Pam, 1365
Ward, Philip, 1175
Wardell, Patrick, 1464
Warden, Gail L., 1245
Ware, Richard A., 217
Warhurst, Ron, 1468
Waring, Mike D., 1171
Warmels, Daniel, 1316
Warmels, Daniel J., 406
Warren, Chris, 1483
Warshay, Nathaniel, 1421
Wascoe, Thomas M., 933
Washabaugh, Cathy, 1087
Washburn, Ruth, 695
Washington, Shawn, 1140
Wasilewski, Peter, 129
Watchowsky, Dale L., 1106
Waters, Susan, 786
Watkins, Gregg D., 180
Watkins, Walter, 158
Watson, Alan D., 1249
Watson, Evona, 851
Watson, Milton H., 597
Watson, Richard T., 1164
Wattles, Charles D., 299
Wattles, John C., 577
Watts, Arleuh, 144
Watts, Christine, 144
Watts, R., 1332
Watts, Tim, 1113
Watz, Janet L., 1141
Wavering, Albert, 1402
Wawrowski, Kara, 1522
Wayne County Department of Child and
    Family Services, 1485
Wayne, Jim, 1430
Wazniak, Gary, 1362
Weatherhead, Diane, 1417
Weatherholt, Sara, 1365
Weathers, Frank, 1436
Weatherspoon, Donald, 1028
Weatherwax Trust I, K.A., 852
Weaver, John F., 459, 460
Weaver, Karen Williams, 1107
Weaver, Kathy, 1410
Weaver, Pam Perri, 1195
Webb, Jan, 1195
Webb, Jon, 1123
Webb, Thomas J., 122, 955, 961
Webber, Eloise, 392
Webber, Richard, 392
Weber, Allen, 1402
Weber, Doug, 1083
Weber, Sharon, Sr., 557
Webster Residual Trust, Lorraine, 854
Webster, Jeffrey, 1040
Webster, Sarah, 853
Webster, Steven, 1094
Weddle, Matilda, 1269
Wedel, Greg, 1011
Weeks, Errolyn, 770
Weeldreyer, Robert, 131
Wege, Christopher, 856
Wege, Diana, 856
Wege, Jonathan C., 856

Wege, Marjorie R., 190
Wege, Peter M., 856
Wege, Peter M., II, 856
Wegman, Patrick, II, 1168
Wehmeier, Helge H., 484
Wehner, Brent, 1133
Weideman, William H., 973
Weidemann, Barbara J., 857
Weidenbach, Robert, 395
Weidner, Ann, 1462
Weidner, Jack, 1462
Weidner, Matt, 1462
Weigel, Raymond A., Jr., 858
Weigel, Wavelet M., 858
Weighner, Philip J., 647
Weikart, David, 859
Weikart, Phyllis S., 859
Weill, Douglas M., 1233
Weinand, Clarence E., 181
Weiner, Josephine S., 860
Weinfeld, Arnold, 1459
Weir, Deierdre L., 1206
Weisberg, Bernard, 862
Weisberg, Helen, 862
Weisberg, Shelli, 1204
Weisblat Foundation, 1502
Weisblat, Christine, 863
Weisblat, David A., 863
Weisenbach, Christy, 680
Weisenbach, Paul, 1053
Weisner, Thomas S., 1401
Weiss, Arthur, 1281
Weiss, Arthur A., 1260
Weiss, James D., Sr., 865
Weiss, Janet, 1174
Weiss, Karen, 686
Weiss, Martin E., 1110
Weiss, Robert, 864
Weiss, Robert B., 864
Weiss, Shira, 864
Weiss, Susan, 864
Weissman Charitable Lead Trust,
    Fredrick & Evelyn, 866
Weissman, Margaret, 866
Weissman, Patricia, 866
Weissman, Rebecca, 866
Weitzenhoffer, Max, 867
Welburn, Edward T., Jr., 990
Welch, Andrew M., 647
Welch, Dennis E., 937
Weldy, Judy, 45
Weller, Bradley E., 145
Weller, Danielle, 1007
Wellman, Adam, 1554
Wells Fargo Bank Michigan, N.A., 272
Wells Fargo Bank, N.A., 439
Wells, Bill, 1224
Wells, Chuck, 1412
Wells, Leeroy, Jr., 961
Wells, Leon, 869
Welsh, Alise, 620
Welsh, Lorie Jo, 871
Welsh, Michael J., 1505
Welsh, Sean, 1277
Welsh, Thomas S., III, 871
Welter, Edward P., 1571
Welter, Wilhelmina J., 1571
Welty, Joy, 1397
Wend, Gary, 1250
Wendler, Paul, 19
Wendling, John C., 418
Wenham, Charlotte, 1412
Wenick-Kutz, Bonnie, 1100, 1112
Wentworth, Elizabeth B., 78
Wenzel, Sharon R., 1573
Wenzlick, Vearn, 1168
Werdlow, Sean K., 1106
Werth, Thomas L., 1420
Wertheimer, Barbara, 967
Weschler, R. Ted, 573
Wesley, Robert, 1185
Wesselhoft, Betsy, 1270
West Co., Inc., The, 1071

West Pharmaceutical Services, Inc., 1071
West Shore Family YMCA, 1102
West, Anna, 474
West, Byron, 1385
West, Christine R., 748
West, Dan, 1144
West, Jeffrey P., 1074
West, Rick, 1232
West, Robin Kinzer, 1145
West, Sherril, 1402
West, Teresa, 1247
Westcott, Julie, 1416
Westerman, Samuel L., 872
Westfall, Harley J., 874
Westfall, Ruthmary, 874
Westgate, Gerald A., 1326
Weston, Herbert E., 381
Westrate, Richard, Jr., 1381
Wettlaufer, Ann, 1263
Wey, Matt, 1275
Weyand, Florence H., 875
Weyand, Louis F., 875
Weyerhaeuser Company, 1234
Weyhing, Bob, 980
Wharton, Laurie, 1043
Wharton-Bickley, Stevens, 42
Wheeler, David, 1388
Wheeler, Dean, 1319
Wheeler, Robert L., 1154
Wheeler, Tina, 1350
Wheeler, W., 1332
Whipple, Ken, 1106
Whirlpool Corp., 1072
White, Al, 1429
White, Ashley, 1141
White, B. Joseph, 1451
White, Betty Lou, 460
White, C. Edward, Jr., 346
White, Carolyn, 1456
White, Claire, 1255
White, Claire M., 587
White, Claire Mott, 346, 409
White, David, 762
White, Gilbert M., 877
White, Glenn, 762
White, Greg, 460
White, Gregory D., 459
White, Jill, 1177
White, Jodi, 1080
White, Linda V., 639
White, Lorlie, 1526
White, Lynn T., 816
White, Miles D., 933
White, Richard, 1028
White, Ridgeway H., 409
White, Ridgway H., 346, 587
White, Ruth E., 762
White, Sarah, 557
White, Shannon M. Easter, 1107
White, Steve, 949
White, William S., 346, 409, 587
White, Woodie T., 1195
Whitehouse, Fred, 683
Whitelaw, Anne, 1455
Whitfield, Donald B., 1249
Whitfield, Leon, 879
Whitham, Mark, 1018
Whiting, Gregory, 1405
Whiting, Harriet Clark, 881
Whiting, Helen Dow, 202
Whiting, Macauley, Jr., 202
Whiting, Scott, 1291
Whitlock, Louis, 1382
Whitman, John, 1100
Whitman, Lars, 448
Whitman, Susan T.K., 448
Whitmire, Lynne, 1121
Whitmore, Robin, 1548
Whittington, Jerry, 1432
Whittlesey, Steven B., 1082
Whitton, Cheryl A., 1113
Whitworth, Larry, 1180
Wichman, Gary, 1119

Wickens, Jeanne, 1436
Wickes, Harvey Randall, 882
Wickson, James, 883
Wickson, Meta, 883
Widder, Steve, 1414
Widlak, Becky, 1093
Wiedlea, John, 1114, 1175, 1178
Wiedmeyer, Jill, 183
Wierda, Carolyn, 1087
Wierenga, Janelle, 884
Wierenga, Jud, 1268
Wierenga, Pamela, 884
Wierenga, Stacy, 1268
Wierenga, Wendell, 884
Wierman, Denise, 1500
Wiersba, Abha, 1258
Wiersma, Robert, 1291
Wiggins, Don, 1185
Wigginton, Ruth, 885
Wigler, Lori, 1321
Wiklanski, Mary, 1456
Wilbanks, Laura, 1180
Wilbur, Clarence, 1372
Wilburn, Walt, 1089
Wilcox, Beverly, 1116
Wilcox, Priscilla, 1354
Wild, Michael M., 234
Wilder, Kurtis T., Hon., 1410
Wiley, Alfredine J., 1465
Wiley, Tyrone, 1454
Wilk, Stanley J., 181
Wilkerson, Marie, 1159, 1513
Wilkie, David, 1201
Wilkins, Zelene, 448
Wilkinson, Cathy, 1110
Willard, Gregory D., 1257
Willet, Vern, 184
Willey, Ann, 561
Willey, Mark, Rev., 761
Williams, Addie, 1408
Williams, Arlene, 1389
Williams, Betty J., 888
Williams, Carolyn H., Hon., 1138
Williams, Charlie J., 36, 1470
Williams, David, 1100, 1383
Williams, Deborah, 1403
Williams, Douglas, 1370
Williams, Elaine, 1240
Williams, Erick, 1202
Williams, Heather, 111
Williams, Jeffrey, 1250
Williams, Joanne, 964
Williams, John P., 42
Williams, Joyce G., 307
Williams, Margaret, 729
Williams, Mary, 990
Williams, Mary Alice, 275
Williams, Michael, 1307
Williams, Michael E., 1374
Williams, Michael P., II, 948
Williams, Patricia M., 887
Williams, Paul, 1323
Williams, Pete, 1021
Williams, R. Jamison, 888
Williams, R. Jamison, Jr., 888
Williams, Robert J., Jr., 948
Williams, Robert J., Sr., 948
Williams, Robert T., 1402
Williams, Roger K., 948
Williams, Ronald A., 887
Williams, Ronald K., 280
Williamson, Barbara, 1168
Williamson, D., 1332
Williamson, Dean, 1043
Williamson, Donald, 1417
Williamson, Judith Cole, 1086
Williamson, Tonya, 402
Willis, Beverly, 1410
Willis, Elizabeth A., 1077
Willis, Kirsten, 677
Willis, Sandy, 1165
Willit, Meg Miller, 1328
Willman, Rob, 1084
Willming, Karen, 1169

Willoughby, Elizabeth L., 485
Willyard, Barbara A., 1104
Wilmers, Adam, 1279
Wilmont, Tracy L., 1185
Wilson, Alfred G., 891
Wilson, Chris A., 133
Wilson, Don, 391
Wilson, J. Richard, 69
Wilson, Joyce R., 1407
Wilson, Karen M., 890
Wilson, L. James, 683
Wilson, Leon E., 1361
Wilson, Linda, 1376, 1568
Wilson, Lula C., 893
Wilson, Mark, 1376, 1568
Wilson, Mark K., 1239
Wilson, Mary Elizabeth, 889
Wilson, Matilda R., 891
Wilson, Rodney B., 892
Wilson, Ron, 1449
Wilson, Ryan M., 1094
Wilson, Steven M., 588
Wilson, Thomas J., 935
Wilson, Thomas S., 1046
Wilson, Tracy, 885
Wilson-Oyelaran, Eileen, 1282
Wilson-Oyelaran, Eileen B., Dr., 1138
Wilson-Thompson, Kathleen, 1015
Wilton, Kathy, 1432
Wiltse, Tom, 1128
Winans, Michael L., 895
Winans, Michael, Jr., 895
Winbush, William, 1171
Winchester, Joyce, 1212
Wind, David, 210, 355
Wind, Kathie, 1125
Windemuller, Debra, 426
Windemuller, Steven C., 426
Wine, Larry, 561
Winer, Donald, 896
Wing, Keith, 1129
Wingert, Dale, 1177
Winget, Alicia J., 1326
Winkle, Beverly L., 1572
Winkle, Gerard I., 1572
Winkler, Dennis, 1321
Winn, John A., 899
Winn, June C., 898
Winn, Mary Jo, 899
Winn, William H., Sr., 898
Winnell, Todd, 1162
Winowiecki, Ronald L., 1045
Winquist, Thomas R., 847
Winship, Virginia, 900
Winslow, Linda, 1329
Winter, Erik, 325
Winter, Mathew E., 935
Wintermute, Timothy, 1511
Winters, Barbara, 396
Wirtz, Barbara, 1414
Wirtz, Jason T., 903
Wirtz, John O., 903
Wirtz, John W., 902
Wirtz, John W., II, 903
Wirtz, Wanda A., 902
Wisconsin Energy Corp., 1074
Wisconsin Public Service Corp., 1075
Wise, Leslie, 242
Wise, Robert G., 959
Wiseman Seminoff, Nancy, 1148
Wiskur, Christina, 1099
Wisne, Kathryn, 1088
Wisner, Donald, 798
Wisner, Joyce S., 798
Wisner, Leslie, 798
Wiswell, James, 1000, 1378
Witmer, Jean Hudson, 392
Wittenberg, Joel, 1013
Wittenberg, Joel R., 450
Wllliams, Robert, 1417
Wodzinski, Rick, 1166
Wojan, Connie, 1096
Wolanin, Craig, 1053
Wolf, Barth J., 1075

Wolf, Kaitlin Hennessey, 362
Wolf, Lawrence M., 376
Wolf, Robert, 1476
Wolfe, C. Christopher, 906
Wolfe, Howard H., 906
Wolfe, Janet, 1372
Wolff, Amy Zimmerman, 927
Wolff, Jean, 907
Wolff, Keith, 907, 927
Wolff, Kevin, 907
Wolff, Lewis, 907
Wolff, Paula, 427
Wolfinger, Mary, 931
Wolfson, Jeffrey A., 647
Wollack, Judy, 1364
Wollack, Robert E., 1468
Wollenweber, Mark, 1240
Wolohan, James L., 1237
Wolohan, Sean, 1164
Wolters, Kate Pew, 908, 1058
Wolters, Richard, 908
Wolverine Sign Works, 147
Wolverine World Wide, 1076
Wolverton, Charles, 1417
Wong, Laura, 909
Wong, Lawrence, 909
Wong, Michael, 909
Wong, Sylvia, 909
Wong, Tammy, 1556
Wood, Cele, 1440
Wood, Chuck, 605
Wood, Dean, 1112
Wood, Elaine, 1391
Wood, Jacqueline, 1338
Wood, Robert, 1124
Wood, Rodney P., 262, 263, 264
Wood, Sylvia Upton, 833
Woodbeck, Jan, 1232
Woodhouse, Robert C., Jr., 42
Woodruff, Barb, 1432
Woods, Stephen K., 1151
Woodside Credit, 1228
Woodside, Leonard, 1082
Wooley, Charles, 1273
Woolhiser, Michael, 628
Woolson, Tyler, 992
Wooster, Jeff, 595
Wooten, Fred, 1269
Word, Carl, 1407
Worden, Catherine, 1097
Worden, Joe, 1122
Worgess, Andrew, 629
Worgess, Rachel E., 629
Worsham, Richard B., 912
Worst, Jamison, 825
Worthington, Doug, 1225
Worthy, Mik, 722
Wright, Albert F., 1402
Wright, Daniel, 1480
Wright, Dave, 1091
Wright, Gail, 1145
Wright, J. Patrick, 1386
Wright, Joe, 1384
Wright, John, 1321
Wright, Julie, 1327
Wright, Mary, 1248
Wright, O'Neal O., 36
Wright, Terrence P., 647
Wright, V. Ennis, 913
Wright, William, 1340
Wrigley, Benham R., 384
Wroblewski, D.M., 1552
Wroten, Linda L., 289
Wruble, Ron, 1286
Wudcoski, Karen, 849
Wurst, Lisa, 1394
Wurzer, Robert, 1158
Wyers, Kirk, 1124
Wyett, Pamela Applebaum, 26
Wynalda Litho, Inc., 914
Wynalda, Connie, 7
Wynalda, Patricia, 914
Wynalda, Robert, 7, 914
Wynalda, Robert, III, 7

Wynalda, Robert, Jr., 914
Wynn, Angela Patrick, 1171
Wynsma, James B., 1291
Wyrick, Jermaine A., 1470

Xcel Energy Inc., 1077

Yadavalli, Somayajulu, Dr., 1292
Yaffe, Frederick, 915
Yaffe, Katherine, 915
Yagiela, Dale, 1383
Yalamanchi, Ravi, 1388, 1431
Yankama, Andrew S., 916
Yankama, Rachel D., 916
Yankie, Karen, 1078, 1230
Yantz, Jeff, 1087
Yantz, Jerome L., 434
Yatooma, Norman A., 1222
Yaw, Carol K., 905
Yaw, James J., 905
Yaw, William Rumer, 905
Yeager Trust, Charles F., 918
Yeager, John, 1128
Yeager, Thomas C., 917
Yeckel, Catherine L., 859
Yeo, Judith N., 919
Yeo, Lloyd J., 919
Yeo, William E., 919

Yoe, Timothy C., 757
York, Eilene M., 920
York, Jerome B., 920
Yorston, Carolyn, 875
Youmans, Marvin R., Dr., 1485
Young, Carlito H., 1470
Young, Donna H., 921
Young, Gladys M., 723
Young, Harry, 1353
Young, Linda, 1263
Young, Mark, 921
Young, Michael, 1146
Young, Pareese, 557
Young, Rick, 1167
Young, Sue, 1247
Young, Walter R., Jr., 921
Young-Bueltel, Michelle, 921
Youngquist, Kevin, 1324
Youra, Andy, 358
Yuhas, Barbara G., 1253
Yuhn, Daniel, 1204

Zachry, Sarah Skiles, 754
Zack, Marilyn, 1127
Zadora, Ronald J., 713
Zadvinskis, Ivars, 647
Zale, Deborah J., 160
Zampetis, Ann J., 924
Zampetis, Callie A., 924

Zampetis, Constantine T., 924
Zampetis, Theodore K., 924
Zandstra, Ray, 1527
Zappa, Roger, 1148
Zaskowski, Bonnie, 384
Zavitz, Darrell, 1441
Zeddies, Fanny Boone, 727
Zeese, Craig, 1129
Zeff, Lester, Dr., 928
Zehnder, Karen, 1123
Zehnder, W. Don, 625, 1123
Zehr, Tim, 1150
Zeitlin, Froma I., 897
Zeldenrust, Robert, 1124
Zelt, Beverly A., 925
Zemke, Martha, 926
Zemke, Mary, 926
Zerbo, John, 1246
Zerinque, Tony, 1405
Zernicke, Sue, 997
Zietz, Lonny E., 1238
Zikakis, Stephanie, 1353
Zimmer, Rick, 1177
Zimmer, Scott, 1123
Zimmerman, Charles, 488
Zimmerman, Nellie M., 878
Zimmerman, Ron, 1397
Zimmerman, William, 139
Zink & Triest Co., 1064
Zionkowski, Ed, 772

Zionkowski, Edward, 606
Ziraldo, John, 1321
Zitner, Ricki Farber, 657
Zitzlesberger, Terri, 1154
Zocher, Bryan, 627
Zoller, Howard L., 929
Zoller, Lawrence C., 929
Zoller, Walter F., 929
Zondervan, Mary, 930
Zondervan, Peter J., 930
Zondervan, Robert Lee, 930
Zonta Club of Muskegon, 931
Zuberi, Habib, 1383
Zuberi, Sajid, 1493
Zurek, Mark, 918
Zurschmiede, Thomas, 981
Zurschmiede, W. Thomas, 932
Zurschmiede, W. Thomas, Jr., 932, 981
Zurvalec, Susan, 1253
Zutter, Steve, 1139
Zuzga, Eric, 1210
Zwier, Daniel, 1111
Zwiers, James D., 1076
Zylstra, Betty, 215
Zylstra, Joel M., 314
Zynda, David P., 1575
Zynda, James K., 1575
Zynda, Stephen R., 1575
Zynda, Virginia, 1575